THE PAPER REPUBLIC

The Struggle for Money, Credit and Independence in the Republic of Texas

bright sky press
HOUSTON, TEXAS

2365 Rice Boulevard, Suite 202,
Houston, Texas 77005

10 9 8 7 6 5 4 3 2

Bevill, James P., 1959-
The paper republic : the struggle for money, credit and independence in the Republic of Texas / James Bevill.
p. cm.
Includes bibliographical references and index.
ISBN 978-1-933979-25-0 (hardcover)
1. Texas--History--Revolution, 1835-1836--Finance. 2. Capitalists and financiers--Texas--History--19th century.
3. Numismatics--Texas--History--19th century. 4. Money--Texas--History--19th century. I. Title.

F390.B497 2009
976.4'03--dc22 2009024429

Book and cover design by Marla Garcia
Edited by Carlyn Kahl
Printed in China through Asia Pacific Offset

THE PAPER REPUBLIC

The Struggle for Money, Credit and Independence in the Republic of Texas

James P. Bevill

bright sky press
HOUSTON, TEXAS

ACKNOWLEDGEMENTS

It would have been difficult to take on a work of this magnitude without the help and support of my wife Jodie. She encouraged me to write this book to share my passion and knowledge of the history of early Texas with you, the reader, which follows a trail of silver, gold and paper money over the period. Most importantly, I thank her for believing in me and encouraging me to move forward with the project. She is my best friend, and my first line editor and closest advisor. She made numerous astute recommendations for the manuscript and suggested that I inject a human element into the story for appeal to a much broader audience.

After Jodie completed her initial review, our good friend and former Language Arts teacher Barbara Upchurch edited the work for grammar, punctuation, content and readability. Her revisions were then looked over by my father-in-law, Paul L. Springer (Yale, Class of 1941), who caught several typographical and grammatical errors while proofing and polishing the manuscript. I thank them both for their time and efforts.

Dr. Bruce Winders, the Historian and Curator of the Alamo, first suggested that I write a book about the money of the Republic of Texas when we discussed a possible exhibit of the money in November 2005. He also referred me to some key sources of material on the finances of the Republic of Texas which would have been much more difficult to find without his collaboration. I thank him for his continuous support in getting this book completed.

The chapters on Spanish and Mexican Texas would have been impossible for me to put together without the guidance and organizational skills of my good friend and enthusiastic Mexican coin collector, Ricardo de león Tallavas. Ricardo helped me see the origins of the early money that flowed into colonial Texas from the Mexican perspective and was instrumental in helping me put these pieces into their historical context. Pat Johnson, owner of Houston Numismatic Exchange, also offered several of his coins for imaging and some helpful suggestions on the first three chapters after an initial review of this portion of the manuscript. After the pictures were added, Ricardo (an instructor on Mexican Coins at the American Numismatic Association's Summer Seminar) and Mike Dunigan (author, coin dealer and an authority specializing in Mexican coinage) each proofread this section independently of each other. Both were instrumental in helping me make this portion of the book historically accurate, and I am grateful for their help.

Along the same lines, Darrel Brown (who held one of the largest private collections of Texana in private hands) helped me tremendously by offering over two dozen images from his personal collection. He doggedly researched several exceedingly rare and interesting items via his voluminous personal library. His loan (and ultimately the gift) to me of a four volume set of the Texas Treasury Papers was a key factor in deciphering the inner workings of the treasury department. Although most of Darrel's own authoritative research work has not been previously published, there are several instances in which it is referenced and noted as such throughout this book.

The subject of Texas paper money is a very specialized field. I would also like to thank Richard Laster (a thirty-year Texas currency collector) for his technical review of the manuscript. Richard's intense focus on the accuracy of the voluminous Texas paper varieties and their respective descriptions was a technical task all unto itself. Jeff Dunn, a Dallas attorney and the founder of the Battle of San Jacinto Symposium, also gave an important historical review of the manuscript and offered several suggestions, often challenging me to confirm my original sources to verify the accuracy of my text.

John N. Rowe not only helped me acquire many of the pieces in my private collection, he previously owned the most complete collection of Texas currency and bonds ever assembled. John then donated his collection to the DeGolyer Library at Southern Methodist University in Dallas for scholarly research. John, and Russell Martin, the library's director, gave me unprecedented access to the Rowe collection. They shared dozens of hours of commentary with me regarding rarity, varieties and the origins of many of the pieces. John was one of the final proofreaders of the manuscript for accuracy in regards to the Texas documents and paper money before it was turned over to the publisher. With John's guidance and help, the book is as accurate and complete as it could be.

Imaging the various coin and currency collections proved to be a Herculean task. I thank John Barber and Ricardo de león Tallavas for their help in photographing and editing several of the pieces. Their collective efforts are both noteworthy and appreciated. I give special thanks to David Lisot and Steve Ivy at Heritage Auction Galleries for arranging the professional photography of over a hundred coins from several private collections used in this book by the staff at Heritage Auctions without a charge. Their time, interest and generosity is greatly appreciated. Q. David Bowers of Stack's graciously allowed me to publish images of several unique pieces from the archives of the American Bank Note Company related to the Republic of Texas era and unobtainable from any other source. Cartographer and fellow historian Jim Glass helped me with maps and other illustrations, and directed me to several sources which enabled me to fill in some of the gaps.

To my assistant, Angela Vincent, I say thank you for your patience and understanding as I undertook this project over the last three years. Theresa and Manuel Cavasos were of tremendous help in translating several of the old Spanish documents. Sue Y'Barbo helped me by organizing the appendix, processing and cataloging the images and freeing up hundreds of hours of my time to concentrate on my business during each and every weekday. The moral support and encouragement which all of my friends, clients and co-workers showed will always be remembered.

There are numerous illustrations from research libraries and museums included in the work and I thank the staff members of these institutions who were extraordinarily helpful in the pursuit of various images and items of research. Special thanks goes to Lisa Struthers at the San Jacinto Museum of History, John Anderson at the Texas State Library, Elaine Davis and Warren Stricker at the Daughters of the Republic of Texas Library at the Alamo, and Russell Martin at the DeGolyer Library at SMU in Dallas.

It would have been difficult, if not impossible to amass the content for this book without the assistance of many friends who shared their knowledge and allowed me to obtain the images contained herein from their per sonal collections. I thank the following group of friends who came together for the common good and allowed me to use images from their private collections of coins, currency, documents, and pictures for this book:

Sue Brinkman Alston
John and Eve Barber
Darrel and Caroline Brown
David and Martha Kerr Burke
Greg Cooper
Ricardo de león Tallavas
Michael Doyle
Kenny Duncan, Sr.
Mike Dunigan
Jeff Dunn
Jean Epperson
Sebastian Frommhold
Jim Glass
Joseph and Joanne Hayes
Pat Johnson
Max Keech
Richard Laster
Kirk Menczer
Mike Niebriegge
Joseph D. Olson
Dick Osburn
Joseph G. Putman III
John N. Rowe III
Bob Shelton
Ed Stephens
Alvin L. Stern

To everyone at Bright Sky Press: Carly Kahl, Rue Judd, Ellen Cregan, Lucy Chambers and Marla Garcia, you did a fabulous job. Your gifts of creativity, design, technology and your relentless pursuit of perfection have helped me make this book a stunningly beautiful tribute to the Republic of Texas era. There are many other friends and colleagues which have not been named here but helped me in other ways. Your contributions to the work are priceless and your friendship will be treasured always. It's been quite a journey for all of us.

Sincerely,

James P. Bevill

TABLE OF CONTENTS

PREFACE

This book was written to tell the story of early Texas through the money and paper documents which were used from 1535-1846. No prior knowledge of the history of the Republic of Texas era, or the collecting of coins or paper money is needed. This work is intended for the enrichment of the widest possible audience.

The reader may notice that virtually all of the paper money and other Texas obligations are numerically denoted and cross referenced into the standard guides for paper money collectors of the Texas series. This was done for the benefit of the aspiring collector. Many of these varieties were previously catalogued by major design and paper type by researchers, including the late Grover C. Criswell, Bob Medlar, Joseph D. Olson, and most recently, Hugh Shull. Although both the Criswell and Olson numbers were used where applicable, these notations are barely noticeable to the casual reader.

The Criswell numbers were updated in 2007 by Hugh Shull in *A Guide Book of Southern States Currency, History, Rarity and Values*. This numbering system uses letter prefixes to divide the Republic and government obligations by place of issue. For instance, the prefix "H" denotes Houston, "A" denotes Austin, etc. In several cases, where Shull has updated and re-numbered a note from the original Criswell guides, the original number "Cr. XX" is denoted first, followed by Shull's updated number which is followed in parentheses "(YY)". These updated number changes appear in chapters 4, 11 and 14.

Olson, in his 2006 book, *Texas Currency: A Catalogue, 1813-1868*, scrapped the Criswell system entirely and presents a numbering system which also includes issues from the colonial period. Olson provides a logical numbering sequence which is for the most part in the chronological order of issue. Colonial and provisional government issues are numbered in single or double digits, and the remainder is organized by the place of issue. For example, the 100 series is used for Velasco, 200 series for Columbia, etc., and the examples of these pieces will be noted as "O-109" or "O-203" respectively. Each Criswell number is followed by the Olson number.

All identifying numbers regarding bonds and other debt obligations of the Republic were noted as catalogued in Grover Criswell's *Confederate and Southern States Bonds*, second edition, published in 1980. Advanced collectors may notice that not all of the numerous paper types of money and varieties of bonds previously catalogued were included in this book. Private, city or county issues were not included (with the exception of three city notes in Chapter 10), as the scope of the work would have taken on an unwieldy size.

Most importantly, the examples within this book were selected for their content and historical significance rather than for the variety of paper on which they were printed or written. While a pricing guide on the market value of a collectable series of paper money can quickly become outdated, understanding the factors which drove the issuance and created the scarcity of the surviving pieces is of greater importance in estimating their value. This also gives the reader a greater understanding of the history and the economic struggles of the Republic of Texas.

INTRODUCTION

As any good detective will tell you, "just follow the money and you will find the truth." This is the story of the Republic of Texas as told through the money that was used from the colonial period through annexation. This paper trail of obligations was once scattered across the old Republic of Texas. It has been woven together to illustrate this fascinating and remarkably accurate picture of one of the most colorful chapters in American history. The enthralling history of Texas, once an independent nation, has captured the imagination of millions with its struggles and triumphs. Surprisingly, many historians simply skip over the study of the money and finances of the Republic era. But the history of early Texas was as much of an economic struggle as it was a military one. It is a story not only of the greed and politics of the times, but also of a unique cast of characters whose influences forever changed the world in which we live.

The factors that surrounded the issue of various forms of money during this period provide us with hard evidence of what transpired in the region long before the first shots were fired in the Texas revolution. By studying the coinage of this explosive period, we can trace the expansion of the Spanish empire into the New World, the establishment of the first mints in North America, the rise of Mexico as a regional power and its separation from Spain in 1821. We can witness the birth of the five-pointed lone star symbol for Texas, which was coined for the use of daily commerce in San Antonio de Béxar in 1817-1818 when Texas was still known as a province of New Spain. By contrast, the various forms of money that circulated in the Republic of Texas also tell a story about the people who founded a nation with a rich and turbulent history as old as Texas itself.

The founders of the Republic of Texas were no less daring than those leaders who declared independence from Great Britain in 1776 and were no doubt inspired by them as they shook themselves free from Mexico. In a short period of only seven months, from the Consultation of political leaders at San Felipe de Austin in the fall of 1835 to the lightning victory of Sam Houston and the Texas army at San Jacinto on April 21, 1836, the Texians achieved the independence of a country larger than France. Barely a year after Texas severed its ties with Mexico, a global credit crisis known as the Panic of 1837 swept through the U.S. and the American Southwest. The financial panic and subsequent depression decimated the economy of the young nation, forcing Texas to rely on a paper money system and the extension of credit for economic survival. Functioning without any banks in the new republic, Texas maintained that independence for a decade without any meaningful assistance from foreign governments, and in complete defiance of a hostile neighbor to the south who made repeated military harassments and incursions.[1]

The Texians' violent struggle with Mexico was funded almost entirely on credit. The provisional government rose to function as a sovereign nation, overcoming almost impossible odds in the process.[2] The desperate financial measures undertaken by revolutionary Texas and the borrowing of funds to finance the war were necessitated because money was needed to build an army, purchase guns, ammunition, tents, horses and supplies. The procurement of funds was also necessary to launch and maintain the first Texas Navy, an indispensable force in protecting Texas ports and capturing merchant ships loaded with supplies for the Mexican armies. The provisional government issued handwritten drafts to acknowledge contributions of money and goods and used these to finance the war on credit. Officials also issued paper certificates to acknowledge bounty payments of land as a recruitment bonus for soldiers. These early Texas obligations were written as evidence of a rebellious new nation, a seat of Government on the run and a quest for diplomatic recognition. Yet the early auditors, treasurers and controllers were no less essential than any officer or soldier, for without the money and the credit to keep the government functioning, the

Republic of Texas would have ceased to exist.[3]

These old scraps of paper, many of which were cancelled by the government and discarded, have now been placed in sequence. They form a trail though a secret door to the past. This doorway, now opened for all, reveals the grave condition of early Texas finances and the desperate military struggle during the war for independence. From this prolific series of paper issues, we can learn about the political and financial struggles of the people and about the events which earned Texas her independence. The early pay certificates and warrants not only reference soldiers and sailors by name, but also their commanding officers and various government officials. Pay warrants often tell us the salary of executives and their specific duties. Some pay warrants relate to Indian wars, the Texas Navy and the first Texas Rangers. This paper trail also documents the frequent relocation of the seat of government, first as a game of chase by the Mexican Army and then as a game of tug-of-war by Presidents Houston and Lamar. Serving as silent witnesses to history, these issues recorded many key events and signatures of the period along with the city or town of issue. This information was once available only to sophisticated collectors, but it is now open to a much wider audience of social, financial and military historians with an interest in this fascinating period of Texas history.

A much broader study of Texas money provides a unique perspective into the economy, daily life and finances of the early Texans. Looking beyond the artistic designs on the coinage and the allegorical vignettes on the paper money, there is evidence of an economy that was run entirely on credit, a series of devaluations versus the U.S. dollar (then denominated in gold and silver), a battle against counterfeiting, a scramble for hard assets, as well as a multitude of re-financings. Texas was perennially broke and desperate to stay afloat during the years that it was a free and independent republic. Credit was stretched to the limit and then exhausted to an extreme. Although Texas pledged its public faith for the repayment of these debts, in the back of the mind, every holder of Texas paper saw the millions of acres of public land that would somehow, someday, be available for the eventual repayment of those obligations if all else failed. It was an economy run almost entirely on faith and credit—without one, the other would not exist. Collectively, these pieces tell the story of the ongoing financial crisis of a new nation struggling to defend itself in the midst of runaway inflation and an economic collapse of epic proportions.

During the writing of The Paper Republic, every effort has been made to set the record straight regarding the various types and major varieties of currency, warrants and certificates issued by the Republic of Texas. Rather than focus on the different varieties of paper that were used, the emphasis is on the history of each piece, places of issue, factors that created scarcity, acceptance in the marketplace during the time of issuance and how the pieces were interwoven into the society and daily transactions of the people. In that sense, understanding the political, economic and historical context of the period is imperative to understanding how the various forms of money and credit were reflective of the course of history.

Whether you are fascinated with the Texas struggle or interested in a compelling story, or are a student of financial history, a casual collector, or a serious numismatist, you will thoroughly enjoy this epic tale of the finances behind the scenes of history. The stunning visual images and exhaustive study of the financial instruments and the monetary system of the Republic of Texas create an invaluable guide to understanding the key figures, events, places, commerce and financial circumstances which forever changed the map of the North American continent. The crushing series of economic events and the lack of hard money during the era of the Republic of Texas eventually led to annexation by the United States in 1846, an event that became the pivotal detonator of the Mexican War (1846-1848).

This unique perspective on the financial transactions of the Republic of Texas is a story that has never been told before. As much about personalities and hardships as it is about money and finances, it reveals the good, the bad and the often humorous history of the people and the policies of a well intentioned but desperate and fragile government. As you follow this paper trail across the Republic of Texas, you will find many heretofore undiscovered truths, as told by the money.

---

1 William M. Gouge, *The Fiscal History of Texas* (New York: Burt Franklin, 1852; rpt. 1969), 5.

2 Ibid.

3 Ibid.

FOREWORD

Most people think of history as something decided on battlefields under the direction of great men. Authors tend to give readers what they want: tales of battles with well known names and commanders with recognizable faces. The demand for epic stories and heroic deeds has dominated much the literature on Texas history. Much of human existence, though, is filled with the mundane task of just getting by in life. Government, commerce, society, and family history—necessary studies in history—seem to lack the thrill that draws readers other than academics. It is just the reality of writing history.

Several years ago, I was approached by Jim Bevill, a numismatist from Houston, Texas. Jim broached the idea of displaying a collection of rare artifacts and documents from members of an organization to which he belonged, the Texas Numismatic Association. He proposed bringing together pieces that would tell the history of early Texas through its money. As our conversations progressed over the next few months, I was impressed with his dedication to the project. I was also impressed by the pieces that Jim and other collectors were offering for the exhibit. I quickly realized that Jim had hit on an effective way to literally piece together the story of early Texas. The common thread that ran through Texas whether under the control of Spain, Mexico, or the Republic was its money.

The story uncovered by Jim is fascinating. At one point I suggested that he put it down in book form. This volume is a result of that suggestion. Like me, readers will have a chance to be impressed by the pieces that Jim has assembled for this study and the story he has been able to tell from them. Who, after all, isn't at least a little interested in the topic of money? And although they may not expect it, readers will find plenty of drama in this tale.

Jim's research connects the somewhat abstract topic of finance with the real world. How did the coins used by Spaniards on the Texas frontier reflect their place in the larger Spanish empire? How did a credit system based on a man's word operate? Where did the funds come from to finance the Texas Revolution? What role did Texas' lack of solvency play in her ultimate annexation to the United States? These are important questions and Jim answers them and more.

The Paper Republic is history on both the grand and small scale. Moreover, it presents readers with valuable insight into the Republic of Texas that will forever change their view of the revolution and its aftermath. This volume is destined to become a classic. Although the exhibit is still several years off, luckily we have Jim's book now. I congratulate him on a job well done.

Dr. Richard Bruce Winders
Historian and Curator at the Alamo

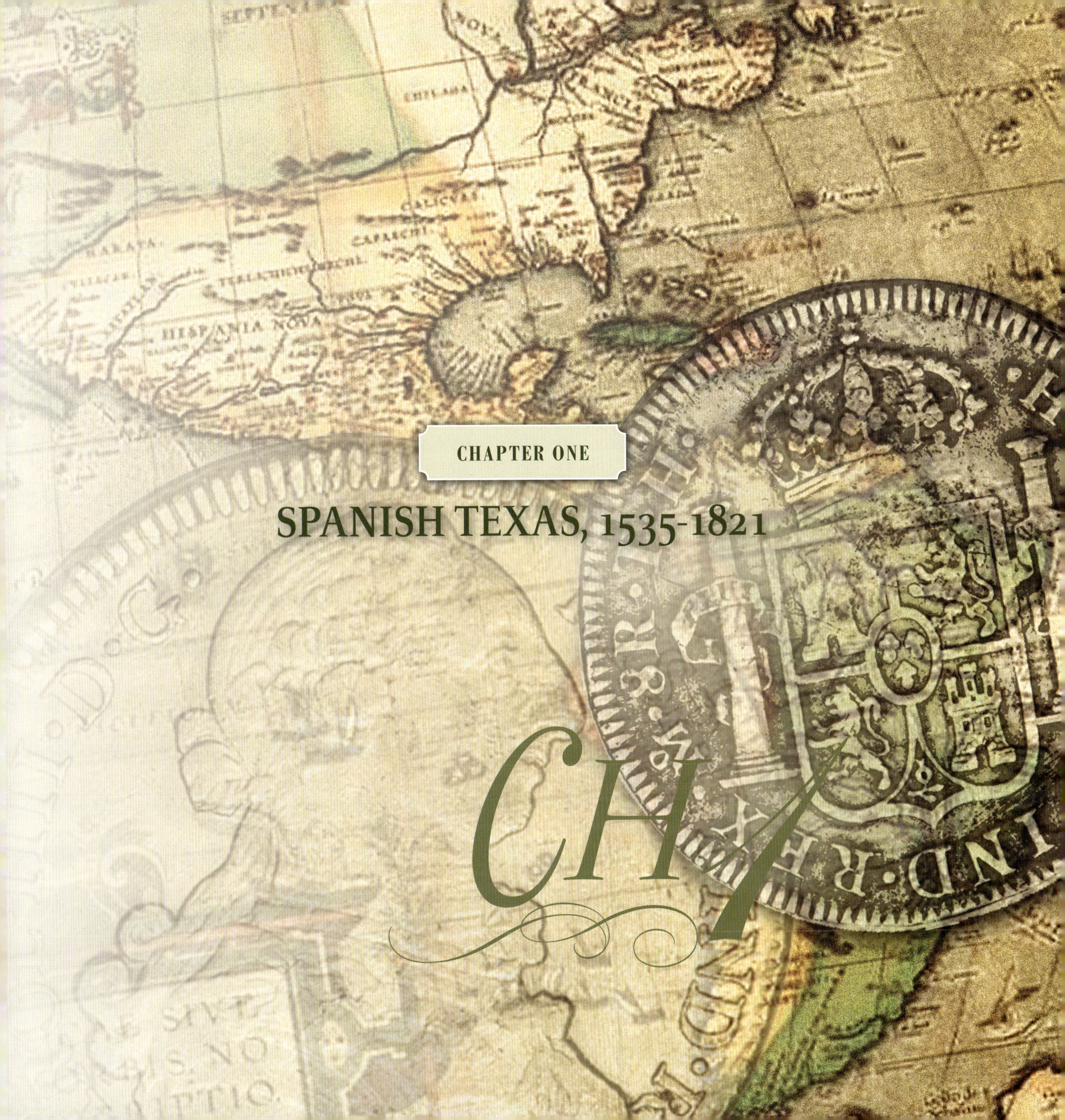

CHAPTER ONE

SPANISH TEXAS, 1535-1821

A NEW WORLD OF SILVER AND GOLD

Fig 1.1, Columbus Discovers America.

American Bank Note Company Vignette, Author's Collection.

Soon after Christopher Columbus claimed the New World for the Kingdom of Spain on October 12, 1492, European establishments began to appear over the Native American settlements. Shortly thereafter, Santo Domingo, Cuba, and Puerto Rico materialized on the map of America. It took only forty-four years after Columbus' first trip to the Antilles for the Spanish to mine the silver and gold ore deposits discovered in the Western Hemisphere and to refine and process the metals into coins for export to Europe.

Fig 1.2, Hernando de Cortés.

The San Jacinto Museum of History, Houston, Texas.

Twenty-nine years after Columbus first set foot in America, Hernando de Cortés and his men conquered the vast Aztec empire and established Mexico City as the Spanish capital of the New World. Cortés befriended Malintzin, the daughter of a local lord of a village island near the Tabasco River who was previously enslaved and sold to merchants. Cortés discovered that she spoke both the Nahuatl and Mayan languages. Malintzin became his mistress and interpreter, assisting the Spanish in communicating with the local tribes and the Aztecs.[1] Due to Malintzin's love for Cortés and her invaluable translations, advice, diplomacy and wisdom, the Aztecs fell to a coalition of native groups led by the Spaniards. The lands were then re-named *Nueva Espania* or New Spain.

Around 1536, the first mint in New Spain was established in Mexico City by the Spanish Crown. Antonio de Mendoza, the First Viceroy of New Spain, had been an administrator of the Granada's Mint prior to his appointment in the New World.[2] The former mint director's position over the area rich in gold and silver ore was a strategic one since Mendoza carried the royal written decree for the opening of Mexico's mint. This transcendental document was signed by Queen Johanna of Spain on May 11, 1535. Mendoza assigned Francisco del Rincón as the first Assayer for the Mexico City mint. Rincón oversaw the refining of silver paste produced

Fig 1.3, Map of the New World, c. 1587, by Abraham Ortelius.

Courtesy, Virginia Garrett Cartographic History Library, Special Collections, The University of Texas at Arlington Library, Arlington, Texas.

from the mines into the metal base needed to meet the legal standards for striking coins.[3]

The Spanish expansion quickly extended into what later became known as Texas. This expanded area received its first Spanish expedition within twenty years of the conquest of Mexico City. After several excursions, villages started to appear in the acquired area. On April 30, 1598, Juan de Oñate took formal possession of what is now western Texas for King Philip II of Spain. Subsequently, Oñate crossed the Rio Grande River just west of present-day downtown El Paso, which he named *El Paso del Rio del Norte,* meaning the "crossing to the north of the river." This was the first use of the name "El Paso."

Fig 1.4, Carlos & Johanna (Early Series) 1 *Real*, Mexico City, c. 1536-1538

Fig 1.5, Carlos & Johanna (Early Series) 2 *Reales*, Mexico City, c. 1541.

Fig 1.6, Carlos & Johanna (Early Series) 3 *Reales*, Mexico City, c. 1536.

Fig 1.7, Carlos & Johanna (Early Series) 4 *Reales*, Mexico City, c. 1541.

Courtesy of ANA Museum, Colorado Springs, Colorado.

CARLOS AND JOHANNA (EARLY SERIES 1536-1541)

The first money officially minted in New Spain came from the Mexico City mint in 1536. These silver coins became known as the Carlos and Johanna pieces, named for King Carlos I and his mother Johanna. Johanna was the daughter of Ferdinand and Isabella and heir to the Spanish throne. Although Johanna was the royal figurehead of the Spanish monarchy, her unstable mental state was such that after the untimely death of her husband, Philip the Handsome, her son was called upon to co-reign with her. The queen later became known as Johanna "The Mad" or "*La Loca.*"

While the minting of money was already well developed in Europe during this period, creating a minting facility in the raw landscape of early Mexico was a formidable task. The coins had one engraved die (carrying an inverse of the design) in an anvil, and another die carved into a large hammer-like tool (carrying the other design). A blank piece of silver was inserted between the two and struck with a sharp blow, impressing the design on the coin.

The early silver pieces in figures 1.4 through 1.7, coined in Mexico City in the sixteenth century, represent the first money struck for circulation in New Spain. On the smaller pieces, the denomination was expressed in "dots" rather than Arabic numbers, which were foreign to the native Aztecs. The assayer's initials "R" for Rincón, and "P" for Pedro de Espina, are also plainly visible. Although the 3 *reales* denomination is the rarest, several sea-salvaged examples have been recovered from shipwrecks near Padre Island, Texas.[4]

These coins carry a simple, yet uniquely Spanish design. The obverse (or "heads" side) depicts the Spanish coat of arms with two lions and two castles representing the united medieval reigns of Castille and León, a result of the marriage of Queen Isabella and King Ferdinand. Seven centuries of Arabic presence in Spain (711-1492) came to an end when Ferdinand and Isabella reestablished the influence of the Catholic Church in Spain. The complete legends on both sides of the coin read "CAROLVS ET IOHANNA HISPANIARVM ET INDIARVM REGES" which translates "Charles and Johanna, King and Queen of Spain and Indies." Also included are a mint mark "M" for Mexico City and the initial of the assayer "R" or "P" to certify the silver content of the coin.[5]

The reverse (or "tails" side) portrays the "Crowned Pillars," representing the Pillars of Hercules, also known as the gateway from the Mediterranean Sea to the unknown. The early series (1536-1541) can be distinguished by the lack of water between the pillars on the coin. The legend "PLVSVLTR" means "more beyond" and the legend "HISPANIARUM ET INDIARUM," or "of Spain and the Indies represents all of Spain's holdings in the New World. These early pieces were struck in denominations of ¼, ½, 1, 2, 3, 4 and 8 *reales*. The Spanish *real* (12 ½ cents), or the plural *reales*, soon became the dominant denomination of silver coins in the Western Hemisphere. The 8 *reales* pieces in this series were only struck for a brief period. The silver content of an 8 *reales* coin later became the standard on which the U.S. silver dollar was based (8 *reales* and silver dollar will later be used interchangeably in this book). Because the native Aztecs could not read the Arabic numbers used by the Spaniards, dots between the pillars rather than numbers were used to represent the denominations. One dot for 1 *real*, two dots for 2 *reales*, three for the short-lived 3 *reales* (also seen with arches) and the number "4" between the pillars on the 4 *reales* coin.

CARLOS AND JOHANNA (LATE SERIES 1542 – 1555)

The later series shows distinctive waves between the pillars, a design which resurfaced several issues later with widespread acceptance. These later Carlos and Johanna pieces were struck in denominations of ¼, ½, 1, 2 and 4 *reales*. As time passed, the spelling of the name of the King evolved into "CAROLVS," and Spanish royalty continued to assert their influence as they added the word "REGES," meaning "rulers" after "CAROLVS ET JOHANNA."

Figures 1.8 through 1.11 show the later series of coins, differentiated from the earlier series by the appearance of water between the pillars. This design became known as the "pillars and waves." These coins were struck from 1542-1555. Note the denomination of the dots between the pillars on the ½, 1 and 2 *reales* pieces. Also included are a mint mark "M" or "Mo" for Mexico City and the initial of the assayer "L" to certify the silver content of the coin.

The ½ *real* also has distinctively different obverse design, with the initials "K" for Karolvs (Carlos) and "I" for Joanna. Because there is no Latin "J," it was substituted by an "I." These coins were very small and easily recognized by the locals due to the different design.

The Spanish found a new source of wealth in the vast silver mines of the New World, and were determined to politicize their success by stamping their claim on each piece of money exported back to Europe. The Spanish kingdom's extension reached well into the area now known as Texas. These early silver coins from Mexico City were the forerunners of the famous milled Spanish pillar dollars, which established the standard of exchange in the New World, Europe and Asia for the next 250 years.

During this early period in New Spain no banks existed. Commerce was often conducted on credit or the exchange of goods or property. The introduction of hard money was well received in the region. While most wealth was concentrated in land holdings, cattle, horses and other property, gold and silver coins were the most widely accepted medium of exchange for large transactions. The practices of hoarding money, stacking it in a coffer or chest, or simply burying it became common. To this day, early Spanish silver coins are still discovered in thick walls, wells, or underground in parts of the old Spanish settlements in Texas.

Fig 1.8, Carlos & Johanna (Late Series) ½ *Real*, Mexico City, c. 1542-1555.

Fig 1.9, Carlos & Johanna (Late Series) 1 *Real*, Mexico Citay, c. 1542-1555.

Fig 1.10, Carlos & Johanna (Late Series) 2 *Reales*, Mexico City,a c. 1542-1555.

Fig 1.11, Carlos & Johanna (Late Series) 4 *Reales*, Mexico City, c. 1542-1555.

Fig 1.12, Carlos & Johanna (Early Series) 4 *Reales*, Mexico City, c. 1536-1541, Corroded Reverse.

The coin in Figure 1.12 shows evidence of having been buried. On one side nearly all the design is apparent. On the other side, it is obvious that centuries of running water (perhaps a river or stream) corroded most of the coin's face.

Fig 1.13, Carlos & Johanna (Late Series) 4 *Reales*, Mexico City, c. 1542-1555.

The sea-salvaged piece in Figure 1.13 was reportedly discovered in a small hoard on Padre Island in South Texas by the owner. Since these coins often traveled on the waterways, it is possible that this money found its way into the area after Spanish ships foundered on the coastline of the Gulf of Mexico. Some of the coins washed ashore centuries later by means of the violent tropical storms which periodically struck the coast.

SPANISH COBS – THE "PIECES OF EIGHT"

Silver "cobs" followed the Carlos and Johanna pieces. They were struck at the Spanish Colonial mints in the Western Hemisphere during the late 1500s and early 1600s, with Mexico City striking the first 8 *reales* cobs around 1573. These large silver coins eventually became known as *ocho reales,* or "pieces of eight" due to the largest denomination of "8 *reales*," though they were also struck in 4, 2, and 1 *reales* denominations. These 8 *reales* coins were known in Mexico as *pesos*. Gold coins were called *escudos*, and each *escudo* equaled 16 *reales*.[7] Both the early gold and silver coins were produced from metal ore that was indigenous to the region with crude equipment and somewhat primitive smelting and manufacturing conditions.

Mexico quickly became the most populous of the western economies, though the territory only retained about 2 to 5 percent of the coinage for local commerce, primarily the smaller denominations. Some of these coins found their way into the earliest Spanish settlements in Texas where they were used to pay the soldiers stationed in the remote locations.[7] Since the majority of the coins were struck for export, other Spanish mints were established at Lima and Cuzco (both in Peru), La Plata and Potosi (located in Bolivia), and Cartagena, Colombia. A mint was established in Guatemala in 1731.[8]

King Philip II (1556-1598) focused his attention on expanding the Spanish empire and building another fleet of ships for the navy, all of which required money. The source of funding for Spain's ambitions resulted from the discovery of large ore deposits in South America and the intense mining labor of the native Aztecs. The well-guarded Spanish treasure fleets were laden with silver and gold and regularly crossed the Atlantic ocean.

After departing from Latin American ports, the ships rendezvoused in Havana and then continued their long seafaring journey around the tip of Florida and up the gulf stream, bound for the port of Seville in Spain.

Silver cobs may have originally derived their name from the Spanish phrase "*cabo de barra*" meaning "end of the bar." Another theory suggests the coins received their name from the Old English word "cob" for "cobble," because their hand-cut shapes looked similar to the stones found in a cobbled stone road.[9] Regardless of the origin of the name, the early mint produced refined slabs of silver more than 90 percent pure. After alloyed by the assayer the still warm metal was rolled into a bar, like a long string of dough. Workers cut slices from the end of the bar and then used a tool or shears to trim the crude planchet (a blank disc of metal) down to the proper weight.[10]

These planchets were then re-heated and placed on a die. The die, a hardened metal tool bearing an inverse (or mirror image) design, was mounted on an anvil or another hard object. Another die was placed on the planchet by a rod or a holder, and the image was impressed on the coin by a strong strike of a hammer. After 1572, the design of the cobs was changed to a shield on the obverse and a cross on the reverse. The most interesting aspect of cobs is that they are all unique. If you ever see two cobs of an identical shape, thickness and imprint, then at least one of the two coins is a counterfeit![11]

The well-guarded Spanish treasure fleets were laden with silver and gold and regularly crossed the Atlantic ocean.

Fig 1.14, Cob Coinage, Philip II 1 *Real*, Mexico City, c. 1572-1598.

The 1 real coin in Figure 1.14 depicts the design of Philip II, with the Assayer's letter "O" at left, possibly for Bernardo de Oñate who was assayer from 1590–1605. The mintmark "Mo" is on the right. The religious influences of the Roman Catholic Church in the New World can be seen by the representation of a bold cross on the reverse which had replaced the pillars. This design was also struck in denominations of ½, 2, 4, and 8 reales.

Mexican cobs featured an elaborate shield with the Spanish coat of arms which replaced the pillars. The mintmark, denomination, and assayer letters are located on the obverse or front of the coin. The peripheral legend reads "PHILIPPVS.II.DEI.GRATIA." Literally translated, the phrase means "Philip II, by the Grace of God." The reverse holds an even stronger statement, with the castles of Castilla and León set inside a bold cross representing the Catholic Church, a reminder that all citizens in the Spanish empire held to the Roman Catholic faith. The emblem of the cross dominated the money of the New World for the next century and a half, and was a constant reminder for a century beyond.

Although coins were struck in lands far across the ocean, the Spanish Government required the use of a mintmark and the assayer's initials to trace the coin's origin and to identify who had overseen the production process. Struck in standard units, coins became an efficient way for the Spanish to export large quantities of bullion back across the Atlantic. Some of the imported coinage was re-melted and produced into European silver coins. The surviving specimens retained remarkably accurate weights and detailed information. As a result of shipwrecks, pilfering from the New World mints, and outright piracy on the high seas, some coins eventually found their way into Texas, as well as other Spanish, French, and English settlements in what is now the United States.

Fig 1.15, An Early Map of New Spain, London, c. 1625.

Attributed to Hessel Gerritsz, Courtesy of the San Jacinto Museum of History, Houston, Texas.

The two pieces shown in figures 1.16 and 1.17 are from the reign of King Philip III (1598-1621). These crudely struck silver pieces show dramatic differences in the amount of detail on each coin.

Fig 1.16, "Piece of Eight" Cob, Philip III
8 *Reales*, Mexico City, c. 1598-1605.

Fig 1.17, "Piece of Eight" Cob, Philip III
8 *Reales*, Mexico City, c. 1598-1605.

Figure 1.17 shows the elaborate coat of arms of Spain and around it the partial legend "PHILIPPVS III. DEI.GRATIA" translated as "Philip the Third, by the Grace of God." It is rare to find a piece with the legend spelled in its entirety.

Fig 1.18, "Piece of Eight" Cob, Philip IV
8 *Reales*, Mexico City, 1659/8.

The 8 *reales* cob in Figure 1.18 bears the date of 1659/8. Although very few coins with full dates have survived, this well-struck Mexico City specimen is known as an over date variety. The date was struck over a 1658 date, as the "8" is barely visible under the "9." The shield design is not completely intact on the obverse, but the bold cross representing the Catholic Church is plainly visible on the reverse. This issue was struck under the authority of King Philip IV.

Fig 1.19, Cob Coinage, Philip V
4 *Reales*, Mexico City, 1714.

The cobs from the reign of King Philip V represent the most commonly found coins bearing all four digits of the date as part of the design. The piece depicted in Figure 1.19 is a 4 *reales*. The obverse was oddly stamped with a die for a coin twice its size, while the reverse (with a cross) appears to have been struck by the correct die. Evidence of bent metal from "clipping" can also be seen on the piece, most notably on the reverse. This coin, dated 1714, was struck four years before the founding of San Antonio de Béxar.

Fig 1.20, "Piece of Eight" Cob, Philip V
8 *Reales*, Mexico City, 1714. Struck with "Royal" dies.

Although the 8 *reales* piece in Figure 1.20 is dated 1714, it shows a remarkable level of detail. This cob was struck on specially prepared dies designed for the minting of "Royals." Royals were presentation pieces, made to prove the quality of the minting to the Viceroy of New Spain or perhaps even to the King. The royal coinage was never designed for circulation, and all examples of denominations larger than a ½ *real* are extremely rare. Regular issue coins bearing the strike from a set of royal dies are most unusual. The remarkable specimen in Figure 1.20 was lost in the 1715 fleet wreck off the coast of southern Florida during a violent hurricane. Almost three centuries later, after being recovered by treasure hunters in the mid 1960s, this rare find resides in a private collection in Houston, Texas.

Fig 1.22, Philip V, King of Spain

Portrait attributed to Miguel Jacinto Melendez.

Fig 1.21, Cob Coinage of Louis I ½ *Real*, Mexico City, c. 1724.

The piece illustrated in Figure 1.21 was specifically minted for circulation in everyday commerce and shows the denomination ½. King Louis I authorized the production of the coin during his eight-month reign on the Spanish throne. Louis I was the teenage son of Philip V, who regained the throne upon the untimely death of his son in 1724.

FUNDING THE SPANISH SETTLEMENTS IN TEXAS

It may be difficult to conceive the wide circulation of the silver coins in the mostly uninhabited wilderness of Texas during the colonial period. At the time, commerce in the area was largely nonexistent and the primary use of the coins was for payment of the Spanish soldiers stationed in mission outposts. Most importantly, these silver coins represented the money that funded the first permanent settlements in Texas. Although the Spanish attempted to establish several settlements in the late 1600s, many of these efforts proved unsuccessful and were later abandoned.

Philip V was the grandson of Louis XIV and the first King of the French Bourbon House to sit on the throne of Spain establishing the present-day line of the monarchy. He reigned from 1700 to 1746.

In the early 1700s, under the rule of King Philip V, detailed plans for the colonization of Texas and the subsequent distribution of money were developed. The funding for the colonization plan would require the distribution of large amounts of silver coins for the experiment to be successful. These plans were conceived in a detailed resolution by the King's general council on August 22, 1715.[12] The discussion of how to implement Spain's colonization plan centered around a long-term strategy which was political as well as evangelical. At the time, present-day Florida was firmly under Spanish control. The western port of Pensacola in Spanish Florida bordered on the French post of Mobile (in present-day Alabama). Heavily fortified French conquests extended along the Mississippi River and included posts at Biloxi (in present-day Mississippi) and what would later become the city of New Orleans (in present-day Louisiana) in 1718. It was important for the Spanish to gain a foothold west of the Mississippi River and especially in what is now Texas by establishing their own colonies. These proposed colonies were meant to check the advances of the French from the territories along the Mississippi River and further into the new possessions of Spain.

Another goal of the colonization plan was to establish trade with the Indians who had grown accustomed to European goods and had developed a fondness for blankets, housewares, western clothing, and liquor. By developing ties with the Indians, Spain hoped to control trade and spread the good word of Christianity. As the report outlined, the Indians were to be conquered "in order that we may civilize them and spread the gospel among them." A meeting was held in Mexico City to implement the plan and initiate a substantial effort to occupy the northern states.[13]

Command of the military expedition was given on September 30, 1715, to Domingo Ramón, a son of the commandant at San Juan Bautista. Another man, Louis Juchereau de St. Denis, the founder of Natchitoches, was appointed the commissary officer and guide for what became known as the Ramón expedition. The evangelical Spaniards with St. Denis, their French guide, soon involved themselves in building several fortifications to protect the young Spanish settlements. The long-term strategic plan which originated in Spain determined that a minimum of six new locations would be necessary.[14] The planned locations included the territory known as the San Francisco de los Tejas, an early mission established in 1690 on the upper Trinity River, and inhabited only by the natives. Another mission was planned on the San Antonio River, still another on the River Bravo de Norte at the Bay of Espiritu Santo (near present-day Matagorda), and two others on the Caudachez and Mississippi Rivers. An unintended long-term side effect of trading with the Indians was their development of a fondness for firearms and weaponry, which rogue traders inevitably brought with them into the new territories.

Money would be needed to purchase the goods and supplies required to construct the presidios and pay for the small groups of soldiers stationed in them. The oddly cut silver coins from the mint at Mexico City provided the money which facilitated the funding of these expeditions. If soldiers, missionaries, and would-be colonists ventured into the wilderness of Texas without preparation in an attempt to build the settlements straight from the native timber and rocks, they risked exposure to the weather and attacks from hostile Indians. Any significant delay in the shipment of supplies into Texas could also jeopardize the expedition. To hasten the construction phase, ships carried pre-cut timbers. When the ships arrived, the timbers could be quickly unloaded, fastened together, and reconstructed for the initial dwellings along with slats and posts provided for that purpose. Following the initial construction, plans for permanent buildings made from suitable rock or limestone available in the area were drawn up by the inhabitants.

As planned out beforehand, each settlement included a presidio, a mission, and a colony of settlers consisting of Spaniards and Indians. Salaries for the men were paid in silver coins, mainly with the 8 *reales* coins commonly referred to as *pesos*. Twenty-five soldiers and five missionaries (who were also soldiers) garrisoned the presidio, each with a salary of 300 *pesos* per annum. Each settlement also contained one officer with a salary of 1,000 *pesos* per annum.[15] A colony of Spanish families settled the community with each family receiving 300 *pesos* annually. Another group of families were Indians, either from Tlascala or from Mexico. Although their residences were typically segregated from the Spanish, each Indian family received a salary of 200 *pesos*. The total cost of an individual permanent settlement would be 15,000 *pesos* per year in silver coin. Much like the English who settled the northeast part of the continent, only those persons who were skilled craftsman and well versed in trades and farming were considered. The Spanish crown furnished the newcomers with tools, plows, and all the instruments needed to ply their trades and develop the community. The Indians served mainly in manual occupations, such as the cultivation of the fields, the cutting of wood, and in the construction of houses.

The Spanish crown provided the colonists with sufficient land for cultivation and the raising of livestock. Ample tracts of land were also set aside for the settlement of the people and their housing, mission building and the accompanying presidios. Many soldiers brought their wives with them, and the Spanish crown encouraged the colonists to spread the word of Christianity to the natives. These women became the first Spanish women in Texas. The Spanish colonies in the New World were employed for pay under the authority of Philip V of Spain, the first King of the French Bourbon House to rule in Madrid. Spain's long-term goal was to settle, civilize and eventually rule these largely virgin lands.

The Spanish government's master plan for the settlement of land in Florida, the areas west of the Mississippi River, and the lands in northern Mexico was very straightforward. With an estimated annual cost of 300,000 *pesos* to the soldiers, priests and settlers, the high production of the silver coins continued to flow northward. If these families were given salaries for ten years as a monetary provision for themselves—to cultivate fields and to raise stock—the settlers could eventually acquire the necessary resources to provide for themselves without any further subsidies from the Spanish crown. If the plan proved successful, a new colony could then be founded and provided for in the same manner at a distance of ten or fifteen leagues from the original ones. With a network of communities successfully linked with one another over a period of one hundred years, Spain would have an unimpeachable claim on the land and a substantial cultural barrier to block the expansion of the French. At the same time, it was thought that many of the Indians would find salvation in Christ and be converted to Christianity.

With a network of communities successfully linked with one another over a period of one hundred years, Spain would have an unimpeachable claim on the land and a substantial cultural barrier to block the expansion of the French.

After extensive preparations, the Ramón expedition reached present-day Texas in 1716 and founded the first permanent Spanish settlements.[16] It proved a difficult undertaking, and the expedition experienced a series of physical and cultural handicaps. The supplies which Ramón and St. Denis brought with them included gifts for the Indians, military equipment, hand tools and various kinds of seeds for the planting of crops.[17] The expedition established four missions and the accompanying settlements. One mission settled near the original site of San Francisco de los Tejas, and another, named Nuestra Señora de los Guadalupe, became modern-day Nacogdoches. In early 1717, a mission was founded in present-day San Augustine (Nuestra Señora de los Dolores) and another east of the Sabine River about fifteen miles from Nachitoches, Louisiana, named San Miguel de Los Adeas.

Unfortunately for the expedition, budget cuts from Mexico City soon imposed additional hardships in gaining a foothold for their missionary work and the settlement of the area. An agent for the Spanish crown reduced the expedition's allowance for gifts to the Indians by 40 percent, probably as a result of the loss of the 1715 treasure fleet, which was sunk by a hurricane off the coast of southern Florida. This reduction in the allowance for gifts greatly impaired the initial friendliness of the natives. As any experienced explorer knew, gifts to potentially hostile native peoples were not the area in which expenses should be reduced. While the Caddo Indians at first enthusiastically received their new neighbors, it quickly became apparent that they would not embrace the Roman Catholic faith of the missionaries.

INFLUENCES OF PHILIP V IN TEXAS

The influence of King Philip V of Spain continued to dominate the affairs of the Spanish speaking peoples of the New World. During his rule, a presidio was built in San Fernando de Bejar in 1722, which housed the Spanish military and the presidio captain of the region.[18] Fortunately for these early missions, the Marqués de Valero became the new viceroy over the region in 1717 and made the personal support of the missions one of his primary objectives. He appointed Martín de Alarcón as Governor of Texas in 1717, and directed Alarcón to lead an expedition with the purpose of creating a mission, presidio and a civilian settlement on the banks of the San Antonio River. This new community would hopefully link the new missions to the older Franciscan missions to the east.

Once again, the oddly shaped silver 8 *reales* pieces minted in Mexico City became the funding mechanism for outfitting another expedition to Texas in 1718. Alarcón crossed the Rio Grande in April 1718 with soldiers, missionaries and ten families recruited from other areas in northern Mexico. On May 1, 1718, he founded the mission named San Antonio de Valero, later known as the Alamo. Within days, construction began on a presidio approximately a mile west of the new mission. Alarcón established Presidio de Béxar to protect the Mission de Valero, which served as a home to missionaries and the local Indians whom the Spanish hoped to convert to Catholicism. Presidio de Béxar is the present-day Spanish Governor's Palace. Stonemasons and blacksmiths constructed the mission and were paid with the silver coins appropriated for the expedition. The remnants of a hurricane destroyed the original mission structure in 1724.[19] The work to build a new chapel at the mission began in 1744. The chapel design had an ornamental front and two towers, but the building collapsed twelve years later. The work on what is now the Alamo chapel began in 1758. This structure survived to become the scene of the famous siege in 1836. Homes were built around the presidio, and the little community named itself Villa de Béxar.

In order to ensure the villa's long-term survival, the king financed a later settlement expedition which included a volunteer group from the Canary Islands, sent for the purpose of asserting Spain's claims in the New World. The group arrived at the Spanish presidio in 1731 after a journey which lasted almost a year, with stops by boat in Havana and Vera Cruz. The colonists then traveled overland through the Mexican town of Saltillo to San Antonio de Valero. Upon arrival at the mission, they were provided with supplies, livestock and allowances of goods for one year. The villagers named their new settlement Villa de San Fernando in honor of Philip's son, Don Fernando, the Prince of Asturias who succeeded his father in 1746. The portrait of Don Fernando, better known as King Ferdinand VI, was immortalized on the gold coins issued from 1747-1759 during his reign. The name of the little township of San Fernando de Béxar which grew around the early mission was legally changed to San Antonio de Béxar in 1837.

Fig 1.23, "Piece of Eight" Cob, Philip V 8 *Reales*, Mexico City, c. 1730.

The well-struck example in Figure 1.23 portrays the mintmark "Mo," and the assayer's initial "G" to the left of the shield. The bold cross representing the Catholic Church with the familiar castles and lions dominates the reverse. The excessive wear is indicative of decades of circulation.

Fig 1.24, "Piece of Eight" Cob, Philip V 8 *Reales*, Mexico City, c. 1700-1732.

The sea-salvaged piece in Figure 1.24 was found on South Padre Island, Texas. King Philip V added the trademark French Fleur-de-Lys to the Spanish coat of arms (visible at the bottom of the shield). This cob represents a long-forgotten example of original Spanish "Texana."

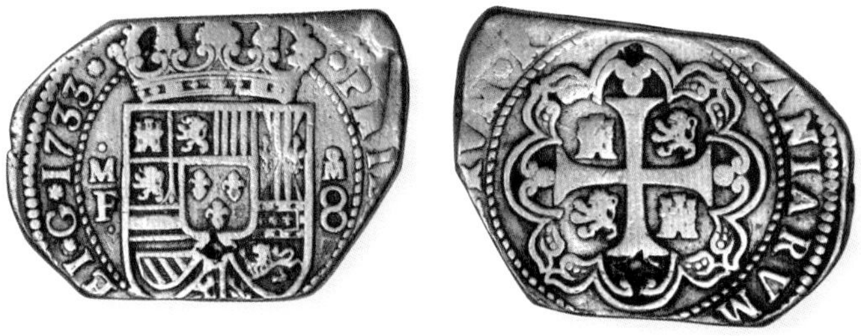

Fig 1.25, "Piece of Eight" Klippe, Philip V 8 *Reales*, Mexico City, 1733.

Mexico began to implement a much higher standard for manufacture of silver coins in 1733. Figure 1.25 shows these machine-stamped coins, a dramatic improvement over the old hand-stamped silver coinage. These coins are known as "klippes" because their edges were trimmed to conform to the standard weight in silver which was required by the assayer. The assayer's initials "MF" and denomination "8" were also standardized on the reverse. Figure 1.25 shows one of the first examples of machine-stamped money in the New World.

Fig 1.26, Casting the Ingots.

An Illustrated History of the U.S. Mint.

Fig 1.27, Rolling Machine.

An Illustrated History of the U.S. Mint.

THE MILLED SPANISH PILLAR DOLLAR

Under the influential rule of Philip V, the first milled coins were struck at the Spanish mints in the New World.[20] This practice refined the standard of exchange for the export of silver coinage from Mexico and South America, and these coins, along with their smaller 4, 2, and 1 *real* pieces, circulated throughout the world. In addition to staking their claim to vast regions in the Americas, the Spanish crown gave birth to the first round coins of the New World, the *Columnario* or Pillar Dollar, marking the beginning of a new era. Since there had been widespread tampering with money through the clipping of the edges, the coins were to be made almost exactly the same so evidence of tampering would be much easier to detect. In essence, the introduction of a milled edge was designed as a security feature for the coins.

Great attention to detail was made in the casting of the ingots and the rolling of the strips of silver from which the planchets were cut. The precision manufacturing process for the planchets (from which the coins were struck) can be seen in figures 1.26 through 1.29. The Spanish colonial mints in Latin America produced high-quality silver coins that were readily accepted around the world. Six decades later, the first U.S. mint in Philadelphia replicated this process for the first silver coins produced by the United States.

The precision manufacturing process insured the security edge, uniformity, and the subsequent worldwide acceptance of the pieces as a world trade coin. These milled Spanish dollars were not really dollars at all, but had the standardized size and weight upon which the United States later modeled their silver dollars in 1794. Although the U.S. coins were of similar size,

Fig 1.28, Cutting Machine.

An Illustrated History of the U.S. Mint.

Fig 1.30, Milled Spanish Pillar Dollar (Shown 1.5 x actual size) 8 *Reales*, Mexico City, Philip V, 1735.

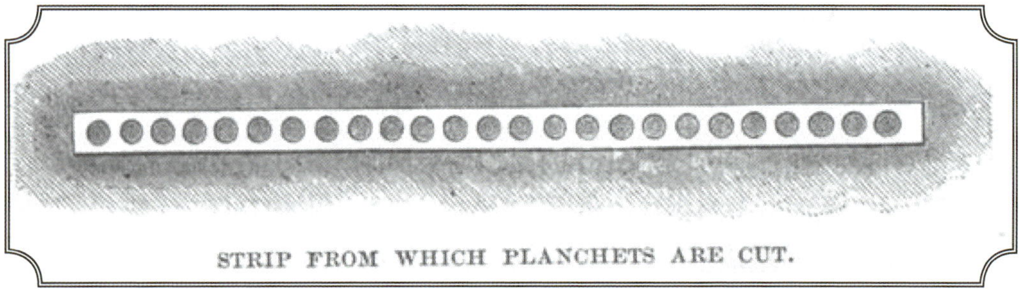

Fig 1.29, Planchet Strip.

An Illustrated History of the U.S. Mint.

they contained a slightly lower content of silver and were met with some reluctance as a world trade coin in the first decade of their existence.

The piece in Figure 1.30 is an example of the first type of round milled coinage struck exclusively in the New World from 1732-1772.[21] Note the name of the king (Philip V) boldly displayed on the reverse. The coin is dated 1735 and was struck in Mexico City. Note the fancy script for the number "5" and the attractive color toning or patina which the coin acquired over time.

Pillar Dollars were so named because the obverse features the Pillars of Hercules (the cliffs of North Africa and the Rock of Gibraltar), the entrance to the Atlantic Ocean, once believed to be the limits of the world.[22] At the center of the obverse are two globes, representing the old and new worlds, with a crown symbolizing the Spanish kingdom above. The pillars are draped with the words "PLUS" and "ULTRA," meaning "more beyond." Early European maps often inscribed "ne plus ultra" or "no more beyond," as the Atlantic often stood for an exit to the unknown. Underneath the pillars are waves which represented the distance between the worlds.

The coin in Figure 1.30 makes a clear statement: Over the waves, and beyond the Pillars of Hercules, a new world exists, and it lies under the rule (or the crown) of the Kingdom of Spain. The legend towards the top of the obverse side reads "VTRAQUE VNUM" or "both make one." This was a warning to other world powers not to trespass in Spain's New World, united with the old. The reverse (or tails side) message is even stronger. Similar to the design on the cobs, the crowned coat of arms of Castilla and León is depicted, but set inside a Bourbon Shield. The name of the king (Philip V) dominates the beginning of the encircling legend around the periphery of the reverse. When translated into English the legend, including all abbreviations, reads: "Philip V, by the Grace of God, King of Spain and the Indies." The Assayer's initials "MF" and denomination "8" can be seen to the left and right of the shield.

Figure 1.31 shows an example dated 1757 and was struck in Mexico City. As noted on the reverse, it now reads "Ferdinand VI, by the Grace of God, King of Spain and the Indies." Ferdinand VI was the son of Philip V, whose reign ended in 1746. After Maria Barbara of Braganza, Ferdinand's loyal wife and companion of twenty-nine years, died in 1758, the King was left in a melancholy depression. He refused to dress or shave, and wondered around his park in a nightgown, refusing to pay attention to matters of state.[23] Ferdinand died in 1759, almost exactly a year following the death of his beloved wife. Ferdinand was succeeded by his half brother, who took the name of Charles III.

Fig 1.31, Milled Spanish Pillar Dollar (Shown 1.5 x actual size) 8 *Reales*, Mexico City, Ferdinand VI, 1757.

Fig 1.32, Milled Spanish Pillar Dollar (Shown 1.5 x actual size) 8 *Reales*, Mexico City, Charles III, 1761.

The example in Figure 1.32, dated 1761 from Mexico City, bears the name of "Carlous III, King of Spain and the Indies." Charles III was the son of Philip V and a half brother of Ferdinand VI. He was the last of the Spanish Kings to have his name grace the pillar coinage. Charles III later replaced the familiar pillars and waves design with a portrait of himself. The milled Spanish 8 *reales* pieces were issued from the Mexico City mint until 1771.

SPANISH INFLUENCES ON AMERICA

As the Spaniards gained new wealth from the ore deposits in Mexico and South America, they minted massive amounts of milled coins under improving technology. Mexico in particular led the world in silver production for centuries, and virtually all of the silver for 285 years was struck into the form of coins under Spanish law.[24] These coins were widely circulated and became the monetary standard worldwide for hundreds of years.

CURRENCY OF THE CONTINENTAL CONGRESS

Spanish Texas changed very little from the time of the Ramon and St. Denis expeditions in the early 1730s, to the days of the early 1760s.[25] While the mission settlement of San Antonio de Béxar thrived, it only contained about one thousand residents. In the east, the communities around the missions at Nacogdoches, San Augustine, and Los Adaes held fewer than five hundred residents and had little success in converting the Indians to Christianity. Mexico became a tremendous source of economic wealth to its mother country across the Atlantic, while Texas served primarily as a buffer zone against French Louisiana and as a field for Spain's missionary work. By contrast, England's North American colonies prospered. Due to their relatively short supply of silver, the colonists used paper money as a substitute for hard currency. The acceptance of Spanish silver coins became so widespread that the thirteen original American colonies issued their first Federal paper money as promises to pay in Spanish Milled Dollars.

This "Continental Currency" commenced with notes authorized by the May 10, 1775, session of the Continental Congress.[26] The notes were essential for financing the American Revolution, and were to be redeemed with taxes levied by the individual United Colonies. The resolution determined eleven issue dates and the Continental Currency circulated side-by-side with the colonial paper money issued by the individual colonies and later by individual states. The denominations issued were numerous. Between 1775-1778, denominations of $1, $2, $3, $4, $5, $6, $7, $8, $20, $30, $40, $50, $60 and several fractional notes were issued, resulting in hundreds of varieties.[27] All these pieces were replaced by federally-backed state issues on March 18, 1780, guaranteed by the United States.

The notes in figures 1.33 and 1.34 were printed by Hall and Sellers in Philadelphia. They used various combinations of border cuts, emblems, hand-set type and nature back print designs popularized by Ben Franklin in the mid-1750s. The thick rag paper had mica flakes and blue fibers imbedded in it as anti-counterfeiting device.

While Continental Currency circulated widely in the East, these notes quickly lost their purchasing power because of the inability of the colonial governments to deliver the promised pieces of Spanish silver on demand. Because the people much preferred payment in the large silver coins, the chronic depreciation of the paper medium in the newly formed United States of America resulted in the phrase "not worth a Continental." It was a hard lesson which was destined to be forgotten and then learned again two generations later by the Republic of Texas.

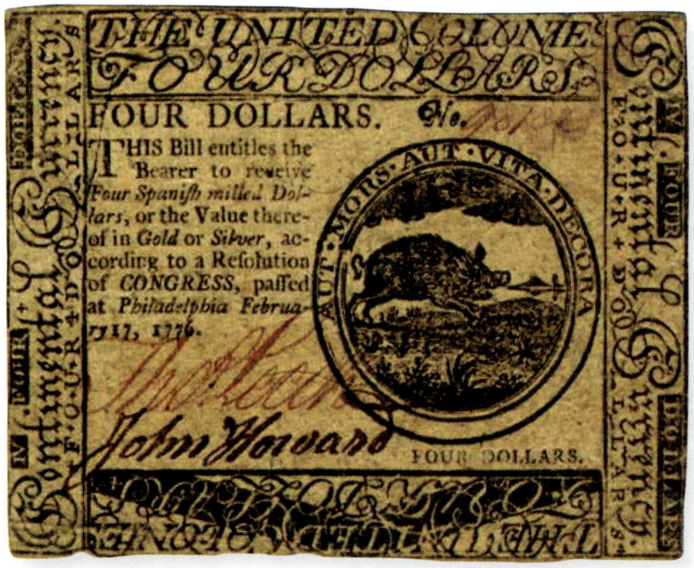

Fig 1.33, $4 Continental Currency The United Colonies, February 17, 1776.

THE UNITED COLONIES, FOUR DOLLARS
This Bill entitles the Bearer to receive Four Spani[s]h Milled Dollars, or the Value thereof in Gold or Silver, according to a Re[s]olution of CONGRESS, Pa[ss]ed at Philadelphia February 17, 1776. Signed by Tho[mas] Leech and John Howard.

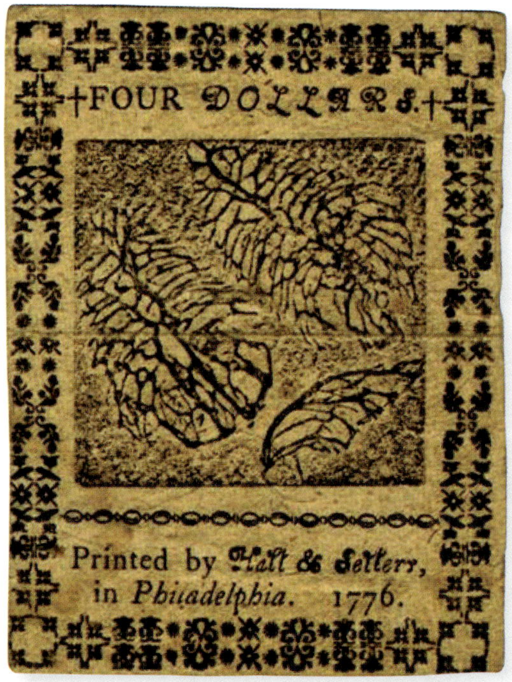

Fig 1.34, $4 Nature print reverse:

FOUR DOLLARS, Printed by Hall and Sellers, in Philadelphia, 1776.

INFLUENCES ON THE UNITED STATES

The Spanish 8 *reales* pieces were so widely accepted as the monetary standard of the time period that in 1792, when the New York Stock Exchange was founded under a buttonwood tree at the corner of Wall and Broad Street, a system was devised for stock prices to be denominated and quoted in "eighths of a dollar." This reference to the "pieces of eight" is still used on Wall Street more than 200 years later. The American expression "two bits" (for $0.25) references the Spanish standard as well. If a Spanish dollar was split into quarters, each part would consist of two "bits" or *reales*.[28] All sports fans remember the phrase: "Two bits, four bits, six bits a dollar…all for our team stand up and holler!"

THE ORIGINS OF THE DOLLAR SIGN

Upon close examination of the Pillar Dollars, it is widely thought that the familiar dollar sign ($) had its origin from a portion of the design on these coins. The symbol was first used in North America in the late 1760s.[29] In the following decade, the dollar sign became widely used as a symbol for the 8 *reales* pieces used by English-speaking merchants conducting business in the ports of New Orleans, Mobile and Pensacola. These merchants carried out much of their business in Spanish milled dollars, the standard method of cash payments for trade in the Americas.

In Figure 1.37, notice the scroll on the Pillars of Hercules, wrapped in an "S" fashion, bearing the legend "Ultra" at right. Although this evidence is not conclusive, the lasting influences of these early Spanish "pieces of eight" or "pillar dollars" seems to have transcended through the generations.

From the earliest U.S. dollars to references on Wall Street more than 200 years later, the pieces of eight influenced not only the founders of the United States and the Republic of Texas, but virtually the entire Western Hemisphere. Even something as familiar as the dollar sign is thought to trace its roots back to these early silver pieces of eight.[30] The familiar design features, strict standards for weight and fineness of the silver content as well as their wide circulation, made the milled Spanish Pillar Dollar widely accepted in world commerce. These coins were recognized as legal tender in the United States until the year 1857.

Although these coins represented the Spanish King's warning to other nations not to trespass in Spain's New World, the warning went unheeded in the struggle for riches and new land. In the late 1700s, the three largest powers in Europe (Spain, France, and England) had extensive holdings in the Americas and the West Indies. The Europeans routinely attacked and preyed on each other, especially the Spanish, whose ships were the fattest, richest trade ships on the seas. The vessels carried sugar, coffee, and spices from the Indies, cotton and large quantities of freshly minted silver, and gold booty from the port of Vera Cruz. The ships traveled across the Gulf of Mexico, around the tip of Florida, and across the Atlantic Ocean before reaching Europe, giving pirates and marauders ample time to seize the wealthy vessels.

Charles III is often regarded as the greatest Bourbon King of Spain and was quite popular with the people. During much of his adult life he worked diligently on the affairs of state, which had long-lasting implications for Mexico and Texas.

Fig 1.37, Origins of the $ Sign.

NEW SPAIN UNDER CHARLES III

In 1759, Charles III was thrust onto the world stage when he succeeded his half brother, Ferdinand VI, to the throne. He initiated several foreign policy initiatives which had lasting effects on northern Mexico, including present-day Texas. Charles was a strong, intelligent ruler who renewed a strategic military alliance between France and Spain in 1761 known as the Bourbon Family Contract.[31] Spain declared war against the English on January 11, 1762, resulting in a shift of power on the map of America. In order to preserve the claim on Cuba following the war, Spain willingly ceded all interests in Florida to England upon the signing of a peace treaty on November 3, 1762. On the same day, as part of a broad settlement, King Louis XIV of France transferred all of French Louisiana to Spain. Although French citizens and militia units in New Orleans opposed the transfer of power and resisted Spanish rule, it soon became apparent that reorganizing the northern frontier of New Spain (including present-day Texas) became strategically important in creating a buffer zone against the English.

Fig 1.38, King Charles III of Spain.

The San Jacinto Museum of History, Houston, Texas.

Charles III realized that only sweeping reforms would protect Spain's expanded interests in the Western Hemisphere. Among the king's most significant undertakings in New Spain following the war was the organization of a regular army in Mexico, structured into colonial militia units. This initiative was followed by Charles' insistence that Marqués de Rubí visit the southwest and report on the state of the Spanish missions. The mission system had been established in Texas more than four decades before, but no comprehensive report on their status had ever been generated.

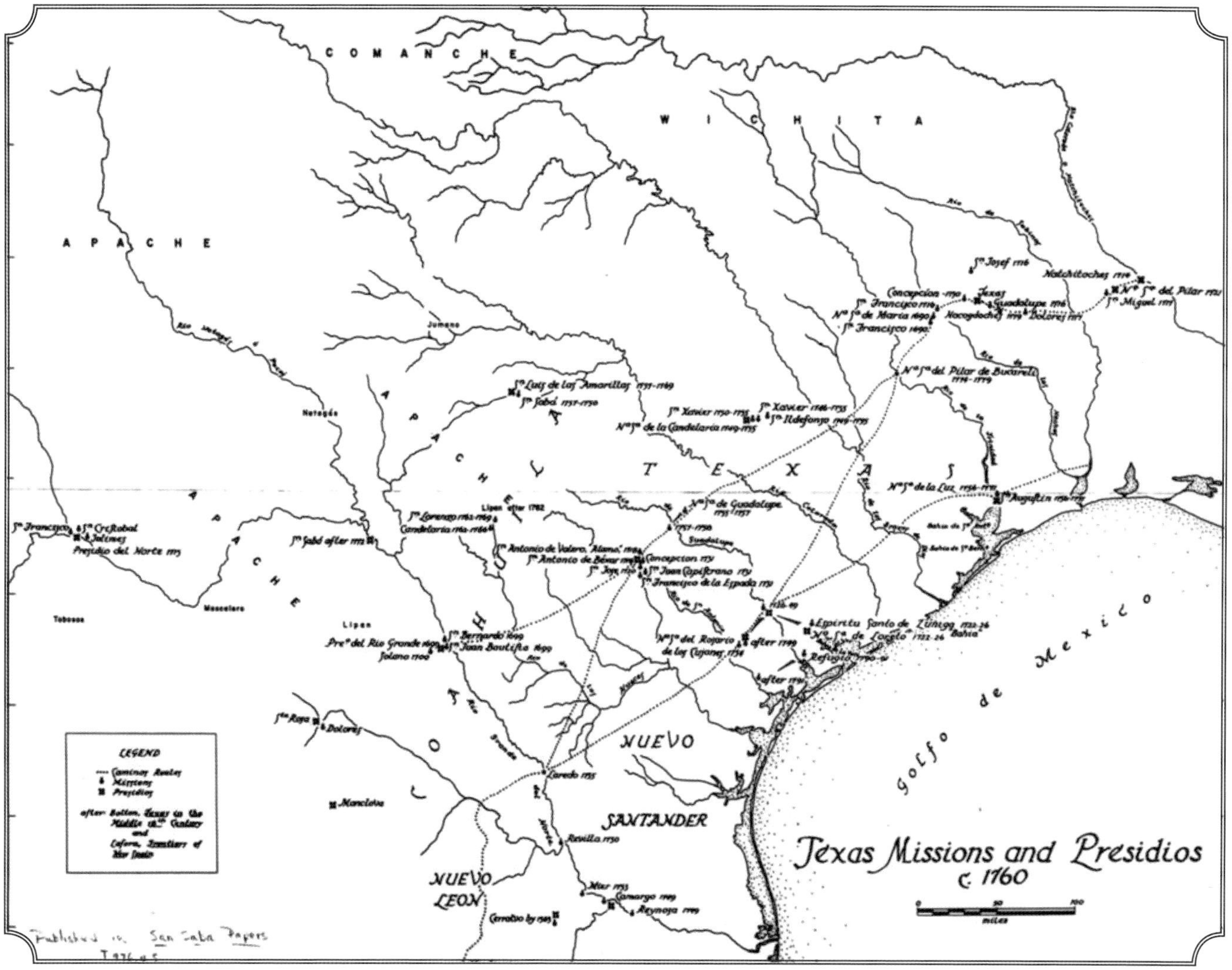

Fig 1.39, Texas Missions and Presidios c. 1760 (Map).

Courtesy of the Houston Metropolitan Research Center, Houston Public Library, Houston, Texas.

The map in Figure 1.39 illustrates the extensive network of missions and presidios in Texas which were visited by the Rubí expedition beginning in 1767. The dotted lines mark the long dusty road which traversed the land from Laredo through San Antonio de Béxar and Nacogdoches to Natchitoches, Louisiana. The upper path became known as the old San Antonio Road.

Rubí was charged by the king to inspect the presidios in Spain's holdings from the Gulf of California to Louisiana. Charles instructed Rubí to report on the garrisons, the status of the guards, and to determine the fairness of prices and the economic structure surrounding each mission and settlement in the area. He was also to examine and determine whether the remote military outposts remained in the best interests of the government, if the locations seemed effective in the defense against hostile Indians, and whether or not the missions successfully converted the native Indians to Christianity. After first visiting New Mexico, Sonora and Coahuila, the Marqués de Rubí arrived at the mission of San Sabá in July 1767. He then proceeded to the heart of the mission system in San Antonio de Béxar on August 24, 1767.

He found the presidio at Béxar to be surprisingly well maintained, with each of the five nearby missions to be substantial hubs for the small but distinct settlements which had grown around them. By contrast, he found the missions in the eastern region deplorable with ineffective military strength, widespread corruption, and no evidence of any converted Indians.

In short, Rubí determined that the mission system was a drain on the financial resources of Spain, much of which now originated from the mints in Mexico City and in South America. Rubí also found the settlements to be completely ineffective at defense, and predicted that the region would be vulnerable to the aggressive Anglo settlers moving westward from the English settlements of the northeast.

After his lengthy journey through Spain's holdings, Rubí filed a detailed report, the basis of which brought a royal order from Charles III and sweeping changes for northern Mexico. Charles issued the "New Regulations for Presidios" on September 10, 1772. The regulations called for the abandonment of all missions and presidios in Texas except for those at San Antonio de Béxar and La Bahía, the strengthening of San Antonio by designating it as the capital of the state, and the removal of soldiers and settlers from the eastern portion of the region. The document also implemented a new Indian policy aimed at establishing good relations with the northern nations at the expense of the Apaches. The removal of soldiers from the east had the long-term effect of ensuring an unimpeded gathering place for Anglo revolutionaries in Nacogdoches.

Although the inspection of the mission system was of the utmost importance to Charles III, his strong interest in the northern province of New Spain was not limited purely to political and military matters. Charles was not only a capable administrator, but he also possessed a wide range of other interests including the native flora of the conquered lands. As the King, he developed a particular interest in the native plants and animals of Texas.[32] In the mid 1770s, the King commissioned Teodoro de Croix on at least two occasions to send domesticated buffalo from the area to Spain at the king's expense. A male and female, both presumed to be calves, died in transit across the Atlantic in 1778. Croix tried again in 1779, after both male and female specimens about six months in age were captured and transported to Chihuahua, Mexico. These Spanish explorers were undoubtedly the most rugged of characters to have fulfilled the assignment, and this exercise of roping and capturing two live buffalo on the plains of Texas may have been the first rodeo event in Texas. As if capturing the buffalo wasn't difficult enough, Charles' agents also captured deer in New Mexico and shipped them southward with the buffalo. These unusual examples of native wildlife were intended purely for the King's pleasure.

These Spanish explorers were undoubtedly the most rugged of characters to have fulfilled the assignment, and this exercise of roping and capturing two live buffalo on the plains of Texas may have been the first rodeo event in Texas.

PORTRAIT COINAGE OF NEW SPAIN

In 1772, Spain re-designed the 8 *reales* pieces so that not only the name of the king appeared on them, but the familiar "Pillars and Waves" were replaced by a portrait of King Charles III wearing a Roman style armor and a hair ribbon.[33] The Latin spelling of Charles (Carolus) was used on the coins. This new design was also imprinted on the heavier gold coinage (the 8 *escudos* denomination) which are commonly called *doubloons*.[34] The legend formerly on the reverse, now surrounds the portrait on the obverse of the coin: "Carolus III, by the Grace of God, King of Spain and the Indies."

Fig 1.40, 8 *Reales*, Mexico City, Charles III, 1788.

The boldly struck, uncirculated example shown in Figure 1.40 was made in Mexico City in 1788. The portrait of Charles (Carolus) III appeared from 1772-1789, while the portrait of his son and successor, Charles (Carolus) IV, appeared on the coins from 1789-1808.

When Charles III died on December 14, 1788, his second son Charles IV, was elevated to the throne after the elder son was declared an imbecile. The younger Charles did not possess his father's keen intellect and strong grasp of world affairs.[35] He was also said to be intellectually sluggish and quite credulous. As happens so often in history when a strong ruler is succeeded by a weak one, the balance of power continued to shift away from Spain, with ramifications for both Europe and North America. The emergence of the United States, finalized by the Treaty of Paris in 1783, brought an influx of Anglos into the vital port city of New Orleans during the next two decades. Following the death of Charles III, it took more than three months for word of his death to reach New Spain. From 1789-1790, the mint at Mexico City continued to strike coins with Charles III's portrait, but changed the legend on the coins to "CAROLUS IIII" to mark the reign of the new king.

Fig 1.41, 8 ***Reales***, **Mexico City, Charles IIII, 1791.**

The example of an 8 *reales* piece in Figure 1.41 exhibits the portrait of Charles' son, who was crowned as the new King of Spain in late 1788. Although his name graced the money in Europe immediately following the death of his father, his portrait was not received by the people through the coinage in New Spain until 1791.

Fig 1.42, 8 *Reales*, Mexico City, Charles IIII, 1805.

Figure 1.42 shows a later portrait of Charles IV. He was perceived as a weak king in the eyes of the people, and popular protests were later held in Spain to renounce his rule.

SPAIN LOSES ITS GRIP ON MEXICO AND TEXAS

As king, Charles IV developed only a passing interest in the affairs of state and was not a very active or competent leader. Consequently, his wife, Maria Amelia of Saxony, a vicious and coarse woman, and her lover, Minister Manuel de Godoy, largely attended to the king's policy decisions. Surprisingly, the king seemed to accept the situation, and he had an amicable relationship with his wife's lover for most of his life.

Following a palace revolution at the city of Aranjuez in March 1808, an unruly mob forced Charles IV to abdicate the throne to his son, the young prince of Asturias, who took the name of Ferdinand VII.[36] After years of rule by a useless Charles IV, the handsome twenty-four-year-old Ferdinand was enthusiastically acclaimed by the Spanish people as their king. The deposed Charles IV sought a reinstatement of the crown and appealed to Napoleon Bonaparte, the Emperor of France for help. Unknown to Charles IV, Ferdinand VII had already conspired against his father, and in an effort to form an alliance with France was persuaded to cross the French border and meet with Bonaparte. It was a poor decision that created an opportunity for Napoleon to envelope Spain in turmoil that had far reaching consequences across the Atlantic Ocean.

Fig 1.43, Napoleon Bonaparte.

Author's Collection.

In early 1808, the French maintained a seaport in Perpignan, a town in the Pyrenees-Orientales area of southern France, located a few miles west of the Mediterranean Sea. France was at war with the British, but remained friendly with Spain. Napoleon Bonaparte sought to close the ports in Portugal, which were still open to trade and supplying England.[37] Knowing that the Spanish kingdom had no love for their western neighbor, Napoleon sought permission from Manuel de Godoy to move French troops across Spain to effectively blockade Portugal. Napoleon used this ruse to create an illusion of being a strong military ally of Spain and Charles IV. Moving ships from Perpignan in France to Barcelona, on the Spanish coast, with an additional 100,000 troops marching through the mainland, the French seized the forts on the Spanish frontier.[38] By February 29, 1808, rather than capturing the Portuguese ports, French troops instead captured Barcelona. Within days French soldiers had entered Madrid and seized control of the city. Although Ferdinand VII ascended to the throne under pressure from Napoleon, the young king was forced to abdicate the throne back to his father only a few months later on May 6, 1808. In turn, Charles resigned his rights to Joseph Bonaparte, the brother of the Emperor of France.

By June 6, 1808, Napoleon claimed Spain in the name of France, imprisoned Ferdinand VII and installed his brother Joseph on the throne of Spain. The invasion of Spain and the imprisonment of the young king sparked a broad European conflict known as the Peninsular War (1808-1814). Given the lack of high-speed communication during the period, it was more than a month before news of the coup reached Mexico City and the other mints in the Americas. The French occupation of Spain sparked a bloody war of resistance in Spain, and the government operated through a central *junta* (or government) in Seville, acting in the name of Ferdinand VII. While this exiled government governed in the name of Ferdinand, the principals established a new Constitution in 1812 which reduced the king's absolute power, and granted freedom of the press in all matters except religion.[39] These events in Spain threw the political system in Mexico into a state of flux, and provoked mixed reactions among the largely Mexican-born population of New Spain known as the *criollos*.

Predictably, the Spanish colonies in the New World never recognized the rule of Joseph Bonaparte as the King of Spain. Throughout the Spanish empire, the name of the beloved but untested Ferdinand VII became the rallying cry of the royalists (those loyal to the mother kingdom). The Spanish mints in the Western Hemisphere responded to this political crisis in Europe by stamping a likeness of Ferdinand on the coins, although engravers had no official portrait of Ferdinand upon which to base their design. These coins represented the mints defiance of Bonaparte and their unity towards the mother country and its true king. These coins are now known as the fantasy portraits of Ferdinand VII.

Fig 1.44, Ferdinand VII.

Benson Latin American Collection, University of Texas Libraries.

Fig 1.45, Armored Bust or "Fantasy" Portrait

8 *Reales*, Mexico City, Ferdinand VII, 1809.

Sometimes called an armored bust or "fantasy" portrait, Figure 1.45 displays a coin bearing a portrait of the imprisoned king based on a painting of him as a young boy. It was struck in Mexico City in 1809. A variety of likenesses of Ferdinand VII appeared on Mexican coins from 1808-1821.

Fig 1.46, Young Bust or "Proper" Portrait 8 *Reales*, Mexico City, Ferdinand VII, 1811.

Fig 1.47, 8 *Escudos* Cob, Mexico City, Philip V, 1714.

The coin in Figure 1.46 portrays Ferdinand VII, "King of Spain and the Indies," showing a young bust or "proper" portrait of the king. The image on the obverse was taken from a canvas portrait shipped to the New World for use by the engravers. It depicts a much more realistic likeness of the revered but untested young king. Ferdinand was restored to the throne of Spain in 1813.

GOLD IN THE SPANISH EMPIRE

The use of gold coins in the northern areas of Mexico began much later than the use of the silver coins. The first gold coins were struck on December 22, 1679, under the authority of King Charles II of Spain who ruled until 1700. Very few, if any, of the earlier coins circulated into the area which later became Texas since the region was primarily populated by Indians at that time. The early scattering of Spanish missions did not begin in earnest until the following century with the founding of Nacogdoches in 1716, San Fernando de Béxar in 1718, and the original site of Presidio La Bahía in 1721.

The earliest 8 *escudo* cobs were first struck in Mexico City in 1691 for export to Spain. None of these coins were ever intended to circulate or be used in any Mexican states. Upon reaching Spain, Philip V and his predecessors claimed a large percentage (usually 20 percent) of the incoming treasure as taxes.[40] This percentage became known as the Royal Fifth. As the production of gold coins continued into the early eighteenth century, pirating, shipwrecks and other events caused many of the gold pieces to find their way into commerce along the Gulf Coast. It was not uncommon for the manifests of the treasure fleets to routinely understate the value of their precious cargoes. The routine bribery of Spain's port officials became a way of life, as it did in major ports around the world.

The 8 *escudo* gold cob in Figure 1.47 bears the legend and a full date around the shield. The mint mark "Mo" and the assayer initial "J" for José de León, is plainly visible at left. The detailed relief of the Spanish Crown can be seen atop the intricate Bourbon shield, a rarity on these crudely struck coins. At right is the denomination, VIII. The reverse features the bold cross of the Catholic Church with a partial legend around the periphery. This *doubloon* was recovered from the 1715 wreck of the Spanish treasure fleet off the coast of southern Florida in the 1960s.

The 1715 Spanish fleet, loaded with almost two years of production from the mints, sailed from the Mexican port of Vera Cruz along the Gulf Coast past the present locations of Corpus Christi and Galveston. The ships continued east to rendezvous with other Spanish vessels in Havana, Cuba. This long and circuitous route allowed the fleet to avoid the dangerous infestation of pirates then active and rampant in the western Caribbean. Once in Cuba, the ships were loaded with supplies and readied for the long trip across the Atlantic to Spain.[41] Following their departure from Cuba in late July 1715, a powerful hurricane devastated the fleet and wrecked ten of the eleven ships, sending more than $14,000,000 in registered treasure to the bottom of the sea. The event became one of the greatest maritime disasters of all time. Although salvage teams recovered part of the treasure, the financial loss to Spain plunged the economy of Europe into a two year depression.

Following a design change in 1732, the images of the Spanish kings remained on the gold 8 *escudos* coinage for many years, and the coins circulated as *doubloons*. In the Americas, the term *doubloon* refers to the larger, 8 *escudos* gold coins. The word *doubloon,* derived from the Spanish word *doblón,* means "double." This term was the ratio between the *reales* denomination in silver and the *escudo* denomination in gold: two 8 *reales* coins equaled one *escudo*, four 8 *reales* coins equaled two *escudos*, and so forth until sixteen large silver 8 *reales* coins (locally called *pesos*) could be traded for one gold *doubloon*.[42]

These 8 *escudo* pieces, or gold *doubloons,* were widely accepted throughout the world. The coins portrayed the busts of Philip V from 1732-1747, Ferdinand VI from 1747-1759, a short-lived bust of Charles III from 1760-1761, Charles III from 1762-1789, Charles IIII from 1789-1808, and Ferdinand VII from 1808-1821.

Fig 1.48, 8 *Escudos*, Mexico City, Philip V, 1744.

The obverse of the 8 *escudo* coin in Figure 1.48 bears the portrait of Philip V, the dominant king who ushered in Spain's role as a world superpower in the first half of the eighteenth century. The reverse depicts the familiar shield set inside a chain of the Order of the Golden Fleece. The reverse legend, "INITIUM SAPIENTIAE TIMOR DOMINI," translates as "the beginning of wisdom is the fear of the Lord."[43]

Fig 1.49, 8 *Escudos*, Mexico City, Ferdinand VI, 1755.

Figure 1.49 presents the obverse of an 8 *escudo* coin bearing the portrait of Ferdinand VI, for whom the town of San Fernando de Béxar was named. On the reverse, we again see the familiar shield set inside a chain of the Order of the Golden Fleece. The reverse legend was changed under Ferdinand to "NOMINA MAGNA SEQUOR," which translates as "I succeed great names."

Fig 1.50, 8 *Escudos*, Mexico City, Charles III, 1761.

The obverse of the 8 *escudo* coin in Figure 1.50 bears the portrait of Charles III. This "young bust" portrait was only used in 1760-1761 and was replaced with a larger portrait of the king in 1762. Like the gold pieces which preceded it, this coin was manufactured for export to Spain. It also bears the legend "NOMINA MAGNA SEQUOR," or "I succeed great names" on the reverse. Charles III is perhaps best remembered as the last of the great Spanish Kings of the era.

Fig 1.51, 8 *Escudos*, Santiago, Chile, Charles IIII, 1791
With portrait of Charles III.

The 1791 8 *escudos* piece in Figure 1.51 was struck in Santiago, Chile. It bears the name of Carlos, or Charles IV (abbreviated as Carol IIII) and the incorrect portrait of his father, Charles III. Although the monarch had changed, it was indicative of the glacial speed with which a portrait of the current king could be transported across the Atlantic for use by the engravers. Several early gold coins from South American mints have been discovered by metal detectors in Texas.[44]

Fig 1.52, 8 *Escudos*, Mexico City, Charles IIII, 1806.

The obverse of the 8 *escudo* coin in Figure 1.52 bears the correct portrait of Charles IIII, the inept King of Spain who succeeded his much respected ancestors to the throne. The reverse legend reads "IN UTROQ FELIX AUSPICE DEO," which translates as "Both happy under God's guidance."

Fig 1.53, 8 *Escudos*, Mexico City, Ferdinand VII, 1810.

In Figure 1.53, the obverse of the 8 *escudo* coin bears the "fantasy" portrait of Ferdinand VII, who was imprisoned in France at the time this coin was struck in Mexico City. The reverse legend again reads "IN UTROQ FELIX AUSPICE DEO," or "Both happy under God's guidance." By the time this coin was minted, rebel factions were fighting the Spanish-controlled government in a war of independence, determined to form an independent Mexican Republic.

Fig 1.54, Father Miguel Hidalgo y Costilla.

The San Jacinto Museum of History, Houston, Texas.

Although there were shorter-lived gold 8 *escudos* coins bearing the portrait of Agustín Iturbide in 1823, and gold eagle 8 *escudos* pieces from the northern Mexican mints during the period of Mexican control beginning in 1821, the coins bearing portraits of the old Spanish rulers were mass produced and had the highest survival rate. These coins paid for the importation of European goods. In Spanish Texas, they were most likely used for larger transactions and important acts of bribery among the bureaucrats and military officials which dominated the system of missions.

THE MEXICAN WAR FOR INDEPENDENCE, 1810-1821

Beginning in 1811, a proper canvas portrait of King Ferdinand VII was made available to the die engravers in Mexico and new designs were used on coins struck at the Mexico City mint. By this time, Mexicans had grown tired of centuries of Spanish rule, and the war for independence had already started. But the Mexican mints continued to use the portrait of the Spanish king until 1822, when they were changed to reflect the dawn of a new political landscape.[45]

Although the Spanish colonial mints may have been loyal to Spain, the people of Mexico and the rest of Latin America were much less so than the images on their money would suggest. The seeds of revolution had already been sown in Mexico by the events which took place in Europe. The imprisonment of the king initially provoked mixed reactions among the political leaders in Mexico. Some believed that the power resided originally in the people who gave it to the king, and once the king was gone, the power reverted back to the people.[46]

Spanish natives, who typically held the most powerful offices in Mexico, insisted that the status quo be maintained in Mexico City out of loyalty to Ferdinand VII. By contrast, the Spanish born in Mexico (*criollos*) argued that a *junta,* or a small council of political leaders, should govern. The *criollos* outnumbered their Spanish-born political counterparts (known as *peninsulares*) by about ten to one. A failed attempt by Viceroy Jose de Iturrigaray to unite the *criollos* in a quest to make himself the independent ruler of Mexico resulted in his arrest by royalist troops on September 15, 1808, and his deportation back to Spain via Vera Cruz. A dangerous precedent was set as the royalist *peninsulares* angered their more numerous Mexican-born counterparts. Although the attempt by de Iturrigaray failed, it gave the *criollos* their first taste of real power and politics.

During the following two years, the *criollos* who resided north of Mexico City planned an uprising against the ruling *peninsulares* who controlled the government of New Spain from Mexico City. By 1810, the *criollos* found an unlikely candidate to lead their rebellion in a parish priest named Miguel Hidalgo y Costilla. In the eyes of the church, Father Hidalgo was hardly an exemplary figure. He questioned celibacy for the priesthood, kept a mistress, fathered three daughters and even challenged the infallibility of the Pope.[47] Hidalgo's biggest strength was that he was seen as a man of the common people. As a parish priest for seven years, he taught his largely Indian parishioners such practical skills as carpentry, wool weaving, silk raising and wine making, then forbidden in Mexico. With widespread dissatisfaction brewing among the people, and the *criollos* outnumbering the ruling party by about ten to one, it did not take long to realize the makings of an independent government in Mexico City. As external influences in Europe became intertwined with the internal conflicts in Mexico, the controversial *padre* soon found himself at the center of a firestorm of discontent.

On the morning of September 16, 1810, Father Hidalgo delivered his *Grito de Dolores,* a cry for social and economic justice and good government for the people. In large part due to Hidalgo's cry for social and political changes, a mob of several thousand insurgents overwhelmed royalist forces and captured the town of Guanajuato in late September. The loosely banded insurgent army began to exploit their long-standing hatred of the wealthy and the ruling class. They descended on Mexico City and defeated a garrison of royalist forces outside the capital. At this critical juncture, Hidalgo's forces failed to seize the moment and occupy the city. Although there seemed to be widespread discontent between Hidalgo and his *criollo* commanders, the two factions eventually formed an 8,000-man army which created widespread havoc in Mexico. The last major battle of the Hidalgo revolt was fought on January 17, 1811, about thirty miles east of Guadalajara. After being defeated by both royalist forces and a massive grassfire which spread through their ranks, Hidalgo and his followers retreated northward. By the summer of 1811, Hidalgo and most of the important insurgent leaders were captured and summarily executed.

MEXICAN WAR FOR INDEPENDENCE: "HAMMERED MONEY" FROM THE EMERGENCY MINTS

During the turbulent times of the Mexican War for Independence, various mints were created to strike coins for regional use.[48] The violent rebel factions (initially led by Father Hidalgo) and the subsequent infighting with royalist troops (those loyal to Spain) kept Mexico in a state of political and military turmoil for another decade. The *peninsulares* became increasingly concerned that the rebels would hijack and plunder the raw silver shipments transported from the mining areas to the production facilities in Mexico City. As journeys to the central mint became too risky, branch mints were established near the sources of the lucrative silver mines. Several of these mints were established by a royal decree on October 8, 1810. These branch mints became known as emergency mints. Facilities sprung up in Monclova, Chihuahua, Guadalajara, Guanajuato, Sombrerete, Zacatecas, Durango and other towns located near the mines. The production quality of these mints was generally not as good as in Mexico City, which resulted in many crudely made coins entering circulation. The early coins from Zacatecas were particularly crude and often significantly off center, though the quality of the finished product began to improve over time. Because of their northern proximity, many of these emergency mint coins eventually found their way into Texas, where they were known among the colonists as "hammered money."

Fig 1.55, The Mints of Mexico.

The illustration in figure 1.55 shows the location of the various mints where coins were produced in Mexico. Reprinted from Standard Catalog of World Coins: Spain, Portugal and the New World, *by Chester L. Krause and Clifford Mishler, with permission from Krause Publications (www.krausebooks.com).*

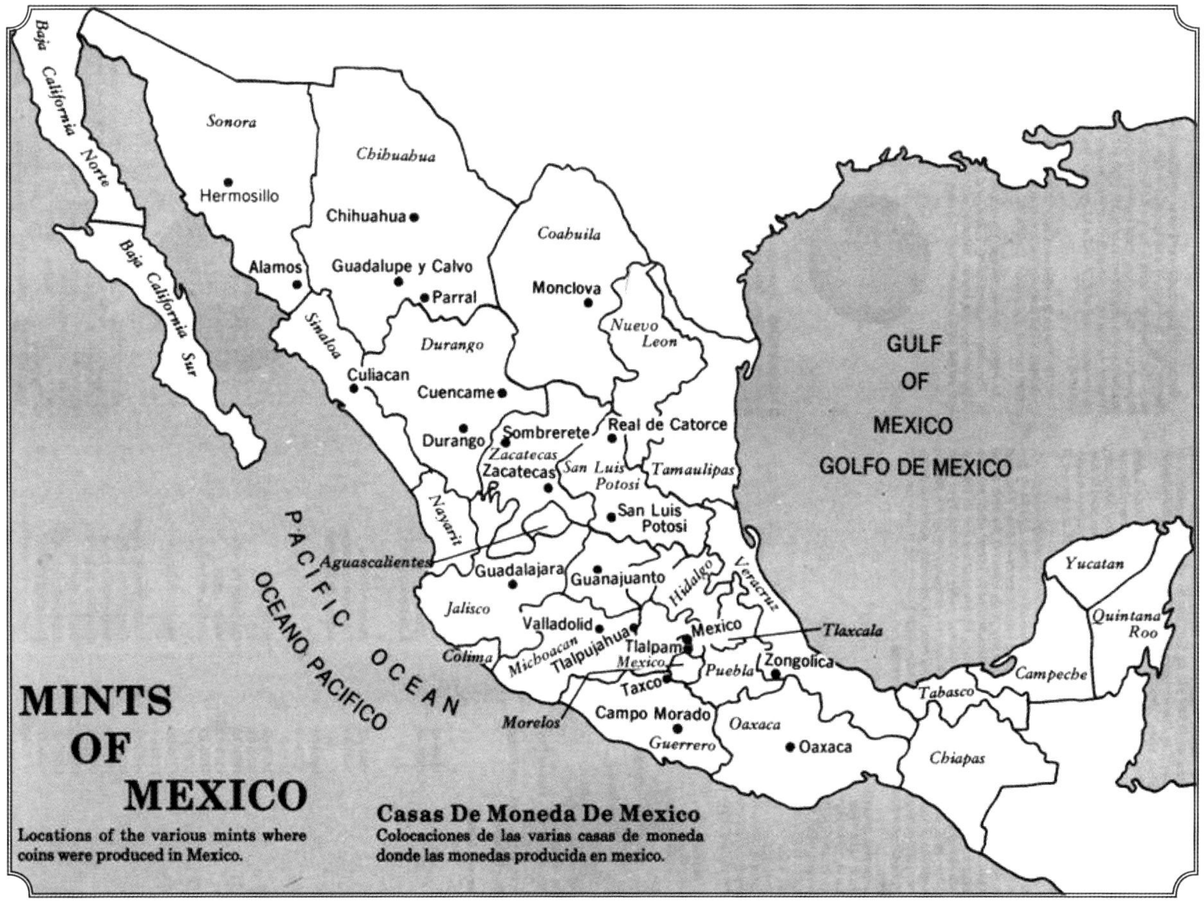

ROYALIST COINAGE

Fig 1.56, 8 ***Reales***, **Mexico City "Stamped 1812," 1812. Monclova mintmark over a cast coin dated 1809.**

Fig 1.58, 8 *Reales*, Sombrerete, 1811. Vargas, Punched Type.

The dates which appear on some of the coins from this era can be deceiving. Much of the money from this tumultuous period was cast rather than struck with prepared dies. The example displayed in Figure 1.56 was cast in silver in the year 1812 from an 1809 host coin struck in Mexico City. The mintmark "MVA" (for Monclova) and the date "1812" were punched in with a hammer. The purpose of the mintmark was to certify the silver content of the coin. Although the host coin was dated 1809, this coin can be dated from the year it was cast and the mintmark applied, which was 1812.

The Sombretete Mint opened on October 8, 1810, in an area that boasted some of the richest mines in Mexico.[49] The mint was operated sporadically between 1810-1812 by Gen. Fernando Vargas, the Superintendent of the mine, who also oversaw the coining operations. The example in Figure 1.58 bears the punch mark "VARGAS," and was found near Presidio la Bahía at Goliad in the 1960s, indicating that it once circulated in Spanish Texas.

Fig 1.57, 8 *Reales*, Chihuahua, 1811.

The obverse of the Chihuahua coin in Figure 1.57 was countermarked with a "T" to the left of the bust designating receipt by the Royal treasury. To the right of the bust is a second countermark indicating the comptroller's inspection. This northern Mexican mint produced cast coins and changed the mint mark to "CA" in the mold prior to casting. This mint mark can be seen on the reverse of this early example. At the time this issue was made, Father Hidalgo and his insurgent generals were awaiting trial only three blocks away for their role in the populist uprising. All of the insurgent rebels were executed.

Fig 1.59, 8 *Reales*, Zacatecas, LVO, 1811.

Moneda Provisional De Zacatecas.

Figure 1.59 exhibits one of the first coins produced at the emergency mint of Zacatecas. On the obverse is a mountain of silver with the initials "LVO" underneath. "LVO" is the Latin abbreviation for "Labor Vincit Omnia" or "all effort/work succeeds." Around the perimeter is the legend "MONEDA PROVISIONAL DE ZACATECAS," or "Provisional money of Zacatecas." On the reverse is the familiar shield, with the date incorporated into the legend: "1811 FERDINANDUS.VII . DEI GRATIA. 8R"

The city of Zacatecas is located in a rich mining region of Mexico, and provided silver for the mints in New Spain since the mid-1500s.[50] The Zacatecas mint was the most prolific producer of coins during the War of Independence and was briefly captured by insurgents in 1811. The mint was a large provider of coins to the northern provinces of Mexico including Zacatecas, Nuevo Leon, Coahuila and Texas. The production from this mint would later play a key role in financing the Mexican Army during the Texas Revolution.

Fig 1.60, 8 *Reales*, Zacatecas, 1812.

Figure 1.60 shows a crudely made coin minted in Zacatecas in 1812 and later counterstuck at a facility in Monclova, Mexico. This example was discovered almost 150 years later in a hoard of old coins near the bank of the San Antonio River. The area of the find, discovered during excavation work in 1959 in San Antonio, was once a nineteenth century campground used by cowboys who passed through the area.

Fig 1.61, 8 *Reales*, Chihuahua, 1812.

Another example of the crudely cast Chihuahua 8 *reales* is represented in Figure 1.61, showing the uniformity of the countermarks by the royal treasurer "T" (left of bust) and the comptroller (right of bust). Standard dies for producing the official coins were not made available until 1815, and 8 *reales* pieces were produced at Chihuahua until 1822.

Fig 1.62, 8 *Reales*, Chihuahua, 1816

Struck over an earlier dated cast coin.

Some of the most fascinating examples of money from the turbulent period is the 1816 piece shown in Figure 1.62 from Chihuahua, which was struck over an earlier dated cast 8 *reales* coin. On the obverse, the periphery of the original portrait of Ferdinand VII can be seen above and to the left of the newly struck portrait.The treasurer's countermark "T" can be seen to the left of the portrait. On the reverse, the "crooked" pillar at right is a remainder of the original design, with the coin having been rotated and overstruck.

INSURGENT COINAGE

There was a series of copper 8 *reales* pieces struck in the region south of Mexico City beginning in 1811 and continuing until October 1814.[51] These issues from the Oaxaca and Morelos regions were struck by insurgents under dire circumstances and made of copper. The insurgents intended the coins to be redeemed at face value in gold or silver once they captured the precious metals.

The instigator of the copper coinage in this region was José María Morelos y Pavón. Born in 1765, Morelos was a priest who studied under Father Hidalgo at St. Nicolás' Seminary in Michoacán. The city was then named Valladolid, but changed in 1828 to the name of Morelia to honor Morelos. Much of the copper insurgent coinage of the period bears an "M" indicating that it was struck in the region by Morelos, who was later executed by the Royalist government in December 1815. Many of these coins found their way into the northern province of Texas.[52]

Fig 1.63, 8 *Reales* (Copper), off-center strike, 1812. "SUD" Insurgent coinage w/ Morelos Countermark.

The obverse of the large copper coin in Figure 1.63 bears the countermark "M" for Morelos, "8.R." for 8 *reales,* and the year of issue "1812." On the reverse is the old Aztec symbol of a bow. Although it is weakly struck, it represents that this was a true Mexican issue. The word "SUD" means "South," indicating the region south of Mexico City and assigned to Morelos by Hidalgo in favor of the revolution. These symbols are framed inside the reverse by a circle of dots.

Fig 1.64, 8 *Reales* (Copper), 1813 "SUD" Insurgent coinage from Morelos.

The obverse of the 1813 issue in Figure 1.64 is awash in symbolism of the Mexican War of Independence. In addition to the monogram "M" of Morelos, the denomination of "8.R." and the date, there are a series of circles representing olives and grapes, both of which were forbidden to be harvested in New Spain by the Spanish Crown. As a protectionist policy against cheap foreign imports, it had been decreed that no wine or olive oil from New Spain would be allowed to compete against the products of Spain. This copper coin reminded the Mexican people of the many reasons for independence. The reverse of this issue contains a sharply struck Aztec symbol of the bow and the word "SUD" or south with a more decorative border. Regardless of their unique symbolism, some of these coins found their way north. At least one of which was found in small hoard of coins recovered at the site of Jane Long's old tavern in Brazoria.[53]

Since these crudely struck coins were the most recently issued, they became the primary currency in Texas during the time until they were replaced by the "eagle money," or silver pesos of the *Republica Mexicana* in 1823. The defacing of the pieces also served to devalue the coins to 90 percent of face value, thereby keeping them in the country. Many of the coins, predominantly from Chihuahua, were actually cast rather than struck. Although no coins were minted in Monclova, many of the cast coins of Chihuahua were counterstruck there. Due to their proximity to northern Mexico, a multitude of coins found their way into the early trade centers of Texas. As Americans settled the land in the early 1820s, a good part of the money in circulation consisted of these "hammered dollars," the common name for the counterstamped 8 *reales* pieces from the War of Independence.[54]

PROVINCE OF TEXAS – ROYALIST COUNTERMARKED COINAGE

The hammered dollars still circulated in Texas until the late 1850s. James Ross Snowden, Director of the U.S. Mint in 1857, wrote: "There is a class of dollars which is generally mistaken for the true Spanish pillar dollar, but is decidedly inferior, being worth only 101 cents on the average, and withal [*sic*] very irregular. They were coined by the royal party in the revolutionary times of Mexico, and may be known by their defaced appearance, which is not due to wear, but to blows of the hammer, by which they were coined, whence they are called '*hammered* dollars.'"[55]

The term "hammered dollars" sometimes described an 8 *reales* silver coin which had been "hammered" or punched with a countermark to authenticate the silver content of the coin. The action of the stamp was to punch through the surface and determine the origin of the base metal underneath, therefore validating the money. This confirmation was important in the last few years of Spanish Texas, as counterfeiting was rampant, especially in the northern province of Texas.[56] The most significant of these stamps originated in San Antonio de Béxar under the authority of Manuel Maria de Salcedo, who served as the Spanish Governor of Texas from 1808-1813. His counterstamp, exclusive to the state, validated legitimate silver coins against those struck or cast in copper by counterfeiters and plated with a thin layer of silver.

Fig 1.65, 8 *Reales*, Mexico City, 1809
Manuel Salcedo "Countermark."

Figure 1.65 shows a coin bearing the monogrammed countermark of Manuel Salcedo. Very few of the originals have survived. Although many of the Mexican War of Independence coins found their way into Texas, these monogrammed pieces were the only ones countermarked exclusively in the area.[57] These pieces circulated in Texas and also in other northern provinces of Mexico.

Indians primarily populated the interior of Texas in the early 1800s, except for areas surrounding the Spanish missions at Nacogdoches, San Antonio de Béxar and La Bahía near the coast. Despite the enormous size of the territory under Governor Salcedo, in 1809 only 352 veteran soldiers and 3,122 civilians resided in the state.[58] Because the population remained relatively poor, bartering for goods continued as the order of the day, and the large silver coins purchased primarily European goods imported into the presidios and surrounding missions. As present-day Texas lay largely uninhabited, a trickle of Anglo-American traders routinely passed through this neutral zone. Governor Salcedo found that the American merchants were particularly industrious, and he perceived them to be good for the commerce of Béxar. Sensing their desire for ownership of the Spanish land, he also warned others that "they are not to be underestimated as enemies."

1 "Malintzin," PBS.org, http://www.pbs.org/opb/conquistadors/mexico/adventure2/pop-malintzin.htm (accessed September 25, 2008).

2 Porrúa Miguel Angel, "La Casa de Moneda de México a más 450 Años de distancia," *Editorial Porrúa,* Mexico DF (1988): 8-10.

3 Porrúa Miguel Angel, "La Casa de Moneda de México a más 450 Años de distancia," *Editorial Porrúa,* Mexico DF (1988): 8-10.

4 Chester L. Krause and Clifford Mishler, *Standard Catalog of World Coins: Spain, Portugal and the New World (Iola, WI:* Krause Publications, 2002), 304.

5 The location of the Assayer's initial can sometimes be confusing on this early transitional series. The initial "R" appears between the pillars on some coins and "P" to the right of the shield (replacing the mintmark "M") on others. On the late series, both the mint mark "M" and the Assayer's initial "L" appear on both sides of the shield, but are sometimes indiscriminately transposed.

6 Colin R. Bruce, III, *Standard Catalog of Mexican Coins, Paper Money, Stocks, Bonds, and Medals* (Iola, WI: Krause Publications, 1981), 29-31.

7 J. Villasana Haggard, "Spain's Indian Policy in Texas," *SHQ,* vol. 44 (April 1904), 2: 232-44, viewed on-line at: http://www.tsha.utexas.edu/publications/journals/shq/online/v044/n2/contrib_DIVL3544.html.

8 Pradeeau Francisco, "Historia Numismática de México, 1823-1950," *Ed. Stylo,* vol. 2, Mexico DF (1950): 41-42.

9 Ricardo De Leon Tallavas, "Cob *Coins of Mexico's Mint,* c. 1572-1733," (unpublished, August 2006).

10 Frank Sedwick, *The Practical Book of Cobs* (self-published, 2nd ed., 1990), 18-21.

11 Sedwick, *The Practical Book of Cobs,* 18.

12 Haggard, "Spain's Indian Policy in Texas," 232-44.

13 Donald E. Chipman, *Spanish Texas, 1519-1821* (Austin: University of Texas Press, 1992), 111-17.

14 Haggard, "Spain's Indian Policy in Texas," 232-44.

15 Haggard, "Spain's Indian Policy in Texas," 232-44; "The Report of Don Juan Manuel de Oliván Rebolledo, August 22, 1715," translations from the Béxar Archives.

16 Randolph B. Campbell, *Gone to Texas: A History of the Lone Star State* (Oxford University Press, 2003), 55-57.

17 Chipman, *Spanish Texas, 1519-1821,* 112.

18 Spanish Governor's Palace, "Presidio de Bejar, La Commandancia, 1722-1772," brochure.

19 Lon Tinkle and James M. Day, "The Alamo," *Six Missions of Texas* (Waco: Texian Press, 1965), 1-48.

20 Francisco, "Historia Numismática," 51.

21 R.S. Yeoman, ed. by Ken Bressett, *A Guide Book of United States Coins* (New York: St Martin's Press, 2002), 3.

22 Francisco, "Historia Numismática," 53-56.

23 "Biography of Ferdinand VI," The Millennia Collection, Catalogue Three: The New World Including Africa, Asia & Oceana, Auction book (Ira and Larry Goldberg, Auctioneers, Beverly Hills, California, sale date May 26, 2008), 201.

24 Richard A. Long, *"Mail Auction Sale 99, Mexican Coins," Auction book* (December 12, 2006), 65.

25 Campbell, *Gone to Texas,* 71-75.

26 "Coins, Medals and Currency Part XVII, The Paper Money of the Continental Congress," The John J. Ford, Jr., Collection, Auction book (Stack's, March 21, 2007), 231-72.

27 Robert Friedberg, *Paper Money of the United States: A Complete Illustrate Guide with Valuations,* 14th ed. (Clifton, NJ: The Coin and Currency Institute, Inc., 1963), 207.

28 Arthur A. Nussbaum, *A History of the Dollar* (New York: Columbia University Press, 1957).

29 Eric P. Newman, *"The Dollar Sign, Its Written and Printed Origins,"* (lecture, Coinage of the Americas Conference at the American Numismatic Society, New York, October 30, 1993), reprinted in *American Numismatic Society Journal* (1993), 1-17.

30 Glyn Davies, *A History of Money: From Ancient Times to the Present Day,* 3rd. ed. (Cardiff: University of Wales Press, 2002; rpt. 2005).

31 Chipman, *Spanish Texas, 1519-1821,* 171-79.

32 Chipman, *Spanish Texas, 1519-1821,* 8.

33 Bruce, *Standard Catalog of Mexican Coins,* 45-46.

34 Francisco, "Historia Numismática," 60-62.

35 Chipman, *Spanish Texas, 1519-1821,* 195.

36 "Charles IV Abdication," "The Braganzas," "Ferdinand VII," and "José Napoleón I," *The Columbia Encyclopedia,* 6th ed. (Columbia University Press, 2001).

37 French Military Organizational Chart, March 21, 1808, Signed, ap/.NP, also countersigned "Clarke" as Minister of War, "Autographs, Rare Books, and Manuscripts," Auction book (Heritage Grand Format Auction, October 12-13, 2006), lot # 25424.

38 French Military Organizational Chart, lot #25424.

39 Campbell, *Gone to Texas,* 96.

40 Kip Wagner, as told to L.B. Taylor, Jr., *Pieces of Eight: Recovering the Riches of a Lost Spanish Treasure Fleet* (New York: E.P. Dutton & Co., 1966), 54.

41 Wagner, *Pieces of Eight,* 56-61.

42 Bruce, *Standard Catalog of Mexican Coins,* 70-74, 88, 137.

43 Krause, *Standard Catalog of World Coins,* 10.

44 Bobby J. McKinney, *A Search for Texas: The Revolution, the Republic, the Relics, 1836-1846* (Mouth of Caney, 2006), 2-10.

45 Bruce, *Standard Catalog of Mexican Coins,* 79.

46 Campbell, *Gone to Texas,* 89-91.

47 Chipman, *Spanish Texas, 1519-1821,* 218-21.

48 Francisco, "Historia Numismática," 59-63.

49 Krause, *Standard Catalog of World Coins,* 401.

50 Krause, *Standard Catalog of World Coins,* 411-13.

51 Chester L. Krause and Clifford Mishler, *Standard Catalog of World Coins: Spain, Portugal and the New World (Iola, WI:* Krause Publications, 2002), 398.

52 Bobby J. McKinney, *A Search for Texas: The Revolution, the Republic, the Relics, 1836-1846* (Mouth of Caney, 2006), 7.

53 McKinney, *A Search for Texas,* 8.

54 William M. Gouge, *The Fiscal History of Texas* (New York: Burt Franklin, 1852; rpt. 1969), 227-29.

55 Letter from James Ross Snowden, Director of the U.S. Mint, to Hon. James Guthrie, Secretary of the Treasury, Philadelphia, dated February 6, 1857. Included in a letter from the Secretary of the Treasury, communicating, in obedience to law, a report of the Superintendent of the Mint, on the fineness and value of certain foreign gold and silver coins. U.S. Senate, 34th Cong., 3d sess., February 10, 1857, Ex. Doc. 42.

56 Noah Smithwick, compiled by his daughter Nanna Smithwick Henderson, *The Evolution of a State or Recollections of Old Texas Days* (Austin: Gammel Book Company, 1900; rpt. 1993).

57 Author's Note: Although highly desired by numismatists, many of these countermarks are still being stuck over legitimate host coins in Mexico and are being sold to unsuspecting collectors.

58 Chipman, *Spanish Texas, 1519-1821,* 231.

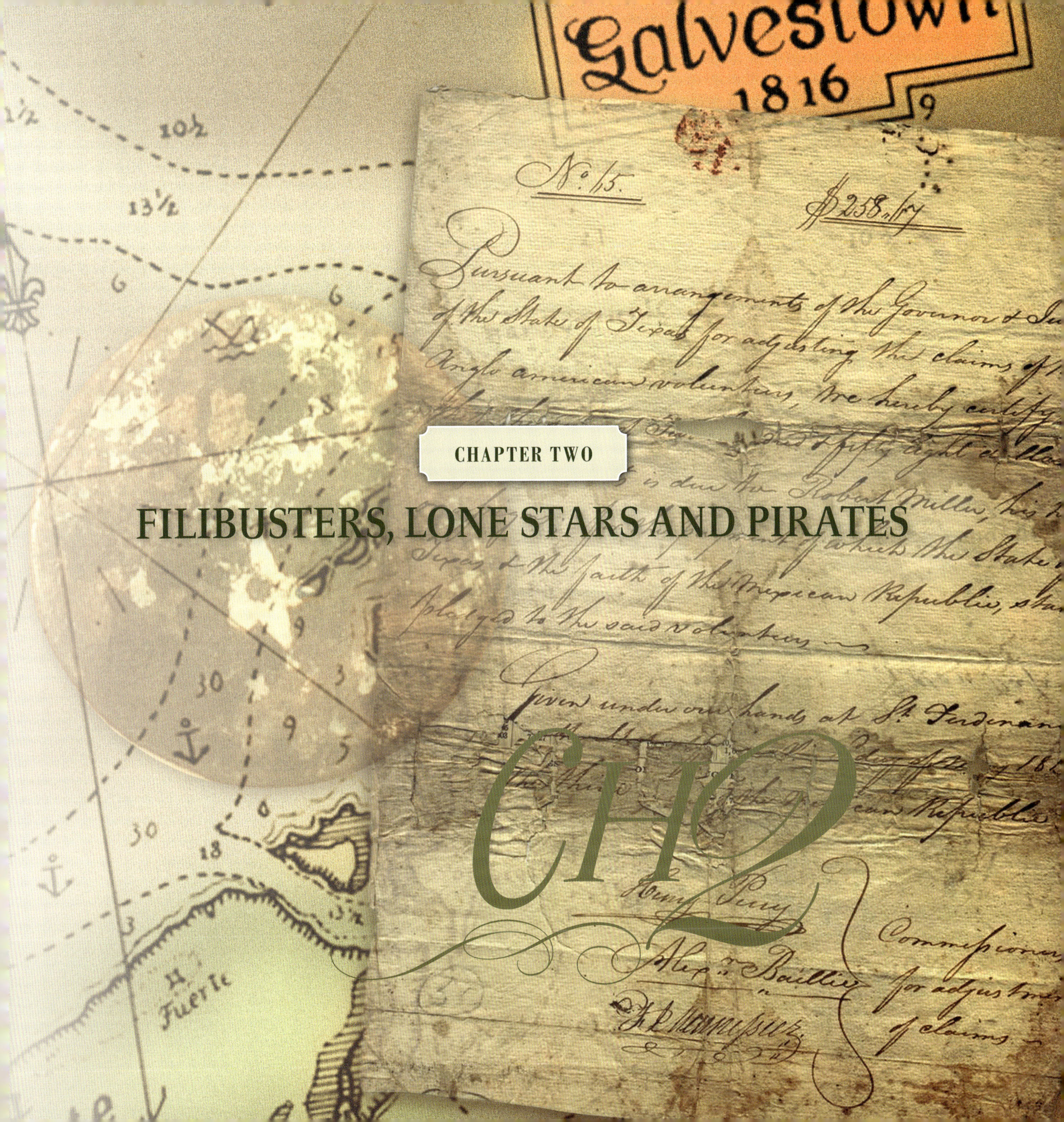

CHAPTER TWO

FILIBUSTERS, LONE STARS AND PIRATES

CH2

There was a growing social and political unrest in Mexico which had originated with the imprisonment of Ferdinand VII by Napoleon Bonaparte. Several factions competed for power in the vacuum left by the jailed monarch, resulting in intense fighting throughout parts of Mexico. To a large degree, the violence in Mexico had been successfully and forcefully dealt with by troops loyal to the Spanish crown. Although much of the civil unrest in Mexico had been concentrated far to the south of Texas, Gov. Manuel Salcedo had correctly perceived the vulnerability of his northern frontier province. To protect Texas, Salcedo requested new regiments of infantry, cavalry and mounted artillery from Mexico totaling four thousand men. Although he was well aware of the growing unrest against Spanish rule in Mexico, even he could not have foreseen the firestorm of Anglo-American revolution which would suddenly be thrust upon Texas from the East.

Although he was well aware of the growing unrest against Spanish rule in Mexico, even he could not have foreseen the firestorm of Anglo-American revolution which would suddenly be thrust upon Texas from the East.

THE GUTIERREZ-MAGEE EXPEDITION OF 1811-1813

José Bernardo Gutiérrez de Lara was a merchant, blacksmith, Mexican revolutionary and diplomat. A good-looking man of medium stature, keen eyes and black hair,[1] he led a filibustering expedition into Texas against the backdrop of mounting opposition to Spanish rule.[2] During the Mexican War of Independence, led by Miguel Hidalgo y Costilla, the amiable Gutiérrez and his brother were successful in instigating a revolution in the Mexican state of Nuevo Santander. Afterwards, Gutiérrez was sent by Father Hidalgo to recruit troops along the Rio Grande River and later in the United States. Gutiérrez left Saltillo, Mexico, for the United States on March 17, 1811, by way of Natchitoches, Louisiana. He arrived in Washington, D.C., on December 11, 1811. He was received by Secretary of State James Monroe who wanted to hear about Gutiérrez's plans for establishing a republican government in Texas and for the use of Texas as a base for securing the eventual liberation of Mexico from Spain. While Monroe offered no assistance on behalf of the U.S., he did provide Gutiérrez with a letter of introduction to the governor of New Orleans.[3] Monroe also hinted that the U.S. would not hinder the progress of the expedition.

Augustus Magee was a Boston native who graduated third in his class from the U.S. Military Academy on January 23,1809.[4] He was a distinguished officer and was recommended for a promotion in the Army by his commander, though the promotion was refused. Magee, still smarting from the denial of his promotion, resigned from the U.S. Army on June 22, 1812. He was joined by Gutiérrez in a collaborative effort to recruit an armed force for the first attempted liberation of Texas from Spain. The expedition was organized in New Orleans and assembled at or near Natchitoches, Louisiana. This is where the nucleus of an invading army was formed and readied for the task of liberating Texas from Spain.

The impromptu rebel army crossed the Sabine River with 130 men on August 8, 1812. The Magee forces advanced to Nacogdoches four days later, uniting with the forces of Gutiérrez. Many of the townspeople abandoned their Spanish loyalties and cast their lots with the liberating army. The army advanced down the Gulf Coast to La Bahía, near Goliad, where they met little resistance. The rebel numbers swelled to more than 300 men as the sweet smell of success filled the salt-laden air. While at La Bahía, Magee died, thus depriving the expedition of its primary Anglo military leader. While Governor Salcedo ordered his troops to guard San Antonio de Béxar, the rebel army had grown to more than 800 as volunteers flowed in from Louisiana to participate in the uprising. The two forces met at the intersection of Salado Creek and the San Antonio River on March 28, 1813. Here, a royalist army of 1,200 men was defeated by the largely Anglo force in the battle of Rosillo over the next two days. Having lost control of San Antonio to the filibusters, Governor Salcedo surrendered on April 1.

Gutiérrez and the rebel force were now firmly in control of the city. They immediately tried Governor Salcedo and thirteen of his officers for treason against the revolutionary *junta*, sentencing them to death. Although Gutiérrez assured several Anglo-American leaders that Salcedo and the others would only be held as prisoners, his men had other plans for them. On April 3, after being taken out to the site of the battle on Salado Creek, Gov. Manuel Salcedo and thirteen of his officers were dismounted from their horses. With their hands still bound, the prisoners were then stabbed to death with knives by their captors. Although a declaration of independence was proclaimed on April 6, 1813, this first Republic of Texas was short lived. As the executioners returned to San Antonio to brag about what they had done, the horrific deaths of Governor Salcedo and his thirteen officers began to tarnish the legitimacy of the expedition. The incident caused a public outcry against the rebels in the United States. With the loss of additional men through attrition and the lack of political support for their cause, a large portion of the Anglos deserted the force in disgust and began the long journey back to Louisiana.

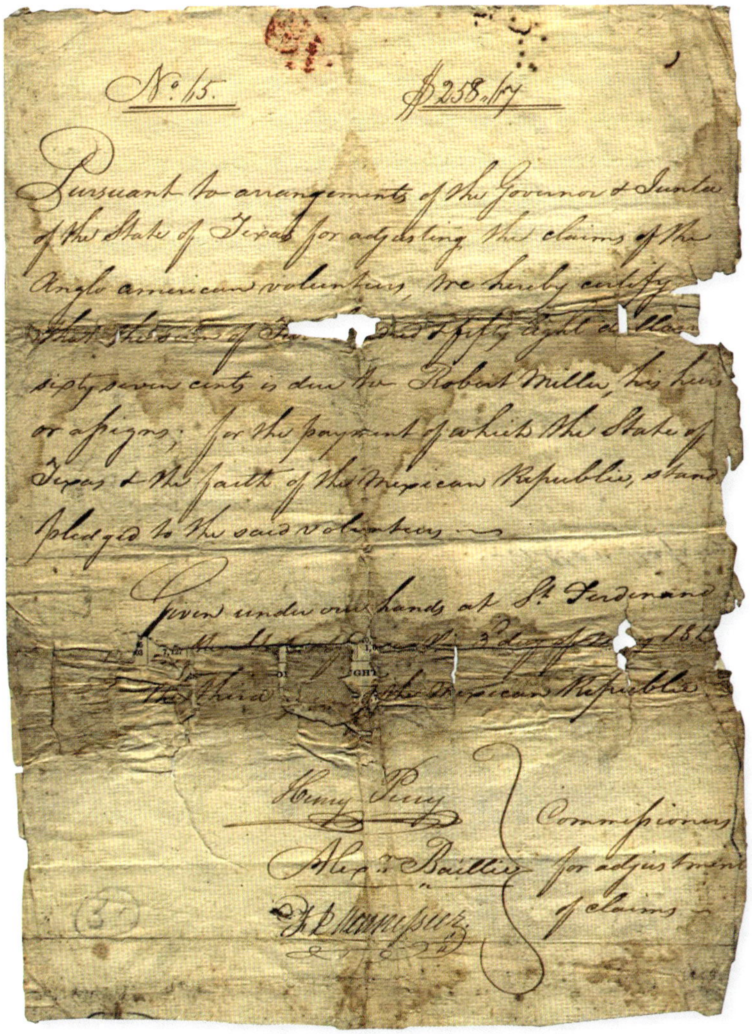
No. 15 $258.67
Pursuant to arrangements of the Governor & Junta of the State of Texas for adjusting the claims of the Anglo american volunteers, we hereby certify that [illegible] fifty eight dollars sixty seven cents is due to Robert Miller, his heirs or assigns; for the payment of which the State of Texas & the faith of the Mexican Republic, stand pledged to the said volunteers —
Given under our hands at St. Fernando [illegible] the third [illegible] the Mexican Republic
Henry Perry
Alex. Baillie
F L Menepier
Commissioners for adjustment of claims

Fig 2.1, Promissory Note from the Gutiérrez-Magee Expedition, c. 1813.

Private Collection. Cr. Unlisted, O-1.

Miraculously, this lone promissory note of the expedition, shown in Figure 2.1, survived to tell the story of the volunteers who attempted to wrest the Mexican State of Texas away from Spain with disastrous results. The earliest known filibustering expedition by any rebelling faction dates back to the Gutierrez-Magee Expedition of 1811-1813.[5] The note, written entirely in English, is dated at San Fernando de Béxar, May 3, 1813, and reads as follows:

No. 15 $258.67

Pursuant to arrangements of the Government and Junta of the State of Texas for adjusting the claims of the Anglo american volunteers, we hereby certify that the sum of Two Hundred Fifty Eight dollars sixty seven cents is due to Robert Miller, his heirs or assigns; for the payment of which the State of Texas & the faith of the Mexican Republic, stands pledged to the said volunteers...

Given under our hands at S. Fernando... The State of Texas 3'rd day of May, 18[13] ....the Mexican Republic.

Henry Perry	*Commissioners*
Alex Baillie	*for adjustment*
F. L. Menepier	*of claims.*

Although the date is illegible, Henry Perry (the first signature) had joined the expedition at Natchitoches and was promoted to a captain of the expedition while at Béxar in April-May 1813, which dates this piece to that year.[6] F.L. Menepier (the third signature) was the secretary of Bernardo Gutiérrez at the time his command was deposed by José Álvarez de Toledo y Dubois.[7] The note clearly references

Among them was nineteen-year-old Lt. Antonio López de Santa Anna, who was cited for bravery during the battle.

the revolutionary fervor of the insurgents. Their goal was to unshackle the yokes of Spanish rule and declare Texas a free and independent State. The reference to payments in the note came from a promise to the men of a two million dollar appropriation by the U.S. Congress. It was a false promise by Toledo, a self-appointed commander who told the men that the money had been appropriated to pay the soldiers for their service. This promise came with an understanding—that Gutiérrez was to retire and Toledo was to be named as the new commander.[8] Although the piece is dated as No. 15, indicating numerous payments, it is possible that hundreds of notes were originally issued. Only a handful of these specimens are thought to have survived.

The Gutiérrez-Magee expedition of 1811-1813 literally came to a dead end at the battle of Medina, the bloodiest battle ever fought on Texas soil. The rebel expedition was defeated by a Spanish force under the command of Gen. Joaquín de Arredondo. Arredondo was a former governor of Nuevo Santander, and had come to Texas with the goal of crushing the rebels and implementing a policy of deadly revenge in the Texas province. The Spanish force of nearly two thousand men defeated the remaining rebel army in the battle of Medina on August 18, 1813, approximately twenty miles south of San Fernando de Béxar, now known as San Antonio.[9] After defeating the rebel force of about thirteen hundred men, the Spanish cavalry rounded up a detachment of eighty insurgents after the main battle. They perched the rebels on timbers across a large ditch dug by the engineers.[10] The firing squads summarily executed the captives and the Spanish troops covered up the bloody graves of the rebellious filibuster army.

These mass executions ordered by General Arredondo in the aftermath of the battle left a lasting and sobering impression on the young Spanish officers. They witnessed first hand how the royalist commander brutally dealt with the largely American insurgents who had challenged the *status quo*. Among them was nineteen-year-old Lt. Antonio López de Santa Anna, who was cited for bravery during the battle. The impressionable young officer from Vera Cruz would later return to Texas with another army in an attempt to squelch a much stronger rebellion some twenty-three years later. Despite the victory for the royalist troops, the greed of the filibuster expeditions so intensified the rebellious interests in Texas that peace could not be restored until Augustín de Iturbide brought the Mexican revolution to an end in 1821.

The vindictive Arredondo marched his troops into San Antonio de Béxar following the battle of Medina and rounded up three hundred of the town's citizens into a small improvised jail.[11] Many of the civilians were executed the following morning. The merchandise and many of the good-looking women were subsequently taken for the pleasure of the army. The Mexican republicans who had initially resisted the royalist troops fled for their lives.[12] Two of the townspeople who made it to safety were José Francisco Ruiz and José Antonio Navarro. These men would again become revolutionaries as signers of the Texas Declaration of Independence, more than two decades later. At the time of the massacre, San Antonio de Béxar was a little city of small adobe houses clustered around two important buildings. These buildings still stand today. One of them was the low lying Presidio, also known as the Spanish Governor's palace. The other was the old Mission de San Antonio de Valero—the Alamo.

Within sight of the Alamo, another arrest was made during the Arredondo occupation. Lt. Antonio López de Santa Anna was celebrating the occasion of his citation of valor with a group of his comrades, and enjoying a round of drinking and revelry at an improvised gaming table. Having soon amassed a staggering gambling debt of 300 *pesos*, Santa Anna was arrested on the charge of forging his commander's signature on a check for the payment of his debt. Citing his loyalty to his division, the honor of his regiment, and numerous other expostulations, the young lieutenant offered one after another shallow excuse for his dishonesty. It was only after the expedition's surgeon came forward and covered the amount of the forgery that Santa Anna was released. The affair was smoothed over and the focus redirected on the persecution of the townspeople. The belles of the town became the prey for the soldiers' fancy. The less-attractive women were put to work making tortillas for the commissary. Forty men suspected of aiding the rebels were summarily executed. A handful of women and children died of suffocation after being stuffed into an overcrowded jail.[13] Seventy-one civilians who had fled the occupation were executed on the road to Nacogdoches when they were overtaken by Arredondo's forces. The most important civil and economic center of Texas was left a shadow of its former self for several years afterward. When the occupation finally ended, the largely Anglo rebels learned a bitter lesson about their brief quest for independence. According to one historian, Arredondo's vengeance on Spanish Texas was so thorough "that the province was virtually depopulated save for the settlement at Béxar."[14]

Henry Perry, one of the rebel commanders, managed to survive the fighting. He returned to Louisiana and rejoined the U.S. Army from December 15, 1814, to June 15, 1815, probably in the quartermaster corps. He continued his filibustering activities over the next several years. He established a camp overlooking the Trinity River in 1816, which was originally known by the Anglo settlers as Perry's point, but which later became known as Anahuac.[15] In the summer of 1816, Perry joined Louis Michael Aury, who ran a pirating operation in the Gulf of Mexico from Galveston Island.[16] Perry left Galveston and led another group of insurgents into battle against the royalists at La Bahía on June 17, 1817. On June 19, the Spanish army surrounded Perry and his men in the woods, where most were subsequently killed or wounded. Perry himself was wounded, but refused to surrender, preferring death by his own hand. We can only assume that it was with the same hand which signed the early Texas promissory note shown in Figure 2.1.

THE RETURN OF FERDINAND TO SPAIN

After Napoleon Bonaparte's forces received a stunning defeat by the British at the end of the Peninsular War in 1813, Ferdinand VII was released back to Spain. The king soon discovered that there had been turmoil throughout the Spanish empire and that royalists had been carrying out a war of nationalism and liberalism in his name. Once restored to the throne, Ferdinand proceeded to undo every positive development which had taken place during his absence. He discarded the Constitution of 1812, declared himself the absolute ruler of the Spanish empire, and embarked on a program to eliminate liberalism in Spain. Ferdinand VII crushed the wars for independence in America, and opted to share his absolute power with no one. The king's continual firing of ministers and the relentless persecution of his enemies resulted in his being referred to as the "chief jailer" of Spain. Ferdinand's reactionary policies led to increasing discontent by the Spanish citizens on both sides of the Atlantic.[17] It was Ferdinand's approach to government, rather than the threat posed by expansion-minded Anglo-Americans, which would eventually end three centuries of Spanish rule in Mexico and Texas. Within eleven years of Ferdinand's restoration to the throne, all of the former Spanish colonies over the Atlantic, except Cuba and Puerto Rico, would become free and independent republics.[18]

Fig 2.2, 8 *Reales*, Zacatecas, Ferdinand VII, 1821.

Ferdinand VII would be the last of the Spanish kings whose portraits would grace the silver pieces of eight which circulated in New Spain. The portrait on the 1821 8 *reales* piece in Figure 2.2 from Zacatecas shows the king as he appeared near the end of his disastrous reign over Mexico and Texas.

THE ORIGIN OF THE LONE STAR

In the interior of Texas there was a bustle of commerce and daily activity around the early Spanish missions of the early 1800s. The areas of San Antonio, Goliad, and Nacogdoches had flourished and became the most successful of the Spanish settlements. Only four years after the brutal forces of Gen. Joaquín de Arredondo had occupied the city, peace had again been established. The presidio of San Antonio de Béxar was once again thriving, but still boasted a significant number of Spanish troops among its population. Following a succession of interim appointments after the death of Manuel Salcedo, Antonio Martinez began his term as the last Spanish Governor of Texas in 1817. It was in this relatively quiet period during the struggle for Mexican Independence that an obscure but very significant event in the history of Spanish Texas occurred. An impromptu minting of small copper coins in San Antonio de Béxar would mark the first appearance of the five-pointed Lone Star—the symbol for Texas.

Although there were active mints in Mexico, the interior of Texas was far away, and a steady supply of small denomination change was essential for merchants, soldiers and travelers to transact business. Many transactions in those days were relatively small. These ranged from selling goods, replenishing supplies and buying produce and breads in the local market. In 1817, a chronic shortage of low-denomination coins occurred, partly due to the absence of their manufacture by the regional mints during the Mexican War for Independence. These branch mints produced a steady stream of large sized 8, 4, and 2 *reales* pieces. The 2 *reales* coins ($0.25 cents) were the most frequently found in circulation.[19] The lower denomination coins of ½ *real*, and 1 *real* were almost non-existent. The smaller ½ *real* coins (6 ½ cents) were needed for making change and were called *jolas*.

These small silver ½ *real* coins from the Mexico City mint shown in figures 2.3 through 2.7 were of the type that circulated in New Spain up to and including the time that a new series of small copper coins known as *jolas* came into existence in the northern province of Texas in 1817-1818.

Fig 2.3, ½ *Real*, Pillars & Waves, 1736.

Fig 2.4, ½ *Real*, Charles III, 1774.

Fig 2.5, ½ *Real*, Charles IV, 1806.

Fig 2.6, ½ *Real*, Ferdinand VII "Fantasy" Portrait, 1812.

Fig 2.7, ½ *Real*, Ferdinand VII, "Proper" Portrait, 1818.

NEW SPAIN (TEXAS) JOLAS

In order to alleviate the shortage of hard money, acting Spanish Gov. Manuel Pardo authorized Manual Barrera, a local merchant and jeweler, to coin 8,000 jolas and issued a proclamation for the public to accept them in commerce at ½ *real* a piece. The jolas were copper, fifteen to twenty millimeters in diameter, with initials of the "minter" and the value, crudely struck as ½ (*real*) on the obverse. On the reverse was a five-pointed Lone Star with a small denticle or raised "dot" in the middle. This incuse five-pointed star on the blank backs is believed to represent the earliest use of the "Lone Star" symbol for Texas.[20]

Fig 2.8, New Spain (Texas) ½ *Real*, 1817. (Shown 2 ½ x actual size)

The coin in Figure 2.8 was struck in San Fernando de Béxar by Manuel Barrera as ordered by Governor Pardo. The order for the coins is thought to have originated in the Presidio, known today as the Spanish Governor's Palace. On the obverse are Barrera's initials "MB," the denomination "½," and the date "1817." On the reverse is the five-pointed Lone Star symbol for Texas. This coin is one of the five original "discovery" specimens and has been professionally restored by the owner to its original appearance.

Fig 2.9, New Spain (Texas) ½ *Real*, 1817. (Shown 2 ½ x actual size)

The remarkable coin in Figure 2.9 was photographed in exactly the same condition in which it was found. Traces of Barrera's initials "MB," the denomination "½," and the date "1817" can be seen on the obverse through almost two centuries of dirt and corrosion. This coin is also from the five original discovery specimens. On the reverse, the outline of the five-pointed Lone Star can be seen, with the diagnostic dot in the middle of the star.

Seven specimens of the 1817 *jolas* are known to have survived out of the original mintage of 8,000. Some were discovered in a "junk box" of seemingly worthless coins from an old Schulenberg collection in 2004.[21] A 2011 research study using mass spectrometry to compare the ore signatures of all known varieties of the 1817-1818 jolas has validated the authenticity of these coins. Evidence indicates that these coins were released into circulation in San Fernando de Béxar on or about February 29, 1817.

To facilitate their acceptance in the community, the governor had the following notice posted to inform the community these coins were legitimate. The translated notice reads:

> *Public Notice*
>
> *Our neighbor Don Manuel Barrera having petitioned to this government the milling of five hundred* pesos *in total containing his name and surname; This government has accepted this individual's solicitation to mill five hundred* pesos *in total, with a value of half a* real *for each for use in purchases and sales and should circulate in the commerce of this city and no one should decline to accept them. I sign this in San Fernando de Béxar on the 29th day of the month of March in 1817 to advise the public.*[22]

A unique example of a small copper coin with a denomination of "½" was found during an archeological excavation on the grounds of the Presidio La Bahía on December 17, 1963. It was discovered in a trench inside the north wall of the old Spanish fort at Goliad, near the site of the execution of Col. James W. Fannin. Although the coin is permanently in the custody of the Catholic Diocese of Victoria, some believe that the piece is cursed as two deaths have recently been recorded in attempts to have the coin photographed for this publication.[23]

Fig 2.10, New Spain (Texas) ½ *Real*, 1817 Trial strike, Presidio La Bahía Specimen. (Shown 2 ½ x actual size)

Photo by Jim Bevill, Courtesy of Presidio La Bahía.

The obverse of the coin in Figure 2.10 bears the letters "BARR" with an "I" and an "A" to follow, possibly an abbreviation of Barrera. Oddly, the letters and the fraction (½) are inverse, as if they were mistakenly punched into the die only to have the lettering come out backwards when impressed into the planchet. It also displays a date, presumably 1817, with only the number "17" having been struck. The reverse of the coin is blank. The coin appears to be a remarkable find from the period, possibly a trial striking of the 1817 *jolas* by Manuel Barrera in San Fernando de Béxar. It may have been discarded during the minting process following the discovery of the lettering error and mixed in with the previously described specimens.

Barrera's coinage monopoly was later withdrawn by Gov. Antonio Maria Martinez, who then granted a similar coining monopoly to the local postmaster, José Antonio de la Garza, in 1818. De la Garza coined an additional 8,000 specimens which bear the date 1818, and the initials "J.A.G." on the obverse.[24] The initials of Barrera and de la Garza on these small Spanish coins appears to be consistent with the 1817-1818 time period when assayers at the mint were required to place their initials on their work. While widely circulated in the area around San Antonio, these were unknown in the numismatic world until 1959 when a small hoard of sixty coins was unearthed on the banks of the San Antonio River during an excavation.

The low survival rate of the 1817 *jolas* can be explained by their withdrawal from circulation on the order of local authorities dated December 6, 1818. A posted order recalling the Barrera coins translates in part:

> *The circulation of the previously minted coins by D[on] Manuel Barrera should cease today. And with the effect that whoever has the* jolas *minted by Barrera should not lose them and present them to D. Jose Antonio Lagarza [sic] within 12 days. He will receive them and give them the same quantity of the newly minted coins.*[25]

Some of these ½ *real* pieces may have made their way along the trade routes which ran east into Nacogdoches and then to Natchitoches, Louisiana, though there was little to spend them on outside of any of the populated areas. On a trip through Texas in 1821, Stephen F. Austin remarked that money was "tolerably plenty" at La Bahía, because of the trade "from Nachitoches [*sic*] to the coast," but he found that on the whole, the environment was very rural and people lived very poorly.[26]

Fig 2.11, New Spain (Texas) ½ *Real*, 1818. (Shown 2 ½ x actual size)

Photo by Jim Bevill, Courtesy of Presidio La Bahía.

The widespread use of the *jolas* in colonial Texas is confirmed by the 1818 specimen of the de la Garza coins which were found during an archeological dig in the southeast corner of the Presidio La Bahía near Goliad on December 14, 1963. The very rare coin in Figure 2.11, with an extraordinary provenance, was mistakenly identified as a button and resided among a collection of military buttons for a number of years before being correctly identified as a ½ *real* coin of New Spain.

Fig 2.12, New Spain (Texas) ½ *Real*, 1818. (Shown 2 ½ x actual size)

The coin in Figure 2.12 was struck in San Fernando de Béxar by José Antonio de la Garza. It was discovered as part of a hoard of coins found in a 1959 excavation near the bank of the San Antonio River and shows considerable signs of corrosion.

Fig 2.13, New Spain (Texas) ½ *Real*, 1818. (Shown 2 ½ x actual size)

The coin in figure 2.13 was struck in San Fernando de Béxar by José Antonio de la Garza using a different set of dies. It exhibits a much more refined appearance than the earlier, crudely struck *jolas*. This type is known as the small letters variety. The denticle or raised "dot" in the middle of the Lone Star on the reverse is also not as pronounced. There are several distinct varieties of the 1818 coins struck by de la Garza.

In the mid-1960s, a Texas collector found three small copper coins dated 1817 with a metal detector at the site of Mission San Bernardo, adjacent to San Juan Bautista at the present day town of Guerrero, Mexico near Eagle Pass. Spanish explorers used these early missions as a staging area for expeditions into Texas. This numismatic discovery was significant, as this "gateway to Texas" is located where *El Camino Real de los Tejas* (the Old San Antonio Road) crosses the Rio Grande River. This places the discovery coins squarely in the trade route from San Antonio de Béxar to the interior of Mexico. Undoubtedly, these ½ real pieces are also 1817 *jolas,* as they were small copper coins used to make change. All known specimens were struck from crudely cast dies.

Fig 2.14, New Spain (Texas) ½ *Real*, 1817. (Shown 2 ½ x actual size)

Photo by Bob Shelton

On the obverse of the coin in Figure 2.14 is the denomination ½, the date, 1817; and a symbol to the left of the date which appears to be a monogram A.D for *Anno Domini.* A cluster of eight raised dots flank the monogram and date, with the initials "R" and "A" (possibly for "Royal Authority"). On the reverse is a multi-pointed motif that resembles a flower.

Fig 2.15, New Spain (Texas) ½ *Real*, 1817. (Shown 2 ½ x actual size).

Photo by Bob Shelton

The obverse of Figure 2.15 bears the denomination ½; three numerals of the date, 817, and the monogram A.D. Clusters of eight raised dots are found at the left and right, with the initial "R." above, as on the previous specimen. The remainder of the obverse is illegible. There are no distinctive design elements on the reverse. The striking similarities with the previous specimen and their mutual discovery via metal detector in south Texas indicates that these coins were struck under the same authority and circulated side by side.

Reflecting numerous die varieties across their impromptu mintages, the *jolas* were the first and only coins struck in Texas, or in any of the former Spanish Territories (1810-1821) or Mexican areas (1821-1848) which are now part of the United States.The little Texas *jolas,* coined while Texas was still known as New Spain, left a lasting imprint of the "Lone Star" which became, and will forever be, a unique symbol for Texas.

Fig 2.16, The Long Expedition - Filibustering expedition into Texas.

(James Long is pictured with a pipe and top hat) University of Texas at San Antonio, Institute of Texas Cultures, No. 076-0038.

THE LONG EXPEDITION

It wasn't long after the jolas appeared in Texas that the Lone Star began to be manifested on a flag. The Adams-Onís Treaty, signed on February 22, 1819, by John Quincy Adams for the United States and by Luis de Onís for Spain, renounced any United States' claim to Texas and fixed the border of Texas and Louisiana at the Sabine River.[27] This boundary, necessary for the Louisiana Purchase, was viewed by many settlers in the trans-Mississippi as a sellout of their claims to Texas. In fact, the feeling that Texas should belong to the Anglos ran so strong that bands of revolutionaries soon formed a small filibuster army to claim for themselves what the United States had renounced in the Adams-Onís Treaty. The largely uninhabited lands of Texas were loosely held by Spanish troops scattered hundreds of miles apart. If the Spanish could be overthrown, then Texas could be divided among the victors. The movement by Anglo-American settlers to wrest Texas away from Spain was nothing more than a filibustering expedition. Determined leaders used a small mercenary army to accomplish their own political and economic goals of securing valuable real estate in Texas. The most famous of these filibusters was commanded by Dr. James Long in 1819.

Dr. James Long joined the United States Army and served as a surgeon in the War of 1812. After the battle of New Orleans, Long went to Natchez, Mississippi, where he practiced medicine. At the suggestion of his wife, Jane Herbert Wilkinson Long, he bought a plantation near Vicksburg, Mississippi. Long was incensed by what he perceived as the surrender of Texas under the terms of the Adams-Onís Treaty. He was determined to take matters into his own hands and take the Spanish territory by force if necessary and bring it into the United States. "General" Long attracted more than three hundred followers with a promise of a league of Texas land for each of the volunteers who participated in the expedition. Among the protesters who gathered in Natchez were James Gaines, Warren D.C. Hall, and Jim and Rezin Bowie.[28] An advance force, led by Eli Harris, crossed the Sabine River on June 19, 1819, and proceeded to Nacogdoches, flying the first Lone Star flag in open rebellion against the Spanish. The flag bore a white five-point star placed on a red background, and the field consisted of the thirteen alternating red and white stripes like the flag of the United States. Harris was soon joined by an additional force under the command of Long on June 21. While in Nacogdoches, the citizens and mercenary soldiers met to organize a provisional government of Texas with James Long as its leader. The United States government took no official actions to stop or otherwise discourage the incursion into Spanish Texas.

Fig 2.17, Lone Star Flag of the Long Expedition.

Photo by Jim Bevill.

The depiction in Figure 2.17 of a single white five-pointed star set inside a red field was said to have been a proclamation of liberty. Eli Harris, a member of the Long expedition, later claimed to be the designer of the flag.[29]

On June 23, 1819, the rebel government declared

the independence of Texas and voted to provide ten sections of land (6,400 acres) to each private who joined their "army." They soon developed a plan to sell other portions of the seized Spanish territory at fifty cents per acre. John Sibley, Samuel Davenport and Bernardo Gutiérrez (who led the disastrous expedition into Texas in 1811-1813) soon joined the rebel force.[30] This attempt at the liberation of Texas did not last long as an inability to obtain supplies doomed the expedition. Long made a trip to Galveston Island in order to gain assistance from the pirate Jean Lafitte, who was cordial but uncooperative. By the end of September, Governor Martinez sent Col. Ignacio Pérez with more than 500 royalist troops to drive Long's men out of Texas. Pérez moved in on the rebels slowly, capturing a few of the filibusters on his way to Nacogdoches, which he reached on October 28, 1819. By the end of November, Pérez and his men had driven the American settlers out of East Texas and back across the Sabine River.

Fig 2.18, Bernardo de Galvez.

Courtesy of the Rosenberg Library, Galveston, Texas.

GALVESTON, JEAN LAFITTE AND THE PIRATES

While the interior of Texas outside of the Spanish missions was still quite backward and poor, the sandy island at the entrance to the great bay on the upper Texas coast quickly became the largest center of illegal commerce and slave trading on the entire Gulf Coast. "Bahia de Galveztown" was named in honor of Don Bernardo de Galvez, the viceroy of Mexico, by the Spanish navigator Hervia who charted the great bay in 1783. Curiously, Galvez never saw nor set foot on the island.[31] The name of the bay and the island which marked the bay's entrance was later shortened to Galveston. The island named for Galvez soon drew trade money from many nations across the Western Hemisphere. Galveston was dominated by a man whose name was so synonymous with pirating that his economic impact on the times is only overshadowed by his legend. That man was Jean Lafitte—the most notorious pirate on the entire Gulf Coast.

Bernardo de Galvez was appointed by Charles III to command the Spanish forces in the Gulf Coast region, assist the Americans in their cause, and thereby limit the influence of Great Britain in North America. In 1777, he served as the Spanish Governor of Louisiana and secured the port of New Orleans so that only American, Spanish and French ships could traverse the Mississippi River. The great river proved to be an indispensable lifeline of supplies for the revolutionary armies commanded by George Washington.

After the War of 1812, the Gulf of Mexico became a hot bed of activity for pirates and smugglers. There was an important, legal difference between a pirate and a privateer in the early nineteenth century. Pirates operated on their own, robbing and plundering merchant vessels on the high seas. Pirating was a capital offense and was punishable by hanging under the laws of the United States. On the other hand, Privateers operated under what was known as a "Letter of Marque," issued by a host country which authorized them to loot, plunder, and capture as "prizes" any vessel flying the flag of the enemy. Privateers were issued these letters in exchange by host countries for a 20 percent take of the proceeds. Once captured, the enemy ship was sailed to a friendly port and condemned as a "Prize of War" by an Admiralty Court, which had jurisdiction to sanction the capture and subsequently divide the proceeds. The reality of the times was such that these privateers often did not discriminate as to which vessels they were capturing and looting. While patrolling the high seas, they sometimes captured neutral vessels and never bothered to bring these ships into port for condemnation, preferring to keep all of the goods for themselves. This blatant crossing of the legal line into downright piracy on the high seas was rampant in the Caribbean Sea and in the Gulf of Mexico off the coasts of Louisiana and Texas.

The most famous of these pirates on the Gulf Coast was Jean Lafitte, who received a Letter of Marque from Cartagena, Colombia. Lafitte made it his life's work to loot any vessel flying the flag of Spain, his "declared"

Fig 2.19, Isla Serpiente, Map of Galvestown.

Courtesy of the Rosenberg Library, Galveston, Texas.

At the time this map was drawn, the long, cigar-shaped island at the foot of Galveston Bay was still being referred to as Isla Serpiente*, or Snake Island.*

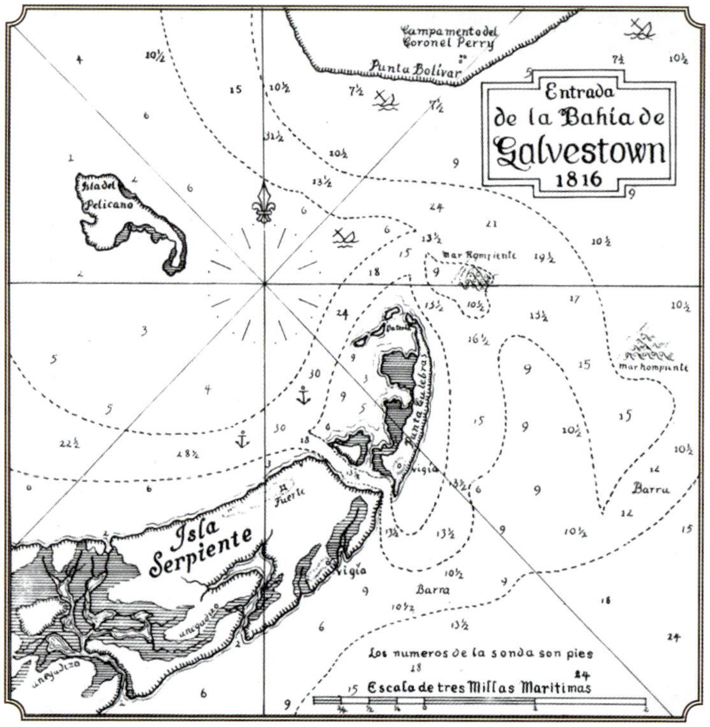

enemy. At the time, Colombia, like Mexico, also sought independence from Spain, and Colombian agents granted daring and colorful filibusters like Jean Lafitte the authority to rob, plunder, and otherwise disrupt the Spanish shipping in exchange for part of the loot.[32]

THE LAFITTE BROTHERS IN NEW ORLEANS

Jean and his brother Pierre were well-known blacksmiths in New Orleans in the early 1800s. They bought slaves at the waterfront and later resold them to Louisiana planters. Many of the slaves were apprenticed in their blacksmith shop which still stands today at the corner of Bourbon Street and St. Philip in the French Quarter. Knowing that a slave with the skills of a craftsman would sell for more than an unskilled one, the brothers Lafitte turned a handsome profit with this venture. Seeking a more adventurous life, they soon changed their emphasis from blacksmithing to smuggling goods obtained from pirates and privateers. They settled on the island of Grande Terre in Barataria Bay near the mouth of the Mississippi River where Louisiana customs officials were easily bribed with stolen goods. In 1808, with the passage of a law banning the importation of slaves to the United States, the shortage of slaves caused a tenfold spike in the price of human goods, which greatly increased the profitability of illegal smuggling of slaves into the United States.[33]

Jean Lafitte's involvement in the War of 1812 made him somewhat of an American hero. Lafitte and his men offered their weapons to Gen. Andrew Jackson, helping to turn the tide in the battle of New Orleans.[34] Lafitte supplied Jackson's men more than two thousand rifle flints prior to the engagement against the English. Many of Jackson's men had worn down their flints from a long campaign in the Creek Indian War, and the fresh pieces greatly improved the reliability of the soldier's weapons. Jean and Pierre Lafitte also served as guides for Jackson's troops through the bayous and backwaters of southern Louisiana as the American force prepared to launch an attack on the British encamped on the Mississippi. After a stealthy move through the swamps, cunning military tactics and skilled artillery honed in with deadly fire on the British officers and men. The British were no match for the skilled gunners, trained to fire with deadly accuracy even on the rolling waters of the high seas. As the guns fell silent and the city returned to normal, the Lafitte brother's long-standing reputation as pirates became socially embarrassing—even in New Orleans!

After a falling out with military personnel in New Orleans—and a personal snub by Andrew Jackson—Jean Lafitte sailed with his own private force of seven ships into the harbor at Galveston Bay. He and his men took control over the base of another pirating warlord, Don Louis D'Aury, who was on an expedition force in Mexico at the time.[35] Lafitte was able to secure the island for himself while under the illusion of aiding the *juntas* in support of the Mexican revolution. He rounded up various members of D'Aury's men who had remained on the island. Lafitte had them take an oath of loyalty to the Mexican Republic and appointed them to important military positions in his fleet. He also established a sham Admiralty Court, bequeathing the puppet agency jurisdiction over maritime matters. The court had the express power to "condemn" a captured vessel as a "prize" of war, thereby granting Lafitte the authority to seize the cargoes of the captured ships in the name of the Mexican *junta*.

To add an even grander air of legitimacy to the operation, Lafitte agreed to withhold a percentage of each prize (as the captured ships were called) to defer expenses on the island. Any surplus left after paying the captains and crews went to satisfy the debt of the Mexican *juntas*—but only those debts owed to the men living on the island. Consequently, the salaries set aside for the Mexican military were reallocated to pay his own men—privateers who fought the Spanish. Once organized, Lafitte's ships set sail from the coast of Texas, capturing and looting Spanish property under a Mexican flag without any intention of aiding the revolution in Mexico or any other Spanish colony in Latin America.[36]

Fig 2.20, Jean Lafitte.

Courtesy of the Rosenberg Library, Galveston, Texas.

Fig 2.21, Andrew Jackson.

Louisiana State Museum, New Orleans.

THE FIRST SETTLEMENT ON GALVESTON ISLAND

Fig 2.22, Lafitte's Maison Rouge in Galveston.

Artist's depiction by Joe W. Carr, Courtesy of Joseph and Joanne Hayes.

Galveston, formerly referred to as "Snake Island" by the local Indians, became Lafitte's base of operations for several years and was the first permanent settlement on the island. Lafitte named the settlement *Campeche* after a prominent Mexican port on the Yucatan Peninsula. The little village contained huts for the pirates, a large slave market, boarding houses for visiting buyers, a shipyard, saloons, stores, gambling houses, and Lafitte's own mansion known as the "Maison Rouge." The remnants of the mansion are still visible under the ruins of a later structure near the foot of present-day 15th Street and Harborside Drive in Galveston. Jean Lafitte built this small fortress town on the east end of the island. The remains of D'Aury's camp and *Campeche* are known today as the "East End Historic District" near "The Strand."

At first the settlement was a community of tents and shelters, except for the impressive masonry house that Lafitte built for himself. From Galveston Island, the pirates launched raiding parties on any straying Spanish ships, plundering their cargos and any gold and silver coins. Lafitte and his men used the money from the sale of cargoes to buy food, wine, guns, furniture, and a host of other goods from New Orleans and other ports on the Gulf Coast. By the end of 1817, approximately 200 buildings speckled the east end of Galveston and a population of almost 1,000 citizens resided in the town. It was said that "*doubloons* ran thick in the streets" with saloons, stores, gambling, and improvised housing. Buyers sailed into Galveston from nearly every port in the United States, buying stolen goods and loot that had been ransacked from Spanish ships. While Lafitte may have hated the Spanish, he was quite partial to their money, as Spanish *doubloons* and pieces of eight were his preferred means of payment.

The Spanish were not the only targets of the privateers. Lafitte and his men also sailed far out into the Indies, capturing slave ships and bringing their human cargo back to the Texas coast, out of the reach of U.S. law. Once in Galveston, slaves were sold and smuggled into Louisiana from the west bank of the Sabine River, about twenty-five miles above Sabine Lake and the Gulf of Mexico. The buyers conducted business on the Texas side of the river, where Lafitte's men sold slaves for one silver dollar per pound. Once the slaves were transported to Louisiana, they could then be re-sold to planters for $1,000 to $1,500 each. Though rooted in illegal activity, these transactions only served to reinforce the widespread acceptance of the Spanish "dollars" in the United States. The upper coast of Spanish Texas and the city of New Orleans soon became another point of entry of the Spanish silver "dollars" into the U.S. and the early Texas economy.

Spanish officials in Havana were keenly aware of the plunder taking place, and expressed their fears to anyone who might listen.[37] As early as January 18, 1818, Texas Gov. Antonio Martinez made plans to send a force from San Antonio de Béxar against Lafitte's force in Galveston. Martinez wished to "rid those scoundrels from their nest." The governor was hampered, however, by a lack of supplies and pack animals, which would be needed to launch a meaningful military expedition. In an effort to curtail the illegal activity occurring off its coastline, the U.S. Congress passed legislation on April 20, 1818, meant to strike a blow at the illegal slave trade. This legislation allowed for the seizure of slave ships and offered a reward of 50 percent of the cargo proceeds from those who assisted in the capture of slave ships or smugglers.[38] The law permitted the sale of captured slaves as a means to raise the funds to pay informants helping the U.S. government.

One of the more active slave traders of the day was Jim Bowie who later died in the defense of the Alamo in 1836. Jim made several trading trips with his brother Rezin to Galveston in 1818-1819. The Bowie brothers bought slaves in lots of up to forty at a time, paying one silver dollar per pound to Laffite. After the transaction, the men crossed the bay to the Bolivar Peninsula, and then followed the coast overland to Louisiana where they informed the local customs inspector of the whereabouts of the smuggled human cargo.[39] The slaves, after being seized by the U.S. government, were then sold at public auction. Half of the proceeds went to the Bowies as "informants" under the new law. Jim and Rezin then bought the slaves at auction, effectively laundering the human goods and receiving half of the bid amount back for their roles as informants.

Thus, one slave bought from Lafitte for $150 would bring $500 or more at auction, with $250 being paid to the informants. Once away from the coastal area with a clear title, a male slave in good health could fetch up to $1,000, turning a handsome, yet dirty profit. The Bowie brothers continued to trade with Laffite as long as the pirate remained in Galveston, and Jim Bowie may have had a friendly acquaintance with the pirate Jean Lafitte.[40] The Gulf Coast of early Texas was a rough place, and for a time, it was the largest slave market in the New World. Regardless of the moral or legal issues, this slave commerce provided an opportunity for the milled Spanish dollars, and later the portrait head silver coins, to become the widely accepted standard of exchange in Spanish Texas.

Late in the summer of 1818, the commerce of Galveston came to an abrupt halt. A powerful hurricane decimated the island, destroying all of the housing and virtually all of the buildings, leaving the community in ruins. The entire island was under water during the storm. After the water receded only piles of debris, splintered ships, and mounds of corpses remained in *Campeche*. Almost half of the inhabitants died in the storm. While this stronghold was eventually re-built, the town became only a shadow of its former self.

Lafitte's reputation as pirate, slave trader and renegade businessman did not escape the attention of Gen. James Long. In an effort to reconcile his forces after being driven from Nacogdoches, Long's men approached Lafitte for a possible alliance in 1819, suggesting that they join forces in the liberation of Texas.[41] Long proposed that an Admiralty Court be set up on the island in the name of the Republic of Texas, and that Jean Lafitte himself would be given the title of Governor of Texas. This posed a dilemma for the Lafitte brothers, as their raiding operation flew the flag of the Mexican insurgency and Long's revolutionaries were trying to sever Texas from both Spain and Mexico. If Long were unsuccessful, the failure might spell an end to the brother's lucrative operation. As the Lafittes' pondered the idea, Long set up headquarters at Point Bolivar across the entrance to Galveston Bay and began to reassemble his troops and plan for another invasion of Texas.[42]

By 1821, Mexico had won its independence from Spain. Lafitte stayed on Galveston Island and continued raiding operations under the flag of the Mexican *juntas*. Although Lafitte was well liked by his men and had a gift for charming his adversaries, in many ways he was the equivalent of a nineteenth-century Mafia don. The economic impact from the sale of pirated goods or "prizes" significantly influenced the fortunes of all who made or lost money as a result of the dealings. Lafitte accelerated the introduction of slaves into Louisiana and the resulting profits from this operation attracted so many men to Galveston Island that the settlement of *Campeche* was, for a time, the second largest city in Texas. As a result of rampant pirating, the gold and silver which crossed the warm waters of the Gulf of Mexico was up for grabs and Lafitte had secured one of the biggest shares. But he was not immune to the federal crackdown on organized pirating, even to the extent that he operated largely outside of the U.S. After one of Lafitte's ships attacked an American vessel, the United States Navy forced the privateer to abandon his operation on the Gulf Coast. Because the Adams-Onís Treaty was not yet ratified, the U.S. Navy threatened to seize Galveston Island for the United States if Lafitte remained in port. He was subsequently issued an ultimatum by the U.S. Navy to destroy his settlement at *Campeche* and leave the Gulf Coast for good. If he refused, he would be arrested for piracy and the U.S. Navy would take care of the demolition of *Campeche* for him.

In May 1821, Lafitte readied his three remaining ships, held a huge party for his pirates with wine and whiskey and then burned his settlement of *Campeche* to the ground. On the last evening before his departure, he invited James Long and his lovely young wife Jane aboard his flagship, the *General Victoria*, for a farewell dinner in the harbor. His guests had been camped on Point Bolivar, across the narrow inlet where the great bay meets the Gulf of Mexico. Lafitte charmed the couple with his many tales of adventure and discussed his lifelong hatred of the Spanish. Mrs. Long found him to be exceptionally conversational, almost like a woman. While Jean Lafitte was known for his exceptional manners, his outgoing demeanor concealed a much deeper sense of secrecy. He deftly avoided any mention of his future plans and left Jane Long "with as little knowledge as she came."[43] After bidding his guests goodnight, Lafitte retired for one last moonlit night off the sandy island that he had

Fig 2.24, Jim Bowie.

The San Jacinto Museum of History, Houston, Texas.

Fig 2.25, Rezin Bowie.

Antiquarian Antique Print & Map Gallery, Houston, Texas.

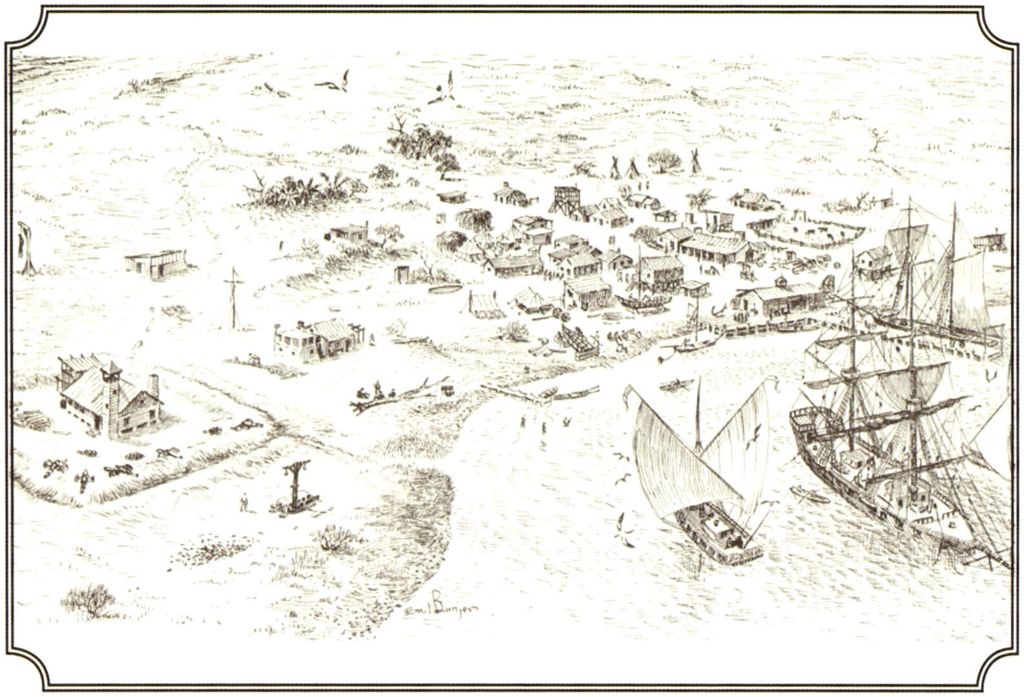

Fig 2.23, Campeachy, Pirate Stronghold.

Courtesy of the Rosenberg Library, Galveston, Texas.

dominated for almost four years. Having lost any authority for privateering under the Colombian or Mexican flags, on the following morning the pirate sailed his small fleet into the warm waters of the Gulf of Mexico, never again returning to the Texas Gulf Coast.

THE TWILIGHT OF SPANISH TEXAS

The concept of the land *empresarios* in Texas began under Spanish rule by a man named Moses Austin. Once a successful lead miner from Missouri, Austin traveled to San Antonio de Béxar in December 1819 and requested a meeting with Spanish Governor Martinez for the purpose of bringing settlers to Texas. He was initially denied the meeting and was ordered to leave the province. While crossing the plaza, he came across on old acquaintance, the Baron de Bastrop whom he had last seen in New Orleans several years before. After becoming reacquainted, Bastrop took Austin's documents to Governor Martinez and intervened on his behalf. Missouri was under the Spanish crown prior to the French ceding of Louisiana to the United States in 1803. Austin declared "that he was fifty-three years old, a Catholic, and a former subject of the King of Spain."[44] Governor Martinez was intrigued with Austin's request to bring families to settle in Texas, as the Spanish had been largely unsuccessful in this venture over the preceding 250 years. Austin's statement of faith in the Catholic Church was a condition of citizenship in New Spain, and he made the declaration in order to provide a basis for his request to bring families to settle in Texas.

After three days of discussion, the application of Moses Austin to settle 300 Catholic families from the former province of Spanish Louisiana into Texas near the mouth of the Colorado River was submitted. The request was forwarded to the commandant general of the Eastern Interior Provinces in Monterrey with a recommendation for approval.[45] Ironically, the approval was signed and granted on January 17, 1821, by none other than Joaquín de Arredondo, the fearsome royalist military leader who inflicted the punishing defeat of the Anglo-led filibustering army at the battle of Medina only eight years before.

Only two weeks after returning from Texas to Missouri in 1821, Moses Austin found a great interest among local businessmen in his proposed colonization plan. Before even learning that his application to settle 300 families had been granted, Austin wrote, "I have been offered as many names of respectable families as will make up the number."[46] The long and difficult journey from San Antonio to Potosi, Missouri, had taken a heavy physical toll on Moses Austin. He continued his journey to St. Louis to wrap up his lead mining business with a bank, wiping out all liability for his family and leaving the bank owing him $5,000. He fell ill and had to rest at three different homes on his return journey.[47] By the first part of June 1821, Austin's wife Maria reached his deathbed in just enough time to receive his last instructions. Moses

Fig 2.26, Moses Austin.

Courtesy of the Rosenberg Library, Galveston, Texas.

pulled his wife close and said, "tell dear Stephen that it is his dying father's last request to prosecute the enterprise he had commenced." As Maria later explained to her son, "he had set his heart too much on it, but for some wise purpose God had prevented his traveling the road he had planned out." Moses Austin had opened the path for the Anglo-American colonization of Texas, and on his deathbed begged his son Stephen Fuller Austin to carry the torch of the colonization plan into Spanish Texas. Maria began to prepare her sons for the task ahead. It would fall upon Stephen F. Austin, then only twenty-seven-years old, to carry on his father's real estate venture and fulfill his own destiny with the task of settling Texas.

---

1 The Papers of Mirabeau Buonaparte Lamar, ed. Harriet Smither, Texas State Library & Archives, 6:339;

2 *Handbook of Texas Online*, s.v., "José Bernardo Maximiliano Gutiérrez de Lara," http://www.tsha.utexas.edu/handbook/online/articles/GG/fgu11.html (accessed November 29, 2006).

3 Randolph B. Campbell, *Gone to Texas: A History of the Lone Star State* (Oxford University Press, 2003), 91.

4 *Handbook of Texas Online*, s.v., "Augustus William Magee," http://www.tsha.utexas.edu/handbook/online/articles/MM/fma12.html (accessed November 29, 2006).

5 Joseph D. Olson, *Texas Numismatic History: A Catalogue*, 1st ed. (Texas Numismatic Heritage Press, 2006), 12-13.

6 *Handbook of Texas Online*, s.v., "Henry Perry," http://www.tsha.utexas.edu/handbook/online/articles/PP/fpe42.html (accessed September 15, 2006).

7 Robert Thonhoff, "People Associated with the Republican Army of the North," *Forgotten Battlefield of the First Texas Revolution*, also found in Linda Ericson Devareux's *Tales From the Old Stone Fort* (Pineywood Printing, 1976); the 1815 Jose Toledo report, translated by Robert Benavides with additions and details added by Tom Green, non-published.

8 The Papers of Mirabeau Buonaparte Lamar, ed. Harriet Smither, Texas State Library & Archives, 6:396-97.

9 *Handbook of Texas Online*, s.v., "Battle of Medina," http://www.tsha.utexas.edu/handbook/online/articles/MM/qfm1.html (accessed November 29, 2006). San Fernando de Béxar officially became San Antonio de Béxar in 1837, though the community had been known as San Antonio for some time beforehand. For clarity, the author will only use San Antonio de Béxar since that is the most common name for the community.

10 Frank C. Hanighen, *Santa Anna: The Napoleon of the West* (Coward-McCann, Inc., 1934), 4-6.

11 Ibid., *Santa Anna*, 5-6.

12 Richard Bruce Winders, *Crisis in the Southwest: The United States, Mexico and the Struggle over Texas* ((New York: Scholarly Resources, Inc., 2002), 76.

13 Campbell, *Gone to Texas*, 93.

14 Donald E. Chipman, *Spanish Texas, 1519-1821* (Austin: University of Texas Press, 1992), 237.

15 *Handbook of Texas Online*, s.v., "Anahuac," http://www.tsha.utexas.edu/handbook/online/articles/AA/hja8.html (accessed December 24, 2006).

16 Campbell, *Gone to Texas*, 93.

17 Chipman, *Spanish Texas*, 238.

18 Chester L. Krause and Clifford Mishler, *Standard Catalog of World Coins: Spain, Portugal and the New World* (New York: Krause Publications, 2002), 10.

19 Q. David Bowers, *American Coin Treasures and Hoards* (Bobers and Merena Galleries, Inc., 1997), 184.

20 Walter H. Breen, *Walter Breen's Complete Encyclopedia of U.S. and Colonial Coins* (Doubleday, 1988), 108.

21 Alvin L. Stern, "History of the Texas *Jolas*," non-published, 2005, 2.

22 Béxar Archive, SF de BX, 3/29/1817 058:0227, trans. Ernesto Rodriguez, document provided by Alvin L. Stern, AM.

23 An associate of the author who lives near Corpus Christi attempted to make several appointments to photograph the coin in 2006 and 2007, but all were unsuccessful. Two associates who lived in the area and agreed to take the photos of the coin recently died and yet another prospective photographer required a kidney transplant. The coin was finally photographed by the author and his wife on March 6, 2008, due to the generosity of Mr. Newton Warzecha, the Director of the Presidio La Bahía. Within an hour of the photo session on the drive to Refugio, we encountered a violent tornado and accompanying hailstorm, which soon forced our vehicle off the narrow road in the pitch black afternoon conditions to seek shelter from the harrowing storm.

24 Stern, "History of the Texas *Jolas*," 1.

25 Béxar Archive, SF de BX, 12/6/1818 062:0463-64, trans. Ernesto Rodriguez, document provided by Alvin L. Stern, AM.

26 Eugene C. Barker, *The Life of Stephen F. Austin, Founder of Texas, 1793-1836: A Chapter in the Westward Movement of the Anglo-American People* (Austin: University of Texas Press, 1969), 34; Stephen F. Austin, "Journal of Stephen F. Austin on His First Trip to Texas, 1821," *Southwestern Historical Quarterly* (herein cited as *SHW*), vol. 7 (April 1904), 4:298.

27 *Handbook of Texas Online*, s.v., "Adams-Onis Treaty," http://www.tsha.utexas.edu/handbook/online/articles/AA/nba1.html (accessed September 15, 2006).

28 William C. Davis, *The Pirates Lafitte: The Treacherous World of the Corsairs of the Gulf* (New York: Harcourt, Inc., 2005), 394.

29 Robert Maberry, Jr., *Texas Flags* (College Station: Texas A&M University Press, 2001), 21-22.

30 Chipman, *Spanish Texas*, 237.

31 Don Bernardo de Galvez did much to advance the cause of his American friends during the American Revolution. Gary Cartwright, *Galveston: A History of The Island* (New York: MacMillan Publishing Company, 1991), 3.

32 Ibid.

33 Ibid., 41.

34 Ibid., 43.

35 Davis, *The Pirates Lafitte*, 324-25.

36 Ibid.

37 Bill Doree, *Profiles in Pillage: The Galveston Pirateers, 1816-1822* (Self-published), 24.

38 Davis, *The Pirates Lafitte*, 411-12.

39 Ibid., 361-62.

40 Ibid., 411-13.

41 Ibid., 397.

42 Campbell, *Gone to Texas*, 96.

43 Davis, *The Pirates Lafitte*, 430-31.

44 Barker, *The Life of Stephen F. Austin*, 23-25.

45 Campbell, *Gone to Texas*, 101.

46 Barker, *The Life of Stephen F. Austin*, 83, see Moses Austin to J.E.B. Austin, April 8, 1821.

47 Maria Austin, "Maria Austin's letter to her son Stephen F. Austin," as reprinted in the *Herculenium*, August 25, 1821.

q
Pa
de
dis
ya
sejo
da,S
do de

CHAPTER THREE

MEXICAN TEXAS, 1821-1836

CH3

Fig 3.1, Agustín Iturbide, Emperor of Mexico.
Benson Latin American Collection, University of Texas Libraries.

Agustín de Iturbide was born on September 27, 1783, at Valladolid near present-day Michoacán, Mexico. He joined the provincial regiment of his native city in 1797. He first opposed the revolutionaries, but in 1820 Iturbide formed an alliance with Gen. Vicente Guererro and strengthened the rebel movement against the liberal Spanish Constitution of 1812. They issued the Plan de Iguala for a Mexican empire on February 24, 1821, and created the Army of the Three Guarantees: Union, Religion and Independence. After the treaty of Córdoba formally gave Mexico its independence on August 24, 1821, Iturbide triumphantly entered Mexico City as a liberator in September 1821. An independent Mexican government was firmly established and Iturbide was crowned Emperor of Mexico on July 21, 1822.[1] Once swept into power, Don Agustín Iturbide instituted a short-lived imperial government which pledged to support the constitution composed by the Mexican Congress.[2]

Fig 3.2, Stephen F. Austin.
The San Jacinto Museum of History, Houston, Texas.

Iturbide realized that vast portions of the Republic of Mexico, mainly areas northeast of the Rio Grande River and known by the name of Texas, were still occupied by various tribes of hostile Indians. These Indians repeatedly raided Mexican citizens in the territory and had to a large degree prevented the Mexican population from colonizing Texas. Iturbide ascertained that Mexicans had a natural dread of Indians, and they could not be induced to venture into or settle the vast wilderness of Texas. At the time, Texas was largely an agricultural land with large crops of cotton and sugar cane. Iturbide, like the Spanish viceroy before him, correctly surmised that the enterprising Anglos to the east would be much more motivated by the offerings of land on which to build settlements, and much less intimidated by the Indians.

Iturbide also validated Stephen F. Austin's role as a land *empresario*. An *empresario* operated in much the same way as a real estate agent who brings in potential residents for a new development, except that in this instance the settlers were given a land grant by the government in exchange for developing the location. The *empresario* had to settle a minimum of 100 families during a six-year period in order to fulfill the contract with the Mexican government.[3] In exchange for this service, *empresarios* received large bonuses paid to them in money as well as in land. The men who were granted these early *empresario* contracts included Austin, Martín de León, Green DeWitt, Haden Edwards, Frost Thorn and Robert Leftwich.[4] Each agent received five leagues of grazing land and five leagues of farmland for settling 100 families. Each family who settled in Texas paid a fee of $50 for the agent's services in translation, surveying, registration, obtaining clear title, and in locating suitable land for their family.[5] This system was instigated in order to stimulate commerce and improvements in the sparsely populated northern state, eventually building a tax base in the area.

With Iturbide's recommendation and sanction, the colonization law was adopted by the national council on January 3, 1823. This opened the legal immigration of foreigners into the Mexican state of Texas, who gladly took an oath to observe the federal and state constitutions and join the Catholic Church in exchange for the generous grants of land. After an immigrant was accepted into the colony, he would select any un-appropriated land and formally petition the *empresario* for a title, then pay the fees for surveying as well as the other associated fees.

Stephen F. Austin was particularly successful at bringing families to the northern Mexican state. He settled 297 families in colonial Texas by 1836, thereafter known

Fig 3.3, New map of Texas, with the contiguous American & Mexican states, by J.H. Young. *Courtesy, Virginia Garrett Cartographic History Library, Special Collections, The University of Texas at Arlington, Arlington, Texas.*

This early map of Texas illustrates the important role that the land empresarios *played in regards to the settlement of the Mexican state of Texas. Each colony is labeled with the names of the men in which the contracts were made for the settlement of the land.*

as Austin's "Old Three Hundred." Much to the credit of Austin, it was said that "he conscientiously endeavored to comply with his contract with Mexico to settle none but respectable families on the land allotted to his colony."[6] Among the men who laid the foundation for the nation, Stephen F. Austin became the central figure in this early period. At the time the colonization law was adopted in 1823, Austin was barely thirty years old. He had a tremendous amount of energy, although there was little in his outward appearance which would suggest the caliber of his personality. He had dark hair and eyes, was sparsely built and quite unassuming in his manner. Yet he possessed the patience and perseverance of a skilled diplomat. He walked a fine line between the interests of his colonists and his Mexican superiors, ever mindful of both those who had settled the land with him, and those who had made it possible.

It was the colonists who cleared the timber, built the houses, cultivated the soil and planted the crops that made life manageable and sustainable in the interior of Texas.[7]

These are the circumstances which brought the largely American immigration into Texas from the East, including several families of Irish, Scottish, German and French origin. In essence, these new settlers paid for their land as a result of their labor. It involved incredibly hard physical work to make this previously uninhabitable buffer zone of rolling hills, prairie and thick wooded forests between Mexico and Louisiana into a home.

When Iturbide became emperor, the portrait of Ferdinand VII then being imprinted on the money was replaced with his own portrait. The monarchy of Agustín de Iturbide, brought to power through fraud and force, was a short-lived experiment in a Mexican monarchy styled after its Spanish predecessors. Iturbide lasted less than two years.[8] With the change in leadership, the silver and gold mines (along with the various mints) came under Mexican, rather than Spanish control. Under Iturbide's rule, Mexico City coined the first national silver pieces of Mexico in denominations of ½ *real*, 1 *real*, 2 *reales*, and 8 *reales*. These coins bore Iturbide's portrait on the obverse and a Mexican eagle on the reverse—the first for a federal issue from Mexico. Some smaller copper coins were also struck under the emperor's authority at a smaller mint in the town of Durango, Province of Nueva Vizcaya.

THE MEXICAN EMPIRE

During Iturbide's short rule of twenty-two months, the vanity of the new ruler was seen by Mexican citizens through a changing series of portraits on the silver coinage. Gold 4 *escudos* and 8 *escudos* pieces were also produced bearing the portrait of Iturbide in 1822 and 1823, though these coins found little circulation in Texas because of their limited mintage. There were no less than four major designs of the 8 *escudos* and five major designs of the 8 *reales* pieces which bore the emperor's portrait. The splendid gold and silver coins bearing his portraits offer the historian a fascinating record of this oft-forgotten liberator of Mexico.

Fig 3.4, Agustín Iturbide, Small Portrait. 8 *Reales*, Mexico City, Small Eagle Reverse, 1822.

This deeply toned example shown in Figure 3.4 exhibits a series of striking colors, a result of the oxidation of silver when it is exposed to warm, moist air. The obverse displays a small portrait of Agustín Iturbide (the short-lived Emperor of Mexico), the date 1822, and the mint mark "Mo" for Mexico City. The legend on the obverse reads "Augustin I by God's Providence." On the reverse is a small crowned eagle, perched on a cactus and surrounded by the legend (translated): "First Constitutional Emperor of Mexico," followed by the denomination, 8R, and the assayer's initials "JM," for Joaquin Davila Madrid.

The sharply struck large portrait of the Emperor of Mexico in figure 3.5 is set in a background of deeply reflective fields. These proof-like surfaces indicate that it was among the very first of this type to be struck, before the dies exhibited any signs of wear. On the reverse, the large eagle wears a crown with a small cross of Christianity planted on top, a subtle reminder of the lasting influences of the Catholic Church even in these early days of the Mexican Empire. The reverse legend is identical to the others, with the exception of the denomination and assayer's initials having been moved under the eagle.

Fig 3.5, Agustín Iturbide - Large Portrait. 8 *Reales*, Mexico City, Large Eagle Reverse, 1822.

The brilliant, uncirculated specimen in Figure 3.6 bears a large portrait of Augustín Iturbide, the date 1823, and the mint mark "Mo." The legend on the obverse reads "AUGUSTINUS.DEI. PROVIDENTIA," translated as: "Agustin I by God's Providence." On the reverse is a large crowned eagle, perched on a cactus and surrounded by the legend, "First Constitutional Emperor of Mexico." The denomination, 8R, and the designer's initials "JM," have been moved to the center at the base of the coin.

Fig 3.6, Agustín Iturbide - Large Portrait. 8 *Reales*, Mexico City, Large Eagle Reverse, 1823.

Fig 3.7, Agustín Iturbide - Small Bust.
8 *Escudos*, Mexico City, 1822.

The beautiful gold specimen in Figure 3.7 bears the "small" portrait on the obverse, with the legend around the perimeter: "AUGUSTINUS.DEI. PROVIDENTIA," or "Augustin I by God's Providence." On the reverse is a crowned eagle on a cactus, with a trophy of weapons and the legend, "First Constitutional Emperor of Mexico," followed by the denomination, 8S (for *scudi*, Latin for *escudos*) and the requisite assayer's initials "JM."

Fig 3.8, Agustín Iturbide - Large Bust.
8 *Escudos*, Mexico City, 1823.

The obverse of the brilliant gold specimen shown in Figure 3.8 features a large portrait of Iturbide, with the identical legend found on the previous specimen (Figure 3.7). The reverse features a crowned small eagle perched on a cactus, set inside a shield, with a cache of weapons at the bottom. Once again, the legend on the reverse reads "First Constitutional Emperor of Mexico," followed by the denomination "8S" and the requisite assayer's initials "JM."

THE MEXICAN REPUBLIC

The Mexican nation quickly grew tired of the self proclaimed emperor and deposed Iturbide. The ruling council replaced the supreme executive with a governing body of individuals and drafted a new federal constitution in 1824. This document united the Mexican provinces of Nuevo León and Coahuila y Tejas as one state. Nuevo León was later separated from Coahuila y Tejas on May 7, 1824. After his banishment from power, Iturbide traveled to Europe for a year-long sabbatical. He returned to Mexico in July 1824 upon learning of a plot to re-conquer Mexico by Spain and arrived in the port city of Soto La Marina. He was unaware that a death sentence had been imposed on him and was recognized, captured and shot at the village of Padilla Viejo on July 19, 1824.[9]

Following the death of Iturbide, the new rulers again addressed the immigration issue concerning colonial Texas. They adopted a colonization law on August 10, 1824, which guaranteed the protection of persons and property for the settlers. In accordance with this law, the state of Coahuila y Tejas adopted another colonization law on March 24, 1825, for the purpose of augmenting the population, promoting the cultivation of lands, expelling the savages, and promoting commerce.

The Colonization Act of 1825 had the same effect on Texas as did the discovery of gold in California nearly a generation later.[10] New settlers began pouring into the area as the land *empresario* contracts were validated. Although the lands granted to new settlers were mostly located in the wilderness, the pioneers obtained the land on generous terms. The woods were filled with an abundance of wild game: turkey, deer, buffalo and antelope. Since the Mexican government had never taken possession of these lands, by offering the new Anglo citizens land grants the government could validate their claim to the sprawling northern state of Coahuila y Tejas as part of the new Mexican Republic.

THE CONSTITUTION OF 1824

While validating the immigration policy of Iturbide, the new Mexican Republic rejected the idea of adorning the nation's money with the heads of rulers as was previously done under Iturbide's rule and the host of Spanish rulers before him.[11] This was a common practice for many countries over the last 2,000 years, as even the earliest Roman coins bore the likenesses of the Caesar. The Mexican Republic re-designed the money in 1823 to be symbolic of the nation itself and its new liberty, rather than depicting a ruler or a tyrant.

Fig 3.9, 8 *Reales*, Durango, "Hook Neck Eagle," 1824.

Fig 3.10, 8 *Reales*, Mexico City, "Hook Neck Eagle," 1824.

The design selected for the new money shown in figures 3.9 and 3.10 featured a "Liberty Cap" with *Libertad* boldly emblazoned across a "Phrygian Cap" set in a starburst of "Rays." For the reverse, the designers reached back to the traditional Aztec image of an eagle clutching a snake. For the Aztecs this image symbolized the eternal struggle of day and night and the fulfillment of the Aztec prophecy on which Mexico City was founded. By revisiting their earliest native roots, these coins became the symbol of the new Mexican Republic. This design is commonly known by collectors as a "Hook Neck Eagle" 8 *reales* and is found in several different varieties.

Known as a "Phrygian Cap," the symbol (shown in Figure 3.9) dates back to the Roman Empire. Former slaves wore this emblem as a sign that their descendants were considered citizens of Rome. During the eighteenth century, the "Phrygian Cap" evolved into a symbol of freedom and was held aloft atop a pole during the American Revolution as a representation of liberty. In the United States, this symbol became known as a "Liberty Cap." The Republic of Texas used this same symbol of freedom to adorn their own series of money a little more than a dozen years after Mexico adopted the symbol for their money.

This hand-on-book design in Figure 3.11 first appeared in 1823 and marked the beginning of the Mexican Republic, established under the Constitution of 1824. When translated to English, the inscription at the top reads "Liberty in Law." In the hand is a "Liberty Cap" on a pole, a universal symbol of freedom. The book represents the constitution itself, the governing document which provided the protections of property and law for the Anglo-American colonists who immigrated to Mexican Texas. This design was used on the gold coins of Mexico until 1873.

Fig 3.11, Hand-on-Book, 8 *Escudos*, Guanajuato, 1832.

Fig 3.12, Hand-on-Book, 8 *Escudos*, Mexico City, 1836.

The gold coin shown in figure 3.12 is of the same type as the coin shown in figure 3.11. It was struck in Mexico City in 1836. It was during this year that Santa Anna would bring his armies to Texas in an effort to crush the rebellious American colonists who had settled there and were seeking independence. Santa Anna had abolished the protections which were provided under the Constitution of 1824.

REPUBLIC OF MEXICO – CAP & RAYS, EAGLE COINAGE

The introduction of the "Cap & Rays" design (shown in Figure 3.13), also known as the "eagle coinage" in colonial Texas, marked the single longest era of consistency of the Mexican monetary system. This design for the 8 *reales* pieces of the Mexican Republic continued with only minor variations until the 1890s and appeared on the silver *pesos* until 1909.

Fig 3.13, 8 *Reales*, Mexico City, Cap & Rays, Eagle Coinage, 1825.

The Mexican "eagle coinage" was first produced in Mexico City in 1824, and minted the following year at Zacatecas, Durango, Guadalajara, and Guanajuato. The pieces were struck with the "Cap and Rays" design on the obverse and the Mexican Eagle perched on a cactus, holding a snake in its mouth on the reverse. These 8 *reales* pieces, known as *pesos* or Mexican "dollars," were frequently encountered in parts of Texas. The new money was mass produced as the immigration under the Texas colonization plan began to gather steam under Stephen F. Austin, Green DeWitt, Lorenzo de Zavala, and the other land *empresarios*.

The "Cap and Rays" design was the most prolifically produced coin of the Mexican Republic and circulated widely in Mexico, Texas and the United States. It remained legal tender coinage in the U.S. until 1857. The production of these coins by Mexico lasted well into the last half of the nineteenth century when the denomination of 8 *reales* was officially changed into one *peso*, and a *peso* was further divided into one hundred *centavos*.

Fig 3.14, 8 *Reales*, Guanajuato, Cap & Rays, Eagle Coinage, 1836.

In figures 3.14 and 3.15 are two examples of the coins from the Mexican mints at Guanajuato and San Luis Potosi, both of which were produced and dated in the year 1836. The brilliant uncirculated specimen in

Fig 3.15, 8 *Reales*, San Luis Potosi, Cap & Rays, Eagle Coinage, 1836.

Figure 3.14 was minted in the year that Texas won its independence, and appears very much like it did on the day in which it was minted. The 8 *reales* piece in Figure 3.15 was minted in the central Mexican city of San Luis Potosi. Many of these older silver coins are "toned," and bear a colored patina, which results from the oxidation of the silver with moist air over an extended period of time—sometimes a hundred years or more.

THE INFLUENCES OF ANGLO-AMERICAN IMMIGRATION

Anglo immigrants soon began staking their own claims of sovereignty in colonial Texas. The financial panic of 1818 and later the panic of 1823 largely drove the settlers westward. These severe economic downturns were fraught with several high-profile bank failures in the United States. Many of these banks were funded with a combination of gold and silver coin (also referred to as specie), with the balance of the bank's capital often secured by government bonds or stock notes. These were promissory notes which had been collateralized by shares. Given that many of the banks were only capitalized by as little as 10 percent in specie and the balance in paper obligations, any excessive leverage of their loan portfolios often resulted in a disastrous run on the bank, leaving their own ornately printed bank notes selling for a significant discount to gold and silver coin. For some of the settlers who had obtained the notes through loans, they simply spent the remainder of the money and moved out West. Texas had become a debtor's paradise. Under these circumstances, the offer of significant land grants to new settlers in 1823 was quite an inducement to begin a new life.

THE FIRST PAPER MONEY USED IN TEXAS

The establishment of the *Banco Nacional de Texas* in 1822 was the first attempt to use paper money as a common medium of exchange in Texas. Upon his arrival in San Antonio de Béxar, Gov. José Felix Trespalacios discovered that shipments of specie from the subtreasury in San Luis Potosi intended for military payroll were arriving on an irregular basis.[12] This irregularity resulted in long delays between paydays for the Mexican troops, many of whom lived on credit extended to them by local merchants. When a shipment of coins arrived, many of the soldiers celebrated in local saloons, leaving the merchants to wait for the next shipment of specie. This system resulted in a low morale among the troops and their families and caused a stagnation of credit in the town.

In order to expedite the payment process and alleviate the miseries of the existing system, Governor Trespalacios issued a decree on October 21, 1822, to establish a bank to issue notes fully redeemable in specie from the central government as wages to the soldiers.[13] The *Banco Nacional de Texas,* or Texas National Bank, located in San Antonio was Governor Trespalacios' solution to the credit problem. Although it was subject to official approval by Agustín Iturbide, the plan was presented to the city council and unanimously approved, with several members of the council installed as officers of the bank. This plan created the first chartered bank west of the Mississippi River. Four soldiers were given the task of hand producing the notes, since there was no press in San Antonio at the time. The issue of notes was regulated by the amount of money needed to meet the payroll in the province, which would be redeemable for specie upon its arrival.

Similar to the Texas *jolas*, which were issued five years earlier, these notes were declared legal tender for public and private debts. This declaration was followed by a Treasury circular specifying that the notes were not to be redeemed in specie, but by another national issue of paper money.[14] The bank issued less than 12,000 *pesos* of the new paper money in two installments, the first on November 1 and the second on December 1, 1822. Perhaps afraid of similarities with the banking panic in the United States, the local populace refused to accept the paper money in place of coins, and the operations of the bank were summarily suspended.[15]

Unfortunately, there are no known specimens of the "Trespalacios Notes." They were all manuscript notes (handwritten) and most likely written on poor quality paper. By estimate, there were probably less than 200 pieces issued. Although no specimen of the notes has survived, there is a document evidencing this issue of early paper money in the state of Coahuila y Tejas known as the *Lista que Manifiesta el Prestamo*.

The *Lista* is dated October, 14, 1825, and describes the establishment of a tobacco factory at Saltillo and

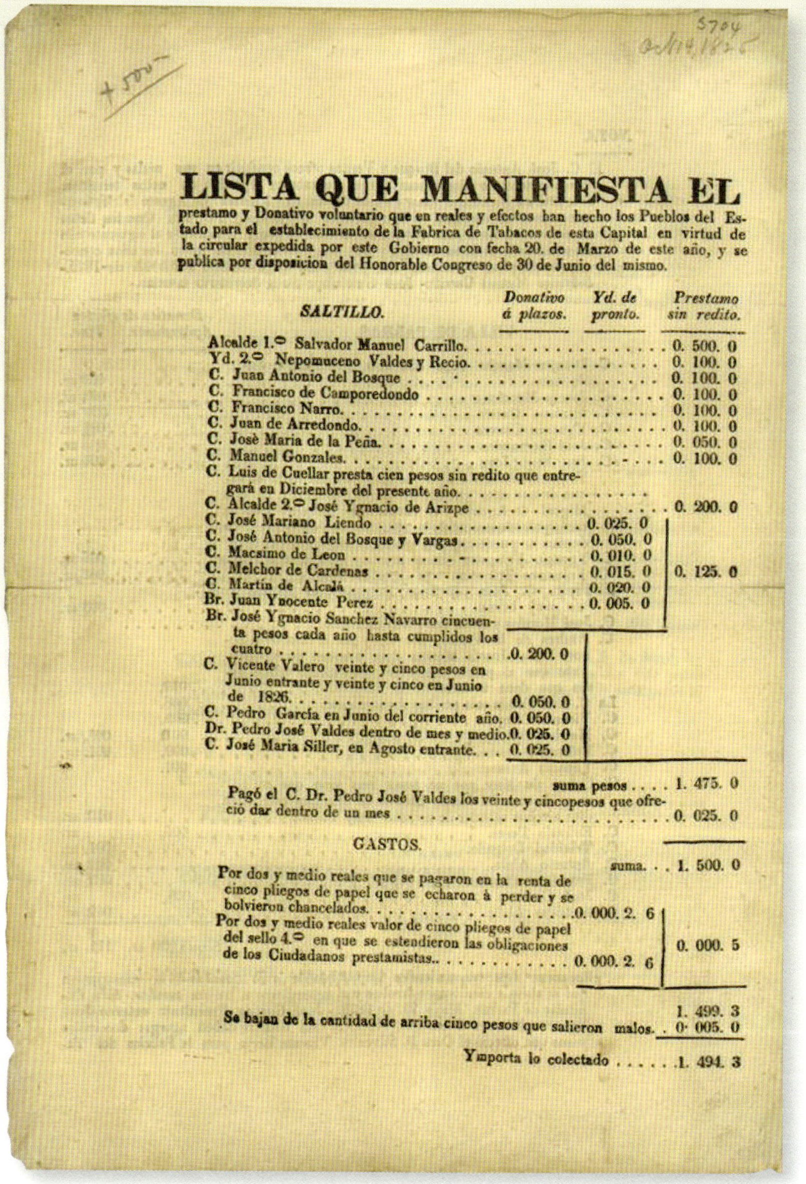

LISTA QUE MANIFIESTA EL

prestamo y Donativo voluntario que en reales y efectos han hecho los Pueblos del Estado para el establecimiento de la Fabrica de Tabacos de esta Capital en virtud de la circular expedida por este Gobierno con fecha 20. de Marzo de este año, y se publica por disposicion del Honorable Congreso de 30 de Junio del mismo.

SALTILLO.	*Donativo á plazos.*	*Yd. de pronto.*	*Prestamo sin redito.*
Alcalde 1.º Salvador Manuel Carrillo			0. 500. 0
Yd. 2.º Nepomuceno Valdes y Recio			0. 100. 0
C. Juan Antonio del Bosque			0. 100. 0
C. Francisco de Camporedondo			0. 100. 0
C. Francisco Narro			0. 100. 0
C. Juan de Arredondo			0. 100. 0
C. Josè Maria de la Peña			0. 050. 0
C. Manuel Gonzales			0. 100. 0
C. Luis de Cuellar presta cien pesos sin redito que entregará en Diciembre del presente año			
C. Alcalde 2.º José Ygnacio de Arizpe			0. 200. 0
C. José Mariano Liendo		0. 025. 0	
C. José Antonio del Bosque y Vargas		0. 050. 0	
C. Macsimo de Leon		0. 010. 0	
C. Melchor de Cardenas		0. 015. 0	0. 125. 0
C. Martin de Alcalá		0. 020. 0	
Br. Juan Ynocente Perez		0. 005. 0	
Br. José Ygnacio Sanchez Navarro cincuenta pesos cada año hasta cumplidos los cuatro	0. 200. 0		
C. Vicente Valero veinte y cinco pesos en Junio entrante y veinte y cinco en Junio de 1826	0. 050. 0		
C. Pedro García en Junio del corriente año	0. 050. 0		
Dr. Pedro José Valdes dentro de mes y medio	0. 025. 0		
C. José Maria Siller, en Agosto entrante	0. 025. 0		
suma pesos			1. 475. 0
Pagó el C. Dr. Pedro José Valdes los veinte y cincopesos que ofreció dar dentro de un mes			0. 025. 0
suma			1. 500. 0

GASTOS.

Por dos y medio reales que se pagaron en la renta de cinco pliegos de papel que se echaron à perder y se bolvieron chancelados	0. 000. 2. 6	
Por dos y medio reales valor de cinco pliegos de papel del sello 4.º en que se estendieron las obligaciones de los Ciudadanos prestamistas	0. 000. 2. 6	0. 000. 5
		1. 499. 3
Se bajan de la cantidad de arriba cinco pesos que salieron malos		0· 005. 0
Ymporta lo colectado		1. 494. 3

Fig 3.16, Lista Que Manifiesta, Page 1.
Private Collection.

various contributions of capital by the partners to the venture in varying amounts of wine (111 barrels), brandy (30 barrels), and *reales* pieces totaling 3,388.2 *pesos*. More importantly, it references the paper money of the *Banco Nacional de Texas* and its lack of acceptance by the organizers of commerce in early Texas. An English translation of the entire document can be found in Appendix C.

The second page of the *Lista* included a contract for a shipping arrangement for the finished product (presumably cigars) made by Jose Antonio del Bosque y Vargas. In the contract, Vargas "offers to drive his mules with eighty loads of tobacco, for a term of five years, distributing such under these terms...." This contract provides clear evidence of bartering and documentation which references the bank described previously and the reluctance of the group to accept the bank's payment in paper money.

The *Lista* has a statement on page four dated at Sala Capitular de Bejar on May 8, 1825, giving an account of contributions made at Béxar "en papel del Banco Nacional de Texas" for the factory. Clearly referencing the contributions in "paper funds of the Bank of Texas," the document also provides verification of the problems that the organizers foresaw if they accepted the paper money in lieu of silver *pesos*. The men were afraid the bank's paper issue could not easily be converted to the coveted silver coins.

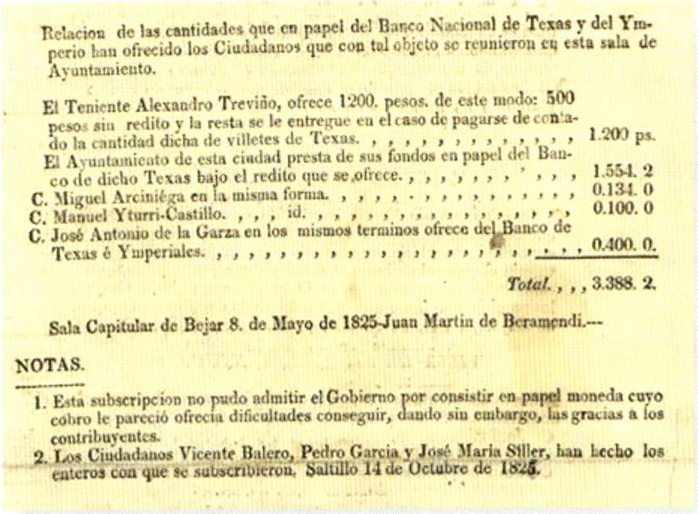
Relacion de las cantidades que en papel del Banco Nacional de Texas y del Ymperio han ofrecido los Ciudadanos que con tal objeto se reunieron en esta sala de Ayuntamiento.

El Teniente Alexandro Treviño, ofrece 1200. pesos. de este modo: 500 pesos sin redito y la resta se le entregue en el caso de pagarse de contado la cantidad dicha de villetes de Texas. , , , , , , , , , , , , 1.200 ps.
El Ayuntamiento de esta ciudad presta de sus fondos en papel del Banco de dicho Texas bajo el redito que se ofrece. , , , , , , , , , , , 1.554. 2
C. Miguel Arciniéga en la misma forma. , , , , , , , , , , , , , , , 0.134. 0
C. Manuel Yturri-Castillo. , , , id. , , , , , , , , , , , , , , , , 0.100. 0
C. José Antonio de la Garza en los mismos terminos ofrece del Banco de Texas é Ymperiales. , 0.400. 0.

Total. , , , 3.388. 2.

Sala Capitular de Bejar 8. de Mayo de 1825-Juan Martin de Beramendi.--

NOTAS.

1. Esta subscripcion no pudo admitir el Gobierno por consistir en papel moneda cuyo cobro le pareció ofrecia dificultades conseguir, dando sin embargo, las gracias a los contribuyentes.
2. Los Ciudadanos Vicente Balero, Pedro Garcia y José Maria Siller, han hecho los enteros con que se subscribieron. Saltillo 14 de Octubre de 1825.

Fig 3.17, LISTA QUE MANIFIESTA, Excerpts from Page 4.
Private Collection.

When translated into English, the *Notas* at the end of the agreement read as follows:

> *Notes:*
>
> 1. *The Government could not admit this subscription because it constitutes paper money which cashing seemed to them to be difficult, although, thanks were given to the donors*
>
> 2. *The Citizens Vicente Balero, Pedro Garcia and Jose Maria Siller, have made the payments with which they subscribed. Saltillo 14th day of October, 1825*[16]

One may find this type of arrangement strange or even bizarre today, in that the organizers of the factory clearly state that while the payments in paper money were not acceptable, there was no question about significant contributions which were made to the venture in brandy and wine. As was true in many parts of colonial Texas, payments were made in specie, and bartering with goods was the order of the day.[17]

Not long after the *Banco Nacional de Texas* was founded, Mexican emperor Agustín Iturbide issued a decree in Mexico authorizing the government to produce a national issue of paper money.[18] By this time, the portrait of Iturbide already graced the silver and gold coins of Mexico, and the populace had a strong prejudice against anything that was not backed by specie. This meant that the Texas notes of *Banco Nacional de Texas* were no longer backed by gold or silver, and on February 5, 1823, a circular was issued in Mexico by the Secretary of the Treasury ordering that the Texas paper money be replaced by new notes issued by the central government, the "Imperio Mexicano" notes. This order was unacceptable to the people who held the "Banco Nacional" notes. The Government of Mexico eventually issued a decree on May 8, 1829, ordering the treasury to liquidate the amount due the citizens of San Antonio de Béxar for any paper money issued from the defunct *Banco Nacional de Texas*. Following their redemption, the retired notes were ultimately destroyed by the Mexican government.[19]

THE "IMPERIO MEXICANO" (MEXICAN EMPIRE) NOTES OF ITURBIDE

The "Imperio Mexicano" notes were issued in January 1823 in denominations of 1, 2 and 10 *pesos*. They were printed on the face of a rectangular piece of white paper. They bear the legend "IMPERIO MEXICANO" or "Mexican Empire." The reverse (or back) is blank. Although designed for widespread circulation in Mexico, they were also issued as payment to Mexican troops stationed in Texas. The notes were only accepted in payment for private transactions, and even then with great reluctance if at all. These "Empire Notes," as they are sometimes called, were most likely printed by Samuel Bangs in Saltillo, a well-established printer in the region who had numerous government printing jobs in 1822 and 1823.[20] They may have come from the Imperial Palace in Mexico City, however, where most of the official paper documents of the period were printed. The paper is high quality and appears to be a cotton or linen blend. The printing created a slight raising of the lettering on the reverse. The facsimile signatures were stamped on each note after their printing, rather than included in the printing process.

These notes were issued in denominations of 1, 2 and 10 *pesos*. According to the Decree of December 20, 1822, the 1 *peso* notes were to be issued in the amount of four million *pesos*, the 2 *peso* notes issued in the amount of two million *pesos*, and the 10 *peso* notes issued in the amount of 100,000 *pesos*.[21] Despite the large number originally authorized, the surviving specimens are scarce in any condition, with the 10 *peso* notes being the rarest.

Examples of the 1, 2, and 10 *peso* notes are shown in Figures 3.18 through 3.20 with each example translated to English. The language in the notes are identical, and all are dated January 1, 1823, with the denominations and serial numbers being the only change in the design.

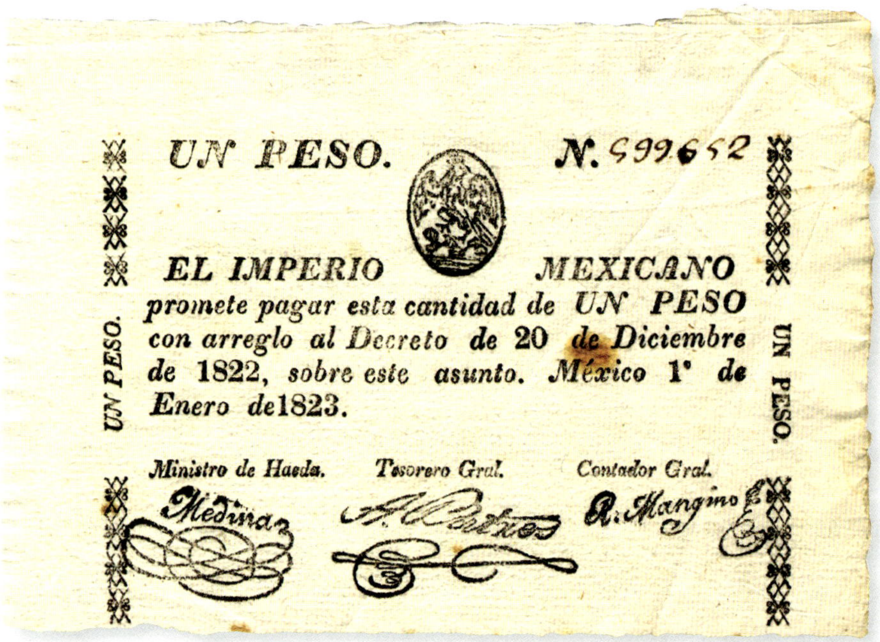

Fig 3.18, ***Un Peso IMPERIO MEXICANO.***
Private Collection, Cr. Unlisted, O-10.

ONE PESO N.599652 *THE MEXICAN EMPIRE*

Promises to pay the amount of ONE PESO in agreement with Decree of the 20th of December of 1822, in regards to this matter. Mexico 1st of January 1823.

Minister of Revenues	*Treasurer General*	*Accountant General*
Medina	*A. Batres*	*R. Mangino*

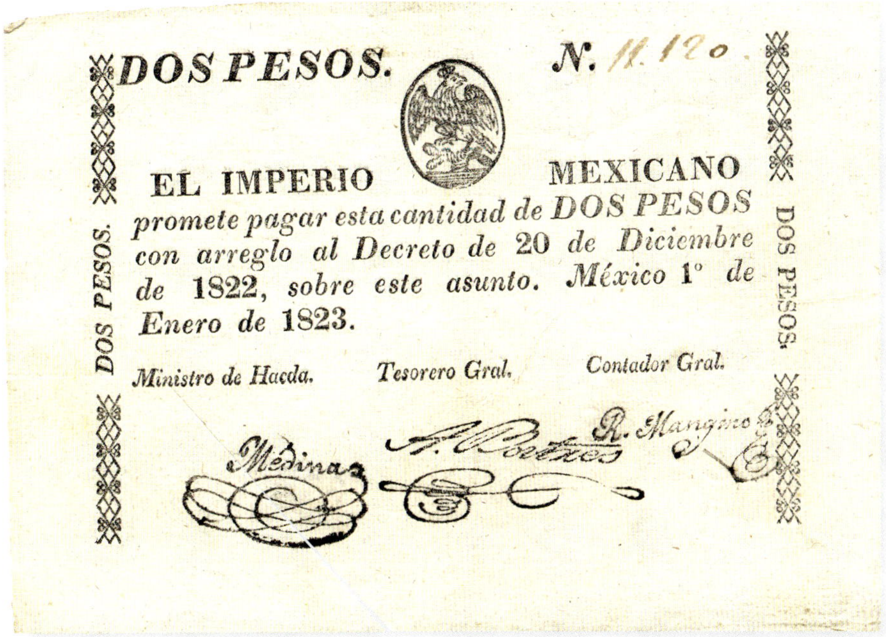

DOS PESOS *N. 11.120.* *THE MEXICAN EMPIRE*

Promises to pay the amount of TWO PESOS in agreement with Decree of the 20th of December of 1822, in regards to this matter. Mexico 1st of January 1823.

Minister of Revenues *Treasurer General* *Accountant General*
Medina *A. Batres* *R. Mangino*

Fig 3.19, *Dos Pesos IMPERIO MEXICANO.*
Private Collection. Cr. Unlisted, O-11.

DIEZ PESOS *N. 2156* *THE MEXICAN EMPIRE*

Promises to pay the amount of TEN PESOS in agreement with Decree of the 20th of December of 1822, in regards to this matter. Mexico 1st of January 1823.

Minister of Revenues *Treasurer General* *Accountant General*
Medina *A. Batres* *R. Mangino*

Fig 3.20, *Diez Pesos IMPERIO MEXICANO.*
Private Collection. Cr. Unlisted, O-12.

THE MEXICAN REPUBLIC BANKNOTES OF 1823

When Mexico became a Federal Republic in 1823, the new government tried to correct the treasury mistakes made by Iturbide and restore the public trust in the government's financial management. They withdrew Iturbide's "Empire Notes" from circulation and began to issue new notes.[22] The new design was meant to compel the public's acceptance of the pieces by playing on their religious convictions. The money was printed on the backs of several different varieties of cancelled "papal bulls" (an official proclamation from the Vatican). The Catholic Church originally issued the "papal bulls" between 1784-1785. These notes were met with widespread skepticism because of their large size (12 $\frac{1}{2}$" x 8 $\frac{1}{2}$") and a general reluctance to accept paper issues. The "papal bull" notes were subsequently withdrawn from circulation in favor of the silver coins which followed. These notes were made in denominations of 1, 2 and 10 *pesos* as shown in Figures 3.21 through 3.23 with each example translated to English.[23] The language in the notes are identical, and all are dated May 5, 1823, with the denominations and serial numbers being the only change in the design.

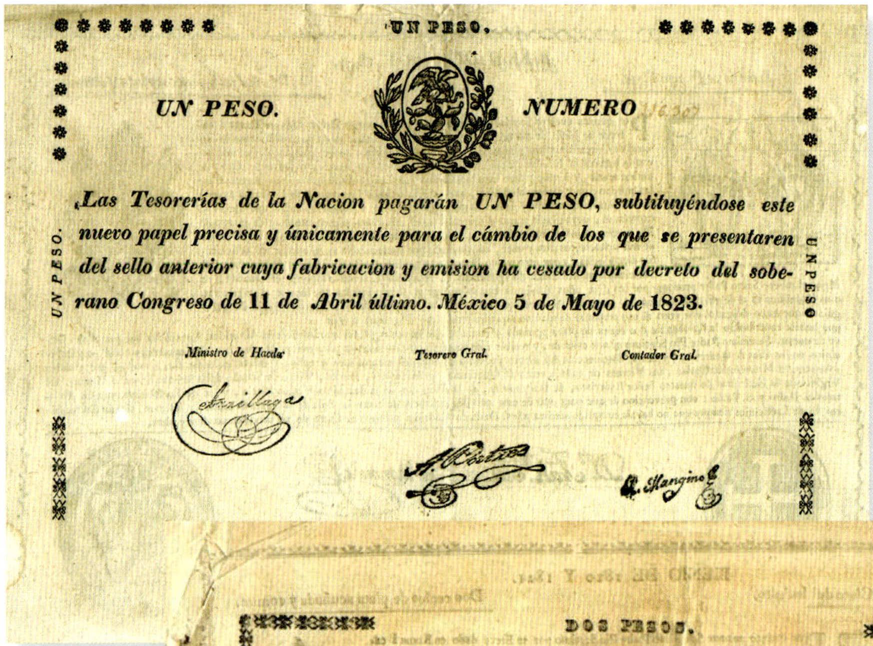

ONE PESO, NUMBER 116.307, *The Treasuries of the Nation will pay ONE PESO, substituting this new paper precisely and exclusively for the exchange of those presented with the before shown seal which fabrication and issuance has ceased by decree of the sovereign Congress of the past 11th of April. Mexico, 5th of May 1823.*

Minister of Revenue	General Treasury	General Accountant
Arrillaga	A. Batres	R. Mangino

Fig 3.21, *Un Peso*, Mexican Republic Banknote.
Private Collection, Cr. Unlisted, O-15.

DOS PESOS, NUMBER 77.205, The Treasuries of the Nation will pay DOS PESOS, substituting this new paper precisely and exclusively for the exchange of those presented with the before shown seal which fabrication and issuance has ceased by decree of the sovereign Congress of the past 11th of April. Mexico, 5th of May 1823.

Minister of Revenue	*Arrillaga*
General Treasury	*A. Batres*
General Accountant	*R. Mangino*

Fig 3.22, *Dos Pesos*, Mexican Republic Banknote.
Private Collection, Cr. Unlisted, O-16.

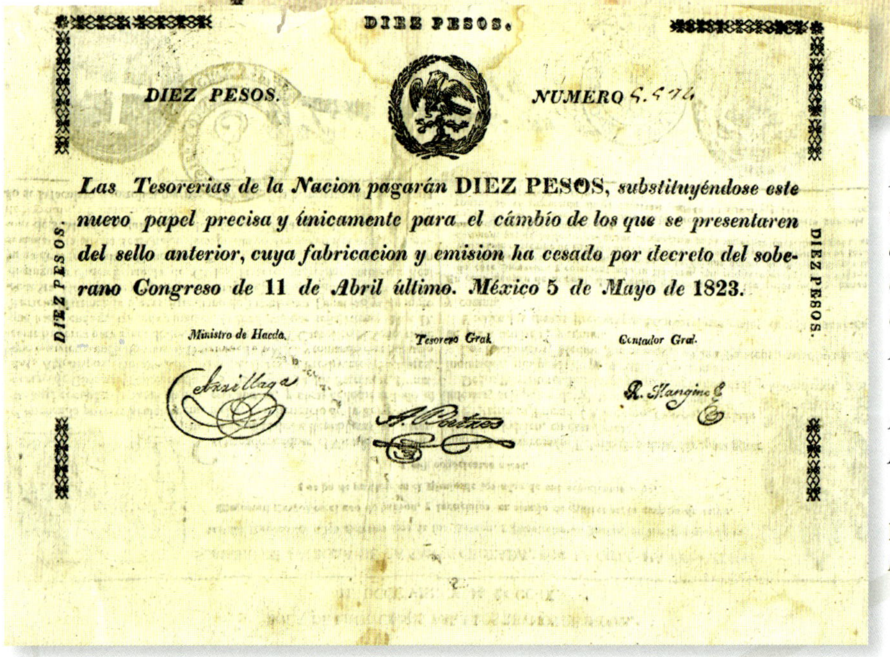

DIEZ PESOS, NUMBER 5.574, The Treasuries of the Nation will pay DIEZ PESOS, substituting this new paper precisely and exclusively for the exchange of those presented with the before shown seal which fabrication and issuance has ceased by decree of the sovereign Congress of the past 11th of April. Mexico, 5th of May 1823.

Minister of Revenue	General Treasury	General Accountant
Arrillaga	A. Batres	R. Mangino

Fig 3.23, *Diez Pesos*, Mexican Republic Banknote.
Private Collection, Cr. Unlisted, O-17.

BULA DE LACTICINIOS PARA LOS REYNOS DE INDIAS.
M. DCCC VIII, Y M. DCCC IX.

SUMARIO DE LA BULA DE LA SANTA CRUZADA, POR LA QUAL HA CONCEDIDO la Silla Apostolica á los Eclesiasticos de los Reynos, y Provincias de Indias, de los Dominios de su Magestad Catholica el uso de huevos, y lacticinios en tiempo de Quaresma, la qual ha de servir, y se ha de publicar en el Bienio de los años de mil ochocientos ocho, y mil ochocientos nueve.

Compadeciendose el Vicario de Christo de la necesidad de las Republicas Christianas, y queriendo proveer benignamente á ella, con beneficio de la Religion Catholica, concedió la facultad de comer huevos, y cosas de leche en todo el tiempo de Quaresma (exceptuada la Semana Santa) á los Patriarcas, Primados, Arzobispos, Obispos, Prelados inferiores, y Presbyteros Seculares, que estuvieren en los Reynos, y Dominios de S.M.C. y tomando este Sumario contribuyeren para ayuda de los gastos, que el REY Catholico N. Señor tiene que hacer en la guerra contra Infieles, la limosna, que señalaremos Nos D. Patricio Martinez de Bustos, Arcediano de Trastamara, Dignidad y Canonigo de la Sta Metropolitana Iglesia de Santiago, Caballero Gran Cruz de la Real distinguida Orden Española de Carlos Tercero, Individuo nato de la Real Junta de la Inmaculada Concepcion, Exactor y Colector de las Pensiones consignadas á la misma Real Orden, Juez privativo del nuevo Rezado, del Consejo de S.M. y Comisario Apostolico General de las Tres Gracias de Cruzada, Subsidio, y Escusado, en todos los Reynos, y Señorios, de S.M.C. que usando de la facultad Apostolica, que nos [illegible], hemos tasado lo que cada uno de los expresados Eclesiastico debe dàr, para gozar de dicho Indulto, en esta forma.

El Patriarca, Primado, Arzobispo, Obispo, y Prelado inferior, seis pesos de plata acuñada, y comun.

De los Presbyteros Seculares, el que tenga Dignidad, ó Canonicato, ó sea Inquisidor, tres pesos de plata acuñada, y comun.

Los Racioneros, Medios Racioneros, y Curas Parrocos, peso y medio de plata acuñada, y comun.

Y todos los demas Presbyteros Seculares, tres reales de plata acuñada, y comun.

En consequencia de lo qual, declaramos, que cada uno de los arriba dichos, tomando este Sumario, y contribuyendo la limosna, que respectivamente va señalada, y no de otra suerte, puede comer huevos, y lacticinios dentro de dichos Reynos de Indias, en el tiempo de Quaresma (excepto en la Semana Santa) durante dicha predicacion, que se ha de contar desde la proxima publicacion de esta dicha Bula, en sus Lugares. Y porquanto vos [illegible] tomasteis este Sumario, dando para dicha guerra [illegible] de plata acuñada, comun, os es permitida dicha facultad. Dada en Madrid á primero de enero de mil ochocientos y seis.

Fig 3.24, ***Diez Pesos***, **Mexican Republic Banknote, "Papal Bull" reverse.**
Private Collection, Cr. Unlisted, O-15 (reverse).

The old "papal bull" on the back of this 10 *pesos* note provides an interesting insight into how the declarations of the Catholic Church were interwoven with the financial transactions of early Spanish and Mexican Texas. Although there are several varieties of the papal bulls, the bizarre pronouncement shown below and dated 1806, declares that for a prescribed "donation" to the church in silver *pesos*, priests and parishioners have the blessing of the church to consume eggs and dairy products during the season of Lent. The English translation reads:[24]

AUTHORIZATION OF LACTOSE FOR THE KINGDOM OF THE INDIES.
M. DCC VIII, Y M.DCCC IX.

SUMMARY OF THE ORDER OF THE HOLY CRUSADE, BY WHICH IS CONCEDED by the Apostolic Chair to the Eclesiastics of the Kingdom of the Indies and other parts of his Catholic Majesty's Domains, the use of eggs and dairy products during lent. This will be in effect and be published during the years of 1808 AND 1809.

The Vicar of Christ feeling empathy for the needs of the Christian Republics and wanting to provide them with the benefits of Catholicism, conceded the right to consume eggs and dairy products during lent (except Easter week), to the Patriarchs, Archbishops, Bishops, inferior priests and secular Presbyterians that reside in the kingship and domains of His Majesty. In order to take advantage of this summary they shall contribute to the expenses that the Catholic King, our Lord, incurs to battle the infidels. The donation established by Don Manuel Ventura Figueroa, Arcediano de Nendo, Dignity of the Saint and Apostolic Metropolitan Church of Santiago, Knight of the Great Cross of the distinguished order of Charles III, Council Governor, Castilla Chamber, General Apostolic Commissary of the Holy Crusade and other graces in all the Catholic kingships of His Majesty. By using the appointed apostolic faculty, we have set the amount that each ecclesiastic shall pay in order to enjoy the above privileges.

The Patriarch, Archbishop, bishop and inferior priest shall pay four silver coins pesos.

Secular Presbyterians, dignitaries, those ordained to say mass and the Inquisitionist, two silver coin pesos.

The remaining Presbyterians one silver coin peso.

Consequently, we declare that each one of the above mentioned, adhering to this summary and paying the established donation may eat eggs and dairy products in these provinces during lent (except Easter week). This summary will take effect starting on it's fifth publication. Madrid, January 1st, 1806.

Fig 3.25, Green DeWitt.

Texas State Library & Archives Commission, Austin, Texas.

For the citizens of Mexico and Texas, the pronouncement on the back of the "papal bull" shown in Figure 3.27 amounted to a voluntary tax on the consumption of eggs during Lent. The ban would have been very difficult to enforce, however. Although these peculiar notes found little acceptance outside of the soldiers stationed in the missions of Texas, they serve as an important reminder of how closely the Catholic Church and the Mexican Government were intertwined in the eyes of early Anglo-American colonists of Texas.

COLONIAL TEXAS AND THE LAND *EMPRESARIOS*

The steady stream of American immigrants arriving in colonial Texas under the *empresario* system made their transactions in dollars, rather than in *pesos* or *reales*. The currency primarily consisted of the old pillar coinage, portrait coins, hammered dollars and bank notes from the United States. There are several references to hammered dollars in period writings, primarily because many of these crudely made coins from the Mexican War of Independence era were made in close proximity to Texas. The panic of 1823 and the banking collapse that followed brought an influx of settlers westward into Alabama, Mississippi and eventually Texas. The settlers also carried American bank notes that were denominated in dollars. Even the heavy Spanish and Mexican silver coins had become known as silver "dollars." The silver dollars of the United States were made of similar size and feel as the Mexican 8 *reales* coins, although their silver content was slightly less. The bank notes brought in by the settlers were also used, but only to the extent to which these banks were known to be solvent, as many of the banks had defaulted on their obligations during the financial panic. Hence the name "broken bank notes" is used by collectors to describe many of the obsolete issues. Silver and gold coins were the preferred means of payment, as the specie of several countries was used interchangeably and readily accepted.

As Stephen F. Austin brought settlers to colonial Texas, Green DeWitt—a Kentucky native inspired by the stories of Moses Austin's successes—traveled to Mexico City and applied for an *empresario* contract. When he was a small boy, DeWitt's father had moved his family to the Spanish-held territory of Missouri and had become a citizen of Spain. Like Moses Austin, his first *empresario* request was unsuccessful. Having passed through Texas on his journey to Mexico City, DeWitt again ventured to Saltillo, the capital of the Mexican state of Coahuila y Tejas, but this time he was accompanied by Stephen F. Austin and the Baron de Bastrop.[25] DeWitt then received a grant to settle "four hundred industrious Catholic families" in a tract adjacent to Austin's first grant, centered in present Gonzales County. DeWitt's Colony was subject to the colonization laws of 1824.[26]

For the early settlers in DeWitt's Colony, life was nothing more than just an existence. As described by an early settler, the colonists—consisting of about a dozen families—lived in rude log cabins, windowless and floorless, and often described as the "abode of the pioneer."[27] These cabins gave the settlers some shelter from the sun and the rain but were devoid of comfort. Several families huddled together for protection against the hostile Karankawa Indians. Subsistence farming was the order of the day and game was plentiful. Although food was abundant, there was a shortage of "civilized" items. As one old lady remarked, Texas was "a heaven for men and dogs, but a hell for women and oxen." The women talked sadly of the homes they left behind, for in these early days there was no spinning wheel or loom for making new clothes and nothing to spin. There was no poultry, no garden, no books, newspapers, schools or churches. Not only was there very little money, there was even less to spend it on, unless it was for the purchase of additional land. As the land *empresario* and administrator of his colony, Green DeWitt offered a partial solution to the money shortage by issuing his own private currency in payment for goods. It is important to note that these issues were denominated in dollars rather than *pesos* or *reales* as was customary in other parts of Mexico.

THE NOTES OF GREEN DEWITT'S COLONY

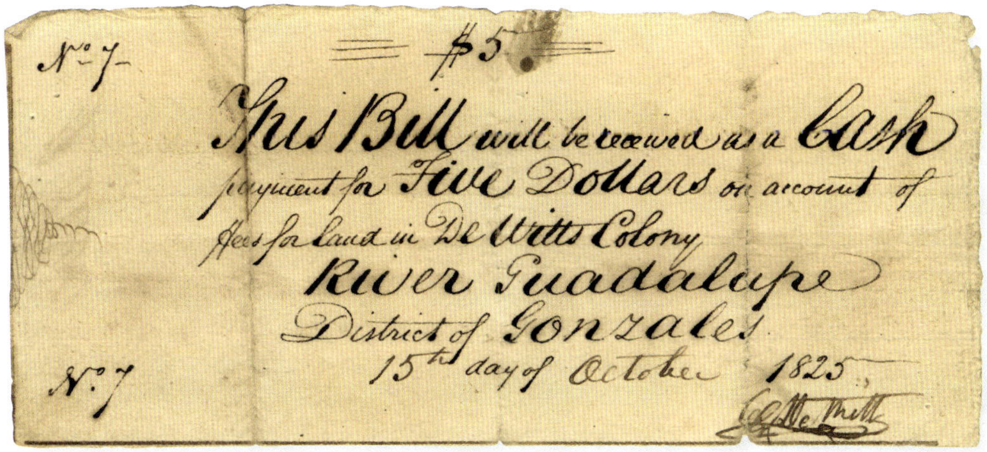

No. 7 — $5
This Bill will be received as a Cash payment for Five Dollars on account of fees for land in De Witts Colony
River Guadalupe
District of Gonzales
15th day of October 1825
No. 7
G. DeWitt

No. 7, $5, This Bill will be received as a Cash payment for Five Dollars on account of fees for land in De Witts Colony. River Guadalupe, District of Gonzales. 15th day of October, 1825.
No. 7. Signed: G. DeWitt

Fig 3.26, $5 DeWitt Colony.

River Guadalupe, District of Gonzales, October 15, 1825, John N. Rowe III Collection of Texas Currency, DeGolyer Library, Southern Methodist University, Dallas, Texas, Cr. Unl, O-20.

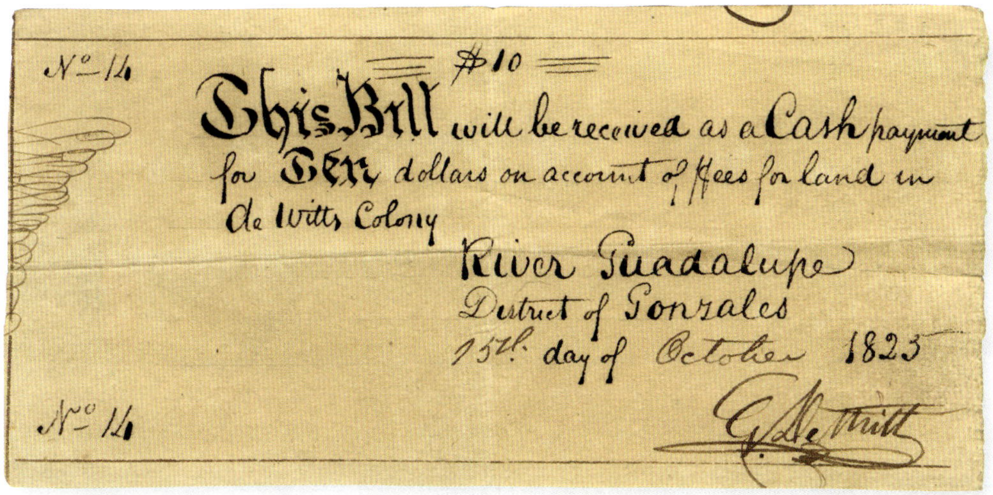

No. 14 — $10
This Bill will be received as a Cash payment for TEN dollars on account of fees for land in de Witts Colony
River Guadalupe
District of Gonzales
15th day of October 1825
No. 14
G. DeWitt

No. 14, $10, This Bill will be received as a Cash payment for TEN dollars on account of fees for land in de Witts Colony. River Guadalupe, District of Gonzales. 15th day of October, 1825.
No 14. Signed: G. DeWitt

Fig 3.27, $10 DeWitt Colony.

River Guadalupe, District of Gonzales, October 15, 1825, John N. Rowe III Collection of Texas Currency, DeGolyer Library, Southern Methodist University, Dallas, Texas, Cr. Unl, O-21.

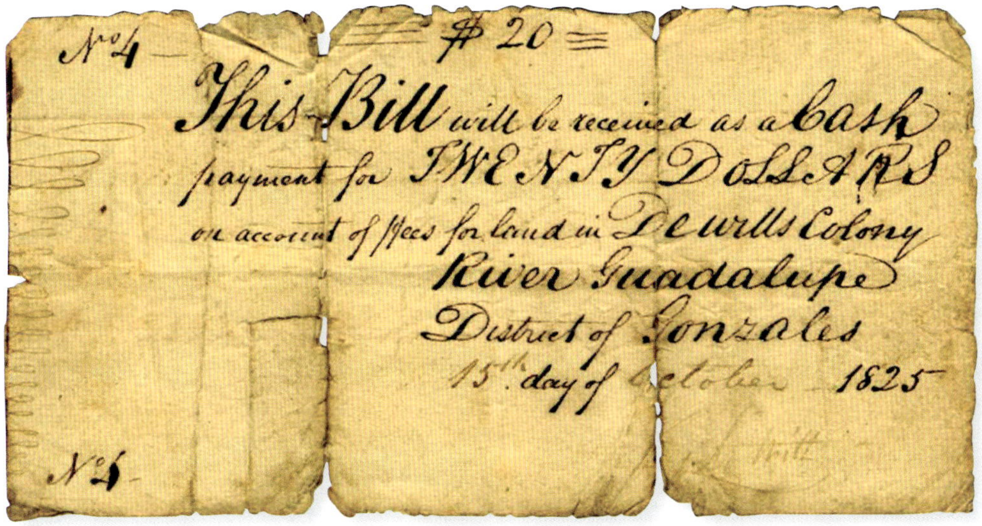

No. 4 — $20
This Bill will be received as a Cash payment for TWENTY DOLLARS on account of fees for land in Dewitts Colony
River Guadalupe
District of Gonzales
15th day of October 1825
No. 4

No. 4, $20, This Bill will be received as a Cash payment for TWENTY DOLLARS on account of fees for land in Dewitts Colony. River Guadalupe, District of Gonzales. 15th day of October, 1825.
No. 4. Signed: G. DeWitt

Fig 3.28, $20 DeWitt's Colony.

River Guadalupe, District of Gonzales, October 18, 1825, Private Collection, Cr. Unl, O-22.

THE NOTES OF GREEN DEWITT'S COLONY

Being backed by specie was the initial necessity for the acceptance of paper money in Texas. An innovative idea was to make a private issue of currency backed by land to foster its acceptance. The hand-written currency of land *empresario* Green DeWitt was issued in amounts of $5, $10, and $20.[28] These specimens could be redeemed for the purchase of land or in payment of land fees in DeWitt's Colony. Because these notes were used by Anglo-American immigrants, they were denominated in dollars. Although the notes were readily accepted in DeWitt's Colony, the low serial numbers on the surviving specimens indicate that only a few dozen at most ever existed in colonial Texas. The acceptance of a paper draft redeemable for land fees was a unique concept in its day.

NACOGDOCHES "RED HOUSE" NOTES

Haden Edwards was a pioneer settler and prominent land speculator from Virginia who traveled to Mexico City in 1823 to seek an *empresario* contract with Stephen F. Austin and others.[29] Following the passage of the colonization laws, Edwards received a grant in the vicinity of Nacogdoches to locate up to 800 families. Because Nacogdoches had many pre-existing claims to land, Edwards posted notices for landowners to come forward and verify their claims with him or risk losing title to their property. This angered many of the older settlers and Edwards was expelled two years later following an incident involving Edwards' son-in-law and an over-turned election for *alcalde* of the area. Edwards' expulsion resulted in an armed insurrection against the Mexican Government known as the Fredonia Rebellion. Edwards and others attempted to separate the area surrounding Nacogdoches and declared their independence from Mexico on December 26, 1826. Less than a month later the rebels were forced across the Sabine River into Louisiana by Mexican troops.

Following the rebellion, the Mexican Government knew that Nacogdoches still harbored elements from previous filibustering expeditions, so the area was reinforced by the 12th Battalion of the Mexican Army. Col. José de las Piedras took command of the 320-man garrison shortly after his arrival in April 1827. He initially lacked suitable headquarters, but the colonel had a frame and adobe building constructed, with wooden walls plastered over with adobe made from the red clay soil of Nacogdoches. It became known as the "Red House."[30] The large and comfortable dwelling served as headquarters for Piedras and the officers of the 12th Infantry Battalion and became the center of military and social authority in the town.[31]

These ½ *real* paper notes were used by Mexican troops during the occupation of Nacogdoches from 1827-1832 as indicated by the "12th Infantry Battalion" stamp on the reverse. The stamp bears the familiar Mexican eagle perched on a cactus. In many ways, these small paper notes may have been used like a "gift card" of today as the legend on the face of the note indicates it could be redeemed for merchandise. They may have also been handed out as a promotional item to trade in the merchant's store or issued in change for purchases. This place of business was likely the mercantile store established in Nacogdoches in 1831 by Henry and Louis Rueg. The Rueg brothers were Swiss born and had come to the United States in 1818 and traded horses and mules in East Texas before opening their store in the town of Nacogdoches.[32] They likely saw the occupation of the city as an opportunity to trade with the Mexican soldiers for their silver.

Only two signatories are known on this extremely rare series. The first note appears to be "Rueg Lenard," which happens to be the name of the Ruegs' Swiss father. The second example is signed "H. Edwards," undoubtedly the same Haden Edwards who fled across the Sabine River to escape capture by Mexican authorities. Ironically, this indicates that Edwards may have assisted the Rueg brothers in establishing the store which later profited from the trade of the same garrison of soldiers who had been sent to expel him from Texas.

Col. José de las Piedras stayed in Nacogdoches until 1832, at which time he surrendered his command to his officers who declared their allegiance to Santa Anna, the charismatic Mexican political leader who had sworn to uphold the Constitution of 1824. Following a skirmish known as the "battle of Nacogdoches," Piedras withdrew to San Antonio, leaving the town open to newcomers and a center of activity for revolutionaries. The "Red House" was rented to new settlers and in 1835 became the first Texas home of Thomas J. Rusk. One year later, Rusk became the first Secretary of War for the Republic of Texas.

MERCHANT SCRIP, NACOGDOCHES (C. 1827-1832) "RED HOUSE" NOTES

Left Margin: MEDIO REAL

Medio Real, *6 ¼ Cents, Vale por MEDIO REAL, En efectos de nuestra tienda. Rueg Lenard*

Half Real, *6 ¼ Cents, Good for Half* Real, *For merchandise in our store. Rueg Lenard*

Right Margin: NACOGDOCHES

Fig 3.29, Medio *Real* , 6 ¼ Cents, Rueg Lenard.
John N. Rowe III Collection of Texas Currency, DeGoyler Library, Southern Methodist University, Dallas, Texas, Cr. Unlisted, O-35.

Left Margin: MEDIO REAL

Medio Real, *6 ¼ Cents, Vale por MEDIO REAL, En efectos de nuestra tienda. H. Edwards*

Half Real, *6 ¼ Cents, Good for Half* Real, *For merchandise in our store. H. Edwards*

Right Margin: NACOGDOCHES

Fig 3.30, Medio *Real*, 6 ¼ Cents, H. Edwards, c. 1827-1832.
John N. Rowe III Collection of Texas Currency, DeGoyler Library, Southern Methodist University, Dallas, Texas, Cr. Unlisted, O-35.

Fig 3.31, Medio *Real*, Reverse Stamp, c. 1827-1832.
BATALLON. INFANTERIA. DE. LINEA. NUM. 12

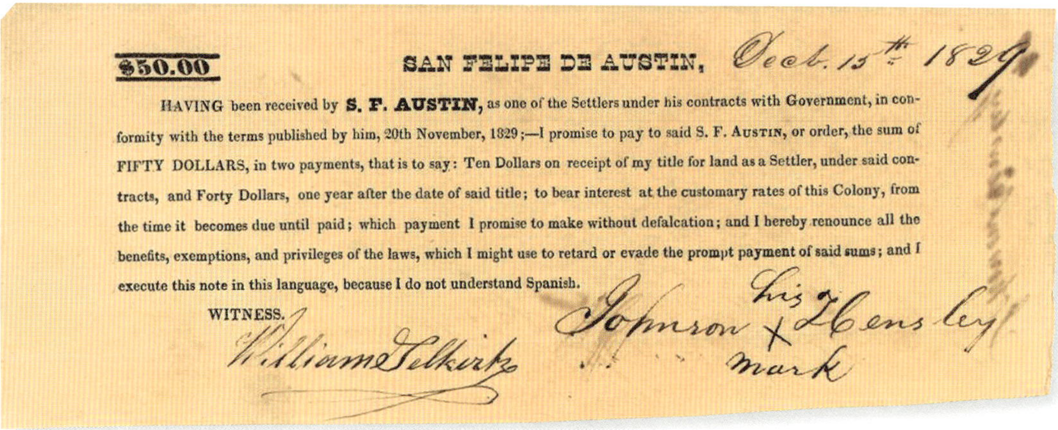

$50.00 SAN FELIPE DE AUSTIN, Decb. 15th 1829

HAVING been received by S. F. AUSTIN, as one of the Settlers under his contracts with Government, in conformity with the terms published by him, 20th November, 1829;—I promise to pay to said S. F. Austin, or order, the sum of FIFTY DOLLARS, in two payments, that is to say: Ten Dollars on receipt of my title for land as a Settler, under said contracts, and Forty Dollars, one year after the date of said title; to bear interest at the customary rates of this Colony, from the time it becomes due until paid; which payment I promise to make without defalcation; and I hereby renounce all the benefits, exemptions, and privileges of the laws, which I might use to retard or evade the prompt payment of said sums; and I execute this note in this language, because I do not understand Spanish.

WITNESS. William Selkirk

Johnson his X mark Hensley

Fig 3.32, $50 San Felipe de Austin, December 15, 1829.

Private Collection, Cr. Unlisted, 0-30.

SAN FELIPE DE AUSTIN

San Felipe de Austin was established by Stephen F. Austin in July 1823 as the epicenter of the first Anglo-American colony in Texas. It was at this small town on the Brazos River, about seventeen miles west of present-day Katy, Texas, that Austin brought the first 297 families to colonize Texas under a contract with the Mexican government. Not to be confused with the city of Austin which did not exist until 1839, San Felipe de Austin was often described as the social, economic, and political center of Texas, as well as the capital of the Anglo colonies during the period of 1824-1836. This was also the home of Stephen F. Austin and other famous pioneers, the home of Texas' first Anglo newspaper (*The Texas Gazette*, founded in 1829), and home of the first postal system in Texas.[33] Both the conventions of 1832 and 1833, and the consultation of delegates met at San Felipe de Austin in the fall of 1835.

Stephen F. Austin was by far the most successful of the land *empresarios* and is now known as the "Father of Texas" for his exhaustive efforts in bringing settlers to the area. In 1829 and 1830, promissory notes were issued by settlers in San Felipe de Austin to the *empresario*, who used them to document payments due for land in his colony on which title had been issued. These $50 obligations were paid to Austin, as his contract with Mexico required his services as the land *empresario*.[34]

Unlike the "Red House" notes of Nacogdoches or the land currency issued by Green DeWitt, the San Felipe issues were not intended to be used as a medium of exchange. These issues were essentially a mortgage on the property of the settlers located in Austin's Colony. These obligations were issued for the purchase of land with $10 down upon receipt of title and required a payment of $40 to "S.F. Austin" in one year, to bear interest "at the customary rates of this Colony." Interestingly, these notes securing land in the Mexican state of Coahuila y Tejas were printed in English for the settlers with a moniker at the end: "and I execute this note in this language, because I do not understand Spanish."

The $50 land note in Figure 3.32 was signed by Johnson Hensley with an "X," indicating that he could not read, write, or sign his name. This document was countersigned by William Selkirk, as a witness to Hensley's mark.[35] Selkirk was one of Austin's "Old Three Hundred" and worked as a surveyor in Austin's colony. Henley was one of several settlers by that name who lived in colonial Texas, some of whom were law clients of William Barret Travis. Travis recorded the death of "Old Hensley" in his diary on May 4, 1834, though he did not indicate which member of the Hensley family had died. It was printed by G.B. Cotton, 1829.

No witness was required for the note in Figure 3.33, as it bears the signature of Amos Gates rather than a mark. Gates was the son of William Gates and Catherine Hardin, who were included in Austin's "Old Three Hundred" colonists. The couple traveled from Kentucky through Arkansas and finally to Austin's colony in 1821 with three sons (including Amos) and a daughter. One of Amos's brothers named Charles died in 1836. Amos's sister Sarah married Abner Kuykendall. Amos Gates lost

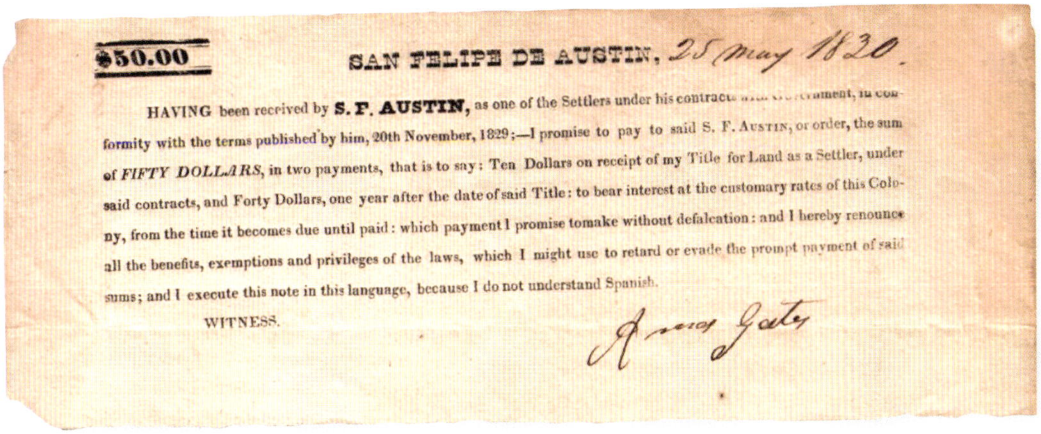

$50.00 SAN FELIPE DE AUSTIN, 25 May 1830.

HAVING been received by **S. F. AUSTIN,** as one of the Settlers under his contract [illegible], in conformity with the terms published by him, 20th November, 1829;—I promise to pay to said S. F. AUSTIN, or order, the sum of *FIFTY DOLLARS*, in two payments, that is to say: Ten Dollars on receipt of my Title for Land as a Settler, under said contracts, and Forty Dollars, one year after the date of said Title: to bear interest at the customary rates of this Colony, from the time it becomes due until paid: which payment I promise tomake without defalcation: and I hereby renounce all the benefits, exemptions and privileges of the laws, which I might use to retard or evade the prompt payment of said sums; and I execute this note in this language, because I do not understand Spanish.

WITNESS.

Amos Gates

Fig 3.33, $50 San Felipe de Austin, May 25, 1830.

Private Collection, Cr. Unlisted, O-30.

his mother Catherine in 1826, and his father William on August 20, 1828.[36] The date on this obligation indicates that Amos had expanded his land holdings following the death of his father. It was printed by G.B. Cotton in 1829.

Many of us might picture an early settler trekking through the piney woods of Texas with a coonskin cap, a gun on his shoulder, a mule in tow, and a family following in a covered wagon several months later. In fact, there is another reality regarding the history of early settlers which was never depicted in this Hollywood-induced image. After searching for land and selecting the appropriate parcel, the settler was required to pledge his faith to the Catholic Church, the Mexican Government and the Constitution of 1824. He was also required to pay a $2 fee to a commissioner for a stamped certificate of title, $10 in administrative fees, an average of $12 for surveying costs and had to execute a $50 mortgage note on his new homestead to the agent of the Mexican Government who brought him to Texas! Regardless of the written rules for emigration, no one was turned away, or ever wanted for his title because he was poor. Stephen F. Austin himself would often lend the settlers money to pay the surveyor. These early San Felipe de Austin issues represent the first printed mortgage notes (versus handwritten) in the English language which were used in Texas.

To a large degree, the settlers of Texas in the late 1820s and early 1830s were few and scattered far between.[37] Although the work was hard, most of them appeared to be contented and satisfied with their newfound lot in life. The almost universal hospitality and friendship amongst the settlers throughout the country continued for several years due to their common cultural background and mutual dependence on each other for protection. The land *empresarios* possessed the sole governing power over the colonists, and enacted a set of colonial laws for their local government. Commerce was limited and money was primarily spent for surveying, title work and for imported goods. Imported goods were of the highest priority, and imported whisky, fine wines, clothing and furniture were among the most sought-after items in making the wilds of Texas into a home.

COUNTERFEITING IN MEXICAN TEXAS

But for every place a dollar can be spent, there is a dishonest person who was willing to cheat that merchant out of those goods. The colony of San Felipe de Austin was no exception. Counterfeiting in San Felipe de Austin was rampant in the heart of colonial Texas, as a notorious counterfeiter had perfected a homespun minting process for the bogus coins. He made a hearty supply of coins similar to those in circulation except that instead of making the pieces entirely out of silver, they were made of copper with a thin coating of silver. The coins were described by Noah Smithwick, an early Texas pioneer, as "His Mexican eagle dollars were as handsome coins as I ever saw, much finer in execution, in fact, than the genuine article, and passed current in the community until the plating began to wear off, when he gathered them in, treating them to a fresh coat, [and] sent them out again."[38] While the counterfeit copper "dollars" were accepted in local transactions, any attempt to pass the coins in a foreign transaction was asking

Counterfeiting in San Felipe de Austin was rampant in the heart of colonial Texas, as a notorious counterfeiter had perfected a homespun minting process for the bogus coins.

The authorities in Mexico City required all couples to be married in a ceremony of the Catholic faith. Since the only Catholic churches in the area were in the mission settlements, rather than requiring that couples be married in the church, the church came to them so to speak.

for trouble. The ambitious counterfeiter attempted to pass his manufactured money in Louisiana and was apprehended. Although the authorities failed to convict him, the exposure of his plated copper "dollars" doomed their future acceptance by the Texas settlers.

HENRY SMITH ARRIVES IN BRAZORIA

One of the more interesting examples of social interaction in colonial Texas was recounted by Henry Smith, an early settler in Brazoria who would later become the first Anglo Governor of Texas.[39] Smith was born on May 20, 1788, in Kentucky, the youngest of ten children.[40] His father, James Smith, had emigrated from Bedford County, Virginia, and joined company with Daniel Boone, one of the great pioneers of the West.[41] James Smith died when Henry was about nine years old. Henry later recalled some advantages to being the youngest and was grateful to have been afforded an education. He began to travel and pursue various businesses at the age of seventeen and traveled through the southern Trans-Mississippi region.

When Smith first considered coming to Texas in 1826, he contemplated the benefits of moving his family to this new, unexplored land by gathering as much information as he could from fellow travelers, particularly in New Orleans. Smith cited in his memoirs that "every person who pretended to know any thing of Texas, either from personal observation or hearsay, depicted it in the most shocking and horrid point of view—cannibals, savage wild beasts of every hue and form were innumerable and in waiting to destroy the deluded emigrant…" He continued, if not, "civil war, then raging, famine or pestilence would surely close the scene." Ignoring the skeptics, Smith and his family arrived in Texas by boat in 1827 and settled in Brazoria, where he farmed, taught school, worked as a surveyor and soon became active in public affairs. Smith recalled that although the imposition of the Catholic faith was tolerated by the Anglo-American settlers, the government was determined to subject the colonists to every possible test of loyalty.

PADRE MULDOON AND THE MARRIAGE TAX

Around 1831, a Roman Catholic priest named Michael Muldoon was sent from Mexico City to Brazoria to reside among the settlers and administer to their spiritual needs.[42] Father Muldoon was described by Noah Smithwick as a "bigoted old Irishman, with an unlimited capacity for drink."[43] Muldoon was born in Ireland and was said to have licked the blarney stone before he left the Emerald Isle. When sober, he cast a sage appearance among the colonists. His white hair and outwardly good manners caused him to be kindly received by the colonists. The *padre* was also viewed by the colonists as a necessary evil, required if they were to continue to live on the cheap land. He had been sent to Texas by Mexican officials to redeem the settlers from heresy and infidelity. Overall, every courtesy and attention was paid to him and for a time, the relationship between the parishioners and the *padre* was quite congenial.

Unlike most priests, the *padre* never troubled the settlers with attending church services, but confined his duties to baptism, marriage ceremonies and funerals. The authorities in Mexico City required all couples to be married in a ceremony of the Catholic faith. Since the only Catholic churches in the area were in the mission settlements, rather than requiring that couples be married in the church, the church came to them so to speak. It was a snug little business for the *padre*, as he collected $2 for each baptism and $24 for each wedding. This amounted to an additional tax on the people, as all immigrant couples were told to come forward and have their unions blessed by the church. Padre Muldoon was also quite lenient with regard to the imposition of the Catholic faith on the largely Protestant settlers—as long as he was able to collect his fee for services. It was not uncommon to see the priest perform the marriage ceremony both for young couples and for those who had been married for years. They often stood at the altar with several children in tow as the white-headed Irishman administered the ceremony and collected his fee. Both young and old were also required to be baptized in the Catholic faith before they could be married, which resulted in an additional fee for each couple. All of this proved to be very inconvenient for the people who lived scattered across a district of several hundred miles. As a general rule, very little attention was paid to the *padre's* edict except for those who lived immediately in his vicinity.

Following the arrival of the Father Muldoon in Brazoria, a number of married couples were determined to save themselves the trouble of having individual marriage rites performed for each of them. Someone had proposed a group wedding by which one grand Roman Catholic ceremony could be performed for all of the "eligible" couples in the area.[44] This would also give the *padre* an opportunity to perform a wholesale business for which he could collect his fee. Padre Muldoon readily agreed. They accordingly set a convenient date and place for the priest to meet the couples and perform the necessary rituals to comply with the spiritual requirements laid down by the Mexican government. The area around the township of Brazoria was soon buzzing with preparations for the big event. The women sprung into action and tried to turn their rural habitat into a center of social and cultural attention in celebration for the special day. The festivities included decorations, a splendid barbeque and abundant quantities of brandy and wine. As the ladies meticulously planned the event, Henry Smith, already an influential settler, readied a snug little house to receive the *padre* and attended to the reception. Smith also created a sort of muster roll of twelve rank-and-file couples who were candidates for baptism and fit to be wed in the ceremony out of the forty or so couples that had originally consented to the nuptials.

The appointed day approached with the eager anticipation of the baptism and the wedding, to be followed by the consumption of imported wines, a splendid dinner and a magnificent community dance. The tables groaned under the weight of the food, including a pyramid of the most translucent and luscious honeycomb in its center. All seemed to not only enjoy the celebration but the rare presence of a Roman Catholic priest in their midst. The *padre* was quite pleased with the preparations, and after a few glasses of generously poured wine, he was ready to administer the rites. Smith, being generally acquainted with the people, was called to act as a kind of precursor. He was asked to write down the names of the candidates for matrimony in order to prepare the necessary certificates for distribution afterward.

As the ceremony began, the mass baptism came first, followed by a brief liturgy and then a short marriage ceremony which was a mere conjoining of lawful wedlock. This amusing scene was truly one to behold and soon became quite ludicrous to an extreme. Most of the nuptial couples had five or six children with them. Several "brides" stood at the altar with their bosoms wide open, nursing a child as the marriage rites were being performed. As the wine continued to flow, other brides were sprawled on the floor during the ceremony and were said to be in situations "too delicate to mention." Smith remarked that "it appeared to be more like a burlesque parody of marriage than a marriage in fact" and "it was a fine scene for a painter as it afforded much for amusement." At the end of the day, the settlers enjoyed the grandiose party and the blessings of the priest who dictated their vows according to the laws of the Mexican Republic. Having collected his fees, Father Muldoon befriended many of the settlers and later parlayed his earnings into land speculation. The *padre* eventually acquired a large tract of land encompassing the entire south shore of Clear Lake, on the western edge of Galveston Bay.[45]

THE SEEDS OF CHANGE

Such was the happy state of existence in Texas in the early 1830s. The small but close-knit communities formed by the work of the *empresarios* offered cheap land, friendship, and a varied array of social outlets. The Texas settlers improved their grants and worked the land. Unfortunately however, this state of being did not exist for long. Soon after the hardy and adventurous pioneers disbursed the cannibalistic Karankawa Indians with the barrel of a gun, cleared the wooded forests, sowed their seeds, and harvested their crops, a new series of political and economic hardships befell them. The seeds of change had already been planted and taken root, not from Brazoria, San Felipe, Nacogdoches or even from San Antonio de Béxar, but instead from the distant port city of Vera Cruz, Mexico. These seeds had grown through the ranks of the military and were about to bloom in the form of a powerful dictator in Mexico City. His subsequent actions would have far-reaching implications for not only Texas, but the entire continent of North America.

Fig 3.37, Antonio López de Santa Anna, the President and Dictator of Mexico.

Author's Collection.

THE RISE OF SANTA ANNA

Antonio López de Santa Anna, the son of Antonio López de Santa Anna and Manuela Pérez de Lebrón, was born in Jalapa, in Vera Cruz, Mexico, on February 21, 1794. His family belonged to the *criollos* middle class, the first generation born of full-blooded Spanish parents. His father served as a mortgage broker in the province of Vera Cruz. After limited schooling, the young Santa Anna worked for a merchant in Vera Cruz and his family wished him to go into business. After a primary school education in Jalapa, Antonio overcame his family's objections and opted for the military academy in the bustling port city of Vera Cruz. In June 1810, he was appointed a cadet in the *Fijo de Vera Cruz* infantry regiment under the command of Gen. Joaquín de Arredondo.

Like most young officers in the Royalist army, Santa Anna remained loyal to Spain for a number of years and fought against the movement for Mexican independence. He received his first wound when an Indian arrow pierced his left arm or hand in 1811. In 1813, he served with Arredondo against the Gutiérrez-Magee expedition and was cited for bravery after the battle of Medina. In the aftermath of the rebellion, the young officer witnessed Arredondo's fierce counterinsurgency policy. Historians have speculated that Santa Anna modeled his policy and conduct in the Texas Revolution on his experience under Arredondo.[46]

Santa Anna soon garnered a reputation as a skilled military officer. He was also said to possess the air and manners of a true gentleman and had a ready elocution which incited patriotic emotions in the masses.[47] At first having fought on the side of the royalist forces in the War for Mexican Independence, he eventually changed his allegiances in the most dramatic of fashions. When Santa Anna served under Gov. José García Davila in Vera Cruz, who was loyal to the Spanish crown, he was known as an accomplished rebel disperser and a highly acclaimed officer. Later, however, his Spanish superiors charged him with insubordination regarding the old affair of the forged check in San Antonio de Béxar.[48] Santa Anna had never paid the obliging doctor the 300 *pesos*, whether through his own stubbornness or a true lack of funds. The surgeon had eventually appealed the matter to the highest Spanish military authorities who then questioned the integrity of the young officer.

On March 23, 1821, Santa Anna commanded a Spanish regiment in Vera Cruz who were charged with routing a small body of revolutionaries. By drawing attention away from the old affair with this successful feat, he was promoted to a lieutenant colonel in the Spanish army. That very same afternoon the rebels persuaded Santa Anna to join their cause, honoring him with the rank of a full colonel under Gen. Agustín de Iturbide. Incredibly, Santa Anna had managed to receive two battlefield promotions by opposing forces on the same day!

Although the Treaty of Cordoba formally recognized the independence of Mexico, several pockets of royalists still remained. Soon after Iturbide was seated on the Imperial throne, Santa Anna led a regiment to crush the centers of opposition in the fortress of Perote, near Jalapa and in the port city of Vera Cruz. These battles pitted Santa Anna's forces against royalist holdouts in his own boyhood province. He again emerged victorious, but Santa Anna was having second thoughts about his allegiance to Iturbide. The emperor's unwillingness to make Santa Anna the military commander and governor of Vera Cruz caused a rift between the Mexican general and the ambitious young colonel. Iturbide eventually promoted Santa Anna to the rank of brigadier general and appointed him as the commanding general of the Province of Vera Cruz, but the damage to the warrior's ego had already been done.[49] Having once toasted Iturbide to his entire regiment and proclaimed "Long live Augustín the first, Emperor of Mexico," Santa Anna broke allegiance with Iturbide over a series of personal grievances regarding his delayed promotion. Within six months, Santa Anna was instrumental in plotting an open political revolt against the self-proclaimed Emperor, even though he played no direct role in Iturbide's actual overthrow and departure into exile once the Army of Liberation marched into the capital on March 27, 1823.[50]

Within a span of only two years, Santa Anna had emerged on the Mexican political scene as a major military figure with considerable influence among members of the armed forces.[51] He transferred his allegiance twice, from royalist to a supporter of Iturbide's empire, and from his initial devotion of the emperor to the promotion of a Republic. After serving as the military governor of the Yucatán and then governor in his hometown of Vera Cruz, Santa Anna was soon recognized as a powerful force by most prominent Mexicans. Among the military and political elite, he quietly developed a reputation for being "a man drunk without doubt of ambition."[52]

Santa Anna's reputation as a daring military commander continued to grow as Spain tried to recapture Mexico in the summer of 1829. Gen. Isidro Barradas landed on the eastern coast at Tampico with a force of more than 4,000 men.[53] While Barradas took three quarters of the force into the interior of the country, Santa Anna, José de Urrea and some 700 men traveled in open boats from Vera Cruz and launched an immediate attack on the remaining garrison of 1,000 Spanish troops on the morning of August 1, 1829. The garrison capitulated to Santa Anna's forces in only four hours. When Barradas returned with his main force, Santa Anna, his retreat blocked by a river, bluffed the opposing commander into thinking that he was surrounded by a superior force and duped him into negotiations. This bought the young Mexican general valuable time to receive reinforcements. His army now strengthened, Santa Anna repeatedly attacked the Spanish force, culminating in a vicious attack on the fort which guarded the bar on September 11, 1829. It was a battle in which the Spanish general eventually capitulated. Surrendering his forces with almost half of them dead or captured, Barradas was allowed retreat by ship to Havana with his remaining force of 2,200 men. Having defeated the last of the Spanish invasions, Santa Anna emerged from the Tampico campaign a national hero.

Santa Anna was elected as President of Mexico, taking office for the first time on May 16, 1833. A dedicated centralist, he made every effort to consolidate his power and increase his authority over the many Mexican states. When a new Congress met on January 4, 1835, the centralists again asserted their authority. State legislatures were disbanded, governors were deposed, and town councils dissolved.[54] Feigning illness, Santa Anna sometimes retreated to his hacienda for weeks at a time and delegated much of his duties to Gomez Farias, his Vice President, in an attempt to manipulate and control the government while gauging the reaction of the people to major changes in the laws. He did this without being publicly responsible for his own acts.

TEXAS ON THE BRINK

As the centralists tightened their controls, the colonists in Texas remained opposed to the political changes. The growing military presence in the region was soon felt, especially in Zacatecas and Coahuila y Tejas. Mexican soldiers had been sent to Texas in a steady stream since the passage of a controversial law on April 6, 1830, which sought to stop the further colonization of Texas by settlers from the United States. To prohibit more settlement, military garrisons were erected in Texas.[55] The ostensible purpose of the law was to guard and protect the colonies from Indian invasion, protect the customs and prevent further immigration. Customhouse officers were then introduced to enforce the collection of duties and tariffs on imported goods. The customs officials were not ordinary bureaucrats but were predominantly Mexican military officers. Many of the soldiers who occupied the various customhouse garrisons were former inmates from the prisons of Mexico who had been released to fill the positions in the ports of Texas. These men were described by Henry Smith as "the most wretched and abandoned set of cutthroats and outlaws that ever made a track on the soil of any country."[56] The settlers desired goods from outside the territory, including dishes, bedding, blankets, furniture, clothing, and many more items. The new Mexican tariffs and their subsequent enforcement seemed unreasonable to many of the colonists. Many of the indispensable articles for day-to-day living soon became contraband. The import duties on the goods became so high that it amounted to a prohibition on these desired items.

The two earliest episodes in this struggle between Federalists and Centralists occurred in Zacatecas and in Texas.[57] In Zacatecas, Gov. Francisco Garcia refused to comply with the decrees coming from Mexico City in early 1835. On April 18, 1835, Santa Anna personally took charge of the military campaign to force the submission of the rebellious state of Zacatecas at the point of a gun. On May 11, 1835, Santa Anna encountered Governor Garcia's forces at Guadalupe, near the city of Zacatecas. The two-hour battle which ensued resulted in an overwhelming victory for Santa Anna whose forces entered the city and began to loot it. Among the spoils were immense quantities of 8 *reales* silver coins struck from the indigenous silver and stored at the Zacatecas mint. As

Fig 3.38, James W. Fannin, Jr.

Courtesy of Dallas Historical Society, Dallas, Texas.

President, Santa Anna confiscated the hoard of freshly minted silver coins. He planned to use the money to finance any future military excursions which may be required to bring the other rebellious factions into line.

Even though Zacatecas was firmly in control, the loosely held state of Coahuila y Tejas refused to fall in line. In September 1835, Santa Anna's brother-in-law, Gen. Martín Perfecto de Cos, was sent to Texas by Santa Anna under the ruse of investigating the citizens of Anahuac who refused to pay the imposed duties. Sailing to Texas, Cos landed 300 men at Copano Bay, established a headquarters in San Antonio, and announced his purpose to end the resistance in Texas. Cos summarily dispersed the legislature of Coahuila y Tejas then in session at Monclova.[58]

By mid-1835, a revolutionary fever swept across Texas as Santa Anna suspended the Constitution of 1824 and discarded the protections previously afforded to the settlers. Aside from cultural differences, the root of the difficulty between Texas and the central government in Mexico City was Texas' desire for self government.[59] Henry Smith, who later became the Provisional Governor of Texas, summarized the oppression of the Texans in his writings: "The military had now become pretty strongly fortified in their various garrisons, and began to show us their true intentions by making us feel their power. The civil arm was paralyzed, our citizens incarcerated for slight and trivial offences, and trial by the civil authorities refused. This state of things could not long be borne by those who considered themselves freemen."[60] These freemen were not exclusively the American immigrants, but also included many *tejanos* (Mexicans born in Texas) with strong family or commercial ties to Texas. Many *tejanos* saw the rebellion as an opportunity to face Santa Anna and free themselves from his reign of tyranny.

THE COMMITTEE OF SAFETY AND CORRESPONDENCE

It wasn't long after the erection of Mexican garrisons at the important ports of entry into Texas that the citizens began to take matters into their own hands. On August, 15, 1835, the citizens of Columbia held a meeting to appoint a Committee of Safety and Correspondence, and resolved "that a consultation of all Texas, through her representatives was indispensable."[61] A clean break from the Mexican state of Coahuila y Tejas was being considered. There was also talk of complete independence from Mexico among the more radical elements in Texas. The letter in figure 3.39, signed by William Austin and Branch T. Archer of Brazoria and sent to James W. Fannin, requested the call for a consultation to form a provisional government for Texas. Fannin was a graduate of the U.S. Military Academy at West Point and an early agitator in the Texas Revolution. He actively worked to form the military response by Texas to the powerful rise of the strong and inflexible Santa Anna.[62]

Committees of Safety and Correspondence were organized in Texas as early as 1832 to secure the organization of the militia for defense against hostile Indians. When the storm clouds of discontent began to gather as a result of centralist rule in Mexico, the emphasis of the committee shifted towards forming an effective military resistance against the central government and organizing political leadership. Fannin was appointed in Columbia and asked to use his influence to call a consultation of all of Texas, for the purpose of forming a provisional government.

An early Texas revolutionary, Fannin's charge, as evidenced in the appointment, was "to persuade Wyly Martin and all other persons whom you may have influence to cooperate with us in the call of a consultation of all Texas, through her representatives." Wyly Martin was the acting *jefe* politico or "political chief" of the Department of the Brazos and had previously served as a delegate from San Felipe to previous conventions in 1832 and 1833.[63] Although the committee was instructed to prepare an address to all the jurisdictions of Texas requesting them to co-operate in the call of a consultation, this letter to Fannin is the only example of a letter bearing this language that is known to have survived. Fannin was not only capable of the assignment but quite persuasive, as Wyly Martin did become a member of the

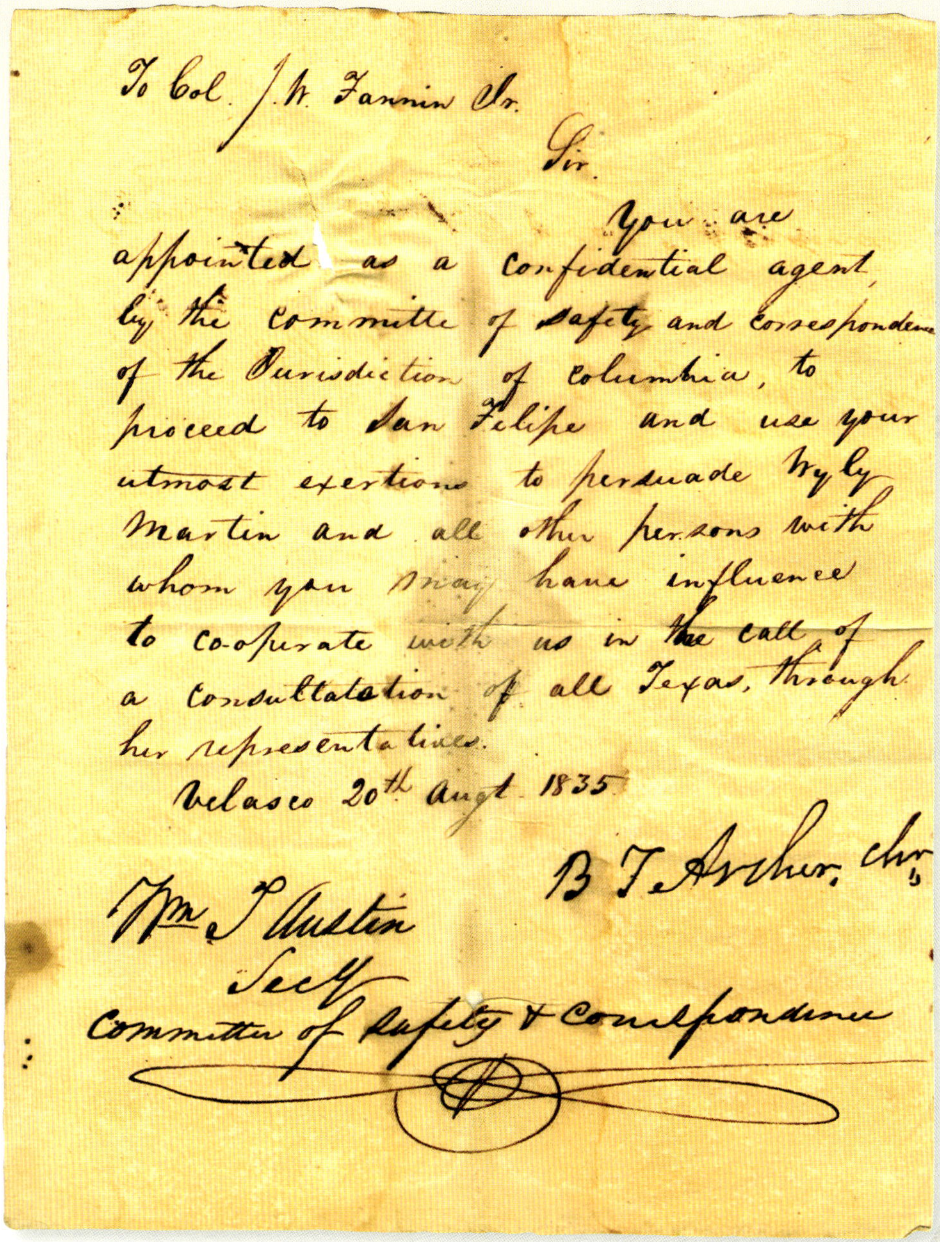
To Col. J.W. Fannin Jr.
Sir.
You are appointed as a Confidential agent, by the committe of safety and correspondence of the Jurisdiction of Columbia, to proceed to San Felipe and use your utmost exertions to persuade Wyly Martin and all other persons with whom you may have influence to co-operate with us in the call of a consultatation of all Texas, through her representatives.
Velasco 20th Augt 1835
B. T. Archer, Chr
Wm T Austin
Secy
Committee of safety & correspondence

Fig 3.39, Appointment of James W. Fannin, Velasco, August, 20, 1835.

Private Collection.

Provisional Council from the municipality of San Felipe de Austin on November 1, 1835.[64]

On August 27, Fannin also wrote to a United States Army officer in Georgia requesting financial aid for the Texas cause and for West Point officers to command the Texas Army. By September, Fannin had become active in the volunteer army and subscribed money for an expedition to capture the *Veracruzana*, a Mexican ship at Copano Bay, though the expedition did not materialize. Fannin returned to Gonzales where, as captain of the Brazos Guards, he participated in the battle of Gonzales on October 2, 1835. In January 1836, he began recruiting volunteers for a military expedition to Matamoros, and the following month was elected colonel of the Provisional Regiment of Volunteers at Goliad.

As the word spread across Texas about the gathering of the consultation, hostilities erupted against Mexican troops on October 2, 1835, at Gonzales. The Mexican cavalry arrived with 200 strong on the banks of the Guadalupe River, but were repulsed by eighteen men under Capt. Albert Martin.[65] On October 9, rebel troops attacked and captured the fort at Goliad, seizing stores, cannon, and arms which would later be used for their cause. Another engagement on October 28, near the mission of Conceptíon under the command of Col. James Bowie and Capt. James Fannin resulted in the defeat of about 400 Mexican soldiers—a decisive victory by the Texians, as the rebels called themselves.

Throughout the fall, hostilities continued to increase, culminating with the siege and storming of Béxar, when an army of Texian volunteers led by Ben Milam laid siege to the Mexican Army in San Antonio de Béxar and forced their surrender and withdrawal from the Alamo on December 9, 1835. It was becoming clear that the raging political climate of hostility against Mexico and the quest for independence by the colonists was rapidly coming to a boil.

To Col. J.W. Fannin Jr

Sir, You are appointed as a confidential agent by the committee of safety and correspondence of the Jurisdiction of Columbia, to proceed to San Felipe and use your utmost exertions to persuade Wyly Martin and all other persons with whom you may have influence to cooperate with us in the call of a consultation of all Texas, through her representatives.

Velasco, 20th August, 1835

Wm T. Austin, *B. T. Archer,*

Sec[retar]y, Committee of safety & correspondence *Cha[irman]*

[1] Eugene C. Barker, *The Life of Stephen F. Austin, Founder of Texas, 1793-1836: A Chapter in the Westward Movement of the Anglo-American People* (Austin: University of Texas Press, 1969), 54, see references to Joshua H. Bell, A. Robinson, and other settlers on the Brazos and Colorado rivers dated July 26, 1822.

[2] John H. Jenkins, ed., The Papers of the Texas Revolution, 1835-1836 (Austin: Presidial Press, 1973), 9:229-30; *A Brief Account of the Origin, Progress and Present State of the Colonial Settlements of Texas* (Nashville: S. Nye & Co., 1836).

[3] Barker, *The Life of Stephen F. Austin,* 121-23.

[4] Randolph B. Campbell, *Gone to Texas: A History of the Lone Star State* (Oxford University Press, 2003), 108.

[5] Barker, *The Life of Stephen F. Austin,* 132-33.

[6] Noah Smithwick, compiled by his daughter Nanna Smithwick Henderson, *The Evolution of a State or Recollections of Old Texas Days* (Austin: Gammel Book Company, 1900; rpt. 1993), 36-37, 51.

[7] The Papers of the Texas Revolution, 9:231-36; *A Brief Account of the Origin.*

[8] Edward L. Miller, *New Orleans and the Texas Revolution* (College Station: Texas A&M University Press, 2004), 19.

[9] *Handbook of Texas Online,* s.v., "Augustín de Iturbide," http://www.tsha.utexas.edu/handbook/online/articles/II/fit1.html (accessed November 29, 2006).

[10] Smithwick, *The Evolution of a State,* 5.

[11] Theodore V. Buttrey and Clyde Hubbard, *A Guide Book of Mexican Coins: 1822 to Date,* 4th ed. (Iola, WI: Krause Publications, 1990), 54.

[12] Joseph M. Grant and Lawrence L. Crum, *The Development of State-Chartered Banking in Texas* (Austin: Bureau of Business Research, The University of Texas at Austin, 1978), 3-4.

[13] "Land, Loans, and Legends," Texas Collection of Darrel Brown, found in Thomas W. Streeter, *Bibliography of Texas* (Harvard University Press, 1960); Carlos E. Castaneda, "The First Chartered Bank West of the Mississippi: Banco National de Texas," *Bulletin of the Business Historical Society* 25 (December 1951).

[14] Grant and Crum, *The Development of State-Chartered Banking,* 5.

[15] Louis Lenz, "Texas Money," *SHQ*, vol. 57 (October 1953),

[16] Translated into English by Manuel and Teresa Cavazos, Houston, Texas, January 2007.

[17] "Land, Loans, and Legends," the Texas Collection of Darrel Brown.

[18] Ibid.

[19] Ibid.

[20] Ibid.

[21] *Historia del Papel Moneda en México* (Fomento Cultural Banamex, 1984), 13.

[22] "Land, Loans, and Legends," the Texas Collection of Darrel Brown, The 1823 Mexican Republic Banknote, non-published.

[23] Translation into English by Teresa Cavazos, Houston, Texas, January 2007.

[24] Translated into English by Manuel and Teresa Cavazos, Houston, Texas, January 2007.

[25] *Handbook of Texas Online,* s.v., "Green DeWitt," http://www.tsha.utexas.edu/handbook/online/articles/DD/fde55.html (accessed May 7, 2007).

[26] Campbell, *Gone to Texas,* 108.

[27] Smithwick, *The Evolution of a State,* 8-9.

[28] Lenz, "Texas Money," 175-80.

[29] *Handbook of Texas Online,* s.v., "Haden Edwards," http://www.tsha.utexas.edu/handbook/online/articles/EE/fed4.html (accessed April 29, 2007).

[30] Lois Foster Blount, "Old Red House at Nacogdoches," *SHQ*, vol. 49 (April 1946), 4:585-92.

[31] *Handbook of Texas Online,* s.v., "José de las Piedras," http://www.tsha.utexas.edu/handbook/online/articles/PP/fpi7.html (accessed April 29, 2007).

[32] *Handbook of Texas Online,* s.v., "Henry Rueg," http://www.tsha.utexas.edu/handbook/online/articles/RR/fru7.html (accessed May 3, 2007).

[33] The old township of San Felipe, now referred to as the San Felipe State Historic Site, is located on the Brazos River adjoining the old ferry site and a part of the Commercio Plaza de San Felipe. This site consists of twelve acres which were set aside in honor of the area's rich Texas heritage. This part of the 633-acre tract was deeded by the San Felipe de Austin Corporation in 1940, and is operated as Stephen F. Austin State Park, located on Hwy 1458, north of Interstate 10, approximately seventeen miles west of Katy, Texas.

[34] Barker, *The Life of Stephen F. Austin,* 132.

[35] *Handbook of Texas Online,* s.v., "James, Hensley," http://www.tsha.utexas.edu/handbook/online/articles/HH/fhe23.html (accessed May 21, 2006).

[36] *Handbook of Texas Online,* s.v., "William Gates," http://www.tsha.utexas.edu/handbook/online/articles/GG/fga43.html (accessed May 21, 2006).

[37] Henry Smith, "Reminiscences of Henry Smith," *SHQ*, vol. 14 (July 1910), 1:24-73.

[38] Smithwick, *The Evolution of a State,* 54-55.

[39] Smith, "Reminiscences," 24-73.

[40] *Handbook of Texas Online,* s.v., "Henry Smith," http://www.tsha.utexas.edu/handbook/online/articles/SS/fsm23.html (accessed November 28, 2006).

[41] Smith, "Reminiscences," 24-73.

[42] Ibid.

[43] Smithwick, *The Evolution of a State,* 41-42.

[44] Smith, "Reminiscences," 24-73.

[45] James L. Glass, From a chart of the Galveston-Houston area c. 1836, 1986.

[46] *Handbook of Texas Online,* s.v., "Antonio López de Santa Anna," http://www.tsha.utexas.edu/handbook/online/articles/SS/fsa29.html (accessed November 29, 2006).

[47] Fay Robinson, "From Mexico and Her Military Chieftains," (1847) found online at www.tamu.edu/ccbn/dewitt/santaanna.htm.

[48] Frank C. Hanighen, *Santa Anna: The Napoleon of the West* (Coward-McCann, Inc., 1934), 15.

[49] Oakah L. Jones, Jr., *Santa Anna* (New York: Twayne Publishers, Inc., 1968), 30-31.

[50] Ibid., 38.

[51] Ibid., 39.

[52] Ibid., 30.

[53] Robinson, "From Mexico and Her Military Chieftains."

[54] Jones, *Santa Anna,* 60.

[55] Smith, "Reminiscences," 24-73.

[56] Ibid.

[57] Jones, *Santa Anna,* 62.

[58] *Handbook of Texas Online,* s.v., "Martín Perfecto de Cos," http://www.tsha.utexas.edu/handbook/online/articles/CC/fco76.html (accessed December 2, 2006).

[59] Jones, *Santa Anna,* 63.

[60] Smith, "Reminiscences," 24-73.

[61] William M. Gouge, *The Fiscal History of Texas* (New York: Burt Franklin, 1852; rpt. 1969), 17.

[62] James Walker Fannin became a key figure in the early days of the Texas Revolution, and was later martyred by his death at Goliad. Fannin was probably born on January 1, 1804, in Georgia. He had been adopted by his maternal grandfather, James W. Walker, and brought up on a plantation near Marion. He entered the United States Military Academy at West Point on July 1, 1819, under the name James F. Walker but withdrew in November 1821. Returning to Georgia, he became friends with Mirabeau B. Lamar, a young aide to the governor whom he would later encourage to come to Texas. In the fall of 1834, Fannin and his family moved to Texas and settled at Velasco where he farmed a small plantation and actively traded slaves.

[63] Heritage Inagural Texana Auction, December 1-3, 2007, Dallas Texas, Heritage Auction Galleries, Auction #661, Page 181, Lot 56322

[64] The Papers of the Texas Revolution, 9:45-247, see Journals of the Consultation, San Felipe de Austin, October 16, 1835.

[65] Gouge, *The Fiscal History of Texas,* 19.

CHAPTER FOUR

FINANCING THE TEXAS REVOLUTION

Fig 4.1, The Town of San Felipe de Austin.

Courtesy of Albert and Ethel Herzstein Library, The San Jacinto Museum of History, Houston, Texas.

In November 1835, the Consultation assembled at San Felipe de Austin with representatives from across Texas to discuss their options and establish a provisional government based upon the principles of the Constitution of 1824. The representatives formed a General Council, which served as a quasi legislative body made up of one member from each municipality of the state. The town of Washington-on-the-Brazos was first considered for the meeting due to its central location, but was later rejected since the community held few if any suitable buildings for public business and no printing establishment.[1]

Fig 4.2, Branch T. Archer.

Texas State Library & Archives Commission, Austin, Texas.

San Felipe also offered few accommodations and many inconveniences to the delegates, but the presence of the printing press of Baker and Borden was the primary inducement for holding the Consultation there rather than in Washington-on-the-Brazos. When arriving in the town, William Fairfax Gray, a land agent and financier, described the site of the meeting as follows: "San Felipe is a wretched, decaying looking place. Five stores of small assortments, two mean taverns, and twenty or thirty mean looking houses, very little paint visible." He lamented that there was "no appearance of industry, or thrift or improvement of any kind."[2] The first order of business by the Consultation was the election of Branch T. Archer of Brazoria as chairman and Henry Smith as Provisional Governor.

Branch Tanner Archer, the son of Francis Tanner and Maj. Peter Field Archer, a Revolutionary War officer, was born in Fauquier County, Virginia, on December 13, 1790.[3] Archer attended the College of William and Mary at Williamsburg in 1804 and received his medical degree from the medical school at the University of Pennsylvania in 1808. He married Eloisa Clark on January 20, 1813, and later returned to Virginia where he practiced medicine and served in the legislature from 1819-1820. In 1828, Archer killed his cousin, Dr. James Crump, in a pistol duel near Scottsville, Powhatan County, Virginia. Arriving in Texas in 1831, he quickly joined a group in Brazoria calling for independence from Mexico. He represented Brazoria at the Convention of 1833 and participated in the battle of Gonzales in October 1835. Having traveled to San Felipe as a representative of Brazoria, Archer was elected by his peers to preside as Chairman of the Consultation.

Henry Smith, the former schoolteacher who once organized the lavish group wedding festivities in Brazoria, had become increasingly active in public affairs in the area during the early 1830s. Smith soon developed a reputation among his peers as both a lover and a fighter. He was married three times and was the father of nine children. All three of his wives were sisters, Harriet, Elizabeth, and Sarah Gillett.[4] Smith was also well known for his combative personality, and became increasingly vocal regarding the escalating oppressive Mexican regime. He called for a surprise attack against the Mexican fort at Velasco in 1832, which guarded the entrance to the Brazos River and Austin's colony. Attacking the fort with John Austin and between 100 and 150 fellow Texians, he was severely wounded in what became known as the battle of Velasco which ended on June 26, 1832.

As tensions grew and the movement towards independence strengthened, Smith became increasingly critical of any Mexican sympathizers, especially Stephen F. Austin. He described Austin to William Fairfax Gray as a "Mexican in his principles and policy, and that he ought to be hung!"[5] The new Provisional Governor of Texas had himself been described by Gray as a "strongly prejudiced party man" and "too illiterate, too little informed, and not of the right caliber for the station he has been placed in."

San Felipe de Austin became the seat of the provisional government from October 16, 1835, to February 16, 1836. Once assembled, the competing factions from across Texas debated their own political agendas. Branch T. Archer, the Chairman of the Consultation encouraged the participants to put aside their differences and concentrate on what was best for Texas. Amid the many debates over the political turmoil in Mexico and the quest for independence, Archer understood the gravity of the situation and he informed the council that "the rights and liberties of thousands of freemen are in your hands and millions yet unborn may be affected by your decisions."[6]

THE TREASURY OF THE PROVISIONAL GOVERNMENT

The Consultation decided that among the highest of priorities was raising the money to finance the war for independence. In addition to the purchase of weapons, money would be needed to feed, pay and clothe the soldiers. To stress his point, Archer declared, "without funds, however heroically your armies may fight, however wisely your councils may legislate, they will erect but a baseless fabric that will fall on its own weight."[7] Texas needed an army, so the council elected agents to procure the funds necessary to finance a military body. The General Council issued an order on October 27, 1835, to close the land offices and halt all further surveys.[8] Although there were some objections to the measure, the council decided that it would be useless to offer new lands to settlers while men were out fighting in the field. A report from the committee on November 13 indicated, "The land offices have been closed, that no advantage should be taken over the soldier in the field in making his selections of lands."[9]

On November 24, 1835, the General Council passed an ordinance to encourage military recruitment by providing 640 acres of land to each man who volunteered for the regular army. This act was later amended on December 8, 1835, to award 320 acres of land to each soldier who served for a three-month enlistment and 640 acres of land for those who served for the duration of the war.[10] The land would be awarded after the war once the land offices reopened. Not only did Texian soldiers fight for the independence of Texas, they literally fought for a piece of it! Realizing that many of the soldiers would likely be killed, a law was passed on December 12, 1835, which provided that the 640 acres should also be awarded to the family or representative of each volunteer who died in battle or in service to Texas.

During the formation of this provisional government, the General Council established a Treasury Department. It was initially composed of a committee on finance, with the offices of treasurer, auditor and controller added shortly thereafter.[11] The Treasury Department was established in spite of a lack of funds. The department had no money on hand and none which could be dispersed. At first, these functions were delegated solely to the committee on finance with an interim treasurer at the head. Henry Smith, the provisional governor, loudly objected to this measure and insisted on establishing the separate offices of an auditor and controller to prevent fraud and the inappropriate disbursement of funds.[12] After a series of heated arguments on the matter, the council eventually recognized Smith's wisdom and agreed that the government be properly audited, regular accounts kept, and a system of checks and balances installed in their new financial system.

Just as the Mexican government had changed the design of the Spanish money years before, Texas was determined to stamp its own identity on the money it

Fig 4.3, Gov. Henry Smith.

Texas State Library & Archives Commission, Austin, Texas.

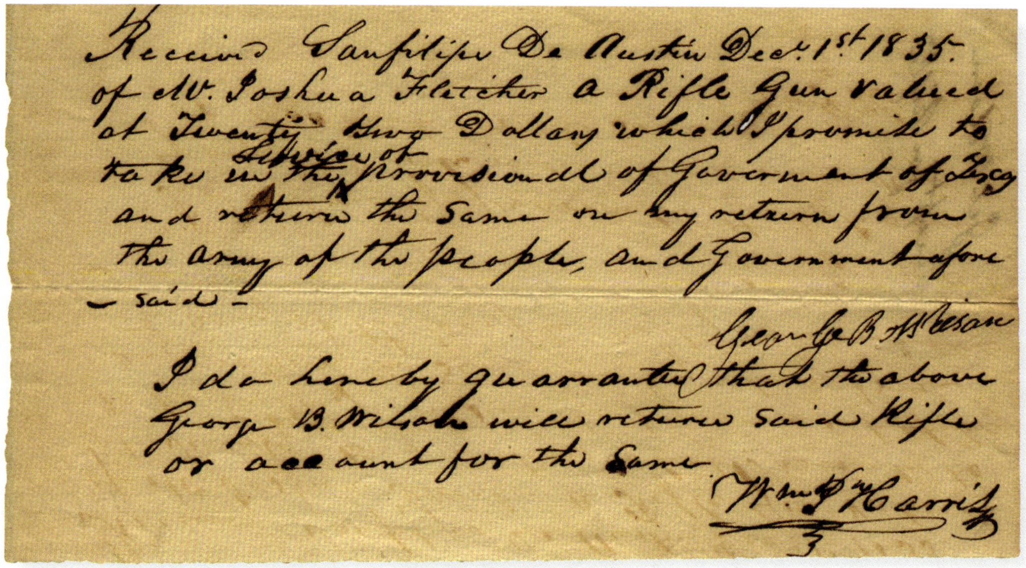

Receivd Sanfilipe De Austin Decr. 1st 1835.
of Mr. Joshua Fletcher a Rifle Gun valued
at Twenty five Dollars which I promise to
take in the Service of provisional of Government of Texas
and return the Same on my return from
the army of the people, and Government afore
- said -
George B. Wilson
I do hereby guarantee that the above
George B. Wilson will return said Rifle
or account for the Same
Wm. P. Harris

Fig 4.4, San Felipe de Austin, December 1, 1835.
Receipt for a rifle by the Provisional Government of Texas.

Private Collection, Cr-Unlisted, O-Unlisted.

issued. Heavily influenced by the growing American presence in the region, and with the General Council comprised of American settlers, the council decided that all money raised or issued by Texas, whether through loans, promissory notes or drafts, would hereafter be denominated in dollars.

The first orders of the government were to make provisions for raising immediate and future revenues. The Treasury spent money as fast as the department received it, and soon developed a propensity to spend nonexistent funds by issuing drafts against future revenues that might later be appropriated to cover their purchases. Wasting little time, these drafts were used to purchase munitions, arms and supplies just days after the Treasury was created. The pledges of faith by the Provisional Government of Texas were absolute. Included in the preamble to the *Plan and Powers of the Provisional Government of Texas* adopted in November 1835 were the following declarations:

> *That Texas is responsible for the expenses of her armies now in the field … That the public faith of Texas is pledged for the payment of any debts contracted by her agents…[and] [t]hese DECLARATIONS we solemnly avow to the world, and call GOD to witness their truth and sincerity; and invoke defeat and disgrace upon our heads should we prove guilty of duplicity.*[13]

Soon after the public faith of Texas was officially pledged, a variety of drafts were issued to acknowledge contributions to the cause. Many of these were merely receipts for guns, horses, or other supplies which were furnished to the volunteer army. They were used to procure food, clothing and munitions, or to acknowledge the receipt of goods that were designated for the army. The public declaration of the *Plan and Powers of the Provisional Government of Texas* assured that these receipts would become bona fide obligations of the new government. The first obligations issued by the Provisional Government of Texas were in the form of receipts, drafts or warrants, drawn against an empty treasury at San Felipe de Austin and Gonzales in November and December 1835. The surviving specimens of these early paper obligations are extremely rare.

> *Received San filipe [sic] De Austin Dec. 1st. 1835. of W. Joshua Fletcher a Rifle Gun valued at Twenty Five Dollars which I promise to take in the Service of provisional of Government of Texas and return the same on my return from the army of the people, and Government afore-said- (Signed) George B. Wilson I do hereby guarantee that the above George B. Wilson will return said Rifle or account for the same.*
> *(Signed) Wm. P. Harris*

The early receipt in Figure 4.4 for a rifle is typical of the type that was issued for supplies by the Provisional Government. Joshua Fletcher, the gun's owner, had just taken an administrative position as acting Treasurer of the Provisional Government of Texas and would not need the weapon in his new capacity. Although George B. Wilson signed for the gun and presumably

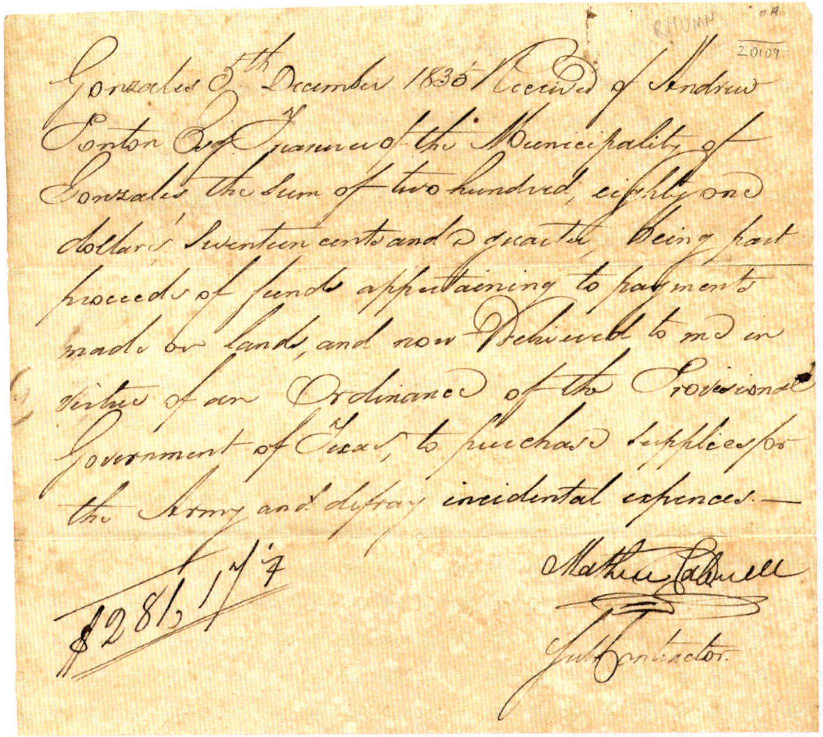

Gonzales 5th December 1835 Received of Andrew Ponton Esq Treasurer of the Municipality of Gonzales the sum of two hundred, eighty one dollars seventeen cents and a quarter, being part proceeds of funds appertaining to payments made on lands, and now Delivered to me in virtue of an Ordinance of the Provisional Government of Texas, to purchase supplies for the Army and defray incidental expences.—

$281,17

Mathew Caldwell
Sub Contractor

Gonzales 5th December 1835. Received of Andrew Ponton Esq. Treasurer of the Municipality of Gonzales, the sum of two hundred, eighty one dollars seventeen cents and a quarter, being part proceeds of funds appertaining [sic] to payments made on land, and now Delivered [sic] to me in virtue of an Ordinance of the Provisional Government of Texas, to purchase supplies for the Army and defray incidental expenses.
$281.17 ¼ (Signed) Matthew Caldwell,
Sub Contractor

Fig 4.5, Gonzales, December 5, 1835.
Receipt for $281.17 ¼ from Andrew Ponton.

Private Collection, Cr. PGG1 (P5), O-50.

used it during the revolution, the note was guaranteed by William Plunkett Harris, who represented the town of Harrisburg at the Consultation.

William Plunkett Harris was born in Cayuga, New York, in 1797 and had run a successful shipping operation on the Mississippi River with his business partner Robert Wilson before arriving in Texas in 1830.[14] John R. Harris, William's brother, founded the town of Harrisburg. William P. Harris served on the General Council and was the chairman of the committee on naval affairs until December 30, 1835, when he left to assume duties as the collector of customs at the port of Galveston Harris was a successful businessman who continued to operate a sawmill and shipping operation in Harrisburg. During the spring campaign of 1836, Harris played a lifesaving role in the Texas Revolution as he transported military supplies and government personnel aboard his steamboat, the *Cayuga*.

Gonzales was a "flash point" in the Texas Revolution. As armies operated in the field, the provisional government sought to purchase supplies or armaments for the soldiers. On December 5, 1835, while the siege and battle of Béxar was fought in nearby San Antonio, this receipt was issued for supplies and incidental expenses for the army.[15] Andrew Ponton, who received this receipt, was the last *alcalde* of Gonzales. Elected to that position in 1835 he was a defender in the battle of Gonzales on October 2, 1835. The receipt is signed by Matthew Caldwell, who became known as the "Paul Revere of the Texas Revolution" by riding from Gonzales to Bastrop with a call to arms before the battle of Gonzales.[16] On March 3, 1836, after the signing of the Texas Declaration of Independence, Caldwell and one courier were dispatched to assess the enemy's strength along the frontier. This example was one of the first issues of this type by the provisional government.

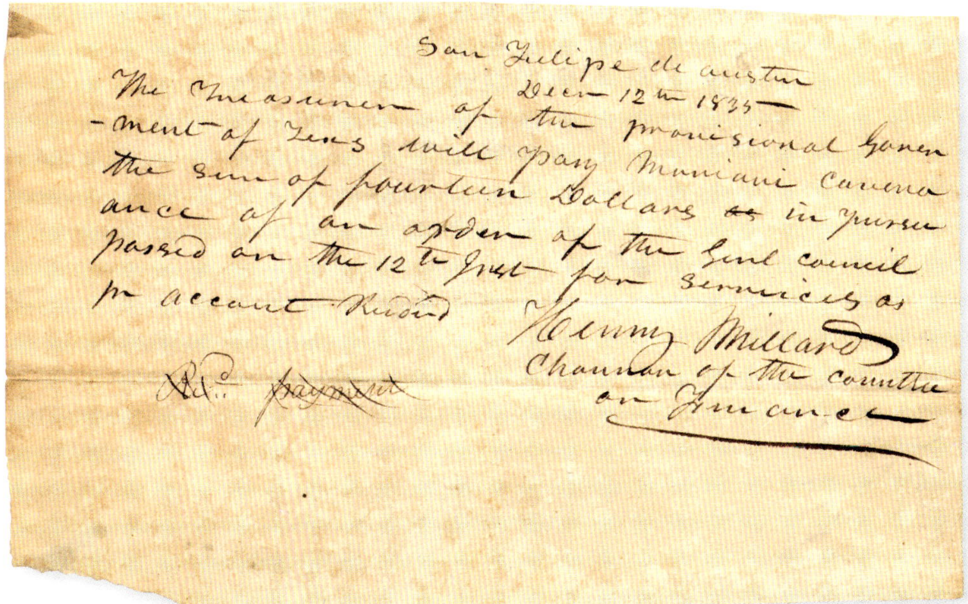

San Felipe de austin
Decr 12th 1835
The Treasurer of the provisional Govern-
-ment of Texas will pay Mariani Carrera
the sum of fourteen Dollars as in pursu-
ance of an order of the Genl council
passed on the 12th Inst for services as
pr accont Rendd
Henry Millard
Chairman of the committee
on Finance
Recd Payment

Fig 4.6, San Felipe de Austin, December 12, 1835.
$14 draft payable to Mariani Carrera. *Private Collection, Cr. Unlisted, O-42.*

Transcription of Figure 4.6:

San Felipe de Austin, Dec[ember] 12th 1835

The Treasurer of the provisional government- of Texas will pay Mariani Carrera the sum of fourteen Dollars in pursuance of an order of the Gen[eral] Council passed on the 12th ____ for services as p[e]r account Received (Signed) Henry Millard Chairman of the committee on Finance

The specimen in Figure 4.6 is among the earliest known drafts of the Texas Treasury at San Felipe. This issuance of payment for services was signed by Henry Millard in his capacity as the "Chairman of the committee on Finance." Millard's influential guidance at the Consultation resulted in many changes—from reducing the price of bread and corn sold to the Republic, to the authorizations for loans to bring money into Texas, and many other revenue raising efforts of the provisional government.[17] Just five months after Millard signed this draft and resigned his committee position, he found himself in the thick of the war as commander of the regulars of the Texas Army at the battle of San Jacinto. Millard's signature on early Texas documents in his capacity as Chairman of the Committee of Finance is extremely rare.

The heading of the early San Felipe de Austin draft shown in Figure 4.7, "In the name of the people Free and Sovereign," serves as an interesting reference to the Journals of the Convention at San Felipe de Austin.[18] This entirely handwritten piece payable to Samuel Stivers for $228.37 ½, seems to have been a reimbursement of sorts, judging by the exact amount which was due to him. This warrant also bears what became the standard language of the Treasury Department "out of any money not otherwise appropriated."

Samuel Stivers was a native of Holland who had come to the U.S. to practice medicine in Philadelphia.[19] After passing through Texas on a visit to Mexico, Stivers arrived near Nacogdoches before the Haden F. Edwards colony was established. After the revolution began, Stivers served as a messenger for Sam Houston. He was placed in the rear guard at San Jacinto and, defying orders, participated in the rout of the Mexicans on April 21, 1836. Standing six-foot four-inches, Stivers was given the name "Big Doctor" by local Indians after helping to treat the wounded following the battle of San Jacinto. Dr. Stivers settled in Nacogdoches and practiced medicine following the war. The draft in Figure 4.7 is signed by John McMullen as Chairman of the Committee on Finance and John W. Moody as Auditor of public accounts, and marked "Cancelled" across the face indicating that Stivers eventually received the funds due him.

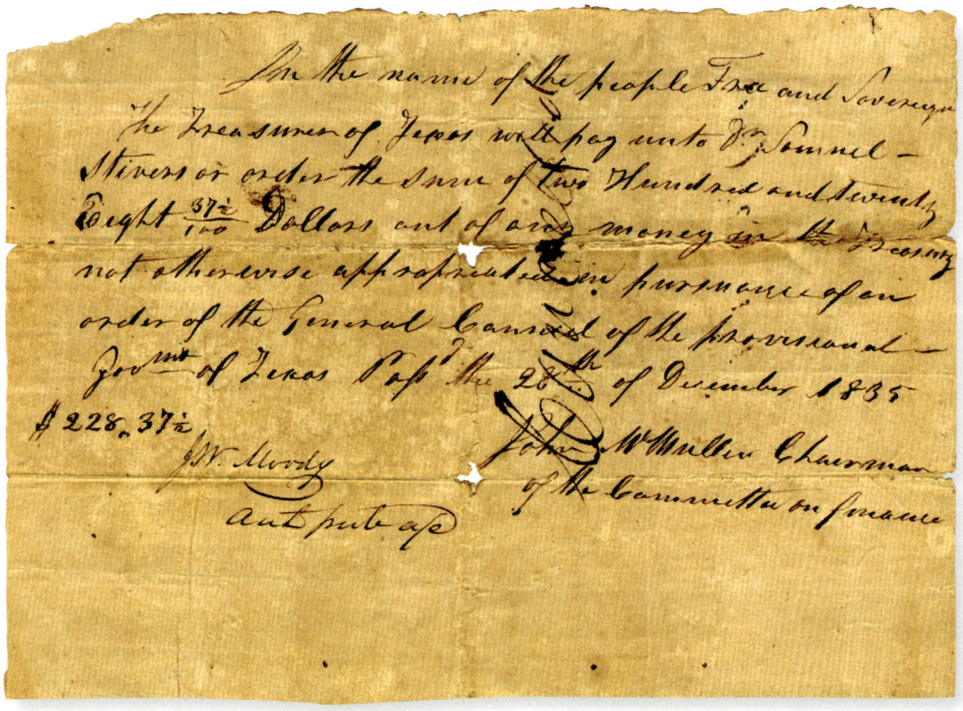

In the name of the people Free and Sovereign
The Treasurer of Texas will pay unto Dr. Samuel -
Stivers or order the sum of Two Hundred and Twenty
Eight 37½/100 Dollars out of any money in the Treasury
not otherwise appropriated in pursuance of an
order of the General Council of the provisional -
Govmt of Texas Pass'd the 28th of December 1835
$228.37½
J.W. Moody
Aud pub ac
John McMullen Chairman
of the Committee on finance

In the name of the people Free and Sovereign. The Treasurer of Texas will pay unto [JM] Samuel Stivers or order the sum of Two Hundred and Twenty Eight 37 ½/100 Dollars out of any money in the Treasury not otherwise appropriated in pursuance of an order of the General Council of the provisional Gov[ernment] of Texas. Pa[ssed] the 28th of December 1835. $228.37 ½ (Signed) J.W. Moody, Aud[itor] [of] Pub[lic] ac[counts]. (Signed) John McMullen, Chairman of the Committee on Finance.

Fig 4.7, San Felipe de Austin, December 28, 1835. $228.37 ½ draft payable to Samuel Stivers.
Private Collection. Cr. P5 (P2), 0-41.

In The name of The people Free and Sovereign
The Treasurer of Texas - will Pay unto H. W. Hanks
or order the sum of Sixty one 67/100 Dollars, out of any money
in the Treasury not otherwise appropriated in pursuance
of an order of the general council of the General Govt of Texas
Pas'd the 28th December 1835
$61,67
John McMullen Chairman of
the committee on finance

Fig 4.8, San Felipe de Austin, December 28, 1835.
Provisional Government of Texas, $61.67 draft payable to H.W. Hanks.

Private Collection, Cr. P4 (P3), 0-40

In the name of the people Free and Sovereign. The Treasurer of Texas will pay unto H.W. Hanks or order the sum of Sixty one 67/100 Dollars, out of any money in the Treasury not otherwise appropriated in pursuance of an order of the General Council of the provisional Gov[ernment] of Texas. Pa[ssed] the 28th of December 1835

$61.67 (Signed) John McMullen, Chairperson of the committee on finance.

The early San Felipe de Austin note (or draft) in Figure 4.8 was issued in "The name of people free and sovereign" to H.W. (Wyatt) Hanks, a judge and a member of the General Council at San Felipe.[20] Around 1820, Hanks married Hannah Gates, the daughter of William Gates and one of Austin's "old three hundred." In 1832, Hanks participated as a captain and camp adjutant in the battle of Nacogdoches which resulted in the permanent removal of all the Mexican federal forces from East Texas.

Hanks operated a ferry where the Coushatta Trace (an old road to Louisiana used by the Coushatta Indians) crossed the Neches River. As an elected delegate from the Bevil District to the Consultation of 1835, he served as one of the committee of twelve that drafted the Declaration of Causes on November 7, 1835, which justified the taking up of arms against Mexico. Hanks was selected as the chairman of the Military Affairs Committee and Finance Committees on the General Council. During the war, he returned to the Bevil District and served as a quartermaster for the Jasper Volunteers for the remainder of the revolution. This note in Figure 4.8 is signed by John McMullen, also on the committee on Finance and marked "Cancelled" across the face, indicating that Hanks received the payment which was due him by the government.

REVENUE-RAISING MEASURES

With any government, provisional or permanent, the raising of revenue to fund its expenditures becomes inherently necessary to ensure its survival. The Provisional Government of Texas was desperate for funds to prosecute the war. As so deftly described by contemporary historian William Gouge, in the throes of the revolution the government was determined to procure the needed funds by "taxing, borrowing, begging, selling, robbing and cheating" if necessary.[21]

The council wasted no time in getting to the business at hand. The need for immediate funds by the government made the assessment and collection of taxes on property too impractical to consider. The provisional government had to look to more immediate means and focused on the collection of import or customs duties based on tonnage brought into Texas ports, primarily in Galveston and Velasco. To accomplish this, the council passed a tariff on imports on December 13, 1835. Another revenue act soon followed on December 15 to tax the value of whiskey, spirits and American gin.

These ordinances were followed by the appointment of collectors of public dues, but this amounted to very little revenue actually received as there were no provisions to enforce their collection. Compounding the problem, because the early obligations of the government were deemed to be assignable, their own treasury drafts were often received in payment. Rather than receiving new revenues in gold or silver, this resulted in the government receiving back and canceling their own recently issued promises to pay.

Borrowing money was seen as the most expeditious method of raising funds for the war. On November 24, Thomas F. McKinney of Velasco was authorized to borrow $100,000 on behalf of the government at a rate

Except for a handful of recruits which had been furloughed from the U.S. Navy, the ships of the first Texas Navy were sailed primarily by ex-pirates and privateers.

not exceeding 10 percent per annum. On January 10, 1836, McKinney and his partner, Samuel May Williams, were further authorized to execute bonds on behalf of the provisional government to secure loans, payable six months from the date of issue. One of the most important acts in this regard was passed on December 4, 1835, which authorized three commissioners to travel to the United States and negotiate a loan for up to $1,000,000 at a rate of interest not exceeding 10 percent per annum. Stephen F. Austin, Branch T. Archer and William Wharton were selected for the task. They were authorized by the decree: "To pledge or hypothecate the public lands of Texas, and to pledge the public faith of Texas, in such manner, and with such restrictions as shall best comport with the honor and dignity of the State, and give effect to the pledges."[22] This ordinance empowered the commissioners to pledge essentially everything that Texas possessed in exchange for the necessary funds to support the cause.

Additional revenues were collected through donations of money and property. There seemed to be no misgivings on the part of the council in regards to soliciting or "begging" for donations. Much of the donated property was sold and the money promptly disbursed to buy weapons and supplies. While some of these contributions only amounted to a few dollars, many of them were significant, as a cadre of early financiers lined up to help the rebel government break Texas away from Mexico. Thomas McKinney and Samuel May Williams, who ran a mercantile firm from the port of Velasco, purchased a schooner—an ex-slaver built in Baltimore for $12,613. Williams' brother-in-law, Samuel St. John, contributed $5,000 towards the purchase in 1835 or early 1836.[23] The men spent approximately $7,500 having the schooner refitted as a warship and commissioned as the Texas warship *Invincible.* The *Invincible* captured and destroyed the Mexican ship *Bravo* on April 3, 1836. When the *Invincible* captured the *Pocket*, a U.S. flagged supply ship headed with supplies for a Mexican port, a political powder keg was ignited with international repercussions.

The United States had maintained a policy of strict neutrality in regards to the Texas and Mexican conflict. Although American sentiments were sympathetic to the Texas cause, Mexico was a major trading partner with the U.S., and sea-faring commerce continued between the southern U.S. ports and those in Mexico. The *Invincible's* crew was later apprehended by the U.S. Navy and transported to New Orleans where they were jailed on charges of pirating. Except for a handful of recruits which had been furloughed from the U.S. Navy, the ships of the first Texas Navy were sailed primarily by ex-pirates and privateers. After a short stint in jail, the Texas sailors were released out of political sympathy to the cheers of onlookers as they defiantly headed back to their ship. The *Invincible* and her crew sailed again and later blockaded the Mexican port of Vera Cruz in July 1837.[24]

Another significant contribution to the Republic was made by John K. and Augustus Allen, two real estate speculators who later founded the city of Houston. They purchased a schooner, the *Brutus*, in New Orleans in 1835 and had her outfitted with armaments. The *Brutus* was commissioned into service as a Texas warship in February of the following year. The *Brutus* measured 180 feet in length, displaced 125-160 tons and was armed with one 18-pound swivel gun, nine smaller guns, with a crew of forty officers and men. The ship blockaded Mexican supply lines along the mouth of the Rio Grande and the port of Matamoros.[25]

Although the provisional government attempted to sell land scrip (paper which could be redeemed for land after the war) they found very few buyers. Money was scarce, the state was in turmoil and the land offices had been closed, effectively ending any presumption of a priority location for the potential buyers.

In regards to robbing, wars are by definition of a predatory nature and everything of value is up for grabs. The provisional government soon turned to procurement as a means of supplying the Texas Army. A resolution was adopted on January 17, 1836, that empowered Lt. Col. James C. Neill at Béxar to procure men "for the purpose of driving up beeves, and procuring provisions for the troops under his command, as many as may be required for that purpose."[26] Soldiers confiscated beef cattle, whiskey, tobacco, guns or horses—whatever they needed to survive—all with the blessings and the authorization of the Provisional Government of Texas.

Among other revenue-raising measures was the implementation of state-sponsored pirating. The members of the General Council knew about the lucrative operations of the pirate Jean Lafitte who operated from Galveston fifteen years before. They passed ordinances and decrees, the first of which was approved on November 27, 1835, granting letters of marque and reprisal to privateers who would attack, pillage and plunder trade ships flying the flags of Mexico in exchange for 20 percent of the captured "prizes."[27] In order to qualify for protection against capital punishment under U.S. laws, privateers had to follow several principles and restrictions, outlined in the following report from James F. Perry from the Committee on Naval Affairs:

> *1st. All persons applying for letters of marque and reprisal should be men of known character, standing and skill as naval tacticians, and no license to cruise as such should be granted to any vessel under eighty tons burthen, or carry less than four twelve pound cannonades, or their equivalent in metal.*
>
> *2nd. All vessels so licensed should cruize [sic] in the Gulf of Mexico, and in no other waters, and should be permitted to war upon, capture or make prize of all vessels sailing under the flag and under commission of the Central Government of Mexico, and no other.*
>
> *3rd. All prizes so captured should be ordered or brought into the ports of Texas, and when there, adjudicated and condemned as prizes to the captors, by the competent tribunals; there should be retained out of the monies arising from the sale of said prize or prizes, twenty-five percent for the use of Texas, and paid forthwith into the public Treasury accordingly, and the balance to be paid over to the captors, or their assigns, or legal representatives.*[28]

Additional ordinances and decrees were issued relating to the use of privateers. Although the percentage of any captured prizes paid to the government was adjusted in the various ordinances, the General Council later agreed that Texas would only take 10 percent of any proceeds. The percentage received by Texas was far less important to the war effort than the potential disruption of Mexican shipping.

As for the last revenue-raising method described by William Gouge as "cheating," he refers to the creation of a paper money system. At the time, the primary currency consisted largely of silver *pesos*, "hammered" Spanish coins and a variety of bank notes from the United States that carried as many different values in the marketplace as the banks that issued them. The General Council realized the urgent need for a uniform national currency to settle the payment of all accrued drafts. Consequently the provisional government passed an ordinance and decree on January 7, 1836, which created a paper money system as follows:

> *That the Treasurer shall immediately cause to be printed in a neat form, and shall issue in discharge of claims against the government and drafts on the treasury, the amount of one hundred and fifty thousand dollars in treasury notes, varying in specified value from one dollar to one hundred dollars, specifying on the face thereof that they will be received in payment for land and public dues, or be redeemed with any moneys in the treasury not otherwise appropriated.*[29]

The ordinance was not signed into law until January 20, 1836, in large part due to infighting between Governor Smith and the General Council. This ordinance effectively laid the groundwork for the paper money system later used during the era of the Republic of Texas. The "cheating" would not occur until a few years later. The government owned plenty of writing pens, but not a suitable printing press, which forestalled the printing of the promissory notes. As a result, the government issued handwritten promises for future payment drawn against a Treasury that could only account for its liabilities. Each draft meticulously recorded the date, payee, and bore the signatures of the auditor and controller that verified the claim. It was a system that became the only functioning issuance of payments for the foreseeable future. Until the government was able to fill its coffers with some badly needed cash via borrowing, the payment of funds "out of any monies in the Treasury not otherwise appropriated" would have to do.

RAISING FUNDS IN NEW ORLEANS

Immediately after Christmas 1835, loan commissioners Branch T. Archer, Stephen F. Austin and William H. Wharton set sail for the port of New Orleans on their fund-raising mission to the United States.[30] The three arrived in New Orleans in January 1836, looking to negotiate a series of loans totaling $250,000. The money was needed to buy munitions and supplies, outfit warships, and recruit volunteers for the war effort. The commissioners were also authorized to receive any donations. After they finished their business in New Orleans, the men were to proceed to Washington, D.C., to raise additional funds and assess the political climate in the United States in regards to the potential annexation of Texas.

By the early 1830s, the port of New Orleans had firmly established itself as the largest commercial hub on the Gulf Coast and carried on a lucrative export market

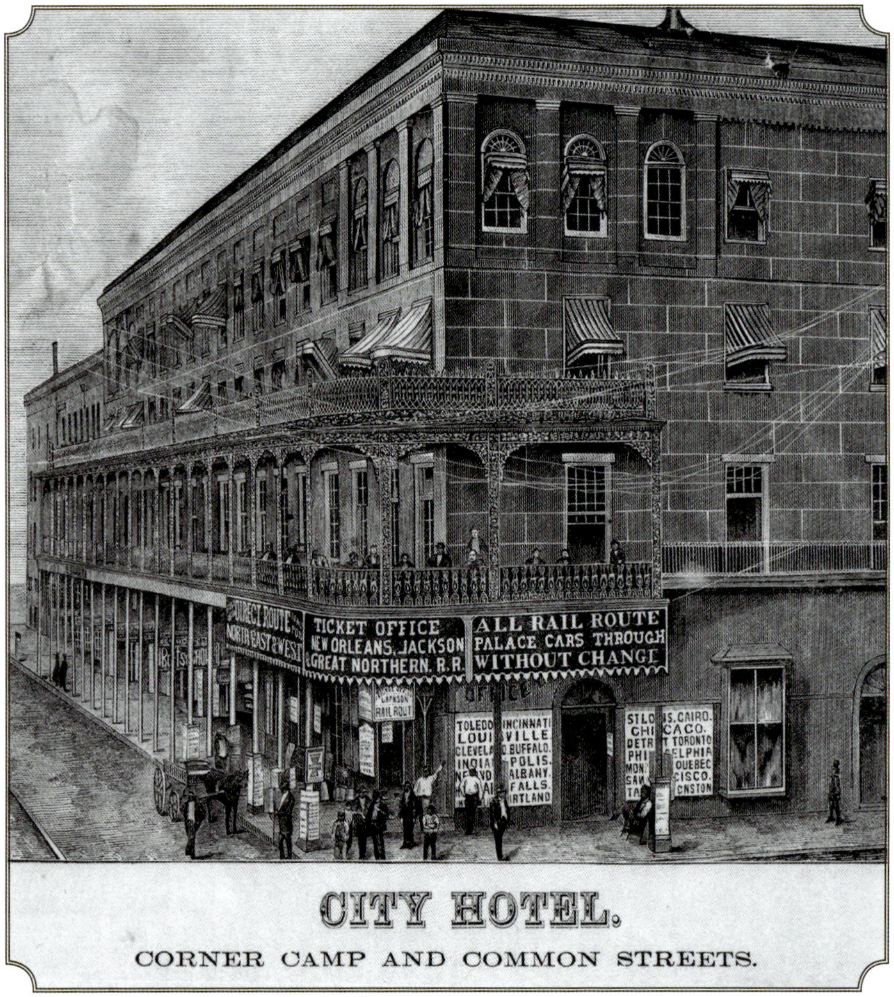

Fig 4.9, Bishop's City Hotel, New Orleans.

Courtesy of the Historic New Orleans Collection

for Texas cotton. The ties between the people of New Orleans and Texas ran deep, and it was viewed by many members of the Consultation as the best place for the commissioners to raise money. In an economy that was largely funded with paper money from private banks and commercial enterprises, there was also a booming sea trade with Mexico which attracted the much-needed silver *reales* and gold *doubloons* in exchange for American dry goods. These goods were brought back via sailing ship to Mexican ports.[31] The New Orleans populace was also well acquainted with the political climate in the Mexican state of Texas as local newspapers paid considerable attention to events in the years preceding the revolution.

A meeting of the commissioners and local businessmen who were sympathetic to the Texas cause took place in the large bar room at Bishop's City Hotel on January 6, 1836, on Camp Street near the French Quarter. Austin, Archer, and Wharton took turns addressing a large gathering of friends, hotel guests, and financiers from the southern part of the United States.[32] The meeting was chaired by William Christy, a New Orleans notary public and attorney, who had become a dominant figure in the commerce and financial dealings of the city.[33] Born in Kentucky in 1793, Christy was studying law when the War of 1812 broke out. He subsequently joined the First Regiment of Kentucky volunteers from Boone County under Capt. Uriel Sebree.[34] Like his Tennessee counterpart Sam Houston, Christy became a war hero and was later sent to New Orleans to serve as the paymaster of his regiment. From 1819 through 1822, Christy participated in rebellious activities in Spanish Texas as part of the Mina Expedition along with James Long, Jose Felix Trespalacios, John Austin, and Ben Milam. In short, William Christy was as sympathetic a chairperson to the Texas cause as anyone could have been at the time.

Fig 4.10, William Christy, engraving, c. 1850.

Center for American History, UT-Austin, CN11529.

Fig 4.11, William Fairfax Gray.

Courtesy of Christ Church Cathedral, Houston, Texas.

Fig 4.12, William H. Wharton.

Center for American History, CN 460, Prints & Photographs Collection, Austin, Texas.

William H. Wharton was an early leader in the Texas Revolution and openly advocated complete independence from Mexico in 1835. He traveled with the army to the siege at Béxar only to resign his commission a few days later to accept his appointment on a fund-raising mission to the United States. Upon completing their travels, the commissioners returned to Texas after the war whereby Wharton and Archer urged Austin to seek the presidency. He lost the 1836 election to Sam Houston. Wharton, appointed by President Houston as the first minister to the United States, successfully pleaded the case for diplomatic recognition in early 1837 with U.S. President Andrew Jackson.

AN IMPASSIONED PLEA FOR TEXAS

The commissioners from Texas soon found they were in friendly company in New Orleans. Many of their new acquaintances were lodgers at the same hotel. Their audience included several noted land agents and financiers, among them William Fairfax Gray and Robert Triplett. Gray had traveled from Virginia to Texas on behalf of his employers—Thomas Green and Albert T. Burnley of Washington, D.C.—in search of land for investment purposes. He was required by his employers to keep a diary and record his dates of travel, expenses, and observations of each area.[35] Leaving Virginia on October 6, 1835, Gray traveled through Ohio, the Carolinas, Kentucky, Tennessee, and later through Mississippi, Louisiana and eventually Texas. Having fortuitously arrived in New Orleans just before New Year's Eve in 1835, he heard an announcement that the commissioners from Texas would be in attendance at the same hotel. Gray attended the meeting to determine what kind of terms the commissioners could offer, and to gain firsthand knowledge of the speculative potential in Texas lands.

Robert Triplett was a wealthy merchant banker and Kentucky native who made his fortune in coal and land speculation.[36] He was also an old acquaintance of Branch Archer. Triplett learned the family business by working at his father's coal yards in Kentucky. He eventually settled in Yellow Banks, Kentucky, where he had accumulated a large amount of land and the rights to several coal deposits. In the late 1820s, Triplett shipped coal to many Louisiana sugar plantations, but when the demand softened due to a drop in the price of sugar, he found his way to New Orleans. There he supplied coal to hotels, cotton mills, and steamboats anchored in the bayou and tied up at the wharves. Triplett's interest in speculative Texas land ventures motivated him to contract for the purchase of lands near Nacogdoches with John Kirby and Augustus C. Allen, two brothers from New York who later founded the city of Houston. Triplett withdrew from the land transaction in late December 1835 when he became concerned about the legitimacy of the title.[37]

As the meeting came to order, the guests of honor—commissioners Austin, Archer, and Wharton—were seated beside William Christy.[38] They took turns addressing the crowd on how the Texians had been wronged, and one written source noted the commissioners "earnest and labored appeals to the feelings and sympathies of the United States."[39] Their resolutions were carried by a loud and enthusiastic applause with unanimous support from their audience. Triplett, in particular was moved by the impassioned pleas of the commissioners and considered the possibilities of their offer.

Even though the audience was sympathetic to the commissioner's plea, the idea of lending money to an interim government in the throes of a revolution was received rather coolly at first.[40] After all, Texas was not even an accredited government. It was well known in New Orleans that Mexican President Antonio López de Santa Anna had pledged to crush the rebellion and treat all those who took up arms against the government as pirates. Any remaining Anglos in Texas would be driven across the Sabine River at the point of a bayonet. Yet the desperate pitch for raising a loan to carry out a war against Mexico was intriguing to some, if proper terms could be had. Later that evening, Branch Archer struck up a conversation with Triplett where the two

It was well known in New Orleans that Mexican President Antonio López de Santa Anna had pledged to crush the rebellion and treat all those who took up arms against the government as pirates.

men discussed some potential terms which might be advantageous for Texas, Triplett, and a potential group of lenders.[41] As the conversations grew more detailed, Triplett and an associate, Thomas D. Carneal of Cincinnati, began to prepare a plan for a loan in the amount of $200,000 bearing interest at 8 percent per annum, but redeemable in land at fifty cents per acre. This plan was submitted to the commissioners and was found acceptable.[42] When it became known that land in Texas could be had at fifty cents an acre, interest in the loan package quickly gathered steam. Details of these Texian loans were worked out on Saturday, January 9, 1836, between the commissioners and the land-hungry investors.[43]

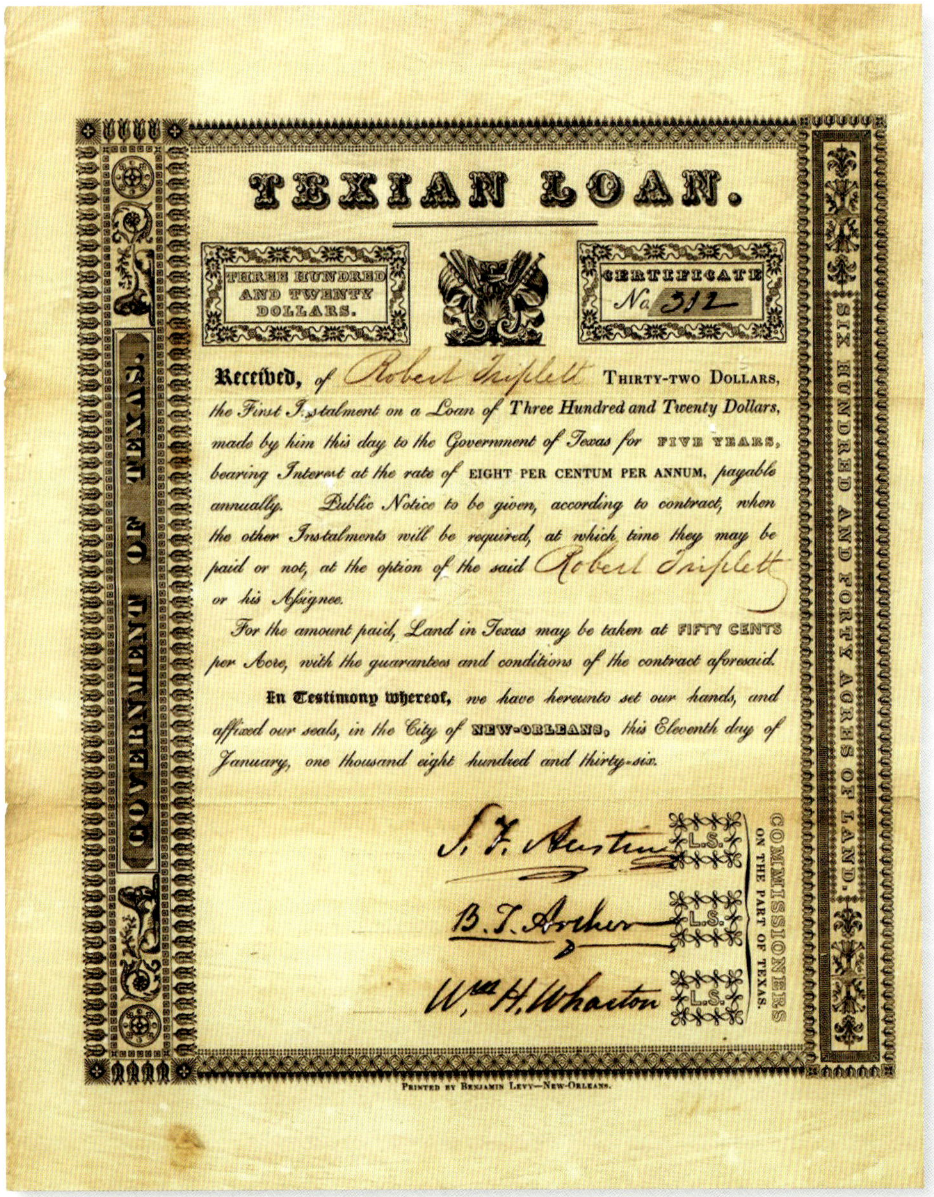
TEXIAN LOAN.

THREE HUNDRED AND TWENTY DOLLARS.

CERTIFICATE No. 312

GOVERNMENT OF TEXAS.

SIX HUNDRED AND FORTY ACRES OF LAND.

Received, of Robert Triplett Thirty-two Dollars, the First Instalment on a Loan of Three Hundred and Twenty Dollars, made by him this day to the Government of Texas for FIVE YEARS, bearing Interest at the rate of EIGHT PER CENTUM PER ANNUM, payable annually. Public Notice to be given, according to contract, when the other Instalments will be required, at which time they may be paid or not, at the option of the said Robert Triplett or his Assignee.

For the amount paid, Land in Texas may be taken at FIFTY CENTS per Acre, with the guarantees and conditions of the contract aforesaid.

In Testimony whereof, we have hereunto set our hands, and affixed our seals, in the City of NEW-ORLEANS, this Eleventh day of January, one thousand eight hundred and thirty-six.

S. F. Austin L.S.

B. T. Archer L.S.

Wm. H. Wharton L.S.

COMMISSIONERS ON THE PART OF TEXAS.

Printed by Benjamin Levy—New-Orleans.

A LOAN FOR TEXAS

The lenders agreed to the terms of the $200,000 loan: five years at 8 percent interest to be repaid in land at fifty cents an acre. An advance of 10 percent of the principal was to be made to Austin, Archer and Wharton, but there was a universal agreement among the lenders that no additional funds would be advanced until a Declaration of Independence was signed and the loan contract ratified by the Convention.[44] Austin assured the investors that a declaration of independence was already planned at Washington-on-the-Brazos in early March. Christy prepared the language for the Texian loan certificates dated Monday, January 11, with the formal loan documents listing the parties dated the following day. The printing and signing of the scrip certificates and the formal loan documents took place on Saturday, January 16.[45]

It was agreed that the lenders would have repayment in Texas lands with a priority of selection over all other parties within six months of the re-opening of the land offices.[46] The loan was soon oversubscribed as demand for prime Texas lands at fifty cents per acre was more than could be accommodated in the loan. The surviving Texian loan certificates bearing the original signatures of the provisional government's three earliest statesmen represent a glimpse into the early finances of Texas in the infancy of the Republic.

Fig 4.13, $200,000 Texian Loan, January 11, 1836.

Typeset Certificate, Private Collection, CR-36A4.

Transcription of Figure 4.13

Left: GOVERNMENT OF TEXAS, flanked on each side by a vignette of a Sphinx.

Right: SIX HUNDRED AND FORTY ACRES OF LAND, with ornamental décor.

Top: TEXIAN LOAN. Three Hundred and Twenty Dollars. Certificate No. 312

Received, of Robert Triplett *Thirty-Two Dollars, the First Installment on a loan of Three Hundred and Twenty Dollars, made by him this day to the Government of Texas for FIVE YEARS, bearing Interest at the rate of EIGHT PER CENTUM PER ANNUM, payable annually. Public Notice to be given, according to contract, when the other installments will be required, at which time they may be paid or not, at the option of the said* Robert Triplett *or his assignee. For the amount paid, Land in Texas may be taken at FIFTY CENTS per Acre, with the guarantees and conditions of the contract aforesaid. In Testimony whereof, we have hereunto set our hands, and affixed our seals, in the city of NEW-ORLEANS, this Eleventh day of January, one thousand eight hundred and thirty-six.*

Signed: S.F. Austin, B.T. Archer, William H. Wharton, *COMMISSIONERS ON THE PART OF TEXAS. Printed by Benjamin Levy-New Orleans.*

These first Texian Loan certificates were issued in amounts of $320 each. They were issued by the "Government of Texas," which had not yet declared independence from Mexico. The certificates were issued upon the payment of $32 down, with the balance of the loan to be paid in installments at a later date, upon the ratification of the loan agreements by the government. An interesting aspect of the loan terms is that the remaining 90 percent of the payment "will be required at which time they may be paid or not, at the option…" of the holder. This clause gave each of the investors an option to withdraw from funding the remainder of the commitment.

The key selling point of the $200,000 loan was that "land in Texas may be taken at fifty cents per acre" for the amount advanced. The commissioners for Texas agreed to withhold all public land from sale until the lenders made their selection.[47] In other words, the new government issued these loan certificates redeemable in land scrip for a price of $320 for 640 acres of land at 10 percent down to help finance the revolution. A second loan of $50,000 was quickly prepared under similar terms to the first. The primary differences were the lenders under the second loan agreed to subordinate their land selections behind the lenders of the first loan and no immediate advance of 10 percent on the second loan would be made to the commissioners of Texas until the terms were ratified by the Convention. Austin wrote on the importance of the $200,000 loan on January 17, 1836: "The enclosed contract contains the terms of the first loan; it will no doubt be ratified by the convention as stipulated. The credit and prospects for the country will be totally ruined if it is not."[48] The vision of this early Texas diplomat was incredibly prophetic.

Fig 4.14, $50,000 Texian Loan, January 18, 1836.

Typeset Certificate, John N. Rowe III Collection of Texas Currency, DeGolyer Library, Southern Methodist University, Dallas, Texas, CR-36A.

TEXIAN LOAN.

THREE HUNDRED AND TWENTY DOLLARS.

CERTIFICATE No. 135.

GOVERNMENT OF TEXAS.

SIX HUNDRED AND FORTY ACRES OF LAND.

Received, of Thomas Banks THREE HUNDRED AND TWENTY DOLLARS, being a Loan to the Government of Texas, for FIVE YEARS, at the rate of EIGHT PER CENTUM PER ANNUM Interest, payable annually, at the Office of WILLIAM CHRISTY, NOTARY PUBLIC, in the City of New-Orleans. For the above amount, Land in Texas may be taken at the rate of FIFTY CENTS per Acre, upon the conditions and with the guarantees contained in a Contract executed this day at the Office of the said Christy, by the undersigned Commissioners and the said Lender.

In Testimony whereof, we have hereunto set our hands, and affixed our seals, in the said City of NEW-ORLEANS, this Eighteenth day of January, one thousand eight hundred and thirty-six.

S. F. Austin (L.S.)

B. T. Archer (L.S.)

(L.S.)

COMMISSIONERS ON THE PART OF TEXAS.

PRINTED BY BENJAMIN LEVY—NEW-ORLEANS.

Transcription of Figure 4.14:

Left: GOVERNMENT OF TEXAS, flanked on each side by a vignette of a Sphinx.

Right: SIX HUNDRED AND FORTY ACRES OF LAND, with ornamental décor.

Top: TEXIAN LOAN. Three Hundred and Twenty Dollars. Certificate No. 135

Received, of Thomas Banks *THREE HUNDRED AND TWENTY DOLLARS, being a Loan to the Government of Texas, for FIVE YEARS, at the rate of EIGHT PER CENTUM PER ANNUM, Interest, payable annually at the Office of WILLIAM CHRISTY, Notary Public, in the City of New Orleans. For the above amount, Land in Texas may be taken at the rate of FIFTY CENTS per Acre, upon the conditions and with the guarantees contained in a Contract executed this day at the Office of the said Christy, by the undersigned Commissioners and the said Lender.*

In Testimony whereof, we have hereunto set our hands, and affixed our seals, in the said City of NEW-ORLEANS, this Eighteenth day of January, one thousand eight hundred and thirty-six.

Signed: S.F. Austin, B.T. Archer, *COMMISSIONERS ON THE PART OF TEXAS.*

Printed by Benjamin Levy-New Orleans

The second Texian loan certificates were also issued in amounts of $320 each and signed on January 18, while the formal loan documents listing the parties to the second loan were signed on January 20, 1836. An interesting aspect of these certificates is the fact that they are missing the signature of William H. Wharton, who had departed New Orleans in route to Tennessee a few days prior to his colleagues.

Both loans were subject to the ratification of the loan agreement by the Provisional Government of Texas before the remaining money was advanced. The commissioners had pledged 500,000 acres of Texas land for the purpose, the whole of which still belonged to the Republic of Mexico. The lender's claims would supersede all other requests or grants until the whole of the loans were retired. These terms were subject to ratification by the Convention in March at Washington-on-the-Brazos. Both loans were considered highly speculative, for it was widely known that if Santa Anna's forces were to enter and conquer Texas, then all of the money advanced for the loans would be for naught.

When each loan was redeemed for land scrip, it was cut cancelled with a razor in the form of a triangle. These certificates were typically cut in a pile, with a few of the bottom specimens surviving the sharp razor cut or bearing only the smallest outline of a cut from the cancellation process. The most common payee on the loans is Robert Triplett who had the largest stake in the loans—$100,000 of the first loan, and $2,000 of the second. William Fairfax Gray had a $5,000 interest in the first loan with the remaining members of the syndicate pledging the remainder of the loan. With the looming threat of Santa Anna's army entering Texas, some of the participants, including Thomas Whiteman, cancelled their financial obligation and signed over their interest to Triplett, who was by far the most committed of the syndicate lenders.[49] The formal loan documents which established the terms and conditions are shown in Appendix C ($200,000 loan) and Appendix D ($50,000 loan).

A MILITARY SPENDING SPREE

The commissioners appointed William Bryan as their agent in New Orleans to receive the $20,000 advance on the first loan, and Edward Hall as the purchasing agent.[50] Bryan and Hall embarked on a rapid spending spree, and the entire $20,000 was expended on guns, ammunition, military supplies and warships for the first Texas Navy.

While the three commissioners were negotiating the final terms of the loans in New Orleans, the men were introduced to Charles E. Hawkins, a former U.S. Navy midshipman who had spent time in the West Indies before joining the Mexican Navy in 1826. A handsome man who was skilled in naval affairs, Hawkins spent a great deal of his seafaring time as a privateer, with letters of marque and reprisal from a South American republic to prey on Spanish shipping. His notoriety as an aggressive force in the Gulf of Mexico and the Caribbean caused him to be described as "Havana's greatest scourge—his very name was a terror to every master of a vessel that was in the Spanish West Indies trade."[51] In early 1836, Hawkins visited provisional Gov. Henry Smith and offered the services of himself and his men, many of which were ex-pirates, to the cause of Texas freedom. Smith, in turn, wrote a letter of recommendation to the commissioners which Hawkins took with him to New Orleans. The commissioners hired him on the spot. Hawkins was placed in command of the newly acquired warship *Independence* and advanced $500 by Austin and Archer for outfitting the schooner.[52] Hawkins was later promoted to the rank of commodore and given command of the entire Texas Navy.

After wrapping up their affairs in New Orleans, Austin and Archer proceeded to travel up the Mississippi River, meeting up with Wharton in Nashville on February 12 where they were detained by cold, icy weather.[53] The men made numerous speeches in the Nashville area before leaving for Washington, D.C. Following their arrival in the capital, the commissioners were unable to persuade the U.S. Congress to support their cause, or to commit the United States to the recognition, and eventual annexation, of the new Republic should independence be declared in the early spring. As the largest single investor in the Texian loans, Triplett traveled to Texas to represent the lending group at the Constitutional Convention at Washington-on-the-Brazos. He was later joined by William Fairfax Gray, and the two men campaigned tirelessly to have the loan contracts ratified by the new government.

HENRY SMITH AND THE GENERAL COUNCIL

The Treasury of the Provisional Government of Texas recorded the payment of the government's official expenses by the issuance of warrants (also called drafts) and by an entry on the accompanying ledger. These warrants were the government's version of a check drawn against the Texas Treasury which was virtually empty at all times. These early warrants were entirely hand-written promises for future payment by the Provisional Government of Texas. A variety of papers were later purchased from a handful of printers with little regard for uniformity in completing the task. Like the various drafts issued under its authority, the provisional government would have even less uniformity, as a firestorm of discontent swelled at the very head of the temporary government.

Henry Smith, the headstrong provisional Governor of Texas, attempted to disband the General Council and appoint himself as the ruling chief executive of the provisional government. In a scathing address to the General Council at San Felipe on January 9, 1836, Smith chastised the council for dissolving "into low, intriguing, caucusing parties" passing resolutions without a quorum, on false premises, and he continued, by "countenancing, aiding and abetting marauding parties." As the stunned council listened in disbelief, Smith's diatribe continued: "I know you have honest men there, and of sterling worth and integrity; but you have Judas in the camp, corruption, base corruption, has crept into your councils—men who, if possible, would deceive their God."[54]

As the members of the council contemplated the venomous words delivered from this heretofore respected but arrogant man, Governor Smith delivered the directive that in his mind would settle all temporary disagreements in the government: "I consider, as the devisers of ways and means you have done all contemplated by the organic law, and that your services are no longer needed. Until the Convention meets, I will discharge my duties as commander-in-chief of the army and navy and see that the laws are executed."[55]

But Smith soon found that the men who comprised the General Council would not roll over and yield to his whims as easily as the Gillett sisters. The Council referred the transcript of Smith's offending speech to a committee. On January 11, a report was unanimously adopted, together with resolutions which declared the members of the council as the representatives of the people and ordered that Henry Smith "be ordered forthwith to cease the functions of his office," effectively impeaching Smith in favor of Lt. Gov. James W. Robinson. It was Robinson who signed the act of January 7, 1836, which authorized the creation of a paper money system for Texas. Henry Smith would never again play a significant role in the provisional government, although he would later emerge as the powerful Treasury Secretary in Sam Houston's first administration. Ironically, the implementation of the paper money system would later be orchestrated by Smith.

EXPANDING THE TREASURY DEPARTMENT

The creation of the offices of auditor and comptroller of Public Accounts for Texas passed by a constitutional majority on December 29, 1835.[56] Although the offices were the brainchild of Henry Smith, he vetoed the passage of the ordinance to create the appointments, only to be overruled by the majority.[57] The function of

A distinguishing feature of the San Felipe warrants of 1836 is the depiction of the name, Joshua Fletcher, Esq., across the top of the short-lived series.

the offices remained largely unaltered and unchanged following the controversy. This stability would have far reaching implications in the issuance of all Texas paper money in the future. All of the treasury warrants issued from this point forward bore standardized language referencing specific appropriation of funds. If the drafts did not list a specific reference, they were to be paid "out of any monies in the Treasury not otherwise appropriated." While attending the Consultation in San Felipe, Joshua Fletcher was appointed by the council as Treasurer pro tem and he was later elected to that position by a vote on December 5, 1836. A distinguishing feature of the San Felipe warrants of 1836 is the depiction of the name, Joshua Fletcher, Esq., across the top of the short-lived series.

THE AUDITOR

John W. Moody, the first auditor of the Republic of Texas, was born around 1791. As a young man, he moved from Iredell County, North Carolina, to Alabama where he lived in Coosa and St. Clair counties around 1816-1819. In 1824, he settled in Montgomery where he owned a small plantation and several slaves.[58] Sometime during his tenure in Alabama, Moody was in either a local militia or the U.S. Army. He acquired the rank of major and was addressed as Major Moody during his professional life. In 1833, after a brief residence in Creek Indian territory, he became interested in Texas and moved to Bastrop with his wife Mary Baldwin Moody in May 1835.

Moody served as the auditor for the Provisional Government of Texas. He was elected auditor by the General Council on December 20, 1835, and began his service ten days later. Before this, he served as chief clerk of the finance committee and clerk of the committee of State and Judiciary Affairs. His work was considered critical to the early functioning of the provisional government. One of his duties was to evaluate the validity of claims against the treasury. When claims were presented, Moody verified the dates that oxen, horses, wagons and other goods were pressed into service. He required either an affidavit or the testimony of credible witnesses regarding the value of the goods or services that were received.[59] Claimants had to prove the customary price of the goods or services presented in their claim before Moody would verify it by issuing a warrant. Although Moody was often handicapped by a lack of suitable stationery, particularly at San Felipe, his thoroughness in the job led to his appointment as the Auditor of Public Accounts during the two years of Sam Houston's first administration. Moody continued to hold the office of auditor until his death on August 21, 1839.[60]

THE COMPTROLLER

Henry C. Hudson was an early Texas lawyer who was present at the 1835 San Felipe meetings regarding the Anahuac Disturbances. He was appointed as a judge by the provisional government in the fall of 1835. On January 13, 1836, in the infancy of the government, Hudson was appointed as comptroller of the Treasury, where he worked side-by-side with Moody to ascertain the validity of claims, validate the books and establish a system of checks and balances. This was a post he held until October 22, 1836. Following the war, President Sam Houston nominated Hudson as the district attorney of Fayette County in December 1836, and Hudson practiced law in the summer of 1837 with Josiah Crosby in Washington-on-the-Brazos.

Some knowledge of the duties of the auditor and comptroller (or controller) is essential to the understanding of the money and finances of the Republic of Texas. The entire system of auditor's certificates and treasury warrants were based upon the actions of these men. When a claim was presented to the government, the auditor examined the claim for validity through receipts, vouchers, or other evidence and was required to reject or accept the claim.[61] If accepted, an entry was made in the books of the treasury, and no entry was made for a claim which had been rejected. Claims under $4,000 were presented by the auditor to the comptroller, who "approved" the claim if it appeared valid. The claim was subsequently returned to the auditor for his signature.

Once a claim was approved, the auditor issued a draft (a claim on the treasury) which would read as follows:

> *The Treasurer of the Provisional Government of Texas, will pay to ________ or order the sum of ________ dollars, out of any monies in the Treasury not otherwise appropriated.*
>
> *Date, etc...* *Auditor*
> *Comptroller*

This language became the standard on all outstanding drafts issued from January 1836 forward by the short-lived Provisional Government of Texas. This language was also carried over into the era of the Republic. Claims over $4,000 were referred to the governor or the General Council for approval and were signed and approved in the same manner as described previously. While the auditor wrote the checks, it was the comptroller who had the right to approve or reject every claim against the government, and who kept a running total of the balances. The comptroller inscribed "Approved" across each claim before a draft (or warrant) was issued in payment. The first Texas currency which bore this standardized language in the form of warrants was issued at San Felipe de Austin by the Provisional Government of Texas.

These sequentially numbered warrants are entirely handwritten and are predominantly found on buff, pink, blue or yellow paper. The place of issue is not shown on these early drafts, but they can be identified by the dates of issue and the color of the paper. All of the San Felipe issues are referenced to Joshua Fletcher, Esq., who served as the treasurer of the provisional government at the time. Thus began the cycle of credit and borrowing, receipts and payments and a functioning Treasury of the provisional, yet fully operational, government of Texas.

No. 119 To Joshua Fletcher, Esquire $25.00

The Treasurer of the provisional Government of Texas will pay to Erastus Smith or order twenty five dollars out of any monies in the Treasury not Otherwise Appropriated.

$25.00 January 13th, 1836

(Signed) H.C. Hudson, Controller (Signed) J.W. Moody, Auditor

The early San Felipe note in Figure 4.16, made payable to Erastus "Deaf" Smith, places the legendary Texas scout in San Felipe de Austin in January 1836. It also bears the new standard language "out of any money in the Treasury not otherwise appropriated" as well as the signatures of the auditor and the comptroller. An endorsement on the reverse of this warrant reads: "on [sic] of the administrators of the Estate of E. Smith" indicates that the note remained unclaimed by Smith at the time of his death, and the "Cancelled" notation written across the face indicates that it was eventually settled by his family.

Like many early residents in the DeWitt Colony, Erastus Smith's attempts to remain neutral in the growing conflict ended as tensions between the Texians and the Mexican Centralists flared. He sided with the Texians and joined the Texas Army in Gonzales in 1835.[63] Though handicapped by a slight loss of hearing, Deaf Smith quickly became an important scout in the war for Texas Independence and had a peculiar habit of being in exactly the right place at the right time during some of the most pivotal episodes of the revolution. His intelligence gathering was important at the battle of Conception in October 1835. He participated in the fierce battle over the mistaken silver payroll which later became known as the "Grass Fight."

Fig 4.15, Portrait of Erastus "Deaf" Smith.

"Deaf" Smith was in Houston in May 1837 when President Sam Houston ordered him to sit for the painting in Figure 4.15 to "adorn some future hall of fame."[62] A portion of the portrait was later reproduced by the engravers at Rawdon Wright, Hatch & Edson in New Orleans, the inverse of which appears on the Republic of Texas $5 note, issued from Austin.

Courtesy of Albert and Ethel Herzstein Library, The San Jacinto Museum of History, Houston, Texas.

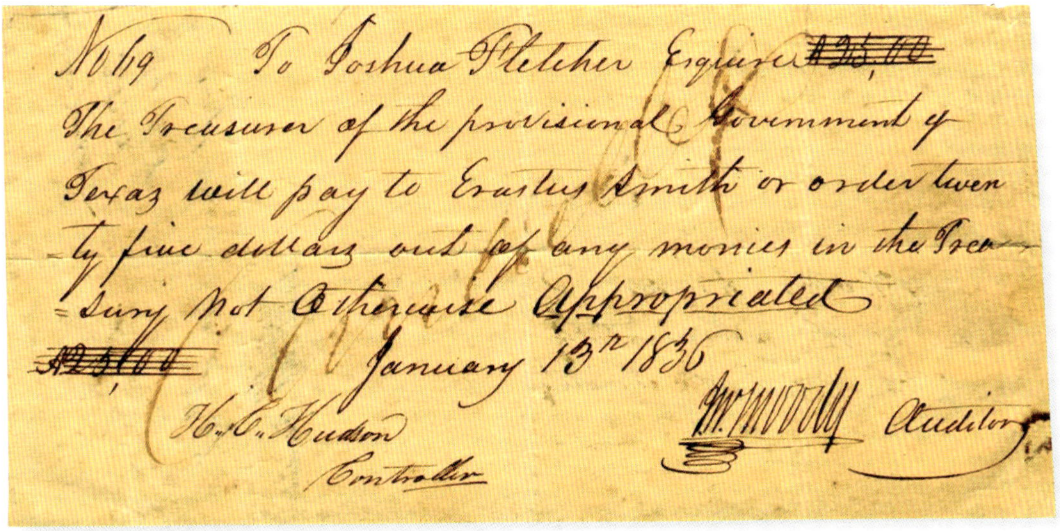

No 119 To Joshua Fletcher Esquire ~~$25,00~~
The Treasurer of the provisional Government of
Texas will pay to Erastus Smith or order twen-
-ty five dollars out of any monies in the Trea-
-sury Not Otherwise Appropriated
~~$25,00~~ January 13th 1836
H.C. Hudson Controller
J.W. Moody Auditor

Fig 4.16, San Felipe de Austin, January 13, 1836. $25 draft payable to Erastus Smith.

Private Collection, Cr. P2 (P1), O-47.

In December 1835, Smith guided troops into San Antonio in the siege and battle of Béxar where he was wounded atop the Veramendi House. He later relocated his family to Columbia and joined Sam Houston at Gonzales after the Declaration of Independence was signed at Washington-on-the-Brazos. Smith was then assigned by Sam Houston to the arduous task of finding the fate of the Alamo defenders. It was Smith who came upon the newly widowed Susanna Dickinson, who had survived the siege along with her infant daughter Angelina. She gave Smith and his companions the terrible news of the massacre, and they subsequently relayed the grim communication to Gen. Sam Houston.[64]

Deaf Smith was revered by his fellow citizens and political leaders for his service accomplishments during the Texas Revolution. He returned to Columbia following the war. Smith raised a company of Rangers in 1837 and defeated a superior Mexican force at Laredo later the same year. He then moved to Richmond in Fort Bend County where he died on November 30, 1837.[65] Smith received a grant of property for his service through a legislative act dated November 11, 1836. The act granted him "any house and lot on the city of Béxar, which may be confiscated for public use." The property was chosen by his widow who lived there until her death on May 1, 1849.

The oddly cut yellow San Felipe specimen in Figure 4.17 was made payable to Caleb M. Tennin or to his legal representative, which represents the assignable nature of these early issues. The standardized language is present along with the signatures of John W. Moody and Henry C. Hudson. Like many early issues, the series of fold marks on the specimen indicates that it was folded and carried around by the payee or his representative.

The nicely preserved yellow specimen of the San Felipe issue in Figure 4.18 was made payable to James S. Lester. The standardized language and the signatures of the auditor and the controller are clearly evident. Lester served as a representative on the General Council from the Municipality of Mina, later known as Bastrop County.[66] At the time

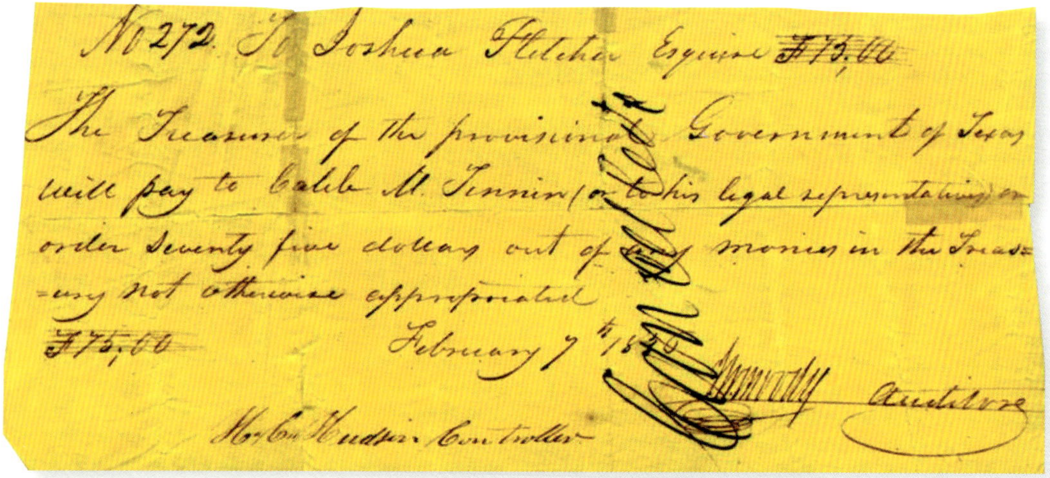

Fig 4.17, San Felipe de Austin, February 7, 1836. $75 draft payable to Caleb M. Tennin.

Private Collection, Cr. P2 (P1), O-47.

No. 272 To Joshua Fletcher, Esquire $75.00
The Treasurer of the provisional Government of Texas will pay to Caleb M. Tennin or To his legal representative or order seventy five dollars out of monies in the Treasury not otherwise Appropriated.

$75.00 February 7th, 1836

(Signed) H.C. Hudson, Controller
(Signed) J.W. Moody, Auditor

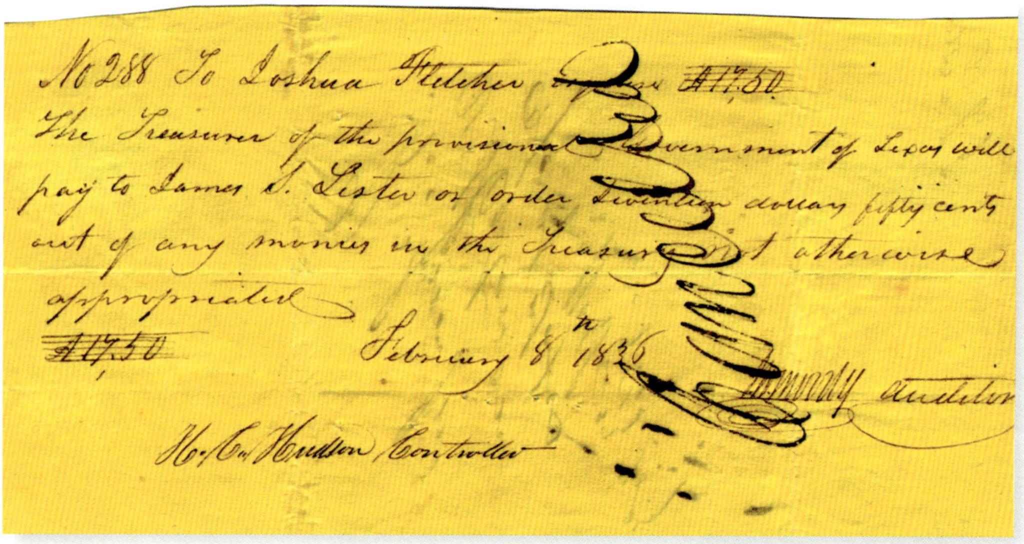

Fig 4.18, San Felipe de Austin, February 8, 1836. $17.50 draft payable to James S. Lester.

Private Collection, Cr. P2 (P1), O-47.

No. 288 To Joshua Fletcher, Esquire $17.50

The Treasurer of the provisional Government of Texas will pay to James S. Lester or order seventeen dollars fifty cents out of monies in the Treasury not otherwise Appropriated.

$17.50 February 8th, 1836

(Signed) H.C. Hudson, Controller
(Signed) J.W. Moody, Auditor

this municipality was formed, only a limited portion of its eastern area had been settled. Lester was present at the third gathering of the General Council in November 1835 where the twenty-one articles were presented. These articles established the *Plan and Powers of the Provisional Government of Texas.*[67]

AGENTS FOR THE PROVISIONAL GOVERNMENT

It became apparent to the representatives of the government that Texas could not wait for supplies to come its way. Agents for the government fanned out across Texas to procure supplies, often issuing little more than a handshake and a receipt for the goods they took. These receipts were of the utmost importance, as they could later be presented as a claim against the government, and exchanged for a draft against the treasury once verified by the auditor.

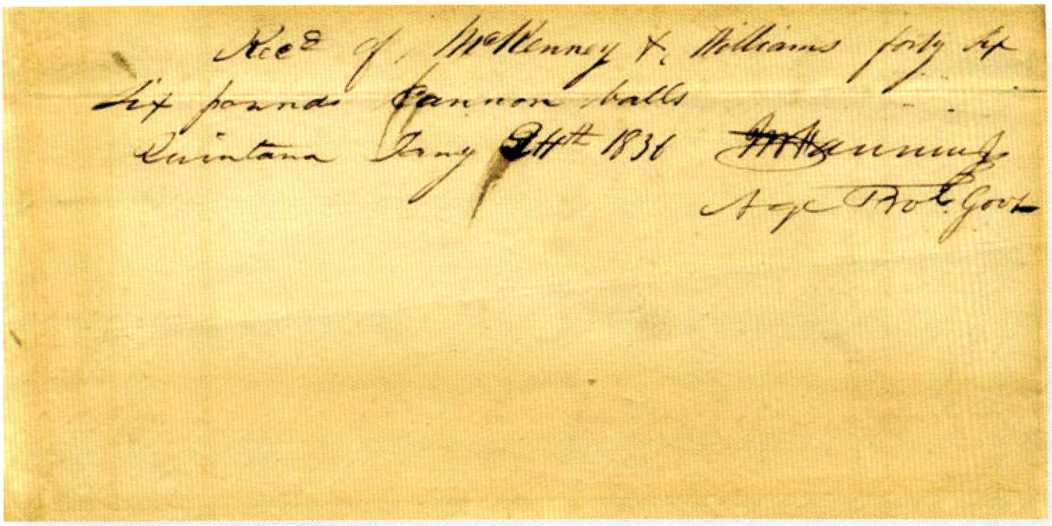

Fig 4.19, Quintana, January 24, 1836. Receipt for cannon balls by J. W. Fannin, Jr, Agent for the Provisional Govt.

Private Collection, Cr. Unlisted. O-Unlisted.

Rec[eive]d of McKinney & Williams forty six, six pound cannon balls, Quintana, Jan[uar]y 24, 1836

(Signed) J[ames] W. Fannin Jr ,

Age[nt] Prov[isional] Gov[ernment]

Fannin's signature as found on the receipt for cannon balls in Figure 4.19 to McKinney and Williams is exceedingly rare, as he met his untimely death only two months after this document was signed. Fannin was referred to as "Fanning" on numerous military documents and official papers. The confusion may have originated from his signature, as he ran the "Jr." onto the end of his name, giving the appearance of the surname "Fanning."

James Fannin was appointed colonel in the Texian Army by General Houston on December 7, 1835.[68] When Col. Francis W. Johnson declined to lead a proposed military expedition against Matamoros, Mexico, Fannin was appointed by the General Council to recruit, collect and concentrate a group of volunteers at or near Copano Bay until the time was right for him to gather additional forces and lead an attack on the Mexican border city.

On January 24, 1836, Fannin was in the coastal town of Quintana, located across the Brazos River from Velasco, where he received munitions from the mercantile firm of McKinney & Williams to whom this receipt was issued. Later that same day, Fannin and his group of 200 armed volunteers embarked by boat into rough seas and landed at Aransas Pass four days later. From there, the troops moved to Copano Bay. When confronted with intelligence that Gen. José de Urrea was advancing a Mexican Army into Texas, Fannin abandoned the planned invasion of Matamoros and began to consolidate his forces in South Texas against the gathering military threat.[69]

The early Texas mercantile firm of McKinney and Williams was a powerful one. They bought ships (from Baltimore), imported hundreds of kegs of first quality gunpowder (from the DuPont Company), furnished ammunition to the Army, and were empowered by an act of the General Council to borrow money on behalf of the provisional government.

Fig 4.20, New Orleans, February 24, 1836.

McKinney & Williams, 8% Government of Texas Bond.

John N. Rowe III Collection of Texas Currency, DeGolyer Library, Southern Methodist University, Dallas, Texas. Cr. 36p, O-Unlisted.

Thomas F. McKinney was a revolutionary leader, prominent businessman, arms dealer and one of the founders of the city of Galveston. He was granted a privateering license in 1835 from the provisional government. He used his firm's credit to buy the schooner *William Robbins,* renamed *Liberty,* which harassed Mexican shipping on behalf of the rebel government. Williams also founded the town of Quintana at the mouth of the Brazos River which was used as a warehouse station for the goods of the McKinney and Williams mercantile firm. Following the war, his business partnership with Samuel May Williams was the most important cotton export business in the Republic.

Samuel May Williams served as land office manager and secretary of Austin's Colony, and was an early confidant of Stephen F. Austin.[70] Beginning in the summer of 1823, Williams prepared the majority of the required titles for Austin's three hundred settlers. The pioneer's skills included his written and verbal command of English, Spanish and French, a fine style of handwriting, the development of meticulous methods for the issuance of deeds and recording of titles, and an enormous capacity for hard work. As the junior partner of the mercantile firm of McKinney & Williams from 1834-1842, his contributions to the Republic of Texas were of a business and financial nature rather than a military one. Williams was in the East when the Texas Revolution broke out, and he acted quickly to gather support and supplies for the Texas Army and Navy. When Williams returned to Texas in May 1836, he brought more than six hundred volunteers, a fleet of three vessels, and a schooner loaded with provisions and arms which he had secured for Texas using his personal credit.

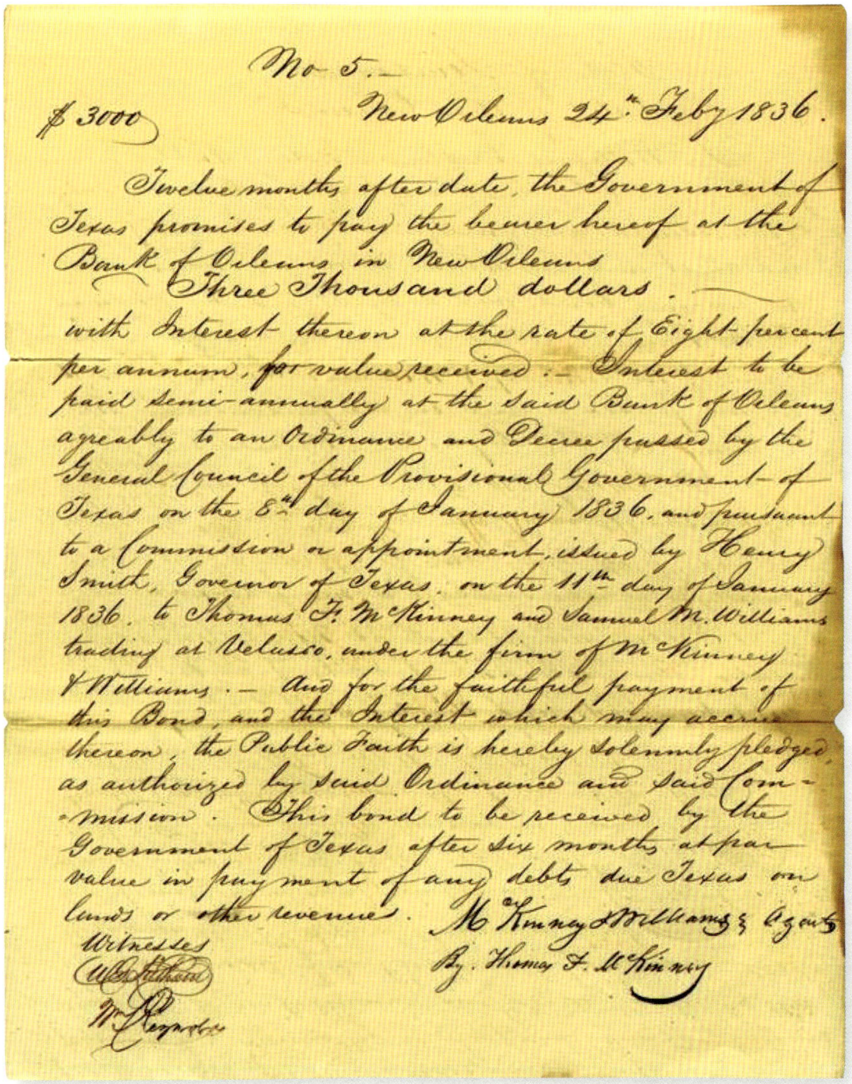

No 5.–
$3000 New Orleans 24th Feby 1836.
Twelve months after date, the Government of
Texas promises to pay the bearer hereof at the
Bank of Orleans in New Orleans
Three Thousand dollars. —
with Interest thereon at the rate of Eight percent
per annum, for value received:– Interest to be
paid semi-annually at the said Bank of Orleans
agreeably to an Ordinance and Decree passed by the
General Council of the Provisional Government of
Texas on the 8th day of January 1836. and pursuant
to a Commission or appointment, issued by Henry
Smith, Governor of Texas, on the 11th day of January
1836. to Thomas F. McKinney and Samuel M. Williams
trading at Velasco, under the firm of McKinney
& Williams. – And for the faithful payment of
this Bond, and the Interest which may accrue
thereon, the Public Faith is hereby solemnly pledged
as authorized by said Ordinance and said Com-
-mission. This bond to be received by the
Government of Texas after six months at par
value in payment of any debts due Texas on
lands or other revenue. McKinney & Williams Agents
Witnesses By: Thomas F. McKinney
W.G. Latham
Wm Reynolds

The primary language of the document in Figure 4.20 reads as follows:

No 5-, $3000, New Orleans, 24th Feb[ruar]y 1836

Twelve months after date, the Government of Texas promises to pay the bearer hereof at the Bank of Orleans in New Orleans Three Thousand Dollars with Interest thereon at the rate of eight percent per annum for value received;... Interest to be paid semi-annually at the said Bank of Orleans agreeably to an ordinance and Decree passed by the General Council of the Provisional Government of Texas on the 8th day of January 1836, and pursuant to a Commission or appointment, issued by Henry Smith, Governor of Texas;on the 11th day of January 1836 to Thomas F. McKinney and Samuel M. Williams trading at Velasco, under the firm of McKinney & Williams. - and for the faithful payment of this bond, and the Interest which may accrue thereon, the Public Faith is hereby solemnly pledged as authorized by said Ordinance and said Commission. This bond to be received by the Government of Texas after six months at par value in payment of any debts due Texas on lands or other revenues. McKinney & Williams, Agents (Signed) By Thomas F. McKinney. Witnesses W.G. Latham, Wm. Reynolds.

The manuscript bond in Figure 4.20 is among the rarest of early Texas debt instruments. The document references the decree of January 8, 1836, which authorized and empowered "Thomas F. McKinney and Samuel M. Williams, of the firm McKinney & Williams, to effect a loan for one hundred thousand dollars...." This bond was one of twelve handwritten issues, ranging in denominations of one thousand to five thousand dollars, which represented the first $30,000 of the loan.[71] Another attempt was made to raise funds under the same act with two bonds of $10,000 each on May 2, 1836, but that attempt also appears to have been unsuccessful.[72]

McKinney traveled to New Orleans to negotiate this first piece of a $100,000 loan for the struggling Provisional Government of Texas. He was concerned that news of Gov. Henry Smith's recent impeachment might hamper his ability to raise the money. On January 25, 1836, McKinney wrote from Quintana: "I leave on tomorrow for N. Orleans hope to be able to do something for the benefit of our country....I much fear the conduct of our Ex Govr [*sic*] and his friends will disgrace us abroad so that on the faith of the country, money cannot be raised."[73] It is clear that these manuscript bonds were created by Thomas F. McKinney while he was in New Orleans in the spring of 1836 as he attempted to raise the loans. Although he tried to sell the bonds in denominations as low as $1,000, he failed to raise the money.[74] It is possible that, like the investors in the Texian loans, any potential lenders were skeptical about advancing their money to a rebel government that had yet to formally declare its independence. Although he failed to raise the needed funds, McKinney did persuade New Orleans merchants William Bryan and Toby & Company to accept McKinney & Williams company drafts for gunpowder and munitions for the Texas Army. He returned to Texas in mid-March with the goods, all of which had been advanced on McKinney & Williams' credit. Unfortunately for Toby & Company, the total of the drafts quickly exceeded McKinney's or the fledgling Republic's ability to repay them. This situation later forced Toby & Company into bankruptcy.

Toby & Company were not the only ones who suffered financially from an arrangement that began or ended with these ill-fated financial instruments. McKinney's partner, Samuel May Williams, noted that his brother-in-law, Samuel St. John of Mobile, Alabama, made a "donation" of $5,000 in 1835 or the beginning of 1836 and another donation in March or April 1836, meant for "the uses and purposes of the revolution."[75] At the time, St. John was considered quite wealthy and a prosperous businessman. Having few concerns about his sister's husband, Williams left these small denomination bearer bonds with St. John for safekeeping. As St. John's fortunes reversed in the economic depression which followed the Panic of 1837, he proceeded to make a claim against the government of Texas under the bearer bonds for his "loan." In 1840, St. John went so far as to grant a power of attorney to Williams to petition the Congress of the Republic on his behalf "asking and praying for Amounts of money advanced by me to the Republic of Texas in the year 1836."[76] The on-going incident caused considerable friction between the two men, resulting in their permanent estrangement. Although Williams demanded the return of the bearer bonds and St. John repeatedly "promised to return them," the bonds remained in St. John's possession. Following the annexation of Texas, the bond shown in Figure 4.20 was one of those presented for a claim against the government by William's sister, Sophia St. John. Her claim was denied by the auditor and comptroller.[77]

NEWS ARRIVES FROM THE ALAMO

The meeting of the General Council in San Felipe began to break up towards the end of February 1836 as delegates left to tend to their families. Arrangements were made for elected delegates to reconvene at Washington-on-the-Brazos for the Convention on March 1. News of the advancing Mexican Army began to trickle into San Felipe. An express message from Col. William Barrett Travis at Béxar was received at San Felipe on the night of February 25, dated two days earlier. It stated that 1,000 of the enemy were in sight of the Alamo.[94] Travis indicated he had only 150 men and was short on provisions and ammunition, but he was determined to defend the Alamo to the last. His letter rang with urgent calls for assistance in his staunch determination to protect the old mission. As William Fairfax Gray described the letter in his diary, "The people now think the wolf has come at last, and are preparing for a march." Gail Borden, the owner of the printing business at San Felipe, began to pack up the papers and records in the land office to remove them to safety in the east, should the enemy continue to advance.

Fig 4.21, Thomas F. McKinney.

Courtesy of the Rosenberg Library, Galveston, Texas.

Fig 4.22, Samuel May Williams.

Courtesy of the Texas Heritage Society.

Fig 4.23,
Col. William Barrett Travis.

Courtesy of the Daughters of the Republic of Texas Library at the Alamo, San Antonio, Texas.

When Jim Bowie's crippling illness left Travis in sole command of the Alamo, William Barrett Travis became one of the youngest leaders of the Texas Revolution.[79] On February 24, 1836, surrounded by the army of Antonio López de Santa Anna, Travis penned this famous appeal for help. He then dispatched Albert Martin on horseback through the Mexican lines to deliver the message. Martin's charge was to deliver the call for help first to Gonzales and then to the gathering at San Felipe for additional reinforcements.[80]

With the Mexican cannons thundering behind him, Martin rode to Gonzales where the call for reinforcements was answered by thirty-two men who rode from Gonzales and entered the walls of the Alamo. James Butler Bonham would join them on March 3. Travis's letter was passed to another courier, Lancelot Smithers, while at Gonzales. Smithers mounted a fresh horse and with a strong south breeze blowing rain in his face, he headed eastward with the desperate appeal for help. At night, the wind from the north blew cold rain on the lone horseman as he crossed the plains and rushed the message to its final destination at San Felipe late on the night of February 26.[81] The remaining council members in San Felipe were alarmed at the gravity of the situation in Béxar. They called an urgent meeting of the remaining members on the morning of February 27. The members discussed Travis' appeal for help and decided to mass distribute Travis' dispatch throughout Texas and the United States in a call to arms. It was decided that a printed broadside would be prepared with the message from the Alamo, which was designed to shock the population into action.

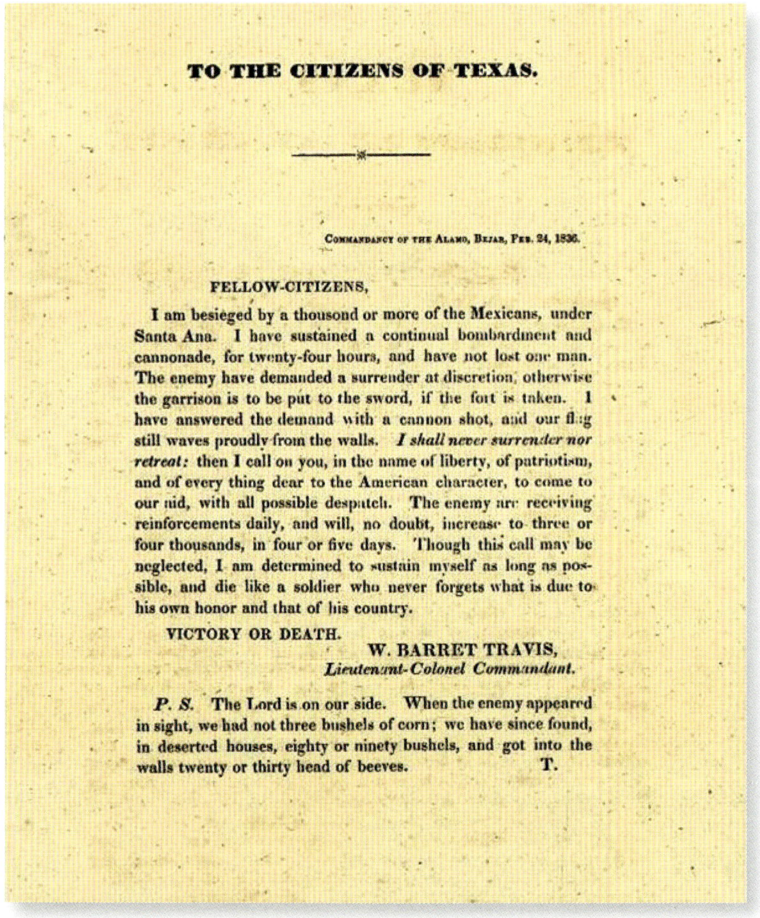

TO THE CITIZENS OF TEXAS.

COMMANDANCY OF THE ALAMO, BEJAR, FEB. 24, 1836.

FELLOW-CITIZENS,

I am besieged by a thousond or more of the Mexicans, under Santa Ana. I have sustained a continual bombardment and cannonade, for twenty-four hours, and have not lost one man. The enemy have demanded a surrender at discretion, otherwise the garrison is to be put to the sword, if the fort is taken. I have answered the demand with a cannon shot, and our flag still waves proudly from the walls. *I shall never surrender nor retreat:* then I call on you, in the name of liberty, of patriotism, and of every thing dear to the American character, to come to our aid, with all possible despatch. The enemy are receiving reinforcements daily, and will, no doubt, increase to three or four thousands, in four or five days. Though this call may be neglected, I am determined to sustain myself as long as possible, and die like a soldier who never forgets what is due to his own honor and that of his country.

VICTORY OR DEATH.

W. BARRET TRAVIS,
Lieutenant-Colonel Commandant.

P. S. The Lord is on our side. When the enemy appeared in sight, we had not three bushels of corn; we have since found, in deserted houses, eighty or ninety bushels, and got into the walls twenty or thirty head of beeves. T.

Fig 4.24,
Col. William Barrett Travis' "Victory or Death," letter from the Alamo.

Printed by Baker & Borden, San Felipe de Austin, 1836. Private Collection.

Exceedingly rare, the hastily printed dispatch in Figure 4.24 from the commander of the Alamo is among a handful of American statements that through the strength and succinctness of their own diction and cadence, defy explication or analysis.[82] William Barrett Travis wrote this desperate appeal for help under the most grave of circumstances and clearly stated his position as "I shall never surrender nor retreat." He was among the first killed at the Alamo when it was overrun by the Mexican Army on the morning of March 6, 1836. The words of the twenty-seven-year-old commander are among the most famous penned in American history.

Working from the handwritten original, Baker and Borden originally typeset Travis' plea underneath a scathing editorial message urging Texans to "rise from your lethargy, and march without a moment's delay to the field of war, or the next Western breeze that sweeps over your habitations will bring with it the shrieks and wailings of the women and children of Guadalupe and Colorado; and the last agonized shriek of liberty will follow."[83] Borden's editorial message was written to stoke the patriotic fires of war in the hearts of all able-bodied men in Texas.

Immediately following the printing of the Travis letter at the end of the above broadside, a separate printing of 300 copies of the letter were prepared on the right-hand side of a proclamation by Gov. Henry Smith titled "Texas Expects Every Man to do his Duty." The two texts, printed side-by-side, were then cut apart, and the plea for help from Travis, including the one in Fig. 4.24, was scattered through the countryside in a rallying cry for the cause. A few days later, the entire contents of the original broadside was reprinted in the *Telegraph and Texas Register* in the March 5, 1836, issue. Travis' original handwritten letter survived and is in the permanent custody of the Texas State Archives.

WASHINGTON-ON-THE-BRAZOS, FEBRUARY AND MARCH 1836

The town of Washington-on-the-Brazos dates from as early as 1822, but was not incorporated until 1834. The delegates to the Convention began to trickle in from across Texas in late February as the Convention date neared and the anticipation of forming a new government filled the air.The officers of the Treasury Department had reconvened a few days earlier and additional drafts against the provisional treasury were issued from February 22, 1836, until March 16, 1836.

Named after Washington, D.C., Washington-on-the-Brazos is considered the birthplace of the Republic of Texas. Located 150 miles east of San Antonio de Béxar, this small town was ill prepared to serve the representatives who arrived to draft a Declaration of Independence from Mexico. The town began as a ferry crossing on the Brazos River in 1822 and had not progressed much in fourteen years. When the delegates to the Convention arrived, the place barely offered the necessities of life, much less any luxuries.

William Fairfax Gray described the town in his diary as having been "laid out in the woods, about a dozen wretched shanties or cabins constitute the city; not one decent house in it and only one well defined street, which consists of an opening cut out of the woods."[84] Gray had become fascinated with the speculative potential of Texas lands and had traveled to the Convention in Washington-on-the-Brazos to make a firsthand observation of the politics and the people that had gathered there. In Gray's words, "It was a rare place to hold a national convention in. They will have to leave it promptly to avoid starvation." A single tavern offered meager lodging that consisted of only a single room with two fireplaces and little more, devoid of doors or windows, with only holes to the outside where they should have been.[85] The wood frame building had once been the home and shop of gunsmith N.T. Byers, though during the Convention it became known as "Independence Hall."[86]

Arriving on February 28, Gray found James W. Robinson, the acting governor, was present with only a handful of the council, including John McMullen who had served on the committee on finance. A number of other members arrived that evening including Lorenzo de Zavala. Gray was quite taken with Zavala, and described him in his diary as "the most interesting man in Texas." Zavala was born in the Yucatan and had served as a representative in the Mexican Congress, a minister of the fiscal department, and as the Republic of Mexico's Ambassador to France. After renouncing his positions in opposition to Mexico and the policies of Santa Anna, he took temporary residence in the United States. Zavala later received an *empresario* grant on March 12, 1829, which authorized him to settle 500 families in a huge tract of land in what is now southeastern Texas. The Convention became a magnet for influential leaders such as Zavala. Men were drawn to the Texian struggle for freedom and the chance to break Texas away from more than three centuries of rule from Mexico City. On February 29, Gen. Sam Houston arrived at Washington-on-the-Brazos creating more sensation than that of any other man at the Convention.[87]

Sam Houston was a towering figure at six foot, two inches tall, and had a reputation for stirring sensations of excitement long before he arrived in Texas in December 1832. Born in Virginia on March 2, 1793, he was the fifth child of Samuel and Elizabeth Houston.[88] After losing his father at the age of thirteen, young Sam moved with his family to eastern Tennessee where they established a farm. He soon tired of farm life and was the least inclined of his siblings to complete his daily chores. Seeking adventure, he ran away from home and crossed the Tennessee River to live with the Cherokee Indians who adopted the sandy-haired lad and nicknamed him the "Raven."

Fig 4.25, Independence Hall.

Texas State Library and Archive Commission, Austin, Texas.

Fig 4.26, Gail Borden, Jr.

Courtesy of the Rosenberg Library, Galveston, Texas.

Gail Borden (pictured here much later in life) printed Travis' letter in handbill form at San Felipe de Austin as a plea for help to shock the people of Texas and the United States into action.

Fig 4.27, Gen. Sam Houston.

Courtesy of Albert and Ethel Herzstein Library, The San Jacinto Museum of History, Houston, Texas.

At the age of twenty, Houston joined the U.S. Army as a private. He soon received a promotion to ensign and later to third lieutenant. Assigned to an army regiment under Andrew Jackson, he fought at the battle of Horseshoe Bend in present-day Alabama. He was recognized for his valor by Jackson, who befriended the young Tennessean and mentored him in politics. In 1818, Houston left the army to study law and began his practice in Lebanon, Tennessee. Houston, a consummate politician and rising star in Jackson's political circle, was elected to the U.S. Congress in 1823. A second two-year term followed in 1825. When his term in the U.S. House of Representatives expired, he was then elected as the Governor of Tennessee in 1827. On January 11, 1829, Sam Houston married nineteen-year-old Eliza Allen of Gallatin, Tennessee, but after only eleven weeks the marriage was dissolved. Houston abruptly resigned from office and lived the life of a reclusive Indian trader among the Cherokees for three years. He took an Indian wife, was granted Cherokee citizenship, and developed such a reputation for drinking that the Indians bestowed upon him the tribal name of "Big Drunk." His relationship with the Cherokees served Houston well, both as an Indian trader and later as a diplomat to the Cherokees for Texas.

After a brief residence in Tennessee, Houston returned to Washington, D.C., where he renewed several old friendships. He actively lobbied for the campaign issues of Andrew Jackson, the seventh U.S. President, then seeking re-election.[89] On March 31, 1832, William Stanberry, an Ohio Congressman, gave a speech in the House of Representatives regarding a contract bid for Indian rations and publicly accused Houston and another man of outright corruption in the matter. Houston, inflamed with rage, tried to settle the score by forcing his way into the House chamber the following day but had to be physically restrained by his friend Congressman James K. Polk. After the local newspapers printed Stanberry's speech, the incident became a magnified public insult of Sam Houston's character. The path of these two men crossed quite by chance on a Washington street on April 13, 1832. Spotting the slanderous congressman, Houston accosted Stanberry for his remarks and flailed him with a heavy hickory cane. When the congressman pulled a pistol, Houston continued to beat him senseless "in an uncontrollable rage" until the representative was severely wounded and heavily bruised.

Houston was arrested for the assault and subsequently tried before the House of Representatives. He was defended by attorney Francis Scott Key. Although he only received a reprimand and a fine, the high-profile incident and month-long trial sparked a feeding frenzy for information on the Tennessean by the newspapers. His name was once again known throughout the country. Seeking a new lease on life and a political fresh start, Houston was intrigued by the stories of land speculation in Texas which he heard from several well-connected sources. Departing Washington, D.C., in the summer, he headed south and crossed the Red River into Mexican Texas on October 2, 1832.

Sam Houston quickly became involved in the politics of Texas by serving as a delegate from Nacogdoches and chairing a meeting in 1835 for the purpose of convening the Consultation. He assembled armed volunteers from Nacogdoches and nearby St. Augustine. Appointed as major general of the Texas Army by the Consultation on November 12, 1835, Houston began to train his troops, consolidate his forces, and instill a sense of discipline in the soldiers. He personally negotiated a peace treaty with the Cherokee Indians to keep them out of the war. With the rapidly deteriorating conditions in Texas, Washington-on-the-Brazos was an entirely different place than its namesake city on the Potomac River that he had frequented only three short years before. Houston contemplated the inevitable meeting of a much larger and stronger enemy and knew that the Mexican Army could not simply be thrashed into submission with a hickory branch. The general was convinced that Texas could not win independence unless the Texas Army was capable of meeting the Mexican Army of Antonio López de Santa Anna and defeating his considerable forces which were already deep in the heart of Texas.[90]

The Mexican Army had been massing in San Antonio de Béxar since February 23. Colonel Travis, commanding the Alamo, wrote his legendary letter to members of the Convention then gathered at Washington-on-the-Brazos stating, "Let the convention go on and make a Declaration of Independence, and we will then understand, and the world will understand, what we are fighting for. If independence is not declared, I shall lay down my arms and so will the men under my command."[91] In response to the urgent plea from Travis received at Goliad on February 25, James W. Fannin headed more than 300 men the 100 miles towards San Antonio.[92] He left behind a garrison of 100 men to guard the old Presidio la Bahía at Goliad. But only a day later when crossing the

San Antonio River, three wagons broke down and their oxen strayed off leaving the reinforcements with no means to transport the cannon and supplies necessary to come to the aid of Travis. Fannin, in turn, ordered his men to halt their advance and fall back to the old stone fort at Goliad.

The same day that Gray arrived in Washington-on-the-Brazos, Travis's dispatch from the Alamo arrived. The "Victory or Death" letter further communicated Travis's desperate plea for help and at the same time indicated that he was determined to defend the place to the last man. Gray described the little town as filled with "considerable excitement prevailing," owing to the news received from Béxar. His partner, Robert Triplett, departed New Orleans and encountered a copy of Travis's appeal while on the road to the Convention. He described it as "one of the most thrilling I ever read."[93] The letter reinforced his belief that the Texians were not afraid to die for their country and that this would ultimately lead to their victory. It was a conviction under which he was determined to get ratification of the Texian loans. These were the tumultuous circumstances swirling around the provisional government in the cold, muddy, destitute little town on the Brazos River.

WASHINGTON ISSUES

Like the provisional pieces issued at San Felipe de Austin, the drafts issued at Washington-on-the-Brazos represent claims against an empty treasury. Since the warrants do not record the place of issue, they can be identified by the issue dates of February 22, 1836, to March 16, 1836. The warrants are entirely handwritten, usually on pink or buff paper. Like the San Felipe notes, each carried signatures by the controller and the auditor, with the numerical denomination in the upper right and lower left hand areas. Because Washington-on-the-Brazos had a much shorter tenure as the seat of government, they are far scarcer than the pieces issued from San Felipe de Austin. They bear a striking resemblance to the San Felipe pieces but lack the reference to Joshua Fletcher, Esq., present on the earlier pieces. Often absent from even the most complete collections, these early Texas obligations carry a special footprint in history. Many were signed in the same one-room building as the Texas Declaration of Independence—some of them perhaps with the same pen!

The lack of a reference to Joshua Fletcher, Esquire, across the top of the draft in Figure 4.28 easily distinguishes it from the earlier San Felipe issues. The date of February 29 indicates that the year of the Texas Revolution was a leap year. Signed only two days before the Texas Declaration of Independence, this $80 payment to Thomas Lobar places him in the provisional capital at the time of the Convention. Lobar had earlier served with Capt. James Bradley in a volunteer unit from the Tunahan District, and had participated in the capture at Béxar on December 10, 1835.[94] Marked cancelled twice across the face, the piece indicates that Lobar eventually collected the payment. Like the previous San Felipe issues, this example bears the standardized language of the Treasury Department and is signed by John W. Moody as auditor and Henry C. Hudson as controller.

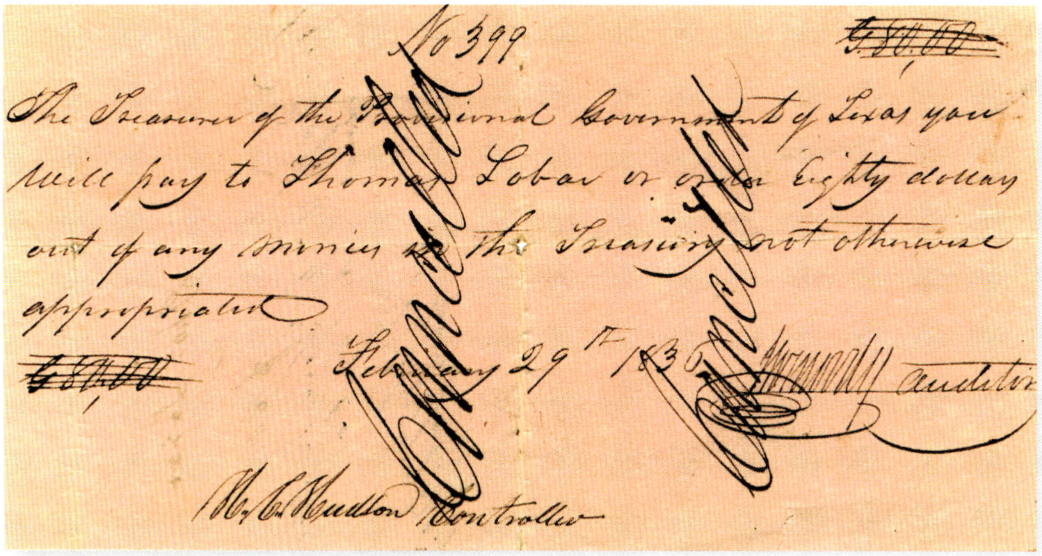

No 399. $80.00 The Treasurer of the Provisional Government of Texas you will pay to Thomas Lobar or order Eighty dollars out of any monies in the Treasury not otherwise appropriated. $80.00 February 29th, 1836. (Signed) J.W. Moody, Auditor, H.C. Hudson, Controller

Fig 4.28, Washington-on-the-Brazos, February 29, 1836. $80.00 draft payable to Thomas Lobar.

Private Collection, Cr. P1 (P4), O-60.

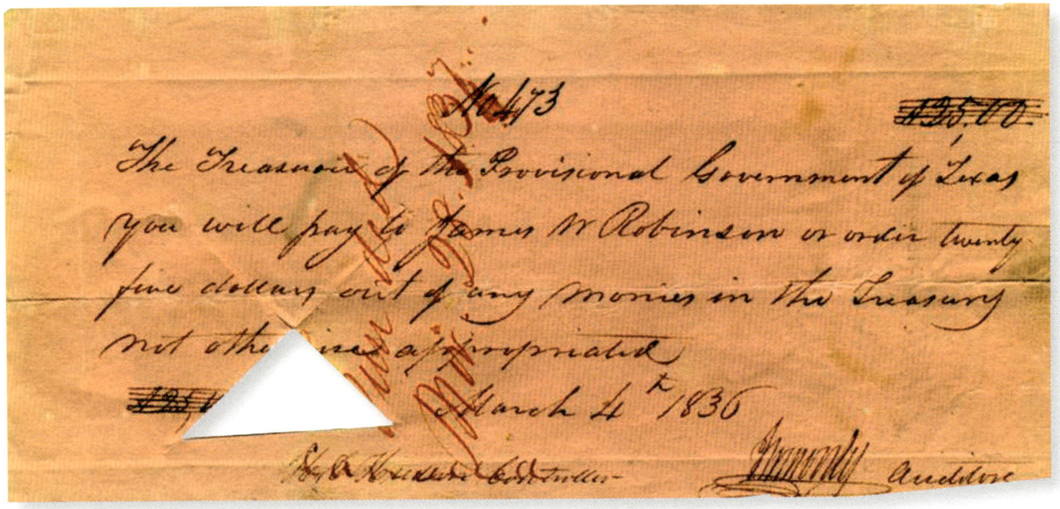

No 473 $25.00
The Treasurer of the Provisional Government of Texas
you will pay to James W Robinson or order twenty
five dollars out of any monies in the Treasury
not othe[...]ise appropriated
March 4th 1836
Auditor

Fig 4.29, Washington-on-the-Brazos, March 4, 1836. $25.00 draft payable to James W. Robinson.

Private Collection, Cr. P1 (P4), O-60.

No 473. $25.00 The Treasurer of the Provisional Government of Texas you will pay to James W. Robinson or order twenty five dollars out of any monies in the Treasury not otherwise appropriated. $25.00 March 4th, 1836. (Signed) J.W. Moody, Auditor, H.C. Hudson, Controller

Fig 4.30, James W. Robinson.

Texas State Library & Archives Commission, Austin, Texas.

The neatly penned example in Figure 4.29 is on the frequently seen pink paper, which dominates the small number of Washington-on-the-Brazos issues. It curiously references the Provisional Government of Texas even though the piece is dated two days after the Declaration of Independence. It was made payable to James W. Robinson, who served as a delegate to the Consultation from Nacogdoches and was elected lieutenant governor of the provisional government.[95] When the executive Council deposed Gov. Henry Smith on January 11, 1836, Smith refused to relinquish the office, claiming the Council did not have a quorum. Afterwards both Robinson and Smith claimed to be governor.

On March 12, shortly after he received the draft in Figure 4.29, Robinson joined the Texas Army and later fought at the battle of San Jacinto as a private in the cavalry company of William H. Smith. Judging by the folds in the paper, he most likely carried this draft in his pocket or knapsack during the battle. Robinson was discharged on September 15, 1836. He was elected as judge of the Fourth Judicial District from Gonzalez in December 1836, and became a member of the Republic's Supreme Court. The warrant is signed on the verso by Robinson and cut cancelled. The piece also sports an unusual pen cancellation indicating he did not receive the payment until November 28, 1837.

THE DECLARATION OF INDEPENDENCE

The delegates to the Convention were forced to meet in the unfinished shack with cotton cloth stretched across the windows in an effort to keep out the bitter cold wind brought in by a northern gale and accompanied by lightning, thunder, rain and hail.[96] The Convention was called to order by George C. Childress, a representative from Milam. Forty-one duly elected representatives were recognized as present—from Nacogdoches to Victoria, Jasper to San Patricio, and all points in between. The House of Representatives was organized and a committee was named and charged with the responsibility of preparing a declaration of independence, and to report back to the House as speedily as practical.

On Wednesday, March 2, 1836, the Convention reconvened and Mr. Childress reported a Declaration of Independence which he read in place to the assembled body. Remarkably, it was received by the House, referred to a committee of the whole, reported without amendment, and unanimously adopted in less than an hour from its first and only reading. The lengthy document underwent no revisions, and no effort or attempt was made to amend the historical work. Following Sam Houston's motion, it was resolved that the Declaration of Independence, reported by the committee of the whole House, be engrossed and signed by the Delegates of the Convention.[97] It was also Sam Houston's forty-third birthday.

Closely modeled after the U.S. Declaration of Independence, the document begins with a summation of the losses of liberty and protection from the abandonment in reference to the Constitution of 1824 stating:

> *When a government has ceased to protect the lives, liberty, and property of the people, from whom its legitimate powers are derived, and for the advancement of whose happiness it was instituted; and so far from being a guarantee for their inestimable and inalienable rights, becomes an instrument in the hands of evil rulers for their oppression.... the first law of nature, the right of self preservation, the inherent and inalienable right of the people to appeal to first principles, and take their political affairs into their own*

> *hands in extreme cases, enjoins it as a right towards themselves and a sacred obligation to their posterity to abolish such government, and create another in its stead, calculated to rescue them from impending dangers, and secure their wealth and happiness…*[98]

Clerks were soon appointed to make handwritten copies of the declaration.

On the following morning, Thursday, March 3, 1836, a clear but cold day, the delegates to the Convention convened at 9 o'clock. Among other business, the Declaration of Independence became the center of attention and was read and signed by all the members present.[99] On the motion of Benjamin Goodrich, it was decided that the declaration was to be printed in handbill form for distribution to all of Texas and the United States. At last, the Republic of Texas had defiantly declared independence from the Mexican Republic.

> *On Motion of Mr. Goodrich*
>
> *Resolved that five copies of the Declaration of Independence, be prepared, and one to be sent forthwith to Bexar, one to Goliad, one to Nacogdoches, one to Brazoria, one to San Felipe, and One to Natchitoches, and that the Printer at San Felipe be requested to print in hand bill form for distribution one thousand copies and that a committee of three be appointed to carry the above resolution into effect.*

On the verso (not pictured) the order reads:

> *Resolution Adopted to print and circulate Declaration of Independence. convention.*
>
> *Commit[tee] Mr. Goodrich, " Palmer," Byrom.*[100]

This hand-written order in Figure 4.31 for the printing of the Declaration of Independence contradicts itself in that five manuscript copies of the Declaration

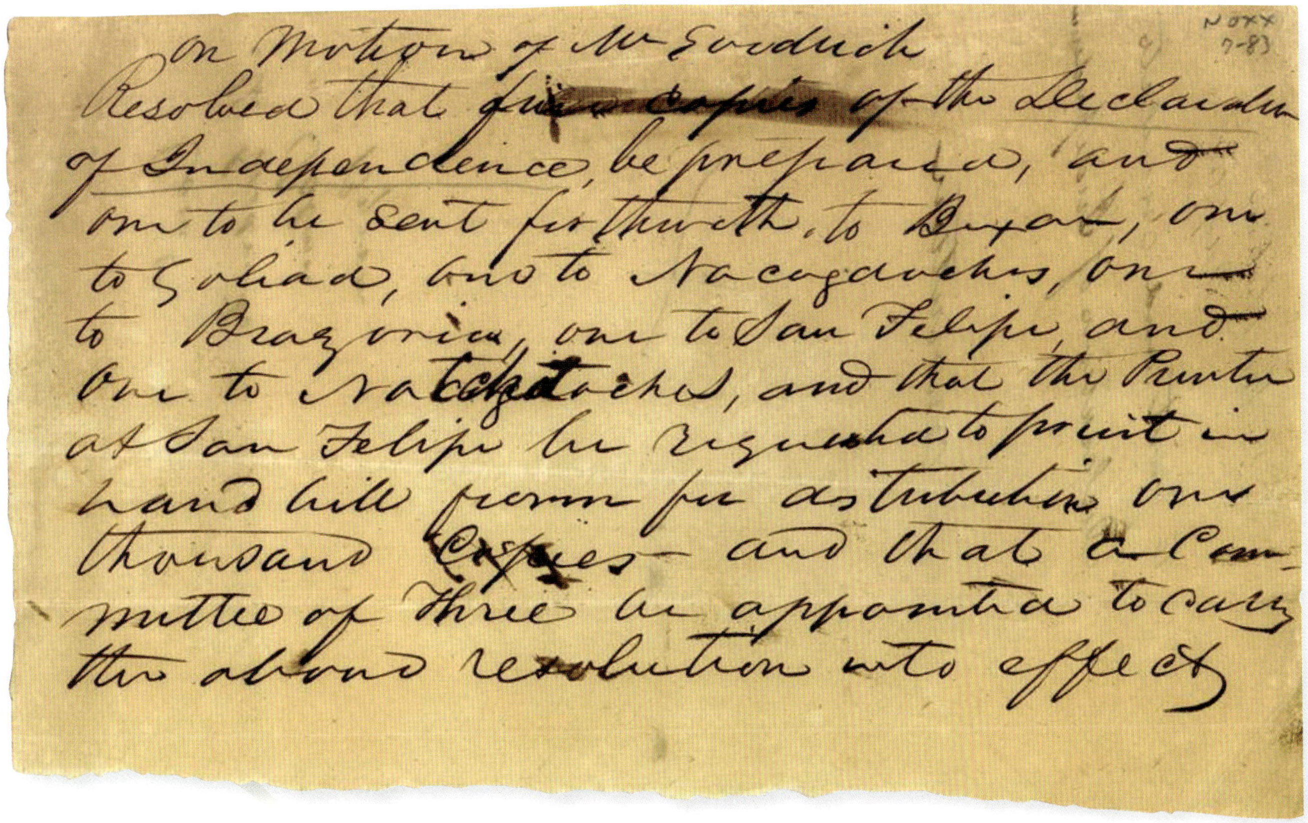

Fig 4.31, Washington-on-the-Brazos, March 2, 1836.

The hand-written order for printing the Texas Declaration of Independence.

Texas State Library and Archives Commission.

were to be dispatched on horseback, yet they are to be sent to six cities. They were to be sent to the Texas towns of Béxar, Goliad, Nacogdoches, Brazoria, San Felipe and one to Natchitoches, Louisiana. Despite the instructions in the order, it is not known if a sixth copy was sent to San Antonio de Béxar, as the Alamo was then under siege by Santa Anna's forces and the town occupied by the Mexican Army. An express rider was dispatched to travel from Washington-on-the-Brazos to the town of San Felipe for delivery to the printer. The messenger arrived at the offices of Baker and Borden, almost forty-eight hours later on Saturday, March 5, with the hand-written declaration dry and intact despite the cold wet weather that he encountered along the way. It was accompanied by orders that the printer publish 1,000 copies in handbill form for distribution.[101]

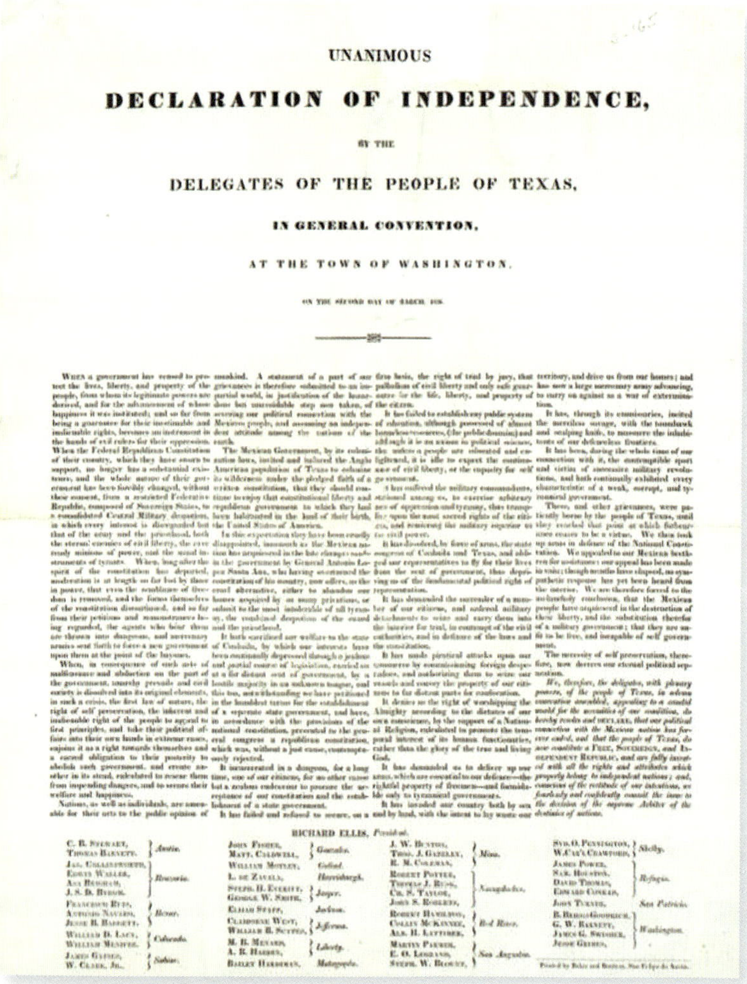
UNANIMOUS

DECLARATION OF INDEPENDENCE,

BY THE

DELEGATES OF THE PEOPLE OF TEXAS,

IN GENERAL CONVENTION,

AT THE TOWN OF WASHINGTON.

Fig 4.32, Washington-on-the-Brazos, March 2, 1836. The Texas Declaration of Independence.

Private Collection.

The handbill copies were designed to tell the people of Texas and the United States that Texas had formally declared independence from Mexico.

PRINTING THE DECLARATION

The printing firm of Baker & Borden in San Felipe undoubtedly did their best to produce the handbills in a hurry while the signers at the Convention were waiting. But unlike a modern press which can generate thousands of sheets of printed paper in a few minutes, a hundred copies from a hand-operated press required each large form of type to be inked by hand and printed on paper that was meticulously dampened by hand before printing.[102] This in itself would have taken several hours of work, and the first printing was produced "in too much haste, and chiefly in the night" on March 5 or early on March 6 according to Gail Borden who commented on the all night work in the March 12, 1836, edition of the *Telegraph and Texas Register.* Upon the printing of the first 100 copies, it was discovered that two of the names of the signers had been left off, including that of George C. Childress, the principal author of the document! These first 100 were sent by dispatch, some of them to Washington-on-the-Brazos the next day with the remainder over the next few days. They were delivered alongside another dispatch from Travis dated March 3.

Figure 4.32 is an original broadside printing of the Texas Declaration of Independence. It is from the first printing of 100 copies in handbill form by Baker & Borden, San Felipe, March 5-6, 1836. The printers then removed the typeset and finished the printing of their newspaper and other pending jobs before completing the printing of the other 900 copies on March 12. This created two distinct issues of the declaration, the second with the names of the original signers that had been inadvertently left off.[103] Of the twelve known copies, ten (including this example) were from the first issue of 100, and two are known from the second printing of 900. A plausible explanation is offered for the disparity in the survival rates. The first 100 printed were sent to the Convention at Washington-on-the-Brazos or back East to the United States where they were read and presumably well kept. The other 900 would have been too heavy to be carried in total on horseback. Given the chaotic state of affairs which occurred after the fall of the Alamo on March 6, 1836, it is very likely that the preservation or even the retention of this second printing of the document became a low priority during the Runaway Scrape.

THE FALL OF THE ALAMO

On the morning of Sunday, March 6, another dispatch was received from Travis while the delegates were gathered for breakfast, dated March 3 from the Alamo.[104] The members of the Convention carefully read it, and all the citizens in the area anxiously gathered in the convention room to hear it. Travis' letter outlined the almost daily reinforcements that were being received by the Mexican Army where he estimated that they numbered from 1,500 to 6,000, and that Santa Anna himself had possibly arrived on the scene.[105] Having largely abandoned hope that Colonel Fannin's forces would be joining him, Travis continued to appeal for further reinforcements and did note that James Butler Bonham had arrived that morning with thirty-two men from Gonzales. In part, his letter also offered a candid observation to the delegates in Washington-on-the-Brazos:

> *The power of Santa Anna is to be met here, or in the colonies; we had better meet them here than to suffer a war of devastation to rage in our settlements. A blood red banner waves from the church at Bejar, and in the camp above us, in token that the war is of vengeance against rebels; they have declared us as such; demanded that we should surrender at discretion, or that the garrison be put to the sword. The threats have had no influence on me or my men, but to make all fight with desperation, and that high souled courage which characterizes the patriot, who is willing to die in defense of his country's liberty and his own honor.*
>
> *God and Texas – Victory or Death*
> *W. Barrett Travis, Lieut. Co. Commander*[106]

It was clear from his writings that Travis knew he was going to die, and that most, if not all, of his 183 brave men at the Alamo would suffer the same fate. What was not clear and would only be known five days later, was that by the time Travis' letter was read at the Convention, the Alamo had already fallen and the dead Texian soldiers at the Garrison were being burned in a funeral pyre in the courtyard of the old mission at San Antonio de Béxar.

Following the reading of the Travis letter, Robert Potter moved that the Convention organize a militia and adjourn to take the field to the Alamo's defense.[107] Although Potter's motion was voted down, a great many people began preparations to leave and ready themselves for the inevitable conflicts of the war.[108] Gen. Sam Houston, Capt. William G. Cooke, most of their staff and many others left that afternoon in an effort to raise men and money for the aid of their country. Robinson and several others would follow suit a few days later.

From the port of Velasco on the Gulf Coast, George W. Poe, Inspector General of the Texian Army, wrote this dispatch on March 6, 1836:

> *Last night an express arrived with the news, that one division of the Mexican Army, 4,000 strong, are now in full march for the interior of Texas, and we hourly expect an attack on this point of the coast, from the Mexicans by sea, under [Gen.] Ugartrecha, 3,500 strong. We have in the field now about 700 men to oppose this force. There is here under my command only 120 men, when we expected at least 2,000; and it is thought the Mexican army is within a few days march of us.*[109]

Although General Poe knew the invading army was advancing deep into Texas, the heroic actions of the Alamo defenders inflicted several hundred casualties on the enemy as they defended the old mission to the last man. Poe also described the widespread fear which had permeated the coastal farms and communities: "The families at a short distance from us are flying before the enemy, and have left their stock, their houses and crops to the mercy of the Tyrant, who is in person at the head of his army." It was a fear which had not only taken root on the Brazos River near the coast, but would soon spread like a wildfire and consume the Anglo population.

SANTA ANNA INTERVIEWS THE WIDOWS

On March 7, as smoke cleared the walls of the old mission at Béxar, Santa Anna had each of the women who had been spared from the massacre brought before him at the Yturri house in San Antonio.[110] The famous chapel at the Alamo was the last point in the Texian stronghold to be taken and it was here that the women and children had been placed for their safety. They were deliberately spared by the Mexican soldiers that had stormed the old mission. Gen. Santa Anna, who proudly referred to himself as the "Napoleon of the West" asked each widow why she had been at the Alamo and whether her husband had been killed or was still at large. After the brief inquiry, Santa Anna dismissed each of the widows, giving them two silver *pesos* from a stack of silver coins and a *serape* to find their way in the now war-ravaged land. The dictator had confiscated a large supply of silver 8 *reales* pieces from the Mexican mint at Zacatecas the previous year and brought these coins with him into Texas. The Texians learned of the massacre from Susanna Dickinson who encountered Deaf Smith, one of Sam Houston's scouts, on her way from Béxar.

Fig 4.33, 8 Reales, Zacatecas, Cap & Rays, Eagle Coinage, 1834.

The coins in Figure 4.33 are dated 1834 from the Mexican Mint at Zacatecas, and are representative of the "two silver *pesos*" which Santa Anna gave to each widow of the Alamo defenders before dismissing them.

DRAFTING A CONSTITUTION

On Monday, March 7, the delegates in Washington-on-the-Brazos returned to business and proceeded to begin the laborious task of drafting a national constitution. Martin Parmer of San Augustine was appointed as chairman of the committee. Another committee was designated to inform the commissioners—Austin, Archer and Wharton—then in the United States, that independence had been declared and to seek recognition for the Republic of Texas by the Congress of the United States which was then in session.[111] The subject of the $200,000 loan that had been negotiated by these same commissioners in New Orleans was again reintroduced, but was then referred to a committee.[112] William Fairfax Gray soon learned that there was serious opposition to the loans, and he later described the sentiment as "arising from the wretched selfishness of members, who regard the terms of the loan as too favorable to the lenders, the land being too low, in their opinion." He added, "To national faith and credit they are insensible." Seeking another opinion, he showed the contract to Lorenzo de Zavala, who thought the interest rate too low and that the price which the lenders were to pay for the land was too high.

With the first printed copies of the Declaration of Independence in hand at the Convention on Wednesday, March 9, Martin Parmer reported that the drafting of the constitution had also been completed. It was then read to the legislative body. The document consisted of six sections or articles, a schedule, a declaration of rights, several general provisions, and a section on slavery.[113] Article I, Section 26, stated that "No money shall be drawn from the public treasury but in consequence of appropriations made by law." This was a provision that would come back to haunt the creditors of the Republic for the next decade, since it sometimes took years for Congress to make good on their paper money promises. In many ways, the constitution echoed the Ordinances and Decrees which had previously been established by the General Council at San Felipe a few months earlier. The ratification of the loan and the question of settling the loan with land scrip again resurfaced, but the Convention was unwilling or unable to decide a course of action. Gray, again writing in his diary, remarked that "such miserable narrow mindedness is astonishing. There is a great want of political philosophy and practical knowledge in the body."[114]

Robert Triplett, the largest lender from the $200,000 loan syndicate, arrived on March 11 and began lobbying members of the loan committee for ratification. He found that his arguments in favor of the transaction largely fell on deaf ears. It was not surprising that the members of the Convention seemed ambivalent about the loan, as they were preoccupied with assessing the military threat and formalizing the new government. Because the ratification of the loan and its terms by the government was required by the lending group before it could be funded, the committee, which had been appointed by Gov. Henry Smith, simply sidestepped the issue. Triplett and Gray offered to render any aid they could to the Convention and found their offer gladly accepted.[115] The legislative proceedings from the day were brought to them to copy at night, which they faithfully executed almost to exhaustion. Triplett also noticed that a strange apathy had become prevalent throughout Texas as to the danger from the advancing Mexicans. Despite the looming threat, the delegates to the Convention went on with their work, although there were almost nightly alarms of the Mexican's approach.

On Thursday, March 14, John Moody, the auditor, reported that the provisional government had issued audited drafts totaling $46,530 through March 10, with $39,835 stipulated for military expenses, $6,053 for civil expenses, and $642 for contingencies. On March 15, a letter was received from Gen. Sam Houston announcing the fall of the Alamo, which was read to the members present. The sad details of the intelligence report confirmed their worst fears. On the following day, an ordinance organizing an *ad interim* government was formally adopted. David G. Burnet was elected President, Lorenzo de Zavala, Vice President, Samuel P. Carson, Secretary of State, Bailey Hardiman, Secretary of the Treasury, and Thomas Rusk was named as the Secretary of War. The new officers, charged with carrying the whole of the business of the Republic through the executive branch, were sworn in at 4 o'clock on the morning of March 17, 1836.

David G. Burnet (1788-1870) was a land speculator, lawyer, and politician, who was born in Newark, New Jersey, and first came to Texas in May 1826 on his way to Saltillo to petition for an *empresario* grant, which he received on December 22.[116] It authorized him to settle 300 families north of the Old Spanish Road around Nacogdoches. He later sold the rights to the colonization contract to a group of northeastern investors who founded Galveston Bay and Texas Land Company. Burnet was orphaned at an early age, and all his life he strove to achieve the prominence of his father, who had served in the Continental Congress and as Surgeon General.

Even though he was known as an articulate man and was well liked, David G. Burnet was an unlikely candidate for the President of Texas. Due to his initial opposition to the independence of Texas in 1835, his more radical neighbors in Liberty did not choose him as a delegate to either the Consultation or the Convention of 1836. He was said to have been a good, honest man, but many questioned his ability for such an important position.[117] Nevertheless, he attended the session on March 10, 1836, and began to successfully lobby the delegation for their support. The delegates, who were opposed to electing one of their number as president of the new Republic, elected Burnet by a majority of seven votes over Samuel P. Carson, a delegate from Pecan Point.

This *ad interim* government had been put in place until the constitution could be incorporated once Texas validated its independence by winning the war. Having achieved his political prominence at last, Burnet and his Cabinet soon discovered they had been elected to the most thankless of jobs. On the morning of March 17, the gravity of their situation became acutely apparent as the affairs of the newly born Republic spiraled downward into a state of military and financial chaos. The Alamo had fallen. It was widely believed that Santa Anna would soon regroup his forces and continue to sweep across Texas, destroying everything in his path. There were no funds for the Texians to purchase weapons and munitions nor to maintain the army. A heightened anxiety permeated the air with the possibility that at any hour they could be attacked and captured. If caught, they would all surely be executed for treason against the Republic of Mexico. Fearing for their safety, the members of the Convention made plans to leave the area.

Texas became an invaded, unarmed and largely un-provisioned country without an organized army to oppose the would-be conquerors. The legislators began to see their folly regarding the pending loan approval as a means to secure a ready source of money to raise new troops or sustain those volunteers in the field. Faced with an impending liquidity crisis, they began to look forward to the possibility of the loans and the opportunity which the influx of money presented. Thomas J. Rusk approached Triplett and said "Well, Colonel Triplett, you and Colonel Gray have labored for us faithfully, and we feel inclined to do what we can for you about this loan." Triplett replied, "If agreeable, Colonel, I would like to address your convention on the subject." Rusk agreed to offer a resolution granting him leave from military service as he was to address the Convention.

Robert Triplett addressed the delegation following breakfast on March 17. He stated that although he had encountered considerable hostility towards the loan among the delegates, he asked them to understand

Fig 4.34, David G. Burnet, the first President of Texas.

From a painting by William H. Huddle, Texas State Library, Austin, Texas.

the position from which the lenders were approached. Referring to Austin, Archer and Wharton, he stated that "on the appearance of the commissioners in New Orleans to obtain a loan, the idea was considered preposterous by most prudent men." Triplett further described the proposition from the lenders side—the loan commissioners did not represent a legitimate government at the time, and the idea of lending money to a government which was not recognized by the United States, and which the loan was payable in land that the government did not even have clear title to was considered to be wildly speculative at best. But the persuasive financier concluded by appealing to the delegates sense of patriotism: "A few of us, however, with a deep sympathy for a young and gallant people, unrestrained by considerations of caution and prudence, which should have been the part of wisdom, believed that Texas should succeed in her struggle, and so believing, doubted not that we should get paid." After stating the most patriotic of reasons for making the loans, he outlined a modification of the loan terms which he would be willing to accept. He took great lengths to point out that he spoke only for himself and he would have to confer with the other lenders. He ended by stating that he would be willing to negotiate with the newly elected chief executive, President Burnet.

After Triplett's speech, a resolution was promptly proposed and passed which authorized the *ad interim* government to exercise their best judgment as to the final terms on the matter. All documents, papers, and matters relating to the loan had now been referred to Burnet and the executive branch for their action. Burnet and his cabinet were given the authority by the Convention to ratify the loans and make any necessary compromises.[118] William Fairfax Gray summed up the attitude of the delegates towards the loan in his diary as: "They have blinked the question."[119] Following the deferral of the loan matter and the morning session, the Convention was adjourned and disbanded. A general panic now set upon the members of the Convention, as their families were largely exposed to Santa Anna's army and quite defenseless. The members dispersed in all directions. Many of them would see to the evacuation of their families and later join the remains of the Texian Army being cobbled together by Sam Houston.

[1] "D.C. Barrett – Report on location of the Provisional Government," Journal of the Proceedings of the General Council of the Republic of Texas, held at San Felipe de Austin, November 14, 1835 (Houston: *National Intelligencer Office*, 1839).

[2] William F. Gray, *Diary of Col. Wm. Fairfax Gray: from Virginia to Texas, 1835-1836* (Houston: Gray, Dillaye & Co Printers, 1909; rpt. 1965), 111.

[3] *Handbook of Texas Online*, s.v. "Branch Tanner Archer," http://www.tsha.utexas.edu/handbook/online/articles/AA/far2.html (accessed November 28, 2006).

[4] *Handbook of Texas Online*, s.v. "Henry Smith," http://www.tsha.utexas.edu/handbook/online/articles/SS/fsm23.html (accessed November 28, 2006).

[5] Gray, *Diary*, 111.

[6] The Papers of the Texas Revolution, 1835-1836, ed. John H. Jenkins (Austin: Presidial Press, Brig. Gen. Jay A. Matthews Publisher, 1973), 9:258, see "Journals of the Consultation, San Felipe de Austin, October 16, 1835."

[7] Ibid., 259.

[8] William M. Gouge, *The Fiscal History of Texas* (New York: Burt Franklin, 1852; rpt. 1969), 21.

[9] Ibid.

[10] Ibid., 27.

[11] Ibid., 23-24.

[12] "Henry Smith to Council," Journal of the Proceedings of the General Council of the Republic of Texas, held at San Felipe de Austin, November 14, 1835 (Houston: *National Intelligencer Office*, 1839).

[13] The Papers of the Texas Revolution, 9:374, see "Declaration of the people of Texas in General Convention Assembled."

[14] *Handbook of Texas Online*, s.v. "William Plunkett Harris," http://www.tsha.utexas.edu/handbook/online/articles/HH/fha98.html (accessed November 13, 2007).

[15] Joseph D. Olson, Texas Numismatic History: A Catalogue, 1st ed. (Texas Numismatic Heritage Press, 2006), 22.

[16] Handbook of Texas Online, s.v. "Matthew Caldwell," http://www.tsha.utexas.edu/handbook/online/articles/CC/fca12.html (accessed June 30, 2006).

[17] "Millard to Council," Journal of the Proceedings of the General Council of the Republic of Texas, held at San Felipe de Austin, November 14, 1835 (Houston: *National Intelligencer Office*, 1839).

[18] The Papers of the Texas Revolution, 1835-1836, ed. John H. Jenkins (Austin: Presidial Press, Brig. Gen. Jay A. Matthews Publisher, 1973), 9:289.

[19] From "The Medicine Man in Texas," author unknown. Biographical information provided by John N. Rowe of Dallas, Texas.

[20] *Handbook of Texas Online*, s.v. "Wyatt Hanks," http://www.tsha.utexas.edu/handbook/online/articles/HH/fha50.html (accessed September 16, 2006).

[21] Gouge, *The Fiscal History of Texas*, 24-27.

[22] The Papers of the Texas Revolution, 9:422, see "Sec. 3, Ordinances and Decrees of the Consultation, Provisional Government of Texas."

[23] Extract of a letter by Samuel May Williams regarding his brother-in-law, Samuel St. John, and the manuscript bonds. Williams to ______, Galveston, February 6, 1849, Samuel May Williams Papers, Rosenberg Library, Galveston, Texas.

[24] David B. Gracy, III, *Ships of the Texas Navy* (Presidial Press, 1978).

[25] Ibid.

[26] Gouge, *The Fiscal History of Texas*, 26.

[27] The Papers of the Texas Revolution, 9:393.

[28] "Report of Mr. Perry, from the Committee on Naval Affairs," Journal of the Proceedings of the General Council of the Republic of Texas, held at San Felipe de Austin, November 14, 1835 (Houston: *National Intelligencer Office*, 1839).

[29] The Papers of the Texas Revolution, 9:499-500.

[30] Eugene C. Barker, *The Life of Stephen F. Austin, Founder of Texas, 1793-1836: A Chapter in the Westward Movement of the Anglo-American People* (Austin: University of Texas Press, 1969), 425.

[31] Edward L. Miller, *New Orleans and the Texas Revolution* (College Station: Texas A&M University Press, 2004), 27.

[32] Gray, *Diary*, 68-69.

[33] Miller, *New Orleans and the Texas Revolution*, 61.

[34] Ibid., 62

[35] Gray, *Diary*, prologue.

[36] Miller, *New Orleans and the Texas Revolution*, 137-38.

[37] Gray, *Diary*, 63.

[38] Miller, *New Orleans and the Texas Revolution*, 131.

[39] Gray, Diary, 69.

[40] Robert Triplett, *Roland Trevor: or, The Pilot of Human Life, being an Autobiography of the Author, Showing how to make and lose a fortune, and then how to make another.* Philadelphia, Lippincott, Grambo, and Co. 1853. Page 335.

[41] Robert Triplett, *Roland Trevor: or, The Pilot of Human Life, being an Autobiography of the Author, Showing how to make and lose a fortune, and then how to make another* (Philadelphia: Lippincott, Grambo, and Co., 1853), 335.

[42] Triplett, *Roland Trevor*, 336.

[43] Gray, *Diary*, 71.

[44] The Papers of the Texas Revolution, 4: 52, see "Austin to Perry, New Orleans, January 18, 1836."

[45] Gray, *Diary*, 77.

[46] "$200,000 Texian Loan Document," signed by William Christy, dated January 1836, John N. Rowe III Collection of Texas Currency, DeGolyer Library, Southern Methodist University, Dallas, Texas, page 1, Article Four.

[47] Barker, *The Life of Stephen F. Austin*, 427.

[48] The Papers of the Texas Revolution, 4:543, see "Austin to Barrett, New Orleans, January 17, 1836."

[49] Texian Loan, No. 444, dated January 11, 1836, Collection of Richard D. Laster.

[50] Gray, *Diary*, 76.

[51] Jonathan W. Jordan, *Lone Star Navy: Texas, the Fight for the Gulf of Mexico, and the Shaping of the American West* (Dulles, VA: Potomac Books, Inc., 2006), 45-46.

[52] The Papers of the Texas Revolution 1835-1836, 4:57, see "Hawkins Receipt, New Orleans, January 18, 1836."

[53] Barker, *The Life of Stephen F. Austin*, 428.

[54] Excerpts from Henry Smith's address to the provisional council as recorded January 9, 1836. Gouge, *The Fiscal History of Texas*, 45-47.

[55] Ibid.

[56] The Papers of the Texas Revolution 1835-1836, 9:469-74, see "An Ordinance and Decree, creating the offices of Auditor and Comptroller of Public Accounts of Texas."

[57] Ibid., 474.

[58] Helen Foster Snow, "John Wyatt Moody of Texas: Notes on Texas," John Wyatt Moody Papers (hereinafter cited as Moody Papers), Woodson Research Center, Fondren Library, Rice University, Houston, Texas, page 2.

[59] Helen Foster Snow, "Major John Wyatt Moody, First Auditor of the Republic of Texas," Moody Papers, page 5; J.W. Moody, Auditor to Mistress A.B. Peyton, San Felipe de Austin, December 30, 1835, as found in W.C. Binkley, ed., *Official Correspondence of the Texas Revolution, 1835-1836* (New York: D. Appleton-Century Company, 1936), 1:259.

[60] Helen Foster Snow, "John Wyatt Moody, First Auditor of the Republic of Texas, 1835-1839," Moody Papers, page 1; Auditor's Office to Sam Houston, Houston, Texas, May 26, 1837, Moody Papers.

[61] The Papers of the Texas Revolution, 9:470-72.

[62] Marquis James, *The Raven: A Biography of Sam Houston* (Austin: University of Texas Press, 1929), 285-86.

[63] Wallace L. McKeehan, "Erastus 'Deaf' Smith," found online at http://www.tamu.edu/ccbn/dewitt/dewitt.htm.

[64] Crystal Sasse Ragsdale, *Women & Children of the Alamo* (Austin: State House Press, 1994), 62-64.

[65] Wallace L. McKeehan, "Erastus 'Deaf' Smith."

[66] *Handbook of Texas Online*, s.v. "Municipality of Mina," http://www.tsha.utexas.edu/handbook/online/articles/MM/usm2.html (accessed July 30, 2006).

[67] The Papers of the Texas Revolution, 9:276-85.

[68] Joseph Milton Nance, *Heroes of Texas* (Waco: Texian Press, 1966), 74-76.

[69] *Handbook of Texas Online*, s.v. "Goliad Campaign of 1836," http://www.tsha.utexas.edu/handbook/online/articles/GG/qdg2.html (accessed May 29, 2007).

[70] Ruth G. Nichols, "Samuel May Williams, 1795-1858," found in the "Calendar to the Samuel May Williams Papers," comp. Ruth G. Nichols and S.W. Lifflander (Galveston: Rosenberg Library Press, 1956), v-xiii.

[71] In a typed letter from the late Tom Bain, dated January 5, 1948, and addressed to Texana Collectors: "A Texas document has been found concerning a $50,000 loan made 24th February, 1836. The Texas Bonds were handwritten and consisted on the following denominations: Bond No. 1-$1,000, No. 2-$1,000, No. 3-$1,000, No. 4-$1,000, No.5-$3,000, No.6-$1,000, No.7-$3,000, No.8-$3,000, No.9-$3,000, No.10-$3,000, No.11-$5,000, No.12-$5,000." These smaller denomination bonds made up $30,000 of the alleged $50,000 loan.

[72] From a manuscript bond, No. 1, $10,000, dated at New Orleans, 2nd May 1836. This instrument was signed by Samuel M. Williams on behalf of McKinney & Williams, notarized on the reverse by Willliam Christy, but no funds were ever reported as being received and there is no evidence that a claim was made following annexation. Bond No. 1 and No 2, both for $10,000 and dated May 2, 1836, were cited as part of the possible $50,000 loan on Tom Bain's letter dated January 5, 1948.

[73] The Papers of the Texas Revolution, 4:143, see "McKinney & Williams to The Provisional Government of Texas, Quintana, January 25, 1836;" Darrel Brown, "McKinney & Williams 8% Government of Texas Bond," non-published, 2007.

[74] Extract of a letter by Samuel May Williams regarding his brother in law, Samuel St. John, and the manuscript bonds. Williams states "In reply I have to say that the provisional Gov[ernment] nor the Gov[ernment] of the Republic of Texas, nor any person for them ever rec[eive]d one dollar for on a/c of said bonds, and of Course [*sic*] in no way shape manner or form liable for the Same." Williams to ______, Galveston , February 6, 1849, Samuel May Williams Papers.

[75] Ibid.

[76] Power of Attorney, Samuel St. John, Jr., to Samuel May Williams, City of Galveston, April 22, 1840, Samuel May Williams Papers, Rosenberg Library, Galveston, Texas.

77 Reverse of manuscript bond, No 5., $3,000, New Orleans, February 24, 1836: "This bond was presented to the Auditor & Comptroller for adjustment by I De Cordova, for Sophia St John, and is rejected for the reason that the Government never rec[eived] any consideration for it. Auditor's office, Austin, July 10th, 1849. J[oh]n Swisher, Auditor, James B. Shaw, Compt[roller]."

78 Gray, *Diary,* 119.

79 "Selby Kiffer, "Remember the Alamo," Auction book (Southeby's, June 18, 2004).

80 W. Thomas Taylor, *Texfake: An Account of the Theft and Forgery of Texas Documents* (Austin: W. Thomas Taylor, 1991), 107-11.

81 This abrupt change in the weather on the night of February 25 was vividly described in the diary of William Fairfax Gray. Gray, *Diary,* 119.

82 Selby Kiffer, "Remember the Alamo," Auction book (Southeby's, June 18, 2004).

83 The Papers of the Texas Revolution, 4:446, see "San Felipe Committee to the Public, February 27, 1836."

84 Gray, *Diary,* 108.

85 Ibid., 120.

86 John Hoyt Williams, *Sam Houston: The Life and Times of the Liberator of Texas, an Authentic American Hero* (New York: Simon & Schuster, Inc., 1993), caption to illustration number 3.

87 Gray, *Diary,* 121.

88 *Handbook of Texas Online,* s.v. "Samuel Houston," http://www.tsha.utexas.edu/handbook/online/articles/HH/fho73.html (accessed February 7, 2006).

89 Williams, *Sam Houston,* 92-96.

90 Marquis James, *The Raven: A Biography of Sam Houston* (Austin: University of Texas Press, 1929), 219.

91 "Texas Declaration of Independence," Auction book (Southeby's, June 18, 2004); The Papers of the Texas Revolution, 4:501-505.

92 Nance, *Heroes of Texas,* 78-79.

93 Triplett, *Roland Trevor,* 336.

94 Index to Military Rolls of the Republic of Texas, Volunteers from Tunahan District at Béxar (capture of San Antonio, December 10, 1835), found on-line at http://www.tshaonline.org/supsites/military/rep_cont.htm.

95 *Handbook of Texas Online,* s.v. "James W. Robinson," http://www.tsha.utexas.edu/handbook/online/articles/RR/fro37.html, (accessed September 16, 2006).

96 Gray, *Diary,* 121-24.

97 The Papers of the Texas Revolution, 9:303-304, see "Journals of the Convention of 1836, The General Convention at Washington-on-the-Brazos, March 1-17."

98 Texas Declaration of Independence, March 2, 1836.

99 Gray, *Diary,* 124.

100 From the reverse of the order for the printing of the Declaration of Independence. The committee of three were Benjamin B. Goodrich , John Smith Davenport Byrom and possibly Martin Parmer. Although the committee member's name was spelled "Palmer," Martin Parmer sometimes spelled his name as "Palmer." He also had ten children who in later years spelled their surname "Palmer."

101 The Papers of the Texas Revolution, 9:303-304.

102 Taylor, *Texfake,* 14-16.

103 "Texas Declaration of Independence," Auction book (Southeby's, June 18, 2004).

104 Gray, *Diary,* 125.

105 The Papers of the Texas Revolution, 9:311-12.

106 The Papers of the Texas Revolution, 4:502-504, see "Travis to Convention, Commandancy of the Alamo, Bejar, March 3, 1836."

107 The Papers of the Texas Revolution, 9:313.

108 Gray, *Diary,* 125.

109 "Perilous conditions of the settlements in Texas," *New York Observer,* April 16, 1836, vol. XIV, no. 16, 3. Courtesy of the Brazoria County Historical Museum, Angleton, Texas.

110 Ragsdale, *Women & Children of the Alamo,* 86.

111 The Papers of the Texas Revolution, 9:314.

112 Gray, *Diary,* 126.

113 The Papers of the Texas Revolution, 9:325-39.

114 Gray, *Diary,* 128.

115 Triplett, *Roland Trevor,* 337-38.

116 *Handbook of Texas Online,* s.v. "David Gouverneur Burnet," http://www.tsha.utexas.edu/handbook/online/articles/BB/fbu46.html (accessed September 17, 2006).

117 Among those who doubted his abilities was William Fairfax Gray. Gray, *Diary,* 129.

118 The Papers of the Texas Revolution, 9:366-70.

119 Gray, *Diary,* 133.

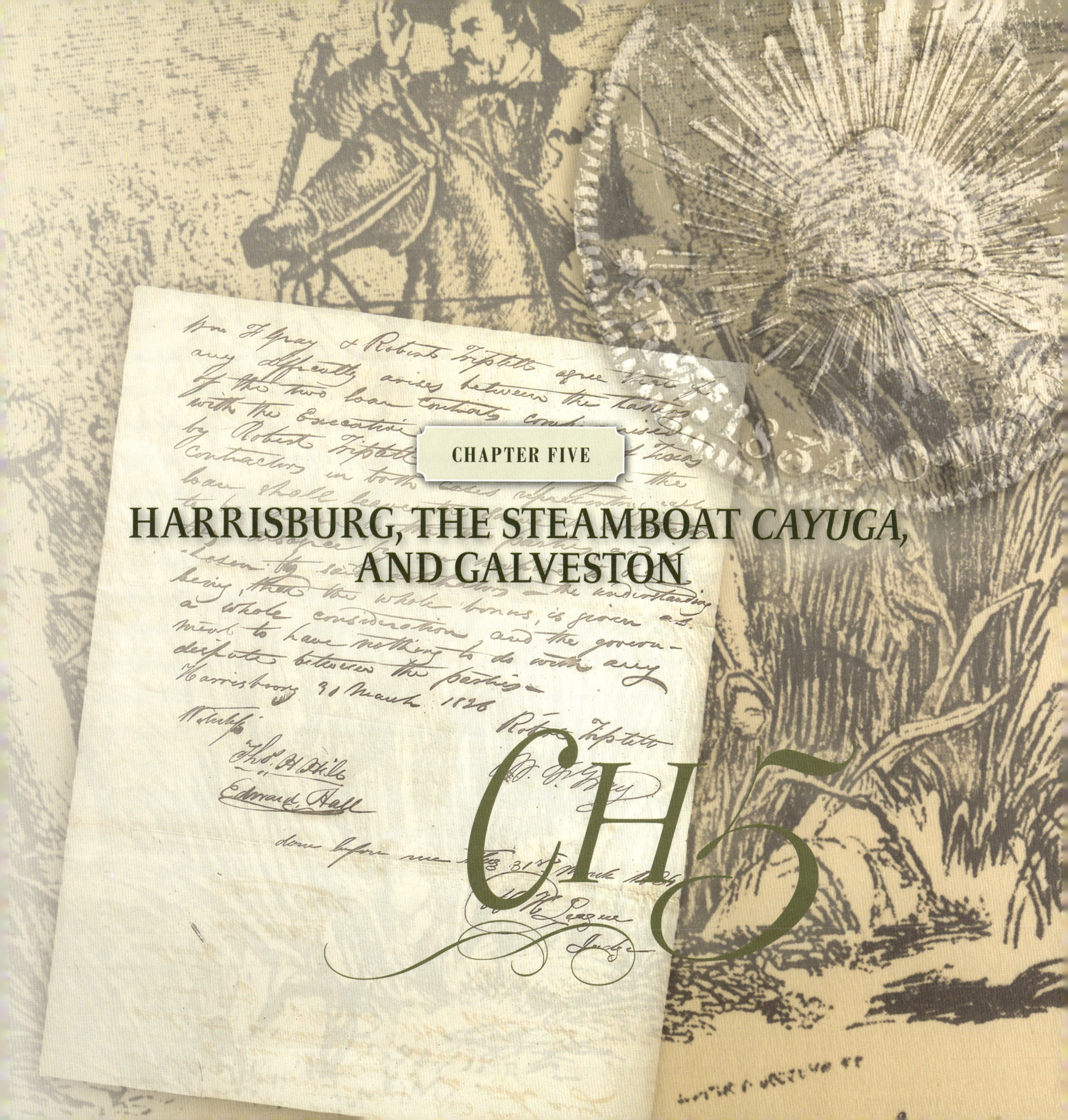

CHAPTER FIVE

HARRISBURG, THE STEAMBOAT *CAYUGA*, AND GALVESTON

CH5

When the Convention disbanded on March 17, 1836, the newly formed Texas government evacuated Washington-on-the-Brazos because of the possibility of death or capture by Santa Anna's advancing forces. The Mexican Army had swept unchecked across Texas, moving eastward from San Antonio de Béxar and crossing the Brazos River near present-day Richmond. The Mexican troops burned and looted everything in their path. President Burnet moved southeast, finally selecting the town of Harrisburg on Buffalo Bayou as the temporary capital. It took about two days for the first members of the cabinet to arrive at this small cluster of wooden-frame houses on the banks of Buffalo Bayou. Harrisburg was the seat of government for the Republic, and the temporary residence of Burnet and his cabinet members, from March 22 to April 13, 1836.

Fig 5.1, The Harris home at Harrisburg.

Texas seat of government, from a photograph of a diorama. Courtesy of the Houston Metropolitan Research Center, Houston, Texas.

Fig 5.2, Lorenzo de Zavala, Vice President.

The San Jacinto Museum of History, Houston, Texas.

Fig 5.3, Thomas J. Rusk, Secretary of War.

Houston Metropolitan Research Center, Houston Public Library, Houston, Texas.

They stayed in the home of Jane Harris, the widow of John R. Harris, who arrived in Texas from New Orleans in 1823. In 1826, Harris received land on Buffalo Bayou, had a survey made, and named the town Harrisburg. Although it was an early Texas port and trading post, by 1828 it only had six to eight houses.[1] The approximate site of this short lived but significant seat of government is near the location of the present-day John R. Harris Elementary School on Broadway Avenue in east Houston.[2] The *ad interim* government adopted the first tri-color Lone Star flag during their stay as the official flag of the Texas Navy. It is thought that the flag was designed in the Harris home by a neighbor, Mrs. Sarah Dodson, during a brief stay in 1835. Harrisburg possessed an important water route down Buffalo Bayou directly to Galveston Bay and onward to the Gulf of Mexico. The bayou ran directly behind the Harris home. This water route offered an escape avenue by boat as well as protection for the government by the fledgling Texas Navy, stationed in the harbor off the island. Present-day Harris County is named for the Harris family and for their contributions to the government at this critical time.

When Burnet called his cabinet together for the first time in Harrisburg, each member in turn rose and expressed his estimate of the situation before them. When the president observed Thomas J. Rusk, the Secretary of War, dozing and looking exhausted, he asked Rusk his opinion of their predicament. Arousing and jumping to his feet Rusk replied, "I think we are in a hell of a fix. We are worked down. Let us go over to the saloon and get a drink, then mount our horses, go fight like the devil, and get out of it."[3] Indeed, one of Burnet's most perplexing problems during his administration was how to get recruits and supplies for the army. Sometimes the troops lived on beef without bread and frequently without salt. Many of the men were barefooted, and most of them were without a change of clothing. Because of the severe shortage of money needed to supply the army and fight the war, Burnet and his cabinet were once again compelled by necessity to address the ratification of the Texian loans.

After the Declaration of Independence was distributed in handbill form, the lending group from New Orleans was willing to negotiate the actual advancement of the money. Two of the principals, Robert Triplett and land agent William Fairfax Gray, followed the government to Harrisburg and waited for the representatives to bring up the subject. On Tuesday, March 29, the steamboat *Cayuga* arrived in the bayou behind the Harris home, bringing several passengers, among them Bailey Hardiman, the acting Secretary of State. Gray and Triplett lamented that Hardiman would retard the negotiations for the loan, although they knew that as Secretary of State he must be aware of the terms.[4]

At last, Secretary Rusk summoned Triplett saying that the cabinet wished to settle the loan business. Triplett recalled the discussion in his autobiography, remembering that Rusk asked him, "what terms we could agree on?"[5] Triplett responded, "What was the current price of lands; at what price could they be bought?" He then continued, "Everybody nearly was now running away from the Mexicans, leaving their lands, and were offering them freely at 12 1/2 cents per acre." "Ah!" said Rusk, "That won't do." Triplett replied, "I do not ask it, although it is very evident if we had our money, that we could buy at those rates. But I am willing to pay double." As Rusk and the cabinet pondered the dilemma, Triplett continued by pointing out that if General Houston had encountered Santa Anna and defeated him, and land had consequently risen to a dollar or two dollars per acre, he would have been bound by his offer to the Convention to buy Texas lands at current prices. On the other hand, given the current state of affairs with Santa Anna terrorizing the country and the population fleeing across the Sabine, land had fallen to 12 1/2 cents an acre. He reasoned that with this extreme, the contract could not be complied without fear that the sacrifice of the government would be too great. Despite his clear advantage, Triplett proposed "to allow double the current prices, and give 25 cents."

"Well," said Rusk, "is there no way to compromise on this matter? What will you relinquish your contract for? Say you take land at 50 cents per acre for what you have paid in, and let go the balance." Triplett, having been advanced $45,890 by the second group of lenders, replied "I would take 135,000 acres." While Rusk objected to this as being unreasonable, upon further discussion it was more than double Triplett's original demand. More importantly, it was the same terms which had been offered in the original negotiations in New Orleans. Yet there were several sticking points, the most critical of which was the location of the lands that would be selected to repay the loans at approximately fifty cents per acre. After lengthy negotiations in the Harris home, a compromise was finally reached. Burnet and the cabinet reasoned that the more desirable tracts of land should be set aside for those soldiers fighting for freedom, and that the land speculators would have to subordinate their locations behind the veterans. As a sweetener to close the deal, the government effectively lowered the price per acre by offering an additional thirty-two leagues of land (142,000 acres) to be distributed pro-rata among the lenders in exchange for the right to the priority locations.[6] Triplett indicated he would advance the money already paid by the lenders of the second loan in exchange for land in Texas at fifty cents per acre. He also informed the government that while he and Gray would accept the new terms of the compromise, he was not authorized to bind the other parties of the first loan, but indicated that he thought they would find it acceptable. If so, the remainder of the $250,000 loan could then be advanced.

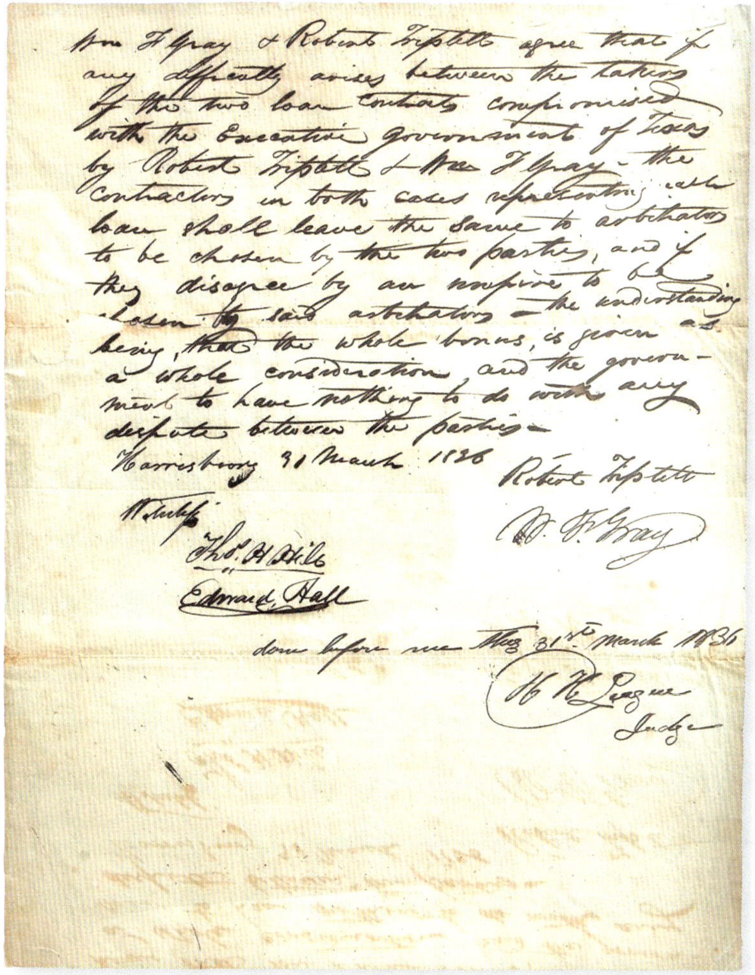
Wm F Gray & Robert Triplett agree that if
any difficulty arises between the takers
of the two loan contracts compromised
with the Executive government of Texas
by Robert Triplett & Wm F Gray - the
contractors in both cases representing each
loan shall leave the same to arbitrators
to be chosen by the two parties, and if
they disagree by an umpire to be
chosen by said arbitrators - the understanding
being, that the whole bonus, is given as
a whole consideration, and the govern-
ment to have nothing to do with any
dispute between the parties -
Harrisburg 31 March 1836

Robert Triplett

W. F. Gray

Witness

Thos. H. Hills

Edward Hall

done before me this 31st March 1836

H. H. League
Judge

Fig 5.4, A manuscript document by Robert Triplett and William Fairfax Gray relating to the compromise of the Texian Loans, Harrisburg, March 31, 1836.

Private Collection.

As widespread panic gripped the countryside, people frantically abandoned their homes and headed east with their wagons and livestock in tow. Their slaves fled with them. The urgency to leave the area was so great that many a house was abandoned with the supper dishes still on the table.

Transcription for Figure 5.4:

W[illia]m F. Gray & Robert Triplett agree that if any difficulty arises between the taking of the two loan contracts compromised with the Executive Government of Texas by Robert Triplett & Wm F. Gray—the contractors in both cases representing the loan shall leave the same to arbitrators to be chosen by the parties, and if they disagree by an umpire to chosen by said arbitrators—the understanding being, that the whole bonus is given as a whole consideration, and the government to have nothing to do with any dispute between the parties- Harrisburg, 31 March 1836. (Signed) Robert Triplett, Wm F. Gray,

Witness, (Signed) Tho[mas] H. Hill Edward Hall, done before me this 31st March 1836

H. H. League, Judge

After lengthy negotiations with the Burnet government, the document in Figure 5.4 was signed in Harrisburg on March 31, 1836, by investors Robert Triplett and William Fairfax Gray and by witnesses Thomas H. Hill and Edward Hall, two clerks in the executive department. Edward Hall also served as the Texas agent in New Orleans. The agreement was signed before Hosea H. League, the first judge of Harrisburg. This document was written in the darkest days of the newly independent Republic and relates to the inner workings of the financing which would propel the Texas Revolution. It is an agreement to arbitrate any difficulty in the compromise loan contract negotiated by Triplett and Gray with the Government of Texas. The driving force behind this agreement appears to be the desire of Triplett and Gray to prevent the Texas government from controlling the division of the land bonus called for in the loan compromise contract.[7] A copy of the printed version of the Texian Loan Compromise Contract has been included in its entirety in Appendix E.

Unknown to the parties at the time the compromise was signed, the remaining investors would later opt out of the balance of the $200,000 loan. Since the original terms of the Texian loans as set forth by the commissioners had been abruptly changed, they refused to pay in the remaining 90 percent of the loan. Even today, the most important valuation measure of real estate is its location. The preferable land selection given in favor of the soldiers caused the lenders to reject the remainder of the deal. This failed transaction caused the beginning of an ongoing liquidity and credibility crisis for the Republic of Texas.[9]

On April 1, 1836, news reached Harrisburg that Santa Anna's army was advancing towards the town. According to the messenger, "The town of San Felipe has certainly been burnt, houses, goods and all. The inhabitants of the west side of the Brazos are all breaking up, leaving their homes and flying east."[10] Secretary Rusk's assessment was correct. They were in a "hell of a fix."[11] The retreating movement of Sam Houston's army also caused great discontent. As widespread panic gripped the countryside, people frantically abandoned their homes and headed east with their wagons and livestock in tow. Their slaves fled with them. The urgency to leave the area was so great that many a house was abandoned with the supper dishes still on the table.[12] Only their meager possessions and necessities were carried with them as they fled east of the Trinity River in the direction of Louisiana.

During this gloomy time, President Burnet and the cabinet officials hunkered down on the edge of Buffalo Bayou with the Mexican Army rapidly advancing on their trail. Burnet later described the finances of the country to be, "in a condition more deplorable than its military equipment." The lending group in New Orleans had already paid the $20,000 installment on the first Texian loan. This money had been exhausted before Austin, Archer and Wharton left for Washington, D.C. With the loan compromise resolved, Triplett advanced the whole of the second loan to the government at Harrisburg on April 1, 1836. The money, amounting to $45,820 was paid entirely by drafts in money of the United States.[13] The second loan infused the government coffers with badly needed cash and represented the only significant money the Republic received for almost two years.[14] So grateful was the President, and so indebted was the interim government to Triplett, that Burnet recalled the perilous funding of this second loan in his address to the First Congress in Columbia, on October 4, 1836.[15]

THE GALVESTON LAND GRAB

While in Harrisburg, President Burnet again came to Triplett and asked him if he could raise an additional two thousand dollars for Texas. Triplett replied that he did not have the money with him, but if Burnet would issue land scrip for that amount, and with the authority to locate the tract, then Triplett would secure the money from a friend. Burnet, in turn, issued the land scrip for 1,920 acres—three grants for 640 acres—in exchange for the funds which Triplett obtained from his friend, Dr. Sterling Neblett.

The document in Figure 5.5 is one of the original manuscript documents signed by David G. Burnet at Harrisburg on April 1, 1836, acknowledging the advance of the private loan from Robert Triplett. The document represents the issuance of land scrip for 640 acres of Triplett's choosing directly from Burnet, the President of the Republic of Texas. It also illustrates the determination of Robert Triplet to secure a prime parcel of Texas real estate for himself in consideration of an additional advance of $1,920. Triplett and Neblett partnered on the deal and the two men left with Gray for Galveston Island in search of lucrative tracts of waterfront property with which to fill their land scrip.

Before leaving for Galveston, Triplett was appointed a general agent for Texas in the U.S. with the power to appoint four secretaries and all local agents.[16] His mission was to locate and purchase supplies to outfit the volunteers and recruits streaming into the ranks of the Texas Army. Soon after arriving in Galveston, Triplett purchased a large cargo of provisions then lying in the harbor at Galveston. He gave the merchants a small down payment, and funded the balance due with a draft on the Texas Treasury recently made solvent.

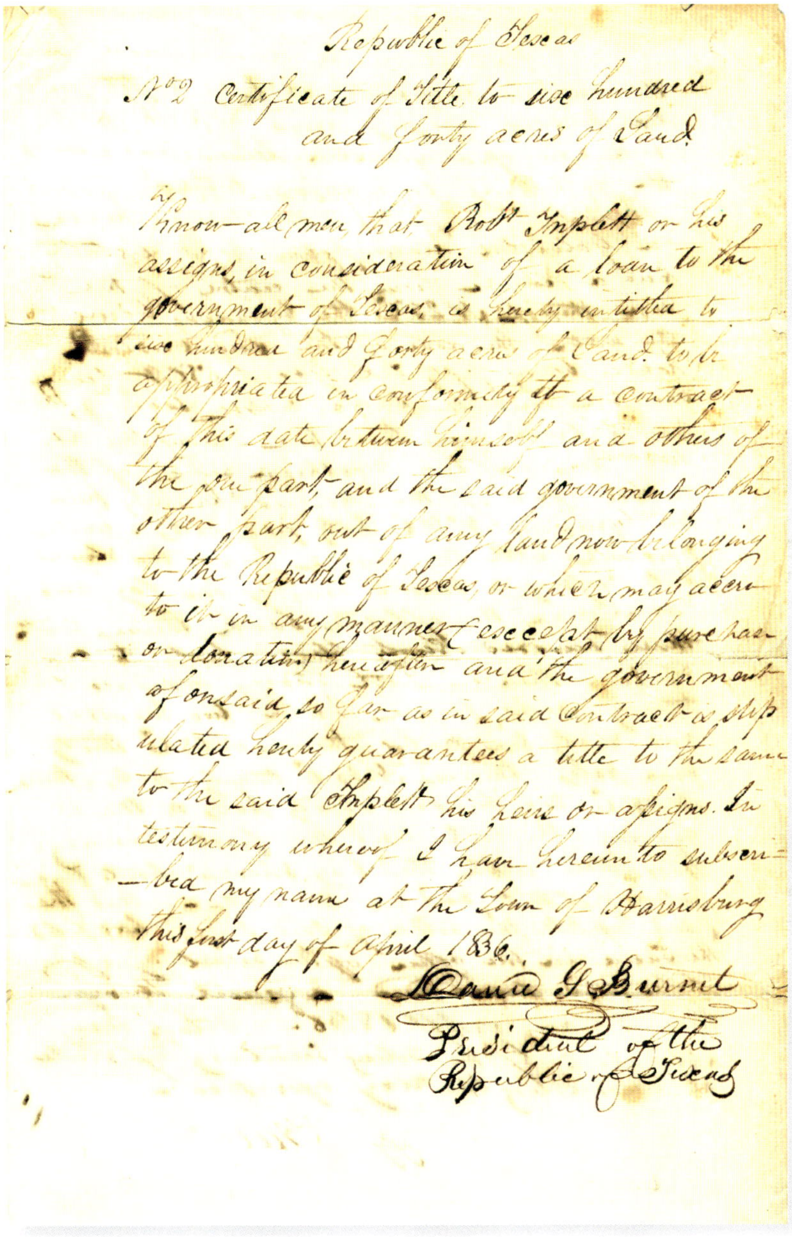

Republic of Texas. No 2 Certificate of Title to six hundred and forty acres of Land

Know all men, that, Rob[er]t Triplett or his assigns, in consideration of a loan to the government of Texas, is hereby entitled to six hundred and forty acres of Land to be appropriated in conformity to a contract of this date between himself and others of the one part, and the said government of the other part, out of any land now belonging to the Republic of Texas, or which may accru[e] to it in any manner—esccept [sic]by purchase or donation, hereafter and the government aforesaid so far as in said contract as stipulated hereby guarantees a title to the same to the said Triplett his heirs or assigns. In testimony whereof I have herein to subscribed my name at the Town of Harrisburg this first day of April 1836.

(Signed) David G. Burnet, President of the Republic of Texas.

Fig 5.5, Harrisburg, April 1, 1836, Republic of Texas, No 2 Certificate of Title to 640 acres of land.

Private Collection.

THE MASSACRE AT GOLIAD

Fig 5.6, The Death March at Goliad.

The San Jacinto Museum of History, Houston, Texas.

On Easter Sunday, April 3, 1836, the news arrived at Harrisburg that Col. James Fannin's forces had been surrounded in an open field at Coleto Creek near Goliad. Some four hundred men were cornered by the Mexican cavalry.[17] Outgunned and outnumbered, Fannin's men spent the night in a cold grassy field, with no food, little water and short on ammunition. On the following day, the Texians surrendered under the belief that their lives would be spared. The prisoners were marched back to Presidio La Bahía where they stayed for seven days. Several of the men were told that a ship was waiting for them at Copano Bay which would take them out of Texas to New Orleans. As the rumor circulated, many were relieved to hear that their fate would not be the same as those who defended the Alamo. The following morning, on Palm Sunday, March 27, almost four hundred Texians were told to pack their belongings. They were then marched out of the presidio in three separate columns. Each column was taken in a different direction, and, after getting to a certain point, they were each halted. A sense of bewilderment quickly turned to horror when guns were pointed at each victim's breast and a volley of deadly fire was unloaded on the unsuspecting prisoners.

On that same Palm Sunday morning, Col. James W. Fannin, Jr., now a wounded prisoner of the Mexican forces at Goliad, awoke in a guarded room at the church to find that rather than being treated as prisoners of war, his men were suffering a far worse fate.[18] Speaking through Joseph H. Spohn, another Texian prisoner who was acting as an interpreter for a Mexican captain, Fannin learned, "That for having come with an armed band to commit depredations and revolutionize Texas, the Mexican Government were about to chastise him." Under direct orders from Santa Anna, Fannin's men were being executed and Fannin and the remaining officers were to suffer the same tragic fate.

As soon as the death sentence was translated for Fannin, he asked to see the commandant. When his request was refused, he offered the captain a valuable gold watch which he said belonged to his wife, for presentation to the commandant as a payment for a proper burial after being shot. Finally, the captain agreed to Fannin's last request. Colonel Fannin then took out a small beaded purse containing gold *doubloons* and gave it to the officer, followed by a double handful of dollars which he retrieved from a piece of canvas in his left overcoat pocket. Spohn, the interpreter, then attempted to bandage Fannin's eyes with a handkerchief. Noticing Spohn's clumsy manner, the officer snatched the handkerchief from his hand, ordered Fannin to sit in a nearby chair, and then stepped behind him to bandage his eyes. After assurances from Fannin that his eyes were properly bound, the captain returned to the front and ordered his men to unfix their bayonets and approach the blindfolded Texian officer. When the muskets were within two feet of Fannin's body, the officer drew forth his handkerchief, signaling the Mexican soldiers to shoot the Texian prisoner.[19]

Fig 5.7, The execution of James Fannin at Goliad. Painting by S. J. Stout at Presidio La Bahia.

Courtesy of Presidio La Bahia, Goliad
Photo by Jim Bevill.

Despite the Mexican captain's promise, all the *doubloons* in Texas could not buy a proper burial for Col. James W. Fannin. As described by Spohn, "Fannin fell dead on the right side of the chair, and from thence rolled into a dry ditch, about three feet deep, close by the wall."[20] Only a handful of men managed to escape the melee at Goliad. As they began to make their way to safety behind the Texian lines, they began to relay their accounts of the indiscriminate slaughter of Fannin's troops by the Mexican Army. The second largest army of Texians had now been destroyed.

THE RUNAWAY SCRAPE

As the government reeled from the terrible news of the massacre at Goliad, a panic gripped the people of Texas as they hurried to escape the advancing Mexican Army. Gray, Triplett and Neblett left Harrisburg the day after Easter, rode to Lynchburg on horseback, then boarded a schooner for the trip to Point Bolivar and Galveston, arriving on April 8. Assuming that previous land grants had not been made in areas adjacent to the coast, Triplett and Neblett measured off two sections of ground on the east end of the island on the site of Jean Lafitte's old fort, the remains of which were still visible.[21] For Triplett, the chance to buy 1,280 acres of waterfront property on Galveston Island at a dollar an acre must have been quite an incentive for him to consummate the funding of the loan. As Triplett and his companions completed the survey of their real estate coup, a dispatch arrived at Harrisburg on April 12 which stated that the Mexican Army had advanced and were crossing the Brazos River at Fort Bend, near present-day Richmond. By April 13, Triplett, Gray, Neblett and the others had returned by boat to San Jacinto Bay with their description and survey of their proposed real estate claims at Galveston and Bolivar. They sailed all the way to Lynch's ferry, with Triplett landing on the south shore and Dr. Neblett proceeding to Harrisburg by horse to get the land grant signed by government officials. Triplett remained at the ferry opposite of San Jacinto. The mass exodus known as the Runaway Scrape was now in full force. Whole towns had been evacuated with families, animals, wagons and slaves desperately heading east to escape the advancing Mexican Army.

As the masses fled in panic to the east, these daring speculators continued to head west in order to get their surveyed sections of land on Galveston Island and Point Bolivar approved by the government. But the *ad interim* President and his cabinet had already abandoned Harrisburg. The old town had now been completely evacuated save for the newspaper office. They boarded the steamboat *Cayuga*, which had been readied with an ample supply of wood in case a sudden departure had to be made. As the steamboat chugged away from the bank an advance party of Mexican scouts appeared and witnessed their escape. The *Cayuga* puffed its billowy white clouds of steam and headed down the murky brown channel to safety.[22] Thus the steamboat *Cayuga* became the *de facto* capital of the Republic as the *ad interim* government proceeded to evacuate down Buffalo Bayou carrying the cabinet members and the remaining national Treasury of Texas to safety.[23]

Capt. William P. Harris and his partner, Robert Wilson, evacuated the town of Harrisburg on the steamboat *Cayuga*, just ahead of Gen. Antonio López de Santa Anna and his troops. The refugees, which included President Burnet, his cabinet and the remaining inhabitants of the town were brought to safety as the steamer made its harrowing escape down Buffalo Bayou.

Robert Wilson was a business partner of William P. Harris and helped develop the town of Harrisburg, where Wilson owned a gristmill and sawmill. Following the death of John R. Harris in 1829, he acquired the nickname of "Honest Bob." It is rumored that he received this nickname because Harris's widow accused Wilson of fraudulently claiming much of her late husband's business as his own.

Fig 5.8, Capt. William P. Harris.

Courtesy of Jean Epperson.

Fig 5.9, Robert (Honest Bob) Wilson.

Courtesy of Jean Epperson.

Fig 5.10, The Steamboat *Cayuga*.

Sketch by Suzanne Wilson, Courtesy of Jean Epperson.

The floating capitol of the Republic depicted in Figure 5.10 was a side-wheel steamer built in Pittsburg, Pennsylvania, in 1832. It had one deck, two boilers, two chimneys, and a high-compression engine.[24] It also contained a cabin on deck, which was used as the executive offices of the government for a brief period of time. Prior to her service in Texas, the *Cayuga* transported cotton along the Mississippi River before it was sold in New Orleans in 1834 to Capt. William P. Harris and Robert Wilson. During 1834, and for several years after, the ship operated on the Brazos River, Galveston Bay and Buffalo Bayou, where Harris and Wilson maintained homes, a store, a warehouse and a sawmill in Harrisburg. With Harris at the helm, the *Cayuga* removed the *ad interim* government to safety and later ferried Texas troops during the war.

As Dr. Sterling Neblett rode from Lynch's ferry towards Harrisburg the road touched upon a bend of the bayou, and he saw the smoke of the steamboat *Cayuga* coming down the bayou.[25] Unaware that the town had been abandoned, he signaled the boat, awaited its approach and found the entire cabinet on board. After boarding, Neblett was determined to get the contract signed. These cunning financiers had risked their lives to locate their prime real estate tracts and nothing, not even an invading army, was going to stand in their way.[26] The speculative nature of their transactions had now become even more precarious, as the fledgling Texas government was only one battle away from being driven into exile.

SANTA ANNA ADVANCES ON HARRISBURG

Santa Anna led a division of his army across the Brazos River near present-day Richmond and then onward to present-day southwest Harris County (then an uninhabited prairie). The main contingent of the Mexican Army arrived in Harrisburg on April 15 where the soldiers proceeded to burn the town of Harrisburg, including the old Harris home where the *ad interim* government had stayed only two days before.[27] The *Telegraph and Texas Register* also met a dramatic end after Gail Borden and Joseph Baker had moved the presses with considerable difficulty to Harrisburg. An issue was printed on April 14 by "a Frenchman and two North Americans" who were left behind by their employers after the town's evacuation.[28] Santa Anna arrived after only a few copies of the paper had been printed and ordered the equipment and the printing presses of Baker and Borden thrown into the muddy waters of Buffalo Bayou. At least one copy of this final newspaper miraculously survived.[29]

But one of the captured print shop workers told Santa Anna that the president had gone to New Washington (now Morgan's Point in present-day La Porte) on the upper end of Galveston Bay, about twenty miles east of Harrisburg.[30] Santa Anna apprised Col. Juan Almonte of Burnet's probable escape route down the bayou. Colonel Almonte and an advance party of dragoons were ordered to New Washington in hot pursuit. Almonte was a good choice for the task, as he was educated in New Orleans and spoke perfect English.[31] He was also familiar with the area, having served on the staff of Gov. José Félix Trespalacios in Texas in 1822. As one of Santa Anna's most loyal commanders, he hoped to cut off the Texas leaders' escape and capture the fleeing rebel government.[32]

NEGOTIATIONS ON BUFFALO BAYOU

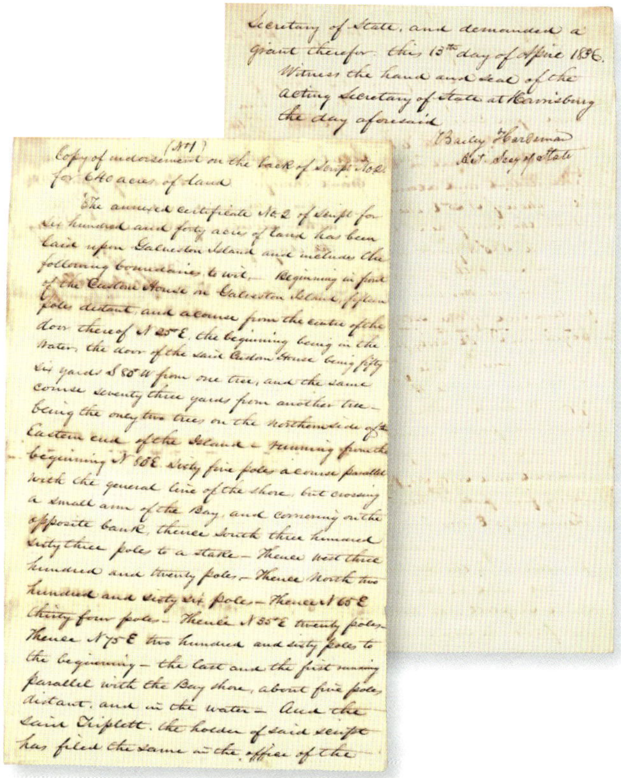
(No 1)
Copy of endorsement on the back of Script No 2 for 640 acres of land
The annexed certificate No 2 of Script for six hundred and forty acres of land has been laid upon Galveston Island and includes the following boundaries to wit — Beginning in front of the Custom House on Galveston Island, fifteen poles distant, and a course from the centre of the door thereof N 25° E. the beginning being in the water, the door of the said Custom House being fifty six yards S 80° W from one tree, and the same course seventy three yards from another tree — being the only two trees on the northern side of the Eastern end of the Island — running from the beginning N 65 E. sixty five poles a course parallel with the general line of the shore, but crossing a small arm of the Bay, and cornering on the opposite bank, thence South three hundred sixty three poles to a stake — thence West three hundred and twenty poles — thence North two hundred and sixty six poles — thence N 65 E thirty four poles — thence N 55° E twenty poles — thence N 75 E two hundred and sixty poles to the beginning — the last and the first running parallel with the Bay shore, about five poles distant, and in the water — And the said Triplett, the holder of said script has filed the same in the office of the Secretary of State, and demanded a grant therefor this 13th day of April 1836.
Witness the hand and seal of the acting Secretary of State at Harrisburg the day aforesaid
Bailey Hardeman
Act. Secy of State

Fig 5.11, Harrisburg, April 13, 1836, (No. 1) Copy of Endorsement on the back of Script No 2 for 640 acres of land.

Private Collection.

The land scrip certificate in Figure 5.11 between Triplett and the Government of Texas for 640 acres of land was presented to the government by Dr. Sterling Neblett on board the steamboat *Cayuga* in Buffalo Bayou while Santa Anna's Army marched on Harrisburg. The city of Galveston now stands on the tract of land described in the survey.[33] Although the piece is dated April 13, 1836, at Harrisburg, it was signed by Bailey Hardiman as acting Secretary of State on the evening of April 15 at Lynchburg.

> *(No 1) Copy of indorsement [sic] on the back of script No 2 for 640 acres of land.*

The text begins:

> *The annexed certificate No. 2 of script for six hundred and forty acres of land has been laid upon Galveston Island and includes the following boundaries to wit, Beginning in front of the Custom House on Galveston Island …*

Note the language at the bottom of the first page and at the beginning of the second:

> *And the said Triplett, the holder of said script has filed the claim in the office of the Secretary of State, and demanded a grant therefore this 13th day of April 1836.*
>
> *Witness the hand and seal of the acting Secretary of State at Harrisburg the day aforesaid. (Signed) Bailey Hardiman, Act[ing] Sec[retar]y of State*

Considering that they were on a steamboat and being chased into exile by the Mexican Army, it is difficult to see how the government could refuse the request by Triplett, Neblitt and Gray for the lucrative parcels of land in consideration for the additional advance of $2,000 at this critical time.

But when Neblett at last presented the precious land scripts to the president, Burnet at first refused to sign them. He then assented, and then repealed his decision and decided to consult with his cabinet. Burnet then signed one grant. Gray wrote of the event in his diary on April 15, 1836. While the land speculators had persuaded the president to sign one script, Gray recalled, "but Hardiman, acting Secretary of State, positively refused. Finally, after coming on shore, he consented to sign for one section, on condition that no more should be asked for at this time."[34] Burnet and Hardiman's reluctance to sign for the land scrip was based on their fear that that the lucrative grants would prove to be unpopular with the troops and would damage their political reputations. As the government discovered when they tried to collect the remaining $180,000 from the lending group, their credibility with the lenders had been tarnished by their reluctance to sign this grant and their refusal to accept the original terms of the Texian loans as negotiated by the commissioners. The investors did not appreciate having the terms of a contract altered. It would be the death knell for any future advances of money from the lending group.

The steamboat passed through the bend in the bayou where it intersects the San Jacinto River. Known as Lynch's crossing because of the ferry boat operation, the *Cayuga* chugged by the marshy plains where the Mexican Army would encamp just a few days later. Even though Mexican scouts were in the area Burnet stopped at Lynchburg to gather his family. They crossed the river on the ferry. Burnet then strapped on his guns, mounted a horse and rode south with his family to the home of Col. James Morgan at the town of New Washington. Burnet planned to board a boat at Morgan's plantation on the bay and evacuate his wife and young son with the *ad interim* government to Galveston.

In the meantime, Juan Almonte's relentless pursuit of Burnet and his cabinet members almost paid off, and Almonte came close to capturing Burnet himself. Burnet and his wife were loading supplies into a boat when a slave shouted a warning that the Mexicans were coming. The Burnets climbed into the small boat and frantically rowed out in the bay where a well-manned schooner, the *Flash*, took them to safety. A patrol of Mexican cavalry raced onto the pier and contemplated firing at them, but the well-bred and American-educated Mexican colonel forbade the soldiers from firing when he spotted a woman on board. The Mexican Army's last attempt to capture the rebel government thus failed, though only by the closest of margins.[35] Santa Anna arrived with the main body of his army on April 18.

The historic moment of Burnet's escape by rowboat was later represented by a vignette on a $10 note (see Figure 5.12), issued by the Government

Fig 5.12, Vignette, "Burnet's escape on Galveston Bay," Government of Texas $10 Note.

Private Collection.

Fig 5.13, Gen. Sam Houston.

Courtesy of Albert and Ethel Herzstein Library, The San Jacinto Museum of History, Houston, Texas.

of Texas from Houston in 1838 on the first series of engraved notes. The vignette shows a man and another companion (presumably Burnet and his wife) in the rowboat, with a steamboat in the background and a schooner (presumably the *Flash*) on the right.[36] The bluff on the right appears to be the red clay bluffs of Morgan's Point, which is just north of the "Red Bluff" which juts into the bay between present-day La Porte and Seabrook, Texas.

The story of the money of the Republic of Texas might have abruptly ended at this moment if Burnet had been shot or captured or the schooner *Flash* intercepted or run aground. After yet another harrowing escape, the parties successfully navigated the great bay and arrived at Galveston to set up their camp without further incident. Following a brief reprise at New Washington, the Mexican army looted Col. Morgan's warehouse of provisions and supplies. Santa Anna also added one of Morgan's servants, a mulatto girl named Emily West, to his entourage. With his female prize in tow, Santa Anna then turned his army northwest in an attempt to secure the ferry boat operation at Lynch's crossing, where Buffalo Bayou flows into the San Jacinto River.

HOUSTON ARRIVES AT SAN JACINTO

In the meantime, Sam Houston's Army crossed the Brazos River on April 13, 1836. The soldiers marched towards Harrisburg and reached the town on April 18 only to find the town burned. That same day, a scouting party led by Erastus "Deaf" Smith captured three Mexican soldiers, including a guide and a courier.[37] These prisoners and their dispatches revealed the location, size, and plans of the Mexican Army. They discovered that Santa Anna had personally marched a column of approximately 750 men, roughly the size of their own army, through Harrisburg and would soon approach Lynch's ferry.[38] With the captured intelligence, Houston's Army was able to intercept Santa Anna's forces on the plains of San Jacinto adjacent to Lynch's ferry on April 20. On the following day, Deaf Smith was sent by Houston to destroy the bridge over Vince's Bayou in order to cut off the Mexican's retreat and the path for additional reinforcements. Deaf Smith later rejoined his unit to fight in the battle of San Jacinto as Houston's Army confronted and defeated the Mexican Army led by Antonio López de Santa Anna on April 21, 1836.

Fig 5.14, The Battle of San Jacinto.

Courtesy of Albert and Ethel Herzstein Library, San Jacinto Museum of History, Houston, Texas.

Fig 5.15, The Capture of Gen. Santa Anna.

Texas Money Collection, Courtesy of Special Collections, University of Houston Libraries, Houston, Texas.

In the confusion of the battle, Santa Anna escaped on horseback but was captured the following day by Texian troops as he hid in a thick scrub of brush and tall grass on the banks of Buffalo Bayou near Vince's Bayou. The once-feared Mexican dictator was cornered by Sgt. James A. Sylvestor of the Texas Army. Sylvestor had joined a scouting party of volunteers led by Col. Ed Burleson in search of generals Santa Anna and Cos, who were believed to be fleeing in the direction of the Brazos River.

When the fleeing dictator was taken into custody his identity was unknown to his captors. Once returned to the battlefield, the other Mexican prisoners revealed his true identity. The dictator was brought before the wounded General Houston, who lay resting beneath the shade of a mighty oak tree. Sam Houston, at first polite, accosted Santa Anna for the massacres of the men at the Alamo and at Goliad. Santa Anna became visibly shaken and to calm his nerves, Houston offered him an opiate.[39] Houston had been chewing the opium to relieve the excruciating pain from the musket ball which had shattered his left leg.[40] Santa Anna accepted his offer and shortly thereafter an armistice, effectively a ceasefire and an agreement for Santa Anna to withdraw his armies from Texas, was signed between the Mexican President and Gen. Sam Houston. The fate of the Republic of Texas had finally been decided, first on the battlefield, and then by two men sitting under a tree, both of whom were stoned on opium as they reached an agreement to end the immediate hostilities. With the greatest battle of the revolution behind them, Santa Anna was now a prisoner of war who had signed an agreement to withdraw his armies in exchange for his life. Learning that there were still two other Mexican armies in Texas, Houston again solicited the aid of Deaf Smith, who he ordered to ride to the southwest and deliver orders from the captured Santa Anna to his second in command, Gen. Vincente Filisola. These orders instructed Filisola to retreat with his armies to Béxar and Victoria while negotiations were under way to bring and end to the war.[41]

Fig 5.16, The Surrender of Santa Anna.

Courtesy of Albert and Ethel Herzstein Library, The San Jacinto Museum of History, Houston, Texas.

BURNET ARRIVES AT GALVESTON

Arriving on the cigar shaped island of Galveston on or about April 22, Burnet took his family and staff and began the arduous task of relocating the government to the only available building—the old Mexican customs house on the harbor.[42] Mexico had previously designated Galveston as a port of entry in 1825 and established a customs house there in 1830. It was here that the members of Burnet's cabinet and their families slept on a sand floor under borrowed blankets in the most primitive of conditions. The new seat of government was not much more than a makeshift shelter comprised primarily of large pieces of driftwood. Some of these were whole logs that had been cut to length, formed and fastened together for stability.[43] The small wooden building was sparsely furnished with two pallets, three boxes, and a barrel turned upside down to serve as a dining table. Many soon suffered from an outbreak of fever, and one of the pallets served as the sick bed for Burnet's ten-month-old son Jacob, the youngest of the party of refugees. The cooking facilities consisted largely of a hole in the ground lined with oyster shells.

The government positioned the three available warships in the area to repel an invasion, which they expected any day. Burnet had fully expected the enemy to soon occupy Galveston Bay and the island.[44] Although three Texas warships were in the harbor, they were armed and ready for action. The only available food had been looted from a Mexican brig by the crew of the schooner *Invincible*, which guarded the approach from the west bay. The Texas warship *Brutus* was anchored off the approach on the east. The *Independence*, waiting off the channel, protected the last point of retreat. The ships waited for an invasion that would never come. Unknown to the refugee government on the island, the war had already been won on April 21 at the battle of San Jacinto.

The news of the victory at San Jacinto took five days to reach Galveston. A small boat departed from the San Jacinto area with news of the victory, but got lost in the great expanse of the bay.[45] On April 23, 1836, Secretary of War Thomas J. Rusk directed captains Robert J. Calder and Benjamin C. Franklin to proceed to Galveston and inform President Burnet and his cabinet of the victory at San Jacinto.[46] The men followed the curve of the shoreline and stopped periodically to rest and prepare meals instead of coming straight down the length of the bay. They first came upon the warship *Invincible* at anchor in the harbor. After boarding the men enjoyed a rest and a meal on the ship. A frenzy of excitement and celebration swept through the wooden vessel as details of the battle arrived along with the news that Santa Anna himself had been captured and taken prisoner on the day following the battle.[47] When the crew fired a cannon in salute, the government on shore was stunned by the outbreak of gunfire, at first thinking the shot was a warning.

When Calder and Franklin came ashore with the ship's captain, President Burnet was initially incensed that he was not informed first. The messengers received a brief scolding from the president, who made it clear that good or bad news should come to the government first. As the temporary rift over the breach in protocol subsided, it was replaced by a wave of joy, as the cabinet members, women and children danced on the beach in celebration of the victory and the capture of Santa Anna. But the celebration was met with mixed emotions, as there were nine reported casualties among the Texas ranks. Many more had been wounded, including Gen. Sam Houston. The military struggle, at least for the time being was over, and the government could temporarily relax from the stress of the conflict as they made preparations to visit the scene of the battle.

Fig 5.17, Galveston Bay, "Receipt for shovels and spades," April 1836.

Private Collection, Cr. Unlisted, 0-85.

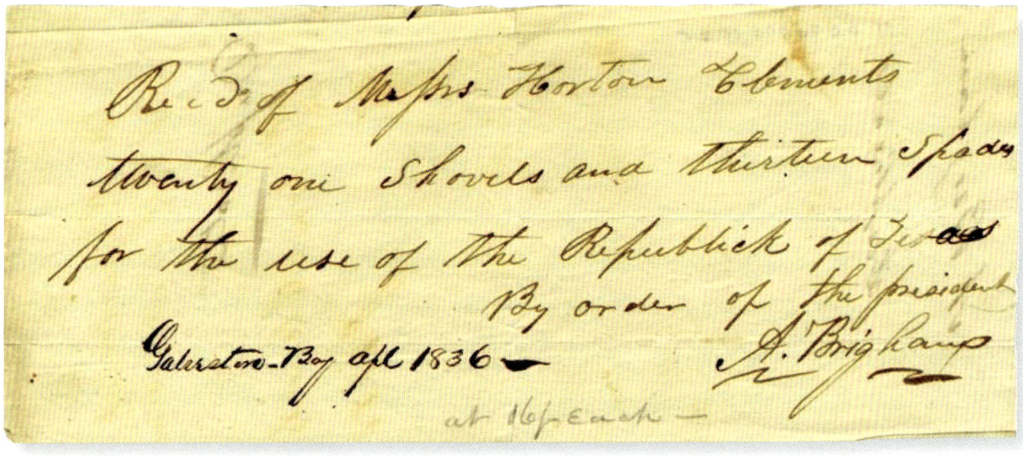
Rec'd of Messrs Horton & Clements
twenty one Shovels and thirteen Spades
for the use of the Republick of Texas
By order of the president
Galveston Bay apl 1836 — A. Brigham
at 16/- Each —

Rec[ieve]d of Mssrs Horton (&) Clements [a mercantile firm headquartered in Matagorda] twenty one shovels and thirteen spades for use of the Republick [sic] of Texas. By order of the president. Galveston Bay Ap[ri]l 1836 – (Signed) A. Brigham

The issue in Figure 5.17 is a receipt for "twenty one shovels and thirteen spades for the use of the Republic of Texas, by order of the President." The receipt was signed by Asa Brigham, the Auditor who accompanied Burnet and the cabinet on the steamboat *Cayuga*. It places the government at Galveston in April 1836. This receipt is a duplicate of a receipt bearing the same language dated April 26, 1836, in the Texas State Archives. This date pinpoints the borrowing of the shovels and spades after the *ad interim* President received the news of the battle of San Jacinto, and before Burnet and the others were transported aboard the steamer *Yellowstone* back up to the battlefield where Buffalo Bayou intersects the San Jacinto River.

This was a heartbreaking moment for Asa Brigham as he issued the receipt for shovels and spades which presumably had been borrowed to bury the Texian dead at San Jacinto. Among those who made the trip to Galveston to inform President Burnet of the battle was Robert James Calder, captain of the Company K, Texas Volunteers.[48] Brigham's son, Benjamin Rice Brigham, served in Calder's company and was among the nine Texians killed at San Jacinto.[49] Brigham undoubtedly received the news from Calder while in Galveston, and used his official post as a high-ranking official in the government to insure that his son and the other dead Texian soldiers at San Jacinto received a proper burial.

BURNET INSPECTS THE BATTLEFIELD

Boarding the steamboat *Yellowstone* at Galveston, Burnet and his entourage took the trip up Galveston Bay to tour the battlefield at San Jacinto. By the time they arrived, the dead Texian soldiers had already been buried. This indicates that none of the borrowed shovels and spades were used, at least not at San Jacinto since no effort was made bury the Mexicans. The Texians summarily stripped their dead counterparts of weapons, watches, money and anything else of value by day, and they were stripped of their flesh by vultures and wolves at night.[50] The dead Mexican soldiers lay rotting in the sun, and no effort was made to remove, burn or bury them. After the battle, the victorious Texian soldiers thought of nothing but reveling in the celebration of victory. Concerned about the lack of discipline among his troops following the battle, the wounded Sam Houston was said to have remarked that "a hundred steady men could wipe us out."[51]

THE SILVER SPOILS OF SAN JACINTO

Thomas J. Rusk fought alongside the other soldiers in the battle and presided over the division of the spoils following the conflict. Among the prizes captured on the battlefield were $12,000 in Mexican silver *pesos*. Some $9,000 was distributed to the soldiers on the battlefield as a bonus, and $3,000 was set aside for the fledgling Texas Navy.[52] Sam Houston, at his own insistence, received none of the cash. The unflappable Rusk, who was trusted by Houston and well liked by the men, reorganized the troops and distributed the captured money and supplies to the appropriate areas.

Much has been written about the silver spoils recovered on the field at the battle of San Jacinto, but the descriptions of the type of money recovered have not been documented until now. Some historians referred to them as silver *pesos* and others as silver dollars, as both of these descriptions had been engrained into the society of the day for the large silver 8 *reales* pieces which were seized after the battle. The coins shown below were recovered in 2004 on the site of the Mexican encampment during an archeological dig at the old battlefield of San Jacinto.

Fig 5.18, 8 Reales, Zacatecas Mint, Found on the battlefield at San Jacinto, 1834.

Courtesy of Moore Archeological Consulting, Inc., and Texas Parks and Wildlife Department.

The coin in Figure 5.18, dated 1834, is from the Mexican mint at Zacatecas and is representative of the large hoard of "silver dollars" taken after the battle of San Jacinto and distributed by Secretary Rusk to the troops, a portion of which was set aside for the government. The absence of wear, the date and the pristine condition in which this coin was found indicates that it was part of the national treasury that Santa Anna seized from the Zacatecas mint in May 1835. He brought some of the money with him to Texas, presumably for the payment of his troops. This is the same type of coin that Santa Anna distributed to each of the widows of the Alamo after their post-battle interview.

Fig 5.19, ½ Real, Charles IIII, Mexico City, 1808, Found on the battlefield at San Jacinto. (1 ¼ x actual size).

Courtesy of Moore Archeological Consulting, Inc., and Texas Parks and Wildlife Department.

By contrast to the larger 8 *reales* piece, the smaller denomination ½ *real* silver coin in Figure 5.19 shows considerable wear. It confirms that many Spanish coins circulated for decades in the Mexican and Texas economies. The portrait of Charles IIII indicates this coin was struck in the first few months of 1808 in Mexico City, shortly before Napoleon Bonaparte invaded Spain and installed his brother Joseph on the throne. It was the installation of Joseph Bonaparte that sparked the Mexican War for Independence. Ironically, this piece was lost on the battlefield in 1836, ending its circulating life twenty-eight years later when the Texian troops defeated the army of the "Napoleon of the West." Santa Anna had met his own Waterloo in Texas on the banks of the San Jacinto River.

TRIPLETT AGAIN MEETS BURNET ON THE BATTLEFIELD

Robert Triplett was near Natchez, Louisiana, when he heard the news about Houston's victory at San Jacinto.[53] Triplett traveled to the scene of the battle and arrived in time to greet his old friend Sam Houston. Triplett described the scene: "General Houston was an old acquaintance, and I met him with a great deal of pleasure. He was flat on his back from a wound he received. I went out on the battlefield to see the scene of the fight. The Mexicans who were killed lay still unburied, about six hundred in number. No buzzards were about, and not much smell, which I thought strange. But this climate is not so putrefying as ours."

Triplett was introduced to Santa Anna and Colonel Almonte, both of whom were prisoners. Triplett recalled the meeting in his autobiography: "Santa Anna is a small man—would probably weigh one hundred and forty pounds; of pale complexion; self possessed, and, I would judge, not wanting in courage. Colonel Almonte is a well educated, well bred gentleman, but seems to be half Indian. The battle cry at San Jacinto was '[R]emember the Alamo! Remember Labordee [LaBahía]!'" He continued, "the poor Mexicans, as they were about to be cut down, would raise their hands, and cry out, 'Me no Alamo!'"

By this time, the *ad interim* government had arrived at the battlefield and surveyed the victory. After touring the corpse strewn plains of San Jacinto, President Burnet called Triplett aside and expressed his misgivings about the land scrip which had been issued to him for the two sections of land on Galveston Island. After making his own observations, Triplett recalled the conversation:

> *I was now prepared to proceed to New Orleans, and the President came to me to say that great excitement had been created in consequence of his having issued to me the grant for a section of land on Galveston Island, and he wished to see me if it could not on some terms be annulled. I replied that I had assigned half of it to Dr. Neblett, who had gone to the United States. The President seemed uneasy, and said he only wanted to suspend it temporarily, until things became more calm and settled, and that he would then reissue it. This I thought a timid dodging of responsibility; but as he very earnestly urged it, I gave him my obligation to suspend the grant for the present, upon condition that it should be reissued hereafter without injury to my rights. This the President used to allay excitement for the time being, and a sale was afterwards made, by the Government of Texas, of a league of land covering the very ground which had been sold to me. This was to me very extraordinary; because it was evident the government had no right to sell it.*[54]

David G. Burnet, having dealt with Triplett, at first refused to remove the wounded Houston from the battlefield as he sensed a growing political rival in the popular military leader. Burnet even denied the revered commander steamboat passage for medical care. But the President was soon overruled by the captain on board the *Yellowstone*, who refused to leave without the severely wounded general.[55] Burnet finally acquiesced and the President and the cabinet boarded the steamboat and headed back to Galveston with the wounded Sam Houston, the captured Santa Anna, and three of his top officers under heavy guard. Robert Triplett returned to New Orleans as a General Agent for Texas and proceeded to deposit the land scrip in the hands of the investors who had already paid-in part of their funds.

Fig 5.20, The Steamboat *Yellowstone*.

Courtesy of Albert and Ethel Herzstein Library, The San Jacinto Museum of History, Houston, Texas.

Once they arrived on the island, Houston addressed the troops, and Burnet made arrangements to pack up and move the *ad interim* government again. Had it not been for the *Liberty*, the first ship ever commissioned in the Texas Navy, Sam Houston may have died after the battle of San Jacinto. The *Liberty*, a 60-ton schooner, convoyed with the *Flora* to carry the wounded Sam Houston to the city of New Orleans, where he arrived on May 22, more than thirty days after the pivotal battle which forever changed the map of North America.

In New Orleans, Houston recovered from his wounds at the opulent home of William Christy, and was attended by several physicians.[56] Christy was one of the New Orleans financiers which had arranged the Texian loans and drafted the documents earlier that year. Houston had Thomas Rusk send Christy the ornate saddle of General Cos which had been taken in the battle as a token of the general's gratitude. While in New Orleans, the recovering general accepted a $2,000 advance fee from a local land company managed by John K. and Augustus C. Allen to act as its representative in Texas, which included the rights for a new city to be named in his honor. While in New Orleans, the *Flora* put in for repairs, but with the Republic unable to pay the bills, the ship was sold in July of that year to cover the claims. In New York, commissioners Austin, Archer and Wharton still sought to raise additional money for the cause. They successfully placed another $100,000 Texian loan with New York financier Samuel Swartwout at the agreed upon terms of 10 percent down and the remaining 90 percent to be funded upon the ratification of the loan contract by the government.[57]

President Burnet departed Galveston by boat in early May with his entourage—Santa Anna and the other captured officers. They traveled a short distance by boat down the sandy, beach-lined Texas coast to the port of Velasco where they established a temporary capital and begin the process of rebuilding the Republic of Texas.

1 "Old Harrisburg," Texas Historical Marker #10680, Houston, Texas, erected 1965.

2 Ibid.

3 Dorothy Louise Fields, "David Gouverneur Burnet," *SHQ*, vol. 49 (October 1945), 2:215-32.

4 William F. Gray, *Diary of Col. Wm. Fairfax Gray: from Virginia to Texas, 1835-1836* (Houston: Gray, Dillaye & Co Printers, 1909; rpt. 1965), 149-50.

5 Robert Triplett, *Roland Trevor: or, The Pilot of Human Life, being an Autobiography of the Author, Showing how to make and lose a fortune, and then how to make another* (Philadelphia: Lippincott, Grambo, and Co., 1853), 342-44.

6 "President Burnet's address to Congress," October 4, 1836, Journals of the House of Representatives of the Republic of Texas, 1st Cong., 1st sess. (Columbia: G & T.H. Borden, Public Printers, 1836), 13-14.

7 Darrel Brown, Analysis of the compromise agreement relating to the first Texian Loans, non-published, 2004.

8 Darrel Brown. Analysis of the compromise agreement relating to the first Texian Loans. Non-published, 2004.

9 Ibid.

10 Gray, *Diary*, 150-63.

11 Fields, "David Gouverneur Burnet," 2:215-32.

12 Gray's description of the Runaway Scrape. Gray, *Diary*, 152.

13 William M. Gouge, *The Fiscal History of Texas* (New York: Burt Franklin, 1852; rpt. 1969), 273. Although Burnet later recalled the funding of the $50,000 loan at Harrisburg by Robert Triplett in a speech before the First Congress at Columbia, the accounting by William Gouge of the actual proceeds which was advanced is deemed to be a more accurate accounting by many historians.

14 The importance of these loans cannot be underestimated as they became the lifeblood of the new government, although they were only partially funded. The eventual proceeds from these Texian Loans (about $65,890), in addition to $25,000 of cash donations by Americans and the $12,000-hoard of Mexican silver pesos captured at the battle of San Jacinto were the only hard currency available to the Republic during its first two years.

15 "President Burnet's address to Congress," Journals of the House of Representatives, 13.

16 Triplett, *Roland Trevor*, 344-45.

17 Ibid., 342.

18 Wallace L. McKeehan, "Colonel James W. Fannin's Execution at Goliad," found online at www.tamu.edu/ccbn/dewitt/goliadspohn.htm .

19 A description of the execution of Colonel James W. Fannin's last moments at Goliad was given by Joseph H. Spohn, one of the Texian survivors. Spohn had been spared execution by the intercession of the Mexican officers for his cooperation as an interpreter. His account of the execution was later published by newspapers in New York and Philadelphia in August 1836.

20 McKeehan, "Colonel James W. Fannin's Execution."

21 Gray, *Diary*, 152-56.

22 The area surrounding old Harrisburg includes the bayou, a reasonably navigable stretch of water averaging twelve to fifteen feet deep with obstructions and sandbars. This section of the bayou was an inlet that ran behind the home of Jane Harris and to the right of the present-day Cypress Street Bridge which crosses onto Brady Island. The inlet empties into the deeper stretch of the main bayou just downstream of the turning basin, which has since been dredged and is now known as the Houston Ship Channel.

23 Triplett, *Roland Trevor*, 345

24 Jean L. Epperson, "*Cayuga*," in the new handbook of Texas, Vol. 1, page 1051.

25 Triplett, *Roland Trevor*, 345.

26 Gray, *Diary*, 160.

27 "Texas Capture of Mexican Dispatches (San Jacinto)," Texas Historical Marker #10791, Bellaire, Texas, erected 1989.

28 W. Thomas Taylor, *Texfake: An Account of the Theft and Forgery of Texas Documents* (Austin: W. Thomas Taylor, 1991), 16.

29 Ibid.

30 Frank J. Tolbert, *The Day of San Jacinto* (New York: The Pemberton Press, Jenkins Publishing Company, 1959), 70-71.

31 *Handbook of Texas Online*, s.v. "Juan Neopmuceno Almonte," http://www.tsha.utexas.edu/handbook/online/articles/AA/fal45.html (accessed November 22, 2006).

32 Steve Goodson, "Retreat to Victory: The Battle of San Jacinto," found online at www.texfiles.com/ERAmar02/sanjacinto.htm (accessed September 30, 2008).

33 Robert Triplett, *Roland Trevor: or, The Pilot of Human Life, being an Autobiography of the Author, Showing how to make and lose a fortune, and then how to make another.* Philadelphia, Lippincott, Grambo, and Co. 1853. Page 345.

34 Gray, *Diary*, 162.

35 Goodson, "Retreat to Victory."

36 It is important to note that the portrait of the steamboat *Cayuga* may not be accurately portrayed in the vignette. The escape was engraved into a steel printing plate by a designer at the firm of Draper, Toppan, Longacre & Company in their New York or Philadelphia offices. The engraver never saw the vessels and therefore took "artistic license" for the depictions of the characters in the incident as they were described to him.

37 "Texan Capture of Mexican Dispatches (San Jacinto)," Texas Historical Marker #10791.

38 John Hoyt Williams, *Sam Houston: The Life and Times of the Liberator of Texas, an Authentic American Hero* (New York: Simon & Schuster, Inc., 1993), 148-49.

39 Marquis James, *The Raven: A Biography of Sam Houston* (Austin: University of Texas Press, 1929), 255.

40 Although this painting of the scene and another both depict Houston with a bandaged right ankle, there were personal letters among his papers in which he described the pain in his left leg from the old would which had been received at San Jacinto. Interview with Madge Thornall Roberts, President General and Historian of the Daughters of the Republic of Texas.

41 Gregory J. Dimmick, *Sea of Mud: The Retreat of the Mexican Army after San Jacinto, An Archeological Investigation* (Austin: Texas State Historical Association, 2004), 153.

42 Gary Cartwright, *Galveston: A History of The Island* (New York: MacMillan Publishing Company, 1991), 66-69.

43 Julia Beazley, "Letters and Documents: David G. Burnet," *SHQ*, vol. 44 (October 1940), 2:245-48.

44 Burnet to Colonel James Morgan, Galveston, April 14, 1836, David G. Burnet Letters, Rice University. The letters were reprinted by the *LaGrange Journal* on July 9, 1936.

45 Cartwright, *Galveston*, 67.

46 *Handbook of Texas Online*, s.v. "Benjamin Cromwell Franklin," http://www.tsha.utexas.edu/handbook/online/articles/FF/ffr2.html (accessed June 3, 2007).

47 Santa Anna had been captured by James Sylvester, a soldier on patrol looking for participants in the battle that had escaped in the confusion. Santa Anna was apprehended on the banks of Buffalo Bayou near the present-day Washburn Tunnel, in the author's hometown of Pasadena.

48 *Handbook of Texas Online*, s.v. "Robert James Calder," http://www.tsha.utexas.edu/handbook/online/articles/CC/fca9.html (accessed October 14, 2006).

49 Index to Military Rolls of the Republic of Texas, R.J. Calder, Company K, 1st Reg. Texan Volunteers, San Jacinto List, Col. Edward Burleson Command (Apr 21, 1836), found on-line at http://www.tshaonline.org/supsites/military/rep_cont.htm.

50 Noah Smithwick, The Evolution of a State or Recollections of Old Texas Days, [Gammel] Book Company, Austin, 1900.

51 Williams, *Sam Houston*, 156.

52 Ibid., 160.

53 Triplett, *Roland Trevor*, 350.

54 Ibid., 351-52.

55 Marquis James, *The Raven: A Biography of Sam Houston* (Austin: University of Texas Press, 1929), 256-58.

56 Williams, *Sam Houston*, 162-63.

57 The Papers of the Texas Revolution, 9:83-84.

CHAPTER SIX

VELASCO AND COLUMBIA: CAPITALS ON THE GULF COAST

Moving approximately forty miles down the Gulf Coast to what is the present-day beachfront community of Surfside Beach, Texas, the new Texas government re-established itself in nearby Velasco in May 1836. First settled in 1821 as the port of entry for Austin's incoming colonists, the community was the scene of the battle of Velasco in 1832 and is often called the "Boston Harbor of the Texas Revolution."[1]

The town was named for a Mexican general, as was nearby Quintana on the opposite side of the Brazos River. Velasco had approximately one dozen houses at the mouth of the river on the east side.[2] Quintana, on the west side of the river, consisted of only four houses and a small store. Fort Velasco was a circular structure built almost entirely out of piled-up wood and sand. The fort lay a few hundred yards inland and was originally built to protect the entrance to the Brazos River. Just inside the fort were three wooden buildings which served as the official place of government, including the Treasury Department. Within these walls, the Government of Texas began to issue the first hand-written and printed obligations of a free and independent Republic of Texas. Inside these same walls, George Jacob Burnet, the President's infant son, died from exposure and the fever that had wracked many of the others during their harrowing ordeal.

Fig 6.1, A Sketch of Fort Velasco on the Texas Gulf Coast. The seat of government resided here from May - October 1836.
Courtesy of Brazoria County Historical Commission, Angleton, Texas.

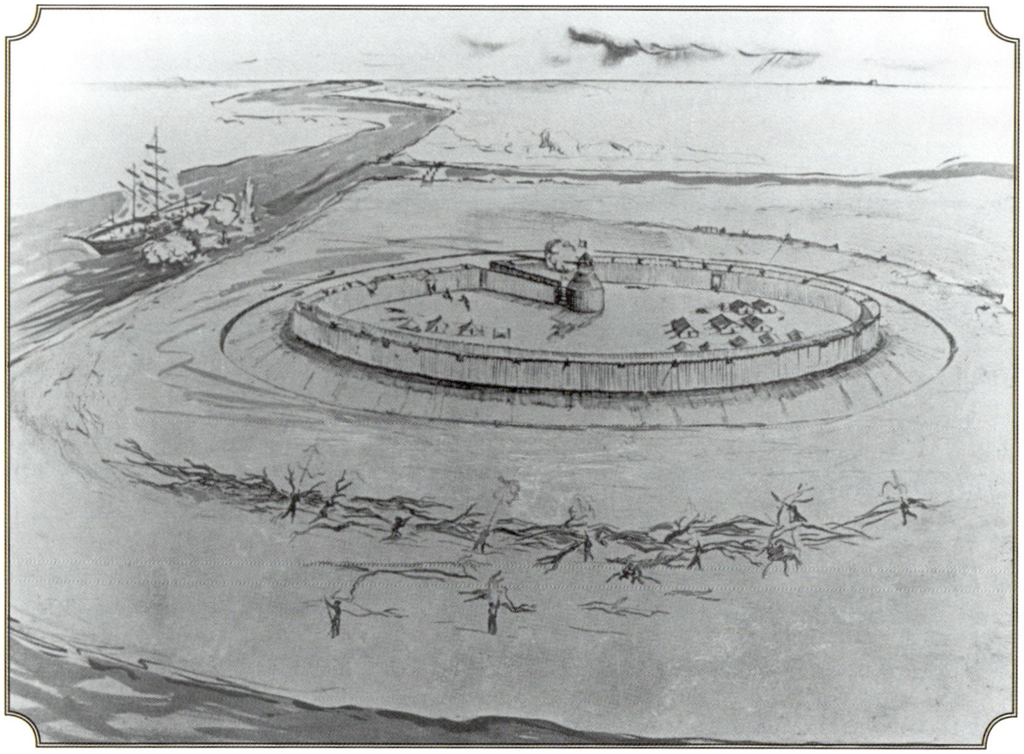

The town of Velasco is best known for the Treaty of Velasco, which was signed on May 14, 1836. The treaty stipulated the terms of Mexico's recognition of the Republic of Texas. Collectively known as the Treaty of Velasco, there were actually two treaties, one public and one secret.[3] These treaties were executed at Velasco between the Texas government and Antonio López de Santa Anna, who signed on behalf of Mexico. It was a longstanding rule of war that a government could not be bound by a treaty made by a head of state while held as a prisoner. Sam Houston, David G. Burnet, and especially Santa Anna were acutely aware of the ramifications of this protocol of nations at war.

The public Treaty of Velasco ceased hostilities and stipulated that Santa Anna would order his forces to withdraw below the Rio Grande River and not take up arms again against Texas. In addition, Santa Anna pledged to restore the property that had been confiscated or destroyed by the Mexicans.[4] Both sides promised to exchange prisoners on an equal basis. This public treaty was signed, and copies were sent to the commanders of the two large Mexican armies still in Texas at the time. There was also a secret treaty drawn up and signed by both parties. According to the terms of the secret treaty, Texas was to transport Santa Anna to the Mexican coastal city of Vera Cruz. In return, Santa Anna agreed to seek ratification of the two treaties by the Mexican government and negotiate a permanent treaty that would acknowledge Texas' independence and recognize the Rio Grande River as Texas' southern boundary. At first Santa Anna balked at signing the secret treaty, alleging that his word of honor and good faith would be sufficient to carry out the agreed upon terms.[5] This act of insolence produced an uproar in the Texian cabinet and those members in favor of Santa Anna's immediate execution began to openly state their opinions. Sensing the inevitability of being summarily taken out and shot, the Mexican President conceded to their demands and affixed his signature to the document. Santa Anna had no intention of keeping his word, however, and was willing to sign virtually any piece of paper in exchange for his life. In turn, the *de facto* Mexican government refused to recognize any treaty signed by Santa Anna while he was a prisoner.

There was a widespread call for the captured Santa Anna to be put to death. The Burnet government quickly lost all credibility with the military by agreeing to release the man who had laid waste to the defenders of the Alamo and executed the Texian prisoners at Goliad. Burnet's cabinet members changed almost daily as he struggled to keep the government together, and his reputation as an incapable administrator grew worse with each passing week. To honor his portion of the treaty, Burnet ordered the man-of-war *Invincible* to set sail in the first days of June for the long trip across the gulf to the Mexican port of Vera Cruz.

Fig 6.3, The Texas Warship *Invincible*.
Detail from the painting "Loss of the Invincible" by Fred Tolar,
Courtesy of Albert and Ethel Herzstein Library, The San Jacinto Museum of History, Houston, Texas.

On June 4, 1836, Santa Anna, his secretary Ramón Martínez Caro, and Col. Juan N. Almonte boarded the *Invincible*. About this time, the steamship *Ocean* entered the port at Velasco with 250 volunteers from New Orleans, who had been recruited in the United States to assist in the fight for the liberation of Texas. Upon landing at the docks, the New Orleans Grays quickly learned that Santa Anna himself was on the ship docked next to the *Ocean*. The crew of the *Invincible* was preparing to spread its canvas to the wind and depart across the open waters in the Gulf of Mexico.

The new recruits, led by Thomas Jefferson Green of North Carolina, stormed the *Invincible* and found the Mexican President lying in a bed. When confronted, he began to beg for mercy from his captors. Santa Anna, sensing that he would be killed, took some opium, so much that it was determined that he might very well die on the ship.[6] Green had his pulse examined and determining his fitness, literally dragged *El Presidente* ashore in iron manacles. Santa Anna was howling and pleading for his life, with his fingers gripping at the rails of the ship, begging that he not be dragged back onto Texas soil.[7] Green continued to humiliate the captured dictator by placing a Texas flag in his hands and practically moving his arms for him while the ship's crew gave three cheers as he was forced to waive the Texas banner over his head. The unruly mob howled its approval as the Mexican President was torn from the ship, defying all the efforts of the *ad interim* President to stop the chaos. Some called for a public hanging of *El Presidente*, but their efforts were stymied by Green's insistence that they keep the distinguished captive alive as a political bargaining chip.

Green thought it safer to move the infamous captives across the river from Velasco to the small hamlet of Quintana. President Burnet then put Green in charge of the prisoners' safety. After another brief but harrowing stay at Velasco, the prisoners were transferred to nearby Columbia where a drunken man approached the building and randomly discharged a revolver into their temporary quarters through a window.[8] Cooler heads eventually prevailed, and Santa Anna and the others were taken by steamer almost thirty miles up the Brazos River to the farm of Dr. James A. Phelps. At the Phelps farm, known as Orozimbo Plantation, Santa Anna was kept under heavy guard during the summer and most of the fall of 1836.[9]

Fig 6.2, Gen. Thomas Jefferson Green.
Courtesy of James L. Glass.

Fig 6.4, The Phelps House on the "Orozimbo Plantation." Santa Anna's Jail in Brazoria
Courtesy of Brazoria County Historical Commission, Angleton, Texas.

Fig 6.5, The oak at Orozimbo Plantation.

Santa Anna was chained to this tree while a prisoner. Courtesy of Brazoria County Historical Museum, Angleton, Texas.

Located nine miles northwest of present-day Angleton in west central Brazoria County, the Orozimbo Plantation was reportedly named for an Indian Chief.[10] The plantation farm was originally acquired by Phelps (one of Austin's Old Three Hundred) in 1824. When Santa Anna's guards learned that a local Mexican boy near the plantation was plotting an escape for the Mexican general, the prisoner was placed in irons and chained to a large oak tree on the farm, said to still be standing on the original site.

Santa Anna grew despondent by the harsh conditions in his new role as the Texian's most famous prisoner. He was befriended by Dr. Phelps, who cared for his mental and physical health while under the watchful eye of his guards. During this time, Phelps once saved the Mexican president from a suicide attempt, as he experienced a severe bout of mental depression during his confinement. Santa Anna was eventually returned to Mexico after spending eight months as a prisoner of war. Some sources claim that for years after Santa Anna's release, he sent presents to the Phelps family at Christmas, which were unusually fine bedspreads. In 1842, Santa Anna saved Phelps's son Orlando, a Mier Expedition member, from execution and returned him to Texas with $500 in gold. As Santa Anna contemplated his fate during the sweltering Texas summer on the mosquito-ridden Phelps plantation, the Texas Government settled in on the beach at Velasco and once again began issuing drafts against the Treasury.

THE TREASURY AT VELASCO

Issued in the name of the Government of Texas, with the "provisional" moniker having been dropped, the issues from Velasco bear dates in the year of 1836 only. The early Velasco warrants were entirely handwritten pro-mises for future payment. There are over a dozen varieties of warrants, certificates and notes, designated by the type of paper that was used, both in the printed and the entirely handwritten form. The signatories included Asa Brigham (signed A. Brigham) as Auditor, Henry C. Hudson (signed H.C. Hudson) as Comptroller, and George Washington Poe (signed Geo.W. Poe), as "acting" Pay Master General. Poe signed many of the notes as acting paymaster before he was officially appointed to the position. David G. Burnet also signed some of these notes in his capacity as President.

The warrant in Figure 6.6, entirely handwritten, was one of the first to be issued at Velasco in June 1836. It is made payable to William P. Brown, possibly for the purchase of supplies. Like the earlier provisional pieces dated in January and February 1836, the now-familiar language appears, "out of any money in [the] Treasury not otherwise appropriated." It is dated and signed by Asa Brigham, the auditor, and counter-signed by H.C. Hudson, the comptroller. This variety is very rare in any condition.

Warrants are most commonly found issued to suppliers of arms, horses, supplies and for uses of various sundry goods by the government. Many of the Velasco issues represent the first payments for military service in the Texian Army during the revolution. The standard pay in the Texas Army for enlisted men was $8 per month (paid every three months) and $25 per month for an officer (paid every three or four months), as evidenced by these early Texas obligations.

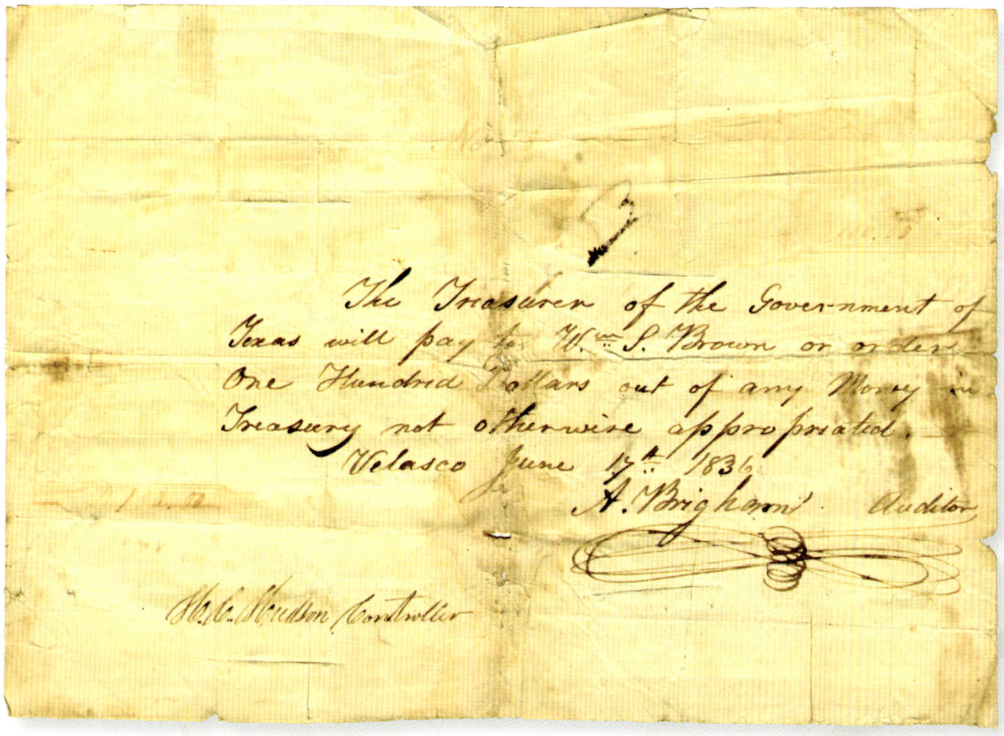

The Treasurer of the Government of
Texas will pay to Wm P. Brown or order
One Hundred Dollars out of any Money in
Treasury not otherwise appropriated.
Velasco June 17th 1836
A. Brigham Auditor
H.C. Hudson Controller

The Treasurer of the Government of Texas will pay to W[illia]m. P. Brown or order One Hundred Dollars out of any Money in Treasury not otherwise appropriated. Velasco, June 17th, 1836

(Signed, below) A. Brigham, Auditor, (Signed, at left) H.C. Hudson, Controller

Fig 6.6, Velasco, June 17, 1836, Treasury Warrant to William P. Brown.

Private Collection, Cr. V-1A, O-103.

No. 107 To The Secr[etar]y of the Treasury $1480.69

The Treasurer of the GOVERNMENT OF TEXAS will pay to Mssrs Howard & Fleming or order, Fourteen Hundred Eighty Dollars, 69 Cents, out of any money In the TREASURY not otherwise appropriated & In[tere]st. 8 pr. ct .pr Annum.

Dated at Velasco June 27th, 1836 (Signed) A. Brigham, Auditor, (Signed, at left) H.C. Hudson Comptroller (Signed, below) Approved David G. Burnet

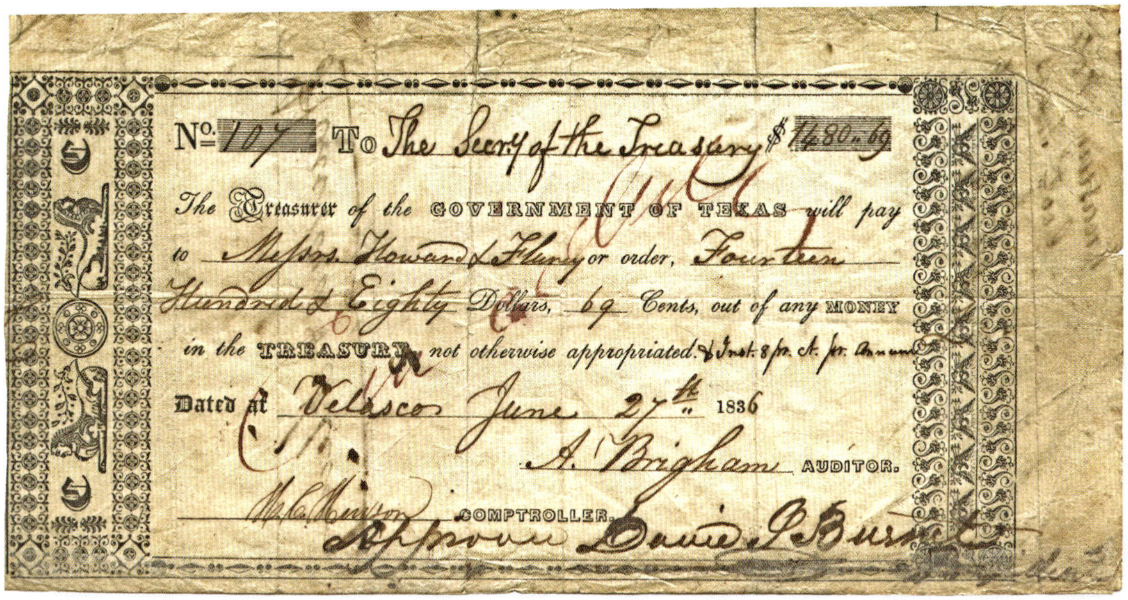

Fig 6.7, Velasco, June 27, 1836, "Sphinx Note," Countersigned by David G. Burnet.

Private Collection, Cr. V2, O-133.

Asa Brigham was perhaps the most prolific signer of these early Texas warrants, as well as a signer of the Texas Declaration of Independence. Brigham was born in Massachusetts around 1790 and arrived in Texas from Louisiana with his wife, Elizabeth, two sons, a daughter, and a son-in-law in 1830. Widowed two years later, he became a major landowner in Brazoria, Galveston and Bastrop counties and served as one of four representatives from Brazoria to the Convention of 1836 at Washington-on-the-Brazos.[11]

He was the first treasurer of the post-revolutionary Republic of Texas and held the position of auditor during the early years of the Republic. Brigham was appointed the first auditor by David G. Burnet, and was later named as treasurer in December 1836 by President Sam Houston. He was reappointed as treasurer by President Mirabeau B. Lamar in January 1839. Brigham married his second wife, Ann Johnson Mather, on July 8, 1839, and died on July 3, 1844, two years after his election as mayor of Austin. He was buried at Washington-on-the-Brazos, where a monument to him was erected by the State of Texas in 1936.

THE SPHINX NOTES OF VELASCO

In late June 1836, the first series of printed paper notes of the Republic arrived at Velasco. These warrants are often referred to as "Sphinx Notes" because of the depiction of the Egyptian Sphinx in the left margin. At the right margin, if turned ninety degrees counter-clockwise, there is a small row of eagles with a shield. The eagles are clutching arrows in their right talons (symbolizing strength) and an olive branch in their left (symbolizing peace). Although there is no indication on the notes as to the printer of origin, they are thought to be printed by Benjamin Levy in New Orleans. This is indicated by the previous use of the Sphinx vignette design on the Texian loan certificates which were printed by Levy earlier in the year.

The note in Figure 6.7, No. 107, for $1,480.69 was countersigned "Approved" by David G. Burnet most likely because of the agreement to pay interest at 8 percent per annum was added as a notation by hand. The irregular margins indicate that although the notes were printed on official paper, the early treasury wasn't particularly concerned about appearance (even though this note was to be countersigned by the President). The word "Cancelled" is written diagonally across the face in red, indicating that the note was eventually paid.

The note in Figure 6.8 is another example of a Sphinx note in the amount of $45.00 and in remarkably clean condition. Again, it is signed by the auditor (Brigham) and by the comptroller (Hudson). While this note is the most frequently seen type from Velasco, the Sphinx notes are difficult to find in nice condition because most have faded over time or have been obscured by heavy pen cancellations. In this case, the cancellation was writ ten through the comptroller's signature.

The payment in Figure 6.9 to Augustus V. Sharpe at Velasco in the summer of 1836 would not have occurred except for Sharpe's harrowing escape from the massacre at Goliad. Sharpe was born on August 10, 1810, in New York and had previously lived in the city of Troy, New York, before coming to Texas.[12] He arrived in Texas

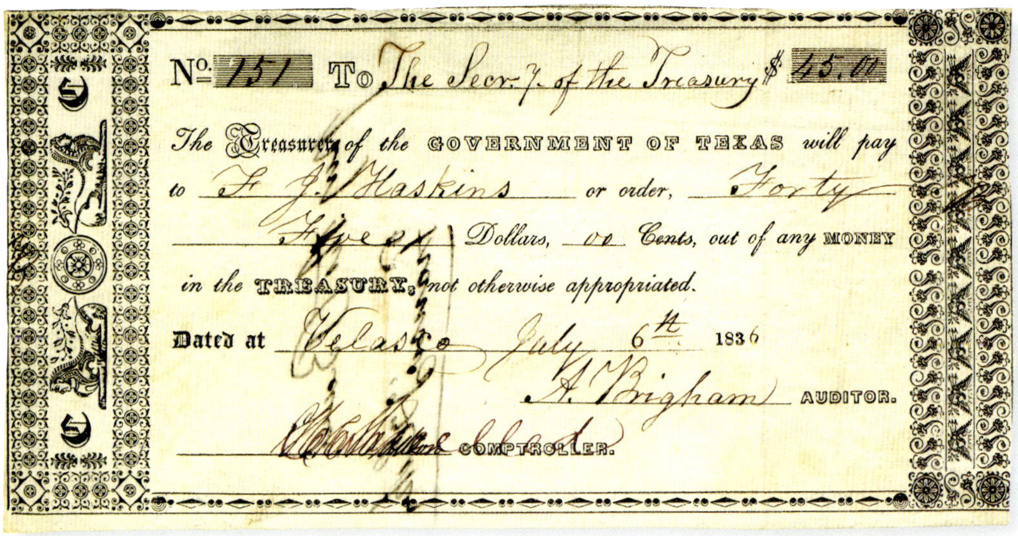

No.151 To The Secr[etar]y of the Treasury $45.00

The Treasurer of the GOVERNMENT OF TEXAS will pay to F.J. Haskins or order, Forty Five Dollars, 00 Cents, out of any money In the TREASURY not otherwise appropriated.

Dated at Velasco July 6th, 1836

(Signed) A. Brigham, Auditor, (Signed, at left) H.C. Hudson Comptroller

Fig 6.8, Velasco, July 6, 1836, "Sphinx Note," Payable to F.J. Haskins.
Private Collection, Cr. V2, 0-130.

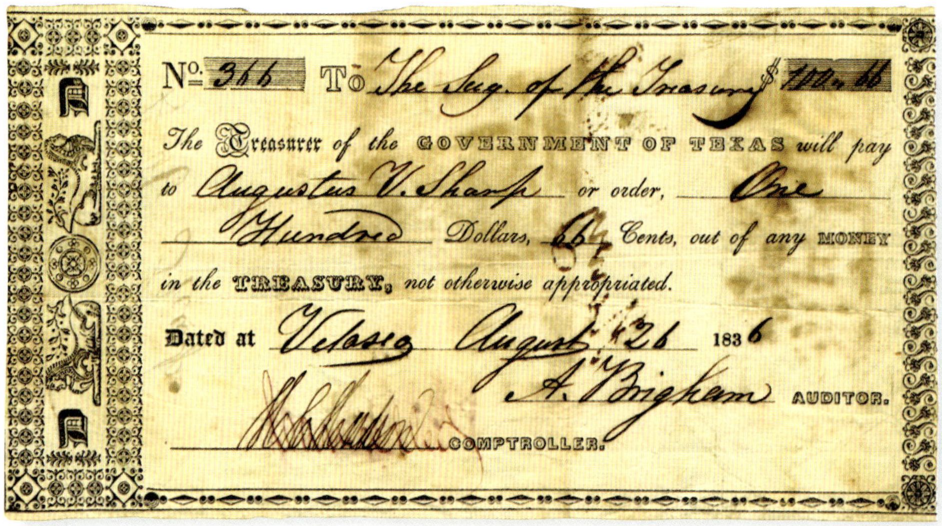

No. 366 To The Secr[etar]y of the Treasury $100.66

The Treasurer of the GOVERNMENT OF TEXAS will pay to Augustus V. Sharpe or order, One Hundred Dollars, 66 Cents, out of any money In the TREASURY not otherwise appropriated.

Dated at Velasco August 26, 1836

(Signed) A. Brigham, Auditor, (Signed, at left) H.C. Hudson Comptroller

Fig 6.9, Velasco, August 26, 1836, "Sphinx Note," Payable to Augustus V. Sharpe.
Private Collection, Cr. V2, 0-130.

on January 17, 1836, and was mustered into service in the Texas Army two days later.[13] Sharpe served in Capt. Isaac Ticknor's Company as a private and then under Capt. B.H. Duval who reported to Col. James W. Fannin, Jr., at La Bahía. Sharpe and his commanders were among the Texian soldiers taken prisoner when Fannin surrendered at Coleto Creek on March 20, 1836. On the morning of March 27, Sharpe and the other prisoners were marched out of the old fort to be executed. While 380 Texian soldiers were cut down by firing squads, Sharpe and twenty-seven others managed to escape. Some ran through the thicket and were shot in the back as they tried to escape. A handful of the soldiers feigned their deaths by lying still amid the heaps of dead bodies. They later rose under the cover of darkness and began their escape.[14]

The details of how Sharpe escaped are unknown, but he made his way to Galveston where he joined Capt. William Graham's Company on May 6, 1836. This Treasury warrant for $100.66 represented his pay for service from January 17 to August 19, 1836, when he was discharged from the army. Like other examples, it is marked "Cancelled" which indicates it was paid. Following the war, Sharpe resided in Harrison County and married a wealthy widow, Emily LeSeur Hayes, on February 8, 1852.[15] He died on March 31, 1868, and is buried in the Sharpe cemetery in Bell County, south of Killeen, Texas.[16]

Although Santa Anna relinquished Texas from Mexican rule by signing the Treaty of Velasco, the Mexican government refused to honor any treaty signed by the president during the time he was held as a prisoner and made plans to avenge his capture. Despite the defeat of Santa Anna's army, there were still two Mexican armies in Texas after San Jacinto. Although these armies had largely withdrawn, rumors began to swell that Mexico was mounting plans for another invasion of Texas with a force of 15,000 men.[17]

THE HORSE MARINES

On May 29, Gen. Thomas J. Rusk, anticipating that Mexican troops might land on the Texas coastline, ordered Maj. Issac W. Burton and twenty mounted rangers to patrol the Texas coast around Copano Bay, near the mouth of the San Antonio River. Several Refugio colonists who were with the Texas Army and familiar with the Matagorda Bay area were enlisted as guides for Burton and his men.[18]

After five days on patrol, the soldiers' worst fears were realized. The *Watchman*, a Mexican schooner, was spotted approaching from the southern coast. Burton and his men quickly formed a plan as the ship approached the area. Hiding most of his men and their horses behind the bushes near the shoreline, Burton had his *Tejano* rangers frantically hail the supply boat in Spanish, as if they were refugees from the Mexican Army. The *Watchman* hoisted American and then Texas colors, which were not answered. When the ship hoisted Mexican colors, the rangers answered as Mexican soldiers in distress. The schooner sent out a small rescue boat with five men to bring the stranded soldiers to "safety." As the boat approached the shore, Burton and his men overpowered the small crew and commandeered the boat. They then slipped sixteen heavily armed rangers in the boat, covered themselves with blankets, and headed back out to the *Watchman*. As the small boat approached the ship in the hazy morning light, the crew realized too late that they had been duped and opened fire at the returning boat with small arms and a cannon. Missing their mark and caught by surprise, the crew of the *Watchman* were overpowered by the rangers. The rangers seized control of the ship loaded with 520 barrels of food and provisions intended for Mexican General Filisola's Army, who, unknown to the Mexican sailors, had already begun his retreat from Texas.

The rangers attempted to sail the ship back to Velasco, but adverse winds prevented the craft from moving in a northeasterly path up the coast.[19] With the ship's crew as prisoners and Burton's men feasting on the captured supplies, the voyage was delayed for nearly two weeks because of the winds. On June 18, two other Mexican supply ships—the *Commanche* and the *Fanny Butler*—were spotted on the approach to Aransas Pass. Burton, local captain James D. Boylan, and six others devised a plan to capture these ships as well. With the crew of the *Watchman* held at gunpoint and the officers locked away in the brig, Burton and his men donned Mexican naval uniforms and ran the ensign up the mast giving the "all clear" signal to the approaching enemy ships. As the ships approached, Burton sent over two rangers dressed as Mexican officers and invited the captains on board for a drink. The two unsuspecting captains fell for the ruse and accepted the devious invitation. Not until they were on board did they realize they had been tricked. The Mexican captains were taken prisoner and their ships surrendered. The *Watchman* was taken to Galveston and the *Commanche* and *Fanny Butler* sailed to Velasco where a local admiralty court condemned them as "Prizes of War." The cargo was sold and a portion of the proceeds was distributed to the men.[20]

The note in Figure 6.10 may be the only surviving example of a payment of "Prize Money" under the letters of marque and reprisal granted by the General Council at San Felipe in 1835. It references a payment of $9,496.36 to Maj. Isaac W. Burton and his men for "the capture of the cargoes of the Schooners *Commanche* and *Fanny Butler*."[21] This payment is thought to be a manuscript copy of the original copied by a clerk in the government or by Lee himself, as indicated by the misspelling of Burnet's name.[22]

Col. Edward J. Wilson of Lexington, Kentucky, one of the original twenty mounted rangers, later said he supposed they would be called the "Horse Marines." No payment was recorded for the seizure of the *Watchman*, as it was an American flagged vessel and was not condemned as a prize of war. Although the cargo of the *Watchman* was seized and distributed to the brig *Pocket*, the admiralty court may have concluded that the rangers ate and drank more than their share of any prize money during the days they were anchored aboard the first captured vessel.[23]

On the reverse of the payment shown in Figure 6.11 to the "Horse Marines" is a calculation, indicating that it may have been Major Burton's copy, showing $2,848.90

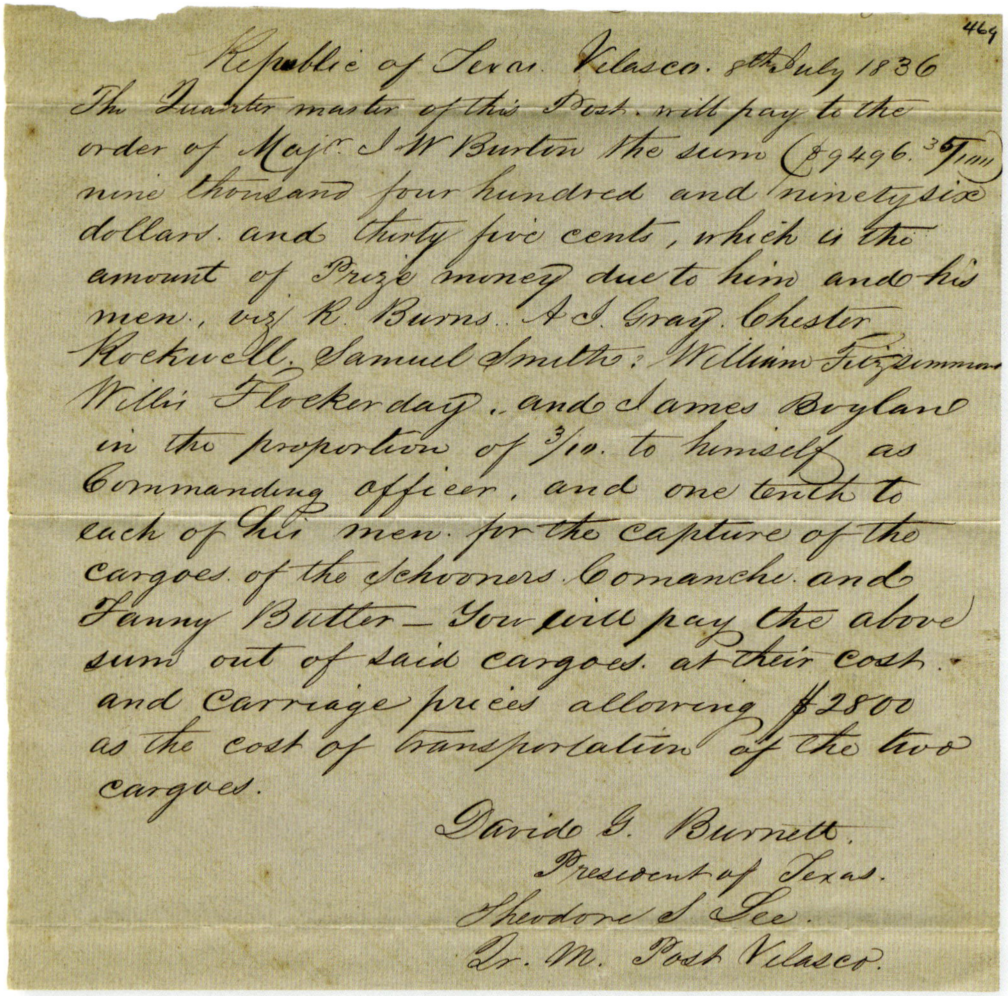
469
Republic of Texas. Velasco. 8th July 1836
The Quarter master of this Post. will pay to the order of Majr. I. W. Burton the sum ($9496.35/100) nine thousand four hundred and ninety six dollars and thirty five cents, which is the amount of Prize money due to him and his men., viz R. Burns. A. C. Gray. Chester Rockwell, Samuel Smith: William Fitzsimmons Willis Flockerday., and James Boyland in the proportion of 3/10. to himself as Commanding officer, and one tenth to each of his men. for the capture of the cargoes. of the Schooners Comanche. and Fanny Butler – You will pay the above sum out of said cargoes. at their cost. and Carriage prices allowing $2800 as the cost of transportation of the two cargoes.
David G. Burnett.
President of Texas.
Theodore S. Lee.
Qr. M. Post Velasco.

Fig 6.10, Velasco, July 8, 1836, Prize Money payment to the "Horse Marines."

Private Collection, Cr. Unlisted, O-185.

Republic of Texas. Velasco. 8th July 1836.

The Quarter master of this Post will pay to the order of Maj. I[ssac] W. Burton the sum ($9496.36/100) nine thousand four hundred and ninety six dollars and thirty five cents, which is the amount of Prize money due to him and his men, viz R. Burns. A.C. Gray. Chester Rockwell, Samuel Smith, William Fitzsimmons, Willis Flockerday and James Boyland in the proportion of 3/10 to himself as commanding officer, and one tenth to each of his men for the capture of the cargoes of the schooners Commanche *and* Fanny Butler. *- You will pay the above sum out of the said cargoes at their cost and carriage prices allowing $2800 as the cost of transportation of the two cargoes. (Signed) David G. Burnett [sic] President of Texas*

(Signed below) Theodore S. Lee, Q[uarte]r M[aster] Post Velasco.

Fig 6.11, The Horse Marines, Maj. Isaac Burton's 3/10 share.

Private Collection.

as his 3/10 share of the "Prize Money." Burton was later appointed as a commissioner to treat with the Indians and served in the Republic of Texas Senate from 1837 to 1840 and on Lamar's committee to select a site for a permanent capital. Burton practiced law in Nacogdoches for several years and died in the town of Crockett in 1843.[24]

Even as U.S. reinforcements arrived daily into Texas due to recruitment efforts from previous months, the landscape of the American southwest could have easily turned out differently. If the Mexican Army had halted its retreat near the town of Refugio (southwest of Victoria) and made successful contact with the three vessels loaded with hundreds of tons of food and provisions, then they may well have contemplated a second assault on Texas forces. As it turned out, General Filisola withdrew his troops below the Rio Grande and was deluged by a series of torrential rains and ran woefully short of reinforcements, food and supplies for his men. The bravery and quick thinking of the legendary "Horse Marines" only served to hasten the Mexican Army's undoing and strengthen the Texas cause.

Following the fiasco of his preparations to return Santa Anna to the port of Vera Cruz under the treaty of Velasco, Burnet became increasingly cautious about his own security. He was perhaps the most unappreciated man of the early Republic for he was neither a skilled politician nor a general, and had failed to earn the respect of his fellow Texians while at Velasco. When a plot was discovered to kidnap and depose him (in which Henry Millard was a conspirator), Burnet welcomed the protection of the Buckeye Rangers who hailed from Cincinnati, Ohio, several of whom served as his personal bodyguards.

The issue shown in Figure 6.12 is an instruction for the government to pay for boarding a member of the President's bodyguard detail (the "Buckeye Rangers") possibly because of an injury which may have left the soldier, Joseph Boyle, an invalid.[25] Most of the volunteer ranger company from Ohio remained in Texas and became citizens of the Republic.

VELASCO - MILITARY PAY CERTIFICATES

A payroll system was soon set up at Velasco to begin paying the war veterans and the active members of the Texas Army. The Consultation in San Felipe created the office of Paymaster General as early as November 13, 1835. The position was one of the five heads of the department under the command of the Texian Army.[26] George Washington Poe was named "Acting" Paymaster General in September 1836 while at Velasco and was charged with the responsibility of establishing a pay department for the Army based on the pay standards of the U.S. Army. There are five major varieties of military pay certificates issued from Velasco, both in handwritten and printed form. These pay certificates were officially known as certificates of military entitlement because they "entitled" the recipient to receive pay.

The entirely hand-written payment shown in Figure 6.13, No. 89, was assigned to two merchants by the payee, Thomas Beckley, a soldier who served for three months as a private in Captain Reeds Company of Texas Volunteers. The assignment of military benefits to others, sometimes at a deep discount, was a common practice by veterans of the war.

Captain Reed organized a volunteer company at San Augustine on June 4, 1836. The men served for three months in the Second Brigade commanded by Brig. Gen. Thomas J. Rusk.[27] Beckley would have served in that volunteer company from its inception, as evidenced by the warrant's description. The pay certificate in Figure 6.13 also depicts the standard private's pay of $8 per month and was signed by George Washington Poe as Acting Paymaster General.

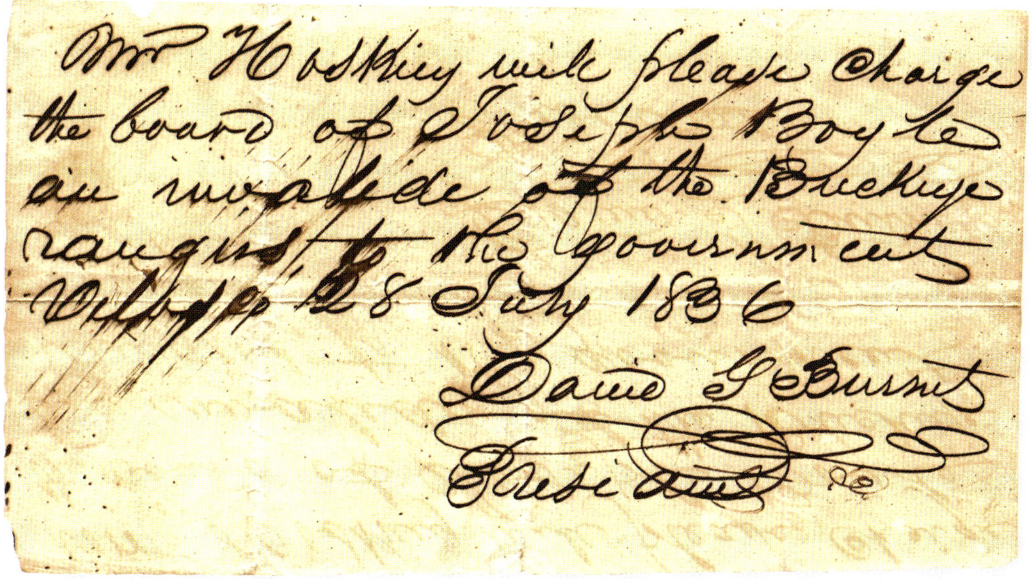

Fig 6.12, Velasco, July 28, 1836, Instruction for the board of a Buckeye Ranger, Signed by David G. Burnet, President.

Private Collection, Cr. Unlisted, O-160.

Mr Hoskiey [?] will please charge the board of Joseph Boyle an invalide [sic] of the Buckeye rangers to the government. Velasco 28 July 1836. (Signed) David G. Burnet, President

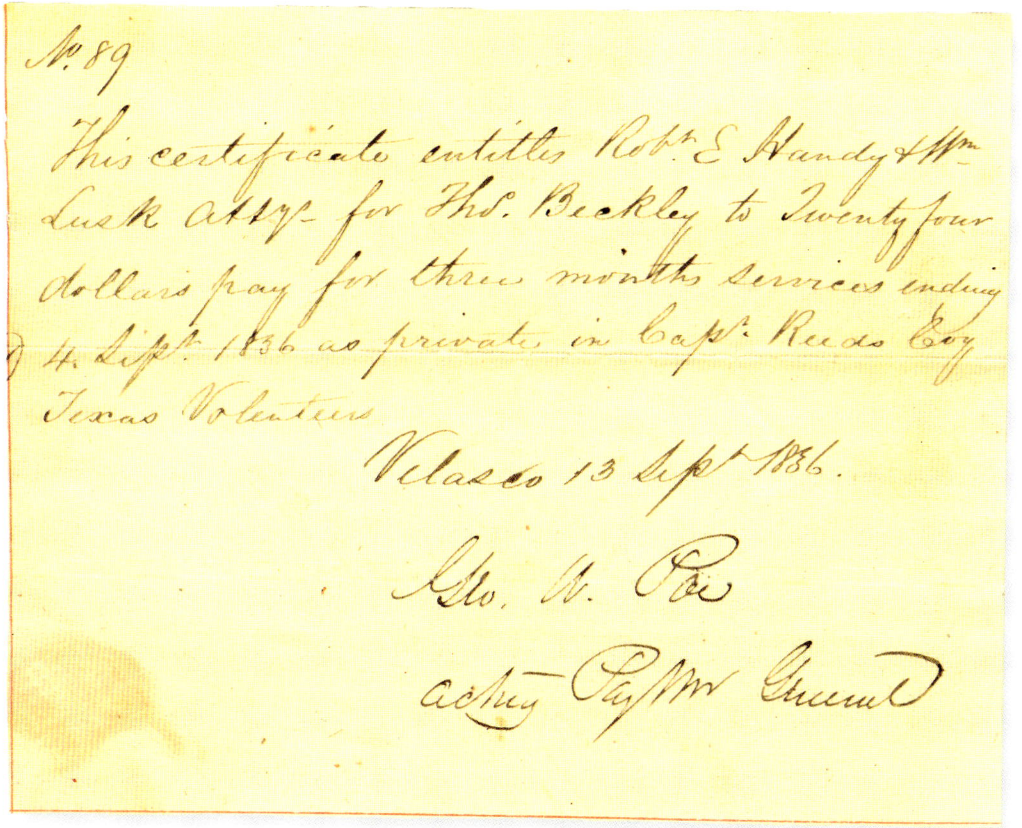

No. 89. This Certificate entitles Rob[er]t E. Handy & W[illia]m Lusk assign[nee]s for Tho[mas] Beckley to Twenty Four dollars pay for three months services ending 4 Sept. 1836 as private in Capt. Reeds Co[mpan]y Texas Volunteers. Velasco 13 Sept 1836. (Signed) George W. Poe

Acting - PayMaster General

Fig 6.13, Velasco, Sept 13, 1836, Military Pay Certificate to Thomas Beckley.

Private Collection, Cr. V7, O-109.

Fig 6.14, Jane Long.
Courtesy of the Rosenberg Library, Galveston, Texas.

This Certificate entitles Mrs James H. Long to Thirty Two Dollars, Fifty Cents, pay per order of Lieut Wm K. Smith and ch[ar]g[e]d to his Acct in this office. Velasco, Sept 24th, 1836

Signed: ________ Act[ing] P[ay] M[aster] Geo[rge] W. Poe, Act[ing] Pay Master General

Fig 6.15, Velasco, September 24, 1836, Military Pay Certificate to Jane Long.
Private Collection, Cr. V3, O-114.

George Washington Poe signed many of the military pay certificates issued from Velasco and later at Columbia, and was an integral figure of the Texas Revolution. Poe served as a volunteer captain in the artillery as early as October 1835. By November 6, he was part of the artillery company engaging the troops of General Cos in the siege of Béxar. By December 30, 1835, Poe was an acting adjutant general of Gen. Sam Houston and was stationed at army headquarters in Columbia. His duties included supervising the construction of fortifications at Galveston and at Fort Velasco. On March 14, 1836, Poe left Velasco with his company and a five-gun artillery battery to join Houston at Beason's Crossing on the Colorado River. On May 3, Poe was at army headquarters near the San Jacinto battlefield. On June 4, Poe commanded the artillery piece that fired a salute over the remains of Fannin's command at La Bahía.[28]

The examples in figures 6.13 and 6.15 were signed by Poe as "Acting" Paymaster General because they predated his official appointment on October 12, 1836. General Poe was also a longtime resident of Brazoria and a friend Stephen F. Austin. So close were the two that Poe served as the marshal and led the funeral procession after the death of his friend on December 27, 1836. Soon afterwards Austin became known as the "Father of Texas."

A military pay certificate to someone other than a member of the military is unusual in itself, but the example in Figure 6.15 is the only known pay certificate to Mrs. James H. Long. She was the young wife of Gen. James Long, the early revolutionary who attempted to gain Texas' independence by occupying Nacogdoches with an "army" in 1819. Long later returned to Texas with Jane to Point Bolivar in 1821 to gain an alliance with Jean Lafitte.[29] The Longs dined with Lafitte aboard the *General Victoria* the night before Lafitte departed from Galveston. Lafitte charmed Mrs. Long with storied tales of his adventures. She described the infamous pirate as being "the very reverse of what her imagination had pictured him" and to be quite conversational, almost like a woman. Following Lafitte's departure, her husband departed for another filibustering expedition at La Bahía, leaving his pregnant wife behind at Bolivar.

Jane stubbornly waited for him to return and gave birth to their third daughter, Mary James, on December 21, 1821. Her husband had been captured and taken to San Antonio as a prisoner and was later transferred to Mexico City.[30] James Long was shot and killed by a Mexican guard on May 28, 1822, reportedly on the order of Gov. Felix Trespalacios. Jane survived the ordeal and raised her children as a widowed mother. She is known as the "Mother of Texas," having given birth to the first reported Anglo baby in Texas. By 1832, she had owned and operated a boarding house for five years in Brazoria.[31] It was during this period of time that the pay order to Jane Long was issued, possibly for providing lodging for officers in the Texas Army. She survived her husband by almost sixty years. Jane Long died on December 30, 1880, at the home of her grandson, James E. Winston, and was buried in the Morton Cemetery in Richmond, Texas.

BURNET CALLS FOR ELECTIONS

David G. Burnet knew that his influence was waning in the military and his presidency had become wholly ineffective. He announced a general election for September 5. The offices of President, Vice President and resolutions to adopt the constitution and approve the annexation of Texas to the United States were to be affixed to the ballot. Stephen F. Austin entered the presidential race, encouraged by Archer and Wharton. Gen. Sam Houston was still recovering from his leg wound in the town of San Augustine and encouraged Thomas J. Rusk to run for the office. Rusk, in turn, encouraged the popular general to run for president.[32] Henry Smith's name was entered as a candidate for president but he asked that his name be withdrawn and, like Rusk, announced his support for General Houston who would not enter the race until late August, a mere eleven days before the election.

For many years after this period the coastal town of Velasco became known as a popular summer resort area. After the Civil War, the town declined and was destroyed by a hurricane in 1875. A new Velasco was built in 1891, four miles upriver from the original site. It too began to grow in population until the Great Storm of 1900 destroyed the beachfront community, along with its more populous neighbor up the coast, the city of Galveston. Velasco is sometimes forgotten as the first capital of a free and independent Republic of Texas. The early treasury warrants and military pay certificates issued from here represent a fascinating yet exceedingly scarce series of paper obligations issued by the young Republic. Velasco was later incorporated into what is today the coastal city of Freeport in Brazoria County.

COLUMBIA: THE FIRST OFFICIAL CAPITAL OF TEXAS

Knowing that Velasco was to serve only as a temporary capital, the government established Columbia (present-day West Columbia in Brazoria County) as their new headquarters. The town officially served as the capital of the Republic of Texas from October 1836 through April 19, 1837. In Columbia the first session of the First Congress met in a wooden clapboard house built in 1833. The Congress formed committees to study an extensive list of topics: foreign relations, ways and means, claims and accounts, the post office, the judiciary, public lands, Indians and Indian affairs, the state of the Republic, county boundaries, roads, bridges and ferries, naval affairs, and military affairs.[33] This Congress also debated the fate of Santa Anna (who was still jailed on the Phelps farm in nearby Brazoria) before ratifying the Treaty of Velasco and finalizing the terms of Santa Anna's release.

Fig 6.16, First Capitol Building of the Republic of Texas, Columbia.
Courtesy Brazoria County Historical Museum, Angleton, Texas.

Fig 6.17, The Old Capitol at Columbia, c. 1900. The ruins of the old Capitol building before its destruction in the Great Storm of 1900.
Courtesy Brazoria County Historical Museum, Angleton, Texas.

The early photos in figures 6.16 and 6.17 are views of the old capitol building in Columbia, taken shortly before it was destroyed by the devastating Hurricane of 1900. The Great Storm obliterated not only the old Capitol building in Columbia, but also any remnants of Fort Velasco and most of the buildings on Galveston Island. From the dilapidated condition of the building shown in these photographs, it probably would not have taken much of a wind to knock down the structure. Of special note is the small lean-to room on the right side of the building which housed the treasury department office. This is where many of the military pay certificates and treasury warrants were written and signed by government officials.

Interim President David G. Burnet gave his "State of the Republic" speech on October 4, 1836, through his personal secretary, John Ricord.[34] This speech outlined the functions of the *ad interim* government in conducting its business "under every imaginable difficulty" during the throes of the revolution. Burnet also described the difficulties under which the Texian loans were obtained and his reasoning for changing their terms. As Burnet publicly lamented that the lenders had refused to advance the remainder of the money, he warned the First Congress about the difficulties that might lay ahead in seeking additional funds from loans. The "paper" Republic continued to fund their operations and debts by issuing a plethora of new obligations while in Columbia.

COLUMBIA ISSUES

Unlike the warrants and pay certificates issued from Velasco, all of the payments issued from Columbia were in printed form. They were printed on a variety of papers and with little regard to their uniformity. The amount, payee, and the date of each certificate or warrant was written in by hand, and all were dated in 1836 or 1837. Treasury warrants were used to pay for the transportation of troops, stores, government expenses, and supplies of every kind. Those that were issued in 1837 reflect a significant number of payments for the military. Since these payments were made payable to a specific person, for a specific amount, and listed the nature of the expense, they disclose an interesting frame of reference for this period of Texas history.

The terms "warrant" and "certificate" are often used interchangeably when describing the various Republic of Texas issues, but there are several distinct and important differences in these obligations. Pay certificates were issued with the distinction that they were certificates evidencing military entitlement, and these would bear the signature of a paymaster.[35] A treasury warrant was merely a government check. To obtain a pay certificate, the soldier would present a written verification showing his rank, enlistment date, discharge date, company or regiment, and commanding officer. This information was given to the paymaster and when approved, entitled him to his pay. These pay certificates were first issued from Velasco in 1836, then at Columbia, and then later at Galveston. Once received, the certificate could then be presented to the auditor's office at the Treasury Department for the issuance of a warrant. The auditor would verify and approve the payment, retain the original paperwork, and then issue a treasury warrant which replaced the certificate (or certificates) in recognition of the obligation. To prevent fraud, the comptroller was required to countersign the warrant before its issuance, but this requirement was dropped by the Treasury Department shortly after the war.

Auditor's certificates represented claims against the government and treasury warrants represented official expenditures of money by the government. During the period of the *ad interim* government there was very little distinction between the two types of payments. While these obligations were initially synonymous, the differences between these obligations became more distinct following the relocation of the government to Columbia. But neither of these government issues were convertible at face value into real money for the recipients.

Regardless of the payment method, many soldiers who fought in the Texas Revolution sold their pay certificates and headright certificates at deep discounts for any gold or silver available. Pay certificates entitled the soldiers to treasury warrants, and headright certificates entitled them to land. With the absence of specie in the Treasury, many of the soldiers sought any source of cash. All of these obligations were assignable. William Fairfax Gray, on his return to Texas in the spring of 1837, reported that he and several of his associates were purchasing soldiers' rights for steep discounts to their land values. One such transaction netted three land certificates of 640 acres each and some pay certificates for a mere $3.50.[36] Since many soldiers lived a hundred miles or more from the available bounty land, they often sold the certificate for cash they could spend locally. Although the bounty law entitled them to the acreage—320 acres of Texas land for a three-month enlistment and 640 acres for a six-month enlistment—many veterans lacked the resources to hire a surveyor to plot a tract of land not previously claimed. A surveyor's field notes were required for the general land office to issue certification. Other soldiers labored through the process and once completed, relocated their families. With no money in the treasury for which these certificates and warrants could be redeemed, many veterans simply signed away a large portion of both their paper and land compensation for just pennies on the dollar.

COLUMBIA – MILITARY PAY CERTIFICATES

No 325 This Certificate $25 21/100 entitles S.O. Pennington as Atty [for] W H Dunn to Twenty five 21/100 dollars, for Three months and four days services, from April 19th 1836 until July 23rd 1836 in Capt. Bradley's Comp[an]y 1836. Columbia, Oct 10th 1836 (Signed) Geo[rge] W. Poe Acting Paymaster General.

Fig 6.18, Columbia, October 10, 1836, Military Pay Certificate. Entitles W. H. Dunn to $25.00 for service in Capt. Bradley's Company.

Private Collection, Cr. C7, 0-230.

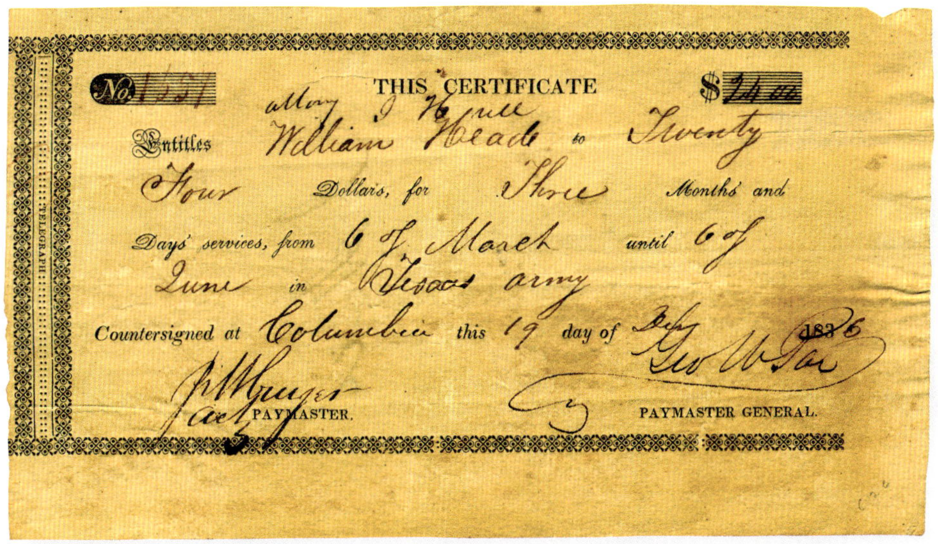

No 1557 This Certificate $24.00

Entitles (Atty H. Howell) William Head to Twenty Four Dollars, for Three months and Days' services, from 6 of March until 6 of June in Texas Army. Countersigned at Columbia this 19 day of July 1836 (Signed, at left) J.M. Cruger, Act[ing] Paymaster, (Signed) George W. Poe Paymaster General.

Fig 6.19, Columbia, December 19, 1836, Military Pay Certificate to William Head for service in the Texas Army.

Private Collection, Cr. C2C, 0-253.

The crisp, almost uncirculated pay certificate in Figure 6.18 entitled William H. Dunn to $25 for three months and four days of military service. Like many early certificates, it was paid to an attorney on the behalf of the soldier, possibly because of the physical location of the paymaster or the Treasury Department. It was common for one attorney to travel and receive the payments for a number of soldiers who had returned home to tend their crops. In this example, Sidney O. Pennington acted as Dunn's attorney to receive the payment. Pennington had been a representative from Shelby to the Convention at Washington-on-the-Brazos and was a signer of the Declaration of Independence. The certificate is signed by George Washington Poe as acting Paymaster General.

The soldier, Pvt. William H. Dunn, served in Capt. John M. Bradley's company of San Augustine Volunteers.[37] In October 1835, Captain Bradley first raised this company in San Augustine and Tenaha. He participated in the Grass Fight on November 26 and later at the siege of Béxar in December.[38] As indicated by the service date on the payment, Dunn was picked up by Captain Bradley and enlisted with the volunteers on April 19, 1836, only two days before the battle of San Jacinto. On May 15, 1836, this company, later known as the San Augustine Cavalry, joined the regular Texas Army at Fort Bend on the Brazos River. The company mopped up the remains of the Mexican Army and expelled them from Texas.

Private Dunn and the remainder of the company were discharged at Victoria on July 23. The note bears Dunn's endorsement on the reverse, indicating that he survived the fighting and received the certificate, although it may never have been redeemed by him as it bears no cut cancellations and is not marked as such. The condition of this pay certificate indicates that it may have been neatly stored in a book and forgotten for generations.

The standard pay certificate in Figure 6.19 was issued to William Head in the amount of $24 for three-months service in the Texas Army. What is unusual about this payment is that it records Head entering the service on March 6, 1836, the very day that the Alamo fell to Santa Anna's forces. This certificate indicates that Sam Houston was actively enlisting troops in the field at the time the Alamo was lost. While this issue reflects the standard private's pay, William Head is listed in the index of military records as a 2nd Sergeant.[39] He served in Capt. Peyton R. Splane's Company and was assigned to guard the sick and baggage opposite Harrisburg prior to the battle of San Jacinto. The certificate is signed by George Washington Poe as Paymaster.

Similar to other soldiers, on April 10, 1838, Sergeant Head received a bounty warrant for 320 acres of land for his three-month service. His land rights were situated in Béxar County, and assigned to an Enoch Jones, indicating that Sergeant Head had sold or otherwise assigned the bounty certificate.[40]

The pay certificate in Figure 6.20 was issued to Isaiah D. Lawson for service in a company of mounted volunteers known as the Red River Blues, organized on July 14, 1836. The unit served along the Lavaca River until the fall of that year. Lawson's commander, Capt. William Becknell, later formed a company of mounted Volunteer Rangers, which was organized twenty-five miles south of the Red River. It was the first company "raised for the protection of the frontiers of Texas, having no laws or rooles [*sic*] to go by." Lawson served in the company of mounted volunteers which patrolled near the Oklahoma border.[41]

Even though this payment was issued from the small wooden building at Columbia in the Gulf Coast area, it illustrates the wide range of geographic regions served by the early treasury and paymaster departments. It is but another variety of the different printed papers on which these early payments were written. The certificate is signed by James W. Scott at left and George Washington Poe as acting Paymaster General.

The Texian Army Certificates or "Black Star Notes" were used exclusively for payments in the military. Much more ornate than other Columbia issues, the certificate in Figure 6.21 is named for the large black star in the top center. Note that the $24 payment was for "Bounty" rather than service in the army. Bounty had two meanings: either as an enlistment bonus or, in this case, as payment for a specific one-time duty or assignment such as transporting prisoners. No listing for George W. Shaw was found on the muster rolls of 1835-1845. This certificate is marked "approved" and countersigned by Bernard Bee, the Secretary of War under President Sam Houston, whose signature accompanies Poe's as Paymaster General.

While having Barnard Bee approve the payment seems to add some credibility to Shaw's assignment, Bee was a poor judge of his creditors in at least one instance. When Antonio López de Santa Anna was released to Washington, D.C., several months after the battle of San Jacinto, George W. Hockley, Reuben M. Potter, and Bee accompanied him. Bee lent Santa Anna $3,000 in return for a draft on the Mexican general's Mexico City bank. When Bee attempted to cash the draft, Santa Anna refused to honor it, insisting that he had signed the draft under duress as a prisoner of war.[42]

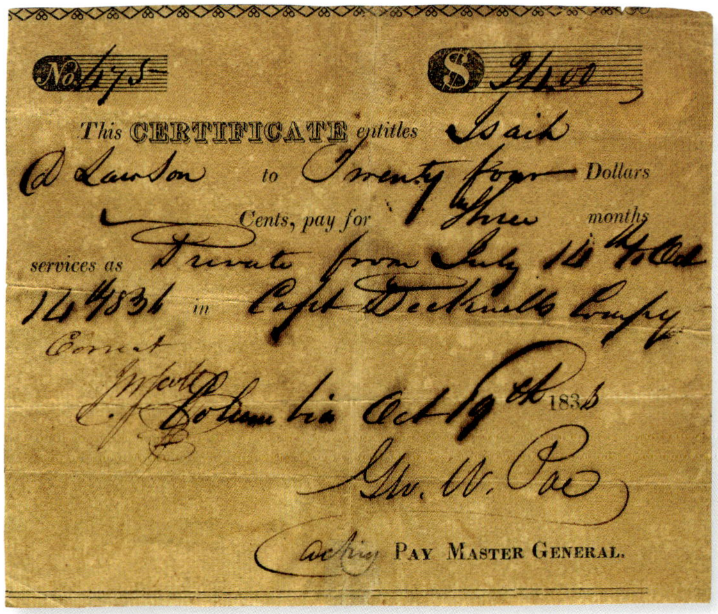

No 475 $24.00

This CERTIFICATE entitles Isaih D. Lawson to Twenty Four Dollars, ___ cents, pay for Three months services as Private from July 14th to Oct 14th 1836 in Capt Becknell's Comp[an]y. Columbia Oct 19th 1836 (Signed, at left) J.W. Scott, (Signed) George W. Poe acting Paymaster General.

Fig 6.20, Columbia, October 19, 1836, Military Pay Certificate to Isiah D. Lawson for service in Capt. Becknell's Company.

Private Collection, Cr. C-8, 0-239.

The payment in Figure 6.22 of $100 for four months service indicates that Michael Goheen drew the officer's pay of $25 per month. This certificate also noted a "substitute J.F. Webber" who may have been entitled to receive the payment on Goheen's behalf. A "substitute" was used to fulfill a military obligation on a soldier's part when that soldier was unable to serve. It was not uncommon for a wealthy man to hire a friend or a poor man to substitute for a portion of his enlistment period. The certificate is signed by Joseph M. Cruger as Paymaster and George Washington Poe as Paymaster General.

The most frequently seen issues from Columbia are for military payrolls. Virtually all of the soldiers who fought at San Jacinto received military pay certificates issued from Velasco or Columbia. The 1836 military pay certificates were issued to document a soldier's service as an entitlement for pay. Most of these certificates were issued from Columbia, which are found on a dozen different varieties of printed paper. Later in 1836 and 1837, detachments of infantry and artillery companies received pay certificates signed and issued on Galveston Island where they were stationed. These certificates offer an interesting glimpse into the lives and circumstances which swirled around these early Texas veterans. A complete listing of the pay scale of the Texian Army can be found in Appendix G.

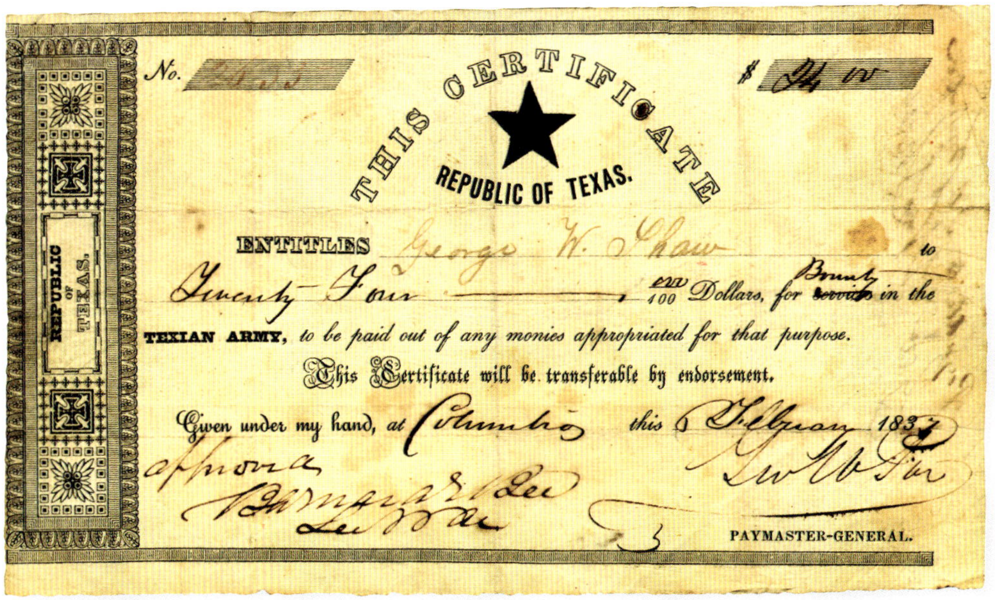

No. 2633 THIS CERTIFICATE REPUBLIC OF TEXAS $24.00

ENTITLES George W. Shaw to Twenty Four 000/100 Dollars for BOUNTY in the TEXIAN ARMY, to be paid out of any monies appropriated for that purpose. This Certificate will be transferable by endorsement. Given under my hand, at Columbia this February 1837. (Signed, at left) approved Barnard Bee, Sec[retary] (Signed) Geo[rge] W. Poe PAYMASTER- GENERAL

Fig 6.21, Columbia, February 1837, Texian Army Certificate to George W. Shaw, for "Bounty" in the Texian Army.

Private Collection, Cr. C16A, O-264.

No 1848 This Certificate $100.00

Entitles (substitute J.F. Webber) Michael R. Goheen to One Hundred Dollars, for Four months and Days' services, from 20 of July until 20th Nov in McGehee's Company. Countersigned at Columbia this 26 day of Dec 1836 (Signed, at left) J.M. Cruger, PAYMASTER, (Signed) George W. Poe PAYMASTER GENERAL.

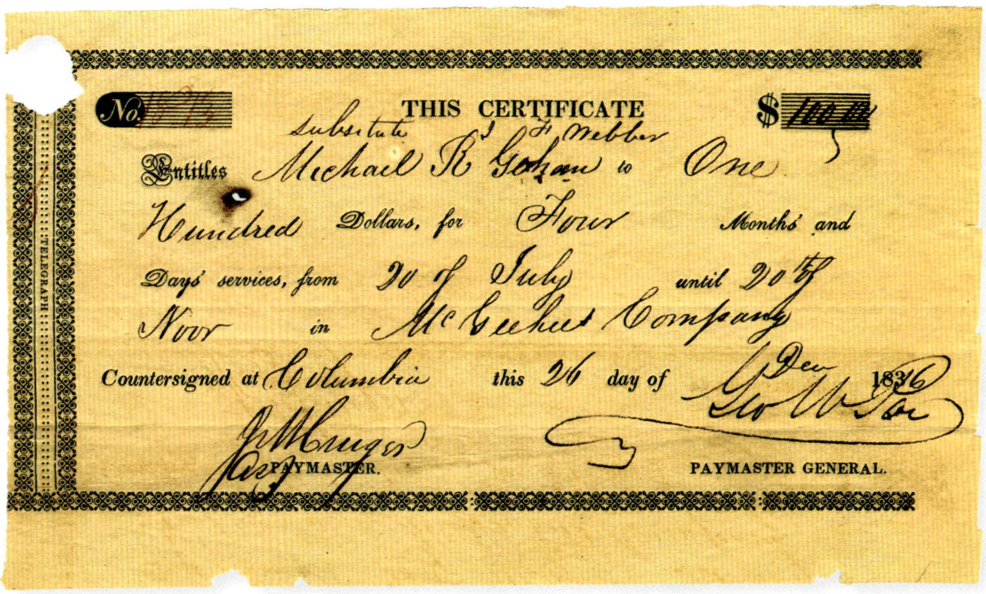

Fig 6.22, Columbia, December 26, 1836, Military Pay Certificate to Michael R. Goheen for service in McGehee's Company.

Private Collection, Cr. C2-C, O-253.

THE OFFICER AND THE SUBSTITUTE

Twenty-six-year-old Michael R. Goheen made the long trek from his native Michigan to arrive in Texas in 1833. Like many others before him, Goheen came to Texas looking for land and instead found a fight. When the revolution broke out, he enlisted in the army and was quickly promoted to Captain. Goheen was one of four commanders who led companies with Jim Bowie and James Fannin on the outskirts of a wooded bend in the San Antonio River near the mission of Concepción on October 27, 1835. There the officers decided to camp for the evening rather than return to the main part of the army as their commanding officer Gen. Stephen F. Austin had directed. The Texans occupied the bend in the San Antonio River protected by an embankment and sent out pickets to warn of a Mexican approach. They were attacked at dawn on the following morning by 275 Mexican troops in what became known as the battle of Concepción.[43] This was the first engagement in the siege which led to the storming and capture of Béxar by Texas forces on December 5, 1835. Surviving the ordeal, Goheen served in the army until December 15, 1835.[44] He returned to the army on March 1, 1836, to fight with James Gillespie's 2nd Regiment of Texas Volunteers under the command of Col. Sidney Sherman at the battle of San Jacinto.

The certificate in figure 6.22 is a payment for Captain Goheen's second and final stint in the army which ended November 20, 1836, after serving in the company of Thomas Gilmer McGehee.[45] Goheen married Dorinda M. Moody on April 25, 1837, the daughter of John W. Moody who served as the auditor for the Republic.[46] Goheen also received a certificate for 320 acres of land for his service in 1835 and 640 acres of land for his service in 1836. He relocated his family to the land in Grimes County where he died on his ranch in 1850.

John F. Webber, Goheen's "substitute," was in Austin's Colony as early as 1826 and received a headright on June 22, 1832. He became entangled in a love affair with a slave girl, Silvia Hector. When she became pregnant, he faced his responsibilities like a man. According to an affidavit by his widow, they were married by Father Michael Muldoon.[47] Rather than abandon his wife and child to a life of slavery, on June 11, 1834, Webber purchased his family from their owner, who took advantage of their situation to drive a steep bargain.[48] John and Sylvia had at least eight additional children together. Beginning in the 1840s newcomers from the southern United States ostracized the family because of their racially mixed marriage, and ultimately Webber moved his household. In 1853, he bought several leagues of land on the Rio Grande River downstream from Hidalgo. There he established Webber's Ranch, where his family farmed in poverty. A Unionist, he fled to Mexico during the Confederate occupation of the Rio Grande Valley and returned home in May 1865. Webber died at his home on July 19, 1882, and was buried in the family cemetery on the levee road, a short distance from Donna, Texas. His widow, known as "Puss," died about 1891. Webberville in Travis County bears his name.

THE DEATH OF THE TEXIAN LOAN

While many of the veterans of the Texas Revolution eventually collected on their military pay certificates and land grants for service, there were a good number who did not. By the end of 1836, some soldiers made their way to New Orleans. The old French city on the banks of the Mississippi River became a primary trading spot for headright certificates and Texas land scrip, some of which sold for as little as twenty-five cents per acre. Compounding the problem for Texas, when Robert Triplett presented the modified Texian loan contract to his fellow lenders for approval, the group balked at the altered terms proposed by Burnet and they unanimously refused to advance the remaining 90 percent of the loan.[49] A key provision of the loan was for the group to be able to buy land in Texas at fifty cents an acre with a priority choice of location over all others. The government arbitrarily changed the terms as had originally been negotiated and attempted to subordinate their priority of claims behind the soldiers. But with many of the former soldiers now streaming into New Orleans, a new opportunity for speculators emerged. Many of the potential lenders bought headright certificates from veterans for less than could be had under the original loan terms. Since the soldier's certificates carried a priority of location, the death of the Texian loan was assured. The remaining balance of the loans was never advanced by the lending group in New Orleans or the individuals in New York.

Robert Triplett returned to his home in Yellow Banks, Kentucky. He wrote to his friend William Christy on

October 4, 1836, about his despair in the repudiation of the loan terms by Texas: "I was one of the warmest advocates for Texas—have written much in her cause, and intended going great lengths for her—such was the feeling of all concerned in that loan." He continued, "No government can exist, with such evidence of palpable faith blazed upon its front—and that too towards its first and best friends."[50] Compounding Triplett's problem, Burnet had authorized Texas officials in New York to sell additional land scrip to pay off the debt of the warships *Brutus* and *Invincible* which had been seized by their creditors for unpaid repair bills.[51] To a large degree, these actions and the alteration of terms of the Texian loans would forever haunt the credit of the Republic.

Even Triplett's claim to the 640 acres on Galveston was now being repudiated by President Burnet. The President admitted the survey and the filing of the boundaries of the section of land was valid, but claimed that he "erred in signing the patent" for the title. Triplett in turn, voluntarily surrendered it.[52] When William Fairfax Gray later asked Burnet who held the title to the lands and where the documents pertaining to them had been filed, he could not even ascertain who owned large parts of the island. In fact, the boundaries of the grant were actually within a tract on the east end of Galveston (4605.5 acres) originally granted to Juan N. Seguin by the State of Coahuila y Tejas in 1832.[53] The significance of this failed transaction is that Triplett was unable to lay out the city which he had planned. He had ventured into a previous land deal with John Kirby and Augustus C. Allen, real estate speculators from New York. The brothers hoped to establish a new city on Triplett's tract of land on Galveston Island, but the flawed title forbid the venture. Their new city, which was to be christened with the name of Houston, would have to find another home elsewhere.

Robert Triplett expressed his own feelings to Christy about his real estate experience and how the Texas Government would be perceived by future lenders. In his letter, Triplett added: "Capitalists will refuse to invest money in her lands, and they will be at so low a price that a few resident monopolizers will get the whole for a song."[54] His prophecy about the finances of the Republic of Texas was already beginning to ring true.

BRIGHAM'S REPORT TO CONGRESS

While the claims for military supplies and service in the Republic were both documented and expected, the new government soon found itself in the throes of a new financial dilemma. In his report as Treasurer on October 10, 1836, Asa Brigham presented to Congress the status of the Treasury from January 1 up to September 27, 1836. The claims outstanding which had been audited and paid by drafts from the empty treasury comprised the following:[55]

Military claims	*$225,154.20*
Naval " "	*27,364.73*
Civil " "	*8,527.92*
Contingent " "	*6,427.84*
Total	*$264,534.69*

In addition to the predominantly military and civil claims, the Treasurer was deluged by a host of additional claims against the new government for "horses and other property lost in the service" and "also for property destroyed by the enemy and by order of the officers of our army to prevent its falling into the hands of the enemy."[56] It seems that during the Runaway Scrape, Sam Houston's Army had either confiscated property or laid waste to everything that could be used by the advancing Mexican Army. Brigham added that until this point, "claims of these descriptions are not provided for by the existing laws, and we have declined acting on them until Congress shall pass some general law on the subject."

When Brigham brought these claims to light, it became clear that while Texas was victorious in its quest for independence, the fledgling nation soon found itself mired in financial claims from the very same war that had set it free. After the soldiers and their families returned to their homes and farms, many consulted attorneys or presented claims on their own behalf to the government for lost, stolen, or destroyed property.

Indeed, the list of claims was quite varied. In addition to lost horses, mules and rifles, the following claims were presented:

Claim No	*1*	*Freeman Wilkinson*	*"tobacco destroyed"*	*$1,543.75*
	4	*Martin Clow & Co*	*"whiskey and brandy destroyed"*	*250.00*
	17	*John L. Sleight*	*"Brandy destroyed"*	*304.00*
	33	*Jacob Eberly*	*"spirits destroyed"*	*362.50*
	48	*Elisha Flack*	*"ferry boat & canoe sunk"*	*65.00*

Fig 6.23, Sam Houston, President of Texas.
Author's Collection.

These ninety-three miscellaneous claims on Brigham's report totaled $28,413 (See Appendix H). These claims put the Treasury Department and the new Congress in an unusual predicament as there was no law in place to validate or even allow such claims against the government for property destroyed by the Texas or Mexican armies. There was also not a way to distribute the appropriate payments to the aggrieved parties from the rapidly shrinking Treasury funds.[57] These claims were eventually satisfied by a special act of Congress, though it is still not clear how or if the Republic settled the accounts for missing or stolen whiskey!

It is out of this dilemma that the payment system of warrants and audited certificates became firmly cemented in the finances of the Republic. A claim for payment was made through the office of the auditor. If validated with proper receipts or evidence, a certificate was issued for payment "out of funds not otherwise appropriated" against public dues when they became available. If a surplus of funds were available the certificate served as a government check. If funds were not available, the certificate served as an I.O.U.[58] This policy held true for all warrants and certificates issued from Columbia, Velasco, Houston, Washington, and eventually Austin as well. Because there were no surplus funds in the Treasury, many of these warrants and certificates went unpaid by the government for years.

SAM HOUSTON, PRESIDENT OF TEXAS

On October 18, 1836, the Speaker of the House of Representatives declared Sam Houston to be the "duly and constitutionally elected president of the Republic of Texas, and Mirabeau B. Lamar Vice President for the term of two years, immediately ensuing from the second Monday in December."[59] In this first national election in September 1836, the people were also asked to vote on a resolution for annexation to the United States of America. It was overwhelmingly passed by the citizens of Texas, most of whom had emigrated from the U.S. Still reeling from unmitigated criticism, David G. Burnet was relieved to hand over the reigns of government to the hero of San Jacinto. On October 22, 1836, Sam Houston was inaugurated in the small wooden capitol building in Columbia as the first elected President of the Republic of Texas. The former Governor of Tennessee had his hands full as a myriad of difficult domestic and diplomatic tasks lay before him, including annexation to the United States, making peace with the Indians, negotiating with Mexico, and an empty treasury. Houston judged the accommodations at Columbia to be wholly inadequate and immediately lobbied for the seat of government to be moved to his namesake town of Houston. The muddy little town had been laid out less than two months before by the Allen brothers at the confluence of Buffalo and White Oak Bayous, several miles upstream from the former site of Harrisburg.

One of the newly elected President's most puzzling dilemmas after his inauguration was what to do with Antonio López de Santa Anna, the Mexican President who was still being held as a prisoner in Brazoria. Santa Anna had written to Houston offering his assistance to negotiate with the United States for its annexation of Texas. Houston dismissed his offer as insincere but was determined to get the infamous prisoner out of Texas.[60] Santa Anna was released through diplomatic channels to Washington, D.C., where he managed to charm the Washington elite. He was hailed by the abolitionists as a crusader who had taken on the breakaway slave-holding Republic, rather than the man who had ordered the massacres of Texians at the Alamo and at Goliad. Houston rationalized, "Restored to his own country [Santa Anna] would keep Mexico in commotion for years, and Texas will be safe." With the treaties of Velasco violated by both governments, Texas independence was not recognized by Mexico and her boundary was not determined until after the U.S. and Mexican War with the Treaty of Guadalupe Hidalgo in 1848.

When the Congress of the Republic met in Columbia to debate the location of a permanent capital, it was John Kirby Allen, a member of the Congress, who argued the case for selecting their new city of Houston as the seat of government. After four ballots and a slim majority over votes for Matagorda, Fort Bend, Washington, Columbia and Nacogdoches, Houston was selected as the new capital until the conclusion of the 1840 legislature, conditional on the Allen brothers themselves erecting a capitol building from their own personal funds of $10,000.[61] This move officially took place on April 18, 1837. The treasury warrants from Columbia continued to be issued until that time. The last of the military pay certificates distributed to the troops stationed on Galveston Island continued to be issued as late as December 1837.

GALVESTON – MILITARY PAY CERTIFICATES

The surviving military pay certificates issued in 1836 and 1837 from Galveston are quite rare, primarily because of the small detachments stationed there. These certificates, along with the earliest issues from Gonzales in 1835, represent an unusual series of payments countersigned in a place other than where the government was headquartered. The Texian troops still occupied the island more than a year after the battle of San Jacinto.[62] They were charged with guarding more than one hundred Mexican prisoners and keeping watch for another invasion by Mexico, which came not by land, but in the form of a naval blockade in 1837. Of the few surviving specimens of this issue, all are known to have been issued to men who were either in Capt. J.M.H. Hall's or Capt. James Jevons' company. These last military pay certificates issued by the Republic were used through the end of 1837. They are of great historical importance and are also the most difficult for collectors to find.

As President, Sam Houston increased the regular army to approximately 2,000 men by December 1836 and appointed Brig. Gen. Felix Huston as temporary Commander in Chief. Entering into 1837, most soldiers were dissatisfied with no war to fight, short rations, meager clothing, and lack of pay. Not surprisingly, the army went into a serious decline, and many men were mustered out of service while others deserted. When a soldier with a grudge murdered Col. Henry Teal in his sleep at Camp Bowie on May 5, 1837, the President was outraged at the heinous act. Colonel Teal was a decorated war veteran, having received a commission from the Convention of 1836 and served at the siege of Béxar.[63] Teal was also sent to Matamoros, Mexico, to negotiate with Gen. José de Urrea for the exchange of prisoners under the treaties of Velasco, only to be imprisoned when he learned of their plans to launch another invasion of Texas. Although Teal escaped from Mexico, delighting Sam Houston, the President was incensed when he learned of Teal's murder by his own troops and ordered Secretary of War William S. Fisher to furlough two-thirds of the army. With two-thirds of the army disbanded, only 500 to 600 men remained to guard the most essential posts of San Antonio and Galveston. It was during this time that Hall's and Jevons' companies were dispatched to Galveston.

The certificate in Figure 6.24 entitled Jacob K. Beaumont to $46.24 for military service from September 6 to December 1, 1836, in Hall's "Company B. Artillery" unit on the island. It was undoubtedly issued as payment for the building of coastal defenses.

While the hostilities on land had effectively come to an end, the erection of shore batteries against an ever imminent Mexican naval threat had become a necessary defense measure in the eyes of the Republic. The Texas Navy had been crippled by a loss of key personnel and ships. The long-range guns erected by Hall's and Jevons' companies were intended to thwart a Mexican threat by water and may have given the appearance of a strong coastal defense—but it was hardly effective. By mid-1837, as many as five Mexican warships had clamped a watertight blockade on Texas shipping, and several American flagged schooners, including the *Champion* and the *Louisiana,* were captured by the Mexican fleet and sent to Matamoros to be condemned as "Prizes of War."[64] Patrolling just twelve miles off the coasts of

No. THIS CERTIFICATE $
Entitles to
Dollars, for Months' and
Days' services, from until
in
Countersigned at this day of 183
PAYMASTER. PAYMASTER GENERAL.

No 25 THIS CERTIFICATE $46.24

Entitles J[acob] K. Beaumont to Forty Six -Twenty Four /100 Dollars, for -one- Months and Twenty Four Days' services, from September 6 until 1st Dec - 1836 in Comp[any] B Artillery

Countersigned at Galveston this 1st day of Dec 1836 (Signed, at left) J[ames].W. Scott, Acting PAYMASTER, (Signed) George W. Poe PAYMASTER GENERAL.

Fig 6.24, Galveston, December 1, 1836, Military Pay Certificate to J. K. Beaumont in Company B Artillery

Private Collection, Cr. G2, O-278.

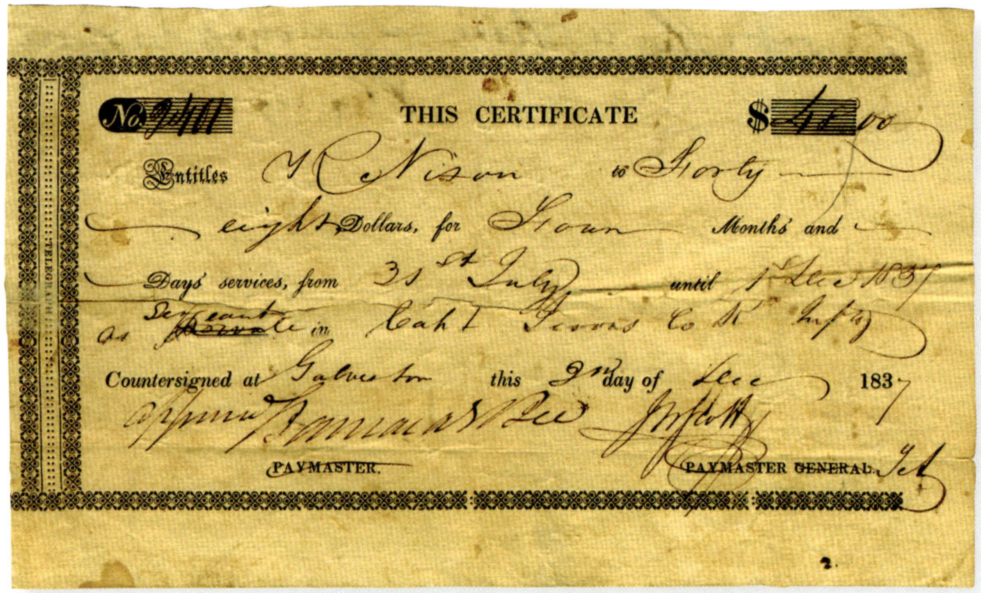
No 2411 THIS CERTIFICATE $48.00
Entitles R. Nixon to Forty-eight Dollars, for Four Months and - Days' services, from 31st July until 1st Dec 1837
as Sergeant in Capt Jevons Co K. Infty
Countersigned at Galveston this 2nd day of Dec 1837
Approved Barnard Bee J W Scott
PAYMASTER. PAYMASTER GENERAL.

No 2401 THIS CERTIFICATE $48.00

Entitles R[ichard] Nixon to Forty - eight Dollars, for Four Months and - Days' services, from 31st July until 1st Dec 1837 as Sergeant in Capt. Jevons Co. K. Inf[antr]y.

Countersigned at Galveston this 2nd day of Dec 1837(Signed, at left) approved, Barnard Bee (Signed) J[ames] W. Scott, PAYMASTER GENERAL.

Fig 6.25, Galveston, December 2, 1837, Military Pay Certificate to Richard Nixon in Capt. Jevon's Co. K. Infantry.

Private Collection, Cr. G1, O-275.

Galveston and Velasco, these hostile Mexican warships were well out of the big gun's reach.

The certificate in Figure 6.25 entitled Richard Nixon to $48 for four-month pay in Capt. Jevons, Company K, Infantry. Nixon had enlisted on February 22, 1837, in New Orleans as a regular in the Texas Army. He served at Camp Chambers near the present site of Inez in Victoria County.[65] Inez was the last of a series of encampments which the Army of the Republic made on the lower Lavaca and Navidad rivers in 1837. According to Republic military archives, Jevons' company then traveled to Galveston in November 1837 where "they built barracks and established a heavy battery" for coastal defense. All the men were discharged in the first week of December. Nixon re-enlisted the following year and served in the frontier regiment until he was discharged by Albert Sidney Johnston in April 1839.

The implications of the naval blockade of Texas were both commercial and financial. Galveston was not only the primary port of entry into Texas, it was here that most of the hard currency or specie was collected at the Customs House after the inspection and unloading of goods in the harbor.[66] Unable to export goods by sea in exchange for hard currency and deprived of the badly needed customs revenue, the blockade of the port of Galveston tightened the financial noose around the neck of the Republic that summer. In a brave effort to break the blockade on August 27, 1837, the Texas warships, *Brutus* and *Invincible*, effectively met their deaths at the hands of a superior Mexican force.[67] The resulting damage to the economy after the Texas naval response to the blockade became even more complete.

COLUMBIA - TREASURY WARRANTS

The $100 payment in Figure 6.26 for the first Texas Navy was funded at a perilous time for the small fleet. A blockade of Texas ports was established by the Mexican Navy on March 11, 1837. Mexican warships were reported cruising within twelve miles of Galveston. At the time this payment was issued, the Texian warships, *Brutus* and *Invincible*, were woefully short of supplies and anchored inside the blockade in the Galveston harbor. The ships' captains, William Hurd and Jeremiah Brown, were immediately dismissed upon their return to Galveston, stemming from their unauthorized visits to the port of New York during the in fall of 1836 where they extended the Republic's credit for the repair and re-provisioning of their vessels. Upon the firing of the popular captains, many of the crew members subsequently deserted. The *Brutus* was placed under the command of Lt. James Boyland of the "Horse Marines" fame. On April 5, 1837, Navy Secretary Fisher ordered this small fleet to Velasco to meet the Mexican naval threat and to defend the Texas coast.[68]

Another problem in restocking the government coffers through tax collection was the lack of a circulating currency, as it rendered tax collection somewhat untenable. The steady flow of Mexican silver coins into Texas during the colonial period had been abruptly halted in 1835 as the war began. A great difficulty in obtaining revenue was brought to the attention of the government when the local Sheriff in Brazoria, Robert Stevenson, attempted to collect taxes from citizens who had audited certificates for a larger amount than they owed in taxes.[69] In writing to Treasury Secretary Henry Smith in the fall of 1837, Stevenson asked for guidance, as there was no way for him to collect the payments unless he were allowed to make change for a warrant whose face value exceeded the taxes that were owed. As a temporary solution, local Sheriffs had been placing a credit for taxes paid on the back of an audited claim, thereby reducing its redemption value accordingly. Although there is no record of Smith's response to Stevenson's inquiry, the need for a circulating currency in Texas became paramount if the new government was to continue to function and maintain its independence.

Many of the payments to Texas veterans were simply endorsed on the reverse and signed over for their taxes. The payment in Figure 6.27 to Holman George illustrates how some Texians chose to assign this illiquid

No. 1050 $100

THE TREASURER of the REPUBLIC OF TEXAS, will pay to the order of Benjamin F. Harrison one hundred – Dollars, out of any money in the Treasury not otherwise appropriated, for the payment of the Navy.

Columbia, March 27th 1837, (Signed) J.W. Moody, AUDITOR

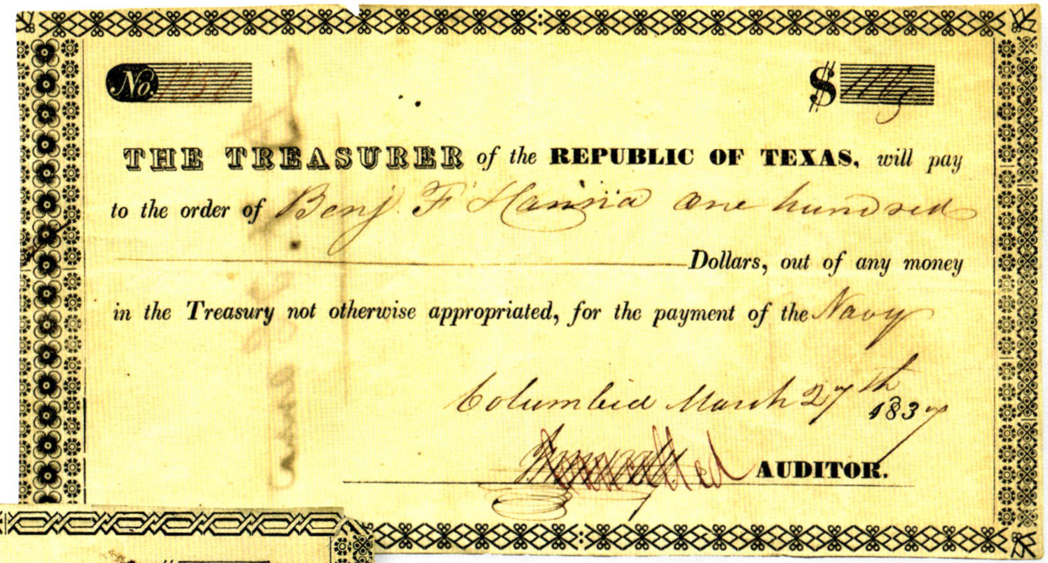
THE TREASURER of the REPUBLIC OF TEXAS, will pay to the order of Benj. F. Harrison one hundred Dollars, out of any money in the Treasury not otherwise appropriated, for the payment of the Navy

Columbia March 27th 1837

AUDITOR.

Fig 6.26, Columbia, March 27, 1837, Treasury Warrant to Benjamin Harrison for payment of the Navy.

Private Collection, Cr. C5, O-210.

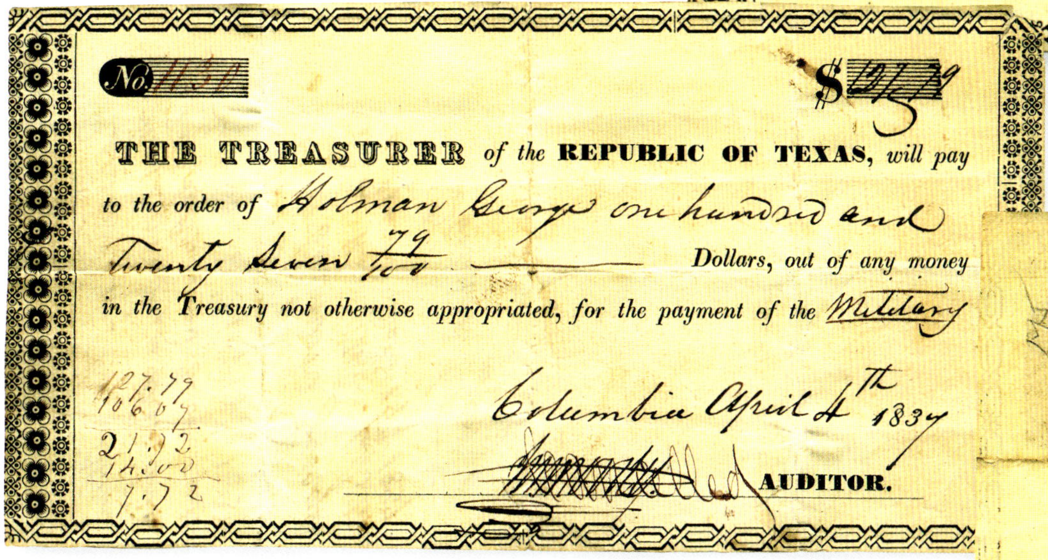
THE TREASURER of the REPUBLIC OF TEXAS, will pay to the order of Holman George one hundred and Twenty Seven 79/100 Dollars, out of any money in the Treasury not otherwise appropriated, for the payment of the Military

Columbia April 4th 1837

AUDITOR.

Fig 6.27, Columbia, April 4, 1837, Treasury Warrant to Holman George for payment of the Military.

Private Collection, Cr. C5A, O-212.

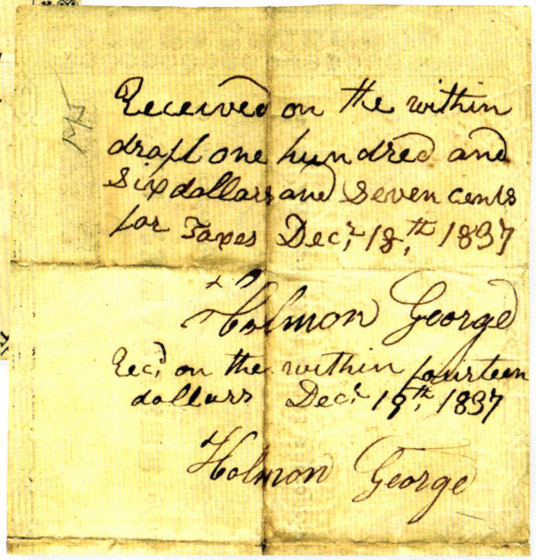
Received on the within draft one hundred and Six dollars and Seven cents for Taxes Dec. 18th 1837

Holman George

Rec'd on the within fourteen dollars Dec 19th 1837

Holman George

Fig 6.28, Columbia, Reverse of Treasury Warrant.

$106.07 for Taxes December 18, 1837.

No. 1130 $127.79

THE TREASURER of the REPUBLIC OF TEXAS, will pay to the order of Holman George one hundred and Twenty Seven 79/100 Dollars, out of any money in the Treasury not otherwise appropriated, for the payment of the Military.

Columbia, April 4th 1837, (Signed) J.W. Moody, AUDITOR

Received in the within draft one hundred and Six dollars and Seven cents for taxes Dec. 18th, 1837. Holman George. Ex[ecute] d on the within fourteen dollars Dec 19th 1837. Holman George.

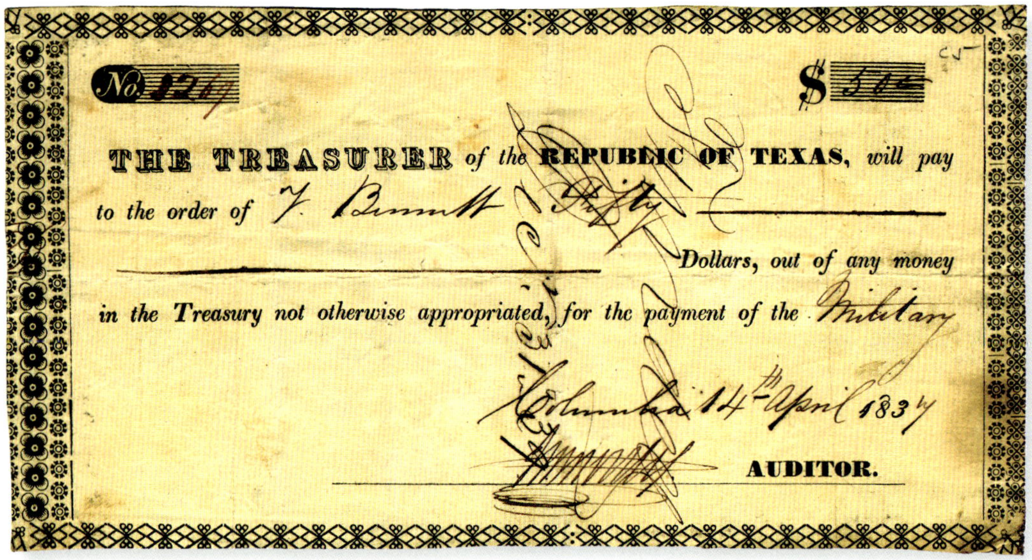
No. 1269 $50
THE TREASURER of the REPUBLIC OF TEXAS, will pay to the order of T. Bennett Fifty Dollars, out of any money in the Treasury not otherwise appropriated, for the payment of the Military
Columbia 14th April 1837
AUDITOR.

No. 2269 $50.00

THE TREASURER of the REPUBLIC OF TEXAS, will pay to the order of T. Bennett Fifty ——Dollars, out of any money in the Treasury not otherwise appropriated, for the payment of the Military.

Columbia, April 14th 1837, (Signed) J.W. Moody, AUDITOR

Fig 6.29, Columbia, April 14, 1837, Treasury Warrant to T. Bennett for payment of the Military.
Private Collection, Cr. C4A, O-209.

paper directly back to the government. When taxpayers paid in receipts and certificates instead of in cash, the fiscal dilemma of the Republic of Texas increased as it had no hard currency in hand. In the left-hand corner on the face is a calculation showing that his taxes of $106.07 had been subtracted from the amount owed to Mr. George. The reverse is shown in Figure 6.28.

In such cases, the tax collector (the sheriff) was authorized to accept the endorsement on the back of the draft for taxes paid and the payee could use the balance for other purposes.[70] It is unclear why an additional $14.00 was signed over on the reverse of the warrant for Holman George bearing the same date. It is possible that this represented two distinct payments to the government and was merely an itemization of his payments. There is a remainder of $7.72 on the face (see Figure 6.27).

Sometimes the payee chose to receive the cash payment which was due him rather than sign over a warrant for taxes. The $50 payment in Figure 6.29 to T. Bennett "for the payment of the Military" is one of the most frequently seen varieties of treasury warrants issued from Columbia during Sam Houston's first term in office. Five days after its issue, the Second Congress convened in the new Capitol building and the government officially relocated to the town of Houston.

Unfortunately for Bennett, the legislators were not in the same hurry to pay his claim, as scrawled across the face of the note are the words "Funded Dec. 31…39." This indicates that not only was Bennett not paid while in Columbia, but the capital had since been moved to Houston, and then to Austin. It wasn't until after a year into the administration of Mirabeau B. Lamar that this payment was funded—approximately two and a half years after it was issued to Bennett.

1 *Handbook of Texas Online,* s.v., "Battle of Velasco," http://www.tsha.utexas.edu/handbook/online/articles/VV/hvv7.html (accessed May 27, 2006).

2 William F. Gray, *Diary of Col. Wm. Fairfax Gray: from Virginia to Texas, 1835-1836* (Houston: Gray, Dillaye & Co Printers, 1909; rpt. 1965), 210.

3 "President Burnet's address to Congress," October 4, 1836, Journals of the House of Representatives of the Republic of Texas, 1st Cong., 1st sess. (Columbia: G & T.H. Borden, Public Printers, 1836).

4 *Handbook of Texas Online,* s.v., "Treaty of Velasco," http://www.tsha.utexas.edu/handbook/online/articles/TT/mgt5.html (accessed July 24, 2006).

5 Frank C. Hanighen, *Santa Anna: The Napoleon of the West* (Coward-McCann, Inc., 1934), 127.

6 Ibid., 129-31.

7 Marquis James, *The Raven: A Biography of Sam Houston* (Austin: University of Texas Press, 1929), 259-60.

8 Hanighen, *Santa Anna,* 132.

9 Wallace L. McKeehan, "Santa Anna's Captivity," found online at www.tamu.edu/ccbn/dewitt/santaanna4.htm.

10 *Handbook of Texas Online,* s.v., "Orozimbo Plantation," http://www.tsha.utexas.edu/handbook/online/articles/OO/aco1.html (accessed July 24, 2006).

11 *Handbook of Texas Online,* s.v., "Asa Brigham," http://www.tsha.utexas.edu/handbook/online/articles/BB/fbr49.html (accessed January 23, 2006).

12 Index to Military Rolls of the Republic of Texas, Augustus V. Sharpe, found on-line at http://www.tshaonline.org/supsites/military/rep_cont.htm.

13 "A.V. Sharpe to Asa Brigham, Auditor," dated at Velasco, August 25, 1836, Texas State Library & Archives, Austin, Texas.

14 Index to Military Rolls of the Republic of Texas, Capt. B.H. Duval's Muster roll notation "Escaped the massacre" found on-line at http://www.tshaonline.org/supsites/military/rep_cont.htm.

15 From biographical information compiled by Jeff Dunn, the owner of Sharpe's pay warrant, non-published.

16 Source: Sharpe's Tombstone and Texas Military Muster Rolls.

17 Jonathan W. Jordan, *Lone Star Navy: Texas, the Fight for the Gulf of Mexico, and the Shaping of the American West* (Dulles, VA: Potomac Books, Inc., 2006), 68.

18 *Handbook of Texas Online,* s.v., "Horse Marines," http://www.tsha.utexas.edu/handbook/online/articles/HH/qjh1.html (accessed May 27, 2006).

19 Jordan, *Lone Star Navy,* 68-69.

20 The Papers of the Texas Revolution, 7:255-56, see "Huston to Burnet, Galveston Bay, June 25, 1836."

21 Joe Olson reserved Olson #185 for this promissory note following the receipt of a high-quality photocopy.

22 After examination of this document, John N. Rowe indicated that it was most likely a contemporary manuscript copy of the original. The sticking point seems to be the misspelling of Burnet's name on the signature line. Most duplicates or copies also have the word "duplicate" written on the reverse, which this one does not. However, James Fannin's surname was frequently misspelled as "Fanning," indicating that spelling errors such as these were quite common, even for high-ranking government officials.

23 The Papers of the Texas Revolution, 7:272, see "Huston to Lawrence, Galveston Bay, June 2, 1836."

24 *Handbook of Texas Online,* s.v., "Isaac Watts Burton," http://www.tsha.utexas.edu/handbook/online/articles/BB/fbu60.html (accessed May 27, 2006).

25 Joseph D. Olson, *Texas Numismatic History: A Catalogue,* 1st ed. (Texas Numismatic Heritage Press, 2006), 35-37.

26 Texas Military Pay Entitlement Certificates, Galveston Issue, The Texas Collection of Darrel Brown, non-published, October 2006.

27 "Henry Reed," Veteran Biographies, San Jacinto Museum of History, Herztein Library, found online at http://www.sanjacinto-museum.org/Herzstein_Library/Veteran_Biographies/San_Jacinto_Bios/biographies/default.asp?action=bio&id=3515; Index to Military Rolls of the Republic of Texas, found online at http://www.tshaonline.org/supsites/military/rep_cont.htm.

28 *Handbook of Texas Online,* s.v., "George Washington Poe," http://www.tsha.utexas.edu/handbook/online/articles/PP/fpo2.html (accessed January 23, 2006).

29 William C. Davis, *The Pirates Lafitte: The Treacherous World of the Corsairs of the Gulf* (New York: Harcourt, Inc., 2005), 430-31.

30 Joe B. Frantz, "La Bah_a," *Six Missions of Texas* (Waco: Texian Press, 1965), 63-64.

31 *Handbook of Texas Online,* s.v., "Jane Herbert Wilkinson Long," http://www.tsha.utexas.edu/handbook/online/articles/LL/flo11.html (accessed September 29, 2008).

32 James, *The Raven,* 265-66.

33 "Brigham's report to Congress," October 10, 1836, Journals of the House of Representatives of the Republic of Texas, 1st Cong., 1st sess. (Columbia: G & T.H. Borden, Public Printers, 1836), 10.

34 Ibid., 11-15.

35 Bob Medlar, *Texas Obsolete Notes and Scrip* (San Antonio, TX: Society of Paper Money Collectors, 1968), 186.

36 Gray, *Diary,* 219.

37 Index to Military Rolls of the Republic of Texas, Company San Augustine Volunteers, found online at http://www.tshaonline.org/supsites/military/rep_cont.htm.

38 *Handbook of Texas Online,* s.v., "John M. Bradley," http://www.tsha.utexas.edu/handbook/online/articles/BB/fbr14.html (accessed August 7, 2006).

39 Index to Military Rolls of the Republic of Texas, P.R. Splane, found online at http://www.tshaonline.org/supsites/military/rep_cont.htm.

40 Thomas Lloyd Miller, *Bounty and Donation Land Grants of Texas, 1835-1888* (Austin: University of Texas Press, 1967), 336.

41 *Handbook of Texas Online,* s.v., "William Becknell," http://www.tshaonline.org/handbook/online/articles/BB/fbe17.html (accessed April 28, 2008).

42 *Handbook of Texas Online,* s.v., "Barnard Elliott Bee, Sr.," http://www.tsha.utexas.edu/handbook/online/articles/BB/fbeaz.html (accessed May 27, 2006).

43 *Handbook of Texas Online,* s.v., "Battle of Concepci_n," http://www.tsha.utexas.edu/handbook/online/articles/CC/qec2.html (accessed November 18, 2006).

44 "Michael R. Goheen," Veteran Biographies, San Jacinto Museum of History, Herztein Library, found online at http://www.sanjacinto-museum.org/Herzstein_Library/Veteran_Biographies/San_Jacinto_Bios/biographies/default.asp?action=bio&id=3167 (accessed September 30, 2008).

45 "Thomas Gilmer McGehee," Veteran Biographies, San Jacinto Museum of History, Herztein Library, found online at http://www.sanjacinto-museum.org/Herzstein_Library/Veteran_Biographies/San_Jacinto_Bios/biographies/default.asp?action=bio&id=2830 (accessed September 30, 2008).

46 Helen Foster Snow, "Captain Michael Roup Goheen: Texas Records," Moody Papers, Woodson Research Center, Fondren Library, Rice University, Houston, Texas.

47 *Handbook of Texas Online,* s.v., "John Ferdinand Webber," http://www.tshaonline.org/handbook/online/articles/WW/fwe59.html (accessed May 3, 2008).

48 Smithwick, *The Evolution of a State,* 140-42.

49 "Brigham's report to Congress," Journals of the House of Representatives, 14.

50 The Papers of the Texas Revolution, 9:59-60, see "Triplett to Christy, Yellow Banks, October, 4, 1836."

51 Jordan, *Lone Star Navy,* 79.

52 Gray, *Diary,* 210-11.

53 "Agreement entitling Robert Triplett to and guaranteeing title for six hundred and forty acres on the east end of Galveston island," manuscript document, Texas Collection of Darrel Brown; Research on the Juan N. Seguin land tract, compiled by Darrel Brown.

54 The Papers of the Texas Revolution, 9:59-60.

55 "Brigham's report to Congress," Journals of the House of Representatives, 23.

56 Ibid., 11-22.

57 Virginia H. Taylor, ed., "Henderson to Moody, Columbia, Texas, January 4, 1837," Texas Treasury Papers: Letters received in the Treasury Department of the Republic of Texas, 1836-1846 (hereinafter cited as Texas Treasury Papers), Texas State Library and Archives, Austin, Texas, 4:3.

58 Ibid.

59 "Brigham's report to Congress," Journals of the House of Representatives, 23.

60 James, *The Raven,* 271-73.

61 Stanley Siegel and John A. Moretta, *Houston: A Chronicle of the Bayou City* (Sun Valley, CA: American Historical Press, 2005), 23.

62 Gary Cartwright, *Galveston: A History of The Island* (New York: MacMillan Publishing Company, 1991), 73.

63 *Handbook of Texas Online,* s.v., "Henry Teal," http://www.tsha.utexas.edu/handbook/online/articles/TT/fte2.html (accessed November 19, 2006).

64 Jonathan W. Jordan, *Lone Star Navy* (Dulles, VA: Potomac Books, Inc., 2007), 81.

65 Texas Military Pay Entitlement Certificate, Galveston Issue, The Texas Collection of Darrel Brown, non-published, October 2006.

66 Medlar, *Texas Obsolete Notes and Scrip,* 63.

67 Jordan, *Lone Star Navy,* 83-89.

68 Ibid., 80-81.

69 "Stevenson to Smith, September 23, 1837," Texas Treasury Papers, 1:62.

70 William M. Gouge, *The Fiscal History of Texas* (New York: Burt Franklin, 1852; rpt. 1969), 25.

CHAPTER SEVEN

HOUSTON: THE GREAT STOCK EXCHANGE

CH7

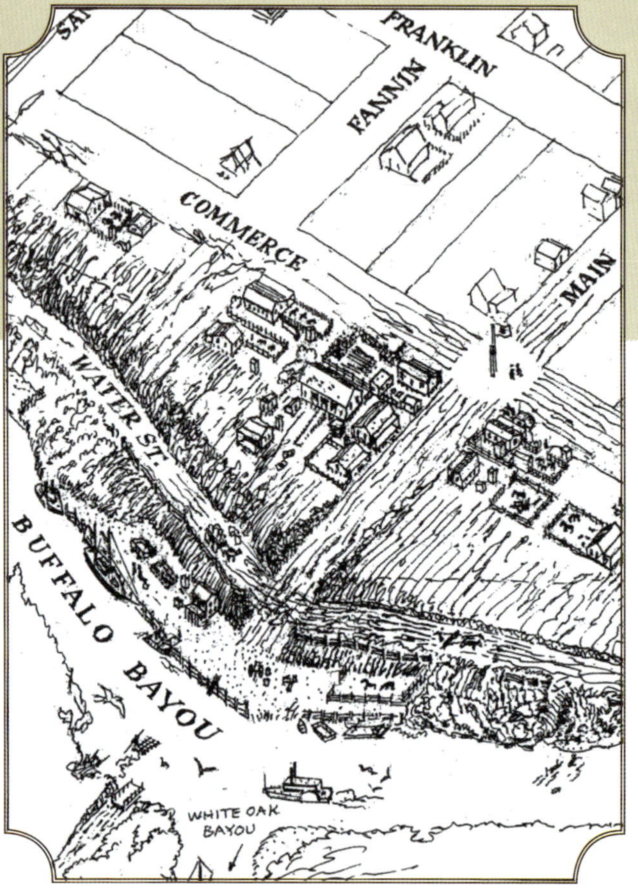

Houston, Texas, was established in the summer of 1836 on the banks of Buffalo Bayou. The town was located several miles upstream from the ashes of Harrisburg, one of many unfortunate targets of a burning rampage conducted by Santa Anna's forces only months before.

Fig 7.1, Allen's Landing, c. 1837, Houston Municipal Wharf.
Courtesy of James L. Glass.

The Bayou City was founded by two land speculators from New York: Augustus Chapman Allen and his brother John Kirby Allen. While the Allen brothers originally sought to purchase land in nearby Galveston and build a port city after the victory at San Jacinto, title problems associated with the Triplett purchase agreement forced them to look further upstream to where Buffalo and White Oak Bayou converged.[1] A title for the land that became the town of Houston was issued to the brothers in August 1836. The Allen Brothers wisely named their new city "Houston" in honor of the hero of San Jacinto, hoping that a name association with the popular general would attract investors. Houston seemed a perfect choice as the new center of commerce because of its direct water route to the sea. It was also centrally located among the population of Texas.

The Allen brothers were so anxious to build their new town that almost no consideration was given to planning the city according to the direction of a compass. The largest streets ran northeast and southwest with the main street extending approximately three quarters of a mile from the wharf on Buffalo Bayou (present-day Allen's Landing) to an area of prairie on which most of the stores were built.[2] The landing itself was littered with cargoes of hogsheads and barrels and other freight stacked up on the docks.[3] Many of the homes were single-story wood-framed houses that were painted white and accompanied with a garden area. The new residents were often irritated with the hot, humid weather and perpetually muddy streets. A plethora of saloons, tents, and numerous drinking establishments greeted investors and visitors to the newly established town. Drunken Indians yelped and stumbled out in the muddy streets, no more than areas of cleared prairie. Among the novelties sold to newcomers were skulls of the Mexican soldiers unscrupulously gathered by entrepreneurs from the battlefields at San Jacinto. In stark contrast to the somewhat uncivilized appearance, Houston proudly carried the name of the hero of San Jacinto and served as Texas' first permanent capital from April 19, 1837, to October 17, 1839.[4]

Fig 7.4, Republic of Texas, Capitol Building.
Courtesy Houston Metropolitan Research Center, Houston Public Library, Houston, Texas.

The new capitol building was constructed by Thomas William Ward at the corner of Main Street and Texas Avenue. The carpenters raced to complete the quarters for the government in the majestic new building which dominated the bustling young town on the bayou. This building represented the pride that radiated throughout all of Texas. It housed an office for the President, members of Congress, and the Treasury Department from which all of the paper money issued from this new capital was signed and issued. With the completion of the capitol building, the new Republic (barely a year old) felt complete and whole as they were at last a sovereign nation. It served as the capitol of the Republic of Texas from 1837-1839. The present-day Rice Hotel now stands on the site of this historic building.

Fig 7.5, Gen. Sam Houston's Old Home.
Courtesy of Richard D. Laster.

The small two-room house shown in Figure 7.5, located near the corner of Caroline and Preston in downtown Houston, was less than two blocks away from the capitol building. It served as Sam Houston's residence and occasional office. This humble abode became known as the "Texas White House" and was next door to the home of John Kirby and Augustus C. Allen.

As the President and members of Congress gathered for their first official function, a buzz of excitement filled the large, wooden building. An extract from the House Journal of May 5, 1837, describes the emotions of Sam Houston's entry into the great hall before the first session of the Second Congress:[5]

> *The Senate then entered the hall, preceded by their Sergeant-at-Arms; the President* pro tem *took his seat on the right hand of the Speaker, and presided jointly with him...The Senators were provided with seats in front of the chair, and the officers of the two Houses associated in their several duties at their respective stations. At twelve o'clock, His Excellency, the President, entered the hall, accompanied by the heads of the several departments, and other officers of the government, and also by Joseph Tucker Crawford, Esq., His Britannic Majesty's Consul, at Tampico, and Commissioner from the British Government to this Republic, and preceded by the joint committee of the two Houses. The President was received by the members of the two houses standing uncovered, and was conducted to a seat between the President* pro tem *of the Senate, and the Speaker of the House.*[6]

At this first address to Congress in his namesake city, Sam Houston must have enjoyed the pomp and celebratory entrance. Although the petition for annexation had been summarily rejected by the United States, the U.S. formally recognized the Republic of Texas in March 1837, on the last day of Andrew Jackson's presidency. As homage to his old friend, Jackson summarily pardoned President Houston for the Stanbery affair and the related fine (which had never been paid) on the same date.[7] The annexation issue was dead, having been soundly defeated by the abolitionists in the U.S. Senate. This vote assured that Texas would remain a "spunky little independent republic" for the foreseeable future.[8]

In this crowning moment of glory and celebration, Sam Houston proudly delivered his speech to the members of Congress and the distinguished guests. With the grand debut in his namesake city behind him, the President and Henry Smith, former provisional governor and newly appointed Treasury Secretary, began to search for solutions to the Republic's looming financial crisis. Both men knew that without money in the treasury and an influx of revenue receipts, the new Republic was headed for insolvency as the government would be unable to function for long without the availability of money and credit.

THE TREASURY DEPARTMENT IS EXPANDED

The Treasury Department also experienced growing pains. Shortly after the capital moved to Houston, it became apparent that auditor John W. Moody was increasingly overwhelmed with work. Sam Houston once referred to Moody as "one of the most capable, industrious and untiring men that I have ever known in any department of business."[9] An avalanche of military and civil claims deluged Moody, and there were not enough hours in the day for him to physically review and audit each item. Although Moody twice tendered his resignation, Sam Houston refused to accept it. Moody, frustrated with the President wrote, "[it is] absolutely necessary that there should be another Auditor; one of

Fig 7.2, Augustus C. Allen.
The San Jacinto Museum of History, Houston, Texas.

Fig 7.3, John Kirby Allen.
The San Jacinto Museum of History, Houston, Texas.

whom should audit the military claims, the other the naval, Civil and Contingent; there should also be a comptroller who should examine the proceedings of both auditors in order that clerical errors should be detected."[10] On May 26, 1837, the same day that Moody's recommendation was written, President Houston forwarded the request to the Texas Congress. Houston also gave his personal endorsement to Moody's recommendation. The Texas Congress quickly granted the approval for an additional auditor and a comptroller of the Treasury. This led to the appointments of J.G. Welschmeyer as a second auditor and Francis R. Lubbock and Elisha Pease as comptrollers.

IN SEARCH OF FINANCING

During the previous few months, agents for the Texas government desperately tried to increase the country's cash on hand by floating a $5 million loan in New Orleans. In February 1837, Smith received a letter from Peter W. Grayson, the Texas Attorney General, describing the stiff resistance from a group of potential lenders.[11] The group cited the Texian loan agreements of the previous year which had been negotiated by the Commissioners of Texas only to have the terms changed by the Burnet government with disastrous results. Their communication with Grayson seemed to be a stall tactic more than anything. The lenders used the Attorney General's office to question the Texas agent's authority to negotiate such a loan, but in reality they had no interest in extending any credit.

A.J. Yates was the newly appointed Commissioner of Loans for Texas. He held several meetings with principals in Philadelphia on the subject of floating a loan for the new government.[12] After several days of interviews and negotiations, Yates began to realize how deep the anti-slavery sentiment ran on the East Coast, and the political fears of the bankers who might be found lending money to a new slave-holding Republic. Even though similar fund raising campaigns had been successful in Charleston and New Orleans, extending credit to this new country outside of the U.S. was deemed excessively risky. Upon traveling to New York, Yates discovered that slavery was already a politically charged issue. He was discouraged by friends from further negotiations regarding a loan for Texas. On April 11, 1837, Yates reported, "that it would be utterly impossible to procure any money in this Country on the Bonds of the Govt. of Texas at any rate of interest or sacrifice at the present crisis… "

Yet Treasury Secretary Henry Smith was a man of relentless determination and appeared unfazed by the reports. His job was to raise funds for the government, support the credit, and keep the country functioning on a sound financial footing. Although he had very little to work with, Smith was determined to overcome the maze of legal, political and credit setbacks which had already befallen the infant Republic.

In anticipation of the opening of Congress in May, Smith prepared a detailed report of the audited claims against the government, issued from January 1, 1836, to April 18, 1837. He cited that of these outstanding claims, $604,985 had been issued and only $1,569 were returned to the government in payment of taxes![13] This amounted to only two and a half cents paid back into the treasury for every $1,000 that had been paid out. In addition to the audited claims, another $1,007,000 had been expended as appropriated by the Texas Congress in 1836.[14] The great majority of this amount ($850,000) was for military and naval expenditures. Making matters worse, virtually all of the revenues that were paid to the government were the Republic's own paper, endorsed back to the government and then cancelled. Smith's alarming report may have been the catalyst that defined Houston's future conservatism, especially regarding the issue of paper money.

Smith presented another report on May 12, 1837, detailing his plan for revenue raising and finance.[15] He suggested a series of new taxes in an effort to raise an additional $200,000 per annum. The proposed taxes were as follows: direct taxes on lands and all other property at one half percent. This *ad valorem* tax was expected to yield $125,000. A license tax on wholesale and retail dealers, public shows, billiard halls, and drinking taverns (of which there were plenty) was expected to produce about $10,000 in revenues. Smith also expected another $40,000 as "present supposed dues on granted lands, and the Republic would have annual revenue of $375,000 per year." The President was quite pleased with Smith's thoroughness and the ambitious plans for revenue raising, but wondered how he planned to pay off the outstanding debts of the Republic. Virtually all of the outstanding drafts written since the early days at San Felipe in 1835 were not accruing interest, and the creditors were now demanding to be paid. Several of them had made a point to travel to the capital and make their position on the matter known to the government. Smith's answer was one of postponement. If he could have all of the outstanding claims or audited drafts consolidated into a common pool or a fund, then the debt would become much more manageable for the young government.

THE CONSOLIDATED FUND OF TEXAS

Encouraged by Houston's endorsement of his taxation plan, Smith then created a plan for funding the public debt. He was careful to offer some relief to the public creditors, and at the same time sustain the integrity of the government.[16] The Treasury Secretary's idea was to call in all the outstanding treasury warrants and audited paper and exchange the odd denominations for certificates of stock in the Consolidated Fund of Texas at $100 per share. These certificates would be redeemable in not less than five years, and would bear an interest rate of 10 percent per annum, payable semi-annually. This would not only result in the redemption and exchange of audited drafts for interest-bearing paper, but it would offer other advantages to the holders of the outstanding paper. For the creditors who had seen their audited drafts and treasury warrants sell at an average of 15 percent of face value, Smith's plan offered them hope of receiving a higher market value. By exchanging their audited drafts and treasury warrants for the new paper, or "consolidating" their debt into an interest bearing fund at 10 percent per annum, the creditors hoped to see their claims trading at or near their par value, thus creating liquidity and a security which could also be used as collateral for loans.

The securitization of the debt was met with overwhelming acceptance in Congress. "An Act to authorize the Consolidation and Funding of the Public Debt" passed Congress on June 7, 1837, and an act for creating revenue from import duties was passed on June 12, 1837. With these two acts, Congress created stock in the Consolidated Fund of Texas in denominations of $100, $500, $1,000, $5,000 and $10,000. In this form, the creditors could be satisfied until the government found itself able to pay off the principal amounts. Until then, the government would only have to provide the interest. The certificates were issued on several different varieties of paper. Small debts or audited certificates of less than $100 would continue to remain outstanding. The amount issued in funding the audited drafts and claims was $771,000, with an additional $66,400 issued for land scrip, making a total of $837,400.[17] The treasury warrants and certificates continued to be funded in this manner until January 1, 1840. While many investors of today may think of stock as an equity stake in a company, this stock was similar to the shares of preferred stock which functions as a debt instrument. True to form, this issue carried a perpetual maturity and could be called, or "redeemed by the government," after five years or on September, 1, 1842.

Fig 7.6, $100 Consolidated Fund of Texas, Houston, September 1, 1837, issued to Lewis A. Collier.

Private Collection, Cr. CF1, O-630.

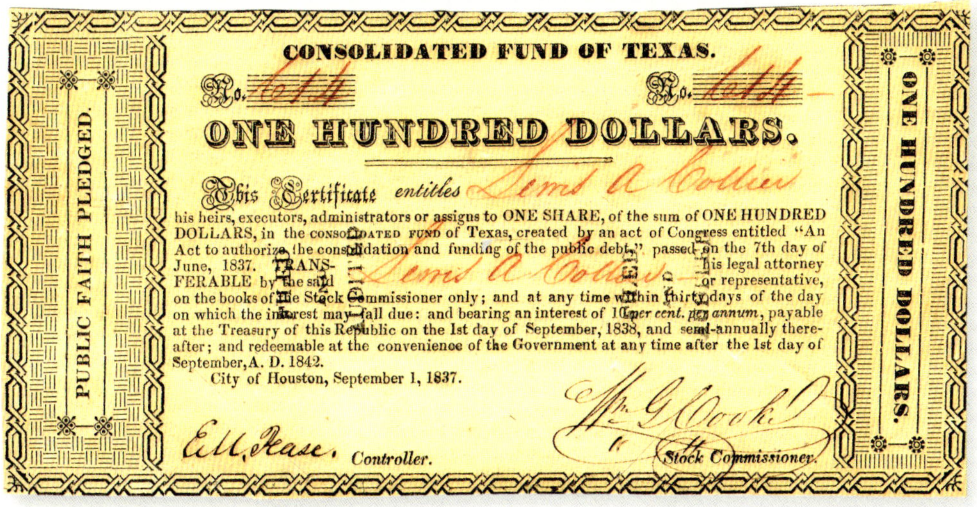
CONSOLIDATED FUND OF TEXAS.

No. 644 No. 644

ONE HUNDRED DOLLARS.

This Certificate entitles Lewis A Collier his heirs, executors, administrators or assigns to ONE SHARE, of the sum of ONE HUNDRED DOLLARS, in the CONSOLIDATED FUND of Texas, created by an act of Congress entitled "An Act to authorize the consolidation and funding of the public debt," passed on the 7th day of June, 1837. TRANSFERABLE by the said Lewis A Collier his legal attorney or representative, on the books of the Stock Commissioner only; and at any time within thirty days of the day on which the interest may fall due: and bearing an interest of 10 *per cent. per annum*, payable at the Treasury of this Republic on the 1st day of September, 1838, and semi-annually thereafter; and redeemable at the convenience of the Government at any time after the 1st day of September, A. D. 1842.

City of Houston, September 1, 1837.

PUBLIC FAITH PLEDGED.

ONE HUNDRED DOLLARS.

E M Pease, *Controller.*

Wm G Cooke *Stock Commissioner.*

The language of the relatively common issue shown in Figure 7.6 references the June 7, 1837, act which created this $100 debt instrument. While the act provided for payment of interest at 10 percent per annum, and a maturity of "not more than ten years" from date of issue, it is important to note the certificate itself plainly states it is "redeemable at the convenience of the Government any time after the 1'st day of September, A.D. 1842." Traces of the "X" cancellation can be seen through the controller's signature, and "FILED AND AUDITED" is stamped twice across the face. It is signed by Elisha Pease, Controller, and William G. Cooke, Stock Commissioner.

On the $500 issue in Figure 7.8, Benjamin Smith endorsed the reverse, indicating that he may have kept

Fig 7.8, $500 Consolidated Fund of Texas, Houston, September 1, 1837, issued to Benjamin F. Smith.
Private Collection, Cr. CF5, 0-655.

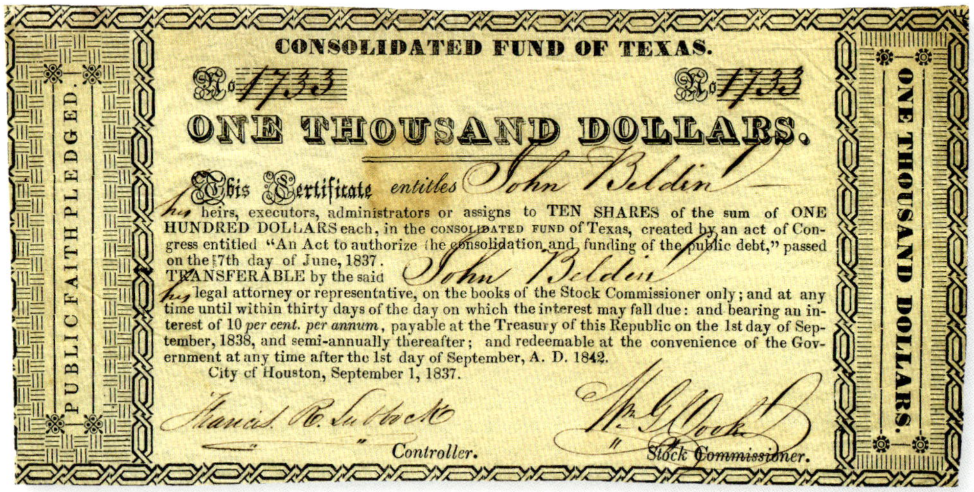

Fig 7.9, $1,000 Consolidated Fund of Texas, Houston, September 1, 1837, issued to John Beldin.
Private Collection, Cr. CF9, 0-675.

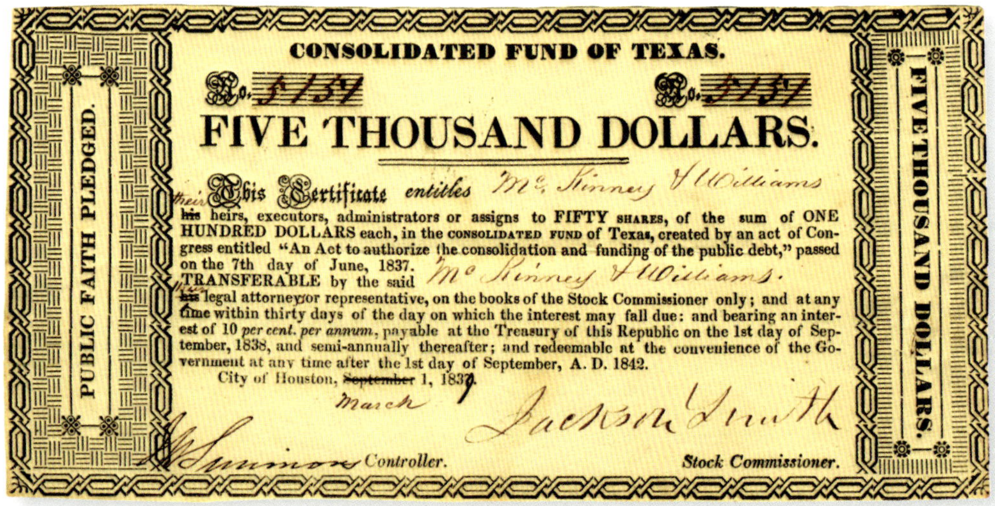

Fig 7.10, $5,000 Consolidated Fund of Texas, Houston, March 1, 1839, issued to McKinney & Williams.
Private Collection, Cr. CF6A, 0-685.

the piece until the ultimate redemption date instead of signing it over to another individual. The left-hand border states "Public Faith Pledged" as do all issues of the 1837 printed series. Like many Texas issues, it also sports a large "X" cut cancellation in the center and is signed by Elisha Pease, Controller, and William G. Cooke, Stock Commissioner.

The $1,000 denomination in Figure 7.9 for ten shares appears to be un-cancelled and does not show any endorsement or other signs that it was ever paid, despite the large amount. The payee, John Beldin, was a veteran of the Texas Army and was listed as having been dangerously wounded during the siege of Béxar from December 5 to December 10, 1835.[18] Beldin eventually recovered from his wounds to become a significant creditor of the Republic whose outstanding warrants were converted into the stock as shown above. The note is signed by Francis R. Lubbock, Controller, and William G. Cooke, Stock Commissioner.

An interesting aspect of the larger denomination Consolidated Fund certificates is that many are found bearing the names of well-known Texans. These persons, or in this case the merchant firm of McKinney & Williams, were owed substantial amounts by the Republic as they made the most significant financial contributions to the cause of the revolution. The $5,000 denomination in Figure 7.10 for fifty shares was not issued until March 1, 1839, as the month and year had been crossed out and re-entered. This crisp un-circulated example is not cancelled, indicating that it may never have been collected. It is signed by James W. Simmons as Controller, and Jackson Smith as Stock Commissioner.

The $10,000 certificate in Figure 7.11 of stock issued to James Love is the highest (and rarest) denomination in the series and reflects Love's significant monetary contributions to the Texas Revolution. Despite their common goals for Texas, Love became a bitter enemy of Sam Houston and later allied himself with Mirabeau B. Lamar and David G. Burnet. Love moved to Houston from New Orleans in 1837 and settled in Galveston in 1838. This issue bears the inscription "This certificate bears an interest of ten per cent from 1st Sept. 1837 payable 1st March 1839. Geor[ge] W. Poe, Stock Comm[issioner]" It is also signed by James W. Simmons as Controller.

Unlike the printed versions which were issued in standard denominations, a partially manuscript issue was used in the spring of 1839 for the consolidation of the public debt which was exchanged into the fund in odd dollar amounts. An example is shown in figure 7.12.

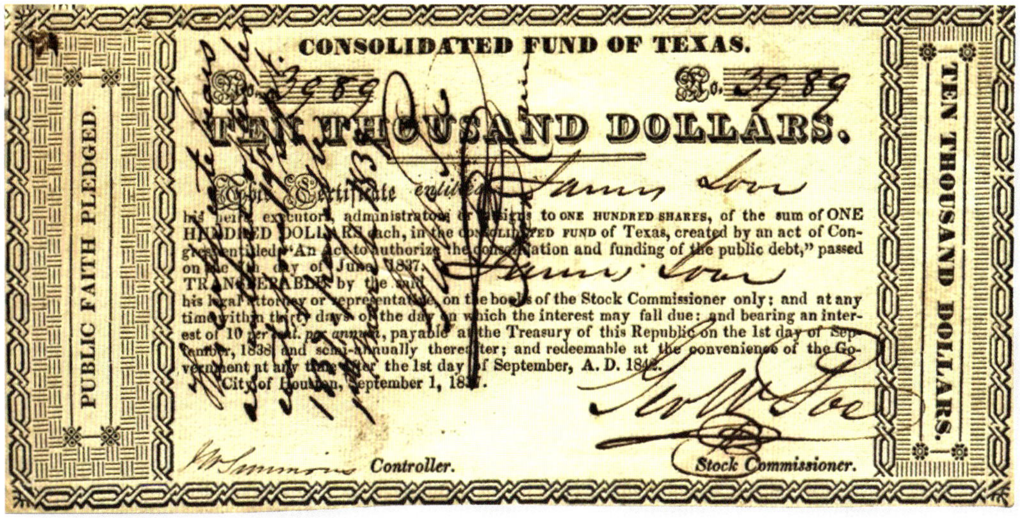
CONSOLIDATED FUND OF TEXAS.

No. 3989 No. 3989

TEN THOUSAND DOLLARS.

PUBLIC FAITH PLEDGED.

TEN THOUSAND DOLLARS.

This Certificate entitles James Love his heirs, executors, administrators or assigns to ONE HUNDRED SHARES, of the sum of ONE HUNDRED DOLLARS each, in the CONSOLIDATED FUND of Texas, created by an act of Congress entitled "An Act to authorize the consolidation and funding of the public debt," passed on the ... day of June 1837. TRANSFERABLE by the said James Love his legal attorney or representative, on the books of the Stock Commissioner only; and at any time within thirty days of the day on which the interest may fall due; and bearing an interest of 10 per cent. per annum, payable at the Treasury of this Republic on the 1st day of September, 1838, and semi-annually thereafter; and redeemable at the convenience of the Government at any time after the 1st day of September, A. D. 184[illegible]. City of Houston, September 1, 18[illegible].

J W Simmons Controller. Geo W Poe Stock Commissioner.

Fig 7.11, $10,000 Consolidated Fund of Texas, Houston, September 1, 1837, issued to James Love.
Private Collection, Cr. CF6B, O-690.

To a large degree, the abundance of stock in the Consolidated Fund explains the relative scarcity of the surviving pieces of early Texas paper. If almost $605,000 of audited drafts had remained outstanding, a plethora of issues would be readily available in the collector marketplace. Instead, the great majority of these issues dated before September 1837 were lost to the ages as they were converted into stock in the Consolidated Fund of Texas. These rather mundane looking printed obligations of the Republic of Texas mask the myriad of handwritten obligations which were issued during and immediately following the revolution. The previous obligations were converted in an effort to realize increased liquidity for the creditors and a better value in the marketplace. Although the funding of the public debt under the Act of June 7, 1837, was set to expire on January 1, 1840, it continued into 1841, long after the capital had been moved to the city of Austin under the direction of President Mirabeau B. Lamar.

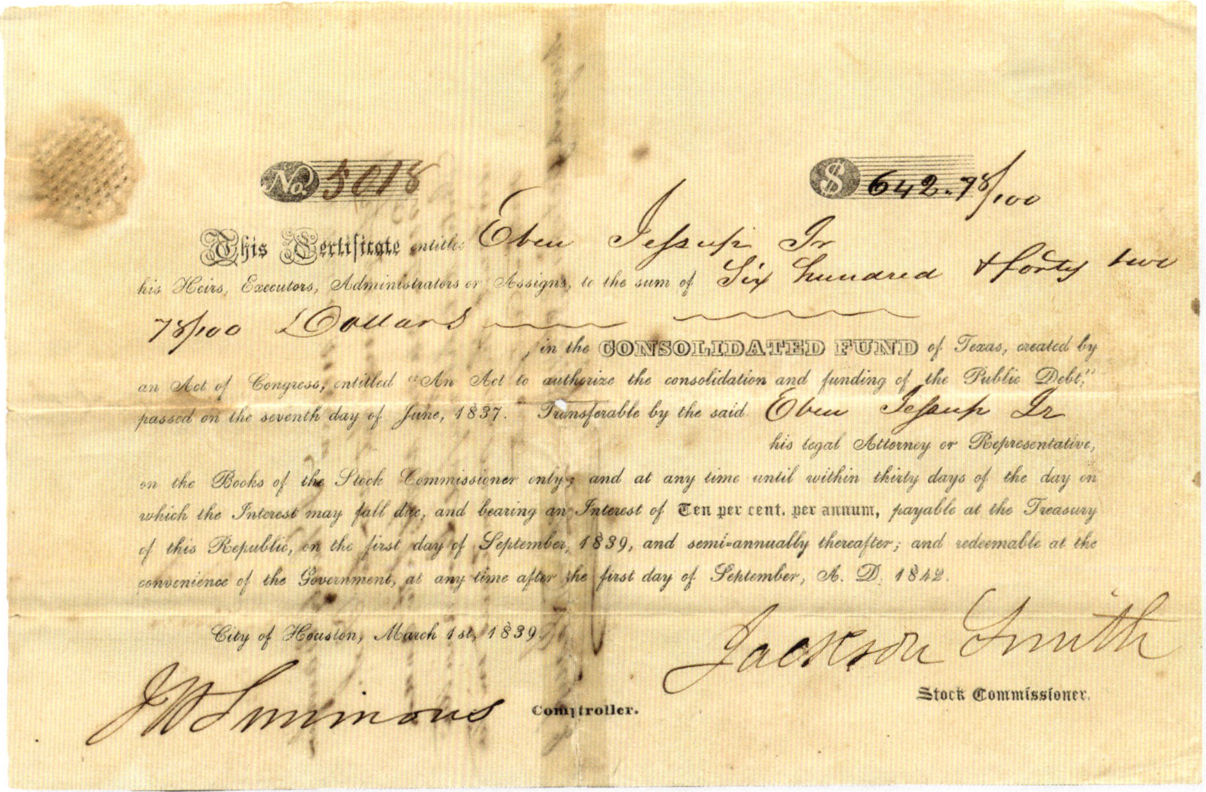
No 5018 $642.78/100

This Certificate entitles Eben Jessup Jr his Heirs, Executors, Administrators or Assigns, to the sum of Six hundred & forty two 78/100 Dollars in the CONSOLIDATED FUND of Texas, created by an Act of Congress, entitled "An Act to authorize the consolidation and funding of the Public Debt," passed on the seventh day of June, 1837. Transferable by the said Eben Jessup Jr his legal Attorney or Representative, on the Books of the Stock Commissioner only; and at any time until within thirty days of the day on which the Interest may fall due, and bearing an Interest of Ten per cent. per annum, payable at the Treasury of this Republic, on the first day of September, 1839, and semi-annually thereafter; and redeemable at the convenience of the Government, at any time after the first day of September, A. D. 1842.

City of Houston, March 1st, 1839.

J W Simmons Comptroller. Jackson Smith Stock Commissioner.

No. 5018 $642.78/100

This certificate entitles Ebner Jessup, Jr, his Heirs, Executors, Administrators or Assigns, to the sum of Six hundred & forty two 78/100 Dollars–

(Signed) James W. Simmons, Comptroller, Jackson Smith, Stock Commissioner

Fig 7.12, $642.78 Consolidated Fund of Texas, Houston, March 1, 1839, issued to Ebner Jessup, Jr.
Private Collection, Cr. CF13, O-695.

Fig 7.13, Elisha M. Pease.
Texas State Library & Archives Commission, Austin, Texas.

Fig 7.14, Francis R. Lubbock.
Courtesy of Albert and Ethel Herzstein Library, The San Jacinto Museum of History, Houston, Texas.

While often described as a somewhat boring series to collectors due to their standardized amounts, the stock of the Consolidated Fund of Texas represents the single most important re-financing during the Republic era. While the measure increased the carrying cost of the debt, it allowed the government to buy something that became even more priceless as the years progressed—it was able to buy time.

Many of the certificates of stock in the Consolidated Fund issued from Houston during Sam Houston's administration were signed by Elisha Pease or Francis Lubbock, as they shared the office of comptroller. Later Consolidated Fund certificates issued from Houston during the Lamar administration were countersigned by James W. Simmons as the comptroller. Pease and Lubbock were anything but ordinary accountants, and their lives took similar yet remarkably different political paths after Texas entered statehood in 1846.

Elisha Marshall Pease was born in Connecticut on January 3, 1812, and educated at Westfield Academy in Massachusetts. He arrived in Texas in 1835 and became engulfed in the developing Texas Revolution.[19] Pease fought in the battle of Gonzales on October 2, and then served as secretary to the General Council of the Provisional Government at San Felipe. He recorded the official proceedings. He later attended the convention that met at Washington-on-the-Brazos in March 1836 and authored a good part of the Constitution of the Republic. Later that same year he served in the *ad interim* government as the chief clerk in the Navy and Treasury Departments.

In the fall of 1836, Pease served as acting Secretary of the Treasury, and in April 1837, he became the Republic's first comptroller of public accounts when the capital was located to Houston. He later practiced law in nearby Brazoria and became well known and respected in the field. Pease was elected governor in 1853 then re-elected in 1855. It was Pease who persuaded the legislature to further the Texas educational system established by Lamar. He helped establish the permanent school fund which has survived and prospered to educate millions to this day. He worked to encourage railroad construction in Texas, instigated the placement of the state penitentiary on a self-supporting basis, and established reservations to civilize and educate the state's Indian population.

As a staunch Unionist, Pease aligned himself with the minority faction in Texas politics in 1859 and remained active into the early months of the Civil War. He then kept a low profile and quietly maintained his loyalty to the Union until the end of the conflict. In 1866, he lost his bid to become governor during Reconstruction, but was later appointed as governor when the democratic candidate was removed from office. In the later years of his life, Pease practiced law in Austin, engaged in various business ventures, and lived a quiet life with his wife and two daughters. Pease died on August 26, 1883, at the age of seventy-one and is buried in Austin.

Pease's counterpart, Francis R. Lubbock, was born October 16, 1815, in Beaufort, South Carolina. He was the brother of Thomas S. Lubbock, after whom Lubbock County is named. Young Frank quit school at the age of fourteen after his father died, and took a job as a clerk in a hardware store. A lifelong Democrat, Lubbock became a prominent political activist at a young age.[20] He was involved in the nullification crisis in South Carolina in 1832, and moved to Houston from New Orleans in 1837 where he opened a general store in the booming new town. While there, his quick mind for business and his strong grasp of finances accelerated his political rise. He was appointed comptroller of the Republic of Texas by President Sam Houston at the young age of twenty-three. Like Pease, his signature graces many of the warrants and certificates issued by Texas during the capital's tenure in Houston.

Lubbock is best known as the Governor of Texas during the Civil War, narrowly defeating incumbent Gov. Edward Clark by only 124 votes in 1861. He presided over Texas's secession from the Union and staunchly supported the Confederacy, constantly working to improve the military capabilities of Texas. He angered the citizens of Galveston when he gave a speech from the steps of the Tremont House advocating laying waste to the island city, except for the existing shore batteries so that when the "vandal hordes arrived they would find neither potable water nor shelter."[21]

After his term ended in August 1864, Lubbock joined the Confederate Army and was appointed aide-de-camp to Jefferson Davis. As an expert on the Trans-Mississippi Department, Lubbock provided Davis with firsthand information on the war west of the Mississippi River. At the end of the war, Lubbock fled Richmond with Davis and was captured by federal authorities in Georgia. After his release, Lubbock returned to Texas and went into business in Houston and Galveston where he served as tax collector. From 1878 to 1891, Lubbock served as Treasurer of the State of Texas. From 1891 until his death, he lived in Austin, where he died on June 22, 1905, at the age of eighty-nine.

Both of these remarkable men rose to dizzying heights and held powerful posts in the fledgling government while still in their early twenties. One became a staunch Unionist and the other a firebrand secessionist. Both served as governor, one during secession and the other during Reconstruction. Although they later grew to be political opposites during Texas statehood, in these early days of the Republic they worked side-by-side in the offices of the Treasury, serving the young country they both adopted.

PROMISSORY NOTES

Even though Congress passed the Act to Consolidate and Fund the Public Debt on June 7, 1837, the new shares of stock would not be issued until the first of September. It is difficult to say how Smith's re-financing plan would have worked if all had gone according to his recommendations. On June 9, 1837, a mere two days after Congress established the Consolidated Fund of Texas they passed an act authorizing an issue of $500,000 in promissory notes bearing 10 percent interest, redeemable in one year. This new legislation effectively increased the national debt and made the notes receivable for all public dues.[22] The notes were to be used by the government to redeem warrants written for the civil and military list of claims and would be received as cash for all public dues. Although President Houston signed the legislation for the new currency in approval, Henry Smith was vehemently opposed to a new issue of interest bearing notes, stating that "the last law virtually repealed the funding law by absorbing all the revenues specially appropriated to pay the interest."[23] He further reasoned that "it places the government under obligations with which she certainly not be able to comply" and warned that "if carried into execution will prove extremely injurious to the government in various ways."[24] Smith's warning was one that would ultimately be ignored by the Congress.

PAYMENTS FOR THE MILITARY

In the meantime, the Treasury Department continued to produce drafts against the empty government coffers. These warrants were issued from Houston in the name of the Republic of Texas to recognize creditors and formalize their claims. As in Columbia, when a claim was presented to the treasury office in Houston, the auditor would examine the voucher or military pay certificate and determine the validity of the claim.[25] He would then reject the claim or issue a warrant or auditors certificate in its stead. These warrants and certificates were also traded or exchanged on the streets of New Orleans for discounts of up to 85 percent. The warrants carried no assurance as to when there would be money to pay them, and their odd amounts kept them from being a circulating medium. Creditors often held on to them, hoping the government finances would stabilize over time. Hence, these drafts or warrants remained a part of the floating debt and changed hands at a substantial discount to their face value unless they were exchanged for stock.

Fig 7.15, John N. Seguin.
Texas State Library & Archives Commission, Austin, Texas.

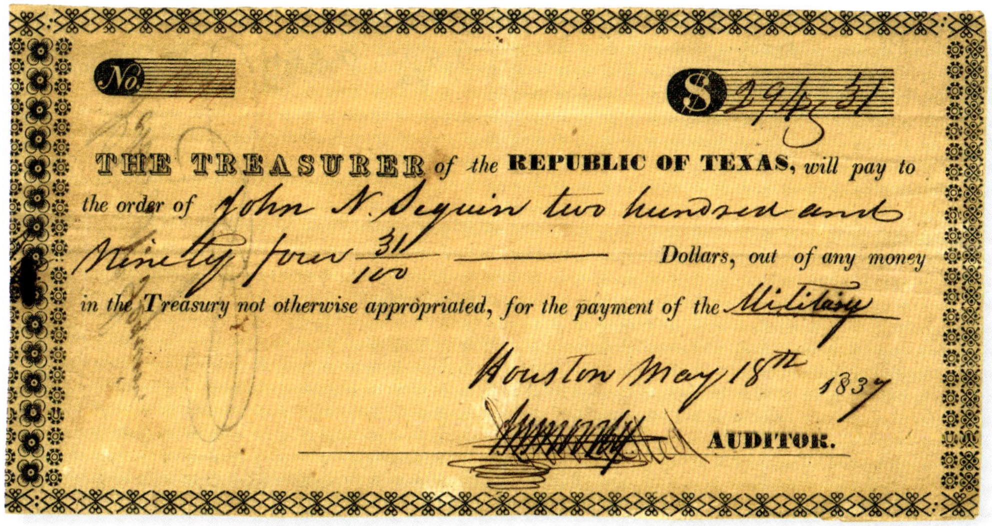
No. $294 31/100
THE TREASURER of the REPUBLIC OF TEXAS, will pay to the order of John N. Seguin two hundred and Ninety four 31/100 Dollars, out of any money in the Treasury not otherwise appropriated, for the payment of the Military
Houston May 18th 1837
AUDITOR.

No. 1696 *$294.31*

THE TREASURER of the REPUBLIC OF TEXAS, will pay to the order of John N. Seguin two hundred and ninety four 31/100 – Dollars, out of any money in the Treasury not otherwise appropriated, for the payment of the Military.

Houston, May 18th 1837, (Signed) J.W. Moody, AUDITOR

Fig 7.16, Houston, May 18, 1837, Treasury Warrant to John N. Seguin for the payment of the Military.
DRT Library Collection, San Antonio, Texas, Cr HW6A, 0-321.

While the payment of $294.31 in Figure 7.16 to John N. Seguin is among the most common paper varieties seen of the Houston warrants, the payee was a most uncommon individual.[26] Unlike many of his American counterparts in the Texas Revolution, Juan Seguin was a native Texan, having been born in San Antonio in 1808. He served on various boards in San Antonio before being elected *alcalde* of Béxar in December 1833. In the spring of 1835, he responded to the Federalist state governor's call for support against the Centralist opposition by leading a militia company to Monclova.

During the Texas revolution, Seguin was promoted to the rank of captain by Stephen F. Austin and raised a company of thirty-seven men. His company participated in the storming of Béxar on December 5, 1835. He returned to the Alamo in February 1836 as the siege began, but was sent out of the old mission as a courier. Upon reaching Gonzales he organized a company of *tejanos* which served as the rear guard to Sam Houston's Army. Seguin later fought at the battle of San Jacinto and afterwards was sent to observe the Mexican Army's retreat. It was Seguin who directed burial services for the remains of the Alamo dead following the war. He returned to San Antonio shortly after this payment was issued and served as the city's military commander until the end of the year. Seguin was the only Texan of Mexican descent to serve in the Senate of the Republic of Texas.

Seguin's warrant is made payable to John N. Seguin, his anglicized name, which he also endorsed in the same manner on the reverse.

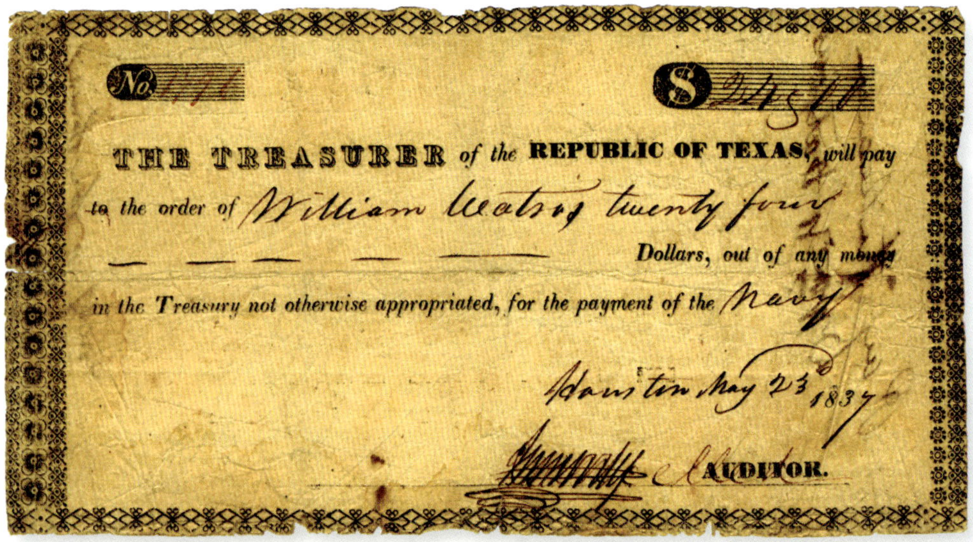

No 1996 $24.00
THE TREASURER of the REPUBLIC OF TEXAS, will pay to the order of William Watson twenty four – Dollars, out of any money in the Treasury not otherwise appropriated, for the payment of the Navy.

Houston, May 23rd 1837, (Signed) J.W. Moody, AUDITOR

Fig 7.17, Houston, May 23, 1837, $24, Treasury Warrant to William Watson for the payment of the Navy.
Private Collection, Cr HW3, 0-321.

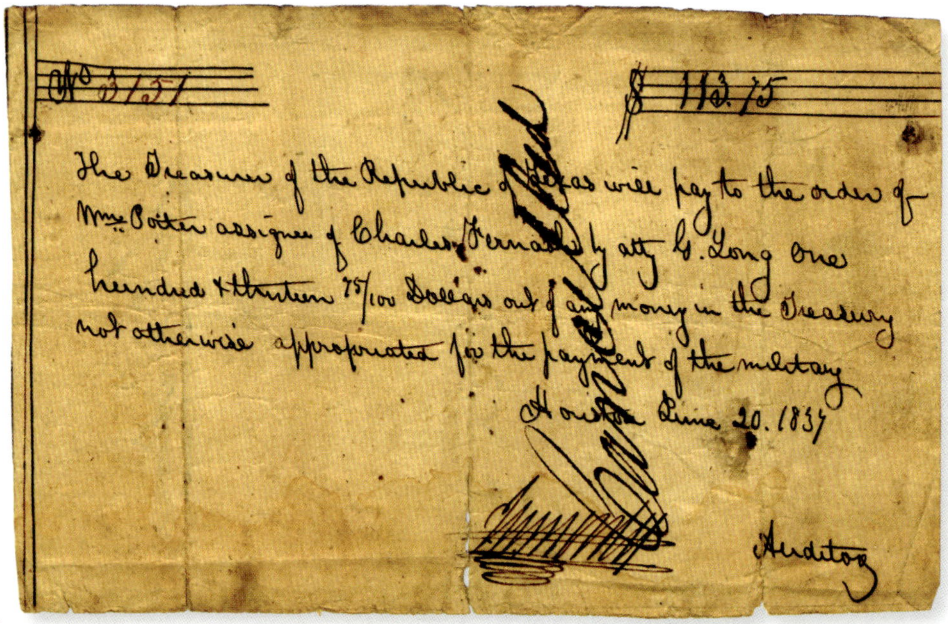

No 3151 $113.75
The Treasurer of the Republic of Texas will pay to the order of W[illia]m Porter assignee of Charles Fernab[le] by att[orne]y G. Long one hundred & thirteen 75/100 Dollars out of any money in the Treasury not otherwise appropriated for the payment of the Military.

Houston, June 20, 1837 (Signed) J.W. Moody, Auditor

Fig 7.18, Houston, June 20, 1837, Handwritten Treasury Warrant to William Porter for the payment of the Military.
Private Collection, Cr. HW1-A, 0-300.

The impact of the Mexican naval blockade was felt by Texas in April and May 1837 when the Mexican Navy sacked or captured four American or Texas vessels, including the grounding and capture of the Texas flagship *Independence* near Velasco. The $24 payment in Figure 7.17 was most likely a "bounty" payment to William Watson, the payee, for enlistment in the first Texas Navy. It was signed the same day that Navy Secretary S. Rhodes Fisher authorized Henry L. Thompson to gather a recruitment of idle soldiers from an army base. Thompson had been described as a "hard-drinking, foul mouth sea dog" and was prone to bravado and carelessness.[27] But Fisher considered him politically reliable, and felt that Watson had burning desire to make the Mexican Navy pay for their actions.

Perhaps having distributed all the leftover printed warrants from Columbia, the Treasury department at Houston issued entirely handwritten pieces from the new capital. In Figure 7.18, note the hand-drawn border at left and the lines for recording the payment number and dollar amount. This payment, No. 3151, is curiously issued as a third party payment "to the order of Wm. Porter assignee of Charles Fernab[le] by atty G. Long." This handwritten treasury warrant is among the scarcest of the early Houston pay warrants.

James A. Sylvester, the payee of the $100 warrant in Figure 7.19, was the soldier who captured Santa Anna following the battle of San Jacinto. Although he was among the most revered of heroes of the Texas Revolution, his name has largely been forgotten to twenty-first century Texans. He was born in Baltimore, Maryland, in 1807 and entered the Texas military through a volunteer company raised in Newport, Kentucky, by Sidney J. Sherman in December 1835.[28] When the Texas Army was reorganized at Gonzales on March 12, 1836, Sylvestor was named as a second sergeant and a color bearer for the company. Not only did he fight in the pivotal battle, it was he who carried the lone battle flag flown by the Texians at San Jacinto.

On the morning of April 22, 1836, Sylvester volunteered for a scouting party of about fifty soldiers led by Col. Ed Burleson in search of General Santa Anna, General Cos and other Mexican soldiers who fled the battlefield the previous day.[29] With a group of four other men, Sylvester departed from the main search party near Vince's Bayou to hunt game. Spotting four deer near the banks of adjacent Buffalo Bayou, Sylvester stopped his horse under a lone tree in the prairie to take a shot when the deer was startled by a Mexican in the grass. Closing in on his new prey, Sergeant Sylvester trained his gun on the fugitive whom he found "lying on his side; with a blanket over his face." Within a few moments of the enemy's surrender, Sylvester was joined by the remainder of the hunting party and escorted the "polite little fellow" back to the site of the battle as a prisoner of war. Unbeknownst to the group, Sylvester had captured Antonio López de Santa Anna. It was almost unprecedented in the annals of warfare for a head of state to be captured fleeing a battlefield. Sylvester's unexpected prize presented Texas with the ultimate bargaining chip, helping to secure its independence.

After several years in Texana, Jackson County, where he worked as a deputy recorder for the county, James Sylvestor left Texas in 1843 for New Orleans. He took a position with the *New Orleans Picayune* newspaper. He periodically returned to Texas for veterans reunions. He never married, but remained a trusted employee of the newspaper until his death on April 9, 1882.

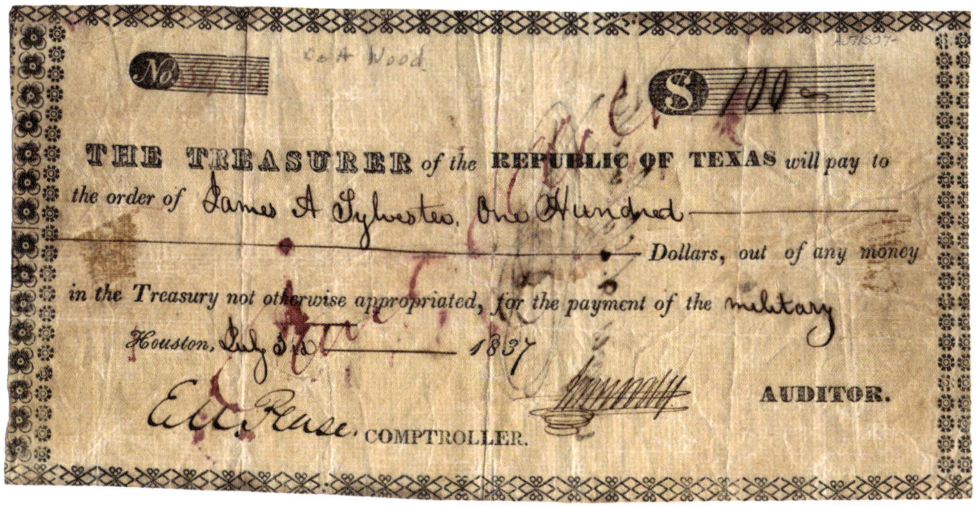

No. 3403 $100 ~

THE TREASURER of the REPUBLIC OF TEXAS, will pay to the order of James A. Sylvester, One Hundred — Dollars, out of any money in the Treasury not otherwise appropriated, for the payment of the Military.

Houston, July 3rd, 1837, (Signed) J.W. Moody, AUDITOR, Elisha Pease, COMPTROLLER

Fig 7.19, Houston, July 3, 1837, Treasury Warrant to James A. Sylvester for the payment of the Military.

Texas Money Collection, Courtesy of Special Collections, University of Houston Libraries, Cr. HW4, 0-342.

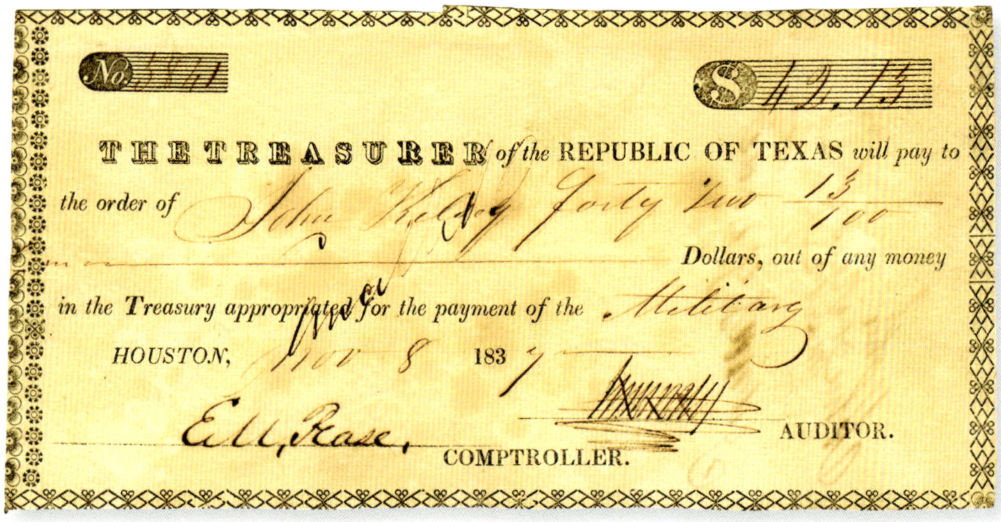

Fig 7.20, Houston, November 8, 1837, Treasury Warrant to John Kelsey for the payment of the Military.

Private Collection, Cr. HW5, 0-393.

No 5841 $42.13
THE TREASURER of the REPUBLIC OF TEXAS, will pay to the order of John Kelsey forty two 13/100 – Dollars, out of any money in the Treasury appropriated for the payment of the Military.

Houston, Nov 8, 1837, (Signed) J.W. Moody, AUDITOR, Elisha Pease, COMPTROLLER,

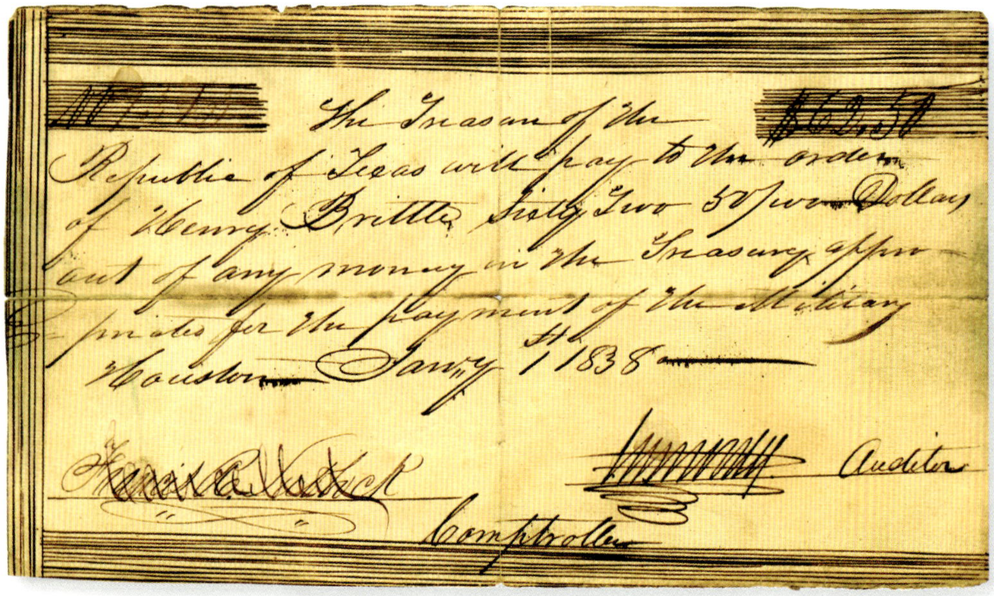

Fig 7.21, Houston, January 1, 1838, Handwritten Treasury Warrant to Henry Brittle for the payment of the Military.

Private Collection, Cr. HW6, 0-312.

No ____ $62.50
The Treasurer of the Republic of Texas will pay to the order of Henry Brittle Sixty Two 50/100 Dollars, out of any money in the Treasury appropriated for the payment of the Military.

Houston, Jan[uar]y 1st, 1838, (Signed) J.W. Moody, Auditor, Francis Lubbock, Comptroller

The payment in Figure 7.20 is very similar in appearance to several of the printed Columbia warrants. It was paid as the Star Money was being issued and began to circulate in the Houston area. This payment of $42.13 to John Kelsey was most likely converted to the new circulating paper money shortly after it was issued. It is one of the most commonly seen varieties of Houston warrants.

Whether it was pure vanity or a lack of printed paper, the most striking appearance of the next series of early Houston warrants is the meticulous way in which the lines were hand drawn with an ink pen and ruler to make it look "official." It was most likely the work of a lone employee who served as the unofficial "graphics department" for the Texas Treasury. The military payment in Figure 7.21 for $62.50 was countersigned by Francis R. Lubbock as Comptroller and John W. Moody as Auditor. A later pen cancellation at left obscures Lubbock's signature. Perhaps even more surprising is the fact that this payment was written and signed by two government officials who were taking care of important government business in their office on New Year's Day in 1838.

No 9355 $24.00

THE TREASURER of the Republic of Texas will pay to the Order of James S. McGahey Assignee of Thos. Dorman twenty four Dollars, out of any money in the Treasury appropriated for the payment of the Military. for bounty

Houston, June 20th, 1838, (Signed) J.W. Moody, 1st Auditor. Francis R. Lubbock Comptroller.

No. $
THE TREASURER of the Republic of Texas will pay
to the Order of
Dollars out of any money in the Treasury appropriated for the payment of the Military.
Houston, 183
1st Auditor.
Comptroller.

Fig 7.22, Houston, June 20, 1838, Treasury Warrant to James S. McGahey for the payment of the Military for bounty.

Private Collection, Cr. HW-10, O-363.

The payment in Figure 7.22 was made to James S. McGahey as an assignee of Thomas Dorman who was another Texas veteran. McGahey joined the Texian Army in the fall of 1835. Aside from serving with distinction in several early battles, McGahey is widely credited with the creation of a blue Lone Star battle flag bearing the word "Independence."

In September 1835, McGahey served as a second lieutenant under the command of William Scott, one of Austin's original colonists.[30] After a brief stop in Lynchburg, Scott delivered to the young lieutenant four yards of blue silk and ordered him to have a battle flag made for the regiment. McGahey enlisted the help of Mrs. Joseph Lynch who cut the silk and sewed it into a flag. He then enlisted a local painter to add a white five-pointed lone star in the center of the flag and McGahey, in burst of inspiration, asked him to paint the word "Independence" under the star. At first, the troops were taken aback by the boldness of the message when McGahey unfurled the flag and planted the staff in the ground for all to see. After gazing upon the bright blue silk cloth flapping in the wind, adorned with the white star and Independence, the soldiers shouted "Hurrah for the Lone Star" and the enthusiasm began to spread. On the march to Béxar, McGahey carried this flag on its staff as far as San Felipe, where he then neatly folded it and placed it in a knapsack. After being seriously wounded at Concepcíon, he then passed the flag to his close friend, Thomas Bell. Bell later displayed the flag at the Grass Fight and he may have carried it during the storming and siege at Béxar. The whereabouts of the original flag are still unknown.

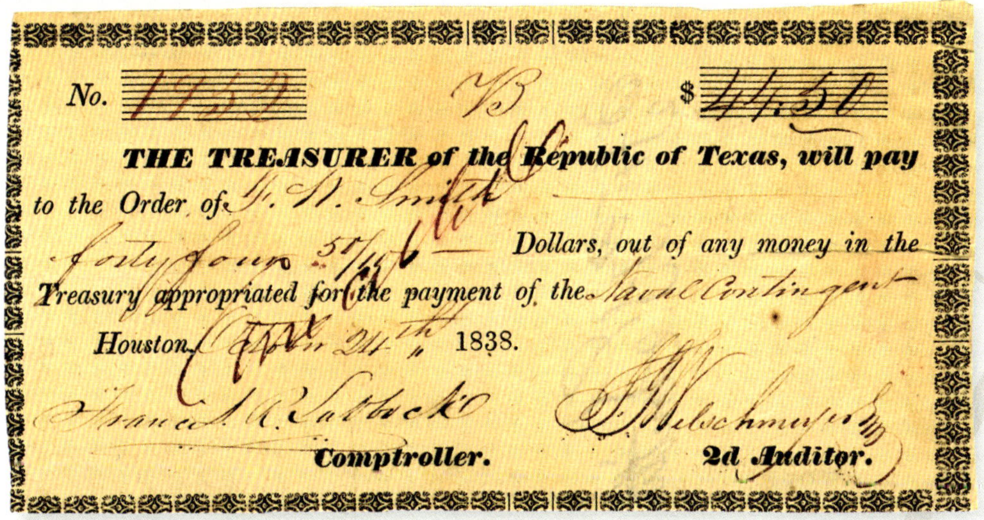
No. $
THE TREASURER of the Republic of Texas, will pay
to the Order of
Dollars, out of any money in the Treasury appropriated for the payment of the
Houston, 1838.
Comptroller. 2d Auditor.

Fig 7.23, Houston, October 24, 1838, Treasury Warrant to F.W. Smith for the payment of the Naval Contingent.

Private Collection, Cr. HW-8, O-408.

No 1952 $44.50

THE TREASURER of the Republic of Texas will pay to the Order of F.W. Smith forty four Dollars, out of any money in the Treasury appropriated for the payment of the Naval Contingent

Houston, October 24th, 1838, (Signed) J.G. Welschmeyer 2nd Auditor. Francis R. Lubbock Comptroller.

The payment in Figure 7.23 for $44.50 relates to the Republic's efforts to rebuild the Texas fleet, both in personnel and in ships. It was signed on the same date that a deal was struck to acquire the steamer *Charleston*. This double side-wheel steamer had been damaged but repaired after being caught in a gale off Cape Hatteras. By the time of this issuance, all the ships of the First Texas Navy had either been captured or grounded by the Mexicans in the blockade of 1837 or seized by creditors. The Texas Congress quickly approved the purchase of the steamer. The *Charleston* was outfitted with armaments under the Lamar administration and rechristened as the Texas warship *Zavala* in honor of the first Vice President of the Republic.[31] These initial steps to build the second Texas Navy involved massive borrowing in the waning months of Sam Houston's first administration. The purchase price for the *Zavala* was $195,907, advanced on credit, to be paid over a ten year period at 5 percent interest.

Although the pay certificates, audited drafts, and Treasury warrants were prevalent in Texas, their odd dollar amounts made them poorly suited for everyday expenditures. Specie, in the form of gold and silver coin both from Mexico and the United States, was widely accepted, but very scarce since all legitimate trade with Mexico had ceased to exist. The stock in the Consolidated Fund, issued to redeem the outstanding warrants and drafts, were only issued in large amounts and were ill suited for day-to-day transactions.

Despite the vehement objections of Henry Smith, Texas was going to have a uniform issue of paper money, backed by the full faith of the Republic and bearing interest at 10 percent per annum. On the face of the newly printed notes was the emblem which had graced the only money issued exclusively for Texas. Similar to the *jolas* of a generation before, this money would also bear the Lone Star symbol of Texas. The "star money" began circulating in Houston immediately after the first pieces were issued in November 1837.

---

1 Stanley Siegel and John A. Moretta, *Houston: A Chronicle of the Bayou City* (Sun Valley, CA: American Historical Press, 2005), 23.

2 Ellen Robbins Red, *Early Days on the Bayou, 1838-1890: The Life and Letters of Horace Dickinson Taylor* (Waco: Texian Press, 1986), 33-36.

3 Gary Cartwright, *Galveston: A History of The Island* (New York: MacMillan Publishing Company, 1991), 75.

4 The date upon which the seat of government moved to Austin is subject to some debate, as the Treasury Department issued currency bearing the word "Austin" in the spring of 1839. October 17, 1839, was the day that President Lamar and his cabinet arrived in Austin. The first session of the Fourth Congress did not meet in Austin until the following month. Larry Willoughby, *Austin: A Historical Portrait* (Norfolk, VA: Donning Company, Publishers, 1981), 15.

5 William M. Gouge, *The Fiscal History of Texas* (New York: Burt Franklin, 1852; rpt. 1969), 63.

6 Ibid.

7 John Hoyt Williams, *Sam Houston: The Life and Times of the Liberator of Texas, an Authentic American Hero* (New York: Simon & Schuster, Inc., 1993), 96.

8 Anson Jones, *Memoranda and Official Correspondence relating to the Republic of Texas its History and Annexation* (New York: D. Appleton & Company, 1859), 29.

9 Amelia W. Williams and Eugene C. Barker, eds., "Sam Houston to the Texas Congress, Houston, May 26, 1837," *The Writings of Sam Houston*, 1813-1863 (Austin: University of Texas Press, 1939), 2:105.

10 Helen Foster Snow, "Major John Wyatt Moody, First Auditor of the Republic of Texas," Moody Papers, page 2; Auditor's Office to Sam Houston, Houston, May 26, 1837, Moody Papers.

11 Seymour V. Conner, ed., "Grayson to Smith, Columbia, Texas, February 12, 1837," Texas Treasury Papers, 1:25-26.

12 Virginia H. Taylor, eds., "Yates to Smith, New York, April 11, 1837," Texas Treasury Papers, 4:7-8.

13 Gouge, *The Fiscal History of Texas*, 64.

14 Report of the Secretary of the Treasury, November 14, 1841 (Austin), 4, Statement of Appropriations made by Congress from 1836-1839, inclusive.

15 Gouge, *The Fiscal History of Texas*, 64-66.

16 Report of the Secretary of the Treasury, October 13, 1837, Second Congress, First Session (Houston: The Office of the Telegraph, 1837), 3.

17 Edmund Thornton Miller, "A Financial History of Texas," *Bulletin of the University of Texas 1916: No. 37* (Austin: University of Texas, 1916), 79.

18 "List of the Wounded during the Storm of Bexar from the 5'th to the 10'th December," Texas State Library and Archives, Austin, Texas, found online at http://www.tsl.state.tx.us/treasures/republic/bexar/wounded.html

19 *Handbook of Texas Online*, s.v., "Elisha Marshall Pease," found online at http://www.tsha.utexas.edu/handbook/online/articles/PP/fpe8.html (accessed January 23, 2006).

20 *Handbook of Texas Online*, s.v., "Francis Richard Lubbock," found online at http://www.tsha.utexas.edu/handbook/online/articles/LL/flu1.html (accessed January 23, 2006).

21 From a historical marker in front of the Tremont House Hotel, Mechanic Street, Galveston Texas. Credited to George L. Hosek.

22 Gouge, *The Fiscal History of Texas*, 65.

23 Report of the Secretary of the Treasury, October 13, 1837, 9.

24 Ibid., 4-5.

25 Seymour V. Conner, ed., "Houston to Moody, May 26, 1838," Texas Treasury Papers, 1:107.

26 Jesús F. de la Teja, ed., *A Revolution Remembered: The Memoirs and Selected Correspondence of Juan N. Seguín* (Austin: State House Press, 1991).

27 Jonathan W. Jordan, *Lone Star Navy* (Dulles, VA: Potomac Books, Inc., 2007), 80-81, 89-90.

28 "Comptroller's Military Service Record No. 1046, James A Sylvester," Texas State Library and Archives, Austin Texas.

29 "James A. Sylvester," Veteran Biographies, San Jacinto Museum of History, Herzstein Library, found online at http://www.sanjacinto-museum.org/Herzstein_Library/Veteran_Biographies/San_Jacinto_Bios/biographies/default.asp?action=bio&id=3632

30 Robert Maberry, Jr., *Texas Flags* (College Station: Texas A&M University Press, 2001), 23-24.

31 Jordan, *Lone Star Navy*, 122-23.

CHAPTER EIGHT

STAR MONEY, ENGRAVED NOTES AND CHANGE NOTES

The first circulating paper currency of Texas was called "Star Money." This issue of promissory notes was authorized by an act of Congress on June 9, 1837, but they were not signed, dated and released into circulation until November 4, 1837. These notes are commonly referred to as "Star Notes" by most collectors today. $500,000 face value was authorized to meet current expenses of the government, though the actual amount issued was $514,510.[1] The House Committee of Ways and Means provided that the issue was to be paid out for the civil and contingent expenses of the government (including salaries, rent, printing, etc.) with the largest amount allocated for military expenses, $100,000 of which was earmarked for the purchase of horses and munitions to be provided for rangers and mounted gunmen to wage a war against the Indians.[2] A large part of this first issue was also used to settle some of the outstanding audited drafts and warrants not large enough to be pooled into the Consolidated Fund.

Fig 8.1, Captain William G. Cooke.

UTSA's Institute of Texan Cultures, Courtesy of the Hearst Corporation.

The laborious task of signing Sam Houston's name on the new currency fell to William G. Gooke, who served as the President's personal secretary during Houston's first administration.

These notes feature a "Lone Star" in the middle of each bill, and were issued in denominations of $5, $10, $20, $50, $100, and $500. They were printed by Cruger & Moore in Houston (who acquired the printing business of Baker & Borden) and were designed to be a temporary issue until a series of engraved notes could be procured.[3] Each note would be numbered, dated, and bear the signature of the Secretary of the Treasurer and the President. The notes could be redeemed with interest at 10 percent *per annum* as is stated on the face of each bill. The bearer could redeem the notes twelve months from the date of issue. The attractive interest rate was intended to support the value of the currency by inspiring confidence in the marketplace. However, it also had the effect of concentrating the notes in the hands of speculators, a fact that became apparent towards the end of their short circulating life.

Sam Houston was reluctant to personally sign such a large number of notes because of an old arm injury sustained during the Creek Indian War when he served under Andrew Jackson. In March 1814 while storming a Creek stronghold, a bullet shattered his right arm and another lodged in his right shoulder which left young Houston nearly dead. Although he eventually recovered from the battle wounds, the injury left his right arm somewhat lame for the rest of his life.[4] Much to the President's relief, Congress passed an act dated October 23, 1837, which allowed the star notes to be signed on his behalf by his personal secretary, William G. Cooke, and countersigned by Secretary of the Treasury Henry Smith.[5] The secretarial signing of the President's name on bills was something that would continue under Lamar's term, even though he had the capacity, but not the time to laboriously sign each note.

Fig 8.2, $5 Republic of Texas "Star Money" c. 1837.

John N. Rowe III Collection of Texas Currency, DeGolyer Library, Southern Methodist University, Dallas, Texas. Cr. H1, 0-440

William Gordon Cooke, Houston's secretary and an eminent soldier and statesman, was born on March 26, 1808, in Fredericksburg, Virginia.[6] Reared and educated there, he later moved to New Orleans where he engaged in the drug business until 1835. In that year Cooke traveled to Texas at the age of twenty-seven with the New Orleans Greys. He was elected first lieutenant at Velasco. The Virginian served under Ben Milam, and was later elected captain. He was in the forefront at the storming of Béxar.[7] Cooke served as quartermaster for the Army and as Sam Houston's aide de camp in 1836, and later fought in the battle of San Jacinto. It was Cooke who accompanied the wounded Sam Houston to New Orleans for treatment of an infectious leg wound he received during the battle.[8] Cooke remained in the Army until 1837 and then opened a drug store in Houston, the recently established new capital. In addition to running a drug store, working in the Treasury Department and serving as Houston's personal secretary, Cooke also acted as the Stock Commissioner from 1837-1838.

It was paramount for Sam Houston's administration to ensure that the interest on these notes could be paid, and that the issue could be maintained at par value—100 cents on the dollar. Houston and Henry Smith regarded the public's faith in the new money as absolutely critical in order to maintain their national existence. The Republic needed to meet the government's expenses in a variety of ways. The government raised funds from donations in the United States, charged tariffs on imported goods and raised cash from the outright sale of Mexican property confiscated during the war. Direct taxes were assessed in sixteen counties, though all of it was expected to be received in audited drafts.[9] Texas also commenced land scrip sales in the U.S. at 50 cents an acre in an effort to boost the revenue, but these sales proved to be difficult.

Most star notes were redeemed at maturity after one year and not re-issued. Although some were hoarded, the great majority were exchanged with interest for the engraved series of notes, cancelled by the government and retired. For this reason, the star notes have a very low survival rate and collectors oftentimes try many years to compile a complete set by denomination. Not only challenging to collectors, but of tremendous historical importance, these Texas star notes hold the prestigious position of being the first circulating paper money issued by the Republic of Texas.

Fig 8.3, $10 Republic of Texas "Star Money" c. 1837.
Private Collection, Cr. H3, O-452.

Fig 8.4, $20 Republic of Texas "Star Money" c. 1837.
Private Collection, Cr. H5, O-458.

Fig 8.5, $50 Republic of Texas "Star Money" c. 1838.
Private Collection, Cr. H8, O-476.

Fig 8.6, $100 Republic of Texas "Star Money" c. 1838, Small "One Hundred Dollars."
Private Collection, Cr. H11, O-492.

Fig 8.7, $100 Republic of Texas "Star Money" c. 1837, Large "One Hundred Dollars."
Private Collection, Cr. H9, O-479.

While the new currency was initially well received, problems soon arose. One of the mysteries surrounding the issue of star notes is why more than 60 percent consisted of $100 and $500 notes, an impractical denomination in a time when the per capita income of Texas was about $200 per year.[10] Although they bore an attractive 10 percent interest rate, the government's ability to pay the interest began to be questioned by the general public. As uncertainty grew, the value of the notes declined in the marketplace against the value of U.S. silver and gold coins. Many travelers and merchants who attempted to pass these notes on the streets of New Orleans encountered wide swings in the exchange rate, much to the detriment of their plans.

Fig 8.9, Henry Austin.
Courtesy of Albert and Ethel Herzstein Library, San Jacinto Museum of History, Houston, Texas.

Henry Austin was a noted lawyer, land dealer, and a cousin of Stephen F. Austin. In May 1838, Austin had trouble passing the star money in payment for steamboat passage to bring his family from New Orleans to Texas. He recounted the experience in a letter to Treasury Secretary Henry Smith, expressing his concern for the sudden depreciation of the Texas notes.[11] Austin explained that on Sunday he was told that the boat would honor his Texas money at 62 ½ cents on the U.S. dollar. But when he attempted to cash the $50 star note the next day, "the highest offers I could get were a 50 to 55% discount." That same Monday he was offered audited drafts (or warrants) of Texas for purchase at 25 percent of face value. In asking about the reason for the rapid decline in the new Texas paper money values, Austin was informed that the Texas Congress passed legislation for an additional million dollar issuance of these notes. This news then depreciated the bills value in the market.

Fig 8.8, $500 Republic of Texas "Star Money" c. 1838.
Private Collection, Cr. H12, O-495.

While Congress had proposed an act to increase the issue by $150,000 and the Senate had increased the amount to $1,000,000, President Houston refused to sign the bill on May 12. In his message to Congress, Houston stated, "That the increased proposal by the present bill will have the effect of depreciating still further the value of the paper, no reasonable mind can doubt."[12] Yet the vicious rumors that the Texas government would issue a large amount of new notes had already swept through the marketplace, depreciating the money, and temporarily thwarting the travel plans of Henry Austin and his family by at least two weeks. Seeking an explanation for the swiftness of the market makers, Smith received this analysis from J.W. Garraty, "the depreciation in our currency is created by a few pedlars [*sic*] (and would be brokers) who has brought a few goods to the place and linked themselves with a few Mexicans that has the principal supplies, with the understanding to sell, for nothing but silver, or to take the currency of our country at the enormous discount of 50 percent."[13]

For a new Republic trying to establish credibility in the financial world, the concern over flooding the market with cheap paper money was not to be taken lightly. As noted by Henry Austin in his letter to Henry Smith, the star notes had been bid as low as 50 cents on the dollar in May 1838 in New Orleans. As speculative fears about an oversupply of the notes began to subside after the news of Houston's veto, the notes recovered to 60 cents on the dollar and word spread that the government planned to redeem the bills at face value along with the interest due.

THE $5 AND $20 DOLLRAS NOTES OF 1837

Several curious errors appear on some of the December 1837 $5 and $20 star notes. The word "dollars" was misspelled and printed instead as "FIVE DOLLRAS" and "TWENTY DOLLRAS" respectively on some December 1837 issues. It was an unconscionable error on the part of the printers. Although an early Treasury department staffed by seasoned professionals would have had a quality control process, there is at least one theory as to how these notes with the egregious spelling errors escaped into circulation. Upon closer inspection (see figures 8.10 and 8.11), all of the known examples of the "DOLLRAS" notes were signed and dated by Henry Smith and William G. Cooke (for Sam Houston) on December 31, 1837.

We can only surmise that Smith and Cooke started their New Year's Eve celebrations a bit early and dated and signed the notes with a drink in one hand and a pen in the other. One of the controllers—Francis Lubbock or John Moody—who were in the Treasury office the following day may have spotted the errors and prevented any more from being issued. Even though the printing error was significant at the time, it probably meant little to those receiving the notes as payment. These star money notes, shown in figures 8.10 and 8.11, offer an interesting glimpse into the quality control process (or lack thereof) of the day.

Fig 8.10, $5 Republic of Texas "Star Money," December 31, 1837, "FIVE DOLLRAS" Variety.
Private Collection, Cr. H2, 0-443.

Fig 8.11, $20 Republic of Texas "Star Money," December 31, 1837, "TWENTY DOLLRAS" Variety.
John N. Rowe III Collection of Texas Currency, DeGolyer Library, Southern Methodist University, Dallas, Texas. Cr. H6, 0-464.

Fig 8.12, $ 50 "Star Money" C ngress Variety, c. 1837 Issue. Close-up of "C ngress,"

Private Collection, Cr. H7, 0-467.

The printing flaw of this $50 note curiously left out the "o" in Congress and gives the appearance that the Republic misspelled an "act of C ngress."

The word "Congress" was also misspelled on some $50 notes (see Figure 8.12). While the spelling of the words "dollars" and "Congress" was corrected on the January 1838 issues, the printers (or perhaps the Treasury department) proceeded to butcher the abbreviation "Sec of the Treas'y" to "Sec. of the Trras'y" on several of the $50 and $100 notes. Notice the differences in the typesetting of the abbreviation for "treasury" on the two genuine $100 notes shown in figures 8.13 and 8.14.

Fig 8.13, $100 "Star Money" TREAS'Y Variety, c. 1837 Issue. Close-up of "Sec of the TREAS'Y,"

Private Collection.

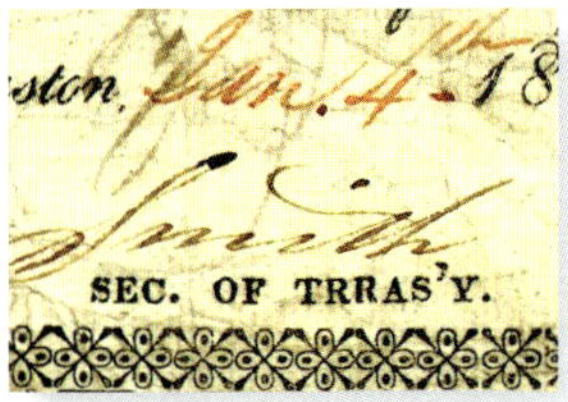

Fig 8.14, $100 "Star Money" TRRAS'Y Variety, c. 1838 Issue. Close-up of "Sec of the TRRAS'Y,"

Private Collection.

COUNTERFEITS AND REDEMPTIONS

Whether trying to capitalize on the printing errors or taking advantage of the newness of the money, counterfeit notes began to appear and circulate in and around the capital. While crudely printed notes were sometimes spotted and refused, other counterfeiting problems began to surface—a cut and paste variety of altered genuine notes were being turned in and offered for full redemption at the Treasury itself.[14]

To pay the interest on the funded debt, Congress pledged one-fourth of the proceeds from the sale of Matagorda and Galveston islands, along with a half million acres of public land and all of the forfeited property in the Republic. Payment in silver coin was still the preferred medium for customs payments and continued to be the most popular form of money with settlers. But the government did not collect even a modest amount of silver in their revenue efforts. With the passage of a bill dated May 1838, the government paid the interest on the stock with the promissory notes, restoring confidence in the money as the announcement of the interest payments appeared in New Orleans newspapers.[15] Speculators jumped into the marketplace to buy what Texas money they could at a discount with the hope of later redeeming them to the government at face value. By November, the Texas government began to retire this first issue of promissory notes. The star notes along with their accumulated interest were then replaced by the new issue of engraved notes, rather than by payment in silver or gold coin.

As one problem was solved, however, another was created. As the old notes were redeemed, the Treasurer's office noticed that a large quantity was missing a portion of the note: one or both signatures, a corner, a left margin, etc. Patched together counterfeits were being presented for redemption at full value! Plying the world's second oldest profession, counterfeiters were taking advantage of the sloppily printed issue. Treasurer Asa Brigham was asked to redeem several notes which were "formed and presented out of fragments not appearing ...as is evident that many have been attempted to foist such notes upon this office ...and it is supposed that counterfeiters would have as few scruples in patching up parts and parcels."[16] In short, pieces of legitimate notes had been taped together and patched up for redemption. Seeking guidance on what to accept, Brigham asked his superior, Secretary of the Treasury R. G. Dunlop, for direction. Dunlop informed Brigham that the responsibility was his alone, and "you will keep in mind that the Govt. is bound to redeem its old issue with the new notes, and that the rights of citizens, or holders of the paper, must be protected as the interest of the Republic."[17] Brigham proceeded to redeem all those notes he thought legitimate.

Only in the most remote instances were treasury warrants or certificates ever paid with *specie* in these early years. The hoard of silver *pesos* captured at San Jacinto had long been exhausted. When a warrant was redeemed "out of the money appropriated by the Treasury," it was paid in star notes. The star money was then redeemed with the engraved notes, and the precedent was set. The redemption of paper for a different form of paper was something that the creditors of Texas learned to live with—or quickly learned to live without, since the money was based on whatever paper the government decided to issue and honor at the given time. The marketplace came to honor the value of the paper money much less than the government did itself.

THE ENGRAVED NOTES OF HOUSTON

In an effort to provide higher quality promissory notes, the year-old government issued a series of engraved notes featuring allegorical figures of Liberty on the face. These were paid out to the redeemers of the star notes, for both the face value and the interest. All denominations of these notes depict a seated portrait of Liberty except the $5, which pictures her standing. These pieces are known to collectors as the "Government of Texas" notes, authorized by an act of Congress on June 9, 1837 (the same act as for the Star Notes), and bear written dates of 1838 and 1839 of which the 18 is printed.[18] Like the previous issue, these notes list Houston as the location of the seat of government.

A total of $650,629 "Government of Texas" notes were printed in denominations of $1, $3, $5, $10, $20, $50 by Draper, Toppan, Longacre & Co. of Philadelphia and New York. Like the star notes, the engraved notes were signed by Henry Smith as Treasurer and by William G. Cooke, signing the name of Sam Houston as President. Under close examination, the quality of the penmanship is remarkably consistent across each bill. Every now and then, the notes contain different inks, and sometimes one signature is missing completely.

Like the previously issued star notes, the "Government of Texas Notes" were redeemable in one year at 10 percent *per annum*. Unlike the American currency of gold, silver and copper coins, these notes represented only a promise to pay. As it became apparent that the Texas government did not possess the gold or silver to back the paper, their value in the marketplace declined from 65 percent of face value in May 1838 to 40 percent of face value by January 1839.[19]

Unlike the star notes, the artistic vignettes on the engraved notes provide a snapshot of the American design influences of the period. The pieces represent the intricate art of engraving, meant not only for its aesthetic appeal, but also to provide the government with a high quality instrument difficult to counterfeit. Allegorical figures of gods and goddesses were quite common on the intricately engraved paper money of private banking institutions at the time.[20] These figures were used by the engravers to adorn the new series of promissory notes which were customized for Texas.

Liberty, representing freedom, was depicted as a goddess with a shield or an eagle nearby. Minerva, the Roman goddess of commerce, industry, and education, was shown with machinery or tools in close proximity. Ceres, the goddess of agriculture and grain, was shown beside plowshares or a sheaf of grain. Justice was represented holding balance scales. These allegorical figures from Roman and Greek culture were woven together with images of Indians, wildlife, steamships, and other elements representative of the early days of Texas.[21] The familiar five-pointed Lone Star appeared in several of the designs. The combination of images resulted in a distinctively ornate series of paper money for Texas. At first, these elaborate designs added an air of legitimacy to the money of the Republic of Texas.

On the left side of the note in Figure 8.15 is Miss Liberty, standing with cap and pole while resting on a shield striped like the flag of the Texas Navy with a lone five-pointed star. The denomination "ONE" is both above and below Liberty. In the center is Minerva (note the crown), seated with a large male lion at her feet. The example is signed by Henry Smith, Treasurer, and Sam Houston, President.

Fig 8.15, $1 Government of Texas, "Engraved Note," c. 1838.
Private Collection, Cr. H14, 0-520.

Fig 8.16, $3 Government of Texas "Engraved Note," c. 1838.
Private Collection, Cr. H15A, O-535.

Fig 8.17, $5 Government of Texas "Engraved Note," c. 1838.
Private Collection, Cr. H16, O-545.

Fig 8.18, $10 Government of Texas "Engraved Note," c. 1838.
Private Collection, Cr. H-17, O-550.

Fig 8.19, $20 Government of Texas "Engraved Note," c. 1838.
Private Collection, Cr. H18, O-560.

In Figure 8.16, the denomination "THREE" is printed across the left margin. In the center of the note is Liberty, seated by the shore, holding a sword with her right hand and resting her left hand on a shield bearing a five-pointed star. The shield represents the strength of the Republic. Behind her is a plume of grain and plowshares which represent agriculture. A steamship and mountains can be seen in the distant background. The note is signed by Henry Smith, Treasurer, and Sam Houston, President.

In the $5 example in Figure 8.17, Liberty is standing with her left foot on a globe and her bare breast exposed as a representation of the beauty of nature. In the center of the note is an Indian on horseback, drawn bow at the ready, chasing a bison already pierced by another arrow. A herd of running bison is in the background. The note is signed by Henry Smith, Treasurer, and Sam Houston, President.

In Figure 8.18, the left side depicts the steamboat *Cayuga*, bearing a striped flag, belching smoke and with the Cabinet members at the rails. In the foreground is a representation of President David G. Burnet escaping with another person in a small rowboat. Another ship, presumably the schooner *Flash*, can be partially seen in front of the red clay bluffs on Galveston Bay. The denomination "TEN" is both above and below the vignette. Note the ornate printing of "The Government of Texas" on the $10 note with the top of the letters of GOVERNMENT in small dots. This differs from the printing found on all other Texas notes. On the right is a maiden, representing Industry, seated with tools at her feet. The note is signed by Henry Smith, Treasurer, and Sam Houston, President.

In Figure 8.19, Liberty is standing with pole and shield bearing a five-pointed star on the left. The denomination "20" is below. Minerva is seated in the center on the seashore with a shield bearing a five-pointed star. A jug is at her left, and mountains and clouds appear in the background. The note is signed by Henry Smith, Treasurer, and Sam Houston, President.

Fig 8.20, $50 Government of Texas "Engraved Note," c. 1838.
Private Collection, Cr. H-21, O-580.

Figure 8.10 shows a $50 note with a seated sailor tipping his hat and holding a flag with a small Lone Star on the left. There is a coil of rope at his feet. The denomination "50" is below. In the center is a maiden, representing Justice (note the scales), seated by the shore. There is a man standing over freight and a horse-drawn cart in the foreground, with a sailing ship in the background. The note is signed by Henry Smith, Treasurer, and Sam Houston, President.

Because the notes were issued in large quantities, they depreciated significantly relative to the value of silver and gold coin. For this same reason many have survived, and the engraved "Government of Texas" notes are reasonably available to collectors today. Of all the denominations, the $1 and $3 are the scarcest and most difficult to locate in uncirculated condition. Since these small denomination bills were frequently passed from hand to hand, very little could be gained (or lost) by holding the notes as a bet on the solvency of the government. Since many were traded for goods and passed to merchants many of the surviving samples are found in a heavily worn condition.

Many of the surviving notes are often found razor cut with an "X" or with a triangle cut cancellation missing from the specimen, similar to many of the star notes and early warrants. The engraved bills were cancelled and retired as they were paid into the Treasury, and as such could not be re-entered into circulation. It is possible that these cancelled notes accumulated in boxes either at the time of redemption or many years later. Some of the specimens were sold or otherwise dispersed as pieces of nostalgia many decades later by state officials who sought to preserve the early Texas culture.

THE FIRST ISSUE OF "CHANGE NOTES" AUTHORIZED DECEMBER 14, 1837

Although the star money was kept nearly at par value for most of its short-lived circulation, problems arose when these notes were used for daily transactions. There was an inability for merchants to make change because the smallest denomination note was $5. A special resolution was passed by Congress on December 14, 1837, which authorized the Treasurer to issue "change notes" in denominations of $1, $2 and $3 in an amount not exceeding $10,000.[22] These notes were the smallest monetary issue of paper money by the Republic of Texas up to that time. Depending on the quantities of each denomination, only an estimated 5,000 notes circulated at any one time.[23] The Treasurer was required to place an equal portion of the $150,000 previous issue in reserve in order to make them freely exchangeable for the larger denomination star notes.[24] Similar to the *jolas* of a generation before, these small bills were produced for the sole purpose of making change from larger denominations.

On the same day the change note resolution was passed, Congress passed an act "to prevent the issuance of individual printed or lithographed notes." This measure was intended to prevent the counterfeit reproductions that had plagued the first experiment with paper money. In an effort to thwart the rampant counterfeiting of the money, these small denomination notes were made from engraved metal plates by Childs, Clark & Company in New Orleans. The change notes themselves are virtually the only record of the existence of the short-lived engraving firm. The circumstances surrounding their work for Texas has been unearthed in large part by researcher Darrel Brown.[25] Brown unearthed a record in the Texas State Archives of an engraver in New Orleans named John V. Childs. This receipt proves that Childs provided the engraving for the consular seal for Nathanial Townsend. On April 2, 1837, Townsend was named consul in New Orleans for the Republic of Texas and served in that capacity until September 20, 1838. Brown speculates that John V. Childs is the Childs namesake of the engraving firm. The other engraver was most likely J.R. Clark, who later became a partner with George Endicott of New York. Under the name of Endicott & Clark of New Orleans, they later produced the change notes issued in 1840 under the Lamar Administration. It was a common practice during that time period for engraving houses and engravers to frequently change affiliations—the partnership of Childs, Clark & Company was one of those brief affiliations.

Interestingly, there were at least two separate printings of this rare series of small denomination notes. One series is shown in the examples for this text (see figures 8.21, 8.22, and 8.23). The second series carries the label, "Niles Print, Houston" in fine print under the left signature line. Although both series were hastily printed on poor quality paper, the change notes found immediate acceptance. They were heavily circulated, and even the best surviving specimens are found in worn and often tattered condition. While not quite the artistic rendition of the following issues, the short-lived series of bills began circulating in the spring of 1838.

On the same day that the first series of change notes was authorized, another act of Congress was passed which declared that "nothing but gold or silver, or promissory notes of this government should be received in payment of duties on goods imported nor shall any bank notes be received in payment of any dues to the Government of Texas." This act was meant to sustain the currency system, though in actuality it cut short the tax revenues of the country for two reasons: outside bank notes were no longer accepted for dues, and audited drafts on the empty Texas Treasury were in odd amounts, making them ill adapted for the payment of taxes.

CHANGE (OR MEDALLION) NOTES

The first series of change notes are often referred to as "Medallion Notes" by collectors. They are easily recognized by the ornate oval medallion on the left border, which frames an engraved vignette of a steamboat. These notes bear written dates of 1838, with the "18" printed and the year handwritten. Usually found in worn condition, often torn, repaired or reinforced, they still remain one of the key series of historical notes from the Republic era. Since no coins were issued by the Republic of Texas, "Medallion Notes" filled the necessary role of making change from the larger-denomination star notes already in circulation.

These change notes were issued concurrently with the star notes and the other engraved notes. Although the change notes did not pay interest and had no maturity or redemption date, they were exchangeable for bills which bore a rate of 10 percent interest, which helped with their immediate public acceptance. Many of these notes circulated for years beyond the redemption dates of both the star notes and the later engraved issues which immediately followed .

The left side of Figure 8.21 shows a steamship framed in an ornate oval "medallion." In the center is a reclining male, pouring water from an urn, above a faint but sharply defined five-pointed star. A small eagle with spread wings is centered at the bottom. On the right is a portrait of Thomas Jefferson, the third President of the United States. The note is signed by A.B. Howe, Chief Clerk, and Asa Brigham, Treasurer.

Fig 8.21, $1 Republic of Texas "Change Note" (Houston).
Private Collection, Cr. H23, O-500.

Fig 8.22, $ 2 Republic of Texas "Change Note" (Houston).
Private Collection, Cr. H25, 0-509.

Fig 8.23, $ 3 Republic of Texas "Change Note" (Houston).
Private Collection, Cr. H27, 0-515.

The left side of Figure 8.22 also shows a steamship framed in an ornate oval "medallion." In the center is Liberty, seated and holding a pole with a liberty cap in her left hand while her right hand rests on a shield, representing strength. An eagle with outstretched wings is beside the shield. On the right is a cotton boll set in a frame. The note is signed by A.B. Howe, Chief Clerk, and Asa Brigham, Treasurer.

Very similar to the $1 note, the left side of Figure 8.23 shows a steamship framed in an ornate oval "medallion." In the center is a reclining male, pouring water from an urn, above a faint but sharply defined five-pointed star. A small eagle with spread wings is centered at the bottom. On the right is a portrait of Thomas Jefferson, the third President of the United States. The note is signed by A.B. Howe, Chief Clerk, and Asa Brigham, Treasurer.

PRODUCING THE THOMAS JEFFERSON IMAGE ON THE 1838 "CHANGE NOTES"

Curiously, the design elements on the $1 and $3 are virtually identical except for the numerical denomination. This is also the first of the Republic of Texas notes to carry an engraved portrait. Thomas Jefferson, the third American President, was given this distinguished honor. It is thought that Jefferson was chosen for this short-lived Texas series because he was the principal author of the U.S. Declaration of Independence and was also credited with the Louisiana Purchase during his administration. Given that the plates for these notes were engraved in New Orleans, a city which became known as the gateway to Texas, Jefferson was both a logical and patriotic choice for the Texian neighbors west of the Sabine River. The image of Jefferson was replaced on the $2 note by a cotton boll.

The "change" or "medallion" notes represent a crude form of portrait art which later appeared on U.S. paper money designs for the remainder of the 19th century. The Texas series displays the first portrait of Jefferson

Fig 8.24, Thomas Jefferson Lithographic Print.
This image was taken from a lithographic print produced by the Boston firm of William and John Pendleton in 1828. Courtesy of Darrel Brown.

Fig 8.25, Portion of the Jefferson engraved plate by Childs & Company, New Orleans.
Courtesy of Darrel Brown.

known to appear on any series of paper money, and the portrait offers a glimpse into the technology and the reproduction methods of the day. In 1828, the U.S. produced a series of prints of the first five American Presidents from the paintings by Gilbert Stuart (1755-1828). The Jefferson portrait shown on the medallion notes was reproduced from the original lithograph by Stuart.[26]

The engravers at Childs & Company selected the bust portrait of Jefferson from the 1828 lithograph print and proceeded to painstakingly engrave the portrait into a steel plate by hand for reproduction on the $1 and $3 denominations. The image that appears on the notes is a mirror or inverse image of the portrait when transferred to the paper via the printing process.

When initially issued during Houston's first administration in 1837, the promissory notes traded nearly at par with silver for several months because of tight controls on the amounts in circulation. Because the interest payments were met on the star money and on the Consolidated Fund stock in a timely manner, the promptness of the interest payments restored confidence in the money for a time. When the star notes were withdrawn and replaced with the engraved (or Government) notes, their purchasing power remained steady for the first few months of 1838 until the reality of additional government borrowing materialized. In an effort to borrow money both in the United States and overseas, an act was passed by the Texas legislature on May 16, 1838, which "authorized the President to negotiate a loan on the bonds of the Government not exceeding five million dollars."[27] It read in part: "Section 7: *Be it further enacted,* that, for the punctual payment of the interest and final redemption of said bonds, the public faith is hereby solemnly pledged."[28] With each additional promise to pay a new obligation, the ability to pay an old obligation decreased. The anticipated passage of the act caused the purchasing power of the engraved notes to depreciate in the spring of 1838, and with each subsequent issuance of bills the depreciation continued. Even the tight-fisted Sam Houston could not resist the temptation to operate the government almost entirely on credit and to raise the credit limit far beyond the limits of prudence. The Texas government did this just as the worldwide depression known as the Panic of 1837 began to spread to the American southwest.

Fig 8.28, The engraved image of Thomas Jefferson as it appears on the $1 and $3 change notes.
Private Collection.

Fig 8.27, An inverse image of the engraved portrait.
Private Collection.

Fig 8.26, An inverse image of the Jefferson portrait.
Courtesy of Darrel Brown.

THE PANIC OF 1837

Although the economic trouble initially seemed a world away, the panic (or financial depression) started with an incident early in 1837 known as the "Flour Riot" which occurred in New York City's Chatham Square.[29] Inflation had been running rampant in the eastern United States and a large crowd gathered in the square to protest the high cost of bread, meat and fuel. A mob descended on a large warehouse of flour and ransacked the stockpile after efforts by the mayor and local police to stop the rioters proved futile. Stock prices on Wall Street soon plummeted across the board. An uneasy anxiety gripped the financial community in the East and it spread to New Orleans, the bustling commerce center of the Gulf Coast. Herman Briggs & Company, a leading cotton brokerage house, failed in March 1837. Other cotton brokers and factors in New Orleans soon followed them into bankruptcy. Several banks in other southern cities experienced severe cash shortages as depositors rushed to withdraw their funds.

On May 10, 1837, New York banks suspended all payments of specie to prevent a run on their reserves, a measure permitted under state law for a one-year period.[30] By this time, approximately 100 banks failed in New York alone, and business conditions went from bad to worse. The run on the banks had a domino effect as depositors rushed to withdraw their funds, and in time virtually every bank in the United States suspended paying out silver and gold coins. By the end of the year over 600 banks had failed, leaving the U.S. in a severe economic depression, brought on by a deadly stagnation of credit, falling real estate prices and a lack of confidence in the banking system. Largely because of the tight money policies which resulted in the economic slowdown, the unbridled speculation by investors in public lands, including those in the newly-born Republic of Texas, quickly came to a screeching halt because there was no hard money in circulation to buy them. Land speculation in Texas had been particularly rampant. Many bankers, businessmen and farmers had over extended themselves, counting on a steady stream of immigrants flowing into Texas to support the prices. Once the restriction of credit and lack of a stable currency took its toll, the Republic was particularly hard hit and land prices fell dramatically. The depression had immediate repercussions for Texas as early as 1837, with the psychological effects coming later and lasting much longer than in the eastern United States.[31] It was precisely during this chaotic period of economic decline that Texas began to leverage its already shaky balance sheet in the name of national defense.

REBUILDING THE TEXAS NAVY

The Mexican naval blockade of 1837 also took its toll on Texas and customs revenues suffered a tremendous shortfall as a result. In an effort to protect the Texas coast from another Mexican blockade, Congress decided that another Texas Navy should be built. John Grant Tod was appointed naval inspector for Texas in 1838 and he oversaw the purchases of maritime equipment in New Orleans for the Texian Navy based in Galveston. The money allotted for the purchase of ships would come from the bonds authorized under the new legislation. Albert T. Burnley, a nephew of Robert Triplett and a former partner in his uncle's Kentucky coal business, was appointed loan commissioner and given the task of raising the necessary funds for Texas.[32] While the full five million dollar goal would never be realized, Burnley possessed his uncle's negotiating skills and was successful in securing a loan commitment from a group of bankers in Baltimore. At that time, the shipyards in Baltimore were heavily involved in building naval vessels for the U.S. military. The Baltimore bankers were much less sensitive to the slavery issue than other East Coast financiers and felt no moral compunction by extending credit to the slave-holding Republic of Texas. Sam Houston, acting under the authority of the appropriation, appointed Samuel May Williams as Naval Agent for the Republic of Texas to negotiate the purchase of one ship, two brigs, and three schooners from a shipbuilder in Baltimore.[33]

The deal was closed on December 3, 1838. Financing for the ships would come from a loan of $280,000 at 10 percent interest with a one-year term made by Frederick Dawson, a Baltimore banker. The loan would be secured by a private placement of Texas 10 percent bonds totaling $280,000.[34] In order to insure the prompt payment of funds, a second bond of $280,000 was pledged to cover the first, increasing the principal amount by double in case Texas failed to pay off the note in twelve

Fig 8.29, John Grant Tod, Sr.

Courtesy of the Rosenberg Library, Galveston, Texas.

John Grant Tod was appointed as a naval inspector in the waning months of Sam Houston's administration and later supervised the building of the second Texas Navy under President Mirabeau B. Lamar.

months. These two bonds totaling $560,000 were deposited in the Bank of the United States in Philadelphia and pledged as security for the loan. At the time the money was borrowed, Burnley knew that Texas did not have the means to pay off the balance within twelve months, but he counted on borrowing the money elsewhere to pay off the amount advanced by Dawson. As naval inspector, John Grant Tod oversaw the construction of the warships and developed a lasting friendship with Dawson, the contractor who helped finance and built the fleet.[35] For the Baltimore bankers who loaned the money, the deal seemed to be a lucrative transaction, backed by the full faith and credit of a sovereign nation. They needed only to remember that borrowers who are unconcerned about the rate of interest at which they borrow often have even less concern as to whether it is paid back.

Sam Houston plunged the Republic into debt in the waning days of his administration, but Texas was about to have its second Navy. In Galveston, Texas continued to build a Navy Yard on the harbor where the new fleet would be headquartered. Thomas Borden, a collector at the port of Galveston, voiced his concerns to Henry Smith in the spring of 1838 about the expense of the military buildup at the navy yard as follows: "The Navy at this place is at present a moth in the national purse which will eat out the filling, and waste the substance of the people."[36] Houston's successor, Mirabeau B. Lamar, took full credit for building the Second Texas Navy, though the associated costs eventually led to Lamar's undoing. Three years later, Houston would successfully blame the mounting debt and the declining values of the paper money on Lamar, although it was Houston who lit the match and started the fire. Virtually everybody who loaned money to Texas or received the new paper money would eventually get burned by the action of the government.

---

1 Report of the Secretary of the Treasury, to His Excellency, Sam Houston, President of the Republic of Texas, City of Houston, *Telegraph Press,* November 3, 1838, 7.

2 William M. Gouge, *The Fiscal History of Texas* (New York: Burt Franklin, 1852; rpt. 1969), 67.

3 Report of the Auditor and Comptroller to the fourth legislature on the Public Debt of Texas (Austin: Printed by Cushney & Hampton, "State Gazette" Office, 1851), 6.

4 Marquis James, *The Raven: A Biography of Sam Houston* (Austin: University of Texas Press, 1929), 32-35.

5 Gouge, *The Fiscal History of Texas*, 69.

6 Mary C. Bond, "Family tree: William Cooke story told," *The Seguin Gazette-Enterprise* [Seguin, TX], December 1, 1982.

7 "Biography of William G. Cooke," DRT Library, San Antonio, Texas.

8 Allen F. Adams, "William Cooke's Career Unusual," *San Antonio Light,* April 21, 1940.

9 Report of the Secretary of the Treasury, 3.

10 Douglas B. Ball, "Lone Star Notes: Early Texas Currency has a Galaxy of Forms," *Bank Note Reporter* (April 1988), 20.

11 Seymour V. Conner, ed., "Austin to Smith, New Orleans, May 15, 1838," Texas Treasury Papers, 1:103.

12 Message from the President of the Republic, May 12, 1838, to the House of Representatives, giving his reasons for not signing the bill entitled, "An Act to Define and limit the issue of Promissory Notes," Printed by order of the Senate (Houston: Telegraph Press, 1838), 6.

13 William Ransom Hogan, *The Texas Republic: A Social and Economic History* (Norman, OK: University of Oklahoma Press, 1946), see "Garraty to Henry Smith, May 6, 1838."

14 Seymour V. Conner, ed. "Brigham to Secretary, Houston, Dec 22, 1838," Texas Treasury Papers, 1.169

15 Seymour V. Conner, ed., "Love to Smith, New Orleans, May 29, 1838," Texas Treasury Papers, 1:109.

16 Seymour V. Conner, ed. "Brigham to Secretary, Houston, Dec 22, 1838," Texas Treasury Papers, 1.169

17 Ibid.

18 Grover C. Criswell, *Confederate and Southern States Currency: A Descriptive Listing, Including Rarity and Values,* vol.1, 4th ed. (1992), 364.

19 Report of the Auditor and Comptroller, 6.

20 "Treasures from the American Bank Note Company," The Old West and Franklin Collection, Auction book (American Numismatic Rarities, Inc., August 11, 2006), 209-10.

21 For the design elements on Government of Texas notes see http://www.unrv.com/culture/major-roman-god-list.php

22 "Joint Resolution Authorizing the Treasurer of the Republic to issue Change Notes, Section 1, Approved, December 14, 1837, Laws of the Republic of Texas.

23 Darrel Brown, "Republic of Texas 'Medallion' Change Notes, 1838 Issue," non-published.

24 Gouge, *The Fiscal History of Texas*, 74.

25 Brown, "Republic of Texas 'Medallion' Change Notes."

26 Darrel Brown, "Producing the Thomas Jefferson image for the Republic of Texas 1838 Medallion Note," non-published.

27 Seymour V. Conner, ed., "Burnley to Smith, Louisville, Kentucky, December 3, 1838," Texas Treasury Papers, 1:159-61.

28 Gouge, *The Fiscal History of Texas*, 220.

29 Q. David Bowers, *Obsolete Paper Money Issued by Banks in the United States, 1782-1866* (Whitman publishing, LLC, 2006), 221.

30 Ibid., 223.

31 Hogan, *The Texas Republic,* 81-83.

32 Martha A. Burnley, "Albert Triplett Burnley," *SHQ,* vol. 14 (October 1910), 2:150-54.

33 Seymour V. Conner, ed., "E.D. Whitney & Co to Anson Jones. Philadelphia, May 8th, 1845," Texas Treasury Papers, 3:1,102-103.

34 Seymour V. Conner, ed., "Burnley to Smith, Louisville, Kentucky, December 3, 1838," Texas Treasury Papers, 1:159-61.

35 Jonathan W. Jordan, *Lone Star Navy: Texas, the Fight for the Gulf of Mexico, and the Shaping of the American West* (Dulles, VA: Potomac Books, Inc., 2006), 148-49.

36 "T.H. Borden to Hon. Henry Smith, Port of Galveston, March 27, 1838," Thomas W. Streeter Texas Collection, Beinecke Rare Book and Manuscript Library, Yale University, New Haven, Connecticut.

CHAPTER NINE

MIRABEAU B. LAMAR: THE GREAT PAPER CHASE BEGINS

CH9

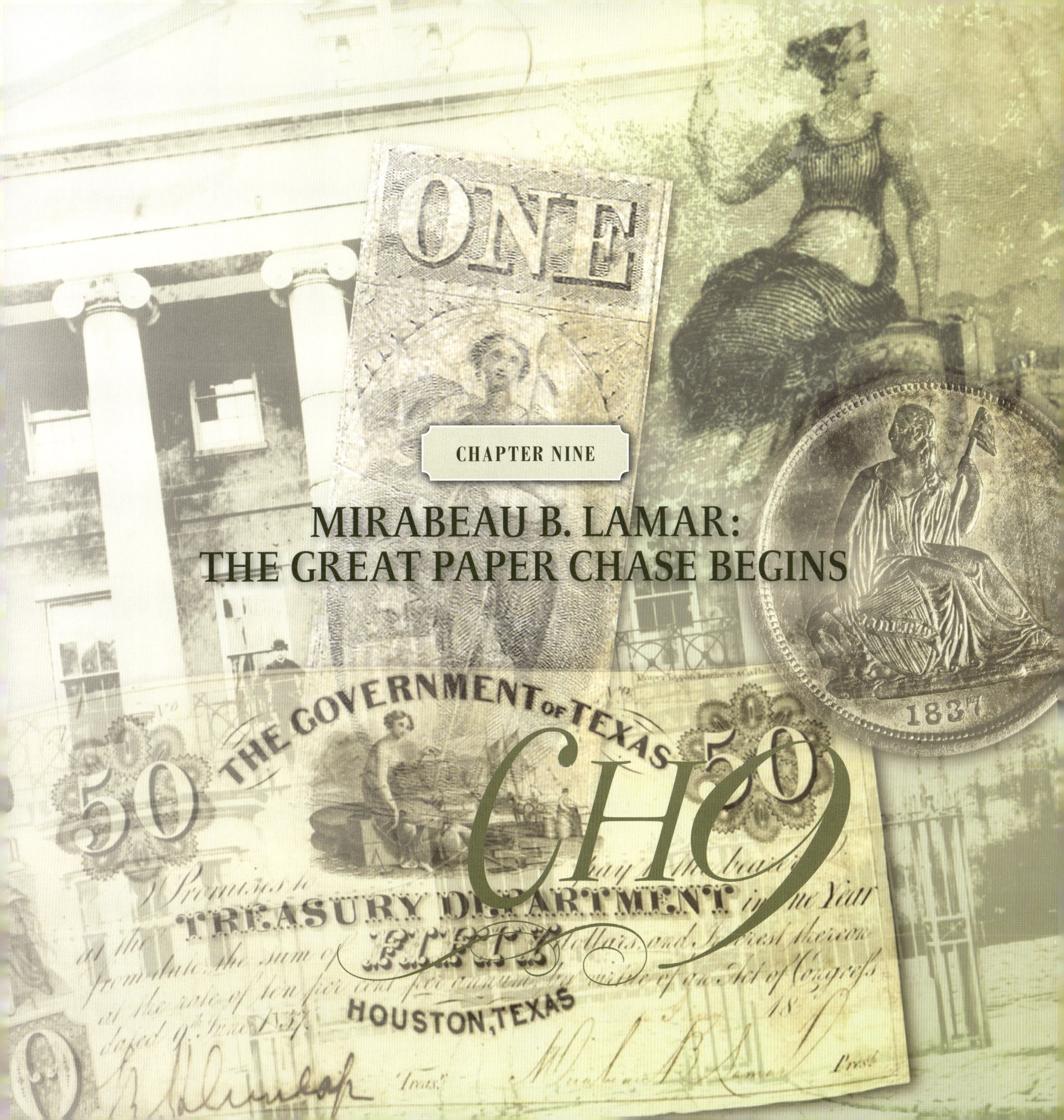

Mirabeau Buonaparte Lamar succeeded Sam Houston as President of the Republic of Texas.[1] Like his namesakes of the French Revolution—Count Mirabeau and Napoleon Buonaparte—his life coincided with revolutionary movements and filibustering expeditions.[2] Lamar began life on the Alabama frontier and entered politics at an early age.[3] He joined the staff of Georgia's Gov. George M. Troup in 1823 as his personal secretary where Lamar learned the rigors and rewards of political office. After two unsuccessful runs for Congress, he came to Texas in July 1835 at the urging of an old friend, James W. Fannin. Lamar soon found that Fannin was openly rebellious along with a host of others in the quest for Texas independence. He briefly returned to Georgia to settle some family affairs, then traveled back to Texas in 1836. Upon his arrival he discovered that Texas was in turmoil after the massacres at the Alamo and Goliad, where Fannin was counted among the dead.

Fig 9.1, Mirabeau B. Lamar, President of the Republic.

The San Jacinto Museum of History, Houston, Texas.

Lamar enlisted in the regular Texas Army as a private. Shortly thereafter, he saved the lives of Secretary of War Thomas J. Rusk and Walter P. Lane in a heated skirmish with Mexican troops. As a result of these high-profile rescues, Lamar was recognized for his quick thinking, bravery, and leadership abilities by Gen. Sam Houston. Lamar was promoted to colonel, and Houston placed him in charge of the cavalry shortly before the battle of San Jacinto. After Lamar's cavalry distinguished themselves at the pivotal conflict, he was befriended by *ad interim* President David G. Burnet. The President attempted to put Lamar in command of the regular army, but Lamar was relieved of the post by a popular vote against him by the troops.

Tossing his hat into the political ring in the fall of 1836, Lamar was elected Vice President of the Republic and served for two years under Sam Houston. But Houston, with his strong personality, had little use for a second in command and subsequently alienated Lamar after they disagreed on several issues. Houston favored the annexation of Texas by the U.S. while Lamar had a vision of expanding the Texas Republic. The distance between these two early Texas leaders grew into such distaste for each other that they eventually became bitter political enemies.

In an effort to keep any one man from becoming too powerful, the constitution was written to prevent Texas presidents from succeeding themselves. Since Sam Houston was not able to run for re-election in the fall of 1838, Lamar began to prepare for the biggest political gamble of his life—a run for the Presidency. As if a harbinger of things to come, Lamar was swept into office to a large degree because his two political opponents in the race killed themselves before the election. Lamar's primary opponent, Peter W. Grayson, the diplomat who also served as Attorney General, had a history of mental illness and committed suicide during a bout of severe depression. The Sam Houston camp chose Chief Justice James Collinsworth, but after a week-long drinking binge, Collinsworth either fell or jumped from a boat in Galveston Bay and drowned. The untimely deaths shocked the young nation as both men were well-known commissioners. Anson Jones, then serving in the Congress, remarked in his memoirs, "I shall be surprised at no one's committing suicide after hearing Col. Grayson's doing so."[4] After the deaths of Grayson and Collinsworth, Lamar faced Texas Sen. Robert "Honest Bob" Wilson who entered the Presidential race only a short time before the election. Against his new opponent, Lamar easily cruised to victory, winning 6,095 votes to Wilson's 252.[5] Lamar began to implement his own political agenda, which included rebuilding the Texas Navy and exploring ways to permanently settle the Texas frontier.

One of the principal issues facing Lamar was the lack of schools in the Republic. Within a month of taking office, Lamar proposed a system of educational funding based on revenues from public land, a program that eventually blossomed into a public school and university system for Texas. While the early revenues from the public land consisted of lease payments from farming and the grazing of cattle, many decades later a public university system was built with the revenues from oil producing properties on the public lands which Texas retained following annexation to the United States in 1845. The setting aside of public lands for the use of public education was one of Lamar's most lasting achievements.

Lamar's long-term vision was to establish a new capital for the Republic, not only to stimulate economic development in the western portion of the country, but to also wrench the seat of government away from the town named after his political rival. Lamar was a visionary and an expansionist who shunned the idea of annexation and was determined to borrow money and build Texas into a great nation. He dreamed of expanding the border of Texas westward. A strong advocate of the military, he was also determined to raise funds—and print additional money if needed—to ensure a strong Texas Navy to protect the coast from another Mexican blockade. With a policy of expansion for Texas, containment of the Mexicans, and a determination to drive the Indians to the fringes of civilization, the free-spending days of the Lamar administration were about to begin.

PRESIDENTIAL TRANSITION NOTES

The majority of the "Government of Texas" notes were issued under the Houston administration and depict the city of Houston as the capital of the Republic. Some of these engraved notes were issued during the first months of Lamar's Presidency in 1839 when the government was still in Houston. One of the most interesting examples of how quickly the Lamar administration issued paper money can be seen in the two $50 engraved notes shown in figures 9.2 and 9.3, each signed on December 10, 1838, Sam Houston's last day in office and Lamar's inauguration day. At the Treasury offices, Henry Smith and William G. Cooke signed one set of notes in the morning with Houston's signature and another set in the afternoon with Lamar's signature. These were undoubtedly signed while Sam Houston, dressed in a white powdered wig in the style of George Washington, delivered a booming, three-hour farewell speech that boasted of his accomplishments, railed against Lamar's platform of hostility towards the Indians, and upstaged the incoming President to the point where Lamar's personal secretary delivered his acceptance speech in absentia.[6]

Fig 9.2, $50 "Presidential Transition Notes," Dec. 10, 1838.
Henry Smith / Sam Houston
Private Collection, Cr. H21A, O-585.

Fig 9.3, $50 "Presidential Transition Notes," Dec. 10, 1838.
Henry Smith / Mirabeau B. Lamar
Private Collection, Cr. H21A, O-585.

The promissory notes issued under President Lamar also reflect somewhat of a revolving door to the office of Treasury Secretary during his three-year administration. As noted earlier, Henry Smith served as the interim Treasury Secretary for the first few days of Lamar's administration and continued signing the notes in that capacity until December 15, 1838. This was one day after his successor, Richard G. Dunlap, was appointed to the office by Lamar. Dunlap served as Treasury Secretary until April 1839. Dunlap fought in the War of 1812 and in the Seminole campaign in 1817 and served in the Tennessee legislature from 1829 to 1831 before coming to Texas in 1837.[7]

Henry Smith continued to work on budgetary matters during the transition. Smith's overbearing nature was apparent to Dunlap, who was greeted with a letter from Smith in early 1839, arrogantly stating, "when I put you in charge of the Department…"[8] Henry Smith was later elected to a term in the House of Representatives in 1840 where he served as the Chairman of the Committee on Finance. Following his term in Congress, he retired to private life and did not seek public office again. Smith lived in retirement until 1849 when he succumbed to the fever of the California gold rush and headed west. Although he reached California, he did not find any gold. Smith died in a mining camp in Los Angeles County on March 4, 1851, as he sought the precious metal that eluded him during his twenty-year tenure in Texas.[9]

Fig 9.4, $1 Government of Texas, "Engraved Note" 1839.
R.G. Dunlap / Mirabeau B. Lamar
Private Collection, Cr. H-14, O-520.

ENGRAVED NOTES (THE GOVERNMENT OF TEXAS)

For the collector, the Lamar notes of 1838-1839 are somewhat rarer than the earlier 1838 counterparts bearing the signatures of Houston. Collecting the series with Sam Houston's signature is more popular, though many novice collectors may not realize that it was actually William G. Cooke who signed Houston's name. While the notes containing Lamar's signature (also signed by his secretary) are scarcer, they are usually offered at only a slight premium if at all. These notes, examples of which are shown in figures 9.4 through 9.9, are more difficult to find because of the smaller number issued. They bear the signatures of Richard G. Dunlap as Treasury Secretary and Mirabeau B. Lamar as President, and were issued from Houston, a city which the new President loathed and soon vacated.

Fig 9.5, $3 Government of Texas, "Engraved Note" 1839.
R.G. Dunlap / Mirabeau B. Lamar
Private Collection, Cr. H-15, O-530.

Fig 9.6, $5 Government of Texas, "Engraved Note" 1839.
R.G. Dunlap / Mirabeau B. Lamar
Private Collection, H-16, O-545.

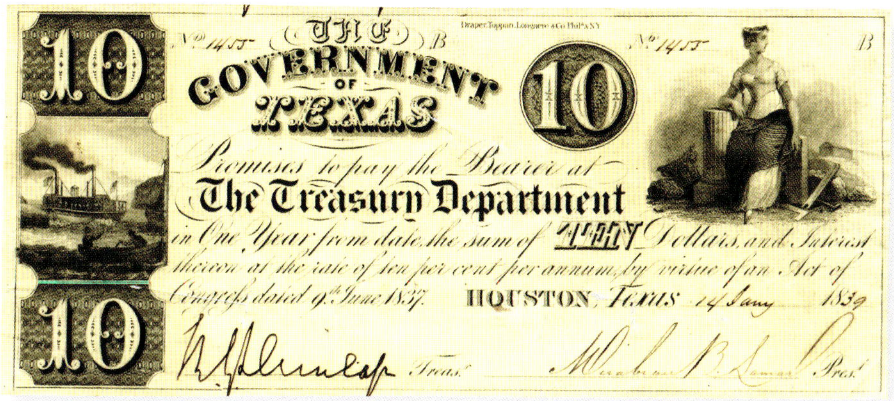

Fig 9.7, $10 Government of Texas, "Engraved Note" 1839.
R.G. Dunlap / Mirabeau B. Lamar
Private Collection, Cr. H-17, O-550.

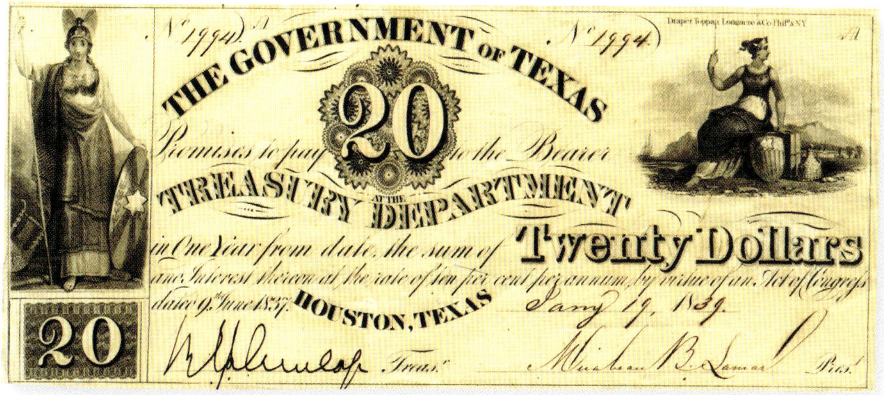

Fig 9.8, $20 Government of Texas, "Engraved Note" 1839.
R.G. Dunlap / Mirabeau B. Lamar, Note the "Six Pointed Star on Shield."
Private Collection, Cr. H-19, O-565.

Fig 9.9, $50 Government of Texas, "Engraved Note" 1839.
R.G. Dunlap / Mirabeau B. Lamar
Private Collection, Cr. H-21A, O-585.

VARIETIES IN THE GOVERNMENT OF TEXAS SERIES

When a person has the opportunity to examine a large number of notes, he or she may notice several small, but distinctive, differences in the design elements. There are only six denominations of the "Government of Texas" engraved notes, but thirteen distinct design varieties in the issues from Houston. They are spread somewhat evenly throughout the notes graced with Sam Houston's or Mirabeau Lamar's signature.[10] In order to gain an understanding of why these design varieties occur, it is important to understand a little bit about the engraving process and how these notes were produced.

A handful of private engraving firms provided the plates and the printing of currency for state-chartered banks in the early part of the nineteenth century.[11] The first series of engraved notes from Houston was produced by Draper, Toppan, Longacre & Co. of Philadelphia and New York. One of the engravers, James B. Longacre, later worked as an engraver of the United

Fig 9.10, James B. Longacre, Self Portrait.
Courtesy of Heritage Auctions, Dallas, Texas.

States Mint from 1844 to1869.[12] He developed several of the long-running designs for coins issued by the U.S. in the nineteenth century. The skillful artistry was engraved and transferred into metal plates which usually consisted of four subjects to a sheet. In other words, each impression of the plate inked a sheet of four notes, which were then shipped to and signed by the issuing bank or entity, which then paid them out for obligations. In the case of the Republic of Texas, this was done by the Treasury officials. These plates were normally used to produce limited runs of currency, typically less than 5,000 impressions, and were usually made of copper. These were referred to as the master set of plates which also carried the name of the engraver. Printing notes in excess of 5,000 impressions would have required using plates made of hardened steel or additional copper master plates.

Fig 9.11, The Engraver, Die Transfer, and Note Printing.

Courtesy of Stack's, New York, from the American Bank Note Co. Archives.

These promotional engravings from the American Bank Note Company, were made on a single steel plate, 6.25" x 4" in size, and show the three stages of the printing process. At left is the engraver, in the center is the transfer of designs from the cylinder dies, and the actual process of printing the notes on a hand-operated "spider" press at right. These photographs are inverse images of the plate vignettes.

Fig 9.12, Hunting the Buffaloe [*sic*] by Peter Rindisbacher c. 1837.

Courtesy of the Amon Carter Museum, Fort Worth, Texas.

The engraved vignette on the $5 promissory note shown in Figure 9.6 was adapted from this 1837 lithograph by artist Peter Rindisbacher.

Fig 9.13, Buffalo Hunt, Steel Vignette Plate 3.5" x 2.25".

Courtesy of Stack's, New York, from the American Bank Note Co. Archives.

This hardened-steel plate was engraved from the Rindisbacher lithograph by Draper, Toppan, Longacre & Co. This photograph is an inverse image of the plate which was used to transfer the final image to the $5 note shown in Figure 9.14.

Fig 9.14, Buffalo Hunt, Vignette on Texas $5 Bill.

Private Collection.

The allegorical features of Liberty, the Indian hunting a buffalo, the steamboat, and other images which appeared on the "Government of Texas" notes were first engraved inversely into a steel plate known as a vignette die. These rectangular plates were then heated and quickly immersed in water to harden them, a process known as tempering.

Fig 9.16, Vignette of Sailor in a different pose, by Rawdon, Wright, Hatch & Edson, New York.

Private Collection.

Fig 9.15, Sailor holding Texas Navy flag, Vignette on Texas $50 Bill, by Draper, Toppan Longacre & Co.

Private Collection.

The vivid images were selected by the engravers based upon their client needs and then transferred to the master plates. Some of the Texas vignettes had been previously used on other bank notes. Other vignettes were copied from bank notes in various parts of the United States. Many of these characters are seen in different surroundings on various banknotes, and there was a distinct effort to customize the designs for the Texas paper. Buffalo hunting was popular in Texas and large herds roamed freely throughout the open plains. The addition of the five-pointed Lone Star to the shield and the sailor holding the striped flag of the Texas Navy are examples of how the designs were customized for the Republic of Texas.

The detailed, intricate engraving process was painstakingly time consuming, but once completed, there were repeated uses of the same designs in different combinations for a variety of issuers. Rather than electronically cutting and pasting these designs as we would today, they were laboriously hand engraved and then physically impressed into the plate which was customized for an issuer using a vignette die made of tempered steel. In addition to the use of the five-pointed Lone Star, the only designs which are known to be completely unique to the Texas series are the engraved portrait of Thomas Jefferson on the $1 and $3 change notes and the portraits of Deaf Smith and Stephen F. Austin on the $5 and $50 redback notes. (Both the Smith and Austin portraits are in the redback series issued in 1839-1841 from the cities of Houston and Austin.)

Once the outline of the initial bank note plate was designed, the appropriate vignettes were applied by the use of a cylinder die. These metal cylinders transferred the images to the master plates. Before tempering, the soft metal was impressed or rolled across the length of a vignette die to pick up the impression of the design. Once hardened by tempering, these cylinders were used to transfer the inverse impression into the soft steel or copper master printing plate. Another cylinder was then used to transfer the impressions of lettering from an additional vignette die and so forth. These cylinders bore around their perimeter a relief impression that was used to make the final impressions of large lettering, denominations, etc. The successive series of transfers to the final plate became the final impression for printing, after which it was hardened, polished, and readied for production.

Fig 9.17, An example of a steel cylinder die, with a representation of Liberty c. 1847.

Courtesy of Stack's, New York, from the American Bank Note Co. Archives.

There are several intriguing features on these notes. While the $1 and $3 had the lowest survival rate in the series, the vignette shown in Figure 9.18 is of a very scarce variety, bearing seven tiny stars around the periphery of the center star in the shield. This was due to a different vignette die which was substituted for the making of a new master plate.

Fig 9.18, $1 Vignette, "Tiny Stars on Shield."

Private Collection.

Fig 9.19, $20 Vignette, "Six Pointed Star on Shield."

Private Collection.

Fig 9.20, $20 Government of Texas, "Star" on Shield.

Private Collection.

Fig 9.21, $20 Government of Texas, "Eagle" on Shield.

Private Collection.

Another interesting example of the engraved notes issued from Houston is the vignette on the $20 note shown in figure 9.19. It is found on notes bearing both the Houston and Lamar signatures. The shield in Miss Liberty's left hand bears a six-pointed star resembling the Star of David, rather than the symbolic five-pointed star for Texas.

It has been said that the New York artisan who engraved the vignette plate may have been Jewish and was attempting to add his own personal touch to the shield, rather than use the traditional five-pointed Lone Star. These early bank note engravers were highly skilled artisans who were very precise in their work. Perhaps this design was not prompted by religious motivation, but ignorance of the five-pointed Lone Star symbol for Texas. It is also possible that the foreman simply used the wrong vignette roller, designed for a different series of private bank notes. The rationale for the six-pointed star instead of the five-pointed version remains unanswered to this day. Many sharp-eyed collectors have been pondering this question for well over a century.

Perhaps the most interesting variety in this engraved series and one of the true rarities is the introduction of an eagle on the $20 note. The engravers in New York made an engraved replacement note plate for the $20 with an eagle on the shield at right, rather than the traditional five-pointed Lone Star. Was this change requested by the Texas government or was it another example of U.S. influence being borne out through the actions of a rogue employee? More likely than not, it was simply the use of an incorrect cylinder die which was destined for a different series of American banknotes when making a new master plate. Whether deliberate or not, the design change gives another reason to pause and reflect upon the politics of the United States and the distinctly American influences of the day.

THE TEXAS COINAGE ACT OF 1839

From the earliest days at San Felipe de Austin, promissory notes issued by Texas were denominated in dollars, rather than in *pesos*. From the beginning of his term, the Lamar administration was awash in paper money. The United States sought to expand the production of gold and silver coins by establishing branch mints in Dahlonega, Georgia, Charlotte, North Carolina, and in New Orleans, Louisiana, in 1838. The New Orleans mint was strategically located at the foot of the French Quarter near the docks on the Mississippi River. Much of the resulting production of silver and gold coins flowing from this southern mint was quickly absorbed by the New Orleans banks. Previously, the coins had to work their way through the economy from distant Philadelphia. Although the arrival of this badly needed specie made it easier for banks and merchants on the Gulf Coast to do business, many of the banks that resumed their specie payments from the suspension a year before were forced to postpone them once again as business conditions worsened.[13] As the U.S. gold and silver coins flowed in a steady trickle from Louisiana, the old Mexican and Spanish coins were still prevalent in many parts of Texas. It was clear that the newest coins from the United States were met with widespread acceptance by those persons in Texas fortunate enough to be paid with them. In an effort to establish a clear monetary standard, the Texas government decided to permanently establish an acceptable gold and silver standard with an act that fixed the standard of silver and gold coins in the Republic. The act read as follows:

> *Be it enacted by the Senate and house of representatives of the Republic of Texas in Congress assembled, that the standard value of silver and gold coins shall be and is hereby declared to be the same as in the United States of America; and the standard by which silver and gold coin is established by the government of the United states, is hereby adopted for the government of this Republic.*

JOHN M. HANSFORD
Speaker of the House of Representatives
DAVID G. BURNETT
President of the Senate
Approved Jan. 15, 1839
MIRABEAU B. LAMAR[14]

Fig 9.22, The New Orleans Mint.
Louisiana State Museum, New Orleans, Louisiana.

Although the gold and silver coins of the United States became the new monetary standard for Texas, it is also important to note that many of the coins were retained by southern banks, in an effort to shore up their reserves. During the period from 1838-1841, the U.S. Mint in New Orleans struck $321,752 in gold coins and $1,039,771.70 in silver coins, a large part of which were held by the banks.[15] Unfortunately, the gold coins were rarely seen by the general public following the passage of the legislation. The silver coins which were released into circulation became increasingly scarce due to hoarding. All of the southern banks routinely paid their depositors in their own bank notes rather than in gold and silver coins, and the coins soon commanded a premium to the paper money. As the banks restricted the flow of specie, real estate prices in Texas continued to plummet and the remaining silver coins in Texas soon disappeared from circulation. With very little money in circulation, commerce slowed and bartering once again became the basis for many transactions in Texas.

UNITED STATES COINS – THE NEW MONETARY STANDARD FOR TEXAS

All of the coins shown in figures 9.23 through 9.41 are representative of the types of U.S. coins which became the monetary standard for silver and gold coins in Texas established by the Act of January 15, 1839. Although copper coins were not a part of the official monetary standard for Texas, they were readily accepted in routine transactions.

Fig 9.23, 1828 Half Cent, Classic Head, c. 1809-1836.

Fig 9.24, 1851 Half Cent, Coronet Head, c. 1840-1857.

Fig 9.25, 1837 Large Cent, Matron Head, c. 1837-1839.

Fig 9.26, 1839 Large Cent, Coronet Head, c. 1839-1857.

Fig 9.27, 1837 Half Dime, Liberty Seated, No Stars, c. 1837-1838.

Fig 9.28, 1838 Half Dime, Liberty Seated, With Stars, c. 1838-1839.

Fig 9.29, 1837 Dime, Liberty Seated, No Stars, c. 1837-1838.

Fig 9.30, 1838 Dime, Liberty Seated, With Stars, c. 1838-1860.

Fig 9.31, 1831 Quarter Dollar, Capped Bust, c. 1831-1838.

Fig 9.32, 1840-O Quarter Dollar, Liberty Seated, c. 1838-1865.

Fig 9.33, 1836 Half Dollar, Capped Bust, c. 1836-1839.

Fig 9.34, 1841-O Half Dollar, Seated Liberty, c. 1839-1865.

Fig 9.35, 1836 Gobrecht Dollar, c. 1836-1839.

Fig 9.36, 1840 Dollar, Seated Liberty, c. 1840-1865.

Fig 9.37, 1834 $2.50 Quarter Eagle, Classic Head, c. 1834-1839.

Fig 9.38, 1852 $2.50 Quarter Eagle, Coronet Type, c. 1840-1865.

Fig 9.39, 1834 $5.00 Half Eagle, Classic Head, c. 1834-1838.

Fig 9.40, 1842-O $5.00 Half Eagle, Coronet Type, c. 1834-1866.

Fig 9.41, 1842-O $10.00 Eagle, Coronet Type, No Motto, c. 1838-1866.

A SHORTAGE OF HARD MONEY

Unfortunately, the Texas government not only didn't possess the necessary equipment to strike the coins, but the Republic had no available stockpile of gold or silver from which to strike the coins. Although there were Mexican coins still circulating in Texas both before and after the revolution, little of the precious specie changed hands in the ten years that Texas was a Republic. In 1838, David G. Burnet wrote: "You are in error as to specie being very abundant with our government. I doubt if the desk of the Treasurer has heard the jingle of it for the past year."[16] The economy of the Republic was run on a barter system and financed by the issuance of paper. This paper had no backing other than the faith and credit of the Republic itself. Although the Coinage Act firmly established the standards of coins in which the government would accept payment, the Treasury records indicate they would accept virtually any form of specie in payment. In the spring of 1839, the value of the engraved notes continued to fall even further, and was widely quoted at forty cents on the dollar throughout Texas.[17]

In nearby Galveston, the blockade ended, commerce resumed and the busy port city became a prime source of customs revenues. Virtually all of these revenues were received in goods or Texas' own discounted paper. With regular steamboat passage to and from New Orleans, and daily runs up the bayou to Houston, business was booming and the island city was soon the largest city in Texas. Galveston had become so culturally developed that the city's first luxury hotel, the Tremont House, was built by McKinney & Williams in 1839. Erected at the corner of Post Office and Tremont streets, the impressive two-story structure had long galleries extending the length of the grand new hotel from east to west. A grand-opening ball was held on April 19, 1839, to coincide with the third anniversary of San Jacinto Day, marked as a celebration across all of Texas. As a testament to the depreciating currency, admission to the grand-opening ball was $25 in gold or $50 in Texas currency.[18] The paper money was cheap, abundant, and readily accepted at the appropriate discount. The opening of the Tremont House hotel would mark the last occasion on which this Texas paper money would be accepted at 50 percent of the value of gold.

---

1. Mirabeau B. Lamar was the third President of the Republic of Texas, though he is sometimes thought of as the second president since David G. Burnet was the *ad interim* President and not elected by the people.
2. Calendar of the Papers of Mirabeau Buonaparte Lamar, ed. by Michael R. Green (Austin: Texas State Library & Archives, 1982), preface.
3. "Mirabeau B. Lamar," Triumph and Tragedy: Presidents of the Republic of Texas, Texas State Library & Archives, found online at http://www.tsl.state.tx.us/exhibits/presidents/lamar/grow.html
4. Anson Jones, Memoranda and Official Correspondence relating to the Republic of Texas its History and Annexation (New York: D. Appleton & Company, 1859), 28.
5. John Nathan Craven, James Harper Starr, Financier of the Republic of Texas (Austin: The Daughters of the Republic of Texas, 1950), 38.
6. John Hoyt Williams, Sam Houston: The Life and Times of the Liberator of Texas, an Authentic American Hero (New York: Simon & Schuster, Inc., 1993), 188-89.
7. Thomas Maitland Marshall, "Diplomatic Relations of Texas and the United States, 1839-1843," *SHQ*, vol. 15 (April 1912), 4:267-93.
8. Seymour V. Conner, ed., "Smith to Dunlop, City of Houston, February 21, 1839," Texas Treasury Papers, 1:188.
9. Handbook of Texas Online, s.v., "Henry Smith," http://www.tsha.utexas.edu/handbook/online/articles/SS/fsm23.html (accessed August 12, 2007).
10. Grover C. Criswell, Confederate and Southern States Currency: A Descriptive Listing, Including Rarity and Values, vol.1, 4th ed. (1992), 364-67.
11. "Treasures from the American Bank Note Company," The Old West and Franklin Collection, Auction book (American Numismatic Rarities, Inc., August 11, 2006), 209-10.
12. Gene Hessler, The Comprehensive Catalogue of U.S. Paper Money, 6th ed. (BNR Press, 1997), 11.
13. Q. David Bowers, Obsolete Paper Money Issued by Banks in the United States, 1782-1866 (Whitman publishing, LLC, 2006).
14. An act fixing the standard of silver and gold coin in this Republic," January 15, 1839, Journals of the Sixth Congress of the Republic of Texas, 42-43.
15. R.S. Yeoman, ed. by Ken Bressett, A Guide Book of United States Coins (New York: St Martin's Press, 2002), 118-64 and 200-24.
16. William Ransom Hogan, The Texas Republic: A Social and Economic History (Norman, OK: University of Oklahoma Press, 1946), 101.
17. Report of the Auditor and Comptroller to the fourth legislature on the Public Debt of Texas (Austin: Printed by Cushney & Hampton, "State Gazette" Office, 1851), 6.
18. From a historical marker in front of the Tremont House Hotel, Mechanic Street, Galveston, Texas. Credited to George L. Hosek.

CHAPTER TEN

AUSTIN: "YOU WILL STRIKE OUT THE INTEREST!"

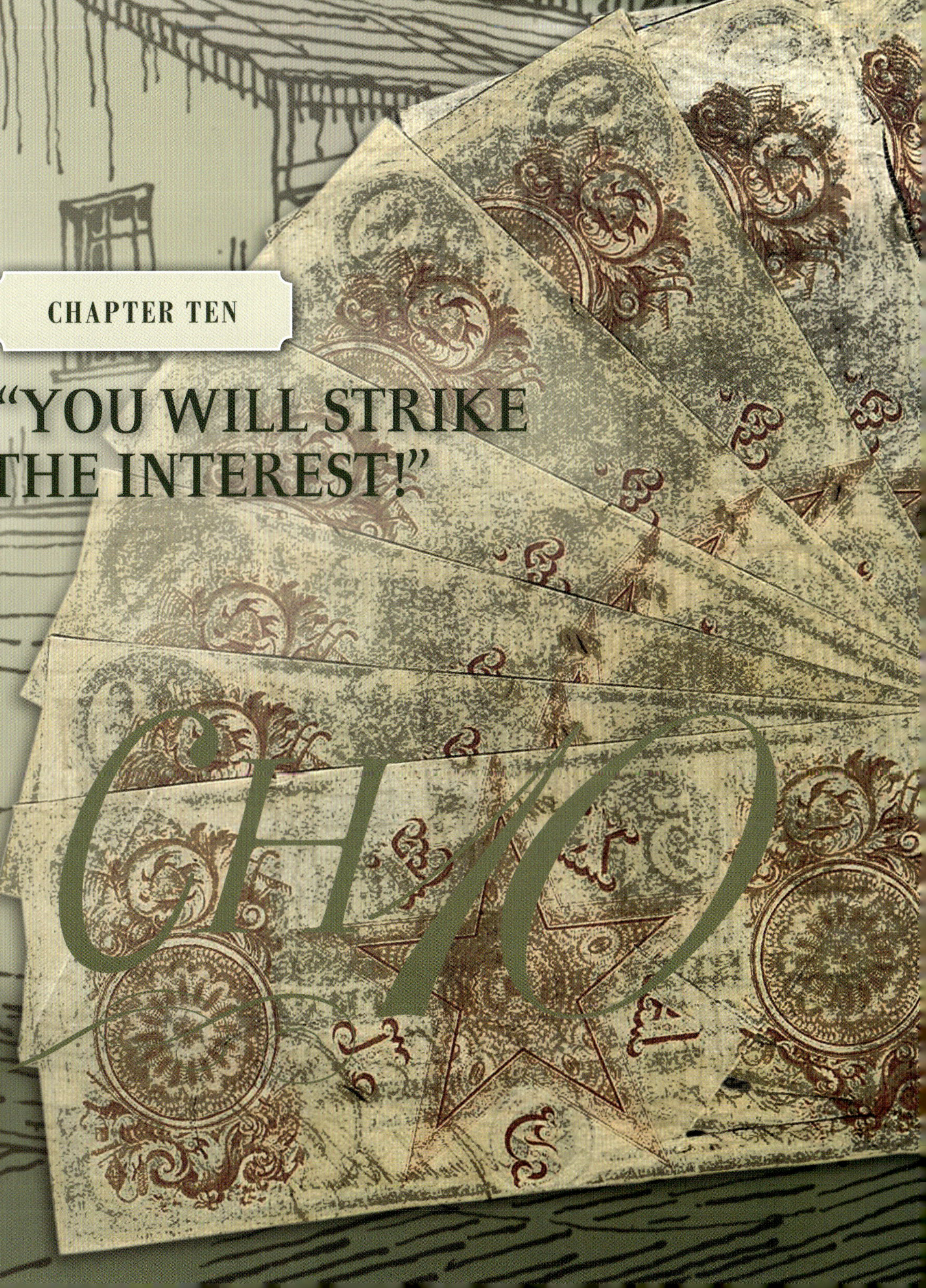

The effort to relocate the capital began in earnest shortly after the election of Lamar in the fall of 1838. It began on January 14, 1839, with the passage of a bill in the Senate entitled "An act for the permanent location of the seat of Government." Following the war, the veterans received headright certificates payable in land as bounty for their military service. Whether these headright certificates were sold and transferred or exercised by the soldiers mattered little, as claims were being made pertaining to areas surrounding the small communities of Columbia, Houston, and Washington. As the land parcels were allocated, many of the properties set aside for veterans were located near the western frontier. American settlers who arrived in Texas after the war began to drift westward even though the eastern area was far from settled. As the populace inched westward, raids by Comanche Indians against the new residents were not uncommon. Noting the westward expansion of the modest population, Lamar surmised that if the government were indeed moved further westward, not only would elected officials and their staffs be forced to relocate, it would also spur construction in the area to provide lodging, trade, printing, and commerce for the new settlers.

Fig 10.1, The Log Cabin Capitol of the Republic, Austin, c. 1839-1842.
Texas State Library & Archive Commission, Austin, Texas.

A committee was formed to survey potential sites, followed by a recommendation to relocate the capital to the east bank of the Colorado River north of the old San Antonio Road on the edge of what is now known as the Texas Hill Country. Formerly called Waterloo, the town was renamed "Austin" in honor of the famous land *empresario,* Stephen F. Austin, who died in December 1836. Much of the furniture and the complete archives of the government were moved from Houston by a caravan of forty to fifty covered wagons in the fall of 1839.

The first capitol in Austin was built on a hilltop at the corner of 8th and Colorado Streets where City Hall is presently located.[1] A log cabin constructed of rough pine wood with two large rooms, one each for the House and Senate, served as the capital offices during the Republic of Texas era until a more permanent structure could be built. The first session of Congress in Austin was held in that building in November 1839, during a time when the capitol building was one of the very few structures in town. In the fall of 1839, Austin was a town very much in the woods, with five or six hundred people in cabins, shanties or camps.[2] The building also served as a community gathering place because of its large rooms and as a refuge against Indian raids because of the eight-foot stockade fence surrounding the structure.

Fig 10.2, The Bullock Hotel, Austin.
Austin History Center, Austin Public Library, Austin, Texas.

Transcription of Figure 10.3:

War Department, Austin 8th Jan[uar]y 1840

THIS IS TO CERTIFY, That D[illard] Cooper Entered the Army of Texas on the Nineteenth – day of January 1836 and was Honorably Discharged. This certificate is given said claimant for the purposes of enabling him to obtain his headright from the Hon[orable] Board of Land Commissioners. (Signed) A. Sidney Johnston, Secretary of War.

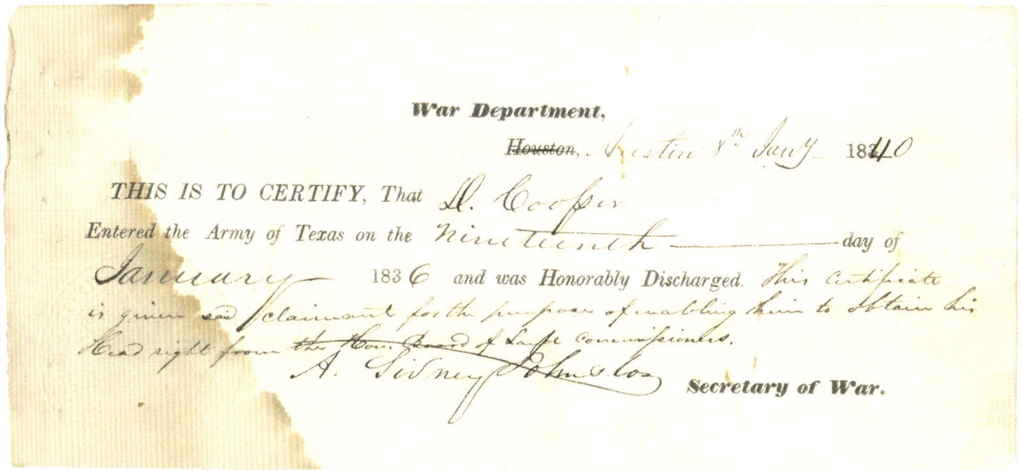

War Department,

~~Houston~~, Austin 8th Jany 1840

THIS IS TO CERTIFY, That D. Cooper

Entered the Army of Texas on the Nineteenth day of

January 1836 and was Honorably Discharged. This certificate is given said claimant for the purpose of enabling him to obtain his Head right from the Hon. Board of Land Commissioners.

A. Sidney Johnston Secretary of War.

Fig 10.3, Austin, Headright Certificate, January 8, 1840.
Private Collection.

Among the little dwellings which dominated the frontier capital was the Bullock House, for a time the only available hotel in town. It was sparsely furnished but offered the largest rooms in the area, and served as a gathering place for public officials and for Presbyterian services on Sundays. It soon proved to be a popular venue for the predominantly protestant government officials.

A law was passed in January 1840 dictating that all future government buildings were to be constructed of stone. The first permanent capitol building was not erected until 1853, long after Texas was annexed to the United States. Not only was moving the capital away from the city of Houston a slap at Lamar's biggest political rival, Sam Houston, it further widened the rift between these two Texas politicians. The town of Houston, located on Buffalo Bayou with its hot, humid climate, muddy streets and ravenous mosquito population, suffered from a yellow fever epidemic that swept through the area in 1838-1839. Among the victims of the fever were John Kirby Allen, co-founder of the city, who died on August 18, 1838, and John Wyatt Moody, the auditor, who died at the age of forty-eight on August 21, 1839.[3] The formerly busy town was, for a while, but a shadow of its former self as many citizens left the coastal areas of Houston and Galveston for the new town of Austin in the interior of Texas.

The headright certificate in Figure 10.3 documents Dillard Cooper's service entry and discharge dates from the Texas Army, and validates his claim to a headright of bounty land awarded to veterans for military service. Dillard Cooper came to Texas from Alabama with Capt. John Shackelford's Red Rovers, landing at Copano Bay on January 19, 1836. Shortly thereafter, he was sent to join the army under Fannin's command. Cooper was slightly wounded at the battle of Coleto but escaped the massacre at Goliad. This certificate is identical to those issued from Houston, but the previous city of issue was struck through and the newest capital city, Austin, was written in its place. Once it was signed and received, individuals were allowed to locate their own land and have it surveyed. This document was printed at the Telegraph office in Houston, by Francis Moore, around 1837-1838. The example was signed by Albert Sidney Johnston, appointed as the Secretary of War by President Lamar.

Fig 10.4, Albert Sidney Johnston.
Courtesy of the Rosenberg Library, Galveston, Texas.

Fig 10.5, $1 Vignette.
Author's Collection.

Fig 10.6, $2 Vignette.
Author's Collection.

Fig 10.7, $3 Vignette.
Author's Collection.

Albert Sidney Johnston was born in Kentucky on February 2, 1803. He attended Transylvania University and graduated from West Point in 1826. In 1834, Johnston left the U.S. Army and took up farming near St Louis.[4] After the death of his first wife in 1835, he moved to Texas where he enlisted as a private in the Texas Army. His leadership skills were quickly recognized and on August 5, 1836, he was appointed an adjutant general by Thomas J. Rusk. He was promoted to senior brigadier general in command of the Army in 1837, but was seriously wounded in a duel with Felix Huston, the man whose command he was to assume. Johnston recovered, but was unable to assume the command. He was appointed as Secretary of War by President Lamar on December 22, 1838, and placed in command of the Texas Army. It was in this capacity that he signed Cooper's headright certificate.

Johnston was a professional soldier with a charismatic personality. He was instrumental in carrying out Lamar's policy of hostility towards the Indians and led a military expedition against the Cherokees in East Texas in 1839. Following the annexation of Texas, he rejoined the U.S. Army. During the Mexican War, his quick thinking saved both his life and that of his friend, Jefferson Davis, who would later become the President of the Confederate States of America.[5] Following the Mexican War, Johnston served as paymaster of the U.S. Army and was assigned to the Texas frontier. During the American Civil War, Johnston was appointed as a full general in the Confederate Army by Jefferson Davis and placed in command of the Western Department. He led his troops through battles in Kentucky and Tennessee, eventually withdrawing to Mississippi. Johnston massed his troops in Corinth, Mississippi, and succeeded in launching a surprise attack on Grant's forces in Tennessee in the battle of Shiloh on April 6, 1862. After overcoming the Union soldiers in the attack, Johnston led the final charge to clear the enemy troops from a peach orchard, only to receive a severe wound in the leg. Johnston bled to death on the battlefield. The loss of the former Texas commander was widely believed to be a negative turning point for the Confederate forces.

AUSTIN CHANGE NOTES

With the seat of government relocating to the small, somewhat primitive, town in the hills, the bureaucrats and printers busied themselves with the business of the government. Before the government was physically able to move, it became apparent that the previous issue of change notes would be inadequate to facilitate the daily commerce of the new capital of Austin. The chronic shortage of coins led to bills printed in $1, $2 and $3 denominations by Endicott & Clark of New Orleans. They were authorized by an act of Congress on December 14, 1838, and were limited to an issue of $150,000. While the legislation authorizing the bills was passed shortly after Lamar took office, the arrangements for having the plates engraved and the money printed took place as the government planned the move westward. The new capital city of Austin was named as the place of issue and embellished on the face of each bill. The public passed off these notes as quickly as possible before they too depreciated against the value of coins. However, the printing quality and the intricate designs of these engraved bills were far superior to the previous issue of change notes, which are now known as the medallion series. Austin officially became the Texas capital in the fall of 1839 and the place of issue is scripted on the $1 note and boldly printed on the $2 and $3.

MICRO VIGNETTES ON THE CHANGE NOTES

The change notes were widely circulated and are often described as the most artistic in the series. They carry a distinct difference from the later series of bills in the form of a miniature vignette located at the center of the bottom of each note. The $1 note features an eagle with spread wings. The $2 note has a steamship belching black smoke and carrying a flag with a Lone Star off the stern. The $3 note features a small boy riding a white pony.

While these miniature vignettes are sometimes obscured by the mark of the comptroller—abbreviated "Comp"—they are a unique design element of these notes in the short-lived series. Notes which have the miniature design elements un-obscured by the writing of the comptroller may carry a small premium to the collector.

SECOND ISSUE OF CHANGE NOTES (AUSTIN)

The second issue of change notes featured allegorical vignettes which reflected the wildlife and western themes of Texas. Similar to all previously issued Texas money, their reverses were blank. True to the previous issue of change notes, these notes bore the signatures of the comptroller and treasurer, rather than the signature of the treasury secretary and President. The signature combinations on the bills further differentiate them from the larger denominations of the "redback" series which were issued concurrently bearing the signature of President Lamar.[6]

On the left side of the $1 note shown in Figure 10.8 is an Indian brave with a bow and a quiver of arrows across his back. In the center is a representation of Ceres as a bare-breasted maiden, seated in agriculture as symbolized by the wheat and plowshares. At the bottom of the note is a small black eagle with outstretched wings, and the right side depicts the denomination 1, with "ONE" superimposed on a five-pointed star, surrounded by a ribbon with microprinting of "ONE DOLLAR" in a continuous loop. The note is signed by James B. Shaw and J.W. Simmons.

On the left side of the $2 note in Figure 10.9 is a stag perched on a bluff overlooking the water. In the center is a cowboy riding a white horse and roping a longhorn steer with a herd of longhorn cattle in the background. At the bottom is a steamship belching black smoke and flying a Lone Star flag off the stern. The right shows the denomination 2, with "TWO" superimposed on a five-pointed star, surrounded by a ribbon with microprinting of "TWO" in a continuous loop. The note is signed by James B. Shaw and J.W. Simmons.

The $3 note in Figure 10.10 has a cotton plant, the primary cash crop of Texas, symbolizing commerce on the left side. In the center is Ceres with an exposed breast, seated on a hay bale with an ax, sickle, and shovel next to a mirror with a reflection of the Lone Star overlooking water. In the distance is a steamer and a sailboat. At the bottom is a small boy riding atop a white pony, and on the right is the denomination "THREE" printed in vertical fashion. The note is signed by James B. Shaw and James H. Raymond.

Austin is known today as a modern, cosmopolitan city and the heart of the University of Texas educational system. However, in the first two years that the government adopted the former town of Waterloo,

Fig 10.8, $1 Republic of Texas (Austin).
Private Collection, Cr. A1, O-750.

Fig 10.9, $2 Republic of Texas (Austin).
Private Collection, Cr. A2, O-753.

Fig 10.10, $3 Republic of Texas (Austin).
Private Collection, Cr. A3, O-756.

it was little more than a remote outpost on the fringe of civilization. Sam Houston described it as "the most unfortunate site upon earth for the seat of Government."[7] The former President predicted that great difficulties would be encountered in having the capital and Treasury Department in such a far flung location. Austin was located far from the center of the population concentrated in the east, prone to frequent Indian attacks, and could only be reached by a long trek over difficult roads by horse or wagon. Although the public buildings in the capital were ready to be occupied, they were largely unfurnished.[8] The Treasury building was a one-story wood-framed structure on the southwest corner of Congress Avenue and Sixth Street. The small wooden abode, which included the comptroller's office, was not large enough to accommodate all of the Treasury's needs, especially when the largest part of the Treasury's furniture and archives arrived from Houston on October 1.[9] Asa Brigham was so offended by the inadequate office space that he requested a room in separate quarters from the main building.

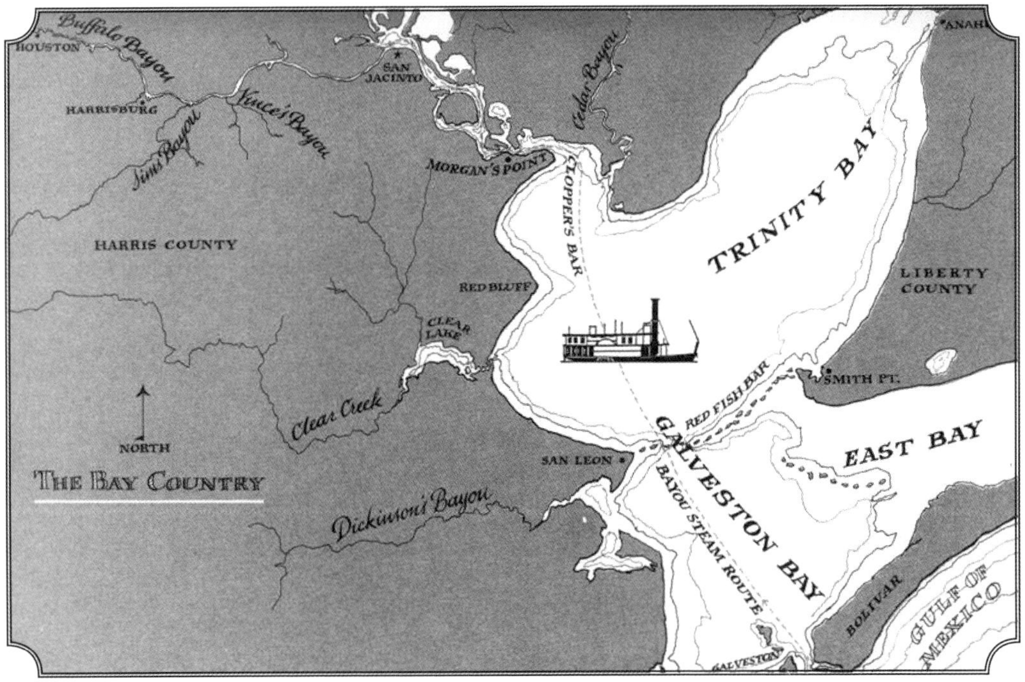

Fig 10.11, Bayou Steamboat Route.
Map by James L. Glass.

STEAMBOATS AND MUDDY STREETS

The relocation of the seat of government to Austin also created a host of logistical problems for the Treasury Department. This was especially true in regards to the ordering of blank promissory notes and their subsequent delivery from New Orleans far into the interior of Texas. Upon their arrival in Austin, the notes were numbered, signed, dated and used for the payment of warrants, which, in turn, released them into circulation. Once the Lamar administration paid out the initial appropriation of change notes, an Act of Congress was passed and signed into law by President Lamar on February 5, 1840, extending the issue of change notes up to an additional $150,000 face value. Lamar made this decision in hopes of alleviating the shortage of the small denomination notes in the western counties.[10] Unfortunately, the production and delivery of the notes was delayed and the problem was not solved.

When the Republic placed an order with the New Orleans printers for these engraved notes, they were printed and readied for delivery (assuming their account with the printers was current). The delivery process involved physically transporting the blank notes in a sealed tin box via sailing ship from New Orleans to Galveston, then via steamship up the vast reaches of Galveston Bay into Buffalo Bayou. The cargo was eventually unloaded at the Houston docks—now known as Allen's Landing—located at the foot of Main Street in present-day downtown Houston.

From the Houston docks, the blank notes were then transported via light wagon or stagecoach under guard to the distant Treasury building in Austin where they were processed by the government. If the logistics of transportation were not challenging enough even in good weather, the cold and heavy rains which often deluged the town of Houston in the winter months presented another set of problems. In the winter of 1840, a "box of promissory notes was received from the steamer *Columbia* on the 19th of February" which made daily runs from Galveston to Houston.[11] As a result of the recent heavy rains, it was concluded that it would be impossible for a light wagon loaded with the box to proceed through the thick, muddy, red clay streets for delivery via the long road to Austin. Other options were discussed, and the Treasury officials concluded that the sealed tin box was also too heavy to be carried on horseback. In other words, the government's latest issue of paper money could not be disbursed into the economy until the roads dried out because the shipment was literally stuck in the muddy, rain-filled streets of Houston.

Fig 10.12, City of Austin, the New Capital of Texas, c. January 1, 1840.

A hand colored plate from the book: Texas in 1840, or the Emigrant's Guide to the New Republic *by A.B. Lawrence. Courtesy of Darrel Brown.*

A picturesque view of Austin in 1840. The capitol building can be seen to the left of the main street part way up the hill, overlooking the center of the town. The small wooden buildings down the hill from the capitol housed the Department of the Navy, the Executive Office, and the State Department.

SHIN PLASTERS

While waiting for the roads to dry out, the shortage of small denomination notes was further exacerbated by the same legislation which brought the change notes into being. The act forbid any corporation or town from issuing private notes over the value of fifty cents, less they be subject to a fine of no less than $500. Some of the larger Texas towns did print notes in denominations of fifty cents and less, and figures 10.13 through 10.15 illustrate some of those examples.

Also referred to as "shin plasters," these small denomination notes were issued to help fill the void of small denomination paper money.[12] The logistical problems of obtaining the newest change notes, combined with the fact that there were never any coins minted by the Republic of Texas, forced the issue of these temporary bills, which effectively replaced the usage of coins in the larger Texas cities. Surviving specimens are extremely rare and are typically found in poor condition because of their extensive use in daily commerce. For some issues, less than a dozen of each denomination have survived in any condition and some examples are unique.

Fig 10.13, 25 Cent, Corporation of the City of Bastrop.

Private Collection, Cr. Unlisted, O-1140.

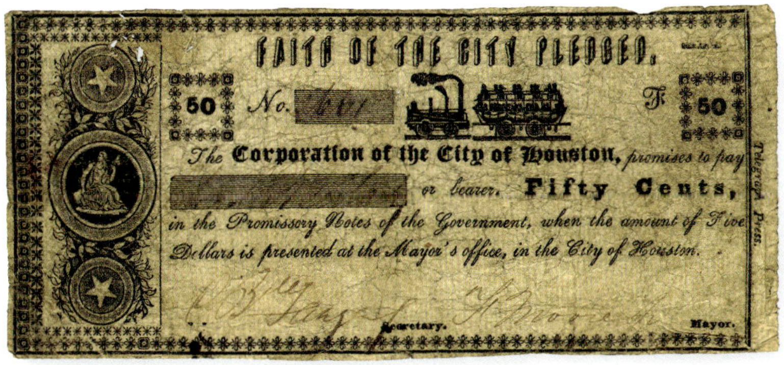

Fig 10.14, 50 Cent, Corporation of the City of Houston.

Private Collection, Cr. Unlisted, O-1180.

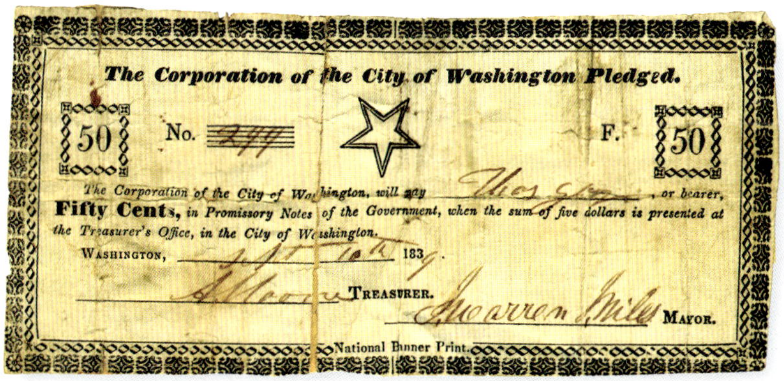

Fig 10.15, 50 Cent, Corporation of the City of Washington.

Private Collection, Cr. Unlisted, O-Unlisted.

REPUBLIC OF TEXAS "REDBACK" NOTES

Fig 10.16, "Redback Notes," The Republic of Texas, Reverse of $10 Bill.
Private Collection.

The appearance of the redbacks marked the first time a design appeared on the reverse of a Texas note. The reverse of the $5, $10, $20, $50, $100 and $500 notes have a distinct burnt orange color with the letters T-E-X-A-S surrounding the five-pointed star. This color on the reverse earned them the nickname "redbacks." The bills were the most prolifically produced and their burnt orange color has remained a popular one in the city of Austin to this day. The University of Texas at Austin later adopted the burnt orange color for its athletic teams more than a century after the first redbacks appeared, although there is no conclusive evidence that the color was adopted from the paper money. Coincidental or not, the burnt orange color of the Texas sunset was first seen not on a football jersey, but on the reverse of these Republic of Texas promissory notes. The redbacks were issued concurrently with the change notes. The $5, $10, $20 and $50 notes are the most frequently seen surviving specimens.

RAWDON, WRIGHT, HATCH & EDSON

It is not known why the government chose Rawdon, Wright, Hatch & Edson of New York and New Orleans as the new firm to engrave the master plates and print the new promissory notes. Perhaps the Government of Texas decided to change printers because their credit with the previous engravers was exhausted. Demands for payment of an invoice from Draper, Topper, Longacre & Co., were dated as late as April 30, 1840.[13] The debt was for the printing of the first series of engraved notes issued from Houston, ordered two years previously by former Secretary of the Treasury Henry Smith. The invoice amounted to only $407.50, but the company asked that payment be met by remitting a draft on a bank in Philadelphia or New Orleans. Despite repeated efforts to collect this payment for their previous work, the last of these invoices was not paid until 1844.[14] It was becoming clear even to the printers of the money that the credit of the Republic was rapidly deteriorating.

The old adage that money will get you through times of no credit better than credit will get you through times of no money was prophetically true for the Republic of Texas. With that in mind, the government was eager to have new money printed. The new bills were authorized by an act of Congress on January 19, 1839, and printed in denominations of $5, $10, $20, $50, $100, and $500. Well known in the southern states for bank note printing, the New Orleans engraving firm placed their artistry and skill on a level comparable to any engraver in the North. The engravers endeavored to take the quality of the new Texas bills to a higher level of the fine arts.[15]

Fig 10.17, Rawdon, Wright, Hatch & Edson, New Orleans.
Courtesy of the Historic New Orleans Collection.
The engraving firm of Rawdon, Wright, Hatch & Edson was located on the second floor of the building pictured in the far left of the 1873 drawing of Canal Street by Marie Adrien Persac shown in figure 10.17. The firm's building was located between Chartres and Royal streets. It was in this building that the last two series of paper money of the Republic of Texas were printed. The streetcar line shown in the drawing was not established until 1861.

In his letter dated March 20, 1839, to the engraving firm, Treasury Secretary R.G. Dunlap instructed the printers to "have the notes embellished with suitable devices and ornaments. Make them as near national as possible. Have the backs of the notes colored, the amounts of the notes cut in water marks, at the lower edge of the notes." He also added the instruction, "Let the notes read as the old or last issue does, except you will strike out the interest."[16] Strike out the interest! Unlike the previous "Star Money" and "Government" issues, this new series of paper money, issued under the Lamar administration in Austin, would not bear interest.

The issue was intentionally designed to influence the public into accepting the new notes through their beauty and aesthetic appeal, even though they did not bear interest. Each design displayed allegorical images of Native Americans, Miss Liberty, scantily clad maidens and even Zeus hurling a thunder bolt. In an effort to promote their acceptance across the country, they were clearly marked "Receivable for all Government dues."

Fig 10.18, Vignette Specimen Plate, Rawdon Wright & Hatch, New York.

Courtesy of Stack's, New York, from the American Bank Note Company Archives.

Many of the vignettes which adorned the new Republic of Texas promissory notes were selected from a specimen sheet printed from the plate shown in figure 10.18. The image is in an inverse of the actual steel plate. Note the rust stains at the bottom.

THE REPUBLIC OF TEXAS – REDBACK NOTES

Fig 10.19, $5 Republic of Texas – Redback Note
Private Collection, Cr. A4, O-759.

Fig 10.20, $10 Republic of Texas – Redback Note
Private Collection, Cr. A5, O-761.

Fig 10.21, $20 Republic of Texas – Redback Note
Private Collection, Cr. A6, O-763.

The Austin change notes and non-interest bearing redbacks are now known as the 4th and 5th series, commonly referred to as the Republic of Texas series. This second series of change notes and the redbacks are often lumped together and collected as a set because of their similar designs and use of allegorical figures. There are differences in paper, designers, engraving firms, and the printed reverses on the denominations of $5 and above which dominate the 5th series. The primary commonality is the similar design of the bills and that both issues bear the wording "The Republic of Texas" across the face.

In an ironic twist, Richard G. Dunlap, who ordered the printing of the notes, never signed any of the redbacks. He was relieved of his duties in the Treasury and appointed by Lamar as the minister from Texas to the United States in April 1839.[17] Dunlap was replaced by James Webb as acting Treasury Secretary in the same month. It was James Webb's signature which graced the earliest issue of redback notes as they began their entry into Texas circulation in April 1839.[18] James Webb was subsequently appointed as Secretary of State and James Harper Starr took over as the Secretary of the Treasury in May 1839. The redback notes bear the signatures of James Webb and James H. Starr in their capacities as Secretary of the Treasury. The signature of Mirabeau B. Lamar was signed on his behalf by a clerk in the Treasury Department for the duration of their issue under different treasury officials.[19]

The $5 note in Figure 10.19 features an Indian brave seated in the center with tomahawk and bow, looking over the ruins of a building. Birds in flight appear in the distance over the ruins. On the right side is a portrait of Erastus "Deaf" Smith, the famed scout in the Texian Army. The Lone Star is located on the bottom in the center of the Republic of Texas Seal. The note is signed by James H. Starr and Mirabeau B. Lamar.

On the left side of the $10 note in Figure 10.20 is Zeus with a Thunderbolt, an eagle above his right foot with a claw on a shield bearing the colors of Texas and the Lone Star. Below the shield are the words "E. Pluribus Unum." In the center of the note is a maiden bust is rising from waters, with a cap on her head. A sailing ship bearing the striped flag of the Texas Navy, passing a building (also with a striped flag) and a flock of birds flying overhead is located on the right of the note.

The Lone Star in the center of the Republic of Texas Seal is at the bottom. The note is signed by James H. Starr and Mirabeau B. Lamar.

The $20 note in Figure 10.21 portrays an Indian warrior with a drawn bow. In the center is a maiden with a liberty cap on a pole, with an Indian holding a rifle, both surrounding a shield bearing a wreath and the Lone Star. Miss Liberty, with Roman-style helmet and armor, stands over a vanquished foe on the right side of the note. The bottom shows the Lone Star in the center of the Republic of Texas Seal. The note is signed by James H. Starr and Mirabeau B. Lamar.

On the left side of the $50 note in Figure 10.22, a nude maiden, representing Venus rising from the sea; note the creatures, resembling both a dog and a dragon. The tribute to Texas warships in the center of the note shows a steamer in the foreground, with a sailboat in the background and a lighthouse off the point of the shore. A portrait of Stephen F. Austin, the "Father of Texas," graces the right side of the note, and the Lone Star in the center of the Republic of Texas Seal is located at the bottom. The note is signed by James Webb and Mirabeau B. Lamar.

The $100 note in Figure 10.23 shows a locomotive with black belching smoke (representing industry) on the left side. In the center, Minerva is seated, with a winged creature to her right, and shown receiving money from the gods. Also shown is Mercury, with winged head and a sack of coins, arrayed with the physician's staff below. On the right is a sailing ship on choppy water. The Lone Star in the center of the Republic of Texas Seal is located at the bottom. The note is signed by James H. Starr and Mirabeau B. Lamar.

In the center of the $500 note in Figure 10.24 are two maidens, one bare breasted and one clothed, representing commerce and industry. One holds a shield inlaid with a wreath and a Lone Star, set against a backdrop of sailing ships and a steamer. On the right is a maiden resting on a shield inlayed with the design of the Texas flag, holding a liberty cap on a pole. Behind her sits an eagle with outstretched wings. The note is signed by James H. Starr and Mirabeau B. Lamar.

Fig 10.22, $50 Republic of Texas – Redback Note
Private Collection, Cr. A7, O-766.

Fig 10.23, $100 Republic of Texas – Redback Note
Private Collection, Cr. A8, O-769.

Fig 10.24, $500 Republic of Texas – Redback Note
Private Collection, Cr. A9, O-772.

CUSTOMIZATION FOR TEXAS

Fig 10.25, This vignette of "Commerce and Industry" was taken from a Rawdon, Wright, Hatch & Edson specimen plate.

Private Collection.

Fig 10.26, The same vignette as customized for the Texas $500 redback, with the addition of the Lone Star on the shield.

Private Collection.

Fig 10.27, This vignette of "Miss Liberty" was taken from a Rawdon, Wright, Hatch & Edson specimen plate.

Private Collection.

Fig 10.28, A similar vignette was reduced into an oval design by the engravers and used on the Texas $20 redback (note that the crown has been moved into the foreground).

Private Collection.

Fig 10.30, A sailing ship bearing the striped flag of the Texas Navy.

Private Collection.

The $10 and $50 redback notes were adorned with symbols of the Republic's impressive warships, christened during Lamar's presidency.

Treasury Secretary Starr's predecessor, Richard G. Dunlap, authorized the engravers at Rawdon, Wright, Hatch & Edson to use their best judgment in designing the redback notes. The engravers took great pains to customize at least three of the new pieces for Texas.

Although some images were customized for the Republic of Texas issues, several of them also appeared on numerous banknotes throughout the United States. These familiar vignettes on southern banknotes initially proved to be a somewhat effective measure to thwart the efforts of counterfeiters. Although the process of transferring the images to the master plates was time consuming and entailed a high degree of skill, it was the early nineteenth century equivalent of using clip art to cut and paste the various designs on different banknotes.

PRODUCING THE PORTRAITS OF DEAF SMITH AND STEPHEN F. AUSTIN

The portraits of Erastus "Deaf" Smith on the $5 and Stephen F. Austin on the $50 are unique to the redback series and were not used to embellish any other series of money. The portrait of Deaf Smith was completed in Houston in 1837 and currently resides in the San Jacinto Museum of History. The portrait of Stephen F. Austin was painted on a window shade canvas and was once owned by his cousin Henry Austin. The shade canvas was hung in the old Austin home in Galveston for several generations before it was donated to the Texas State Library in 1972 by Austin's descendents.

When Treasury Secretary R.G. Dunlap instructed the engravers at Rawdon, Wright, Hatch & Edson to make the new notes "as near national as possible," a high degree of customization was required to represent Texas. Reproducing the painted portraits of Smith and Austin on many thousands of notes in an era which pre-dated the invention of photography required a large degree of skill and ingenuity. Each of these original paintings were placed aboard a ship and physically transported to the engravers in New Orleans. The paintings were unloaded at the docks on the Mississippi River in New Orleans and then taken by coach or wagon to the headquarters of the engravers at Royal and Canal streets. Perhaps because of the tedious work required to reproduce the images, there was only one set of master plates used for the red-back series. Unlike the previous series of engraved notes from Houston, no varieties of the notes exist other than signature combinations and plate letters.

THE DEAF SMITH $5 PORTRAIT

The engravers at Rawdon, Wright, Hatch & Edson selected the bust portrait of Smith from the painting and proceeded to engrave the master plate or transfer die for the $5 denomination. A copy of the portrait in Figure 10.30 was painstakingly engraved into a steel plate by hand. The image on the printed $5 note appears as a mirror image of the painting.

Fig 10.30, Portrait of Erastus "Deaf" Smith, Portion of the portrait engraved by Rawdon, Wright, Hatch & Edson, New Orleans.

Courtesy of Albert and Ethel Herzstein Library, The San Jacinto Museum of History, Houston, Texas.

Fig 10.31, The engraving resulted in a reproduction which would be transferred as an inverse or mirror image to the paper.

Fig 10.32, The engraved mirror image of Erastus "Deaf" Smith as it appears on the $5 note.

Author's Collection.

Fig 10.33, The portion of the $5 note bearing the portrait of Erastus "Deaf" Smith.

Author's Collection.

THE STEPHEN F. AUSTIN, $50 PORTRAIT

Fig 10.34, Portrait of Stephen F. Austin, Portion engraved by Rawdon, Wright, Hatch & Edson, New Orleans.

Texas State Library & Archives Commission, Austin, Texas.

Fig 10.35, The engraving resulted in a reproduction which would be transferred as an inverse or mirror image to the paper.

Fig 10.36, The engraved mirror image of Stephen F. Austin as it appears on this $50 note.

Author's Collection.

Fig 10.37, The portion of the $50 note bearing the portrait of Stephen .F. Austin.

Author's Collection.

The engravers at Rawdon, Wright, Hatch & Edson selected the bust portrait of Austin from the painting and proceeded to engrave the master plate or transfer die for the $50 denomination. Like the image of Deaf Smith, a copy of the portrait in Figure 10.34 was painstakingly engraved into a steel plate by hand. The image on the $50 note appears as a mirror image of the painting.

JAMES H. STARR

Treasury Secretary James Harper Starr was a highly intelligent man, well educated and well liked, but he was an unlikely appointee for the position. He was born in New Hartford, Connecticut, on December 18, 1809. As a young man, he worked on the family farm and read books on a wide range of subjects.[20] At the age of fifteen, he broke his right leg in a farm accident and the resulting botched surgery on his knee left him without the use of the joint for the rest of his life. Consequently, he spent a great part of his young adulthood reading medical books and was granted a medical diploma by the Reformed Medical College of the United States in 1822.

Following an extended stay in Georgia during which time he married, Starr traveled west and practiced medicine near Selma, Alabama, in the summer of 1836. Starr eventually followed his brother, Franklin Starr, to Texas. Franklin arrived in San Felipe in 1835. Hearing that the Texas Revolution had ended, James Starr arrived in Nacogdoches on January 17, 1837. Unfortunately, his brother died in July of the same year. After his brother's death, Starr became engrossed in his medical practice and the settlement of his brother's estate. During this time, he was appointed as the receiver of land dues in Nacogdoches County. In this capacity, he became acquainted with Thomas J. Rusk, Kelsey H. Douglas and other influential citizens. Well liked and well respected, Starr became an ardent political supporter of Mirabeau B. Lamar during the election of 1838 and a good friend of Albert Sidney Johnston. Starr's popularity with Lamar led to his appointment as the Secretary of the Treasury on May 25, 1839.

Starr's duties as Treasury Secretary began by penning his name on $232,400 worth of redbacks before the first day of June 1839. The onerous task grew particularly time consuming as the hot summer months passed.

Although Starr recognized that such routine labor was necessary to the operation of the Treasury, he wryly remarked that the signing of the paper money was laboring for the credit of the country rather than its benefit.[21] Although fiercely loyal to Lamar, he began to realize that the unrelenting issuance of promissory notes would only add to Texas' debt and may not be in its best long-term interests. By September 5, 1839, Starr hand signed more than three quarters of a million dollars worth of redbacks in his official capacity. Consequently, his signature is the most frequently encountered on the surviving specimens. These early redback notes were issued by the Lamar administration as the Treasury Department remained in Houston until the seat of government was relocated to Austin in September 1839.[22]

CONGRESSIONAL CONCERNS

Although the redbacks were strikingly artistic and carried the portraits of two Texas heroes, this was of little consequence to their intrinsic value. By April 1839, even before most of the redbacks were issued, conservative members of Congress were already voicing their concerns about the fiscal state of the Republic. Anson Jones, who later became Secretary of State and the last President of the Republic, observed the following: "The financial affairs of Texas are in the most ruinous train … [and] the recklessness of the present administration is most astonishing in this respect." He continued, "[Congress] has made the most extravagant as well as unlimited appropriations without providing any means" of paying for them. "Their foolish extravagance is incredible, horrible. An unlimited amount of promissory notes have been appropriated for public buildings, when the present ones are sufficient for five or ten years to come, or even twenty if necessary," he concluded.[23] Jones described the prolific issuance of paper money as "the great swindling plan" and noted that "the bubble will burst one of these days."[24] True to Jones' predictions, the redback notes lost their purchasing power almost as soon as they were issued. Many of the notes lost 60 percent or more of their face value against the value of silver and gold coins and were passed off just as quickly as they were received. While the monetary bubble may not have burst in the summer of 1839, it was certainly leaking air.

The Lamar administration was also committed to driving the hostile Indians of Texas away from the western settlements. In the winter of 1839, a group of Texian settlers, including Noah Smithwick, participated in a coordinated attack with the Lipan Apaches against the Comanches. The attack was waged on the banks of the Colorado River near the mouth of the San Saba River in the winter of 1839.[25] This brief but fierce battle resulted in the death of two Texians, several horses, and many Indians, though the government-supported group successfully drove the Comanches away from their encampment. When the Texas Congress passed an act to indemnify Smithwick and the others for the loss of their horses, they were "paid in the commonwealth's paper, worth twenty-five cents on the dollar." The Lamar administration soon began to pay out the redbacks at their discounted rates. In this instance, it was at twenty-five cents on the dollar. Smithwick remarked "for a $100 horse I got $400 which I didn't allow to depreciate on my hands." The depreciation of the paper money was not unknown to the citizens, and their reluctance to hoard the redbacks only served to further devalue the promissory notes and increase the demand for any form of specie which might be available as a store of value.

While Texas had no hard currency reserves, there were still sporadic sums of silver coins available to sellers of hard goods. Gold coins were particularly difficult to find. One of the biggest problems this presented for Texas was in the collection of tax revenues. Citizens were not about to part with their specie when the discounted paper money could be redeemed at face value for taxes. It did not matter whether the coins were of United States, Mexican, French, Dutch or Spanish origin. The citizens refused to part with their coins except for the most essential of goods. The government was awash in its own discounted paper, paid at face value for a laundry list of new taxes implemented by Lamar to raise the government's revenue. Auditor's certificates were cancelled upon receipt and many of the outstanding notes were simply re-issued. Older bills, which bore 10 percent interest, were painstakingly re-issued without interest. The oversupply of promissory notes and their declining value signaled the beginning of the rapid financial decline that Texas was about to experience. Other problems would soon begin to unfold.

Fig 10.38, Dr. James H. Starr.
Texas State Library & Archives Commission, Austin, Texas.

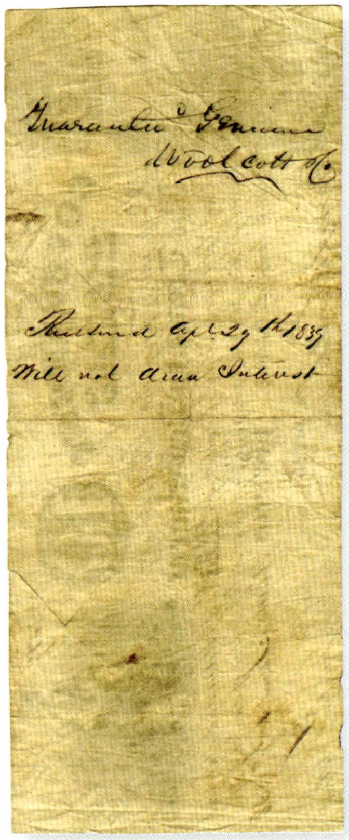

Fig 10.39, $10 Government of Texas, Re-Issued without interest.
Private Collection.

The reverse of the Government of Texas $10 note in Figure 10.39 reads, "Guaranteed Genuine, Woolcott (?) Reissued Apr 29th 1839. Will not draw Interest." This is an example of an engraved note received by the government and subsequently re-issued without interest as the non-interest-bearing redbacks began to enter circulation.

MUSGROVE EVANS AND THE STOLEN BOX OF NOTES

Even though the shipments of blank notes were routinely transported by sailing ship or steamer from the New Orleans printers to Galveston, problems were also encountered in delivering the blank notes to their final destination at the Treasury Department in Austin. Once received in Galveston, they were signed for by a Treasury official who took custody of the parcel, usually at the Customs House on the island. In March 1840, a shipment was received at the harbor by Musgrove Evans, who was then serving as the second auditor. This particular shipment resulted in an escapade that would haunt Evans for the rest of his career.

Musgrove Evans was born on December 17, 1785, probably in New York. He was the son of Gen. Samuel Evans who had served in the colonial army during the American Revolution.[26] Musgrove Evans was living in Jefferson County, New York, as recorded in the 1820 census and was successful in a number of different ventures. As a trained surveyor, Evans executed his trade in the lands around Tecumseh and Detroit, Michigan, and in 1825 he built a gristmill in Detroit. He later established the first mail and stagecoach line from Detroit to Chicago. By 1831, he had obtained land grants in Texas. Following the death of his first wife Abi in 1832, Evans began an exploration of Texas, and moved his five children there in 1834. During the Texas Revolution, one of his sons, Samuel B. Evans, was killed at the Alamo. Evans was heartbroken by his son's death and enlisted in the Texas Army on April 1, 1836. He later fought at the battle of San Jacinto. Following the war, Evans acquired several tracts of land as a bounty payment for his service in the Army. With his skill for business, he eventually relocated to Austin and served in the Treasury Department as the second auditor under Lamar.

In March 1840, Evans received the shipment of blank promissory notes in a sealed box marked "Asa Brigham, Treasure[r], Austin" at the docks in Galveston.[27] The box arrived on the steamer *Neptune,* traveling from New Orleans under the watchful eye of Col. James Love, the customs collector at Galveston. Evans discretely opened the sealed box and checked its contents in the safety of the nearby Customs House. Inside, he found two packages, each marked as 1,000 sheets of $5, $10, $20, and $50 notes. The sheets totaled $170,000 in blank Treasury notes destined for Austin to be numbered and signed into circulation by Treasury officials. Evans carefully nailed the box shut, and it was loaded with his personal bags onto a waiting steamboat. He then proceeded on the long journey up Galveston Bay and around the bend in the San Jacinto River, which led up the narrow passage of the chocolate-colored Buffalo Bayou. The steamboat's final destination was the docks at the head of Main Street in Houston.

Upon his arrival in Houston, Evans was unable to find a vacant room for the night. After several attempts to secure lodging, he was informed by Judge Buckner that room could be made for him at the Houston House. After checking with the clerk, Evans was told that a room might be available later that evening but none could be had at the moment. Returning to the steamboat, he retrieved the box and his remaining bags from the custody of the clerk, and it being nearly sunset, he proceeded to carry them to a back storeroom of the Houston House where the proprietor, a Mr. Walker, told him "[the box] would be perfectly safe." Evans, with the assistance of others, buried the luggage and box under a pile of trunks, saddles, saddle bags and blankets. He then went to supper, after which he went from tavern to tavern searching for the Treasury official who had left him a message that it was not necessary to leave for Austin immediately. Finding that his colleagues had gone to the theatre, he again checked the storeroom and his bags and found everything in order. Not feeling well from the day-long boat trip, and fatigued from his errands, he took a nap in an empty bed upstairs in the tavern. Evans reported that he slept soundly until he was abruptly awakened by the person whose bed he had taken the liberty of "borrowing."

It was indeed a rude awakening. Evans headed downstairs once again to check his belongings and was shocked to find the storeroom ransacked, with his baggage strewn all over the floor. The box containing $170,000 in newly printed blanks was gone! Horrified at this state of affairs, Evans remained in Houston for two additional days and made a report to the *Neptune's* captain. He also interviewed the other passengers on the steamer for clues which might lead to identify the thief, but he found no trace of the culprits. Evans then informed the customs collector in Galveston and the Texas Consul at New Orleans to be on the lookout for the stolen notes should they begin to surface.

Initially, it was believed that the stolen blank notes left Texas and made their way to the United States. The search went out in all directions, but the stash of missing blanks was never recovered. Many of these blanks were illegally dated, had forged signatures added, and were placed into circulation by the culprits. Several were recovered in the same month they were stolen. A group of gamblers on board the steamer *New York* were arrested by an officer who boarded her in Galveston Harbor in an attempt to locate the box of stolen notes.[28] Several of the stolen notes were confiscated in this arrest. William G. Cooke reported that he examined "two or three $50 notes of the second issue, which appeared to be newly signed and hardly dry," with the forged (and incorrect) signatures of Henry Smith and Sam Houston. These notes had been backdated "and the signatures badly done." The signatures of Smith and Houston of course would have shown these notes to be forgeries, for these signatures only graced the bills that were previously issued out of Houston on the prior series.

Other abnormalities in the paper money began to surface, resulting in arrests in Houston. An economic paranoia gripped the citizens and merchants as bills were presented to the Treasury for authentication. The note's signatures were checked with the utmost scrutiny by officials, and the serial numbers were called into question if their numbers were higher than that of those of other bills dated two weeks later.[29] Serial numbers on each bill and their corresponding dates of issue were meticulously checked by Treasury officials against the official records in an attempt to detect forgeries. As members of the second oldest profession continued to ply their trade, the newly countersigned bills surfaced in Galveston in May 1840, then in New Orleans in June 1840.[30] These occurrences further weakened the confidence in the money and injured the marketability of the good notes.[31]

Although a series of legitimate bills were signed by acting Treasury Secretary James Webb and placed in circulation in May 1839 (before the blanks were stolen), a $10 bill was sent to the Treasury Department for examination as late as 1841, because some bills were being rejected in the marketplace due to James Webb's unfamiliar signature and dates of service.[32] While the bills signed by Webb were legitimate, many carrying the signatures of Starr and Lamar were closely examined and withdrawn from circulation. Webb's signature on these bills constitutes a rather scarce subset in the most common series of Texas paper money.

Fig 10.40, Austin, $5 "Stolen Note" marked "Counterfeit" by the Treasury Department.
Private Collection, Cr. A4, O-759.

IDENTIFYING THE "STOLEN NOTES"

For the collector who tires of the Republic of Texas redback series, a renewed interest can be aroused by a keen eye for unusual signature combinations and out-of-date serial numbers. The information on these notes might lead to a seemly discovery of the financial underworld of the past. Regarding the box of stolen notes, the bills themselves were genuine, but the added signatures were forged. Many of these entered circulation, and several were sent to Austin where they were examined by Treasury officials and subsequently marked "Counterfeit." These notes were undoubtedly from the same box of blanks stolen from Musgrove Evans in 1840 on a twilight spring evening in Houston.[33]

Rather than being cut cancelled, the $5 note in

Fig 10.41, Austin, $10 "Stolen Note" marked "Counterfeit" by the Treasury Department.
Private Collection, Cr. A5, 0-761.

Fig 10.42, Austin, $50 "Stolen Note" marked "Counterfeit" by the Treasury Department.
Private Collection, Cr. A7, 0-766.

Figure 10.40 had been marked "Counterfeit" diagonally across the face, followed by "Even" (possibly Evans) "Act Sec Tsy" by the Treasury Department in Austin. It is thought to be from the series of bills stolen from the custody of Musgrove Evans while at the tavern in Houston.

Figure 10.41 shows another example marked "Counterfeit" perpendicular across the face. This otherwise genuine bill, bearing what appear to be legitimate signatures, was rejected by the Treasury Department as belonging to the series of stolen notes.

Figure 10.42 displays another specimen with a marking similar to that on the $5 example in Figure 10.41. This $50 note has also been marked "Counterfeit" in the diagonal manner, followed by "Even" (possibly Evans) "Act Sec Tsy" by the Treasury Department in Austin. It, too, is thought to be from the series of bills stolen from the tavern storeroom in Houston.

Figure 10.43 shows the reverse of the $50 "stolen note" bearing the language "Lamar is fony" (phony), indicating that Treasury officials believed the President's signature to be forged.

Fig 10.43, The reverse of the $50 "Stolen Note."
Private Collection, Cr. A7, 0-766.

NEW WARSHIPS ARRIVE IN TEXAS

By March 1839, the paddlewheel steamer *Charleston* crossed the U.S. border south of the Sabine River with a dismounted cannon stowed below her decks to evade U.S. neutrality laws.[34] Renamed the *Zavala,* this ship of the Second Texas Navy had officially arrived in Galveston on March 22, 1839, and was re-registered as a Texas warship. By the end of June 1839, the first of the Navy vessels contracted from Dawson in Baltimore began to arrive. These included the five-gun schooner *Viper* which was re-christened the *San Jacinto.* Upon arrival in Galveston, some of the ship's passengers included Samuel May Williams, Anson Jones, and Moses Austin Bryan. A second schooner carrying six twelve-pound guns and a pivot gun arrived August 7 and was christened the *San Antonio.* The third sister ship and the last of the three schooners, the *San Bernard,* joined the growing Texas fleet at month's end.

At the beginning of Lamar's term, government revenues from customs, direct taxes, and other sources of income were estimated by outgoing Treasury Secretary Henry Smith to leave a small surplus in the fiscal year that ended September 30, 1839.[35] Perhaps the financial community's confidence was bolstered by Smith's fiscal projections, as a loan of $457,380 was approved and received by Texas from the Bank of the United States in Philadelphia on September 1, 1839. British pound sterling bonds were issued by Texas as collateral under the Five Million Dollar Loan Act—James Hamilton and Albert T. Burnley were finally successful in their efforts to secure a loan for Texas. The proceeds from the loan were paid to Texas with $280,000 in bank notes issued from the Bank of the United States with the balance paid in specie. With the deposit of the notes in the Merchants Bank of New Orleans and the additional gold and silver in hand, the liquidity position of Texas dramatically improved and reduced the financial pressures to a great degree.[36] In light of the successful placement of the loan, the Texas money rose in value at the New Orleans exchange houses from twenty-five cents on the dollar to forty cents.

Rather than using the loan proceeds from the Bank of the United States to retire the $280,000 bond to the Baltimore bankers, the administration chose to issue additional drafts against the loan proceeds in the Treasury. These drafts were then paid by the Treasury with newly printed redbacks. As a result of not paying off the first bond of $280,000, the principal amount of the loan effectively doubled to $560,000 when the failure to pay the first bond triggered the additional debt of the second. Although the interest payments on the Baltimore loan were kept current for a time, it would not be long before the doubling of the principal amount would cripple the Republic's ability to stay current on the interest payments. President Lamar remarked on November 12, 1839, that the prospects of obtaining additional loans were "cheering and satisfactory."[37] Lamar's misguided optimism undoubtedly contributed to the unbridled spending on behalf of Texas in anticipation of future loans from foreign governments which would never materialize.

Fig 10.44, The Bank of the United States, Third Street, Philadelphia.

Courtesy of Stack's, New York.

DIGGING AN EVEN DEEPER HOLE

By the end of 1839, it became increasingly clear that additional loans would not be forthcoming anytime soon. Texas had taken on an additional debt of $280,000 at 10 percent interest through the mere stroke of a pen—a mistake which could have been easily avoided. While Henry Smith initially estimated that the total revenues for the fiscal year 1839 would exceed $1,000,000, the total revenues of the Republic that year were actually $302,166. Almost all of the revenue was in the form of the government's illiquid paper. The collection of import duties became increasingly difficult during these years. When merchants brought goods into Texas, many of the importers posted a bond to secure the payment of their duties at a later date—many of these were never able to be redeemed.[38] Although the more established merchants eventually made good on some of their duties, the bonds which were redeemed by the importers were often paid back with the heavily depreciated Texas paper which the government accepted at face value. With receipts falling woefully short, Lamar, his Cabinet, and the Congress proceeded to pass numerous revenue-raising measures, including many direct taxes on personal property, but they failed to enact the appropriate measures needed to enforce their collection. As a result, the administration proceeded to spend much of the anticipated money on new appropriations even before collecting the $1,300,000 they had expected to receive in taxes for the previous period. The administration hap-hazardly projected that customs revenues and sales of land scrip for the following year would be a full $1 million more than had been received in the previous year.

The cavalier attitude of Treasury officials regarding the Baltimore loan was summed up by James Love in a letter to James Starr on March 21, 1840. Love wrote, "No one has any cause to complain of this government in relation to her financial obligations, because we have done all we could and have done more, and have done it better than any other people under the same circumstances, and because we have not attempted by legislation to violate the faith of the nation." He added, "I do not believe the failure to pay the interest on [the] Dawson bonds will materially effect our credit because no one expects us to pay interest unless the loan should be negotiated. ..." The fact that the creditors expected them to pay the interest as well as the principal seemed lost on Love, who confessed to Starr on the subject of finance, "I am not much skilled in such matters."[39]

Although the Republic lacked much of the requisite gold and silver common to the governments of the day, there was an abundance of paper. Several printing companies stood ready to create a new series of paper money—or so they thought. Due to heavy borrowing to finance the Second Texas Navy and the almost unchecked printing and issuance of the redbacks, the Lamar administration had dug itself into a deep financial hole. The Republic was having trouble paying the outstanding claims of the soldiers, sailors and government officials, everyday supplies, and even for the printing of the money of the Republic of Texas itself.

In a sharply worded letter to Treasury Secretary James H. Starr dated May 7, 1840, from New Orleans, the engraving and printing firm of Rawdon, Wright, Hatch & Edson complained that the Republic's account was past due, and they would no longer accept any redbacks as payment.[40] This letter was dated only one week after another past due notice was sent from Draper, Toppan, Longacre & Co, the government's previous engraver and printer. The firm of Rawdon Wright noted that they had only been paid for their printing efforts in "promissory notes of the Govt. [the same notes they were hired to print] for a portion of the amount due us, yet we hold them still and we have never realized a cent for all we have done, though our bills for work are always considered due on completion of orders." Texas had again fallen behind on its bills, and things had deterio-rated to the point where the Republic could scarcely afford to pay for the printing of its own money. Compounding the Republic's lack of credibility, it also appears that one of Rawdon Wright's representatives, Tracy R. Edson, visited Austin in 1839 and upon collecting a payment at the Treasury, was shortchanged $825.00, which was not discovered until after he left the area.[41] The company diplomatically referred to the incident as a "mistake" and asked Starr for "a rigid examination to be made into this circumstance," meaning they were anxious to be paid in full for the amount of the "mistake" and stated that future printing jobs would need to be paid in specie.

There was a strong need for a radical change if Texas was to stay financially afloat, as the profusely issued redbacks were worth only fifteen cents on the U.S. dollar in New Orleans.[42] Back at home, citizens were keenly aware of the depreciating Texas paper. The downward spiral of Texas' currency in the marketplace continued unabated. Talk began to sweep the city of New Orleans that twelve and a half cents on the dollar was the next stop. With each passing day, another store, saloon, stable, or steamboat would refuse to accept Texas money, or mark it down to an even greater discount, to the detriment of all who presented the notes for payment. The term "passing the buck" soon began to take on a whole new meaning for Texians.

1 "Austin Treasures," Online exhibits from the Austin History Center, Austin Capitols, found online at: http://www.ci.austin.tx.us/library/ahc/capitol/early.htm

2 William S. Red, ed., "Allen's Reminiscences of Texas, 1838-1842," *SHQ*, vol. 15 (January 1914), 3:283-305, found online at: http://www.tshaonline.org/shqonline/apager.php?vol=017&pag=284 (accessed March 31, 2007).

3 Helen Foster Snow, "Major John Wyatt Moody, First Auditor of the Republic of Texas," Moody Papers, page 1.

4 *Handbook of Texas Online*, s.v., "Albert Sidney Johnston," http://www.tsha.utexas.edu/handbook/online/articles/JJ/fjo32.html (accessed August 30, 2007).

5 Angus Konstam, ed., *The Civil War: A Visual Encyclopedia* (New York: Barnes & Noble Books, 2004), 262-63.

6 Bob Medlar cited the signature combinations on the Austin Change Notes as J.H. Simmons –Asa Brigham, J.H. Simmons – D.P. Barhydr, James B. Shaw – J.H. Simmons, James B. Shaw, J.H. Raymond, William H. Abell – J.H. Raymond. Bob Medlar, *Texas Obsolete Notes and Scrip* (Society of Paper Money Collectors, 1968), 6.

7 John Hoyt Williams, *Sam Houston: The Life and Times of the Liberator of Texas, an Authentic American Hero* (New York: Simon & Schuster, Inc., 1993), 201.

8 John Nathan Craven, *James Harper Starr: Financier of the Republic of Texas* (Austin: The Daughters of the Republic of Texas, 1950), 49.

9 Ibid., 49-50.

10 "An Act authorizing the Treasurer of the Republic of Texas to extend the issue of Change notes," Journals of the Sixth Congress of the Republic of Texas, 190-91.

11 Seymour V. Conner, ed., "Jackson to Starr, Galveston, March 12, 1840," Texas Treasury Papers, 1:412.

12 Medlar, *Texas Obsolete Notes and Script,* vii.

13 Seymour V. Conner, ed., "Draper, Topper, Longacre & Co to Secretary, Philadelphia, April 30, 1840," Texas Treasury Papers, 2:457.

14 Douglas B. Ball, "Lone Star Notes: Largest U.S. State Created Currency from Scratch," *Bank Note Reporter* (May 1988), see Part II, "The Third Issue: The Red Backs of Rawdon, Wright, Hatch & Edson."

15 Seymour V. Conner, ed., "Rawdon , Wright, Hatch & Edson to Starr, New Orleans, May 7, 1840," Texas Treasury Papers, 2:464.

16 Virginia H Taylor, ed, "Dunlop to Johnston, March 20, 1839," Texas Treasury Papers, Supplement, 4:45-46.

17 *Handbook of Texas Online,* s.v., "Richard G. Dunlap," http://www.tsha.utexas.edu/handbook/online/articles/SS/fsm23.html (accessed August 12, 2007).

18 From a Republic of Texas $10 Promissory Note, Dated May 15, 1839, Serial Number 14. Signed by James Webb, as Acting Secretary of the Treasury.

19 From an Auditor's Certificate, $96.00 payable to James Izod (?), for "Signing the President's Name to Promissory Notes," Dated October 2, 1840. Signed by Musgrove Evans and James B. Shaw.

20 Craven, *James Harper Starr,* 2-28.

21 Ibid., 42.

22 Seymour V. Conner, ed., "Harris to Secretary, Houston, September 15, 1839," Texas Treasury Papers, 1:271.

23 Anson Jones, *Memoranda and Official Correspondence relating to the Republic of Texas its History and Annexation* (New York: D. Appleton & Company, 1859), 32.

24 Ibid., 33.

25 Noah Smithwick, compiled by his daughter Nanna Smithwick Henderson, *The Evolution of a State or Recollections of Old Texas Days* (Austin: Gammel Book Company, 1900; rpt. 1993), 134-39.

26 Earlayne Chance, "Pioneer Evans Family," found online at: http://www.rootsweb.com/~nyjeffer/evanssp.htm

27 Seymour V. Conner, ed., "Evans to Starr, Austin, June 15, 1840," Texas Treasury Papers, 2:504.

28 Ibid., "Hall to Starr, Houston, March 20, 1840," 2:417.

29 Seymour V. Conner, ed., "Gayley & Robinson to Starr, Houston, May 12, 1840;" Texas Treasury Papers, 2:470.

30 Ibid., "Patterson to Sevey," Galveston, May 23, 1840, Texas Treasury Papers, 2:481.

31 Ibid., "Gayley & Robinson to Starr" Houston, May 12, 1840; Texas Treasury Papers, 2:512.

32 Ibid., "Collins to Secretary, Election Register, 1836-1842," 2:821.

33 Ibid., "Branham to Stickney, Galveston, February 4, 1841," 2:591.

34 Jonathan W. Jordan, *Lone Star Navy: Texas, the Fight for the Gulf of Mexico, and the Shaping of the American West* (Dulles, VA: Potomac Books, Inc., 2006), 130.

35 William M. Gouge, *The Fiscal History of Texas* (New York: Burt Franklin, 1852; rpt. 1969), 98-99.

36 "Report of the Auditor and Comptroller, to the Fourth Legislature, on the Public Debt of Texas," (Austin: Cushney & Hampton, State Gazette Office, 1851), 8.

37 Edmund Thornton Miller, "A Financial History of Texas," *Bulletin of the University of Texas 1916: No. 37* (Austin: University of Texas, 1916), 60-61.

38 Craven, *James Harper Starr,* 55.

39 Seymour V. Conner, ed., "Love to Starr, Houston, March 21, 1840," Texas Treasury Papers, 2:420.

40 Ibid., "Rawdon, Wright, Hatch & Edson to Starr, New Orleans, May 7, 1840," 2:464.

41 Ibid.

42 Ibid., "Bryan, Austin & Co to Evans, New Orleans, May 29, 1840," 2:485.

CHAPTER ELEVEN

AUSTIN: “STOCKS, BONDS, WOODEN SHIPS AND PIGS”

CH 11

Secretary of the Treasury James H. Starr was greatly disturbed by the dilution in value of the currency as the government continued to issue the newly printed redbacks. Although he was concerned about the lack of acceptance of the notes, Starr had been powerless to stop its slide. The representatives in Congress, and the citizens of Texas, were well aware of the falling value of the redbacks. The loss of purchasing power of the Texas paper money had become a political liability for members of Congress. Their constituents voraciously complained that something had to be done about the situation, and legislation was passed on February 5, 1840, which authorized sweeping changes by the Treasury Department. On June 4, 1840, Starr took a page straight out of Henry Smith's playbook. He realized that the unrelenting supply of newly issued notes had to be stopped in order for the currency to stabilize in the open market. In an effort to decrease the supply of outstanding redbacks, Starr ordered the immediate withdrawal from circulation of as many outstanding promissory notes as possible.[1]

Fig 11.1, Mirabeau B. Lamar, President.

Daguerreotype, Late 1840s. Courtesy of Joseph D. Olson.

But Starr was not acting on his own accord. A primary goal of the new legislation was to reduce the number of promissory notes in circulation by replacing them with a new issue of stock in the Consolidated Fund of Texas, which promised to pay semi-annual interest in gold and silver coin.[2] With the Texas economy now in a free fall, the dramatic legislation also prohibited the government from issuing any additional promissory notes.

The Act of February 5, 1840, signed into law by President Mirabeau B. Lamar, authorized sweeping changes regarding the reduction of money in circulation and the issue of stock by the Republic of Texas. Although the issuance of new stock was used to shrink the outstanding supply of redbacks, it did little to increase the exchange rate of the Texas money against the value of specie.

A REVOLVING DOOR OF DECEPTION

While the government publicly halted the issuance of redbacks in February 1840, it was, at the same time, secretly re-issuing many of the notes which had been paid in for various taxes. On February 5, 1840, the same day on which the act was passed to reduce the amount of promissory notes in circulation, Treasury Secretary Starr instructed Asa Brigham, then serving as Treasurer, to re-issue the non-interest bearing promissory notes received into the Treasury for taxes in a sufficient amount to meet the present demands on the Treasury. In his letter to Brigham, Starr cited, "This being under authority of a secret Resolution of Congress you will please not give publicity to the Measure [*sic*]." This secret resolution by the legislature only served to further accelerate the decline in the value of the Texas currency.[3]

Although the re-issued notes were used to redeem the warrants for current appropriations, the collection of the revenue was not sufficient to meet the demands on the Treasury for the redemption of previously issued obligations.

Fig 11.2, Charles DeMorse, Stock Commissioner.

Texas State Library & Archives Commission, Austin, Texas.

By the June 18, Starr informed Charles DeMorse, the Stock Commissioner in Austin, that he would no longer be able to supply the Treasury with promissory notes in amounts sufficient to redeem any outstanding warrants presented to his department for payment.[4] The meager amount of redbacks on hand was insufficient to redeem even the older warrants presented for payment. Because the Treasury Department lacked a funding mechanism from which to pay the obligations, Starr instructed DeMorse to issue new certificates of stock as payment to holders of the warrants. In other words, although the authority to issue stock under the Act of June 7, 1837, expired on January 1, 1840, Starr effectively ordered DeMorse to continue issuing the 1837 stock for warrants issued before January 1, 1840, but not to cancel the warrants as he funded them.

DeMorse was ordered to hold the warrants and have them redeemed at the Treasury in return for the promissory notes which had been deposited in their place. This was merely a bookkeeping ploy, as the treasury didn't have any gold or silver. As a result of this move, even the older treasury warrants and auditor's certificates could not be redeemed for the redbacks. All of the obligations of the government would now be payable in stock. This practice was referred to by Starr as an "investment in the funded debt of Texas."

CONSOLIDATED FUND – AUSTIN ISSUES

The government soon followed one broken promise with another. Even before the new stock certificates could be engraved and printed to facilitate the withdrawal of the currency, a second issue of stock was interspersed with the first one which carried the identical terms of the old Consolidated Fund of Texas issue of June 7, 1837. In essence, because the government no longer issued the redbacks, any outstanding warrants and auditor's certificates were to be redeemed and subsequently "invested" in stock which was originally used to redeem the earliest Texas obligations from the revolutionary period. Unlike the stock created by the Act of February 5, 1840, the certificates issued under the Act of June 7, 1837, made no mention of paying interest in gold or silver. Although interest was accrued up to and including the most recent payment date, no interest was allowed for fractional parts of a six-month period.[5] On many of the certificates, Houston, the original city of issue, was merely marked through and the word "Austin" was written in its place with the new date written by hand.

In 1840, the government had new certificates printed and issued under the same terms as the original 1837 issue. The language of the 1840 version is virtually identical to the 1837 version, except the place of issue was printed as the "City of Austin." The date was written in by hand. The specimen in Figure 11.3 is dated December 19, 1840, and has a handwritten notation near the left margin, underneath the Public Faith Pledged border. It reads: "This certificate bears interest from

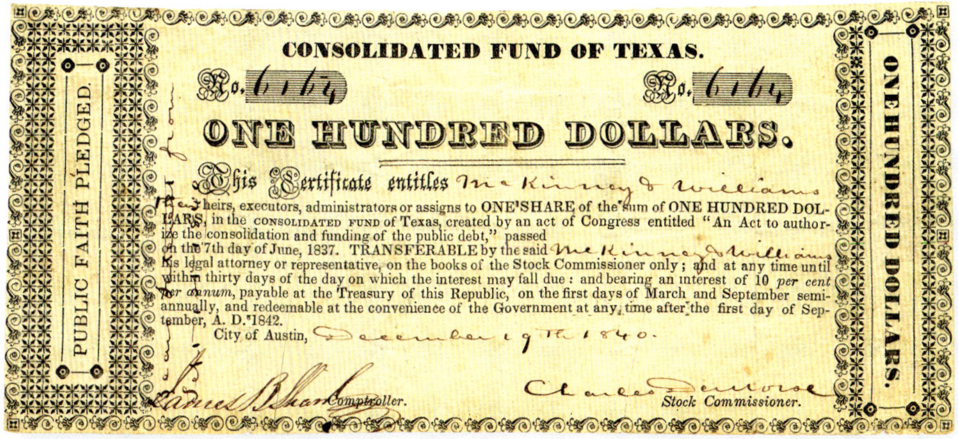

Fig 11.3, $100 Consolidated Fund of Texas, Austin, December 19, 1840, issued to McKinney & Williams.

Private Collection, Cr. CF14, O-720.

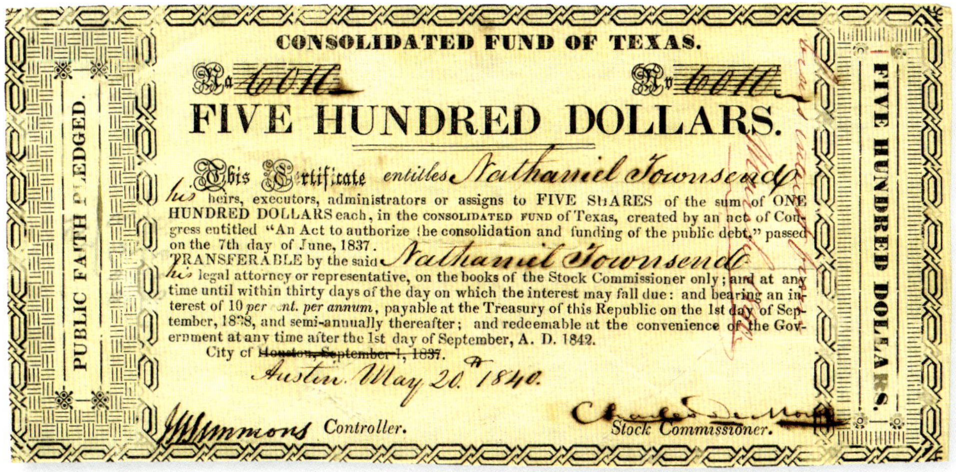

Fig 11.4, $500 Consolidated Fund of Texas, Austin, May 20, 1840, issued to Nathaniel Townsend.

Private Collection, Cr. CF5 (CF17), O-725.

PUBLIC FAITH PLEDGED.

CONSOLIDATED FUND OF TEXAS.

No. 5720 No. 5720

ONE THOUSAND DOLLARS.

THIS CERTIFICATE entitles Isaac McGary heirs, executors, administrators or assigns, to TEN SHARES of the sum of ONE HUNDRED DOLLARS each, in the Consolidated Fund of Texas, created by an Act of Congress entitled "An Act to authorize the consolidation and funding of the public debt," passed on the 7th day of June, 1837. Transferable by the said Isaac McGary legal attorney or representative, on the books of the Stock Commissioner only; and at any time until within thirty days of the day on which the interest may fall due; and bearing an interest of 10 PER CENT. PER ANNUM, payable at the Treasury of this Republic on the 1st day of September, 1838, and semi-annually thereafter; and redeemable at the convenience of the Government at any time after the 1st day of September, A. D. 1842.

City of Houston, September 1, 1837.

Austin Nov 1st

James B. Shaw actg Comptroller.

Joseph Moreland Stock Commissioner.

ONE THOUSAND DOLLARS.

Fig 11.5, $1,000 Consolidated Fund of Texas, Austin, November 1, 1839, issued to Isaac McGary. *Private Collection, Cr. CF12, O-740.*

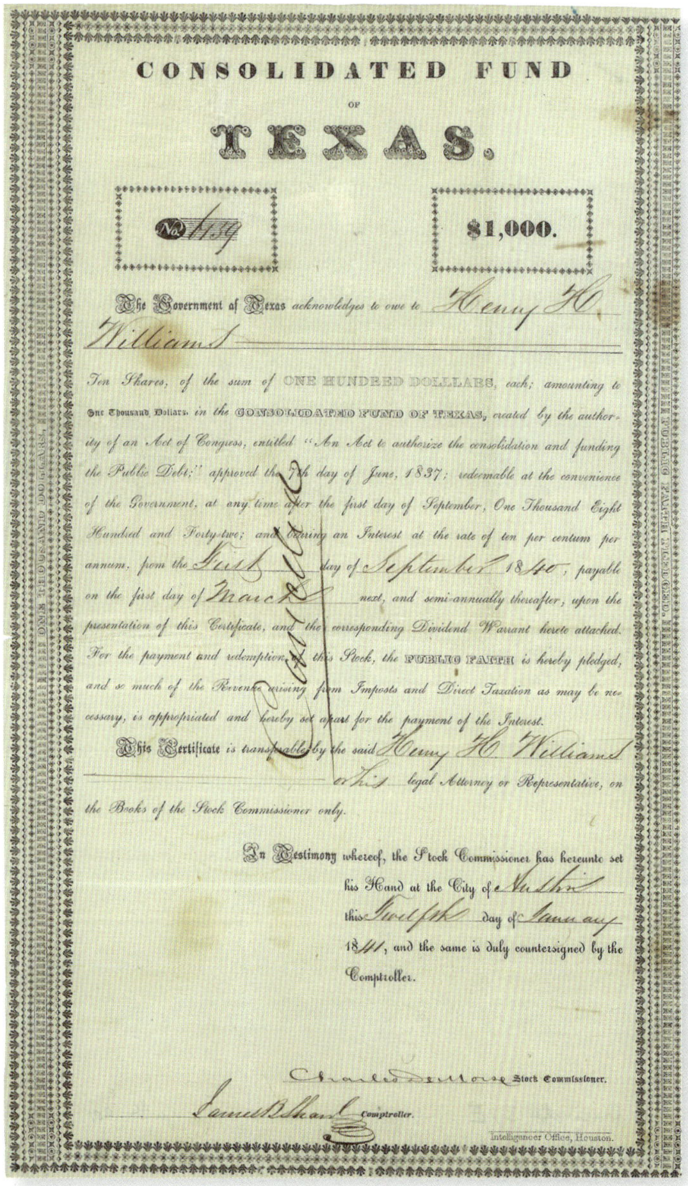
CONSOLIDATED FUND OF TEXAS.

No. 139 $1,000.

The Government of Texas acknowledges to owe to Henry H. Williams Ten Shares, of the sum of ONE HUNDRED DOLLARS, each; amounting to One Thousand Dollars, in the CONSOLIDATED FUND OF TEXAS, created by the authority of an Act of Congress, entitled "An Act to authorize the consolidation and funding the Public Debt;" approved the 7th day of June, 1837; redeemable at the convenience of the Government, at any time after the first day of September, One Thousand Eight Hundred and Forty-two; and bearing an Interest at the rate of ten per centum per annum, from the First day of September 1840, payable on the first day of March next, and semi-annually thereafter, upon the presentation of this Certificate, and the corresponding Dividend Warrant hereto attached. For the payment and redemption of this Stock, the PUBLIC FAITH is hereby pledged, and so much of the Revenue arising from Imposts and Direct Taxation as may be necessary, is appropriated and hereby set apart for the payment of the Interest.

This Certificate is transferable by the said Henry H. Williams or his legal Attorney or Representative, on the Books of the Stock Commissioner only.

In Testimony whereof, the Stock Commissioner has hereunto set his Hand at the City of Austin this Twelfth day of January 1841, and the same is duly countersigned by the Comptroller.

Charles DeMorse Stock Commissioner.

James B. Shaw Comptroller.

Intelligencer Office, Houston.

Fig 11.6, $1,000 Consolidated Fund of Texas, Austin, January 12, 1841, issued to Henry H. Williams. *Private Collection, Cr. 37E, O-Unlisted.*

Sept 12th 1840." These later issues bearing the printed "City of Austin" are among the rarest in the Consolidated Fund series, indicating a very limited number of issues. The document is signed by James B. Shaw, Comptroller, and Charles Demorse, Stock Commissioner.

Much like the previous example, the $500 certificate in Figure 11.4 has the place of issue, Houston, boldly lined through and replaced with "Austin, May 20th, 1840." In the right margin is the consolatory verbiage, "bears interest from March 1840." Although the authority to issue stock under the Act of June 7, 1837, had expired on New Year's Day 1840, the Treasury Department extended the issuance of shares for warrants issued prior to that date. The document is signed by J.W. Simmons, Controller, and Charles DeMorse, Stock Commissioner.

The $1,000 example in Figure 11.5 has Houston, the original place of issue, also lined through. Beneath it was written "Austin, Nov 1, 1839." This indicates that it was funded under the laws governing the first issue of Stock in the Consolidated Fund in 1837. This certificate for ten shares of stock was paid to Issac McGary for $1,000 in previously issued Texas obligations. As a consolation to the payee, there is a handwritten notation near the left margin, underneath the Public Faith Pledged border, that reads: "This Certificate bears interest from September 1, 1837." This certificates accrued interest up to and including the most recent payment date, amounting to $200 at the time it was issued to McGary. The document is signed by James B. Shaw, Acting Comptroller, and Joseph Moreland, Stock Commissioner.

The typeset certificate shown in Figure 11.6 for ten shares of stock in the Consolidated Fund of Texas was printed at the *Intellegencer* Office in Houston. It was completed and countersigned in the City of Austin. As noted in the body of the instrument, interest on the stock would accumulate from "the First of September, 1840," long after the original authority to issue stock under the Act of June 7, 1837, had run its course. These printed certificates, unlike their smaller predecessors, were issued with a series of dividend coupons (or warrants) which have been detached from the left side of the bond. This design was also issued in a $5,000 denomination. The document is signed by James B. Shaw, Comptroller, and Charles DeMorse, Stock Commissioner.

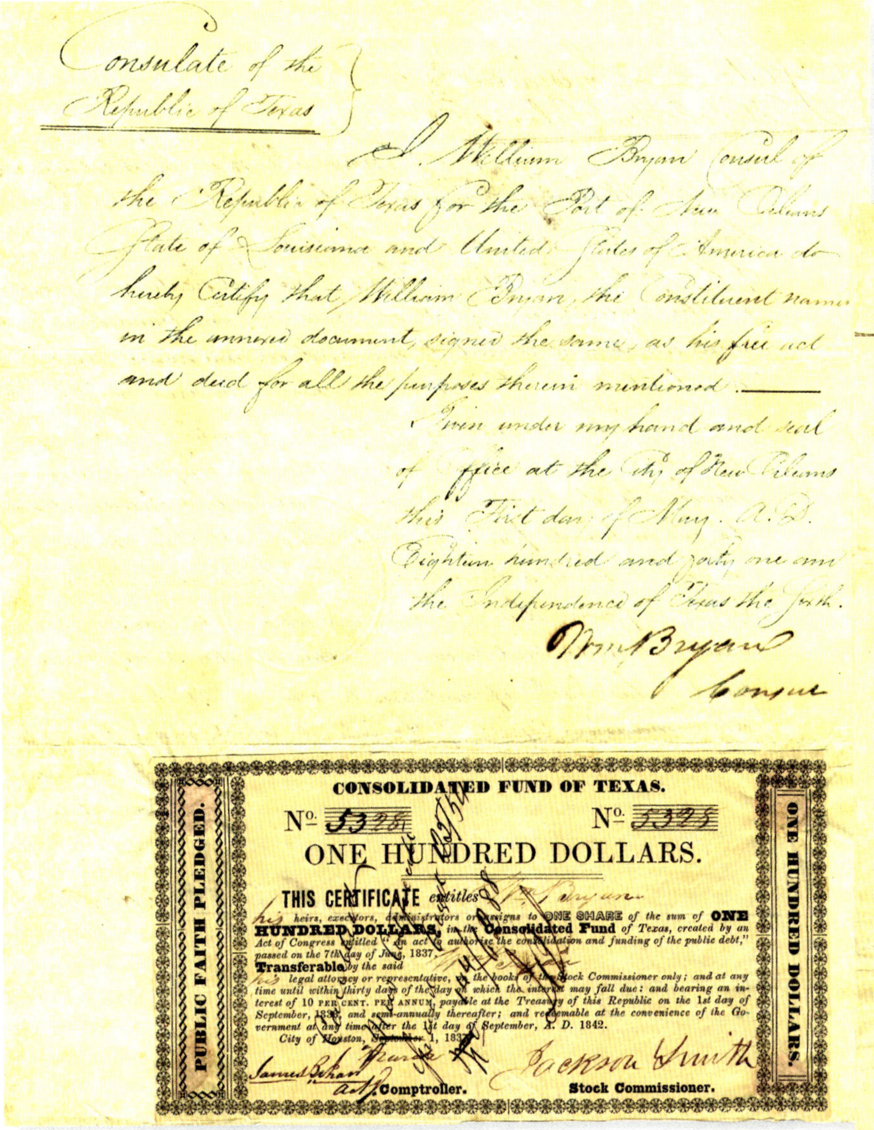

Consulate of the Republic of Texas

I, William Bryan Consul of the Republic of Texas for the Port of New Orleans State of Louisiana and United States of America do hereby Certify that William Bryan the Constituent named in the annexed document, signed the same, as his free act and deed for all the purposes therein mentioned ——

Given under my hand and seal of office at the City of New Orleans this First day of May. A.D. Eighteen hundred and forty one and the Independence of Texas the Sixth.

Wm Bryan
Consul

CONSOLIDATED FUND OF TEXAS.

No. 5328 No. 5328

ONE HUNDRED DOLLARS.

THIS CERTIFICATE entitles Wm Bryan his heirs, executors, administrators or assigns to ONE SHARE of the sum of ONE HUNDRED DOLLARS, in the Consolidated Fund of Texas, created by an Act of Congress entitled "an act to authorise the consolidation and funding of the public debt," passed on the 7th day of June, 1837. Transferable by the said legal attorney or representative, on the books of the Stock Commissioner only; and at any time until within thirty days of the day on which the interest may fall due: and bearing an interest of 10 PER CENT. PER ANNUM, payable at the Treasury of this Republic on the 1st day of September, 1838, and semi-annually thereafter; and redeemable at the convenience of the Government at any time after the 1st day of September, A. D. 1842.

City of Houston, 1, 183

James Behan Act. Comptroller. Jackson Smith Stock Commissioner.

PUBLIC FAITH PLEDGED. ONE HUNDRED DOLLARS.

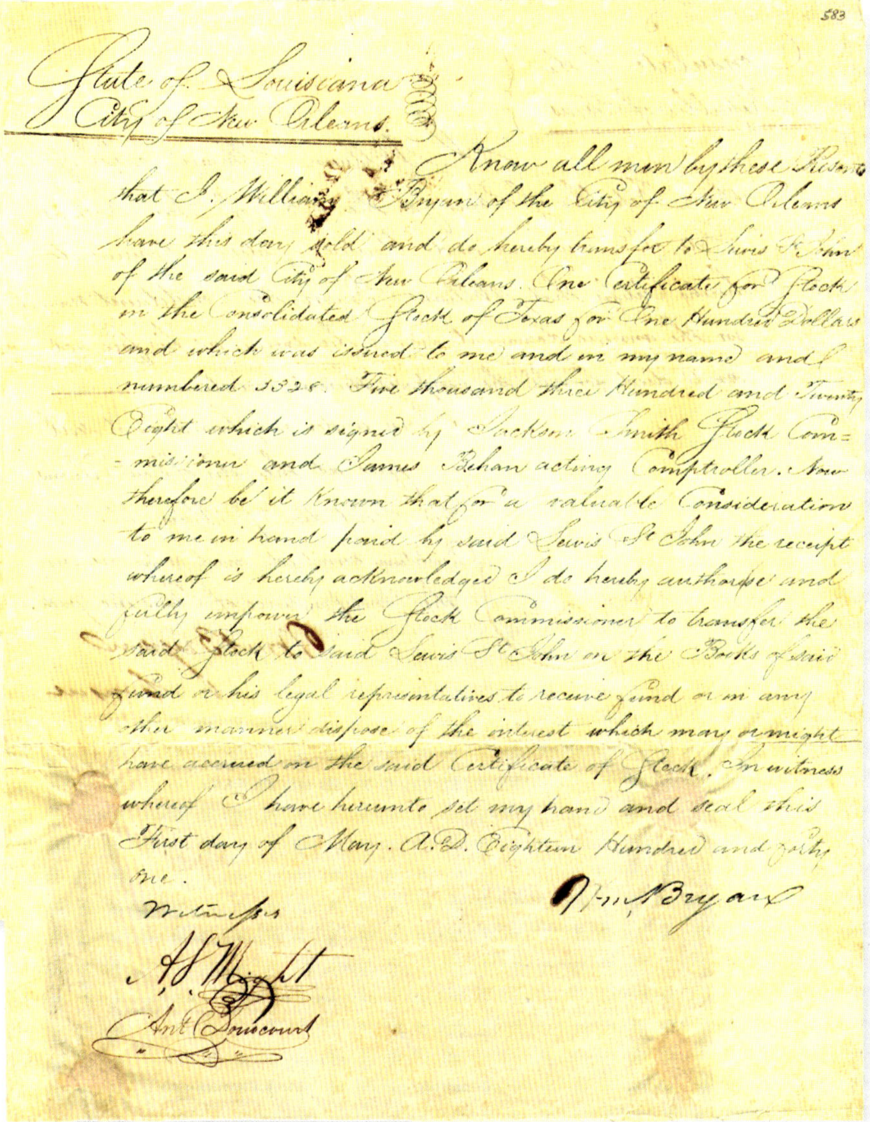

583

State of Louisiana
City of New Orleans

Know all men by these Presents that I, William Bryan of the City of New Orleans have this day sold and do hereby transfer to Louis St John of the said City of New Orleans One Certificate for Stock in the Consolidated Stock of Texas for One Hundred Dollars and which was issued to me and in my name and numbered 5328. Five thousand three Hundred and Twenty Eight which is signed by Jackson Smith Stock Commissioner and James Behan acting Comptroller. Now therefore be it known that for a valuable Consideration to me in hand paid by said Louis St John the receipt whereof is hereby acknowledged I do hereby authorise and fully empower the Stock Commissioner to transfer the said Stock to said Louis St John on the Books of said fund or his legal representatives to receive fund or in any other manner dispose of the interest which may or might have accrued on the said Certificate of Stock. In witness whereof I have hereunto set my hand and seal this First day of May. A.D. Eighteen Hundred and forty one.

Wm Bryan

Witnesses

Fig 11.7, Consulate of the Republic of Texas, New Orleans, May 1, 1841, issued to William Bryan (both sides are shown).

Private Collection, Cr. CF10, O-642.

Of special interest is the $100 Consolidated Fund of Texas certificate in Figure 11.7. It was attached to an original Republic of Texas legal document of transfer drafted by William Bryan, in his capacity as Consul General of the Republic of Texas in New Orleans. The complicated attestation of transfer in the letter illustrates the maddening bureaucracy created by the government to transfer the title of the 1837 stock on the books of the stock commissioner. It is not known how many of these certificates were transferred in this manner. The stock certificate is signed by James B. Shaw, Acting Comptroller and Jackson Smith, Stock Commissioner. The transfer letter is signed on the front and again on the verso by William Bryan.

TWO DISTINCT ISSUES OF THE CONSOLIDATED FUND OF TEXAS

This practice of funding the public debt resulted in two distinct issues of stock in the Consolidated Fund of Texas, issued concurrently from the city of Austin. These are commonly known as the 1837 issue and the 1840 issue. The 1837 stock issue had a special pledge of revenue for the payment of the interest but no stipulation in regard to the medium in which it should be paid.[6] The interest of 10 percent was initially paid to stockholders via the paper promissory notes but these payments were later suspended. These certificates were receivable for dues owed to the government, were only transferable on the books of the stock commissioner, and were not generally used to redeem outstanding promissory notes. There are several different printed varieties and denominations of this issue, ranging from the smaller, currency sized issues, to several larger printed varieties issued in certificate form (most commonly used for the transfer of ownership from a previous holder). This stock was issued from the cities of both Houston and Austin and was primarily used to redeem treasury warrants and audited paper issued before January 1, 1840.

The 1840 issue was initially used to fund the withdrawal of promissory notes from circulation. These ornate stock certificates were later used by the government for the direct redemption of treasury warrants paid out between 1840 and 1841. Although they had no special provision stipulating where the 10 percent interest would come from, the interest was to be paid in gold or silver, although there is no record of the government ever having done so. The stock could not be used for the payment of taxes, was transferable by simple endorsement, and was issued at a substantial discount to its ostensible or face value. The stock was issued in denominations of $100 and $500 with interest warrants attached via engraved certificates. A second issue, with an 8 percent interest rate and otherwise identical terms, was issued for the refunding of notes after July 1, 1840. There is only one variety of the 8 percent issue, which was a printed (rather than engraved) stock certificate with interest warrants attached. All of the 1840 stock originated from the city of Austin. The interest payments on all of these obligations were suspended by the government in 1841.

Fig 11.8, Building Vignette, American Bank Note Company.
An engraved image of the Southern Bank Note Company building in New Orleans. This photograph is an inverse image of the plate. Twenty years later, this firm also printed a series of issues for the Confederate States of America. Courtesy of Stack's, New York, from the American Bank Note Co. Archives.

REFUNDING THE REDBACKS

Since the cities of Galveston and New Orleans had the largest amounts of Texas currency in circulation, the two cities were selected for the initial refunding of the depreciated promissory notes and their subsequent exchange for newly printed stock certificates. James Love was appointed to the stock commissioner's post in Galveston, and William Bryan was appointed to the post in New Orleans. Bryan was also the Texas Consul in New Orleans. These two men were to spread the official word of the refunding to the holders of the depreciating currency and effect the appropriate exchanges. The public was persuaded to surrender their paper money for the newly issued shares of stock which promised semi-annual interest payments in gold and silver.[7] The government was not only short on gold and silver, but undoubtedly used what little they had to cajole the printers into producing the new engraved series of 1840 stock certificates.

By mid June, the 1840 stock certificates were ready, and Bryan and Love sprung into action. Their assignment was to collect the outstanding promissory notes and exchange them into the 10 percent stock created by the act of February 5, 1840. These notes included redbacks, engraved notes, audited paper and old star notes still in circulation. Starr publicly referred to the exchange of the paper money into the new stock as "investing." Love and Bryan were quite persuasive, and many tendered their notes in exchange for the interest bearing stock. This swap of the stock certificates for the promissory notes was seen as a way to pull the depreciated money out of circulation, literally shrinking the money supply. It was hoped that this move would stop the rampant devaluation of the Texas notes with the burnt orange reverses.

For the average Texian on the street, exchanging their depreciated paper money for stock which would pay 10 percent semi-annual interest in specie appeared to be a good move. Although the exchange seemed lucrative, it flew in the face of being a logical transaction for the treasury. There is an old adage in the credit markets about potential borrowers who are unconcerned about the rate of interest at which they borrow. These are usually the ones who are the least likely to pay the money back. Unfortunately for these investors, this old adage rang true. The Treasury of the Republic of Texas had no means to pay the interest on the new stock—and it had no intention of doing so in the first place. It is important to keep in mind that although the purchasing value of the Texas promissory notes was, on average, less than twenty cents on the U.S. dollar, these notes could still be used to pay taxes at full face value. Perhaps many of the holders of these notes had no intention of paying their taxes with them anyway.

The $100 engraved certificate in Figure 11.9 features an allegorical figure of Liberty seated at left, a vignette of an old mill at the center and the traditional five-pointed Lone Star at the bottom.[8] It was engraved by the Southern Bank Note Co. and Endicott & Clark, New Orleans. It should be noted that unlike the stocks of companies listed on the New York Stock Exchange, these securities didn't offer the liquidity of the stocks of railroads, canal companies and the more established northeastern banks of the day.

Fig 11.9, $100 Republic of Texas, Certificate of Stock, 10 Percent Consolidated Fund, Dated June 15, 1840. *Private Collection, Cr. 40E.*

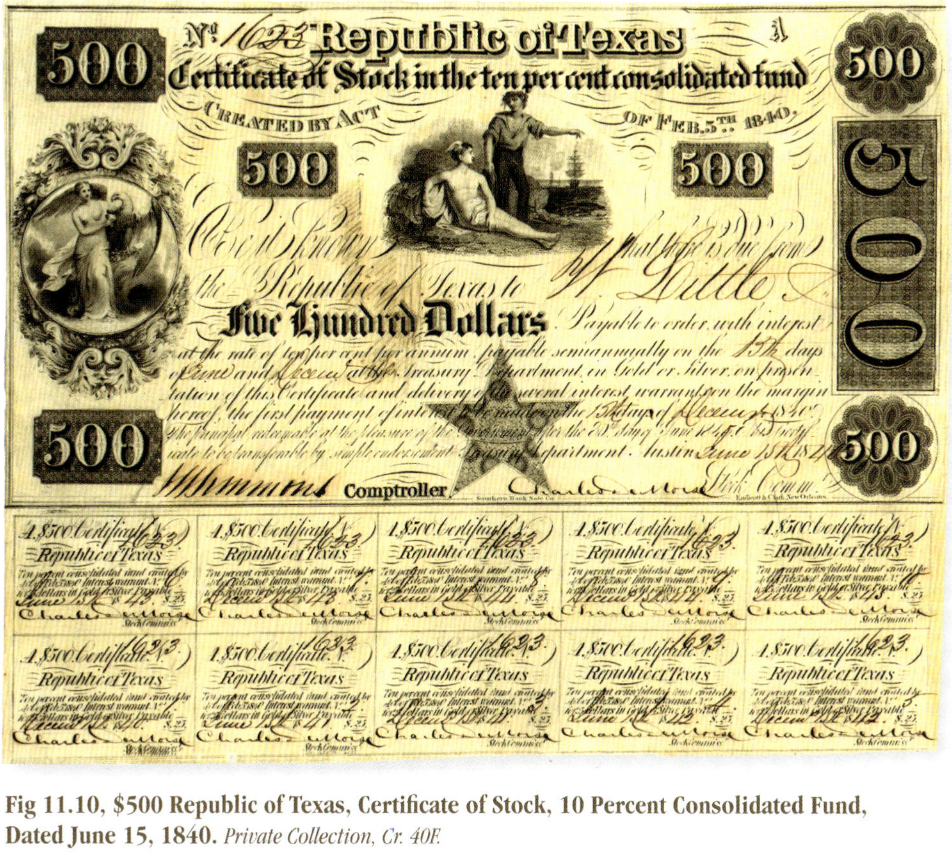

Fig 11.10, $500 Republic of Texas, Certificate of Stock, 10 Percent Consolidated Fund, Dated June 15, 1840. *Private Collection, Cr. 40F.*

Of particular note in Figure 11.9 are the interest coupons which are still attached. These are dated from December 15, 1840 (at lower left). This indicates that Texas never met the obligations on this stock beginning with the first interest payment. The false hope of receiving interest payments in specie was soon shattered, rendering these certificates illiquid. The certificates soon became poorly suited as a medium of exchange for virtually any transaction.

The $500 engraved certificate in Figure 11.10 features an allegorical maiden with an eagle at left, a vignette of Mercury seated before a sailor at center, and the traditional five-pointed Lone Star at the bottom.[9] It, too, was engraved by the Southern Bank Note Co. and Endicott & Clark, New Orleans. These ornate certificates, made by some of the most skilled artisans of the time, stated on the face that they were "payable to order with interest at the rate of ten percent per annum payable semi annually on the 15th days of June and December at the Treasury Department in Gold or Silver on presentation of the certificate…" Like the $100 issue previously mentioned in Figure 11.9, the attached interest coupons are dated from December 15, 1840, indicating that no interest was ever received by the holder of this certificate. As for the final payment date for the face value, the principal was "redeemable at the pleasure of the Government after the 30th day of June 1845." Like many preferred stocks, it was issued with a perpetual maturity, and could not be called by the government until after a period of five years.

For the holders of the stock who exchanged their promissory notes in New Orleans or Galveston, redeeming the attached warrants (today called coupons) in distant Austin was all but physically impossible. Those holders who did manage the long journey to the treasury department never received their interest payments in specie. Instead, the interest due them was acknowledged with another treasury warrant drawn on the empty coffers of Texas. Imagine for a moment that you were a bartender, blacksmith, lawyer, horse trader or a seamstress in Texas during this time period. You may have accepted the engraved notes or redbacks in payment for your trade and then exchanged them for these certificates of stock, in which "there is due from the Republic of Texas" a promise to pay your interest in gold or silver. Imagine again that you made the long, hot, overland trek to Austin to collect your interest in specie. You exchanged your interest warrant on the payment date and you received only another paper warrant for the interest which was due you. Only this time, the warrant would read something like "payable out of funds not otherwise appropriated." This was the financial reality of the day that the Texians had to deal with in regards to the issuance of the various forms of money from the "Paper Republic."

By June 30 a report was sent from New Orleans that the commissioners had successfully taken out of circulation almost $100,000 in redbacks. Included in this amount were several audited drafts and issues of military scrip which they also replaced with the 10 percent stock in the Consolidated Fund.[10] The Texas money had sunk to such an obscene level, that the commissioners gleefully reported as a result of their actions, the Texas "money is ranging at 16 to 18 cents" on the dollar, although "several counterfeits had also gotten into the market, and that had also weakened them." This response is akin to a student, accustomed to seeing his test scores in single digits, proudly reporting to a stunned parent that he had brought his semester grades into the high teens! William Bryan and James Love clearly understood that their goal was to "get as much money out of the market as possible," although they missed the bigger picture. The long-term strategy for the refunding was to stop the depreciation of the currency, and to that extent the extra interest expense and the illiquidity of the stock would make the funding exchange a miserable failure.

William Bryan made a final accounting from New Orleans on July 15, 1840, that $98,493 in promissory notes "without interest" had been turned in for redemption, "to be funded in the ten percent stock payable in gold or silver semiannually."[11] Though many citizens turned in their promissory notes for stock, the general public was skeptical of the government's ability to fulfill what could be another empty promise. While the stock commissioners were busy redeeming all of the available promissory notes in a futile effort to halt the currency's slide against the dollar, another onerous provision of the law was about to take effect. This was the stipulation that any outstanding promissory notes not turned in by July 1, 1840, would not receive the 10 percent stock but would only be entitled to receive certificates of a new issue of 8 percent stock, the interest on that issue to be paid in specie as well.

The $100 printed certificate in Figure 11.11, made payable to Thomas Gardiner, is one of a handful of examples known to have survived. It features a vignette of a sailing ship at left and a U.S. Gobrecht dollar at right, with the five-pointed Lone Star both above and below. The certificate was printed by "Whiting's Press, Austin."[12] Like the previous examples, the original interest warrants (or coupons) are still attached, indicating that not a single payment was ever collected by the owner. The certificate is cut cancelled and triangled, stamped "FILED" and "AUDITED." This indicates that it was eventually redeemed more than ten years after issue following the annexation of Texas by the United States.

Between the various forms of the 10 percent Consolidated Fund created under the Act of February 5, 1840, $754,000 in outstanding promissory notes were eventually refunded and withdrawn from circulation by the Lamar administration.[13] An additional $24,280 was later withdrawn and replaced with the smaller issue of the 8 percent Consolidated Fund for those redback holders who swapped their paper money for stock after the prescribed deadline. Although the interest on the stock was promised in gold or silver, not a single interest payment of this type was ever recorded. In the end, it mattered little as to which form of stock certificate was received in the place of the promissory notes which had been "invested" in the Consolidated Fund. All of these issues would soon suspend any hope of paying the interest for which the public faith had been pledged.

Fig 11.11, Republic of Texas, $100 Certificate of Stock, 8 Percent Consolidated Fund, dated October 15th, 1840.

Private Collection, Cr. 40K.

THE 8 PERCENT TREASURY BOND ISSUE

The legislative Act of February 5, 1840, which authorized the redemption of promissory notes, also authorized an issue of treasury bonds in $100, $500 and $1,000 denominations. Like the 10 percent stock certificates, the $100 and $500 treasury bond denominations were printed on a single plate. The act also required a $1,000 denomination, but the order was "dispensed with" because the treasury lacked a large enough appropriation of specie to even pay for the engraving of an additional plate.[14] That incident itself should have been an indication of things to come.

In a normal bond issue, a government would borrow money by issuing bonds through an underwriter or investment bank for sale to investors. This allowed the treasury to borrow funds and use the money for the good of the state, so long as the periodic interest payments were met. The investors had the promise of a sovereign government that the full face value would be repaid to the holder of the bond at maturity. In this case, the stated maturity date was "redeemable at the pleasure of the Government, after the first day of January, 1846," indicating that the maturity was perpetual, as were the previous stock issues. However, no money could be borrowed through these bonds as there were no investors willing to part with their gold and silver to buy them. Since no investors wanted the bonds, even at a deep discount, the bonds were issued in payment to defray part of the expenses of the Republic for the year. Many of the small denomination bonds were paid out at an average of twenty cents on the dollar in exchange to merchants who provided goods and services to the government. As a practical matter, most were used to fund the treasury warrants issued to judges, diplomats and government officials who were forced to redeem their treasury warrants for treasury bonds in payment of salaries because the redbacks were no longer issued.

Like the stock issue created under the same act, interest on the bonds was to be paid semi-annually in the silver and gold coin. As an added inducement for investors, it was plainly printed on the face of the certificate that funds were appropriated for payment by

Fig 11.12, $100 Government Bond payable to holder, 8 Percent per annum.
Private Collection, Cr. 40A.

Fig 11.13, $500 Government Bond payable to holder, 8 Percent per annum.
Private Collection, Cr. 40B.

"revenue from license tax and tax on personal property" which had been "set apart and specifically appropriated for the payment of the interest on this fund." As if to validate the bond's acceptance, these debentures were personally signed by the President. However, this signature mattered little to the merchant taking the bonds in payment. With the interest payments on the bonds in serious arrears, their depreciation in value was deemed complete when Texas declared that they would not even be receivable for customs dues or taxes after February 1, 1842. Although Congress levied a new series of direct taxes under the Lamar administration, these did little for the government's ability to service their debt. Many of the taxes on billiard halls, drinking establishments and personal property were difficult to collect. Although the taxes may have been due, the local sheriffs had no means to enforce their payment. While the collected taxes were set aside to meet the interest on the bonds, people hoarded their gold and silver and paid their taxes with promissory notes and other forms of the depreciating Texas paper, thus exacerbating the problem even further.[15]

These ornately printed bonds are frequently seen in the collector market and are quite popular because they bear the original signatures of Mirabeau B. Lamar as President or David G. Burnet as acting President, depending upon the date of issue. Each interest coupon was meticulously numbered with the corresponding serial number of the certificate. Although $766,800 in face value was still outstanding at the time Texas was annexed to the United States in 1846, most of the certificates in existence today are found with all ten interest warrants attached, indicating that Texas never paid even one installment of interest in specie, not even for the first six-month period. Un-cancelled bond certificates are somewhat scarce and difficult to locate in nice condition.

The $100 engraved certificate in Figure 11.12 features a vignette of a cow at left, a bull at upper right, a steamboat at lower right and a vignette of a man seated in industry. The five-pointed Lone Star graces the certificate at the bottom. These printed certificates were engraved by the Southern Bank Note Co. and Endicott & Clark, New Orleans.[16] All ten interest coupons are attached, indicating that interest was never paid. The bond also appears to be un-cancelled. It is dated October 1, 1841, and signed by William Sevey as Acting Secretary of the Treasury and Mirabeau B. Lamar as President.

The $500 engraved certificate in Figure 11.13 features a vignette of a man plowing a field at left, and an Indian brave with a bow and a quiver of arrows over his back (same as on the $1 change note from Austin). The five-pointed Lone Star graces the certificate at the bottom. These printed certificates were engraved by the Southern Bank Note Co. and Endicott & Clark, New Orleans.[17] Like the previous example in Figure 11.12, all ten interest coupons are attached indicating that interest was never paid. It also appears to be uncancelled. This specimen is dated January 1, 1841, and signed by William Sevey as Acting Secretary of the Treasury, and David G. Burnet as acting President. At the time, President Mirabeau B. Lamar had taken ill and was recuperating in New Orleans, with David G. Burnet, his Vice President, temporarily assuming the presidential duties.

THE FRENCH CONNECTION

In late 1839, Texas emissaries traveled abroad to explore prospects of obtaining a foreign loan. The most notable of these emissaries was James Hamilton, a former Governor of South Carolina, who had offered his services to negotiate a loan for the financially depressed Republic. He was appointed as a loan commissioner by President Lamar.[18] A report dated February 8, 1840, arrived in Austin indicating that France might be willing to advance up to ten million dollars if certain inducements were made by the Republic.[19] The center of influence in the matter was the French chargé d'affaires Alphonse Dubois de Saligny, who maintained an official residence in Austin.[20] De Saligny agreed to lobby the French government for a loan on behalf of Texas if the import duties on French wines were waived. Although De Saligny also lobbied the Texas Congress for the passage of a Franco-Texian Bill to appropriate lands for French immigration, his diplomatic efforts to obtain the proposed loan was a welcome development.

The French chargé d'affaires acquired a reputation among the Austin elite as a somewhat unsavory individual. On one occasion in 1840, Dubois de Saligny allegedly passed $300 in counterfeit bills to a waggoner in payment of some transportation costs.[21] Saligny refused to redeem the spurious bills he had passed to the waggoner and the injured party proceeded to have the Frenchman prosecuted for the offense. The matter became so politically sensitive that Judge James Webb, accompanied by Vice President David G. Burnet, came to Treasury Secretary Starr's office to see what could be done about the incident. Starr paid the waggoner out of some genuine bills recently received in the treasury from the sale of some Austin lots to quiet the matter and maintain good relations with the influential diplomat.

The foreign loan being lobbied by de Saligny was considered crucial for keeping the finances of the Republic afloat. France was considered Texas's best hope for a financial rescue package and Starr wasn't about to see their funding hopes dashed by prosecuting a diplomat for passing counterfeit bills. As Starr later recalled to Lamar: "This measure was determined upon because of the absence of your Excellency and our great desire to avoid any difficulty with the French Minister at that period and under those circumstances."[22] Although the matter of negotiating the loan would take time, the French wines would flow freely in Texas while diplomats toasted France and courted the devious Dubois de Saligny in Austin.

REDEEMABLE BY INVESTMENT...

By the fall of 1840, printers weren't printing any more Texas money and the government suspended all further issues of promissory notes, though this didn't stop the government from issuing drafts against money that the Republic did not have on hand. With no loan proceeds, the Act of February 5, 1840, prevented the government from paying out any new redbacks, creating a serious problem when the government could not meet the payroll of the Republic's employees. This unusual dilemma resulted in a prolific number of auditor's certificates being issued from Austin for claims against the government. The content on these certificates is sometimes quite interesting, since they demonstrate the illiquidity of the government. The face of the auditor's certificates state that these payments were to be redeemed "by investment in the Funded Debt of Texas, or in payment of certain Dues to Gov't," though citizens could still use the auditor's certificates as payment for their taxes—at least for a while longer.

The certificate in Figure 11.14 for $6.25 to John S. Bryan for "service as witness" was common pay for persons who served as jurors or witnesses for a day. The language under the serial number: "Redeemable by

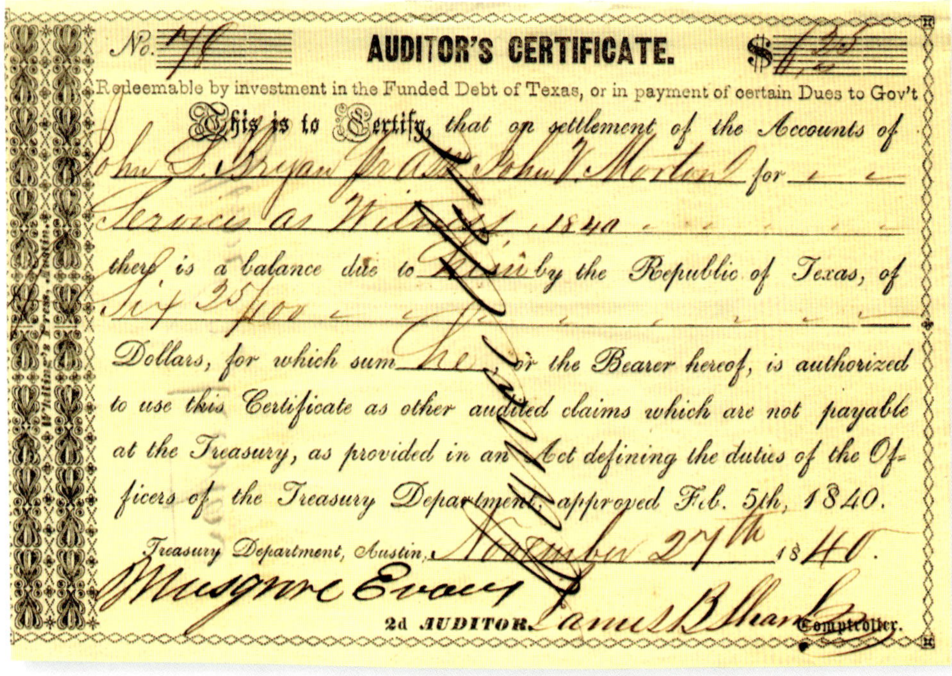
No. 78 AUDITOR'S CERTIFICATE. $6.25
Redeemable by investment in the Funded Debt of Texas, or in payment of certain Dues to Gov't
This is to Certify, that on settlement of the Accounts of John M. Bryan for Ass. John V. Morton for Services as Witness, 1840
there is a balance due to him by the Republic of Texas, of Six 25/100
Dollars, for which sum he or the Bearer hereof, is authorized to use this Certificate as other audited claims which are not payable at the Treasury, as provided in an Act defining the duties of the Officers of the Treasury Department, approved Feb. 5th, 1840.
Treasury Department, Austin, November 27th 1840.
Musgrove Evans
2d AUDITOR. James B. Shaw Comptroller.

No. 78 AUDITOR'S CERTIFICATE $6.25 Redeemable by investment in the Funded Debt of Texas, or in payment of certain Dues to Gov't. This is to Certify, that on settlement of the Accounts of John M. Bryan for Ass[ignee] John V. Morton for Services as Witness, 1840, there is a balance due to him by the Republic of Texas, of Six 25/100 Dollars, for which sum he, or the Bearer hereof, is authorized to use this Certificate as other audited claims which are not payable at the Treasury, as provided in an Act defining the duties of the Officers of the Treasury Department, approved Feb. 5th, 1840. Treasury Department, Austin, November 27th, 1840.

(Signed) Musgrove Evans, 2d Auditor, James B. Shaw, Comptroller

Fig 11.14, Austin, November 27, 1840, Auditor's Certificate to John M Bryan for Service as a Witness.

Private Collection, Cr. AW2 (AW2-1), O-926.

investment in the Funded Debt of Texas, or in payment of certain Dues to Gov't" indicates this certificate could not be redeemed for cash, not even the redbacks, but could be endorsed and paid for taxes or "invested" in the Consolidated Fund of Texas. The fact that it is payable to Bryan "or the Bearer hereof" indicates that the certificate was transferable, and the assignee would hold the same rights as the original payee. Since $6.25 could not be invested in the Consolidated Fund (the smallest denomination being $100), it was good that the bearer could transfer the amount. The pay for a court witness was eventually raised to $10 per day by the Texas State Legislature in 1993, a full 153 years later![23]

For all of its faults, the Treasury Department kept meticulous records, evidenced by the example of an auditor's certificate shown in Figure 11.15. This certificate was issued to replace a lost draft, No. 1099 on the Treasury for $467 as pay for the military service of William Gamble. He had served as a 2nd Lieutenant in the Second Brigade of Texas Volunteers in 1836. Although it had been five years since the original draft was issued, Thomas Ward, in his capacity as Lieutenant Gamble's attorney, was able to get the new certificate issued. Like the previous example, this certificate could only be "invested" in shares of the Consolidated Fund of Texas or paid in for taxes. The certificate is marked "Cancelled" twice across the face and is endorsed by Ward on Gamble's behalf on the reverse. This indicates that it was turned in to the government for redemption.

These auditor's certificates as well as the later treasury warrants are often referred to by collectors as the most boring issues in the entire series, because the majority were routine payments to government officials. In his landmark work entitled *Confederate and Southern States Currency,* Grover Criswell listed fifteen different varieties of paper. The government wasn't choosy as to the type of paper on which they were printed. Many of these issues were printed by Sam Whiting and Company, a local printer in Austin, who along with other suppliers, builders, and boarding house keepers, was happy to have the additional business the government brought to town. For all the lack of hard currency in the economy, it was an excellent time to be in the printing business in Texas. Many of the certificates and warrants payable to government officials were redeemed in exchange for the 1840 issue of stock and the $100 and $500 8 percent treasury bonds.

Even the redemption and payment of interest on outstanding promissory notes became somewhat of a paper farce. James Starr issued instructions to officials in

No. 109 AUDITOR'S CERTIFICATE $467.00 Redeemable by investment in the Funded Debt of Texas, or in payment of certain Dues to Gov't. This is to Certify, that on settlement of the Accounts of William Gamble per attys Tho[ma]s W. Ward for Lost Draft No. 1099 for Military Services there is a balance due to him by the Republic of Texas, of Four Hundred & Sixty Seven Dollars, for which sum he, or the Bearer hereof, is authorized to use this Certificate as other audited claims which are not payable at the Treasury, as provided in an Act defining the duties of the Officers of the Treasury Department, approved Feb. 5th, 1840. Treasury Department, Austin, November 5th, 1841. (Signed) Charles Mason, Auditor and James B. Shaw, Comptroller

No. 109 AUDITOR'S CERTIFICATE. $467
Redeemable by investment in the Funded Debt of Texas, or in payment of certain Dues to Gov't.
This is to Certify, that on settlement of the Accounts of William Gamble pr atty Thos W. Ward for Lost Draft (No 1099) for Military Services there is a balance due to him by the Republic of Texas, of Four hundred & Sixty Seven Dollars, for which sum he, or the Bearer hereof, is authorized to use this Certificate as other audited claims which are not payable at the Treasury, as provided in an Act defining the duties of the Officers of the Treasury Department, approved Feb. 5th, 1840.
Treasury Department, Austin, November 5 1841.
Charles Mason AUDITOR. James B. Shaw Comptroller.

Fig 11.15, Austin, November 5, 1841, Auditor's Certificate to William Gamble for Lost Draft No. 109 for Military Services.

Private Collection, Cr. AW2A, O-910.

the treasury department outlining how future redemptions of the outstanding promissory notes would be handled. Many of the outstanding notes of the engraved type had been previously issued in Houston and still bore interest.[24] Naturally, people were even less inclined to exchange these for stock. Starr's instructions specifically stated, "Hereafter when notes are presented for redemption, warrants will be drawn for the interest only, and the notes themselves, after having been cancelled by the Comptroller will be presented for exchange at your office at the same time that the corresponding is presented for payment." In other words, when older notes were presented for payment, the face amount was to be exchanged into a like face value of stock in the Consolidated Fund of Texas, and any interest due was to be acknowledged by a treasury warrant for the amount which had accrued on the paper money. It soon became apparent to the holders of these notes, warrants, and certificates that it was nothing more than a paper chase being conducted by the Treasury on borrowed time.

There was such a shortage of hard money in the U.S. and Texas during this time period that many merchants resorted to having cent-size copper tokens made for the purpose of making change. These copper coins, known as a "Hard Times" tokens, were routinely used for making change in the depressed economy of the U.S. and Texas following the financial panic of 1837, which resulted in the widespread hoarding of all types of hard currency.

Fig 11.16, 1841 "Hard Times" Token.

Author's Collection.

The obverse of the example in Figure 11.16 is inscribed: "E Pluribus Unum" or "One of Many." The reverse also displays a blunt economic and political message: "Millions for defense. Not one cent for tribute." Although designed for use in the United States, this inscription was quite descriptive of public opinion towards the ongoing expenditures for the Texas Navy.

NAVAL PAYMENT CERTIFICATES, ISSUED APRIL 23, 1841

Unlike his predecessor, Mirabeau B. Lamar had the strategic vision to build and acquire an impressive naval fleet for the Republic. There were actually two Texas navies. The first served in the Texas war for independence and the second was commissioned during the Lamar administration.

As an expansionist, Lamar predicted the strategic military importance of building a strong navy for coastal defenses. However, it became clear that the government lacked the money to maintain the small but impressive fleet of ships. The financing of this second navy had been funded on credit by shipbuilders, a private placement of bonds and the issue of promissory notes. Sailors were recruited at several ports in the United States and signed up with bounty bonuses paid in redbacks. Many were lured into service with dreams of military action and the capture of "prizes" on the high seas. It was common at the time for captured enemy ships to be sold along with their cargoes and the proceeds distributed as "prize money" on a pro rata basis among the crew. With peace at hand in the U.S. and idle sailors seeking adventure on the ocean, the naval agents of Texas embarked on recruitment missions to staff their new fleet with skilled seamen ranging from New York to New Orleans.

Fig 11.17, Texas Navy Vessels, *Austin* and *San Antonio*.
Courtesy of the Rosenberg Library, Galveston, Texas.

Lamar plunged the Republic into an additional $250,000 debt when legislation was passed by Congress on January 26, 1839, for appropriations to fund the Texas Navy.[25] This legislation authorized the Treasury to execute drafts for the entire congressional appropriation. New redback notes were printed to fund the drafts when presented for redemption. With the money approved by Congress and the newly created cash in hand, Texas used these funds to purchase supplies and ships built in Baltimore and New York. The ships were outfitted with armaments and were renamed once they crossed the international boundary into Texas waters west of the Sabine River. The second Texas Navy dominated the Gulf Coast from New Orleans to the Yucatan Peninsula. The Navy was a powerful military deterrent to any naval hostilities on the part of Mexico. The tall wooden warships under the skillful command of Commodore Edwin W. Moore patrolled the Texas and Mexican coasts, wreaking havoc on the enemy as they blockaded ports, interrupted Mexican shipping, captured supplies, and protected the trade routes to and from the Texas ports.

The small but mighty Texas fleet consisted of the sloop of war *Austin*, the steamship *Zavala,* the brigs *Wharton* and *Archer,* three shoal draft schooners built from the Baltimore deal—the *San Jacinto, San Antonio* and *San Bernard*—and the schooner *Louisville.* The *Austin*, a 600-ton sloop, was considered the flagship of the Texas fleet and was placed under the direct command of Commodore Edwin W. Moore.[26] Since military expenditures are among the most expensive for any government, the Republic of Texas was no exception to the massive outlays which were needed to keep the powerful wooden ships in fighting condition. To make matters worse, as the tax and customs revenues fell woefully short of their initial projections, coupled with the incessant spending of the Government, the Republic was unable to meet its obligations and ran short of almost every available method of payment for the fleet.

Due to the inadequacy of funds set aside to pay the Navy, the government resorted to drastic financial measures to meet the long overdue naval payroll. The government had little choice but to pay the sailors with IOU's, since the Treasury was flat broke. As of March

31, 1841, the Treasury reported $135,815.37 in promissory and change notes and only $1,657.10 of specie on hand.[27] Of the specie amount, all except $17.43 was in the form of escrow deposits, leaving the entire Republic of Texas with less than twenty dollars in hard currency. The government issued special pay certificates to meet the overdue wage obligations for the officers, sailors, and marines of the Texian Navy. These certificates could be presented for payment "out of the first appropriation made by Congress to meet said claims."

These pay certificates were perhaps the most egregious examples of several dubious paper obligations issued under the Lamar administration. They remain a haunting reminder of the desperate financial measures taken to avoid an all out mutiny among the sailors. If you can imagine the audacity of a large employer distributing these instruments to an entire division and telling the employees they would be honored "as soon as Congress passes a law to appropriate the money," then you can understand the frustration felt by the hard fighting officers and seamen. When the sailors returned from their service on the high seas of the Gulf of Mexico, they found no payroll funds available to them for distribution.

With the payroll long overdue in April 1841, the sensitive task of meeting the naval personnel in Galveston fell to Charles Mason, the former Stock Commissioner, then serving as an auditor in the Treasury Department. His instructions came from John Chalmers, who succeeded James H. Starr as Treasury Secretary, and were quite explicit. Chalmers told Mason, "proceed to Galveston and settle with the different pursers of the Navy." The ship's purser was a warrant officer who served as the ship's storekeeper and accountant and was most likely the person who distributed the payroll.[28] It was further decreed to Mason, "in paying the officers, seamen and marines of the Navy, you will keep a register of the number and the amount of the certificates and also to whom paid."[29] Chalmers also required that each certificate be endorsed by the payee. Perhaps fearing that the Naval Certificates would not be accepted and knowing how much the Texas money had depreciated, Chalmers further instructed Mason with the following: "In your disbursements for the Navy, you will pay out the Bonds of the Government at two for one, and the promissory notes at three for one in par funds, and not less than that, but if you should find on your arrival at Galveston that our money has depreciated, you will pay it out at its highest rates."

The crew of the *Austin* received their pay certificates during Mason's initial visit to Galveston since the flagship was in port at the time to pick up nautical maps and equipment. The crew was preparing for a long overdue coastal surveying project of the Texas shoreline.[30] After this first payroll was met, other packages of the same $25 and $50 certificates were received in Galveston for the sailors on other ships. One of the packages was destined for the *Zavala,* as Mason had received a request from the ship's purser Fleming T. Wells regarding the payroll, to "send it back" indicating that "it is essential to a settlement of those accounts."[31] Shortly thereafter, Commodore Moore wrote from the *Austin* on May 15, 1841, that he received "two packages of audited certificates each containing twenty thousand dollars."[32] By June 15, Commodore Moore acknowledged the receipt of an additional package from the city of Austin containing additional $25 and $50 certificates amounting to $55,000.[33] Moore signed a letter onboard the *Austin* then moored in Galveston Bay, indicating that the entire payroll process took several weeks and that the crews of multiple ships had been paid aboard the *Austin*.

The Naval Certificates were issued in two denominations, $25 and $50. All specimens are dated April 23, 1841. There are three minor varieties of the $25 issue and only a single known variety of the $50 denomination. None of these issues are particularly rare, except for one variety printed as "Navy" Appropriation rather than as "Naval" Appropriation. All of them represent claims for back pay. The Naval Payment Certificates relate to the claims of officers and sailors of the Second Texian Navy.

The extremely rare example in Figure 11.18 is a $25 Navy Payment Certificate. It differs only from the more common varieties shown in Figure 11.19 with the substitution of the word "Navy," rather than "Naval" on the first line. All of these certificates bear the date of April 23, 1841. This example was payable to a George Stacy, a Master, who endorsed the certificate on the reverse aboard the flagship *Austin*. It is signed by James B. Shaw as Comptroller and J.W. Simmons as Treasurer.

The example in Figure 11.19 is a $25 Naval Payment Certificate, one of thousands issued bearing the date of

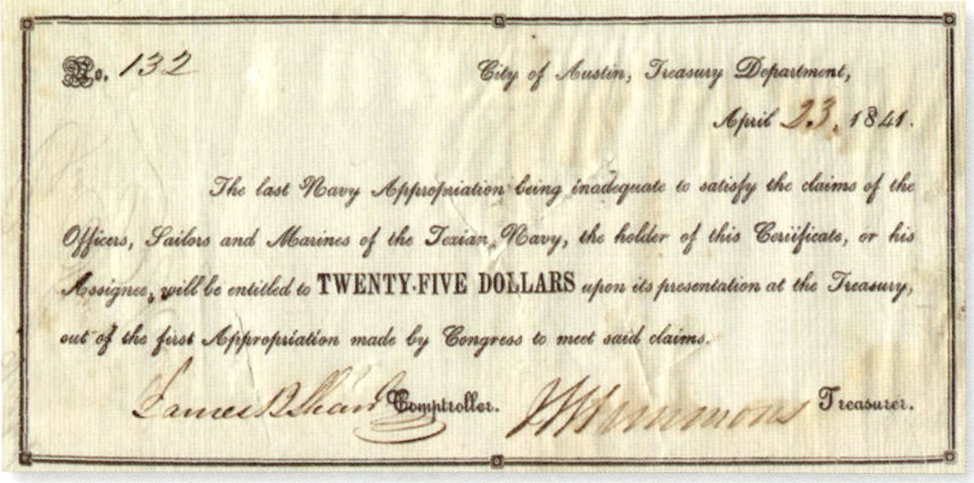
No. 132 City of Austin, Treasury Department,
April 23, 1841.
The last Navy Appropriation being inadequate to satisfy the claims of the Officers, Sailors and Marines of the Texian Navy, the holder of this Certificate, or his Assignee, will be entitled to TWENTY-FIVE DOLLARS upon its presentation at the Treasury, out of the first Appropriation made by Congress to meet said claims.
Comptroller. Treasurer.

Fig 11.18, Austin, $25 Texian Navy Certificate, No. 132.
Texas Money Collection, Courtesy of Special Collections, University of Houston Libraries, Houston, Texas, Cr. AW3B, O-825.

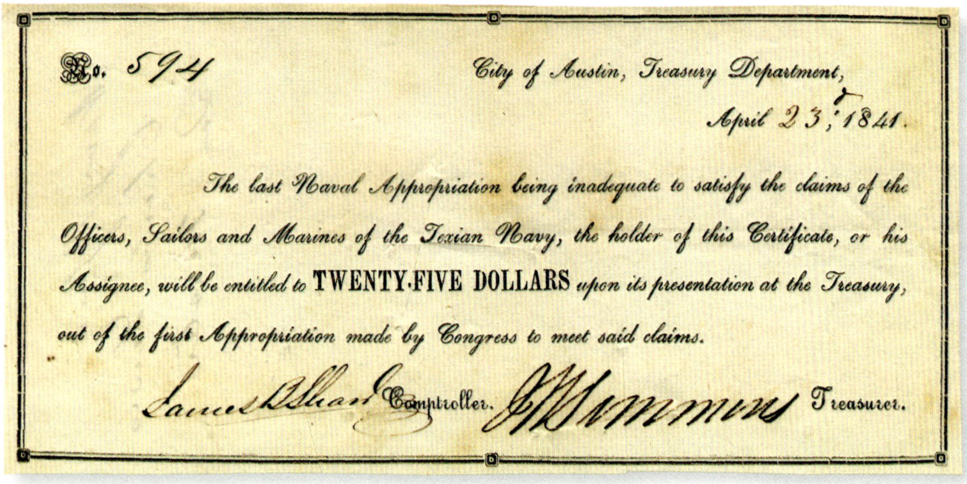
No. 594 City of Austin, Treasury Department,
April 23, 1841.
The last Naval Appropriation being inadequate to satisfy the claims of the Officers, Sailors and Marines of the Texian Navy, the holder of this Certificate, or his Assignee, will be entitled to TWENTY-FIVE DOLLARS upon its presentation at the Treasury, out of the first Appropriation made by Congress to meet said claims.
Comptroller. Treasurer.

Fig 11.19, Austin, $25 Texian Navy Certificate, No. 594.
Private Collection, Cr. AW3A, O-822.

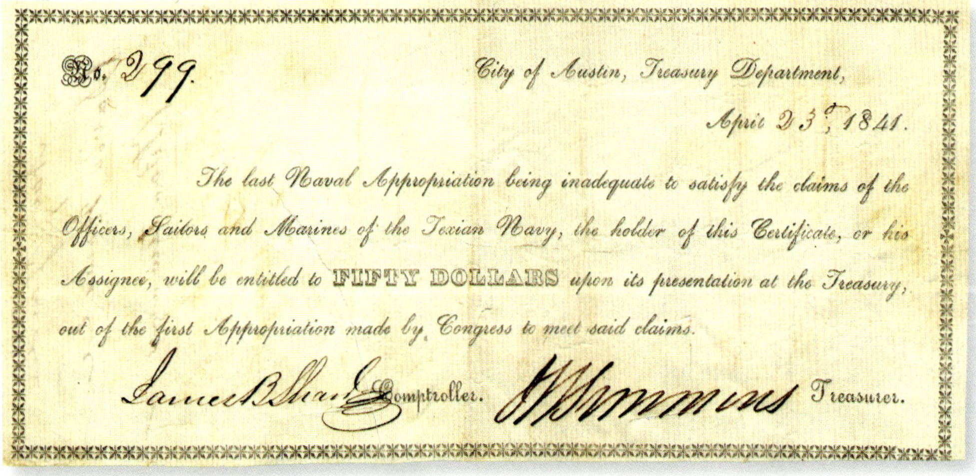
No. 299 City of Austin, Treasury Department,
April 23, 1841.
The last Naval Appropriation being inadequate to satisfy the claims of the Officers, Sailors and Marines of the Texian Navy, the holder of this Certificate, or his Assignee, will be entitled to FIFTY DOLLARS upon its presentation at the Treasury, out of the first Appropriation made by Congress to meet said claims.
Comptroller. Treasurer.

Fig 11.20, Austin, $50 Texian Navy Certificate, No. 299.
Private Collection, Cr. AW4, O-828.

April 23, 1841. This payment was to a Charles Lewis, a Quarter Master in the Navy Yard at Galveston. Two razor cut cancellations above "TWENTY FIVE DOLLARS" and again through Comptroller James B. Shaw's signature indicates that Lewis eventually received the payment after the funds were finally appropriated in July 1842.

The $50 Naval Payment Certificate shown in Figure 11.20 was paid to David Howell, a Boatswain then stationed at the Navy Yard in Galveston. Like the previous specimen, razor cut cancellations appear above the word "DOLLARS" and again through the signatures of James B. Shaw and J.W. Simmons, indicating that Howell eventually collected the payment.

Upon payment to each sailor, the reverse of the certificate was endorsed with each sailor's station, name, and duty. This written account leaves researchers a record of the sailors who received payment, where they received their compensation, and the location of their station. Since many of the reverses are distinctly uniform, it is quite possible that Mason or one of the pursers signed some of the endorsements for the seamen. For both the collector and the historian, it is the endorsements on the reverse of each Naval Payment Certificate which give an interesting glimpse into the daily duties of the officers, sailors, and marines of the Texian Navy. While these certificates were dated at the Treasury Department in Austin, the endorsements on each reverse list the place of issue such as the "Navy Yard" at Galveston or the flagship "Austin" which was in the port of Galveston at the time the certificates were distributed.

While quite ordinary and uniform on the faces, the certificate's reverses appear to be representative only of those sailors stationed in the Navy Yard at Galveston or on board the *Austin*. Since all of the certificates bear a date of April 23, 1841, it appears that the entire naval payroll was dispersed in this newly printed scrip. One of the mysteries regarding this issue is why the *Austin* was the predominant ship of issue for the certificates. It is not possible to state with certainty which ship each sailor served on for the pay period covered by the certificates. For example, the rolls of the *Austin* and the *Zavala,* both dated March 1841, show an almost identical ship's complement. A spot check of where each sailor was stationed at the time of the payroll does provide definitive evidence that the payroll covered sailors stationed on multiple ships, even though most examples show only the Navy Yard and the *Austin* as the place of payment. Pay certificates from the *Steam Ship Zavala* are also known.

The eastern tip of the cigar shaped island of Galveston is shown with the "Navy Yard" located on the inland shore, approximately two thirds down the early sketch shown in Figure 11.21. A marking can be seen in the water directly across showing the area for anchoring of war vessels. Further up the map, there is a notation marking the "Customs House," depicting the approximate location of where the Burnet government set up their temporary capitol in 1836 to avoid capture by Santa Anna's army during the War for Texas Independence.

The naval pay certificate shown in Figure 11.22 was paid to David Howell, a boatswain as well as a naval petty officer. The boatswain took the primary responsibility for the ship's sails and rigging.[34] When a new ship was commissioned, it was the boatswain's duty to see that all stores committed to his charge were on-board as expeditiously as possible and to minutely inspect every fitted rigging before the ship set sail.[35] It was also the boatswain who traditionally administered on board corporal punishment with the cat-o-nine-tails when ordered to do so by the captain.

Alex Collins was stationed at the Navy Yard at the time the certificate in Figure 11.23 was issued. He had previously served on the *Colorado, Wharton,* and the *San Jacinto.*[36] As a gunner, Collins duties went far beyond the loading, aiming, firing, and maintaining the ship's cannon during a battle.[37] The gunner was charged with maintaining the state of the powder magazine, seeing that the powder stayed perfectly dry, and that the supplies were supervised at all times. When gunpowder was loaded on the ship, the gunner had to check that the fire in the galley had been extinguished, that no candles were lighted, and that no man on board was smoking tobacco until the powder was properly stored, the room secured, and the keys to the magazine delivered to the captain or the designated officer.

Charles Lewis worked onshore at the Navy Yard in Galveston at the time the payment shown in Figure 11.24 was issued. As the quartermaster, Lewis distributed rations of goods, clothing, and supplies to the ships. Shortly after Lewis' pay certificate was issued, he was transferred to the brig *Wharton* in June 1841.[38]

Fig 11.21, Plot of Galveston and the harbor showing the Navy Yard around 1836.

Texas State Library and Archives Commission, Austin, Texas.

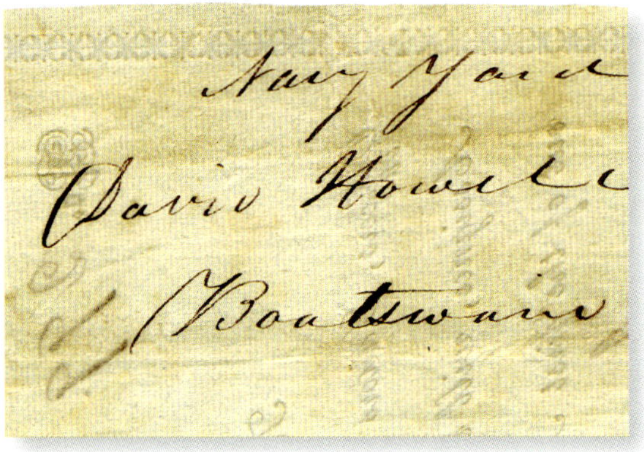

Fig 11.22, Navy Yard, No. 299, $50 (reverse), David Howell, Boatswain.

Private Collection.

Fig 11.23, Navy Yard, No. 556, $25 (reverse), Alex Collins, Gunner.

Private Collection.

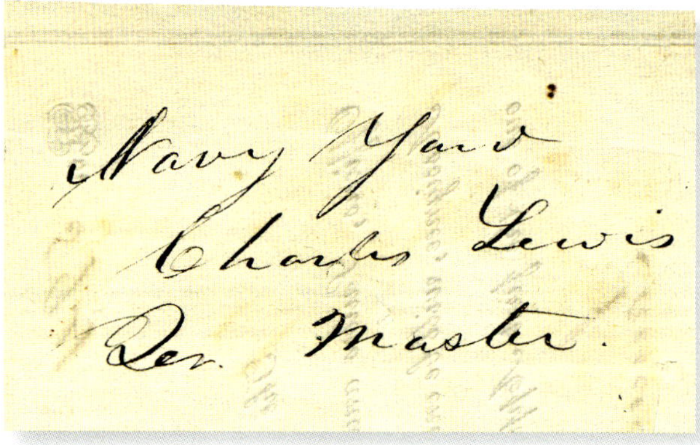

Fig 11.24, Navy Yard, No. 594, $25 (reverse), Charles Lewis, Quarter Master.

Private Collection.

Fig 11.25, Commodore Edwin W. Moore.

Naval Historical Center, Washington, D.C.

Fig 11.26, Texas Sloop-of-War *Austin*.

"Texas Warships," Painting by Fred Toler, Courtesy of the San Jacinto Museum of History, Houston, Texas.

The *Austin*, pictured in Figure 11.26, was the flagship of the second Texas Navy under the Lamar administration. The ship was built in Baltimore and named for Stephen F. Austin, the Father of Texas. The ship was 125 feet in length, displaced 600 tons, and had a thirty-one-foot beam and a twelve-foot-six-inch draft. Commissioned in January 1840, the *Austin* was the fastest ship in the Gulf of Mexico and mounted sixteen 24-pound cannon, two 18-pound cannon, and two 18-pound long range guns. At full staffing (ever difficult for the bankrupt Texian Navy) the ship carried a crew of twenty-three officers and 151 seamen.[39]

It was the *Austin*, accompanied only by the schooner *Wharton*, that broke the Mexican blockade of the Yucatan in May 1843. This attack infuriated President Sam Houston, who considered Commodore E.W. Moore insubordinate for taking action against the blockade without formal authorization. While Moore's actions infuriated the President, they also caused a significant interruption in the plans of the Mexican Navy, keeping them tied up on the Yucatan peninsula rather than allowing them to divert northward and initiate a planned blockade of the Texas coast.[40]

Fig 11.27, Steam Ship *Zavala*.

"Relief on station," Detail from a painting by Fred Toler, Courtesy of the San Jacinto Museum of History, Houston, Texas.

Named for Lorenzo de Zavala, the first Vice President of the Republic, the eight-gun steamer represented in Figure 11.27 was commissioned in the Texas Navy on March 23, 1839. The ship saw numerous actions in the Gulf of Mexico and it blockaded several Mexican ports.[41] For a time, the *Zavala* was considered the most advanced warship in the Western Hemisphere. Along with the *Austin* and the *San Bernard*, the *Zavala* took part in the capture of San Juan Bautista (now known as Villahermosa) in the state of Tabasco, Mexico. Afterwards, the *Zavala*, while patrolling the gulf near the mouth of the Tabasco River, was caught in a violent tropical storm.[42] The crew made a gallant effort to keep the boilers alive while trying to avoid the shallows which would smash the ship to pieces. The *Zavala* miraculously survived the three-day ordeal, but with seasick sailors and a stripped-down ship, it was not able to return to Galveston until February 1841.

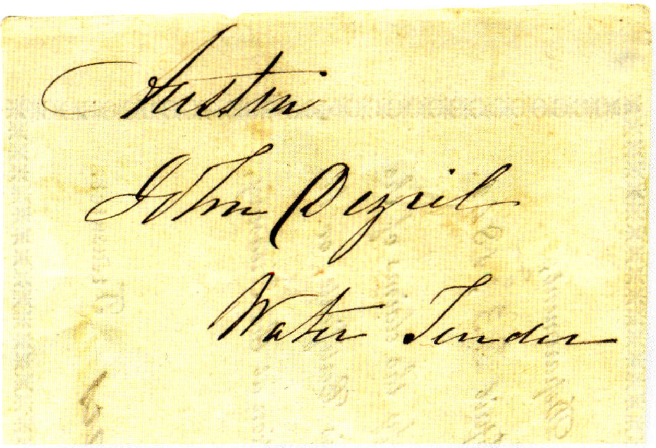
Austin
John Deziel
Water Tender

Fig 11.28, Austin, No. 482, $50 (reverse), John Deziel, Water Tender.

Private Collection.

John Deziel's service record indicates that he was stationed on the steamer *Zavala* for a two-year period except for a brief time in the spring of 1841 when he was aboard the *Austin*.[43] During his time on the *Austin*, Deziel received the pay certificate in Figure 11.28. Deziel's responsibility was that of a water tender, the most critical of tasks in order to sustain life aboard wooden warships on the high seas. His duties included gathering, sanitizing, and storing fresh drinking water and other provisions.

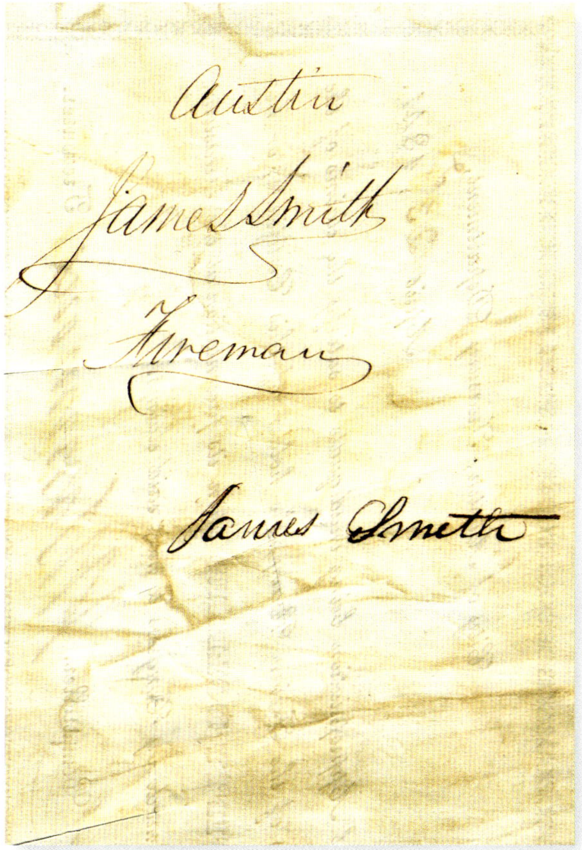
Austin
James Smith
Fireman
James Smith

Fig 11.29, Austin, No. 522, $50 (reverse), James Smith, Fireman.

Private Collection.

As a fireman stationed on the *Zavala*, James Smith, recipient of the pay certificate in Figure 11.29, was responsible for loading the coal in the hot furnaces aboard the steam-powered warship. Smith was stationed aboard the *Zavala* in October 1840 when the ship was caught in the violent storm off the mouth of the Tabasco River in Mexico.[44] After running out of coal, Smith and the rest of the crew burned the mast, doors, furniture, and even the saloon counter to keep the steam engines alive.[45] The *Zavala* was badly damaged, but managed to survive as the crew burned almost everything except the wooden hull in order to generate steam and make headway against the rolling seas during the storm.

Henry Lockwood was listed as a seaman on the *Zavala* in March 1841. At the time of the payment

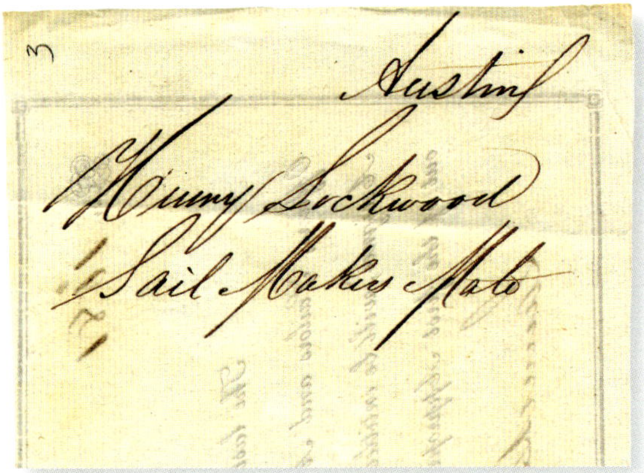

Fig 11.30, Austin, No. 1081 $25 (reverse), Henry Lockwood, Sail Maker's Mate.

Private Collection.

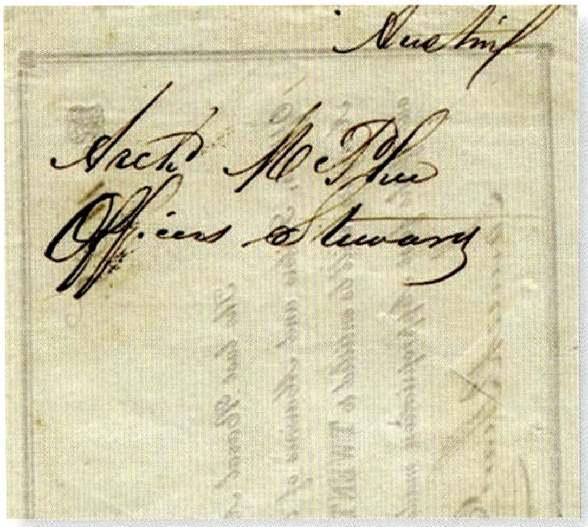

Fig 11.31, Austin, No. 1138 $25, Arch McPhee, Officers Steward (reverse).

DRT Library Collection, San Antonio, Texas.

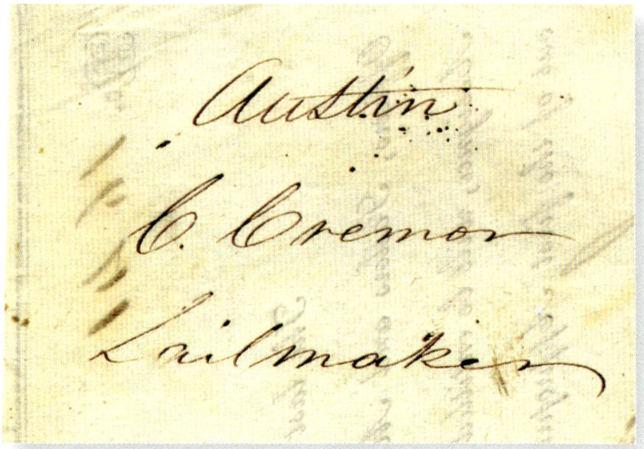

Fig 11.32, Austin, No. 1641 $25 (reverse), C. Cremons, Sail Maker.

Private Collection.

in Figure 11.30, Lockwood, a sail maker's mate, would have assisted in the care and maintenance of the sailing rigs. He frequently inspected the condition of the sails in the sail rooms by checking for damage by water leak or vermin. If conditions were not satisfactory, Lockwood reported the situation to the boatswain, who in turn ordered the sails taken to the deck and dried. As his title implies, Lockwood also assisted the sail maker in his daily tasks.[46] Lockwood learned his craft quickly as the muster roll subsequently lists his position as a sailmaker on the *Austin* and later as a sailmaster on the *Zavala* in 1841.[47]

As an officer's steward, Arch McPhee brings to mind the image of a polished waiter or maitre'd serving dinner and pouring wine to the captain and senior officers of the ship. McPhee's poise and good manners were on display as the senior brass of the *Zavala* gathered for important military or navigational conversations over a meal. Aside from his cabin and dinner duties, the steward was appointed by the purser to distribute provisions for the officers and the crew. It was an important position that required a mate and several assistants. McPhee, the recipient of the pay certificate in Figure 11.31, held the position of officer's steward on the *Zavala* in 1840-1841 and served under Commander John Lothrop.[48]

It was Cornelius Cremons' duty to carefully examine the ship's sails and inform the boatswain of any defects or mistakes in their dimensions. He also checked that the sails were perfectly dry when stored in the sail room. If any part of the sails were damp, Cremons took the first opportunity to dry them.[49] Cremons, the payee of the certificate in Figure 11.32, held several positions in his four-year career with the Texian Navy, serving on the *Colorado* (later renamed the *Wharton),* the *Zavala,* and the *Austin*.[50]

Fig 11.33, Steam Ship Zavala, No 250, $50 (reverse), William Hardy, Qtr Gunner.

Private Collection.

As a quarter-gunner, William Hardy was under the direction of a gunner on the Texas warship *Zavala* and assisted him in every aspect of his duty. The number of quarter-gunners on any given ship was always in proportion to the number of artillery pieces, one quarter-gunner being allowed for every four cannon.[51] Naval Pay Certificates from the *Zavala* are very rare.

Commodore E.W. Moore used the mighty sloop-of-war *Austin* as a floating pay station, distributing the pay certificates from the flagship as other vessels came into port. But instead of being paid in specie, pay warrants, or even redbacks, sailors were handed a bundle of IOU's. The outrage among the ranks was both widespread and immediate. Many of the men had gone several months without pay and harbored doubts about when, or if, they would receive their pay. Letters were sent to the Treasury Secretary from Galveston expressing the concerns of the men about the validity of the Naval Payment Certificates. One letter, sent to the capital at Austin on May 25, demanded to know if the certificates would be paid at all if presented at the Treasury office. Many wondered whether or not a subsequent appropriation of funds was to be made for the Navy.[52] Secretary Chalmers was asked to render an immediate opinion as to "the precise manner in which this scrip is regarded by the Executive and his cabinet." Requesting an immediate response, the ships pursers attempted to extract an endorsement of the pay certificate's validity from no less than President Lamar himself. Lamar was seen by the men as the Navy's staunchest ally and his opinion was sought in an effort to set the men at ease regarding their pay and to prevent an even greater depreciation of the funds.

For the collector, these issues are among the most easily acquired of the military pay certificates because they were issued in large quantities. These naval pay certificates also offer the unique perspective of searching for specific names and stations of early heroes of the Texian Navy. The pieces offer an affordable yet fascinating glimpse into this period of Texas naval history. Like many claimants owed money by the Republic of Texas, it literally took an act of Congress for them to get paid. While there was an act of Congress on January 25, 1842, authorizing and requiring the Secretary of War and Navy to issue certificates for bounty land to the officers, seaman and marines of the Texas Navy, the money was not appropriated to redeem the naval pay certificates until July of that same year.[53]

THE FRENCH LOAN AND THE AUSTIN PIGS

For all the shortcomings of the financial affairs of the Republic, Treasury Secretary James H. Starr had every reason to believe that additional funds were forthcoming to meet the payroll of the Texas Navy and other critical items. The courting of the French minister regarding the proposed loan looked like it was about to pay off.

Besides the obvious trade connections with Texas, the French government had a long-standing hatred of Mexico, and France became the first European power to recognize the Republic of Texas as an independent nation. A Franco-Texian bill was introduced to the Texas Congress on De Saligny's behalf on January 12, 1841, for the purpose of bringing some 8,000 families into Texas in return for a grant of approximately three million acres of land.[54] In addition to the establishment of twenty forts in the region, the proposed bill would exempt the French settlers from all tariffs and taxes for a period of twenty years. In return, de Saligny continued to lobby his government to extend a sizable loan to Texas. Several Texas leaders considered the French diplomat the best hope for an infusion of funds from France.

James Hamilton, the Texas Minister to France, became the bearer of good news when the *Austin City Gazette* reported in April 1841 that Hamilton had negotiated a contract for a sizeable loan between Texas and the French bankers J. Lafite & Co.[55] On May 18, 1841, Hamilton confirmed the completion of the loan contract in a letter to President Lamar.[56] As news began to spread, the market makers for Texian securities in New Orleans and New York were ecstatic about the development. The *New Orleans Bulletin* reported, "The news of the negotiation of a loan for Texas has a most beneficial effect. Texan securities have experienced a sudden elevation (of value) in the market, and the process may be expected to go on until they reach a par quotation."

By May 19, 1841, the loan negotiations with France seemed settled. The *Austin City Gazette* reported that if the guarantee of the French Government were procured, the bonds in the amount of $7 million would be offered at ninety-five cents on the dollar. If the guarantee could not be procured, the bonds would be offered at fifty-five cents on the dollar. The Treasury Department received recommendations for allocation of the expected funds, and discussions were conducted regarding how to pay back the interest on the stock, setting up a sinking fund for the eventual retirement of other debt, and proposing a "dutch auction" to retire a portion of the outstanding redbacks and other promissory notes.[57] At the same time, James Hamilton, with the support of President Lamar, initiated another proposal to plan and administer a national bank for the Republic of Texas.

Lamar previously entertained the prospect of a national bank, and with the potential loan proceeds almost in hand, Hamilton and his contemporaries set their sights on organizing the national bank. The bank's goal was to hold, save, and distribute the Republic's funds into circulation as soon as they were realized.[58] It was not uncommon for banks of the time to loan funds many times in excess of their actual capital. Additionally, extra capital was routinely set aside for the generous salaries the principals of these banks. This planned use of the loan proceeds for even further leverage would certainly have added to the already ruinous destruction of the public credit accumulated in the six short years of the Republic.

In an effort to calm the public apprehension regarding the proposed loan from France, John C. Chalmers, appointed as Secretary of the Treasury in May 1841, released a public statement regarding the status of the loan on June 29, 1841. It read in part: "official communication has been received by the Executive of the positive sale of our bonds by our loan commissioner at Paris; the proceeds of which will, it is confidently expected, be realized in the city of New York in the course of the month of August next." On July 15, 1841, the details of the loan contract, essentially an entire summary of the prospectus, was reproduced and published by the *Austin City Gazette*.[59] In retrospect, the Treasury officials had every reason to believe that the loan would be forthcoming. As the old saying goes, however, they were "counting their chickens before they hatched." In the summer of 1841, the debt of the Republic of Texas was about to be doubled and the financial impact of spending more than three dollars for every dollar brought in would undoubtedly continue. However, the French loan, like the proverbial chickens, would never hatch. The fate of the $7 million loan was not sealed by bankers in New York, Paris, or New Orleans, but instead by a band of marauding Texas pigs in Austin.

Fig 11.34, Alphonse Dubois de Saligny.
Center for American History, University of Texas at Austin, Austin, Texas, CN Number 01265.

Alphonse Dubois de Saligny, the powerful French Charge d'affaires, was a neighbor of Richard Bullock, who maintained a boarding house on the corner of Congress Avenue and Pecan (Sixth) street. Known as the Bullock Hotel, the establishment was the social epicenter at the time, as well as the primary place of entertainment for high-level government officials. Following an extended stay at the Bullock Hotel before his official residence was completed, there was a dispute between de Saligny and Bullock over the Frenchman's hotel bill, which had remained unpaid by the diplomat. It was common in those days for hotels to keep a pen of livestock so that fresh meat would be available for large parties or special occasions, and Bullock kept a large number of pigs on the premises for those purposes. One night in 1841, the pigs escaped and found their way to the neighboring stables of Dubois de Saligny. The pigs then proceeded into de Saligny's house, penetrating into his very bedroom! The pigs devoured the linen on his bed and chewed his official papers. Count de Saligny's servant arrived on scene and killed some of the pigs. To make matters worse, the servant also was the French Ambassador's personal chef, and he reportedly butchered one of Bullock's stray pigs for the official dining room. The resulting political and emotional backlash from a seemingly innocuous incident had profound and lasting financial repercussions on the finances of the Republic of Texas.

Upon hearing the report of the intrusion and slaughter of his pigs, Bullock confronted de Saligny's servant and whipped him senseless. One New Orleans newspaper reported that Bullock had fallen upon the "unlucky murderer" of the pigs, "bunging up his eyes and phlebotomizing his nose in a manner to appease the ghosts of the slaughtered innocents."[60] Bullock even threatened the diplomat himself with a thorough

Fig 11.36, Pigs at the trough.
The French Charge de'affairs was incensed by the actions of Richard Bullock's stray pigs which invaded his temporary quarters in Austin. Undated photo, Author's Collection.

beating. Dubois de Saligny filed a complaint with the district attorney and insisted that Bullock be punished. Secretary of State James Mayfield insisted that the innkeeper could not be punished without the due process of law. Although Bullock's pigs were clearly the aggressors, Bullock had many powerful allies in the government. He played host to top government officials at his boarding house and counted many of these men among his closest friends. These officials strongly defended his personal reputation against the allegations made by the French Charge d'Affairs.

Fig 11.37, Razorback Pig.
A band of Austin pigs similar to this razorback would lead to the undoing of the French loan to Texas. Author's Collection.

It was on this occasion that all of Texas, including the Houstonites, stood by Bullock and his pigs, not anticipating the dramatic fallout on the loan approval from the pig incident and the offending effect it would have on the French Ambassador in Austin. Dubois de Saligny exploited the undignified incident to vent his frustrations with the Lamar administration. When Bullock was finally arrested for the assault, Treasury Secretary John Chalmers naively posted bail for the innkeeper. Chalmers seemed oblivious to the relationship between the pig incident, Dubois de Saligny, the loan funding, and pending Texian bond placement with the French. Dubois de Saligny was incensed at the perceived alliance between Bullock, the pigs who had trashed his home, and the officials in the Treasury Department. Acting without instructions from his government, de Saligny broke off diplomatic relations with Texas and left the country. Upon arriving in New Orleans, de Saligny consulted with his brother-in-law regarding his treatment at the hands of the Texas government officials. Dubois de Saligny and his brother-in-law, who was the Finance Minister of France, officially terminated the $7 million French loan to Texas. Unofficially, everyone realized that it was actually Bullock's pigs that had killed the French loan to Texas. This diplomatic rift between Alphonse Dubois de Saligny and the Lamar administration later became known as the "Pig War."

THE SANTA FE EXPEDITION

One of Lamar's goals as President of the Republic was to expand westward, and the settlement of the frontier was largely successful, though at great expense of the Indians. The city of Austin became a booming frontier community, but the President felt that Texas should reach even further west to validate its boundary claims. With the presidential election of 1841 on the horizon, Lamar tried to boost the chances for his political party by sending a goodwill expedition northwest. He hoped to plant the Lone Star flag in Santa Fe, New Mexico, claiming the town for Texas and thereby incorporating its wealth into the government treasury.

Texas had long claimed all of the territory to the east of the Rio Grande River. Santa Fe, about twelve miles east of the river, was claimed by both the Republic and Mexico. One of the motivations for the expedition was to bring Santa Fe under Texas control, securing the rich supply of silver for the Republic's needs. At the time, Santa Fe was a major export center for gold, silver, and mountain furs with extensive trading connections to St. Louis and Matamoros.[61] If the people of Santa Fe embraced the expedition and acquiesced to the Texas government, the loose claims Texas held on Santa Fe would be materially strengthened. In time, Texas would benefit financially by opening up a new trade route from Santa Fe through Austin and then on to Galveston.

The Santa Fe Expedition proved controversial from the start. President Lamar failed to secure an appropriation to fund the venture from Congress. The Treasury was virtually empty, and invoices had piled up for maintaining the Navy and paying naval personnel. In order to fund the planned Santa Fe Expedition, Lamar circumvented Congress and ordered the Treasury Department to make a $1,000 payment to Rawdon, Wright, Hatch & Edson to print and ship another $500,000 of new redback notes to Galveston in May 1841.[62] The notes were then forwarded to Austin where the blanks were dated, signed and used to outfit the Santa Fe Expedition. As soon as the freshly printed money arrived, new uniforms for the troops were procured. Horses were bought for as much as $1,000 apiece with the depreciated money.[63] When, in turn, these merchants passed the notes to others in payment, the downward spiral of depreciation continued.

Although the journey to Santa Fe began as a mission of good will, the widely publicized expedition ended as a financial, political, and diplomatic disaster. The military command was led by the inept twenty-six-year-old Hugh McLeod. McLeod had previously pleaded with the government for back pay regarding his service in the Army. He discussed the matter with John Chalmers, but the request had been rebuffed. McLeod then appealed directly to President Lamar stating, "I owe money here, & there is at least a possibility of my being killed in this Campaign- I am entitled to pay already, enough to settle my debts- and I therefore asked for enough to do it- I did not think it unreasonable, or I would have not asked for it- If it is not granted, I shall feel myself much lowered in my estimation-leaving creditors who are dunning me, unpaid."[64] Like the others, McLeod received his appropriation in depreciated redbacks.

A column of 275 soldiers and forty-six teamsters and traders departed from Austin in mid-June 1841 with twenty-one wagons filled with supplies and merchandise.[65] Many thought the expedition large and strong enough to handle any military or Indian situation encountered along the way. The campaign was ill planned and poorly executed, however, and with no experienced guides leading the way the caravan of wagons mistook the Wichita River for the Red River, turning the expedition hundreds of miles off course over difficult rocky terrain in the sweltering summer heat.

When an advance party finally entered New Mexico in September 1841, instead of being greeted by the friendly citizens of New Mexico they were greeted by armed Mexican troops. Confronted by the superior Mexican force, and low on food and water, the advance party surrendered without firing a shot on September 12, 1841. Five days later, the inexperienced McLeod surrendered the remainder of his men to a Mexican garrison. The Mexican commander falsely assured McLeod that the Texans would be returned home with adequate provisions. Once the volunteers surrendered, though, they were stripped of their weapons and horses. The Texian prisoners were marched more than 1,000 miles to Mexico City. Many of the men died on the long, hard, dusty march, and the survivors were forced into hard labor. Among the prisoners were such notables as William G. Cooke, Thomas R. Lubbock, and the editor of the New Orleans *Picayune* who had accompanied the expedition to cover the story.[66] The Texians were not heard from again until several months after the presidential election and the close of Lamar's term in office which ended in December 1841.

TREASURY WARRANTS – THE DECLINING ECONOMY

By the second half of 1841, the $500,000 in newly issued redbacks flooded the market. With no prospects of a foreign loan on the horizon, the value of the Texas paper money once again spiraled out of control. Texan securities again plummeted in New Orleans and elsewhere when it became obvious that the interest on the stock could not be paid in specie. By December 9, 1841, government issues were only being accepted for taxes at a rate of 14.28 cents, and claims against the Republic were paid out at seven for one.[67] This forced the Treasury Department to take the unusual step of refusing to honor their own drafts for the payment of taxes. In the waning days of the Lamar administration, the Treasury had run up such huge deficits that even the pay of top government officials was in question.

The rarely seen un-issued example in Figure 11.38 is complete with the pay stub at left, where the warrant number, amount and appropriation number were recorded. The auditor or comptroller would cut the stub portion from the main body upon payment and retain them for Treasury records.

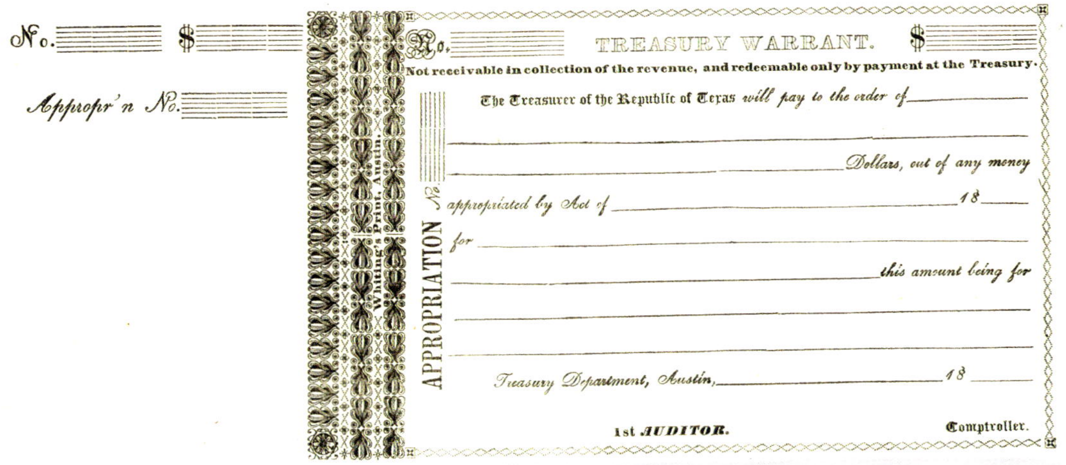
No. $
Appropr'n No.
No. TREASURY WARRANT. $
Not receivable in collection of the revenue, and redeemable only by payment at the Treasury.
The Treasurer of the Republic of Texas will pay to the order of
Dollars, out of any money
appropriated by Act of 18
for
this amount being for
Treasury Department, Austin, 18
1st AUDITOR. Comptroller.
APPROPRIATION No.
Whiting's Print, Austin.

Fig 11.38, Austin, Treasury Warrant, Unissued Blank.
Private Collection, Cr. AW8A, O-865.

A new issue of Treasury warrants from Austin carried the disclaimer line "Not receivable in collection of the Revenue, and redeemable only by Payment at the Treasury." Almost every Treasury warrant during this period referenced the specific congressional appropriation which allocated the funds. In at least one instance, however, a payment was issued without a congressional appropriation, although the piece was written on standard paper designed exactly for that purpose.

The crisp, uncirculated Austin warrant shown in Figure 11.39 is unusual in that the payment referenced was appropriated by "Order of Executive," rather than by an act of Congress (which was lined out). The payment was made to John Pleasants for "Supplies furnished Spies in 1841," the final year of Lamar's Presidency.

John Pleasants joined a company of volunteers led by Capt. William M. Logan on April 16, 1836, and fought at the battle of San Jacinto less than a week later.[68] His name also appears on the "Receipt List for Division of Spoils," dated May 10, 1836, following the battle. Although Pleasants later received a headright certificate for 640 acres of land for his service in the Army, there is little information about any role which he might have held later. It is important for the modern reader to realize that "spies" was also another word for "scouts" which were used in the military. While the "spies" referenced in the certificate may have actually been snooping on the Mexicans or perhaps the French, it is also likely that the men were merely scouts hired for their knowledge of the western landscape. The warrant was signed on December 13, 1841, marking President Mirabeau B. Lamar's last day in office. I will leave this analysis of who was spying on whom and for what reason to the imagination of the reader.

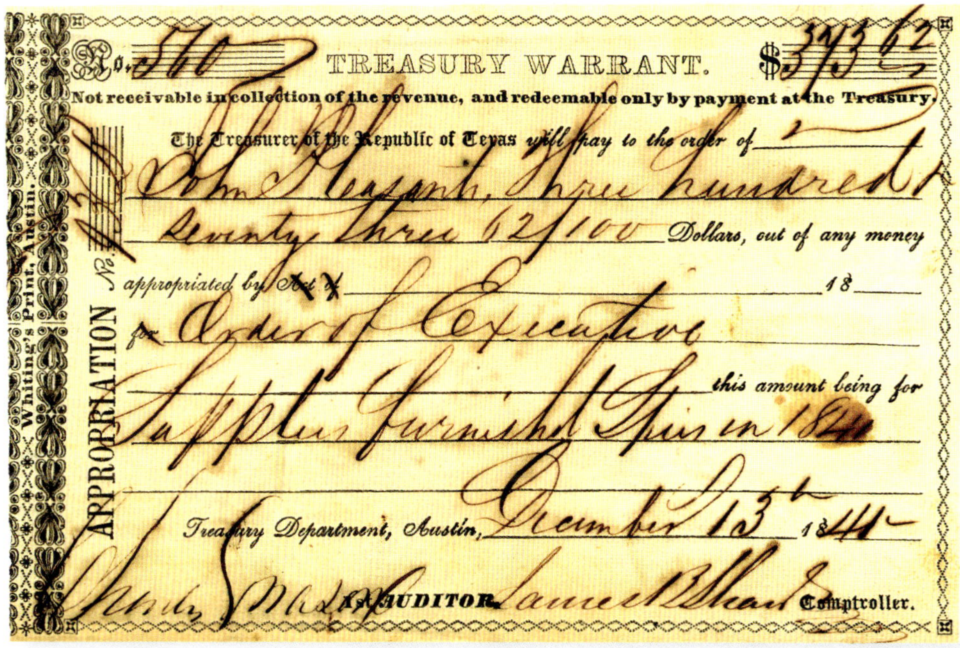
No. 560 TREASURY WARRANT. $373 62/100
Not receivable in collection of the revenue, and redeemable only by payment at the Treasury.
The Treasurer of the Republic of Texas will pay to the order of
John Pleasants, Three hundred &
Seventy three 62/100 Dollars, out of any money
appropriated by Act of 18
for Order of Executive
this amount being for
Supplies furnished Spies in 1841
Treasury Department, Austin, December 13th 1841
Chas. Mason 1st AUDITOR. James B. Shaw Comptroller.
APPROPRIATION No.
Whiting's Print, Austin.

Fig 11.39, Austin, Treasury Warrant, December 13, 1841, John Pleasants, for "Supplies furnished Spies in 1841."
Private Collection, Cr. AW8A, O-863.

No. 560 TREASURY WARRANT $373.62 Not receivable in collection of the revenue, and redeemable only by payment at the Treasury. The Treasurer of the Republic of Texas will pay to the order of John Pleasants, Three hundred & seventy three 62/100 Dollars, out of any money appropriated by 18__ Order of Executive This amount being for Supplies furnished Spies in 1841. Treasury Department, Austin, December 13th, 1841

(Signed) Charles Mason, Auditor James B. Shaw, Comptroller

No. 4029 TREASURY WARRANT. $208 33

Not receivable in collection of the Revenue, and redeemable only by Payment at the Treasury.

The Treasurer of the Republic of Texas will pay to the order of J.B. Ransom Two hundred & eight 33/100 Dollars, out of any money appropriated by Act of Feby 5 1841 for Saly of Presidents Private Secty this amount being for Service as Presidents Private Secty

Treasury Department, Austin, Decemb 16th 1841

Charles Mason 1st AUDITOR. James B. Shaw Comptroller.

APPROPRIATION No.

No. 4029 TREASURY WARRANT $208.33 Not receivable in collection of the revenue, and redeemable only by payment at the Treasury. The Treasurer of the Republic of Texas will pay to the order of J.B. Ransom, Two hundred & eight 33/100 Dollars, out of any money appropriated by act of Feb[ruar]y 5th, 1841 for Sal[ar]y of President's Private Sec[re]t[ar]y. this amount being for Service as President's Private Sec[re]t[ar]y. Treasury Department, Austin, December 16th, 1841

(Signed) Charles Mason, 1st Auditor James B. Shaw, Comptroller

Fig 11.40, Austin, Treasury Warrant, December 16, 1841, J.B. Ransom for Salary of President's Private Secretary.
Private Collection, Cr. AW5 (AW5-1), 0-857.

The payment for $208.33 shown in Figure 11.40 was issued to J.B. Ransom out of any money appropriated by the Act of February 5, 1841. The finances of the Republic became so unpredictable that even Lamar's private secretary could not endorse his own salary back to the Government for his taxes. James Burchett Ransom first appeared in Texas in early 1839, and served as the private secretary to President Lamar from February to November 1839. He later became a reporter to the Texas Senate until February 5, 1840. After his stint as a senate reporter he served as the quartermaster to troops in northeastern Texas, and in 1841 was sent by Lamar to East Texas to recruit volunteers for the Santa Fe Expedition.

Aside from his time as a government official, Ransom became an established writer who penned a novel, published several poems, and other period writings regarding Texas and the settlement of the frontier. Known as a writer of merit and elegance, Ransom's literary productions were much admired, and his pieces "Sunset at Austin" and "Ode to San Jacinto" were printed in the *Austin City Gazette* on May 27, 1840. Someone once described Ransom as "a little erratic, but a man of genius and observation and a pleasing and sprightly writer." The payment to Ransom shown in Figure 11.40 was issued for two-months service during Lamar's administration. Ransom was accidentally killed by his own gun on March 3, 1843, as he was crossing a creek on a buffalo hunt near the Waco Village. The warrant to Ransom is boldly marked "Paid" across the face, indicating that he eventually collected on the warrant.[69]

Despite their non-negotiability for tax payments, even a complaint to the Attorney General would have fallen on deaf ears. The warrant in Figure 11.41 for $397.98 to F.A. Morris for "Salary of Attorney General" was appropriated out of the Act of February 5, 1841. Morris could only receive his salary in Treasury Bonds or stock in the Consolidated Fund, as paper money was no longer being issued. Note that this payment is "not receivable in collection of the revenue." Francis A. Morris served as the Attorney General of the Republic of Texas under President Lamar from May 10, 1841, until his resignation on December 13 of the same year. In 1842, Morris accepted a position as professor of languages at St. Charles College in St. Charles, Missouri, and entered the ministry of the Methodist Episcopal Church, where perhaps the clergy paid better than the government. The countermarking on the face indicates that the warrant was eventually "Paid." There is no official record, however, as to whether this type of treasury warrant was routinely accepted in the offering plates of churches within the Republic![70]

The treasury warrant in Figure 11.42 for $104.21 to E.L. Stickney for "Salary of (the) Commissioner of Revenue" was perhaps the most ironic payment ever issued under the Lamar administration. The above war-

No. 4046 TREASURY WARRANT $397.98 Not receivable in collection of the revenue, and redeemable only by payment at the Treasury. The Treasurer of the Republic of Texas will pay to the order of F.A. Morris Three hundred & ninety seven 98/100 Dollars, out of any money appropriated by act of Feb[ruar]y 5th, 1841 for Salary of Attorney Gen[era]l this amount being for Service as Attorney General to 13 December. Treasury Department, Austin, December 17th, 1841

(Signed) Charles Mason, Auditor James B. Shaw, Comptroller

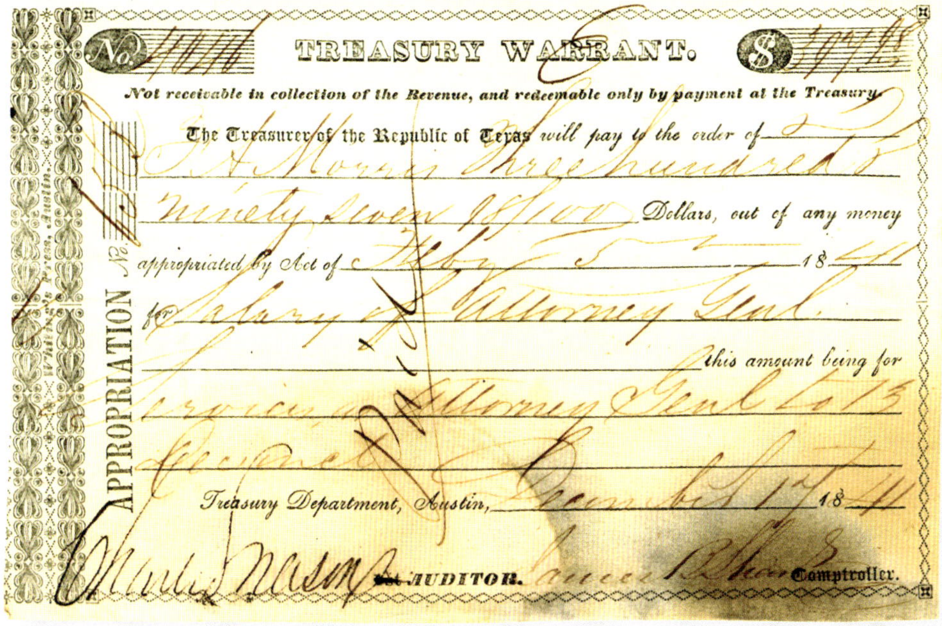

Fig 11.41, Austin, Treasury Warrant, December 17, 1841, F.A. Morris, for Salary of Attorney General.
Private Collection, Cr. AW5, O-851.

No. 4051 TREASURY WARRANT $104.21 Not receivable in collection of the revenue, and redeemable only by payment at the Treasury. The Treasurer of the Republic of Texas will pay to the order of E.L. Stickney, One hundred & four & 21/100 Dollars, out of any money appropriated by Act of Feb[uar]y 5th, 1841 for Salary of Comm[issioner] of Rev[enu]e this amount being for Services as Comm[issioner] of Rev[enu]e. Treasury Department, Austin, December 18th, 1841

(Signed) Charles Mason, Auditor James B. Shaw, Comptroller

Fig 11.42, Austin, Treasury Warrant, December 18, 1841, E.L. Stickney, for Salary of Commissioner of Revenue.
Private Collection, Cr. AW5, O-851.

rant indicates that even the Commissioner of Revenue for the Republic of Texas could not accept his own salary payment in the collection of taxes! This was an ever growing problem for Stickney and other top officials in the Treasury Department as they struggled to bring in hard currency for the critical tax and customs revenue when their own government issued obligations that were no longer accepted. Similar to the treasury warrants of his counterparts, this one too was eventually marked "Paid."

Although E.L. Stickney was the chief tax collector for the government, he was also a staunch supporter of the liberal arts in Austin, presiding over a group known as the Austin Lyceum. The organization's purpose was the cultivation of the minds of young men through a "debating club" and the planning for the private funding of a library and a museum.[71] The lyceums debated popular subjects such as "Ought the Texian government to have put Santa Anna to death in 1836?" and "Which is the stronger passion, love or hatred? "[72] Stickney's ser-

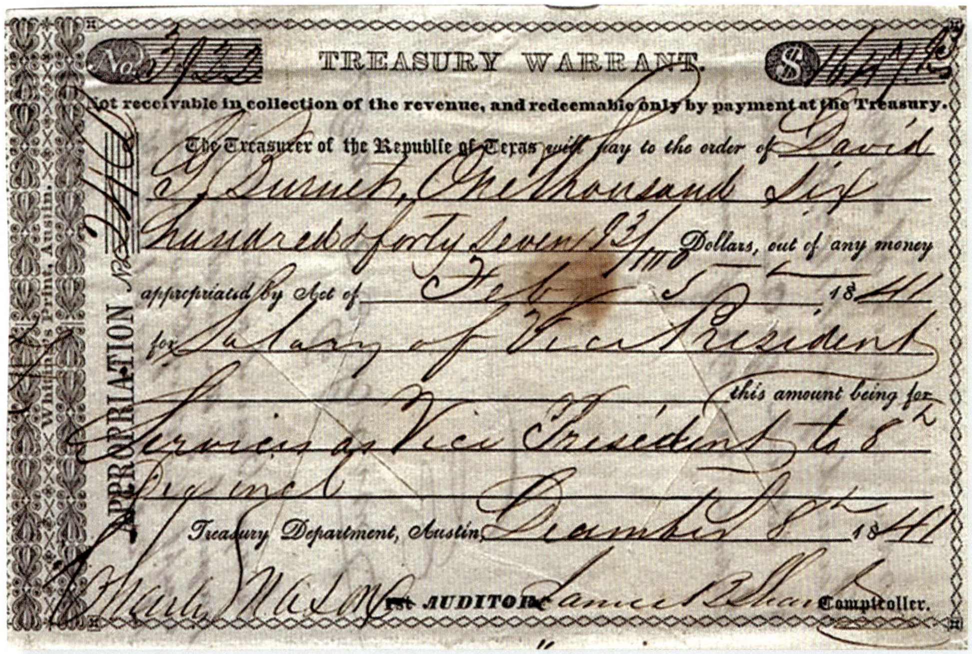

Fig 11.43, Austin, Treasury Warrant, December 8, 1841, David G. Burnet for Salary as Vice President.

John N. Rowe III Collection of Texas Currency, DeGolyer Library, Southern Methodist University, Dallas, Texas, Cr. AW5, 0-851.

No. 3922 TREASURY WARRANT $1647.93 Not receivable in collection of the revenue, and redeemable only by payment at the Treasury. The Treasurer of the Republic of Texas will pay to the order of David G. Burnet, One Thousand Six hundred & fourty [sic] seven 93/100 Dollars, out of any money appropriated by act of Feb[ruar]y 5th, 1841 for Salary of Vice President this amount being for Services as Vice President to 8th Dec[ember] incl[uded]

Treasury Department, Austin, December 8th, 1841

(Signed) Charles Mason, Auditor James B. Shaw, Comptroller

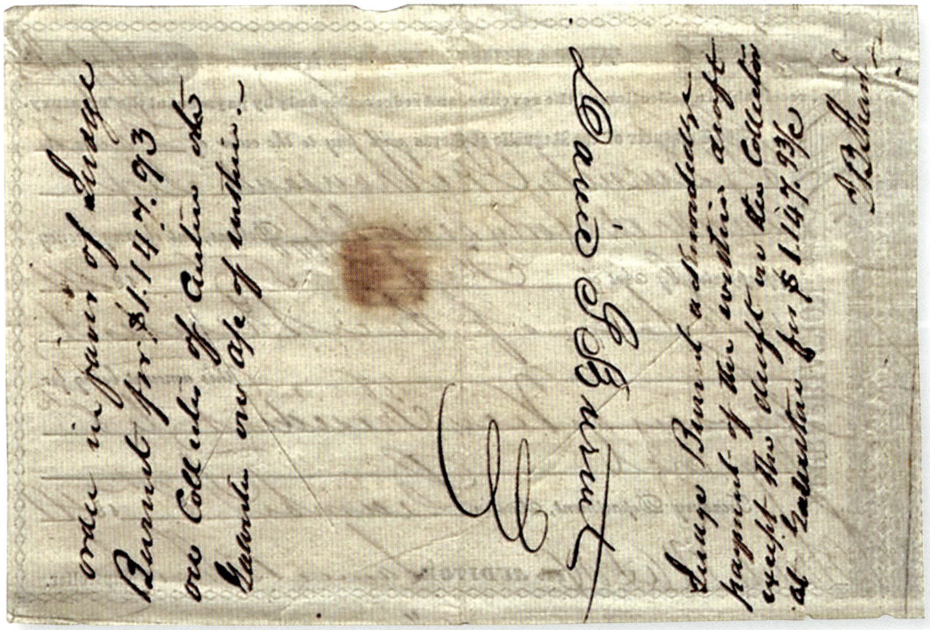

vice as the Commissioner of Revenue under President Lamar continued into Sam Houston's second term.[73]

The treasury warrants in figures 11.40, 11.41 and 11.42 payable to Ransom, Morris, and Stickney are distinctive from other Austin issues. Each of them bear a large purplish stain in the lower right-hand corner of the note as if a cup of coffee or red wine had been set upon a blank stack of the warrants and dripped onto the blank paper. These warrants were completed on the disfigured paper before they were dated and signed. They show no sign of smeared ink on the date or signature. The three issues were acquired from three different collections, indicating that all of them were stained before they were completed and signed by Mason and Shaw.

The President's personal secretary, the Attorney General, and the Commissioner of Revenue could not use their warrants to pay their own taxes. At least one exception was made, however, for a high-ranking government official in regards to his taxes. The exception was for David G. Burnet. He had previously made his own arrangements with the Treasury Department, keeping silent about the agreement to the other cabinet officials.

During his service as ad interim President of the Republic of Texas, David G. Burnet angered Sam Houston, the army, the vice president, many cabinet members, as well as the general public.[74] He particularly alienated the original investors of the Texian loans which were negotiated in New Orleans. A former judge of the Brazos District Court and a lawyer by profession, Burnet was forced to turn to farming for subsistence after the war. In 1838, he was elected Vice President, and the warrant in Figure 11.43 was issued in Burnet's last days as the Vice President under Lamar. The endorsement on the reverse reads as follows:

"order in favor of Judge Burnet for $1147.93 (ou)? collectors of Austin and Galveston on a/c[count] of within." "Judge Burnet authorized payment of the within draft except the draft on the collector at Galveston for $1,147.93. J.B. Shaw" David G Burnet.

Fig 11.44, Austin, Treasury Warrant, December 8, 1841 (Reverse).

John N. Rowe III Collection of Texas Currency, DeGolyer Library, Southern Methodist University, Dallas, Texas, Cr. AW5, 0-851.

Although the draft clearly states, "Not receivable in collection of the revenue" on its face, James B. Shaw, then serving as comptroller was, "authorized" to accept it in payment for taxes by the Vice President during his last days in office. This is a prime example of a high-ranking government official bending the rules for his own benefit. It is possible that Burnet received another draft for the $500 difference.

In the last few months of Lamar's Presidency, the great paper chase caused the Texas economy to spiral out of control. There was no longer any public market where money could be borrowed. The paper money system had run its course. The purchasing power of the currency had fallen to the point where even the government would no longer accept its own paper money for the payment of taxes. Payments to individuals had originally been made by issuing treasury warrants, but these were eventually redeemed by promissory notes bearing interest as Congress appropriated the money. The engraved notes bearing interest were replaced by another series of paper money which didn't pay interest. Neither issues were backed by gold or silver, however, and they continued to depreciate against the value of coin. When obligations which paid interest in other paper obligations fell in value, they were exchanged into the stock of the Consolidated Fund, which supposedly paid interest in gold and silver. But the interest was instead paid with a treasury warrant, or another paper promise. The Republic had fallen into a vicious paper cycle that it could not break. Paper chased paper, with no end in sight.

The extravagances of the Lamar administration extracted a huge economic cost to Texas and further depreciated the purchasing power of the paper currency. At the close of Lamar's three-year term, the public debt of Texas had swollen from less than $2 million to more than $7 million.[75] The congressional appropriations during this time period, according to the Treasurer's Report, were as follows:[76]

Congressional appropiations under Lamar

Year ending December 31,	*1839*	*$ 1,618,000.00*
" "	*1840*	*2,060,162.53*
" "	*1841*	*800,651.31*
Total Appropriations:		*$ 4,478,813.84*

When the un-appropriated amount of $500,000 in redbacks for the Santa Fe Expedition is added to this amount, the Lamar administration spent more than $1,659,000 on average each year. This sum exceeded the amounts appropriated under the Houston administration of 1837-1838 by more than 440 percent per annum. As Anson Jones so deftly predicted in 1839, the bubble had indeed burst. The money became nearly worthless and the people of Texas were ready for a change. For all the faults that can be found with the Lamar administration—the hostile Indian policy, the Santa Fe Expedition, and other flawed policy initiatives—it was the total failure of the financial system which caused more discontent among the people than all the other matters put together.

As the election of 1841 approached, Sam Houston, serving as a representative in the Texas Congress from San Augustine, continued to assail Lamar and his administration for the extravagances which brought the commerce of the country to a grinding halt. Ever the deft politician, Houston successfully pinned the blame for the debt buildup and the failure of the paper money system on Lamar and declared himself as a candidate for the Presidency. Old Sam was about to have his second calling as a financial, rather than a military, savior of the Republic of Texas.

[1] Seymour V. Conner, ed., "Starr to DeMorse, Treasury Department, Austin, June 4, 1840," Texas Treasury Papers, 2: 497.

[2] "An Act to Provide for the Redemption of Promissory Notes of the Government," Journals of the Sixth Congress of the Republic of Texas, 279-80.

[3] Seymour V. Conner, ed., "Starr to Brigham, Treasury Department, Austin, February 5, 1840," Texas Treasury Papers, 1: 374.

[4] Ibid., "Starr to DeMorse, Treasury Department, Austin, June 18, 1840," 2: 506-507.

[5] Ibid., "Starr to DeMorse, Treasury Department, Austin, June 4, 1840," 2: 496-97.

[6] Edmund Thornton Miller, "A Financial History of Texas," *Bulletin of the University of Texas 1916: No. 37* (Austin: University of Texas, 1916), 80.

[7] William M. Gouge, *The Fiscal History of Texas* (New York: Burt Franklin, 1852; rpt. 1969), 194.

[8] Grover C. Criswell, *Confederate and Southern States Currency: A Descriptive Listing, Including Rarity and Values,* vol.1, 4th ed. (1992), 342.

[9] Ibid., 343.

[10] Seymour V. Conner, ed., "Hall to Starr, New Orleans, June 30, 1840," Texas Treasury Papers, 2: 517-18.

[11] Ibid., "Bryan to Starr, Consulate of Texas, July 15, 1840," 4: 61.

[12] Grover C. Criswell, *Confederate and Southern States Bonds: A Descriptive Listing, Including Rarity,* vol. 2, 2nd ed. (1980), 344.

[13] "Report of the Auditor and Comptroller, to the Fourth Legislature, on the Public Debt of Texas," (Austin: Cushney & Hampton, State Gazette Office, 1851), 3.

[14] Seymour V. Conner, ed., "Starr to Evans, Austin, February 14, 1840," Texas Treasury Papers, 1: 384-85.

[15] Ibid., "Sevey to Simmons, Austin, January 9, 1841," 2: 575.

[16] Criswell, *Confederate and Southern States Bonds,* 340.

[17] Ibid., 341.

[18] *Handbook of Texas Online,* s.v., "James Hamilton," http://www.tsha.utexas.edu/handbook/online/articles/HH/fha35.html (accessed January 7, 2007).

[19] Seymour V. Conner, ed., "Hamilton to Starr, Charleston, February 8, 1840, and Austin, July 1, 1840," Texas Treasury Papers, 2: 377.

[20] *Handbook of Texas Online,* s.v., "Pig Wars," http://www.tsha.utexas.edu/handbook/online/articles/PP/mgp1.html (accessed December 7, 2006).

[21] Harriet Smither, ed., "James H. Starr to M.B. Lamar. Austin, Nacogdoches, May 15, 1841," The Papers of Mirabeau Buonaparte Lamar, Texas State Library & Archives, 3: 2,022.

[22] Ibid.

[23] Witness Fees, (a) Except as provided by Section 22.002, a witness is entitled to 10 dollars for each day the witness attends court. This fee includes the entitlement for travel and the witness is not entitled to any reimbursement for mileage traveled. Acts 1985, 69th Leg., ch. 959, § 1, eff. September 1, 1985. Amended by Acts 1993, 73rd Leg., ch. 103, § 1, eff. January 1, 1994; Acts 1993, 73rd Leg., ch. 449, § 16, eff. September 1, 1993, found online at: http://www.txhima.org/laws/currlaw7.htm

[24] Seymour V. Conner, ed., "Starr to Simmons and Evans, Starr to Barhydt, Austin, July 1, 1840," Texas Treasury Papers, 2: 525-26.

[25] "An Act Making Appropriations for Naval Service for the Year 1839," Journals of the Sixth Congress of the Republic of Texas, 1: 116.

[26] Douglas V. Meed, *The Fighting Texas Navy, 1832-1843* (Plano: Republic of Texas Press, 2001), 110-12.

[27] "Annual Report of the Treasurer of the Republic of Texas for 1841," by order of the House of Representatives (Austin: S. Whiting, Public Printer, 1842), 4-5.

[28] Jonathan W. Jordan, *Lone Star Navy: Texas, the Fight for the Gulf of Mexico, and the Shaping of the American West* (Dulles, VA: Potomac Books, Inc., 2006), 43.

[29] Seymour V. Conner, ed., "Chalmers to Mason, Austin, April 25, 1841," Texas Treasury Papers, 2: 649.

[30] Jordan, *Lone Star Navy,* 184.

[31] Seymour V. Conner, ed., "Moore to Chalmers, Texas Sloop of War Austin, May 15, 1841," Texas Treasury Papers, 4: 232.

[32] Ibid., "Wells to Mason, Navy Yard, Galveston, May 12, 1841," 4: 231.

[33] Ibid., "Moore to Swisher, Texas Sloop of War Austin, Galveston Bay, June 15, 1841," 4: 234.

[34] Jordan, *Lone Star Navy,* 43.

[35] "An Act, Establishing regulations and instructions for the government of the naval service in Texas, December 15, 1836, Boatswain," Laws of the Republic of Texas, 1: 120-21.

[36] "Archive Staff to James Bevill, January 23, 2007," Texas State Library & Archives Commission, regarding the findings from the Republic Navy Muster Roll database search for Alex Collins.

[37] "An Act, Establishing Regulations and Instructions for the Government of the Naval Service in Texas, December 15, 1836, the Gunner," Laws of the Republic of Texas, 1: 116-17.

[38] "Archive Staff to James Bevill, January 23, 2007," Texas State Library & Archives Commission, regarding findings from the Republic Navy Muster Roll database search for Charles Lewis.

[39] David B. Gracy, III, *Ships of the Texas Navy* (Presidial Press, 1978).

[40] Jordan, *Lone Star Navy,* 259-63.

[41] *Handbook of Texas Online,* s.v., "Zavala," http://www.tsha.utexas.edu/handbook/online/articles/ZZ/qtz1.html (accessed August 8, 2006).

[42] Jordan, *Lone Star Navy,* 162-65.

[43] "Archive Staff to James Bevill, January 23, 2007," Texas State Library & Archives Commission, regarding findings from the Republic Navy Muster Roll database search for John Deziel.

[44] "Archive Staff to James Bevill, January 23, 2007," Texas State Library & Archives Commission, regarding findings from the Republic Navy Muster Roll database search for James Smith.

[45] Jordan, *Lone Star Navy,* 163-64.

[46] "An Act, Establishing Regulations and Instructions for the Government of the Naval Service in Texas, December 15, 1836, The Sail Maker," 1: 119.

[47] "Archive Staff to James Bevill, January 23, 2007," Texas State Library & Archives Commission, regarding findings from the Republic Navy Muster Roll database search for Henry Lockwood.

[48] "Archive Staff to James Bevill, January 23, 2007," Texas State Library & Archives Commission, regarding findings from the Republic Navy Muster Roll database search for Arch McPhee.

[49] "The Sail Maker," Laws of the Republic of Texas, 1: 119.

[50] "Archive Staff to James Bevill, January 23, 2007," Texas State Library & Archives Commission, regarding findings from the Republic Navy Muster Roll database search for C. Cremons.

[51] William Falconer's Dictionary of the Marine, London: 1880, Page 226, http://southseas.nla.gov.au/refs/falc/1013.html

[52] Seymour V. Conner, ed., "Edmunds to Chalmers, Galveston, May 25, 1841," Texas Treasury Papers, 4: 232.

[53] Journals of the Sixth Congress of the Republic of Texas, 1: 422.

[54] *Handbook of Texas Online,* s.v., "Pig War," http://www.tsha.utexas.edu/handbook/online/articles/PP/mgp1.html (accessed November 10, 2006).

[55] Gouge, *The Fiscal History of Texas*, 106-11.

[56] Harriet Smither, ed., "James Hamilton, London to Mirabeau B. Lamar, Austin, May 18, 1841," The Papers of Mirabeau Buonaparte Lamar, Texas State Library & Archives, 3: 2,027.

[57] Seymour V. Conner, ed., "Bucker to Starr, New Orleans, April 7, 1841," Texas Treasury Papers, 3: 629.

[58] Gouge, *The Fiscal History of Texas*, 108.

[59] Harriet Smither, ed., "From the Austin City Gazette, Texian Loan, July 15, 1841," The Papers of Mirabeau Buonaparte Lamar, Texas State Library & Archives, 3: 2,068.

[60] William Ransom Hogan, *The Texas Republic: A Social and Economic History* (Norman, OK: University of Oklahoma Press, 1946), 167.

[61] A. K. Christian, "Mirabeau Buonaparte Lamar," vol. 24, SHQ (October 1920), 2: 87-139.

[62] Seymour V. Conner, ed., "Rawdon, Wright, Hatch & Edson to Chalmers, New Orleans, May 6, 1841," Texas Treasury Papers, 2: 659-60.

[63] Marquis James, *The Raven: A Biography of Sam Houston* (Austin: University of Texas Press, 1929), 317-18.

[64] Harriet Smither, ed., "H. McLeod, Camp (Near Austin, Texas) to M.B. Lamar (Austin, Texas), June 10, 1841," The Papers of Mirabeau Buonaparte Lamar, Texas State Library & Archives, 3: 2,049.

[65] Richard Bruce Winders, *Crisis in the Southwest: The United States, Mexico and the Struggle over Texas* (New York: Scholarly Resources, Inc., 2002), 49-50.

[66] James, *The Raven,* 317-18.

[67] Seymour V. Conner, ed., "Chalmers to Mason, Treasury Department, City of Austin, December 9, 1841," Texas Treasury Papers, 2: 809.

[68] "John Pleasants," found online at: www.sanjacinto-museum.org/Herzstein_Library/Veteran_Biographies/Browse_Biographies/biographies/default.asp?action=bio&id=3496

[69] *Handbook of Texas Online,* s.v., "J.B. Ransom," http://www.tsha.utexas.edu/handbook/online/articles/RR/fra56.html (accessed July 13, 2006).

[70] *Handbook of Texas Online,* s.v., "Francis Asbury Morris," http://www.tsha.utexas.edu/handbook/online/articles/MM/fmo55.html (accessed July 13, 2006).

[71] Louise Jarrell, "The Austin Lyceum, 1839-1841" (M.A. Thesis, University of Texas, 1941).

[72] Hogan, *The Texas Republic,* 164.

[73] Seymour V. Conner, ed., "G.W. Terrell to E.L. Stickney, Esq., February 7, 1842," Texas Treasury Papers, 3: 840.

[74] *Handbook of Texas Online,* s.v., "David Gourvernour Burnet," http://www.tsha.utexas.edu/handbook/online/articles/BB/fbu46.html (accessed September 17, 2006).

[75] Gouge, *The Fiscal History of Texas*, 126.

[76] "Annual Report of the Treasurer," November 10, 1841, 4-5.

CHAPTER TWELVE

OLD SAM AND THE EXCHEQUER BILLS

Fig 12.1, Sam Houston, President of the Republic of Texas.
Photo by Matthew B. Brady, c. 1848-1850.

As in many elections, in 1841 the people of Texas voted with their wallets as they reached for a strong leader to stabilize the country. The campaign issues of the day included the protection of the frontier, reforms for the proper titling of land grants, continued Mexican aggression, and the substantial depreciation of the Texas paper money. Texas citizens witnessed how the freely printed money under Lamar's administration depreciated so steeply that even government officials could scarcely live on their salaries. In the election of 1841, Sam Houston ran for another term as President against David G. Burnet, the Vice President under Lamar.

Sam Houston successfully created the impression that only "old Sam" could save the country. He also succeeded in pinning the failures of the Lamar administration on Burnet's candidacy. Houston's political strength was built by exploiting the weaknesses of his opponents and distancing himself from their actions.[1] It was rumored that he learned this technique from Old Chief Bowles, the Cherokee Indian who tutored the young Houston many years before. Houston was also a master of taking credit for every positive development in Texas. With Santa Anna again rattling his saber towards Texas and the paper money almost worthless, the people elected Sam Houston by an overwhelming majority to a second term as their President. Houston, along with San Jacinto-veteran Ed Burleson as Vice President, was sworn in at the Capital of Austin on December 13, 1841.[2]

While Lamar's financial policies failed drastically, he had made tremendous strides in education and westward expansion during his administration. Upon taking office, Sam Houston made it his sovereign duty to undo as many of Lamar's policies as possible. He acted to take a hard line defensive stance against Mexico, sought peace treaties with the Indians, and encouraged trade along the western and southern borders to bring more hard currency into the country. On the financial front, Houston began by relieving John G. Chalmers of his duties a Secretary of the Treasury within hours of taking office. Houston appointed E. Lawrence Stickney, the former Commissioner of Revenue, to the office as Acting Secretary until a permanent appointment could be made.[3]

The harsh reality of the day was that commerce in the Republic was practically at a standstill. From the Rio Grande to the Sabine, the country was experiencing the long-term fallout from the deep depression that began with the Panic of 1837. Land prices fell, real estate became un-saleable due to a lack of hard money, and bartering was once again the order of the day. Doctors and newspaper editors advertised that produce of all sorts could be exchanged for medical services and newspaper subscriptions.[4] The captain of a visiting French warship stated that the only market in Texas was for hard liquors.[5] Tax collection came to a halt following the refusal of the government to accept its own paper in payment. J.H. Money, a receiver of public accounts in Austin County, reported to Stickney on December 31, 1841, that "I have received no Govt dues on lands ending the Quarter with 31st December 1841 – neither have I received a Single Dollar in like manner during the last Twelve months."[6] Indeed, the collection of public revenues slowed to a trickle in even the most populous of counties due to the severe shortage of money. Although the customs received in ports were still a significant source of revenues, even those had dropped off dramatically. Customs revenues were reported as $59,284.36 during the second quarter of 1841.[7] During the third quarter, following the failure of the proposed French loan to Texas, imports dropped and the customs revenues amounted to only $22,775.40.[8] It was clear to the citizens of Texas that something had to be done.

The Houston administration immediately proceeded to assess the damage, and it was soon determined that without a functioning currency and a method to pay its bills, the wheels of government would soon grind to a halt, taking down the rest of the country as well. Even though Sam Houston loathed the capital city of Austin, he spent the first several months of 1842 there in his new quarters. He sometimes resided at the homes of friends and in boarding houses. The Bullock Hotel, well known for the pig incident, became a favorite of the President. Establishments such as the Bullock Hotel routinely hosted visitors to the frontier capital. The Sixth Congress was already in session when Sam Houston took office for the second time. Houston and the members of the Sixth Congress searched for a solution to the looming fiscal crisis. Among Houston's most significant appointments was Dr. Anson Jones, appointed to the critical post of Secretary of State.

Anson Jones was born in the township of Great Barrington, Massachusetts, on January 20, 1798, the son of Solomon and Sarah Jones.[9] Like several influential leaders in the Republic of Texas, Jones' father was a veteran of the American Revolution. The elder Jones volunteered in 1775, spent five years in the Army, and was engaged in the defense of Bunker Hill. He was at Saratoga when British General Burgoyne surrendered. As a young boy,Anson attended a school run by his sister, about a mile from the family farm. He later completed studies in English at the Episcopal Church in Great Barrington and by 1812, commenced the study of languages and higher mathematics at the Lenox Academy in the same county.

Jones planned to pursue a career as a printer, but his father persuaded him to study medicine instead. Jones obtained a license as a physician in New York in 1820, and moved to Philadelphia in 1827 where he practiced medicine. Jones moved to New Orleans and worked for a while as a commission merchant before he found his way to Texas in October 1833. At the urging of John A. Wharton, Jones built a successful medical practice in Brazoria until the Texas Revolution called him to arms. Jones enlisted in the company of Robert J. Calder and soon found himself on the plains of San Jacinto. He fought as a private in the infantry during the pivotal campaign, and following the battle, he tended to the wounded until the sun rose the following morning. In the aftermath of the battle, Dr. Jones discovered Juan N. Almonte's *Journal and Order Book* lying in the field, which he sent to the *New York Herald* for publication in June 1836.[10]

Returning to his medical practice in Brazoria following the war, Jones became increasingly interested in public policy and critical of congressional practices. He was elected a representative to the Second Congress and chaired committees on Foreign Relations, Privileges and Elections, and Ways and Means. Jones advocated a withdrawal of the Texas proposal for annexation to the United States. A fiscal conservative, he quickly drew the attention of Houston as he railed against Lamar's fiscal policies and introduced a Senate resolution on November 20, 1840, to repeal all the laws authorizing the issue of promissory notes of the government.[11] It was soundly defeated by a vote of ten to two, but Jones's political star began to rise as Lamar's came crashing down.

Fig 12.2, Anson Jones, Secretary of State.

Courtesy of Albert and Ethel Herzstein Library, The San Jacinto Museum of History, Houston, Texas.

Sam Houston's administration needed a plan to raise funds and implement a stable currency system after efforts to secure another foreign loan fell through. The outstanding Texas promissory notes were only accepted at steep discounts to their face value in gold or silver coin, and the downward spiral of the paper money values was an ever increasing problem. The government proposed a new series of bills named "exchequers." The name change was most likely done as a name association with the department of the British government which dealt with public money. An Exchequer Bank had also been proposed by U.S. President John Tyler, popularizing the term in the U.S. though the bank never materialized.[12]

Anson Jones later summed up the solution to the financial crisis which faced Sam Houston's new administration, "I must, in the language of scripture do evil, that good may come. But the evil is small, and the good may be great."[13] Ground-breaking legislation soon came before Congress. The most important objective of the legislation was to complete the salvation and safety of the country and accomplish no less than a complete restoration of its finances. The essence of the legislation stated that after the first day of February 1842, the customs collectors at the ports could only accept payments in silver or gold coins or exchequer bills.[14] While that may have been acceptable to many of the representatives, a debate soon raged in the Senate over the issuance of these new bills, as the second section of the legislation authorizing the issue reads as follows:

> *Be it further enacted- That it shall not be lawful for the Sheriffs and Collectors of direct or license*

taxes to be assessed for the year 1842 and all subsequent years, to receive anything in payment of such taxes except gold or silver or the Exchequer Bills authorized to be issued by the provisions of this Act.[15]

The mere introduction of the legislation caused the existing redbacks to depreciate further from the recently established value of sixteen to one. One source reported, "neither washerwoman, landlord nor grocery keeper, would now touch it [redbacks] at even one cent on the dollar."[16] Commerce essentially froze in anticipation of the outcome. Lawmakers rushed to add amendments to the bill, but to no avail. Sen. Francis Moore, Jr., representing Harris, Liberty and Galveston, in an attempt to stabilize the matter, moved to amend the act by allowing the acceptance of all promissory notes or audited drafts for taxes or one sixth of the amount in gold or silver. This would have the same effect as the proposed second section of the bill, only it would lower the government revenues and add what would amount to a statutory devaluation of the currency.

Sen. Robert Potter of the Red River and Fannin districts summed up the situation in *The Daily Texian* on January 11, 1842 by stating: "Today, we pay out notes at four or six for one, and tomorrow we refuse to receive them for taxes. Last month, our notes were worth six for one, and now not worth more than from eight to sixteen to one, and refused by many at any rate of per cent." He added, "I would say to the gentlemen from Harris, that the present situation in Texas, is very different from that in 1837, when the promissory notes were first issued—they were for the payment of the civil department—our streets were full of penniless and destitute soldiers, crying give, give—the mania of speculation raged—civil officers, senators and representatives, engaged in buying up the soldiers claims, at ten cents on the dollar—the funding law was gotten up to the great detriment of the country."

George W. Barnett, representing the districts of Washington and Montgomery, was appalled by the gravity of the financial crisis which had been presented to him in the President's message and the debates between his colleagues. Barnett remarked, "the picture was so terrific in relation to Texas, that his blood was well nigh chilled in his veins." Although it was clear that the finances of the Republic were in a sad condition, the system of exchequer bills proposed to Congress was the only means by which Texas could pay its ongoing obligations. Barrett eloquently stated the situation to his colleagues on the House floor, "When the mariner is in a storm, if the vessel must be lightened or lost, the cargo is thrown over. Texas must be dissolved, or means must be obtained." The paper money system, estimated by the lawmakers at about $1,500,000 then in circulation, was about to be jettisoned overboard at great detriment to those holding the notes.[17]

Despite heated objections from several lawmakers, the act creating the "Exchequer Bills" was passed on January 19, 1842.[18] In an attempt to stabilize the latest issue of Texas currency, the exchequer bills would be accepted at full face value at par with gold or silver for payment of taxes and other government debts. The legislation also effectively rendered every other form of previously issued Texas currency almost worthless. The stinging impact of the legislation was felt immediately by anyone possessing the promissory notes or other securities. (See Appendix I for a copy of the legislation which authorized the issuance of Exchequer Bills).

In the waning days of the Lamar administration, Texas money was quoted at between fifteen and twenty cents on the dollar. The money then fell to ten cents, five cents, then three and two cents if any takers could be found. The currency fell so low in value that several uses for the paper money became laughable. One gentleman was quoted as saying that he had spent $15 dollars in treasury bills "for three glasses of brandy and a glass of water without sugar." Keep in mind that a glass of brandy during this time was typically only a dime. There was at least one instance where a $50 treasury note was used to light a cigar![19] The soft paper bills were said to have also been used for more hygienic purposes, the description of which will be left to the imagination of the reader.

A LIFELINE FOR THE TEXAS NAVY

Aside from the domestic implications of the new money, the bankrupt Texas Navy was fighting what amounted to a war on two fronts—the Mexican Navy in the Gulf of Mexico and Congress in Austin. On January 25, 1842, at the same legislative session, James W. Byrne, the Chairman of the Committee on Naval Affairs, reported to Congress that the following sums were needed to continue to operate the Navy: $151,108 for the men who died in the service and for improvements at the Galveston Navy Yard through December 31, 1841; $58,200 for service in the current year and for repairs at the Navy Yard. There was a debit of $10,000 to Commodore Edwin W. Moore for personal advances made out of his own funds to keep the Navy afloat; and $40,000 still owed to the officers, sailors and marines in the form of un-cashed Treasury Certificates and Navy scrip.[20]

The Navy presented these obligations totaling $259,308 to Congress for payment. The Congress grudgingly complied with an appropriation of $20,000 in exchequer bills on February 3, 1842.[21] The tight-fisted Houston asked Congress for an appropriation of less than half of that owed in wages under the Naval Payment Certificates issued by the Lamar government the previous April. Compounding the injury to the Navy, the exchequer bills were not ordered by the President for distribution until the following July.[22]

Putting aside the ramifications of the new issue, the exchequer bills were simply treasury notes in a new form. This series of bills was issued in various denominations and later in fractions of a dollar, with no other purpose than to fund the specific appropriations as made by Congress. While up to $200,000 was initially authorized, the total production of the notes amounted to only $150,490. All exchequer bills were accepted for payment of taxes.[23] Having learned their lesson with previous issues, many merchants declined to accept exchequer bills. The exchequer bills initially saw their values trade at between thirty and fifty cents on the dollar, though the value of the currency eventually stabilized and the exchequers briefly traded at their par value in January 1843.[24] Thereafter, customs officials at the port of Galveston reported that the value of exchequer bills abruptly fell to seventy-five cents on the dollar and were likely to trade at a discount as long as the Congress was in session.[25] The people had no confidence in the legislative body of Texas and this was directly reflected in the declining value of the currency. Not surprisingly, with no new notes being printed, virtually all of the outstanding issue of exchequer bills were eventually redeemed at face value and then subsequently destroyed by the government. As a result, very few of these notes are known to have survived at all. Any exchequer bills are extremely rare in any condition.

To put this low survival rate into perspective, only the notes issued in denominations of 12 ½ cents, 25 cents, 50 cents, 75 cents, $1 and $5 are known to exist today. To date, there is not a single example of an exchequer bill of $2, $3, $10, $20, $50 or $100 denomination known in any collection, public or private. Of the remaining notes, the 12 ½ cent note is the most "common" with fewer than a dozen surviving. This small denomination may not have been worthwhile to be redeemed for full face value and some were set aside and saved. Despite a long standing belief on the part of many collectors that Sam Houston personally signed each note, the President's name was signed to the smaller denomination bills by W.D. Miller, his personal secretary.[26] The larger denominations of $5 and above bear a lithographed signature of Sam Houston, also signed on his behalf by Miller.

Initially, the act authorizing the exchequer bills called for denominations of $100, $50, $20, $10 and $5. The exchequer bills were conceived in three separate printings, the first being the larger denomination bills. Of the entire series of large bills printed, 300 were $100 bills, 499 were $50 bills, 899 were $20 bills, 2,698 were $10 bills, and 7,196 were $5 bills. Of these printings, only three specimens from the $5 issue survived. Notice that the $5 differs materially in design and appearance from the smaller denomination bills.

Rather than being printed from an engraved plate, the $5 and larger bills were printed by lithograph by Sam Whiting & Co. as evidenced by "S. Whiting, Printer" on the notes. Sam Whiting, the owner of the printing company, took great pains to see that the bills were not overproduced. In February 1842, he informed the government that "every possible care has been taken to prevent the printing of more than were ordered."[27] We can only surmise that if a larger denomination bill surfaces, the design elements would be similar to those on the $5 specimen, rather than the smaller-denomination engraved pieces.

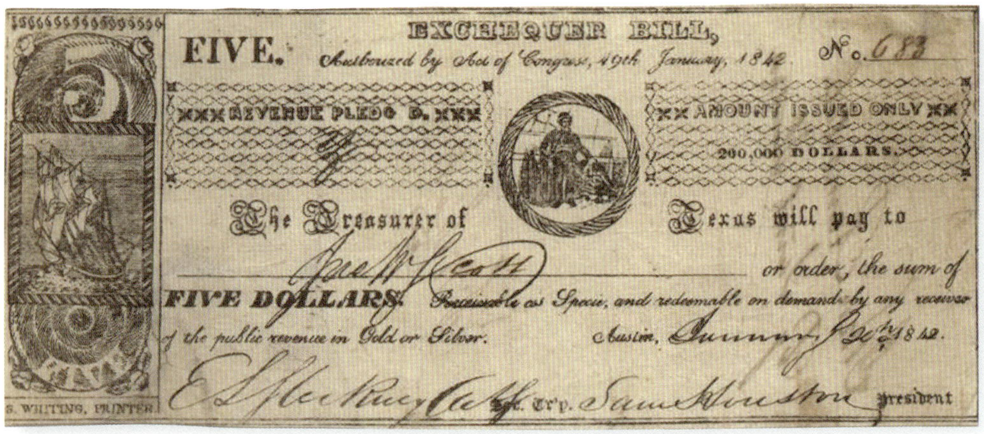

Fig 12.3, $5 Republic of Texas - Exchequer Bill, dated January 20, 1842.

John N. Rowe III Collection of Texas Currency, DeGolyer Library, Southern Methodist University, Dallas, Texas, Cr. A-17, 0-800.

Portrayed on the $5 exchequer bill in Figure 12.3 is a sailing ship at left. In the center is a sailor set in a wreath and the text (known as the legal line) reads: "The Treasurer of Texas will pay to James W. Scott or order, the sum of FIVE DOLLARS. Receiveable [*sic*] as Specie, and redeemable on demand by any receiver of the public revenue in Gold or Silver. Austin, *January 20th, 1842.*" At the bottom are facsimile signatures of E.L. Stickney, Acting Secretary of the Treasury, and Sam Houston, as President.

Although the bill was payable to James W. Scott, the Comptroller of the Treasury Department, it was also endorsed by him on the reverse. His signature was an additional anti-counterfeiting measure. The face of each bill was also completed in a peculiar manner, as Scott signed the last four letters of his last name on the face of each bill.[28] Although they were initially paid out at the same value as specie, contrary to what is stated on the face of the bill, these printed bills were never backed by specie or exchangeable for gold or silver coins at the Treasury. When the bills were presented at the customs house for duties, they were accepted not at their face value, but at the exchange rate they bore in the market which was considerably less.[29]

The second printing of the exchequer bills in $3, $2, and $1 denominations resulted when Congress again repudiated its own legislation.[30] A law was passed at a special session of the Sixth Congress in Houston on July 23, 1842, authorizing an engraved series of small-denomination bills along with a series of fractional currency. Not surprisingly, the market value of the bills began to fall with nearly every session of Congress as the people greatly feared that another ruinous issue of paper money would be forthcoming. Treasury Secretary Henry Dangerfield traveled to New Orleans where he signed a contract for printing the new exchequer bills with Rawdon Wright, Hatch & Edson.[31] After the firm was paid a portion of the invoice in exchequers and the balance in a draft on the Customs House, the printers happily churned out the new money. Similar to previous printing jobs, the collection by the firm of Rawdon, Wright proved difficult. Invoices dated as early as December 1841 were still unpaid on June 6, 1843.[32] The exchequer bills which the printers held for payment could not be exchanged for gold or silver at face value or they would have done so. Not only did the Customs House refuse to cash their draft, but the Treasury Department still lacked the specie to pay the remainder of the invoice.

At the top central device of the $1 exchequer bill in Figure 12.4 is a vignette of Ceres seated beside a bale of cotton. On the right is a vignette of a steamboat, and at the bottom center is a small eagle. The text of the note reads: "The Republic of Texas will pay ONE DOLLAR on demand to J.W. Scott or bearer, in Exchequer Bills. Austin. Receivable in Sums of Five Dollars." At the bottom are signatures of James B. Shaw, Secretary of the Treasury, and Sam Houston, President.

Differing materially in quality and design from the lithographed notes, one is initially struck by the slightly larger size of the engraved $1 exchequer bill, making it different from any previously issued Republic notes. Of the smaller-denomination printing, 1,000 were $3 bills, 1,000 were $2 bills, and 2,000 were $1 bills.[33] Of the limited issue, only the $1 note is known to have survived. These smaller denomination bills served the same purpose as the prior issues of change notes issued first from Houston and then from Austin. Many merchants at first refused to accept them. When they could get paid with nothing else, the bills were quickly passed them off to

Fig 12.4, $1 Republic of Texas - Exchequer Bill, dated April 1, 1842.

John N. Rowe III Collection of Texas Currency, DeGolyer Library, Southern Methodist University, Dallas, Texas, Cr. A-14, 0-792.

other merchants or paid in as soon as possible for taxes. President Houston was rightfully afraid that the new money would depreciate much like the previous issues. He determined to keep in circulation only the minimum amount of bills required for the government to function. To a large extent, these smaller-denomination engraved bills replaced the printed bills in circulation. Instructions were given for officials to cancel the larger-denomination printed exchequer bills as soon as they were paid back into the treasury by writing "Cancelled" across the face of the bill and signing their name underneath.[34] As the printed bills were exchanged for the smaller-denomination engraved bills, the words "Redeemed and Cancelled" were written across the face of each bill and the Treasury official signed each accordingly.

By August 1842, Houston ordered the Treasurer to suspend any additional issue of exchequer bills until further instructions were received from him.[35] There was such a shortage of small circulating coins at the time that it was deemed necessary to issue a short series of fractional currency to provide change for small transactions. The President exercised such rigorous control over the issuance of new money that he personally oversaw much of their disbursement up to the last issue on December 4, 1843.[36] The smallest denomination of 12 ½ cents was a throwback to the days of Spanish rule as it represented exactly the value of one-eighth of a milled Spanish dollar.

On the left side of the 12 ½ cent exchequer bill in Figure 12.5 is a train, consisting only of the engine and caboose. A worker in the foreground with large staves and bales of cotton represents agriculture. In the center is a farmer planting seed and a horse pulling a plow, with a man and a house in the background. On the right-side of the bill is Liberty standing in agriculture. At the bottom are signatures of James B. Shaw, Secretary of the Treasury, and Sam Houston, President.

On the left side of Figure 12.6 is an identical vignette of the train pictured on the 12 ½ cent bill. The center of the bill differs, however, as Liberty is seated with a scepter in her right hand and her left arm resting on a mirror reflecting a building. The right side of the bill displays Liberty in agriculture, with wheat and sickle. The small yellow spots on the note are part of a reinforced backing which was applied to the piece many decades ago by the owner as the result of a framing. At the bottom are signatures of James B. Shaw, Secretary of the Treasury, and Sam Houston, President.

Fig 12.5, 12 ½ Cent, Republic of Texas - Exchequer Bill, dated May 1, 1843.
Private Collection, Cr. A10, O-780.

Fig 12.6, 25 Cent, Republic of Texas - Exchequer Bill, dated May 1, 1843.
Private Collection, Cr. A11, O-783.

On the left side of the 50 cent exchequer bill in Figure 12.7 is a steamship. The center shows a farmer with horses, pulling a plow to the right. At the bottom are signatures of James B. Shaw, Secretary of the Treasury, and Sam Houston, President.

The left side of the 75 cent exchequer bill in Figure 12.8 displays a winged cherub. In the center is a bearded man rising from water, with a bridge at the left, and a sailing ship in the distance. The right side of the bill shows Minerva seated, and at her right is a portrait of George Washington on the bust of an eagle. In her left hand is a scroll of paper. At the bottom are signatures of James B. Shaw, Secretary of the Treasury, and Sam Houston, President.

Not only did Sam Houston attempt to tightly control the release of the exchequer bills, he also oversaw much of the destruction of the money after it was paid in for customs and taxes. Because Congress mandated

Fig 12.7, 50 Cent, Republic of Texas - Exchequer Bill, dated April 1, 1843.

Private Collection, Cr. A-12, O-786.

Fig 12.8, 75 Cent, Republic of Texas Exchequer Bill, dated May 1, 1843.

The City of Omaha, in the permanent collection of the Durham Western Heritage Museum, Omaha, Nebraska. Cr. A-13, O-789.

that no more than $50,000 of exchequer bills would ever be outstanding at any one time, the printed larger denomination bills were withdrawn from circulation and replaced with the smaller $1, $2, and $3 bills which were slow to arrive from the printers in New Orleans.

The government later pledged to keep the circulating amount under $30,000, reducing the need for the $3, $2 and $1 bills. They, too, were eventually replaced with the fractional bills. All of these bills were eventually taken out of circulation as they were paid in for customs and taxes, cancelled, and subsequently burned. The issuance of the exchequer bills began in Austin, and continued as the seat of government moved back to Houston and then Washington-on-the-Brazos. It was rumored that Sam Houston delighted in watching the destruction of the exchequer bills—as if the free money policies of the Lamar administration were being burned in effigy.

Largely because of Houston and Jones's tight-fisted monetary policies, the economy strengthened, tax revenues increased, and the exchequer bills eventually reached par value. The record grain harvest of 1843 resulted in a boom to the farming economy and shipping was again bringing goods out of Texas and gold and silver into government coffers.[37] By December 15, 1845, only $14,518 in exchequer bills were reported outstanding by the government.[38] With the exchequer bills accepted at 100 percent of face value, virtually all of these notes were paid into the Treasury for taxes and subsequently destroyed.

From the standpoint of the collector, this has made the "Exchequer Series" of notes by far the most difficult to obtain, and therefore the most expensive to acquire. Of the fractional bills printed, 7,600 were 12 ½ cent bills, 7,600 were 25 cent bills, 3,800 were 50 cent bills and 3,800 were 75 cent bills.[39] Their scarcity is a result of their almost complete destruction by Treasury officials. The most complete set of notes in existence today was assembled by Mr. John N. Rowe, III, and the five-note set is currently part of the permanent collection of the DeGolyer Library at Southern Methodist University in Dallas. The following report, dated December 4, 1843, helps to put this low survival rate into perspective.

TABLE 12.1 REPORT OF THE TREASURER TO THE HOUSE OF REPRESENTATIVES SHOWING THE WHOLE AMOUNT OF EXCHEQUER BILLS ISSUED BY THE TREASURY DEPARTMENT.

Number of Bills.	Denomination.	Amount Issued.
300	$ 100.00	$30,000.00
499	50.00	24,950.00
899	20.00	17,980.00
2,698	10.00	26,980.00
7,196	5.00	35,980.00
1,000	3.00	3,000.00
1,000	2.00	2,000.00
2,000	1.00	2,000.00
3,800	75 cents	2,850.00
3,800	50 cents	1,900.00
7,600	25 cents	1,900.00
7,600	12 ½ cents	950.00
		—————
	Total amount issued,	$150,490.00
From which must be deducted the following amounts, viz: amount destroyed at different times under the provisions of a joint Resolution, approved Jan. 29, 1842.	$64,865.00	
Amt. in the Treas. at this time Probable amt. in the hands of Receiving officers.	17,600.00 54,816.71	——— 137,281.71
Probable balance in circulation.		$13,208.29
TREASURY DEPARTMENT, J. B. MILLER, Washington, Dec. 4, 1843. Secretary Treasury.		

Even though none of these larger denomination notes are thought to have survived, it is possible that one or more specimens may indeed exist in some previously un-searched collection of old papers. For example, the lone surviving specimen of the 75 cent exchequer bill surfaced in 2001. It was discovered attached to the back of an engraving of Sam Houston in the Byron Reed Collection at the Durham Western Heritage Museum in Omaha, Nebraska—a full 110 years after it was bequeathed by Reed to the City of Omaha.[40] Two specimens of the extremely rare 12 ½ cent and 25 cent exchequer bills were recently discovered by the author, hanging in a picture frame on the wall of a fashionable home in a Houston suburb—preserved in the owner's family Bible for more than 150 years! Just because these bills may be presently "undiscovered," it does not mean that they don't exist.

BACK TO HOUSTON: THE SUMMER OF 1842

Fig 12.9, Allen's Landing, Buffalo and White Oak Bayous, Houston, Texas, c. 1860 (Houston Public Library).

Author's Collection.

Fig 12.10, Sam Houston's modest two room home, the "Texas White House."

Texas State Library & Archives Commission, Austin, Texas.

President Houston was deeply concerned about controlling any further issuance of paper money and putting the wheels of commerce back on track in Texas. He was also obsessed with moving the capital away from Austin and back to the city of Houston, which was much more central to the population of the country. Remotely located on the outskirts of the frontier, Austin was subject to frequent Indian attacks. Although the town was still sparsely populated, Austin financially benefited from the printing, lodging, saloons and other businesses spawned by housing the Republic's capital. By the early 1840s, Houston was the most important shipping center in Texas because of the town's accessibility to the port of Galveston.[41] A brisk trade with the cotton-growing area of Brazoria sprang up, causing the city and the population to grow to more than two thousand people. By 1841, wagons loaded with merchandise bound for the interior crowded the streets of Houston. Visitor Josiah Gregg noted that by November 1841, the town had, "a brisk trade supporting from a dozen to twenty dry goods stores. It has indeed several tolerably extensive foreign importing houses." With the city having largely recovered from the yellow fever epidemic just two years before, Sam Houston crafted plans to relocate the seat of government back to the banks of Buffalo Bayou.

Driven by a deep-seated hatred for Lamar's chosen capital, Sam Houston moved the executive branch back to his namesake city in the summer of 1842. He arrived at his modest two-room house in May. Since the owners of the Capitol building converted the establishment for use as a hotel, President Houston largely operated the government from this "Texas White House." With summer temperatures averaging from the very humid mid-90s to more than 100 degrees on the majority of summer days, one can only conclude that Sam Houston hated residing in Lamar's chosen capital of Austin so much that he preferred Houston during the hottest months of the year. Always the smooth politician, Sam Houston justified the move back to his namesake city for reasons of safety, driven largely by the continued Mexican aggression. Mexico again invaded Texas in March 1842 when Gen. Rafael Vasquez crossed the Rio Grande River with 700 troops and occupied San Antonio.[42] Houston declared Austin unsafe, as it lay a mere seventy miles from the path of an invading Army. He then recommended returning the seat of government to Houston.

TROUBLE BREWING IN THE NAVY

On March 26, 1842, Sam Houston sent orders to Galveston for the Texas Navy to blockade Mexican ports. The new assignment for the Texas Navy would have to wait until Commodore E.W. Moore returned from Campeche where Texas warships were busy capturing Mexican prizes off the coast of Yucatan. Moore was not due back to Galveston until the end of April. Moore and the Navy also rescued several survivors from the Santa Fe Expedition, including Thomas R. Lubbock, the brother of former comptroller Francis R. Lubbock. Moore and his associate, Samuel R. Fisher, found Thomas Lubbock to possess a "considerable knowledge of the geography and Statistics [*sic*] of Mexico," which they expected would assist the Republic in its military efforts. Although the Navy lacked funds, Moore and Fisher were so determined to continue their seafaring adventures that Fisher wrote, "[we] will have a very favorable tendency of prosecuting an offensive war against Mexico, in the midst of an exhausted public treasury."[43]

Upon Moore's return to Galveston, Navy Secretary George Hockley handed the commodore Houston's orders to implement a naval blockade of Mexican ports. After reviewing the dispatch, Moore felt hopeful that the Navy was finally being recognized—at long last, the Navy was given an important military assignment. His officers, however, reacted quite differently. The men had gone for a long period without pay, and on May 7, 1842, the sailor's pent-up frustration regarding their chronic lack of pay exploded like the burst of a naval artillery shell. When confronted with the order to return to sea without any hope of receiving their back pay, virtually every officer of the Texas Navy handed in his resignation. Sympathetically, Moore forwarded their complaints to President Houston through Navy Secretary George Hockley stating, "None of them have received one dollar from the Government for twelve months, and they have nearly two years pay due them."[44] Sam Houston had not received the enthusiastic response that he had anticipated. It became even more evident that the Republic of Texas could not remain independent if it did not secure the financial means to maintain a strong military and defend itself against foreign aggression.

In the interim, Moore continued to fund the daily operations of the Navy through the revenues he received from a steamboat operation that he ran between New Orleans and Galveston. The commander kept a careful accounting of the debts that he was incurring in the name of the Republic, and scrambled to keep his men fed and clothed from his own personal funds. Arriving in New Orleans on May 29, Moore found that President Houston refused to release the original $20,000 in exchequer bills previously appropriated for the Navy in February 1842, citing a campaign promise not to place any new exchequer bills into circulation until the next session of Congress.[45] Moore was furious at Houston's refusal to release the appropriated funds. In a concerted effort not to issue any new money unless funds were received by the government, Houston dispatched his Secretary of State, Anson Jones, on a new fundraising mission to the United States on June 10, 1842.[46] Jones was granted full powers as a commissioner to negotiate a loan of up to $1,000,000 under the legislation previously approved by Congress on January 22, 1839.

A LEGISLATIVE CIRCUS

Although Sam Houston's attempts to return the government to Houston are but a footnote in the study of the Republic of Texas, the political shenanigans and resulting legislation which took place had far-reaching implications for the currency, the citizens who used the currency, and the subsequent fate of the Texas Navy. The location of the government in the city of Houston during the summer of 1842 left yet another paper trail of warrants. President Houston was determined to bring as many members of the government with him to the Bayou City, and for a time, it was as if old Sam had never left. He called a special session of Congress, issued executive orders, and housed the members of Congress at the old Capitol-building-turned-hotel.

The appointment of a senior Treasury official in Houston is evidenced by the warrant shown in Figure 12.11 issued from Houston and made payable to William G. Crump, Acting Secretary of the Treasury. It references his position and the amount being for "Payment on order of the President" for his service during the time period. Houston appointed William G. Crump as Acting Treasury Secretary on May 17, 1842, in an attempt to maintain closer control over the issuance of the exchequer bills, as the Treasury Department and Congress were still located in Austin. Houston instructed Crump to "forth-

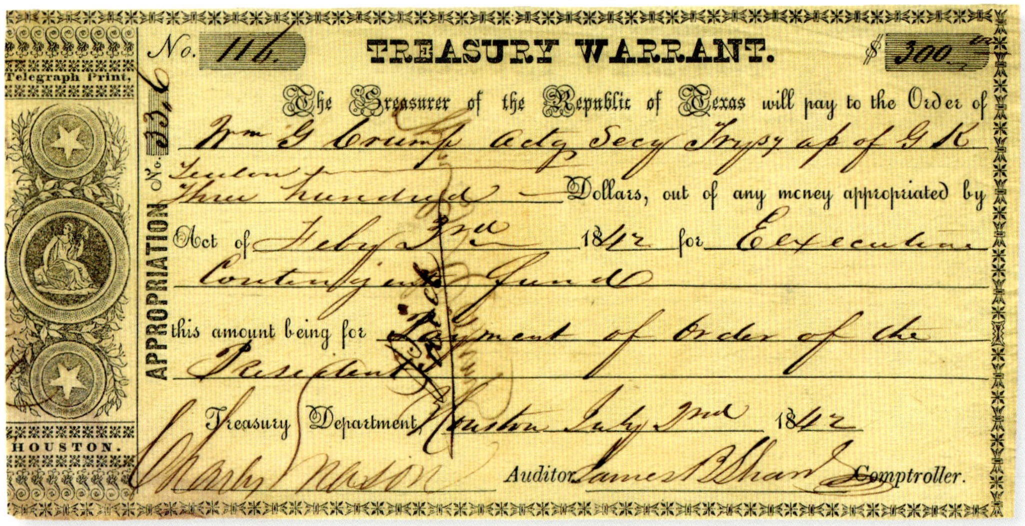
Telegraph Print.
No. 116. TREASURY WARRANT. $300.
The Treasurer of the Republic of Texas will pay to the Order of
APPROPRIATION No.
Dollars, out of any money appropriated by
Act of 1842 for
this amount being for
Treasury Department, 1842
HOUSTON.
Auditor Comptroller.

No. 116 TREASURY WARRANT $300.00

The Treasurer of the Republic of Texas will pay to the Order of W[illia]m G. Crump act[in]g Sec[retar]y Tr[easur]ysy as[signee] of G.K. ______ Three Hundred Dollars, out of any money appropriated by act of Feb[ruar]y 3rd, 1842 for Executive Contingent fund this amount being for Payment of order of the President. Treasury Department, Houston, July 2nd 1842

(Signed) Charles Mason, Auditor James B. Shaw, Comptroller

Fig 12.11, Houston, July 2, 1842, Treasury Warrant to William G. Crump, acting Secretary (of the) Treasury.

Private Collection, Cr. HW13, O-420.

with proceed in the performance of your appropriate duties."[47]

For the collector, this example is among the scarcest of the Houston warrants. It was written on printed paper which bears the seated liberty design (shown at left and flanked by the five-pointed Lone Stars) which first appeared on U.S. coins in 1836, the year of Texas Independence.

Fig 12.12, 1836 U.S. Silver "Gobrecht" Dollar.

Private Collection.

Fig 12.13, 1842 Republic of Texas, "Gobrecht" Design.

Private Collection.

The seated liberty design in Figure 12.12 first appeared on regular issue U.S. silver dollars dated 1836. The design is unique for regular issues due to the lack of thirteen stars (representing the thirteen original colonies) on the obverse. The coin was appropriately dubbed the "Gobrecht Dollar," as it bears the name of the principal designer, Christian Gobrecht, on the base of the design. The image of this coin on the Republic of Texas warrants is unique to this issue of paper, with one other minor variety, and was used in the cities of Houston and Washington, Texas.[48] The image of the Gobrecht dollar was also used by the printer Telegraph Print on small denominations of paper money issued by the city of Houston and from the town of Harrisburg.

The $93.00 warrant for "Pay & mileage as member of Senate Extra Session" shown in Figure 12.14 bears evidence that Sam Houston was trying to wrench the seat of government from Austin. Houston called a special legislative session of Congress to deal with the Mexican incursion into San Antonio. While Congress was in session, he introduced legislation to permanently move the capital back to Houston. There were loud protests from the western counties, however, and Congress rejected the President's proposal. The physical division of the government can be seen on this (and other) Houston warrants as a different color ink was used to write the payment information (completed in Houston) than was used for the signatures (finished in Austin). This indicated that the official Treasury offices were still located in Austin, where the warrant was signed by Mason, the comptroller, and Shaw, the treasurer.

Oliver Jones, the payee, was a Senator representing the district of Austin, Colorado, and Fort Bend in the Sixth Congress, 1841-1842, when the warrant was issued.[49] Jones had previously made a name for himself by opposing an 1840 bill to outlaw the practice of dueling in the Republic.[50] When his efforts to block the offending legislation failed, he moved that the caption of the bill be changed to "An Act for the Protection of Cowards" and later moved to strike out the provision

No. 158 TREASURY WARRANT $93.00

The Treasurer of the Republic of Texas will pay to the Order of Oliver Jones, Ninety Three Dollars, out of any money appropriated by act of Feb[ruar]y 3rd, 1842 for Pay & Mileage of Members of Congress, this amount being for Pay and mileage as Member of Senate Extra Session. Treasury Department, Houston, July 25th, 1842

(Signed) Charles Mason, Auditor James B. Shaw, Comptroller

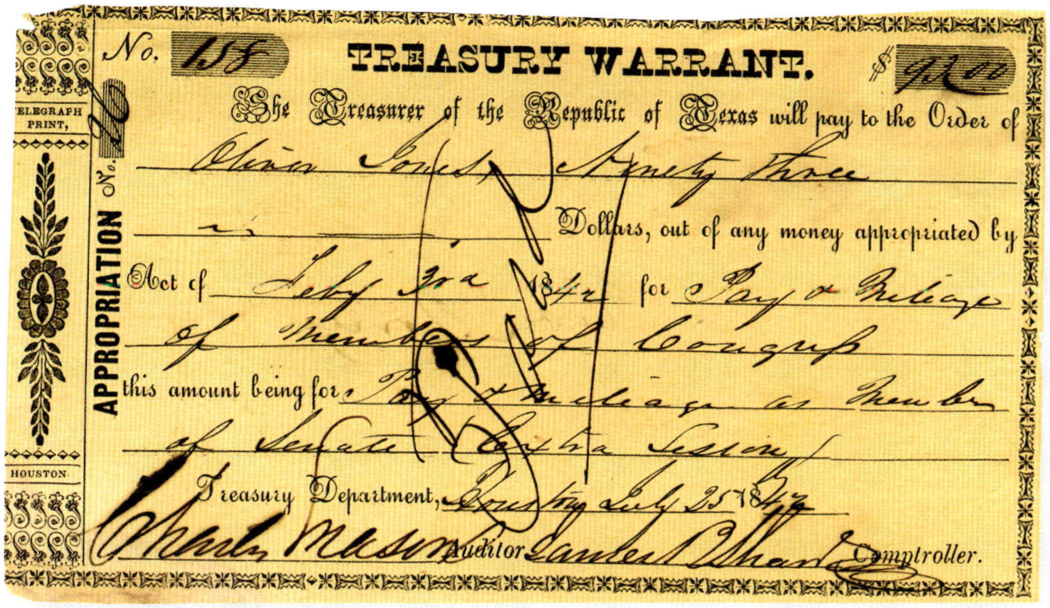

Fig 12.14, Houston, July 25, 1842, Treasury Warrant to Oliver Jones for Pay & Mileage of Member of Congress.

Private Collection, Cr. HW14, O-425.

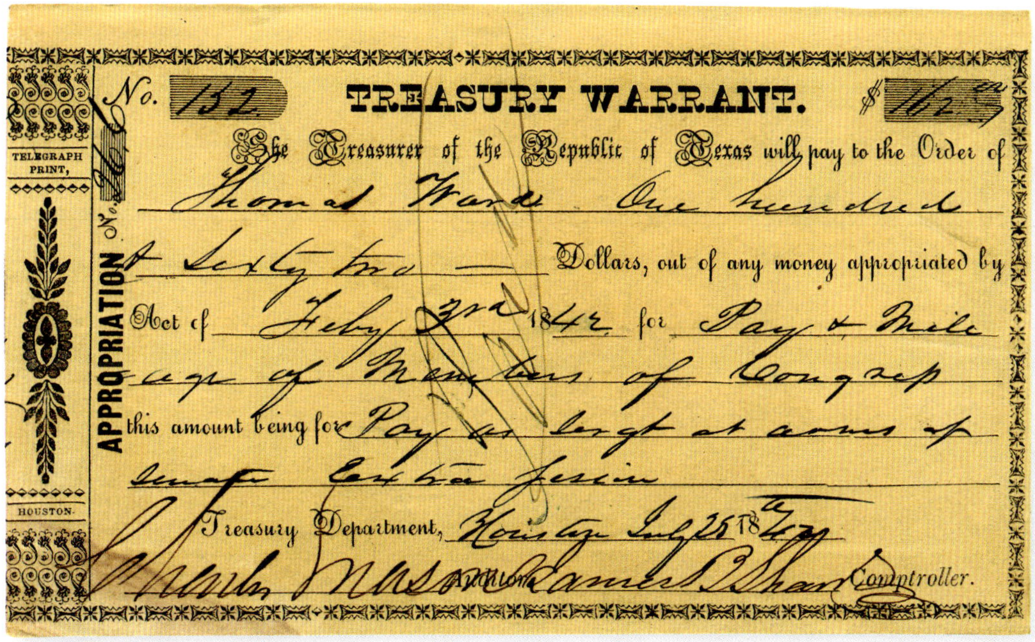

No. 152 TREASURY WARRANT $162.00

The Treasurer of the Republic of Texas will pay to the Order of Thomas Ward, One Hundred & Sixty two – Dollars, out of any money appropriated by act of Feb[ruar]y 3rd, 1842 for Pay & Mileage of Members of Congress, this amount being for Pay as Sergeant at arms of Senate Extra Session. Treasury Department, Houston, July 25th, 1842

(Signed) Charles Mason, Auditor James B. Shaw, Comptroller

Fig 12.15, Houston, July 25, 1842, Treasury Warrant to Thomas Ward for Pay & Mileage of Members of Congress.

Private Collection, Cr. HW14, O-425.

that disqualified duelists from holding public office. It is not known whether Jones supported the relocation of the government to Houston.

The $162.00 payment to Thomas Ward in Figure 12.15 was for "Pay & Mileage of Members of Congress" and demonstrates that Sam Houston had indeed called a session of Congress in Houston. Similar to the previous draft to Oliver Jones shown in Figure 12.14, Ward's payment for "Pay as Sergeant at arms of senate extra session" was also written in one ink and countersigned in another. Unlike the appropriations for the Texas Navy, these payments to government officials were written and issued to the legislators for their expenses while Congress was still in session.

In many ways, this emergency legislative session backfired on Sam Houston. The smaller denomination exchequer bills were authorized on July 23, 1842, during the special session, and despite the President's heated objections, a law was passed requiring sheriffs, clerks, postmasters, and the other collectors of taxes to realize only their current exchange rate in gold and silver when accepting the exchequer bills.[51] Like the previous paper money issues, the holders of the exchequer bills now saw their purchasing power dramatically reduced.

With the naval blockade of Mexican ports, Congress also focused on the precarious financial situation of the Texas Navy during this special session. The Navy had operated without any government-supplied funding for almost two years. The long-awaited relief came on the last day of the Congressional session when $15,000 was appropriated for the repair of the *Zavala* (which had run aground in a tropical storm off the Mexican coast); $25,000 was allotted for naval provisions; $28,231 for back pay through July 1, 1842; and $29,428 for the current pay period.[52] Following the Congressional appropriation, Commodore Edwin W. Moore called on President Houston at his office in Houston. Although the Congress had just appropriated $97,659 for the Navy, Houston refused to release the $20,000 previously appropriated, and suggested that Moore instead use a bond to raise the money in New Orleans. Moore finally lost his temper. According to historian Jonathan W. Jordan, "In an exchange that obliterated any civil feelings between the two men forever, Moore charged that, given the worthlessness of Houston's last two promises, it was clear that Houston was trifling with a matter that disparaged Moore's reputation as well as that of the Navy." The increasingly vindictive President was taken aback by the commander's bold comments, and the verbal confrontation would have serious consequences for both Moore and the Texas Navy in the future.

While members of Congress had been called to session in Houston in the summer of 1842, the remainder of the government remained firmly entrenched in Austin. Officially, the reason for not relocating the capital was cited as "objections from the western counties," though it may have been partly due to the stifling heat found in Houston.[53] Throughout this special session, the legislature endured a scorching Texas summer, and Congress refused to pass the legislation relocating the capital back to Houston. A compromise was eventually established, and the Capital was to be "temporarily" transferred to the Town of Washington. As Secretary of State, Anson Jones had been appalled by Lamar's removal of the seat of government from Houston to Austin and was equally appalled that it would be moved away from Austin to Houston, stating "as so much money had been expended [in Austin]."[54] In a sense, Jones was the perfect cabinet member for Sam Houston. He was diplomatic, intelligent, loyal, and publicly supportive. The tight-lipped Secretary of State never publicly opposed any of President Houston's actions, nor any part of his policy regardless of how much he was opposed to them privately.[55] His policy of cool thinking, fiscal conservatism, and verbal restraint was one that would elevate him to the highest office in the land. But for now, there was much work to be done for General Houston, as Jones often referred to the President.

1 Anson Jones, *Memoranda and Official Correspondence relating to the Republic of Texas its History and Annexation* (New York: D. Appleton & Company, 1859), 2: 35, November 19, 1839.

2 Bob Medlar, *Texas Obsolete Notes and Scrip* (Society of Paper Money Collectors, 1968), 204.

3 Seymour V. Conner, ed., "Houston to Stickney, Executive Department, City of Austin, December 13, 1841," Texas Treasury Papers, 2: 811.

4 William Ransom Hogan, *The Texas Republic: A Social and Economic History* (Norman, OK: University of Oklahoma Press, 1946), 95.

5 Marquis James, *The Raven: A Biography of Sam Houston* (Austin: University of Texas Press, 1929), 320-21.

6 Seymour V. Conner, ed., "Money to Secretary, Republic of Texas, County of Austin, December 31, 1841," Texas Treasury Papers, 2: 819.

7 "Annual Report of the Treasurer of the Republic of Texas for 1841," by order of the House of Representatives (Austin: S. Whiting, Public Printer, 1842), 7.

8 Ibid., 9.

9 Jones, *Memoranda and Official Correspondence,* 1-6.

10 *Handbook of Texas Online,* s.v., "Anson Jones," http://www.tsha.utexas.edu/handbook/online/articles/JJ/fjo42.html (accessed August 8, 2006).

11 Jones, *Memoranda and Official Correspondence,* 3: 38.

12 John Rowe and John Davis, Jr., "Texas Heritage," *Texas Historical Foundation* (Winter 2002), 54.

13 Jones, *Memoranda and Official Correspondence,* 3: 40.

14 William M. Gouge, *The Fiscal History of Texas* (New York: Burt Franklin, 1852; rpt. 1969), 116-17.

15 "Endorsed: Bill to authorize issuing Exchequer Bills," Journals of the Sixth Congress of the Republic of Texas, January 10, 1842, Bill No. 1,820.

16 "January 10, 1842," Journals of the Sixth Congress of the Republic of Texas, 218. As re-printed in *The Daily Texian,* January 11, 1842.

17 The actual amount of promissory notes in circulation was much greater than was estimated by the lawmakers. The amount of notes which were later presented for claims following annexation totaled $1,869,822. The various forms of stock, bonds and other Republic obligations suffered a similar fate.

18 Gouge, *The Fiscal History of Texas,* 116-17.

19 Ibid., 117.

20 "Byrne to Committee, January 25, 1842," Journals of the Sixth Congress of the Republic of Texas, 308-309.

21 Jonathan W. Jordan, *Lone Star Navy: Texas, the Fight for the Gulf of Mexico, and the Shaping of the American West* (Dulles, VA: Potomac Books, Inc., 2006), 211.

22 Seymour V. Conner, ed., "Houston to Crump, Executive Department, City of Houston, July 26, 1842," Texas Treasury Papers, 3: 867.

23 Gouge, *The Fiscal History of Texas,* 279.

24 Ibid., Appendix L, Rates of Value of Exchequer Bills, July 31, 1843 to July 31, 1844.

25 Jones, "James H. Cooke, Esq. Collector at Galveston to Anson Jones, Customs House, Galveston, January 30, 1844," *Memoranda and Official Correspondence,* 305.

26 From a Treasury Warrant, No. 861, payable to W.D. Miller, for $230.21 "out of any money appropriated by Act of February 3, 1842, for Signing Exchequer Bills, this amount being for Signing President's name to Exchequer Bills. Treasury Department, Washington, May 13th, 1843." From the Texas Money Collection, Special Collections, University of Houston Libraries.

27 Seymour V. Conner, ed., "Whiting to Dangerfield, Austin, February 11, 1842," Texas Treasury Papers, 3: 846.

28 Treasury Warrant for $89.93, to James W. Scott, dated August 1, 1843. Payment issued for "Endorsing Exchequer Bills," John N. Rowe III Collection, Southern Methodist University, DeGolyer Library.

29 Gouge, *The Fiscal History of Texas,* 124.

30 Douglas B. Ball, PhD. "Lone Star Notes: Largest U.S. State Created Currency from Scratch," *Bank Note Reporter* (May 1988), part II.

31 Ibid.

32 Seymour V. Conner, ed., "Rawdon, Wright, Hatch & Edson to Miller, New Orleans, June 6, 1843," Texas Treasury Papers, 3: 928-29.

33 "Report of the Secretary of the Treasury, Statement No. 6, Showing the whole amount of Exchequer Bills issued by the Treasury Department," (Washington: Vindicator Office, December 4, 1843), 5.

34 Seymour V. Conner, ed., "Woodhouse to Brigham, Shaw, Houston, September 12, 1842," Texas Treasury Papers, 3: 875-76.

35 Seymour V. Conner, ed., "Woodhouse to Shaw, Houston, August 20, 1842," Texas Treasury Papers, 3: 870.

36 Gouge, *The Fiscal History of Texas,* 122.

37 James, *The Raven,* 337.

38 Ball, "Lone Star Notes," part II.

39 "Report of the Secretary of the Treasury, Statement No. 6, Showing the whole amount of Exchequer Bills issued by the Treasury Department," (Washington: Vindicator Office, December 4, 1843), 5.

40 William Gibbs, "Byron Reed Collection worth $7.9M," *Coin World* (August 6, 2001), 3, 18.

41 Hogan, *The Texas Republic,* 67.

42 *Handbook of Texas Online,* s.v., "The Republic of Texas," http://www.tshaonline.org/handbook/online/articles/RR/mzr2.html (accessed December 6, 2008).

43 Jones, "Col. George Fisher to Anson Jones, Off Campeche, April 25, 1842," *Memoranda and Official Correspondence,* 194-95.

44 Jordan, *Lone Star Navy,* 212-13.

45 Ibid., 215.

46 Jones, "Houston to Jones, City of Houston, June 10, 1842," *Memoranda and Official Correspondence,* 203.

47 Seymour V. Conner, ed., "Houston to Crump, May 17, 1842," Texas Treasury Papers, 3: 858.

48 Grover C. Criswell, *Confederate and Southern States Currency,* vol. 1 (1957), 359; Joseph D. Olson, *Texas Numismatic History: A Catalogue,* 1st ed. (Texas Numismatic Heritage Press, 2006), 126.

49 "Roll of Senators," Journals of the Sixth Congress of the Republic of Texas, vol. 1.

50 Hogan, *The Texas Republic,* 283-84.

51 Gouge, *The Fiscal History of Texas,* 118.

52 Jordan, *Lone Star Navy,* 215-18.

53 James, *The Raven,* 329-30.

54 Jones, "September 16, 1839," *Memoranda and Official Correspondence,* 2: 34.

55 Ibid., "December 31, 1843," 3: 40.

CHAPTER THIRTEEN

WASHINGTON: TEXAS POLITICS IN TURMOIL

Fig 13.1, Washington on the Brazos - Street Scene
Texas State Library & Archives Commission, Austin, Texas.

HATFIELD'S SALOON

Houston's policy of relocating the seat of government back to Washington-on-the-Brazos breathed new life into the little community, though the lack of suitable buildings to house a legislative session presented a problem. The President proposed commandeering Hatfield's Saloon as the meeting place for the House of Representatives, but objections were soon sounded as the legislators claimed this would leave them without a suitable place to have a drink.[1] A gambling establishment which had occupied the second floor agreed to relocate to another building, and their space was used as the meeting chamber for the legislative sessions. Members of Congress entered the upstairs legislative chamber using a stairway from the barroom below. While the arrangement was not perfect, it proved a reasonable compromise as it offered the convenience of having a full service saloon on the first floor. This convenience became problematic, however, as the Speaker of the House had trouble maintaining a quorum with sober participants. President Houston then ordered the interior staircase removed and relocated to the outside of the building.

Nearby, the Senate met over a grocery store where the principal staple was liquor. The Department of War and Marines met in a log cabin with one window, while the Treasury Department (with no hard currency reserves) begged for similar accommodations. It was in these stark, wooden buildings near the banks of the Brazos River that the representatives of the Republic of Texas assessed the harsh economic and military realities of the day. Texas faced a hostile neighbor to the south, held a strained diplomatic relationship with France, opposed a growing abolitionist movement in the United States, and maintained a Treasury Department whose reserves consisted almost entirely of worthless paper instruments.

THE ARCHIVE WAR

In October 1842, the remaining government officials arrived in Washington. For the vindictive Sam Houston, having the government relocated from Austin to Washington-on-the-Brazos might have been victory enough, yet he still wanted to strip one more jewel from Lamar's capital of Austin. The National Archives, which dated back to the earliest Spanish settlements, were located at the land office in Austin. Sam Houston wanted them relocated to Washington, but the Austin residents refused to comply with the President's request. The documents were considered national treasures, and Houston wanted them in the same place as the seat of government.

Sam Houston campaigned for the removal of the archives as early as February 5, 1842, even while Austin remained the capital. In an effort to convince the legislature to remove the historical papers, he argued in a written communication: "I deem it my impervious duty to present to your consideration the exposed condition of the National Archives."[2] Citing the obvious threat of another Mexican invasion of Texas, he penned, "I have every reason to believe that the available force remaining at Austin will not be such as to guarantee the undoubted safety of the archives, and other public property. The loss of the archives would be an irreparable injury to the country. Therefore, to the representatives of the people, I submit the question as to the measures proper to be adopted for the protection and security of an object so important to the whole nation." A group of Austin residents, particularly the boarding house keepers, feared that the archives removal from Austin foreshadowed the permanent move of the capital, a decision which would cause their businesses to suffer. Despite the protests from Austin, once the capital was temporarily re-established in Washington, Sam Houston ordered his trusted friend Thomas W. Ward, the Land Commissioner, and a team of Texas Rangers led by Thomas I. Smith and Eli Chandler to move the archives from the land office in Austin to the new capital.

Thomas William "Peg Leg" Ward, the second commissioner of the General Land Office of Texas, was born in Dublin, Ireland, in 1807 to Mr. and Mrs. Henry Ward, landowning English immigrants. In 1828, Ward emigrated to Quebec and then to New Orleans, where he studied engineering and architecture.[3] During the Texas Revolution, Ward was one of the organizers of the New Orleans Greys which fought at the siege of Béxar in December 1835. Captain Ward, an artillery commander, followed Benjamin R. Milam into San Antonio. During the ensuing battle, Ward lost his right leg to a Mexican cannonball and Ben Milam was killed by a sniper's bullet. Legend has it that Milam's body and Ward's leg were buried in the same grave. Ward returned to New Orleans for medical care and was fitted with a peg leg. He returned to Texas in the spring of 1836, settled in Houston and worked as a general contractor. On February 18, 1837, Augustus C. Allen signed a contract with Ward to build the Texas capitol in Houston. Despite missing the initial deadline due to material delays, Ward completed the building in time for the Second Session of the First Congress.

In January 1841, Ward was appointed as Commissioner of the General Land Office, succeeding John P. Borden. Ward presided over the land office for the next seven years. As he struggled to combat rampant fraud and conflicting surveys and titles, he discovered that even his ceremonial duties were somewhat hazardous for him. On April 21, 1841, as he presided over the official celebration of San Jacinto Day, a cannon misfired and took off his right arm. The fact that Thomas Ward lost an arm and a leg to artillery fire and survived both incidents earned him an additional nickname of "Lucky."

After Sam Houston ordered Ward to remove the archives from Austin, "Peg Leg" and several Texas Rangers traveled the long, winding dirt road from Washington to Austin, arriving on December 13, 1842. Once in Austin, they waited until darkness fell before opening the General Land Office and removing several boxes of the coveted historical papers. Around midnight, a boarding-house keeper named Angelina Eberly noticed the men loading the wagons behind the land office.[4] Determined to keep the capital and the archives in Austin, and hence her boarding house full, Eberly made haste to the top of Congress Avenue where a six-pound cannon had been kept loaded with grapeshot by city officials in the event of an Indian attack. She turned the muzzle towards the land office and fired, peppering the building with shot, scattering the removal party, and awakening the town.

Fig 13.2, Thomas William Ward.
Texas State Library and Archives Commission, Austin, Texas.

Fig 13.3, Angelina Eberly: The Archive War.

Texas State Library and Archives Commission, Austin, Texas.

Thomas Ward, having previously lost two limbs to cannon fire, understandably called off the affair upon seeing the flash of the cannon and the land office peppered with shot! The Rangers, including Thomas I. Smith and Eli Chandler, escaped from the scene with three wagons filled with the priceless archives. They were overtaken on the road by Austin vigilantes near present-day Round Rock the following day where they surrendered the papers. The archives landed in Mrs. Eberly's boarding house, where they were guarded day and night for a time. Although President Houston railed against the citizens of Austin for blocking their removal, the vigilantes publicly offered to exchange the archives for the President. The National Archives have resided in Austin to this day.

THE MIER EXPEDITION

Following Mexican Gen. Adrian Woll's brief capture of San Antonio in September 1842, Sam Houston found himself under intense political pressure to retaliate against the repeated Mexican aggression. Albert Sidney Johnston was particularly angry with Houston's indecisiveness, and finally sent the President a hand-written challenge to a duel.[5] Sam Houston gave the letter to his Secretary, W.D. Miller, saying, "File this. Angry gentlemen must wait their turn." Houston then ordered Gen. Alexander Somervell to organize a retaliatory force of 1,000 volunteers in a show of strength against Mexico.[6] The Mier Expedition, as the force became known, included such notables as Thomas Jefferson Green, Orlando Phelps, Ben McCulloch, John C. Hays, and future Gov. Peter H. Bell. Since little funds were available to purchase supplies for the expedition, the adventurers were to loot supplies from captured towns along the way. The eventual goal was to capture the Mexican town of Mier, located about ninety miles southwest of Laredo.

Fig 13.4, Map of the Border Wars of the Republic of Texas, culminating in the Santa Fe and Mier Expeditions, 1841-1842.

Cartography by James L. Glass.

The expedition reached Laredo by December 7, 1842, and camped two miles outside of town. Sixty soldiers proceeded to loot and plunder the largely *tejano* town on December 9, even though it was on the Texas side of the Rio Grande.[7] The troupe then proceeded to the town of Guerrero and crossed the river into the Mexican settlement, though the town held little supplies for the weary travelers. On December 11, about 187 disillusioned volunteers turned back and headed for home. By December 19, hampered by cold winter, rain, a freak south Texas snowfall, and a further lack of supplies, Somervell called off the raid into Mexico and ordered the rest of his men to return home by way of Gonzales.

Seeking adventure, glory, and a chance for revenge against Mexico, many of the headstrong men refused to turn back to Texas—a decision that was met with disastrous consequences. The men reorganized under Col. William S. Fisher, who proceeded to lead 308 Texians another seventy miles down the Rio Grande River to the Mexican town of Mier. Leaving a base camp behind in Texas, Fisher and a force of 261 men crossed the river and entered Mier on December 23 without opposition.[8] Fisher gave an ultimatum to the local *alcalde* to round up supplies, but the Texians had no way to transport the goods back across the river to their camp and soon returned to their base.

The next day, the Mier Expedition members discovered that Mexican Gen. Pedro de Ampudia had arrived from Matamoros.[9] Accompanying him were more than 2,000 Mexican troops, cavalry, and an artillery regiment. Desperate and famished, on Christmas Day 1842, the Texians again crossed the Rio Grande and engaged the Mexicans in a fierce gun battle, killing 600 and wounding 200 others, while losing only thirty of their own. Outnumbered almost ten to one, they were hungry for food and water and running short on ammunition. Although they had inflicted heavy casualties, the Texian party surrendered to the superior Mexican force.

The captured soldiers were sentenced to death by firing squad, but on December 27, General Ampudia reversed the execution order. Mexican soldiers escorted the prisoners to Matamoros, and then on to Mexico City. While in route to the Mexican capital, the Texians escaped their captors at Salado on February 11, 1843. The rugged terrain and the harsh exposure of the dry, rocky soil eventually took its toll on the men, however, and 176 of the invaders were eventually recaptured and returned to Salado for punishment. President Antonio López de Santa Anna ordered the captured Texians executed, but Gov. Francisco Mexia of the State of Coahuila intervened on the prisoners behalf.

Fig 13.5, The Execution of the Mier Prisoners.

Texas State Library & Archives Commission, Austin, Texas.

The sketch was made by Charles McLaughlin, one of the Mier prisoners who drew a white bean and managed to survive the ordeal.

While in the Mexican town of Salado, Mexican leaders determined that one out of every ten prisoners would be executed. In what became known as the black bean episode, 159 white beans and 17 black beans were placed in a jar. Each man was blindfolded and forced to draw a bean from the jar. Those unlucky men which drew the black beans were summarily executed by a firing squad at Salado, Mexico, on March 25, 1843. The remaining prisoners were marched more than 450 miles to Mexico City. Some were imprisoned in the nearby Perote Prison. Many worked on the hot, dusty, Mexican roads in the summer of 1843 and subsequently died in captivity from wounds, disease, and starvation.

The capture of the Mier Expedition was a political nightmare for Sam Houston, who later conceded that the men had acted without the authority of the government. Without the necessary funds to raise, outfit, supply, and pay an army, Houston knew that the continuation of any military conflict based solely on volunteers would be sheer folly. Although several men escaped or were released at the request of U.S. officials, the last of the Mier prisoners were not set free by Santa Anna until September 16, 1844, when he eventually bowed to diplomatic pressures from England and the United States.

THE PAPER TRAIL CONTINUES THROUGH WASHINGTON

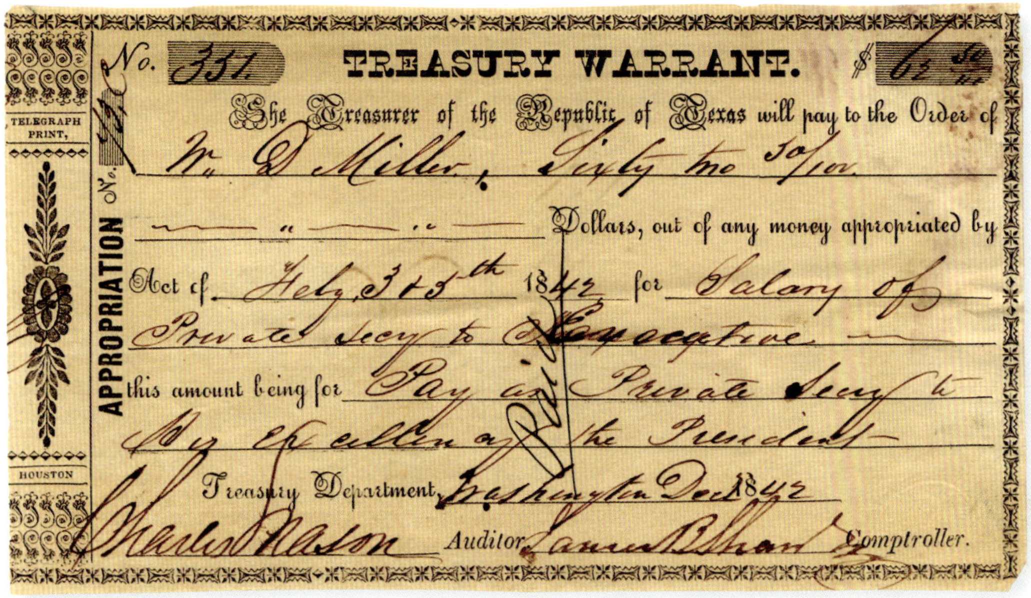
No. 357 TREASURY WARRANT. $62 50/00

The Treasurer of the Republic of Texas will pay to the Order of W. D. Miller, Sixty two 50/100

Dollars, out of any money appropriated by Act of Feby 3 & 5th 1842 for Salary of Private Secy to Executive

this amount being for Pay as Private Secy to His Excellency the President

Treasury Department, Washington Dec 1 1842

Charles Mason Auditor James B. Shaw Comptroller.

TELEGRAPH PRINT, HOUSTON

APPROPRIATION No.

No. 357 TREASURY WARRANT $62.50

The Treasurer of the Republic of Texas will pay to the Order of W.D. Miller, Sixty Two 50/100 – Dollars, out of any money appropriated by act of Feb[ruar]y 3& 5th 1842 for Salary of Private Sec[retar]y to Executive, this amount being for Pay as Private Sec[retar]y to His Excellency the President.

Treasury Department, Washington Dec. 1, 1842 (Signed) Charles Mason, Auditor James B. Shaw, Comptroller

Fig 13.6, Washington, Treasury Warrant, December 1, 1842, W.D. Miller, for "Pay as Private Secretary to His Excellency the President."

Private Collection, Cr. W3, O-1015.

It was under these brazen political circumstances that the late series of treasury warrants were issued from Washington-on-the-Brazos. While no circulating currency was issued from Washington-on-the-Brazos, this series of treasury warrants is among the most colorful issued during the Republic period—not only because of the paper, but also for their content. Each note is a hand written record of the political times. They not only list the date, number, payee, and amount, but also two full lines on which the nature of the expense is described. There are nine major varieties of the paper, all of which were printed: two bear the heading "This Certificate entitles…" and seven with the heading "Treasury Warrant." Many of these drafts were made payable to government officials instrumental in the founding of the Republic, though many of these names have fallen into obscurity. A little bit of detective work on the part of the historian can unearth some interesting discoveries.

Washington D. Miller was an early legislator and lawyer who came to Texas in 1837 from Alabama and settled in Gonzales to practice law.[10] Originally trained as an engineer, he represented Gonzales County in Congress from November 1840 to February 1841. He began serving as Sam Houston's personal secretary shortly afterwards in Austin, and later followed him to Houston and then to Washington where this payment was issued. Fiercely loyal to Sam Houston, Miller's payment for service documents his "Pay as Private Sec(retar)y to His Excellency the President." The chief executive was always referred to as "His Excellency the President" in official proceedings. This address was certainly more flattering than the "Big Drunk" name which the Cherokee Indians bestowed upon Sam Houston in his earlier days.

In March 1842, Miller participated in repelling the incursion of the Mexican Army which had recaptured San Antonio de Béxar. Shortly after this payment was issued, he joined the Mier Expedition which was well under way in South Texas. Miller was among those who continued into Mexico and was captured and held as a prisoner following their surrender on December 26, 1842.[11] He was fortunate enough to draw a white bean during the selection process for the subsequent execution. Following his release to Texas, Miller also served as Postmaster General, Secretary of the Senate in the Seventh Congress, and an assistant to former Comptroller James B. Shaw in preparing a report on the Public Debt of Texas in 1851.[12] In 1861, Miller relocated to Galveston where he died on September 19, 1866.

No. 409 TREASURY WARRANT $10.00

The Treasurer of the Republic of Texas will pay to the Order of Gail Borden, Jr, Ten – Dollars, out of any money appropriated by Act of Feb[ruar]y 3rd 1842 for Contingent Expenses of Treasury Department this amount being for Transportation.

Treasury Department, Washington Dec. 17th, 1842

(Signed) Charles Mason, Auditor James B. Shaw, Comptroller

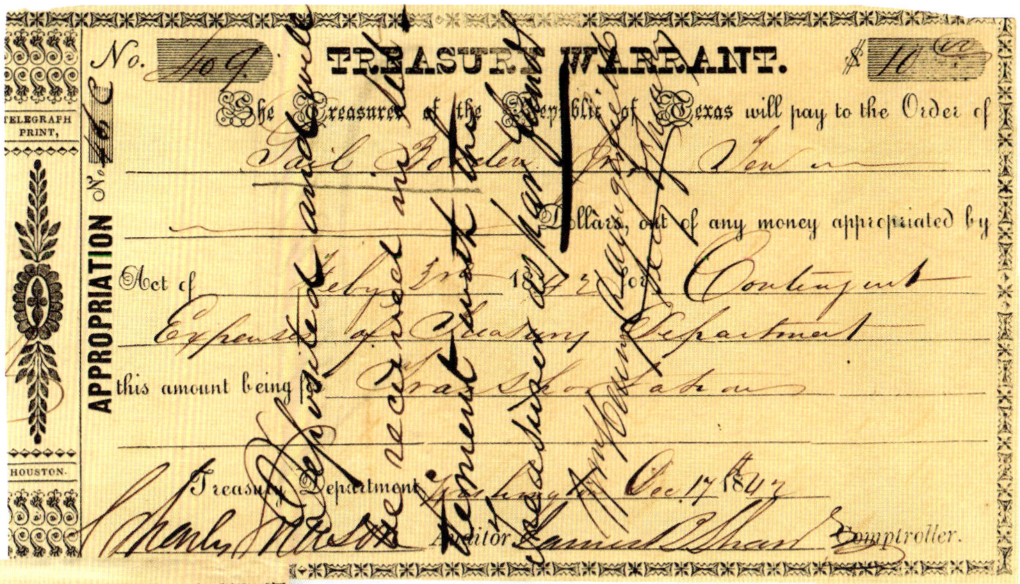

Fig 13.7, Washington, Treasury Warrant, December 17, 1842, Payable to Gail Borden, Jr. for "Transportation."

Private Collection, Cr.W3, O-1015.

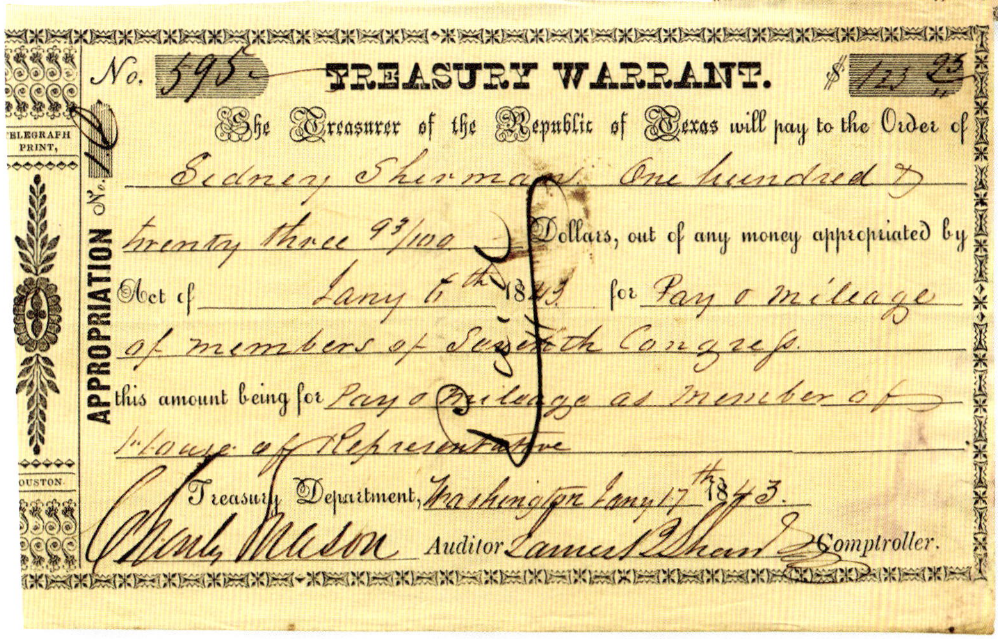

No. 595 TREASURY WARRANT $123.95

The Treasurer of the Republic of Texas will pay to the Order of Sidney Sherman, One Hundred & Twenty three 93/100 Dollars, out of any money appropriated by Act of Jan[uar]y 6th 1843 for Pay & Mileage of members of Seventh Congress this amount being for Pay & mileage as member of House of Representatives.

Treasury Department, Washington Jan[uar]y 17th, 1843

(Signed) Charles Mason, Auditor James B. Shaw, Comptroller

Fig 13.8, Washington, Treasury Warrant, January 17, 1843, Payable to Sidney Sherman , for "Pay and Mileage of members of Seventh Congress."

Private Collection, Cr. W3, O-1015.

The payment in Figure 13.7 was issued to Gail Borden, Jr., for $10 and reflects contingent expenses of the Treasury Department for "transportation." While this is a relatively common warrant, Gail Borden, Jr., was a most uncommon man. He arrived in Texas by way of Galveston on December 24, 1829, farming and raising livestock in Fort Bend.[13] By 1830, he succeeded his brother, Thomas H. Borden as a surveyor in Stephen F. Austin's colony. On October 10, 1835, the first issue of his *Telegraph and Texas Register* newspaper was published in partnership with his brother and Joseph Baker at San Felipe de Austin. Because of the war, the press moved to Harrisburg in April 1836, to Columbia from August 1836 to April 1837, and finally in Houston from May and June 1837. As mentioned earlier in the text, it was Borden who printed several significant broadsides for the Texas government. His skills as a surveyor were still viable, and he helped lay out the site of Houston for the Allen brothers in the fall of 1836. At the time of this payment, he served as the collector of duties at the Port of Galveston. The inscription across the face reads "Deposited and will be received in settlement with the Treasurer as par funds. (signed) W[illia]m H. Dangerfield, Sec of Treas[ur]y."

Outside of Texas, Borden is best remembered as the inventor who developed and patented a process for condensing milk. Having established factories in Connecticut and New York, the Civil War intensified

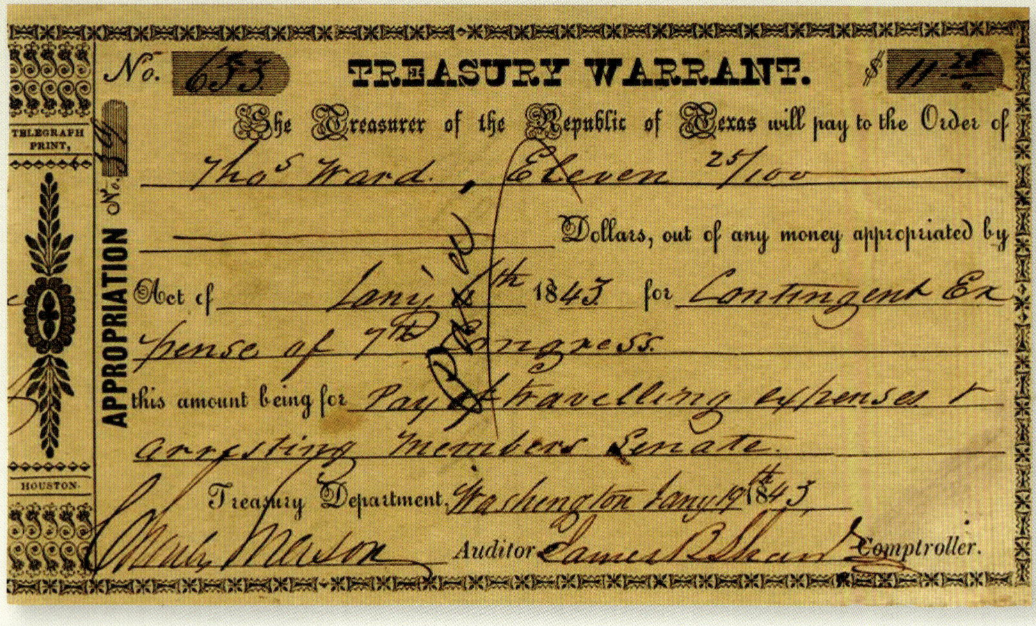
TELEGRAPH PRINT,
No. 653 TREASURY WARRANT. $11.25
APPROPRIATION No.
The Treasurer of the Republic of Texas will pay to the Order of Thos Ward, Eleven 25/100 Dollars, out of any money appropriated by Act of Jany 6th 1843 for Contingent Expense of 7th Congress this amount being for Pay of travelling expenses & arresting Members Senate.
HOUSTON.
Treasury Department, Washington Jany 19 1843
Chas Mason Auditor James B. Shaw Comptroller.

No. 653 TREASURY WARRANT $11.25

The Treasurer of the Republic of Texas will pay to the Order of Tho[ma]s Ward, Eleven 25/100 – Dollars, out of any money appropriated by Act of Jan[uar]y 6th 1843 for Contingent Expense of 7th Congress this amount being for Pay of traveling expenses & arresting Members (of the) Senate.

Treasury Department, Washington Jan[uar]y 19th, 1843

(Signed) Charles Mason, Auditor James B. Shaw, Comptroller

Fig 13.10, Washington, Treasury Warrant, January 19, 1843, Payable to Thomas Ward, for "Arresting Members [of the] Senate."

Private Collection, Cr. W3, 0-1015.

Fig 13.9, Sidney Sherman.

The San Jacinto Museum of History, Houston, Texas.

Sidney Sherman was an entrepreneur who came to Texas in 1835 and commanded the left flank at the battle of San Jacinto. He is credited with initiating the immortal battle-cry "Remember the Alamo" as his regiment advanced on the Mexican breastworks.

the enormous demand for canned milk and assured his success as a businessman. He also founded the dairy products company which still bears his name.

Sidney Sherman was born in Marlboro, Massachusetts, on July 23, 1805.[14] One of ten children, he was orphaned at the age of twelve. By the age of sixteen, he was clerking in a Boston mercantile store. He soon moved to Newport, Kentucky, where he started several business ventures including a cotton bagging plant. Sherman became a captain of a volunteer company of state militia in Kentucky in 1835, sold his interest in the business, equipped a company of fifty-two volunteers, and headed to Texas for the revolution.

When Sam Houston organized his first regiment at Gonzales in March 1836, Sherman was promoted to lieutenant colonel. After crossing Groce's Ferry, the army was reorganized, and Sherman was promoted to colonel and placed in command of the Second Regiment of the Texas Volunteers. General Houston described Sherman's actions at the battle of San Jacinto as follows: "Col. Sherman with his regiment, having commenced the action upon our left wing, the whole line, at the centre and on the right, advancing in double time, rung the war cry 'Remember the Alamo,' received the enemy's fire, and advanced within point blank shot before a piece was discharged from our lines."[15] It was Sherman's advance which first broke the enemy lines, drove the enemy into confusion, and continued to pursue them until all resistance ceased.

Following the war, Sherman returned to Kentucky and brought his wife Catherine back to Texas where they maintained an estate on San Jacinto bay. In 1843, at the time this pay warrant (Fig. 13.8) was issued, Sherman served as Harris County's representative in the Seventh Congress, and was the chairman of the committee on military affairs. He was elected as head of the militia, and presided in that capacity over the court martial trial of Texas navy Commander Edwin W. Moore. Sherman later operated a hotel in Galveston and served as the commander of Confederate forces on the island until ill health forced him to resign the position. Sherman died in Galveston on August 1, 1873.

The payment in Figure 13.10 was issued to Thomas Ward for "pay of traveling expenses & arresting Members [of the] Senate." In addition to serving in harm's way as an officer in the Texas Army, he built the Capitol in Houston for the Allen Brothers, and served as General Land Commissioner under Sam Houston. Ward was also elected as Sergeant at Arms for the Sixth and Seventh Congress and served as the doorkeeper for the House of Representatives during these same congressional sessions.[16]

At the time this warrant was issued, the government had commandeered the upstairs floor of Hatfield's Saloon in Washington as a place for Congress to convene.[17] This payment to Thomas Ward as Sergeant at Arms reflects his official duties to "arrest" the members of the Senate by forcibly herding them from the saloon downstairs and bringing them (physically if necessary) upstairs to make a quorum for an important vote. Although the peg-legged Ward (who was also missing his right arm) could not have been much of a deterrent to

No. 861 TREASURY WARRANT $231.21

The Treasurer of the Republic of Texas will pay to the Order of W.D. Miller Two hundred & thirty one 21/100 – Dollars, out of any money appropriated by Act of February 3, 1842 for Signing Exchequer Bills this amount being for Signing Presidents name to Exchequer Bills

Treasury Department, Washington May 13th, 1843

(Signed) Charles Mason, Auditor James B. Shaw, Comptroller

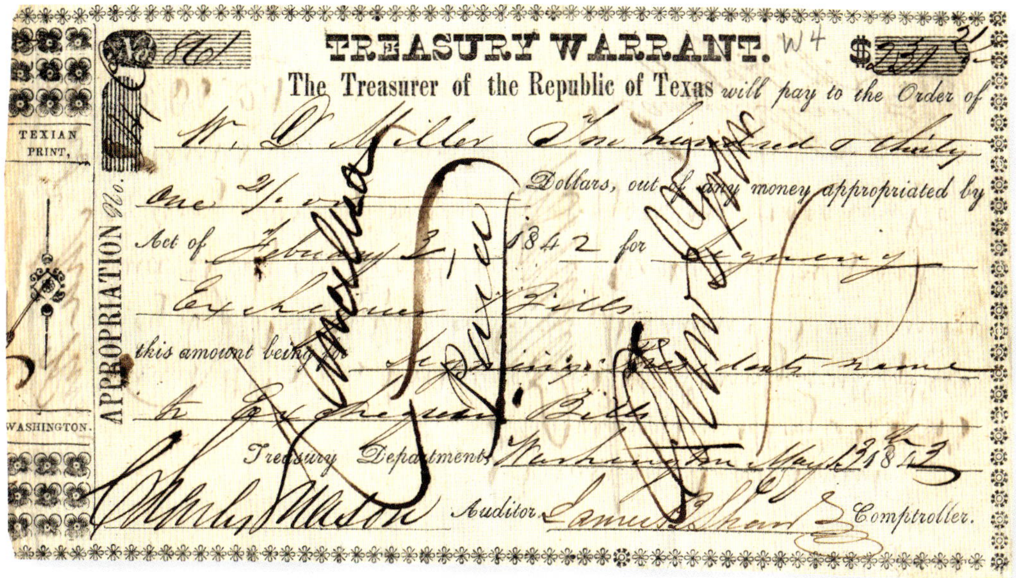
TREASURY WARRANT.
TEXIAN PRINT, WASHINGTON.
APPROPRIATION No.
861 — $231 21
The Treasurer of the Republic of Texas will pay to the Order of W. D. Miller Two hundred & thirty one 21/100 Dollars, out of any money appropriated by Act of February 3, 1842 for Signing Exchequer Bills this amount being for [illegible] name to Exchequer Bills
Treasury Department, Washington May 13 1843
Charles Mason Auditor. James B. Shaw Comptroller.

Fig 13.11, Washington, Treasury Warrant, May 13, 1843, Payable to W.D. Miller, for "Signing President's name to Exchequer Bills."

Texas Money Collection, Courtesy of Special Collections, University of Houston Libraries, Houston, Texas, Cr. W4, O-1020.

(left) Treas Red River (top) Treasury Department, Washington May 31, 1843

James M. Sims, Treasurer of Red County will please pay to W.D. Miller or order the sum of Two hundred and thirty one 21/100 dollars in Exchequer bills out of any money received by you on account of Licenses. $231.21. (signed) James B. Shaw, Act[ing] Sec[retar]y

(endorsed) W.D. Miller

Fig 13.12, Reverse of the treasury warrant to W.D. Miller.

Texas Money Collection, Courtesy of Special Collections, University of Houston Libraries, Houston, Texas.

the men tempted by the saloon, it is a strong reflection of his commitment to serve the Republic in a variety of important roles despite the tremendous physical handicaps that he had to overcome.

As Sam Houston's personal Secretary, Washington D. Miller was assigned the laborious task of affixing Sam Houston's signature to the last currency of the Republic. Miller was paid at the rate of one half cent per signature. Because the Treasury Department had carefully restricted the issue of the exchequer bills, the new money was in short supply even in the spring of 1843. The warrant in Figure 13.11 is marked "Cancelled" and "Paid" across the face.

Miller was unable to redeem the warrant in for the new currency at Washington. The exchequer bills were mandated to be cancelled and destroyed as soon as they were paid into the Treasury. However, with a little influence from his friend James B. Shaw, the Acting Treasury Secretary, the solution to Miller's problem can be determined by the manuscript writing on the reverse of the warrant (see Figure 13.12).

Shaw simply instructed his friend James M. Sims, a county Treasurer, to cash the warrant out of funds received by Red County, thereby funding and canceling Miller's warrant. When the exchequer bills were spent by Miller, they would eventually find their way back to the Treasury where they could be cancelled and destroyed. This is a classic example of one government official taking care of another.

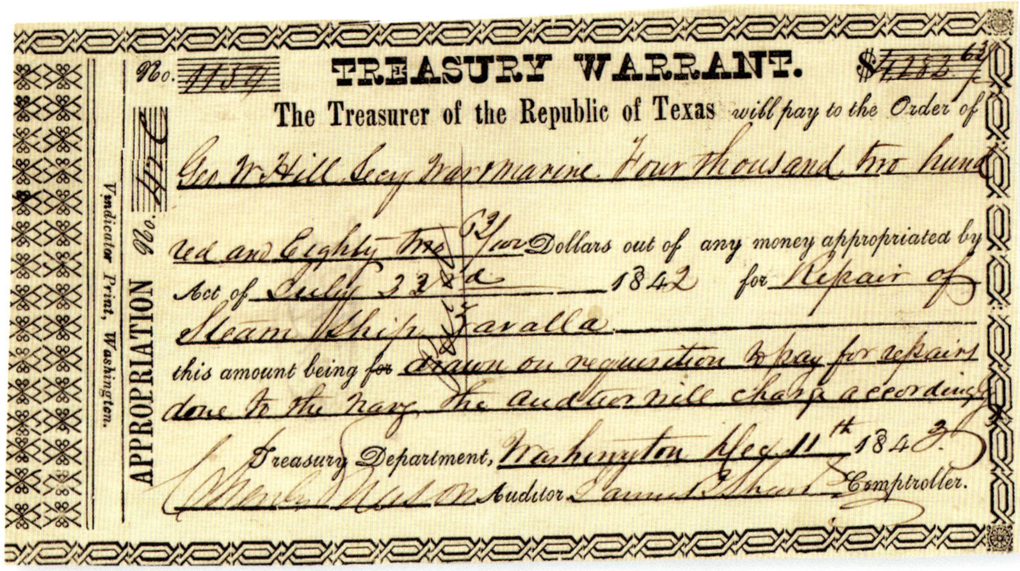

Fig 13.13, Washington, Treasury Warrant, December 11, 1843, Payable to George W. Hill, Secy War & Marine, for "Repair of (the) Steam Ship Zavalla."

Private Collection, Cr. W7, O-1050.

No. 1154 TREASURY WARRANT $4282.63

The Treasurer of the Republic of Texas will pay to the Order of Geo. W. Hill, Sec[reta]y [of] War & Marine. Four thousand, two hundred and Eighty-two 63/100 Dollars, out of any money appropriated by Act of July 23, 1842 for Repair of Steam Ship Zavalla. this amount being drawn on requisition to pay for repairs done to the Navy, the auditors will charge accordingly.

Treasury Department, Washington Dec. 11th, 1843

(Signed) Charles Mason, Auditor James B. Shaw, Comptroller

Fig 13.14, Edward Burleson, Vice President.

The San Jacinto Museum of History, Houston, Texas.

The payment in Figure 13.13 for $4,282.63 for the repair of the *Zavala* was issued almost two years after the ship returned to port and well over a year after Congress appropriated the funds during a legislative session in Houston in the summer of 1842. This delayed payment for the badly needed overhaul underscores the lack of importance that President Sam Houston gave to maintaining a strong Texas Navy. This payment and others which were made for the repairs were deemed inadequate to restore the once mighty warship to service. Congress was notorious for appropriating inadequate sums for the maintenance of the Texas Navy under Houston. Having successfully survived an assault from the Mexican Navy, and later the fury of a violent tropical storm, the ship's eventual undoing was an inadequate congressional appropriation for badly needed repairs.

The *Zavala* was put out of commission due to a lack of funds and was allowed to rot. By May 1842, the ship was in such poor condition that it was run aground at the edge of Galveston harbor to prevent it from sinking. In 1844, the *Zavala* was broken up, and its engines sold for scrap.[18] By 1862, the ship had sunk below the surface with just a single smokestack above the water that warned other vessels of her location on the north side of Galveston Island.[19] In November 1986, a joint archeological expedition between the National Underwater and Marine Agency and the Texas Antiquities Committee located the wreck of the *Zavala*.[20] After a century and a half of being shifted around by hurricanes, the team identified the *Zavala*'s grave underneath a present-day parking lot for a grain elevator under Twenty Ninth Street in the city of Galveston.

Edward Burleson served as Vice President under Sam Houston's second term. Born in North Carolina in 1798, he enlisted as a private in an Alabama regiment in the War of 1812.[21] Burleson came to Texas in 1830, received title to land in Austin's colony and served as a delegate to the convention at Mina. On October 10, 1835, in Gonzales, he was elected as lieutenant colonel in the army under Stephen F. Austin. On December 1, 1835, Burleson was commissioned as commander in chief of the volunteer army by the provisional government. He fought in the siege at Béxar with Ben Milam and commanded the First Regiment at the battle of San Jacinto, where he was placed opposite the Mexican breastworks and was the first to charge them. It was Burleson who accepted the sword and surrender of Col. Juan N. Almonte following the battle.

Burleson is also remembered as one of the few men who easily moved between the political parties of Sam Houston and Mirabeau B. Lamar. In the spring of 1838, Burleson, a trained surveyor, laid out the town of Waterloo which later became the city of Austin. On October 17, 1839, he presided over the ceremonies welcoming Lamar and establishing Austin as the capital of the Republic of Texas. He was elected to the Senate of the Third Congress, but resigned the seat at the request of President Lamar to command the Frontier Regiment in a war against the Indians. On Christmas Day 1839, his men defeated the Cherokees, killing Chief Bowl's son and another chief during the battle. He sent Chief Bowl's "hat" to Sam Houston as a gift, enraging his friend who was raised with the tribe. In 1841, Ed Burleson was elected Vice President of the Republic of Texas for which the $150 payment for "Compensation of Vice President" was issued. He assigned the payment to his friend George D. Hancock before it was issued, as noted by the listing of both names on the payment line.

George D. Hancock was also a significant Texas personality in his own right. Hancock served as a private

No. 1001 TREASURY WARRANT $150.00

The Treasurer of the Republic of Texas will pay to the Order of Edward Burleson per G.D. Hancock, One hundred & fifty Dollars, out of any money appropriated by Act of January 6th 1843 for Compensation of Vice President this amount being for Pay of Salary as Vice President

Treasury Department, Washington July 31, 1843

(Signed) John M. Swisher, act. Auditor James B. Shaw, Comptroller

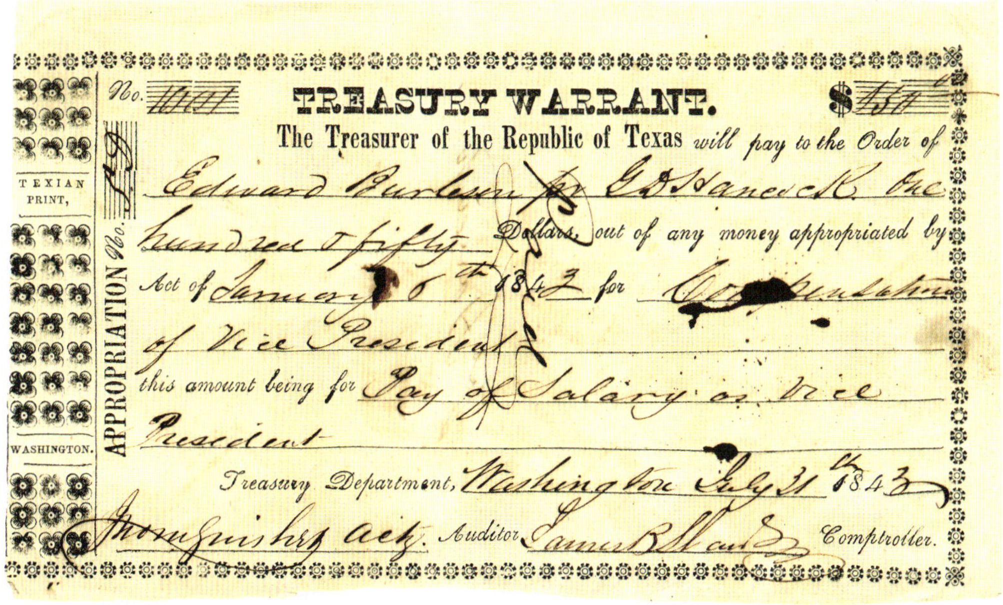

No. 1001 TREASURY WARRANT. $150

The Treasurer of the Republic of Texas will pay to the Order of Edward Burleson per G. D. Hancock One hundred & fifty Dollars, out of any money appropriated by Act of January 6th 1843 for Compensation of Vice President this amount being for Pay of Salary as Vice President

Treasury Department, Washington July 31 1843

John M. Swisher act. Auditor James B. Shaw Comptroller.

TEXIAN PRINT, WASHINGTON.

APPROPRIATION No.

Fig 13.15, Washington, Treasury Warrant, July 31, 1843, Payable to Edward Burleson per George D. Hancock for "Salary as Vice President."

Private Collection, Cr. W5, 0-1025.

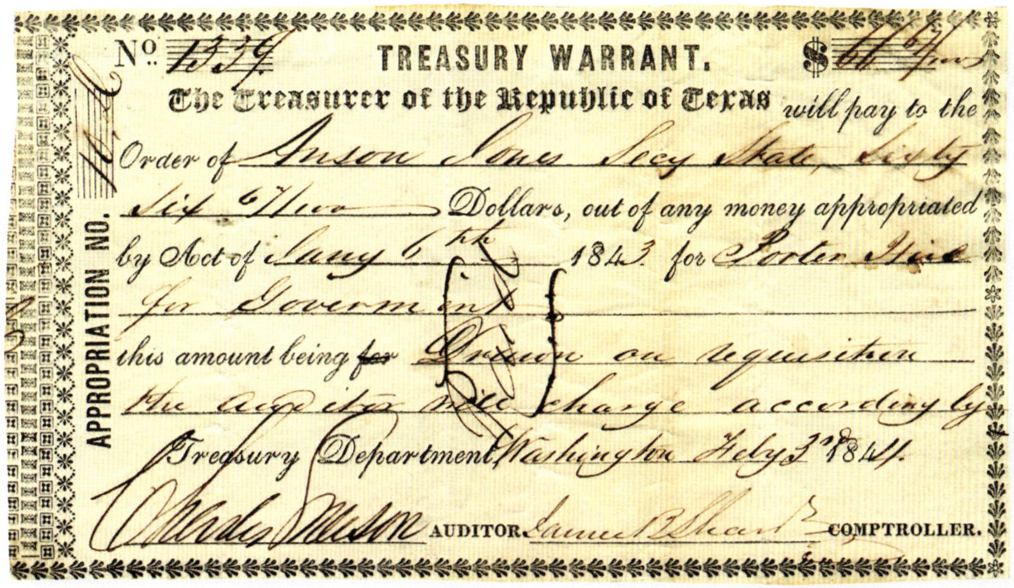

No. 1339 TREASURY WARRANT. $66 67/100

The Treasurer of the Republic of Texas will pay to the Order of Anson Jones Secy State, Sixty Six 67/100 Dollars, out of any money appropriated by Act of Jany 6th 1843 for Porter Hired for Government this amount being Drawn on requisition the auditors will charge accordingly

Treasury Department Washington Feby 3rd 1844.

Charles Mason AUDITOR. James B. Shaw COMPTROLLER.

APPROPRIATION NO.

No. 1339 TREASURY WARRANT $66.67

The Treasurer of the Republic of Texas will pay to the Order of Anson Jones, Sec[retar]y [of] State, Sixty Six 67/100 – Dollars, out of any money appropriated by Act of Jan[uar]y 6th, 1843 for Porter Hired for Government this amount being Drawn on requisition the auditors will charge accordingly.

Treasury Department, Washington Feb[ruar]y 3rd, 1844

(Signed) Charles Mason, Auditor James B. Shaw, Comptroller

Fig 13.16, Washington, Treasury Warrant, February 3, 1844, Payable to Anson Jones, Secretary of State.

Private Collection, Cr. W6A, 0-1030.

in Capt. William Kimbro's company of Texas Volunteers under Sidney Sherman in 1836. He was one of the five men who accompanied "Deaf" Smith in the destruction of Vince's Bridge and afterwards fought at the battle of San Jacinto.[22] Although Hancock worked as a surveyor and participated in the Somervell expedition, he is best remembered for the advancement of the retail trade in the city of Austin. He founded a highly successful store in LaGrange in 1843, later moved it to Bastrop and then again to Austin in 1844. His Austin store was established at the corner of Congress and Pecan (now Sixth Street). The editor of the *Texas State Gazette* regarded Hancock as "an experienced merchant of acknowledged good taste in the selection of goods" and offered "as large and complete a stock…as has ever been brought to the city."

The payment in Figure 13.16 to Anson Jones as Secretary of State for $66.67 is noted as being for a "Porter Hired for Government" and is marked "paid" across the face. Ever a hard money man, Anson Jones carefully pointed out in an interview with biographer William Gouge, for Gouge to make a special record of the fact that "his signature was never affixed to a paper bill of credit."[23] However, his endorsement can be found on the reverse of this warrant from Washington as payment in his official capacity.

As Secretary of State, Jones was largely responsible for assisting Sam Houston in the tight money policies

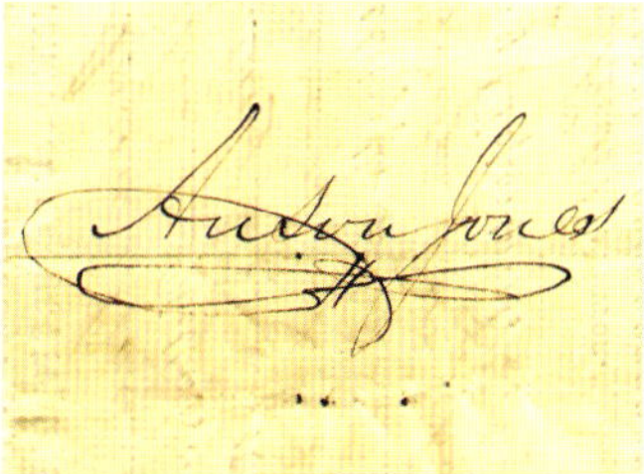

Fig 13.17, Signature on reverse side of Anson Jones' pay warrant.

Private Collection.

during Houston's second administration. Jones successfully managed the foreign relations of Texas through a series of diplomatic crises. He was charged with negotiating the Treaty of Annexation with the United States on April 12, 1844, and gauging the political climate towards annexation in Washington, D.C. It was also Jones who originated as well as controlled and managed much of the domestic and foreign policy of the country for three years. His legacy included returning Texas to a sound financial footing and laying the groundwork with moderate elements in Mexico for an eventual, but short-lived, peace between the two countries.

While the men of the Texas Navy were still at sea in March 1844, Sam Houston proclaimed the officers to be pirates, and requested any friendly country to capture the ships and return them to Galveston.[24] The shortage of funds in the Treasury Department under Lamer had demoralized their ranks, and Sam Houston personally withheld a distribution of exchequer bills originally appropriated for the Navy in 1842.[25]

The payment in Figure 13.18 to Armstrong I. Lewis was authorized by an act of Congress on February 5, 1844, as an appropriation for back pay long overdue the Navy. Lieutenant Lewis served on the *San Bernard* and the *Zavala* and had commanded a group of Yucatan warships which had sided with Texas during the battle of Campeche in May 1843.[26] Despite the officers courageous service to the Republic, this appropriation of funds sparked a protest from the Secretary of War and Marine who submitted a list of officers to the Treasury Department "not entitled to pay" for reasons of being cited for disciplinary violations or infractions "of the known rules and regulation of the service."[27] Lewis, who had once been cited for opening a storeroom and distributing liquor to himself and his fellow shipmates without the consent of the purser, apparently survived the political backlash and received the warrant for back pay.

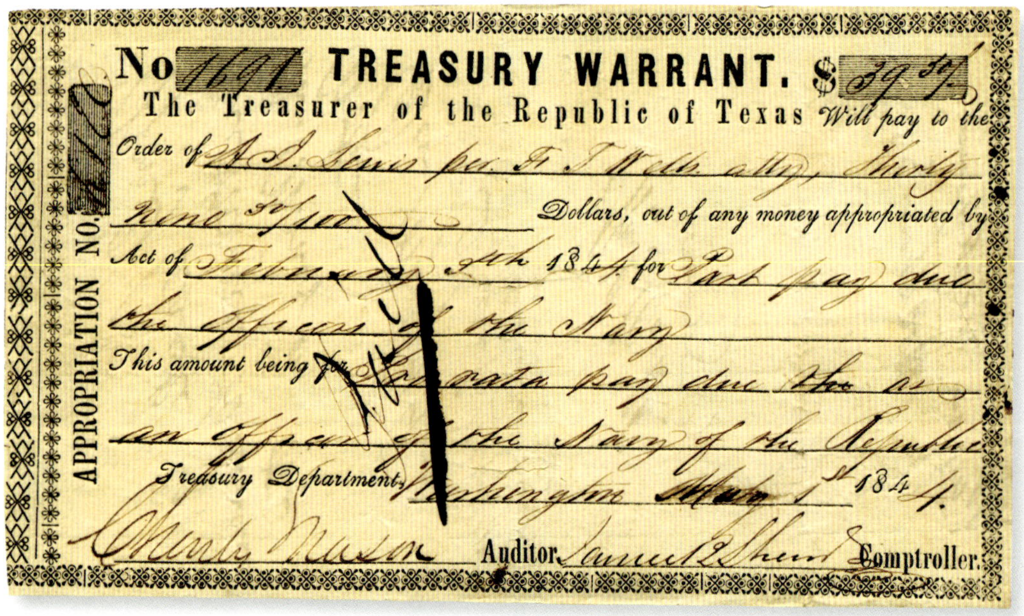
No. TREASURY WARRANT. $

The Treasurer of the Republic of Texas Will pay to the Order of

Dollars, out of any money appropriated by Act of

This amount being for

Treasury Department,

Auditor. Comptroller.

APPROPRIATION NO.

Fig 13.18, Washington, Treasury Warrant, May 1, 1844, Payable to A.I. Lewis per F.T. Wells, Attorney, for "Pro rata pay due as an officer of the Navy of the Republic."

Private Collection, Cr. W8, 0-1045.

No. 1691 TREASURY WARRANT $39.50

The Treasurer of the Republic of Texas will pay to the Order of A.I. Lewis per F.T. Wells att[orney]y, Thirty Nine 50/100 Dollars, out of any money appropriated by Act of February 5th, 1844 for Past pay due the officers of the Navy. This amount being for Pro rata pay due as an officer of the Navy of the Republic.

Treasury Department, Washington May 1st, 1844

(Signed) Charles Mason, Auditor James B. Shaw, Comptroller

Lewis' commander Edwin W. Moore was not so lucky. The payment in Figure 13.19 to William A. Tennison, for "Expenses of the Court Martial to try E.W. Moore, et al," reflects his role as a witness in the most politically charged trial in the history of the Republic. Lieutenant Tennison was a veteran officer of both Texas navies and was considered politically stable by his commanders. He kept a detailed diary or series of notes on his firsthand marine experiences, including the exploits of the Texas flagship *Independence,* as the ship "cruised throughout the Gulf, boarding and burning a number a small Mexican supply vessels" between January and March 1836.[28] Tennison was also onboard the *Zavala* during her furious encounter with a tropical storm. He recorded the ship's return to port as follows: "we came in here all well and hearty on the 7th of October. The Hull of the Vessel and engines being not hurt at all [*sic*]."[29]

Lieutenant Tennison also served directly under Commodore Moore aboard the sloop-of-war *Austin* off the coast of Vera Cruz in 1842. The *Austin* captured the 180-ton brig *Progreso* on February 5 as the ship attempted to sail from Vera Cruz to Matamoros.[30] After Moore sent a detachment of marines onboard the *Progreso* to search and secure the ship, Lieutenant Tennison and Midshipman Robert Clements commanded a prize crew which sailed the captured vessel to Galveston for condemnation by a Texas admiralty court. Although Tennison was not directly implicated in the charges against Moore, his detailed written accounts and descriptions of the various naval engagements were undoubtedly used as fodder by the prosecutors.

The payment in Figure 13.20 to James Reily for "Services as a Members of the Court" demonstrates the enormous political lengths that were taken to prosecute the former Naval Commander. The warrant was dated a

No. 1832 TREASURY WARRANT $43.92

The Treasurer of the Republic of Texas will pay to the Order of W[illia]m A. Tennison Forty three 92/100 – Dollars, out of any money appropriated by Act of February 5th 1844 for Expenses of the Court Martial to try E.W. Moore et al.. This amount being for Pay and Mileage as Witness

Treasury Department, Washington June 4th, 1844

(Signed) Charles Mason, Auditor James B. Shaw, Comptroller

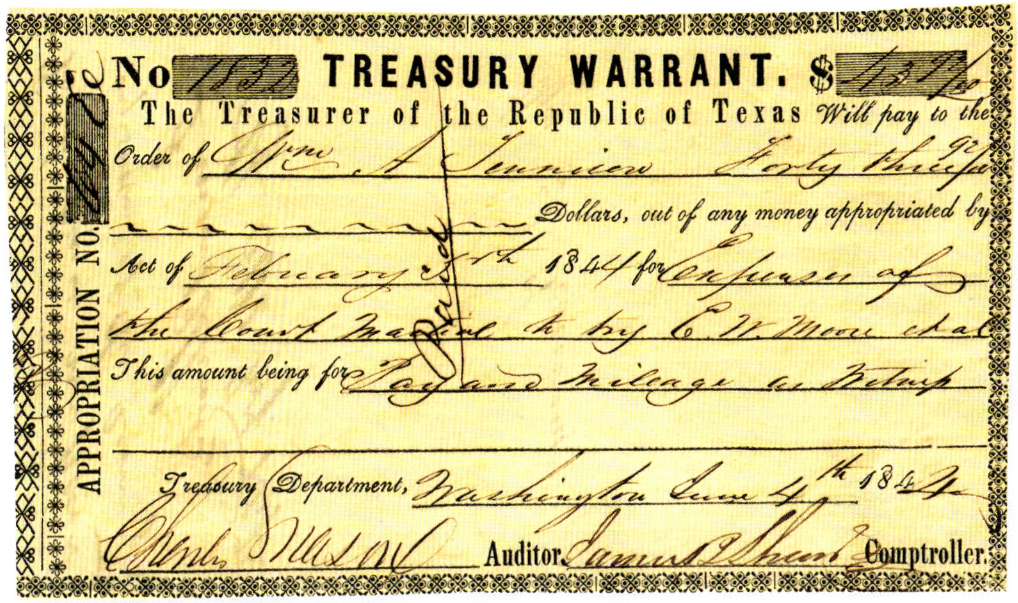

Fig 13.19, Washington, Treasury Warrant, June 4, 1844, Payable to William A. Tennison, for "Expenses of the Court Marshal to try E.W. Moore et al."

Private Collection, Cr. W8, O-1045.

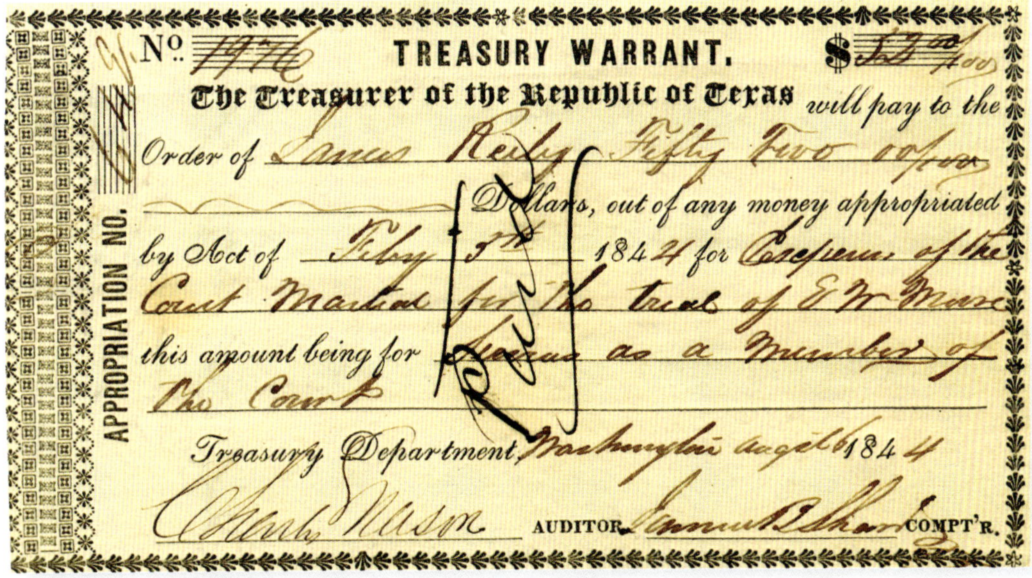

No. 1976 TREASURY WARRANT $32.00

The Treasurer of the Republic of Texas will pay to the Order of James Reily Fifty Two 00/100 – Dollars, out of any money appropriated by Act of February 5th 1844 for Expenses of the Court Martial for the trial of E.W. Moore this amount being for Services as a Members of the Court

Treasury Department, Washington August 6, 1844

(Signed) Charles Mason, Auditor James B. Shaw, Comptroller

Fig 13.20, Washington, Treasury Warrant, August 6, 1844, Payable to James Reily, for "Expenses of the Court Martial for the trial of E.W. Moore."

Private Collection, Cr. W6, O-1035.

full sixty-three days after Lieutenant Tennison's similar payment for his services as a witness on June 4, 1844.

Sam Houston had dishonorably discharged Navy Commodore Edwin W. Moore and two of his top officers, John Lothrop and C.B. Snow.[31] Moore, the commander of the flagship *Austin,* and Lothrop, the commander of the *Wharton,* had just returned from a bitter engagement near Telchac off the coast of the Yucatan. In the battle with the Mexican Navy, the Texians were successful in tying up the Mexican's resources and thwarting a planned blockade of Texas seaports and shipping. On the following day, all of the officers of the Texas Navy, save for two, resigned their commissions in protest of Houston's treatment of their beloved commander Moore. The discharge of Moore, Lothrop, Snow and the subsequent firing of Col. James Morgan from his post as Naval Commissioner effectively disbanded the second Texas navy.

Incensed at his dismissal, Moore demanded his right to trial and in February 1843, a joint committee of Congress granted his request. A proud veteran of the sea, the former naval commander was tried by court martial "on charges of misapplication of funds, embezzlement of public property, neglect of duty, disobedience to orders, contempt and defiance of law, treason and murder."[32] The trial lasted for seventy agonizing days with a parade of witnesses, lengthy examinations of Naval orders and a study of the withholding of naval appropriations by President Houston while Moore pleaded for operating funds.[33] Commander Moore was eventually acquitted of all the charges.

THE IMPROVING ECONOMY

The economy of the Republic of Texas had materially improved under the second administration of Sam Houston and continued to improve as his Secretary of State, Dr. Anson Jones, was elected in his own right succeeding Houston as the President of the Republic of Texas. The primary source of revenues for the country consisted of customs revenues, with land sales and property taxes representing only a small portion of the income. Realizing the past problems of posting bonds for customs duties, the Republic implemented a warehousing system for imported goods. For example, a Texas merchant importing $1,000 of goods with duties at 25 percent would have to pay the duty in cash at time of import or "warehouse" 25 percent of the inventory as payment of duties.[34] This inventory was retained under the watchful eye of the government until it could be sold to pay the import duty. This system eventually brought significant hard money into government coffers, as import duties could only be paid with exchequers or in gold or silver coin. The exchequer bills had first been issued from Austin, then Houston, and later from Washington as the seat of government was moved. This was despite the fact that all of them denote Austin as the place of issue. Over time, the exchequers ran the complete course of circulation: first as payments to government employees and for official expenditures, then into the economy as they were used to pay for goods and services, and eventually back to the government for payment of taxes at face value. Shortly after the exchequer bills were used to pay taxes, they were transported to the Treasury Department where officials cancelled and destroyed the notes.

In sharp contrast to the Lamar administration, the second administration of Sam Houston managed to cut government spending to the bone. Salaries were slashed, offices were eliminated, the navy was disbanded and the Texas army was largely furloughed. In the three full years of 1842 through 1844, the Treasury department managed to run the government with the following expenditures.[35]

For the year of 1842		*$198,051.00*
" "	*1843*	*147,274.38*
" "	*1844*	*147,850.32*
Total disbursed appropriations:		*$493,175.70*

Even with the expenditures for tax collection and mail service (totaling $17,907.30) added back in as expenses, the second Houston administration operated the government on about 10.53 percent of what the Lamar administration spent over the same length of time. Surprisingly, net revenues from customs duties in the period ending July 31, 1844, was nearly $178,000, resulting in a small budget surplus.[36]

Because exchequer bills were only used for expenses appropriated by Congress, their primary use was for the redemption of warrants written to various government officers, clerks and judges. As these notes found their way into the treasury for payment of taxes or duties, they were subsequently destroyed. This limited circulation resulted in a strengthening of the remaining exchequer bills versus the value of specie. The improving economy and the resumption of the flow of silver and gold coins in Texas can be ascertained by examining the reverses of treasury warrants issued from Washington in late 1844 and into 1845. Many of these warrants are still found in old collections, bearing the endorsement of the payee and the type of payment made (usually in "specie," "par funds," or "exchequer bills").

The payment in Figure 13.21 to H.W. Raglin, an assistant clerk, is marked "Paid" on the face. It bears his endorsement on the reverse with the word "specie," indicating that this draft was paid in silver coins, most likely those of the United States which was the official

Fig 13.21, Washington, Treasury Warrant, December 3, 1844, Payable to H.W. Raglin for "Pay as assistant clerk in the State Department."

Private Collection, Cr. W6, O-1035.

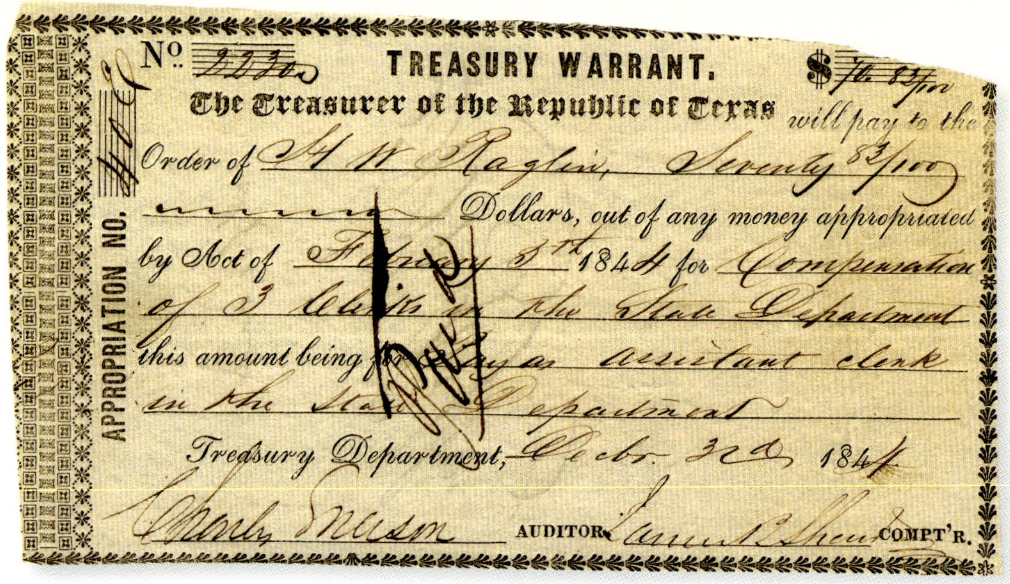
No. ____ TREASURY WARRANT. $70.83/100

The Treasurer of the Republic of Texas will pay to the

Order of H. W. Raglin, Seventy 83/100

Dollars, out of any money appropriated

by Act of February 5th 1844 for Compensation

of 3 Clerks in the State Department

this amount being for Pay as assistant clerk

in the State Department

Treasury Department, Decbr. 3rd 1844

Charles Mason AUDITOR. ____ COMPT'R.

APPROPRIATION NO.

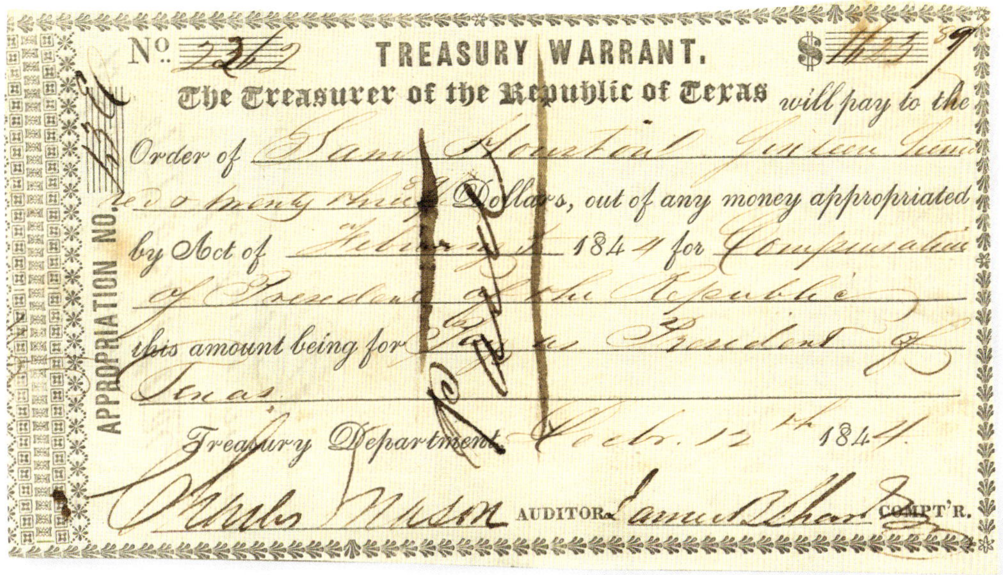
No. 2262 TREASURY WARRANT. $1623 89
The Treasurer of the Republic of Texas will pay to the Order of
Dollars, out of any money appropriated by Act of 1844 for
this amount being for
Treasury Department 1844.
AUDITOR. COMPT'R.
APPROPRIATION NO.

Fig 13.22, Washington, Treasury Warrant, December 12, 1844, Payable to Sam Houston for "Pay as President of Texas."

Private Collection, Cr. W6, O-1035.

No. 2262 TREASURY WARRANT $1623.89

The Treasurer of the Republic of Texas will pay to the Order of Sam Houston Sixteen hundred & twenty three 89/100 Dollars, out of any money appropriated by Act of February 5th 1844 for Compensation of President of the Republic This amount being for Pay as President of Texas.

Treasury Department, December 12th 1844
(Signed) Charles Mason, AUDITOR James B. Shaw, COMPT'R

Pay in Gold coin —
13th December 1844.
Secretary of Treasury

Fig 13.23, The reverse side of Sam Houston's pay warrant.

Private Collection.

monetary standard. This example also indicates that even the lowly government bureaucrats now received legitimate payments in specie for their services.

Culminating his second term as chief executive, His Excellency Sam Houston received the payment shown in Figure 13.22 for "Compensation of President of the Republic," the amount being for "Pay as President of Texas." Unlike the government clerks, President Houston was able to turn his treasury warrant over in exchange for gold coins at the Republic Treasury on his last day in office—remaining a "hard money" man to the end.

Figure 13.23 shows the reverse of Sam Houston's treasury warrant:

> *Paid in gold coin 13th December 1844 by W[illiam] B[eck] Ochiltree, Secretary of the Treasury. (Endorsed below) Sam Houston.*

OVERTURES FOR ANNEXATION

In early 1844, the last year of his Presidency, Sam Houston again proposed a Treaty of Annexation to the United States. With the Texas economy improving, Mexican incursions across the border subsiding, and a substantive peace made with the Indians, Texas would now bring considerably less baggage than in the previous decade. The proposed treaty of annexation with the United States centered around the protection of the Texas coast from Mexico, the validity of land titles for citizens, and an agreement to pay the public debts and liabilities of Texas. Abel P. Upshur, the U.S. Secretary of State, was keenly interested in the proposal and indicated the treaty could be expected to gain approval in the United States Senate. This would present another opportunity to expand the United States which was still hungry in

Fig 13.24, Abel P. Upshur.
U.S. Secretary of State under John Tyler. Once considered Texas's staunchest ally in her quest for annexation by the United States, Secretary of State Abel P. Upshur met an untimely death aboard a U.S naval vessel. His passing abruptly ended the momentum towards annexation which Sam Houston had initiated in order to erase the debt of the Republic of Texas.

its quest for continued westward expansion through its policy of Manifest Destiny.

In a bizarre twist of fate, the annexation of Texas would be delayed by an event on February 28, 1844 as an experimental cannon was being demonstrated aboard the *U.S.S. Princeton* for President John Tyler and a contingent of cabinet members.[37] When Tyler and his wife slipped below deck to have their champagne glasses refilled, the cannon exploded. It instantly killed Secretary Upshur and the President's father-in-law, David Gardier, who was America's richest man at the time. Only the night before he was blown to pieces, Secretary Upshur had penned a draft of the treaty of annexation. With the sudden death of Upshur, who was the treaty's biggest political ally, it would take months for President John Tyler to locate a political replacement.

The original Treaty of Annexation was written and presented to the United States on April 12, 1844. The reason behind the unbridled excitement which followed in Texas can largely be traced to Article V of the proposed Treaty. It reads in part:

The United States assumes and agree to pay the public debts and liabilities of Texas, however created, for which the faith or credit of her government may be bound at the time of the exchange of the ratification of the treaty; which debts and liabilities are estimated not to exceed, in the whole, ten millions of dollars, to be ascertained and paid in the manner hereinafter stated.[38]

A primary motive for annexation, at least to the citizens of the Republic of Texas, was a financial one. Republic officials had been unable to procure the funds to maintain an army and protect the country's borders from repeated Mexican aggression for almost a decade. The government's second attempt at building a meaningful naval force had been a financial disaster, with officers and sailors deserting over a lack of pay and several of the ships left to rot in the harbor. Texas needed money to survive as an independent Republic. The recent trickle of silver and gold through the ports had allowed Texas to barely maintain an existence, let alone borrow the significant sums of money that would be needed to sustain its sovereignty.

Although it was widely known that the paper money and securities of Texas had become almost worthless, the full faith and credit of the Republic had been pledged for their redemption. With the sudden possibility looming that Texas could be annexed to the United States and their funds recovered from the resulting payment, the holders of these securities unanimously praised the wisdom of the potential union. The originally proposed treaty of annexation also included a provision to pay $250,000 to Frederick Dawson, the Baltimore banker, for the naval vessels which had been contracted during Sam Houston's first administration in 1838.[39] Dawson and his firm never received the payment for the warships, initially secured by Texas bonds. Dawson's proposal was in addition to a $100,000 payment to be used by Texas to retire any remaining exchequer bills in circulation. For the citizens and holders of Texian securities, bonds, and promissory notes, the proposed annexation treaty offered a way for them to recover all of their money—or so they thought.

President Houston, ever the deft political wrangler, wrote to his old friend Andrew Jackson on the matter, "Texas is presented to the United States as a bride, adorned for her espousal. But if so confident of the union she should be rejected, her mortification would be indescribable."[40] He continued, "were she now to be spurned...she would seek some other friend." Great Britain had made substantial diplomatic overtures to Mexico, an important trading partner, trying to persuade the Mexican government to recognize Texas and negotiate a lasting peace. If a peace between Texas and Mexico could be negotiated, England's plan was to persuade Texas to remain an independent republic, thereby blocking the westward expansion of the United States. Houston's offer to the United States for the annexation of Texas had considerable strings attached. As diplomats on both sides of the Atlantic debated the issues, the U.S. Senate rejected the initial Treaty of Annexation on June 8, 1844. The speculators in Texian securities would later discover that their rich Uncle Sam would subsequently amend the proposed treaty and attach a few strings of his own.

1 Marquis James, *The Raven: A Biography of Sam Houston* (Austin: University of Texas Press, 1929), 329-30.

2 "Houston to the Senate and House of Representatives. February 5, 1842," Journals of the Sixth Congress of the Republic of Texas.

3 *Handbook of Texas Online,* s.v., "Thomas William Ward," http://www.tsha.utexas.edu/handbook/online/articles/WW/fwa52.html (accessed July 8, 2007).

4 James, *The Raven,* 329.

5 Ibid., 323.

6 John Hoyt Williams, *Sam Houston: The Life and Times of the Liberator of Texas, an Authentic American Hero* (New York: Simon & Schuster, Inc., 1993), 218-19.

7 Mary Margaret McAllen Amberson, *A Brave Boy and a Good Soldier: John C.C. Hill & The Texas Expedition to Mier* (Austin: Texas State Historical Association, 2007), 12.

8 *Handbook of Texas Online,* s.v., "Mier Expedition," http://www.tsha.utexas.edu/handbook/online/articles/MM/qym2.html (accessed July 22, 2007).

9 Amberson, *A Brave Boy and a Good Soldier,* 16-17.

10 *Handbook of Texas Online,* s.v., "Washington D. Miller," http://www.tsha.utexas.edu/handbook/online/articles/MM/fmi29.html (accessed August 3, 2006).

11 Williams, *Sam Houston,* 220.

12 "Report of the Auditor and Comptroller, to the Fourth Legislature, on the Public Debt of Texas," (Austin: Cushney & Hampton, State Gazette Office, 1851).

13 *Handbook of Texas Online,* s.v., "Gail Borden, Jr.," http://www.tsha.utexas.edu/handbook/online/articles/BB/fbo24.html (accessed September 16, 2006).

14 *Handbook of Texas Online,* s.v., "Sidney Sherman," http://www.tsha.utexas.edu/handbook/online/articles/SS/fsh27.html (accessed July 21, 2007).

15 "Documents of Major Gen. Sam Houston, Commander in Chief of the Texian Army, to his excellency, David G. Burnet, President of the Republic of Texas; Containing A Detailed Account of the Battle of San Jacinto," (New Orleans: John Cox & Co., Printers, Bulletin Office, 1836), 4-5.

16 "As noted on a Treasury Warrant, payable to Thomas Ward, for Pay of Doorkeeper, Serg[ean]t at Arms for Senate & House of Rep[resentative]s, Washington, Dated February 7, 1842," Journals of the Sixth Congress of the Republic of Texas.

17 James, *The Raven,* 329-30.

18 *Handbook of Texas Online,* s.v., "Zavalla," http://www.tsha.utexas.edu/handbook/online/articles/ZZ/qtz1.html (accessed August 8, 2006).

19 Jonathan W. Jordan, *Lone Star Navy: Texas, the Fight for the Gulf of Mexico, and the Shaping of the American West* (Dulles, VA: Potomac Books, Inc., 2006), 304.

20 The wreck of the Zavalla was designated as Archeological Site 41GV95.

21 *Handbook of Texas Online,* s.v., "Edward Burleson," http://www.tsha.utexas.edu/handbook/online/articles/BB/fbu40.html (accessed September 29, 2007).

22 *Handbook of Texas Online,* s.v., "George Duncan Hancock," http://www.tsha.utexas.edu/handbook/online/articles/HH/fha45.html (accessed September 29, 2007).

23 William M. Gouge, *The Fiscal History of Texas* (New York: Burt Franklin, 1852; rpt. 1969), 129.

24 *Handbook of Texas Online,* s.v., "Texas Navy," http://www.tsha.utexas.edu/handbook/online/articles/TT/qjt2.html (accessed August 8, 2006).

25 Jordan, *Lone Star Navy,* 215-16.

26 Ibid., 159, 221, 270.

27 Seymour V. Conner, ed., "Hamilton to Mason, Washington, March 9, 1844," Texas Treasury Papers, 4:257.

28 Jordan, *Lone Star Navy,* 55.

29 Ibid., 164.

30 Ibid., 199.

31 Douglas V. Meed, *The Fighting Texas Navy, 1832-1843* (Plano: Republic of Texas Press, 2001), 220.

32 Ibid., 221-22.

33 Jordan, *Lone Star Navy,* 284-86.

34 Anson Jones, "Col. M.L. Smith to Anson Jones, Columbia, October 1, 1843," *Memoranda and Official Correspondence relating to the Republic of Texas its History and Annexation* (New York: D. Appleton & Company, 1859), 256-57.

35 Gouge, *The Fiscal History of Texas,* 127.

36 Ibid., 124.

37 Williams, *Sam Houston,* 237.

38 "Treaty of Annexation, Submitted April 12, 1844, by J.C. Calhoun, Issac Van Zant, J. Pickney Henderson."

39 Dawson and his associates agreed to grant a $30,000 concession from the $280,000 principal amount owed by Texas if a provision to pay the original amount due them plus interest was included in the Treaty of Annexation to the U.S. Seymour V. Conner, ed., "E.D. Whitney to Jones, Philadelphia, May 8, 1845," Texas Treasury Papers, 3:1,103-104.

40 Williams, *Sam Houston,* 236.

CHAPTER FOURTEEN

THE ARCHITECT OF ANNEXATION

CH 14

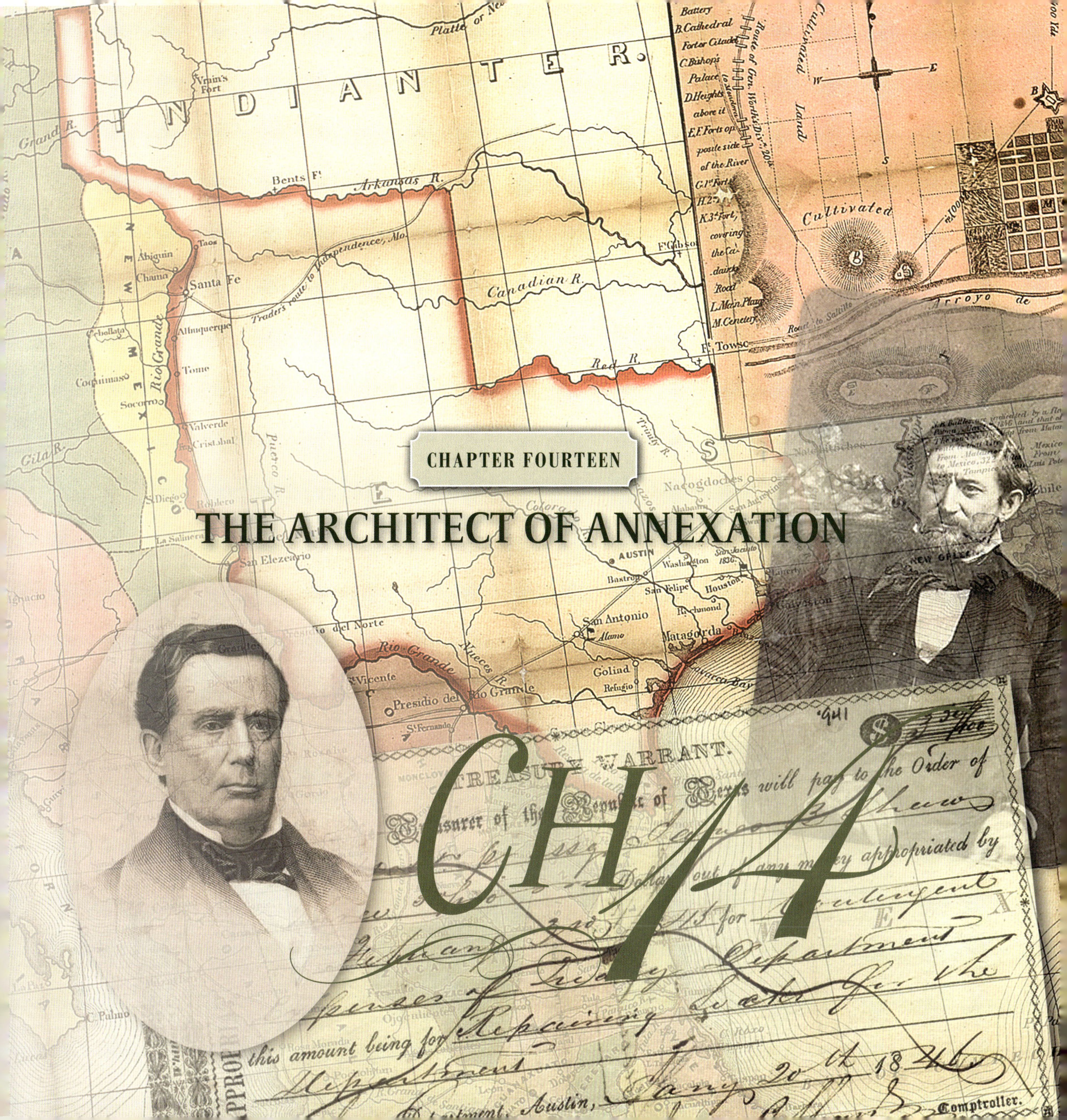

The Texas economy was recovering from the extreme economic depression as the election of 1844 approached. Another proposed treaty of annexation to the United States had again been formally submitted to the U.S. Congress by Texas President Sam Houston. In the public eye, Anson Jones was perceived as a loyal Houston man, but in reality the Secretary of State and the President began to drift apart by the close of 1843.[1] With the improving economy and a rosier outlook for the country, Jones expressed his views to Houston on his moving the capital. As a result of Jones' opposition to having the seat of government moved away from Austin, the President ceased to consult with him on a number of important items. Jones privately cited the President's "system of petty and vindictive warfare upon individuals" as a way to make political allies for himself, and felt Houston's maneuverings were injurious to the interests and character of the Republic.[2]

Although Jones had dutifully played to Houston's vanity and served as a capable and loyal Secretary of State, Jones became more and more alienated from his boss. The distance between the two men became even more evident when Vice President Ed Burleson was hand picked by Houston to be his successor in the election of 1844. Burleson ran against Jones for the Presidency, but despite the favoritism, Jones defeated Burleson and was elected as the President of Texas on September 2, 1844. As Sam Houston's administration drew to a close in October 1844, exchequer bills were received at ninety cents on the dollar for customs at the port of Galveston.[3] Their carefully controlled issue had limited any further depreciation of value. Jones took office on December 9, 1844, in the town of Washington.[4] In his inaugural address to the nation, Jones called for "the entire abolishment of paper money issues by government, corporations, or individuals and the consequent introduction of an exclusive hard money currency."[5]

President Jones' proclamation effectively ended the paper money system in Texas. The entire series of paper obligations issued under Anson Jones' administration was limited to a modest number of treasury warrants and auditors certificates, distributed from Washington-on-the-Brazos and later from Austin, when the capital was moved there for the last time in July 1845. The warrants and auditor's certificates issued during Jones' presidency dated before July 4, 1845 were issued from Washington, and those after this date were issued from Austin. Treasury warrants from this period reflect official government expenditures by money appropriated by Congress. On the other hand, the auditors certificates reflect those claims validated by the auditor, but not yet appropriated by Congress.

Fig 14.1, Washington, Treasury Warrant, January 30, 1845, Payable to Torrey & Brother for "Redemption of Jane & William Simpson."
Private Collection, Cr. W6, O-1035.

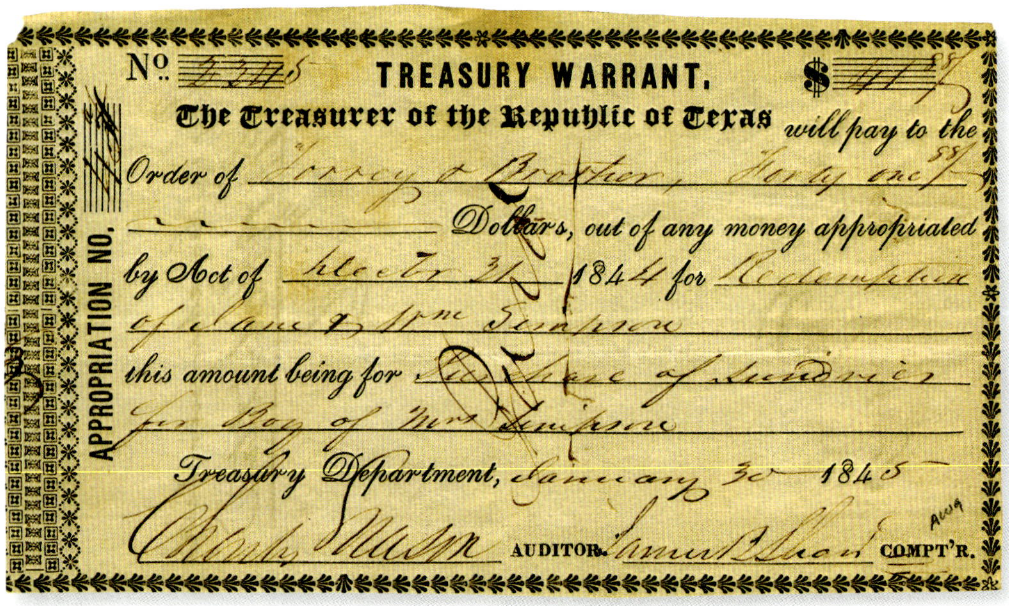
No. TREASURY WARRANT. $
The Treasurer of the Republic of Texas will pay to the
Order of
Dollars, out of any money appropriated
by Act of 1844 for
this amount being for
Treasury Department, 1845
AUDITOR COMPT'R.
APPROPRIATION NO.

No. 2245 TREASURY WARRANT $41.88

The Treasurer of the Republic of Texas will pay to the Order of Torrey & Brother, Forty one 88/100 – Dollars, out of any money appropriated by Act of December 31, 1844 for Redemption of Jane & W[illia]m Simpson. This amount being for Purchase of sundries for Boy of Mrs. Simpson

Treasury Department, January 30, 1845

(Signed) Charles Mason, AUDITOR James B. Shaw, COMPT'R

While most of these issues were paid to clerks and government officials, some reveal a wealth of information about the times and the political and social landscape of the day. In at least one such instance, the story of a notorious kidnapping by hostile Indians can be traced.

THE SIMPSON CHILDREN

The payment in Figure 14.1 for $41.88 issued on January 30, 1845, to Torrey & Brother, an Indian trading company, for the "Redemption of Jane and Wm. Simpson." The purchase of sundries was essentially a ransom payment for the release of kidnapped children. The payment was signed on the reverse by the Secretary of the Treasury, W.B. Ochiltree, with an order to "Pay in Exchequer Bills," the last currency of the Republic. It is also endorsed by "Torry & Bro."

Under the administrations of both Houston and Jones, the Republic expended a great deal of effort in developing a peaceful relationship with the Indians located on the western frontier edges of the primary Texas settlements.[6] This area included the city of Austin. Peace was shattered on Sunday morning, November 3, 1844, when Mrs. Simpson's children, ages twelve and fourteen, were taken captive by Indians while driving in cows for milking. The children were abducted three blocks west of Congress Avenue on West Pecan Street. As quickly as possible, a body of men went out from Austin to overtake the kidnappers, and if possible regain the captives.[7] Unfortunately, the trail was lost, and the men were compelled to return to the bereaved mother with news of the whereabouts of her loved ones. Eventually, it was learned that her daughter was murdered. After two months and seven days of captivity, her son was ransomed from the Waco Indians.

Many elements of the story show through in the draft in Figure 14.1. On December 31, 1844, a Joint Resolution of Congress appropriated $300 to be "placed at the disposition of the President, for the redemption of William and Jane Simpson, now held in captivity by the hostile Indians." This particular amount was the standard ransom cost at the time. The money purchased various clothes, foodstuff, and tobacco products used to facilitate the captives release through negotiations with the Comanche Chiefs.[8] Upon William's liberation, Thomas W. Ward took charge of the boy and escorted him back to his mother.

The efforts to find and rescue the Simpson children had political as well as humanitarian concerns for the government. The Republic needed settlers in its vacant lands, and could not afford future depredations and bad publicity regarding the kidnapping of children by hostile Indians in the Austin area. It was feared that another such incident would hamper further settlement by frontier families in the region.

FRONTIER PROTECTION

Many treasury warrants were paid to Texas Rangers for their services in protecting the frontier. John Coffee "Jack" Hays was a trained surveyor, Texas Ranger, and a veteran of the Mexican War. He was born in Wilson County, Tennessee, on January 28, 1817.[9] His father, Harmon Hays, fought with Andrew Jackson in the War of 1812. In 1836, Jack traveled to New Orleans and entered Texas through Nacogdoches. He then joined the Texian troops under Thomas J. Rusk, and helped bury the remains of the victims at Goliad. In 1837, he fought with a company of rangers under "Deaf" Smith in an engagement with Mexican cavalry near Laredo and rose to the rank of sergeant.

The pay warrant in Figure 14.4, for the "Protection of the Frontier," references Captain Hays' service in ranger companies where they often engaged the Comanches and Mexicans in small skirmishes and major battles. During this time, Hays was involved in military actions at Plum Creek, Canon de Ugalde, Bandera Pass, Salado Creek, and Painted Rock. In an encounter at Enchanted Rock, Hays made a lone stand that enhanced his reputation as a fearless Indian fighter. In these battles, Hays and his rangers were usually outnumbered and their effective use of revolvers revolutionized warfare against the Texas Indians. Following his service in the Mexican War, Jack Hays traveled to California and was elected sheriff of San Francisco County in 1850. He was appointed the U.S. Surveyor General for California in 1853, helped found the city of Oakland, and also ran successful enterprises in real estate and ranching. Hays died on April 21, 1883, and is buried in California.

Fig 14.2, Jack Hays of the Texas Rangers.

Antiquarian Antique Print and Map Gallery, Houston, Texas.

Jack Hays is among the most colorful Texas Rangers of the day. His stature of five feet, nine inches, fair-haired complexion and mild manners did not match the looks and actions of his legendary fame.

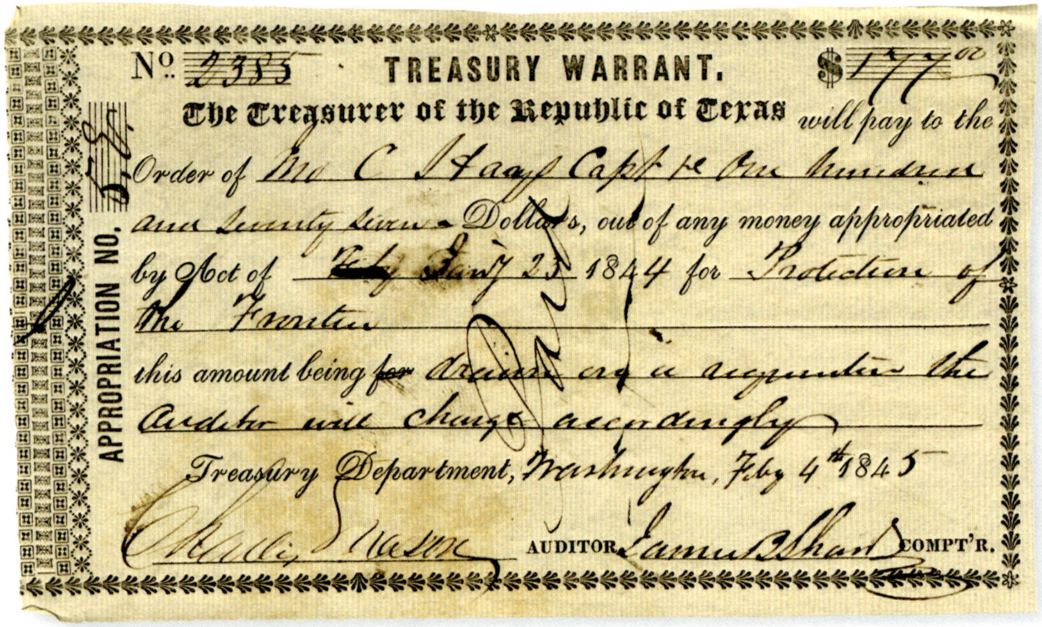

No. 2385 TREASURY WARRANT $177.00

The Treasurer of the Republic of Texas will pay to the Order of Jno [John] C Hays Capt[ain] re One hundred and seventy seven Dollars, out of any money appropriated by Act of Jan[uar]y 23, 1844 for Protection of the Frontier this amount being drawn on a requisition the auditor will charge accordingly.

Treasury Department, Washington, Feb[ruar]y 4th, 1845

(Signed) Charles Mason, AUDITOR James B. Shaw, COMPT'R

Fig 14.4, Washington, Treasury Warrant, February 4, 1845, Payable to John C. Hayes, Capt. for "Protection of the Frontier."

Private Collection, Cr. W6, O-1035.

Fig 14.3, Unidentified Texas Ranger with Knife.

Daguerreotype, c. 1840s, Courtesy of Joseph D. Olson.

A MORATORIUM ON PAPER MONEY

A little more than a year after Jack Hays received the treasury warrant shown in Figure 14.4, the legislation which formalized President Jones' moratorium on the paper money system in Texas was passed.[10] The act, dated February 3, 1845, repealed the law authorizing any future issuance of exchequer bills. It also forbade the Secretary of the Treasury and other officers of the government from issuing bonds, notes, bills, or any other form of circulating paper money, or receiving anything other than gold, silver or exchequer bills in payment for any class of revenue due to the government. The exchequer bills remaining in circulation would continue to be received at par until the whole amount of them had been redeemed.

This legislation also required the Secretary of the Treasury to destroy all the exchequer bills received by the treasury department. Not surprisingly, a report arrived on February 10, 1845, from the Customs House at Galveston stating that the exchequer bills were trading at par with specie. This trend continued for the remaining days of the Republic.[11] Another report came from Velasco on February 25, 1845, that "$604.00 in exchequer bills, 86 'hammered' dollars and $13.66 in silver change" had been paid in on a single day, reflecting the variety of money pouring into government coffers.[12] The treasury department continued to record their ongoing expenses by issuing warrants for current appropriations. When the current supply of authorized exchequers was exhausted, however, nothing but gold or silver could be paid out or received by the government. The only exception to the rule regarded land patents and other land office dues, which could still be received in the audited drafts.[13] These actions effectively wound down the paper money system in Texas and largely accounts for the scarcity of any surviving exchequer bills.

The Act of February 3, 1845, not only drove a legislative nail in the paper money coffin, it also effectively slammed the door on the creditors of the Republic of Texas. It was obvious that while the government was finally able to function on a hard money basis, it still lacked the millions of dollars in hard currency required to pay its creditors. Previously issued paper obligations were held not only by ordinary citizens, but by virtually all of the men who served as members of Congress. The government continued to issue payments and recognize its obligations by issuing drafts (treasury warrants) or certificates against the treasury. These drafts would only be paid out of appropriated funds. For those who still held older forms of currency, stocks, bonds, loans, drafts or audited paper issued "out of funds not otherwise appropriated" by Congress, they were left holding the bag and would later stand in line with the other creditors looking to somehow collect their funds.

LEANING TOWARDS ANNEXATION

As creditors pondered their long-term options, the possible annexation of Texas by the United States seemed a financially viable alternative. Although the voters had overwhelmingly approved the annexation as a referendum in the Presidential election of 1836, it was not a realistic proposition at the time, as the U.S. was rightfully cautious of being drawn into a war with Mexico. In the 1836-1839 time period, the tables of the U.S. Congress were loaded with petitions against the admission of Texas and a subsequent expansion of slavery.[14] During the administration of Mirabeau B. Lamar, the issue of annexation could not be considered as Lamar was determined to keep Texas an independent Republic and expand her boundaries. With her warships waging battle in the Gulf of Mexico and the government sinking into a quagmire of unsustainable debt service, this "spunky little republic," as Anson Jones once referred to Texas under President Lamar, could hardly be described as being groomed for the altar. It was not until the financial and political maneuvering under the later administrations of Sam Houston and Anson Jones that the long suffering Texas economy began to improve. As the record corn crop was harvested and the substantial cotton crop was exported, the jingle of specie was again heard in the barrooms, storefronts and customs houses of Texas. As the wheels of commerce got back on track, the political climate also began to improve.

In many respects, the stewardship of Anson Jones, first as Secretary of State and later as President, brought a level of peace and prosperity to Texas that it had not known before. For the first time in the history of the country, the expenses of the government were brought within the limit of annual receipts.[16] There were no new debts incurred and a modest amount of the outstanding debt was retired during Jones' presidency. The exchequer bills rose to par value verses gold and silver shortly after the beginning of his administration and held steady at substantially the same rate until the last day of the Republic. During this time, Texas did not issue a single dollar of credit or new paper money, and the currency of Texas transitioned from a paper system to one of copper, silver, and gold coins. The only paper which was issued by the government were limited amounts of treasury warrants and auditors certificates. By the close of the Jones administration, there was a specie surplus in the Treasury estimated to be enough to support the Government for at least an additional two years.

Aside from the various monetary issues, two other significant events marked President Anson Jones' administration. After ten years of cross-border incursions, a preliminary treaty of peace was signed with Mexico. Mexico agreed to acknowledge the independence of Texas and recognize the Rio Grande River as the boundary on March 29, 1845. Both governments also recognized that the preliminary treaty would become null and void if Texas was annexed by the United States.[17] Peace was finally at hand in Texas, and new waves of immigrants began to arrive. Rather than focusing on sectional strife between the eastern and western counties, the executive and legislative branches of the Republic focused their attention on building a public school system, and advancing education in the fields of science, religion, and morality. Even the vexing question regarding the "Seat of Government" was harmoniously settled when Jones proposed moving the capital back to Austin.

By early 1845, the people of Texas had long suffered through the financial and military turmoil of previous administrations. They were anxious for rest and the comfort of long-term security that the United States could provide.[18] After careful review, the language from the revised Treaty of Annexation was incorporated into a joint resolution for the annexation of Texas by the United States. On January 25, 1845, the resolution passed in the U.S. House of Representatives. The public approval rate was overwhelming towards annexation and excitement filled the streets of Texas when it was realized that the hitherto sealed doors of the United States were now opened wide. The Texas politicians took advantage of this feeling of euphoria to sway the public opinion even further in favor of annexation. They seized upon another issue to excite the public but which was of direct financial interest to them. This was the false assurance by politicians that the land owned by many of their constituents would suddenly become more valuable if the annexation took place.

Historians have long cited that Texas sought the protection of the United States as the primary driver for annexation. This is largely because Texas did not have the funds to raise and sustain an adequate military force to protect her borders. The reality of the day was that the driver for annexation by the people of Texas was largely a financial one. After Anson Jones took office Texas never actually "needed" the military protection of the United States.[19] The offer for the protection of Texas from the U.S. had come to Anson Jones from Ebenezer Allen, then serving as Attorney General and acting Secretary of State for Texas. Allen was thus urged to accept the "protection" of the United States and was persuaded by his American counterparts.[20] By the time U.S. troops were ready to occupy Texas, President Jones stated that the matter had gone so far that he could not refuse a compliance. Jones later reflected that "owing to the excitement at the time, and to my embarrassment, I yielded a reluctant assent."[21]

The excitement concerning annexation which Jones referred to was widespread in both Texas and the United States. Although the British Government lobbied Texan Minister Ashbel Smith for Texas to remain independent, the voice of the people of Texas largely echoed those of the United States.[22] The political climate was ripe for a vote on the resolution of annexation. As the enthusiasm spread through the eastern United States, massive political rallies were organized in which thousands of supporters voiced their approval for the annexation of Texas. The Democratic party led by James K. Polk overwhelmingly favored the proposal. The various creditors of the Republic of Texas, many of which were located in cities outside of Texas, continued to fan the flames of public opinion for the merger. As various speeches supporting the proposed union were heard, the representatives of the U.S. Congress readied themselves for the all important vote on the matter.

Fig. 14.5 The Republic of Texas, c. 1845.

From a Map of Mexico Including Yucatan & Upper California Exhibiting the Chief Cities and Towns, by S.A. Mitchell, 1847. Courtesy, Virginia Garrett Cartographic History Library, Special Collections, The University of Texas at Arlington, Arlington, Texas.

Fig 14.6, Texas Demonstrations, Jersey City.

Author's Collection.

Newspapers across the U.S. carried the news of the proposed annexation. A Harper's Weekly *artist sketched an imposing demonstration in Jersey City, New Jersey, on Monday evening, February 24, 1845. At the instigation of the Polk and Dallas Club (named for the current U.S. President and Vice President), "one hundred guns were fired" in favor of the immediate annexation of Texas "amid the cheers of a considerable chorus of persons assembled on the occasion."*[23]

Fig 14.7, Great Texas Meeting at New York.

Author's Collection.

In New York City, another large political demonstration was organized in February 1845 to show support for the pending vote on the annexation of Texas. Unlike the large demonstration which gathered across the Hudson River in Jersey City, the New York City mayor prohibited the firing of cannons.

PROVISIONS TO PAY THE PUBLIC DEBT

On February 27, 1845, a joint resolution for the annexation of Texas with amendments still to be voted on by the House passed the U.S. Senate. The following day, the House adopted the senate version to annex the Republic of Texas. President John Tyler signed the resolution to adopt the merger on March 1. The ball was now back in Texas' court, and the resolution was sent back to Anson Jones for his approval. Almost a year had elapsed since the submission of the original proposed treaty of annexation by President Sam Houston. The amended Resolution of Annexation, as presented to Jones, addressed the payment of the public debt as follows. The Republic of Texas:

> *shall retain funds, debts, taxes and dues of every kind which may belong to, or be due and owing to the said Republic; and shall also retain all the vacant and unappropriated lands lying within its limits, to be applied to the payment of the debts and liabilities of said Republic of Texas, and the residue of said lands, after discharging said debts and liabilities, to be disposed of as said State may direct; but in no event are said debts and liabilities to become a charge upon the Government of the United States*[24]

Although the provision to pay off the public debt of the Republic had been removed from the treaty of annexation by the U.S. Senate, the alternate provision that Texas would retain its public lands "to be applied to the payment of the debts and liabilities of said Republic of Texas" gave creditors hope that the long period of payments in arrears would finally be brought current and subsequently made whole. It was widely thought that Texas had plenty of land, which would eventually be used to pay off its debts.

It wasn't long before another group of interested citizens surfaced to help fan the flames in this financial firestorm of anticipation for the union. This group was composed of those who were speculating in the public debt of Texas. They were insistent in their public clamor that annexation be consummated "instantly, on any terms," and it was said that they "would embrace the offer of the United States, if one of the conditions accompanying it had been that every man, woman and child in the country should be stripped and receive thirty-nine lashes on their bare backs." Letters poured into the Treasury Department in the spring of 1845. One of these inquired as to the 8% and 10% stock, the amount of Treasury Notes issued, specifically those that "bear interest and the rates," and "if there is any means of detecting any forgeries."[25] Although the dispersal of Texian securities had been widespread, their ownership became increasingly concentrated in the hands of merchants, storekeepers and speculators in the cities of New Orleans and Philadelphia, and a market was being made for them on the Philadelphia Stock Exchange.[26] Such was the speculative fever in Texian securities in the spring and summer which preceded the annexation of Texas.

The possibility of the sale of public lands in payment of the debt was inducement enough to garner the support of the people, notwithstanding the fact that Texas had been unable to reduce its public debt through land sales during the previous decade. Despite the specific wording of the amended treaty, the citizens of Texas expected the U.S. Congress to somehow take measures to obtain control of the public lands by purchase or by some conveyance in trust, with the proceeds first applied to the payment of debts and the excess handed over to the state.[27] It was also a widely held belief that if Texas were to remain an independent Republic, the Texian securities would never be paid off.

When the Texas Congress met in a special session at Washington-on-the-Brazos on June 16, 1845, their constituents were clamoring to be paid the money that was owed them by previous administrations. While in Washington, the Ninth Congress of the Republic of Texas had to decide the outcome of two very important issues. In addition to the Treaty of Annexation by the United States, they were to consider the Cuevas-Smith treaty of peace between Mexico and Texas. Although the preliminary treaty was in place, subject to ratification by the Congress of the Republic, the terms which Mexico offered Texas were conditional. In exchange for the formal acknowledgement of Texas independence and a permanent peace, Texas was to agree not to annex itself or become the subject of another country. Great Britain was also opposed to the annexation of Texas, and had encouraged Mexico to make peaceful negotiations with the Republic. The British were a major trading partner with Mexico and did not wish to see a further westward expansion of the United States. After ten years of intermittent war with Texas, both across the borders and on the high seas, Mexico had finally made peace with Texas—conditionally. Rather than share a common border with the United States, Mexico preferred sharing a border with the Republic of Texas, which Mexican leaders viewed as being too financially crippled to pose a military threat.

After significant courting of Texas by the administrations of John Tyler and James K. Polk, it became quite apparent that the leaders of Texas trusted the intentions of the United States over those of the Mexican government. The resolution to join the Unites States through annexation was overwhelmingly passed by the Congress of Texas on July 4, 1845, and the Cuevas-Smith treaty with Mexico was subsequently tabled. As a precursor to any anticipated troubles with Mexico, several units of the United States Army moved to Texas under the command of Gen. Zachary Taylor. With a U.S. force of 3,400 troops camped near the mouth of the Nueces River, the small village of Corpus Christi reaped an economic bonanza as merchants and vendors flocked to the area and sold goods to the friendly U.S. soldiers, who paid with U.S. coins.[28] By December 1845, the number of barrooms in Corpus Christi increased from two to more than two hundred in response to the drinking demands of the U.S. troops.[29] This feeling of increased security and change of financial circumstances was certainly a welcome addition to the southern area of Texas. And despite the diplomatic efforts of the Cuevas-Smith treaty, Mexico now had thousands of U.S. soldiers camped just north of the border.

DRAFTING A STATE CONSTITUTION

As the United States government positioned the army to protect their proposed acquisition, the officials and lawmakers in Texas were busy with important tasks of their own. A committee in Austin was formed to draft a state constitution, which was submitted to Texas voters for approval. Although many of the provisions of the state constitution mirrored those of the national constitution adopted March 17, 1836, there was one proviso in the State's document adopted August 27, 1845, which testified to the Republic's recent paper money troubles. The provision declared that "In no case shall the Legislature have power to issue treasury warrants, treasury notes or paper of any description intended to circulate as money."[31]

Other provisions of the original constitution adopted into the state constitution included Section 14 of the Bill of Rights: "No bill of attainder, Ex post facto law, retroactive law, or any law impairing the obligation of contracts, shall be made; and no person's property shall be taken, or applied to public use, without adequate compensation being made, unless by the consent of such person."[32] This statement seemed to be a solemn pledge that the contracts for money made by the Republic of Texas would ultimately be honored.

PRELUDE TO STATEHOOD

As the legislators labored over the document and submitted it to the Texas voters for approval, the Treasury Department proceeded to issue warrants from Austin, the last capital of the Republic. Figures 14.8 through 14.14 are examples of the treasury warrants issued during this period. These are reflective of an interesting set of government expenses which Texas had appropriated during the administration of Anson Jones.

The warrant in figure 14.8 reflects one of the most routine but important expenses incurred by the government offices of the day. With the seat of government moved back to Austin, local printing presses were once again kept busy with government business.

The $95.63 payment in Figure 14.9 to George W. Terrell as *Charge d'affaires* to France and England references the international nature of Terrell's diplomatic assignment. George W. Terrell was born in Kentucky in 1803 and moved to Tennessee as a youth, where he practiced law and was appointed as a district attorney in 1828 by Sam Houston, then the Governor of Tennessee.[33] A reversal of his fortunes brought him to Texas in 1837, where Lamar appointed him first as a district attorney and later as a judge in St. Augustine. He also served briefly as Secretary of State for David G.

No. 3139 TREASURY WARRANT $17.00

The Treasurer of the Republic of Texas will pay to the Order of Miller & Cushney, Seventeen 00/100 Dollars, out of any money appropriated by Act of February 1st, 1844 for Contingent Expenses of Treasury Debt this amount being for Printing for office.

Treasury Department, Sept[ember] 9th, 1845

(Signed) Charles Mason, AUDITOR James B. Shaw, COMPT'R

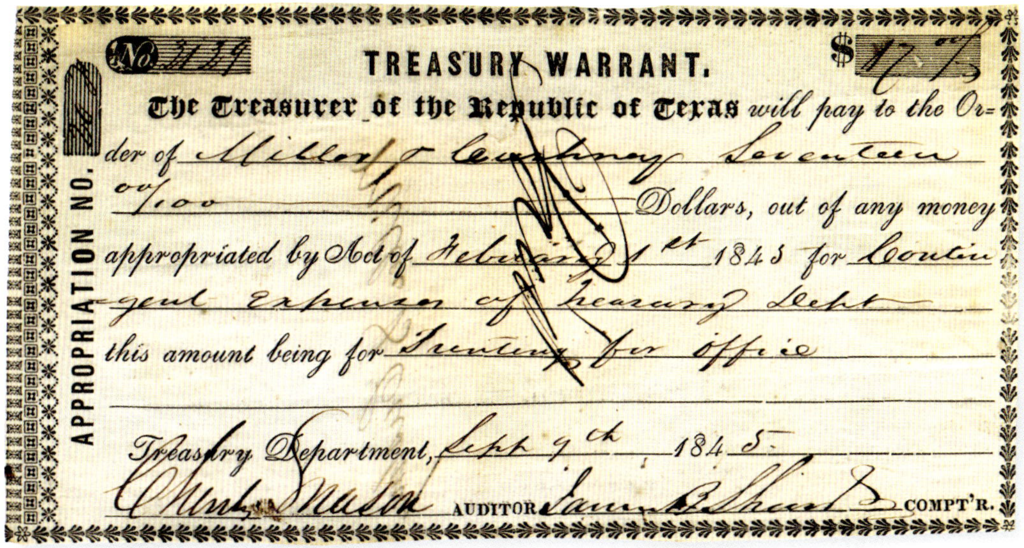
No. 3139 TREASURY WARRANT. $17.00
The Treasurer of the Republic of Texas will pay to the Order of Miller & Cushney Seventeen 00/100 Dollars, out of any money appropriated by Act of February 1st 1845 for Contingent Expenses of Treasury Debt this amount being for Printing for office
Treasury Department, Sept 9th 1845
Chas. Mason AUDITOR Jam B. Shaw COMPT'R.
APPROPRIATION NO.

Fig 14.8, Austin, Treasury Warrant, September 9, 1845, Payable to Miller & Cushney for "Printing for Office."

Private Collection, Cr. AW9, 0-883.

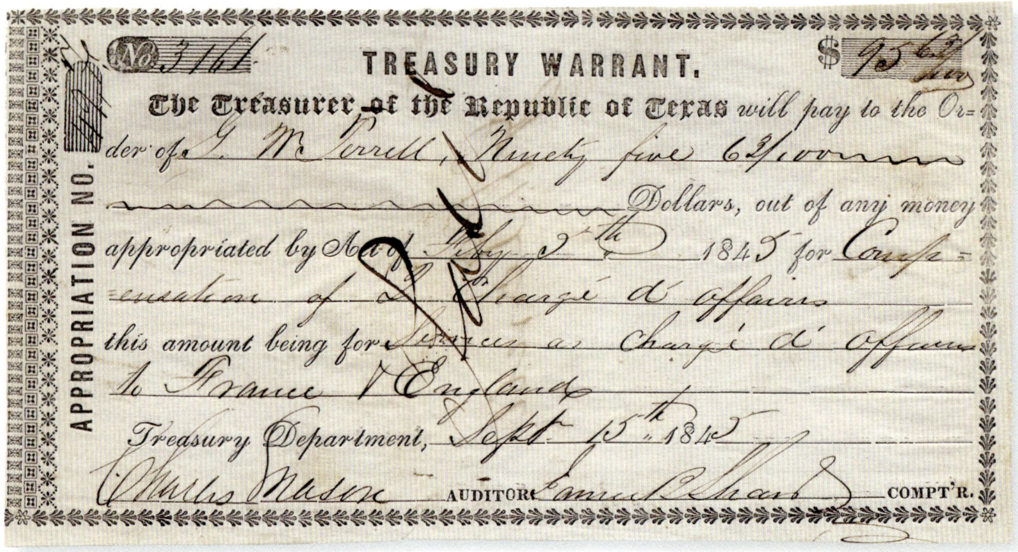

No. 3161 TREASURY WARRANT $95.63/100

The Treasurer of the Republic of Texas will pay to the Order of G.W. Terrell Ninety five 62/100 — Dollars, out of any money appropriated by Act of February 5th, 1845 for Compensation of 2 Charge' d'affaires this amount being for Services as Charge d'affaires to France & England

Treasury Department, Sept[ember] 15th, 1845

(Signed) Charles Mason, AUDITOR James B. Shaw, COMPT'R

Fig 14.9, Austin, Treasury Warrant, September 15, 1845, Payable to G.W. Terrell for "Services as Charge d'affaires to France & England.

Private Collection, Cr. AW9, O-883.

No. 3328 TREASURY WARRANT $25.00

The Treasurer of the Republic of Texas will pay to the Order of W.G. Scott per att[orne]y Francis Hughes Twenty Five 00/100 Dollars, out of any money appropriated by Act of February 1st, 1844 for Relief of Mier Prisoners this amount being for Expenses incurred in returning to Texas from Mexico.

Treasury Department, Austin, Nov[em]ber 20th, 1845

(Signed) Charles Mason, AUDITOR James B. Shaw, Comptroller

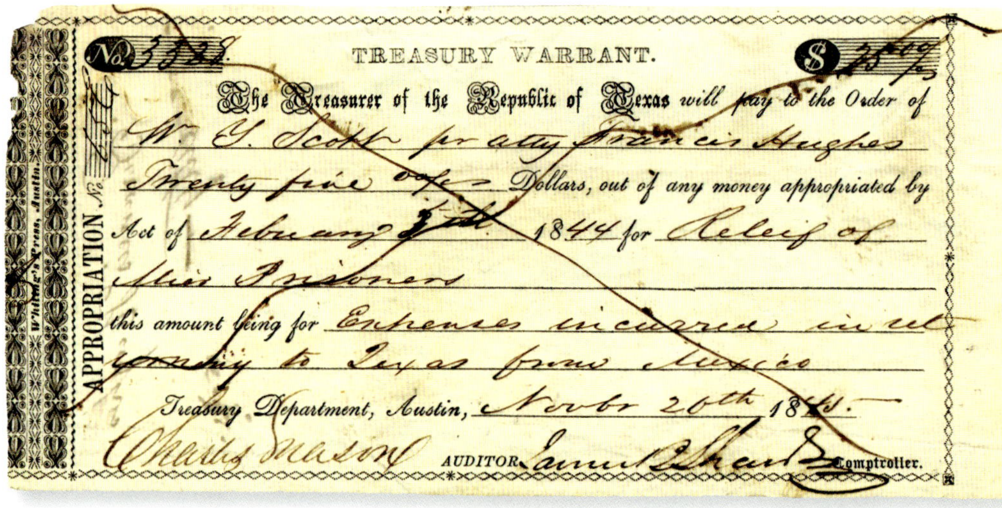

Fig 14.10, Austin, Treasury Warrant, November 20, 1845, $25.00 Payable to W.Y. Scott per attorney Francis Hughes for "Relief of Mier Prisoners."

Private Collection, Cr. AW5B, O-870.

Burnet in 1841, and later as the Attorney General for Sam Houston in December 1841. Terrell was appointed as *Charge d'affaires* to France, England and Spain in 1844 by President Anson Jones.

In early 1845, U.S. newspapers reported stories of the British courting President Jones in an attempt to block the annexation of Texas by the United States. By the summer of 1845, when the ratification of the resolution of annexation appeared to be imminent, the British continued to court Terrell and other diplomats with promises of a permanent peace treaty Mexico if Texas were to reject the Resolution of Annexation. When it became clear that the people of Texas favored annexation, Terrell's English counterparts suggested to editors of several major newspapers that Texas should compel the United States to "pay the private debts of its citizens, as well as the public debts of her states."[34] This later attempt to sway public opinion focused on the large public debt which the Republic of Texas had acquired but did not have the means to repay. Perhaps because of the influence of his English counterparts, Terrell was known as an opponent of the annexation of Texas.

Almost three years after the capture of the Mier Expedition members, Mexico released William Y. Scott, Francis Hughes and the remaining prisoners through diplomatic efforts by the U.S. and Great Britain.[35] Although Scott paid his own expenses to return to Texas, he was required to submit the formal documentation necessary

No. 3371 TREASURY WARRANT $19.00

The Treasurer of the Republic of Texas will pay to the Order of D.C. Sullivan, Nineteen 00/100 – Dollars, out of any money appropriated by Act of Feb[ruar]y 1st, 1844 for Relief of Mier Prisoners this amount being for Passage from Vera Cruz to New Orleans.

Treasury Department, Austin, Dec[ember] 10th, 1845

(Signed) Charles Mason, AUDITOR James B. Shaw, Comptroller

Fig 14.11, Austin, Treasury Warrant, December 10, 1845, $19.00 Payable to D.C. Sullivan for "Relief of Mier Prisoners."

Private Collection, Cr. AW5B (AW5B-1), O-875.

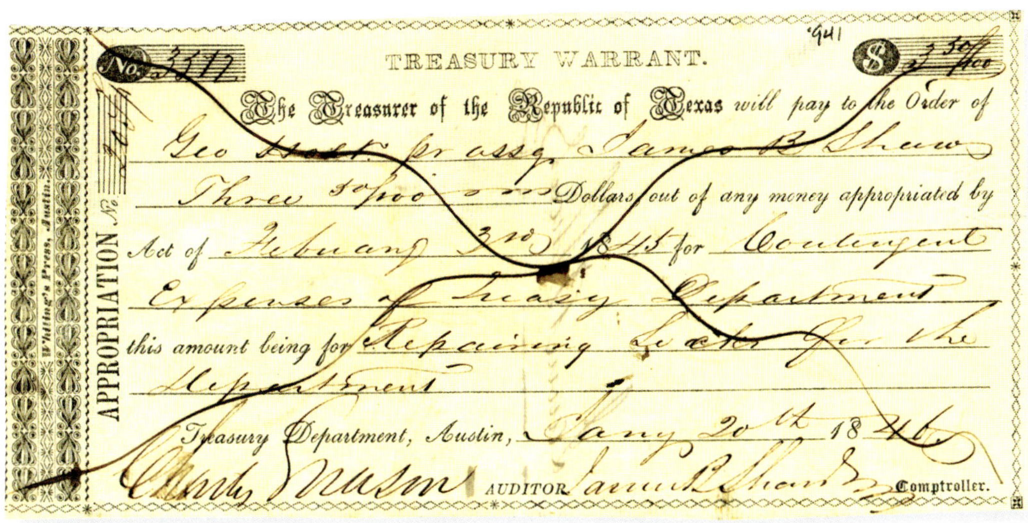

No. 3572 TREASURY WARRANT $3.50

The Treasurer of the Republic of Texas will pay to the Order of Geo[rge] Holt per assign[nee] James B. Shaw, Three 50/100 – Dollars, out of any money appropriated by Act of Feb[ruar]y 3rd, 1844 for Contingent Expenses of Treasury Department this amount being for Repairing Locks for the Department.

Treasury Department, Austin, Jan[uar]y 20th, 1846

(Signed) Charles Mason, AUDITOR James B. Shaw, Comptroller

Fig 14.12, Austin, Treasury Warrant, January 20, 1846, $3.50 to George Holt for "Repairing Locks for the Department."

Private Collection, Cr. AW5B, O-870.

to receive a portion of the appropriated funds from the government.[36] The payment in Figure 14.10 reflects the reimbursement for money expended by Scott to return to Texas. Scott granted a power of attorney to another former Mier prisoner, Francis Hughes, to assist him in collecting the appropriated funds as noted on the warrant.[37]

Although the Mier prisoners found their way back to Texas in a variety of ways, some were transported by ship from Mexican ports following their release. Daniel C. Sullivan took part in the armed expedition under the command of Col. William S. Fisher and was held as a prisoner until he was liberated on September 16, 1844.[38] The $19.00 payment shown in Figure 14.11 payable to Sullivan indicates that he was among the final group of prisoners released and then sent by ship from the port of Vera Cruz to New Orleans.

TEXAS JOINS THE UNITED STATES

The Constitution of the State of Texas was ratified by popular vote in October 1845. On December 16, 1845, the U.S. House of Representatives voted to annex Texas, and the U.S. Senate followed suit on December 22. The United States Congress approved the Texas state constitution, and President James K. Polk signed the act admitting Texas as the twenty-eighth state of the United States on December 29, 1845. James K. Polk, who once restrained Sam Houston from a physical altercation inside the U.S. House of Representatives, now oversaw a physical military presence in Houston's beloved Texas. As the formal process of annexation drew to a close, Polk's vision of Manifest Destiny was close to reality.

THE REPUBLIC OF TEXAS IN 1846

The paper trail of money suggests that the transfer of the government during this time was anything but complete, as Texas still functioned as a sovereign entity until the formal transfer of government on February 19, 1846. Figures 14.12 through 14.14 reflect the continued activity of the government in these final days of the Republic.

With the Treasury Department now abundant in specie, it became important to keep the money under lock and key. This payment for "Repairing Locks for the Department" indicates that James B. Shaw, the Comptroller of the Treasury, may have paid for the repairs out of his own pocket and subsequently had the payee, George Holt, assign the "official" payment for the repairs back to him.

This certificate dated February 12, 1846, was made payable for $16.50 to "Henry B. King" for "services in Capt. Callahan's Comp[an]y of minute men in 1841." King rode with Capt. James Callahan in Guadalupe County as they chased and fought Indians and Mexicans

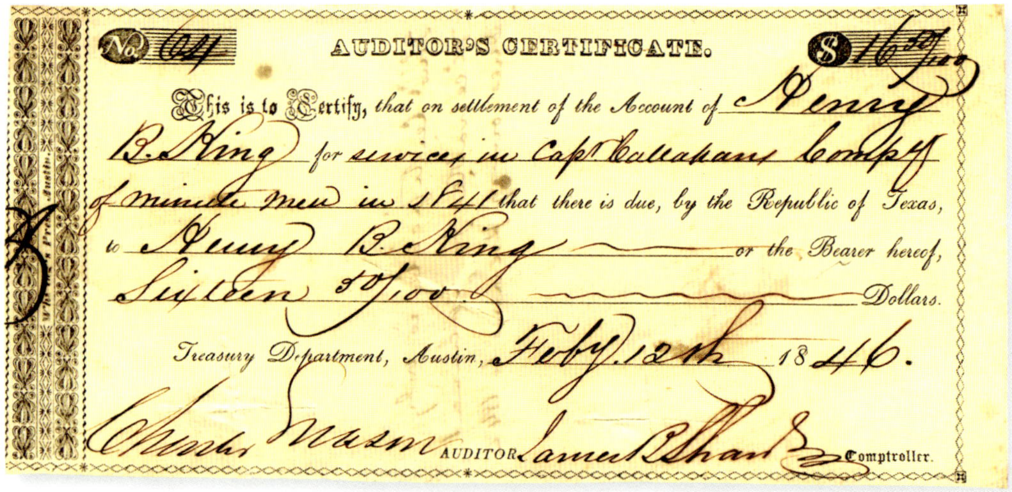
No. 64 AUDITOR'S CERTIFICATE. $16 50/100

This is to Certify, that on settlement of the Account of Henry B. King for services in Capt. Callahans Compy of minute men in 1841 that there is due, by the Republic of Texas, to Henry B. King —— or the Bearer hereof, Sixteen 50/100 —— Dollars.

Treasury Department, Austin, Feby 12th 1846.

Charles Mason AUDITOR James B. Shaw Comptroller.

No. 64 AUDITOR'S CERTIFICATE $16.50

This is to Certify, that on settlement of the account of Henry B. King for services in Capt. Callahan's Comp[an]y of Minute Men in 1841 that there is due, by the Republic of Texas, to Henry B. King – or the Bearer hereof, Sixteen 50/100 – Dollars.

Treasury Department, Austin, Feb[ruar]y 12th, 1846

(Signed) Charles Mason, AUDITOR James B. Shaw, Comptroller

Fig 14.13, Austin, Auditor's Certificate, February 12, 1846, $16.50 to Henry B. King, for "service in Capt. Callahan's Company of Minute Men" in 1841.

Private Collection, Cr. AW10, O-930.

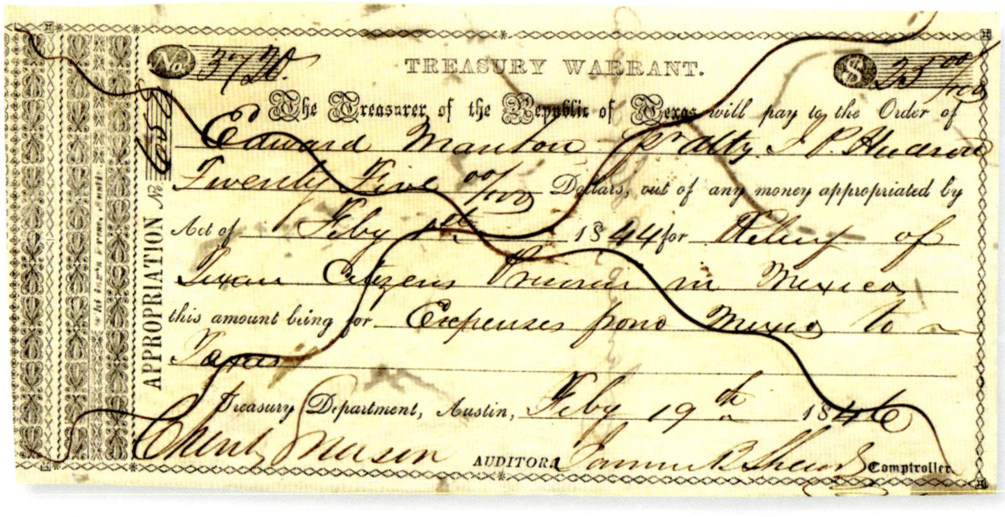
No. 3720 TREASURY WARRANT. $25 00/100

The Treasurer of the Republic of Texas will pay to the Order of Edward Mantou pr atty J. P. Hud Twenty Five 00/100 Dollars, out of any money appropriated by Act of 1 Feby 1844 for Relief of Texan Citizens Prisoner in Mexico this amount being for Expenses from Mexico to Texas

Treasury Department, Austin, Feby 19th 1846

Charles Mason AUDITOR James B. Shaw Comptroller

APPROPRIATION №

No. 3720 TREASURY WARRANT $25.00

The Treasurer of the Republic of Texas will pay to the Order of Edward Mantou per att[orne]y. J.P Hud____ Twenty Five 00/100 Dollars, out of any money appropriated by Act of Feb[ruar]y 1st, 1844 for Relief of Texan Citizens Prisoner in Mexico this amount being for Expenses from Mexico to Texas.

Treasury Department, Austin, Feb[ruar]y 19th, 1846

(Signed) Charles Mason, AUDITOR James B. Shaw, Comptroller

Fig 14.14, Austin, Treasury Warrant, February 19, 1846, $25.00 to Edward Manitou for "Relief of Texas Citizens Prisoner in Mexico."

Private Collection, Cr. AW5B (AW5B-1), O-875.

accused of stealing cattle and horses from settlers.[39] In an effort to protect the frontier, the company also fought during the incursion into Texas by Mexican commander Rafael Vasquez in 1841. Not only is this draft of interest because it documents King's service in a local militia, but it took almost five years for him to get paid for his services as he did not receive this certificate until a week before the formal annexation!

The payment in Figure 14.14 for the "Relief of Mier Prisoners" was made on the last day of the Republic of Texas. It was undoubtedly written as a large crowd gathered in front of the Capital building for the ceremonial admission of Texas as the twenty-eighth state.

Although the Texas Congress made appropriations for the relief of the prisoners at the Perote Prison near Mexico City, the money never reached the prisoners. Instead, these warrants only reflect payments to those prisoners who returned to Texas or assisted others in returning. The late date of the warrant indicates the long process involved in receiving recognition of the claim, even for specific appropriations made more than two years before.

On February 19, 1846, a formal ceremony took place in front of the Capitol building in Austin to consummate the annexation of Texas into the United States. Preparations were made for the event by decorating the Capitol with flags and other adornments. The Texas President and the Governor-elect made their appearance, attended by a joint committee of both Houses, and escorted by officers of the United States.[40] Following a benediction given with the rich fervor of Christian patriots, President Anson Jones rose to give his farewell address. It was on this date that Jones delivered his closing address for which he will forever be remembered:

> *May the union be perpetual, and may it be the means of conferring benefits and blessings upon the people of all the States is my ardent prayer. The final act in this great drama is now performed; the Republic of Texas is no more.*[41]

With these words, many a man's head was bowed, sighs were heaved, and many cheeks were wet with tears.[42] Most of the witnesses to the emotional ceremony were natives of the United States. As the crowd looked up at the flag, the Lone Star shone like a signal light in a field of blue. It was the emblem of the sovereignty of Texas. The Texas flag was taken down and furled away. After the Lone Star banner was retired, the stars and stripes, the flag of their fathers, was raised above the crowd. As it caught the breeze and unrolled its red, white and blue colors in the light of the bright Texas sun, a chorus of cheers filled the capitol. With the formal admission of Texas to the U.S., and the star spangled banner proudly waving above, the celebration concluded with the swearing in of the first governor of the State of Texas, James Pickney Henderson. He closed the ceremony with his inaugural address to the citizens of the newest state in the Union.

Fig 14.15, Anson Jones lowering the Texas Flag.
Texas State Library & Archives Commission, Austin, Texas.

Anson Jones was thereafter known as the Architect of Annexation as he shepherded the acceptance of Texas through the delicate and complicated diplomatic process with the United States. Texas took its place among the United States that brisk February day in 1846 as a proud equal, rather than as a humble inferior. Many felt that Texas was conferring a favor to the United States, rather than receiving one.[43] The U.S. managed to absolve itself of the debt issue and had dodged the question as to what would become of the obsolete stock, bonds, loans and promissory notes of the late Republic of Texas. This financial predicament was soon found too big to ignore as the public anticipation for its final resolution continued to build. The story of the paper republic continues…

1 Anson Jones, *Memoranda and Official Correspondence relating to the Republic of Texas its History and Annexation* (New York: D. Appleton & Company, 1859), 3: 39, December 31, 1843.

2 Ibid.

3 Seymour V. Conner, ed., "Shaw to Mason, October 28, 1844," Texas Treasury Papers, 3: 1,051.

4 *Handbook of Texas Online,* s.v., "Anson Jones," http://www.tsha.utexas.edu/handbook/online/articles/JJ/fjo42.html (accessed August 8, 2006).

5 William M. Gouge, *The Fiscal History of Texas* (New York: Burt Franklin, 1852; rpt. 1969), 122.

6 Dorman H. Winfrey, ed., "Letter from Thomas G. Western to M.C. Hamilton, Act. Secretary of War, Washington, November 21, 1844," Texas Indian Papers, 1844-1845 (Austin: Texas State Library, 1960), No. 104, Courtesy of Darrel Brown.

7 John Holland Jenkins, as stated in "Recollections of Early Texas" courtesy of Darrel Brown.

8 Dorman H. Winfrey, ed., "Letter from Thomas G. Western to Banjamin Sloat, Washington, December 14, 1844," Texas Indian Papers, 1844-1845 (Austin: Texas State Library), No. 112, Courtesy of Darrel Brown.

9 *Handbook of Texas Online,* s.v., "John Coffee Hays," http://www.tsha.utexas.edu/handbook/online/articles/HH/fhabq.html (accessed July 21, 2007).

10 Gouge, *The Fiscal History of Texas,* 129.

11 Jones, "James H. Cooke, Esq. to Anson Jones, Customs-House, Galveston, February 10, 1845," *Memoranda and Official Correspondence,* 422.

12 Seymour V. Conner, ed., "Toler to Shaw, Galveston, February 25, 1845," Texas Treasury Papers, 3: 1,085.

13 Edmund Thornton Miller, "A Financial History of Texas," *Bulletin of the University of Texas 1916: No. 37* (Austin: University of Texas, 1916), 66.

14 Jones, "February 1, 1849," *Memoranda and Official Correspondence,* 5: 46.

15 Anson Jones, Memoranda and Official Correspondence relating to the Republic of Texas its History and Annexation. New York, D. Appleton & Company, 1859. Memorandum Book No. 2. P. 34, August 15, 1839.

16 Ibid., "February 12, 1849 and December 31, 1843, Resume by Anson Jones," 5: 59-60.

17 Ibid., "February 11, 1849, Resume by Anson Jones," 5: 58.

18 Ibid., "February 13, 1849, Resume by Anson Jones," 5: 62-63.

19 Ibid., "February 2, 1850," 5: 53.

20 Ibid., "A.J. Donaldson to Anson Jones, Galveston, May 2, 1845," 457-58.

21 Ibid., "Ebenezer Allen to Anson Jones, Galveston, May 3, 1845," 457-58.

22 From the *Mobile Register,* February 8, 1845.

23 From text accompanying the illustration as printed in *Harper's Weekly,* February 1845.

24 "Joint Resolution for Annexing Texas to the United States, Approved March 1, 1845," Article 2.

25 Seymour V. Conner, ed., "Wickersham & Son to Miller, Philadelphia, April 9, 1845," Texas Treasury Papers, 3: 1,097.

26 Holman Hamilton, "Texas Bonds and Northern Profits: A Study in Compromise, Investment, and Lobby Influence," *The Mississippi Valley Historical Review,* vol. 43 (March 1957), 4: 579-94.

27 Jones, "William D. Lee to Anson Jones, October 20, 1845," *Memoranda and Official Correspondence,* 499.

28 Richard Bruce Winders, *Crisis in the Southwest: The United States, Mexico and the Struggle over Texas* (New York: Scholarly Resources, Inc., 2002), 92.

29 William Ransom Hogan, *The Texas Republic: A Social and Economic History* (Norman, OK: University of Oklahoma Press, 1946), 41.

30 Anson Jones, Memoranda and Official Correspondence relating to the Republic of Texas its History and Annexation. New York, D. Appleton & Company, 1859. Page 477. James R. Wilson to Anson Jones, July 6, 1845.

31 Gouge, *The Fiscal History of Texas,* 231.

32 Constitution of the State of Texas, 1845, Article I, Bill of Rights.

33 *Handbook of Texas Online,* s.v., "George Whitfield Terrell," http://www.tsha.utexas.edu/handbook/online/articles/TT/fte22.html (accessed November 4, 2007).

34 "Ledger & Transcript," *Public Ledger,* vol. 19 (Philadelphia, Thursday, June 5, 1845), 63: 4.

35 From an affidavit in the Texas State Archives stating that Francis Hughes, one of the Mier prisoners, paid his own expenses from the Republic of Mexico to the Republic of Texas. By J.F. Smith, William Hughes, Washington, June 17, 1845.

36 From a document in the Texas State Archives stating that "W.Y. Scott, one of the Mier prisoners and that he came home on his own and Not (sic) at Government Expense." By John D. Owen, County of San Patricio, October 24, 1845.

37 From a document in the Texas State Archives, granting Francis Hughes a power of attorney signed by Wm. Y. Scott and two other individuals. By J. Briddler(?), Wm. Y. Scott, Cyrus K. Gleason, dated at County of San Patricio, October 20, 1845.

38 From an affidavit in the Texas State Archives regarding the service of D.C. Sullivan's military service and his date of liberation from confinement. By William G. Cooke, Secretary of War & Marine, Austin, December 10, 1845.

39 *Handbook of Texas Online,* s.v., "James Hughes Callahan," http://www.tsha.utexas.edu/handbook/online/articles/CC/fca16.html (accessed July 21, 2007).

40 Eugene C. Barker, "The Annexation of Texas," vol. 50, *SHQ* (July 1946), 1: 49-74.

41 Anson Jones, "Valedictory Speech, February 19, 1846," (Austin: Texas State Library & Archives Commission), found online at: http://www.tsl.state.tx.us/treasures/earlystate/nomore-3.html

42 Noah Smithwick, compiled by his daughter Nanna Smithwick Henderson, *The Evolution of a State or Recollections of Old Texas Days* (Austin: Gammel Book Company, 1900; rpt. 1993), 178.

43 Jones, "February 15, 1850," *Memoranda and Official Correspondence,* 5: 53.

CHAPTER FIFTEEN

THE GOLDEN SHOWER

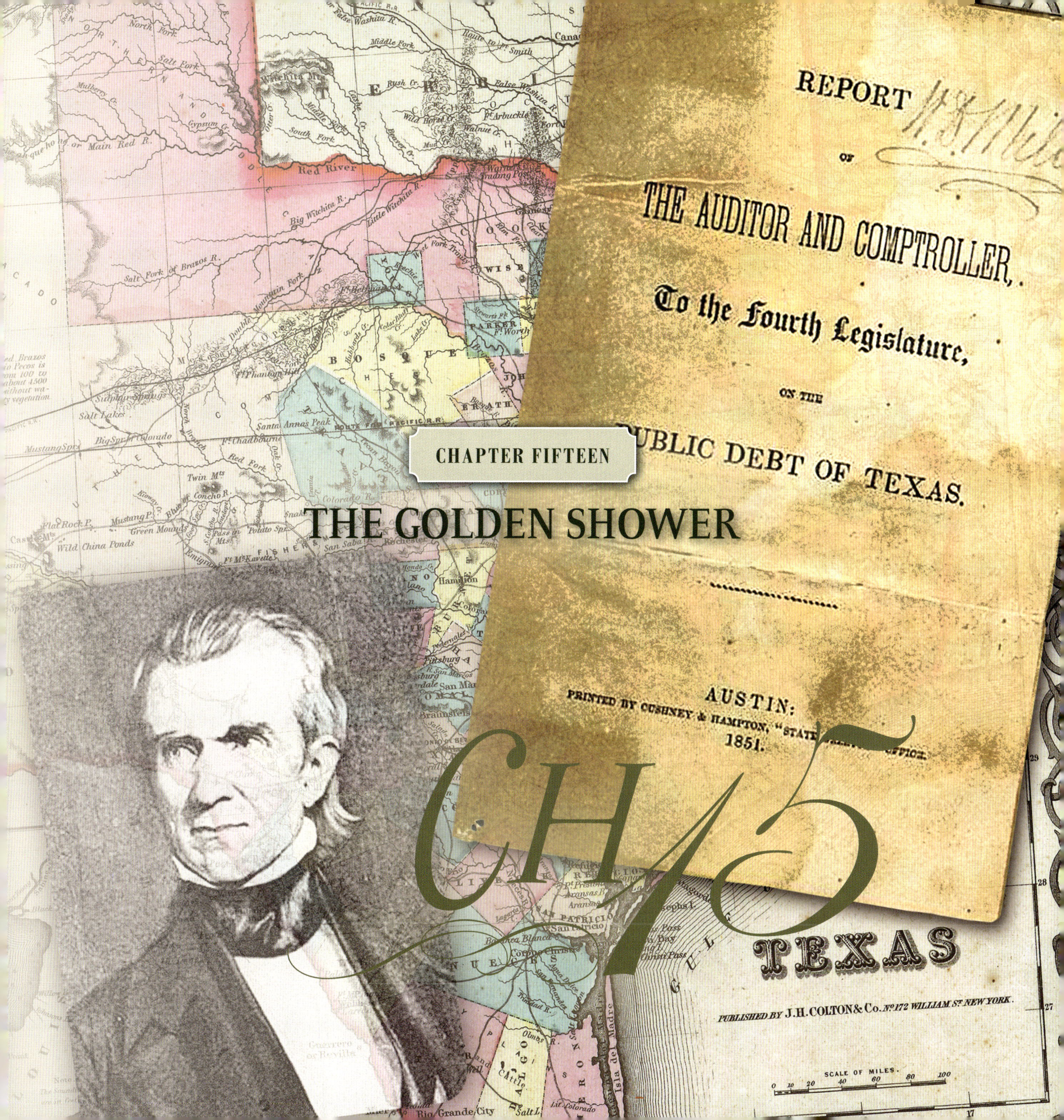

Fig 15.1, James K. Polk, U.S. President, 1845-1849.

From a painting by G.P.A. Healy.

Annexation of the Republic to the United States was a joyous occasion for the people of Texas. Most of the adults inhabiting Texas at the time of annexation had been born somewhere other than the Republic of Texas. Due to the annexation, European immigrants living in Texas consequently became citizens of the United States. For those American-born Texans, the adoption by their mother country elicited a feeling of being brought back home. The financial benefits of annexation were immediately felt in Texas through increased immigration and the resulting trade.[1]

THE MEXICAN WAR

While the annexation of Texas proved beneficial to most of its citizens, the merger shattered any feelings of peace that previously existed between Mexico and Texas during the administration of Anson Jones. Fortunately, Texas no longer had to scrape together a militia to defend its borders. The United States Army, led by generals Zachary Taylor and Winfield Scott, stood on Texas soil, ready to defend their newest state and implement President James K. Polk's strategy of expansionism for the United States.

A brief Mexican incursion across the Texas border in 1846 sparked an invasion of Mexico by U.S. forces and marked the beginning of the two-year Mexican War. The resulting commerce during the war boosted the Texas economy even further. The U.S. made massive expenditures to merchants for the purpose of Texas's defense and for the procurement of supplies for the troops. Within two years, the U.S. Army captured the key Mexican seaport of Vera Cruz, occupied Mexico City, and secured the whole of Texas from any future Mexican claims. The ramifications of the annexation of Texas and the Mexican War which followed had far-reaching consequences for all of North America. James K. Polk, in a single term as President of the United States from 1845-1849, added more land to the United States than did the purchase of Louisiana from the French. The areas which today comprise the states of New Mexico, California, Nevada,

Fig 15.2, Map of North America, c. 1846, Showing the Recent Annexation of the Republic of Texas.

The San Jacinto Museum of History, Houston, Texas.

Utah, nearly half of Colorado, three-fourths of Arizona, and a portion of Wyoming were taken from Mexico as a result of the war.[2] For a $15,000,000 payment to Mexico as compensation for its "ceded" territory and the assumption of $3,250,000 in U.S. claims against Mexico, the Treaty of Guadalupe Hidalgo between Mexico and the United States effectively ended the conflict on February 2, 1848.[3]

THE FIRST STATE LEGISLATURE

During the first assembly of the state legislature on February 16, 1846, Texas lawmakers acknowledged the public debt acquired during the years of the Republic as their own. The U.S. had absolved itself from the liabilities of Texas by amending the proposed treaty of annexation in 1845. In turn, Texas was allowed to keep her public lands so they could be used to pay the public debt. The debt consisted of two major types of obligations: the ordinary or non-revenue debt, consisting primarily of treasury warrants, military scrip, and audited paper; and the revenue debt, consisting of promissory notes and securities with both principal and interest due. The revenue debt was to be secured by the import duties and various taxes, but with the customs revenue transferred to the United States, there was little sustainable cash flow to retire the debt other than the potential sale of public lands. Fortunately, the lands were substantial as Texas contained 133,379,310 square miles, more than 254 million acres of land.[4]

To put this amount in perspective, at the time of annexation in 1845, the portion of Texas lands appropriated by Spanish, Mexican, and Texan authorities exceeded the combined acreage of the states of New York, New Jersey, Maryland, Pennsylvania, and the District of Columbia.[5] While these U.S. states contained approximately 6.5 million people, Texas had a population of roughly 100,000. As the second land rush ensued after annexation, the reality of the available land's location became evident. Many of the prime lands in the eastern portion of the state had already been claimed, and overall, the un-appropriated public lands were far less desirable. For the most part, the vacant public lands were in desolate areas in the western parts of Texas, populated by hostile Indians and far from the centers of population.

In an 1845 report, the Commissioner of the General Land Office stated that almost 182 million acres could be earmarked to pay Texas' debt. When this report reached the Congressional committee at the convention to decide the question of annexation, the committee took into account all the "headright" certificates and settler's claims, soldier's rights, and fraudulent claims, as well as the sizeable grants made by the Mexican state of Coahuila y Tejas. This combined total reduced the available land to 102 million acres. The committee also reasoned that as much as half of the available real estate was wasteland, but the residue of 56,365,126 acres appeared to be an abundant amount of land from which the public debt could eventually be discharged.

Texas' list of unpaid creditors ranged from the shipbuilders in Baltimore, to merchants in Matagorda, Houston, and Nacogdoches, and included former Presidents of Texas and the blacks on the streets of New Orleans. On May 2, 1846, Mirabeau B. Lamar sent a special request to Gov. James Pickney Henderson for unpaid salary accumulated during his presidency.[6] Although Congress appropriated $10,000 for his salary in early 1841, Lamar explained; "When I retired from office, I left a portion of the salary un-drawn; not suspecting for a moment that I might be arbitrarily deprived of it; or that I should forfeit my right to the money by permitting it to remain temporarily in the Treasury." He further stated in his letter to Henderson: "On application for it, the Executive forbid its payment."[7] Whether it was Sam Houston or Anson Jones who denied the salary to Lamar mattered little. The former president was getting a taste of his own medicine and would have to wait in line like everyone else while the process of paying Texas' creditors ran its course. It was to be a long, drawn-out process that tried everyone's patience to an extreme.

LAND SCRIP DEEMED INSUFFICIENT

It was soon determined that the sales of land scrip by the state would be insufficient to retire the public debt. Even if the land could be sold at 65 cents per acre (the going rate for improved property), the resulting revenue based on recent sales would be insufficient even to retire the $331,371 in outstanding engraved notes and $41,630 in star money. But these early debt issues were just the tip of the proverbial iceberg. The early estimates of the "Public Debt" of Texas ran between $9 and $12 million, including the estimated accrued interest. While this may seem like a small sum in financial circles today, it was an enormous and almost

Fig 15.3, Gov. George T. Wood.
Antiquarian Antique Print & Map Gallery, Houston, Texas.

incomprehensible amount in its day. To put the debt into perspective for the modern reader, we shall equate this into 2007 dollars (the date of this writing). Adjusted for inflation at 2.5 percent per annum for 162 years, the $9.6 million debt has an equivalent purchasing power in 2007 of roughly $527 million, or well over half a billion dollars today. The debt had been accumulated from the first promises to pay issued from San Felipe in the fall of 1835 and had been continuously issued, recycled and transferred to others via the paper money system of the Republic of Texas. With each successive issue of new Texian securities, the indebtedness grew, and the outstanding issues sank further from their face value, or what Texas had promised to pay.

During the last three years of its existence, the Republic made no effort to address the outstanding claims against itself. With the sole exception of the exchequer bills, Texas refused to accept its own money for the payment of taxes after January 19, 1842. The debt problem was the focus of the first legislature of the State of Texas. A committee was formed to ascertain the most effective way to sell the public lands for repayment of the debt.[8] Because the collection and receipt of customs revenues had been transferred to the United States in October 1845, the committee concluded that Texas lacked even the $500,000 necessary to survey the tens of millions of acres of vacant land. The committee also reported that for both political and financial reasons, it would be to Texas' advantage for the United States government to purchase the lands, discharging the debt in one fell swoop. Although a similar proposal had been rejected by the U.S. in the amended Treaty of Annexation in 1845, the idea was introduced again over the course of the following year.

LEGISLATIVE SELF-INTERESTS

As the dilemma of how to retire the debt of the late Republic of Texas was debated, the self interests of the early state legislators began to emerge. The committee members appointed to oversee the problem of the public debt soon began to show their true colors. John C. Chalmers, the former Secretary of the Treasury under Lamar (who infamously posted bail for Richard Bullock during the Pig War) served as the chairman of the committee. In section two of the report on the ascertainment and classification of the public debt, Chalmers wrote: "The fact that the debt was contracted during a revolutionary struggle constitutes no reason, in the opinion of the committee, why we should not pay it honestly and in good faith." By this statement, Chalmers acknowledged that the debt was valid. He continued:

> *They, nevertheless, think that she should be bound to return to the public creditors only what, according to just average, they paid for her securities, with the rate of interest stipulated in the bond, or other evidence of the debt; they have endeavored to place the scheme of classification on the broad basis of paying back interest to every man every dollar that he advanced to her service or invested in the faith of her securities.*[9]

In summary, the committee proposed that Texas should pay the creditors only what the government actually received, based upon the estimates of the committee. Since so many different issues of promissory notes, stocks, bonds, and certificates were outstanding, it would be impossible to determine what people paid for them, or what the Republic had received. The wording of this report struck a blow to the very foundation of public credit. Securities are often discounted for those entities deemed the most risky. To not pay the amount promised would amount to a complete breach of faith. It was no small wonder that the committee was composed primarily of holdovers from the Lamar administration, under whose governance the most risky of the Texian securities were issued. But the reasoning of the committee mattered little at the time, as Texas did not have the money to retire even a part of the outstanding debt.

When the second legislature assembled on December 13, 1847, the unresolved question of how to pay the public debt still lingered. Gov. George T. Wood called for a massive public sale of lands to the United States. The first legislature had recommended making a distinction between the original holders and the assignees of the debt and arbitrarily reducing the interests of the non-Texas creditors by half. Although the promissory notes and audited paper could have been handed in at face value for taxes, another holder was now being penalized for accepting them in payment—not to mention all the pay certificates, warrants, and stock issued by the Republic of Texas that were assignable by nature. What good would it do to accept a $20 bill in payment that cannot be spent? This is the mockery of logic which pervaded the question of the Texas debt and the outstanding paper money and securities which represented it.

The once proud nation that had shaken itself free from Mexico in 1836 was now being referred to as the "Late Republic of Texas".

ASCERTAINING THE PUBLIC DEBT

On March 20, 1848, an act was passed by the State Legislature "to provide for ascertaining the debt of the late Republic of Texas."[10] This act was two-fold: it provided a means for creditors to file their claims against the state, and also required the auditor and comptroller to estimate the actual par value realized by the Republic at the time each security or promissory note was issued and then reduce the amount of the claims accordingly. These powerful bureaucrats, Auditor John M. Swisher and Comptroller James B. Shaw, emerged from the process as the financial hatchet men for the state of Texas. Their assignment as defined by the act was to do "as they may deem best calculated to preserve the rights of the State and to do equity to the holders of the claims." They were given sweeping powers to ascertain the value of each claim presented and then reduce it according to their estimates, subject to the revision of the legislature.

With the passage of the act to "Ascertain the Public Debt of Texas," newspaper advertisements advised holders to travel to Austin and file their claims. A deadline was imposed, and all creditors who did not come forward by the second Monday of November 1849 would have their claim postponed. The auditor and comptroller then divided the claims into three distinct classes: the first class included all the promissory notes and stock, bonds, treasury notes, military scrip, or any other audited or government ascertained claim; the second class included all claims with sufficient evidence or vouchers to authorize them into audit—in other words, claims sufficiently documented to merit an auditor's certificate under the laws of the late Republic; in the third class consisted of all the other claims not sufficiently supported by vouchers or evidence which did not fall into the two previous categories.

The auditor and comptroller meticulously accounted for the various claims, which initially totaled more than $7,000,000. As each claimant was audited, it became apparent that only about 10 percent of the original holders of Texian securities, promissory notes, and the like were still residing in Texas.[11] The other 90 percent of claimants were living outside the state and were referred to by the legislature as "outside creditors." Although many of these individuals possessed only small sums of Texian securities and lived far from the centers of influence, there were also substantial holdings concentrated in the hands of men with great financial means. These influential men and their lobbyists often came to Washington, D.C., and enjoyed personal friendships with members of the U.S. Congress.[12]

Barely 1 percent of the warrants or auditor's certificates were still in the hands of the original payee. The rest had been transferred to others, as had many of the old certificates for military pay. As for the paper money, every piece was presumed to have changed hands. Many of the certificates of stock in the Consolidated Fund and Treasury Bonds had found their way into the hands of brokers and speculators. These financiers in Baltimore, Philadelphia, New York, and New Orleans were scoffed at by the bureaucrats in Austin as "not having contributed one cent to the cause of freedom for Texas." The lawmakers forgot that it was the lenders and speculators who had kept the financial system of the Republic of Texas operating for a decade. This paper economy was kept afloat entirely on the belief that someday the holders of the money and securities would receive their money back with the interest as promised.

The initial claim process was followed by another attempt to induce the holders of the audited paper to exchange their certificates for land scrip at fifty cents an acre. At first glance, the offer seemed reasonable as the average value of Texas land in 1850 was approximately sixty-six cents an acre. The offer had few takers, however, as the purchase of land required transfer fees and surveying costs.[13] If the claim holder opted to take the land, property taxes would be applied, requiring yet more additional money. The geographic vastness of Texas made it all but impossible for out-of-state holders to effect anything but a blind real estate transaction through the land scrip offer.

The auditor and comptroller issued another report on December 27, 1849. The report found that despite the threat of forfeiture, large amounts of the old money remained outstanding and had not been presented for audit. The report recommended an extension of time for the holders of any Texas paper so they would not be excluded from the pool of claimants. The recommendation seemed to be a good faith effort, made to accurately assess the debt of the former Republic of Texas. Gov. Peter H. Bell concurred with Swisher and Shaw's report and approved their recommendation for

Fig 15.4, John M. Swisher.
Texas State Library & Archives, Austin, Texas.

an extension. As the State of Texas did not possess the money to pay even the reduced claims, the counting process continued.

THE BOUNDARY BILL

On January 16, 1850, the cold winter winds swept across the plains of Texas, bringing with them the sudden news of change. Like a great thunderclap from the sky, this news shook the very foundation of bankers in New York, Philadelphia, Baltimore, New Orleans, and all of Texas. It resonated not from the small wooden capitol in Austin, but from the distant city of Washington, D.C. Sen. Thomas H. Benton of Missouri introduced a bill into the United States Senate that would, among other things, cede to the United States a certain portion of territory and relinquish all claims on the United States "for liability of the debts of Texas."[14] This blessed thunderclap was the long-awaited sound of hard money that was about to rain down on the creditors of Texas. It was heard loud and clear across the land. The bill was introduced for the purpose of redrawing the boundaries of Texas to exclude all of New Mexico and parts of present-day Oklahoma, Kansas, Colorado, and Wyoming, then contained within Texas' borders. The U.S. Government proposed to purchase tens of millions of acres of public land from Texas, although much of the boundary was the subject of dispute and had only recently been occupied by the Americans following the Mexican War. The map of Texas would be redrawn forever, and the bill would require the federal government to pay the State of Texas $15 million in bonds to settle the outstanding public debt. The very introduction of the legislation swept the price of Texas bonds upward from four to five cents to fifty cents on the dollar in the spring of 1850.[15] The long monetary drought in Texas seemed at an end. Known as the "Boundary Bill," the legislation was also a way for the U.S. to whitewash the title to land which had been taken by conquest in the Mexican War by "purchasing" it from Texas.

There was a tremendous influence in the U.S. Congress by speculators in Texas securities for passage of the bill. One Texas bond lobbyist of prominence was Gen. James Hamilton, the former Texas Minister to France during the Lamar administration. On February 11, 1850, he sponsored a bondholder's meeting at the National Hotel on Pennsylvania Avenue, some six blocks away from the nation's Capitol.[16] Although there is no record of the minutes or discussions which took place at the meeting, Hamilton's newspaper advertisement announced that the group would consider "matters of essential importance to their interests."[17] Partially due to the efforts of Hamilton and others, it appeared that the skies were about to open and shower the creditors with the long-awaited gold and silver which had been promised to them but

Fig 15.5, Map of Texas following the Purchase via the Boundary Bill.
Texas, by J.H. Colton and Co., 1855. Courtesy, Virginia Garrett Cartographic History Library, Special Collections, The University of Texas at Arlington, Arlington, Texas.

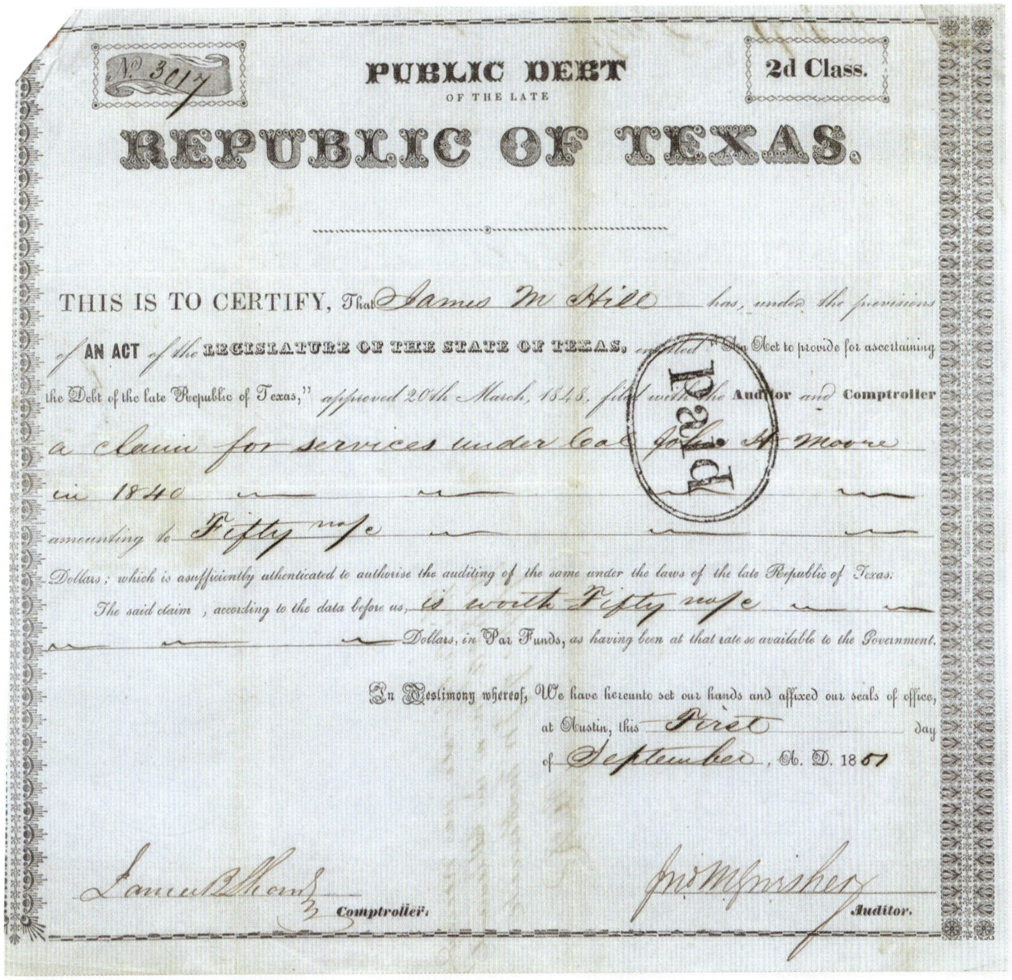
No. 3017

PUBLIC DEBT OF THE LATE REPUBLIC OF TEXAS.

2d Class.

THIS IS TO CERTIFY, That James M Hill has, under the provisions of AN ACT of the LEGISLATURE OF THE STATE OF TEXAS, entitled "An Act to provide for ascertaining the Debt of the late Republic of Texas," approved 20th March, 1848, filed with the Auditor and Comptroller a claim for services under Col. John H. Moore in 1840 amounting to Fifty no/c Dollars; which is sufficiently authenticated to authorise the auditing of the same under the laws of the late Republic of Texas. The said claim, according to the data before us, is worth Fifty no/c Dollars, in Par Funds, as having been at that rate so available to the Government.

In Testimony whereof, We have hereunto set our hands and affixed our seals of office, at Austin, this First day of September, A. D. 1851

Paid

James B. Shaw, Comptroller. Jno. M. Swisher, Auditor.

Fig 15.6, Public Debt of the late Republic of Texas, 2nd Class, No. 3,017, September 1, 1851.

Private Collection, Cr. 48A4.

never paid. In conjunction with the anticipated passing of the Boundary Bill, another act was passed by the Texas Legislature on February 8, 1850, extending the time for creditors to present their claims until the first Monday in September 1851.

The introduction of the "Boundary Bill" and the subsequent legislation regarding the cessation of interest accruing past July 1, 1850, resulted in a flood of demand for the Texas securities. The center of trading was the Philadelphia Stock Exchange, whose quotations shed light on their rising value during the year of the Compromise.[18] As of February 1, 1850, Texas 10 percent bonds were making a "tremendous bound" to 29 cents on the dollar, up more than 20 percent. Those same bonds were being sold at 40 cents in April and 54 cents in May. In mid-June, the Philadelphia *Public Ledger* pointed out that Texas securities had advanced more than 100 percent in the expectation that the Compromise of 1850 would become law.[19] Bolstered by the good news in the East, the creditors burst forth on the capital at Austin and presented their claims in all kinds and types of the old money of the Republic of Texas. Each note and instrument was meticulously checked for previous evidence of cancellation and rightful ownership. If deemed valid, each certificate or promissory note was surrendered to the auditor and exchanged for a certificate evidencing ownership in the appropriate class of the Public Debt of the late Republic of Texas. These certificates were to be held by the owner in lieu of the original obligation until the sale of land to the United States was consummated and funded.

The certificate in Figure 15.6 was issued by the auditor and comptroller as evidence of a claim. James M. Hill submitted the "claim for services under Col. John H. Moore in 1840." The claim was recorded by the State of Texas on September, 1, 1851, indicating that the payment due Hill for an auditor's certificate was outstanding and had remained unpaid for more than a decade since the claim was presented.

Like many other claimants for military pay under the former Republic, Hill was required to submit proof of his service record for his service. In this case, an affidavit

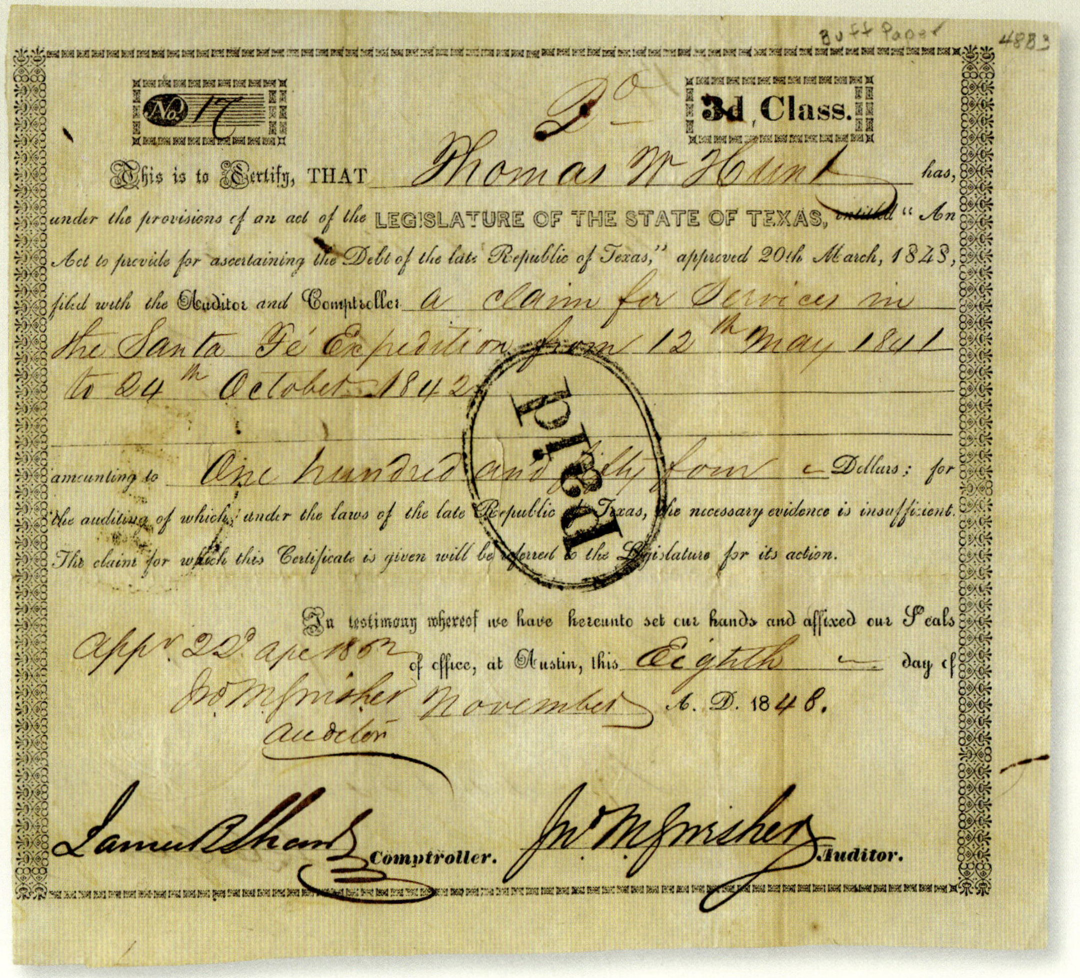

No. 17 3d 3d Class.

This is to Certify, THAT Thomas W Hunt has, under the provisions of an act of the LEGISLATURE OF THE STATE OF TEXAS, entitled "An Act to provide for ascertaining the Debt of the late Republic of Texas," approved 20th March, 1848, filed with the Auditor and Comptroller a claim for Services in the Santa Fé Expedition from 12th May 1841 to 24th October 1842 amounting to One hundred and fifty four Dollars; for the auditing of which, under the laws of the late Republic of Texas, the necessary evidence is insufficient. The claim for which this Certificate is given will be referred to the Legislature for its action.

Paid

In testimony whereof we have hereunto set our hands and affixed our Seals of office, at Austin, this Eighth day of November A. D. 1848.

Jno M Swisher Auditor

James B Shaw Comptroller. Jno. M. Swisher Auditor.

Fig 15.7, Public Debt of the late Republic of Texas, 3rd Class, No. 17, November 8, 1848.
John N. Rowe III Collection of Texas Currency, DeGolyer Library, Southern Methodist University, Dallas, Texas, Cr. 48B.

(now in the Texas State Library) was presented by his former commanding officer, John H. Moore certifying that "I was colonel Commanding [sic] the expedition against the Comanches in the Fall of 1840; that James M. Hill was a member of the company commanded by Captain Nicholas Dawson in Said Expedition; that he served in said from about the 18th day of September to about the 18th of November, and that said James M. Hill was honorably discharged."[20]

Hill's late date of surrender for back pay in the military resulted in its admission as a claim under the 2nd class of claimants. These certificates were assignable financial instruments, with many being endorsed to a third party. The certificate is stamped "PAID" and an attached affidavit indicates that the pending $50 payment was assigned by Hill to the State of Texas (possibly for taxes) on February 16, 1852.

Like many of the public debt claims included in the second and third classes of claims, the certificate in Figure 15.7 was issued for a long overdue claim for military service. The claim was recorded on the "Eighth day of November A.D. 1848" for Thomas W. Hunt, for "a claim for services in the Santa Fe Expedition from 12th May 1841 to 24th October 1842 amounting to One hundred and fifty four Dollars." Unlike a claim which was supported by a previously issued auditor's certificate, the claimant was required to furnish official documentation sufficient to verify the claim against the government.

In order to make this claim, the payee, Thomas W. Hunt, was required to produce proof of his military service in the form of a military discharge certificate (now in the Texas State Library). This certificate verified his service as entering "Captain M. Caldwell's company D. of the Santa Fe Pioneers who was enlisted the 12th day of May 1841" until his formal discharge on August 24, 1842.[21] It was signed by William N. Henry, his commanding officer and marked "approved" by Hugh McLeod, who had led the ill-fated expedition. Hunt resided in Gonzales following the annexation of Texas. Like many veterans, it was impractical for him to personally present his claim to Austin. Therefore, his claim was presented to the state and processed under a power of attorney granted to Charles Mason and W.D. Miller for the purpose of securing his funds.[22]

While the bureaucrats in Austin meticulously recorded and classified each claim, several versions of the Boundary Bill were introduced in the U.S. Senate. Details of the purchase offer were then debated in both Houses of Congress. The final version of the bill, proposed by Sen. James A. Pearce of Maryland, offered Texas $10,000,000 in U.S. Government 5 percent stock in exchange for ceding sixty-seven million acres of land to the federal government. This would include all land north and west of a boundary beginning at the 100th meridian where it intersects the parallel of 36 degrees, 30 minutes, then running west along that parallel to the 103rd meridian, south to the 32nd parallel, and from that point west to the Rio Grande (also see Figure 13.14). On the very day that the vote was taken on the bill, lobbyists representing the Texas bondholders "pressed around the desks of the representatives in such force that one of the members asked for their removal from the floor."[23] The Boundary Act and four additional bills dealing with controversial sectional issues were passed by the U.S. Congress at about the same time.[24] These bills collectively were known as the Compromise of 1850.

With the disastrous Santa Fe expedition still fresh on their minds, the residents of New Mexico had never accepted Texas' longstanding claim to the area. The legislation would permanently settle the boundary dispute between Texas and New Mexico, as much of the latter had been acquired through conquest in the Mexican War. The federal government also recognized that Texas had no effective means to discharge its public debts because customs revenues had been transferred to the United States under the resolution of annexation in 1845. The reality of the day was that Texas had a legal obligation, and the U.S. now had a moral obligation, to see that the debt was paid. It can be best summed up in the words of Senator Pearce in a message to Congress: "I think I am perfectly safe in saying that the Congress of the United States need never expect to get rid of the claims of these creditors of Texas until they are paid."

The terms which had been proposed in the Boundary Bill offered the U.S. and Texas an opportunity to wipe the debt slate clean. The bill was signed into law by President Millard Fillmore on September 7, 1850, and the provisions were approved by the Texas state legislature in Austin on November 25, 1850.[25] In an address to the people of Galveston, former President Sam Houston,

Fig 15.8, $100 Texan Indemnity Stock Certificate, United States of America.
Texan Indemnity 5 Percent Stock, by an Act of September 9, 1850, Private Collection.

then serving as a U.S. Senator from Texas, called the legislation, "the best sale ever made of land of a worthless quality, and a disputable title."

The $100 issue in Figure 15.8, a proof specimen, is an example of the stock certificates the U.S. paid to the State of Texas for the Compromise of 1850. The stock matured in fourteen years at 5 percent interest, payable semi-annually. On the left of the stock is an allegorical representation of Liberty with a shield, and a cap and pole draped across her lap. In the center is an allegory of War with shield and fasces, and at the right is a representation of a woodsman with a dog. At the bottom left is a portrait of George M. Dallas, and at bottom right is a portrait of James K. Polk. It was under the Polk administration that Texas formally joined the U.S. on February 19, 1846. Across the face in bold red is written "100" as an anti-counterfeiting protector. At the bottom center is a dog with a ribbon in its mouth bearing the inscription "ONE HUNDRED." The issue was printed by Toppan, Carpenter, Casilear & Co., of Philadelphia and New York, and contains no coupons.

The $500 issue in Figure 15.9, a proof specimen, is another example of the certificates the U.S. paid to the State of Texas for the Compromise of 1850. The stock matured in fourteen years at 5 percent interest, payable semi-annually. On the bottom left is a woodsman with a dog. Liberty is seated in the top center with a shield, and a cap and pole draped across her lap. On the bottom

Fig 15.9, $500 Texan Indemnity Stock Certificate, United States of America.

Texan Indemnity 5 Percent Stock, by an Act of September 9, 1850, Private Collection.

Fig 15.10, $1,000 Texan Indemnity Stock Certificate, United States of America.

Texan Indemnity 5 Percent Stock, by an Act of September 9, 1850, Private Collection.

right is a vignette of a farmer with a scythe. A portrait of Thomas Corwin, the Secretary of the Treasury under President Millard Fillmore, is on the left. A portrait of Thomas H. Benton, the U.S. Senator from Missouri who introduced the Boundary Bill to Congress, is on the right. "500" is written across the face in bold red as an anti-counterfeiting protector. A dog is in the bottom center carrying a ribbon in its mouth bearing the inscription "FIVE HUNDRED." The issue was printed by Toppan, Carpenter, Casilear & Co., of Philadelphia and New York, and contains no coupons.

The $1,000 issue in Figure 15.10, an un-issued face specimen on special bond paper, is the last example of the certificates the U.S. paid to the State of Texas displayed in this work. The stock matured in fourteen years at 5 percent interest, payable semi-annually. A vignette of a Sailor and Plenty is on the left, and Liberty with a shield, and a cap and pole draped across her lap is in the top center. An allegorical representation of the Arts is on the right of the issue, with a portrait of Gen. Zachary

Taylor, who led U.S. forces into Mexico at the start of the Mexican War, on the left. A portrait of President Millard Fillmore is also on the right.[26] "1,000" is written across the face in bold blue as an anti-counterfeiting protector. A small eagle is in the bottom center of the certificate. The issue was printed by Toppan, Carpenter, Casilear & Co., of Philadelphia and New York. The first and last interest coupons (all of which are attached to this certificate) are shown in figures 15.11 and 15.12. This extraordinary stock certificate is unique.

Fig 15.11, $25 Texan Indemnity Coupon, due July 1, 1851.
Private Collection.

Fig 15.12, $25 Texan Indemnity Coupon, due January 1, 1865.
Private Collection.

The specimens shown in figures 15.11 and 15.12 are the first and last semi-annual interest coupons for the $1,000 denomination. Each certificate of Texan Indemnity 5 percent stock had twenty-eight semi-annual interest coupons attached. Each coupon is identical except for the due date of the interest payment and is adorned with a series of small vignettes, centered at the top by a small eagle and flanked by Presidents Jefferson and Washington. These coupons were removed with scissors and redeemed for payment in silver or gold coins of the United States. The face amount of the stock was paid at maturity upon redemption of the final interest payment on January 1, 1865, upon surrender of the certificate. These stock certificates were interchangeably referred to as bonds, because of the fixed 5 percent coupon. The last known outstanding issues of these bonds were relinquished to the U.S. Treasury in 1869. They were all destroyed.[27]

CALCULATING THE PAYOFF

As John M. Swisher, James B. Shaw, and the staff in the comptroller's office worked to total the various claims and calculate what was owed, they presented a series of reports to the Texas Congress on the subject. According to their final report, $373,001 of interest bearing Star Notes and engraved notes were still outstanding. Many holders of these notes had refused to exchange the 10 percent interest notes for the Consolidated Fund series in 1840. In order to cut their liability, the Texas Congress passed a law on February 11, 1850, declaring that "all liabilities of the late Republic of Texas shall cease to bear interest from and after the 1st day of July, 1850."[28] For the holders of the Star Notes and engraved notes, another provision of the same legislation was even harsher, declaring that these old issues would not bear any interest after January 1, 1841.[29] This was the date which these interest bearing notes were to be exchanged for the certificates of Stock in the Consolidated Fund issued from Austin.

With regard to the Consolidated Fund, the outstanding 8 percent and 10 percent issues totaled $1,418,769.[30] Their interest had been arbitrarily cancelled by the legislature as of July 1, 1850. By taking these actions, the state legislature violated Article 1, Section 14 of the Texas Constitution, which stated "No bill of attainder, Ex post facto law, retroactive law, or any law impairing the obligation of contracts, shall be made; and no person's property shall be taken, or applied to public use, without adequate compensation being made, unless by the consent of such person."[31] Added to the total debt calculation were $766,800 in treasury bonds, $1,828,192 in redbacks and $42,387 in auditor's certificates. When other outstanding liabilities of $475,907 for naval vessels and various miscellaneous items were taken into account, the total amount of the public debt of Texas as validated under the claims process, with accumulated interest, totaled a staggering $9,647,253 on July 1, 1850.

Although the pending $10,000,000 payment from the federal government would retire this amount in full, the legislature continued to argue that Texas should only repay what was actually received by the government, rather than the promised amount. The officials validated their decision because the Republic of Texas had issued many obligations at deep discounts to their face value. This twisted philosophy struck at the very heart of the concept of public credit as it was the government's

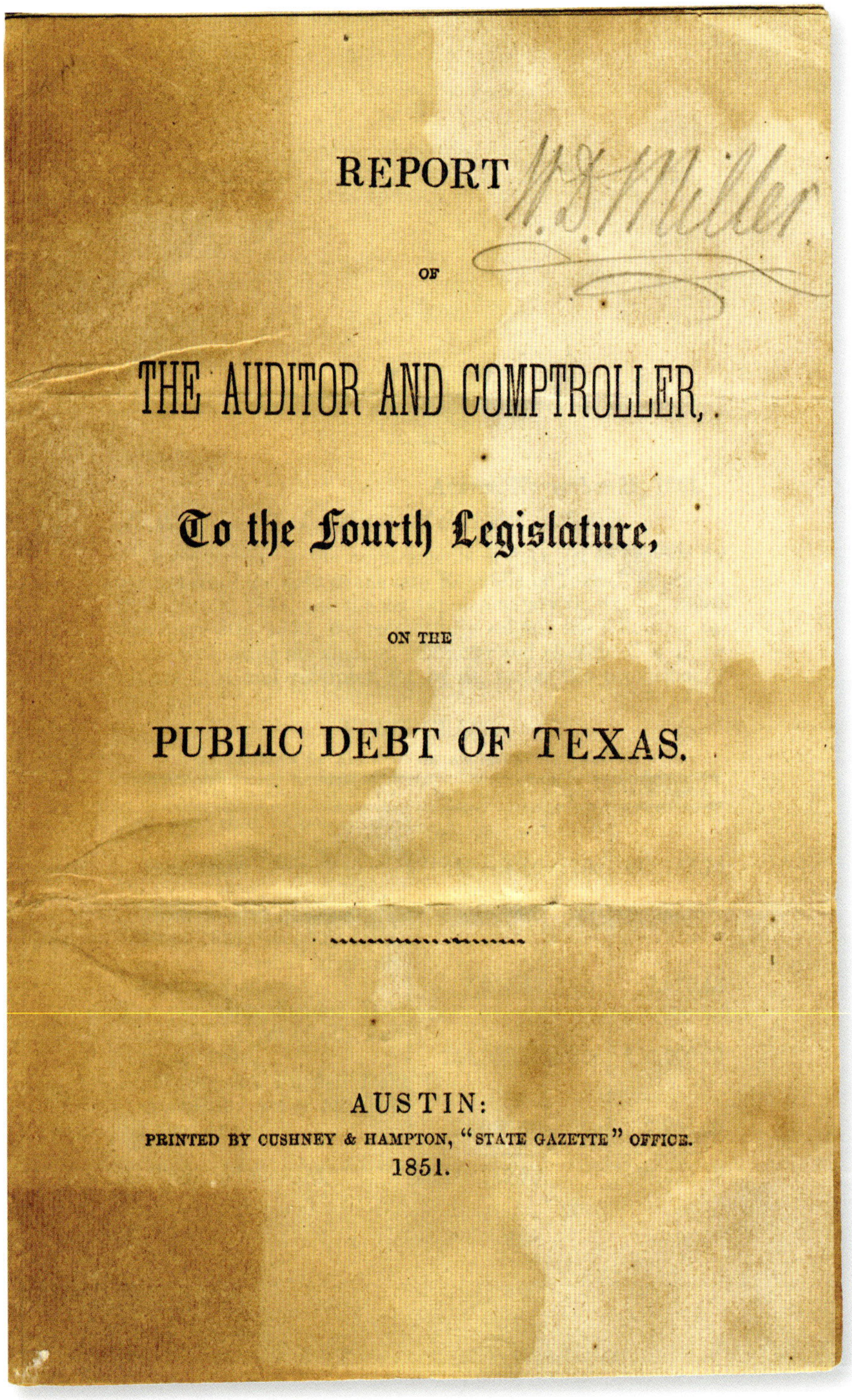
REPORT

W. D. Miller

OF

THE AUDITOR AND COMPTROLLER,

To the Fourth Legislature,

ON THE

PUBLIC DEBT OF TEXAS.

AUSTIN:

PRINTED BY CUSHNEY & HAMPTON, "STATE GAZETTE" OFFICE.

1851.

Fig 15.13, Report of the Auditor and Comptroller on the Public Debt of Texas.

Courtesy of Richard D. Laster.

The Report of the Auditor and Comptroller on the Public Debt of Texas was released in 1851 and was the basis for the scaling system. This copy bears the autograph of W.D. Miller, who assisted the auditor and comptroller in preparing the document. The entire text of the report can be found in Appendix J.

decision to issue the securities at a discount. If the lenders expected to be paid only what they advanced, and not what was promised, they would have advanced nothing. Given its perilous financial condition, the Republic was fortunate to receive what it did, for when interest is not paid on obligations in a timely manner those obligations always decline in value. In terms of raising money through loans, if Texas' creditors had the remotest suspicions that their claims would subsequently be scaled down and reduced on such an arbitrary basis, the Republic would not have been successful in securing the few loans it was able to negotiate.[32]

The congressional committee in charge of determining the payment scale decided that higher payments should be made to the original holders of Texas obligations, rather than the people who ended up with the notes. The reasoning behind the committee's thinking can only be interpreted as the most selfish of political motives. Why would a soldier accept a promissory note as payment for his services if he could not transfer it to another for provisions? What farmer would accept the payment if he could not pass it off to the merchant, who in turn could not use the note for other purchases? Why would anyone accept payment of any kind if they knew it would lose its value once transferred? Paper money, stock certificates and treasury bonds are by their very nature designed to be transferable. In fact, the Treasury of the Provisional Government of Texas at San Felipe de Austin designated that all obligations of Texas were assignable. This concept was acknowledged by the government as being valid for the entire ten years that Texas was a free and independent Republic. Unfortunately for those left holding the various obligations, the committee overseeing the final payoff began to reason otherwise.

As the creditors waited for payment, the auditor and comptroller applied the somewhat arbitrary principle of scaling to the outstanding issues. Most of the creditors had the value of their claims reduced. For instance, those holding Star Notes and audited paper had their claims reduced by only a nominal amount, while other creditors possessing redbacks and 8 percent treasury bonds had their claims reduced by 80 percent with the average claim being reduced to under fifty cents on the dollar. Others had their claims rejected outright! The Auditor and Comptroller summarized the recommended payoff amounts in a report to the fourth legislature.

THE SCALING SYSTEM

The report was prepared by John Swisher and James B. Shaw, who attested to its accuracy. Their job was to verify the amounts which, according to their estimates, Texas had originally received from each issue and to assign a value to each class of the debt. In the beginning, this impossible task had been mandated by Congress with the realization that Texas did not have the means with which to retire her public debt in full largely because of the loss of customs revenues. Nonetheless, the estimates made in the report had been dictated by the Texas Congress. A summary of the report follows, with the headings of each classification re-labeled to more closely correspond to those used in this text.

PAPER MONEY

Audited Paper ($74,441 outstanding): These represent the government paper issued under various enactments, many of which were owned by lawmakers and other employees of the government. The language of the report indicates that both unpaid treasury warrants and outstanding audited paper are included in this category. The report reasoned that these paper issues were issued at par (face value). However, the issues were audited at less than par, and a value of 93.29 cents on the dollar was assigned to this class, a discount of only 6.71 percent.

Star Notes ($41,630 outstanding): The notes in this category include the 10 percent interest bearing treasury notes issued under the act of June 9, 1837. This paper money was placed in circulation during the fall and winter of 1837-1838 until the engraved series of notes could be procured. This issue had run its course before any meaningful depreciation of the currency occurred. These notes were to be repaid at 100 cents on the dollar, although the 10 percent interest only accrued until January 1, 1841 (the date the legislature stated all outstanding promissory notes should be exchanged into stock).[33]

Medallion Notes: The first issue of change notes were not specifically mentioned in the report, possibly because of the relatively small amount issued. Although they were issued to provide change for the Star Notes and engraved series because they did not pay interest, it is thought that they were included under the category of "miscellaneous liabilities" or with the other interest bearing notes.

Government of Texas Notes ($331,371 outstanding): Also known as the engraved notes, this second series of notes was issued under the act of June 9, 1837. Since they began depreciating shortly after their issue in the spring of 1838, a value of 50 cents on the dollar was stipulated by the committee. Like the Star Notes, the engraved notes accrued interest only until January 1, 1841. The promised 10 percent interest was further reduced to 50 percent of the accumulated amount through the cutoff date, since the interest was also calculated at the scaled or reduced rates.

Redback Notes ($1,828,192 outstanding): These notes were issued from Houston and Austin to supersede the first engraved issue of notes. In the spring of 1839, these notes were worth about 37 1/2 cents on the dollar. The unabated and continued issuance of money exacerbated the depreciation of the notes until the Government finally paid them out at between 12 and 15 cents on the dollar. The committee assigned the redbacks a "equitable" value of 25 cents on the dollar. The committee denied any claims of interest on the notes.[34] Although these notes quickly lost their purchasing power, citizens could still use these notes to pay their taxes at 100 percent of face value until 1842. Although the report does not specifically mention the second issue of change notes from Austin, it is thought that they are included in this classification.

Exchequer Bills: There were no exchequer bills mentioned in the report. The committee presumed all exchequer bills had been paid in for taxes at 100 percent of face value, and were subsequently cancelled and destroyed upon receipt.

Miscellaneous Liabilities ($42,387 outstanding): This category includes everything that did not fall under the other groups of audited paper. These liabilities may have included an incremental amount of the first series of change (medallion) notes which were not otherwise mentioned in the report. This category is thought to include various payments to the firm of McKinney & Williams and other individuals who advanced funds during the struggle for independence. McKinney & Williams settled claims of $54,401.11 in land scrip at the rate of 50 cents per acre and other obligations such as treasury notes and bonds.[35] The recognition of an early or "par" payment to the government, and strong political connections, may have allowed these claims to be valued at 100 cents on the dollar.

VARIOUS LOANS, THE CONSOLIDATED FUND AND GOVERNMENT BONDS

Texian Loans: There were no Texian Loans of 1836 outstanding at the time of annexation. All of the loans had been settled in exchange for land under the revised terms dictated by the ad interim government. $20,070 had been advanced under the Triplett loan and $45,820 under the Erwin loan in 1836.[36] The outstanding balance of $7,970 remaining under the $10,000 advanced from Samuel Swartwout had been "funded" by a special issue of shares in the Consolidated Fund of Texas in 1837.

Consolidated Fund of Texas, 1837 Issue ($632,526 outstanding): This is the first issue of the 10 percent stock in the Consolidated Fund of Texas conceived by Henry Smith and created by an Act of June 7, 1837. It was funded by liabilities of the government in the form of drafts on the treasury and audited paper for which Texas received par value.[37] Although the majority of this stock was issued when the Star Notes were in circulation, the committee assigned a value to the Consolidated Fund of only 70 cents on the dollar upon its redemption. Although the holders of the stock expected whole payment, the committee reasoned: "as it [the issue] is now generally in the hands of third parties, who, in most instances, acquired it at a much less value from the original investor than now assigned it."[38]

Consolidated Fund of Texas, 1837 Special Issue ($7,940 outstanding): This was a special issue of the 10 percent stock in the Consolidated Fund created by an act of June 7, 1837, for the relief of Swartwout and others. This amount was for the unused portion of the $10,000 which Swartwout and his friends advanced to Texas in May 1836. The committee assigned this stock a value of 100 cents on the dollar as it was cash money advanced to the government during the early part of the revolution. The report also noted that Swartwout was still the original owner at the time of redemption.[39]

Consolidated Fund of Texas, 1840 10 Percent Issue ($754,000 outstanding): This group included the 10 percent Consolidated Fund created by an act of February 5, 1840. At the time these engraved certificates were issued for the refunding of the promissory notes, the people of Texas could redeem their paper money at 100 cents on the dollar for the payment of taxes. By exchanging their paper money for the stock in the funded debt of Texas, the people were promised interest at 10 percent per annum payable in gold and silver. Unfortunately, the committee assigned this stock a value of only 30 cents on the dollar, reasoning, "the value attached to this stock may act onerously on some holders, but it will fully remunerate a large majority." The interest payments were also reduced to the same rate of 30 cents on the dollar. This is among the most blatant examples of broken promises on the part of the Republic of Texas.

Consolidated Fund of Texas, 1840 8 Percent Issue ($24,280 outstanding): This was the 8 percent stock in the Consolidated Fund created by an act of February 5, 1840, for those citizens who did not exchange their promissory notes by July 1, 1840. The committee assigned this stock a value of 30 cents on the dollar, even though the security had been outstanding more than ten years. The interest payments were also reduced to the same rate of 30 cents on the dollar.

Government Bond, 1840, Payable to Holder ($766,800 outstanding): This was the engraved issue of 8 percent treasury bonds issued in $100 and $500 denominations during the Lamar administration. These bonds were issued by the government in exchange for services and supplies. The bonds were "Receivable for all Government Dues," a fact that was boldly printed on the face of each certificate. The interest was payable in "gold and silver." A U.S. treasury bond is among the safest of investments as 100 percent of the principal is returned if held to maturity. The holders of these Republic of Texas treasury bonds suffered a completely different experience from the bondholders of the United States when the committee assigned a value of only 20 cents on the dollar, with the interest also reduced to the same rate. Imagine today, buying a treasury bond from the U.S. Government only to be later informed that you would only receive one-fifth of your money back and one-fifth of the interest promised.

FOREIGN LOANS

Loan from the Bank of the United States ($457,380 outstanding): This loan from the Pennsylvania Bank of the United States was made to Texas in the fall of 1839 for which 10 percent British pound sterling bonds were issued as collateral. $280,000 was advanced to Texas in bank notes and the balance of $177,380 was advanced in specie. The committee assigned this loan a value of $400,000 or 87.45 cents on the dollar. The report classified this amount as "what the Government actually received," indicating that the bank notes were valued at 79.5 cents on the dollar and the specie at par, with the average of the two resulting in the "scaled" rate. The principal and accumulated interest on this loan amounted to $960,498 by July 1, 1850, at which point it would no longer accrue interest. The significant amount due indicates that any excuse for scaling or reducing the claim to those creditors outside of Texas was deemed plausible by the committee.

LOANS FOR BUILDING THE TEXAS NAVY

Loan for Purchase of Naval Vessels ($560,000 outstanding): This obligation was secured by the placement of two bonds of $280,000 each. These obligations were to James Schott and E.D. Whitney, who filed their claims as partners of Frederick Dawson of Baltimore. In reviewing this claim, the Government dismissed any obligation for payment of the second $280,000 bond because "the Government was unable to meet the payment at the time specified," although the first bond could have easily been retired from the proceeds of the loan from the Bank of the United States. The committee valued the original $280,000 bond at 50 cents on the dollar or $140,000. This loan was as solemn a contract as could have been written for the purchase of the warships *San Jacinto, San Antonio,* and *San Bernard,* contracted by Samuel M. Williams on behalf of Texas.[40] Thirteen long years had passed since Texas entered into this contract with Dawson. The *San Antonio* had been lost at sea, and the other two schooners were allowed to rot in Galveston from a lack of repairs. While the ships were not valuable at the time the debt was repaid, they certainly had value at the time they were contracted and received by the government. They also had value to the shipyard which built and sold them to Texas, as the schooners could have easily been built, sold and delivered to another government. The default on the loan by Texas exhausted the shipbuilder's private fortunes and utterly destroyed their profitable business.[41]

Any obligation for the second $280,000 bond was dismissed entirely, presumably on the grounds that Dawson, Schott, and his associates had lobbied President Anson Jones in 1845 for a provision in the original Treaty of Annexation to settle for the original principal amount of $280,000 and accumulated interest paid to them by the United States within 90 days of ratification of the treaty.[42] Although this provision was included, the first treaty of annexation had been rejected. In addition to the $280,000 principal amount still due on the first loan, the unpaid interest accumulated to $325,577 by July 1, 1850.[43] This amount was also to be scaled down to the same reduced rate of 50 cents on the dollar.

Loan for Purchase of the Steamer *Zavala* ($195,907 outstanding): This debt had long ago been owed to James Holford & Asscociates for the purchase of the paddle wheel steamer *Charleston* under Sam Houston's first administration. Re-christened the *Zavala* upon its delivery to Texas, the committee arbitrarily decided to repay this debt at 50 cents on the dollar on the grounds that the terms of the contract were "similar to that entered into with Mr. Dawson." Like the Dawson loan, this obligation accumulated substantial interest that remained unpaid. The interest stopped accumulating on July 1, 1850, also at the reduced a rate of 50 cents on the dollar. It was obvious that the lenders could not foreclose on their property and seize the collateral, as the *Zavala* had become worm-eaten, damaged beyond repair, and sunken in the muddy harbor at Galveston.

REJECTIONS OF CLAIMS

In addition to the multitude of claims subjected to the scaling system, many claims against the Republic were denied outright if they lacked appropriate documentation or showed previous evidence of cancellation. Others were rejected since the committee decided that the government never received any value for the items presented. The item in Figure 15.14 is one of these examples.

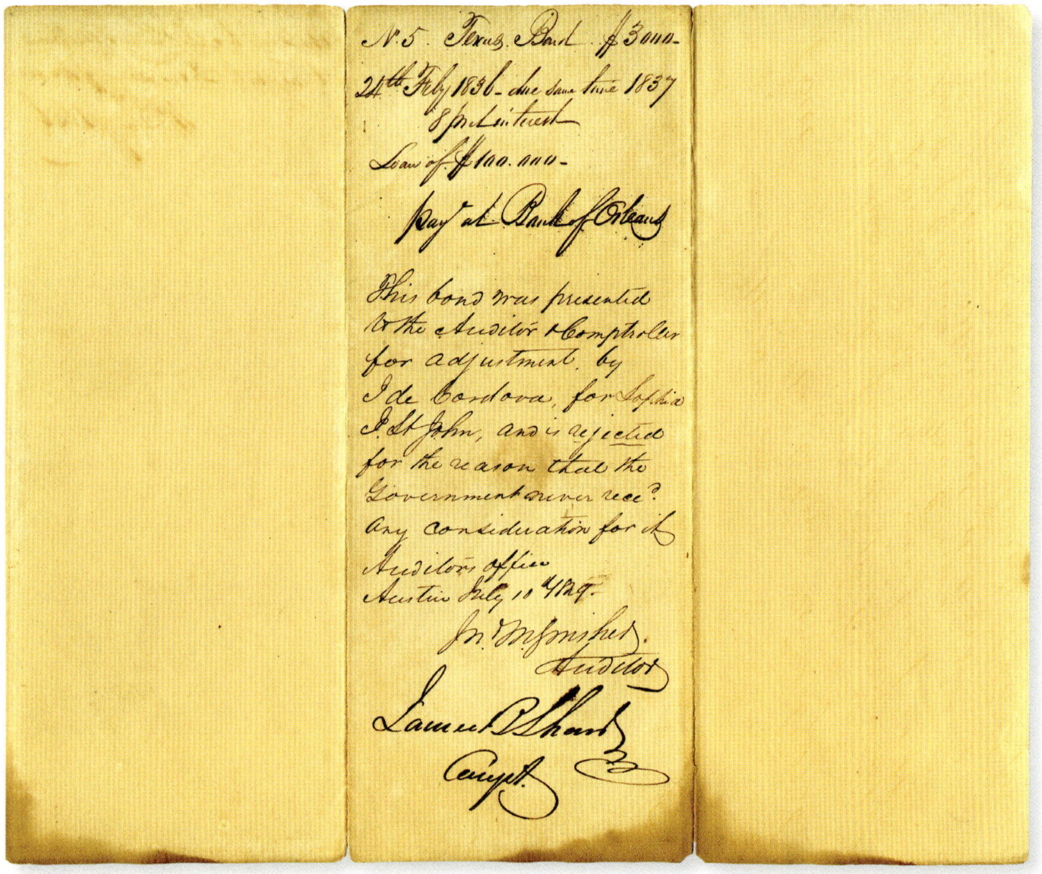

Fig 15.14, The reverse of the No. 5. Texas Bond $3,000, February 24, 1836, due same time 1837, 8 Percent Interest.

John N. Rowe III Collection of Texas Currency, DeGolyer Library, Southern Methodist University, Dallas, Texas, Cr. 36P.

Following the annexation of Texas, Mr. T.J. Teague and Mr. J. de Cordova of Galveston presented the handwritten bond in Figure 15.14 for a claim against the government by William's sister, Mrs. Sophia St. John (these bonds were discussed in Chapter 4). Her claim was denied by the committee as the claim was rejected by the auditor's office on July 10, 1849.[44]

THE PENDING $10 MILLION PAYMENT

It became increasingly apparent that the U.S. Government did not want to be held liable for the debt of the late Republic of Texas. As part of the "Boundary Bill," the federal government agreed to advance only $5,000,000 of the 5 percent stock to Texas for the initial settlement with the creditors of Texas. The second $5,000,000 payment of stock would not be paid to the State of Texas until the release of claims were filed at the Treasury of the United States. The U.S. Treasury reasoned that this procedure would absolve the federal government from any future claims by the creditors of Texas holding bonds and certificates "for which duties and imports were specifically pledged." The U.S. Treasury feared legal repercussions from Texas' creditors. By transferring $10,000,000 to the State of Texas, and by insisting that releases be filed by the creditors, the United States sought to settle the matter and to absolve itself of any future liability from the late Republic.

THE GOLDEN SHOWER

As the creditors eagerly presented their claims in anticipation of their shower of gold from Washington, the fourth legislature of the State of Texas continued to debate the proposed legislation for the most equitable way to repay the debt. Political greed was rampant among the Austin legislators, and the true colors of the elected representatives soon emerged. Hiding behind the "Report of the Auditor and Comptroller" (prepared only to show that Texas did not have the means to repay its debt in total), the legislature twisted its findings to their liking, and rained their interpretation down with devastating authority on the creditors of Texas. The creditors had eagerly anticipated a long-awaited shower of gold from Washington, D.C., via the land sale. They got their golden shower alright, but it would only be a sprinkle compared with the much saltier variety which emanated from the lawmakers in Austin.

In late November 1851, despite the pending payment of $10,000,000 from the United States, the Texas Congress decided to reduce the payoff amount owed to the creditors to less than half of what the Republic of Texas had promised to pay. Rather than using the proceeds from the land sale to make the creditors whole, the Texas Congress decided to take a more underhanded approach. The old report which had begun in 1848 and adopted the scaling system was resurrected and brought under debate. A new piece of legislation was introduced, entitled "An act confirming the action of the auditor and comptroller, under the provisions of an act of the Legislature to provide for the ascertaining the debt of the late Republic of Texas, approved March 20, 1848, and the act supplementary thereto, approved February 8, 1850."[45] The legislature had manipulated the contents of the report to cheat the legitimate creditors of the late Republic and divert the excess proceeds to the State of Texas.

The lawmakers ignored the circumstances under which the original report had been prepared. They equally ignored the disposition of the land proceeds as determined at the time of annexation.[46] Like many legislative bodies, they viewed the people's money as their own. The proposed legislation soon passed both houses.[47] In short, despite having enough money from the proceeds of the land sale to the United States to pay the debt in its entirety, the Representatives of the State of Texas decided to only pay the reduced amounts as outlined in the auditor and comptroller's report, $4,807,764 rather than the face value of $9,647,253.

When the bill was presented to Texas Gov. Peter H. Bell on January 23, 1852, he was furious with its presumptions and refused to sign the act. Instead, he returned it to the Texas Congress for revisions on January 29, with a strong message regarding what he perceived as the swindling of the creditors of Texas by the state. Aiming at a reconciliation of the matter, Governor Bell closed his remarks with the following statement:

> *It is my anxious wish to see the State of Texas, at this time attracting universal attention, assume a position of reference to her debt which will not only command the admiration of her Sister states and of foreign powers, but save her also from any just charge of repudiation. So far as it lies in my power, I desire every creditor of Texas to have what in justice and equity is due him. Such, too, I believe is the sentiment of the people at large, and of the Legislature.*[48]

Despite Governor Bell's wishes, the bill adopting the recommendations to pay off the creditors under the scaling system as outlined by Shaw and Swisher was passed in opposition to his veto by the Senate vote of twenty-nine to five and the House vote of forty-seven to twelve. Consequently, the creditors and the holders of the paper money were defrauded by the state. While there is little question that the legislature had the authority to pass such a law, it violated the law of contractual promises. This legislation amounted to a massive theft of money due the legitimate creditors of the Republic by the State of Texas. While written in paper, this theft by the stroke of a pen was no less than robbery than if Congress itself has stuck a gun in the back of each holder of the old Texas paper money. For ten long years, the people of Texas had endured delayed payments, economic hardship, and broken promises from the Republic of Texas. In the back of every creditor's mind were the untold millions of acres of land which, if everything else failed, might still be available for Texas to make good on its promises. Now that the excess land had been sold, and the State of Texas decided to keep the remaining $4,839,488 which should have been paid to the creditors. Their dreams of receiving some comparable payment for their investments were gone. It was a sorry reflection of the words "Public Faith Pledged," the phrase that graced the obligations of the Republic of Texas for a decade.

A DERELICTION OF LEGISLATIVE ENACTMENT

Since the U.S. Congress clearly stipulated that the second payment of $5,000,000 would not be forthcoming until all of the remaining creditors filed the appropriate release of claims to the U.S., a bill was brought before the legislature to compel the creditors to sign releases to the United States. Although this measure was rejected as being too bold, the resulting legislation that derived from this debate was almost as onerous and conniving as the act which had passed over Governor Bell's veto only a few days before. Rather than providing a means for immediate payment of the $4,807,764 as estimated under the "scaled" or "reduced" rates, a provision of the new law effectively divided the outstanding audited debt into two additional classes—debts payable and debts suspended. The law passed on January 31, 1852, and was entitled "An act for the Liquidation and payment of the Debt of the Late Republic of Texas."

The first class of debt payable was owed primarily to those persons who still lived in Texas and was considered to be the non-revenue debt.[49] The second class of debt was primarily owed to creditors outside of Texas, and those debts for which the customs revenues had been specifically pledged. Texas officials restricted the definition of revenue debt to those securities specifically stating that they would be paid by import duties.[50] Thomas Corwin, the U.S. Treasury Secretary, thought otherwise, stating that the Republic of Texas had pledged these revenues for the redemption of all loans negotiated by the Republic by an Act of Congress on January 14, 1840. Corwin's ruling was affirmed by President Millard Fillmore on September 13, 1851. Although Texas appropriated $2,000,000 of the U.S. 5 percent bonds for the liquidation of the debt for this first class of creditors, the legislation passed on January 31 suspended the payments for the second class of creditors until the additional $5 million in bonds were received from the U.S. (See table 15.1)

Fig 15.15, Gov. Peter H. Bell.
Texas State Library & Archives Commission, Austin, Texas.

Fig 15.16, Millard Fillmore, U.S. President, 1850-1853.
Engraving by Henry B. Hall, Jr.
President Millard Fillmore signed the Boundary Bill into law on September 7, 1850. It was under his administration that the first payments were made to the creditors of the late Republic of Texas in February 1852.

Table 15.1 The various items of debt for which the payments were suspended under the Act of January 31, 1852.[51] Note the heavy use of the "Scaling rate" in the third column (accumulated interest is not included in the table).

	ORIGINAL AMOUNT.	SCALING RATE.	SCALED AMOUNT.
Ten per cent. consolidated fund, created by act of 7th June, 1837	*$632,526.80*	*70 cents*	*$442,768.76*
Ten per cent. consolidated fund, created by act of 7th June, 1837, issued under an act for the relief of Swartwout and others	*7,970.43*	*100 cents*	*7,970.43*
Eight per cent. treasury bonds, created by act of 5th February, 1840	*766,800.00*	*20 cents*	*153,360.00*
Ten per cent. treasury notes issued under act of 9th June, first issue	*41,630.00*	*100 cents*	*41,630.00*
Ten per cent. treasury notes issued under act of 9th June, second issue	*331, 371.00*	*50 cents*	*165,685.50*
Treasury notes, without interest, issued under act of 19th Jan. 1839, third issue	*1,828,192.00*	*25 cents*	*457,048.00*
Ten per cent. bonds issued by commissioners to negotiate a loan for $5,000,000, viz.:-			
For loan obtained from Bank of United States	*457,380.00*		*400,000.00*
For purchase of steamer "Zavala"	*195,907.00*	*50 cents*	*90,014.84*
For purchase of naval vessels under contract with F. Dawson, now owned by James Schott and E. D. Whitney	*280,000.00*	*50 cents*	*140,000.00*
Total of debt suspended	*$4,541,777.23*		*$1,898,477.53*

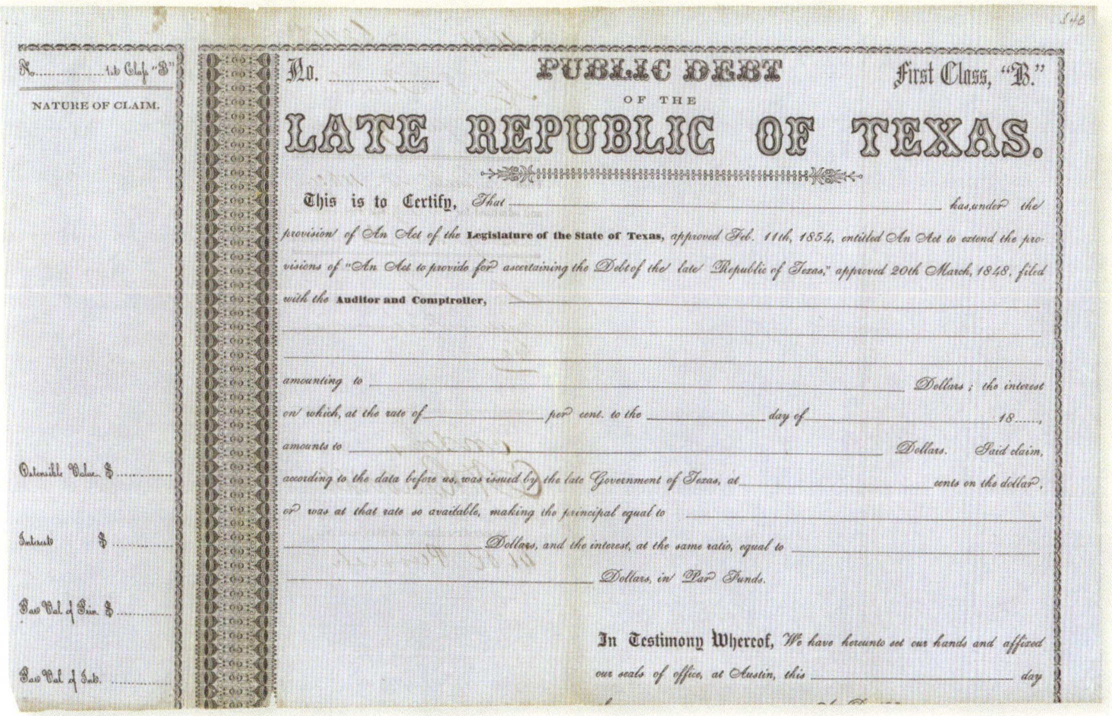

No. .... Aud. Cert. "B"

NATURE OF CLAIM.

Ostensible Value $ ....

Interest $ ....

Par Val. of Prin. $ ....

Par Val. of Int. $ ....

No. .... PUBLIC DEBT OF THE LATE REPUBLIC OF TEXAS. First Class, "B."

This is to Certify, That ________ has, under the provision of An Act of the Legislature of the State of Texas, approved Feb. 11th, 1854, entitled An Act to extend the provisions of "An Act to provide for ascertaining the Debt of the late Republic of Texas," approved 20th March, 1848, filed with the Auditor and Comptroller, ________ amounting to ________ Dollars; the interest on which, at the rate of ________ per cent. to the ________ day of ________ 18____, amounts to ________ Dollars. Said claim, according to the data before us, was issued by the late Government of Texas, at ________ cents on the dollar, or was at that rate so available, making the principal equal to ________ Dollars, and the interest, at the same ratio, equal to ________ Dollars, in Par Funds.

In Testimony Whereof, We have hereunto set our hands and affixed our seals of office, at Austin, this ________ day

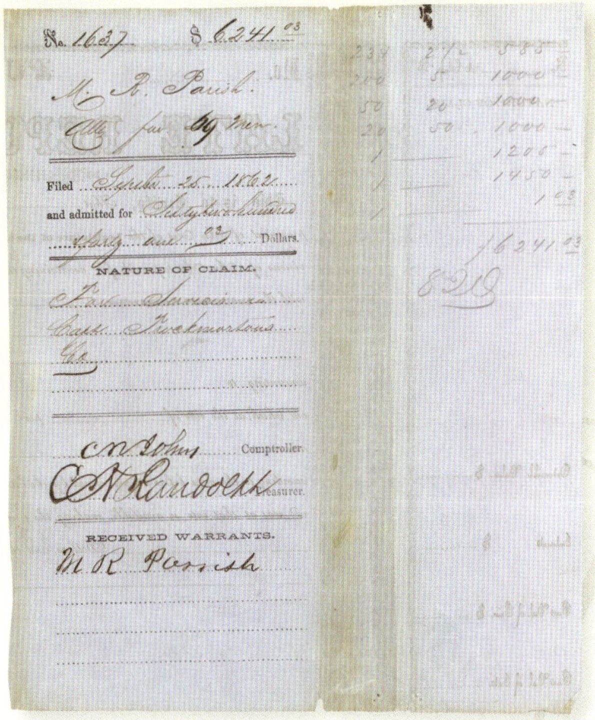

No. 1637 $6241.03

Filed .... and admitted for .... Dollars.

NATURE OF CLAIM.

.... Comptroller.

.... Treasurer.

RECEIVED WARRANTS.

Fig 15.17, Public Debt of the Republic of Texas, First Class, "B," Act of February 11, 1854 (Auditor's Stub attached at left).

Private Collection, Cr. 54D.

Fig 15.18, Texas, 1862 Civil War Claim (Reverse of First Class, "B" Certificate).

Private Collection.

The blank certificate in Figure 15.17 represents a claim under the First Class ("B") of claimants of Late Republic of Texas is indicative of the reluctance of the claimants to accept the terms and conditions dictated to them for settlement. The delays in the payments of this class of certificates is clearly seen, as they were not printed until 1854, indicated by the reference on the second line of the text to "the provision of An Act of the Legislature of the State of Texas, approved Feb.11th, 1854, entitled An Act to extend the provisions for . . . "

On the left of the rarely seen stub is the location of the number and nature of the claim, along with the ostensible (or stated) value of the claim and the interest thereon. Below this, and also noted on the right of the certificate, is a line for the par (or reduced) value of the claim and the corresponding reduction of the interest. This certificate, and perhaps hundreds of others, was defaced along the lower edge with a portion having been cut and removed.[52]

Hundreds of these certificates were possibly defaced and the reverses used as blank paper. The example in Figure 15.18 was later overprinted on the reverse and used for the filing of claims for military pay of Texans who fought for the Confederacy during the Civil War. The claim for $6,241.03 was filed September 25, 1862, on behalf of sixty-nine men in the services of Capt. James Throckmorton's Company of mounted riflemen in Collin County in 1862.

Although the reduced claims under the "plan of settlement" for the public debt only amounted to $4,807,764, Texas had received $5,000,000 in 5 percent U.S. bonds with which it could retire the scaled amounts in full. Rather than retiring the debt on its own terms, the state of Texas set aside $2,000,000 of the bonds to pay some of the creditors, but refused to pay the additional $2,807,764 to the remaining claimants. Instead, these creditors were coerced to file their releases of claim with the United States before the additional money would be released. The intent was to put political pressure on the U.S. to transfer the remainder of the indemnity bonds to the state of Texas. It was a strategy that would later explode in the faces of the lawmakers like the experimental cannon which killed U.S. Secretary of State Upshur. Having now suspended payments to the remaining creditors, the remaining $3,000,000 of bonds were considered by the state to be a revenue windfall. Various internal uses for the money were debated in the Congress, none of which involved paying the debt of the late Republic of Texas for which it was intended.[53] The representatives decided that $2,000,000 should be given to the general school fund, $100,000 to the university fund, and the remainder used to meet the current expenses of the state. In an effort to bolster their chances for re-election, the lawmakers decided that the taxes collected between 1852 and 1858 would be relinquished to the respective counties.

As the legislative session ended, the Texas Congress dispatched James B. Shaw to Washington, D.C., to receive the first $5,000,000 payment in stock and the $250,000 in gold (the accrued interest). When Shaw returned to Austin, the $250,000 in gold was used to pay the members of the Texas Congress their salaries for their efforts in passing these creative pieces of legislation.[54] As the members of Congress headed to their homes, their pockets jingling with their salaries, the creditors remained unsure as to when, and even if, they would receive their long-overdue payments. The State of Texas now possessed the money to initiate the payments, but only a portion of the funds were set to be released.

THE SCALED PAYOFFS BEGIN

Although the liabilities of the Republic of Texas would cease to bear interest on July 1, 1850, the first payments to the creditors under the scaled-down rates did not begin until February 1852, nineteen months later. The first creditors to receive payment were the holders of audited paper, miscellaneous liabilities, the amounts filed as Second Class and Third Class debts. There were also various amounts audited by special acts of the legislature which included the unpaid claims for military pay. These payments were largely considered to be to claimants still living in Texas and commenced in February 1852 with $997,684 distributed before the end of 1852. The face value of the debts totaled $1,678,242, but the scaled rate amounted to only $1,058,778, effectually giving the state a confiscated amount of $619,464. (See table 15.2)

Table 15.2[55] The debt which was made payable immediately after the passage of the act embraced the following items. Note the "scaling rate" in the third column (accumulated interest is not included in the table):

	ORIGINAL AMOUNT.	SCALING RATE.	SCALED AMOUNT.
Ten per cent. funded debt created by act of Feb. 5, 1840	*$754,000.00*	*30 cents*	*$226,200.00*
Eight per cent. funded debt created by act of February 5, 1840	*24,280.00*	*30 cents*	*7,284.00*
Audited paper issued under various enactments	*74,441.26*	*Various*	*69,451.12*
Miscellaneous liabilities	*26,129.87*	*100 cents*	*26,129.87*
Amount filed and receipted for as second class debts	*748,899.89*	*Various*	*679,222.50*
Ditto, third class, since recognized as second class	*16,467.95*	*100 cents*	*16,467.95*
Amount audited by special acts	*34,023.55*	*100 cents*	*34,023.55*
	$1,678,242.52		*$1,058,778.99*

The bulk of this confiscation was borne by those who exchanged their promissory notes for stock during the era of the refunding efforts by W.J. Bryan, James Love, and other officials in 1840. Although Texas argued that these securities were issued at a deep discount, those individuals who exchanged their notes for them could have used those notes for the payment of taxes at face value. As shown in table 15.2, this stock was only redeemed at 30 cents on the dollar. When the supply of gold and silver ran dry with which to pay these, Texas sold $800,000 of the U.S. indemnity stock at premiums as high as 5 percent over their face value and pocketed the difference. As the state of Texas shifted the burden of filing the releases with the U.S. Treasury to the remaining creditors as a condition of payment, a group of creditors in the city of New Orleans began to organize, taking their case directly to the United States Congress.

THE NEW ORLEANS PETITION

A petition by the citizens of New Orleans as creditors of the former Republic of Texas was presented to the Thirty-second Congress of the United States in 1852. In many ways, the petition resembled a modern-day class-action lawsuit. It outlined the grievances of the creditors who, "having been for many years holders of the bonds, and other evidences of debt, of the said late Republic" had not yet been paid one dollar of their funds.[56] The New Orleans petition stipulated that they, like the other creditors of Texas, had waited patiently for as long as sixteen years to be paid the money owed to them. Following the annexation of Texas, the identity of the sovereign government which had pledged its public faith, customs and import duties, and all available resources at its disposal had been obliterated.

In the six years following the annexation of Texas by the United States, the creditors had patiently followed the process of the disposal of excess public lands specifically pledged for the repayment of the public debt under the terms of the Resolution of Annexation. The petition further cited that they had been victims of "a dereliction of legislative enactment" whereby the $10,000,000 payment from the United States was being diverted from its intended purpose and the availability of these funds was lost to the creditors.[57] The petition railed against the ambiguity of the "scaling system," a method of estimation adopted when Texas was nearly bankrupt and had no means to pay its debt, yet had been adopted into law even though the means for complete repayment were now available.[58] The petition rejected the scaling system outright and pointed out that although Texas now had the funds to pay the reduced or scaled amounts according to their own terms, they declined to do so with a large portion of the debt until the remaining creditors bowed to the state's terms and filed the appropriate release of claims.

In summary, the petitioners in New Orleans and elsewhere refused to file the release of claims as dictated by the State of Texas and the United States.[59] Instead, they began to press their case to the U.S. Senate and House of Representatives.[60] By refusing to pay even the scaled amount of the so-called revenue debts, the State of Texas opened up a financial can of worms. Although the ships of the Texas Navy had long ago been sunk, sold, or forgotten, the shipbuilders and financiers who advanced those wooden vessels to the late Republic on credit also joined the lobbying efforts of the New Orleans petitioners in 1852 in an effort to recover their money. By this time, the Auditorial Board of Texas released an updated report estimating the whole of the debt to be $12,436,991, which included the interest up to July 1, 1850. The updated amount had subsequently been reduced to the sum of $6,827,278 under the scaling system. Texas had picked a fight with the very group of people that had staunchly stood by its side in good times and bad, and now Uncle Sam was being forced to step into the ring and act as a referee.

PASSING THE BUCK TO UNCLE SAM

The creditors of Texas had long contended that by gaining the customs revenue and import duties of the Republic prior to annexation, the United States had assumed responsibility for the payment of the debt for which those revenues were pledged. Although the Resolution of Annexation specifically disclaimed any U.S. responsibility for the debt, the creditors of Texas further contended that the responsibility for the debt was virtually admitted to by the provisions in the Boundary Act.[61]

Facing a desperate group of creditors on one hand, and an irresponsible, runaway state legislature on the other, the United States had no choice but to intervene and settle the matter. The creditors continued to lobby the U.S. Congress for repayment. Many of these creditors were influential northern men, including the

Drexel's of Pennsylvania, the Millbank's of New York, and noteworthy Philadelphians Thomas A. Biddle and Charles Macalester, a close friend of future President James Buchanan.[62] Counted among the Texas bondholders was Ohio Sen. Bejamin Tappan, who cast a decisive vote in support of the annexation of slave-holding Texas. Tappan's vote came as a surprise to his northern colleagues, which included his law partner, Edwin M. Stanton and his brothers Lewis and Arthur Tappan, both militant abolitionists. Other politicians with a significant financial stake in the matter were John Slidell of Louisiana and Sen. James A. Bayard of Wilmington, Delaware.[63] Despite the numerous creditors and influential persons within their ranks, Congress was hopelessly deadlocked.

The first thaw in the ice occurred during the hot summer months of 1852. On August 26, the U.S. Senate proposed an amendment to a foreign relations bill to permit the issue of bonds to Texas as soon as the respective claims releases were filed. The amendment failed, in part because it was thought the creditors would not be satisfied with the scaled-down amount of the claims and would continue to seek relief from the U.S. Congress.[64] Another impasse was broken when a bill was introduced in the same month to substitute $8,555,000 in 5 percent bonds in lieu of the $5,000,000 original bonds. These bonds were to be divided equally among the holders of the revenue debt. These proposed amendments died in committee and the Thirty-second Congress adjourned without taking any action on the matter. It was becoming increasingly evident that the burden of payment for the public debt of Texas had now fallen on the United States.

The question on the public debt of Texas was reopened on December 12, 1853, in the First Session of the Thirty-third Congress by Sen. Thompson of Kentucky.[65] Thompson proposed the distribution of $8,333,000 in 3 percent bonds to settle the matter. But on June 15, 1854, after lengthy debate in the Senate Finance Committee, the proposed payment was reduced to $6,500,000 in cash. This amount was also deemed unacceptable, and the debates continued in various committees in the House and Senate. Another bill passed the Senate on July 21, 1854, recognizing that the interest on the debt should be regulated by the existing laws of Texas. This stipulation, known as the Bright amendment, was a major breakthrough for the U.S., as it relieved the United States from making interest payments accrued since July 1, 1850. Although this amendment was deemed favorable to settling the matter, no further action was taken by the House before the session ended.

As the Second Session of the Thirty-third Congress of the United States opened, the eagerly awaited resolution gathered steam. The end of the great debates on the debts of the former Republic of Texas was summarized in a speech by the Honorable G.W. Jones of Tennessee in the House of Representatives on February 6, 1855. Jones summarized the realities of the case in a language that even the most hardened of critics could understand:

> *By the terms of annexation resolutions of 1845, Texas entered into a solemn compact with this Government, that her invaluable public lands should be retained by her, and appropriated to the payment of her debts. By the boundary act of September, 1850, the United States purchased of Texas her claim- and it was a bare claim, the most worthless of all her public lands - for which the United States agreed to pay Texas $10,000,000. This was for only a part of the pledged public lands of Texas, but for which the United States agreed to pay an amount sufficient to pay the entire debt of Texas, or very nearly so, leaving her all the most fertile and desirable lands within her present boundaries relieved and unembarrassed. Not only so, but Texas being annexed and made one of the United States, thousands of our people were induced to go there who never would have identified their fortunes with the Republic of Texas. . We bought her worthless lands to free her from debt, and furnished her with many of the best of our people as purchasers of her better lands and permanent citizens.*[66]

As the debates in the U.S. House of Representatives drew to a close, the Texas Debt Bill passed by a vote of 163 to 43 on February 7, 1855.[67] The bill was sent to the U.S. Senate, where it went to conference, was debated, and all disagreements to the House amendments were withdrawn. The bill was passed in the Senate by a vote of 30 to 14. On February 28, 1855, "An Act to provide for the Payment of such Creditors of the late Republic of Texas..." was signed into law, and an additional $7,750,000 was appropriated by the United States of America to pay off the debt of the former Republic.[68] The paper trail had finally come to an end in the city of Washington, D.C., almost a full generation after the Republic of Texas declared independence from Mexico in an old wooden blacksmith shop at Washington-on-the Brazos.

REDEMPTION

Fig 15.19, Franklin Pierce, U.S. President, 1853-1857.
Courtesy of James L. Glass.

With the signing of the Texas Debt Bill into law by President Franklin Pierce on February 28, 1855, the creditors had good reason to rejoice. Although passed into law, a provision of the act dictated that it would not go into effect until approved by an act of the Legislature of Texas. After lengthy debates, the Texas Legislature adopted the controversial measure on February 1, 1856. The additional $7,750,000 allocated by the federal government was pro-rated among the holders of the various classes of the revenue debt. Under this settlement method, the scaling system was largely abolished. This pro-rata plan provided each creditor approximately 76 9/10 cents on the dollar with a proportionate amount of interest. The settlement was deemed acceptable by the majority of the creditors which now resided outside of Texas and were concentrated in Delaware, Kentucky, Pennsylvania, South Carolina and Louisiana.

Those creditors who hoped to redeem their star notes at par under the new law were sadly disappointed and penalized by the pro-rata distribution. Those who held the redbacks, engraved notes and various issues of stock in the Consolidated Fund, various bonds and loans which had been heavily scaled saw their fortunes improved considerably, although they were deprived of six years of interest payments on the various holdings. Certain holders of the non-revenue debt were later compensated by the state for the difference they received under the scaled amounts in 1852 and the new settlement amounts which made them whole in 1856. Some holders of the redback notes waited as long as sixteen years without interest to receive their principal.

Following the first wave of repayments in 1852, the bulk of the debt was not settled until 1856, by which time six years of interest had been lost. Congress again extended the time for presenting the revenue debt claims to January 1, 1861, as there remained an unclaimed balance on the books of $101,113. By 1881, $45,000 was paid out of this balance, and the unclaimed balance was turned over to the state. The series of payments continued for various claims against the late Republic during the 1880s and continued into the dawn of the twentieth century. The United States finally closed the matter of the public debt of the late Republic of Texas under the administration of President Theodore Roosevelt when the last payment of $15,000 was made in 1902.

Fig 15.20, President Theodore Roosevelt at the Alamo.
Postcard Collection, DRT Library at the Alamo, San Antonio, Texas.
Teddy Roosevelt used the Alamo as a backdrop for a massive political rally in 1904, only two years after the federal government retired the last of the debts it had acquired from the late Republic of Texas. The Alamo continues to stand as symbol of Texas liberty.

1 William M. Gouge, *The Fiscal History of Texas* (New York: Burt Franklin, 1852; rpt. 1969), 146.

2 Noah Smithwick, compiled by his daughter Nanna Smithwick Henderson, *The Evolution of a State or Recollections of Old Texas Days* (Austin: Gammel Book Company, 1900; rpt. 1993), 179.

3 Richard Bruce Winders, *Crisis in the Southwest: The United States, Mexico and the Struggle over Texas* (Scholarly Resources, Inc., 2002), 136-37.

4 Gouge, *The Fiscal History of Texas,* 131.

5 Ibid., 132.

6 "M.B. Lamar to J.P. Henderson, Austin, May 2, 1846," The Papers of Mirabeau Buonaparte Lamar, ed. Harriet Smither, Texas State Library & Archives, 4:133.

7 Ibid.

8 Gouge, *The Fiscal History of Texas,* 145-49.

9 Ibid., 148.

10 Ibid., 182.

11 Ibid., 163-65.

12 Holman Hamilton, "Texas Bonds and Northern Profits: A Study in Compromise, Investment, and Lobby Influence," *The Mississippi Valley Historical Review,* Vol. 43 (March 1957), 4:582.

13 Gouge, *The Fiscal History of Texas,* 166-78.

14 "The 1850 Boundary Act," Texas State Library & Archives Commission, Austin, Texas, found online at www.tsl.state.tx.us/treasures/earlystate/boundary.html

15 Hamilton, "Texas Bonds and Northern Profits," 581.

16 Ibid., 582-83.

17 Austin, *Texas State Gazette,* January 12, 1850.

18 Hamilton, "Texas Bonds and Northern Profits," 588.

19 Ibid. Reference to the Philadelphia *Public Ledger,* February 1, April 2, May 10, and June 14, 1850.

20 From an affidavit of military service by John H. Moore, LaGrange, August 26, 1851, marked "Approved" for service date from September 20, 1840, through November 9, 1840, from the Texas State Library & Archives Commission, as listed under Public Debt Claims.

21 From a military discharge certificate for Thomas W. Hunt, dated August 24, 1842, at Houston, from the Texas State Library & Archives Commission, as listed under Public Debt Claims.

22 From a power of attorney, State of Texas, County of Gonzalez, by T.W. Hunt, dated July 14, 1848, from the Texas State Library & Archives Commission, as listed under Public Debt Claims.

23 Hamilton, "Texas Bonds and Northern Profits," 581, Hamilton quotes Charles A. and Mary R. Beard on the possible effects of speculation on both the annexation of Texas and the Compromise of 1850.

24 Darrel Brown, "Compromise of 1850," non-published 2007.

25 Gouge, *The Fiscal History of Texas,* 179-80.

26 The reader may notice that the words "Taylor" and "Fillmore" have been carefully written on the face of the stock directly beneath the respective portraits. This writing is believed to be in the hand of John J. Ford, the previous owner of this extremely rare $1,000 certificate before it was acquired by Darrel Brown in 2004.

27 Darrel Brown, "Compromise of 1850," non-published 2007. Brown cites these $100 and $500 proof specimens as among only a handful of surviving specimens of the Texas Indemnity Bonds issued under the Compromise of 1850. He cites the $1,000 specimen bond with coupons attached as "Fully Rarity 8, and no doubt unique."

28 Gouge, *The Fiscal History of Texas,* 202.

29 Ibid.

30 "Report of the Auditor and Comptroller, to the Fourth Legislature, on the Public Debt of Texas," (Austin: Cushney & Hampton, State Gazette Office, 1851), 3-5.

31 Constitution of the State of Texas, 1845, Article I, Bill of Rights.

32 Gouge, *The Fiscal History of Texas,* 151.

33 Ibid., 201.

34 "A Report by James B. Shaw, Comptroller to the Hon. Volney E. Howard, Chairman of a Select Committee of the House of Representatives," Austin, March 28, 1846.

35 Edmund Thornton Miller, "A Financial History of Texas," *Bulletin of the University of Texas 1916: No. 37* (Austin: University of Texas, 1916), 81.

36 Gouge, *The Fiscal History of Texas,* Appendix, "Schedule E. Kinds of Funds Received."

37 "A Report by James B. Shaw."

38 "Report of the Auditor and Comptroller," 7.

39 "A Report by James B. Shaw."

40 "Report of the Auditor and Comptroller," 9.

41 Gouge, *The Fiscal History of Texas,* 198-99, from a letter by Messrs. Scott and Whitney, to the Governor of Texas, dated October 9, 1851.

42 Seymour V. Conner, ed., "E.D. Whitney & Co to Jones, Philadelphia, May 8, 1845," Texas Treasury Papers, 3:1,102-104.

43 "Petition of Citizens of New Orleans, Creditors of the Late Republic of Texas, to the Thirty-Second Congress," (New Orleans: Hinton & Bro. Print, 1852), 50.

44 Reverse of manuscript bond, No 5. $3,000, New Orleans, February 24, 1836, "This bond was presented to the Auditor & Comptroller for adjustment by I De Cordova, for Sophia St John, and is rejected for the reason that the Government never rec[eived] any consideration for it. Auditor's office, Austin, July 10th, 1849. J[oh]n Swisher, Auditor, James B. Shaw, Compt[roller]."

45 Gouge, *The Fiscal History of Texas,* 202.

46 Joint Resolution for Annexing Texas to the United States, Approved March 1, 1845, Article 2.

47 Gouge, *The Fiscal History of Texas,* 202-203. The bill was entitled "An act confirming the action of the auditor and comptroller, under the provisions of an act of the Legislature to provide for the ascertaining the debt of the late Republic of Texas, Approved March 20, 1848, and the act supplementary thereto, approved, February 8, 1850."

48 Gouge, *The Fiscal History of Texas,* 203.

49 Ibid., 204-206.

50 Miller, "A Financial History of Texas," 122.

51 Gouge, *The Fiscal History of Texas,* 206.

52 There is an identical example of this certificate (without the auditor's stub) which was used as the plate specimen on page 353 in Grover Criswell's book, *Confederate and Southern States Bonds,* Second Edition, page 353, which has an identical removal of the bottom portion of the certificate.

53 Miller, "A Financial History of Texas," 86-87.

54 Gouge, *The Fiscal History of Texas,* 207.

55 Ibid., 204.

56 "Petition of Citizens of New Orleans," 3-4.

57 Ibid., 18.

58 Ibid., 12.

59 Ibid.

60 Ibid., 19.

61 Gouge, *The Fiscal History of Texas,* 314.

62 Hamilton, "Texas Bonds and Northern Profits," 587-88.

63 Ibid., 590-91.

64 Miller, "A Financial History of Texas," 124.

65 Ibid., 124-25.

66 Appendix to the Congressional Globe, 33rd Congress, Second Session, House of Representatives, Texas Debt Bill, "Remarks of Hon. G.W. Jones of Tennessee, in the House of Representatives," February 6, 1855, 372-73.

67 Miller, "A Financial History of Texas," 125-26.

68 Appendix to the Congressional Globe, 33rd Congress, Second Session, House of Representatives, Laws of the United States, Public XLIX, "An Act to provide for the Payment of such Creditors of the late Republic of Texas as are comprehended in the act of Congress of September nine, eighteen hundred and fifty," February 28, 1855, 383.

CHAPTER SIXTEEN

EPILOGUE – UP IN SMOKE

This story should have had a happy ending. The paper trail of money which extended across the Republic of Texas for the decade of its existence culminated in being only a paper trail of broken promises. The State of Texas had adequate funds from the sale of public lands to the federal government to pay for virtually all of its outstanding debt, a requirement under the terms of annexation. Surprisingly, they declined to do so.

During the glory days of the Republic, money was raised by Texas in every conceivable way in order for the government to function. Texas pledged its public faith for the repayment of those obligations. Although this faith was repeatedly called into question, the almost unlimited amount of land that could someday be available for settlement of those debts offered the holders of Texas paper a glimmer of hope for their eventual repayment. The Texas economy was run entirely on faith and credit, for without one the other would not exist.

From the standpoint of numismatists, it is interesting to note that the money of the Republic of Texas is among the scarcest of collectable paper money. The exchequer bills are extremely rare because they were destroyed by the government upon their redemption to prevent reissue. Although there were hundreds of treasury warrants issued from San Felipe de Austin, Washington-on-the-Brazos and Velasco, these were recalled by the Government of Texas in the summer of 1837 and replaced with stock in the Consolidated Fund of Texas. The stock is among the easiest found in the collector markets except for the two largest denominations. With the plethora of star money, engraved notes, change notes, and redbacks which once flooded the country, one has to wonder what happened to all that money?

The answer lies, in part, to a fire which consumed the office of the Treasury at about two o'clock in the morning on September 9, 1845.[1] The office had been temporarily moved to the wooden home of Dr. Moses Johnson, the current treasurer. Dr. Johnson was later quoted in a local newspaper as saying, "that the whole Treasury Department is burnt, together with a cart load of redbacks."[2] Destroyed in the fire were the archives of the Treasurer's office from the commencement of the government to January 1, 1840. Although copies of the Treasury records were held elsewhere, it appears that a large amount of cancelled promissory notes, audited paper and treasury warrants were destroyed in the fire. A letter discovered by historian E.W. Winkler shed some light on the contents of the wooden building:

> *It appears that a large package of Promissory Notes that had been redeemed was in the Office [sic] at the time it was burned. These notes belonged to the Office of the Secretary of the Treasury, but had been removed to the Treasurer's Office by the request of the Secretary. We understand that these notes had been marked across the face with a pen and had been clipped in one or two places with scissors to denote that they had been cancelled. They were not deposited in an iron safe, but in a wooden box.*[3]

During the process of assessing the outstanding public debt, the Treasury Department worried that critical treasury records had also been destroyed by the fire. Treasury Secretary J.A. Greer elaborated on the contents of the building in the annual report for the year ending October 31, 1845:

> *For the satisfaction of the public, I will here mention that such is not the case. A large amount of promissory notes, and audited drafts were there consumed, but they had all been previously cancelled, they are, moreover, on register in other offices, among the other liabilities of that class issued—though in the sum registered, it would be difficult to identify the separate bills of the amount destroyed, since the detailed register of their cancelment [sic] was burnt with them. The other papers consumed, all of which belonged exclusively to the Treasury Bureau, have in other offices either duplicates or a detailed registry which will answer the same purpose.*[4]

According to Greer's description, many of the promissory notes and drafts were very similar to those shown as examples in this text.

Following the annexation of Texas, as the creditors and merchants relinquished their Republic of Texas promissory notes to the auditor and comptroller as part of the claims process, they were meticulously counted, cancelled, and stored in various government facilities. The largest amount was stored in the basement of the new limestone capitol building in Austin, which was completed in 1853.[5]

The State of Texas had long ago outgrown the original wooden capitol in Austin, and the government was relocated to its new quarters upon its completion. The new structure was a large, impressive limestone building with a wooden interior. Millions of dollars of the old Texas money lay quietly in storage here for another twenty-eight years. Newly elected Gov. Elisha M. Pease and the fifth state legislature were the first to occupy the building in 1853. On December 21, 1859, Sam Houston was sworn in as Governor of Texas and delivered his inaugural address to a large audience, some seated on the steps and others stood in the yard around the capitol. It was also in this impressive edifice that the 180-member Secession Convention met in the Hall of Representatives on January 28, 1861, and debated the inevitable conflict. Their acts, in conjunction with the state legislature, withdrew Texas from the Union to join the Confederate States of America. When Governor Houston refused to swear allegiance to the Confederacy, Lt. Governor Edward Clark took his place and addressed many of the problems brought about by secession. Francis R. Lubbock, the former comptroller of the Republic, took his seat as Governor in the building only eight months after Clark succeeded Houston.

On November 9, 1881, the historic capitol building caught fire, and the wooden interior was gutted in the resulting inferno. It was an accidental fire, caused when a worker extended the exhaust pipe from a wood burning stove into a partition wall, thinking that it vented to an external chimney flue. Instead, the hot pipe showered burning ashes into an adjacent book and paper storage room, sparking a fire which quickly spread to the rest of the building. According to Gov. O.M. Roberts, "Most of the record books and papers of the executive offices were removed from the house before the fire reached them."[6] Roberts remarked that the greatest loss was that of the State Library and the collection of geological specimens in the building. He made no mention of any efforts to rescue the enormous hoard of old paper money that had long ago been stored in the limestone building. Thus to ashes had passed the great saga of the money of the Texas Republic.[7] On this cold, rainy November morning, these long forgotten relics of the old Republic of Texas literally went up in smoke.

Fig 16.1, The Limestone Capitol Building, Austin, Texas

Texas State Library & Archives Commission

Some of the partially charred bills from the old capitol fire were given to individuals and schools by the state officials who supervised the salvage efforts following the fire. A small number of notes were placed in the Alamo, where a bill of any denomination could be purchased for five cents by visitors. One of those visitors, Dr. William E. Howard, bought several of the charred promissory notes as a child. He later donated his modest collection to the Daughters of the Republic of Texas Library at the Alamo shortly before his death in 1948. Several of Dr. Howard's collection pieces are featured as examples in this book.

Fig 16.2, The Old Limestone Capitol After the Fire.
Texas State Library & Archives Commission, Austin, Texas.

Fortunately for collectors and historians of today, there were several thousand pieces of the obsolete money stored in various county depositories. Many families, stuck with the worthless bills following the depreciation of the money in the mid 1840s, tucked them away and passed them down through the generations. It wasn't until the beginning of the twentieth century that these bills began to be seen in anything that approached a collectable condition. Another large hoard of the bills was stored in the archives of the state comptroller's office, and these were distributed through the state representatives to the high schools in Texas around the time of World War I.[8] Many state and county officials, including judges and at least one state treasurer, helped themselves to the old bills from the archives and storage rooms of their respective facilities and discretely sold them to collectors.[9]

Other officials were even more brazen in their attempts to profit from the nostalgic interest in the old Republic of Texas in the early part of the twentieth century. Rather than preserving their heritage, many of these relics of the late Republic were undoubtedly removed from the various archives and sold with the blessings of the state. In a letter on official "State Of Texas, Marion County" letterhead dated March 21, 1915, a county official wrote to B. Max Mehl, a well-known Ft. Worth coin dealer of the day, "I have the following cancelled Republic of Texas bills which I will sell to the highest bidder."[10] The seller lists 5,722 individual pieces plus 334 un-cancelled bills and 6 uncut sheets containing two $1, a $2, and $3. Also offered for sale in the letter were nine $500 bonds and five $500 stock certificates. Although it is not known if Max Mehl bought the pieces, it is believed that the letter originated from his files.

Today, the heritage of that long-forgotten paper trail across the Republic of Texas has been preserved by numismatists for future generations. As collectors of coins and paper money, numismatists often search for these rare and elusive items, not merely for the thrill of the hunt, but for the intellectual reward which comes from discovering new and exciting clues to the past which can often be discerned when a promissory note, warrant, or coin comes under close examination. Surprisingly, most of the obsolete paper money and securities of the Republic of Texas can often be found at coin and currency shows across the country as well as at public auctions. Not surprisingly, the State of Texas is still the home for most of these long-lost paper treasures which collectively represent the entire monetary history of the Republic of Texas.

If you have an interest in collecting rare coins and paper money, I invite you to explore the possibility of joining a collector organization to expand your knowledge and build your own collection as did most of the contributors for this book. The Texas Numismatic Association maintains a website at www.TNA.org with information on coin and paper money shows across Texas as well as links to other numismatic organizations nationwide. Coin and paper money collecting is an interesting, enjoyable and rewarding hobby. It can also be a worthwhile research endeavor and is especially useful for those avocational historians who wish to seek the truth by following a trail of money through the past.

---

1 E.W. Winkler, "Destruction of Historical Archives of Texas," vol. 15, *SHQ* (October 1911), 2:148-55.

2 *The Morning Star*, November 8, 1845.

3 Winkler, "Destruction of Historical Archives of Texas," 150.

4 Ibid., 151.

5 William E. Howard, *The Romance of Texas Money: The Story of Texas Money from Early Colonial Days to the Last Issue of the Money of the Republic* (Dallas, TX: 1946), 15.

6 O.M. Roberts, "The Capitals of Texas," vol. 2, *SHQ* (October 1898), 2:117-23.

7 Howard, *The Romance of Texas Money*, 15.

8 From a typed letter, signed by a J.T. Hamilton. The portion at the top bearing the customary date was torn off. The letter reads in part: "It [the currency] has been kept in the archives of the Comptroller's office for seventy years more or less and is now being distributed through the Representatives of the legislature to the High schools of the state; having been divided in equal denominations of five hundred, one hundred, fifty, twenty, ten, five, three, two and one dollar bills. It has the autographs of Lamar, Houston and others."

9 From a Temple, Texas, affidavit by Alex Diest, dated October 26, 1916. Diest references his letter files and an expense book which contains receipts for Texas currency and bonds. He states that he purchased these "Texas Currency bills lawfully from Don A. Chambers, Belton-Prof[essor] Miengan(?), Belton, Van Nichols, Belton, Hon[orable] Judge, Dyers, Temple, Mr. Terrell, State Treasurer, and a Prof[essor]. Blair, San Marcos State."

10 Letters from The State of Texas, Marion County and Jefferson County Commissioners Era Johnson (Precinct No. 1), F.R. Grubbs (Precinct No. 2), Bedford Bailey (Precinct No. 3), J.G. Morris (Precinct No. 4), to B. Max Mehl, Ft. Worth, Texas, dated March 21, 1915.

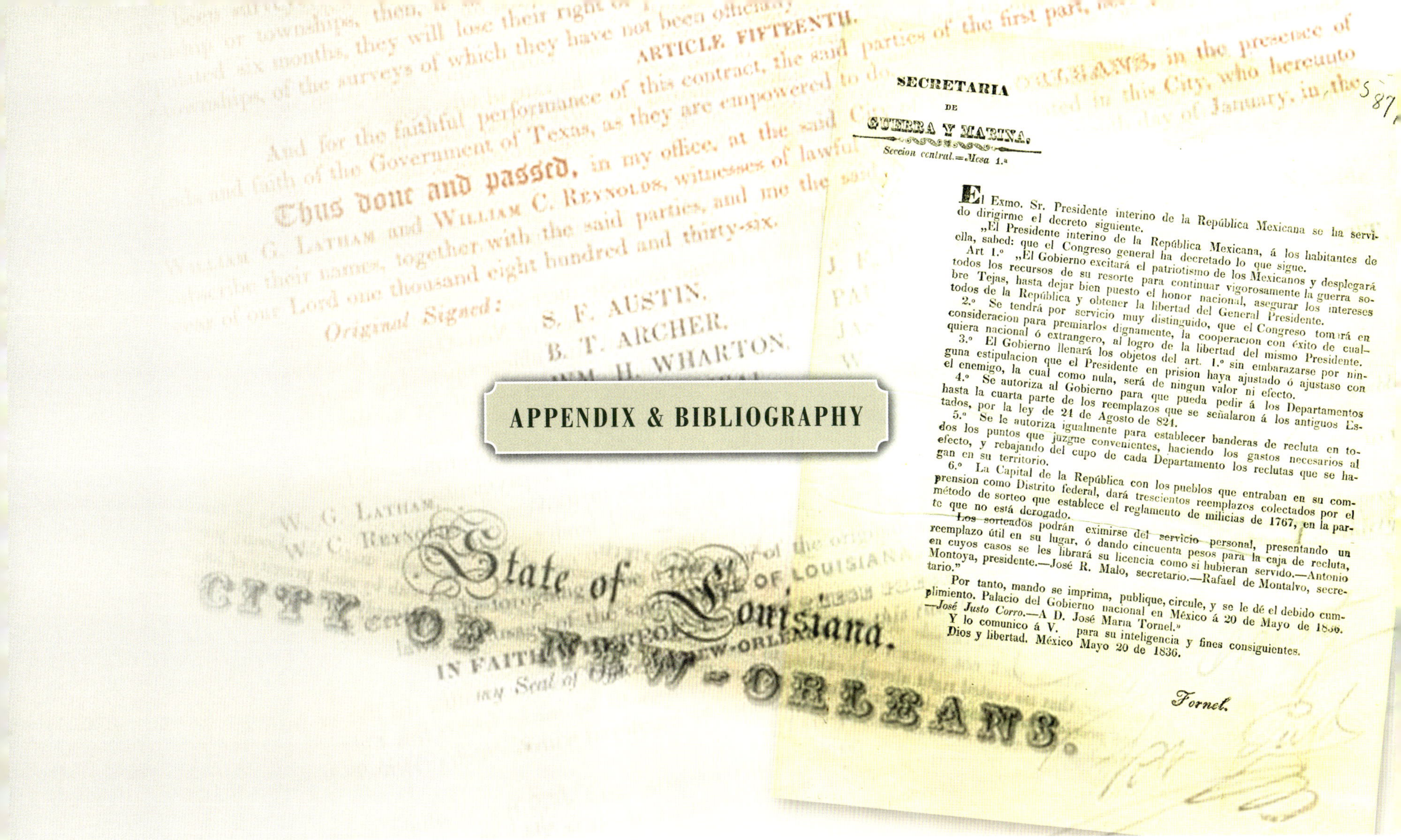

APPENDIX A:

1) Spanish Kings during the colonization of Texas

1474-1504	Ferdinand II & Isabella	
1504-1556	Charles I & Johanna,	CARLOS & IOANNA
1556-1598	Philip II,	PHILLIPPVS
1598-1621	Philip III,	PHILIPPVS
1621-1665	Philip IV,	PHILIPPVS
1665-1700	Charles II	CARLOS II
1700-1724	Philip V	PHILIPPVS V
1724	Louis I,	LVIS I
1724-1746	Philip V	PHILIPPVS V
1746-1759	Ferdinand VI	FERNANDVS VI
1759-1788	Charles III,	CAROLVS III
1788-1808	Charles IV,	CAROLVS IIII
1808-1833	Ferdinand VII	FERNANDVS VII

2) Mint marks on Mexican coins mentioned in this book.

C,CH,CL, CA	: Chihuahua
D, Do	: Durango
Ga	: Guadalajara
GC	: Guadalupe y Calvo
Go, G	: Guanajuato
Ho, H	: Hermosillo
M, Mo, oMo	: Mexico City
OA, O	: Oaxaca
SLP, PI, P, I/P	: San Luis Potosi
Z, Zs	: Zacatecas

APPENDIX B: LISTA QUE MANIFESTA EL PRESTAMO (ENGLISH TRANSLATION)

MANIFEST LIST OF THE LOAN AND VOLUNTARY DONATIONS that in currency and assets have been done by the towns of the State for the establishment of the Tobacco Factory of this Capital in accordance to the ordinance issued by this Government issued on March 20th (1825). And is published by disposition of the Honorable Congress on the 30th of June (1825).

SALTILLO	DONATIONS ON TERMS	CASH DONATIONS	0% Interest Loans
Mayor 1. Salvador Manuel Carrillo			0.500.0
Cash Pymt. Nepomuceno Valdes y Recio			0.100.0
C. Juan Antonio del Bosque			.0.100.0
C. Francisco de Camporedondo			0.100.0
C. Francisco Narro			0.100.0
C. Juan de Arredondo			0.100.0
C. Jose Maria de la Pena			0.050.0
C. Manuel Gonzalez			0.100.0
C. Luis de Cuellar loans one hundred pesos without interest in the month Of December of this year.			
C. Mayor 2nd., Jose Ygnacio de Arizpe			0.200.0
C. Jose Mariano Liendo		0.025.0	
C. Jose Antonio del Bosque y Vargas		0.050.0	
C. Macsimo de Leon		0.010.0	
C. Melchor de Cardenas		0.015.0	
C. Martin de Alcala		0.020.0	
Br.Juan Ynocente Perez		0.005.0	
Br.Jose Ygnacio Sanchez Navarro fifty pesos each year until Four are completed	0.200.0		
C. Vicente Valero twenty five pesos in June of the coming year And twenty five pesos in June of 1826	0.050.0		
C. Pedro Garcia in June of this running year	0.050.0		
Dr.Pedro Jose Valdes during the next month and one half	0.025.0		
C. Jose Maria Siller, in August next month	0.025.0		
		Sum pesos	1. 475.0
C. Dr. Pedro Jose Valdes paid the twenty five pesos that he Offered to give in one month			0.025.0

EXPENSES

Sum 1.500.0

For two and one half reales that were paid on the rent of five sheets of paper That were ruined and were returned cancelled0.000.2.6

0.000.5

For two and one half reales the value of five sheets of paper of seal 4, in which The obligations of the grantor citizens were extended...... 0.000.2.6

1.499.3

We subtract from the quantity above five pesos that proved to be defective 0.005.0

Sum of the collected 1.494.3

NOTE:

The C. Jose Antonio del Bosque y Vargas offers to drive his mules with eighty loads of tobacco, for a term of five years, distributing such under these terms: He offers to forty loads in this capital during the months of August and September and the other forty in the following January and February; That the corresponding shipping costs for the first trip, shall be paid the following year on the same month as his delivery the previous year, and so, progressively in all the years granting terms for each one.-Saltillo, June 13, of 1825.- Salvador Manuel Carrillo- Jose Guadalupe Solis Interim Secretary.-

Objects Donated

VILLA DE PARRAS		Brandy	Wine
C. Dionisio Mancha has offered fifty barrels of wine		050	Br.
C. Josefa Menchaca		.002	Br.
C. Mariano Garcia		.020	Br.
C. Ygnacio Chaves		.001	Br
C. Jose Hernandes		.003	Br.
C. Jose Maria Jove		.005	Br.
And in regards to the Hacienda he said: "that he can not give anything for it, since it belongs to Sr. Marquez de San Miguel de Aguayo and other creditors that own it, thus, he can not list it as his.			
C. Ygnacio Velaustre five barrels of regular raw wine		.005	Br.
C. Francisco Tolentino three barrels of wine		.003	Br.
C. Jose Morelos y Artia two pesos in reales		———	
C. Andres de la Viesca, for himself, and for the family of Senora Dona Josefa Montes, twelve barrels of Brandy that according to current prices are worth one hundred twenty pesos and are being donated in favor of the plant	012.		
Sra. C. Ana Fabila six barrels of Brandy	006.		
C. Vicente Campos	003.		
C. Melchor Bracho	000	......001.	Br.
C. Estevan Navarro	000	001	Br.
C. Ygnacio Arzave	001.		
C. Cosme de Mier, claims that because not having any more wine, except for a little bit from the house Of the deceased Estrada, donates ten barrels known to be of poor quality,		.010	Br.
C. Eufrasio Peres	005		Br.
C. Trinidad Delgado		.001	Br.
C. Antonio Abila		.002	Br.
C. Francisco Flandes		.002	Br.
C. Jose Cortinas	003		Br.
C. Anacleto Abila		.002	Br
Sums	030 Br	111.	Br.

As far as we can see, the wine barrels that were donated in the subscription are increasing, that one hundred eleven barrels and the Brandy at thirty barrels.-Sala Capitular de Parras . May 21. of 1825.- Jose Cortina President interim.- Jose Ygnacio Mixares Secretary.- Note.- To this list we shall add two hundred pesos that was offered by the Priest D. Silvestre Vicente Borja for the Tabacco Manufacturing Plant

And that he offered in form of a loan, in way of a Mortgage that was issued against the house of Marquez de San Miguel de Aguayo; whose administrator has offered to pay in the term of two months starting from June 13 200
Also, we add two pesos that according to this list are offered by the C. Jose Morelos y Artia 002

Sum 202

VALLEY OF THE CAPLLANIA

C. Jose Ygnacio de Alcocer has offered one thousand pesos in this manner:
That this amount be deducted from the income from the fruit sales of the Hacienda Santa Maria; and that one half of this amount be rendered the first of June and the rest as soon as the honor pledges that in previous months were made: according to the statement of the Ayuntamiento (City Hall), of the 10 of May 1.000

VILLA OF SANBUENAVENTURA

Itemization of the loan that has been collected in this Villa for the establishment of the Tabacco Factory
without any interest charged.

C.Jose Cayetano Ramos 100pesos
C.Pedro de la Garza 100pesos
C.Juan Nepomuceno Ramos 100pesos

Sum 300pesos

This notice is in accordance with the document from City Hall dated April 5, warning that the last of the grantors has offered the 100 pesos with which he pledges 200 and also more carved cigars that have been placed in safekeeping with the trustee of that Villa for further sale.

VILLA OF CUATRO CIENEGAS

C. Francisco de Cardenas, according to de City Hall document dated April 14, offered 100 pesos as a loan without interest 100pesos

GENERAL SUMMARY	Loans No-Interest	Donations In Cash	Offerings Brandy	Offerings Wine
Saltillo	1.450	475.0		
Parras	0.200	002.0	030 Br	111 Br
Capellania	1.000			
San Buenaventura	0.300			
Quatro Cienegas	0.100			
Sum Totals	3.050	477.0	030 Br	111 Br

Summary of the amounts that in paper of the Banco Nacional of Texas have been offered by the Citizens and for this objective they have met in this room of City Hall.

The Lieutenant Alexandro Trevino, offers 1200 pesos, in this manner: 500 pesos without interest and the balance to be paid to him, in case it is paid cash, the said amount in paper money of Texas .... 1.200 pesos
The City Hall of this city loans it's paper funds of the Bank of said Texas under the interest offered 1.554.2
C. Miguel Arciniega in the same manner 0.134.0
C Manuel Yturri-Castillo 0.100.0
C. Jose Antonio de la Garza offers the same terms as The Bank Of Texas and Imperial 0.400.0

Total 3.388.2

Capitular de Bejar Room, May 8, 1825 - Juan Martin de Beramendi.—

NOTES:

1. The Government could not admit this subscription because it constitutes paper money which cashing seemed to them to be difficult, although, thanks were given to the donors
2. The Citizens Vicente Balero, Pedro Garcia and Jose Maria Siller, have made the payments with which they subscribed. Saltillo 14th day of October, 1825.

Printing done by the Government in charge of C. Jose Maria Praxedis Sandobal

Translation into English by:

Teresa Ginsburg and Manuel Cavazos-Siller, Houston, Texas.

May 18, 2006

APPENDIX C:

An original $200,000 loan document used to establish the terms of the first Texian Loans to the Government of Texas, New Orleans, 1836. Also known as the Triplett Loan, because Robert Triplett was a subscriber to $100,000 or 50% of the loan amount. Signed at the conclusion of the second page by William Christy Not(ary) Pub(lic).

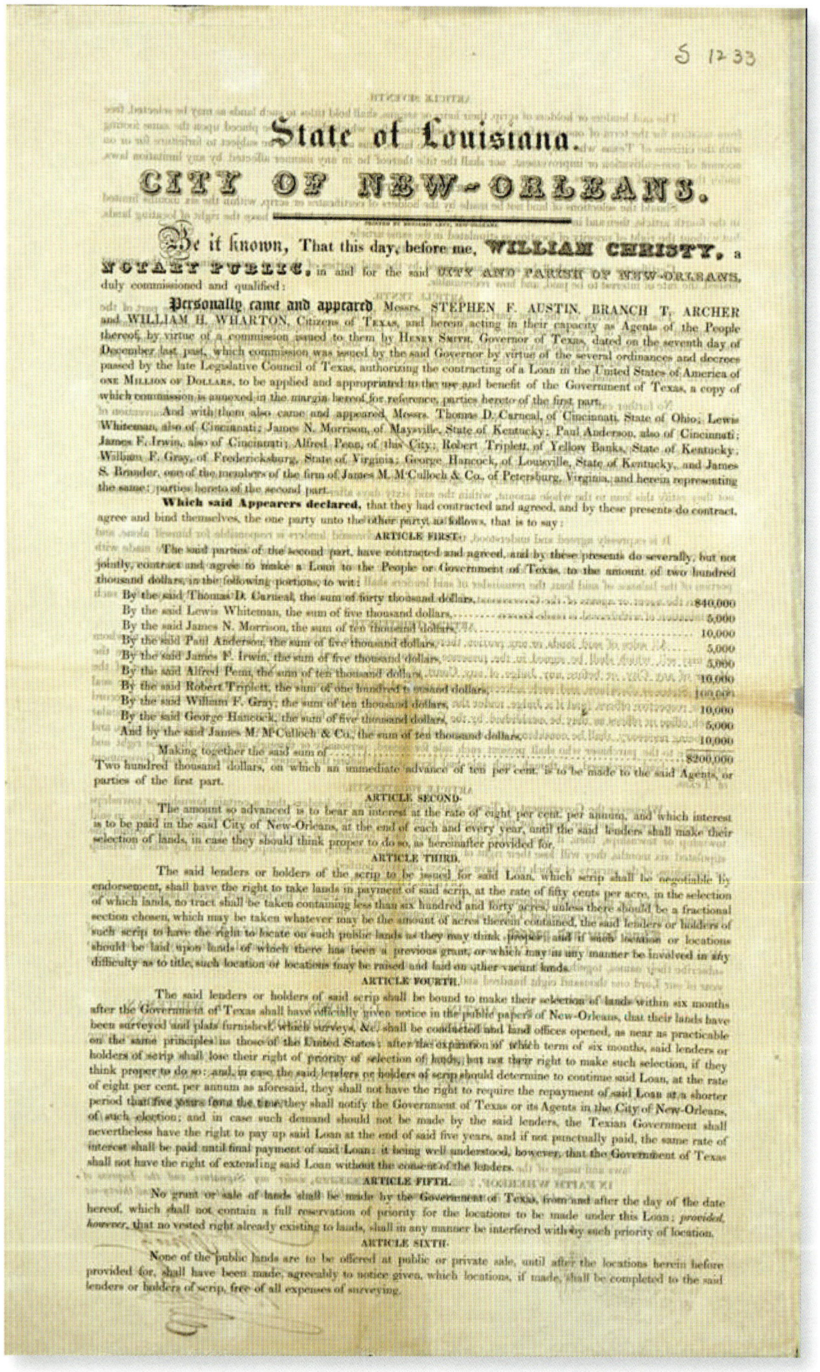

S 12-33

State of Louisiana.

CITY OF NEW-ORLEANS.

Be it known, That this day, before me, **WILLIAM CHRISTY,** a **NOTARY PUBLIC,** in and for the said CITY AND PARISH OF NEW-ORLEANS, duly commissioned and qualified:

Personally came and appeared Messrs. STEPHEN F. AUSTIN, BRANCH T. ARCHER and WILLIAM H. WHARTON, Citizens of Texas, and herein acting in their capacity as Agents of the People thereof, by virtue of a commission issued to them by Henry Smith, Governor of Texas, dated on the seventh day of December last past, which commission was issued by the said Governor by virtue of the several ordinances and decrees passed by the late Legislative Council of Texas, authorizing the contracting of a Loan in the United States of America of one Million of Dollars, to be applied and appropriated to the use and benefit of the Government of Texas, a copy of which commission is annexed in the margin hereof for reference, parties hereto of the first part.

And with them also came and appeared Messrs. Thomas D. Carneal, of Cincinnati, State of Ohio; Lewis Whiteman, also of Cincinnati; James N. Morrison, of Maysville, State of Kentucky; Paul Anderson, also of Cincinnati; James F. Irwin, also of Cincinnati; Alfred Penn, of this City; Robert Triplett, of Yellow Banks, State of Kentucky; William F. Gray, of Fredericksburg, State of Virginia; George Hancock, of Louisville, State of Kentucky, and James S. Brander, one of the members of the firm of James M. M'Culloch & Co. of Petersburg, Virginia, and herein representing the same; parties hereto of the second part.

Which said Appearers declared, that they had contracted and agreed, and by these presents do contract, agree and bind themselves, the one party unto the other party, as follows, that is to say:

ARTICLE FIRST.

The said parties of the second part, have contracted and agreed, and by these presents do severally, but not jointly, contract and agree to make a Loan to the People or Government of Texas, to the amount of two hundred thousand dollars, in the following portions, to wit:

By the said Thomas D. Carneal, the sum of forty thousand dollars	$40,000
By the said Lewis Whiteman, the sum of five thousand dollars	5,000
By the said James N. Morrison, the sum of ten thousand dollars	10,000
By the said Paul Anderson, the sum of five thousand dollars	5,000
By the said James F. Irwin, the sum of five thousand dollars	5,000
By the said Alfred Penn, the sum of ten thousand dollars	10,000
By the said Robert Triplett, the sum of one hundred thousand dollars	100,000
By the said William F. Gray, the sum of ten thousand dollars	10,000
By the said George Hancock, the sum of five thousand dollars	5,000
And by the said James M. M'Culloch & Co., the sum of ten thousand dollars	10,000
Making together the said sum of	$200,000

Two hundred thousand dollars, on which an immediate advance of ten per cent. is to be made to the said Agents, or parties of the first part.

ARTICLE SECOND.

The amount so advanced is to bear an interest at the rate of eight per cent. per annum, and which interest is to be paid in the said City of New-Orleans, at the end of each and every year, until the said lenders shall make their selection of lands, in case they should think proper to do so, as hereinafter provided for.

ARTICLE THIRD.

The said lenders or holders of the scrip to be issued for said Loan, which scrip shall be negotiable by endorsement, shall have the right to take lands in payment of said scrip, at the rate of fifty cents per acre, in the selection of which lands, no tract shall be taken containing less than six hundred and forty acres, unless there should be a fractional section chosen, which may be taken whatever may be the amount of acres therein contained, the said lenders or holders of such scrip to have the right to locate on such public lands as they may think proper; and if such location or locations should be laid upon lands of which there has been a previous grant, or which may in any manner be involved in any difficulty as to title, such location or locations may be raised and laid on other vacant lands.

ARTICLE FOURTH.

The said lenders or holders of said scrip shall be bound to make their selection of lands within six months after the Government of Texas shall have officially given notice in the public papers of New-Orleans, that their lands have been surveyed and plats furnished, which surveys, &c. shall be conducted and land offices opened, as near as practicable on the same principles as those of the United States; after the expiration of which term of six months, said lenders or holders of scrip shall lose their right of priority of selection of lands, but not their right to make such selection, if they think proper to do so: and, in case the said lenders or holders of scrip should determine to continue said Loan, at the rate of eight per cent. per annum as aforesaid, they shall not have the right to require the repayment of said Loan at a shorter period than five years from the time they shall notify the Government of Texas or its Agents in the City of New-Orleans, of such election; and in case such demand should not be made by the said lenders, the Texian Government shall nevertheless have the right to pay up said Loan at the end of said five years, and if not punctually paid, the same rate of interest shall be paid until final payment of said Loan: it being well understood, however, that the Government of Texas shall not have the right of extending said Loan without the consent of the lenders.

ARTICLE FIFTH.

No grant or sale of lands shall be made by the Government of Texas, from and after the day of the date hereof, which shall not contain a full reservation of priority for the locations to be made under this Loan: *provided, however*, that no vested right already existing to lands, shall in any manner be interfered with by such priority of location.

ARTICLE SIXTH.

None of the public lands are to be offered at public or private sale, until after the locations herein before provided for, shall have been made, agreeably to notice given, which locations, if made, shall be completed to the said lenders or holders of scrip, free of all expenses of surveying.

Fig A-1.2, $200,000 Texas Revolution Loan Document, Page 1

Private Collection

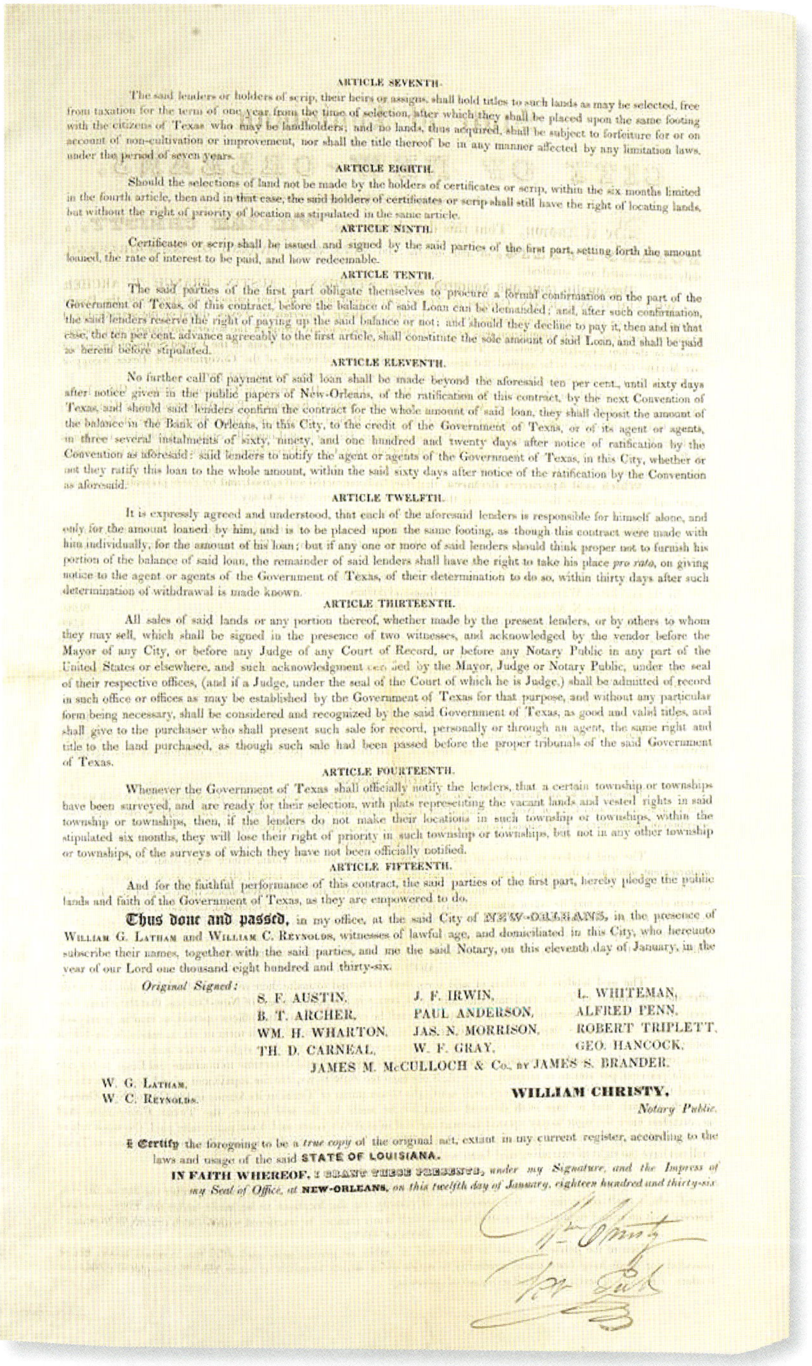

ARTICLE SEVENTH.

The said lenders or holders of scrip, their heirs or assigns, shall hold titles to such lands as may be selected, free from taxation for the term of one year from the time of selection, after which they shall be placed upon the same footing with the citizens of Texas who may be landholders; and no lands, thus acquired, shall be subject to forfeiture for or on account of non-cultivation or improvement, nor shall the title thereof be in any manner affected by any limitation laws, under the period of seven years.

ARTICLE EIGHTH.

Should the selections of land not be made by the holders of certificates or scrip, within the six months limited in the fourth article, then and in that case, the said holders of certificates or scrip shall still have the right of locating lands, but without the right of priority of location as stipulated in the same article.

ARTICLE NINTH.

Certificates or scrip shall be issued and signed by the said parties of the first part, setting forth the amount loaned, the rate of interest to be paid, and how redeemable.

ARTICLE TENTH.

The said parties of the first part obligate themselves to procure a formal confirmation on the part of the Government of Texas, of this contract, before the balance of said Loan can be demanded; and, after such confirmation, the said lenders reserve the right of paying up the said balance or not: and should they decline to pay it, then and in that case, the ten per cent. advance agreeably to the first article, shall constitute the sole amount of said Loan, and shall be paid as herein before stipulated.

ARTICLE ELEVENTH.

No further call of payment of said loan shall be made beyond the aforesaid ten per cent., until sixty days after notice given in the public papers of New-Orleans, of the ratification of this contract, by the next Convention of Texas, and should said lenders confirm the contract for the whole amount of said loan, they shall deposit the amount of the balance in the Bank of Orleans, in this City, to the credit of the Government of Texas, or of its agent or agents, in three several instalments of sixty, ninety, and one hundred and twenty days after notice of ratification by the Convention as aforesaid: said lenders to notify the agent or agents of the Government of Texas, in this City, whether or not they ratify this loan to the whole amount, within the said sixty days after notice of the ratification by the Convention as aforesaid.

ARTICLE TWELFTH.

It is expressly agreed and understood, that each of the aforesaid lenders is responsible for himself alone, and only for the amount loaned by him, and is to be placed upon the same footing, as though this contract were made with him individually, for the amount of his loan; but if any one or more of said lenders should think proper not to furnish his portion of the balance of said loan, the remainder of said lenders shall have the right to take his place *pro rata*, on giving notice to the agent or agents of the Government of Texas, of their determination to do so, within thirty days after such determination of withdrawal is made known.

ARTICLE THIRTEENTH.

All sales of said lands or any portion thereof, whether made by the present lenders, or by others to whom they may sell, which shall be signed in the presence of two witnesses, and acknowledged by the vendor before the Mayor of any City, or before any Judge of any Court of Record, or before any Notary Public in any part of the United States or elsewhere, and such acknowledgment certified by the Mayor, Judge or Notary Public, under the seal of their respective offices, (and if a Judge, under the seal of the Court of which he is Judge,) shall be admitted of record in such office or offices as may be established by the Government of Texas for that purpose, and without any particular form being necessary, shall be considered and recognized by the said Government of Texas, as good and valid titles, and shall give to the purchaser who shall present such sale for record, personally or through an agent, the same right and title to the land purchased, as though such sale had been passed before the proper tribunals of the said Government of Texas.

ARTICLE FOURTEENTH.

Whenever the Government of Texas shall officially notify the lenders, that a certain township or townships have been surveyed, and are ready for their selection, with plats representing the vacant lands and vested rights in said township or townships, then, if the lenders do not make their locations in such township or townships, within the stipulated six months, they will lose their right of priority in such township or townships, but not in any other township or townships, of the surveys of which they have not been officially notified.

ARTICLE FIFTEENTH.

And for the faithful performance of this contract, the said parties of the first part, hereby pledge the public lands and faith of the Government of Texas, as they are empowered to do.

Thus done and passed, in my office, at the said City of NEW-ORLEANS, in the presence of William G. Latham and William C. Reynolds, witnesses of lawful age, and domiciliated in this City, who hereunto subscribe their names, together with the said parties, and me the said Notary, on this eleventh day of January, in the year of our Lord one thousand eight hundred and thirty-six.

Original Signed:

S. F. AUSTIN,	J. F. IRWIN,	L. WHITEMAN,
B. T. ARCHER,	PAUL ANDERSON,	ALFRED PENN,
WM. H. WHARTON,	JAS. N. MORRISON,	ROBERT TRIPLETT,
TH. D. CARNEAL,	W. F. GRAY,	GEO. HANCOCK,

JAMES M. McCULLOCH & Co., by JAMES S. BRANDER.

W. G. Latham,
W. C. Reynolds.

WILLIAM CHRISTY,
Notary Public.

I Certify the foregoing to be a *true copy* of the original act, extant in my current register, according to the laws and usage of the said **STATE OF LOUISIANA.**

IN FAITH WHEREOF, I GRANT THESE PRESENTS, *under my Signature, and the Impress of my Seal of Office, at* **NEW-ORLEANS,** *on this twelfth day of January, eighteen hundred and thirty-six*

Fig A-1.2, $200,000 Texas Revolution Loan Document, Page 2

Private Collection

APPENDIX D:

An original $50,000 loan document used to establish the terms of the second Texian Loan to the Government of Texas, New Orleans, 1836. Also referred to as the Erwin Loan because one of the principal subscribers of $5000, James Erwin, negotiated the terms and was placed at the top of the list of subscribers. Signed at the conclusion of the second page by William Christy as Notary Public.

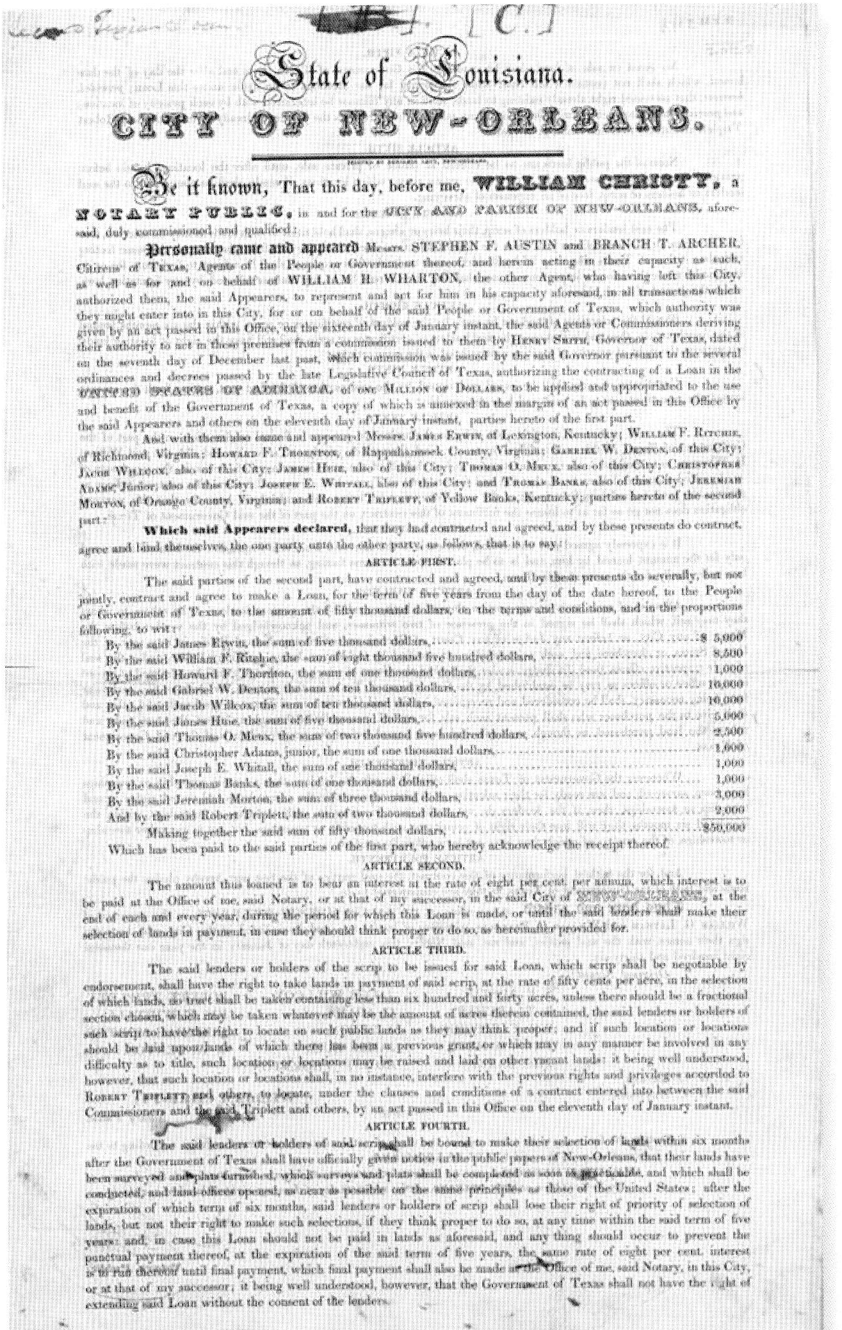

[C.]

State of Louisiana.

CITY OF NEW-ORLEANS.

Be it known, That this day, before me, WILLIAM CHRISTY, a NOTARY PUBLIC, in and for the CITY AND PARISH OF NEW-ORLEANS, aforesaid, duly commissioned and qualified:

Personally came and appeared Messrs. STEPHEN F. AUSTIN and BRANCH T. ARCHER, Citizens of Texas, Agents of the People or Government thereof, and herein acting in their capacity as such, as well as for and on behalf of WILLIAM H. WHARTON, the other Agent, who having left this City, authorized them, the said Appearers, to represent and act for him in his capacity aforesaid, in all transactions which they might enter into in this City, for or on behalf of the said People or Government of Texas, which authority was given by an act passed in this Office, on the sixteenth day of January instant, the said Agents or Commissioners deriving their authority to act in these premises from a commission issued to them by Henry Smith, Governor of Texas, dated on the seventh day of December last past, which commission was issued by the said Governor pursuant to the several ordinances and decrees passed by the late Legislative Council of Texas, authorizing the contracting of a Loan in the UNITED STATES OF AMERICA, of one Million of Dollars, to be applied and appropriated to the use and benefit of the Government of Texas, a copy of which is annexed in the margin of an act passed in this Office by the said Appearers and others on the eleventh day of January instant, parties hereto of the first part.

And with them also came and appeared Messrs. James Erwin, of Lexington, Kentucky; William F. Ritchie, of Richmond, Virginia; Howard F. Thornton, of Rappahannock County, Virginia; Gabriel W. Denton, of this City; Jacob Willcox, also of this City; James Huie, also of this City; Thomas O. Meux, also of this City; Christopher Adams, Junior, also of this City; Joseph E. Whitall, also of this City; and Thomas Banks, also of this City; Jeremiah Morton, of Orange County, Virginia; and Robert Triplett, of Yellow Banks, Kentucky; parties hereto of the second part:

Which said Appearers declared, that they had contracted and agreed, and by these presents do contract, agree and bind themselves, the one party unto the other party, as follows, that is to say:

ARTICLE FIRST.

The said parties of the second part, have contracted and agreed, and by these presents do severally, but not jointly, contract and agree to make a Loan, for the term of five years from the day of the date hereof, to the People or Government of Texas, to the amount of fifty thousand dollars, on the terms and conditions, and in the proportions following, to wit:

By the said James Erwin, the sum of five thousand dollars,	$ 5,000
By the said William F. Ritchie, the sum of eight thousand five hundred dollars,	8,500
By the said Howard F. Thornton, the sum of one thousand dollars,	1,000
By the said Gabriel W. Denton, the sum of ten thousand dollars,	10,000
By the said Jacob Willcox, the sum of ten thousand dollars,	10,000
By the said James Huie, the sum of five thousand dollars,	5,000
By the said Thomas O. Meux, the sum of two thousand five hundred dollars,	2,500
By the said Christopher Adams, junior, the sum of one thousand dollars,	1,000
By the said Joseph E. Whitall, the sum of one thousand dollars,	1,000
By the said Thomas Banks, the sum of one thousand dollars,	1,000
By the said Jeremiah Morton, the sum of three thousand dollars,	3,000
And by the said Robert Triplett, the sum of two thousand dollars,	2,000
Making together the said sum of fifty thousand dollars,	$50,000

Which has been paid to the said parties of the first part, who hereby acknowledge the receipt thereof.

ARTICLE SECOND.

The amount thus loaned is to bear an interest at the rate of eight per cent. per annum, which interest is to be paid at the Office of me, said Notary, or at that of my successor, in the said City of NEW-ORLEANS, at the end of each and every year, during the period for which this Loan is made, or until the said lenders shall make their selection of lands in payment, in case they should think proper to do so, as hereinafter provided for.

ARTICLE THIRD.

The said lenders or holders of the scrip to be issued for said Loan, which scrip shall be negotiable by endorsement, shall have the right to take lands in payment of said scrip, at the rate of fifty cents per acre, in the selection of which lands, no tract shall be taken containing less than six hundred and forty acres, unless there should be a fractional section chosen, which may be taken whatever may be the amount of acres therein contained, the said lenders or holders of such scrip to have the right to locate on such public lands as they may think proper; and if such location or locations should be laid upon lands of which there has been a previous grant, or which may in any manner be involved in any difficulty as to title, such location or locations may be raised and laid on other vacant lands: it being well understood, however, that such location or locations shall, in no instance, interfere with the previous rights and privileges accorded to Robert Triplett and others, to locate, under the clauses and conditions of a contract entered into between the said Commissioners and the said Triplett and others, by an act passed in this Office on the eleventh day of January instant.

ARTICLE FOURTH.

The said lenders or holders of said scrip shall be bound to make their selection of lands within six months after the Government of Texas shall have officially given notice in the public papers of New-Orleans, that their lands have been surveyed and plats furnished, which surveys and plats shall be completed as soon as practicable, and which shall be conducted, and land offices opened, as near as possible on the same principles as those of the United States; after the expiration of which term of six months, said lenders or holders of scrip shall lose their right of priority of selection of lands, but not their right to make such selections, if they think proper to do so, at any time within the said term of five years: and, in case this Loan should not be paid in lands as aforesaid, and any thing should occur to prevent the punctual payment thereof, at the expiration of the said term of five years, the same rate of eight per cent. interest is to run thereon until final payment, which final payment shall also be made at the Office of me, said Notary, in this City, or at that of my successor; it being well understood, however, that the Government of Texas shall not have the right of extending said Loan without the consent of the lenders.

Fig A.2.1, $50,000 Texas Revolution Loan Document, Page 1

Private Collection

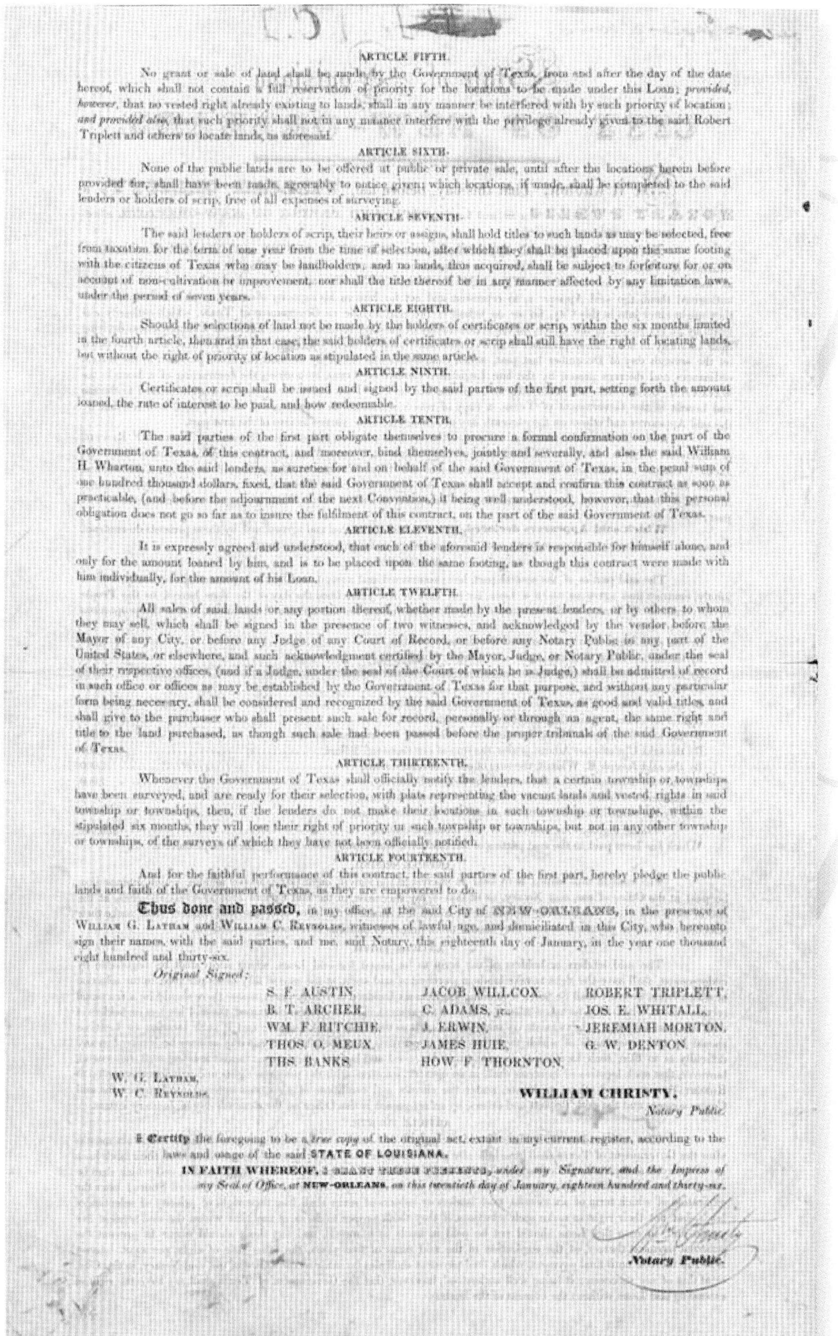

ARTICLE FIFTH.

No grant or sale of land shall be made by the Government of Texas, from and after the day of the date hereof, which shall not contain a full reservation of priority for the locations to be made under this Loan; *provided, however*, that no vested right already existing to lands, shall in any manner be interfered with by such priority of location; *and provided also*, that such priority shall not in any instance interfere with the privilege already given to the said Robert Triplett and others to locate lands, as aforesaid.

ARTICLE SIXTH.

None of the public lands are to be offered at public or private sale, until after the locations herein before provided for, shall have been made, agreeably to notice given; which locations, if made, shall be completed to the said lenders or holders of scrip, free of all expenses of surveying.

ARTICLE SEVENTH.

The said lenders or holders of scrip, their heirs or assigns, shall hold titles to such lands as may be selected, free from taxation for the term of one year from the time of selection, after which they shall be placed upon the same footing with the citizens of Texas who may be landholders, and no lands, thus acquired, shall be subject to forfeiture for or on account of non-cultivation or improvement, nor shall the title thereof be in any manner affected by any limitation laws, under the period of seven years.

ARTICLE EIGHTH.

Should the selections of land not be made by the holders of certificates or scrip, within the six months limited in the fourth article, then and in that case, the said holders of certificates or scrip shall still have the right of locating lands, but without the right of priority of location as stipulated in the same article.

ARTICLE NINTH.

Certificates or scrip shall be issued and signed by the said parties of the first part, setting forth the amount loaned, the rate of interest to be paid, and how redeemable.

ARTICLE TENTH.

The said parties of the first part obligate themselves to procure a formal confirmation on the part of the Government of Texas, of this contract, and moreover, bind themselves, jointly and severally, and also the said William H. Wharton, unto the said lenders, as sureties for and on behalf of the said Government of Texas, in the penal sum of one hundred thousand dollars, fixed, that the said Government of Texas shall accept and confirm this contract as soon as practicable, (and before the adjournment of the next Convention,) it being well understood, however, that this personal obligation does not go so far as to insure the fulfilment of this contract, on the part of the said Government of Texas.

ARTICLE ELEVENTH.

It is expressly agreed and understood, that each of the aforesaid lenders is responsible for himself alone, and only for the amount loaned by him, and is to be placed upon the same footing, as though this contract were made with him individually, for the amount of his Loan.

ARTICLE TWELFTH.

All sales of said lands or any portion thereof, whether made by the present lenders, or by others to whom they may sell, which shall be signed in the presence of two witnesses, and acknowledged by the vendor before the Mayor of any City, or before any Judge of any Court of Record, or before any Notary Public in any part of the United States, or elsewhere, and such acknowledgment certified by the Mayor, Judge, or Notary Public, under the seal of their respective offices, (and if a Judge, under the seal of the Court of which he is Judge,) shall be admitted of record in such office or offices as may be established by the Government of Texas for that purpose, and without any particular form being necessary, shall be considered and recognized by the said Government of Texas, as good and valid titles, and shall give to the purchaser who shall present such sale for record, personally or through an agent, the same right and title to the land purchased, as though such sale had been passed before the proper tribunals of the said Government of Texas.

ARTICLE THIRTEENTH.

Whenever the Government of Texas shall officially notify the lenders, that a certain township or townships have been surveyed, and are ready for their selection, with plats representing the vacant lands and vested rights in said township or townships, then, if the lenders do not make their locations in such township or townships, within the stipulated six months, they will lose their right of priority in such township or townships, but not in any other township or townships, of the surveys of which they have not been officially notified.

ARTICLE FOURTEENTH.

And for the faithful performance of this contract, the said parties of the first part, hereby pledge the public lands and faith of the Government of Texas, as they are empowered to do.

Thus done and passed, in my office, at the said City of NEW-ORLEANS, in the presence of William G. Latham and William C. Reynolds, witnesses of lawful age, and domiciliated in this City, who hereunto sign their names, with the said parties, and me, said Notary, this eighteenth day of January, in the year one thousand eight hundred and thirty-six.

Original Signed:

S. F. AUSTIN,	JACOB WILLCOX,	ROBERT TRIPLETT,
B. T. ARCHER,	C. ADAMS, jr.,	JOS. E. WHITALL,
WM. F. RITCHIE,	J. ERWIN,	JEREMIAH MORTON,
THOS. O. MEUX,	JAMES HUIE,	G. W. DENTON.
THS. BANKS,	HOW. F. THORNTON,	

W. G. Latham,
W. C. Reynolds,

WILLIAM CHRISTY,
Notary Public.

I Certify the foregoing to be a *true copy* of the original act, extant in my current register, according to the laws and usage of the said STATE OF LOUISIANA.

IN FAITH WHEREOF, I GRANT THESE PRESENTS, *under my Signature, and the Impress of my Seal of Office, at* NEW-ORLEANS, *on this twentieth day of January, eighteen hundred and thirty-six.*

Notary Public.

Fig A.2.2, $50,000 Texas Revolution Loan Document, Page 2

Private Collection

APPENDIX E:

A copy of the printed Texian Loan "Compromise Contract" as agreed to by Robert Triplett, William F. Gray and the Government of Texas at Harrisburg on April 1, 1836.

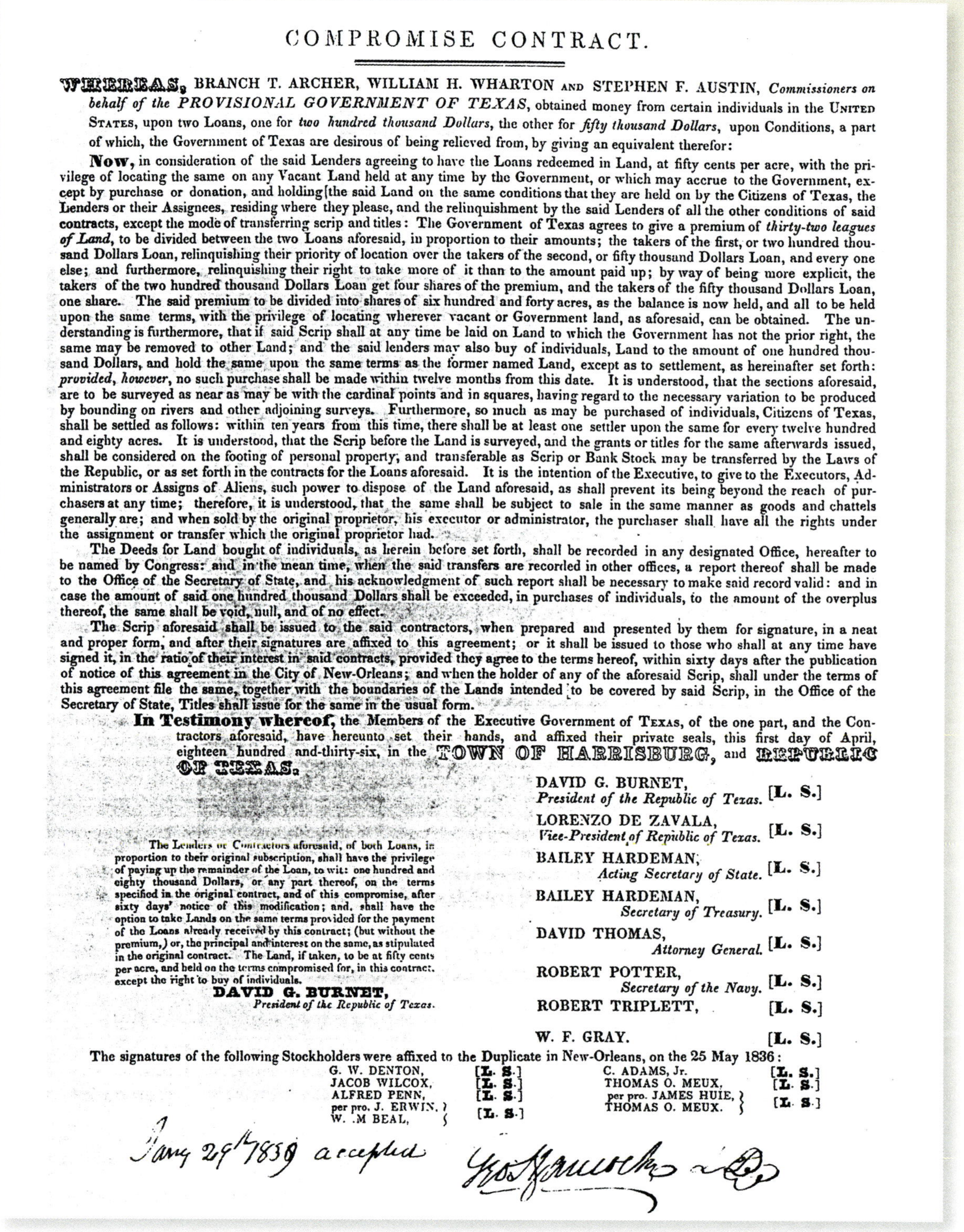

COMPROMISE CONTRACT.

WHEREAS, BRANCH T. ARCHER, WILLIAM H. WHARTON AND STEPHEN F. AUSTIN, *Commissioners on behalf of the PROVISIONAL GOVERNMENT OF TEXAS*, obtained money from certain individuals in the UNITED STATES, upon two Loans, one for *two hundred thousand Dollars*, the other for *fifty thousand Dollars*, upon Conditions, a part of which, the Government of Texas are desirous of being relieved from, by giving an equivalent therefor:

Now, in consideration of the said Lenders agreeing to have the Loans redeemed in Land, at fifty cents per acre, with the privilege of locating the same on any Vacant Land held at any time by the Government, or which may accrue to the Government, except by purchase or donation, and holding the said Land on the same conditions that they are held on by the Citizens of Texas, the Lenders or their Assignees, residing where they please, and the relinquishment by the said Lenders of all the other conditions of said contracts, except the mode of transferring scrip and titles: The Government of Texas agrees to give a premium of *thirty-two leagues of Land*, to be divided between the two Loans aforesaid, in proportion to their amounts; the takers of the first, or two hundred thousand Dollars Loan, relinquishing their priority of location over the takers of the second, or fifty thousand Dollars Loan, and every one else; and furthermore, relinquishing their right to take more of it than to the amount paid up; by way of being more explicit, the takers of the two hundred thousand Dollars Loan get four shares of the premium, and the takers of the fifty thousand Dollars Loan, one share. The said premium to be divided into shares of six hundred and forty acres, as the balance is now held, and all to be held upon the same terms, with the privilege of locating wherever vacant or Government land, as aforesaid, can be obtained. The understanding is furthermore, that if said Scrip shall at any time be laid on Land to which the Government has not the prior right, the same may be removed to other Land; and the said lenders may also buy of individuals, Land to the amount of one hundred thousand Dollars, and hold the same upon the same terms as the former named Land, except as to settlement, as hereinafter set forth: *provided, however*, no such purchase shall be made within twelve months from this date. It is understood, that the sections aforesaid, are to be surveyed as near as may be with the cardinal points and in squares, having regard to the necessary variation to be produced by bounding on rivers and other adjoining surveys. Furthermore, so much as may be purchased of individuals, Citizens of Texas, shall be settled as follows: within ten years from this time, there shall be at least one settler upon the same for every twelve hundred and eighty acres. It is understood, that the Scrip before the Land is surveyed, and the grants or titles for the same afterwards issued, shall be considered on the footing of personal property, and transferable as Scrip or Bank Stock may be transferred by the Laws of the Republic, or as set forth in the contracts for the Loans aforesaid. It is the intention of the Executive, to give to the Executors, Administrators or Assigns of Aliens, such power to dispose of the Land aforesaid, as shall prevent its being beyond the reach of purchasers at any time; therefore, it is understood, that the same shall be subject to sale in the same manner as goods and chattels generally are; and when sold by the original proprietor, his executor or administrator, the purchaser shall have all the rights under the assignment or transfer which the original proprietor had.

The Deeds for Land bought of individuals, as herein before set forth, shall be recorded in any designated Office, hereafter to be named by Congress: and in the mean time, when the said transfers are recorded in other offices, a report thereof shall be made to the Office of the Secretary of State, and his acknowledgment of such report shall be necessary to make said record valid: and in case the amount of said one hundred thousand Dollars shall be exceeded, in purchases of individuals, to the amount of the overplus thereof, the same shall be void, null, and of no effect.

The Scrip aforesaid shall be issued to the said contractors, when prepared and presented by them for signature, in a neat and proper form, and after their signatures are affixed to this agreement; or it shall be issued to those who shall at any time have signed it, in the ratio of their interest in said contracts, provided they agree to the terms hereof, within sixty days after the publication of notice of this agreement in the City of New-Orleans; and when the holder of any of the aforesaid Scrip, shall under the terms of this agreement file the same, together with the boundaries of the Lands intended to be covered by said Scrip, in the Office of the Secretary of State, Titles shall issue for the same in the usual form.

In Testimony whereof, the Members of the Executive Government of TEXAS, of the one part, and the Contractors aforesaid, have hereunto set their hands, and affixed their private seals, this first day of April, eighteen hundred and-thirty-six, in the **TOWN OF HARRISBURG,** and **REPUBLIC OF TEXAS.**

DAVID G. BURNET, *President of the Republic of Texas.* [L. S.]
LORENZO DE ZAVALA, *Vice-President of Republic of Texas.* [L. S.]
BAILEY HARDEMAN, *Acting Secretary of State.* [L. S.]
BAILEY HARDEMAN, *Secretary of Treasury.* [L. S.]
DAVID THOMAS, *Attorney General.* [L. S.]
ROBERT POTTER, *Secretary of the Navy.* [L. S.]
ROBERT TRIPLETT, [L. S.]
W. F. GRAY. [L. S.]

The Lenders or Contractors aforesaid, of both Loans, in proportion to their original subscription, shall have the privilege of paying up the remainder of the Loan, to wit: one hundred and eighty thousand Dollars, or any part thereof, on the terms specified in the original contract, and of this compromise, after sixty days' notice of this modification; and, shall have the option to take Lands on the same terms provided for the payment of the Loans already received by this contract; (but without the premium,) or, the principal and interest on the same, as stipulated in the original contract. The Land, if taken, to be at fifty cents per acre, and held on the terms compromised for, in this contract, except the right to buy of individuals.

DAVID G. BURNET,
President of the Republic of Texas.

The signatures of the following Stockholders were affixed to the Duplicate in New-Orleans, on the 25 May 1836:

G. W. DENTON, [L. S.]
JACOB WILCOX, [L. S.]
ALFRED PENN, [L. S.]
per pro. J. ERWIN, W. .M BEAL, [L. S.]
C. ADAMS, Jr. [L. S.]
THOMAS O. MEUX, [L. S.]
per pro. JAMES HUIE, THOMAS O. MEUX. [L. S.]

Jany 29th 1839 accepted

Fig A.3.1, "Texian Loan" Compromise Contract
Private Collection

APPENDIX F: MEXICAN BROADSIDE REPORTING THE CAPTURE OF SANTA ANNA (ENGLISH TRANSLATION)

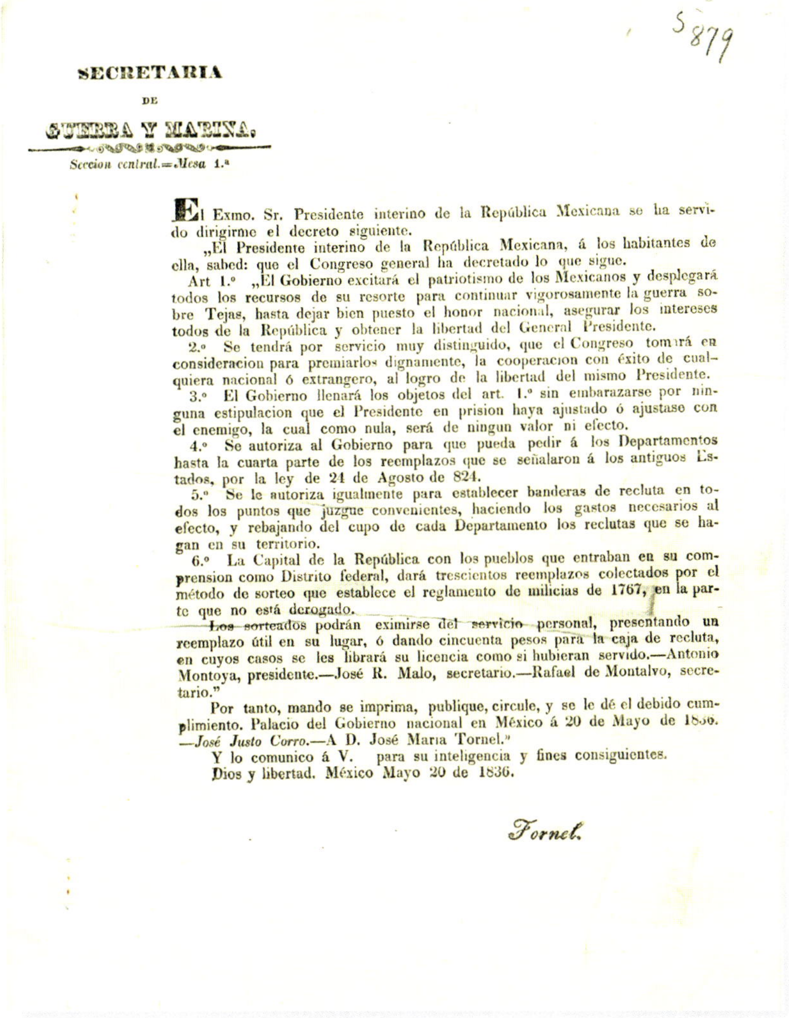

S879

SECRETARIA

DE

GUERRA Y MARINA.

Seccion central.=Mesa 1.ª

El Exmo. Sr. Presidente interino de la República Mexicana se ha servido dirigirme el decreto siguiente.

„El Presidente interino de la República Mexicana, á los habitantes de ella, sabed: que el Congreso general ha decretado lo que sigue.

Art 1.º „El Gobierno excitará el patriotismo de los Mexicanos y desplegará todos los recursos de su resorte para continuar vigorosamente la guerra sobre Tejas, hasta dejar bien puesto el honor nacional, asegurar los intereses todos de la República y obtener la libertad del General Presidente.

2.º Se tendrá por servicio muy distinguido, que el Congreso tomará en consideracion para premiarlos dignamente, la cooperacion con éxito de cualquiera nacional ó extrangero, al logro de la libertad del mismo Presidente.

3.º El Gobierno llenará los objetos del art. 1.º sin embarazarse por ninguna estipulacion que el Presidente en prision haya ajustado ó ajustase con el enemigo, la cual como nula, será de ningun valor ni efecto.

4.º Se autoriza al Gobierno para que pueda pedir á los Departamentos hasta la cuarta parte de los reemplazos que se señalaron á los antiguos Estados, por la ley de 24 de Agosto de 824.

5.º Se le autoriza igualmente para establecer banderas de recluta en todos los puntos que juzgue convenientes, haciendo los gastos necesarios al efecto, y rebajando del cupo de cada Departamento los reclutas que se hagan en su territorio.

6.º La Capital de la República con los pueblos que entraban en su comprension como Distrito federal, dará trescientos reemplazos colectados por el método de sorteo que establece el reglamento de milicias de 1767, en la parte que no está derogado.

Los sorteados podrán eximirse del servicio personal, presentando un reemplazo útil en su lugar, ó dando cincuenta pesos para la caja de recluta, en cuyos casos se les librará su licencia como si hubieran servido.—Antonio Montoya, presidente.—José R. Malo, secretario.—Rafael de Montalvo, secretario."

Por tanto, mando se imprima, publique, circule, y se le dé el debido cumplimiento. Palacio del Gobierno nacional en México á 20 de Mayo de 1836. —*José Justo Corro.*—A D. José María Tornel."

Y lo comunico á V. para su inteligencia y fines consiguientes.

Dios y libertad. México Mayo 20 de 1836.

Fornel.

Fig A- 4.1 Mexican broadside reporting the Capture of Santa Anna.
Private Collection

SECRETARY

OF

WAR AND NAVY

Central Section = Table 1st.

The most Excellent Interim President of the Republic of Mexico, has directed the following decree to me:

Let it be known, from the Interim President of the Republic of Mexico:

That the Congress has decreed the following:

1st. Article - The Government will call on the patriotism of the Mexicans and will make available all it's resources to vigorously continue the war over Texas, until our National honor is well put in place, to insure the Republic's interest and secure the liberty of the President General.

2nd. Article - It will be noted as distinguished service by consideration of the Congress, to highly praise the successful cooperation of any citizen or foreigner, that obtains the liberty of said President.

3rd. Article - The Government will act upon the objective of Article 1, without shame for any stipulation, made by the President while in prison, that may have consequences or favorable consequences for the enemy, which being null will not have any value or effect.

4th. Article - It is authorized that the Government can ask from the Departments up to a fourth of the recruits that were assigned to the previous States, by the law of August 24, of 1824.

5th. Article - It is also authorized to install recruiting centers in all zones that are deemed convenient, making the necessary expenditures, and subtracting from each Department's quota the number of recruits that are recruited in that Department's territory.

6th. Article - The Capital of the Republic, with the towns that comprise it, like the Federal District, will give three hundred back-up recruits made up of a draft by lottery that is established in the Regulation of Militias of 1767, in the part that is not null.

The draftees can appoint another person from their personal service staff, this way making a suitable substitute for them, or giving fifty pesos for the coffers, in which case, they will be discharged as if having served.

— Antonio Montoya, President, — Jose R. Malo, Secretary, — Rafael de Montalvo, Secretary

Therefore, I order printing, publication, circulation and due compliance. Palace of the National Government in Mexico on May 20th, of 1836.

— Jose Justo Corro, — A.D. Jose Maria Fornel

And I communicate to you, for your intelligence and end results.

God and Liberty. Mexico, May 20th, of 1836,

Fornel

APPENDIX G: PAY SCALE FOR THE TEXAS ARMY 1835-1836.

Table of Military Pay for the Texas Army
From the Telegraph and Texas Register, Vol. 1, No. 28 September 06, 1836.

Table of Pay, Subsistence, Forage, &c. allowed to Officers, Soldiers, &c, copied from the regulations of the United States Army and by which our own is governed.

GRADE.	*Pay per month.*	*No. of Rations per day.*	*No. of Horses allowed.*	*Servants No. allowed.*
Major General, - - - - - -	$200	15	7	4
Aide-Camp to to Major General, in addi-tion to his pay in the line, - - - -	24	1	2	
Brigadier General, - - - -	104	12	5	3
Aide-Camp to Brigadier General in addition to his pay in the line, - - - -	20		2	
Adjutant General, - - - -	90	6	5	2
Inspector General, - - - -	90	6	5	2
Quarter Master General, -	104	12	5	3
Quarter Master, - - - - - -	60	4	4	2
Assistant Quarter master in addition to his pay in the line, - - - - - - - -	20			
Pay Master General, $2,500 per annum, Pay Master, - - - - - - - -	50	4	3	2
Commissary General of Purchase $3,000 Commissary General of Subsistence,	90	6	4	2
Commissary of Subsistence,	60	4	4	2
Commissary of Subsistence, in addition to his pay in the line, - -	20		2	
Assistant Commissary of Subsistence in addition to his pay in the line,	10 to 20			
Store Keeper, not to exceed pay of Capt. of Infantry.				
Topographical Engineer,	60	4	4	2

GRADE.	*Pay per month.*	*No. of Rations per day.*	*No. of Horses allowed.*	*Servants No. allowed.*
Assistant Topographical Engineer, - - - - - - - -	40	4		1
Surgeon General, - - - - -	50	8	3	2
Surgeon of 10 years standing, - - - - - - - -	50	4	2	1
Surgeon under 10 years standing, - - - - - - - -	40	8	2	1
Assistant Surgeon of 10 years standing,	40	8	2	1
Assistant Surgeon of 5 years standing,	40	4	2	1
Colonel, - - - - - - - -	75	6	4	2
Lieutenant Colonel, - - -	60	5	3	2
Major, - - - - - - - -	50	4	3	2
Captain, - - - - - - - -	40	4		1
1st Lieutenant, - - - - -	30	4		1
2nd Lieutenant, - - - - -	25	4		1
1st Sergeant Artillery and Infantry,	15	1		
Other Sergeants, - - - -	12	1		
Corporals, - - - - - - - -	8	1		
Privates and Musicians, -	6	1		
Dragoons 1st Sergeant, -	15	1		
Dragoons, other Sergeants, - - - - - - - -	12	1		
Dragoons, Corporals, - - -	10	1		
Dragoons, Privates, - - - OFFICERS OF DRAGOONS, - - - - - -	8	1		

GRADE.	*Pay per month.*	*No. of Rations per day.*	*No. of Horses allowed.*	*Servants No. allowed.*
Colonel, - - - - - - - -	90	6	5	2
Lieutenant Colonel, - - -	75	5	4	2
Major, - - - - - - - -	60	4	4	2
Captain, - - - - - - - -	50	4	3	1
Lieutenants, - - - - - - - -	33	4	2	1
Sergeant Major, - - - - -	16	1		
Quarter Master Sergeant, -	16	1		
Bugler, (Chief), - - - - -	16	1		
Bugler, - - - - - - - -	9	1		
Farrier and Blacksmith, -	10	1		

APPENDIX H: LIST OF CLAIMS FILED DURING ASA BRIGHAM'S REPORT TO CONGRESS, 1836

Brigham's report to Henry Smith, Secretary of the treasury

***

No.2
Nov. 4

BRIGHAM TO THE SECRETARY

Auditor's Office
Columbia Nov 4. 1836

To the Hon Secretary of the Treasury

Sir

Individuals are d[a]ily presenting to this office claims for horses and other property lost in service, – property destroyed by our own army and that of the enemy and of various other descriptions, which are not provided for by the existing laws. Many of these claims have been filed in this office to wait the action of Congress on the subject. You will find annexed a list of such as have been filed with their several amounts.

I would respectfully suggest the propriety of recommending Congress to pass some general law for the settlement of all such claims upon just and equitable principles- - and also the propriety of revising generally the laws for the government of this office.They were enacted at an early period, when the business of the office was small and are inadequate for the the[sic] mass and variety of claims that now come before it.

I have the honor to be very respectfully

Your obt Servt
A. Brigham
Auditor

[Endorsed:] List of Claim filed with original letter

***

List of Claims filed during Asa Brigham's report to Congress, 1836

No. 2(Encl. 1)
Nov 4

LIST OF CLAIMS

No. 1	Freeman Wilkinson "tobacco destroyed"	$1543.75
2	George W. Shelton "horse lost"	40.00
3	Joseph Henry Bernard "clothing lost"	150.00
4	Martin Clow & Co. "whiskey and brandy destroyed"	250.00
5	John W. Hall "money expanded proof wanted by proper vouchers"	670.00
6	T. J. Golitchley "horses for several persons, lost"	500.00
7	T. J. Golithchley "Rifle &c for sundry persons lost"	75.00
8	Samuel M. Davis "lost horse"	200.00
9	William H. Moore "lost horse"	250.00
10	Richard Barrington "lost horse"	175.00
11	Johnson Holcombe "lost horse"	35.00
12	Stephen Doram "lost horse"	250.00
13	Richard Slack "lost horse"	75.00
14	Thomas Robinson "expenses whilst a prisoner"	150.00

15	A. J. Dixon "Lost horse"	200.00
16	Walter L. Mann "lost horse"	250.00
17	John L. Sleight "Brandy destroyed"	304.00
18	Richard Conine "2 horses lost"	100.00
19	William Brennan "Horse lost"	50.00
20	James Waugh "lost horse"	125.00
21	M. Perry, Assignee of Wm F. Halsey "order on a/c lost horse" returned to Perry –	70.00
22	Thomas A. Thomson "lost horse"	55.00
23	J. W. Stoddard " lost horse"	110.00
24	J. E. Flowers "lost horse and damaged pistols"	315.00
25	Josiah Hogan "lost horse"	40.00
26	Hugh Morgan "lost horse"	70.00
27	Jesse C. Bartlett "lost horse"	200.00
28	S. Booker "lost horse"	200.00
29	Horton & Clements "sundry property burnt"	1139.38
30	Walter Little "two horses lost"	70.00
31	J. H. Scaggs "horse lost"	50.00
32	P. B. Dexter "horse lost"	70.00
33	Jacob Eberly "spirits destroyed"	362.50
34	J. W. Bower "horse stolen"	75.00
35	F. Y. Duffau [?] "pistol and horse lost"	170.00
36	Haden Arnold "lost horse	100.00
37	Thomas Jackson "Horse lost"	250.00
38	George Brown "liquors destroyed"	150.00
39	William H. Moore "horse lost"	150.00
40	John D. Rainy "mule lost"	150.00
41	J. B. Bryan "lost horse"	120.00
42	Jesse McEllery "lost horse"	85.00
43	John Watson "lost horse"	200.00

44	Members of Capt. W. Becknell's Company. a. James Pierce "horse &c lost" $127.00 b. Henry R. Latimer "horse & mule lost" 75.00 c. William King "horse lost" d. James Jackson "horse & gun lost" 30.00 e. Richard Overton "rifle lost" 20.00 f. Isaac H. Johnson "rifle lost" 40.00 g. Benjamin J. Jeffeer "horse lost" 80.00 h. Samuel Wilson "horse lost" i. Edward West "two horses lost" j. J. C. Stout "lost horse" k. Preston Blount "lost horse" 75.00	447.00
45	Pascal E. Wayland "lost horse"	100.00
46	Arthur Gamble "lost horse"	35.00
47	Hugh Henderson "lost rifle"	25.00
48	Elisha Flack "ferry boat & canoe sunk"	65.00
49	Joel Leaky "two horses & eight bales cotton destd.	350.00
50	Ralph Wright "mare &c. lost	50.00
51	Joseph S. Morgan "lost horse" William Kerr "lost horse"	250.00 350.00
52	D. L. Kokernot "horses & saddles impressed	160.00
53	Henry Wyland "rifle && furnished Govt.	70.00
54	John Foster "services as courier"	143.00
55	H. Griffith &co "wagon &c furnished army"	400.00
56	Jesse McCelvery "horse lost"	85.00
57	Mr. Boyd "horse impressed	120.00
58	R. J. W. Reed [?] "board for couriers"	119.50
59	Leiper Willoughby "rifle lost"	25.00
60	H. H. Hoay "horse lost"	100.00
61	James Morgan "Merchandize, some vouchers wanting	1818.10
62	Nicholas Lynch "arms and ammunition"	374.00
63	Benjamin S. Reed "horses furnished (returned)	899.00
64	Paul Scarborough "horse lost"	150.00
65	Robert O. Lusk "cash advanced &c"	262.50
66	John English "Services"	60.00
67	Richard Haley "cash advanced, horse lost"	75.00

68	John Lawrence "mule died"	90.00
69	William H. Dunn "horses lost & rifle broke	140.00
70	J. M. Bradley "cash advanced &"	339.00
71	John Seldon "boat impressed & lost"	180.00
72	Samuel Whiting "damages & cattle killed"	600.00
73	J. J. Linn "supplies furnished"	794.00
74	John Sutherland "Cash advanced &c"	225.62
75	Estate N. B. Williams, "horse & equipments lost	60.00
76	David Davis "hauling provisions", no price fixed Per day by law.	41.00
77	Andrew Cloppin "no price established by law as courier	
78	Schooner Columbus, "wants the Commissary General's approval, charter & demurrage	[erased]
79	Samuel Barton "carpenteer's [sic] tools"	500.00
80	Charles DeMorse "services" We wish Govt. to say at what time The services of this corps shall commence.	
81	Handy & Lusk "Merchandize lost"	633.86
82	Archibald Smith "Cash advanced & horse lost"	120.00
83	M. W. Brigham "shot gun lost"	25.00
84	A. L. Harrison "services as Courier"	
85	Elizabeth Powell "property used"	4454.12
86	Rebecca Westover "property abandoned & destroy'd by the enemy	1200.00
87	James P. Caldwell "mule furnished"	70.00
88	Wm. H. Patton "Cash advanced"	21.00
89	E. Waller "Wood furnished steam boat"	52.00
90	Major Diggs "Express"	
91	James C. Little & J. T. Page "horse & furnished"	175.00
92	Robert Stephenson "arms lost"	65.00
93	R. J. Mosley "Cotton destroyed"	2500.00
	Amount I hereby certify this to be a correct list of claims remaining unsettled in this office Columbia, Nov. 4th 1836 A. Brigham Auditor ***	$28,413.33

APPENDIX I: AN ACT TO AUTHORIZE THE PRESIDENT TO ISSUE EXCHEQUER BILLS, AND TO DECLARE WHAT SHALL BE RECEIVABLE IN PAYMENT OF TAXES AND DUTIES ON IMPORTS.

AN ACT

To authorize the President to issue Exchequer Bills, and to declare what shall be receivable in payment of taxes and duties on imports.

Sec. 1. Be it enacted by the Senate and House of Representatives of the Republic of Texas in Congress assembled, That from and after the first day of February next, it shall not be lawful for any Collector of Customs of this Republic to receive in payment of imposts or duties upon goods, wares and merchandize imported into this Republic, after the day above specified, any thing but gold or silver, or the Exchequer Bills hereinafter authorized to be issued.

Sec. 2. Be it further enacted, That it shall not be lawful for the Sheriffs and Collectors of direct or license taxes to be assessed for the year one thousand eight hundred and forty-two, and all subsequent years, to receive anything in payment of such taxes except gold or silver, or the Exchequer Bills authorized to be issued by the provisions of this act.

Sec. 3. Be it further enacted, That the President be, and he is hereby authorized to issue Exchequer Bills, payable on demand, and receivable in payment of all public dues, to an amount not exceeding two hundred thousand dollars, to be signed by the President and countersigned by the Secretary of the Treasury; keeping a record in each Department, specifying the amount of each denomination of bills, their number and date, and payable to, and endorsed by such person as the President may direct, keeping a record as above, which shall be filed in the Comptroller's office.

Sec. 4. Be it further enacted, That the President be, and he is hereby authorized to procure, so soon as may be, lithographed or engraved bills, for the purpose of carrying out the provisions of this act, of such form and with such suitable devices, as he in his judgment may think proper; and that until he can procure such lithographed or engraved bills, it shall be lawful for him to issue such Exchequer Bills printed in such manner as he may direct, and that such printed bills shall be made payable to and endorsed as provided in section third: provided, that such endorsement shall in no case be held or adjusted to make such endorser liable or responsible for the payment of the same.

Sec.5. Be it further enacted, That the President's-Private Secretary be, and he is hereby authorized to sign the President's name to the above contemplated Exchequer Bills, and that he be allowed half a cent for each signature.

Sec. 6. Be it further enacted, That it shall be the duty of the Secretary of the Treasury, whenever any of said printed Exchequer Bills shall be redeemed and returned to the Treasury, to cause the same to be cancelled.

Sec. 7. Be it further enacted, That it shall be the duty of the Collector of Customs, Sheriffs, and other receiving officers of this Republic, whenever any gold or silver may be received by them in payment of government dues, to apply the same to the redemption, upon presentation for that purpose, of any of the Exchequer Bills authorized to be issued by the provisions of this act: provided, that such officers shall in no case redeem the same at a less sum than it represents on its face.

Sec. 8. Be it further enacted, That the Exchequer Bills authorized to be issued by the provisions of this act, shall be paid out for no other purpose than that of carrying out the objects of the general appropriation acts of Congress.

Sec. 9. Be it further enacted, That all land dues (except the land tax) and all payments for patents be made receivable, as heretofore, in the liabilities of the Governement.

Sec. 10. Be it further enacted, That all laws heretofore passed authorizing the issue and re-issue of Promissory Notes, and their reception in payment of duties or taxes hereafter to be assessed, be, and the same are hereby repealed.

Sec. 11. Be it further enacted, That this act take effect from and after its passage.

Approved, 19th January, 1842.

APPENDIX J: REPORT OF THE AUDITOR AND COMPTROLLER ON THE PUBLIC DEBT OF TEXAS 1852.

REPORT
OF
THE AUDITOR AND COMPTROLLER,
TO THE FOURTH LEGISLATURE,
ON THE
PUBLIC DEBT OF TEXAS.

AUSTIN:
PRINTED BY OUSHNEY & HAMPTON, "STATE GAZETTE" OFFICE.
1851.

JOINT REPORT,

AUSTIN, November 12, 1851.

To the Honorable Legislature of the State of Texas:

In conformity to the requirements of "An act to provide for ascertaining the debt of the late Republic of Texas," approved 20th March 1848, and the act supplementary therto, approved February 8th, 1850, we respectfully submit the following report_exhibiting the amount, character and classification of the claims filed and receipted for by us, under the provisions of said acts:

FIRST CLASS
Consisting of Audited or Ascertained Claims.

Character of Liabilities receipted for.	OSTENSIBLE	RATE	PAR VALUE.
Ten per cent. Consolidated Fund, created by act of 7th June, 1837,	632,526.80	at 70c.	442,768.76
Ten per cent. Consolidated Fund created by act of 7th June, 1837, issued under an act for the relief of Swartwout and others,	7,970.43	1.00	7,970.43
Ten percent. Funded Debt created by act of 5th February, 1840,	754,000.00	at 30c.	226,200.00
Eight per cent. Funded Debt created by act of 5th February, 1840,	24,280.00	at 30c.	7,284.00
Aren't carried forward,	$1,418,789.23		$684,223.19
Aren't bro't forward,	$1,418,787.23		684,223.19
Eight per cent. Treasury Bonds created by act of 5th February, 1840,	766,800.00	20	153,360.00
Ten per cent. Treasury Notes issued under act of 9th June, 1837, first issue,	41,630.00	1.00	41,630.00
Ten per cent. Treasury Notes issued under act of 9th June, 1837, second issue,	331,371.00	50	165,685.50

Character of Liabilities receipted for.	OSTENSIBLE	RATE	PAR VALUE.
Treasury Notes, without interest, issued under act of 19th January, 1839, third issue	1,828,192.00	25	457,048.00
Audited Paper issued under various enactments,	74,441.26	v'rs.	69,451.52
Miscellaneous Liabilities,	42,387.73	1.00	42,387.73
Ten per cent. Bonds issued by Commr's to negotiate a loan for $5,000,000, viz:			
For loan obtained from Bank United States,	457,380.00		400,000.00
For purchase of st'm'r Zavalla,	195,907.00	50	97,953.50
" " Naval vessels under contract with F. Dawson, now owned by James Schott and E. D. Whitney,	280,000.00	50	140,000.00
Interest on the above liabilities issued subject to interest,	$5,436,886.22		$2,251,739.44
as stated in the face of the certificates,	2,927,365.50	v'rs	1,468,185.26
Additional interest to 1st July, 1850, allowed by act approved 11th February, 1850, on claims which had been audited prior to its passage,	$8,364,251.72 239,139.06	v'rs	$3,719,914.70 113,664.80
Total amount filed of 1st class, including interest due thereon to 1st July, 1850,	$8,603,390.78		3,833,579.50
Less amount redeemed by issue of Land Scrip,	16,257.86	1.00	16,257.86
Total Amount 1st Class Debt filed, and unredeemed,	$8,587,132.92		$3,817,321.64

SECOND CLASS

Consisting of Claims sufficiently authenticated to admit them to audit under the laws of the late Republic.

	OSTENSIBLE AMOUNT.		PAR VALUE.
Am't filed and receipted for,	$755,218.05		$682,672.57
" " " as 3rd, Class Claims since recg'z'd,	16,467.95		16,467.95
Am't audited by special acts of Legislature,	72,077.28		72,077.28
Estimated amount on file not acted on,	125,000.00		125,000.00
	$968,763.28		$896,217.80
Less, Am't redeemed by the issue of Land Scrip and in payment of Revenue that accrued under the late Republic,	6,318.16		3,450.17
Total Am't of 2nd Class Debt filed,	$962,445.12		$892,767.63

THIRD CLASS

Consisting of Claims not sufficiently authenticated to authorize their being audited under the laws of the late Republic.

	OSTENSIBLE AMOUNT.		PAR VALUE.
Am't filed and receipted for, *less* $16,467.95, recognized and included in the preceding statement of 2d Class Claims,	47,675.10		47,675.10
Estimated amount on file not acted on,	50,000.00		50,000.00
Total Am't 3rd Class filed,	$97,675.10		$97,675.10

RECAPITULATION

	OSTENSIBLE AMOUNT.	PAR VALUE.
Amount of 1st Class,	$8,587,132.92	$3,817,321.54
" 2nd "	962,445.12	3,817,321.54
" 3rd "	97,675.10	97,675.10
Totals,	$9,647,253.14	$4,807,764.37

From the foregoing statement, it will be perceived that the entire amount of claims filed, including interest on all liabilities stipulated to bear interest, amounts to nine millions six hundred and forty seven thousand two hundred and fifty-three dollars fourteen cents: and, according to the value we have assigned them, they were worth to the Government four millions eight hundred and sixty four dollars thirty-seven cents.

As nothing has occurred since our report of 27th December, 1849, to include a change in our opinions respecting the rule which governed us in assigning an equivalent value to each class of liabilities filed, we will repeat the substance of the remarks in said report, as the reasons which guided us in the discharge of that part of our official duty.

TREASURY NOTES

The first issue of this character of indebtedness is known as the printed interest notes. They were put in circulation during the fall and winter of 1837, for a temporary purpose, and until the engraved notes could be procured: as soon as they were received, the further issue and re-issue of the former ceased. This occurred before any perceptible depreciation had taken place, and it was the usage of the Department to cancel them as they were received. Hence, the Government, for this class of liability, received full consideration, and we have so rated it.

To the engraved interest notes, we have assigned an average value of 50 cents on the dollar. These notes were issued under the provisions of the same act that the printed bills were, and took their place: about the time of the first issue of these notes (the spring of 1838) this species of the government paper commenced depreciating in value, so that when the act of 19th of January, 1839, prohibiting their further issue went into operation, they were worth but about 40 cents on the dollar.

To the treasuray notes not bearing interest, generally known as Red Backs, we have assigned an average value of 25 cents on the dollar. These notes superceded the engraved interest notes abouve referred to, and the first issue of them was made during the spring of 1839, when they were worth about 371/2 cents on the dollar. They continued depreciating, so that in 1841, the Government was compelled to pay them out at from 12 to 15 cents on the dollar. The value which we have given them is conceived to be equitable, as an average, both to the Government and the holders. It is impossible to ascertain from the date of the issue of these bills, as shown on the face, what they were worth when last paid out. For instance, a bill issued in 1839, at, say 371/2 cents on the dollar, and after having been returned to the treasury in collection of revenues, may have been re-issued the year following at 25 cents on the dollar, and so on; and in 1841, when it may have been last paid out at one-eighth of its ostensible value.

CONSOLIDATED FUNDED DEBT OF 7TH JUNE, 1837

The stock known by this title was issued under the provisions of an act of Congress approved June 7th, 1837, and could it be analyzed, would be subject to the greatest variety of equivalent rates. We found it impracticable to refer, in each instance, to the original records, to ascertain at what rate each claim had been audited, for which this stock was issued. Even had, or could we have done so, we would have failed to a great extent in acquiring this information, for the reason that Government, for a long time, would not acknowledge any discount on her paper; and the result was, that accounts were made out, augmented in amount, so as to make good the deficit in the value of currency. Hence, the only practicable mode which suggested itself, was to make an average of what the stock availed the Government; which we accordingly did, and assigned to it a value of 70 cents on the dollar. It is believed that this average is about what the Government received in the main, and will, with a few exceptions, (which will be alluded to hereafter,) fully remunerate the present holders, as it is now generally in the hands of third parties, who, in most instances, acquired it at a much less value from the original investor than that now assigned it.

EIGHT & TEN PER CENT. FUNDED DEBT OF 5TH FEBRUARY, 1840

We have assigned to this class of securities an average value of 30 cents on the dollar. This stock was issued under the authority of an act of Congress approval February 5th, 1840, and was created for the purpose of withdrawing and lessening the the amount of revenue currency then in circulation, with a view of enhancing the value of the residue. The inducements held out to the creditors to surrender a revenue currency, and to take one which could not be used in that way, was the promise of the Government to pay the stipulated interest semi-annually in specie; which, is well known, she was unable to do. The value attached to this stock may act onerously on some holders, but it will fully remunerable a large majority. It would be much more difficult in this fund than any other, to ascertain the exact value the Government received for the investments in it, as it is composed of interest notes, red backs and audited paper.

EIGHT PER CENT. TREASURY BONDS

Twenty cents on the dollar is the average equivalent value assigned this class of the government paper. These bond were issued to supercede, to some extent, and take the place of treasury notes. There is less danger of individual hardship growing out of the assignment of an average equivalent value to these bonds, than that of any other of the government securities: they were seldom ever issued at more than 25 cents on the dollar, and rarely less than 15 cents on the dollar. The value assigned them is deemed equitable.

AUDITED PAPER

When issued at par, has been allowed accordingly; when less than par, a corresponding deduction has been made; the records and vouchers showing the rate at which it was audited.

In the first class, are included the bonds issued to the Bank of the United States for a loan of $400,000 obtained from that institution in the year 1839; also, the claim of James Holford and associates, for the purchase of the steamer Zavala. A value corresponding to what the Government actually received, has been assigned to each.

Since our last report, Messrs. James Schott and E. D. Whitney have filed their claims, composed of one of the bonds issued to Frederick Dawson, of Baltimore, in payment for the navy. These gentlemen, although not known in the contract, are acknowledged by Mr. Dawson to have been equally interested in that transaction; and the readiness manifested in aiding the cause of Texas, by undertaking and carrying out a contract requiring a large pecuniary outlay at a time when the public credit was at an exceeding low stage, procured for the contractors the commendations of the late Republic. In assigning to this claim 50 cents on the dollar, as the value received by the Government, we have been governed by the law making the appropriation, and the contract entered into by the agent of the Government and Mr. Dawson. This contract, subsequently recognized by Legislative enactment, (a copy of which accompanies,) stipulates the price of the vessels at $280,000; to secure the payment of which, two bonds of the Republic for $280,000 each were deposited with the President of the Girard Bank at Philadelphia, with the understanding that they could be redeemed at the end of 12 months, by the payment of $280,000 and ten per cent. interest on the two bonds; otherwise the said bonds to become the property of Mr. Dawson. The Government was unable to meet the payment at the time specified; and the President of the Bank, according to instructions, delivered the bonds, amounting to $560,000, to Mr. Dawson. We accompany this statement with a communication form Messrs. Schott and Whitney, explanatory of their claim which is market "B."

It may be proper to remark, that the terms of the contract between the Government and James Holford and associates, for the purchase of the steamer Zavala, are similar to that entered into with Mr. Dawson.

In the average value assigned to the consolidated fund of 7th June, 1837, there came to our knowledge a few cases of hardship, where the Government had received full consideration for the original obligation which had been converted into this fund, and yet owned by the original investor. Had we departed from the rate we had assigned to this or any other character of liability in one instance, no matter how justifiable, others not processing the same merit would have claimed it; and the consequence would have been, that but few claimants would have been satisfied with any other classification than that of par.— For this reason we determined, in all instances, to adhere to the rate affixed to each class, and report such cases of hardship as might arise, to the Legislature, in order that such relief may be awarded in the premise as appears to be just. We therefore accompany this report with a statement marked "C," of such cases, and hope the same will receive your favorable consideration. In this connection, we refer you to the communication of Dr. John W. King, upon the subject of his claim, which is enclosed in the statement last named.

On the liabilities stipulated to bear interest, we have calculated it from the date of last payment to the 1st of July, 1850, in accordance with an act approved February 11th, 1850, except the interest treasury notes, on which we have allowed interest to the 1st of January, 1841; as all holders of this character of notes were required to fund them by that time, and the appropriation for the further payment of interest on said notes was cancelled.

It may be proper to remark, that we have attached the same value to the interest which had accrued on the several classes of liabilities that we attached to the liabilities themselves.

THE SECOND CLASS

Is composed of claims against the late Republic of Texas which had not previously been audited, but contracted under the sanction of law. We have assigned to this class of claims, as we did to the first class, an equivalent value proportionate to what each claim availed the Government in gold and silver, as far as it was in our power to do. Owing to the large number of claims filed immediately preceding the expiration of the law under which we acted, we have been unable to complete the examination and registration of the second and third classes.— We have therefore ascertained as nearly as practicable, the amount of unexamined claims filed, and report them in bulk.

THIRD CLASS

This class is composed of claims, for the auditing of which the existing laws have made no provision, or where the proof is insufficient. In it, however, are many meritorious claims, which will require special legislation to place them on the same footing with valid and authorized claims against the Government. A number of claims have been filed for losses sustained during the revolution and subsequent invasions, being caused by the destruction of property by our own army and that of the enemy. On this character of claims, we have declined taking any action; informing the claimants that the same would be referred to the Legislature, for their consideration and action thereon. These claims, numbered from 1 to 71, amounting to $426,314.03, will be found accompanying, marked "D."

It is necessary that some mode of assignment of the certificates of indebtedness issued, should be prescribed by law.

We have audited the claims of those who performed military service, where the needful evidence was on file, regardless of any application of the claimants holding the certificate, subject to his order or that of his legal representative: as many of these parties are now deceased, the proceeds of these claims should inure to the benefit of the heirs of the deceased; we, therefore, respectfully recommend the enactment of the necessary law to protect the rights of the widows and orphans of those who may have fallen in the defence of the country, by prescribing the necessary regulations to prevent person's from administering for the purpose of speculations. A law of this character was enacted by Congress of the late Republic, for the protection of the estaes of deceased soldiers of the George battalion. — [See article 1053, Hartley's Digest.]

Statements of several claims that would come under the 2nd class were presented within the term of limitation, but unaccompanied with the needful proof. This the claimants not being able to procure before the expiration of the limit, desire the privilege of producing hereafter. The statements have been filed, but could not be acted on; and it may be a subject worthy of consideration, whether additional time should not be allowed for the presentation of testimony in such cases, if a general extension of the limit be not granted.

Supporting that all the claims against the late Government, as shown by the official records, including the amount of supposed unaudited claims outstanding, had been filed as required by law, and assigning each class of those not filed the same equivalent value we have to those filed, the debt would then be as follows:

	OSTENSIBLE.	PAR.
Claims filed of all descriptions, including interest as before stated, _	$9,647,253.14 ___	$4,807,764.37
Claims not filed, of all descriptions, including interest, ______________	2,789,738.20	2,019,514.27
Total debt with interest, including the amount filed and unfiled, _____	$12,436,991.34 ___	$6,827,278.64

All of which will more fully appear by reference to the accompanying statement, market A.

Accompanying this report, is a register of the several claims acted on by us, which we respectfully request may be returned when it shall no longer be required by your Honorable Body.

JNO. M. SWISHER,
Auditor.
JAMES B. SHAW,
Comptroller.

BIBLIOGRAPHY

ARCHIVAL SOURCES (PUBLISHED)

Jones, Anson, *Memoranda and Official Correspondence relating to the Republic of Texas its History and Annexation.* New York, D. Appleton & Company, 1859. Memorandum Books No.1, 2 and 3.

The Papers of Mirabeau Buonaparte Lamar, Edited from the original papers in the Texas State Library by Charles Adams Gulick, Jr. with the assistance of Katherine Elliott, Archivist, Texas State Library. Volumes I, II, III, IV, V and VI.

The Papers of the Texas Revolution 1835-1836, John H. Jenkins, General Editor. Volumes 1- 9, Presidial Press, Brig. Gen. Jay A. Matthews, Publisher, Austin, 1973.

The Samuel May Williams Papers, Compiled by Ruth G. Nichols and S.W. Lifflander, Rosenberg Library, Galveston, Texas.

The Writings of Sam Houston, 1813-1863, Edited by Amelia W. Williams and Eugene C. Barker, University of Texas Press, 1939, Volume II, Page 105, Sam Houston to the Texas Congress, Houston,

Texas Indian Papers 1844-1845, Edited from the original manuscript copies in the Texas State Library Archives by Dorman H. Winfrey. Austin. Texas State Library. 1960.

Texas Treasury Papers, Letters Received in the Treasury Department of the Republic of Texas 1836-1845. Volume 1, Letters 1-620. Edited from the originals in the Texas State Library by Seymour V. Conner. Texas State Library. Austin 1955

Texas Treasury Papers, Letters Received in the Treasury Department of the Republic of Texas 1836-1845. Volume II, Letters 621-1346. Edited from the originals in the Texas State Library by Seymour V. Conner. Texas State Library. Austin 1955

Texas Treasury Papers, Letters Received in the Treasury Department of the Republic of Texas 1836-1845. Volume III, Letters 1347-1814. Edited from the originals in the Texas State Library by Seymour V. Conner. Texas State Library. Austin 1955

Texas Treasury Papers, Letters received in the Treasury Department of the Republic of Texas 1836-1846. Volume IV, SUPPLEMENT AND LETTERS RECEIVED FROM THE MILITARY DEPARTMENTS, Edited from the originals in the Texas State Library by Virginia H. Taylor, Austin, 1956.

The JOHN WYATT MOODY PAPERS, compiled by Helen Foster Snow. Woodson Research Center, Fondren Library, Rice University.

Gray, William Fairfax, *From Virginia to Texas, 1835, Diary of Col. Wm.F. Gray. Gray,* Dillaye & Co Printers, Houston, Texas 1909, Reprinted by The Fletcher Young Publishing Co, 1965.

ARCHIVAL SOURCES (NON-PUBLISHED)

Beinecke Rare Book and Manuscript Library, Yale University, New Haven, Connecticut. Various manuscript letters relating to the era of colonial Texas, the Texas Revolution and the finances and annexation of the Republic of Texas. From the Thomas W. Streeter Texas Collection.

Bexar Archives, Translations by Ernesto Rodriguez, Assistant to the curator at the Alamo.

Daughters of the Republic of Texas Library at the Alamo. Various military pay certificates, treasury warrants, and other documents of the Republic of Texas which were used as illustrations in this book as noted. From the collection of the late Dr. William Howard.

DeGolyer Library, Southern Methodist University, Dallas, Texas. Various military pay certificates, auditor's certificates, treasury warrants, promissory notes and other documents of the Republic of Texas which were used as illustrations in this book as noted. From the John N. Rowe III collection of Texas Currency.

Durham Western Heritage Museum, Omaha Nebraska. A promissory note from the collection of the City of Omaha Nebraska used as an illustration in this book as noted. From the collection of the late Byron Reed.

Museum Collections - Spanish Colonial, Mexican and United States coins used as illustrations in this book from the Presidio La Bahia, Goliad, Texas and the American Numismatic Association (ANA) Money Museum in Colorado Springs, Colorado

Other Collections – Spanish Colonial, Mexican and United States coins used as illustrations in this book from other collections as noted, including Heritage Galleries from their permanent auction archives and the Texas Numismatic Association, through a gift by Paul N. Garner.

Private Collections – Promissory notes, documents and paper money of the Texas colonial period under Spanish and Mexican rule used as illustrations in this book from numerous private collections as noted.

Private Collections - Military pay certificates, auditor's certificates, treasury warrants, promissory notes, stocks, bonds, printed broadsides and other documents from the Provisional Government of Texas, the Republic of Texas, the Late Republic of Texas and the United States used as illustrations in this book from numerous private collections as noted.

University of Houston Libraries, Special Collections, Texas Money Collection. Various military pay certificates, auditor's certificates, treasury warrants and other documents which were used as illustrations in this book as noted. From the collection of the late Frell Albright.

Texas State Archives – Various manuscript documents, affidavits, military service records, military discharge certificates, powers of attorney, and documents relating to the settlement of public debt claims of the Republic of Texas.

OFFICIAL RECORDS

Documents of MAJOR GEN. SAM. HOUSTON, Commander in Chief of the Texian Army, to his excellency, David G. Burnet, President of the Republic of Texas; Containing A Detailed Account of the BATTLE OF SAN JACINTO. New Orleans; John Cox & Co., Printers, Bulletin Office, 1836.

Journals of the Senate of the Republic of Texas, First Congress, First Session, Columbia, G.&T.H. Borden, Public Printers, 1836

Journals of the House of Representatives of the Republic of Texas. First Congress- First Session, G& T.H. Bordon, Public Printers, 1836.

Laws of the Republic of Texas. Printed by the order of the Secretary of State. Volume I. Houston, Office of the Telegraph, 1837.

Report of the Secretary of the Treasury, October 13, 1837. Second Congress, First Session. Printed by order of Congress. Houston. The Office of the Telegraph, 1837.

Message from the President of the Republic, May 12th, 1838, to the House of Representatives, giving his reasons for not signing the bill entitled, "An Act to Define and limit the issue of Promissory Notes". Printed by order of the Senate. Houston. Telegraph Press, 1838.

Report of the Secretary of the Treasury, to His Excellency, Sam Houston, President of the Republic of Texas. City of Houston, November 3, 1838. Telegraph Press.

Communication from the Secretary of the Treasury, with an accompanying document, in answer to a Resolution of Congress. By order of Congress. City of Houston, November 29, 1838. Telegraph Power Press.

Journal of the Proceedings of the General Council of the REPUBLIC OF TEXAS, held at San Felipe de Austin, November 14, 1835. National Intelligincer Office-Houston, 1839

Laws of the Republic of Texas, Passed at the first session of the Third Congress. Houston, Telegraph Power Press. 1839

Annual Report of the Treasurer of the Republic of Texas for 1841. By order of the House of Representatives, Austin. S. Whiting, Public Printer-Congress Avenue. 1842. Treasurer's office, March 31, 1841.

Annual Report of TREASURER of the REPUBLIC OF TEXAS for 1841, By order of the House of Representatives, Austin, S. Whiting, Public Printer - Congress Avenue. 1842, Treasury Department, July 1, 1841

Annual Report of the Treasurer of the Republic of Texas for 1841. By order of the House of Representatives, Austin. S. Whiting, Public Printer-Congress Avenue. 1842. Comptroller's Office, November 10, 1841.

Journals of the Sixth Congress of the Republic of Texas. 1841-1842, Edited by Harriett Smither, Archiver, Texas State Library, Volume 1, Von Bockman-Jones Co. Austin, Tx 1940

Report of the Secretary of the Treasury. Printed at the Vindicator Office, Washington. Dec. 4th, 1843.

Treaty of Annexation. Submitted April 12, 1844. J.C. Calhoun, Issac Van Zant, J. Pickney Henderson.

The Constitution of the State of Texas, 1845

A report by James B. Shaw, Comptroller to the Hon. Volney E. Howard, Chairman of a Select Committee of the House of Representatives. Austin, 28th March, 1846.

Report of the Auditor and Comptroller to the fourth legislature on the Public Debt of Texas. Austin: Printed by Cushney & Hampton, "State Gazette" Office, 1851

Report to the President, on the condition and amount of the debt of the late republic of Texas, by Thomas Corwin, U.S. Secretary of the Treasury. Washington, Sept. 13, 1851.

Petition of Citizens of New Orleans ,Creditors of the Late Republic of Texas, to the Thirty-Second Congress. New Orleans: Hinton & Bro. Print, No. 52 Gravier Street. 1852

Memorial of a Committee Appointed at a Meeting of the Creditors of Texas. U.S. Senate, 32d Congress, 1st Session, Misc. No 72. Referred to the Committee on Finance and ordered to be printed, April 20, 1852.

Appendix to the Congressional Globe, 33rd Congress, Second Session, U.S. House of Representatives, February 6, 1855

Appendix to the Congressional Globe, 33rd Congress, Second Session, U.S. House of Representatives, Laws of the United States, Public XLIX, February 28, 1855.

BOOKS

Amberson, Mary Margaret McAllen, *A Brave Boy and a Good Soldier, John C.C. Hill & The Texas Expedition to Mier*. 2007 Texas State Historical Association.

Barker, Eugene C, *The Life of Stephen F. Austin, Founder of Texas, 1793-1836*. University of Texas Press, Austin and London, 1926

Bolenger, Milton H., *The United States Early Silver Dollars, Krause Publications*

Bowers, Q. David, *American Coin Treasures and Hoards and caches of other American Numismatic items*, Bowers and Merena Galleries, Inc 1997.

Bowers, Q. David, *Obsolete Paper Money Issued by Banks in the United States, 1782-1866.* 2006, Whitman publishing, LLC.

Breen, Walter H., *Walter Breen's Complete Encyclopedia of U.S. and Colonial Coins*, F.C.I. Press, Inc., 1988, Doubleday.

Campbell, Randolph B., *Gone to Texas, A History of the Lone Star State*. Oxford University Press, 2003

Carefoot, Jean, Gen Editor, *Calendar of the Papers of MIRABEAU BUONAPARTE LAMAR*, Compiled and Edited by Michael R. Green, Texas State Library, Austin, Texas 1982.

Chipman, Donald E., *Spanish Texas 1519-1821*, University of Texas Press, Austin.

Craven, John Nathan, *James Harper Starr, Financier of the Republic of Texas*, The Daughters of the Republic of Texas, Austin, 1950, Page 38.

Criswell, Grover C., *Confederate and Southern States Currency,* Vol.1, 4'th edition 1992,

Davies, Glyn. *A History of money from ancient times to the present day*, 3rd. ed. Cardiff: University of Wales Press, 2002.

de la Teja, Jesús F. ed., *A Revolution Remembered: The Memoirs and Selected Correspondence of Juan N. Seguín* (Austin: State House Press, 1991).

Dimmick, Gregory J., *Sea of Mud, The Retreat of the Mexican Army after San Jacinto, An Archeological Investigation*, Texas State Historical Association, Austin, 2004.

Doree, Bill, *Profiles in Pillage: The Galveston Pirateers, 1816-1822*. Self Published.

Duke, Marc, *The du Ponts: Portrait of a Dynasty*, Saturday Review Press. 1976.

Dunigan, Mike, *Resplandores*, 1997. Superior Stamp Ed, Beverly Hills, Ca. Library of Congress: 97-61923.

Evans, George G., *Illustrated History of the United States Mint with Short Historical Sketches and Illustrations of the Branch Mints*. Philadelphia, George G. Evans. 1893.

Frantz, Joe B., *Six Missions of Texas, La Bahia, Texian Press, 1965.*

Friedberg, Robert, *Paper Money of the United States*, Fourteenth Edition, The Coin and Currency Institute, Inc. Clifton, N.J.

Gammel, Hans Peter Mareus Neilsen and Raines, Cadwell Walton, *The Laws of Texas, 1822-1897*. Austin, Gammel Book Co. 1898.

Grant, Joseph M, and Crum, Lawrence L., *The Development of State-Chartered Banking in Texas*, Bureau of Business Research, The University of Texas at Austin, 1978.

Gouge, William M., *The Fiscal History of Texas*, Burt Franklin, New York. 1852. Reprinted: 1969

Gracy, David B. III, *Ships of the Texas Navy*, A limited edition portfolio of fine prints. Presidial Press. 1978

Hanigan, Frank C., *Santa Anna, The Napoleon of the West*, Coward-McCann, Inc. 1934.

Hardin, Stephen L., *Texian Iliad, A military history of the Texas Revolution, 1835-1836*, University of Texas Press, Austin. 1994.

Hessler, Gene, *The Comprehensive Catalogue of U.S. Paper Money*, Sixth Edition, 1997. BNR Press.

Highfill, John W., *The Comprehensive U.S. Silver Dollar Encyclopedia, , Highfill Press, 1992.*

Hogan, William Ransom, *The Texas Republic, A Social and Economic History*, University of Oklahoma Press, Norman, 1946.

Howard, Dr. William E., *The Romance of Texas Money, The story of Texas money from Early Colonial days to the last issue of the money of the Republic*, Dallas, Texas, August 1946.

Hubbard, Clyde and David O'Harrow. *Hookneck*, El Aguila de Perfil, 1997, , ISBN 96—44471. Millcross Litho, Inc. Portland Or.

Jordan, Jonathan W., *Lone Star Navy*, Potomac Books, Inc. 2006.

Konstam, Angus. General Editor, *The Civil War, A Visual Encyclopedia*, Barnes & Noble Books, New York, 2004, Pages 262-263

Krause, Chester L. and Clifford Mishler, *Standard catalog of world coins. Spain, Portugal and the New World,* Colin R. Bruce, Senior Editor. 2002 Krause Publications.

Madis, Franklin, *The Taking of Texas*, First Edition, 2002 by Franklin Madis, Eakin Press, USA.

Mayberry, Robert Jr., *Texas Flags*, Texas A&M University Press, College Station in association with the Museum of Fine Arts, Houston. 2001, Pages21-22.

McKinney, Bobby J., *A Search For Texas, the Revolution-the Republic-The Relics 1836-1846,* Mouth of Caney, 2006.

Meed, Douglas V., *The Fighting Texas Navy 1832-1843*, Republic of Texas Press, Plano, Texas 2001.

Medlar, Bob, *Texas Obsolete Notes & Script*, Society of Paper Money Collectors, San Antonio, Tx 1968.

Miller, Thomas Lloyd, *Bounty and Donation Land Grants of Texas*, 1835-1888., University of Texas Press, Austin & London.

Miller, Edmund Thornton, *Bulletin of the University of Texas 1916: No. 37. A Financial History of Texas,* Austin, Texas.

Nance, Joseph Milton, *Heroes of Texas, Featuring Oil Portraits from the Summerfield G. Roberts Collection.* Texian Press, 1966, Waco, Texas.

Nussbaum, Arthur A., *History of the dollar*. New York : Columbia U.P., 1957.

James, Marquis, *The Raven, A Biography of Sam Houston*, University of Texas Press, Austin. Copyright 1929, by Marquis James; copyright renewed 1956 by Jacqueline Mary Parson James

Nesmith, Robert, *The Coinage of the First Mint of the Americas at Mexico City*, 1536-1572. Reprint of Sanford J. Durst. 2001. Rockville Center, NY. ISBN: 1-886720-10-X

Nichols, Ruth G., *Samuel May Williams, 1795-1858* in *Calendar to the Samuel May Williams Papers*, Compiled by Ruth G. Nichols and S.W. Lifflander, Rosenberg Library Press, Galveston, Texas 1956.

Olson, Joseph D., *Texas Numismatic History: A Catalogue 1813-1868*, 1st Edition, 2006. Corporate Image, Texas Numismatic Heritage Press

Porrúa Miguel Angel, *La Casa de Moneda de México a más 450 Años de distancia*. Editorial Porrúa, Mexico DF. 1988.

Pradeeau, Alberto Francisco, *Historia Numismática de México*, 1823 - 1950. Volume II, Ed. Stylo, Mexico DF. 1950.

Ragsdale, Crystal Sasse, *Women & Children of the Alamo*, State House Press, 1994.

Red, Ellen Robbins, *Early Days on the Bayou 1838-1890, The Life and Letters of HORACE DICKINSON TAYLOR*, Texian Press, Waco, Texas. 1986.

Rosas, Alejandro y José Manuel Villalpando, *Los Presidentes de México*, Ed. Planeta, 2001. ISBN: 970-690-507-3

Sedwick, Frank, *The Practical Book of Cobs,* Second Edition, Frank Sedwick, 1990

Siegel, Stanley and John A. Moretta, *Houston, A Chronicle of the Bayou City*, American Historical Press, Sun Valley, California, 2005.

Shull, Hugh, *A Guide Book of Southern States Currency, History, Rarity and Values*. Whitman Publishing, LLC, 2007.

Smithwick, Noah. *The Evolution of a State or Recollections of Old Texas Days*, compiled by his daughter Nanna Smithwick Henderson, Gammel Book Company, Austin. Austin, Texas, W. Thomas Taylor, 1995

Taylor, W. Thomas, *TEXFAKE, An Account of the Theft and Forgery of Texas Documents*, Austin, W. Thomas Tayor, 1991

Tinkle, Lon, *The Alamo*, from the book *Six Missions of Texas*, Texian Press, 1965, Waco Texas

Tolbert, Frank J., *The Day of San Jacinto,* The Pemberton Press, Jenkins Publishing Company, Austin and New York. 1959.

Triplett, Robert, *Roland Trevor: or, The Pilot of Human Life, being an Autobiography of the Author, Showing how to make and lose a fortune, and then how to make another*. Philadelphia, Lippincott, Grambo, and Co. 1853.

Vázquez, José Antonio Bátiz, Fomento Cultural Banamex, *Historia del Papel Moneda en México*. 1984. ISBN 968-7009-05-5

Wagner, Kip, as told to L.B. Taylor, Jr, *Pieces of Eight, Recovering the Riches of a Lost Spanish Treasure Fleet*, Page 54. New York, , E.P. Dutton & Co, 1966. Eight Real Company.

Williams, John Hoyt, *Sam Houston, The Life and Times of the Liberator of Texas, an Authentic American Hero*. Simon & Schuster, Inc. 1993.

Willoughby, Larry, *Austin, A Historical Portrait*, Donning Company, Publishers, Norfolk, Virginia Beach 1981

Winders, Richard Bruce, *Crisis in the Southwest, The United States, Mexico and the Struggle over Texas*. Scholarly Resources, Inc. 2002.

Yeoman, R.S., *A Guide Book of United States Coins,* 2003, Edited by Kenneth Bressett. 2002 St Martin's Press.

JOURNAL ARTICLES

Ball, Douglas B. PhD., *"Lone Star Notes, Early Texas currency has a galaxy of forms"*. Bank Note Reporter, April 1988

Ball, Douglas B. PhD., *"Lone Star Notes, Largest U.S. state created currency from scratch"*. Bank Note Reporter, May 1988. Part II, The Third Issue. The Red Backs.

Bevill, James P. and Alvin L. Stern, *"Lone Stars Rising, a missing numismatic link"*, The Numismatist, May 2011.

Blount, Lois Foster, *"Old Red House at Nacogdoches"*, Volume 49, Number 4. Southwestern Historical Quarterly.

Epperson, Jean L. *"Cayuga",* in the New Handbook of Texas, Vol. 1.

Gibbs, William, *"Byron Reed Collection worth $7.9M"*, Coin World, Monday, August 6, 2001.

Haugh, John J., *Heritage Insider, July/August 1998, Volume 1, No. 4,*

Rowe, John and John M. Davis, *Jr, "Necessary Paper, Republic of Texas Currency",* Texas Heritage, Texas Historical Foundation, Winter 2002,.

Hamilton, Holman, *"Texas Bonds and Northern Profits: A Study in Comprimise, Investment, and Lobby Influence"*, The Mississippi Valley Historical Review, Vol.43, No. 4.(March 1957), Page 581.

Lentz, Lewis, *"Texas Money", Reprint from The Southwestern Historical Quarterly, Vol. LVII, No. 2, October 1953.*

Kingston, Mike, *"The Capitals of Texas"*, Texas History Highlights, Texas Almanac 1986-1987 edition

Marshall, Thomas Maitland , *"Diplomatic Relations of Texas and the United States, 1839-1843"*, Southwestern Historical Quarterly 15, April 1912.

Newman, Eric P., *"The Dollar Sign, Its Written and Printed Origins"*, Coinage of the Americas

Conference at the American Numismatic Society, New York, October 30, 1993. ANS 1993

NEWSPAPER SOURCES

The Herculenium, August 25, 1821.

The New York Observer, Saturday, April 16, 1836.

The Daily Texian, January 11, 1842

The LaGrange Journal, July 9, 1936.

The San Antonio Light, April 21, 1940.

The Seguin Gazette-Enterprise, Seguin, Texas. December 1, 1982.

The *Mobile Register*, February 8, 1845.

Harper's Weekly, February 1845.

Public Ledger, Vol. XIX.-No.63, Philadelphia, Thursday, June 5, 1845. Austin, *Texas State Gazette*, January 12, 1850

The Morning Star, November 8, 1845

ONLINE SOURCES

Austin Treasures, Online exhibits from the Austin History Center, http://www.ci.austin.tx.us/library/ahc/capitol/early.htm

Handbook of Texas Online, http://www.tsha.utexas.edu/handbook/online

Index to Military Rolls of the Republic of Texas 1835-1845, www.mindspring.com/~dmaxey/l/bradjm91.htm

Pioneer Evans Family, by Earlayne Chance http://www.rootsweb.com/~nyjeffer/evanssp.htm

San Jacinto Museum of History, Herzstein Library, Veteran Biographies, Reed, Henry.

http://www.sanjacinto- seum.org/Herzstein_Library/Veteran_Biographies

Seven Oceans Video & Digital Media Production www.sevenoceans.com

Sons of DeWitt Colony Texas, www.tamu.edu/dewitt/main.htm

Southwestern Historical Quarterly Online, http://www.tsha.utexas.edu

PBS.org http://www.pbs.org/opb/conquistadors/mexico/adventure2/pop-malintzin.htm

Retreat to Victory, The Battle of San Jacinto, by Steve Goodson www.texfiles.com/ERAmar02/sanjacinto.htm

Texas HIMA, Texas Laws affecting HIM Professionals http://www.txhima.org/laws/currlaw7.htm

Texas State Library - Texas Treasures www.tsl.state.tx.us

UN RV History – Roman Empire http://www.unrv.com/culture/major-roman-god-list.php

William Falconer's Dictionary of the Marine, London: 1880, Page 226, http://southseas.nla.gov.au/refs/falc/1013.html

THESES, DISSERTATIONS, LETTERS AND OTHER PAPERS

Bain, Tom, Typewritten letter to "Texana Collectors" dated January 5, 1948.

Bevill, James P. and Dr. Garth Clark, *Authentication Study of the 1817 New Spain (Texas) Jolas using X-Ray Florescence (XRF) Analysis,* Non-Published. March 2012.

Brown, Darrel, *"Land, Loans, and Legends"*, Non-Published. 2005-2007.

Brown, Darrel, *"Texas Military Pay Entitlement Certificates. Galveston Issue."* Non-published. October 2006.

Brown, Darrel, *"Agreement entitling Robert Triplett to and guaranteeing title for six hundred and forty acres on the east end of Galveston island"*. Analysis of a manuscript document dated April 1, 1836. Non-published 2006.

Brown, Darrel, Republic of Texas *"Medallion Change Notes. 1838 Issue"*. 2006. Non-published.

Brown, Darrel, *"Producing the Thomas Jefferson image for the Republic of Texas 1838 Medallion Note"*, Non-published, November 2006.

Brown, Darrel, *"Compromise of 1850"*, non-published. 2007

Glass, James L., *"Replica chart of the Galveston-Houston area circa 1836"*. Completed in 1986.

Frommhold, Sebastian, *"Spanish Colonial Coins used in Texas"*, Non-published, 2005

Hamilton, J.T., A signed typewritten letter. Undated.

Jarrell, Louise. *"The Austin Lyceum"*, 1839-1841, M.A. Thesis, University of Texas, 1941.

Laster, Richard, *"Paper on Texas Appropriations"*, Non-published, November 2005.

Snow, Helen Foster, *"Major John Wyatt Moody, First Auditor of the Republic of Texas"*, Woodson Research Center, Fondren Library, Rice University.

Snow, Helen Foster, *"Captain Michael Roup Goheen", Texas Records.* Woodson Research Center, Rice University.

State of Texas, Marion County, Jefferson. A letter from County Commissioners Era Johnson, Precinct No 1, F.R. Grubbs, Precinct No. 2, Bedford Bailey, Precinct No 3, J.G. Morris, Precinct No 4, dated 3/21/1915, addressed to B. Max Mehl, Ft. Worth Texas.

Stern, Alvin, *"History of the Texas Jola's"*, Non-Published, November 2005

Tallavas, Ricardo De Leon, "Cob *Coins of Mexico's Mint C. 1572-1733*", Non-published, August 2006.

Temple Texas affidavit by Alex Diest, dated 10-26-1916

Texas State Library & Archives Commission. Letter from Archive Staff dated Jan. 23, 2007

the Author regarding findings from the Republic Navy Muster Roll database search for Charles Lewis.

Thonhoff , Robert. *People Associated with the Republican Army of the North.* Taken from *"Forgotten Battlefield of, the First Texas Revolution"* Original List compiled by Robert Thonhoff, and *"Tales From the Old Stone Fort"* by Linda Ericson Devareux. The 1815 Jose Toledo report, Translated by Robert Benavides. Additions and details added by Tom Green, 2008. Non-published.

Unknown Author, Biography, *"William G. Cooke"*, William G. Cooke File, DRT Library, San Antonio, Texas.

Unknown Author, *"The Medicine Man in Texas"*, Biographical information provided by John N. Rowe of Dallas, Texas.

AUCTION CATALOGS AND OTHER SOURCES

American Numismatic Rarities, Inc. Auction Catalogue, *The Old West and Franklin Collection*, August 11, 2006. Treasures from the American Bank Note Company.

Brochure - Spanish Governor's Palace, Presidio de Bejar / La Commandancia 1722-1772

Historical marker in front of the Tremont House Hotel, Mechanic Street, Galveston Texas. Credited to George L. Hosek.

Heritage Grand Format Auction. *Autographs, Rare Books, and Manuscripts. Oct 12 & 13, 2006.* 2006 Heritage Auctions, Inc.

Southeby's Auction Catalogue. R*emember the Alamo*, Sale date, June 18, 2004

Stack's, *The John J. Ford, Jr. Collection , Coins, Medals and Currency Part XVII*,

March 21, 2007,

Texas Historcal Marker, *Texan Capture of Mexican Dispatchers (San Jacinto)*, Bellaire Blvd at Second Street. Bellaire, Texas. Erected in 1969.

Texas Historical Marker, *Old Harrisburg*, 8100 Block of Lawndale near Broadway, Erected 1965.

The Columbia Encyclopedia, Sixth Edition. Copyright 2001-05, Columbia University Press.

The tombstone of Augustus V. Sharpe.

INDEX

Prologue

Illustrated Periodontal Microsurgery Advanced Technique-Soft tissue management for the ultimate esthetic result- is the advanced version of "Periodontal Microsurgery~Total perio dontal tissue surgery with microscope~" published in 2002.
At that point, I used to face clinical difficulties and doubt since I had just started to perform periodontal microsurgery then. I don't think that all the questions and doubt about the procedure haven't become totally clear even now. However, at the same time I strongly feel that my questions and doubt have been somewhat answered by observing 10 years great clinical success of my procedures.

In this new edition book, I tried to explain the current concept, fundamental theory and clinical procedures with detail illustrations and clinical photos for the better understanding. Also I added on my own post clinical evaluation for the each clinical cases. I hope that those will also help the readers to enhance the clinical understanding.

It has been more than 35 years has passed since my mentor Dr. Dennis Shanelec had introduced the periodontal microsurgery. Dr.Shanelec always states " It is the strong conscience for the dentist to use the microscope." The author thinks that using the microscope for the dental treatment shouldn't be the search for the most current technology, but for the method to go back to the basic. Nowadays also "Security in Dentistry" can be enhanced by using a current devices such as microscope, CT scan, piezosurgery. It is my great pleasure that my new book can become a reference as a concept of "Security in Dentistry" with periodontal microsurgery.

At the end, I would like to thank Mr. Kazutaka Sasaki, the chairman of Quintessence publishing Japan, Mr. Yasumichi Kitamine, the president of Quintessence publishing Japan, Mr. Hiroki Tada, the editor at Quintessece publishing Japan, Dr. Masao Yamazaki, my mentor, Dr. Kenji Tsuchiya, my dear friend, Dr. Masayuki Okawa, my dear friend and our clinical staff at Suzuki dental clinic.

CONTENTS

Part 2 Basic of incision, Flapping, Suturing

CONTENTS

PART 3 Clinical application : Natural teeth

Part 4 Clinical approach : Implant

PART 1

Diagnosis

1. What is the gingival esthetic?
2. Basic concept of the gingival esthetic
3. Fundamental examination

1. What is the gingival aesthetic?

Gingiva and alveolar mucosa covers alveolar bone and a couple of mm of the root that is exposed from the alveolar bone. The gingival architecture can be dictated by those hard tissue anatomy. How can the gingival aesthetic be defined?

Generally, perception of "beautiful or unappealing gingival appearance" can be defined by the condition of the gingiva, such as gingivitis, periodontitis or simply color of the gingiva.

However, the evolution of the dental aesthetic treatment makes people aware more defined gingival esthetic. Cervical 1/3 of tooth anatomy can be attributed by the gingival architecture.

Therefore, if the gingival architecture is not appealing, consequently, the ideal aesthetic restoration cannot be achieved.

The author thinks that due to those reasons, the definition of gingival aesthetic can include the meaning of "well balanced gingival architecture". Therefore the author identifies that the gingival aesthetic is the gingiva which presents healthy and well balanced cervical gingival architecture.

2. Fundamental concept of gingival aesthetic

1) Exam of the gingival architecture from the aesthetic point of view

The gingival architecture can be generally examined from the horizontal and vertical point of views. What should we pay attention during this exam? During the vertical view exam, tooth width, tooth length and papilla anatomy should be assessed. During the horizontal view exam, gingival contour should be assessed. Gingival symmetry should be assessed by the vertical and horizontal view exams. However, the author thinks it is beneficial to have simpler method of gingival architecture assessment in the everyday clinical situation. The method is explained as follows.

● Vertical gingival line (*Fig A,B*)

The balance of the vertical gingival line can be assessed by comparing the adjacent teeth's and contra-lateral tooth's scalloped gingival architecture. The scalloped gingival architecture can be determined by the location of the gingival zenith, tooth width and the tip of the papilla location. Therefore those element need to be carefully evaluated.

● Horizontal gingival line (*Fig C*)

The horizontal gingival line should be evaluated with gingival contour comparison with the adjacent teeth and contra lateral teeth. Gingival contour can be changed by the abnormal tooth position or missing tooth.

2) What is the aesthetically problematic gingival architecture?

The aesthetic gingival architecture is considered to be well balanced with teeth alignment. Then how this balance can be evaluated?

Let's say that there is a case of the maxillary left central incisor that has unbalanced gingival scallop architecture due to the gingival recession. It is important to have the criteria that will give a determination of either restoring gingival architecture or not. The dentists generally would like to restore the symmetrical gingival architecture.

Fig Z : Evaluation method of the gingival esthetic (Vertical and horizontal gingival line evaluation)

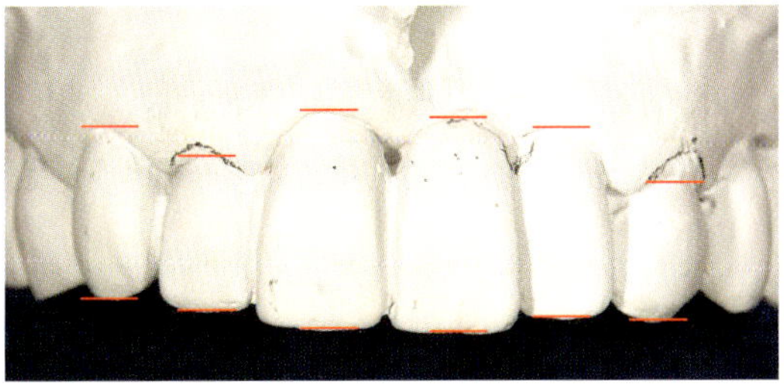

Fig A : #7, 10 and #6,11 Vertical gingival lines are not asymmetrical.

Vertical Gingival line	#6	#7	#8	#9	#10	#11
Balance with djacent teeth		X				X
Balanco with contra lateral teeth	X	X			X	X
Vertical Gingival line	**#6**	**#7**	**#8**	**#9**	**#10**	**#11**
Balance with djacent teeth				X		
Balance with contra lateral teeth				X		

Problematic areas were marked X

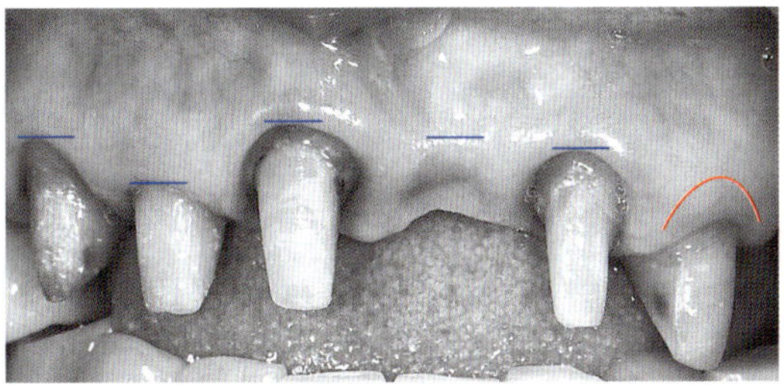

Fig B : Plan to correct the gingival gap on #7 and #11 by moving both gingival lines cervically.

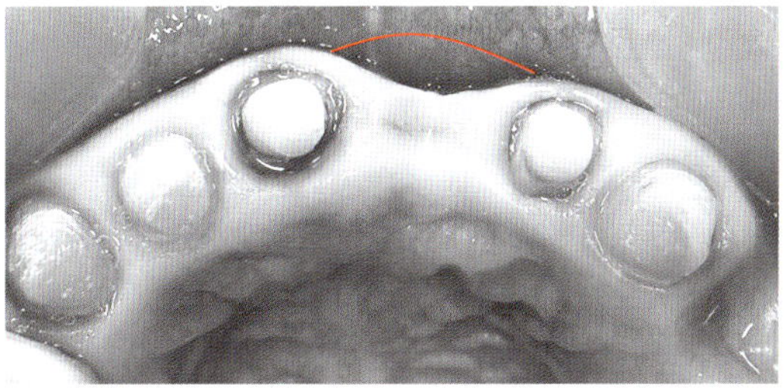

Fig C : Horizontal gingival defect on #9 is appreciated.

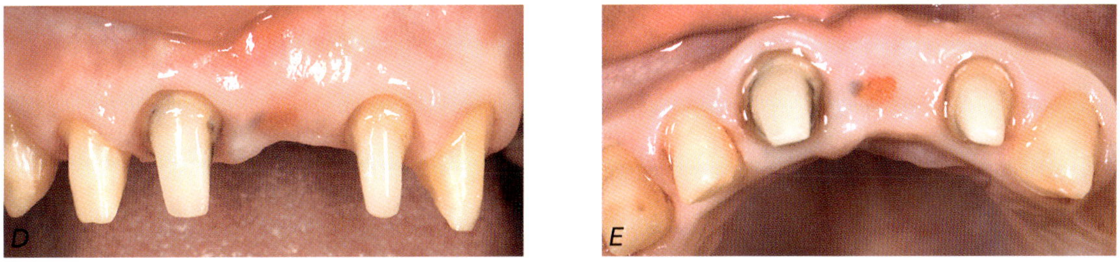

Fig D, E : Vertical gingival level has been relatively improved after the surgery. Also horizontal gingival defect has been corrected and horizontal gingival symmetry has been achieved.

As this case shows that #7,10's and #6,11's vertical gingival levels are asymmetrical and also gingival level gap with adjacent teeth are significant, it is difficult to acquire the ideal vertical gingival esthetic only by the surgery. Therefore the compromised treatment plan approach needs to be taken. The author has planned to keep gingival line discrepancy between contralateral teeth and adjacent teeth within 1.5mm. However, since the gingival line of the maxillary lateral incisor locates slightly coronally compared to the central incisor and canine, the lateral incisor's gingival line gap with the adjacent tooth can exceed 1.5mm with the exception.
This 1.5mm gap is stated from the Kokich's reference. In other words, the importance of the treatment is to acquire the esthetic gingival level that the patient wouldn't be aware. Therefore the treatment plan goal that can be set to acquire 1.5mm gingival gap is theoretically acceptable. In this clinical case, the goal of the treatment is to acquire the well balanced vertical gingival esthetic limiting 1.5mm gingival discrepancy, so the coronally advanced flap technique has been applied on #7,11. The soft tissue augmentation has been done on #9 due to the 3~4mm horizontal tissue loss. For the esthetic treatment, the tissue level control has an important role. The appropriate tissue level evaluation and diagnosis are essential to develop the treatment plan. The author believes that tissue classification and horizontal and vertical tissue evaluation is fundamental to achieve the correct diagnosis.

Reference from Dr. Kokich : The general public pay more attention on the tooth morphology than tissue morphology

Dr. Kokich sent inquiries about the dental esthetic issues to the orthodontists, the general dentists and the general public. There are 8 subjects in the inquiry in 1996 and 7 subjects in the inquiry in 2006. The author especially focused on the part of the result of this inquiries that the gingival level gap on the central incisors can be perceived by the orthodontist with 1mm gap, by the general dentist with 1.5mm gap and the general public with 2mm gap. However none of those 3 category of people didn't perceive the gingival gap with 2mm cervically on the lateral incisors. But this gingival gaps were made bilaterally. In the 2006 data, the inquiry was made by showing the gingival gap on only maxillary left central incisor. The orthodontists perceived the gingival gap when the gap is 0.5mm and the general dentist and the general public perceived the gingival gap when it is 1.5-2.0mm. Through those inquires, it is understood that the gingival gap on the central incisors is more perceptible than on the lateral incisors and also unilateral gingival gap is more perceptible than bilateral gingival gap. This perception can be also similarly applied on the papilla hight gap.

The orthodontists and the general dentists can perceive the gingival gap difference on the bilateral asymmetry but the general public perceive the gingival gap difference in the opposite way. Probably the unilateral gingival gap change appears to have more coronal tooth shape change, but the gingival gap change on only left central incisor or left lateral incisor appears not to have much coronal tooth shape change. So the general public didn't perceive much of those differences. In other words, the general public pay more attention to the tooth morphology than the gingival architecture.

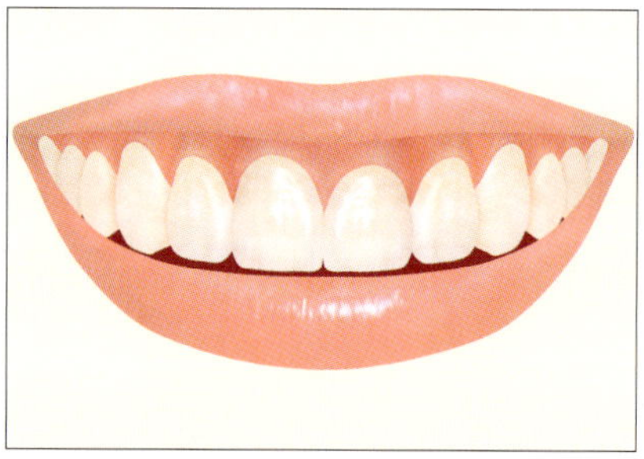

Fig F : Tooth length on #8 seems longer than #9. This can be perceived easily even by the general public.

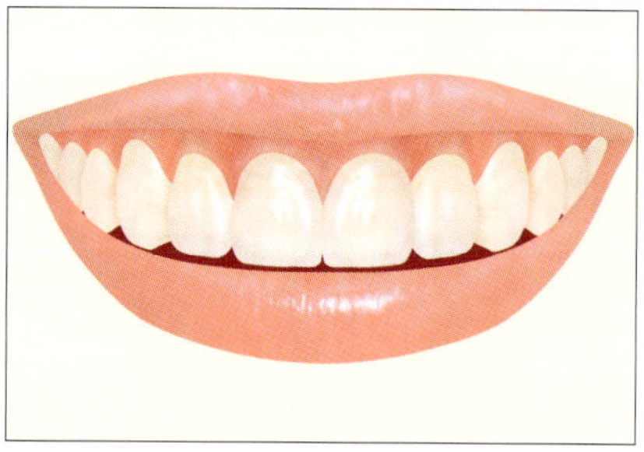

Fig G : Papilla between #9 and 10 is shorter but the general public didn't perceive the difference.

But the dentists don't know how the patient thinks. Does the patient think that a couple of mm gingival gap is unaesthetic? Kokich , reported that the patient wouldn't 1 2 notice 1.5mm gingival gap. (*Fig F, G*)

3) Evaluation of the resorbed alveolar ridge

Generally, the evaluation of the resorbed alveolar ridge can be done by the inverse calculation.

In other words, it should be evaluated by depending on the future treatment such as either implants, bridge or RPD. Of course this evaluation is considered to be the esthetic gingival morphology evaluation, so this evaluation should be for the treatment of either implants or bridge.

The alveolar ridge evaluation has been established by Seibert who 3 evaluates horizontal resorption type, vertical resorption type and horizontal & vertical (mixed type) type. Afterwards, Wang4 and et al established the evaluation method by the resorption quantity. However the measurement method was unclear and the clinical application of those evaluation methods hasn't been clear.

Now the author established the evaluation method of the resorbed alveolar ridge and the method of clinical application as follows. (*Table 1, Fig H, I*)

Classification of the augmentation methods depending on the shape of the alveolar ridge (Suzuki classification)

There are several reports of the classification of the edentulous alveolar ridge, but those tend to just describe the simple edentulous alveolar ridge shapes. It seems that those are not good reference to the clinicians. The goal of the dental treatment should focus on both function and esthetic and it is important to give a comparison between the fixed bridge treatment and implants treatment for the edentulous alveolar ridge restoration. The prosthetic requirements and esthetic requirements of the implants treatment should be fulfilled in order for the implants treatment to provide physiologically acceptable function to the patients.

Recently, the dental implant treatment becomes one of the most important treatment options and it has been applied to the difficult cases. On the other hand, there are a lot of reported implants cases that couldn't fulfill functions and esthetic even though those are not so complicated cases. Those failures are primarily caused by the clinician's inability but partially the reason for those failures can be that there is no appropriate clinical implant treatment guidelines available.

Therefore, the author would like to present the classification of the augmentation methods depending on the shape of the alveolar ridge on Table 1. This classification can be applied to the fixed bridge cases.[5]

Table 1 : The classification of the augmentation methods depending on the shape of the alveolar ridge

	convex(1)	level(2)	concave(3)
hill(a)	no augmentation(1a)	no augmentation or hard tissue(2a)	soft tissue or hard tissue or soft & hard tissues(3a)
level(b)	no augmentation or soft tissue(1b)	soft tissue or soft & hard tissues(2b)	soft tissue or soft & hard tissues(3b)
valley(c)	soft & hard tissues(1c)	soft tissue or soft & hard tissues(2c)	soft & hard tissues(3c)

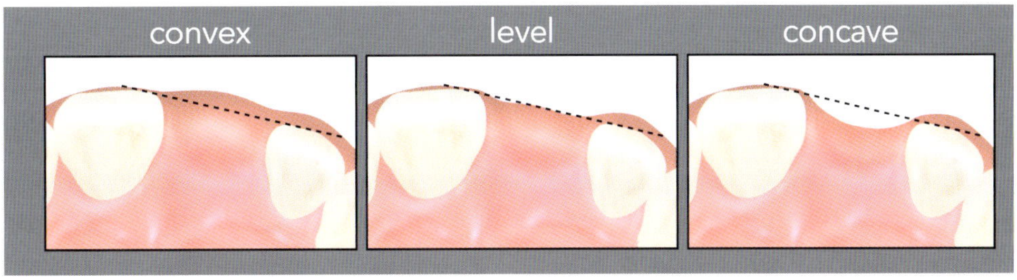

Fig H : horizontal classification

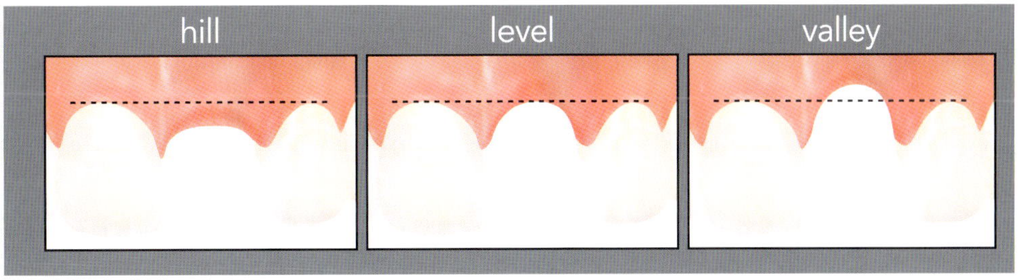

Fig I : vertical classification

Clinical cases : Cases were treated by using Suzuki's classification

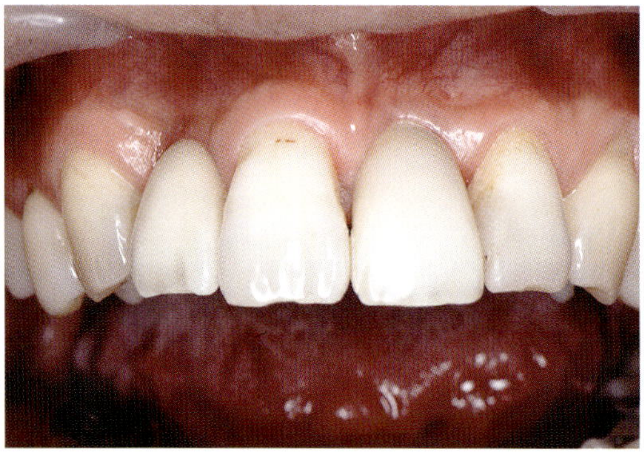

Fig J : #7,9 received implants already and custom abutments and provisional restorations have been inserted.

Vertical Gingival line	#6	#7	#8	#9	#10	#11
Balance with djacent teeth		X				
Balance with contra lateral teeth		X				
Vertical Gingival line	**#6**	**#7**	**#8**	**#9**	**#10**	**#11**
Balance with djacent teeth		X		X		
Balance with contra lateral teeth		X		X		

Problematic areas were marked X

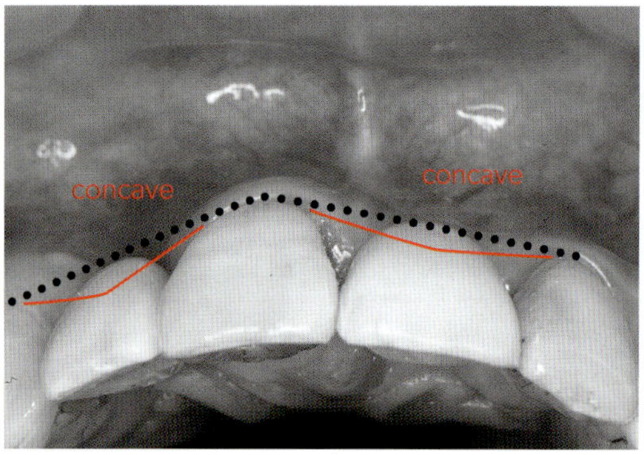

Fig K : Horizontal gingival level on #7 and 9 is located palatally from the reference line (level).
This is concave type.

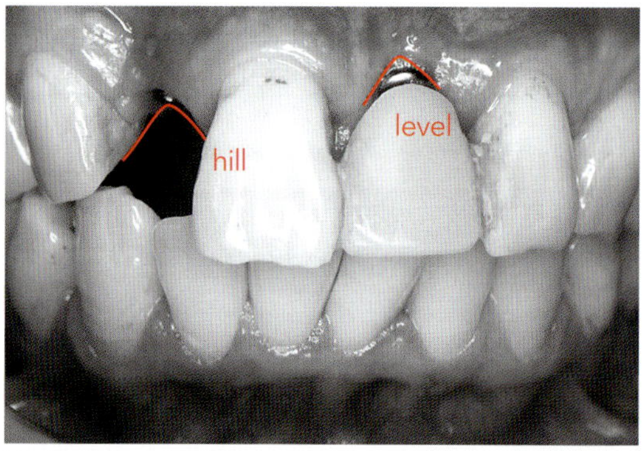

Fig L : #7 vertical gingival line is hill type and #9 vertical gingival line is hill or level type.
Therefore, #7 is concave-hill type and #9 is concave-hill type.

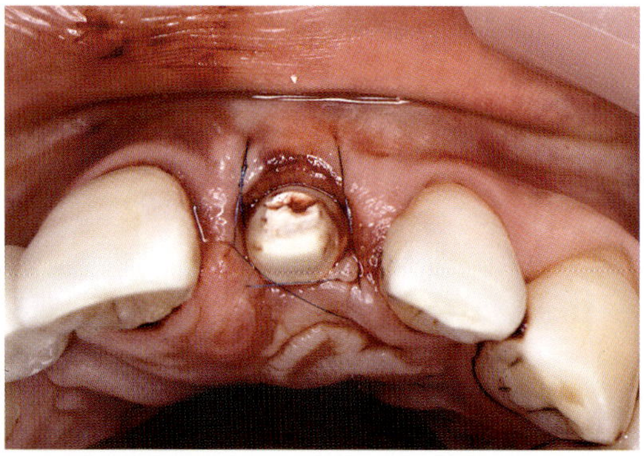

Fig M : Connective tissue augmentation has been performed on #9.

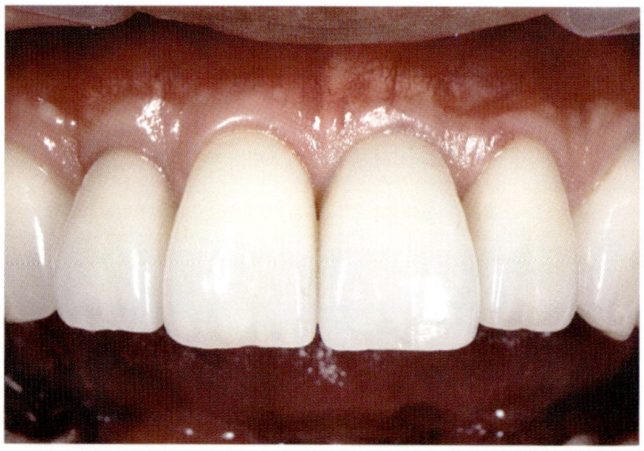

Fig N : Final restorations after #7,9 connective tissue augmentation.

3. Fundamental examination

1) Examination for soft tissue augmentation

The examination for the surgical periodontal treatment requires more details and localized examination along with the generally required fundamental examination for the periodontal treatment. This is not what needs to be explained into details in this book, however the important points that the author wants to emphasize will be discussed as follows.

The purpose of the soft tissue augmentation is to improve the gingival level balance. It isimportant to understand the patient's demand on this part of the treatment. The treatment plan needs to be developed according to this patient's demand. The procedures need to be selected according to this treatment plan, then this examination will dictate if those procedures can be performed or not.

The importance of the examination elements would be varied depending on the procedures, but items on Table 2 are necessary.

Initially, the entire gingival level condition needs to be evaluated. Then the unbalanced areas such as gingival recession areas and edentulous areas need to be identified. Also the condition of teeth and surrounding tissue such as the condition of adjacent teeth, probing depth, bone level and the condition of bone and gingiva of the edentulous area need to be well evaluated.

The most difficult condition to be identified is the tissue biotype. Generally the biotype is classified in thin-scallop type and thick-flat type but it is very difficult to comprehend. The author thinks that this is only categorized by the clinician's clinical judgement with the experience.

Those two types seem to be categorized simply by the thickness of the tissue, however we have to understand why this classification is important.

Table 2 : Examination items for soft tissue augmentation

- Balance of the gingival level
  - Horizontal
  - Vertical
- Focused examination
- X-ray examination
- Evaluation of occlusion
- Teeth - Teeth alignment examination
- Probing depth
- Mobility evaluation
- Evaluation of size of the edentulous area
- Evaluation of gingival biotype

The gingival thickness is determined by the amount of collagen fibers. The collagen fiber matrix encompass blood vessels and nerves. Since there are a lot of bold vessels, the gingiva is considered to have high immunity. Therefore, the thin gingiva is considered to have less immunity so it is not suitable for the periodontal surgery. It is important to identify the gingival biotype for this reason.

The treatment plan needs to be developed by assessing the condition of the surgical area. The insufficient evaluation and examination can cause unforeseen trouble during the surgery. The through examination is the key for success.

2) Image development for the surgical procedure (*Fig O~Q*)

The periodontal plastic surgery for the esthetic dental restoration cannot be successful unless the final restoration's image is clear. In other words, the surgeon needs to understand the appropriate final restoration for the patient. Also the prosthodontist needs to understand the surgery part of the treat-

3 important elements for the image development for the surgical procedure

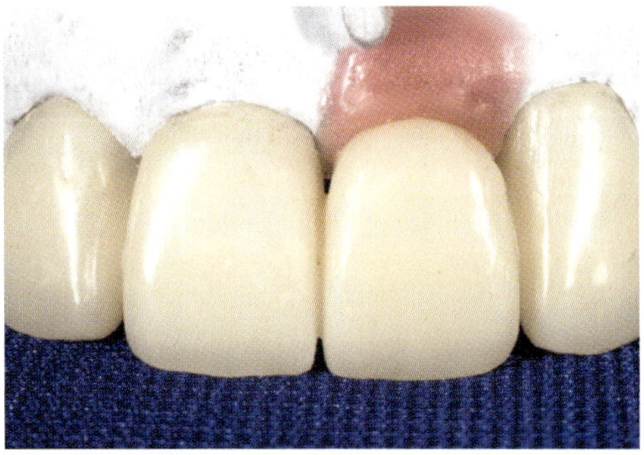

Fig O : Waxed up

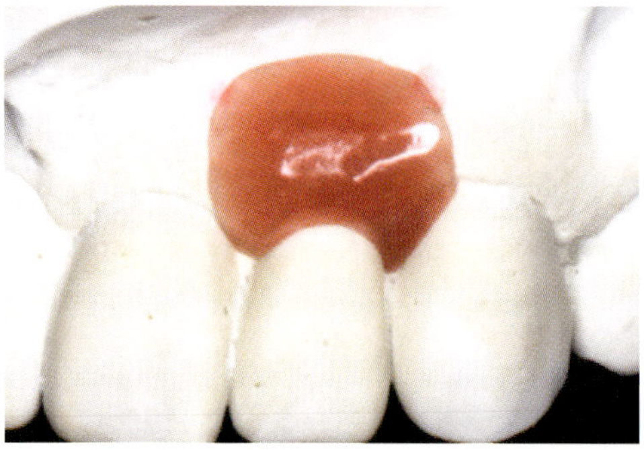

Fig P : Resin replacement from the waxed up

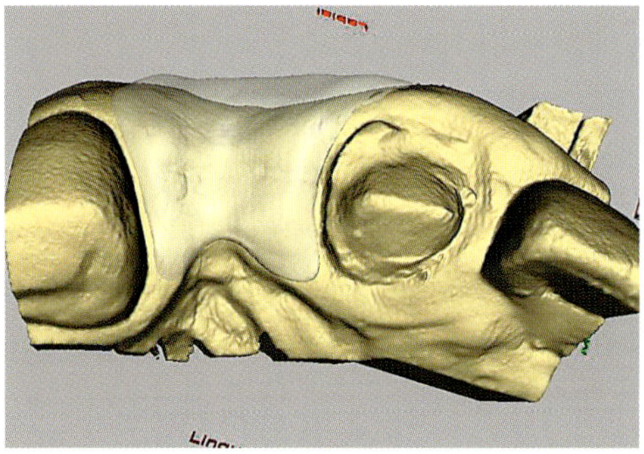

Fig Q : Image from the 3D simulation software

ment and surgical outcome. This is so called "The interdisciplinary treatment approach." The author believes that the appropriate gingival esthetic treatment or soft tissue augmentation cannot be achieved without this interdisciplinary treatment approach.

Pre-operatively the surgeon and prosthodontist should discuss the goal of the surgical and prosthetic treatment. Then the patient's treatment consent should be acquired by showing waxed up model. Usually the prosthodontist uses this waxed up model for the prosthetic treatment, but the conventional waxed up model doesn't include surgical part of the treatment outcome. The waxed up model that the author expresses is the work to verify the final treatment after the through examination. Initially waxed up should be done to the surgical area, then waxed up of the prosthesis follows. After the evaluating waxed up model and finalizing the treatment plan, the surgical treatment plan sequence should be reviewed. If waxed up can be replaced with resin, the actual tissue augmentation amount can be measured.

The author uses 3D simulation software in order to comprehend the detail of the treatment on the computer.

1. Waxed up
2. Resin replacement from the waxed up
3. 3D simulation software

PART 2

Basic of incision, Flapping, Suturing

Fundamental principal of periodontal microsurgery

1. Incision basic
2. Flapping basic
3. Tissue reflection to harvest the connective tissue
4. Suturing basic
5. Basic technique of geometric suture with the enlarged figures

Fundamental principal of periodontal microsurgery

Generally the periodontal microsurgery is the periodontal surgery performed under the microscope. There are 2 purposes of using a microscope.[6 7 8 9 10 11 12] One is to support deteriorating eyesight and the other is to obtain more details of operating area. This book explains the second purpose. The periodontal micro surgery is to achieve the faster procedure, esthetic and predictable outcome by obtaining more detail view with the microscope.[13 14 15 16 17 18 19 20 21 22] Therefore, the different technique and procedure from the conventional periodontal surgery should be developed.

From now, the author explains the fundamental periodontal microsurgery technique by modifying the conventional periodontal surgery technique.

1. Incision Basic

There are 2 elements of incision procedure. One element is the method of primary incision and movement of the scalpel. Other element is the design of the incision. Those are the very important elements that will determine the success of the surgery.

Prior to the surgery, the first thing that needs to be considered is the purpose of the surgery.

Then the incision design must be developed. This needs to be determined by the surgeon who understands the procedure theory.

1) Vertical incision and oblique incision

Generally, the method of incision is classified into the vertical incision and the oblique incision by the scalpel angle towards to the tissue. Basically, the incision should be placed perpendicular to the tissue since this incision needs to be accurately sutured at the end of the procedure. The flap produced by the 90 degree incision can be sutured simply by joining both flaps' butt joint.

But on the other hand, the flap produced by the oblique incision can be very thin, fragile and easily becomes necrotic. Also it is very difficult to suture those flaps back together since the flap's split joint characteristic makes those to be unstable during the suturing procedure.

When the operator predicts the difficulty to reconnect the flaps together for suturing, the oblique incision can be selected as a safety measure since this type incision makes easier for the operator to reconnect those flaps together for incision. The oblique incision can provide more connecting surfaces between flaps; therefore, suturing failure can be easily prevented.

Fundamental principal of Incision, Flap, Suturing

1. Simple incision, suturing

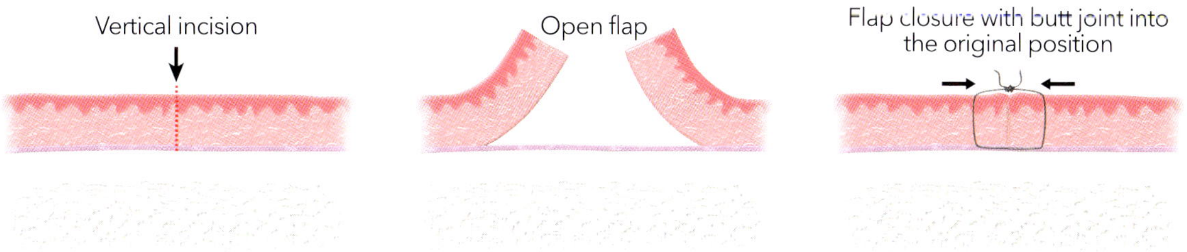

Fig A : This is the most basic incision and flap. Secure flap closure with suturing.

2. Suturing after complicated procedure

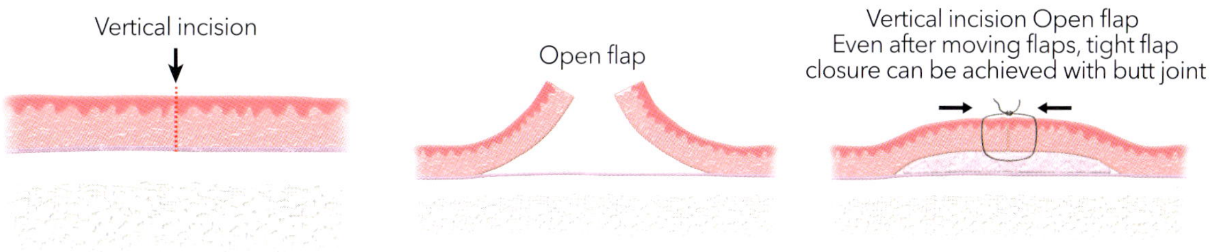

Fig B : Even after connective tissue augmentation or bone augmentation, tight flap suturing closure can be achieved with butt joint.

3. Flaps cannot completely cover the surgical area.

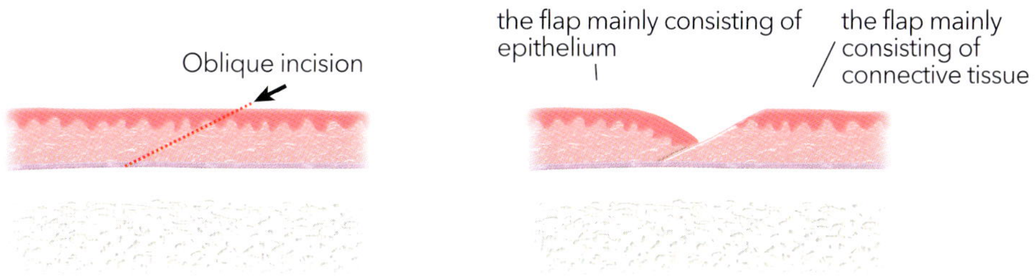

Fig C : This kind of incision can be designed if the flaps can be closed without exposing bone or periosteum even though flaps cannot be placed back to the original position. This incision is made with the flap mainly consisting of the epithelium and the flap mainly consisting of the connective tissue. The flap mainly consisting of the connective tissue is supposed to heal well. But the flap mainly consisting with the epithelium can be easily lost afterwards. The area of papilla or inter-implants considered to be weak for surgical procedures, therefore the post suturing unsatisfactory result may happen. So for those areas, the oblique incision is applied and most papilla tissue tries to be preserved on the palatal position.

Clinical approach for the case that the flap cannot completely cover the surgical site

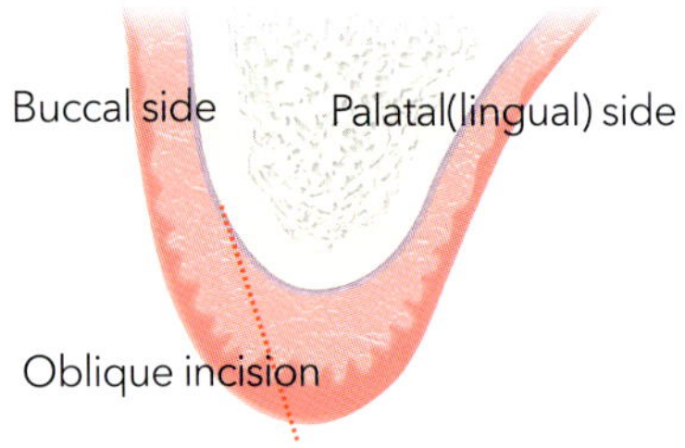

Fig D : Buccal flap is thinly created by placing the oblique incision. Palatal flap becomes quite thick and strong. Therefore, even suturing cannot be completed quite successfully, papilla wouldn't be lost. The author performs this technique quite often for the implant second surgery.

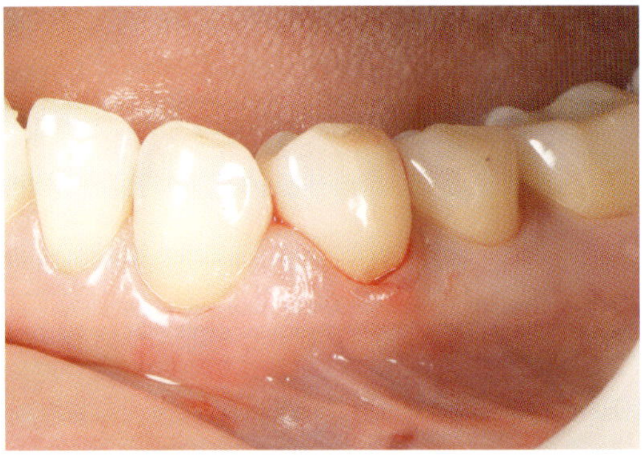

Fig E : Pre-ope picture. #22 has 6mm periodontal pocket.

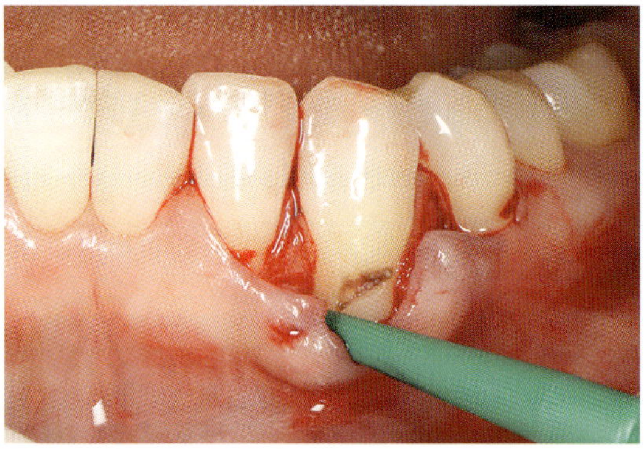

Fig F : After opening the flap. Entire papilla can be appreciated.

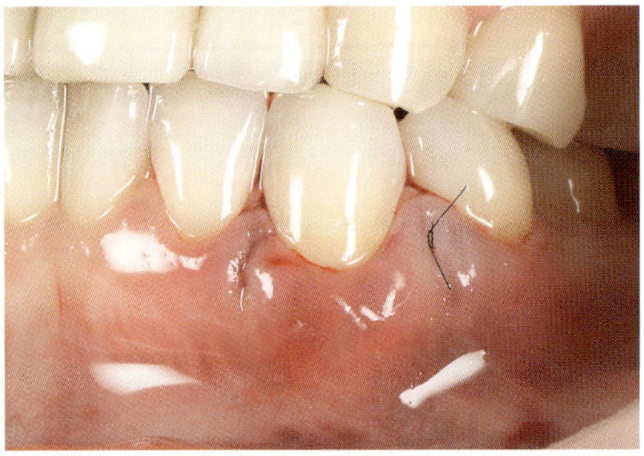

Fig G : Vertical sling mattress suture method was performed.

The open flap technique was performed on #22. The thin buccal papilla incision should be the oblique incision for the esthetic case like this. This type of incision allow papilla to be well preserved.

The important factors to be considered for the incision design.

- **Aquire good surgical site**
- **Blood supply**
- **Possibility of suturing**
- **Safety of suturing**
- **Post-operative esthetic outcome**

2. Flapping basic

Gingival flap can be largely classified into the full thickness flap that encompasses periosteum and the partial thickness flap that doesn't encompass periosteum. The technique should be selected depending on the purpose of the procedure. Usually the full thickness flap should be preformed when the bone procedure is required. The partial thickness flap should be performed for the soft tissue procedure. So the full thickness flap procedure will not be discussed in this book.

1) Partial thickness flap (*Fig H*)

Generally the partial thickness flap should be performed when soft tissue procedure is needed. Especially for the connective tissue augmentation procedure, the partial thickness flap needs to be performed on both donor and recipient sites. The reason is that the full thickness flap doesn't give appropriate healing process after the augmentation procedure.

Healing process after the augmentation procedure

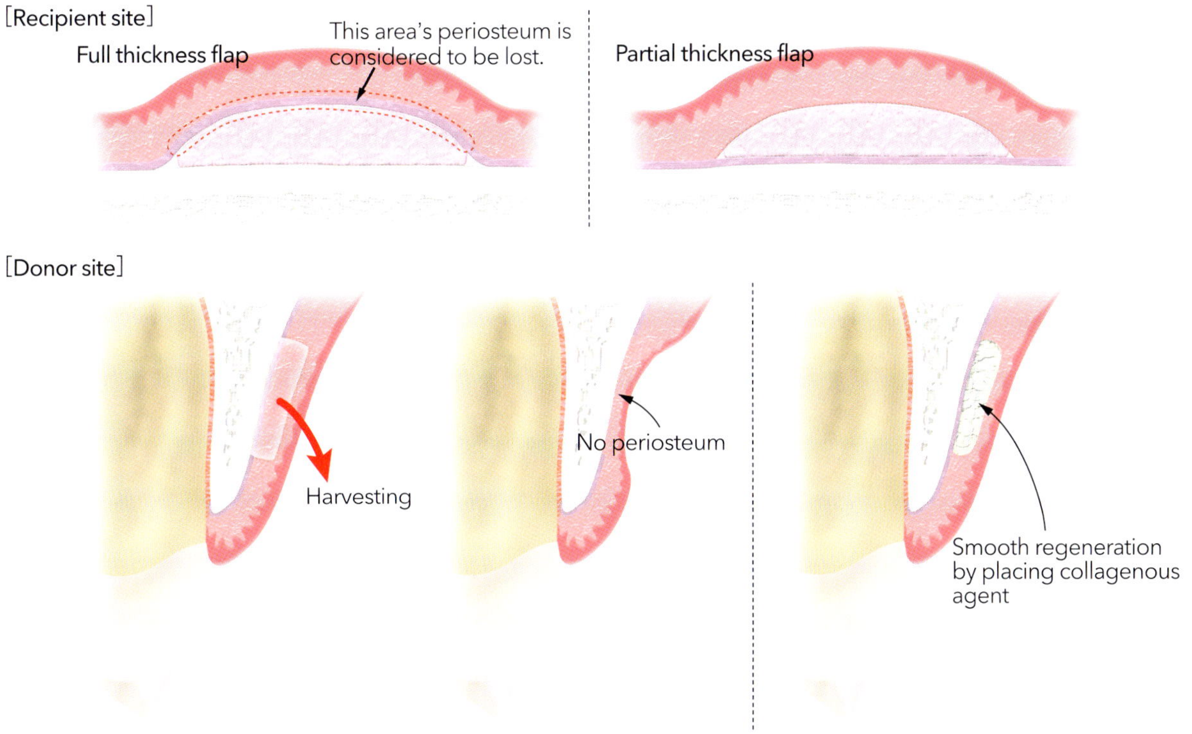

Fig H : If the connective tissue harvested from the palate is augmented under the full thickness flap, it is unknown that new periosteum is created on top of the bone surface. And the periosteum located on top of the harvested connective tissue is supposed be resorbed since it has nowhere to go. Probably, this kind of physiologically unstable the surgical site condition wouldn't heal smoothly and it will take a long time for the tissue to become stable condition. On the other hand, the harvested connective tissue placed on the periosteum after the partial thickness flap was opened, it is supposed to heal smoothly since the connective tissue is placed in the same physiological condition as before.

2) Partial thickness flap technique

(1) Open flap procedure (*Fig I~K*)

One of the most frequently performed periodontal surgical procedures should be the open flap procedure. Generally it is performed with the thin tip #15C scalpel but in periodontal micro surgery procedure, careful crevicular incision and papilla incisions are placed with a micro blade and a micro blade should be proceeded on top pf the periosteum carefully. Sometimes in general surgery, the scissors can be used to open flaps. But the author only uses the scissors for tissue trimming during the periodontal micro surgery, especially during open flap procedure hose are used for tissue trimming inside of the flap or alveolar ridge tissue trimming.

The important points for open flap procedure

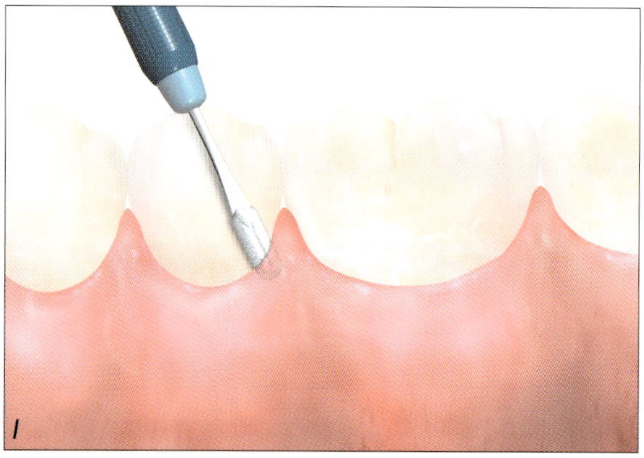

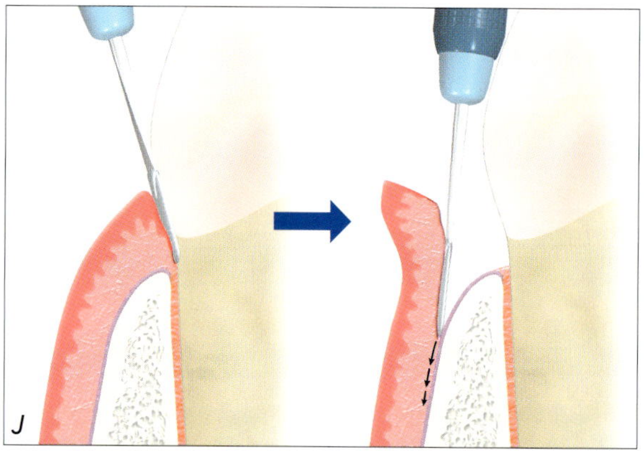

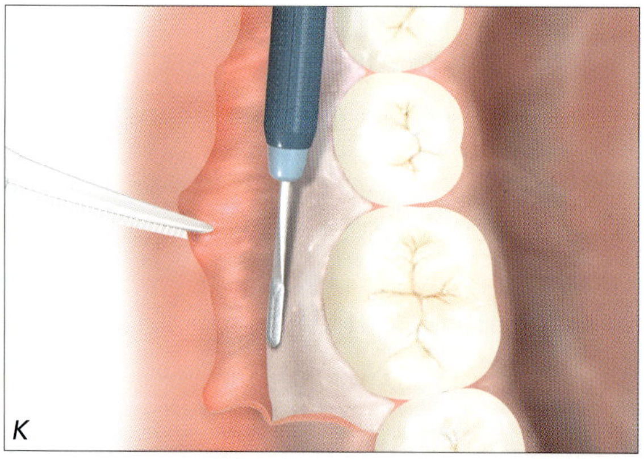

Fig I~K : Careful approach from the alveolar crest. Once the micro blade touches the bone, tissue needs to be lifted by the micro blade proceeding along the bone surface with the light touch. The flap needs to be created with minimum invasive manner by moving the micro blade carefully in one direction. After sufficient flap has been prepared, Inner tissue of the flap should be trimmed.

(2) Envelop flap creation (*Fig L~O*)

The envelop flap is a partial thickness flap as same as the open flap. Since the envelop flap creation is a quite technique sensitive procedure, it is quite suitable to the periodontal micro surgery.

The envelop flap is released with a linear fashion at the gingival margin but has no vertical incisions. Since the approaching direction is restricted, there is a disadvantage for the flap to be easily damaged. However the flap is not completely reflected , so the suturing becomes easy.

This technique is quite stable as part of the augmentation procedure.

The important points for the envelop flap creation

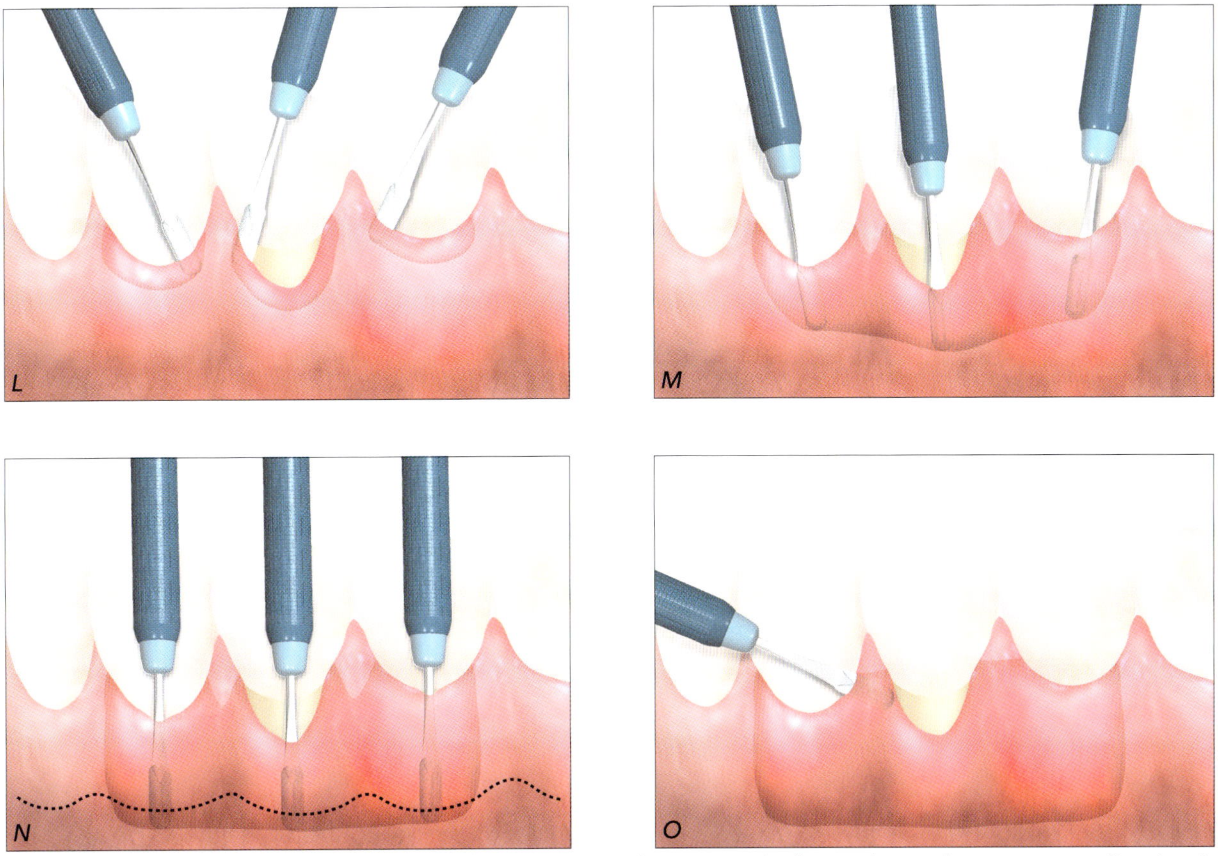

Fig L~O : The micro blade is slowly inserted from the gingival margin and advanced towards to root apex direction. It reaches to the alveolar crest shortly, but the tissue needs to be reflected carefully along the bone contour. There can be an occasional bone eminence on the alveolar crest, the micro blade should be advanced horizontally. Vertical advancement of the micro blade may cause the tissue perforation so the close attention needs to be paid. The tissue reflection on the papilla area should be done with the extra caution. This is the only area that the micro blade should be advanced coronally. If the micro blade slips, the papilla can be cut and it may become open flap. It is essential for the clinician to pay extra close attention not to slip the micro blade and advance it with fine movement.

3. Tissue reflection to harvest the connective tissue

Generally, the connective tissue is harvested from the palatal mucosa. Harvesting enough thickness and size of connective tissue from the other area can be possible, but in this section the method of harvesting the connective tissue from the palatal mucosa will be explained.

1) Harvesting the connective tissue with the epithelium

The connective tissue with epithelium is used for the reconstruction of the keratinized gingiva.

Generally, the epithelium of palatal mucosa layer is thicker than that of buccal mucosa, therefore it can reconstruct the stronger keratinized tissue on the buccal surface.

However there is significant color difference between the palatal keratinized tissue and the buccal keratinized tissue. So the application of the palatal keratinized tissue for the esthetic anterior teeth area should be avoided.

The important points for harvesting the connective tissue with the epithelium

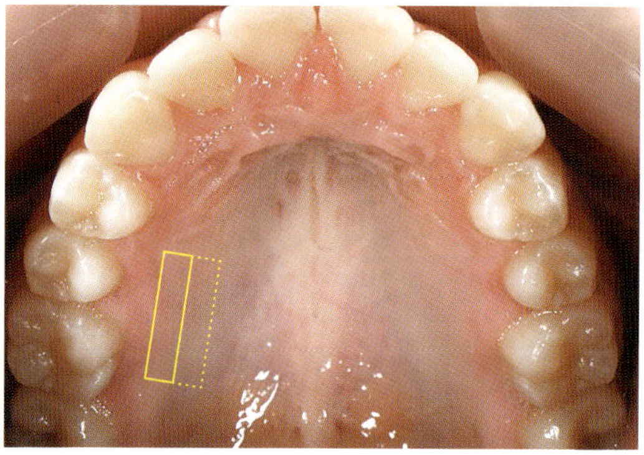

Fig P-1 : Generally the connective tissue is harvested from the palatal area of canine to the second molar.

Horizontal incision is performed on 4mm away from the gingival margin area where there is good underlining alveolar bone.(1) The second incision is performed in the 1.5mm depth parallel to the initial incision with the width of the epithelium tissue that needs to be preserved.(2) The third incision is performed by maintaining the equal thickness.(3) Then the forth incision is performed either parallel to the third incision or along with the alveolar bone.(4) Finally, the fifth incision that connects the third and forth incision is performed vertically and horizontally to acquire the connective tissue.(5)

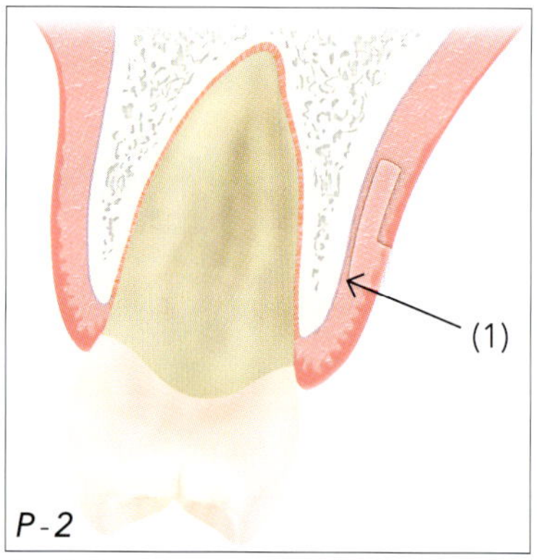

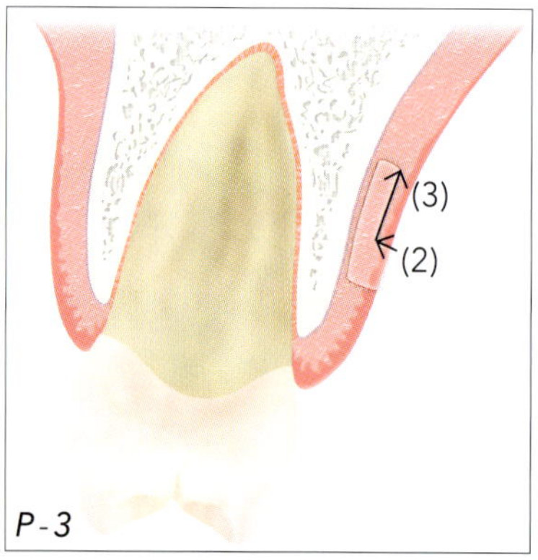

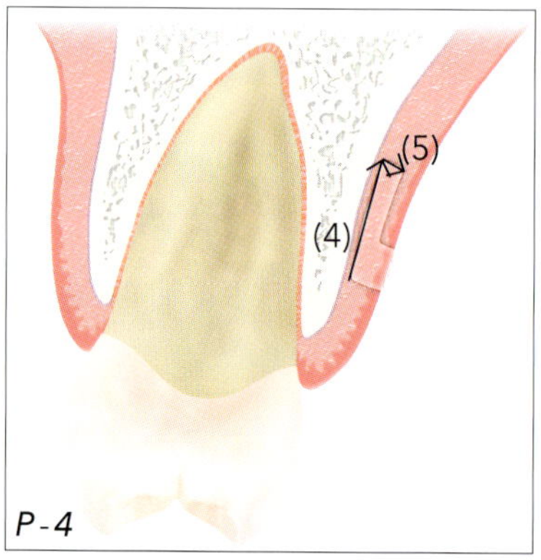

Fig P-2~4 : Harvesting the connective tissue partially including the epithelium.

2) Harvesting the connective tissue without the epithelium

For the esthetic area, the connective tissue without the epithelium can usually be harvested.

However harvesting the connective tissue without the epithelium can be more difficult than harvesting the connective tissue with the epithelium. When only the connective tissue is harvested, the epithelium is left on the palate, since it is quite difficult to remove only epithelium from the harvested connective tissue with epithelium.

The important points for harvesting the connective tissue without the epithelium

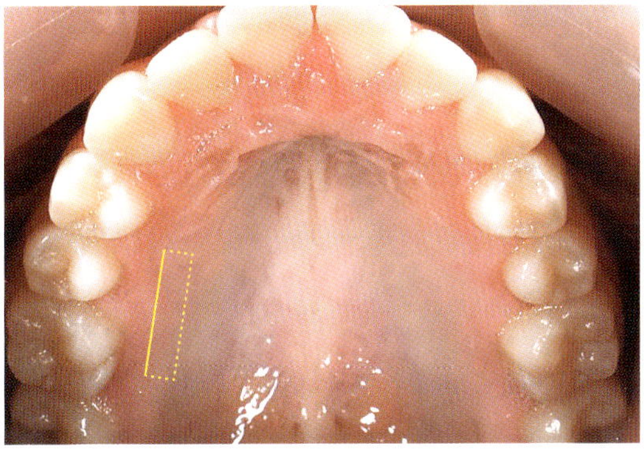

Fig Q-1 : The connective tissue alone is harvested with the single horizontal incision.

Horizontal incision with the right angle to the gingival surface is performed on 4mm away from the gingival margin area where there is good underlining alveolar bone.(1) The second incision is performed by keeping 1.5mm tissue thickness and horizontal to the gingival surface.(2) The third incision is performed with parallel to the second incision or along to the alveolar bone surface by considering the appropriate tissue thickness. Since Japanese patient's palatal tissue is extremely thin, the incision usually performed along to the alveolar bone surface.(3) Finally, the forth incision that connects the second and third incision is performed vertically and horizontally to acquire the connective tissue.(5)

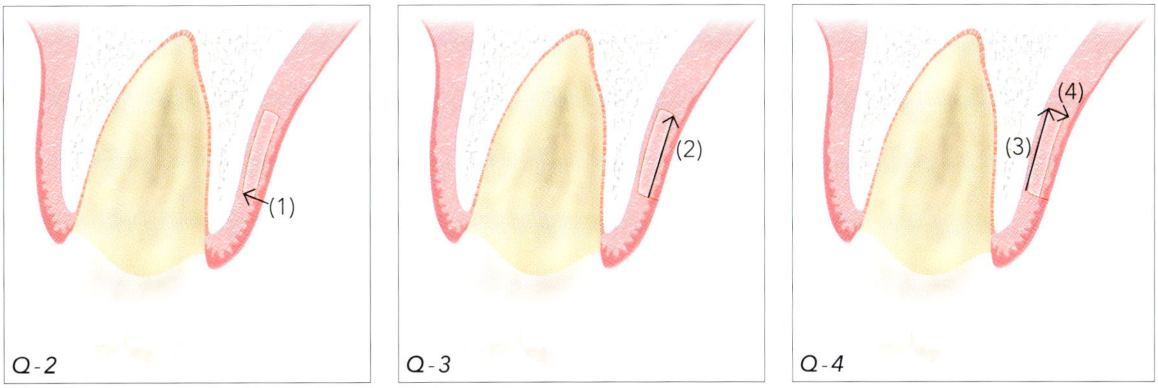

Fig Q-2~4 : The incisions for the harvesting the connective tissue without the epithelium.

4. Basics of suturing

Suturing has purposes of closing flaps and securing and fixation of flaps. Accurate and precise suturing technique is required to achieve successful surgical procedure. A lot of factors needs to be taken into consideration for suturing, such as selection of suture, needle and needle forceps, the technique of holding a needle, the method of using needle forceps and tissue forceps, suturing techniques and methods of knot tying. There are so many methods, so in this section those methods only for periodontal micro surgery will be briefly explained.

1) Suturing technique and methods of knot tying.

Suturing technique shouldn't be different from that of the regular periodontal surgery. There are different kind of suturing techniques such as simple suturing, mattress suturing, continuous suturing, sling suturing and so on. These technique should be selected according to the purpose of the treatment. In this section, detail of the suturing technique will not be explained, but clinical suturing technique will be introduced after Part 3.

Knot tying should be basically so called "surgical knot". Knot tying should be securely tightened and not to have slippage. Occasionally too tight knot tying can be appreciated. If knot tying is too tight, tissue ischemia can happen. This can interfere the tissue healing. Under the magnified view, extremely tight knot tying can be appreciated well, so adjustment of knot tying can be done easily. However since knot tying should be secure and no slipping, knot tying can easily becomes too tight. Therefore the author usually uses the geometric suture recommended by Dr. Shanelec.

Geometric suture

Generally, knot tying should be quite tight as represented by the surgical knot. Under the magnified view during the micro surgery, the process of the knot tying can be closely appreciated very well. The tension between sutured flaps can be carefully appreciated. If the suture is pulled too much, two flaps are bound too close together so tissue ischemia can occur. However under the magnified view, the right amount of force to pull suture can be applied by looking closely during the knot tying. the appropriate force is applied to the suture to bind flaps together then knot tying should be completed under the magnified view.

The author called this technique "geometric suture" that is done by adjusting the suture tension under the magnified view. This technique should be performed with nylon or monofilament suture that has high elasticity.

5. Basic technique of geometric suture under magnified view

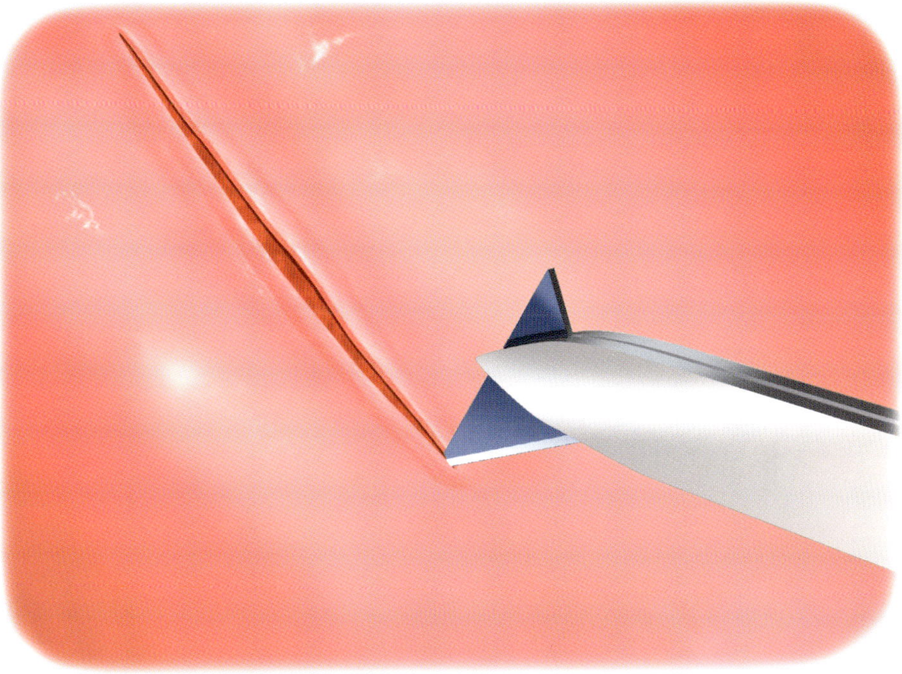

Fig a : Sharp vertical incision is applied on the mucosa

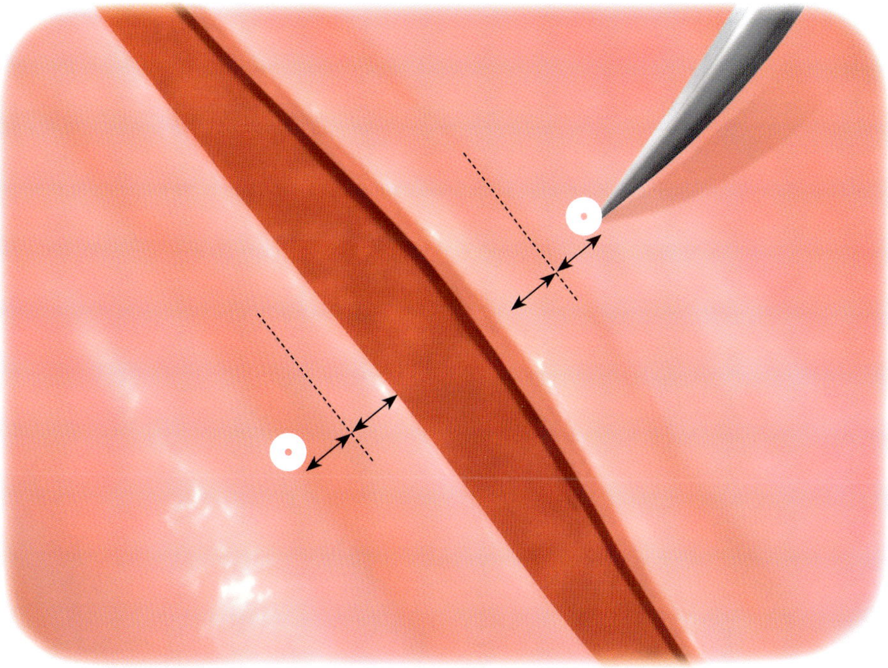

Fig b : Needle placing point should be twice diameter of the needle from the incision so same length should be maintained between incision to each needle penetration point.

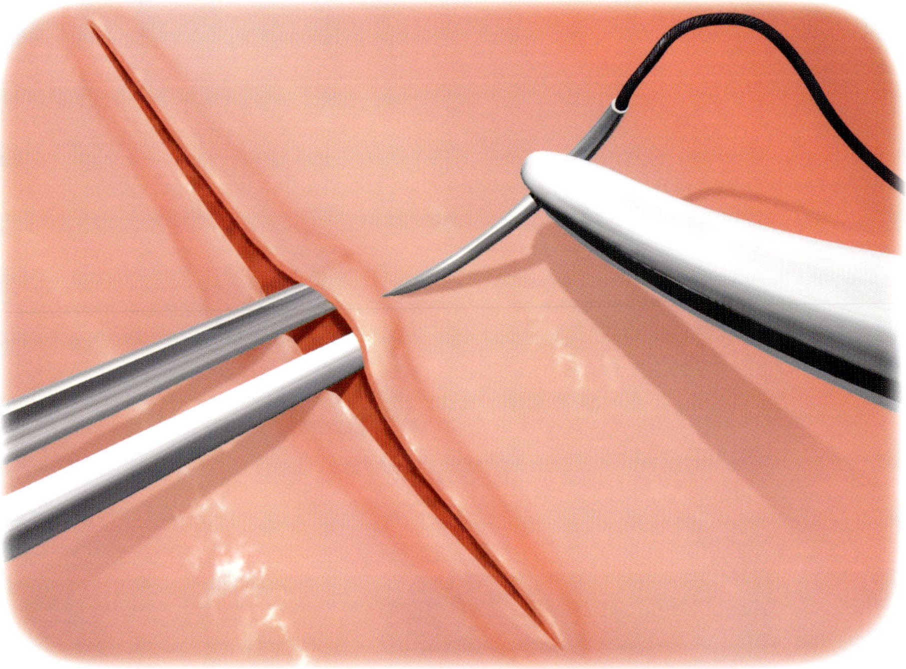

Fig c : Tying forceps is inserted under the flap to support the needle penetration for more accuracy.

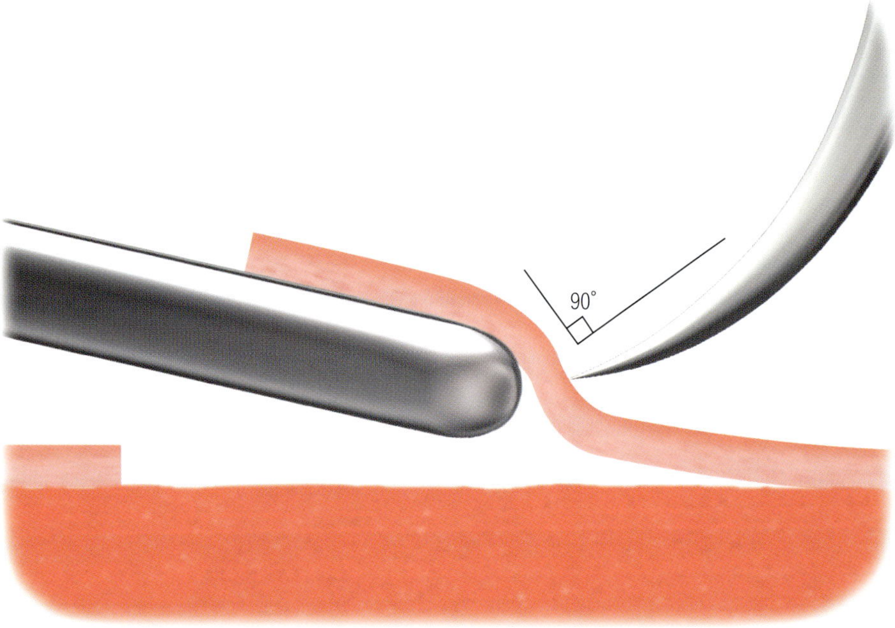

Fig d : The fundamental rule of needle penetration is perpendicular to the tissue surface.

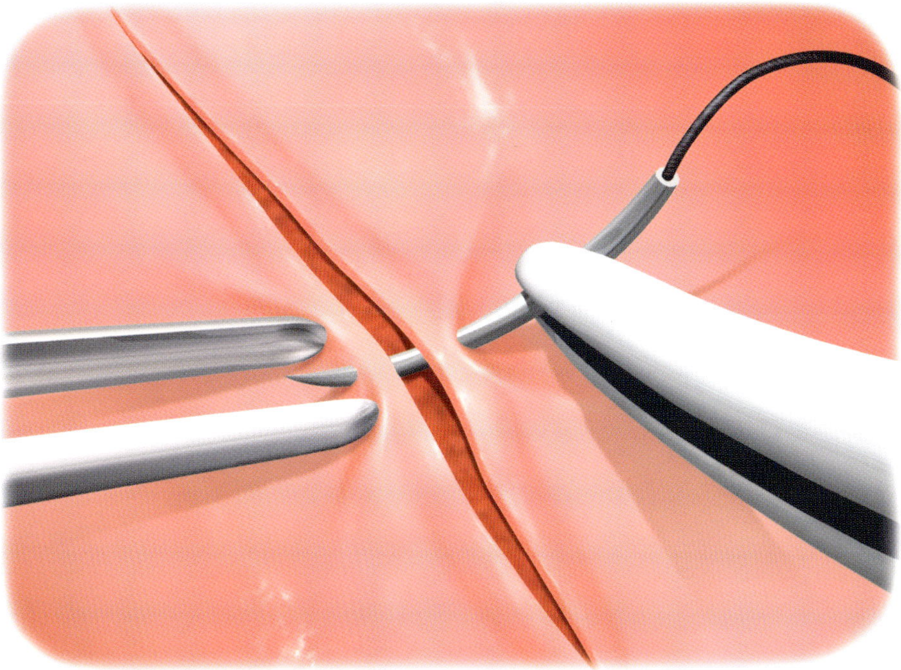

Fig e : When the needle is penetrated the tissue, the tying forceps should be placed lightly on the tissue to guide the needle direction.

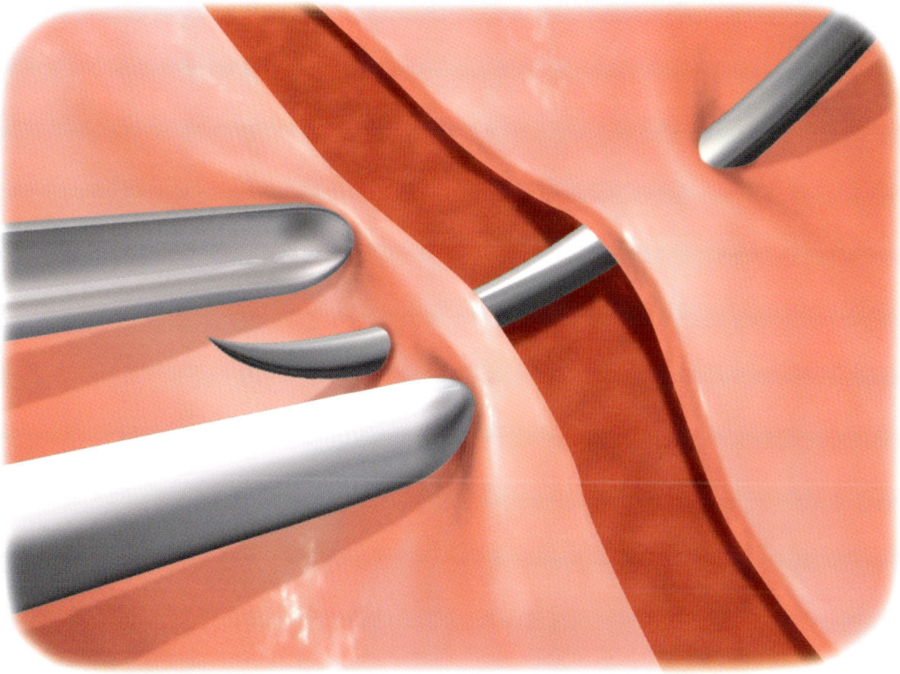

Fig f : The magnified view of *Fig e*. The needle penetration point is located between the peak of the tying forceps.

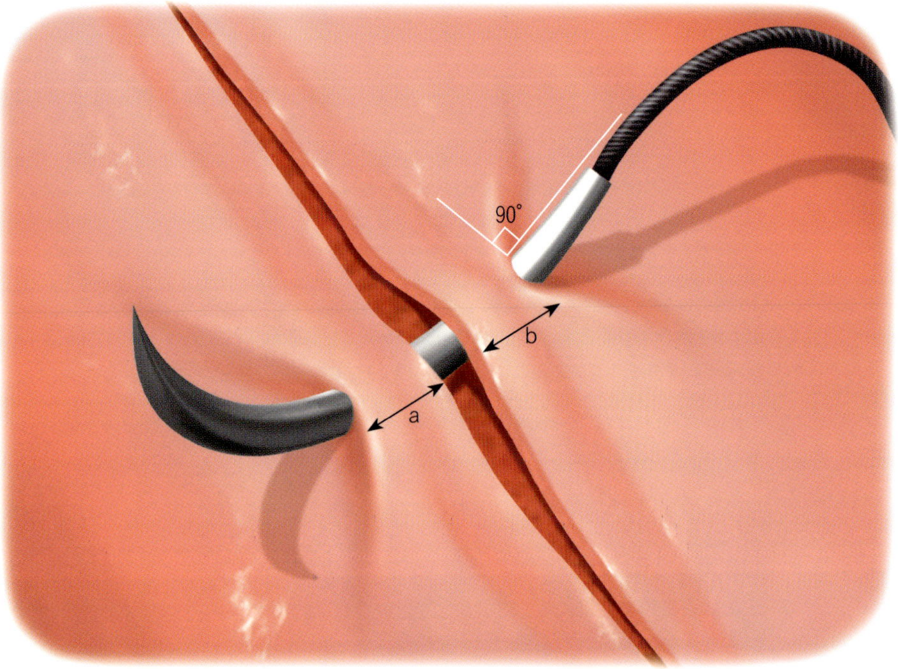

Fig g : The distances between needle penetration points and incision are equal.(a=b) The needle should be out once the needle position is confirmed.

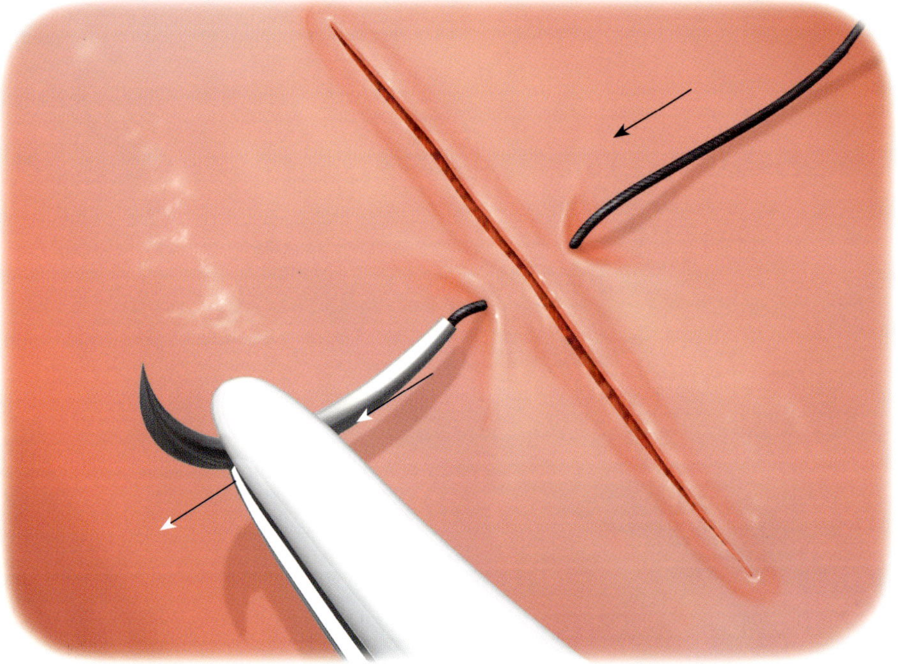

Fig h : When the needle is out and the suture is pulled, the suture pulling direction should be paid an extra attention not to apply too much tension on the flaps.

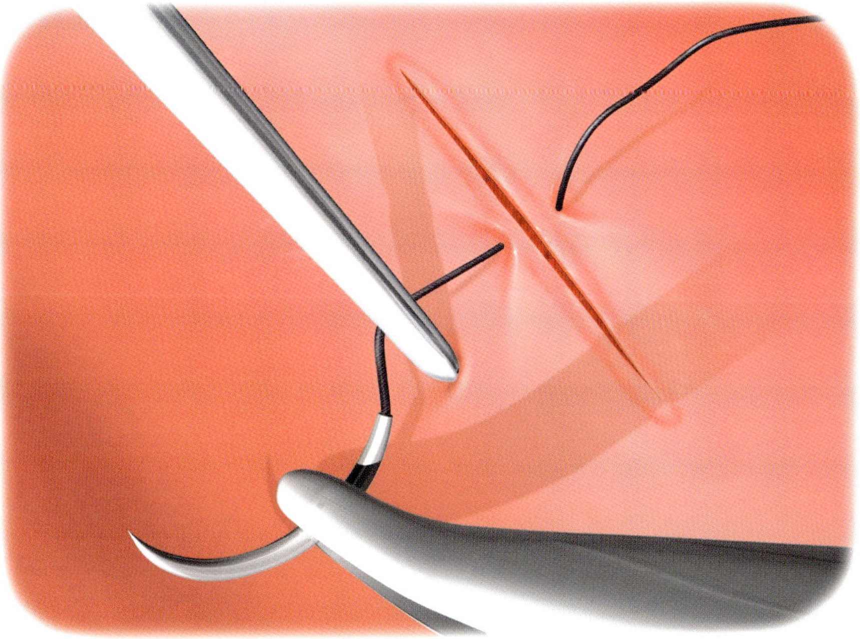

Fig i : The flap should be supported with the tying forceps while the needle and suture are pulled out of the tissue in order not to damage or dislocate the flaps during the procedure.

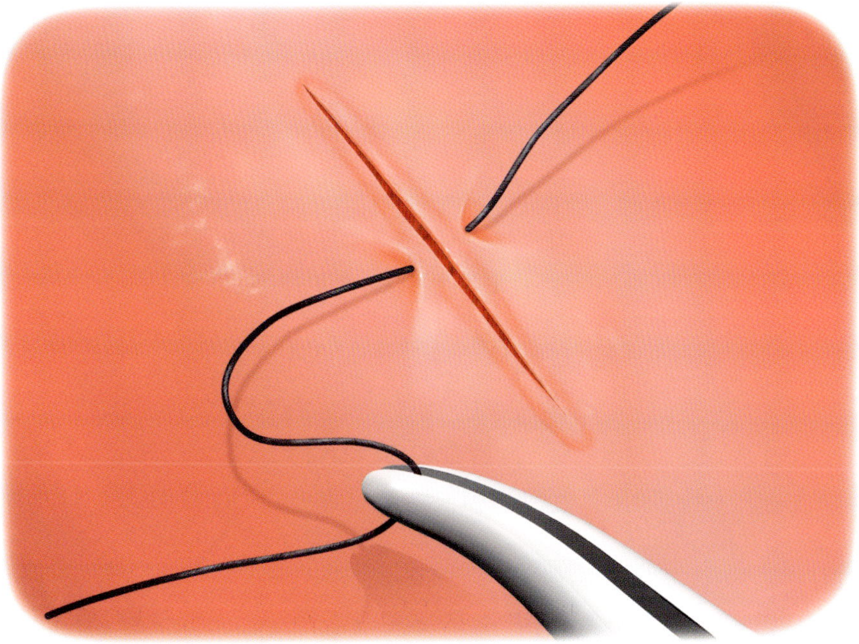

Fig j : The suture should be slowly pulled until the other end length becomes appropriate to knot tying.

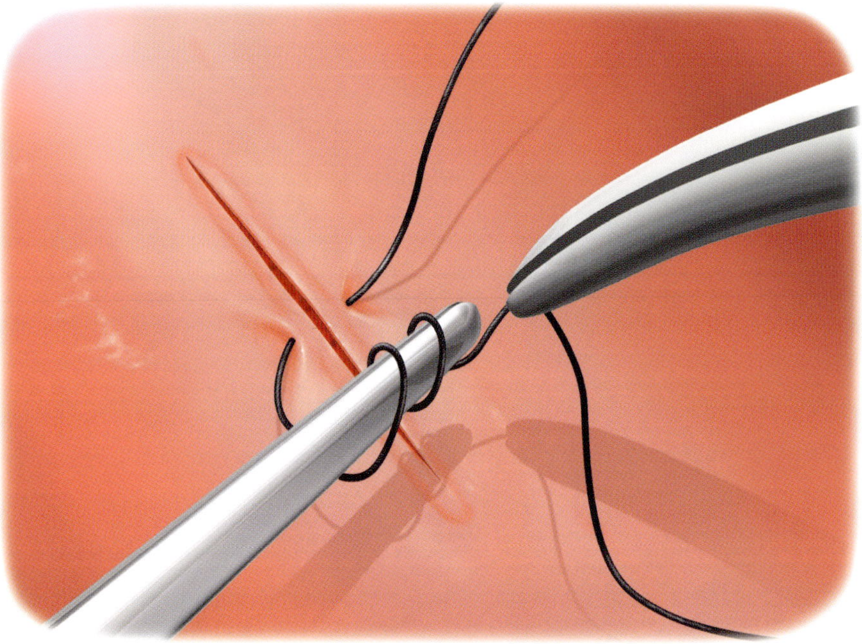

Fig k : The tying forceps should be positioned on top of the incision and the suture should be tied twice to the tying forceps from the top.

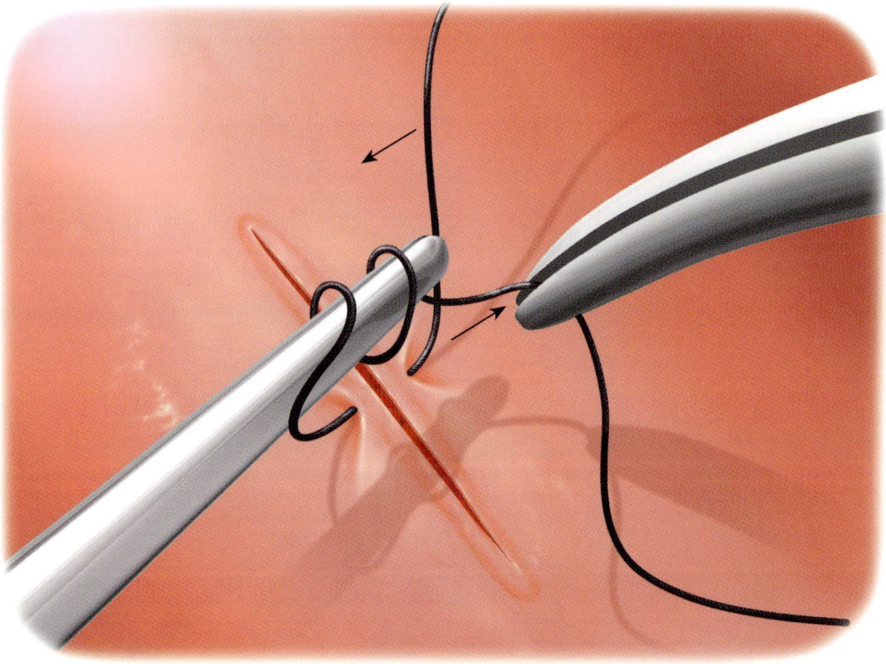

Fig l : The other end of the suture should be secured by the tying forceps with tied suture.

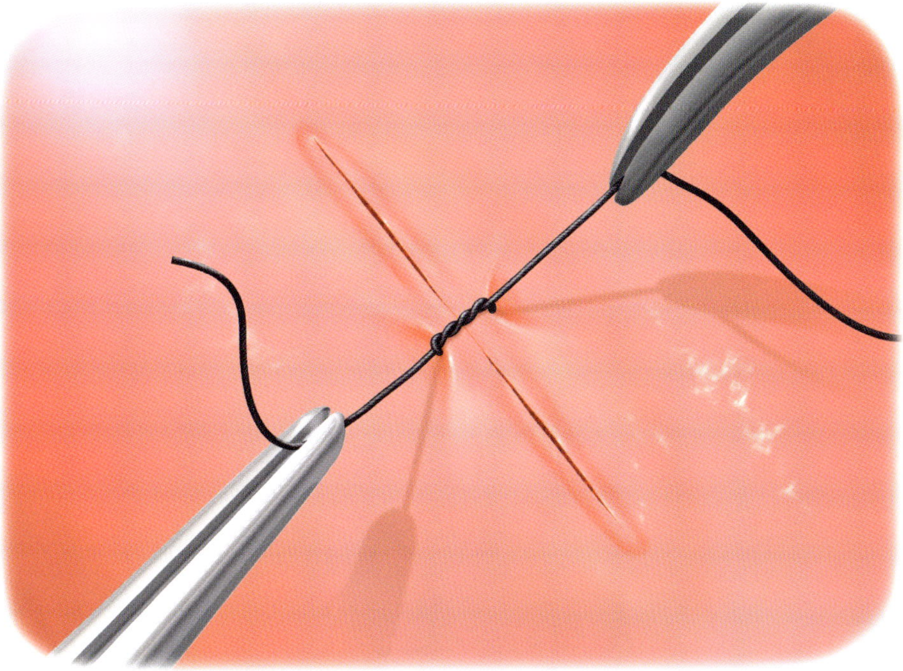

Fig m : Both sides of the suture are pulled to the opposite direction to connect the flaps.

Fig n : The magnified view of *Fig m*. The suture is spirally twined nicely.

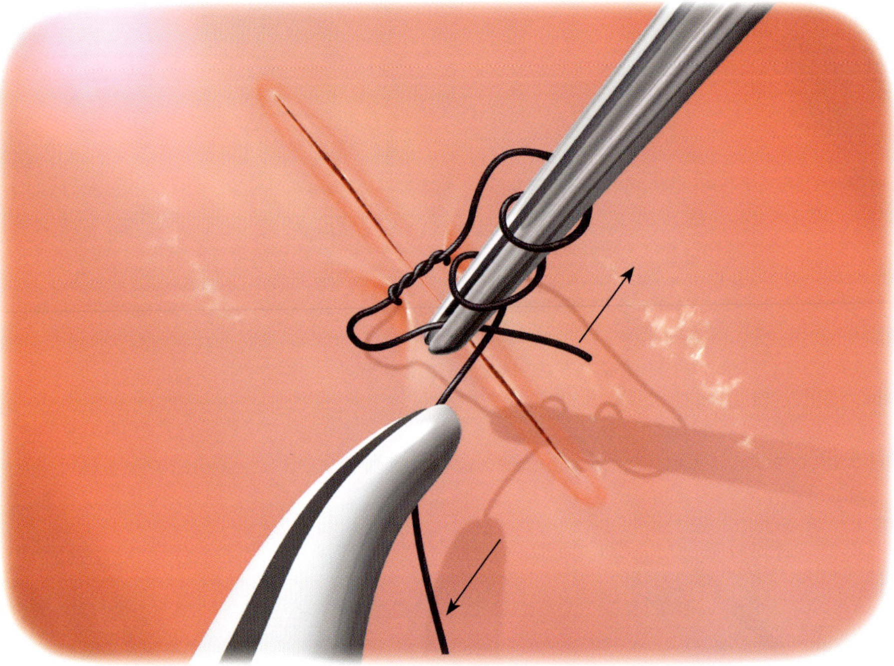

Fig o : Repeat the procedure of *Fig k~m*.

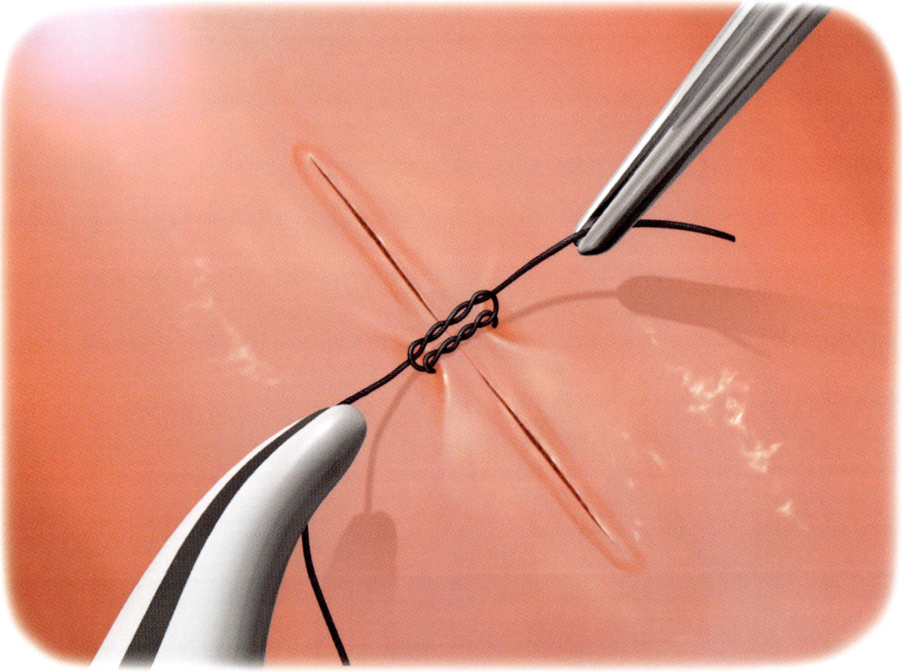

Fig p : It is very important to carry on those procedures slowly in order not to create the tissue tension on the flaps when the suture is pulled.

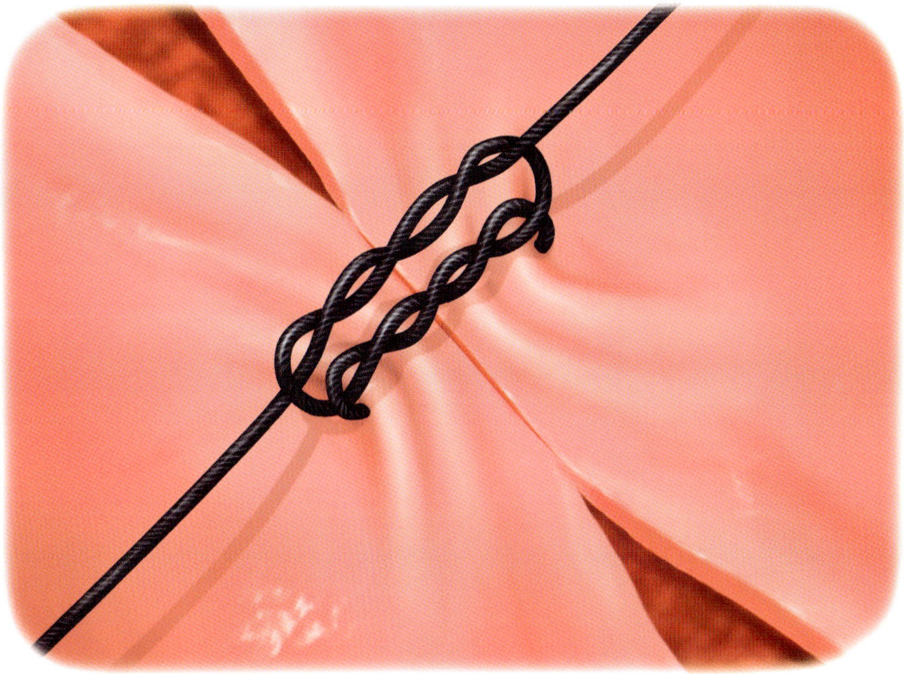

Fig q : The ideal condition is to create the beautiful loops by the suture spirally twined twice.

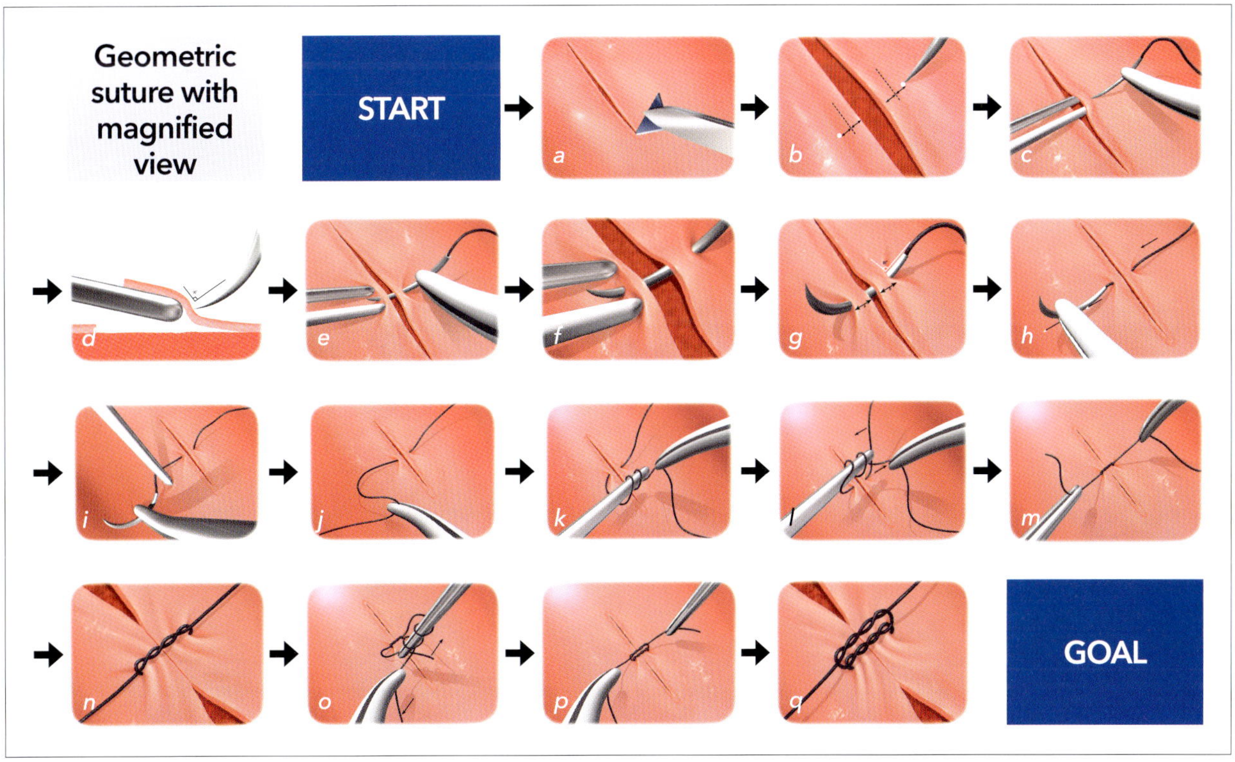

PART 3

Clinical application : Natural teeth

Root coverage procedure : the concept of envelope technique
Root coverage procedure : the concept of modified Langer technique
Root coverage procedure : the concept of subpedicle connective tissue graft
The concept of ridge expansion procedure : basics
The concept of ridge expansion procedure : advanced 1 preprosthetic treatment
The concept of ridge expansion procedure : advanced 2 postprosthetic treatment
The concept of ridge expansion procedure : advanced 3 recovery after prosthetic treatment
The concept of reconstructive surgery of interdental papilla

Root coverage : Concept of envelop technique

Envelope technique is the technique for root coverage procedure by connective tissue graft forming the partial thickness flap from the gingival sulcus[23,24]. Smooth healing process is the advantage of this technique because interdental papilla is preserved with no horizontal and vertical incision. The disadvantages on the other hand are that forming the partial thickness flap is technique sensitive and coronal flap repositioning cannot be performed compared to Langer technique. Micro surgery makes flap forming easier and 2~3 mm of repositioning is possible by extending the flap. This is and advantage in regards to blood supply to the graft, which makes this technique superior.

Root coverage procedure : Envelope technique

Pre-op

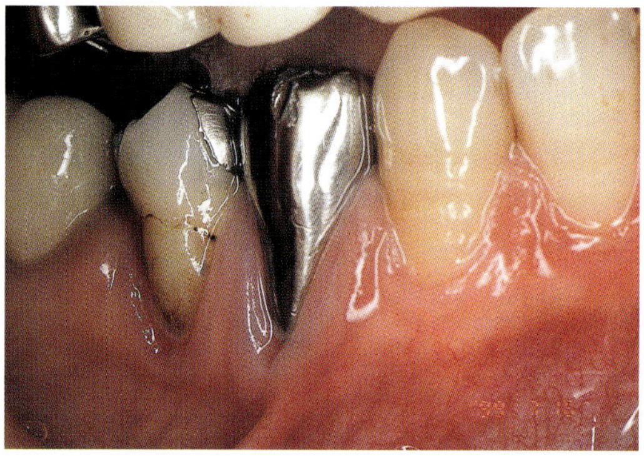

Fig 1a : Pre-op condition. Defective restoration are appreciated on premolars.

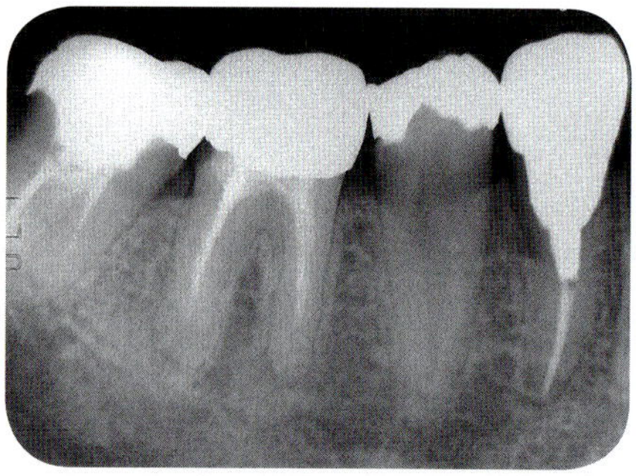

Fig 1b : Pre-op peri-apical x-ray.

Vertical gingival line	6	5	4	3
Balance to the adjacent tooth		X	X	
Balance to the same tooth on the contra lateral side				

*mark [X] in problematic area

Important points of this case

Problems

- Discrepancy is appreciated in vertical gingival level compared to adjacent canine and first molar.
- Restorations extending to root surface exist and secondary caries lesions are appreciated on the first and second premolars.

Purpose and technique of the periodontal surgery

1. Treatment of caries lesion of first and second premolars.
2. Extrusion of first premolar.
3. Root coverage procedure using connective tissue graft with aenvelope technique after completion of pre-surgical treatment.

Surgery (1999. 10.1)

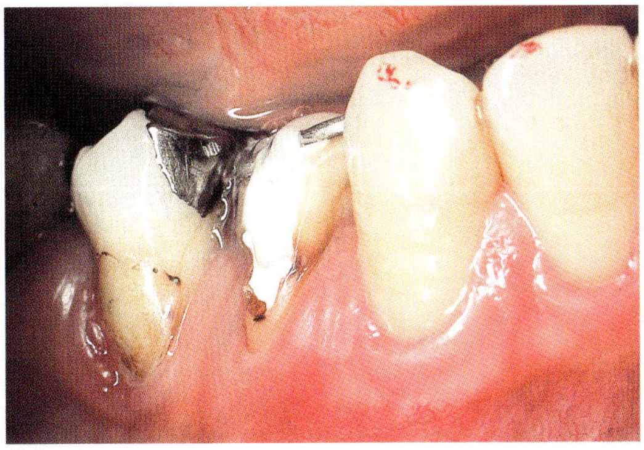

Fig 1c : Completion of extrusion. Extrusion was performed due to extensive root caries.

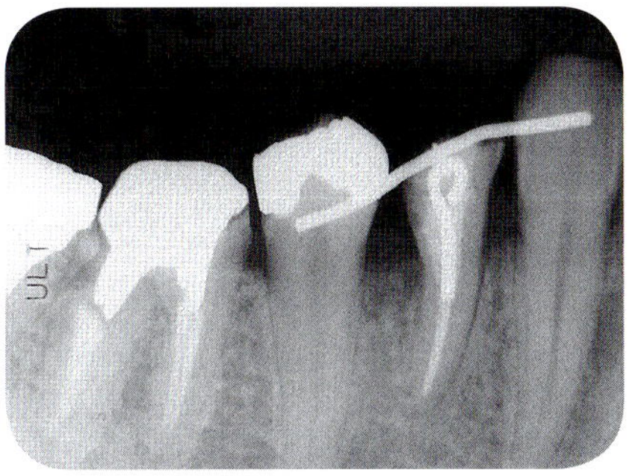

Fig 1d : Peri apical x-ray at the completion of extrusion of the first premolar.

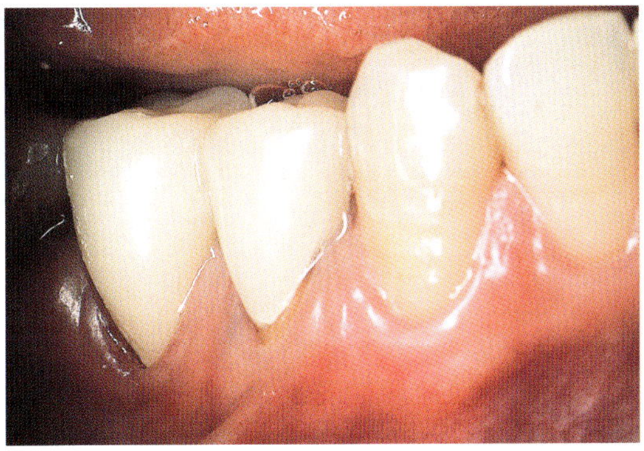

Fig 1e : After completion of extrusion. Provisional restorations are inserted for the purpose of fixation.

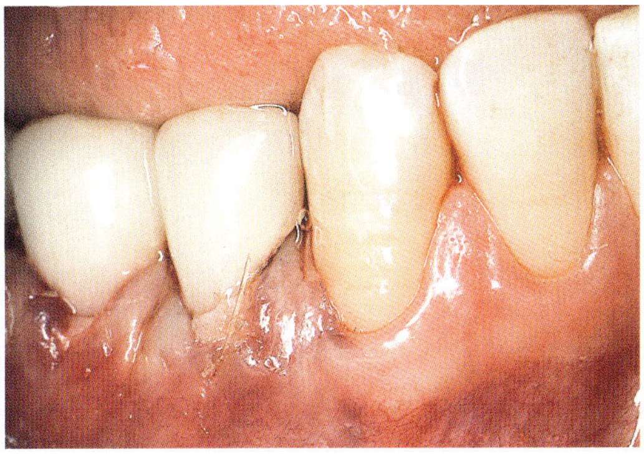

Fig 1f : right after suturing. Root coverage was performed with two teeth continuous envelope technique according to the desired cervical line designated by the trimmed provisional restorations.

Important points

The graft is embedded int the area of the first and second premolars and two sling sutures were performed at interproximal areas between #27-28-29 and #28-29-30. The graft should be stabilized on to the gingival flap by simple interrupted suture if it is not stable.

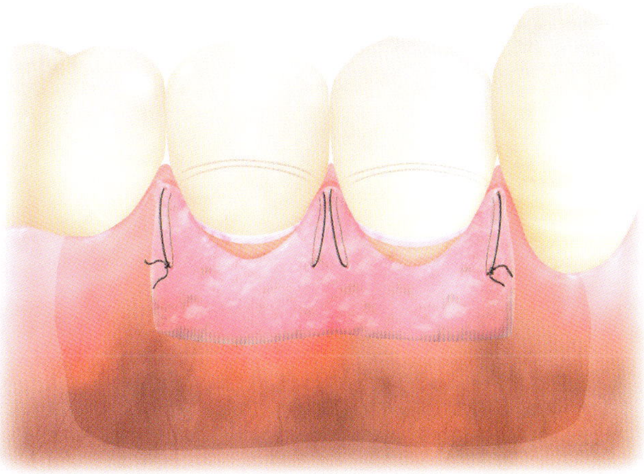

6 months post-op

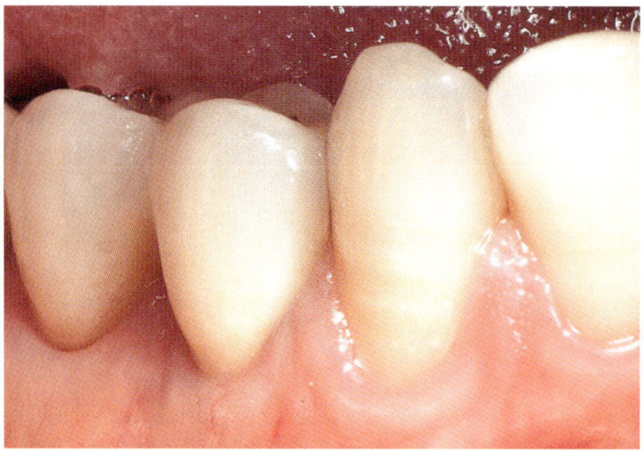

Fig 1g : 6 months post-op. Esthetically acceptable prosthesis are appreciated.

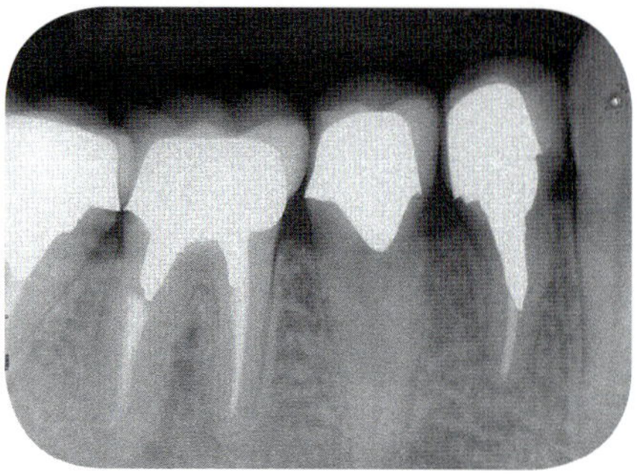

Fig 1h : Peri-apical x-ray at 6 months post-op.

11 years post-op

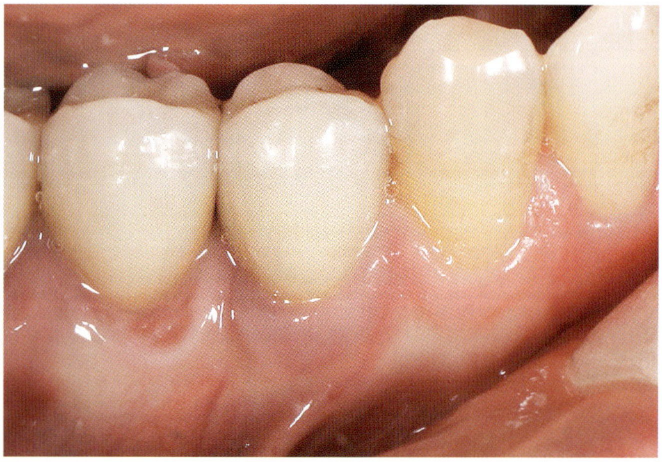

Fig 1i : 11 years post-op.

Evaluation of the case

Gingival architecture at the second premolar has changed after second year post-surgery. Gingival level has not changed and root is not exposed, though gingival step at 2~3 mm from cervical area has emerged, which is constant now at the 11th year. The cause seems to be the remnant of epithelium from the grafted connective tissue. This tissue change has been seen in other cases as well. Thorough removal of epithelium seems to be essential to prevent this phenomena.

Root coverage procedure : Concept of modified Langer technique

Esthetic result of the root coverage procedure with sub epithelial connective tissue introduced by Langer[25] has not been ideal due to forming the flap with vertical incision on medial and distal aspect of adjacent teeth and horizontal incision at interdental papilla. On the other hand, Bruno[26] introduced the root coverage technique with connective tissue graft forming the horizontally extended flap without vertical incision. More blood supply is possible with this technique by additional horizontal incision (originally single incision) enabling coronal repositioning of the flap. The author often use oblique incision in papilla area to avoid esthetic complication by the horizontal incision.

Root coverage procedure : Modified Langer technique

Pre-op

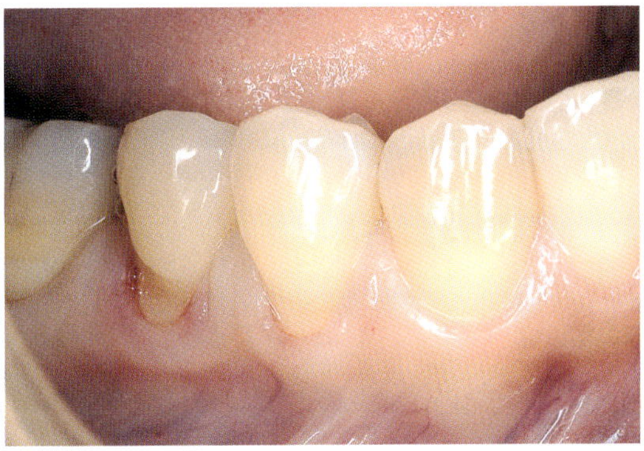

Fig 2a : Pre-op, mandibular right lateral view. Root exposure with wedge-shaped defect is appreciated on both premolars. The defect on the second premolar is more extended.

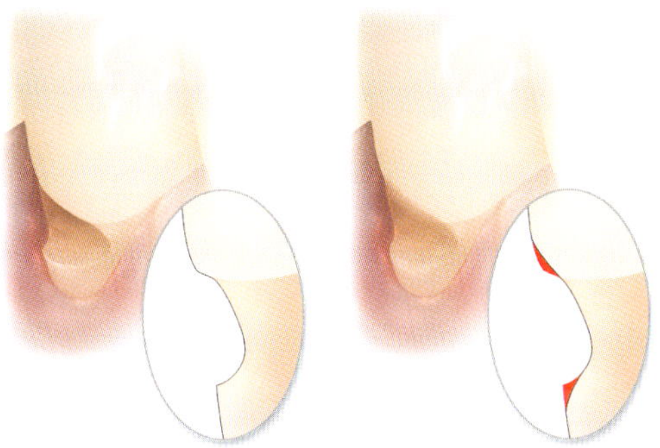

It is important to create smooth curved surface with the rotary instrument.

Vertical gingival line	6	5	4	3
Balance to the adjacent tooth		X	X	
Balance to the same tooth on the contra lateral side				

*mark [X] in problematic area

Points of this case

Problems

- Discrepancy of vertical gingival level of premolars is about 1mm compared to the adjacent teeth.
- Wedge-shaped defect is appreciated. The defect of the second premolar is more extensive than that of the first premolar.

The purpose and procedures of the surgery

1. Root surface is recontoured as pre-surgical procedure.
2. Root coverage procedure with connective tissue graft is performed by modified Langer technique.

Surgery (2000.4.22)

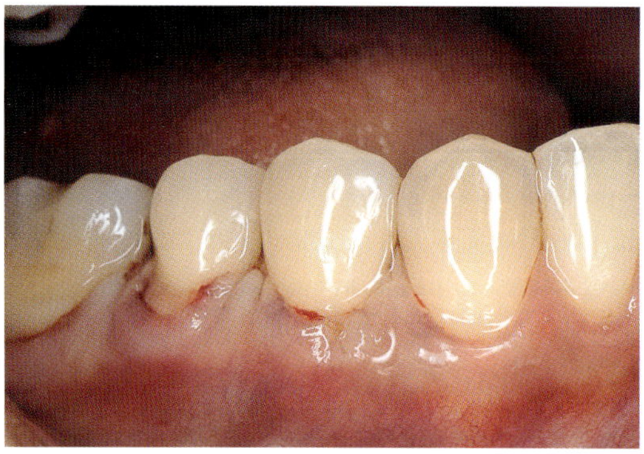

Fig 2b : Condition right after suture. The soft tissue is barely damaged.

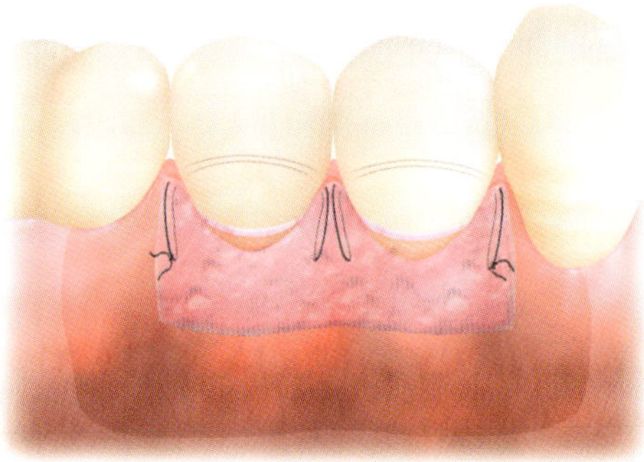

Gingival flap is sutured at the original position. This is the sling suture. If the wound does not match well with the sling suture alone, tight suture is added using size 7-0 or 8-0.

Important points

Difference in degree of wedge-shaped defect between premolars makes this case more difficult. Since the defect of second premolar is extensive, forming gingival flap with the envelope technique is more difficult and the amount of coronal repositioning is more than that of simple vertical repositioning. Therefore, releasing incision is added on the gingival flap. More over, the size of gingival grafts are different between the first and second premolars. Thicker graft is required for the second premolar with more extensive defect. It should be planned ahead and the graft with designated thickness should be taken from the palate.

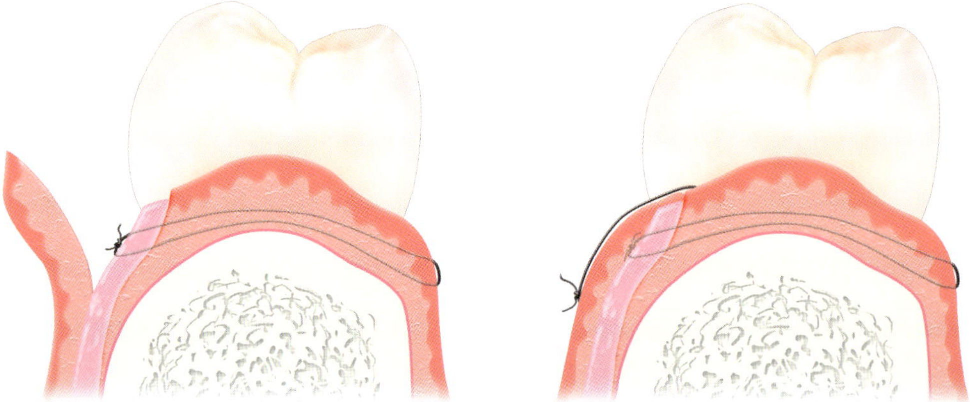

The graft is sutured at interdental papilla using reservable suture. Positioning of the flap needs to be carefully confirmed since it is easy to slip away at the time of suture due to the slip joint intentionally formed by trimming the tip of the graft obliquely.

3 months after the surgery

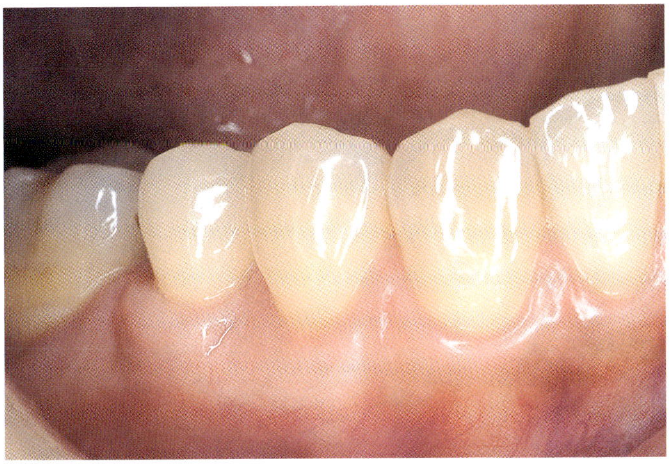

Fig 2c : 3 months after the surgery. Well healed esthetic result is appreciated.

10 years after the surgery

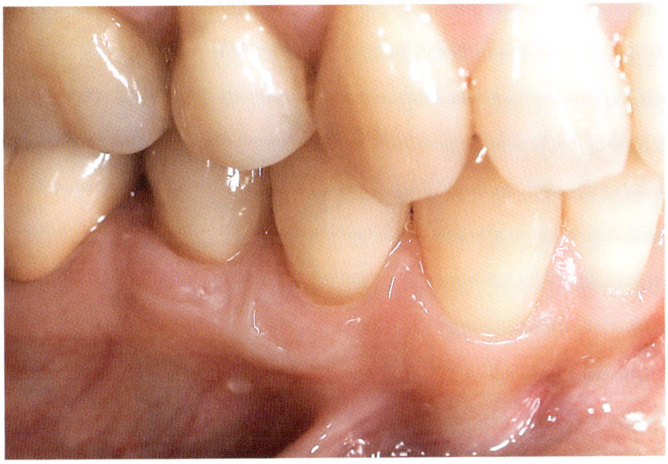

Fig 2d : 10 years after the surgery. Well maintained condition.

Evaluation of the case

The indication of connective tissue graft to the wedge-shaped defect should be carefully considered. It is important to recontour sharp edges to smooth curved surface. If recontour alone is not enough to make smooth surface, composite resin should be used in combination. Slight root surface exposure is appreciated 10 years after the surgery. It is not clear if they are caused by progression of the defect, gingival recession or both, but they all are not at the level that any treatment is indicated. Even after creating the resistant environment by connective tissue graft, the prognosis is somewhat unpredictable because the cause of the wedge-shaped defect is not resolved.

Root coverage procedure : the concept of subpedicle connective tissue graft

Harris and Nelson introduced the combination technique of the gingival flap lateral repositioning and sub-epithelial connective tissue graft procedures[27, 28]. The advantage of this technique is high success rated due to rich blood supply from the pedicle flap to the connective tissue graft. The author apply this technique when enough keratinized tissue is not expected to be obtained with the coronal flap repositioning procedure such as Langer technique.

Root coverage procedure : subpedicle connective tissue graft 1

Pre-op

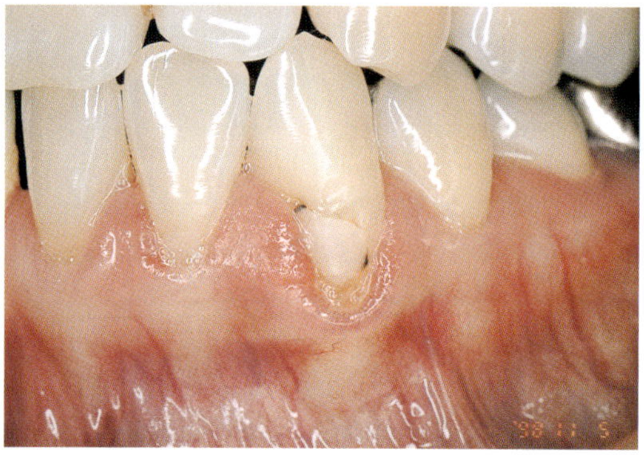

Fig 3a : Pre-op lateral view of mandibular left side. Recurrent caries around the existing restoration and root exposure are appreciated.

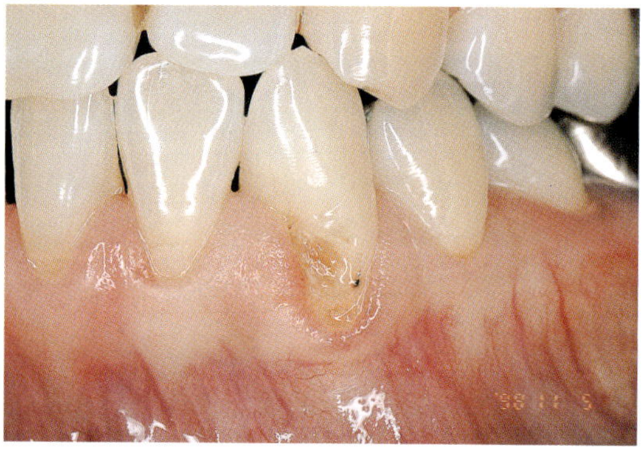

Fig 3b : Large enamel defect and root surface caries were appreciated after removal of the existing composite resin restoration.

Vertical gingival line	2	3	4	5
Balance to the adjacent tooth		X		
Balance to the same tooth on the contra lateral side		X		

*mark [X] in problematic area

Important points of this case

Problems

- Discrepancy of vertical gingival level to adjacent teeth and the root exposure.
- Defective restoration at the cervical area with recurrent caries lesion. Strong hypersensitivity.

The purpose and procedures of the surgery

1. Composite resin restoration prior to the surgery.
2. Root coverage procedure using subpedicle connective tissue graft.

Surgery (1998. 11. 26)

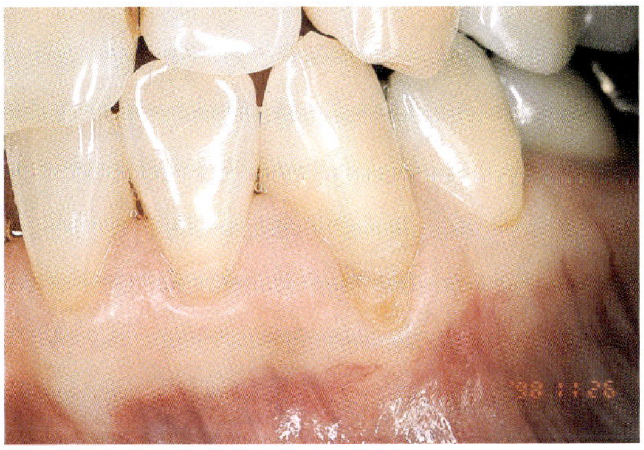

Fig 3c : Right after composite resin restoration. Cement-enamel junction : CEJ) is restored with composite resin.

‖ Point ‖

The reason subpedicle connective tissue graft was chosen over the envelope technique or modified Langer technique is to securely obtain wide keratinized gingiva by covering the exposed root surface with abundant keratinized tissue in the area of mandibular left lateral incisor and canine. Hence, root coverage was successfully performed without changing the level of muco-gingival junction (: MGJ). In other words, the width of keratinized tissue was increased by the size of the covered root surface.

Fig 3d : Vertical incision was made from the spot slightly coronal to the exposed root surface of mesial aspect of mandibular left canine obliquely to apical of the mandibular left lateral incisor. Next, small vertical incision is made in the deepest area of the gingival scallop of mandibular left canine slightly over the MGJ (muco-ginigval junction). Additionally, gingival crevicular incision if made from mesial to distal aspect of mandibular left canine removing crevicular epithelium. Partial thickness flap is extended considering the size of the graft.

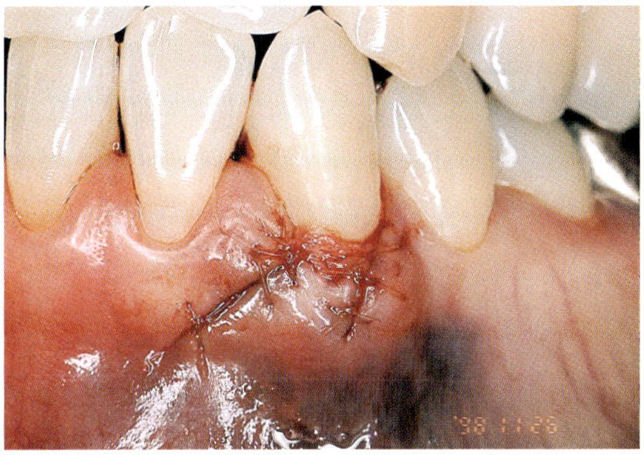

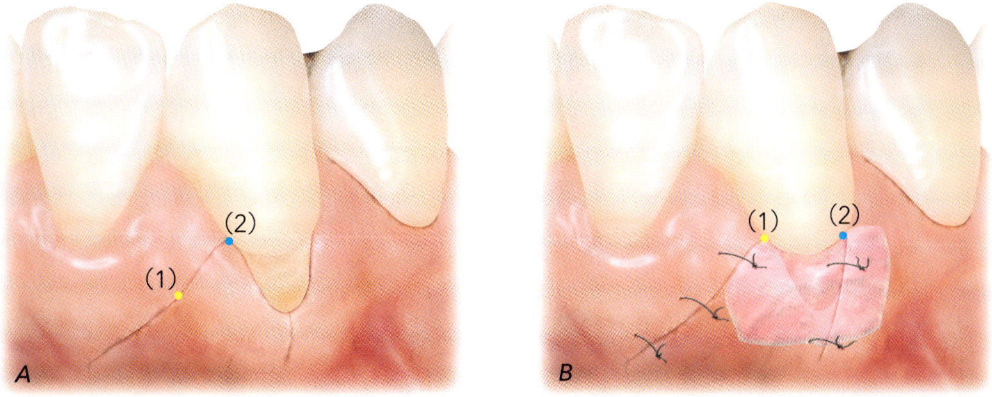

The graft covering the root surface is securely sutured at the medial and distal papilla area of mandibular left canine. Next, the gingival flap is rotated and repositioned, then sutured described in *B*. Please refer to the change of positions of 1・2 indicated in the illustration *A* and *B*.

1 year and 7 months after the surgery

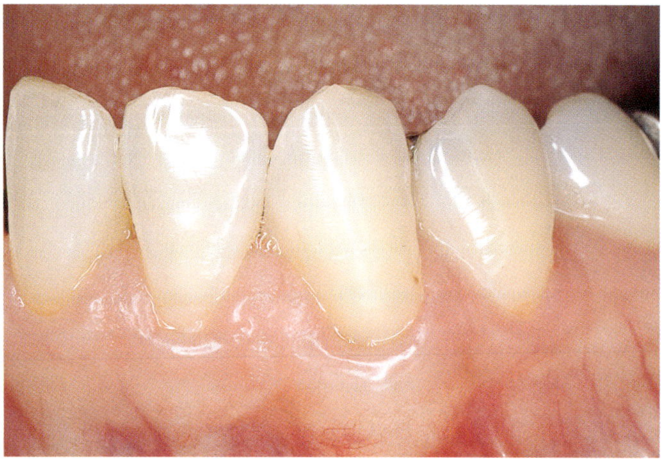

Fig 3e : 1 year and 7 months after the surgery. Esthetic cervical line is reconstructed without scarring of vertical incision.

12 years after the surgery

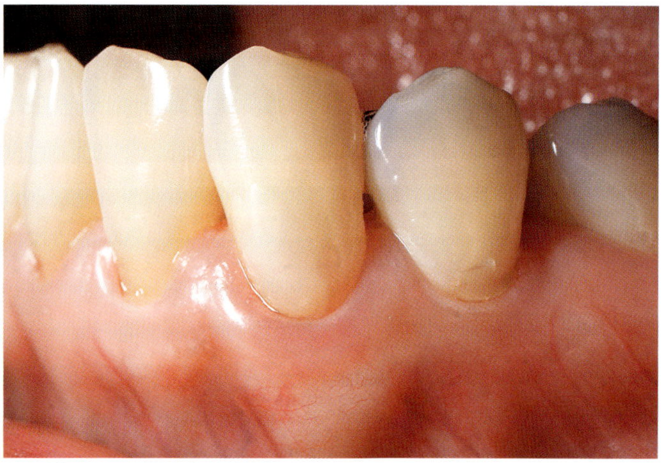

Fig 3f : 12 years after the surgery. The soft tissue appears even more esthetic at this point. It is due to proper maintenance.

Evaluation of the case

The advantage of subpedicle connective tissue graft utilizing rotation graft is that the root surface is covered without changing MGJ creating more keratinized gingiva as a result. This technique is considered more effective compared to the envelope technique because it creates wider keratinized gingiva which leads to more stability.

Subpedicle connective tissue graft 2

Pre-op

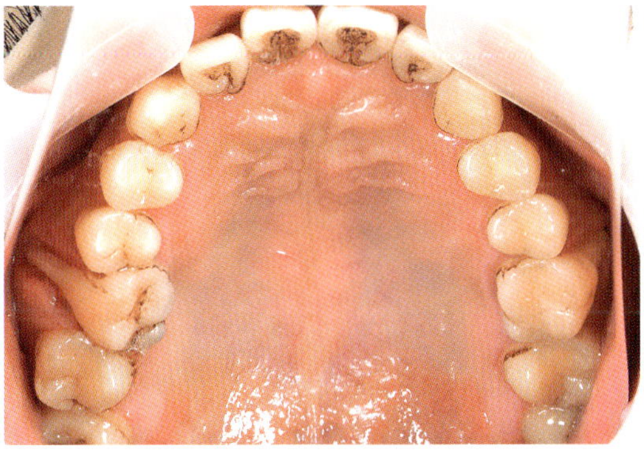
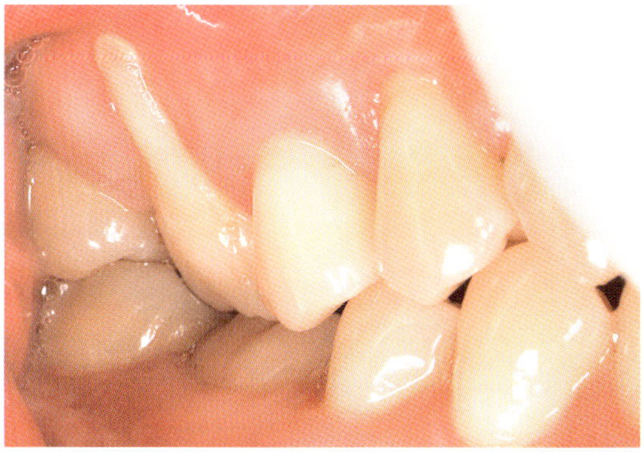

Fig 4a, b : Pre-operative occlusal and right lateral view. Maxillary right first molar is lingually tilted extensively exposing the medial buccal root close to the apex area. Orthodontic treatment is indicated for stability and better occlusion.

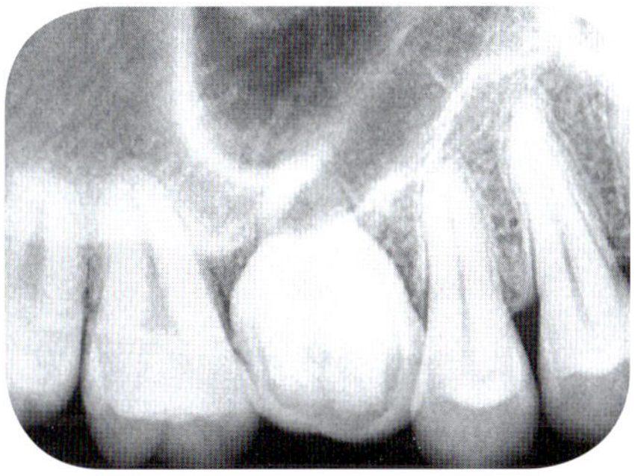

Fig 4c : Pre-op peri-apical x-ray.

Vertical gingival line	7	6	5	4
Balance to the adjacent tooth		X		
Balance to the same tooth on the contra lateral side				

*mark [X] in problematic area

Important points of this case

Problems

- Large vertical gingival level discrepancy at maxillary right first molar, Miller Class III root exposure.

The purpose and procedures of the surgery

1. Root coverage procedure as pre-orthodontic treatment.
2. Subpedicle connective tissue graft with rotated graft was used due to the size of vertical gingival level discrepancy.

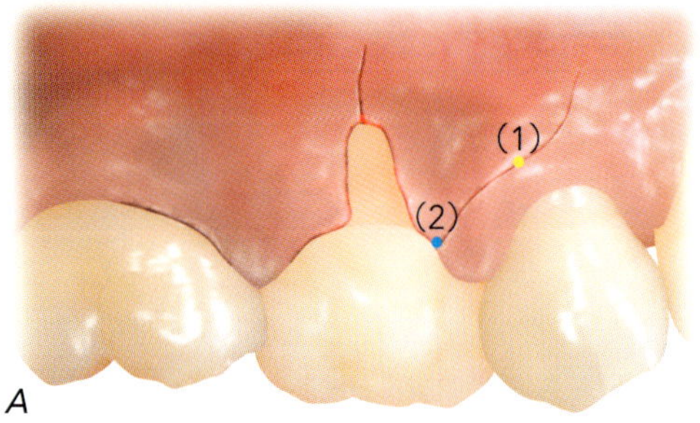

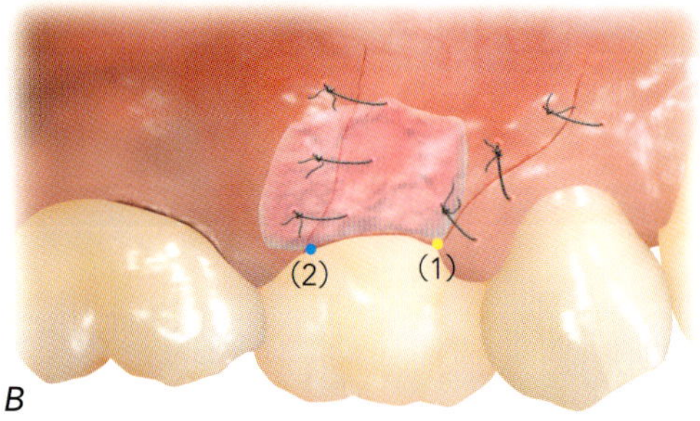

The gingival flap is rotated and sutured as illustrated in *B*. Please refer to the change of positions of 1・2.

Surgery (2009. 10. 22)

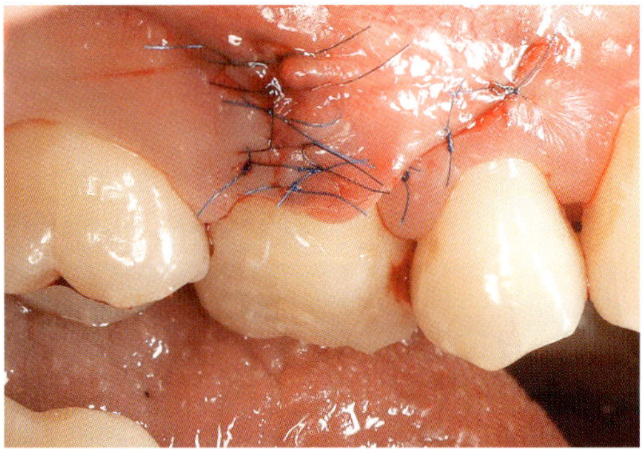

Fig 4d : Right after the sure. Exposed root surface is completely covered.

Point

One simple index to evaluate difficulty of root coverage procedure is exposed area[28]. The shape of exposed area should also be carefully evaluated. Vertical repositioning of the flap is indicated when the defect is wide horizontally. Horizontal (rotational) repositioning is indicated when the defect is wide vertically. Thicker connective tissue graft is utilized as the area is wider.

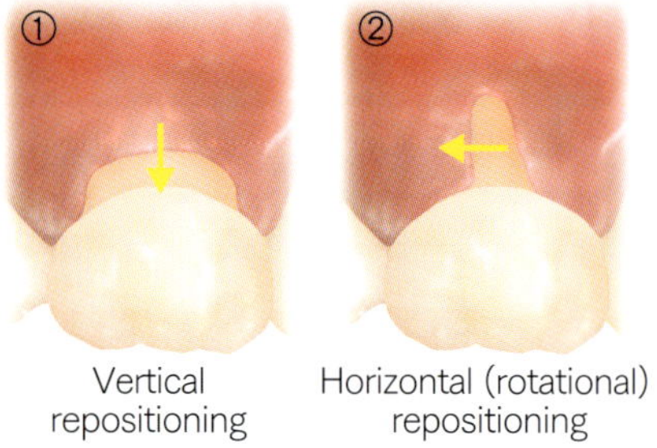

After surgery

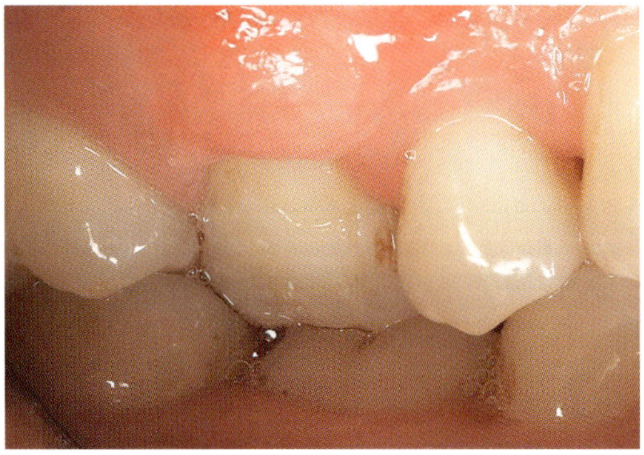

Fig 4e : Post-surgery condition.

Evaluation of the case

Root coverage procedure should be rendered prior to orthodontic movement so that the orthodontic treatment is carried out safely without compromising the periodontal condition.

Root coverage procedure : Modified envelope & Langer technique

Pre-op

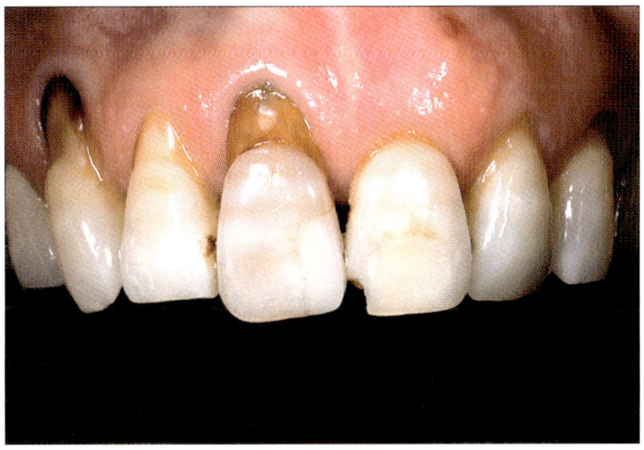

Fig 5a : Vertical gingival recession is appreciated on maxillary right central incisor to canine. Coronal morphologic imbalance is appreciated in maxillary anterior area.

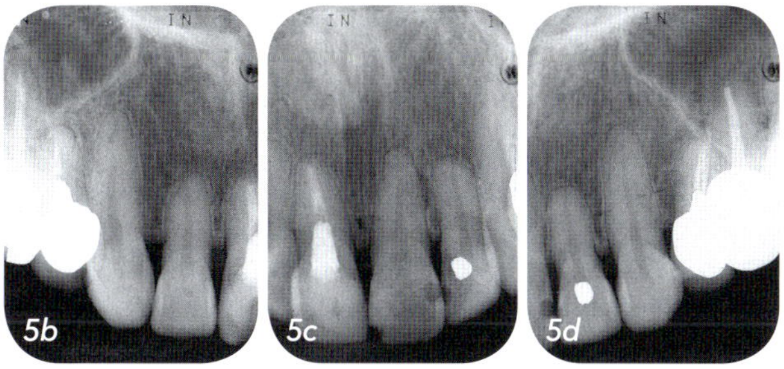

Fig 5b~d

Vertical gingival line	3	2	1	1	2	3
Balance to the adjacent tooth	X	X	X		X	
Balance to the same tooth on the contra lateral side	X	X	X			

*mark [X] in problematic area

Point of this case

Problems

- Asymmetric vertical gingival level is appreciated.
- More extensive gingival recession is appreciated on maxillary right central incisor and canine compared to that of the lateral incisor.

The purpose and procedures of the surgery

1. Vertical gingival level will be improved prior to esthetic restorative treatment.
2. Envelope technique for the central and lateral incisors and Langer technique of the canine are applied.

First surgery (2006 10. 26) : Root coverage procedure by envelope technique for maxillary right central and lateral incisors

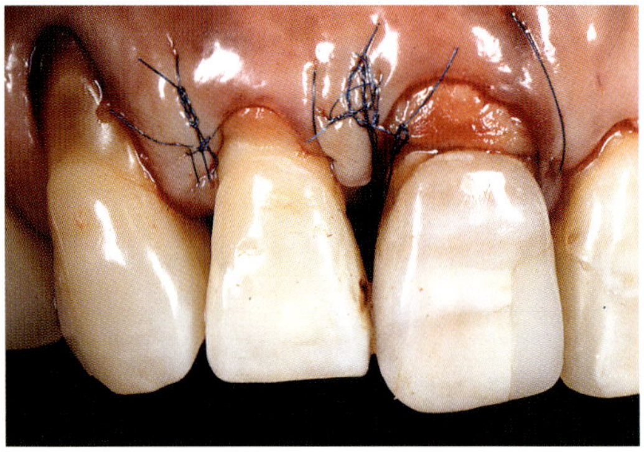

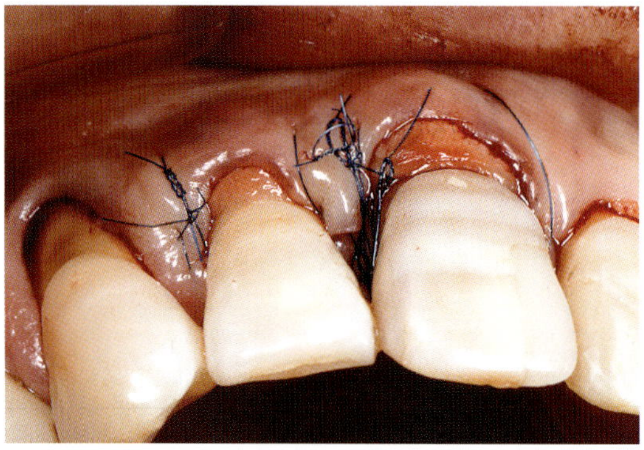

Fig 5e, f : Right after the suture. Envelope technique is applied continuously for the central and lateral incisors. Sling suture is tied. Simple sutures are tied at the distal corner of the central incisor and distal papilla area of the lateral incisor for stability of the graft after the sling suture is tied.

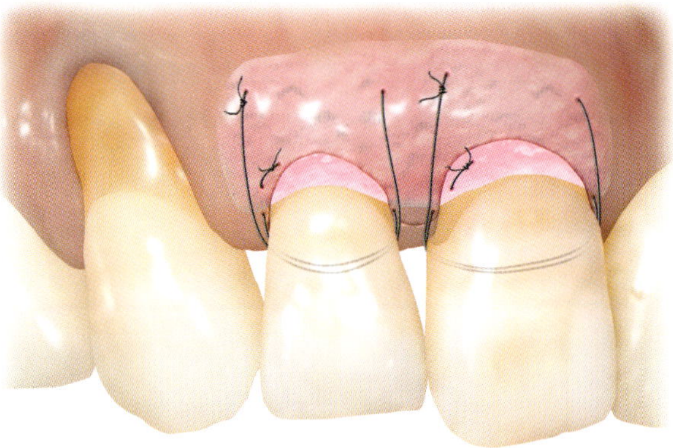

Sling sutures are applied at both central and lateral incisors. The needle is inserted at the flap of distal aspect picking up the graft and then emerge from the papilla area. It is slung around palatal side back to the mesial aspect. Likewise, the needle is inserted in the mesial flap picking up the graft and then emerge from the papilla area. The suture is slung around the palatal side toward distal aspect then tied. This sling suture is performed twice on the central and lateral incisors in this case. This suture alone seems to be sufficient enough to stabilize the graft.

Second surgery (2007. 3. 14) : Root coverage procedure of maxillary right canine by modified Langer technique

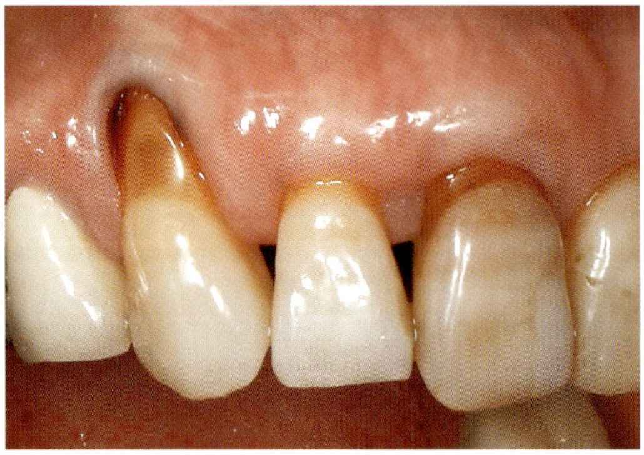

Fig 5g : 3 months after the surgery. Coronal repositioning of vertical gingival level is achieved as planned.

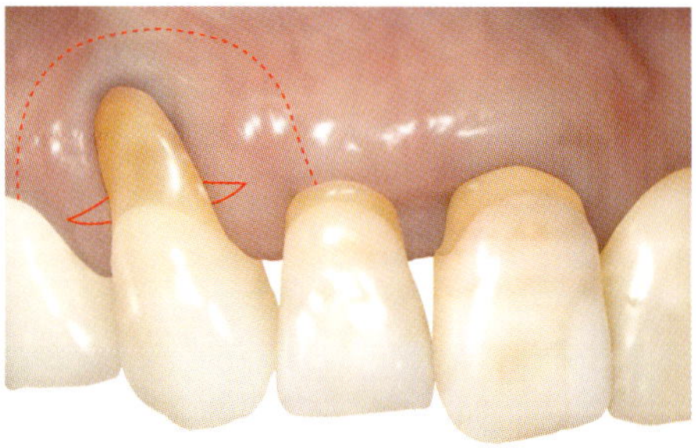

V shaped horizontal incision is placed as illustrated.

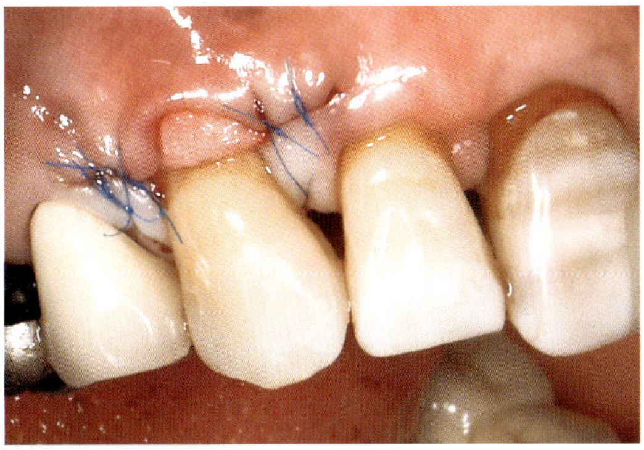

Fig 5h : Right after the suturing. Since the right canine presented relatively large root exposed area, modified Langer technique was utilized considering the amount of coronal repositioning of the gingival flap. Sling suture is tied along with simple loop suture to assure tight but joint gingival joint.

Point

Regarding the insertion technique and the shape of the graft, the edge of the exposed part of the graft is straight, which is different from the scallop shape of CEJ. However, well scalloped gingival healing creeping up to CEJ is appreciated. It is more important to consider the surgical procedure including the initial incision paying attention to the vertical level of the graft than to consider providing scallop shape edge on the graft.

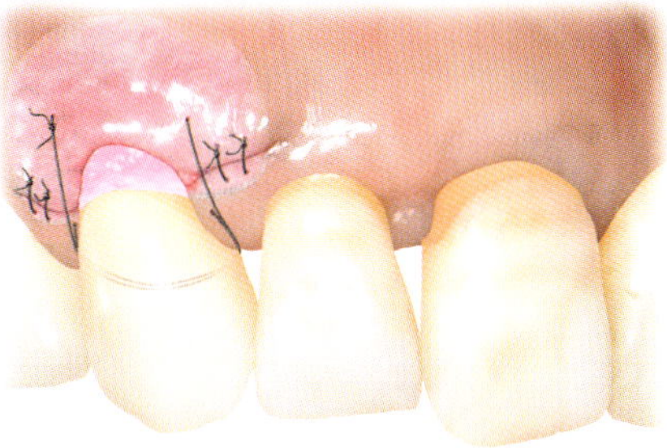

3 months after the surgery / time of insertion of the final prosthesis

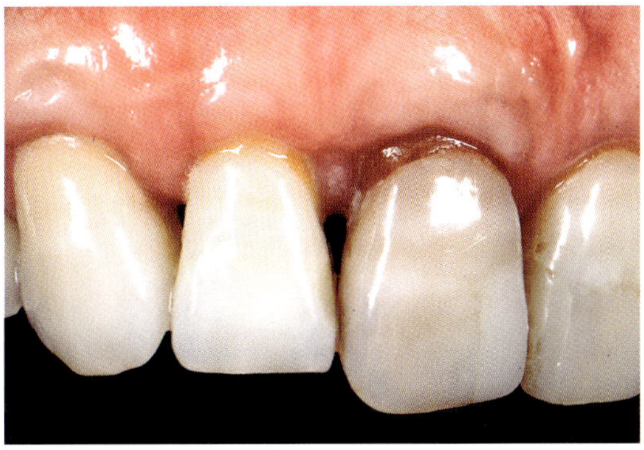

Fig 5i : 3 months after the surgery. Gingival level is more coronal than expected.

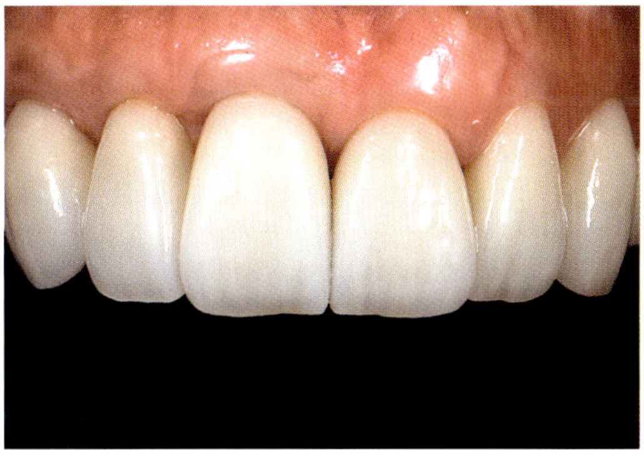

Fig 5j : At the time of insertion of the final prosthesis. Satisfactory esthetic restorative treatment is achieved with improved balance of gingival level and gingival scallop (prosthetic treatment by Dr. Masayuki Okawa).

Evaluation of the case

The graft is positioned coronal to CEJ to cover the root surface completely in root coverage procedure with connective tissue graft. It is true that some recommends overcorrection. However, the author positions the graft at the target level without overcorrection because the epithelium grows crawling up the connective tissue as long as the graft procedure is successful as shown in this case.

The concept of alveolar ridge augmentation : Basics

Alveolar ridge augmentation[29~32] is the procedure applied to defective alveolar ridge to reconstruct the proper alveolar ridge for esthetic and functional purpose. It includes expansion of soft tissue (gingiva), hard tissue (bone) and both depending on the treatment plan. Ridge augmentation mainly by soft tissue is indicated when the edentulous area is restored by fixed prosthesis. On the other hand, reconstruction by hard tissue often used when the edentulous area is restored by implant supported prosthesis.
Basic concept and procedure of ridge augmentation by soft tissue restored by the conventional prosthesis is reviewed through 3 clinical cases. Advanced cases will be discussed according to 'Suzuki's classification' (refer to P13) afterwards.

Alveolar ridge augmentation procedure : The pontic site for the conventional fixed prosthesis 1

Pre-op

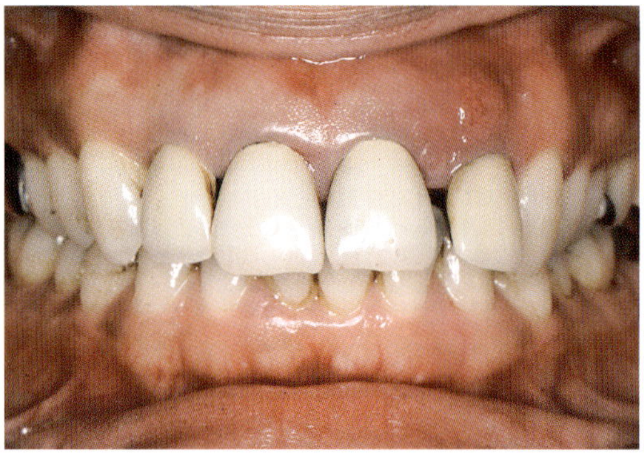

Fig 6a : Pre-op intra-oral frontal view.

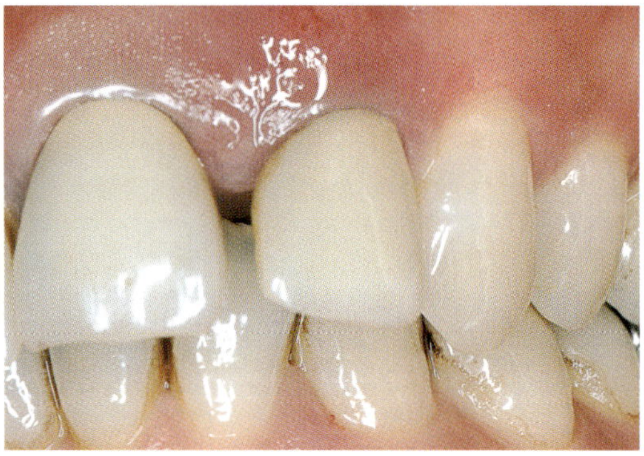

Fig 6b : Pre-op maxillary left lateral incisor. Redness and swelling of gingiva and purulent discharge from the cervical area of maxillary left lateral incisor are appreciated.

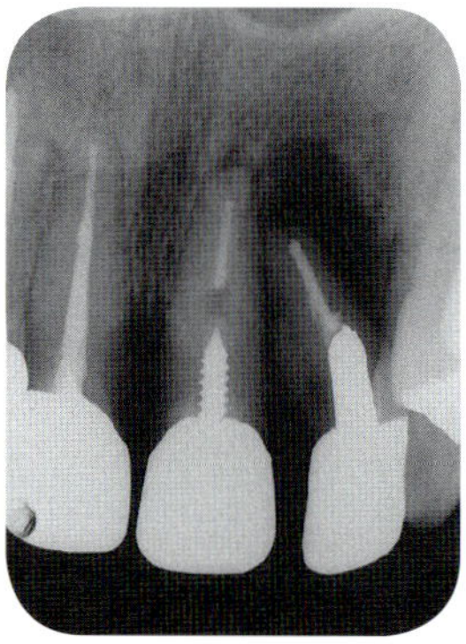

Fig 6c : Pre-op peri-apical x-ray. Large peri-apical radiolucency is appreciated and extraction of maxillary left lateral incisor was indicated.

After Extraction

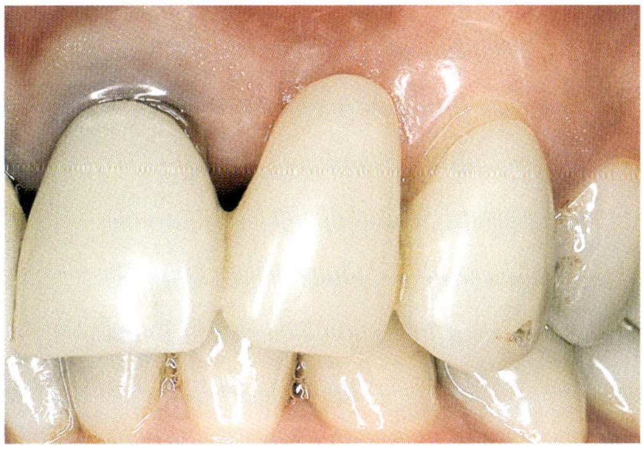

Fig 6d : Frontal view, 6 months after extraction of the lateral incisor.

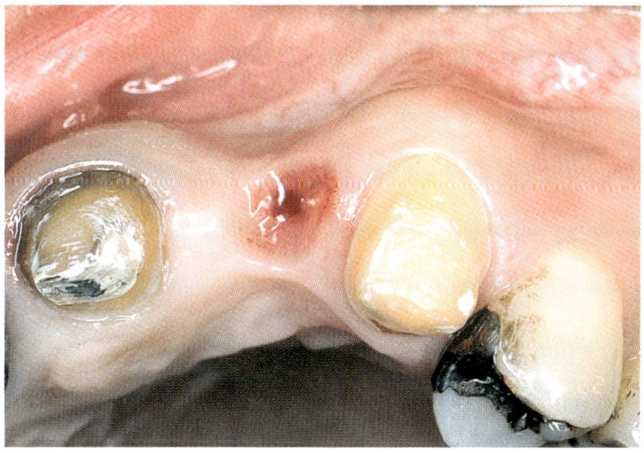

Fig 6e : Occlusal view, 6 months after extraction of the lateral incisor. Remarkable alveolar ridge defect is appreciated. Esthetic restorative treatment is impossible with this condition.

Vertical gingival line	3	2	1	1	2	3
Balance to the adjacent tooth						
Balance to the same tooth on the contra lateral side						
Horizontal gingival line	**3**	**2**	**1**	**1**	**2**	**3**
Balance to the adjacent tooth					X	
Balance to the same tooth on the contra lateral side					X	

*mark [X] in problematic area

Point of this case

Problems

- Discrepancy in horizontal gingival level of maxillary left lateral incisor causing esthetic problems of asymmetry and continuity.

The purpose and procedures of the surgery

1. Provisional restoration as pre-surgical procedure.
2. After pre-surgical procedure, ridge expansion by soft tissue using connective tissue graft is rendered.

Fabrication of the provisional restoration

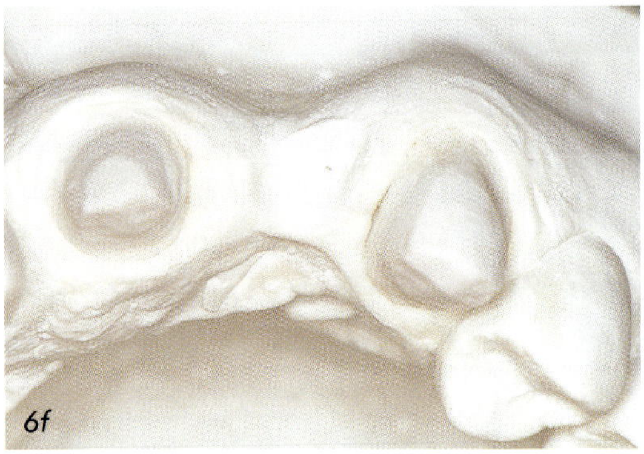

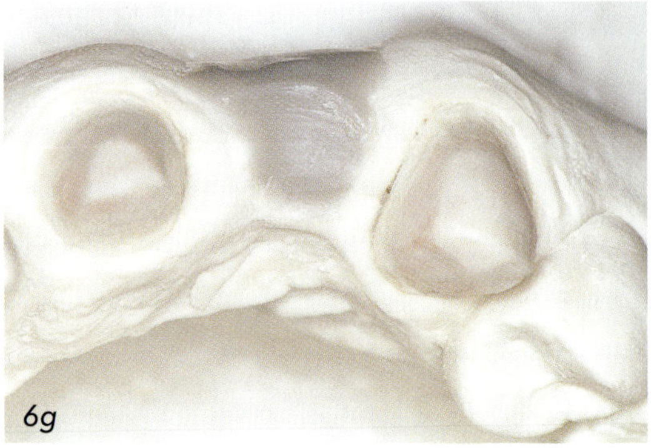

Fig 6f, g : *f* is the pre-op study model (working model). Ideal ridge shape is waxed up and the necessary graft size is estimated. In this case, 5mm thick graft is required (*g*).

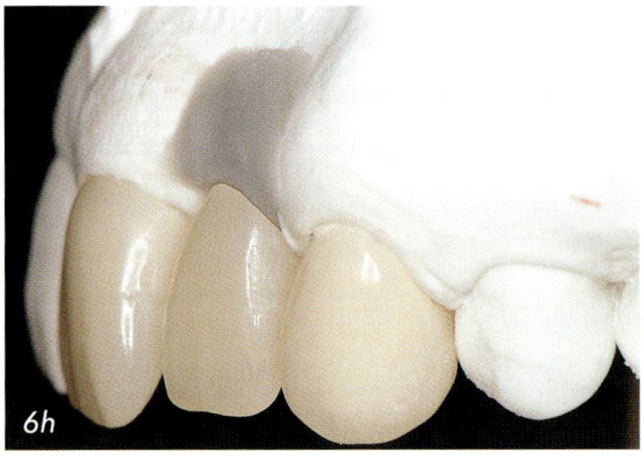

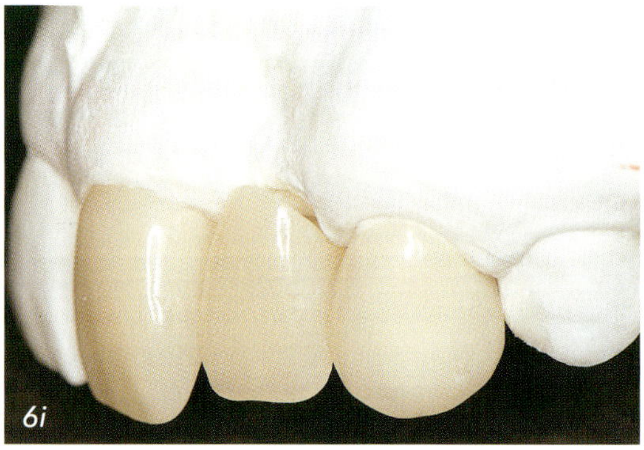

Fig 6h, i : The provisional restoration of *h* is fabricated according to the diagnostic wax up on the working model. Tissue surface of the pontic is formed in ovate shape on the diagnostic wax up. The wax up is reduced by 1mm so that the pontic applies pressure on the grafted ridge. i shows the provisional restoration on the model with the gingival wax up removed.

Surgeray (1999. 5. 22)

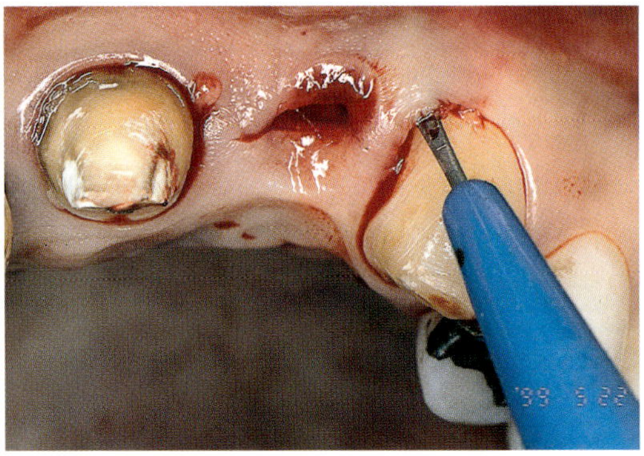

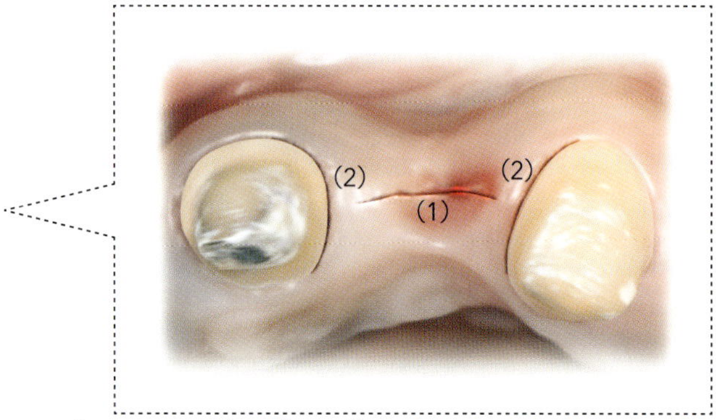

Fig 6j : First, horizontal incision is made on the alveolar crest leaving interdental papilla area intact to prevent cutting off of blood flow (1). Next, incision is made in the gingival sulcus of the central incisor and the canine and make baglike flap on the buccal aspect of the area of lateral incisor (2). The mucotome is used for elevation of the flap.

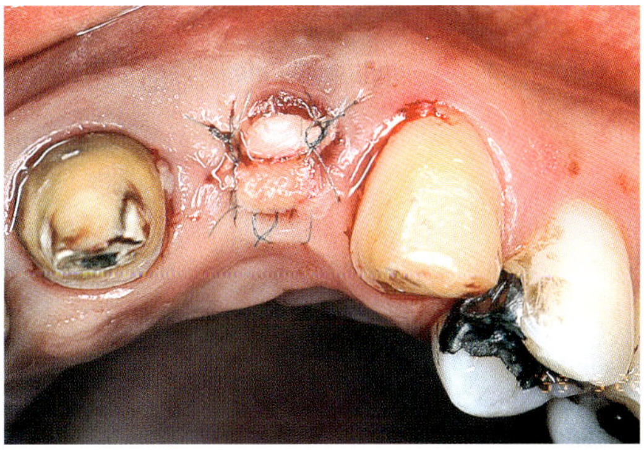

Fig 6k : The connective tissue from the palate is inserted and sutured.

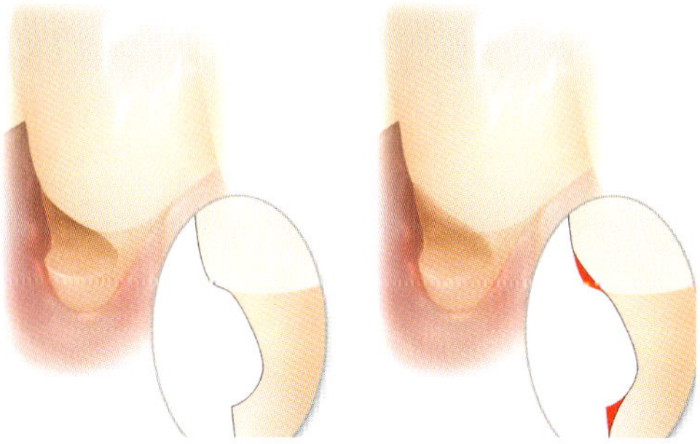

Point

Three 2~3 mm thick connective tissue pieces are trimmed, layered and sutured, since it is not practical to take 5~6 mm thick connective tissue in one piece.

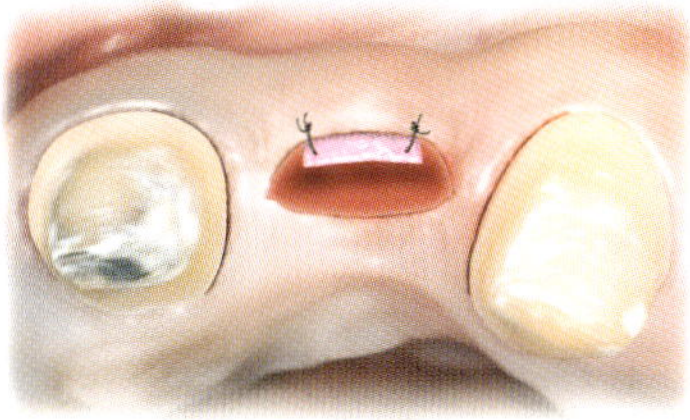

The first layer of the connective tissue graft is sutured on the gingival flap.

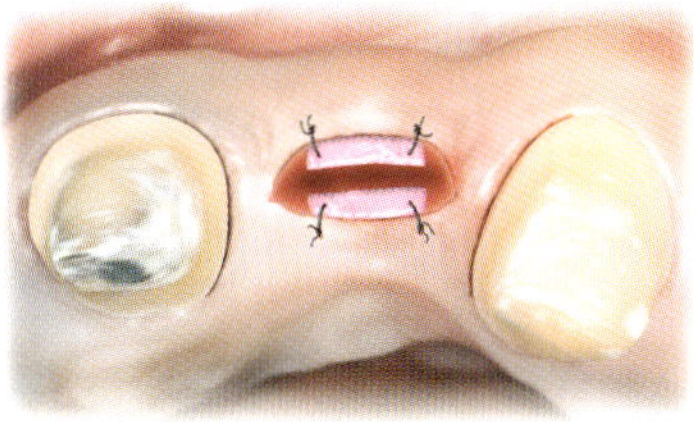

The second layer of the connective tissue graft is sutured on the palatal side.

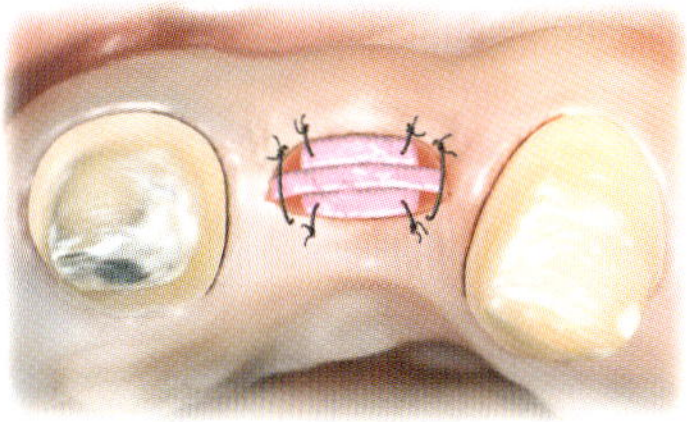

The third layer of the connective tissue graft is inserted in the middle and sutured.

Insertion of the provisional restoration

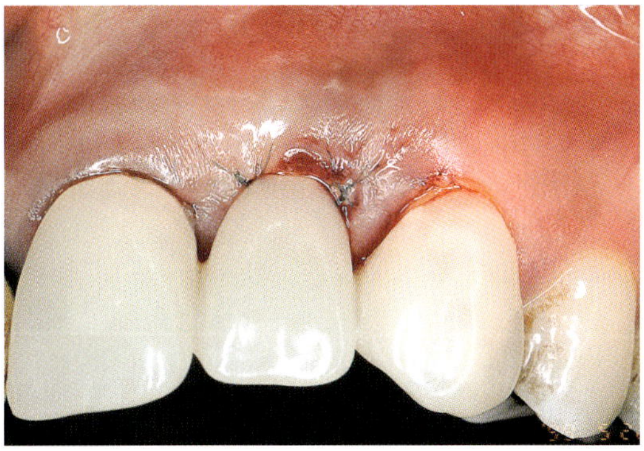

Fig 6l : Right after suturing, pre-fabricated provisional restoration is inserted.

6 months after the surgery

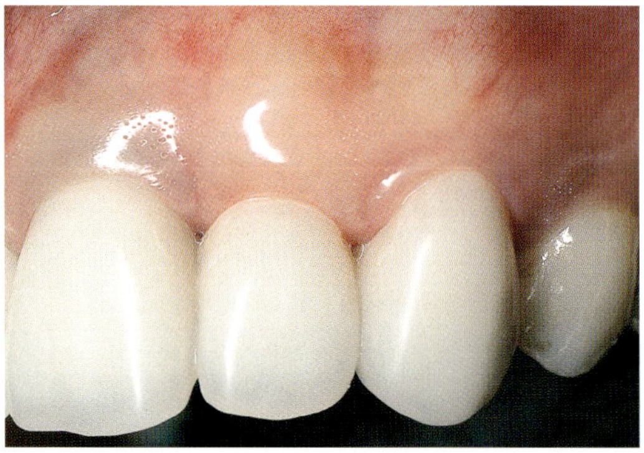

Fig 6m : 6 months after the surgery with the provisional restoration. It was decided to fabricate the final prosthesis, since the soft tissue is matured and stable. The final prosthesis is fabricated 3 months after the surgery these days.

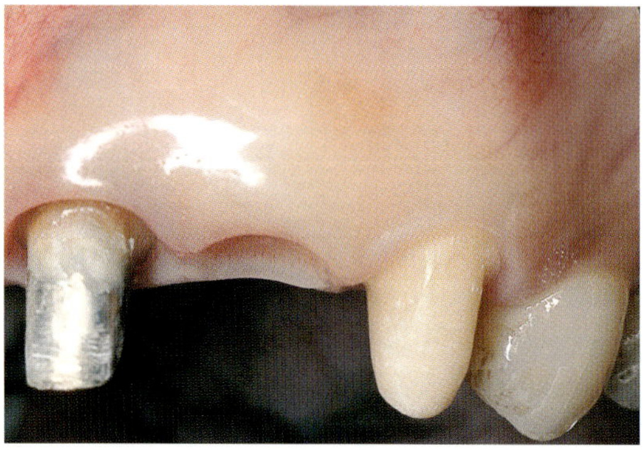

Fig 6n : The condition of the gingiva without the provisional restoration. The gingiva is free of redness and maintaining healthy condition.

Insertion of the final prosthesis

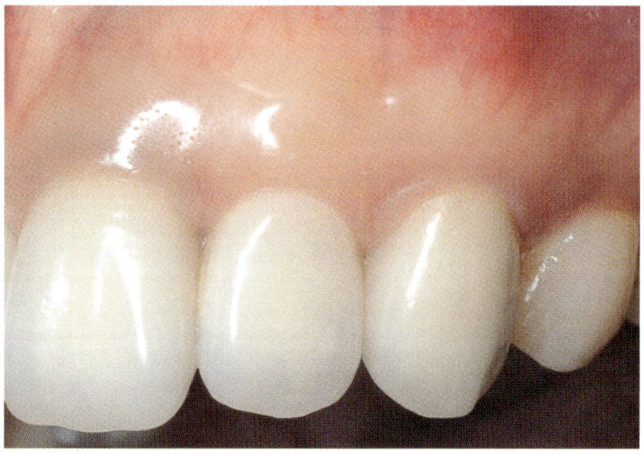

Fig 6o : 9 months after the surgery. The time of insertion of the final prosthesis. Continuity of gingival line and proper gingival contour of the lateral incisor is well reconstructed esthetically satisfying prosthesis.

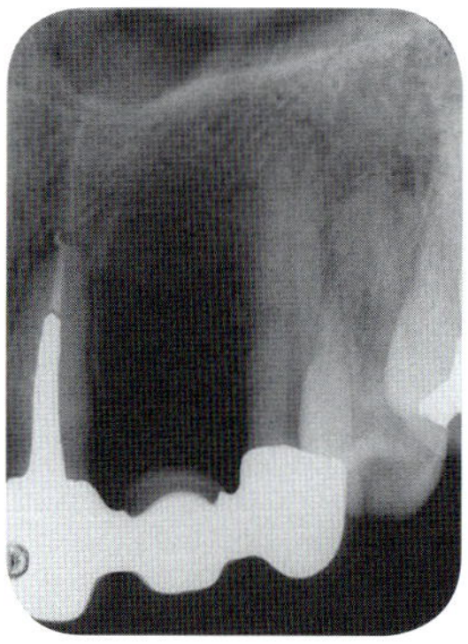

Fig 6p : The peri-apical x-ray at 9 months after the surgery. Gradual maturation of the alveolar bone is appreciated.

10 years after the surgery

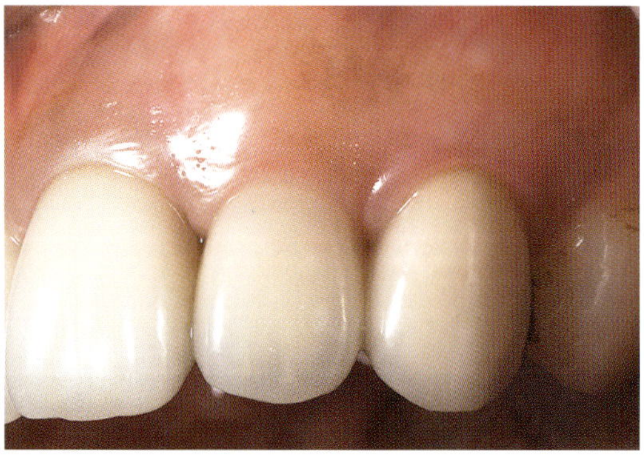

Fig 6q : 10 years after the surgery. Well maintained esthetic condition is appreciated.

Evaluation of the case

This case is the author's first ridge augmentation case with 3 connective tissue grafts layered. Since it was not clear that if the morphology of grafted area would be maintained, the area was was monitored for 6 months with the provisional restoration before final prosthesis. It is clear that good condition has been maintained even after 10 years. The same kind of results have been seen in other cases and the author is confirmed of the effectiveness of this technique from clinical experience.

Alveolar ridge augmentation procedure : The pontic site for the conventional fixed prosthesis 2

Pre-op

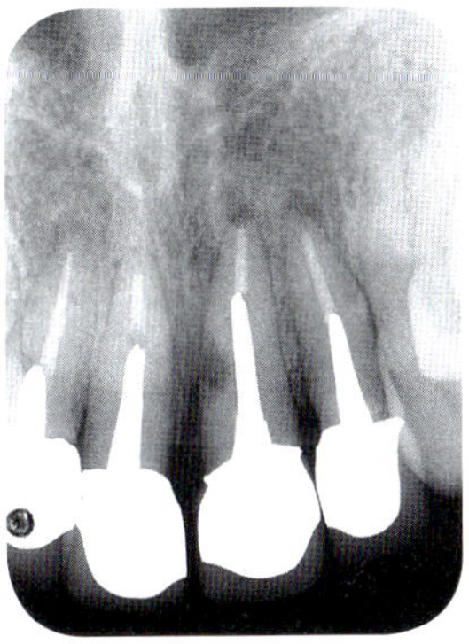

Fig 7a : At the first visit, peri-apical x-ray of maxillary left central incisor before extraction.

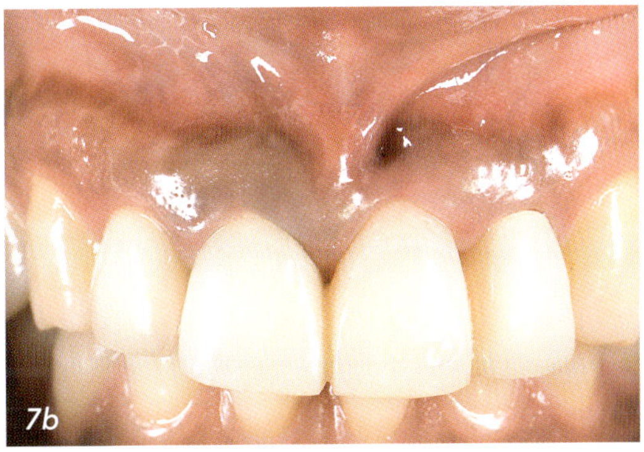

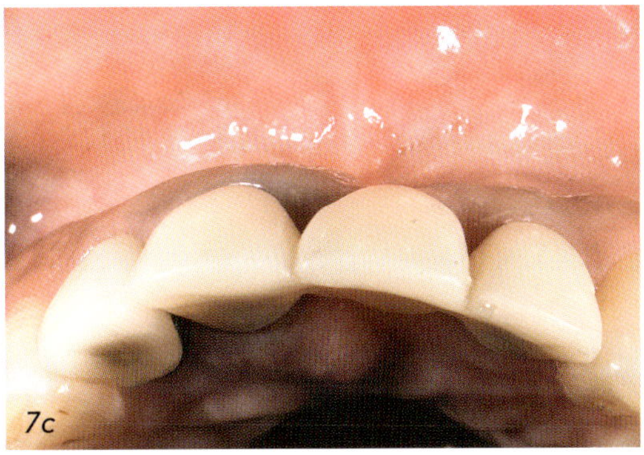

Fig 7b, c : Pre-op frontal view of maxillary anterior teeth. The removal of the provisional restoration.

The removal of the provisional restoration

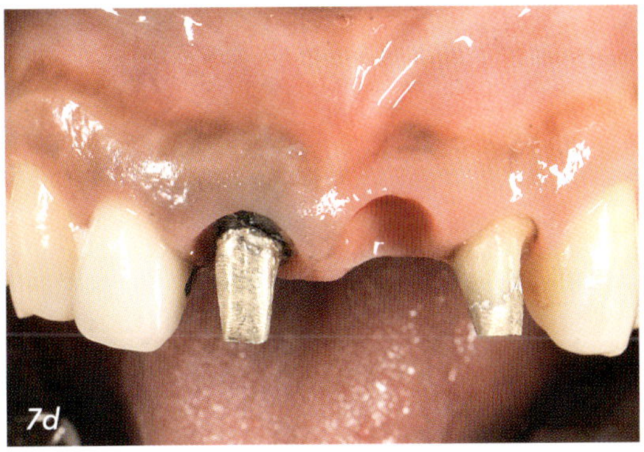

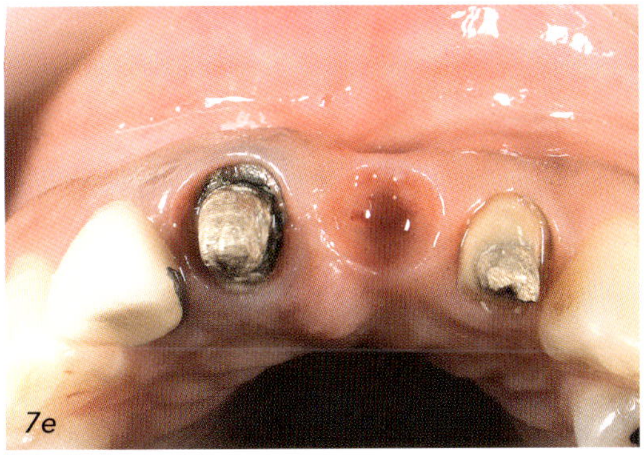

Fig 7d, e : Frontal and occlusal view at the removal of the provisional restoration.

Vertical gingival line	3	2	1	1	2	3
Balance to the adjacent tooth				X		
Balance to the same tooth on the contra lateral side				X		
Horizontal gingival line	**3**	**2**	**1**	**1**	**2**	**3**
Balance to the adjacent tooth				X		
Balance to the same tooth on the contra lateral side				X		

*mark [X] in problematic area

Point of this case

Problems

- Horizontal and vertical gingival discrepancy is appreciated at maxillary left central incisor.
- Strong upper lip frenum between maxillary incisors is appreciated, which would affect the coronal repositioning of the gingival flap.

The purpose and procedures of the surgery

1. Soft tissue ridge expansion with 2 connective tissue grafts is applied to improve the continuity of horizontal•vertical gingival level.
2. Frenectomy is performed simultaneously to improve the prognosis of the graft procedure.

Collecting connective tissue graft (2009. 10.20)

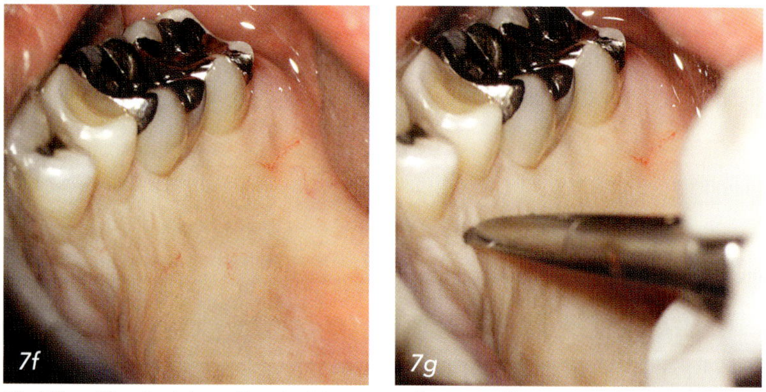

Fig 7f, g : First incision. First incision is made vertically against the palatal mucosa.

The incision to harvest the connective tissue graft

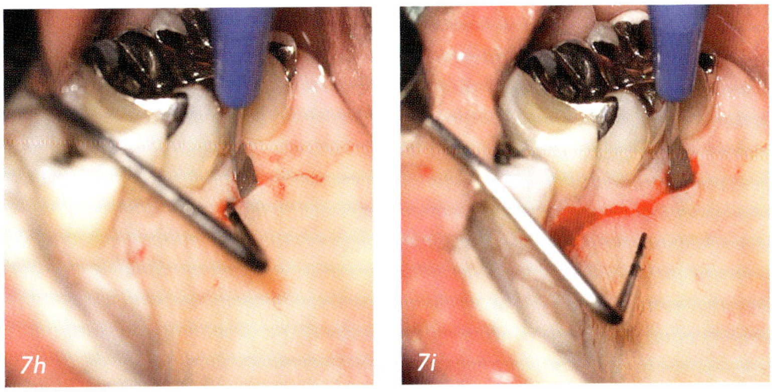

Fig 7h, i : The secondary incision. The secondary incision is made parallel to the surface of the mucosa in 1 mm thickness.

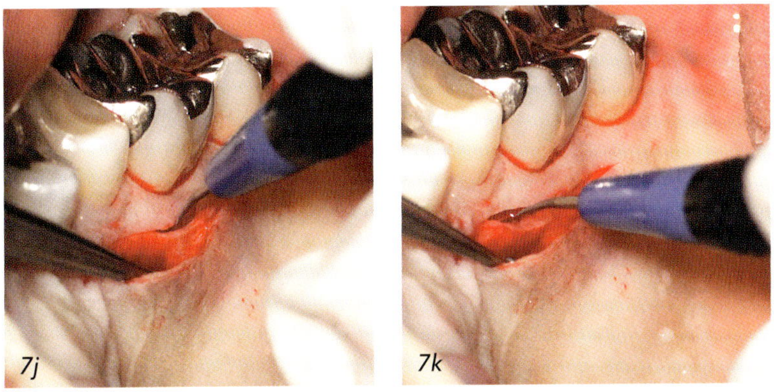

Fig 7j, k : The tertiary incision. The tertiary incision is made parallel to the secondary incision leaving the periosteum intact.

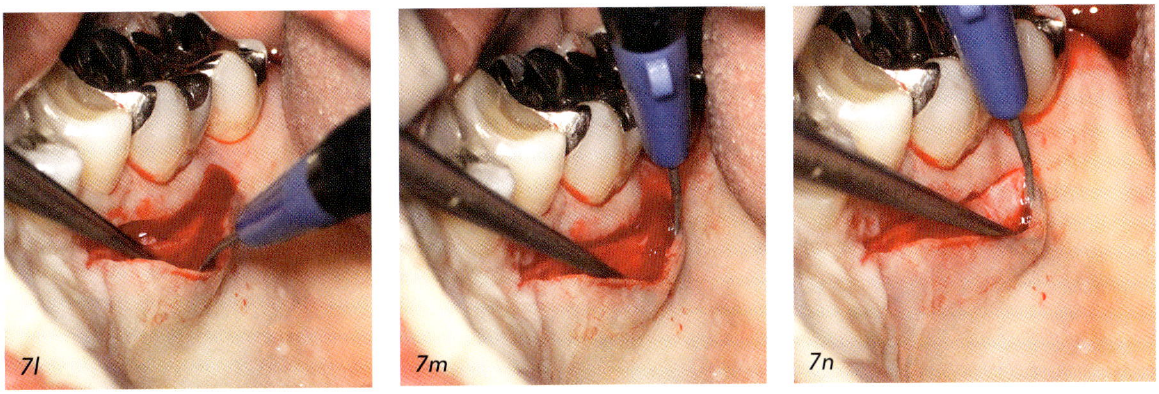

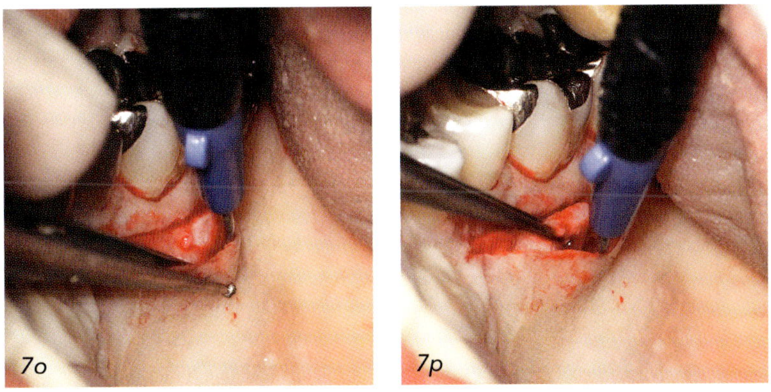

Fig 7 l~p : The incision to cut off the connective tissue graft. It is accomplished by connecting the secondary and tertiary incisions. This incision is approached from the sedentary incision side to the tertiary incision side. However, this approach is reversed if the large artery is suspected to exist in the apex area.

Detachment of the tissue graft

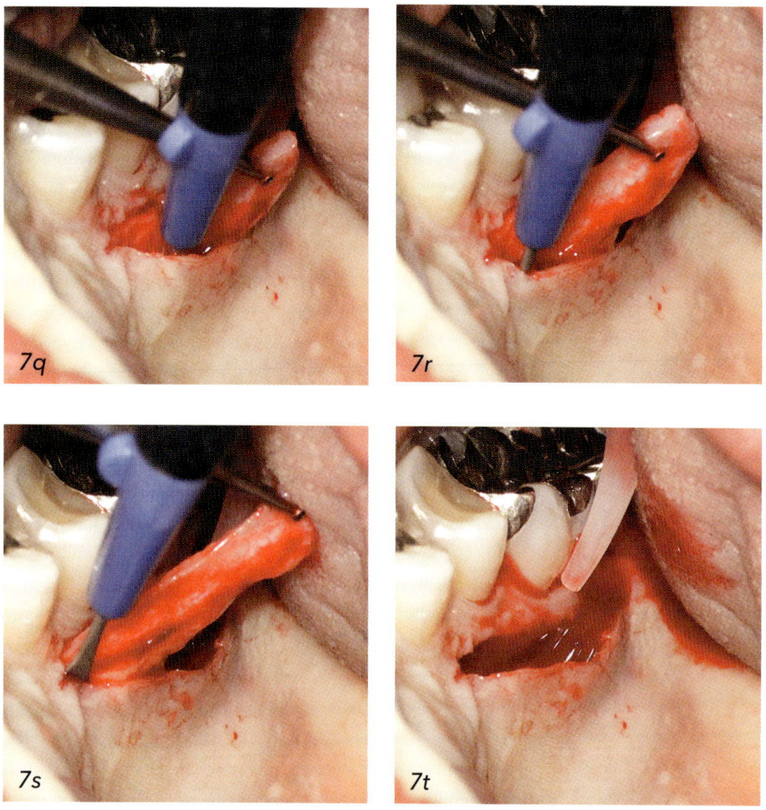

Fig 7q~t : Once the detachment of the graft is progressed to some extent, the graft is pulled with the forceps which cutting the graft confirming the attachment area.

Insertion of the collagen material

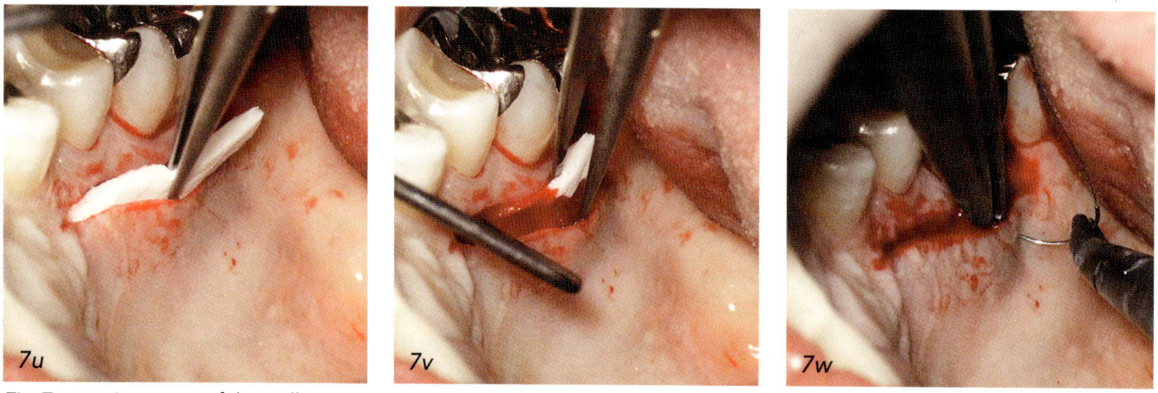

Fig 7u~w : Insertion of the collagen material. The collagen material is inserted to fill the donor site where the connective tissue graft was taken. It is trimmed in the shape of the tissue graft.

Suturing of the donor site

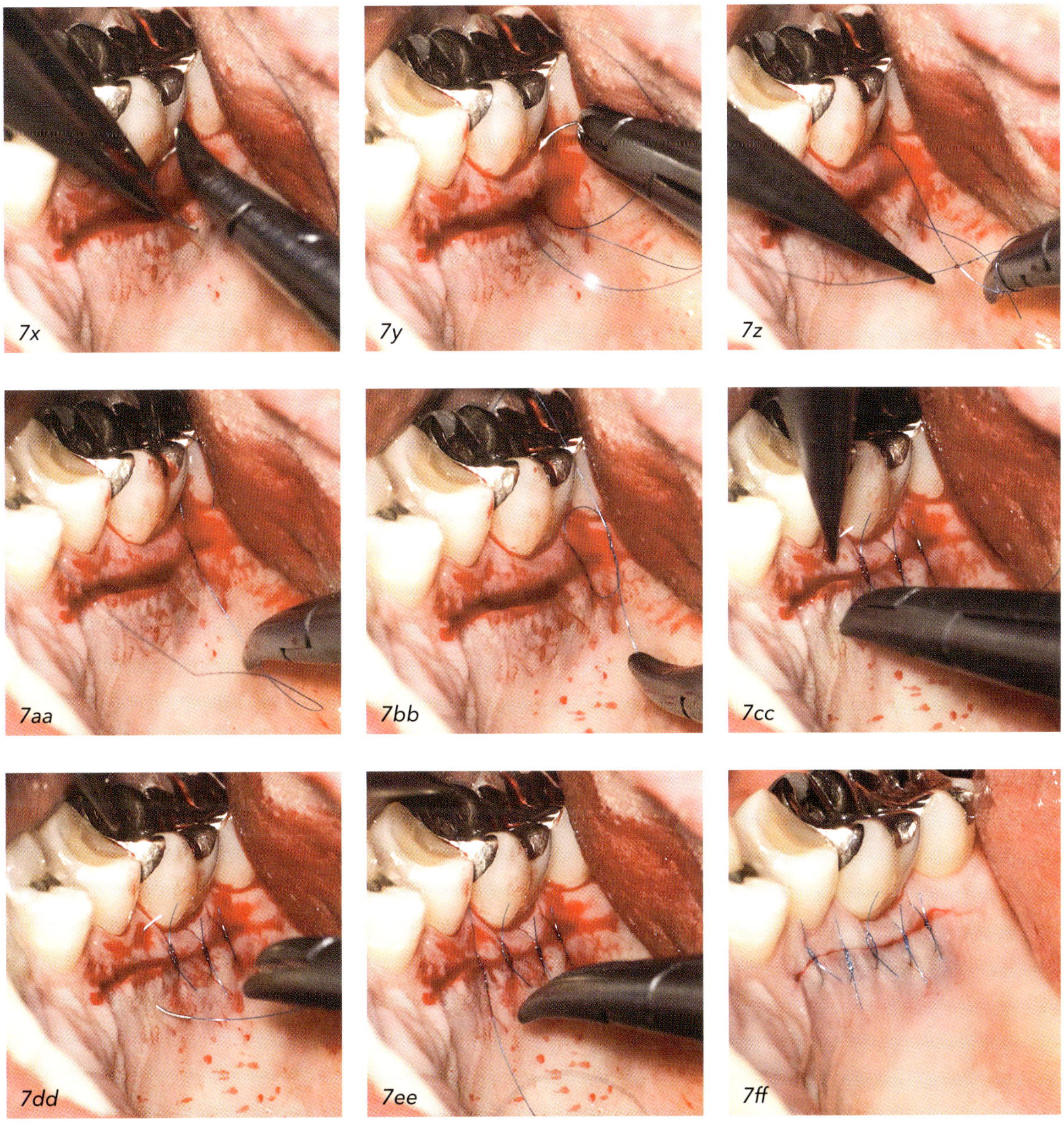

Fig 7x~ff : Simple loop suture is utilized in this case, but continuous suture or mattress suture technique could be applied as well.

Incision for preparing the gingival graft

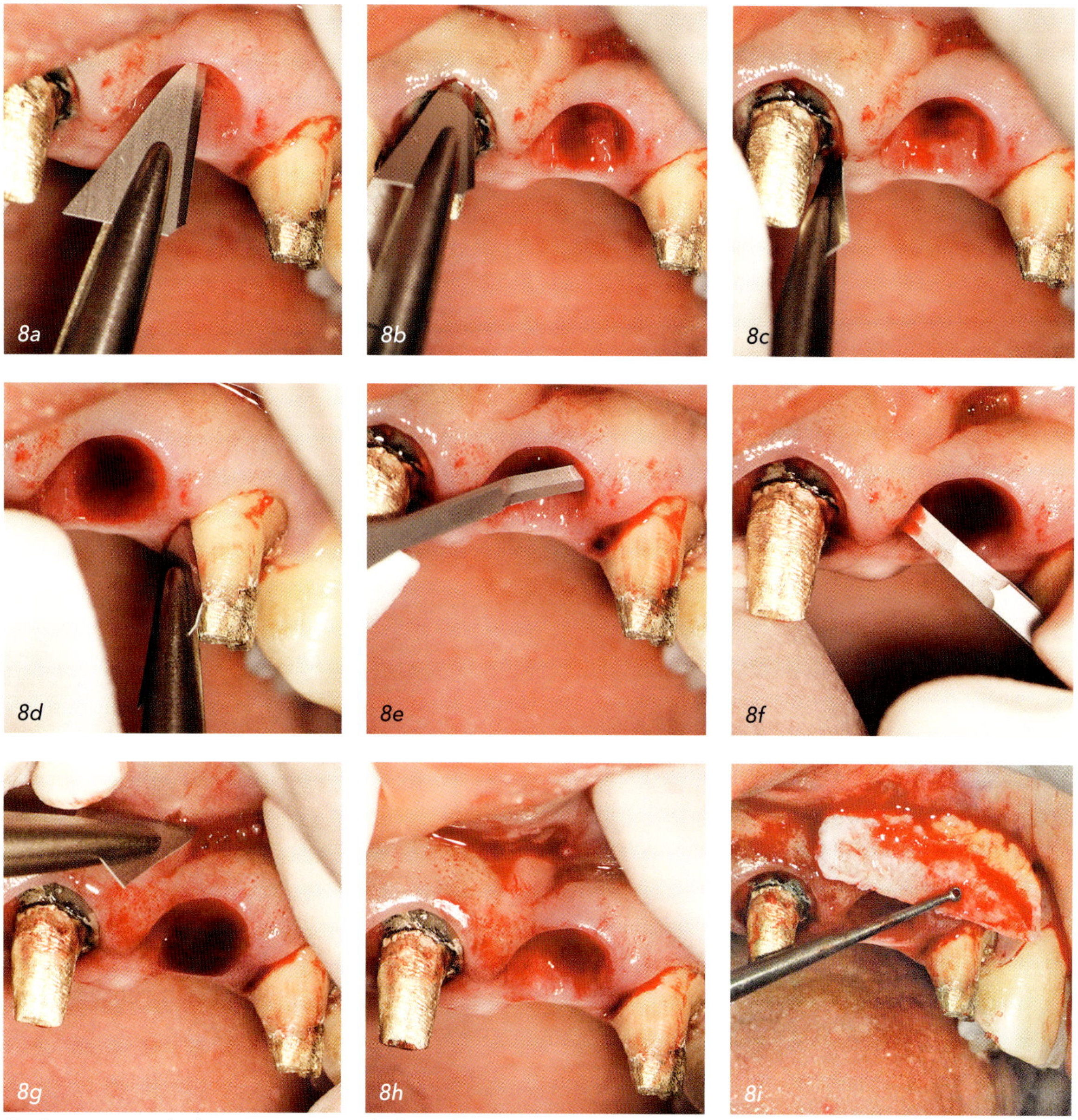

Fig 8a~i : gingival sulcus incision is made from distal buccal corner of both adjacent teeth with the incision scalpel (feather razor blade). Incision of the pontic area is proceeded from palatal corner along the cervical line formed by the pontic imitating the gingival sulcus incision. After the outline is incised, the envelop flap is made carefully using elevating scalpel (CK2). The envelop flap is extended over the MGJ until the flap becomes mobile. Upper lip frenectomy was performed accordingly after the envelop flap is completed.

Trimming and suturing of the connective tissue graft

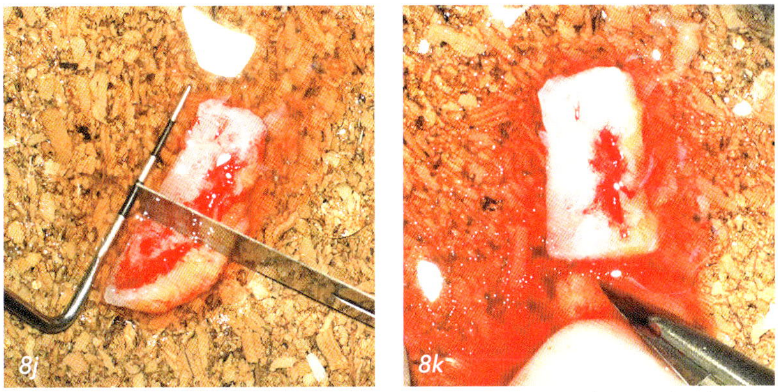

Fig 8j, k : Harvested graft is cut into two pieces and trimmed accordingly.

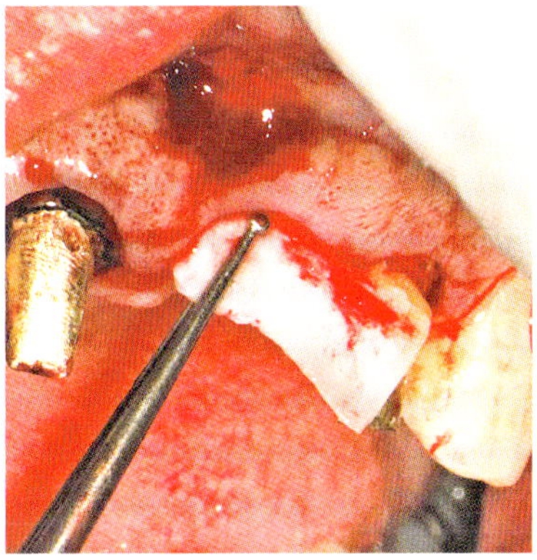

Fig 8l : Insertion of the first graft.

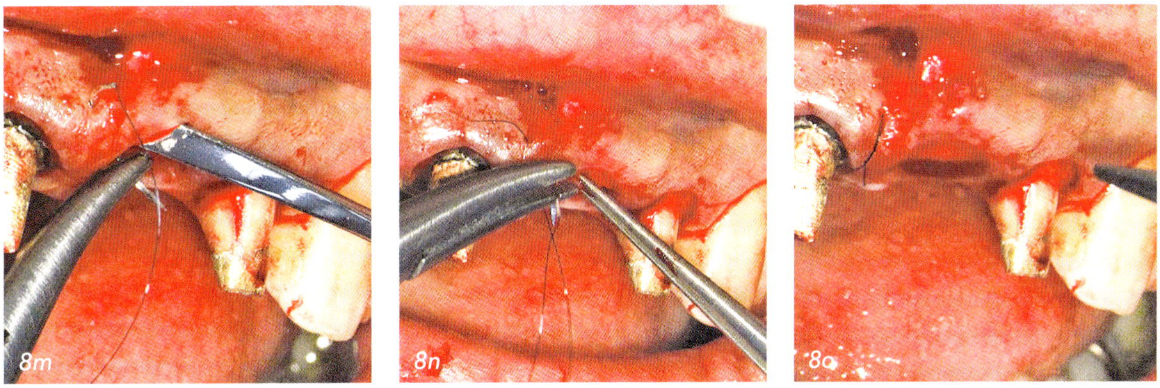

Fig 8m~o : The first graft is inserted in the flap and suture stabilize it by simple sutures at mesial and distal aspect. 2 mm of the graft is kept exposed coronally.

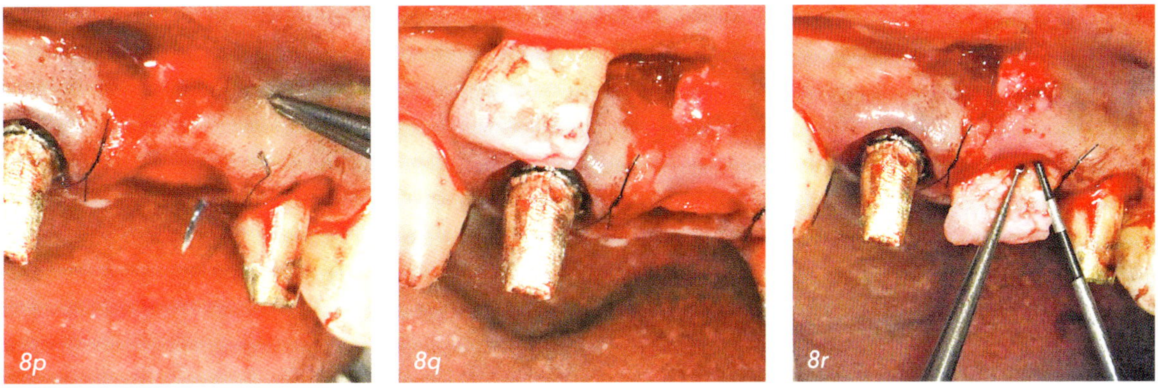

Fig 8p~r : Suturing of the second graft. Buccal volume of the ridge is further increased by the second graft. The contour of the root is reproduced by the vertically long graft.

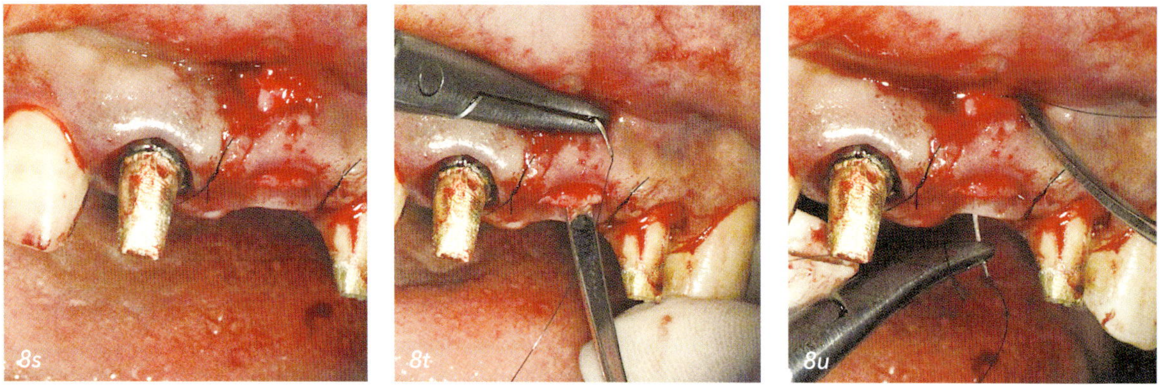

Fig 8s~u : The needle is inserted from the labial side to pick up the graft, then pulled out of the gingival flap. It is then inserted again picking up the second graft, and then the first graft to be tied at the labial side.

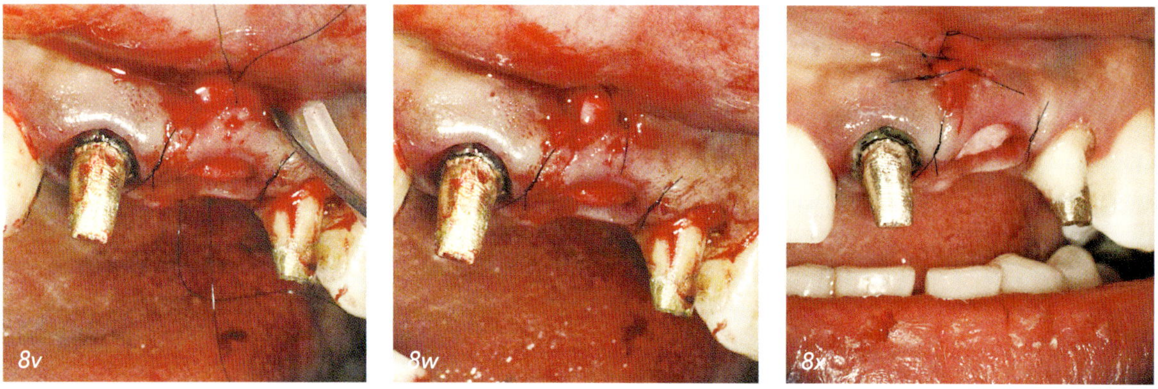

Fig 8v~x : Subsequently, the edge of the second graft and the frenum is trimmed off and the suture is tied covering the open wound area.

Point

The purpose of the 2 mm of exposed first graft when it is sutured is to increase the vertical gingival level. This procedure was performed applying the rational of root coverage procedure to the ovate pontic. It is not practical technique for the usual alveolar ridge.

Right after the surgery

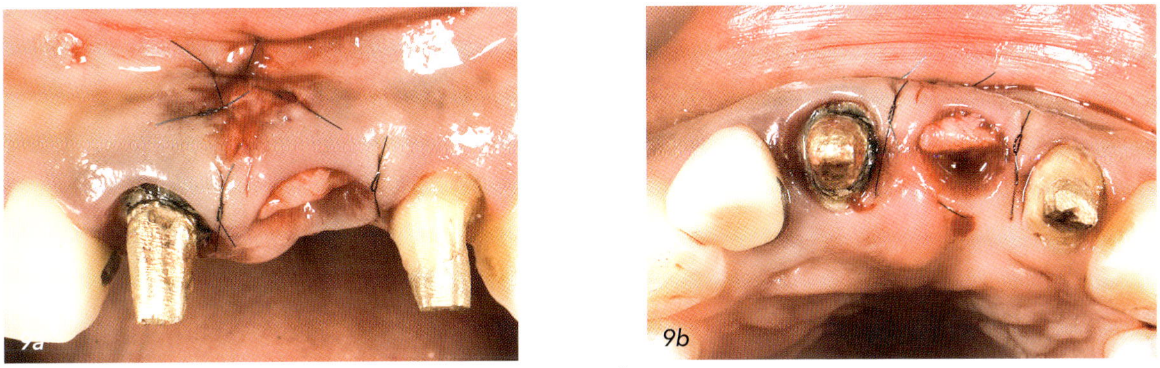

Fig 9a, b : Frontal and occlusal view of maxillary anterior area after suturing.

Removal of sutures

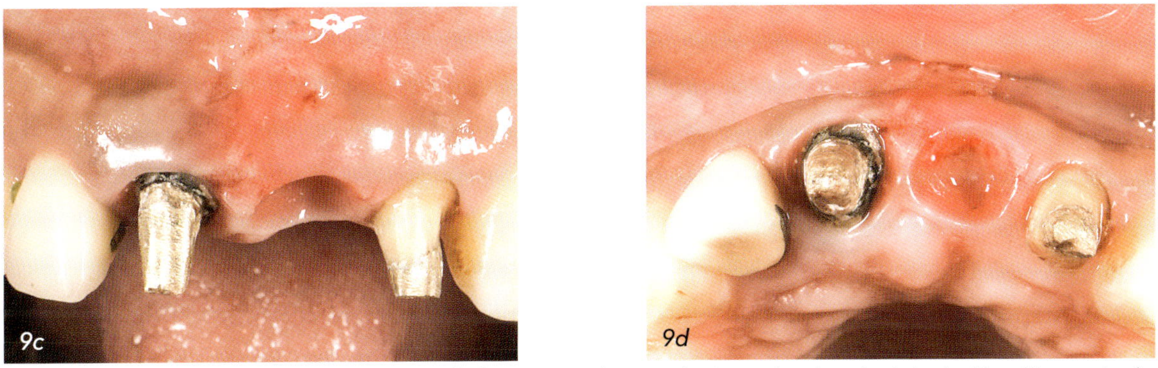

Fig 9c, d : Frontal and occlusal view at removal of sutures. Adequate horizontal and vertical gingival level is acquired.

The provisional restoration in place

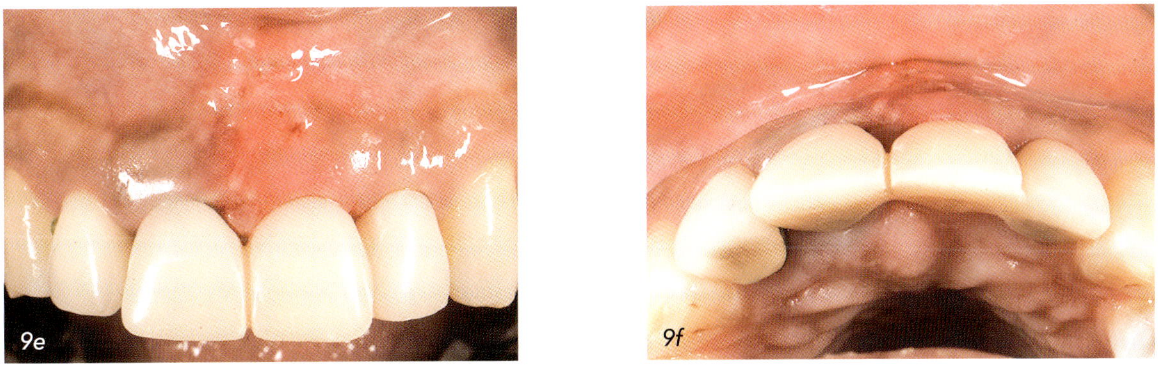

Fig 9e, f : Frontal and occlusal view with the provisional restoration in place.

After the surgery

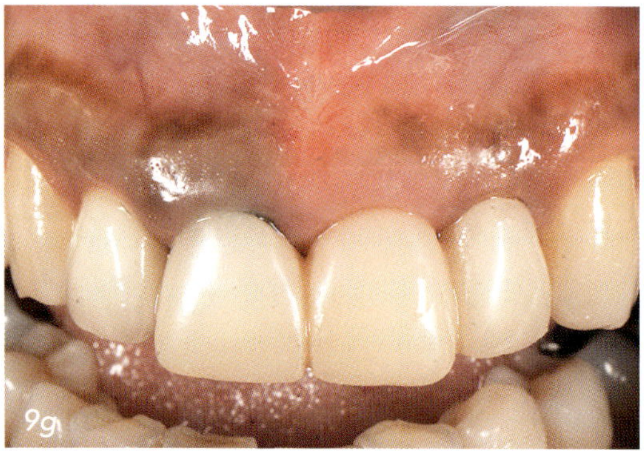

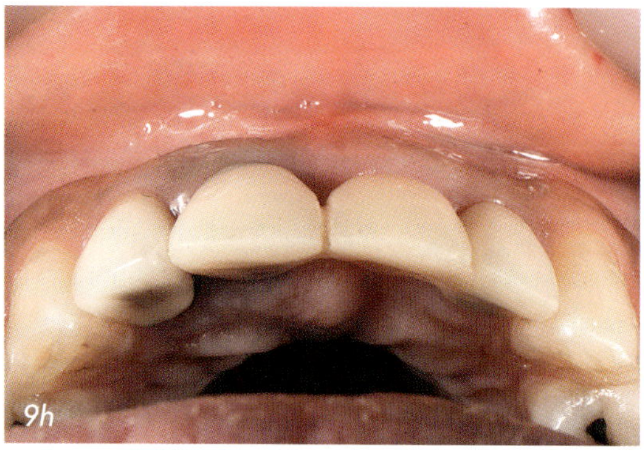

Fig 9g, h : Healing was monitored with the provisional restoration.

Time of insertion of the final prosthesis

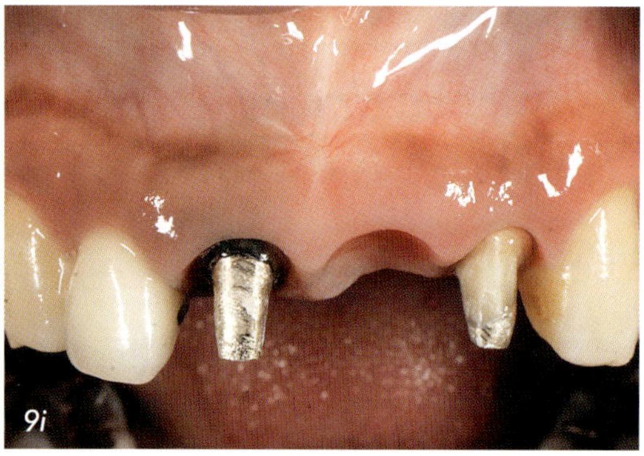

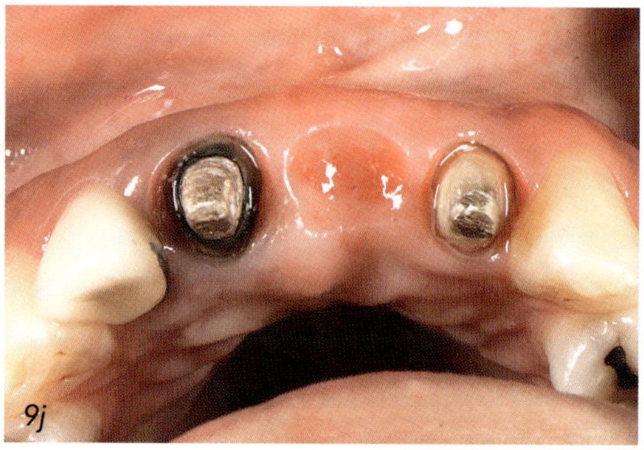

Fig 9i, j : Frontal and occlusal view at the time of insertion of the final prosthesis.

1 year after the procedure

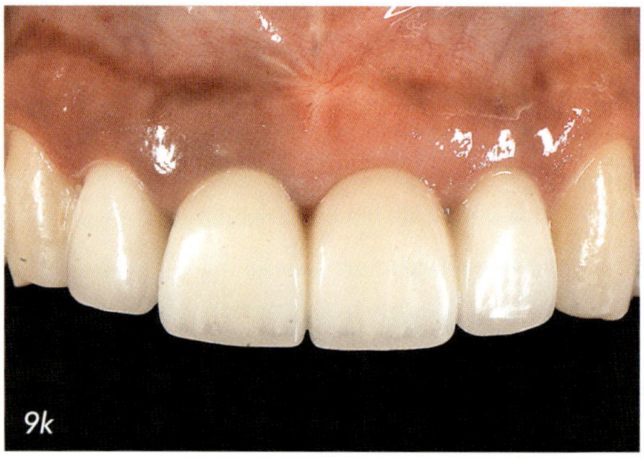

Fig 9k, l : 1 year after the procedure was completed. Esthetically well balanced gingival level has been maintained.

Evaluation of the case

It is well documented through this case that connective tissue graft for the edentulous ridge expansion succeeds against the acrylic resin surface of the pontic as well as against composite resin, which is proven to be biocompatible material. The soft tissue is well adapted to the surroundings indicating that the shape of soft tissue is controlled by the adjacent prosthesis.

Alveolar ridge augmentation procedure : Pontic site of the conventional fixed prosthesis 3

Pre-op

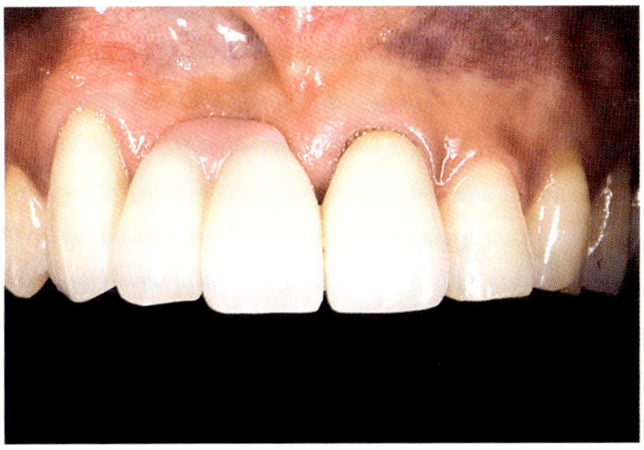

Fig 10a : The patient is not happy with esthetics of the fixed bridge from the maxillary right canine to the left central incisor.

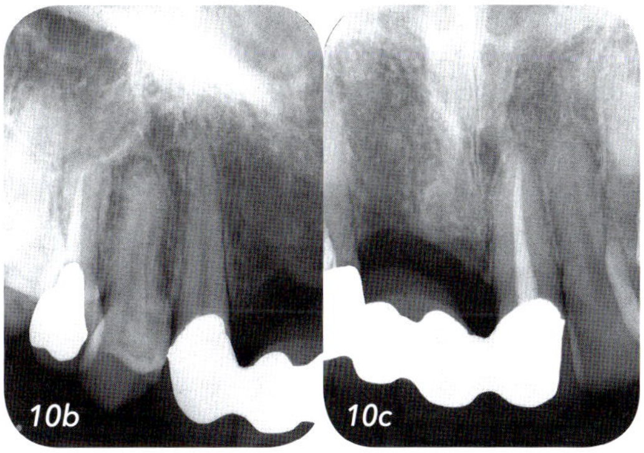

Fig 10b, c : Alveolar bony defect at pontic area of lateral and central incisor is not too extensive.

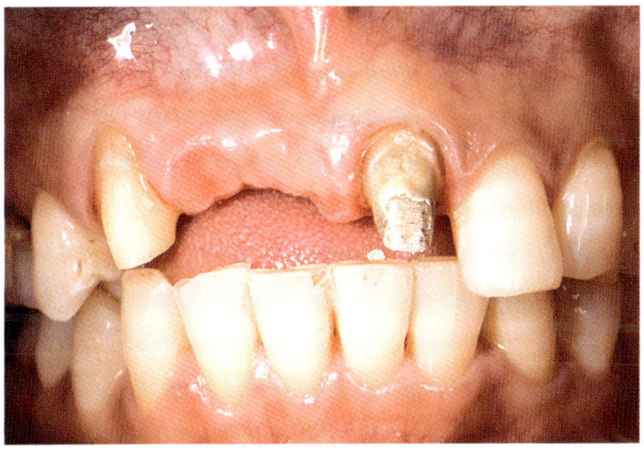

Fig 10d : Decreased vertical gingival level in the area of the right canine to the right central incisor is appreciated.

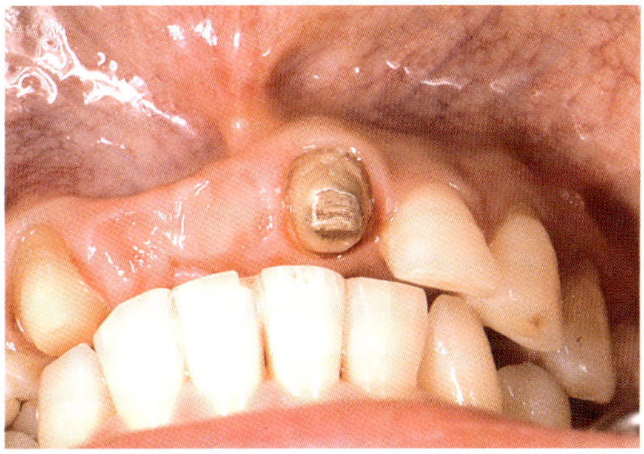

Fig 10e : Decreased horizontal gingival level in the area of the right lateral and central incisor is appreciated.

Vertical gingival line	3	2	1	1	2	3
Balance to the adjacent tooth	X	X	X			
Balance to the same tooth on the contra lateral side	X	X	X			
Horizontal gingival line	**3**	**2**	**1**	**1**	**2**	**3**
Balance to the adjacent tooth		X	X			
Balance to the same tooth on the contra lateral side		X	X			

*mark [X] in problematic area

Points of this case

Problems

- Decreased vertical • horizontal gingival level.
- The most extensive defect is at the proximal area between the lateral and the central incisors.
- Decreased vertical gingival level is appreciated at the right canine and abutment preparation has been performed according to that level.

The purpose and procedures of the surgery

1. Vertical and horizontal gingival level at the area of maxillary right lateral and central incisors is recontoured by two connective tissue graft procedures.
2. The right maxillary canine needs to be extruded orthodontically as a presurgical procedure.

Diagnostic wax up

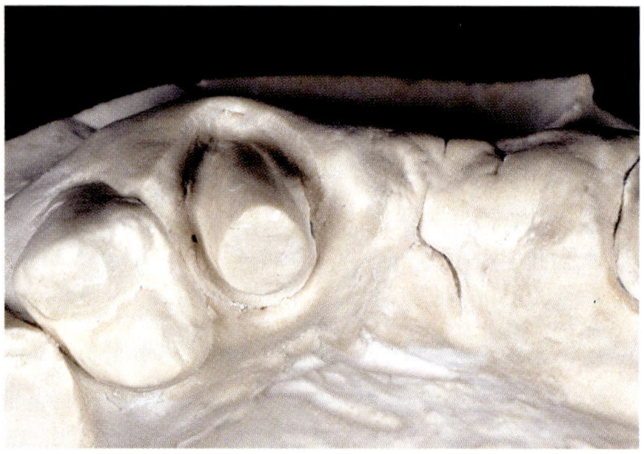

Fig 10f : Study model. Close observation of the study model is essential step to plan the surgery.

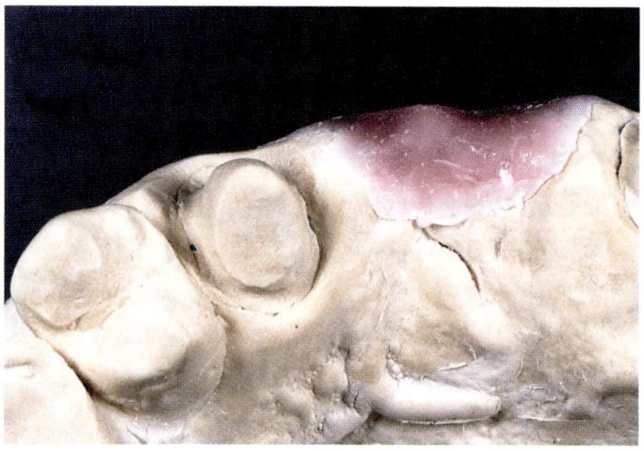

Fig 10g : Ideal contour is waxed up on the study model.

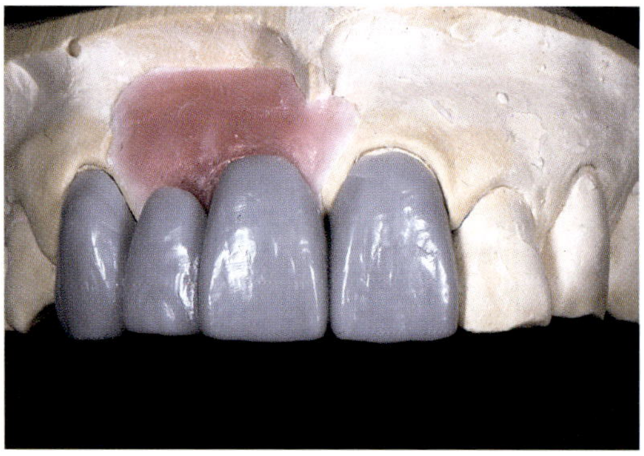

Fig 10h : The soft tissue is waxed up first and then the prosthesis is waxed up.

First surgery (2005. 11. 17)

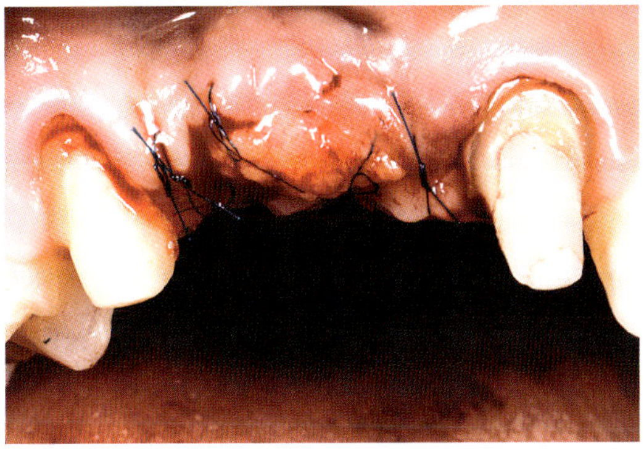

Fig 10i : Onlay graft is performed on the area of the maxillary right lateral and central incisors with the thick graft from the palate.

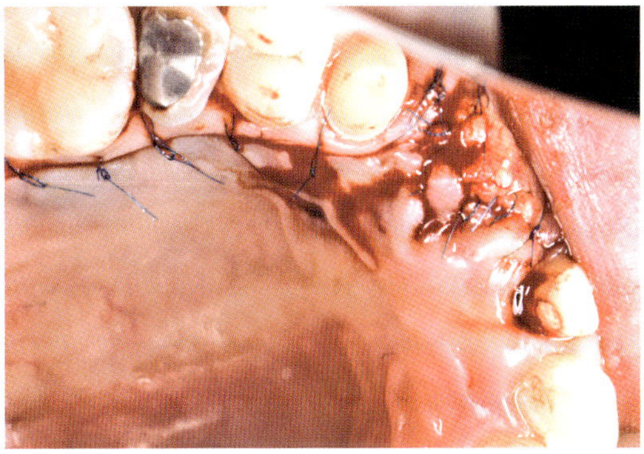

Fig 10j : Suturing. The graft is inserted into the opened partial thickness gingival flap and then closed.

Point

[Incision]

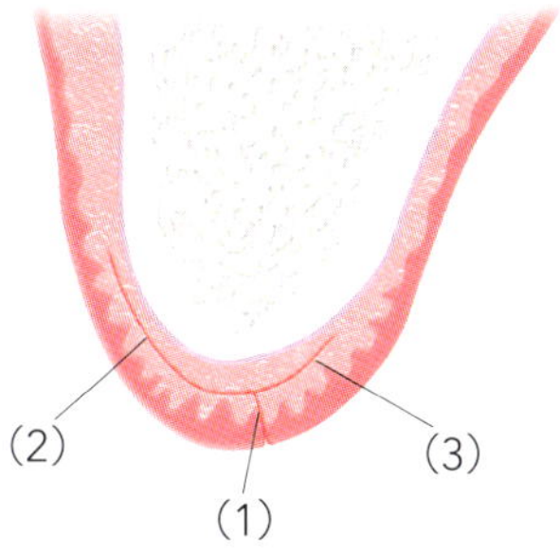

[Suture]

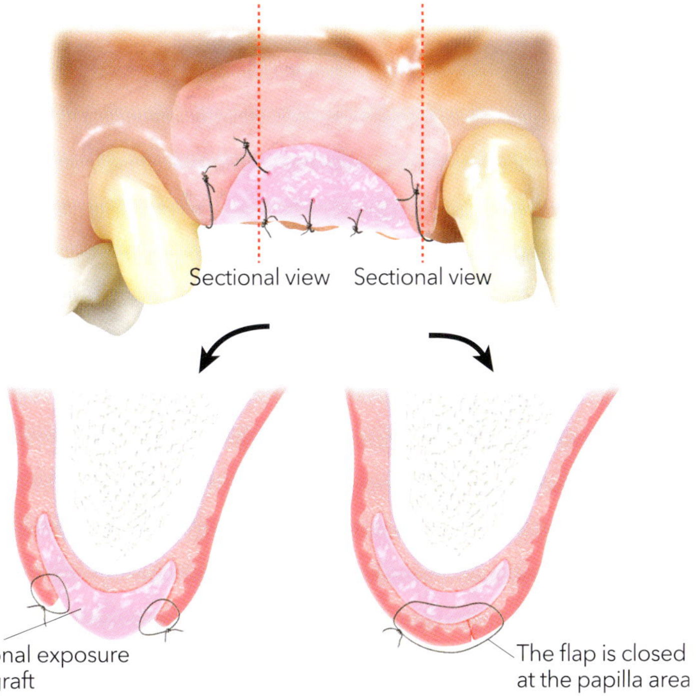

- **Incision** · Gingival sulcus incisions are made from distal labial corner of maxillary right canine and left central incisor to each mesial corner. Alveolar peak incision is made vertically by about 1.5mm (1). The partial thickness flap is made toward labial aspect from the this incision with the same thickness (2). The incision is extended over MGJ to make the gingival flap mobile. The incision is made in the same thickness toward palatal aspect with about 3~5 mm extension (3).
- **Suture** · The connective tissue graft is sutured to the palatal flap. The labial flap is sutured next. First, both papilla areas are sutured to the palatal flap together with the graft. The middle area between the right lateral and central incisors, where the interdental papilla is intended to be reconstructed is sutured with the graft left exposed to facilitate keratinization of the mucosa.

Time of the provisional restoration is inserted / 1 month after the first surgery

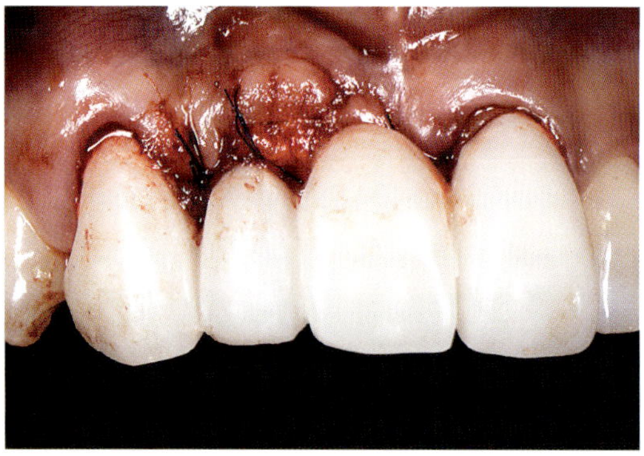

Fig 10k : Right after suturing. Pre-fabricated provisional restoration is inserted.

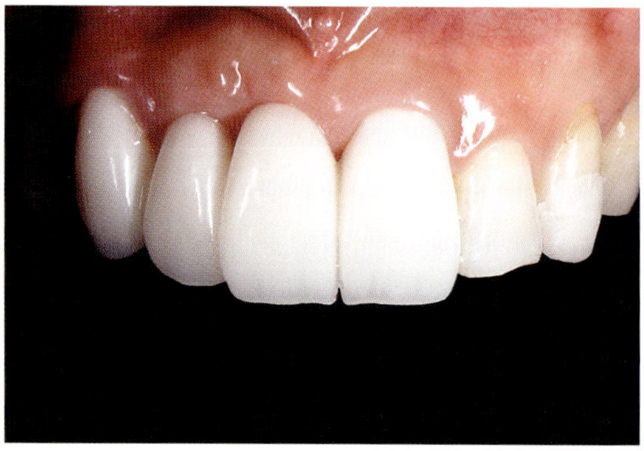

Fig 10l : One month after insertion of the provisional restoration. The soft tissue is healing well.

Second surgery (2006. 4. 6)

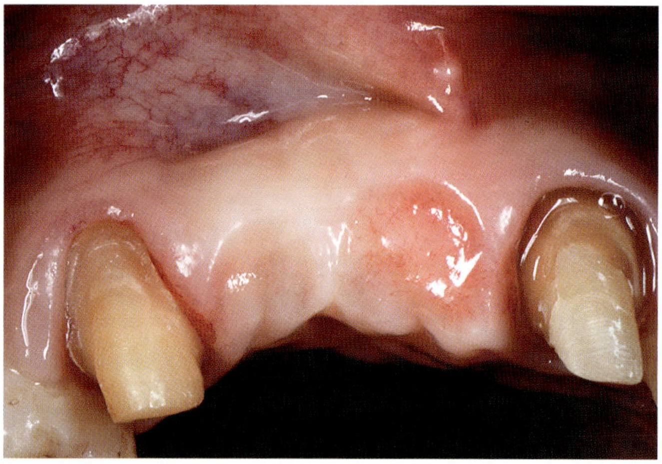

Fig 10m : Enough horizontal gingival level is acquired.

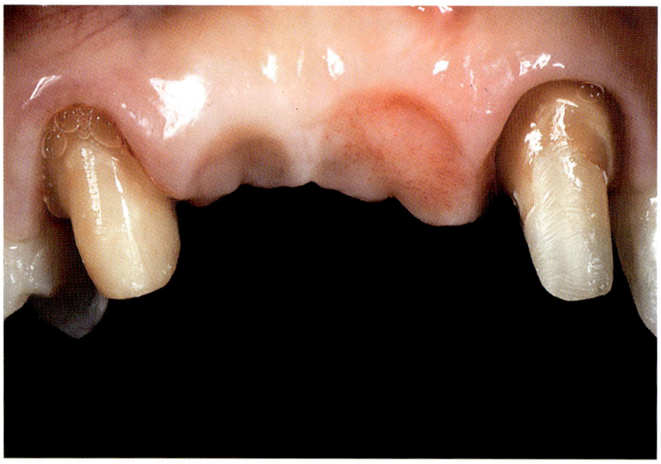

Fig 10n : Vertical gingival level at the interdental papilla area between lateral and central incisors is lacking.

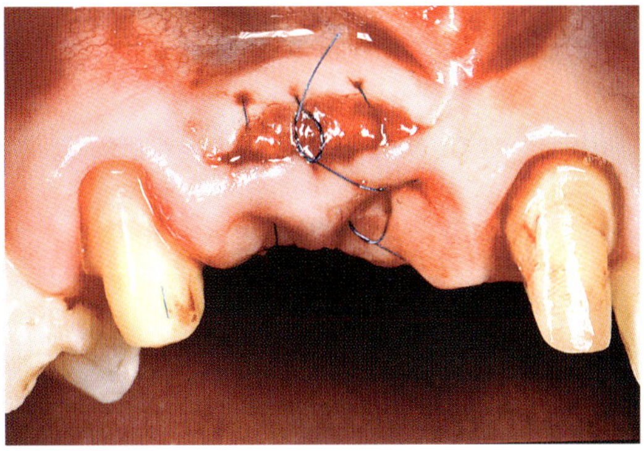

Fig 10o : Inlay graft was performed to increase vertical gingival level of the papilla area. The graft was stabilized with only 3 sutures with support of the provisional restoration.

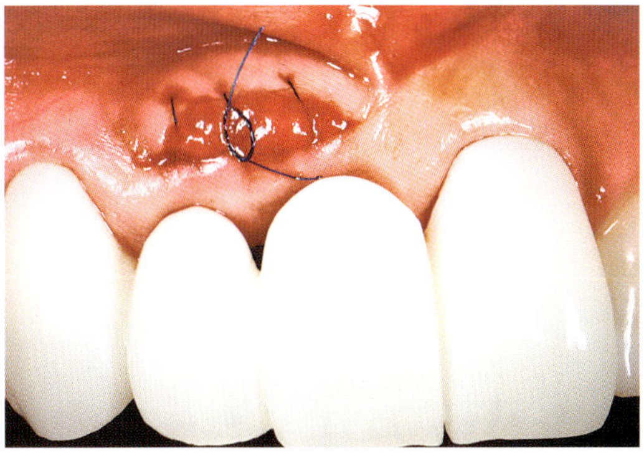

Fig 10p : The shape of the pontic is modified and the provisional restoration is re-inserted after the suture. The pontic is modified so that the base portion presses the gingiva.

Point

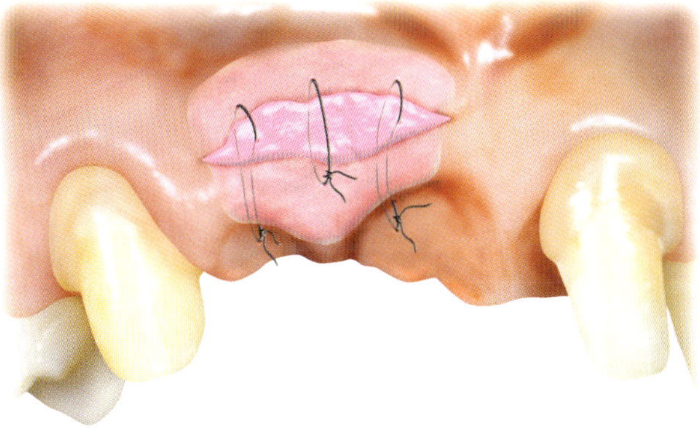

Simple inlay graft was performed for the purpose of increasing vertical gingival level without considering horizontal gingival level, even though it was increased as a result. If the purpose of the surgery is simplified, the procedure is simplified as well.

Try-in

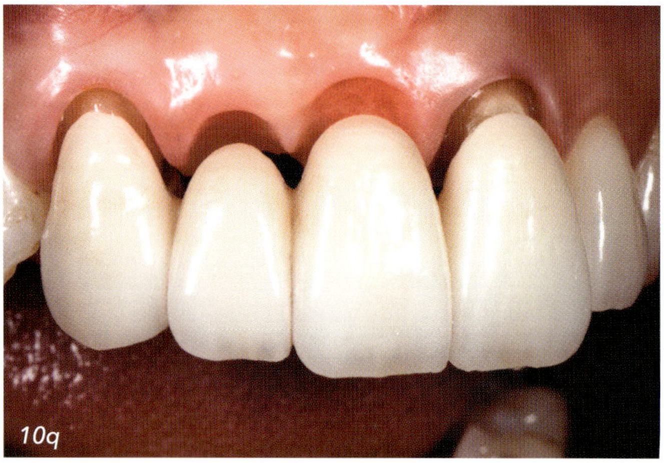

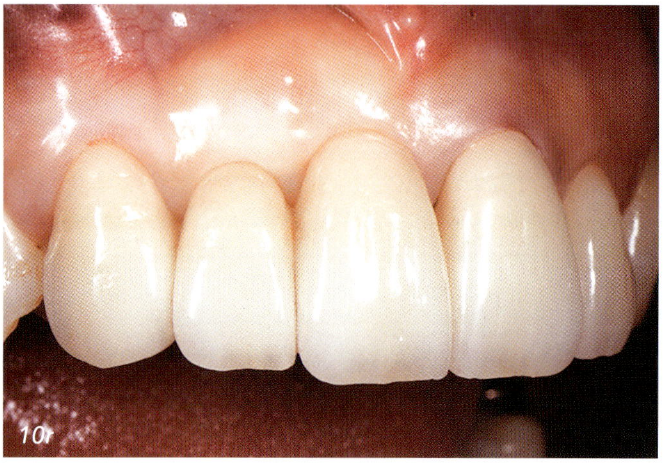

10 q, r : The pontics and gingiva are well harmonized.

Time of insertion of the final prosthesis

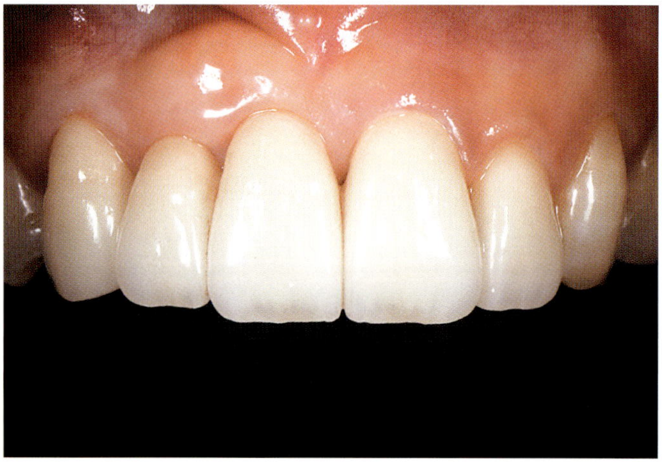

Evaluation of this case

Natural looking gingival level was acquired by reconstructing width and hight of keratinized gingiva through two surgeries.

Fig 10s : Time of insertion of the final prosthesis. Esthetic prosthesis is accomplished with successful expansion of vertical・horizontal gingival level (prosthodontic treatment by Dr. Masayuki Okawa).

The concept of alveolar ridge augmentation procedure : Advanced 1 Pre-prosthetic treatment

[Basic] concept of alveolar ridge augmentation was explained through 3 clinical cases in the previous section. [Advanced] application of alveolar ridge augmentation procedure for pre-, post-prosthetic treatment and recovery is discussed through 8 clinical cases along side with [Classification of augmentation procedure according to the type of alveolar ridge (classification of Suzuki)], which was shown in p13.

- Alveolar ridge augmentation procedure as pre-prosthetic treatment
- Alveolar ridge augmentation procedure as post-prosthetic treatment
- Alveolar ridge augmentation procedure as recovery

Alveolar ridge augmentation procedure as pre-prosthetic treatment 1

Pre-op : concave-hill

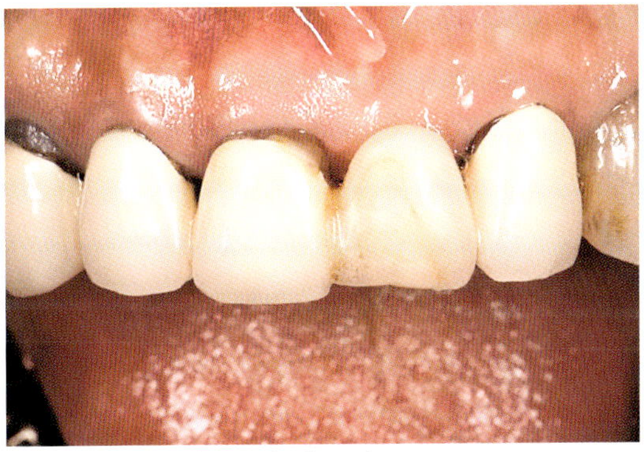

Fig 11a : Frontal view before the surgery.

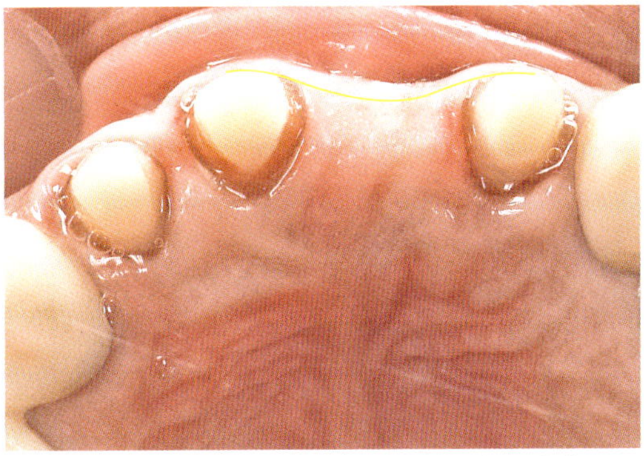

Fig 11b : Concave-hill type alveolar ridge defect at the area of maxillary left central incisor is appreciated. Alveolar ridge augmentation procedure with connective tissue graft was indicated.

Vertical gingival line	3	2	1	1	2	3
Balance to the adjacent tooth						
Balance to the same tooth on the contra lateral side						
Horizontal gingival line	**3**	**2**	**1**	**1**	**2**	**3**
Balance to the adjacent tooth				X		
Balance to the same tooth on the contra lateral side				X		

*mark [X] in problematic area

Points of this case

Problems

- The ridge type is considered concave-hill rather than level-hill with enough vertical gingival level and decreased horizontal gingival level.

The purpose and procedures of the surgery

1. The defect is limited to simple horizontal gingival level and the size is limited as well. One thick connective tissue graft is considered enough to reconstruct the area. Envelope flap was chosen since the amount of repositioning is relatively small due to the small defect size.

The surgery (2003. 12. 11)

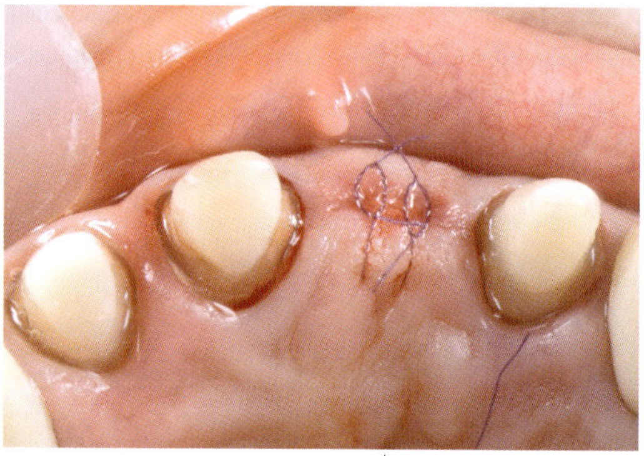

Fig 11c : The envelope flap was formed with the tunneling technique. The connective tissue graft taken from the palate was inserted inside the envelope flap and sutured at the incision area with 7-0.

Point

1

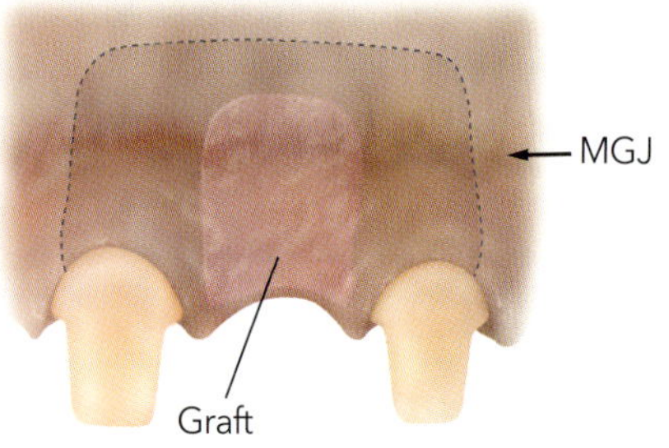

2

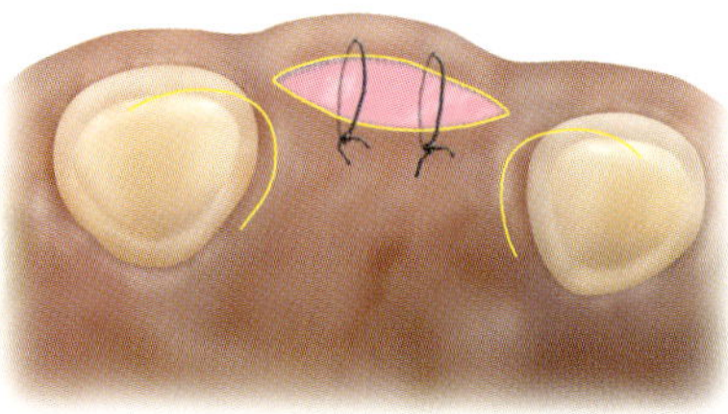

Incision : Gingival sulcus incisions are made from labial distal corner to palatal medial corner of the maxillary right central incisor and the maxillary left lateral incisor. Following alveolar ridge incision is made toward labial side without extending to papilla area. The gingival flap is formed extending beyond MGJ by tunneling technique (1 note : incisions and elevation is extended enough so that the gingival graft is mobile enough including labial papilla area).

Suture : Relatively thick graft (connective tissue) taken from the palate is trimmed according to the condition of the defect and tied at two places with simple loop suture (2).

The time of insertion of the provisional restoration

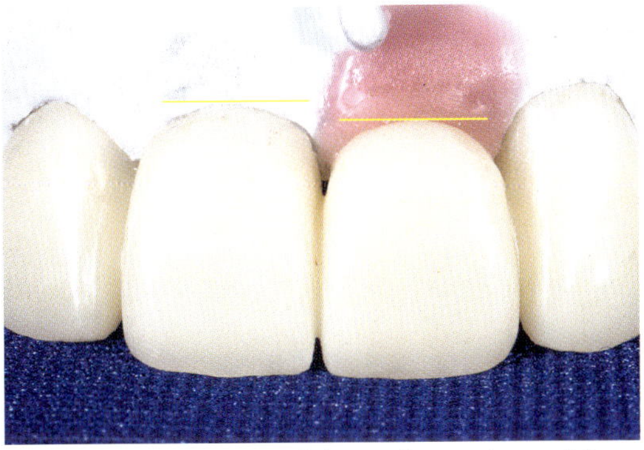

Fig 11d : The amount of the graft is estimated from the diagnostic wax-up.

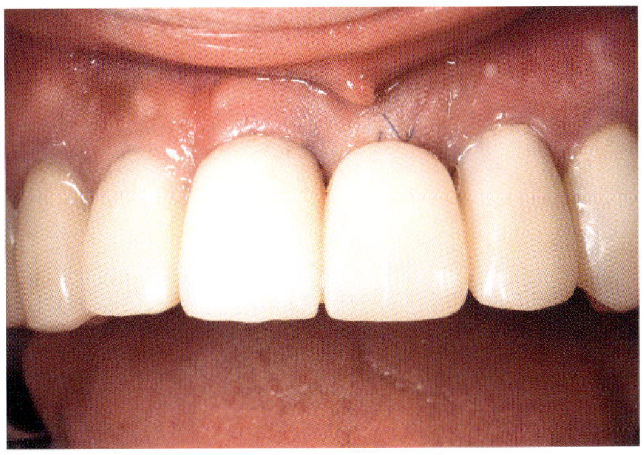

Fig 11e : Insertion of the provisional restoration.

Point

Discussion with the restorative dentist (Dr. Masao Yamazaki) took place in detail using the diagnostic wax-up. According to the request from the restorative dentist, it was planned to increased the hight of the alveolar ridge by 1 mm. Ideal alveolar ridge shape was waxed-up and the provisional restoration was fabricated accordingly. At the time of insertion of provisional restoration after suture, close contact between the base of the pontic area of the provisional restoration and the alveolar ridge. The author usually confirm it by slight blanching on the gingiva of the pontic area.

The time of insertion of the final prosthesis

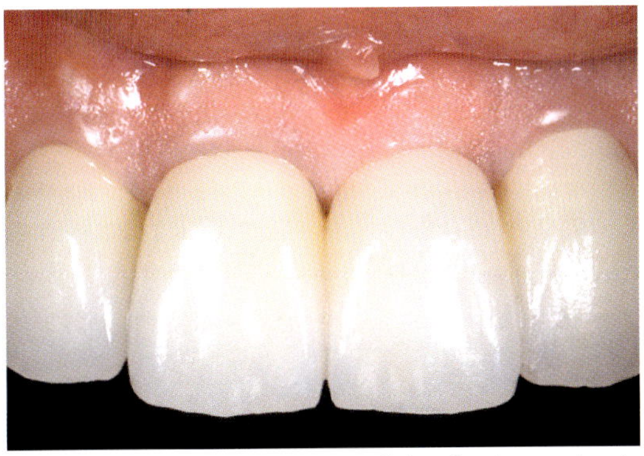

Fig 11f : The time insertion of the final prosthesis (prosthetic treatment by Dr. Masao Yamazaki).

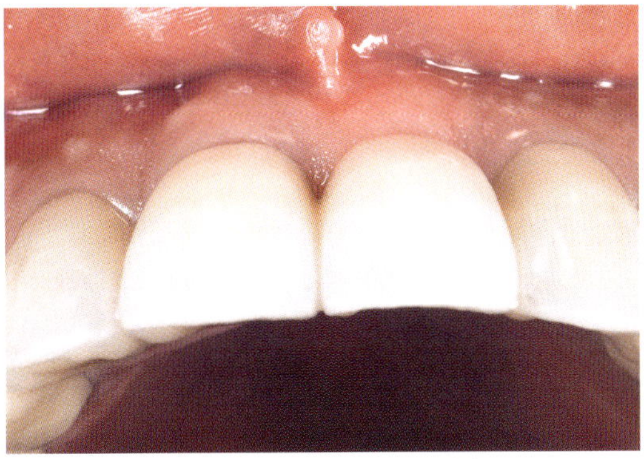

Fig 11g : Well matured and stable gingiva is observed.

2 years post-op

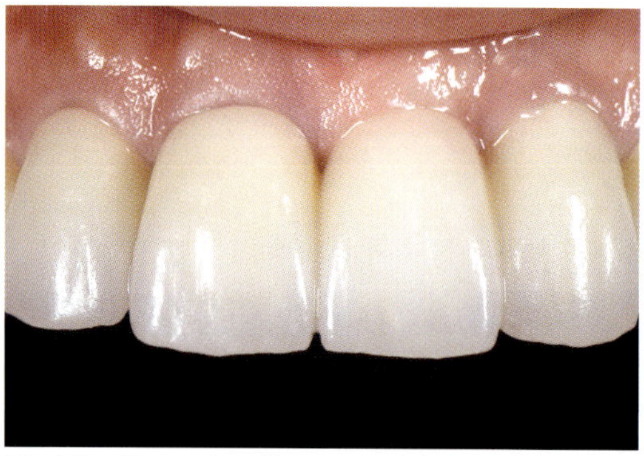

Fig 11h : Gingival scallop around the pontic is stable and well balanced.

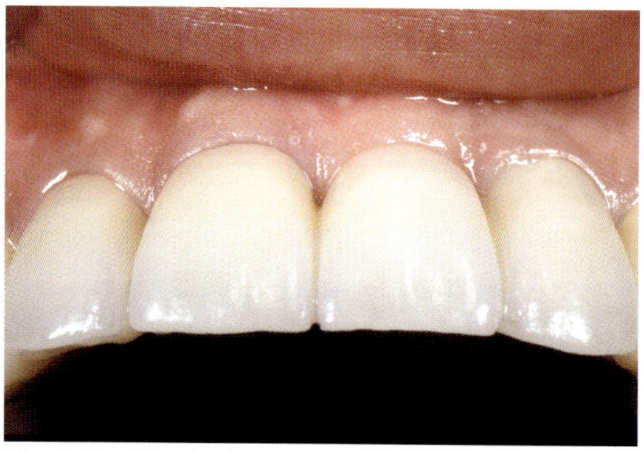

Fig 11i : Gingival contour is stable as well and symmetric.

3.5 years post-op

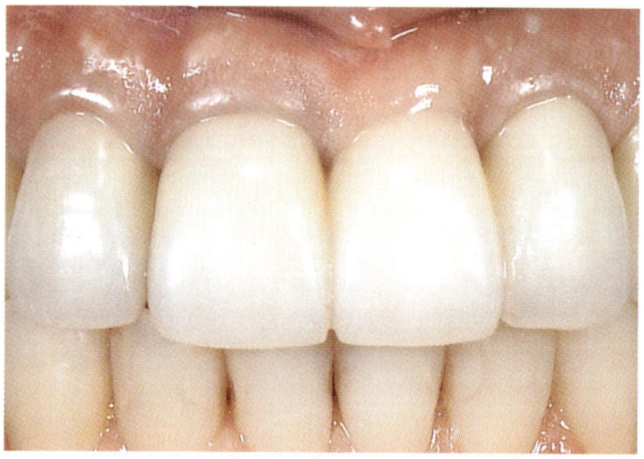

Fig 11j : 3.5 years after the procedure. Gingival condition is well maintained.

Evaluation of the case

The hight of the alveolar ridge was designed 1 mm higher than that of contralateral side. The restorative dentist requested that extra tissue available for adjustment. Proper diagnostic wax-up and pre-op discussion was inevitable. The concept of overcorrection is helpful for esthetically demanded case.

Alveolar ridge augmentation procedure as pre-prosthetic treatment 2

Pre-op : convex-valley

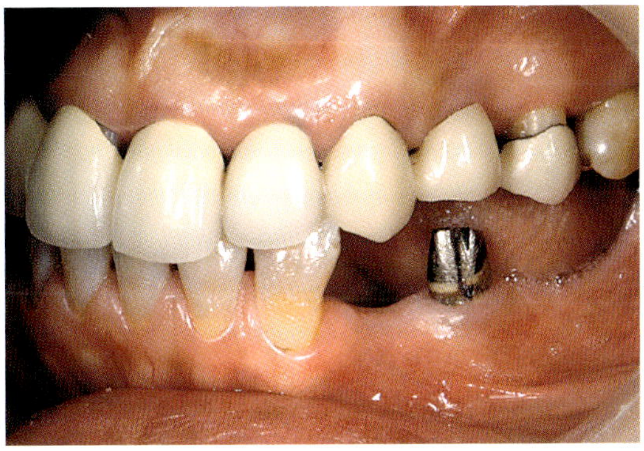

Fig 12a : Pre-op left side view.

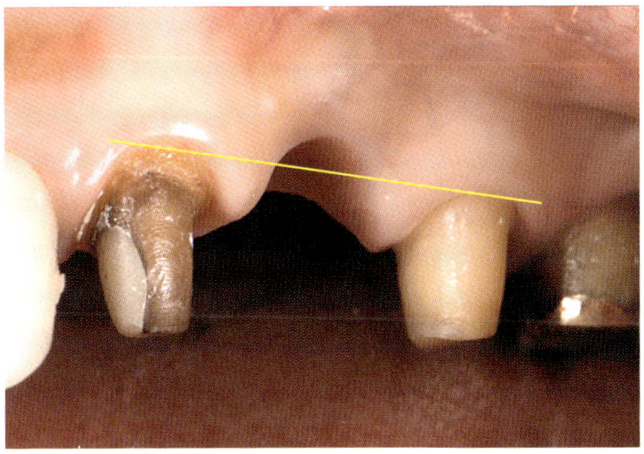

Fig 12b : About 3 mm of vertical defect is appreciated at the ridge of maxillary left first premolar area. Connective tissue inlay graft was indicted.

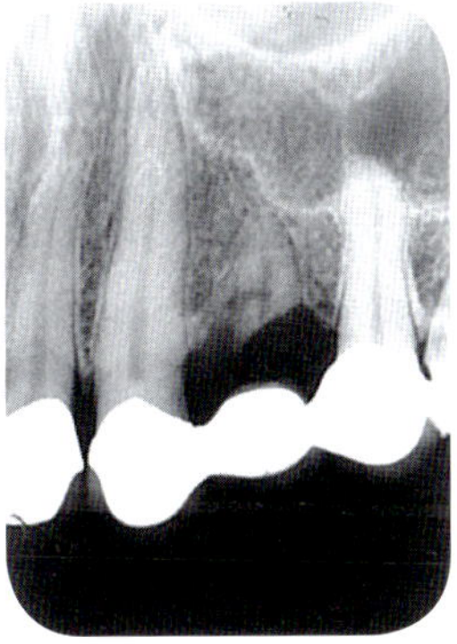

Fig 12c : Pre-op peri-apical x-ray.

Vertical gingival line	3	4	5	6
Balance to the adjacent tooth		X		
Balance to the same tooth on the contra lateral side		X		
Horizontal gingival line	**3**	**4**	**5**	**6**
Balance to the adjacent tooth				
Balance to the same tooth on the contra lateral side				

*mark [X] in problematic area

Points of this case

Problems

- Vertical gingival level is apical to that of both adjacent teeth (convex-valley). Gingival tissue is edematous.

The purpose and procedures of the surgery

1. This was very rare case of reconstruction of vertical gingival level alone since the connective tissue graft was previously perfomed on buccal aspect at the time of extraction. Connective tissue inlay graft procedure was utilized to increase buccal gingival level vertically.

The surgery (2002. 7. 25)

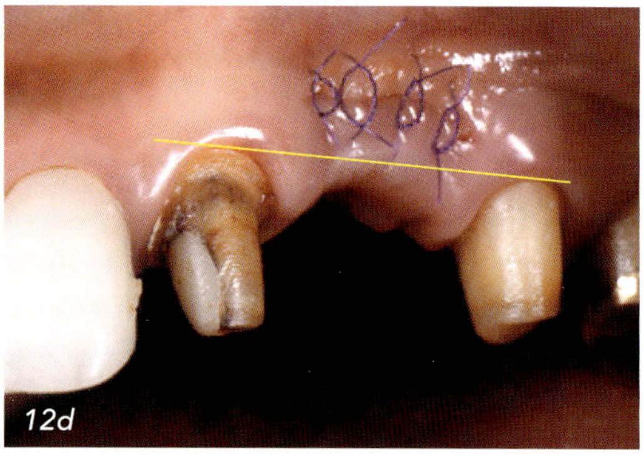

Fig 12d : The graft, which was trimmed in the exact same size as the formed gingival flap was sutured on horizontal incision area with 6-0.

Incision : 1. Gingival sulcus incisions are made on distal aspect of maxillary left canine and medial aspect of left second premolar, 2. Alveolar ridge incision is made down to the bone at about 1/3 towards palatal aspect, 3. Followed by the incision from facial aspect connecting to the alveolar ridge incision (1). Then, the gingival flap is formed by the incision from the incision 3. forming a tunnel to underneath the both papillae using the micro blade (CK2). Attention should be paid not to extend the horizontal incision 2. beyond MGJ keeping it in keratinized gingiva yet obtaining enough mobility of the gingival flap.

Suturing : Inlay graft procedure is performed raising the buccal 2/3 of the alveolar ridge cornily (2). The alveolar ridge incision area is not sutured because it will be pressed by the base of the pontic area of the provisional restoration 4.

Point

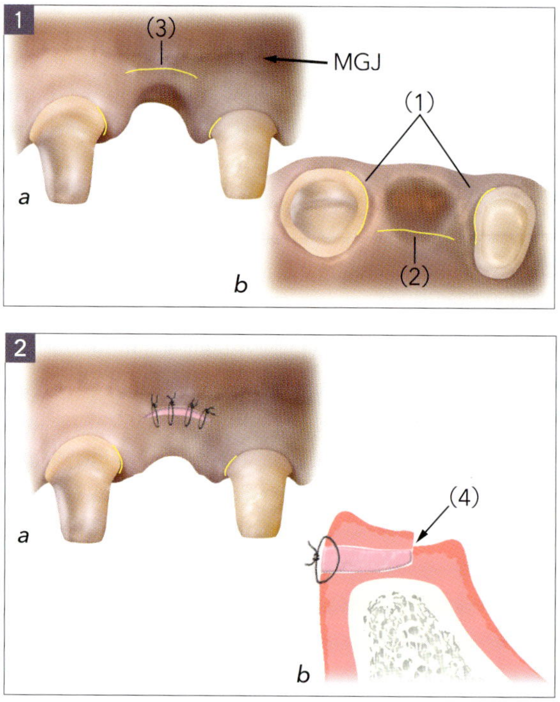

The time of insertion of the provisional restoration

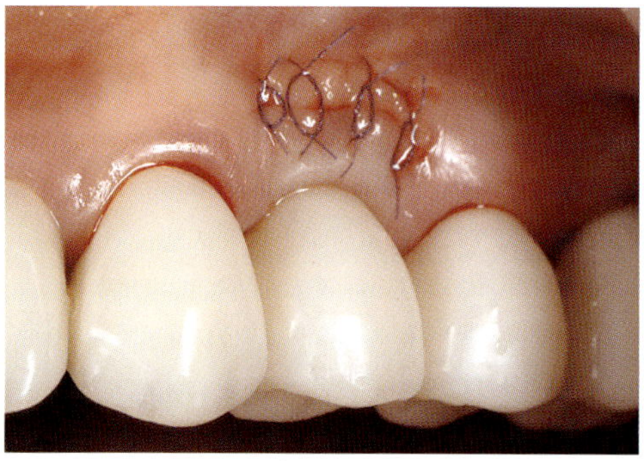

Fig 12e : Insertion of the provisional restoration after suturing. Slight blanching is observed in the gingiva around the pontic area. It suggests close contact between the pontic and the alveolar ridge area.

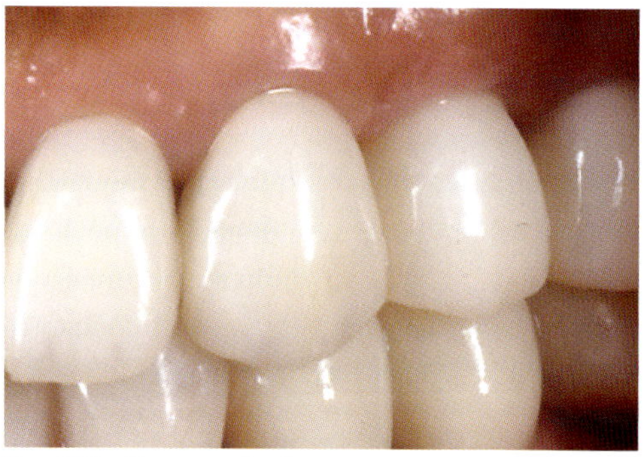

Fig 12f : One week after the surgery. Favorable healing process is observed.

Since the gingiva of this patient presents some edematous condition, the gingival level was elevated coronally by about 1 mm expecting some shrinkage.

3 months post-op

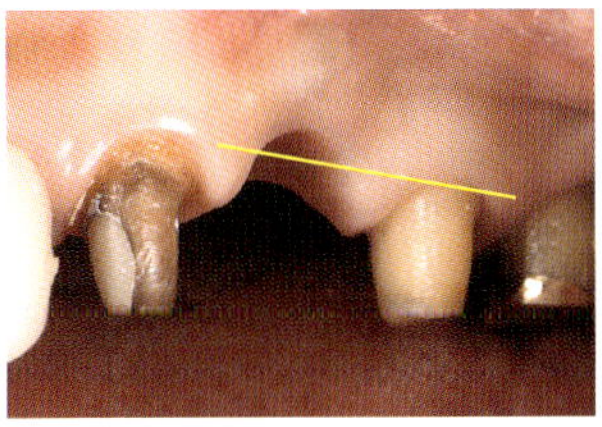

◀ Pre-op

‖ Point ‖
The alveolar ridge was augmented vertically to balance the gingival level. The increase is required only on labial aspect, but not on palatal aspect. Hence, it was planned to increase the hight only on labial aspect. It is practical approach when limited amount of connective tissue is available for graft at the donner site.

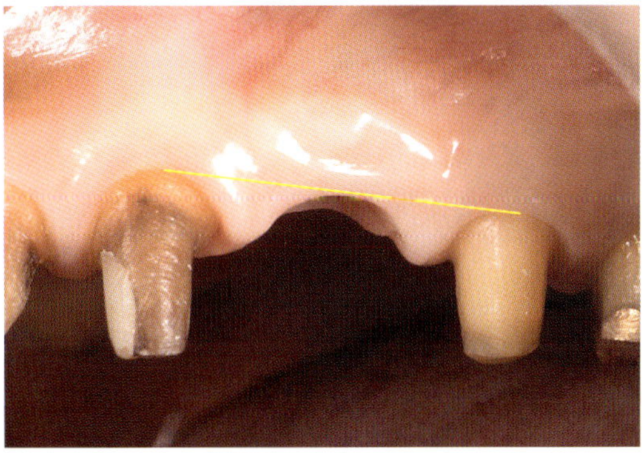

Fig 12g : Pre- and post-op comparison of gingival level. Well balanced and continuous gingival level is reconstructed.

6 months post-op / 2 years post-op

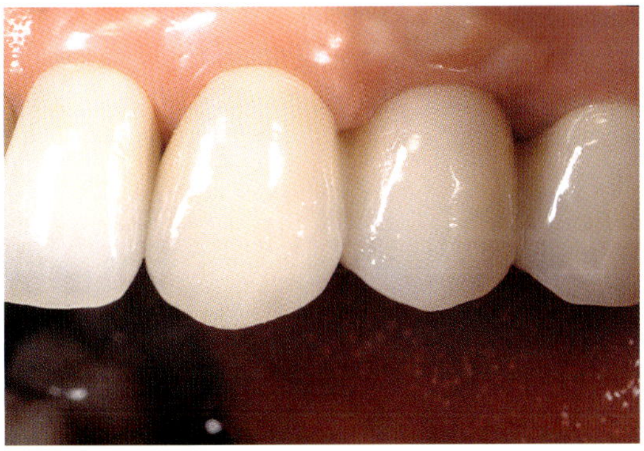

Fig 12h : 6 months post-op. Well balanced final prosthesis is inserted (prosthetic treatment by Dr. Masao Yamazaki).

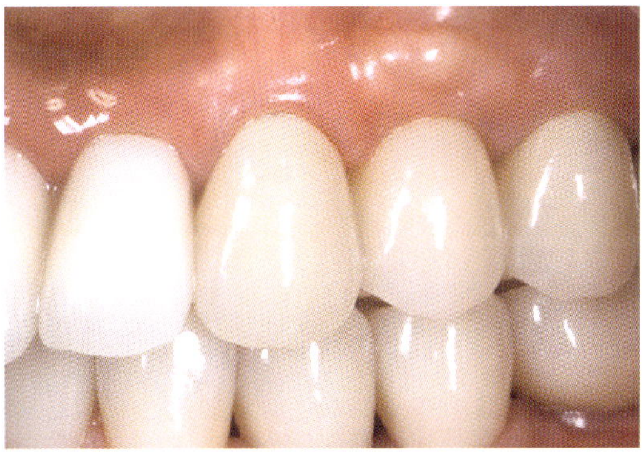

Fig 12i : 2 years pot-op. Grafted area of maxillary left first pre-molar area is well maintained without recession.

Evaluation of the case

Pre-op alveolar ridge type of this case was convex-valley. If an implant is indicated in this area, both hard and soft tissue graft would be indicated. Only soft tissue graft was applied to this case since conventional fixed bridge was the choice of treatment. It was requested to the restorative dentist to monitor the condition of grafted area longer so that stable gingival level is well maintained.

Alveolar ridge augmentation procedure as pre-prosthetic treatment 3

Pre-op : concave-hill

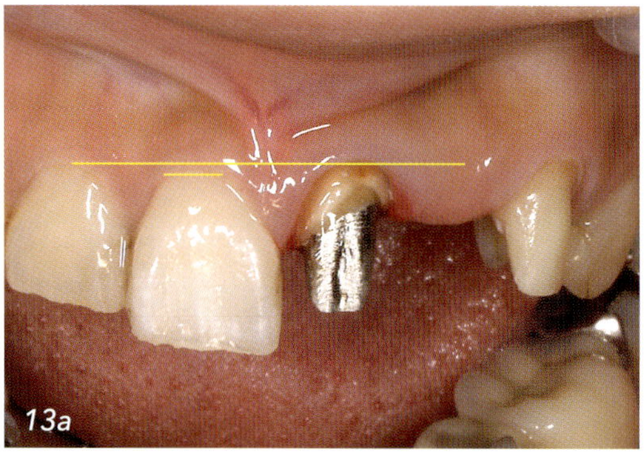

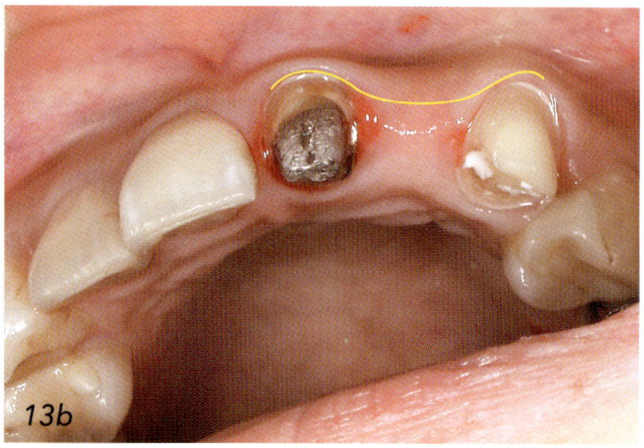

Fig 13a, b : Horizontal gingival level is about 3 mm defective at the area of maxillary left lateral incisor.

Vertical gingival line	3	2	1	1	2	3
Balance to the adjacent tooth			X			
Balance to the same tooth on the contra lateral side			X			
Horizontal gingival line	**3**	**2**	**1**	**1**	**2**	**3**
Balance to the adjacent tooth				X		
Balance to the same tooth on the contra lateral side				X		

*mark [X] in problematic area

Points of the case

Problems

- About 3 mm of horizontal gingival level defect at the area of maxillary left lateral incisor is appreciated.
- The concave defect is extensive from most contoured buccal area toward apical aspect.
- Vertical gingival level of right maxillary central incisor is coronal to that of left central incisor.

The purpose and procedures of the surgery

1. Apical repositioning of vertical gingival level of maxillary right central incisor and expansion of vertical gingival level of maxillary left lateral incisor area.
2. Alveolar ridge eaugmentation procedure and crown lengthening procedure are performed in adjacent areas in this case. Envelope flap is applied for alveolar ridge expansion of maxillary left lateral incisor area and open flap is applied for crown lengthening procedure of maxillary right central incisor.

Surgery (2007. 10. 11)

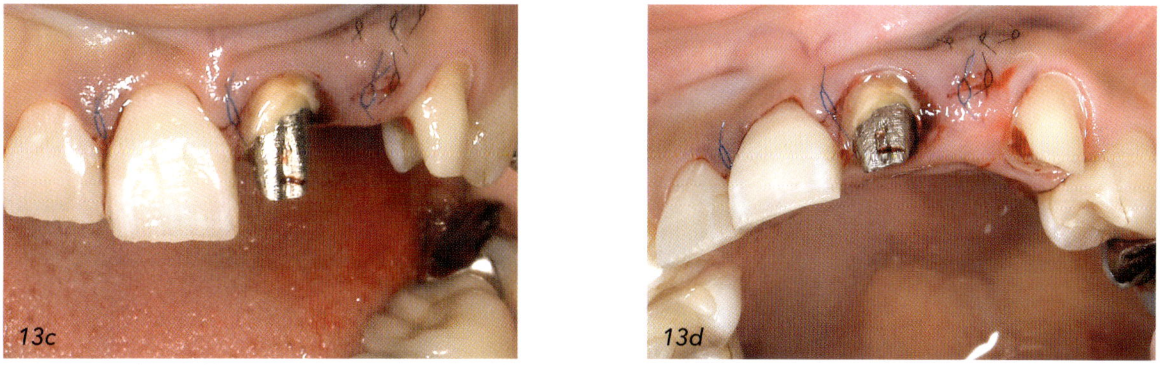

Fig 13 c, d : planned horizontal gingival contour of maxillary left lateral incisor area was reconstructed and symmetric vertical gingival level was achieved.

Incision・Suture

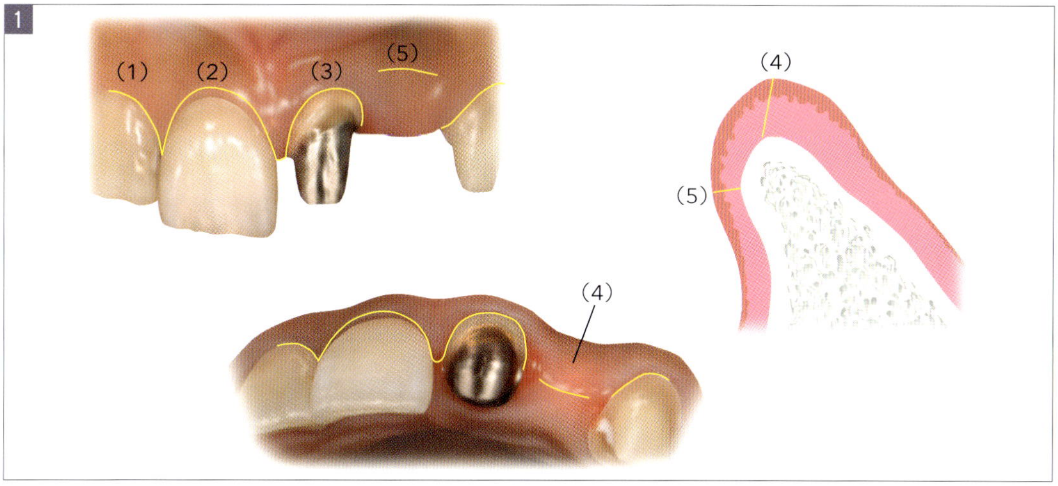

Incision : 1. Gingival sulcus incision from labial distal corner to medial palatal aspect of maxillary left canine, 2. gingival sulcus incision from palatal distal corner to labial medial corner of maxillary left central incisor, 3. Alveolar ridge crest incision from the papilla between central incisors to the papilla between maxillary right lateral and central incisors, 4. Gingival sulcus incision from labial mesial aspect to distal aspect of maxillary left lateral incisor, are made as shown in the diagram 1. Then horizontal incisions is made as shown in 5. This labial incision was made expediently because the undercut area, caused by labial concavity shape of the alveolar bone, was limiting the access with tunneling technique. The alveolar ridge crest incision was made as shown in Case 1.

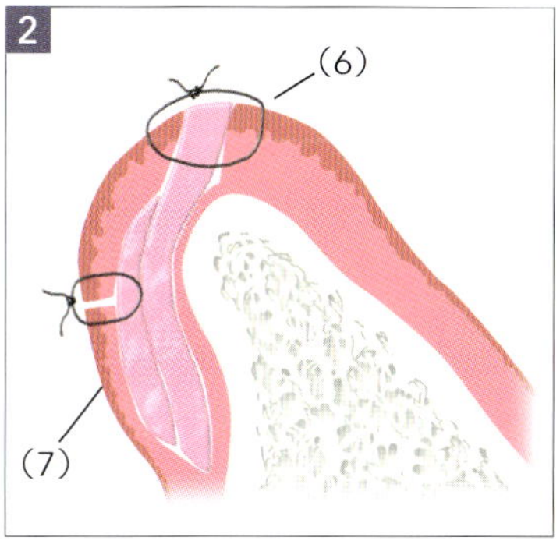

Suture : Two grafts were used in this case. The first graft was sutured at the alveolar ridge crest incision area (6) as shown in 2, then the second graft, which is smaller than the first one, is inserted from the horizontal incision area (7), and sutured.

Post-op・Time of insertion of the provisional restoration

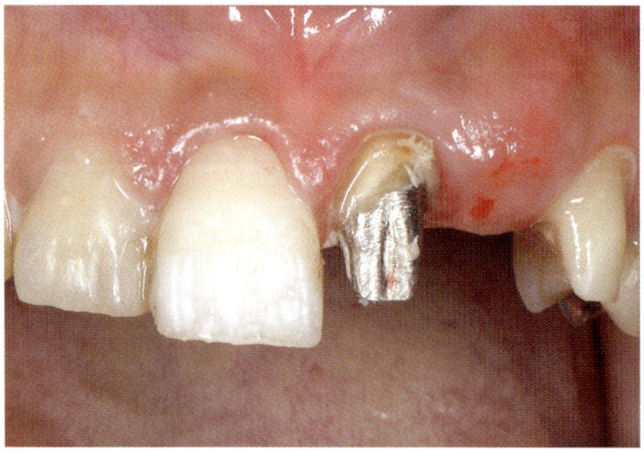

Fig 13e : 1 week post-op. Well healing condition is observed after suture removal since 9-0 was sued fro suturing at the horizontal incision area of maxillary left lateral incisor.

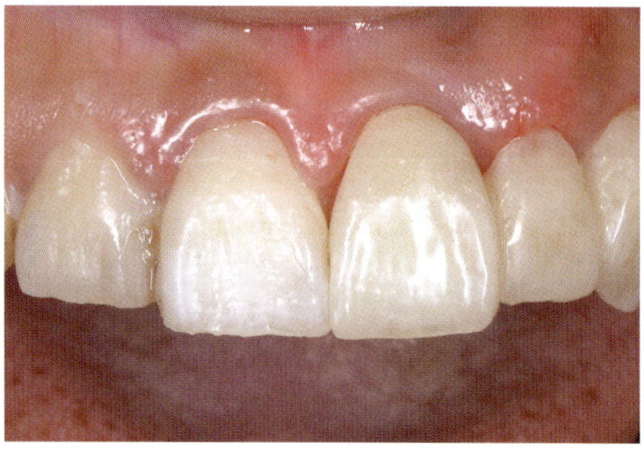

Fig 13f : 1 week post-op. Time of insertion of the provisional restoration. Fast healing of gingiva is observed.

‖ Point ‖

It was difficult to form the envelop flap with regular tunneling technique due to existence of sharp concavity on the labial aspect. The horizontal incision was made at the height of contour area to facilitate forming gingival flap.

1 year post-op

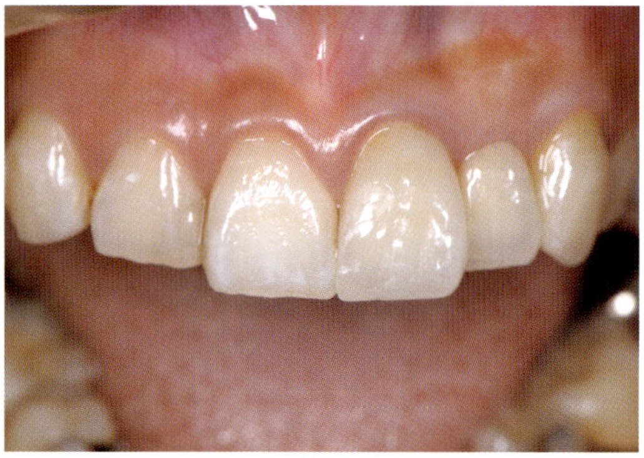

Fig 13g : 1 year post-op. Gingival level has been relatively stable. Difference in scalloping between central incisors are observed (prosthetic treatment by Dr. Masao Yamazaki).

Evaluation of the case

Shapes of gingival scalloping of central incisors are not symmetric in vertical gingival level. During the crown lengthening procedure of the maxillary right central incisor, gingival tissue at the mesial aspect should have been removed more aggressively.

The concept of alveolar ridge augmentation procedure : Advanced 2 Post-prosthetic treatment

The main reason why alveolar ridge augmentation procedure is considered one of pre-prosthetic treatments in general is the difficulty in expecting morphologic and size (resorption) change after the procedure. If this surgical procedure is performed in a way that the final result could be achieved so precisely, it would be possible to perform the surgical procedure according to the prosthesis. The author has been performing microsurgery with the provisional restoration over 11 years. Since the predictable result had been achieved with the provisional restoration constantly, it was started to apply alveolar ridge augmentation procedure after the final prosthesis is inserted. As a result, following advantages are confirmed and this approach has been applied recent years.

1. Over sized augmentation could be avoided because the shape of the final prosthesis is clear.
2. Minimally invasive surgery is possible because minimum required amount of connective tissue graft is accurately estimated from the precise surgical planning.
3. Morphologic change of the augmented alveolar ridge due to breakage or dislodgment of the provisional restoration could be avoided by performing augmentation procedure after the final prosthesis is inserted.
4. Total treatment time is shortened, since waiting period of healing after surgical procedure until the final prosthesis is eliminated.

Alveolar ridge augmentation procedure as post-op treatment 1

Pre-op : concave-hill

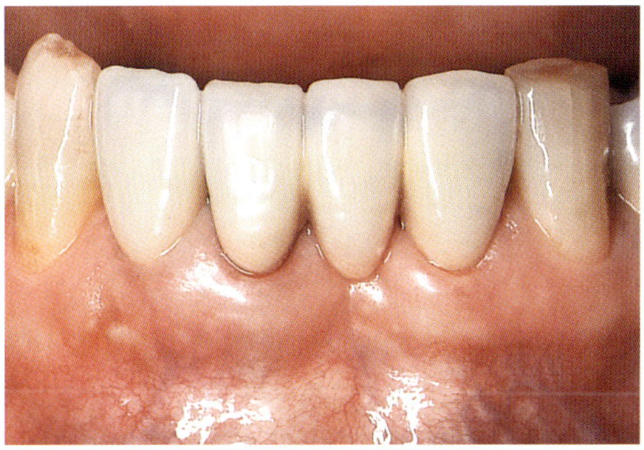

Fig 14a : Temporary cementation of the final prosthesis. This final prosthesis was fabricated on the model, on which diagnostic wax-up of the alveolar ridge was prepared before prior to the surgical procedure.

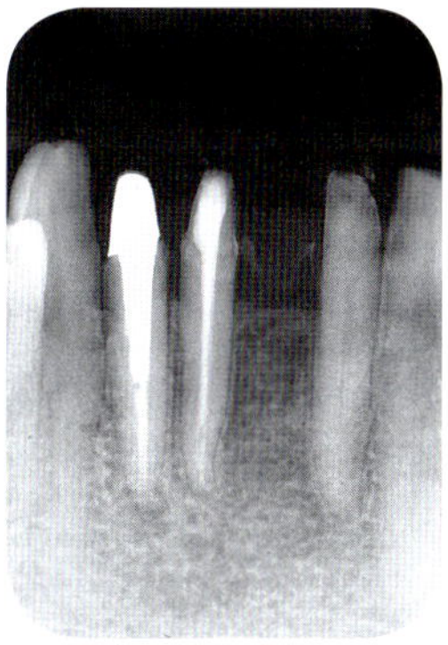

Fig 14b : Pre-op peri-apical x-ray.

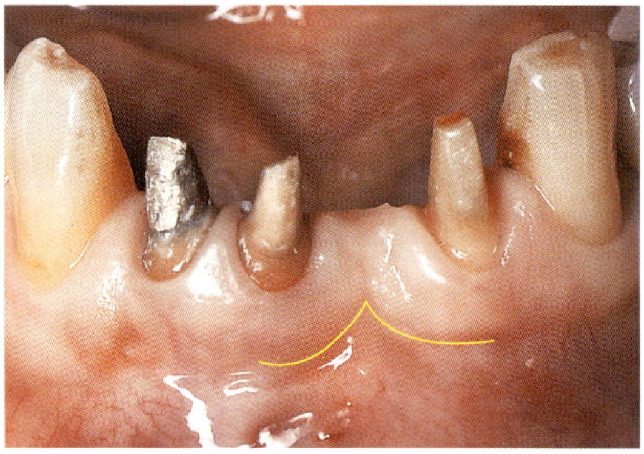

Fig 14c : Condition without the prosthesis. Horizontal defect of the alveolar ridge is appreciated. Defect type is concave-hill and MGJ is located coronal aspect.

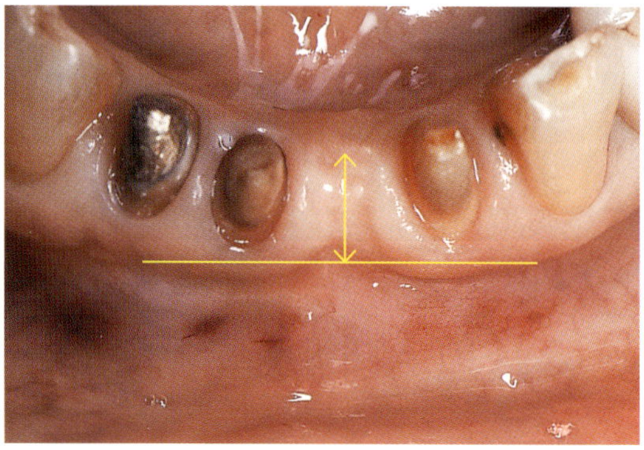

Fig 14d : The width of the defect is relatively narrow, but deep horizontally.

Vertical gingival line	3	2	1	1	2	3
Balance to the adjacent tooth						
Balance to the same tooth on the contra lateral side						
Horizontal gingival line	**3**	**2**	**1**	**1**	**2**	**3**
Balance to the adjacent tooth				X		
Balance to the same tooth on the contra lateral side				X		

*mark [X] in problematic area

Points of this case

Problems

- Horizontal gingival level is relatively narrow, but the defect is deep. MGJ level is located coronal aspect according to that. Root exposure is appreciated on mandibular right central incisor area.

The purpose and procedures of the surgery

1. Soft tissue alveolar ridge augmentation to improve horizontal gingival level of mandibular left central incisor area and root coverage procedure (improvement of vertical gingival level) for root exposure of mandibular right central incisor.
2. Connective tissue graft procedure is performed with two grafts to improve horizontal defect of mandibular left central incisor and horizontal gingival level of both mandibular central incisors.

Surgery (2003. 4. 7)

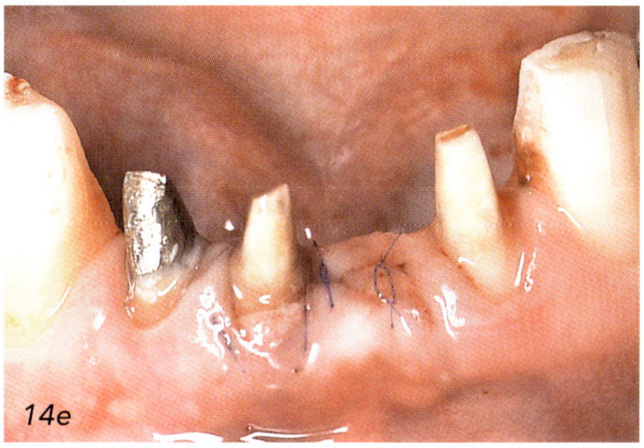

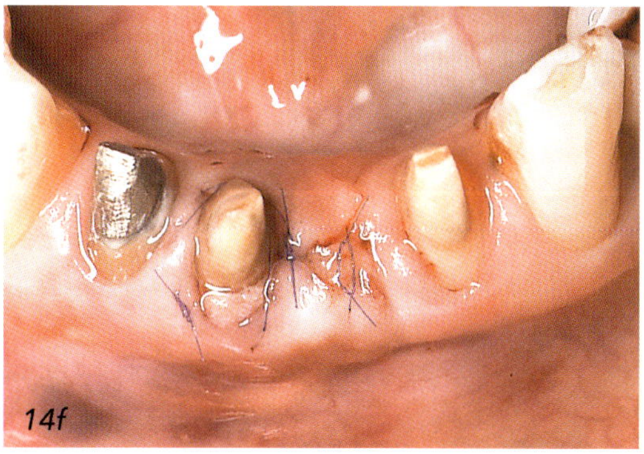

Fig 14e, f : Connective tissue graft was applied to augment the alveolar ridge of mandibular left central incisor area. Root coverage procedure was applied to the exposed root surface of mandibular right central incisor.

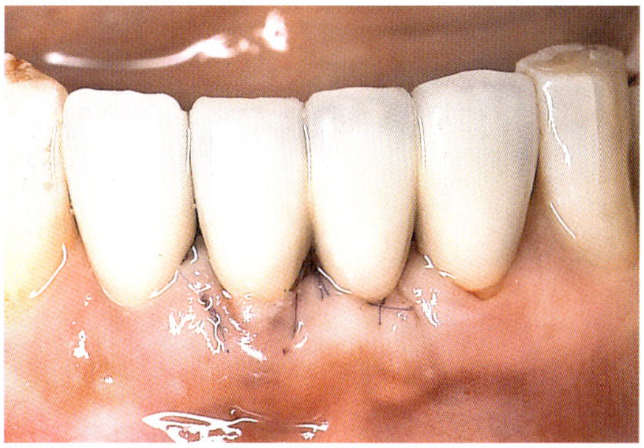

Fig 14g : The final prosthesis is temporarily inserted right after suturing. Pontic area should be in close contact against the alveolar ridge at this point.

‖ Point ‖

Proper contour of the alveolar ridge of mandibular left central incisor is determined by if the pontic is pressuring on the alveolar ridge of the area (slight blanching at the time of insertion of the prosthesis). Proper gingival architecture should be formed by performing the surgical procedure according to the properly designed final prosthesis.

Incision・Suture

1

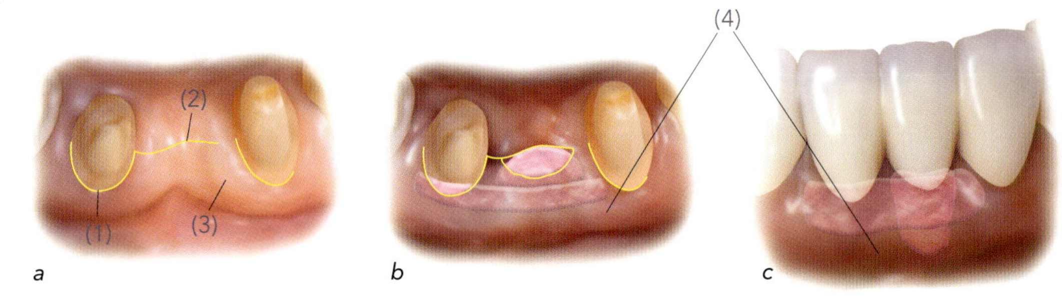

2

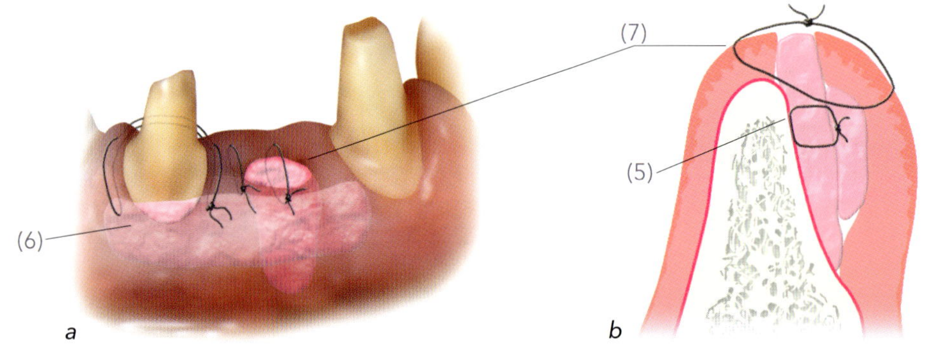

Incision : Gingival sulcus incision is made from distal corner to medial proximal area of mandibular right central incisor as shown in 1 - a (1). Mesial aspect of the alveolar ridge crest incision of mandibular right central incisor area is connected to the gingival sulcus incision of the right central incisor (2), but distal aspect is not connected to the proximal area of left lateral incisor leaving the papilla area intact (3). Lastly, gingival sulcus incision is made from the mesial proximal area of lateral incisor to distal corner.

Suture : Two grafts (connective tissue graft) were used (4). The first graft was sutured through periosteum to the edentulous are of left central incisor using 7-0 resorbable chromic suture (5). Then, the gingival flap and the graft are tied by sling suture for root coverage of the right central incisor (6). Gingival flap was closed tightly by additional simple loop suture at the interdental papilla area between central incisors (7). The second graft is sutured through the gingival flap, the graft and then lingual gingival flap after the sling suture described above as shown in 2 - b.

1 week post-op

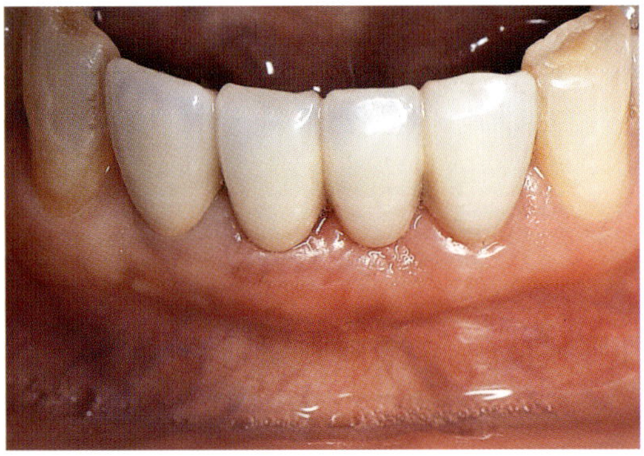

Fig 14h : 1 week post - op. Speedy and good healing is observed.

10 months post-op

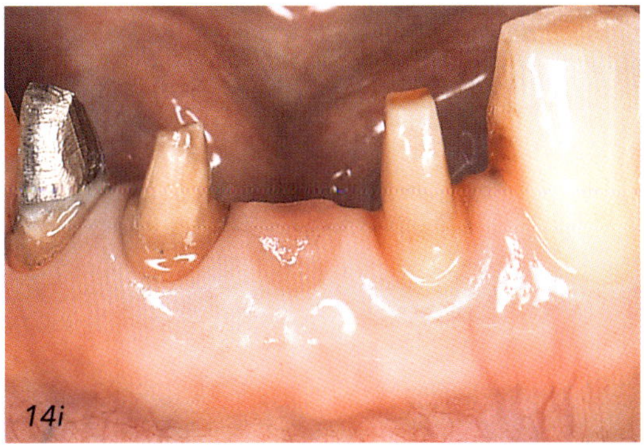
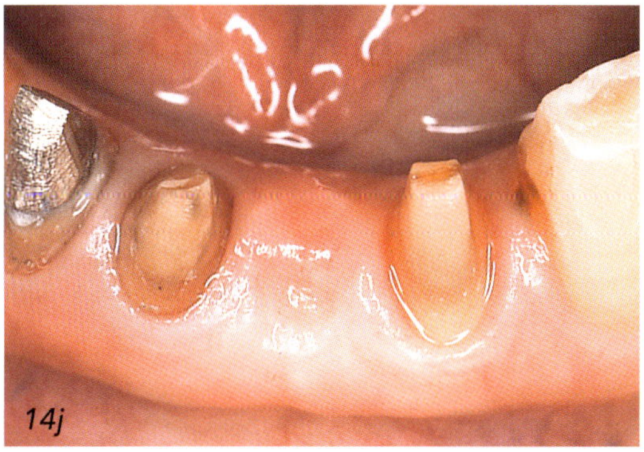

Fig 14i, j : 10 months post - op condition. Well healed and stable gingiva is observed. The final prosthesis was cemented after this condition was checked.

‖ Point ‖
The most important aspect of this surgical procedure is to reconstruct the alveolar ridge, which fits the shape of the pontic of the final prosthesis. Careful and safe surgical procedure following the plan precisely is essential. The author check the proper fit of the pontic area by slight blanching of the alveolar ridge when the final prosthesis is inserted.

2 years post-op/ 7.5 years post-op

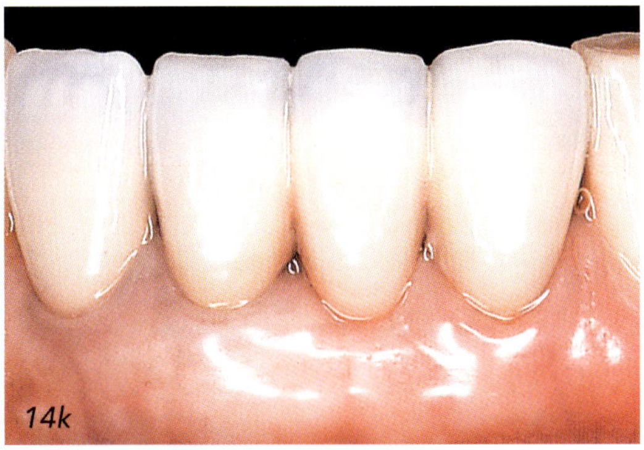
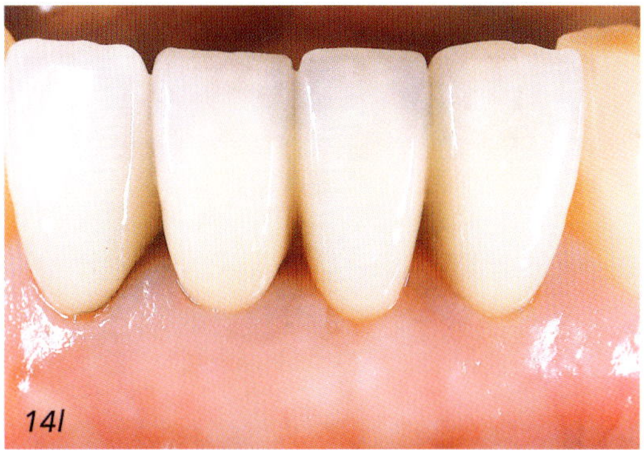
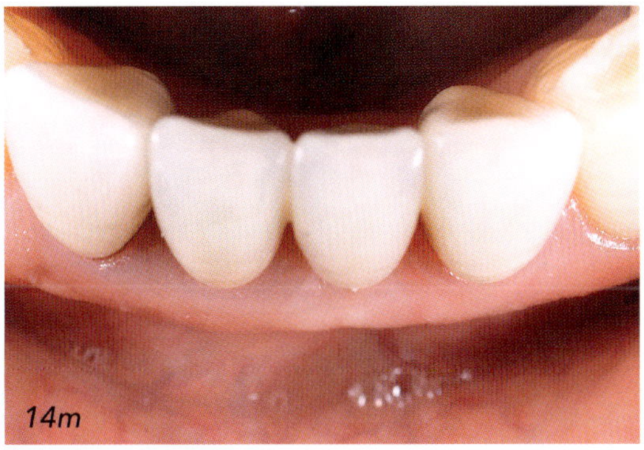

Evaluation of the case

It is confirmed through this case that it is possible thorough examination and precise surgical procedure to reconstruct the gingival architecture according to the final prosthesis using connective tissue graft. This case demonstrates the predictability of this surgical approach.

Fig 14k~m : 2 years post-op (14k) and 7.5 years post-op (14l, m). Stable gingival condition around the pontic is observed.

Alveolar ridge augmentation procedure as post-op treatment 2

Pre-op : concave-hill

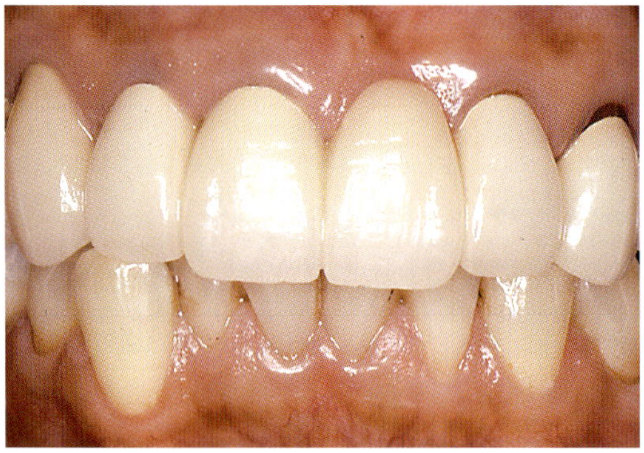

Fig 15a : The chief complaints of the patient are discomfort on the lingual surface of maxillary left central incisor and air leakage. Re-treatment was indicated due to these complaints and other problems observed.

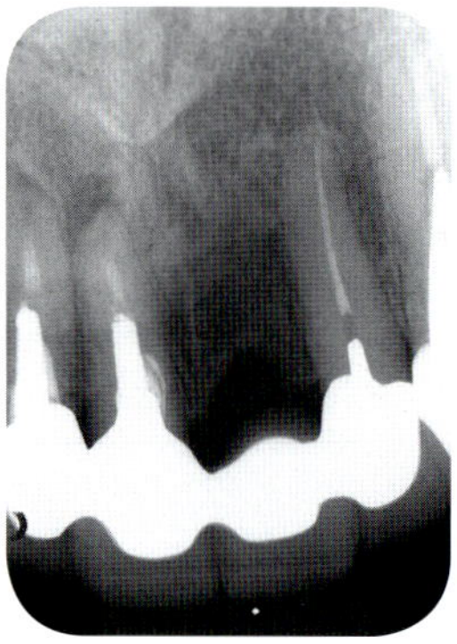

Fig 15b : Pre-op peri-apical x-ray.

Vertical gingival line	3	2	1	1	2	3
Balance to the adjacent tooth						
Balance to the same tooth on the contra lateral side	X					X
Horizontal gingival line	**3**	**2**	**1**	**1**	**2**	**3**
Balance to the adjacent tooth				X		
Balance to the same tooth on the contra lateral side				X		

*mark [X] in problematic area

Points of this case

Problems

- Defective horizontal gingival level of maxillary left central incisor.
- The patient's request to shorten the treatment time.

The purpose and procedures of the surgery

1. Augmentation of horizontal gingival level of maxillary left central incisor.
2. Simple soft tissue alveolar ridge augmentation procedure using envelope flap was indicated. Due to the treatment time constriction upon the patient's request, it was decided to perform the surgical procedure at the time of insertion of the final prosthesis.

Time of insertion of the provisional restoration

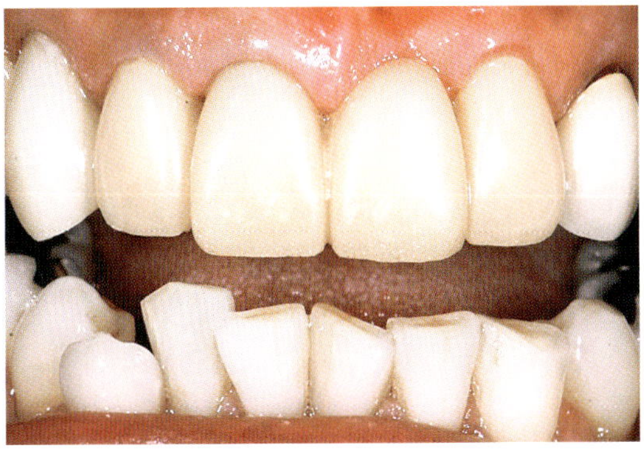

Fig 15c : The pontic of the provisional restoration was shaped so that patient's complaints are resolved.

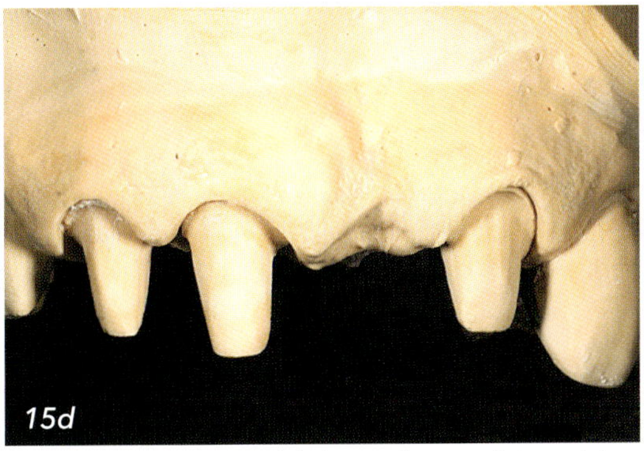

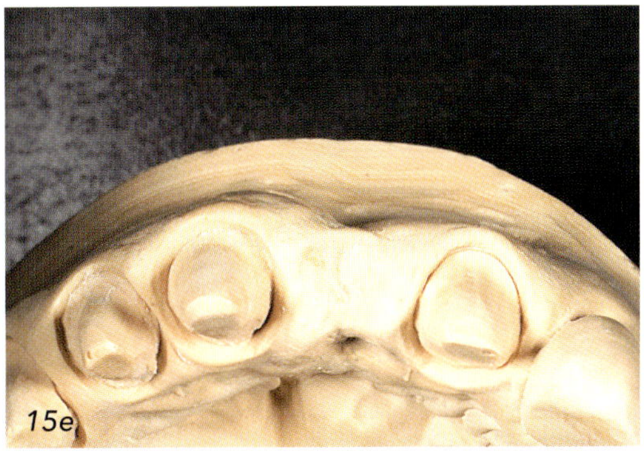

Fig 15d, e : Study model shows the condition of the defect of alveolar ridge more precisely than intra oral photo.

Fabrication of the final prosthesis

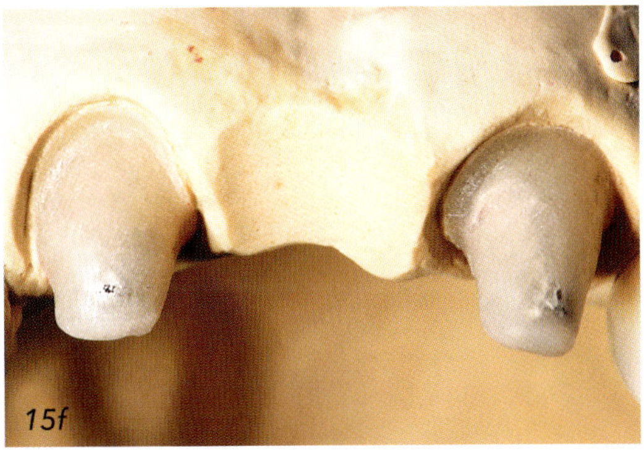

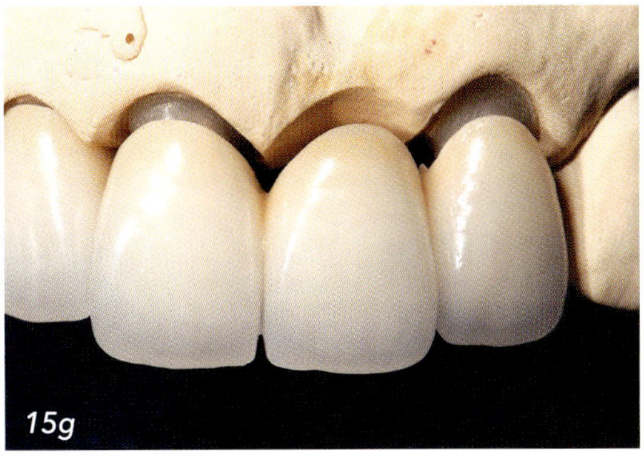

Fig 15f, g : The shape of the pontic area is determined after discussion with the dental technician.

‖ Point ‖

The ovate pontic is usually indicated for this kind of anterior case, but it is not indicated in this particular case because the vertical gingival level is well coronally positioned, which makes it difficult to shape the ovate pontic properly. After careful and thorough examination of the study model and diagnostic waxup, modified saddle pontic was indicated for this case.

Surgery (2007. 10. 25)

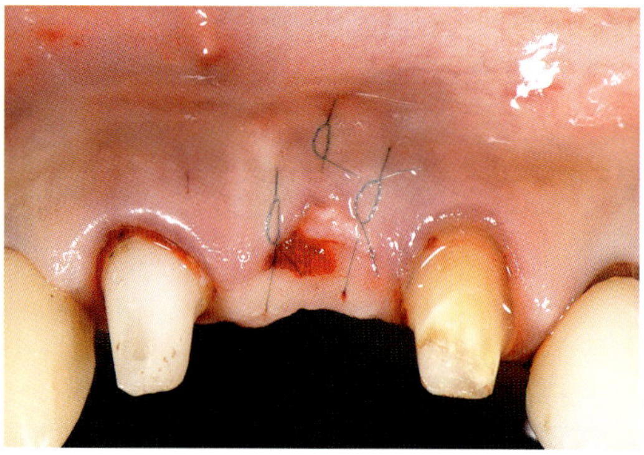

Fig 15h : The contour of the alveolar ridge was formed using 2 grafts (connective tissue) as shown in 2.

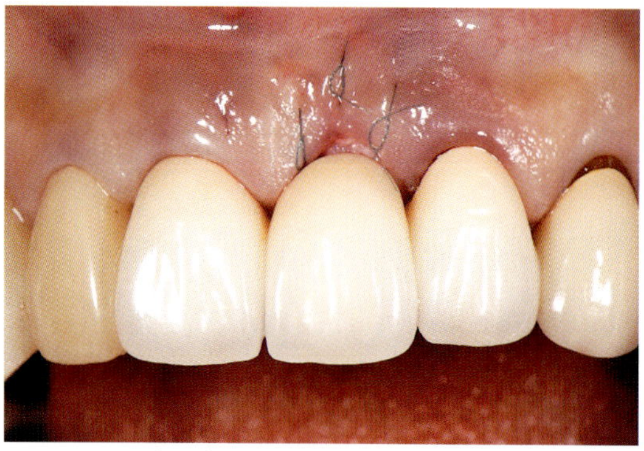

Fig 15i : Right after suturing. The final prosthesis is temporarily cemented.

Incision · Suture

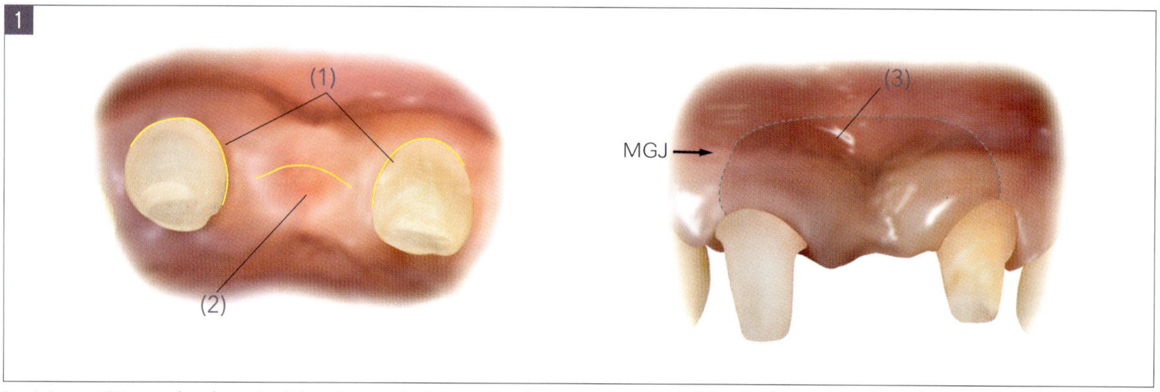

Incision : Gingival sulcus incision is made from distal corner to mesial lingual corner of both maxillary right central incisor and left lateral incisor (1). Then, alveolar ridge crest incision is made at the alveolar crest of left central incisor area along the pontic shape (2). Envelope flap is formed (3).

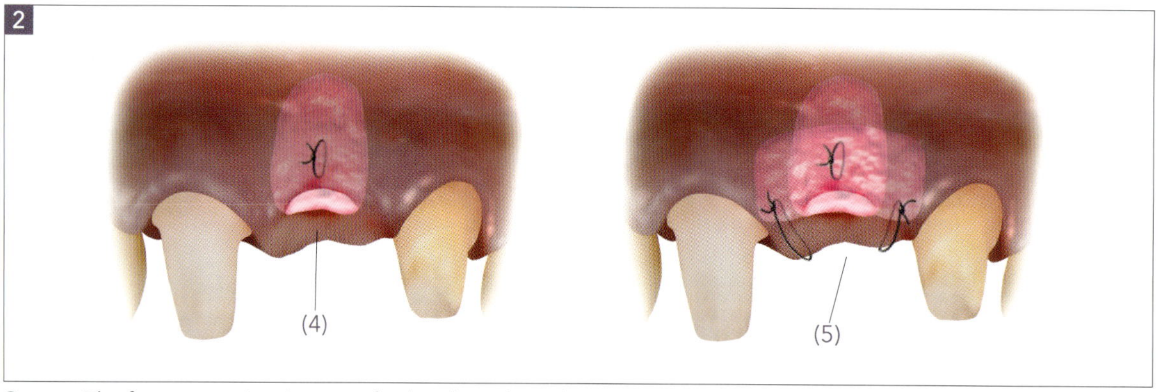

Suture : The first connective tissue graft taken from the palate is sutured to the labial gingival flap after the ridge shape is properly formed (4). Then, the second graft is inserted palatal to the first graft and sutured through the gingival flap at 2 places at mesial and distal aspect (5).

3 months after insertion of the final prosthesis

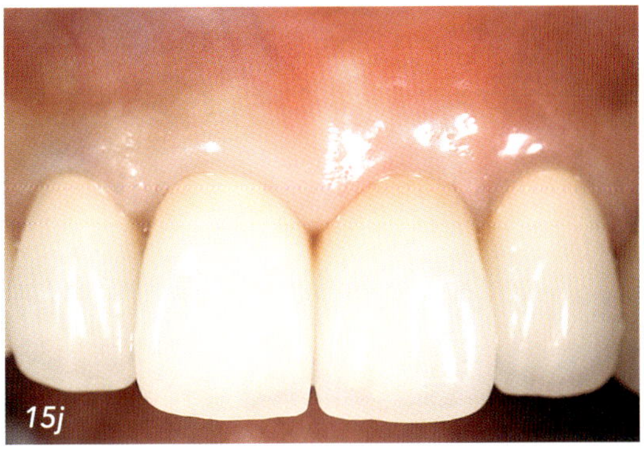

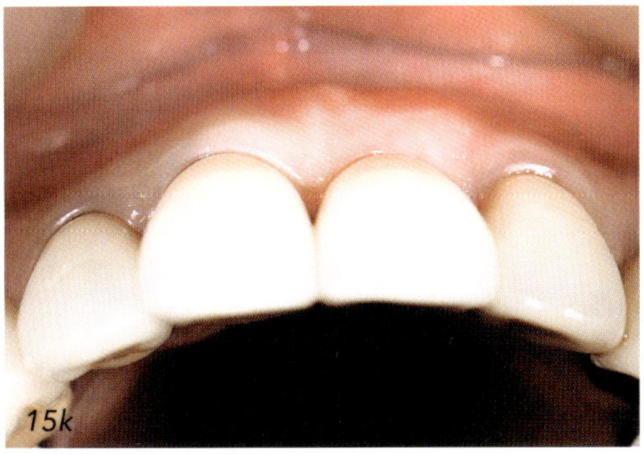

Fig 15j, k : 3 months after insertion of the final prosthesis. Well healed gingiva around pontic area is observed.

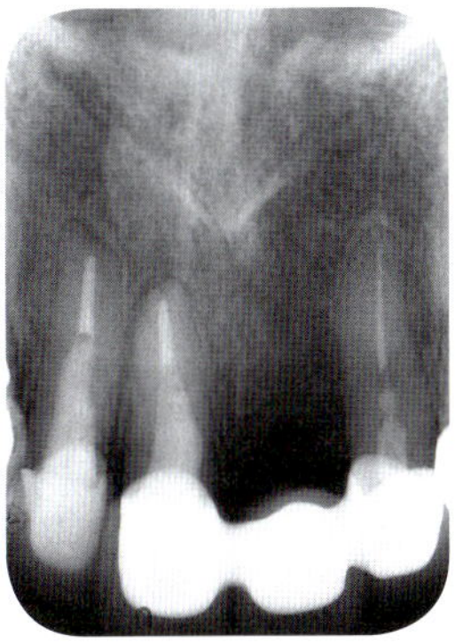

Fig 15l : Peri-apical x-ray of the final prosthesis.

1.5 year post-op

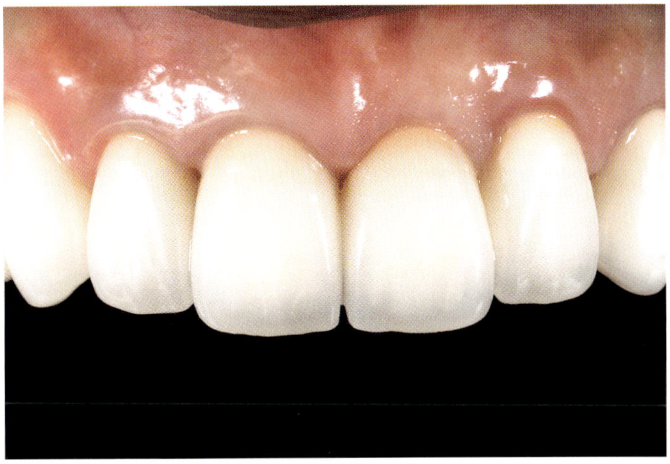

Fig 15m : 1.5 year post-op intra-oral condition.

Evaluation of the case

It is not uncommon that the patient hurries the treatment. The treatment time could be shortened by performing the surgical procedure according to the well planned final prosthesis. This case demonstrates that this prosthesis first approach is as predictable as conventional surgery first approach.

The concept of alveolar ridge augmentation procedure : Advanced 3 post-prosthetic management

Gingival recession happens due to various reasons after prosthetic treatment is completed. It could be seen not only around the tooth or implant, but also around the pontic. Traditionally, new prosthesis would be indicated. If the recession is minor, new prosthesis alone would be indicated. If it is more extensive, alveolar ridge augmentation is indicated prior to the new prosthesis, which would not be favored neither by the patient nor the dentist. If the defect is restored with surgical procedure alone, it would be the simplest solution. Several techniques of root coverage procedure have been established with high predictability in the field of periodontal plastique surgery. The author has been applying the similar theory to the pontic area to reconstruct the soft tissue and established clinically predictable technique. This theory and technique will be introduced in this section.

Alveolar ridge augmentation procedure 1 as post-prosthetic management

Pre-op : concave-hill

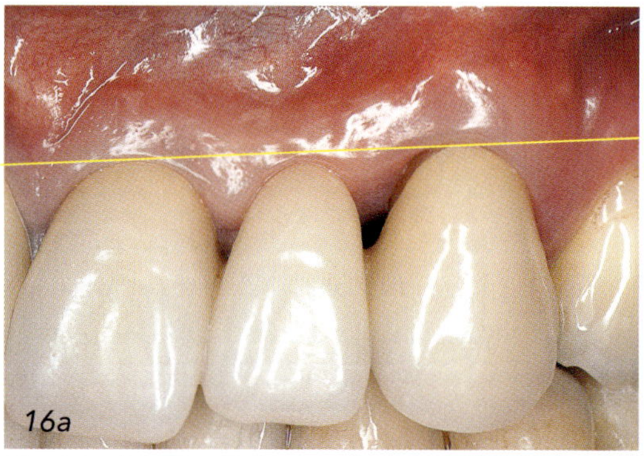

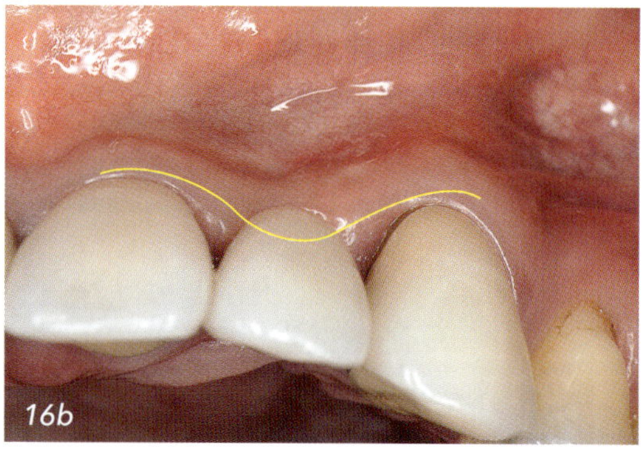

Fig 16a, b : The defect at the inter-dental papilla between maxillary left lateral incisor and canine and gingival recession at the mesial aspect of the canine is appreciated. Horizontal defect of alveolar ridge at the pontic of maxillary lateral incisor is appreciated in occlusal view and it is concave-hill case.

Vertical gingival line	1	1	2	3
Balance to the adjacent tooth			X	X
Balance to the same tooth on the contra lateral side			X	X
Horizontal gingival line	**1**	**1**	**2**	**3**
Balance to the adjacent tooth			X	
Balance to the same tooth on the contra lateral side			X	

*mark [X] in problematic area

Points of this case

Problems

- Root exposure at the canine and black triangle between lateral incisor and canine are appreciated due the defect of horizontal・vertical gingival level at maxillary left lateral incisor.
- The patient refused the option of re-fabricating the prosthesis from the central incisor to the canine after consultation.

The purpose and procedures of the surgery

1. Root coverage procedure of the canine and reconstruction of the papillae between the lateral incisor and the canine is performed improving horizontal・vertical gingival level around the lateral incisor at the same time.
2. Reconstructive surgery is performed with 2 connective tissue grafts forming the envelope flap from the central incisor to the canine without removing the prosthesis.

Pre-op diagnosis with the study model

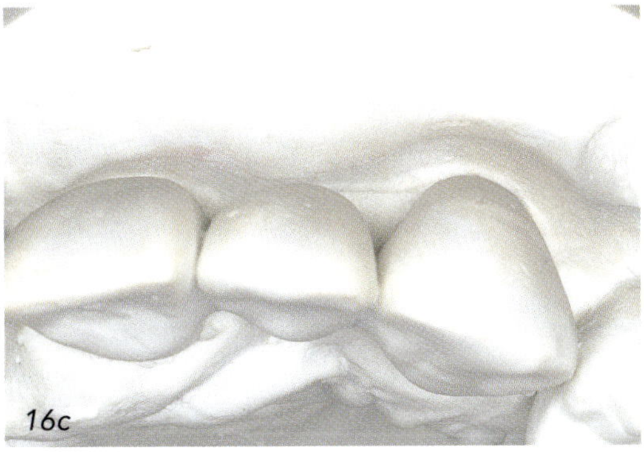
16c

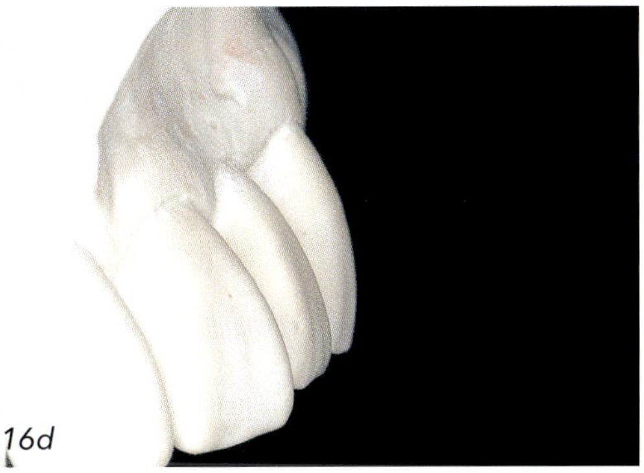
16d

Fig 16c, d : Pre-op diagnosis with the study model. The amount of alveolar ridge and interdental papilla to be reconstruct is determined with pre-surgical diagnostic wax-up.

Simulation of the graft

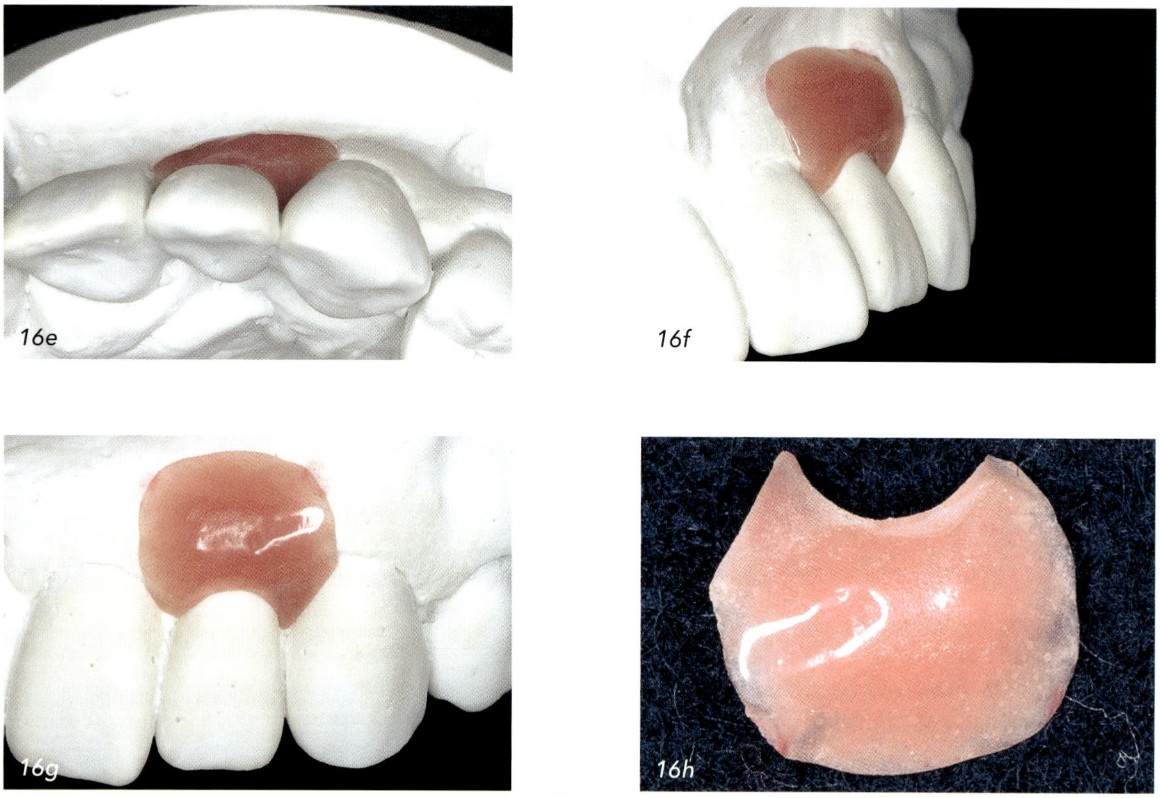

Fig 16e~h : As stated above, the amount of alveolar ridge and interdental papilla to be reconstruct is determined with pre-surgical diagnostic wax-up. This picture shows the tissue model replaced by resin. It could be made of rubber material, which is used for gingival model. This pre-surgical simulation is useful and essential step to estimate the right amount of the graft needed.

‖ Point ‖

The gingival flap of the labial aspect of the lateral incisor of this case needs to be made mobile vertically, since it involves the inter-dental papilla area between lateral incisor and the canine. The gingival flap is repositioned coronally and stabilized by the sling suture when the graft is sutured.

It is possible to increase the width of keratinized gingiva by placing the horizontal incision, for mobility of the flap, coronal to MGJ. Natural gingival shape is formed by simply adapting the graft well to the existing pontic.

Surgery (2000. 5. 1)

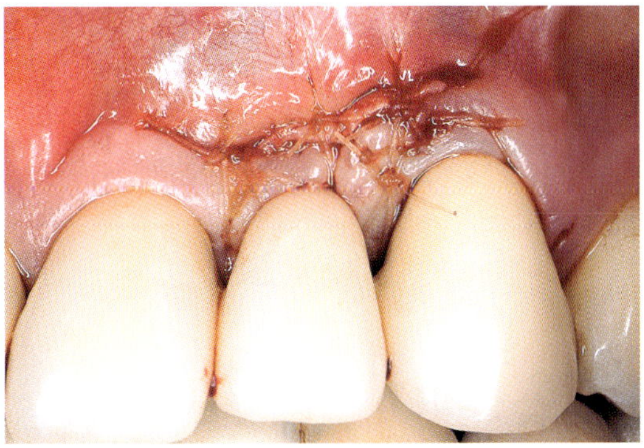

Fig 16i : Right after suturing.

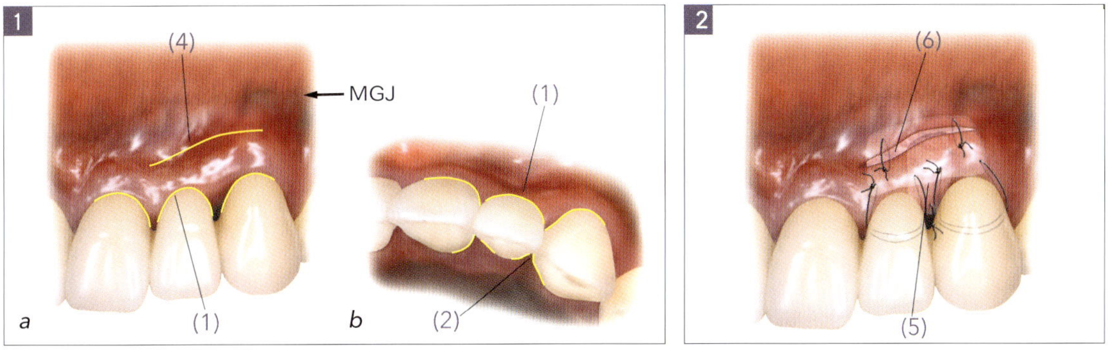

Incision : Gingival sulcus incision is made from mesial aspect of maxillary left central incisor to distal aspect of the left canine. The same continuous incision is made through along the outline of the pontic reaching down to periosteum (1). Gingival sulcus incision is made on the palatal aspect as well from middle to mesial aspect of central incisor connecting to the labial incision. Likewise, gingival sulcus incision to the canine and the same kind of incision for lateral incision are made (2) as shown in 1-b. Then, labial horizontal incision is made coronal to MGJ (4).
Suture : Properly trimmed connective tissue graft is placed under the papilla area between the lateral incisor and the canine, then sutured at the inter-dental papilla area on palatal aspect (5). The connective tissue graft in size of distal aspect of the central incisor to mesial aspect of the canine is tied with sling suture on labial aspect under the same concept of root coverage procedure (6).

3 weeks post-op

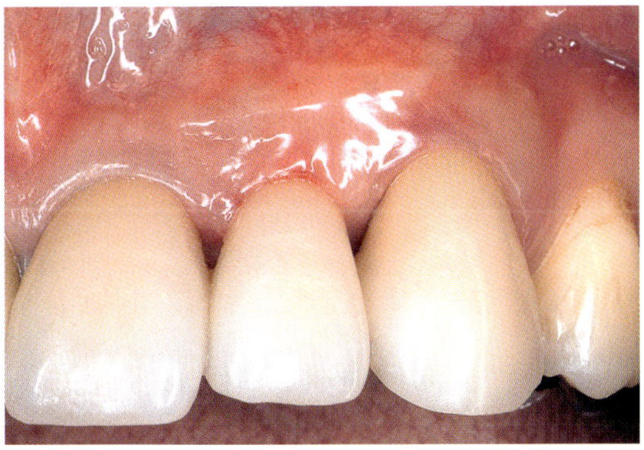

Fig 16j : 3 weeks post-op. Vertical increase of alveolar ridge at the lateral incisor and reconstructed inter-dental papilla between lateral incisor and canine is appreciated.

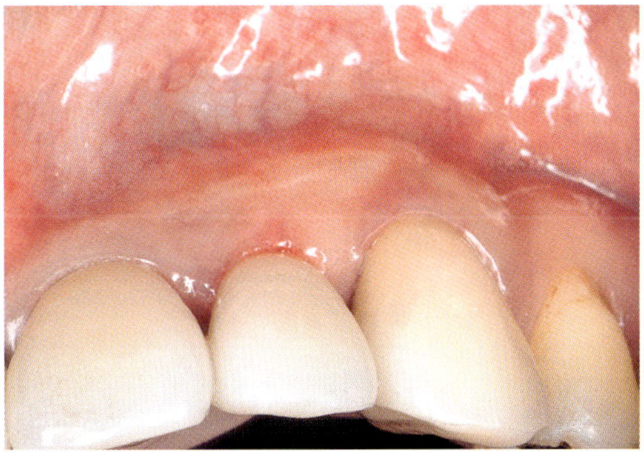

Fig 16k : 3 weeks post-op. Horizontal increase of alveolar ridge is appreciated.

2 years post-op

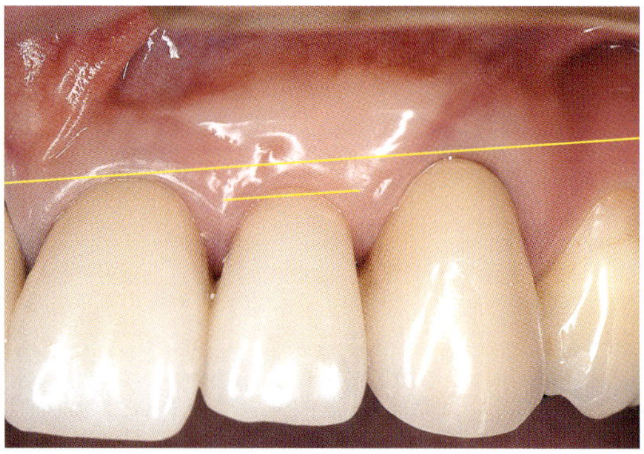

Fig 16l : 2 years post-op. Inter-dental papilla between the lateral incisor and the canine is reconstructed and the cervical line from the central incisor to the canine is natural.

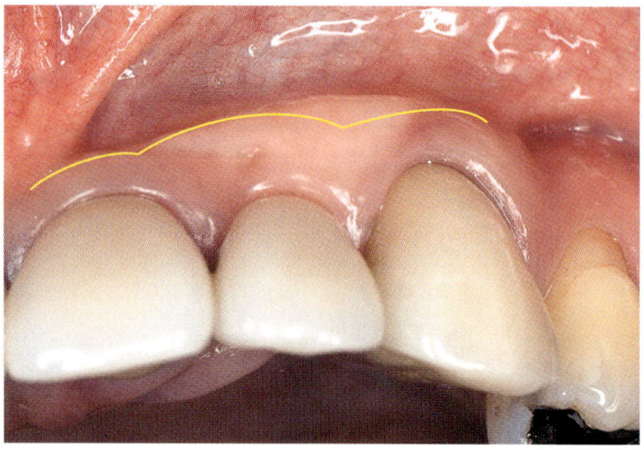

Fig 16m : 2 years post-op. Stable marginal gingiva around the lateral incisor and the canine is appreciated. The pontic area looks more natural than pre-op condition.

7 years post-op

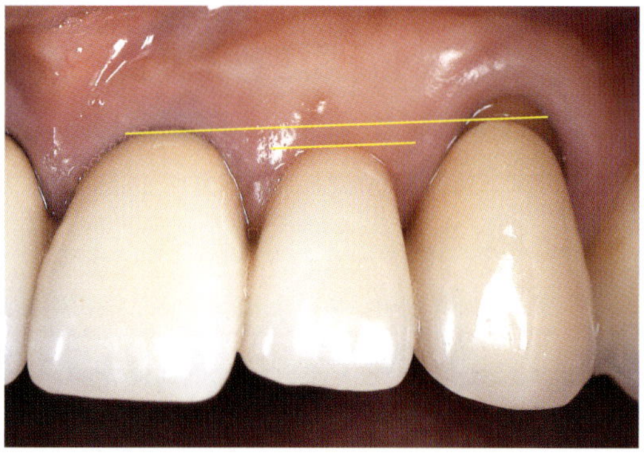

Fig 16n : 7 years post-op. Grafted area keeps stable condition. Gingival recession is appreciated in non-grafted area, especially around the canine.

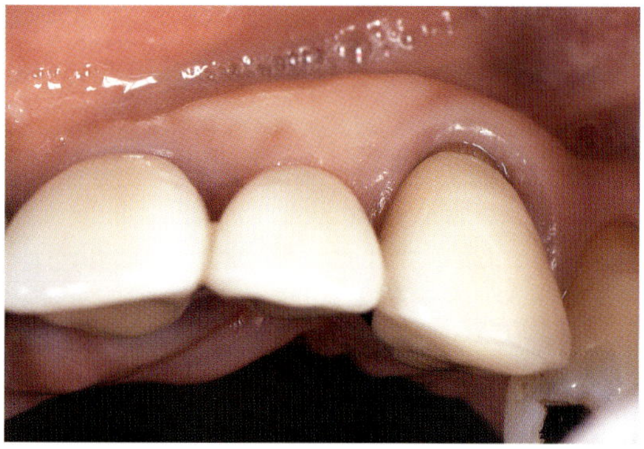

Fig 16o : 7 years post-op.

Evaluation of the case

Recession of the cervical line between the maxillary right central incisor to the left canine is observed as time passes. However, reconstructed inter-dental papilla seems to be stable. There is no histologic consensus for this soft tissue reaction.

Alveolar ridge augmentation procedure 2 as post-prosthetic management

Pre-op : concave-hill

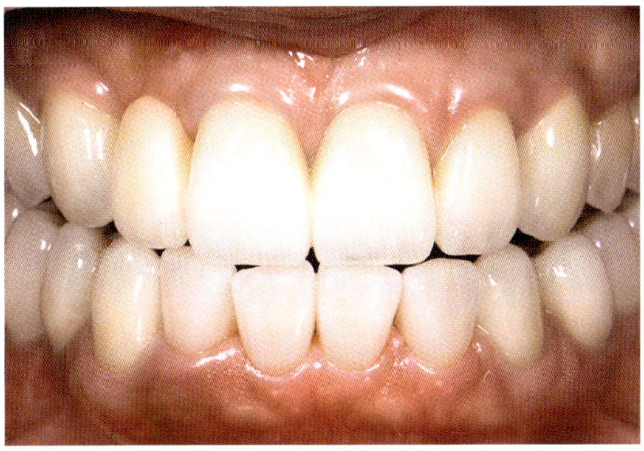

Fig 17a : It seems that there is no problem at a glance, but the patient is concerned about the defective gingival contour around maxillary left lateral incisor hoping for having that area recontoured. Alveolar ridge augmentation with connective tissue graft was indicated.

Vertical gingival line	3	2	1	1	2	3
Balance to the adjacent tooth						
Balance to the same tooth on the contra lateral side		X				
Horizontal gingival line	**3**	**2**	**1**	**1**	**2**	**3**
Balance to the adjacent tooth		X				
Balance to the same tooth on the contra lateral side		X				

*mark [X] in problematic area

Points of this case

Problems

- Defective horizontal gingival level.
- Patient's refusal of re-treatment of the prosthesis.
- Slight defective vertical gingival level (slight space between the alveolar ridge and the pontic).

The purpose and procedures of the surgery

1. Soft tissue alveolar ridge augmentation is applied to the area with the pontic of the final prosthesis. Coronally repositioning of labial gingiva and inlay graft underneath the pontic are performed simultaneously since the augmentation of both horizontal gingival level and vertical gingival level under the pontic are indicated.

Surgery (2005. 10. 20)

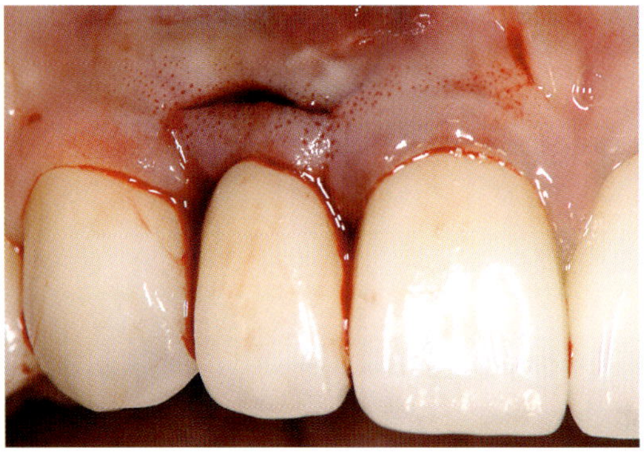

Fig 17b : Incision. Gingival sulcus incision an horizontal incision coronal to MGJ were made.

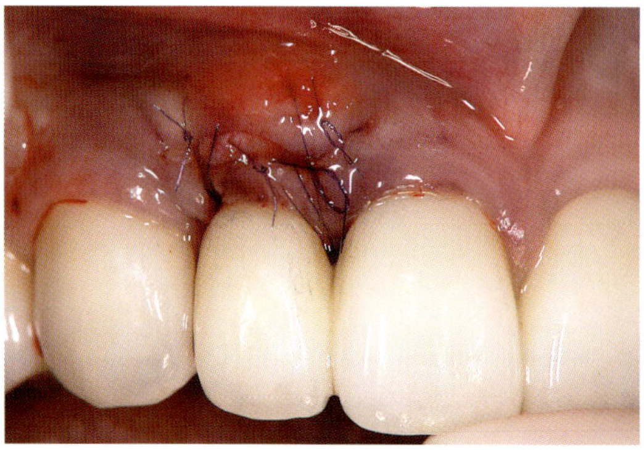

Fig 17c : Suture. Connective tissue graft was inserted inside the gingival flap then sutured as shown in 2. Planned gingival level should be achieved at this point.

1

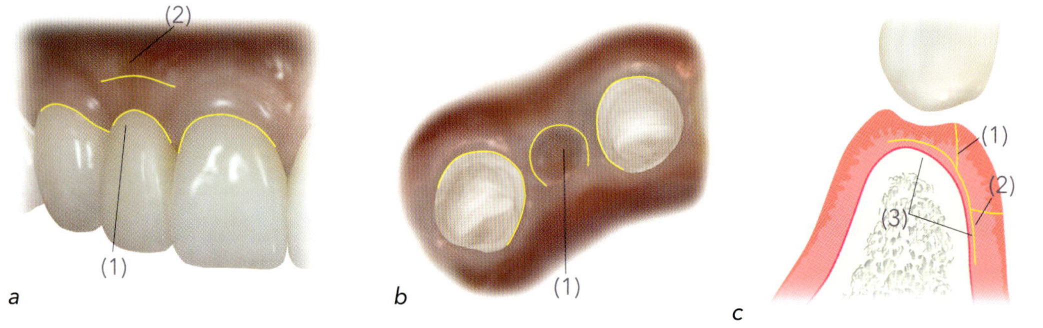

Incision : Gingival sulcus incision is made at the area of the central incisor and the canine as shown in 1-a, b. The incision is made along the outline of the pontic of the lateral incisor reaching down to the alveolar bone (1). Horizontal incision is made coronal to MGJ (2). Then, the envelope flap is formed at labial aspect (3). In this case, incision was made and elevated right under base of the pontic so that the gingiva could be raised up to close the small space between the base of the pontic and alveolar ridge.

2

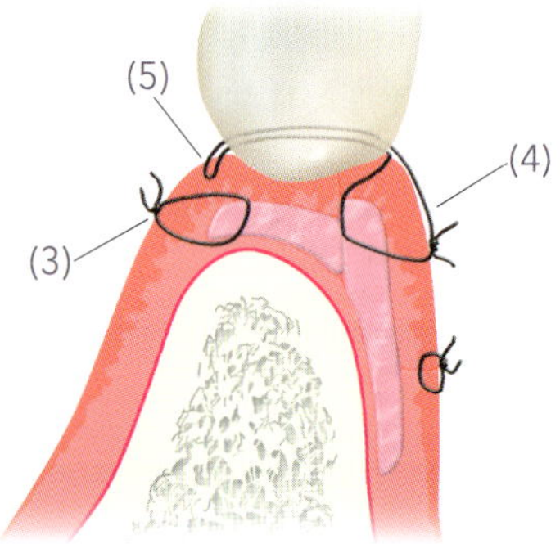

Suture : Small graft with 2mm thickness is inserted in the gingiva right under the base of the pontic with sandwich technique. Then this graft is pulled from palatal aspect and sutured (3). Connective tissue graft is performed on the labial aspect with the same technique as root coverage procedure afterwards. It is tied with sling suture (4) using the palatal gingiva as an anchor since there is no tooth (5).

‖ Point ‖

Approach for the incision at the base of the pontic is difficult. After labial gingival flap is well formed, the blade for microsurgery is used from the horizontal incision area keeping the labial flap pulled up.

6 months post-op

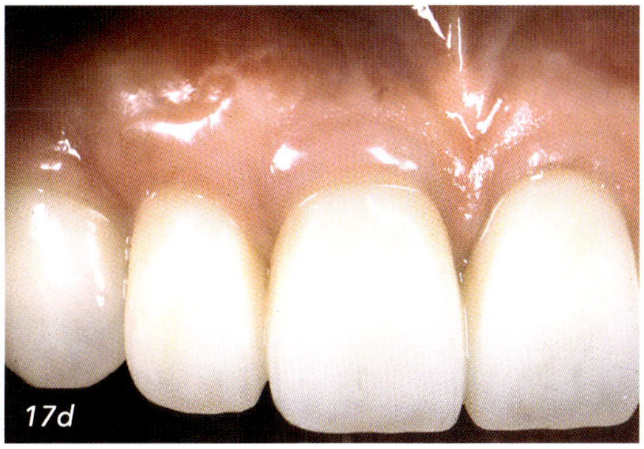

17d

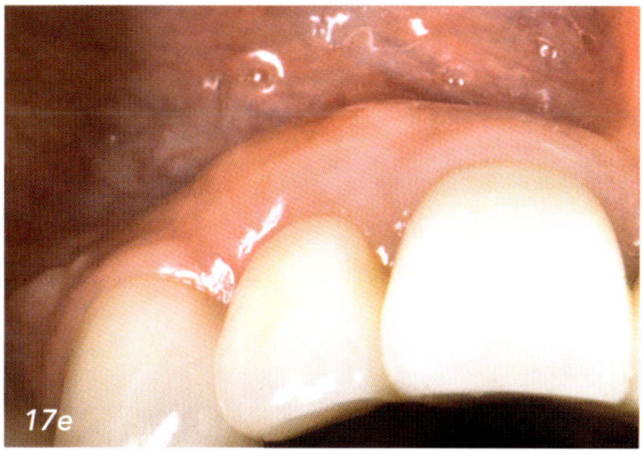

17e

Fig 17d, e : 6 months post-op. Both horizontal and vertical gingival level was improved. Ideal gingival contour was obtained and the patient was satisfied (Prosthetic treatment by Dr. Kenji Tsuchiya).

3 years post-op

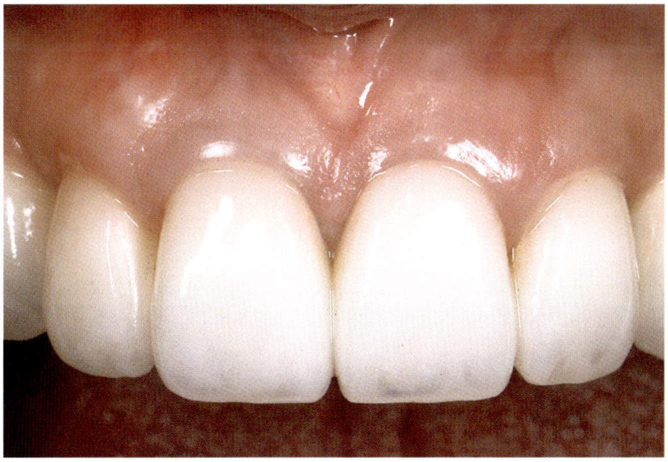

Fig 17f : 3 years post-op.

Evaluation of the case

Labial gingival contour has been well maintained without space between the base of the pontic and alveolar ridge. This is the clinical evidence of predictable gingival augmentation around the pontic area (ceramic surface) using connective tissue graft.

Alveolar ridge augmentation procedure 3 as post-prosthetic management

Pre-op : level-hill or concave-hill

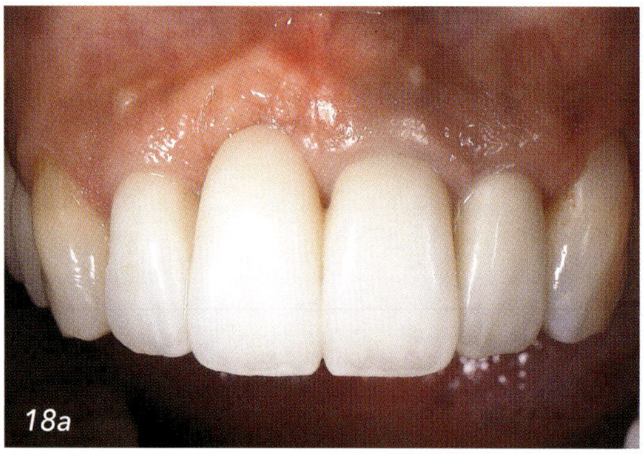

Fig 18a~c : Fixed prosthesis from maxillary right lateral incisor to left central incisor exists. Continuity of gingival line is compromised due to gingival recession at the pontic of right central incisor. Connective tissue graft was indicated to reconstruct the gingival level around the pontic.

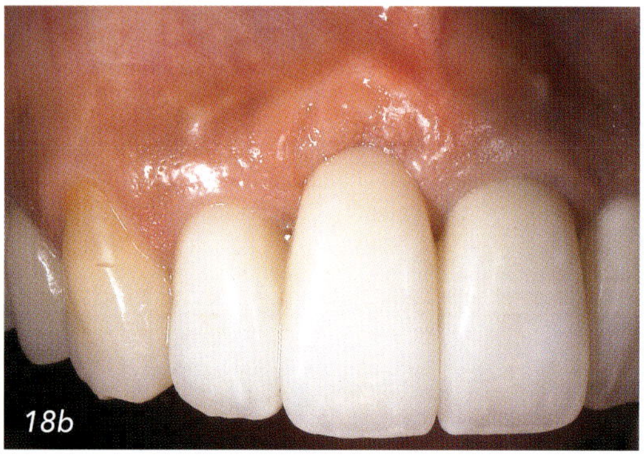

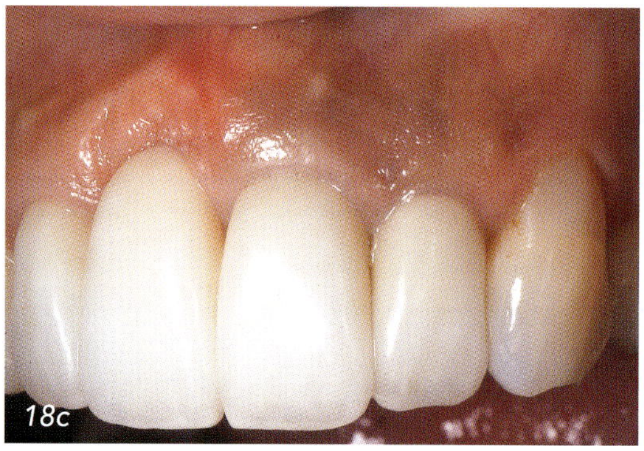

Vertical gingival line	3	2	1	1	2	3
Balance to the adjacent tooth			X			
Balance to the same tooth on the contra lateral side			X			
Horizontal gingival line	**3**	**2**	**1**	**1**	**2**	**3**
Balance to the adjacent tooth			X			
Balance to the same tooth on the contra lateral side			X			

*mark [X] in problematic area

Points of this case

Problems

- Defect of horizontal gingival level at the pontic area of right central incisor is appreciated.
- The pontic of right central incisor is longer than the left central incisor.

The purpose and procedures of the surgery

1. Horizontal and vertical gingival level of the pontic of right central incisor is improved to achieve symmetric crown shape of central incisors. Gingival level is reconstructed on the surface of pontic of right central incisor with connective tissue graft using same technique as root coverage procedure.

Surgery (2007. 4. 16)

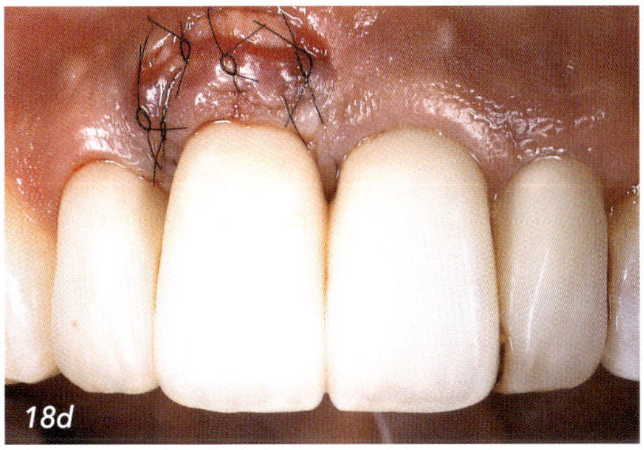

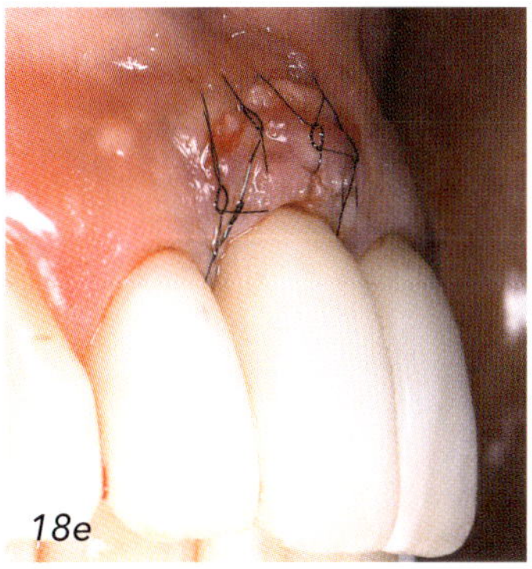

Fig 18d : Horizontal gingival level should be aligned properly at suturing. The author does not typically apply overcorrection.
Fig 18e : Vertical gingival level is aligned according to the left central incisor.

1

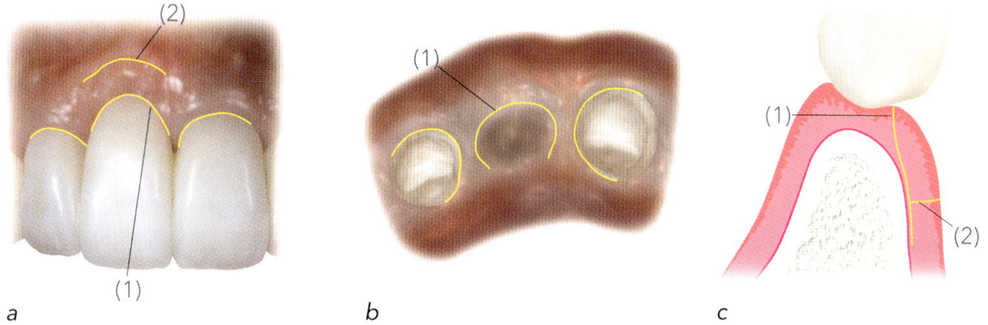

Incision : Almost identical incisions as the case of p97~99 was applied were applied to this case. Gingival sulcus incisions were made from distal labial aspect to mesial palatal aspect of both maxillary right lateral incisor and left central incisor (1-a, b). The incision similar to the gingival sulcus incision was made along the outline of the pontic of right central incisor (1). Then, horizontal incision was made on labial aspect (2), and envelope flap was formed. Since there was intimate contact between the base of the pontic and alveolar ridge in this case, the goal of the procedure was to coronal repositioning of labial gingival level and augmentation of labial gingiva.

2

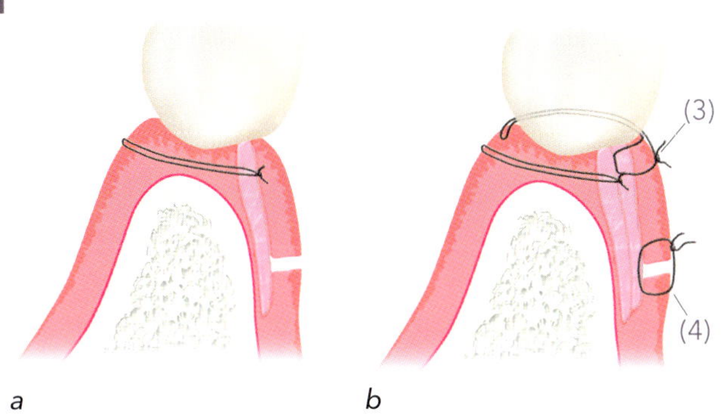

Suture : 2 connective tissue grafts were augmented since the thickness of the connective tissue of the palatal donner site was only about 2 mm. The first graft was placed on the labial aspect of the right central incisor and sutured at papilla areas between right lateral and central incisor and both central incisors as shown in 2-a. Resorbable monofilament (7 - 0) was used. Then, the second graft was tied with sling suture (3), followed by suturing at the horizontal incision area.

‖ Point ‖

The gingival flap is formed right under the papilla with envelope technique, since shape of the prosthesis is square and horizontal width of the gingiva at the area of the papilla is relatively small. Horizontal incision is made at the apex area of maxillary right central incisor to facilitate forming the gingival flap.

3 months post-op

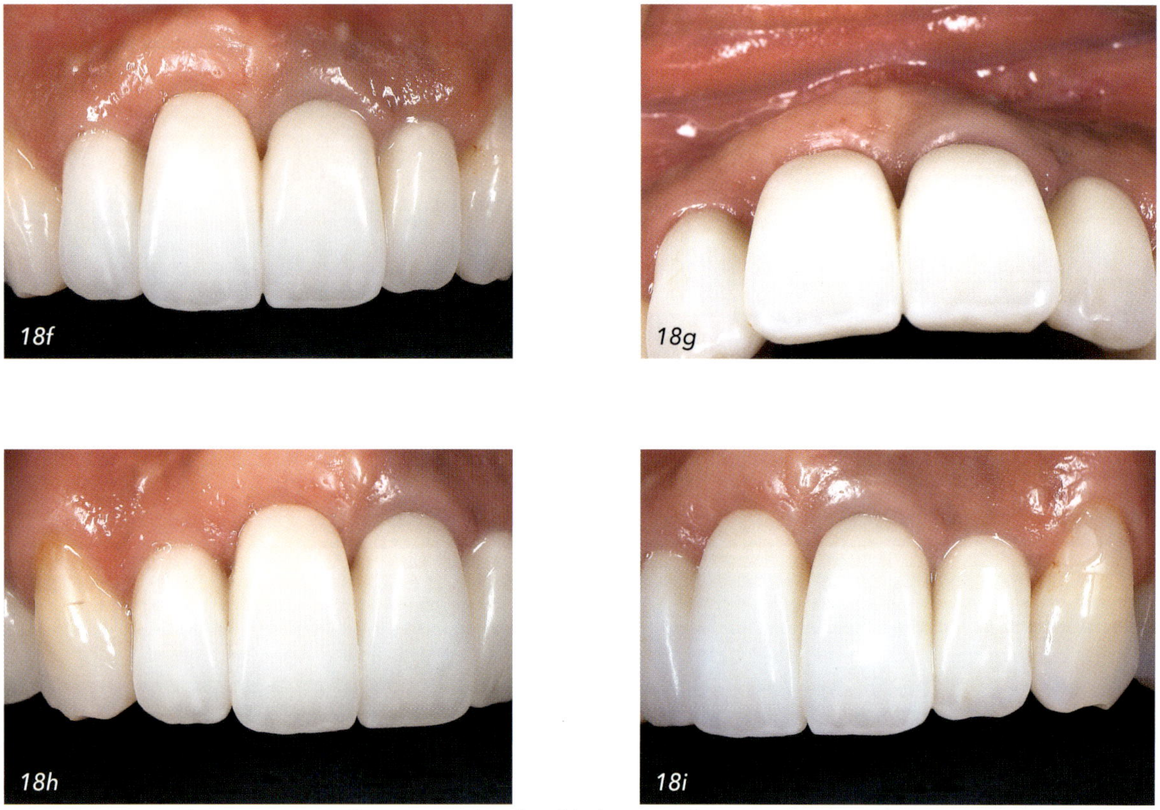

Fig 18f~i : 3 months post-op. Well maintained and stable horizontal・vertical gingival level and harmonized and continuous gingival line is reconstructed (prosthodontics treatment by Dr. Masayuki Okawa).

Eveluation of the case

Coverage procedure pontic is achieved by forming thick keratinized gingiva on labial aspect using thick graft as shown in this case.

The concept of interdental papilla reconstruction procedure

Success of interdental papilla reconstruction depends on secure graft procedure of connective tissue to increase the volume of gingival tissue at the papilla area. Maintaining enough blood supply and minimizing the dead space are especially important to achieve the successful procedure. Minimum incision and management not to interrupt blood supply are essential as well. It is also important to trim the connective tissue graft smooth to match the size and the surface to the recipient site.

Interdental papilla reconstruction procedure 1

Pre-op

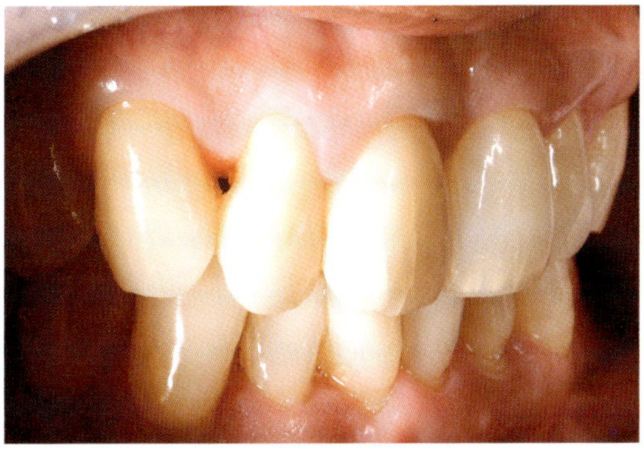

Fig 19a : Pre-op side view.

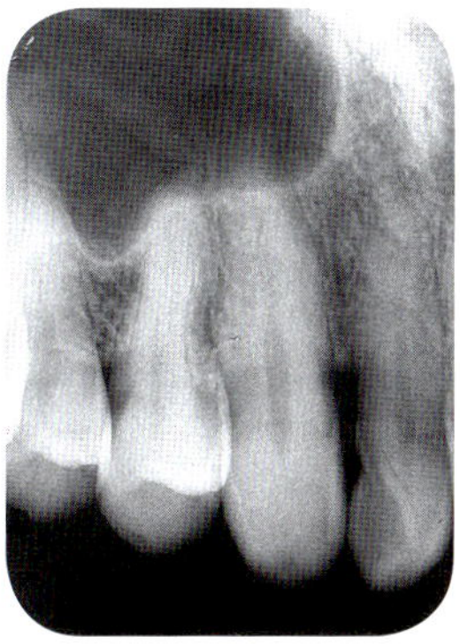

Fig 19b : Pre-op peri-apical x-ray.

Vertical gingival line	3	2	1	1	2	3
Balance to the adjacent tooth	X	X				
Balance to the same tooth on the contra lateral side	X	X				

*mark [X] in problematic area

Points of this case

Problems

- Black triangle is appreciated between maxillary right canine and lateral incisor due to decreased gingival tissue height.
- About 1 mm of root exposure is observed at the right lateral incisor.

The purpose and procedures of the surgery

1. Inter dental papilla reconstruction procedure between maxillary right canine and lateral incisor. Papilla height is improved and labial aspect is thickened by the connective tissue graft to increase the resistance.

Surgery (2008. 6. 22)

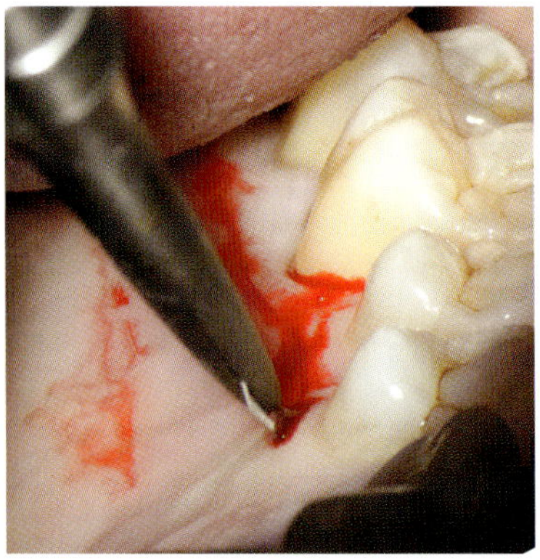

Fig 19c : The first incision: the first incision is made on the palate vertically.

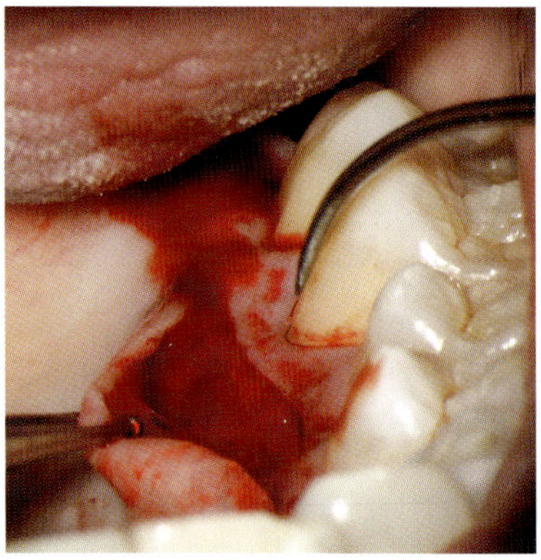

Fig 19d : Second incision: Palatal gingiva is incised keeping 1.5 mm thickness.

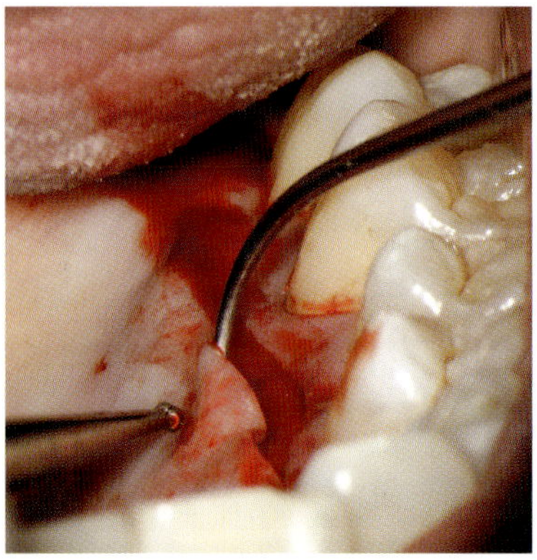

Fig 19e : Third incision: third incision is made palatal to the second incision to make 2 mm thick connective tissue graft.

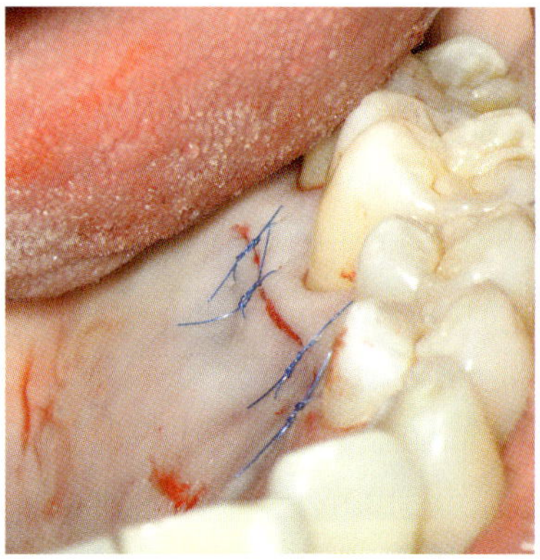

Fig 19f : Right after suturing.

Forming gingival flap at the recipient site

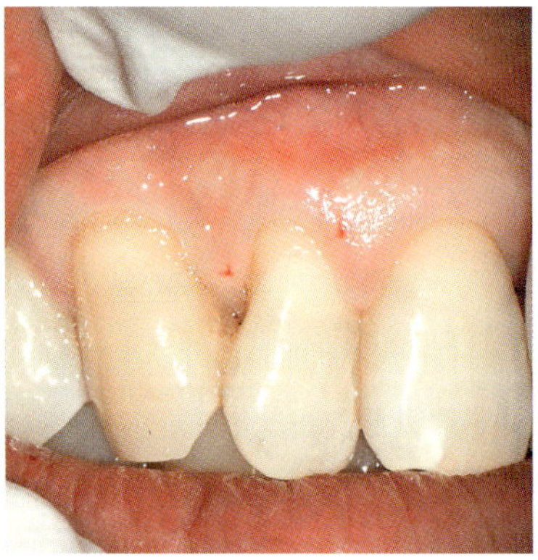

Fig 19g : After local anesthesia is administered.

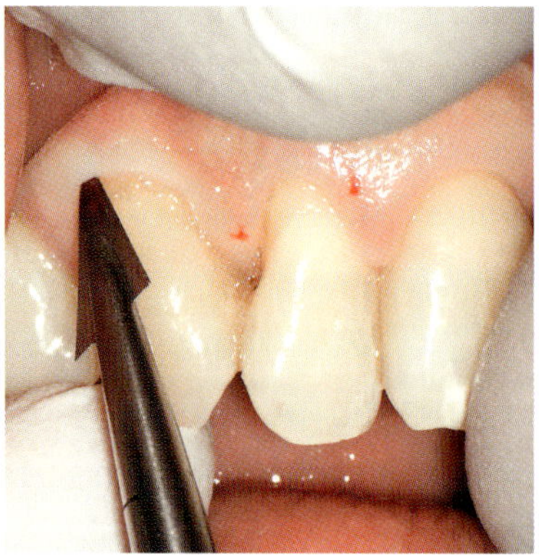

Fig 19h : Gingival sulcus incision is made from distal aspect of maxillary right canine.

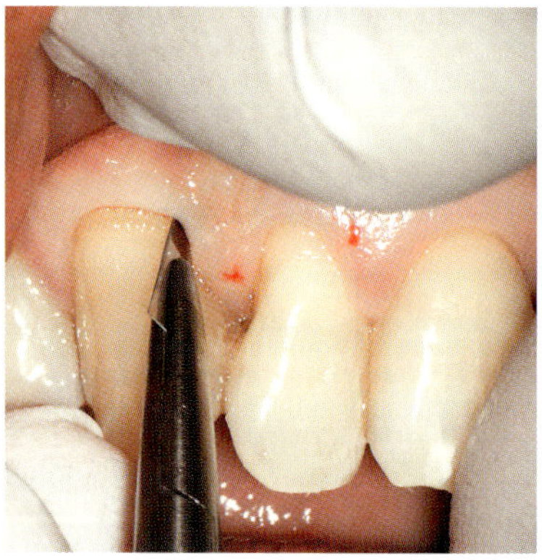

Fig 19i : Gingival sulcus incision at mesial aspect of the canine. The incision is extended as far toward palatal aspect as the blade could reach.

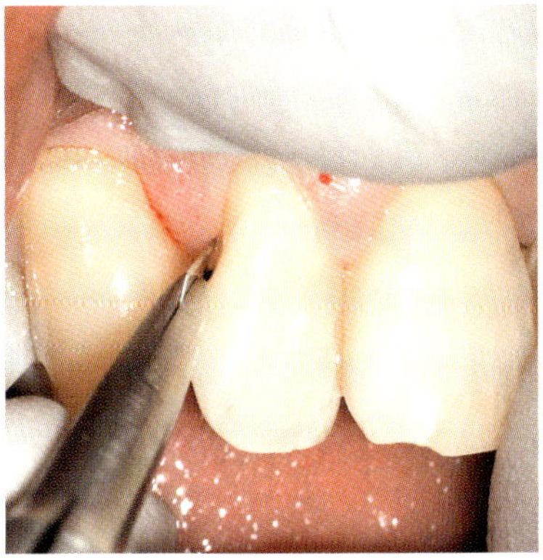

Fig 19j : The incision at distal aspect of maxillary right lateral incisor. Attention must be paid to the direction of the blade due to convicted cervical area.

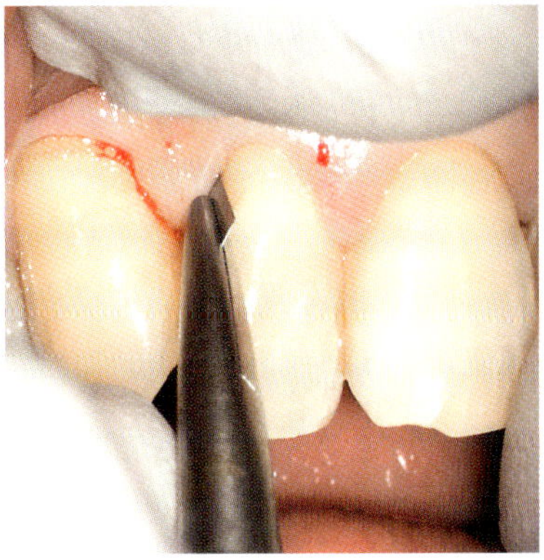

Fig 19k : Gingival sulcus incision is made up to mesial aspect of the lateral incisor.

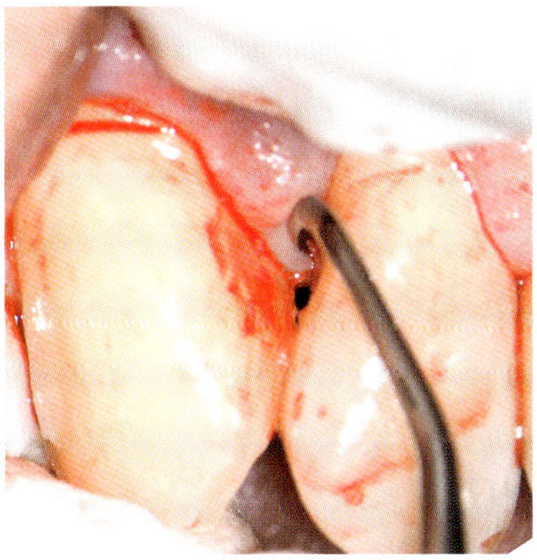

Fig 19l : Periosteum at the papilla area is elevated careful with incision without forcing the area. Horizontal incision is made on labial aspect coronal to MGJ.

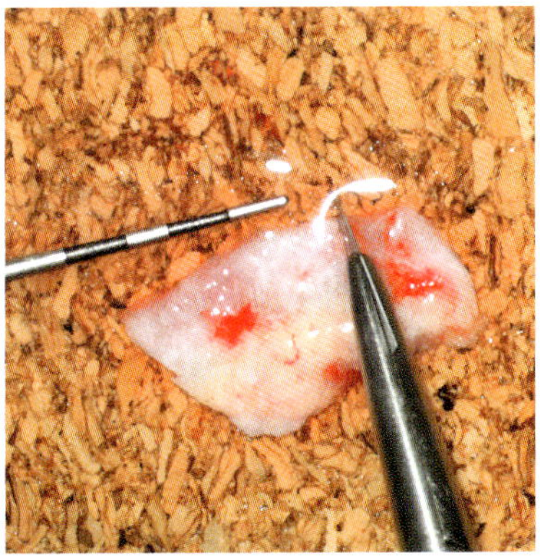

Fig 19m : The graft is trimmed in to desired shape with the sharp blade.

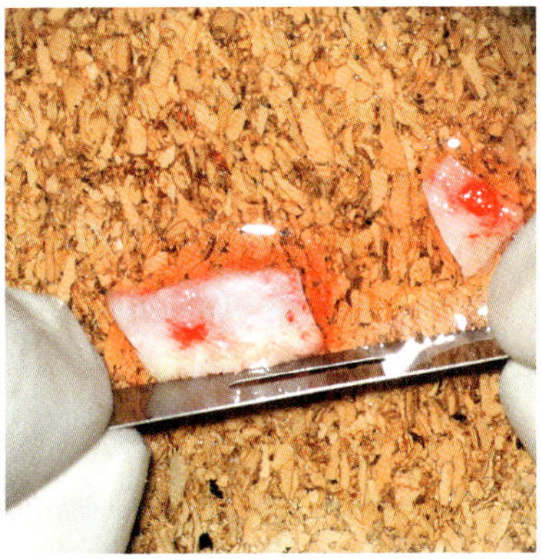

Fig 19n : Razor-shaped blade is used for incision.

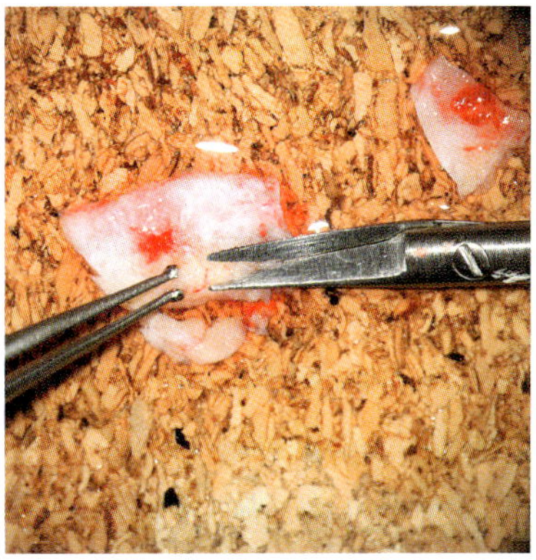

Fig 19o : detailed timmeing. Fatt tissue is removed as much as possible using scissors.

Suture

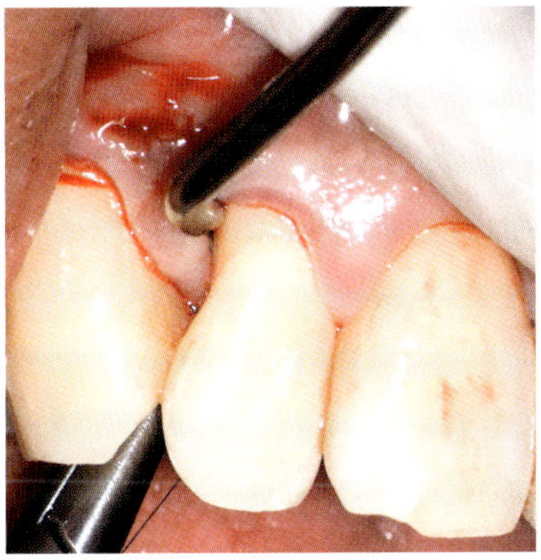

Fig 19p : 2 connective tissue crafts are used. the first graft is sutured at right under the papilla. This photo shows the suture needle, inserted from palatal papilla, pulled out to to distal aspect of the lateral incisor.

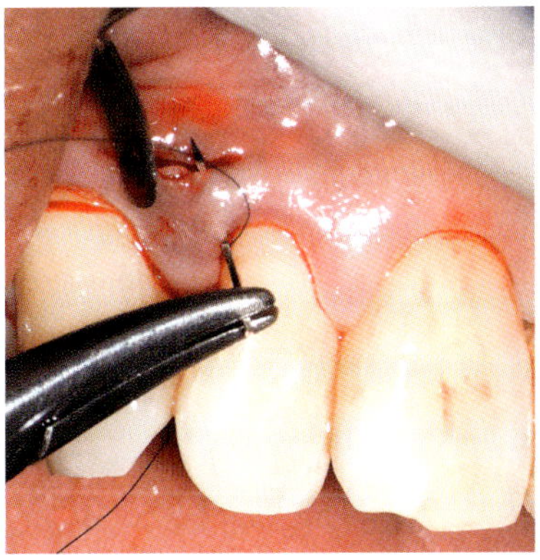

Fig 19q : Pulled needle is inserted through to horizontal incision area.

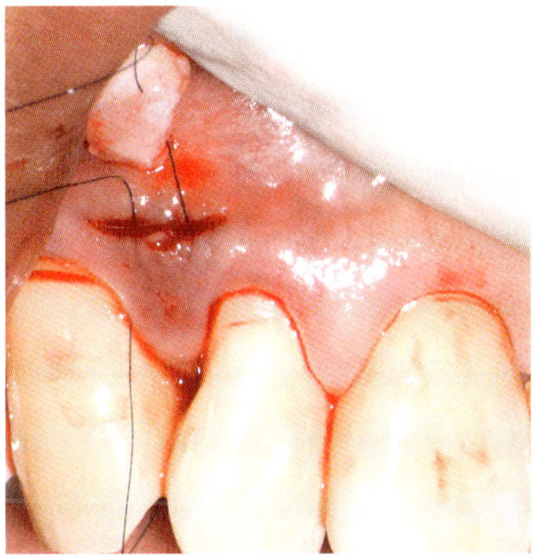

Fig 19r : The needle is inserted to the graft outside of the gingival flap.

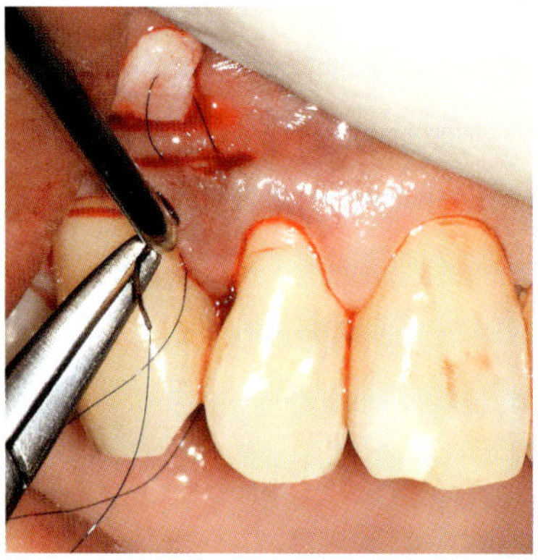

Fig 19s : The needle is made to exit to the palatal papilla through under the gingival flap.

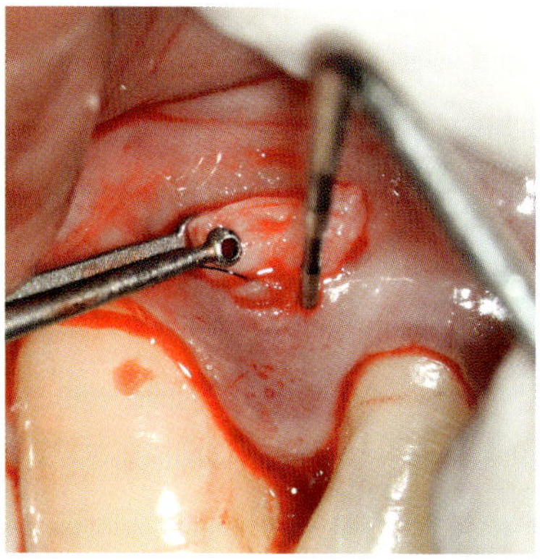

Fig 19t : The graft is inserted under the papillae.

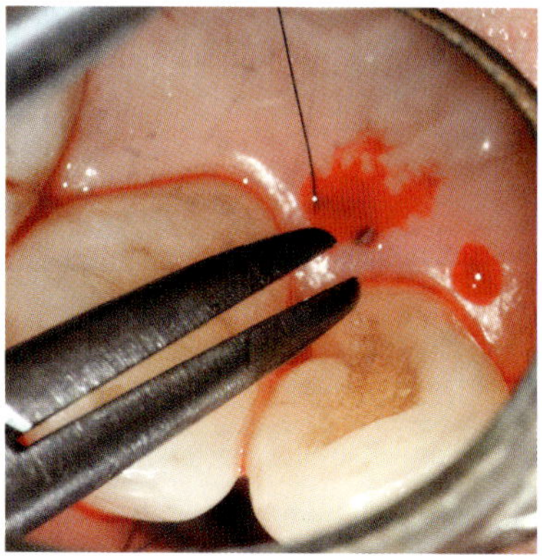

Fig 19u : The suture is pulled from palatal aspect to confirm the position of the graft.

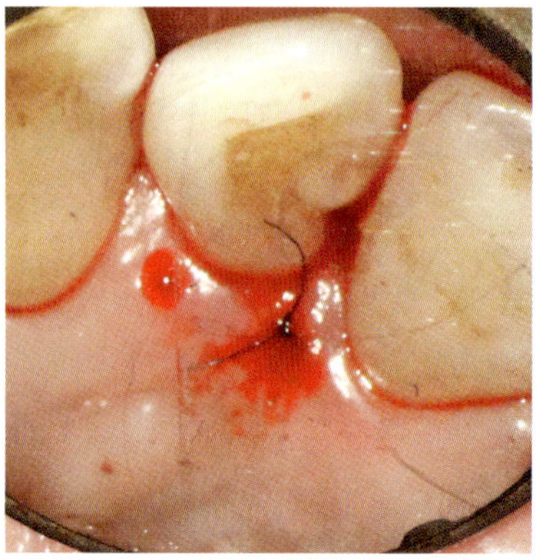

Fig 19v : The graft is stabilized under the papilla by being sutured on the palatal aspect.

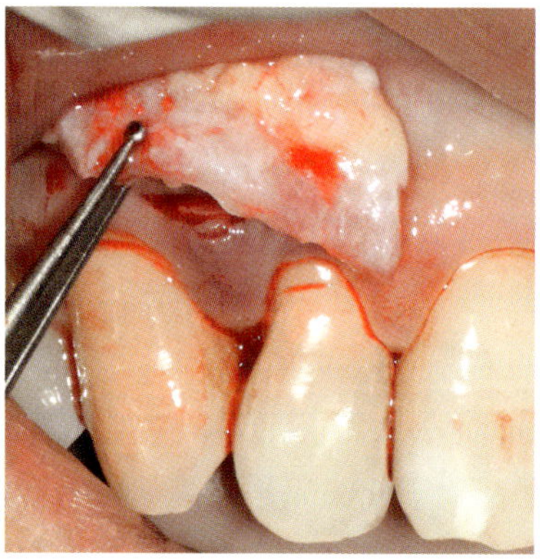

Fig 19w : Size of the second graft for the labial side is confirmed.

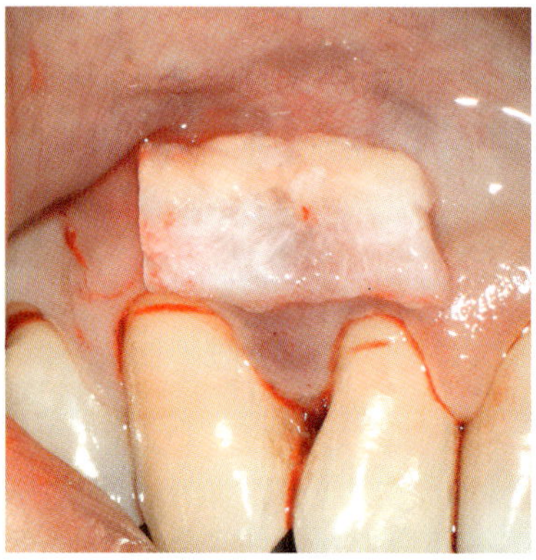

Fig 19x : Size of the graft is confirmed again after trimming. It is re-trimmed to fit the size exactly.

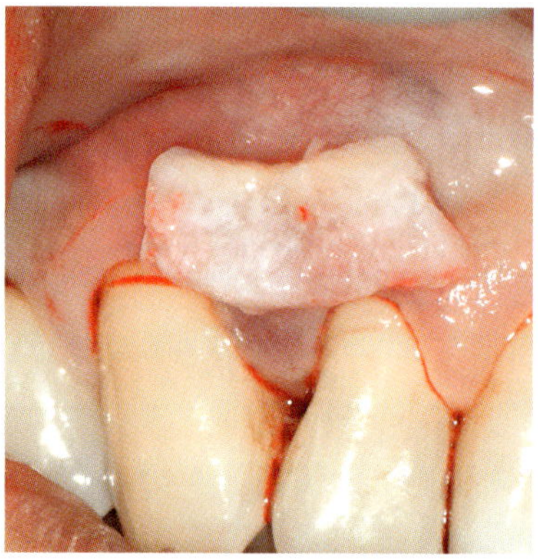

Fig 19y : The graft is trimmed properly.

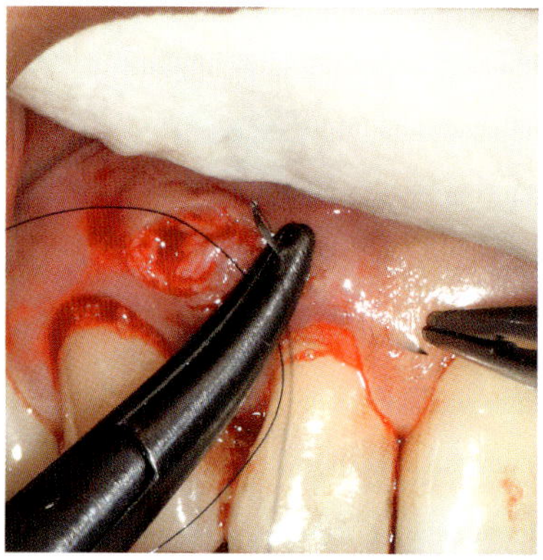

Fig 19z : The graft is inserted in the labial flap and sutured. The graft is sutured at mesial aspect first. The graft is stabilized by suture through the gingival flap and the graft together at mesial aspect of the lateral incisor.

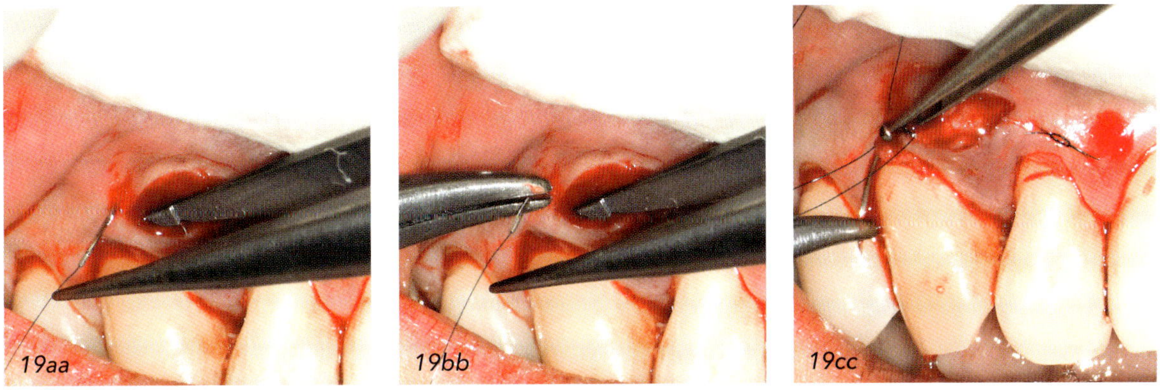

Fig 19aa~cc : Distal aspect is sutured next. It is sutured through the gingival flap and the connective tissue graft together as mesial aspect.

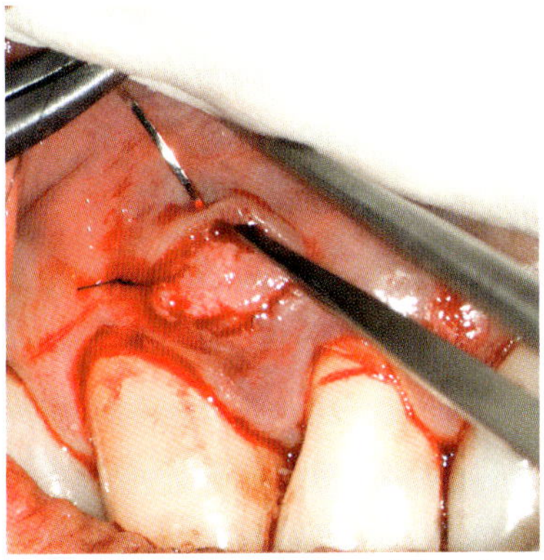

Fig 19dd : The graft is stabilized on both mesial and distal aspect.

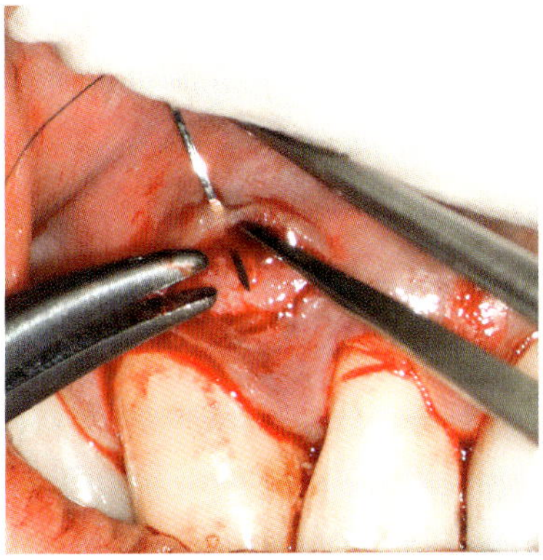

Fig 19ee : The needle is inserted through apical flap.

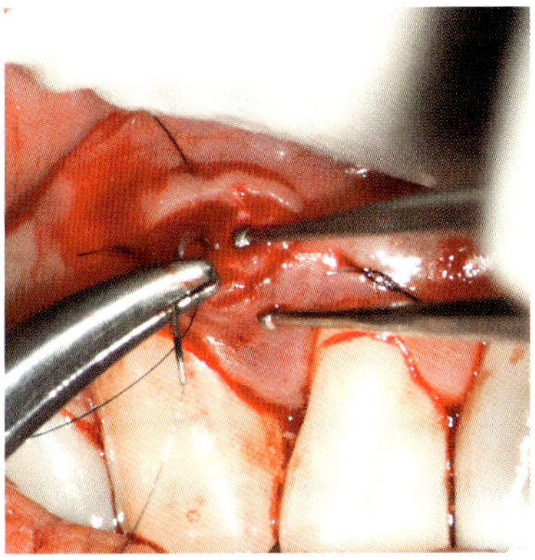

Fig 19ff : The needle is inserted through the graft.

‖ Point ‖

Purposes of this technique are to thicken the labial gingiva and to bring the papilla up. Hence, forming the gingival flap is very important. The gingival flap needs to be formed at the just right condition to host the graft. Apical portion of the flap formation is especially important. If this area is over incised, the graft tends to slip in apically not acting as the stopper to support the flap up coronally and sling suture might have to be employed.

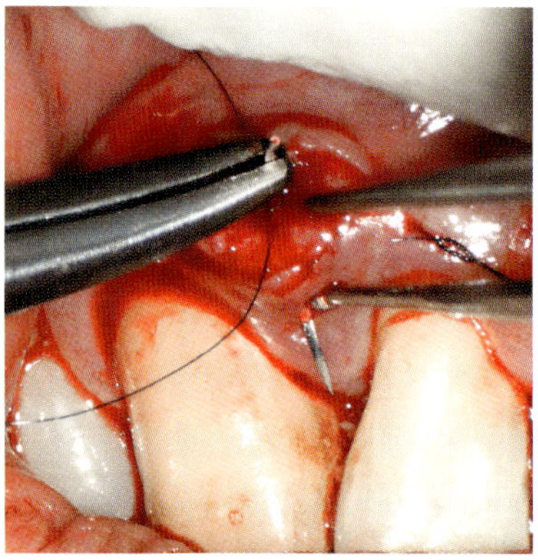

Fig 19gg : The needle is inserted to the labial gingival flap.

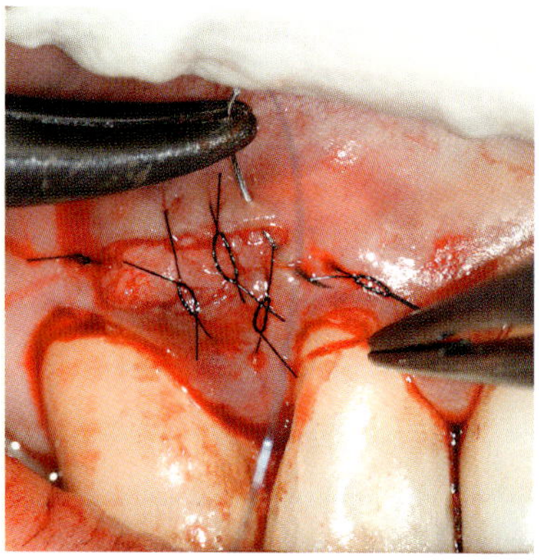

Fig 19hh : Followed by the same suturing.

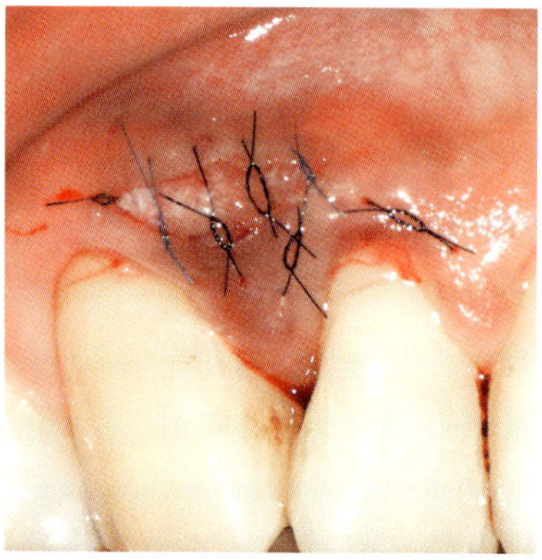

Fig 19ii : Right after suturing. Coronally repositioned papilla is observed.

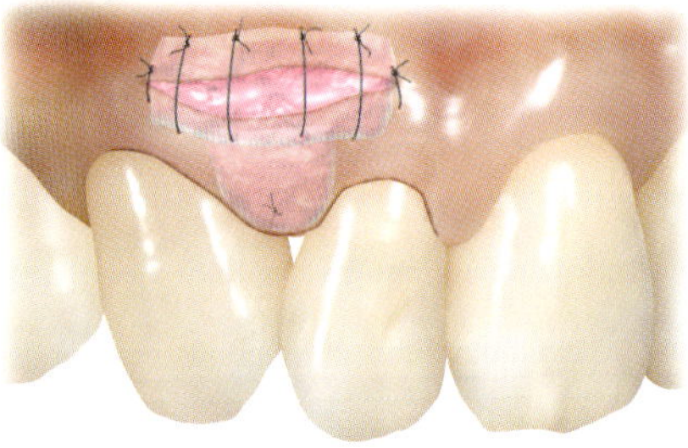

Grafts are positioned and sutured at right under the papilla and labial aspect.

3 months post-op

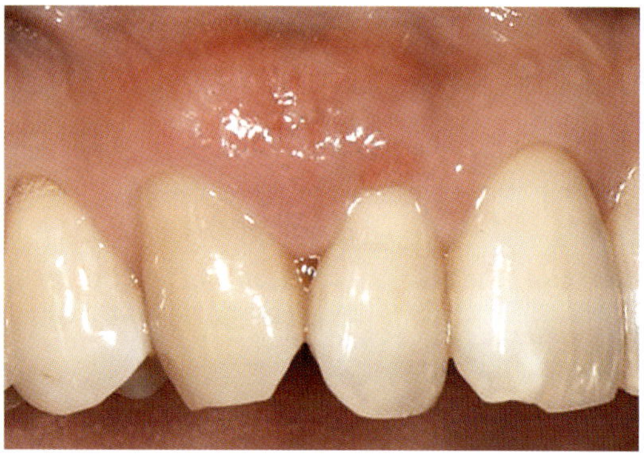

Fig 19jj : 2 weeks post-op. Grafted area is healed already. Papilla area is coronally repositioned and gingival level of distal aspect of the lateral incisor and mesial aspect of the canine are coronally advanced.

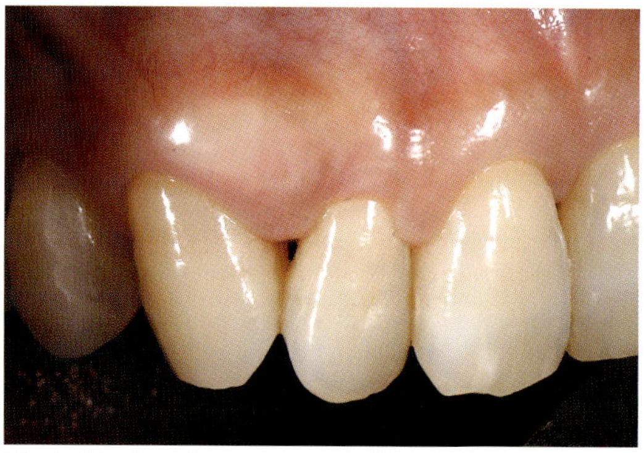

Fig 19kk : Condition at 3 months post-op.

Evaluation of the case

Black triangle has not been eliminated completely with this surgical procedure. However significant improvement is observed in papilla height, gingival level of the canine and lateral incisor area and gingival scallop.

Interdental papilla reconstruction procedure 2

Pre-op

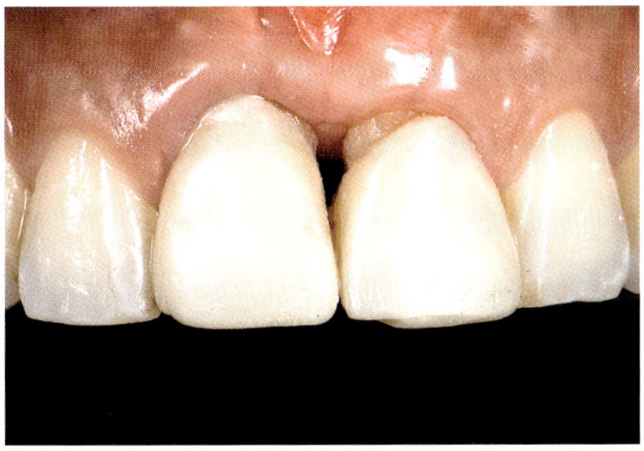

Fig 20a : unbalanced vertical gingival level of central incisors and black triangle is appreciated.

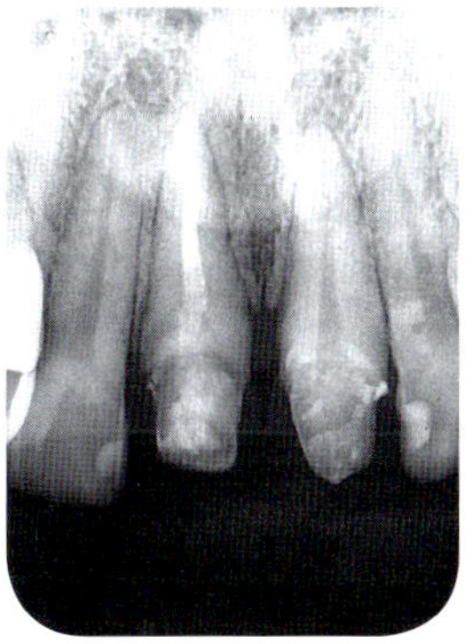

Fig 20b : Slight horizontal bone loss is appreciated around both central incisors.

Vertical gingival line	3	2	1	1	2	3
Balance to the adjacent tooth			X	X		
Balance to the same tooth on the contra lateral side			X	X		

*mark [X] in problematic area

Points of this case

Problems

- Black triangle due to moderate recession of vertical gingival level at central incisors.
- The patient is concerned about discrepancy of midline from the facial midline.

The purpose and procedures of the surgery

1. Orthodontic treatment is planned to correct the midline. It was decided to perform interdental papilla reconstruction procedure with connective tissue graft to the area of central incisors prior to orthodontic treatment.

Orthodontic treatment set-up model

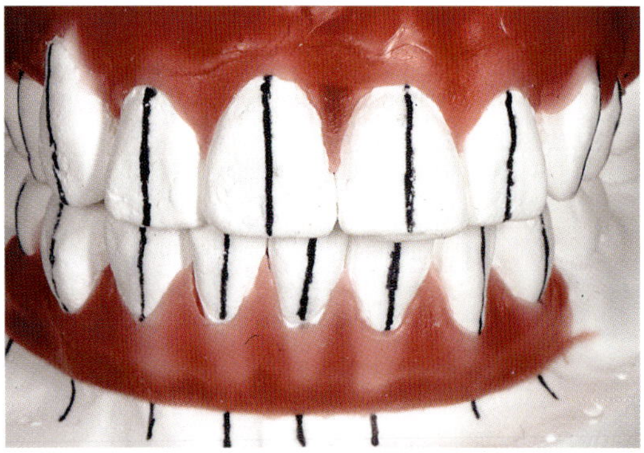

Fig 20c : Orthodontic treatment set-up model (orthodontist : Dr. Toru Hoshino). The set-up model is fabricated prior to the surgical procedure.

Surgery (2004. 1. 29)

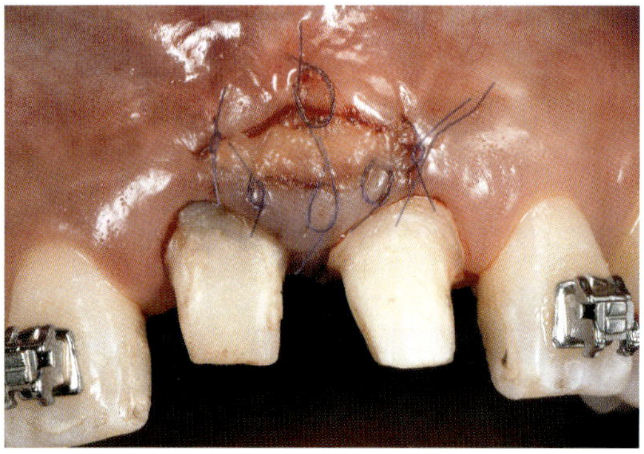

Fig 20d : Suturing. 2 grafts are used. The first graft is augmented right under the papilla and the second on labial aspect.

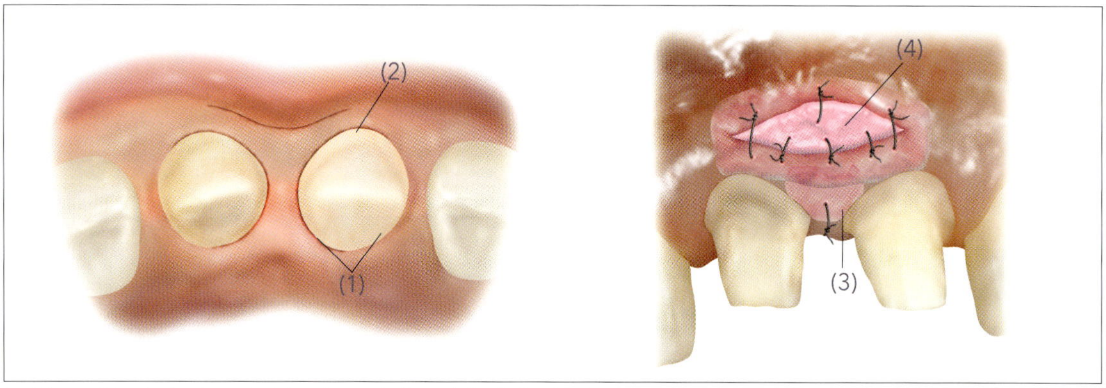

Incision : Gingival sulcus incision is made from labial distal corner to palatal distal aspect of each central incisor (1). Horizontal incision is made in labial keratinized gingiva (2).
Suture : The connective tissue grafts from the palate are trimmed. The first graft is pulled toward palate and sutured (3). The second graft is trimmed in exact size of the labial gingival flap and sutured in order to push the papilla up (4).

Orthodontic treatment

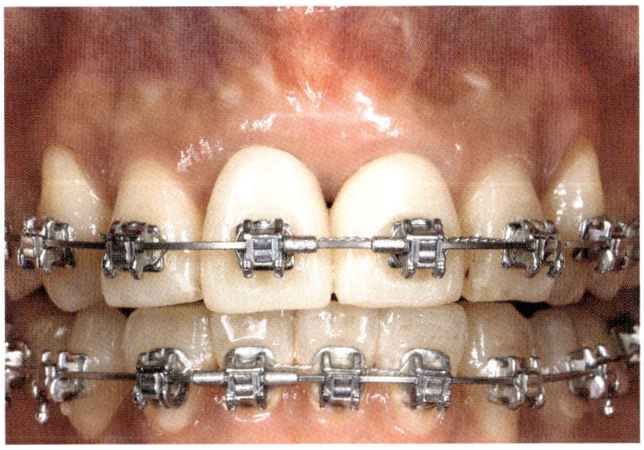

Fig 20e : Orthodontic treatment is activated on central incisors after hearing of the soft tissue.

‖ Point ‖

Thickness of the gingiva could be increased by adding connective tissue graft on labial aspect. This connective tissue graft also serves as the support for coronally raised papilla. It is important not to overly expand apical portion of the gingival flap forming the exact shape so that the graft fits tightly to prevent apical dislocation.

Insertion of the final prosthesis

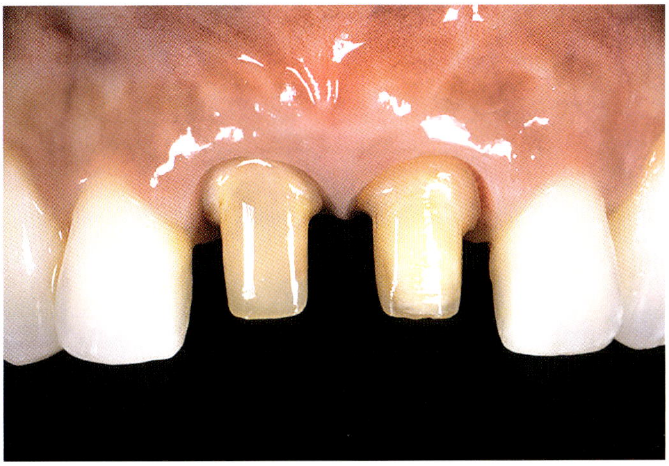

Fig 20f : Tissue condition before insertion of the final prosthesis.

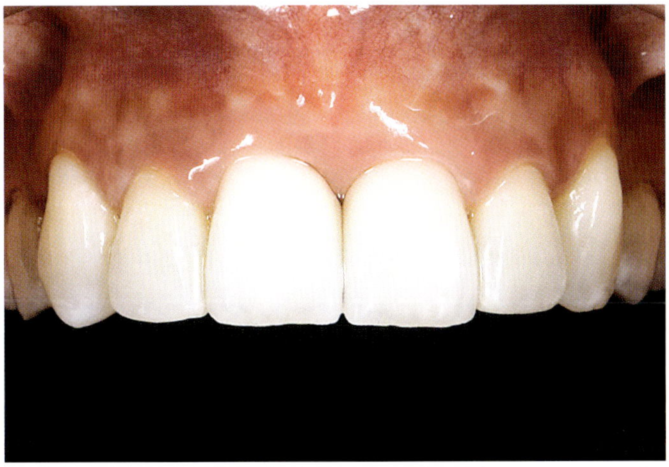

Fig 20g : Insertion of the final prosthesis (prosthetic treatment by Dr. Masayuki Okawa).

Evaluation of the case

Excellent result was achieved with this case through interdisciplinary approach collaborating with Dr. Masayuki Okawa (Daikanyama Address Dental Clinic). Surgical approach, orthodontic approach and prosthetic approach are indicated to treat black triangle. It is rare case that each approach alone could solve the problem. Combination of these approaches are often required to achieve successful result.

PART 4

Clinical approach : Implant

Management of peri-implant soft tissue

Clinicians need to consider good peri-implant tissue management to ensure long-term stability of the implant. The issue is therefore how peri-implant hard and soft tissues can be managed appropriately. The following explanation examines this with a focus on the soft tissues.

The roles of peri-implant soft tissue can be broadly categorized as functional and esthetic. Enhancing functionality means ensuring acquisition of a non-mobile, keratinized mucosa. The general consensus in the past was that acquiring a peri-implant, non-mobile, keratinized mucosa was not essential, but this view has changed, and a non-mobile, keratinized mucosa is now considered essential.

So what techniques should be used to obtain a non-mobile, keratinized mucosa? The author uses a connective tissue graft (CTG) for this. In the CTG procedure, the handling of the epithelium is determined taking esthetic considerations into account. Furthermore, CTG may be divided according to its objective into preventive procedures and recovering procedures. This chapter will look at a number of different cases grouped by objective.

Treatment of peri-implant soft tissue recession

Peri-implant soft tissue recession is a serious problem in esthetic implant treatment, and it is a cause of distress for a great many implant patients. There are broadly three types of methods to resolve the problem of peri-implant soft tissue recession when it occurs:

1. Allow the implant to sleep, and repeat the treatment;
2. Remove the implant and repeat the treatment; and
3. Refabricate the implant abutment and repeat the treatment.

However, there are no clear clinical criteria for selecting the appropriate option. Over the next few pages, we will look at the author's classification and make it a basis for reconstruction.

Classification of peri-implant soft tissue recession

Class Ⅰ Limited to superstructure (including abutment) components

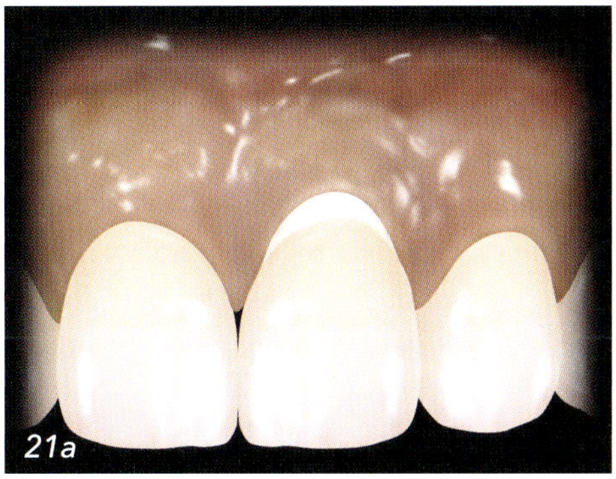

Fig 21a : Does not include recession of neighboring tissue.

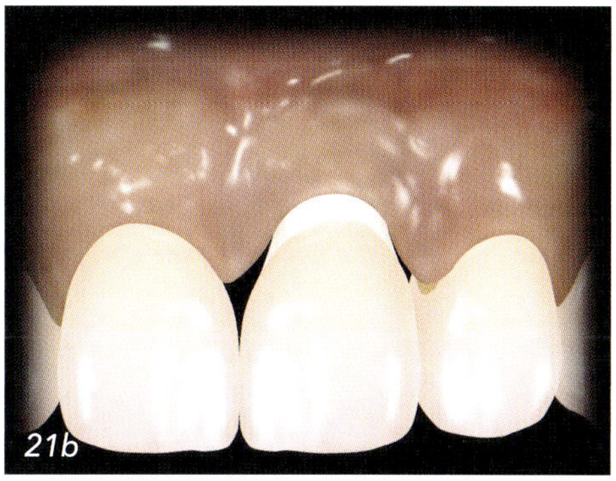

Fig 21b : Includes recession of neighboring tissue.

Class Ⅱ Recession beyond the boundary between the implant platform and the superstructure

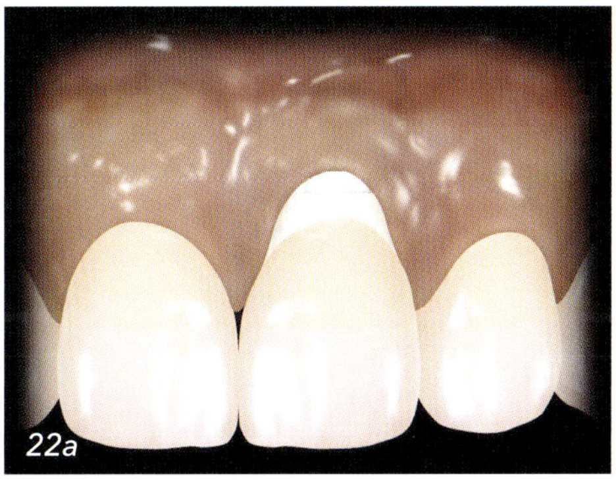

Fig 22a : Does not include recession of neighboring tissue.

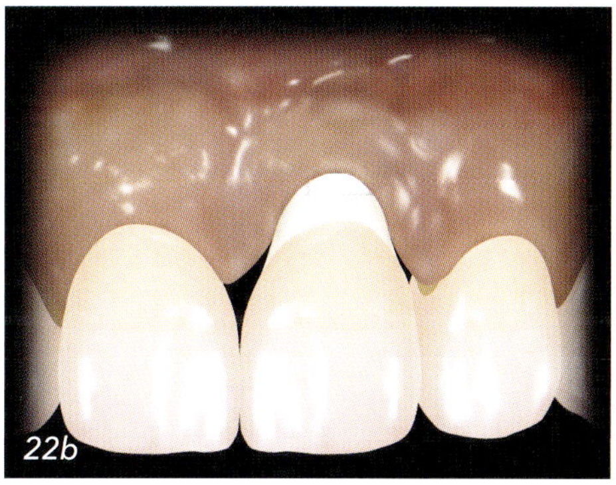

Fig 22b : Includes recession of neighboring tissue.

Class Ⅲ Exposure of osseointegration surface, exposure of components that should be inside the bone (exposure of implant to bone level is Class Ⅲ)

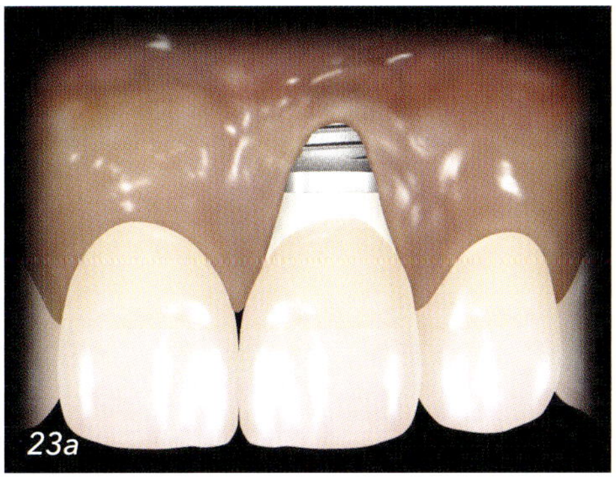

Fig 23a : Does not include recession of neighboring tissue.

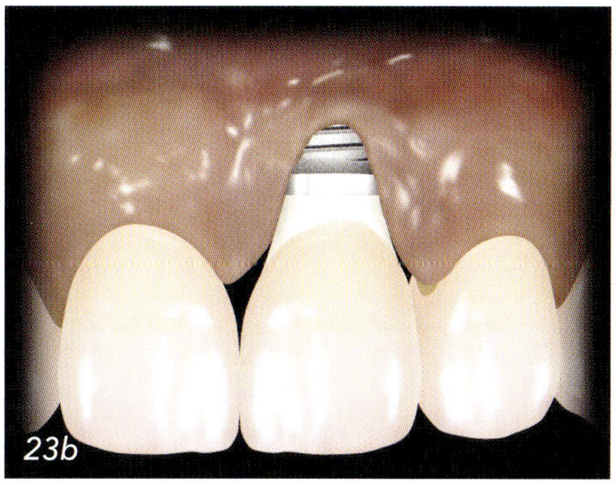

Fig 23b : Includes recession of neighboring tissue.

Philosophy of management of implant problem

Recently, various implant treatment problems can be appreciated. There are various causes for those problems. It is important to prevent those problems from happening but once it happens, we should know how to manage those situations as soon and effective as possible. The 4 implant treatment problem cases that were treated at the author's clinic will be shown in this chapter to review how to manage those issues.

Generally, 3 management techniques for gingiva recession after the implant treatment completion can be explained as follows,

1. Let the implant sleep and re-treatment
2. Remove the implant and re-treatment
3. Remake implant abutment and re-treatment

Probably the most patient's accepted treatment should be 3. Usually the patient would like to keep the implant and work with it. If a new implant needs to be placed to manage the issue, the condition for implant placement can be worse than the first time, therefore the patient burden for the treatment can become very high. So the author thinks that the abutment morphology change and soft tissue augmentation should be the best management of this kind of issue.

The management of implant problem 1

Pre-ope

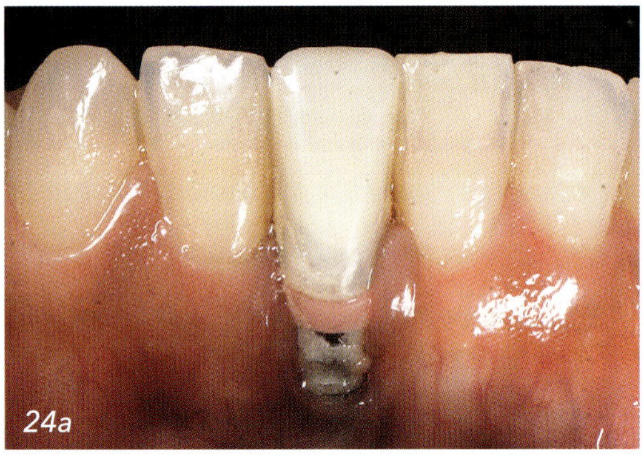

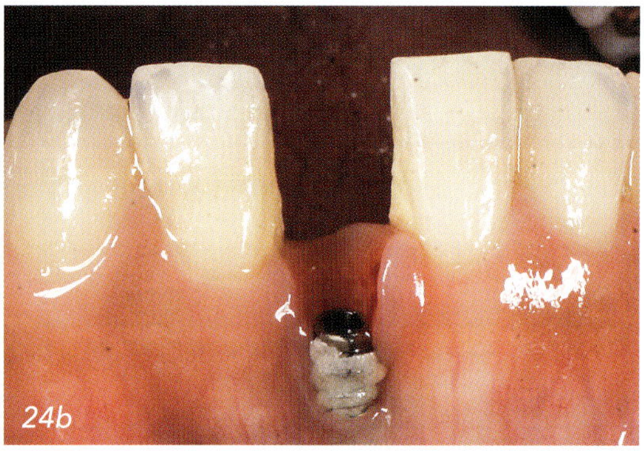

Fig 24a, b : Lower anterior pre-ope facial view.

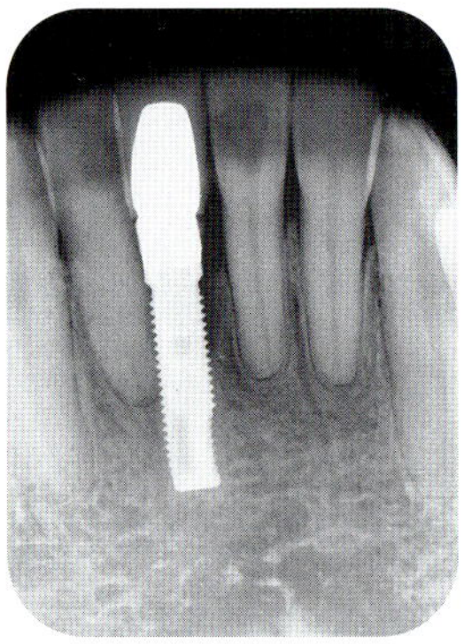

Fig 24c : Lower anterior per-ope x-ray.

Vertical gingival line	#27	#26	#25	#24	#23	#22
Balance with adjacent teeth				X		
Balance with contra lateral teeth				X		
Horizontal gingival line	**#27**	**#26**	**#25**	**#24**	**#23**	**#22**
Balance with adjacent teeth						
Balance with contra lateral teeth						

X is the problematic area

Class III b

Point of this case

Problem

- There is vertical gingival line discrepancy around #24 implant.
- There is implant thread exposure.
- Implant placement is too far buccal.

Purpose and technique of surgery

1. Construct keratinized tissue around the implant with connective tissue graft.

Surgery (5/1/2010)

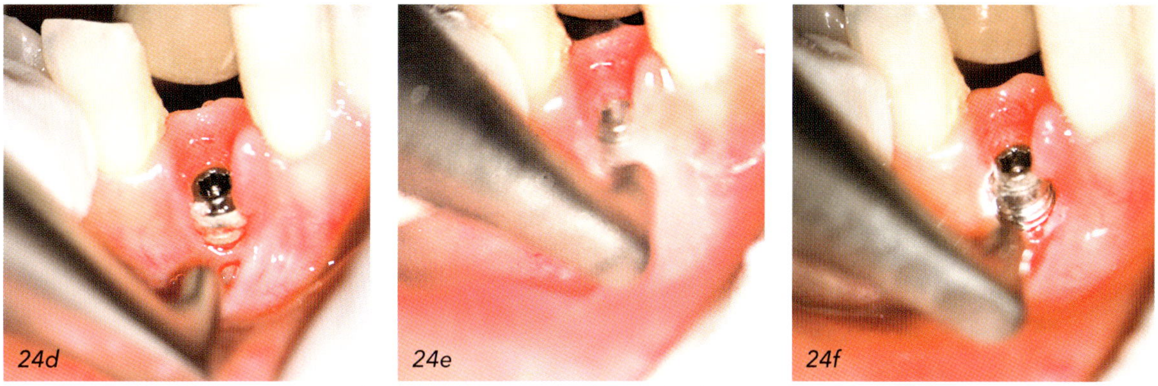

Fig 24d~f : After abutment removal, exposed implant surface debridement is performed with power jet machine. Powder is Amino acid Glycine.

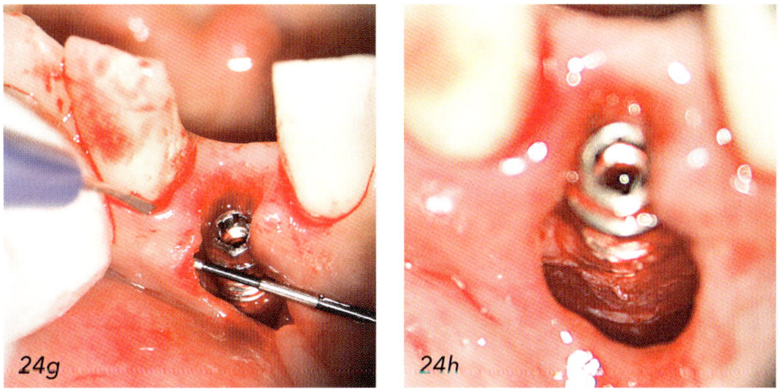

Fig 24g, h : After completion of exposed implant surface debridement, envelop flap is open with the same concept of root surface coverage technique.

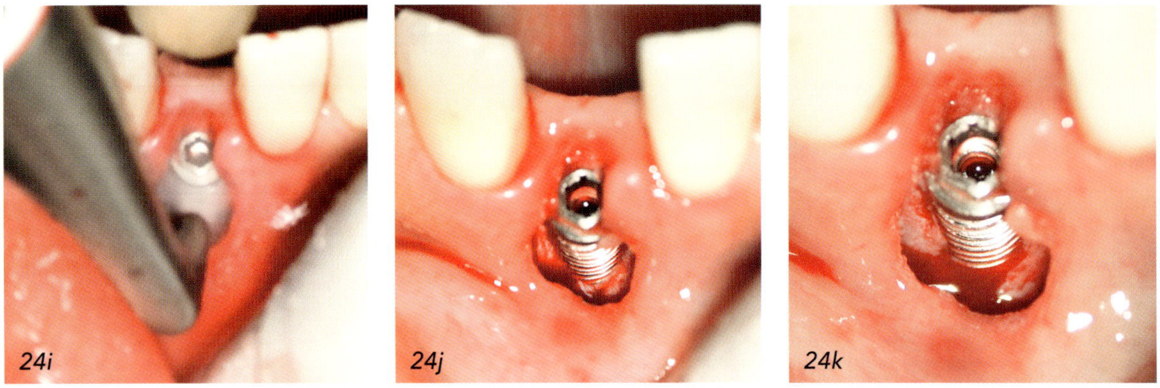

Fig 24i~k : After performing envelop flap opening, exposed implant surface towards to root apex direction debridement is performed with power jet machine.

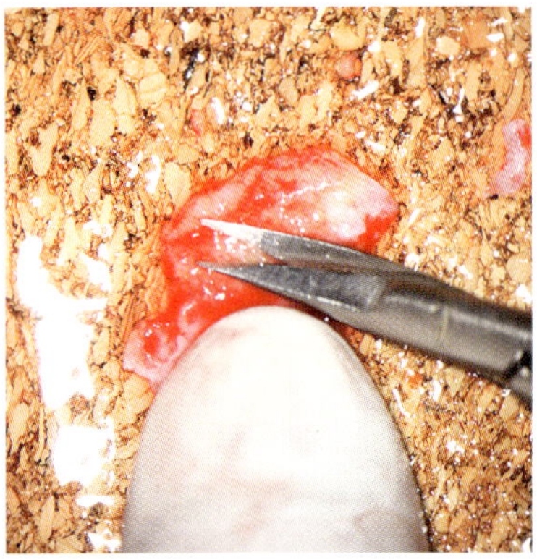

Fig 24l : Connective tissue graft piece is trimmed accordingly.

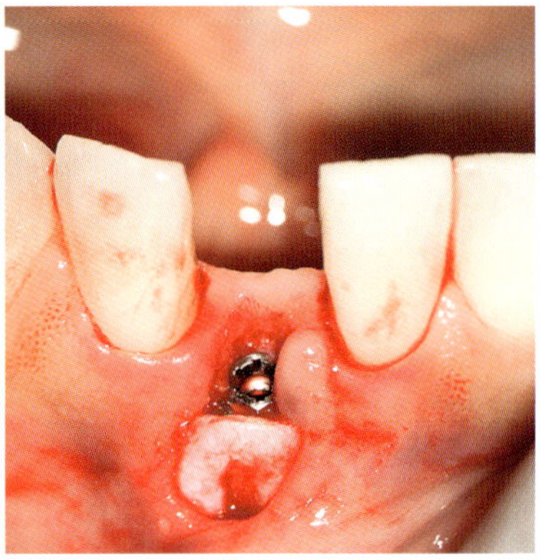

Fig 24m : Try in trimmed connective tissue graft.

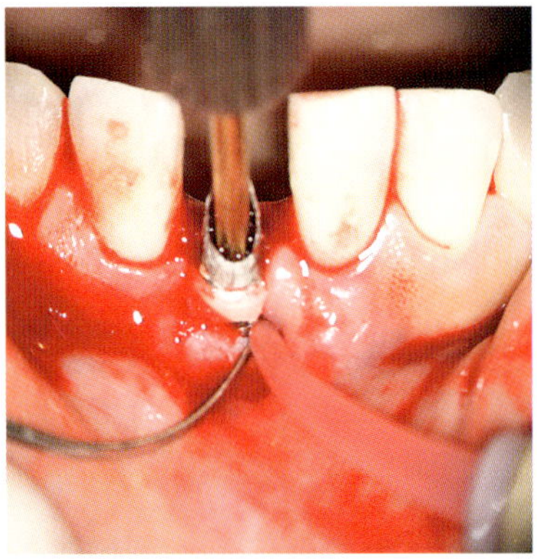

Fig 24n : After connective tissue is inserted under the envelope flap, the abutment should be re-inserted.

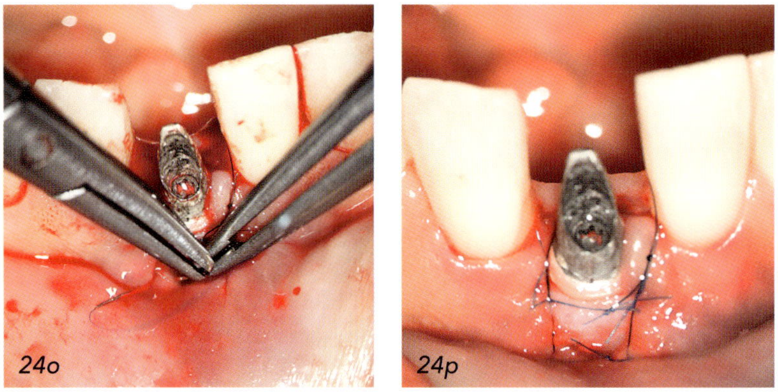

Fig 24o, p : Connective tissue graft is secured with suspensory sling suture.

Point

Peri-implant debridement is done twice with power jet machine. Firstly, exposed thread area with plaque accumulation is cleaned, then secondly the flap is opened and deeper implant body debridement is done. This technique allows the clinician easy approach to the site with the power jet machine and the area of inflammation can be cleaned before the invasive procedure.

Post-ope

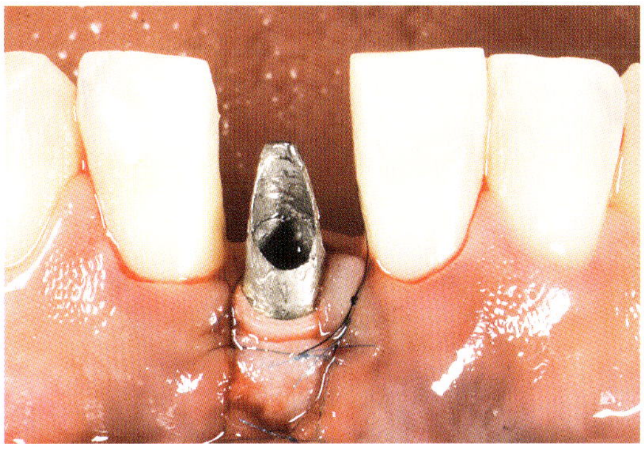

Fig 24q : The vertical gingival level is adjusted to the ideal final restoration gingival level with the suturing technique.

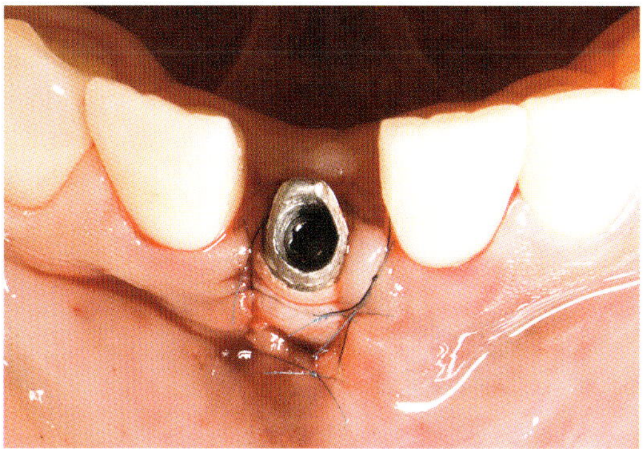

Fig 24r : Horizontal gingival level is created thicker.

3 month post-ope

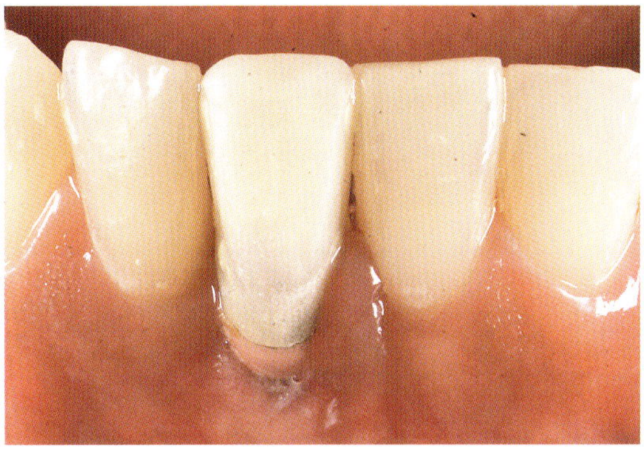

Fig 24s : 3 month post-ope. Soft tissue augmentation has been successfully achieved as planned.

8.5 years post-ope

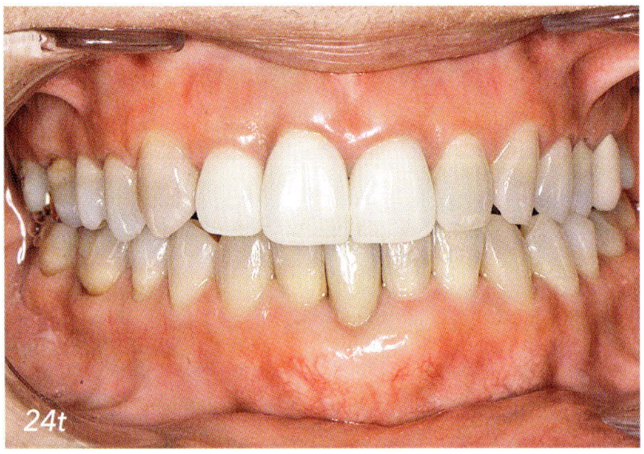

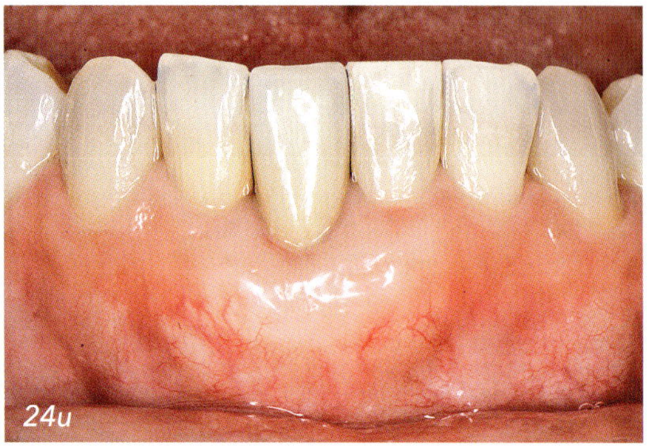

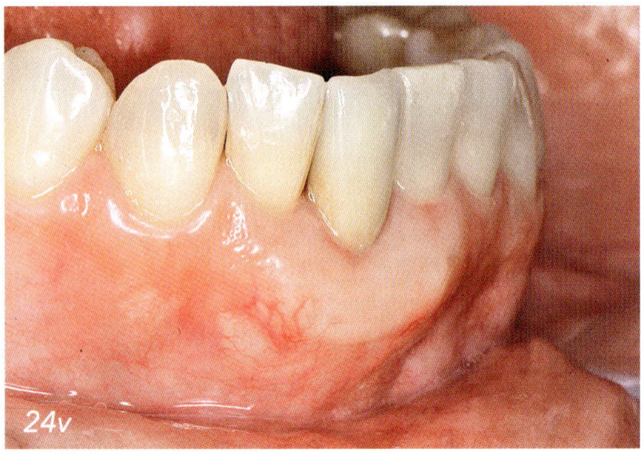

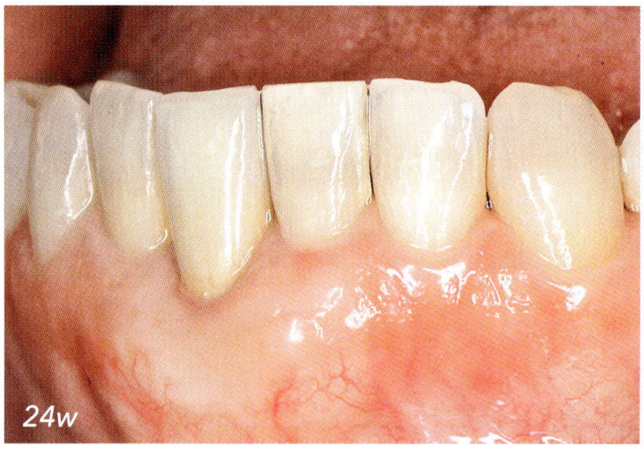

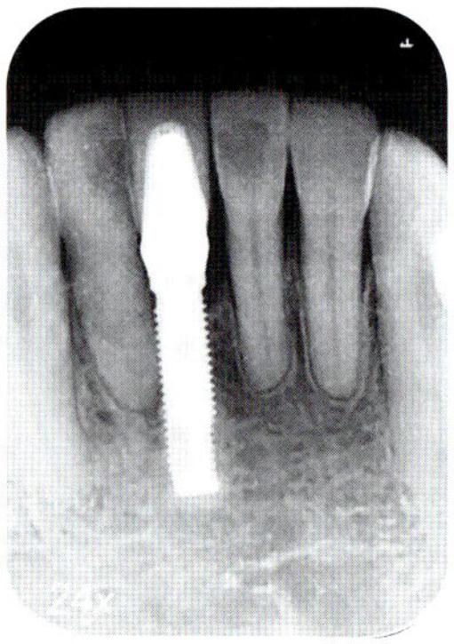

Fig 24t~x : 8.5 years post-ope.

Evaluation

This is the case with minor peri-implantitis due to buccal tissue recession and keratinized tissue loss. The primary issue of this kind of case is whether the exposed implant surface can have a complete debridement or not. If complete debridement can be performed, it is possible to create keratinized tissue by performing connective tissue augmentation. Moreover, once keratinized tissue is created, recreating bone surrounding implant can be possible as a next step. So far there is no well established treatment consensus for management of implant problems. However, success cannot be achieved without re-establishing peri-implant soft tissue.

The management of implant problem 2

Pre-ope

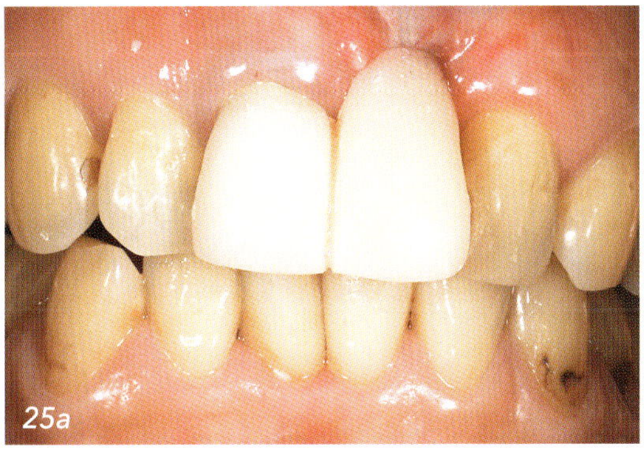

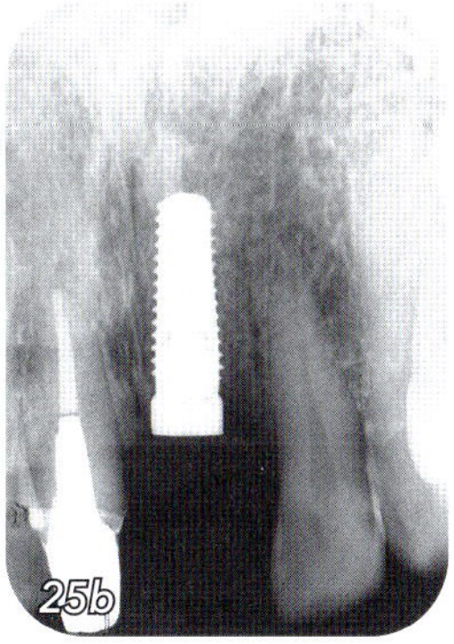

Fig 25a, b : Pre-ope facial view and x-ray. This implant is placed Jan 2007 at the other dental office.

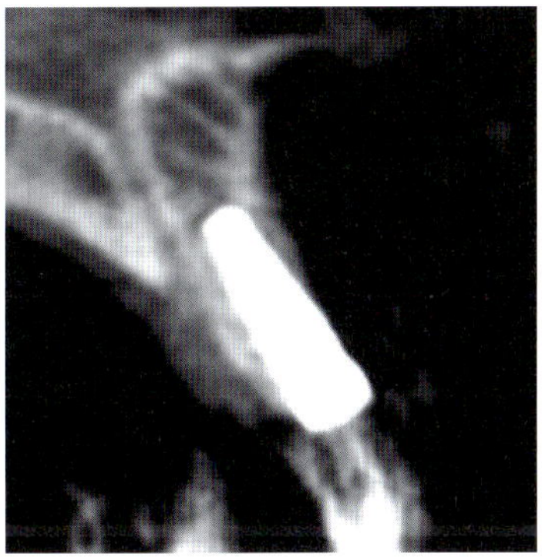

Fig 25c : Pre-ope CT scan.

After removing provisional restoration

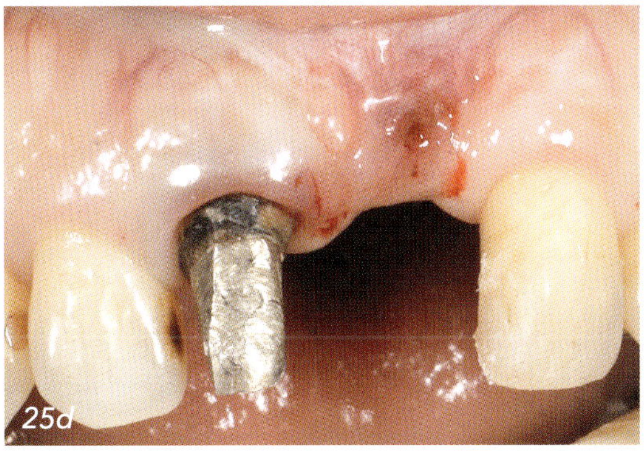

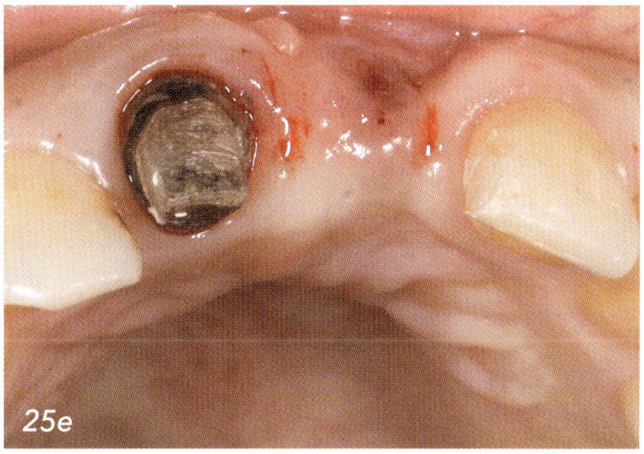

Fig 25d, e : Upper buccal and occlusal view after removing provisional restoration.

Vertical gingival line	#6	#7	#8	#9	#10	#11
Balance with adjacent teeth				X		
Balance with contralateral teeth				X		
Horizontal gingival line	**#6**	**#7**	**#8**	**#9**	**#10**	**#11**
Balance with adjacent teeth				X		
Balance with contralateral teeth				X		

X is the problematic area

Class Ⅱ b

Point of this case

Problem

- There is #9 vertical and horizontal tissue level discrepancy with the provisional restoration.
- #9 MGJ has been migrated coronally. CT scan shows buccally inclined implant.

Purpose and technique of surgery

1. Connective tissue graft has been performed twice since the surgical site needs buccal keratinized tissue and #9,10 papilla vertical hight.
2. Hard tissue augmentation was performed by the GBR technique with non reservable membrane.

Surgery : GBR technique (11/19/2008)

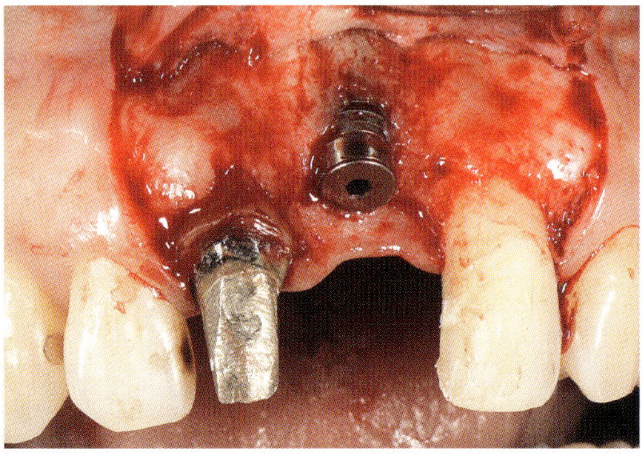

Fig 25f : Buccal bone loss and buccally placed implant are appreciated.

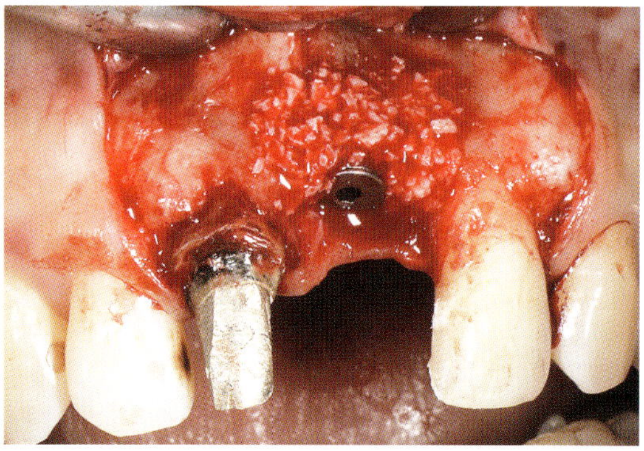

Fig 25g : Bio-Oss is placed in the peri-implant area.

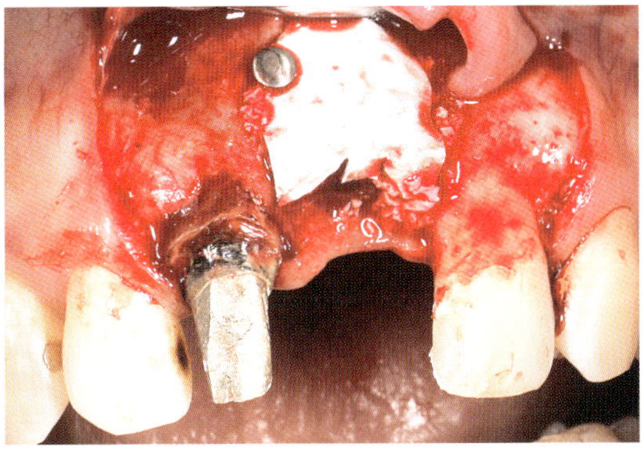

Fig 25h : Bio-Oss is covered with non resorbable membrane.

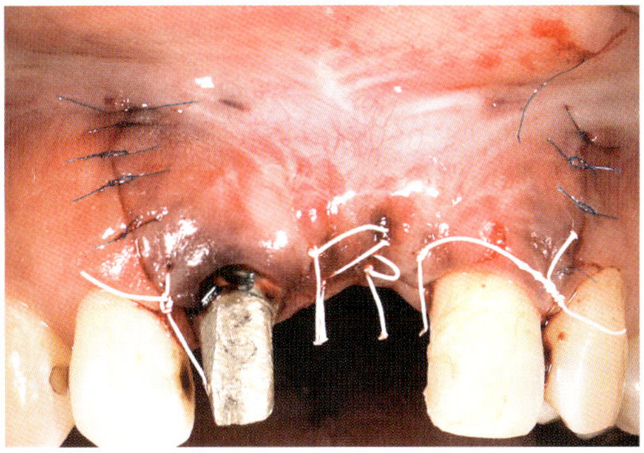

Fig 25i : Post-suturing view. Flap needs to be completely closed. Suture is 8.0, gore-tex suture is 6.0.

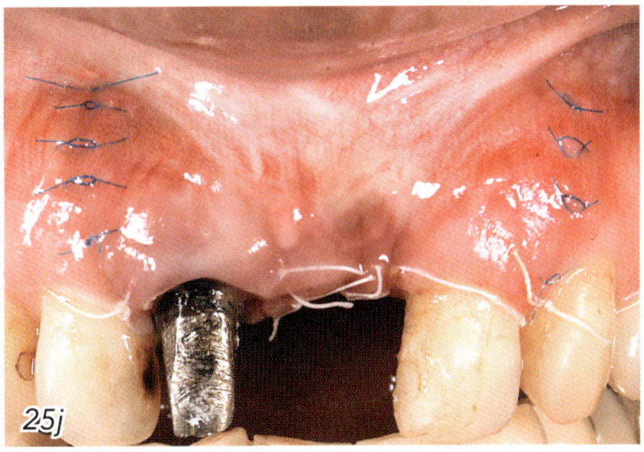

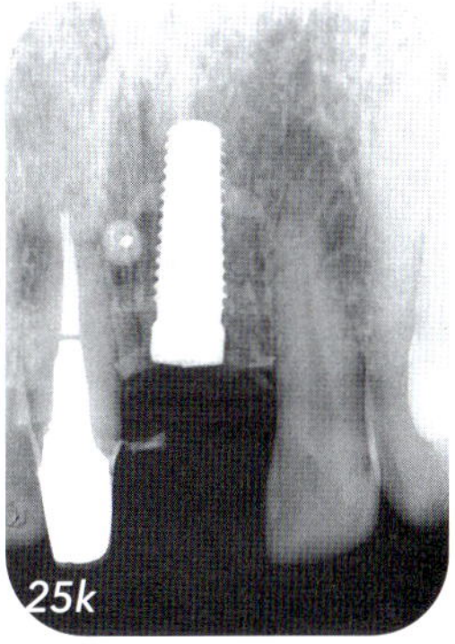

Fig 25j, k : One week after suturing, right before suture removal view. Healing process appears to be in the excellent condition.

Surgery : Connective tissue graft (4/15/2009)

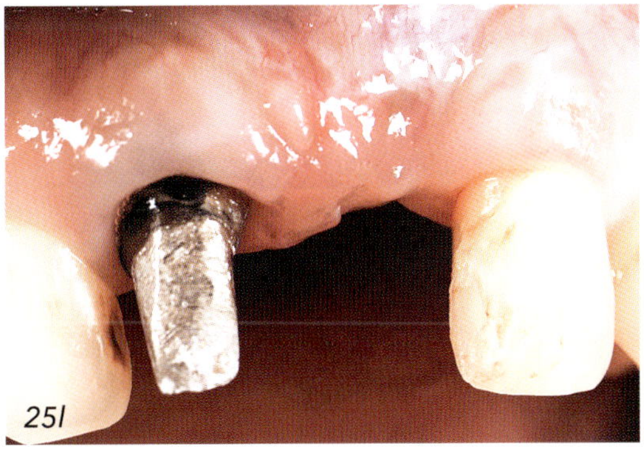

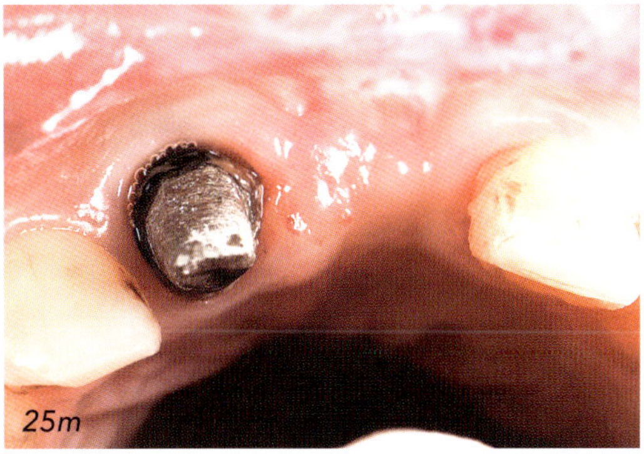

Fig 25l, m : View of 4 months after GBR surgery. Vertical gingival level hasn't been changed, but horizontal gingival level has been improved.

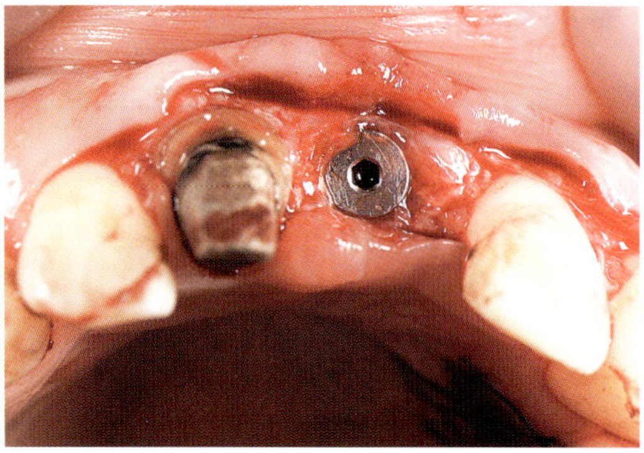

Fig 25n : View of right after membrane removal. Newly developed tissue can be appreciated on the implant buccal area.

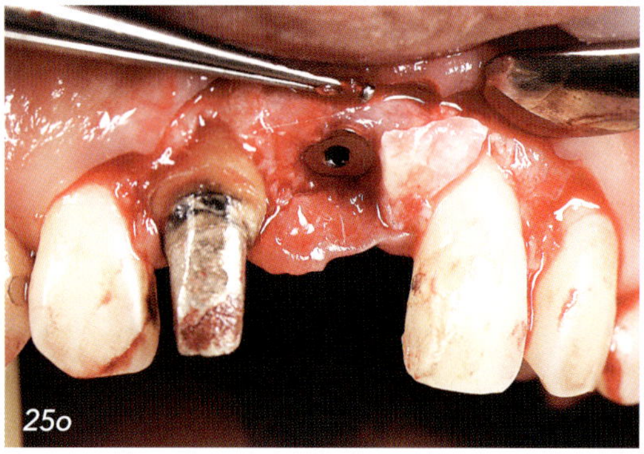

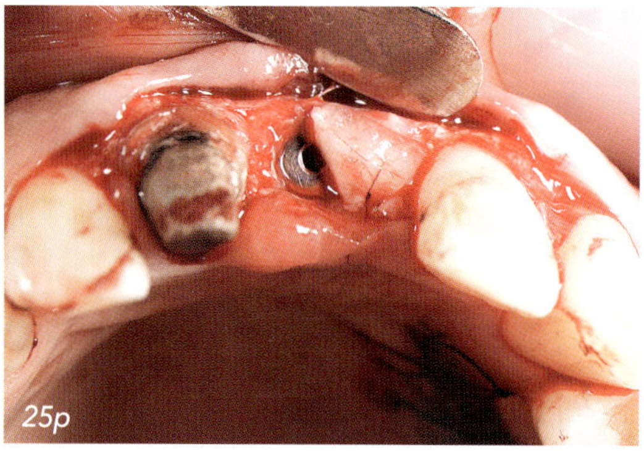

Fig 25o, p : Connective tissue graft is performed after membrane removal. Harvested connected tissue is sutured under #9,10 papilla.

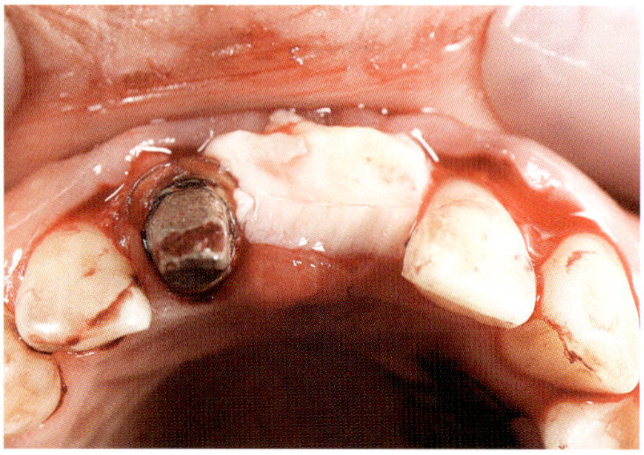

Fig 25q : Second connective tissue piece is sutured by covering alveolar ridge from the buccal aspect.

‖ Point ‖

The technique applied on this case was the connective tissue onlay graft. The important points for this procedure is to secure the harvested connective tissue with suture and during flap suturing, the flap should have releasing incision so the suture wouldn't rip the flap.

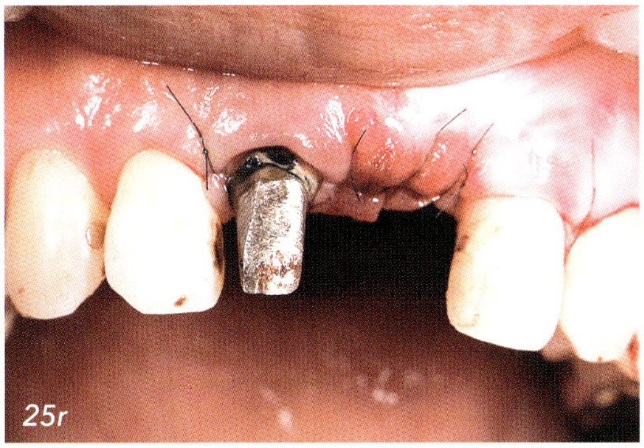

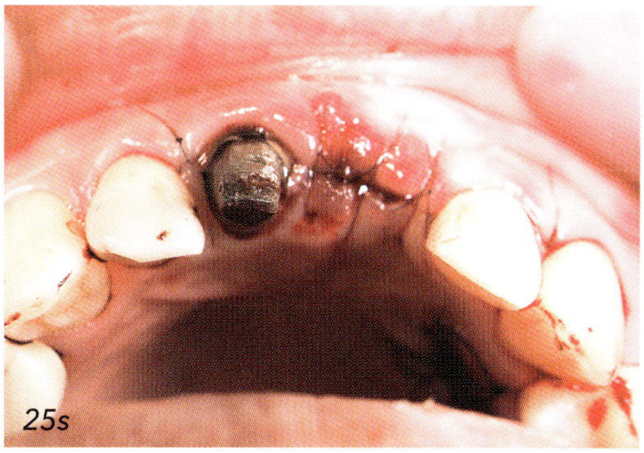

Fig 25r, s : The releasing incision is applied on the flap and suture those flaps tightly. (suture 7.0 is used.)

‖ Point ‖

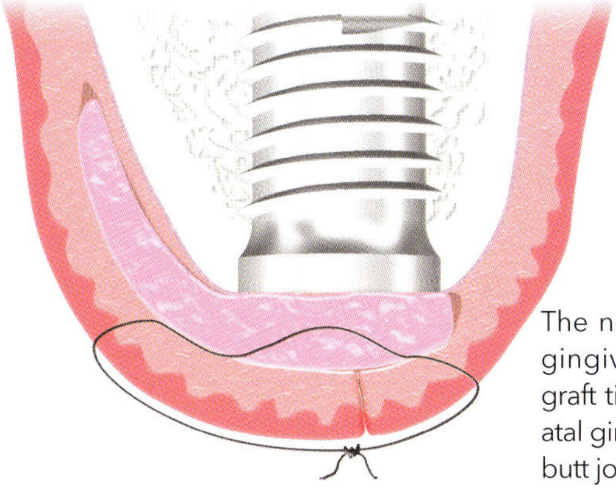

The needle goes through the buccal gingival flap and picked up second graft tissue, then goes through the palatal gingival flap to suture two flaps with butt joint. It is important to apply releasing incision to the flaps not to create too much tension.

Surgery : Papilla reconstruction surgery (7/8/2009)

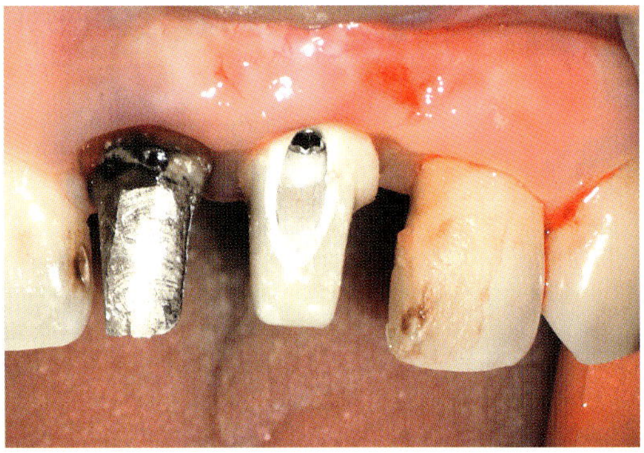

Fig 25t : Pre-ope intra oral photo. The provisional abutment has been already inserted. However, the papilla hight between #9 and 10 wasn't sufficient, so papilla reconstruction surgery is required.

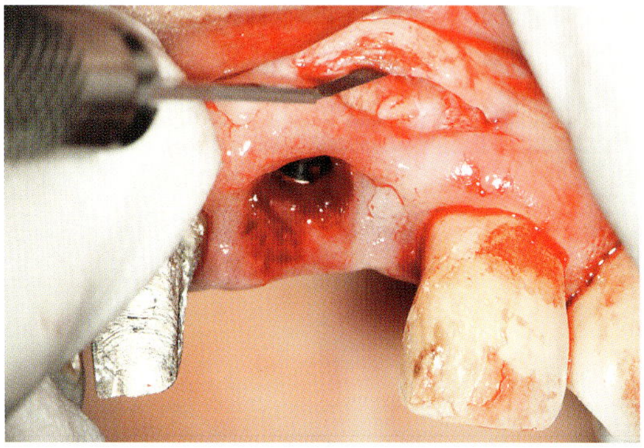

Fig 25u : Incision : Horizontal incision is placed to #9 and 10 inter proximal apical area. Incision is placed from disto-buccal line angle area and palatally, mesio-buccal line angle to disco-buccal line angle with 2mm depth from the free gingival tip. This technique has a purpose to create an envelop flap that enable papilla to be mobile.

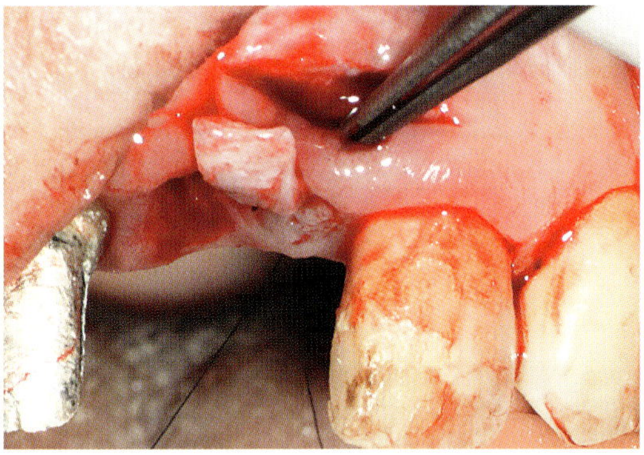

Fig 25v : Suturing the connective tissue graft. 2 pieces of connective tissue grafts were used. The first piece is sutured after being placed under the papilla.

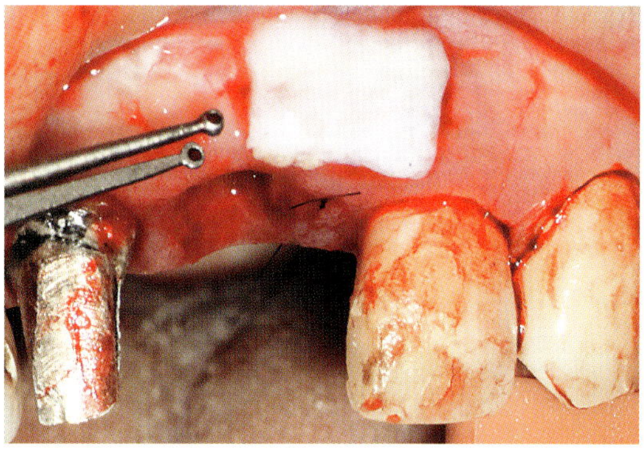

Fig 25w : The second piece is sutured around the buccal papilla area.

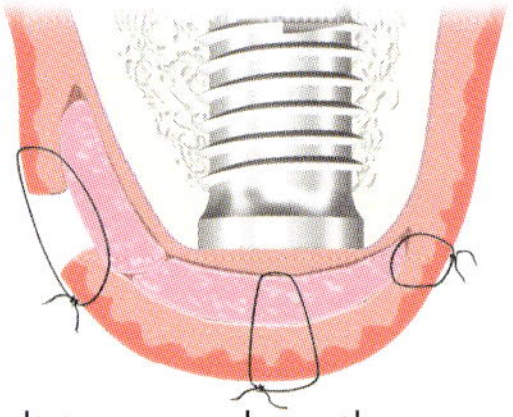

Since It is difficult to reproduce the appropriate gingival morphology with one piece graft tissue, 2 pieces of graft tissue are used for this procedure. The point of this procedure is the technique to create an apical flap after placing horizontal incision. This flap should be created with not too deep incision in order to have the exact fit for the buccal graft piece under the flap. This technique allows the graft tissue piece to be stable and pushed coronally.

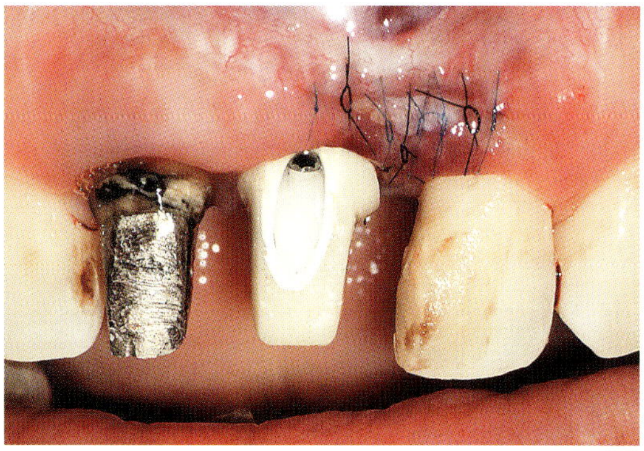

Fig 25x : The view of right after suturing. Papilla is coronally repositioned.

Post-ope/ Insertion of the provisional restoration

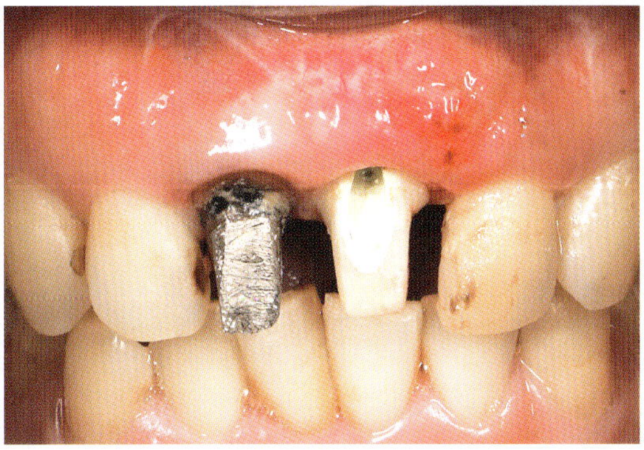

Fig 25y : At the time of the suture removal.

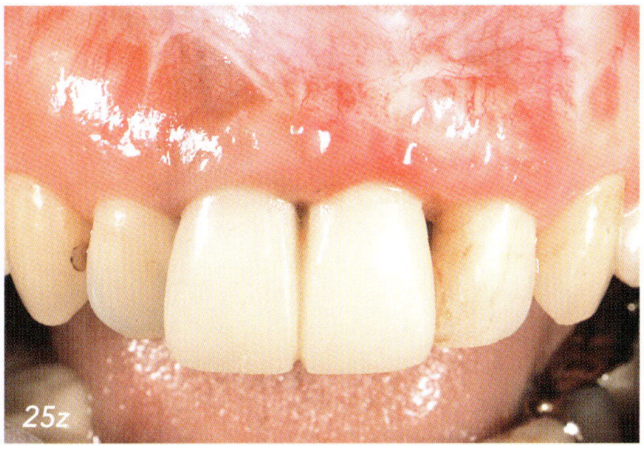

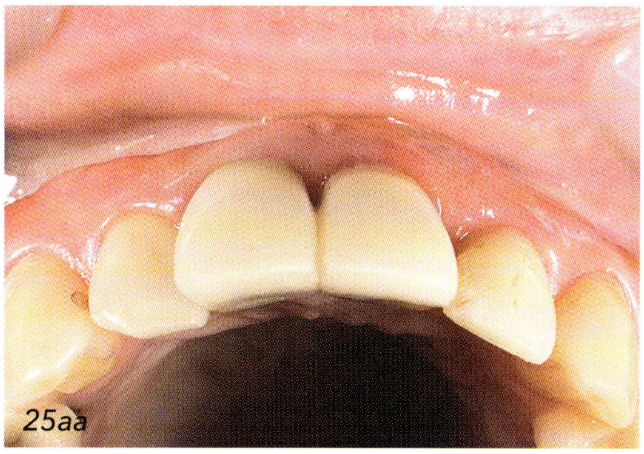

Fig 25z, aa : At the time of the provisional restoration insertion. Provisional restoration morphology changes have been applied several times in order to harmonize with the periimplant soft tissue.

Insertion of the final restoration

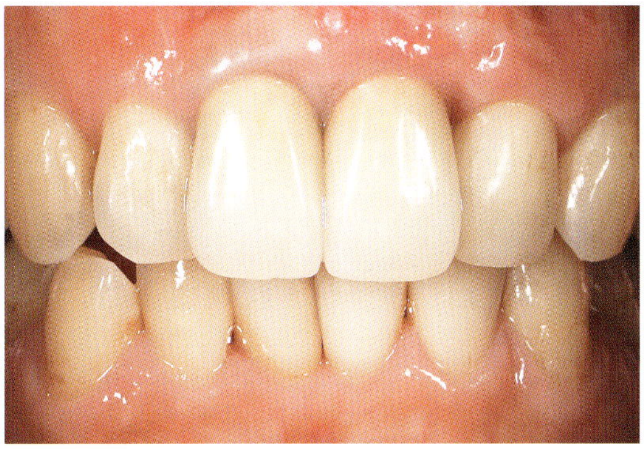

Fig 25bb : At the time of the final restoration insertion. Average gingival level has been acquired.

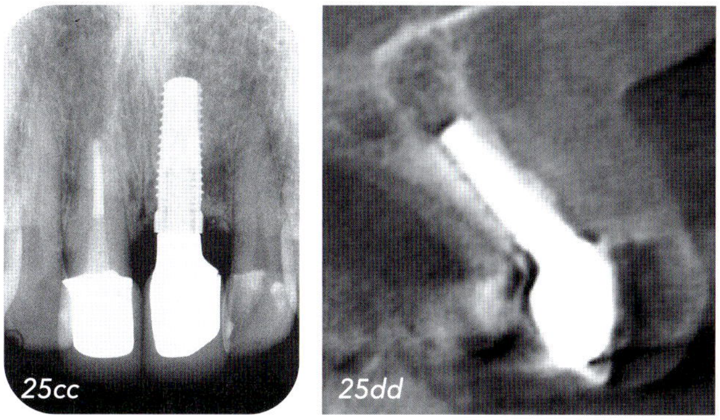

Fig 25cc, dd : Peri-implant hard tissue appears to be in the excellent condition.

12 years post-ope

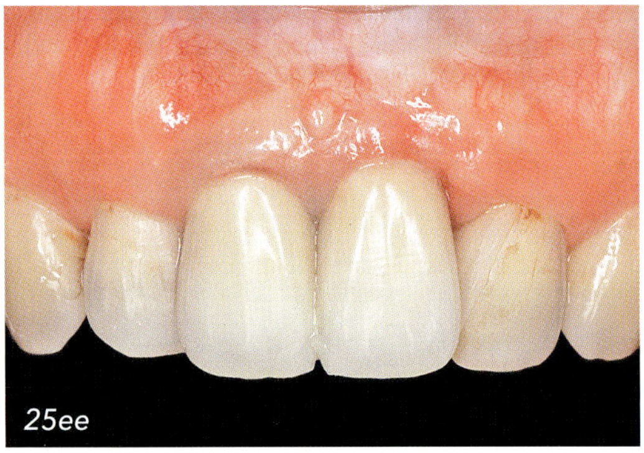

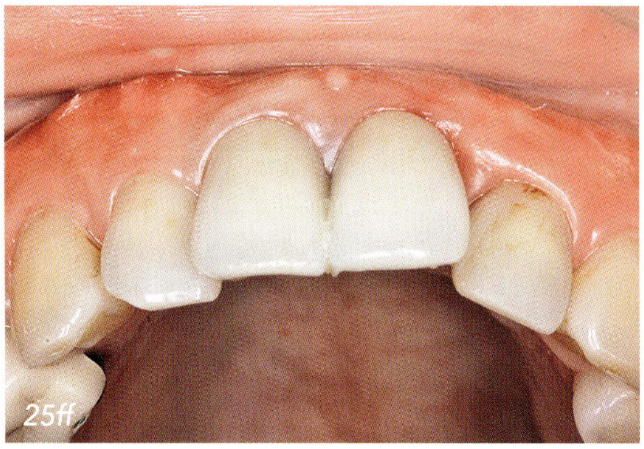

Fig 25ee,ff : 12 years post-ope facial and occlusal view.

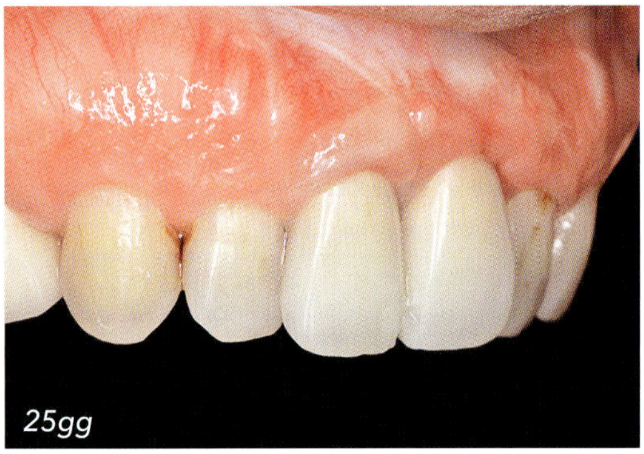

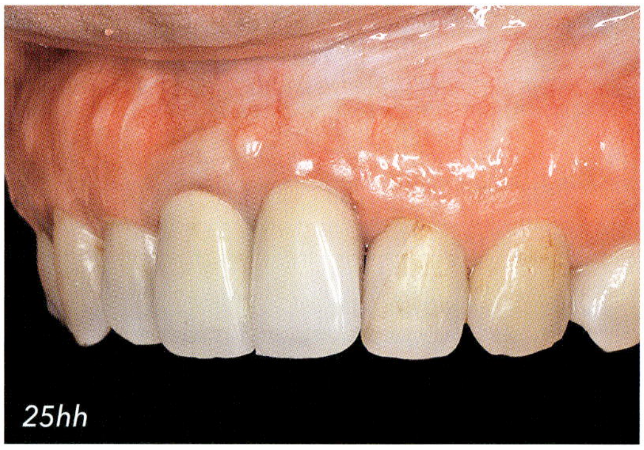

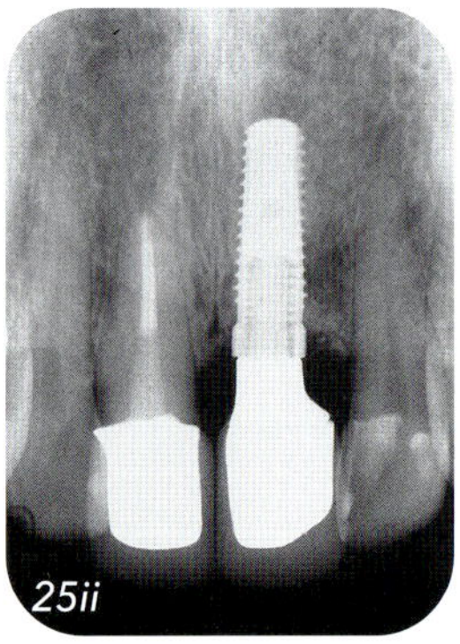

Fig 25gg～ii : 12 years post-ope right and left view.

Evaluation

The patient visited to our office during the implant treatment at the other dental office. This has been a quite challenging case. The soft tissue was very thin and swollen so the soft tissue augmentation was very difficult and challenging. This disadvantageous condition has been well considered pre-operatively, so GBR technique has been selected as a procedure.

This type of thin and swollen type of soft tissue's post-surgical outcome is quite unpredictable, therefore, the hard tissue augmentation should be strongly considered as a treatment choice.

The management of implant problem 3

Pre-ope

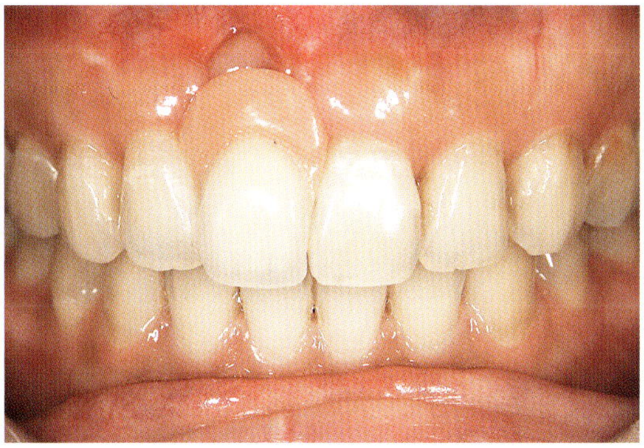

Fig 26a : The patient chief complain is the restoration with pink porcelain

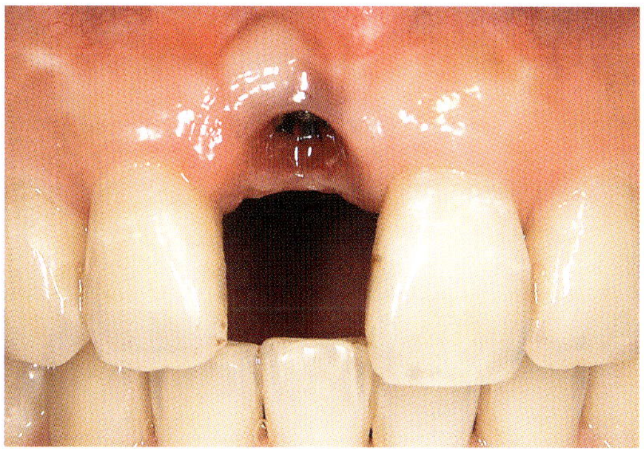

Fig 26b: Intra oral view after removing the restoration. Significant tissue loss can be appreciated.

Vertical gingival line	#6	#7	#8	#9	#10	#11
Balance with adjacent teeth			X			
Balance with contra-lateral teeth			X			
Horizontal gingival line	**#6**	**#7**	**#8**	**#9**	**#10**	**#11**
Balance with adjacent teeth			X			
Balance with contra-lateral teeth			X			

X is the problematic area

Class I b

Point of this case

Problem

- Peri-implant tissue on #8 has vertical and horizontal tissue loss.
- Distal and messiah papilla have been apically migrated.

Purpose and technique of surgery

1. Vertical and horizontal tissue level on #8 will be augmented with the connective tissue to even out with #9 tissue level.
2. Surgery will be performed twice. At the first surgery, tissue thickness is augmented by placing the connective tissue buccally. At the second surgery, this augmented tissue will be moved coronally.

At the time of provisional restoration insertion

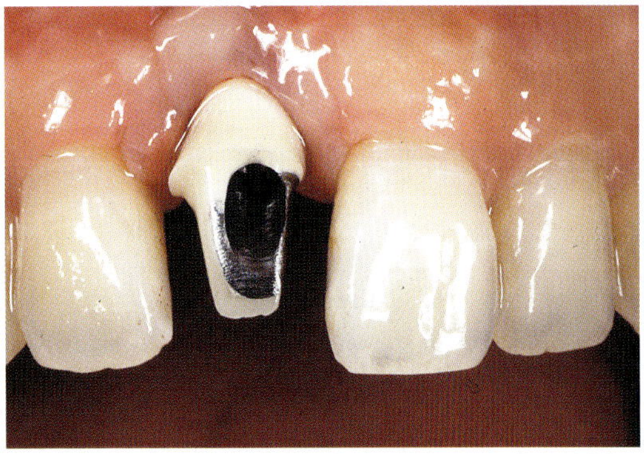

Fig 26c : The abutment finishing line should be placed 1mm coronally compared to #9 vertical gingival level.

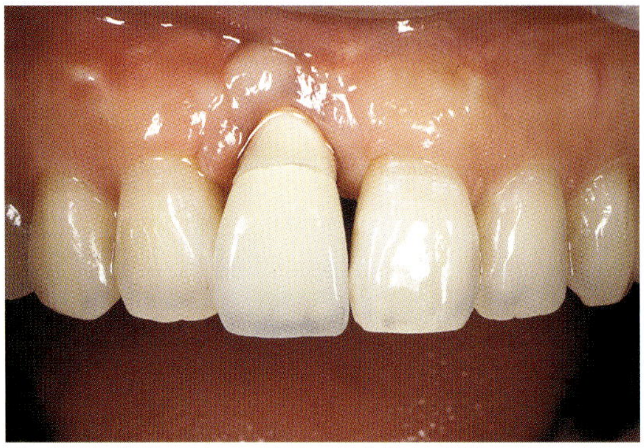

Fig 26d : Inserted provisional abutment and crown. The provisional abutment is made of heatcure resin.

First surgery (7/29/2004)

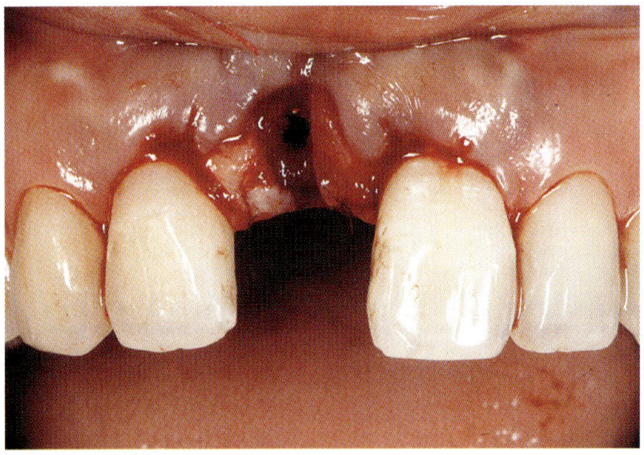

Fig 26e : Partial thickness flap is created from mesial of #6 to distal of #7.

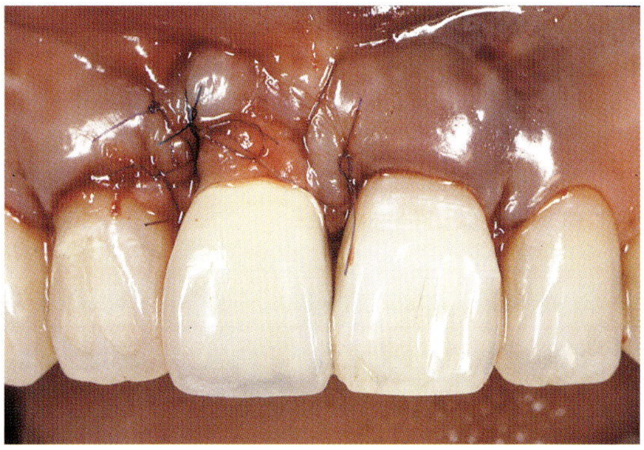

Fig 26f : This connective tissue is augmented buccally and sutured. Simple suturing technique is used through papilla.

Point

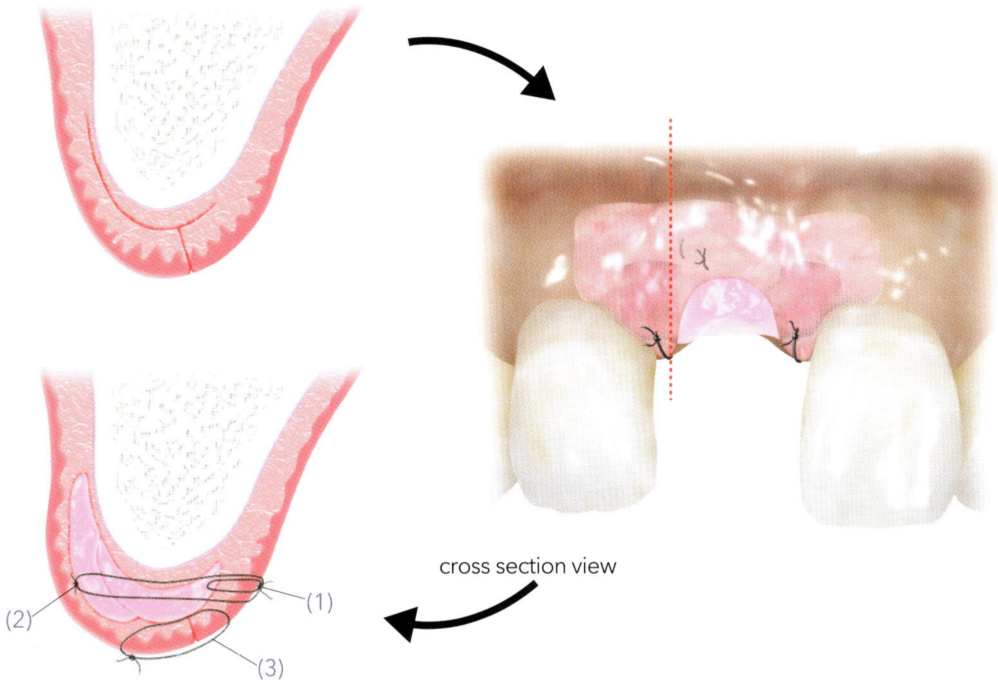

The incision around the papilla should be thin and shallow and then the partial thickness flap is created. The soft tissue on the papilla should be kept thick and connective tissue should be sutured on this area. (1) Then larger connective tissue piece (the width that can cover from #7 mesial to #9 distal) should be placed on the edge of the abutment finishing line buccally and sutured. (2) The suture should be resorbable suture unitl this procedure. The connective tissue should be sandwiched under the flaps and sutured. (3)

One month after the first surgery.

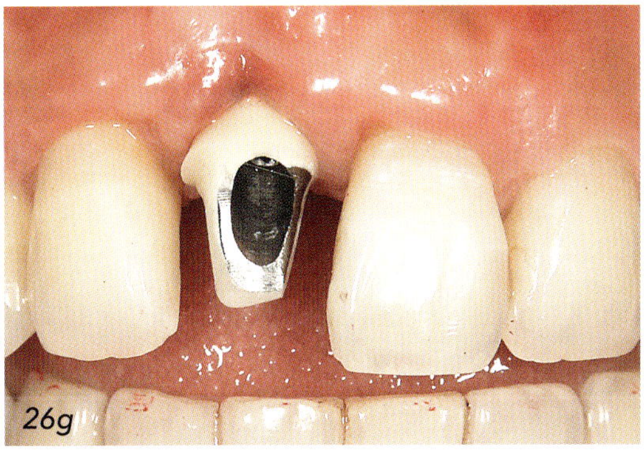

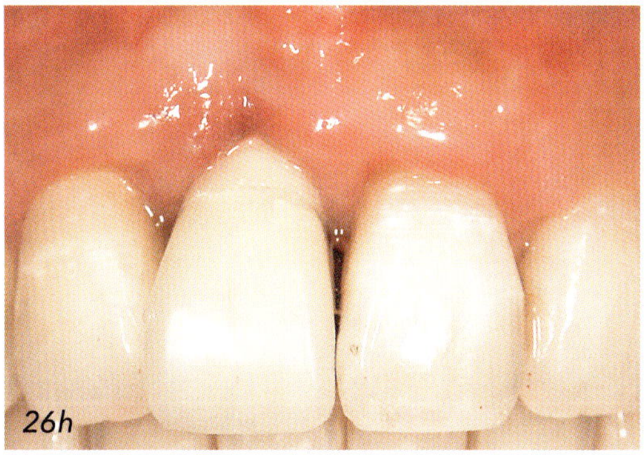

Fig 26g, h : Vertical gingival hight is not insufficient, but horizontal gingival volume is able to be acquired sufficiently. The goal of the first surgery has been achieved.

Second surgery (12/2/2004)

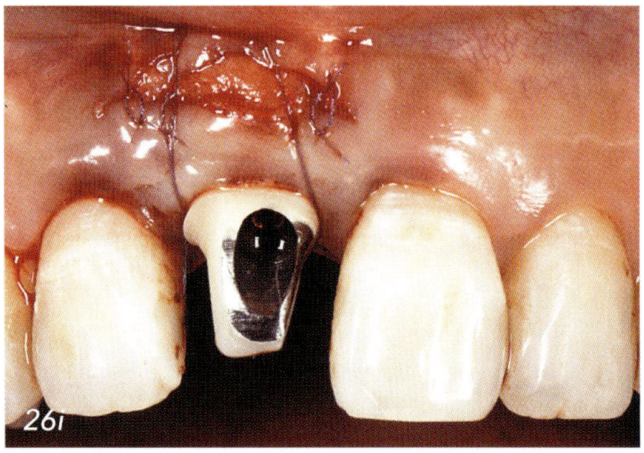

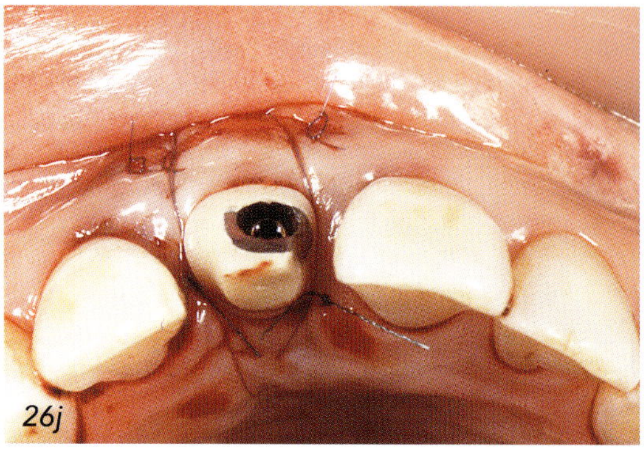

Fig 26i, j : Since horizontal gingival tissue volume is sufficient, coronal advancement procedure of this tissue should be performed. Flap design should be the circular incision from #7 distal angle to #9 mesial angle. #8 implant abutment is removed and circular incision from mesial palatal to disto-palatal is applied. Also horizontal incision is added buccally in order for the flap to move smoothly.

Point

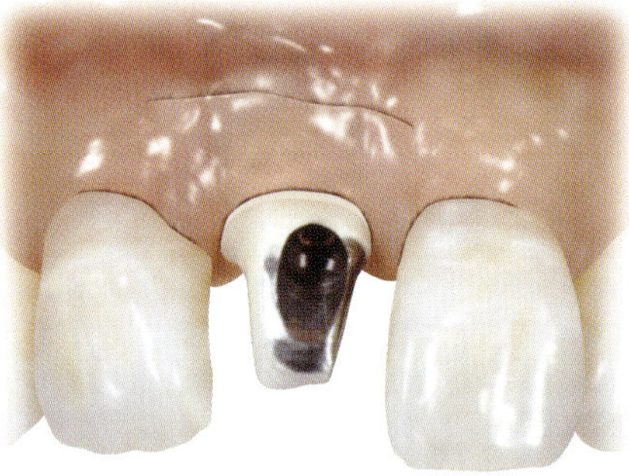

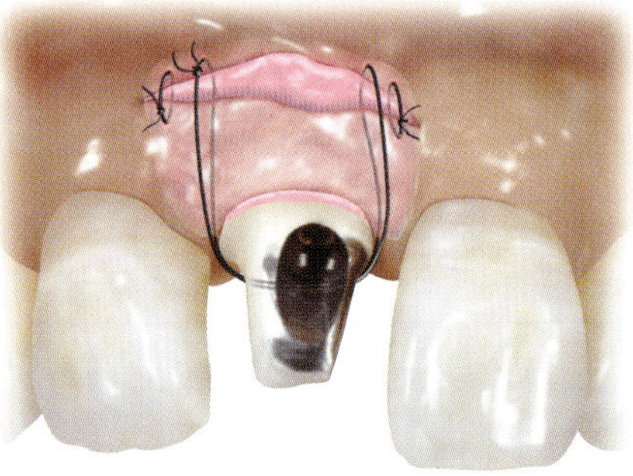

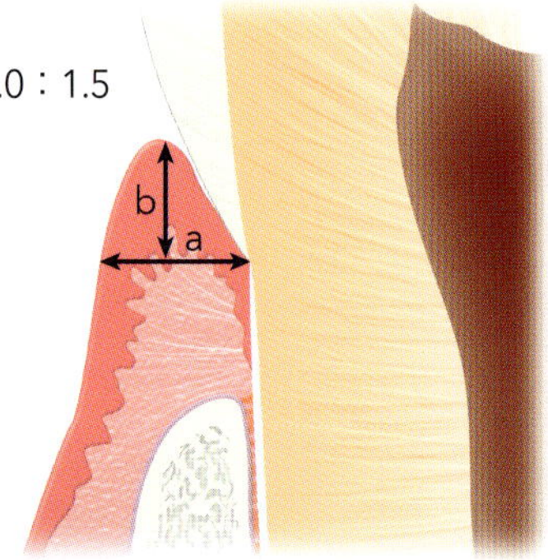

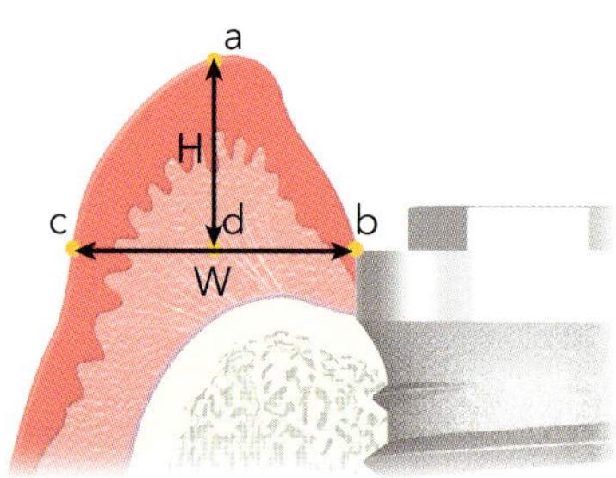

Wennstrom investigated relationships of peri-implant tissues width and hight. Also Nozawa did a similar investigation. As a result, the ratio between peri-implant buccal tissue width and hight is 1.5 : 1.0. However this ratio has the individual variables. The important point of this ratio is that if tissue hight needs to be increased, tissue width needs to be increased together. Therefore, as this case goes, if tissue vertical hight needs to be increased, it is important to consider that tissue width needs to be substantially increased.

3 months after second surgery

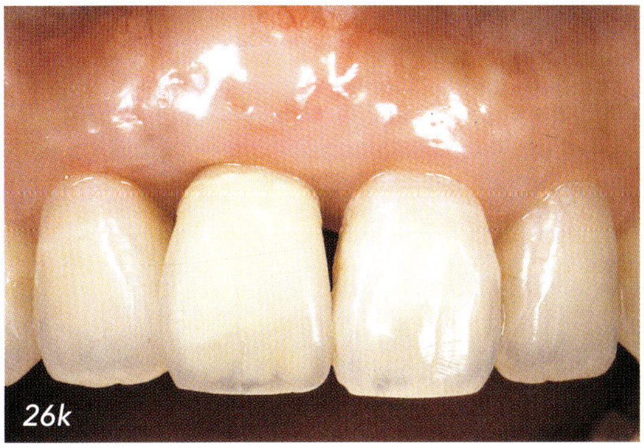

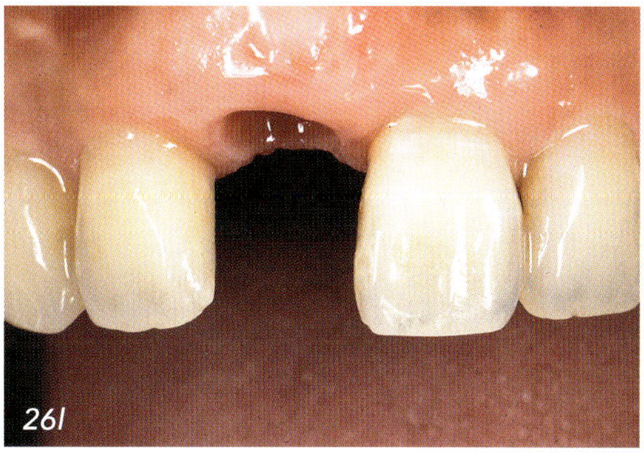

Fig 26k, l : Horizontal and vertical tissue reconstruction has been achieved. However, there is a black triangle between #8 and 9, this needs to be corrected prosthetically.

At the time of the insertion of the final restoration / 10 years after the final insertion

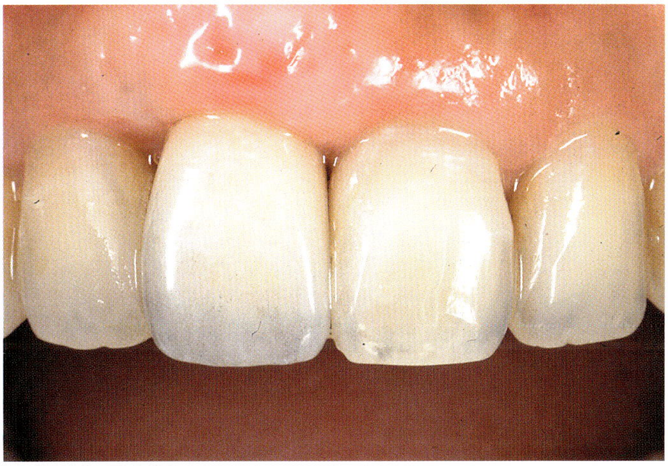

Fig 26m : At the time of the insertion of the final restoration. (Prosthesis's inserted by Dr. Masao Yamazaki.)

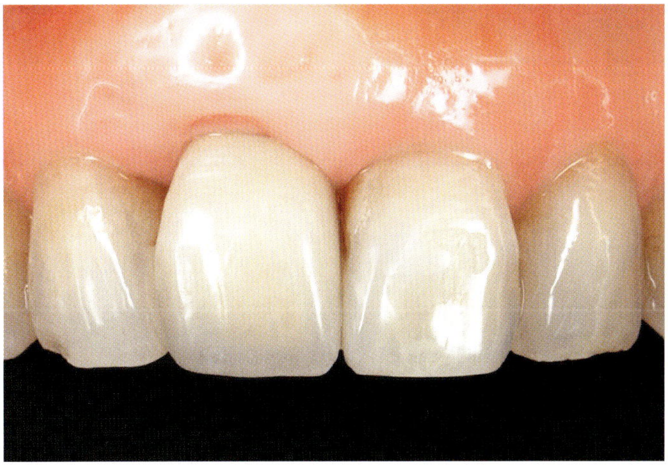

Fig 26n : 10 years after the final insertion.

Evaluation

Once peri-implant soft tissue has recession, the tissue augmentation should be done around the implant abutment. The connective tissue augmentation around the implant abutment can be quite challenging since tissue blood supply has been limited. Therefore planning 2 stage surgery is the right decision and thick tissue coronal advancement is also quite theoretical. The author think that this is the great clinical evidence that the thick keratinized tissue has a high resistance so this allows better outcome on the peri-implant augmentation.

Philosophy of soft tissue augmentation around implant

Regarding to plastic surgery around implant, there are soft tissue procedures and hard tissue procedures. In this book, only soft tissue management will be described. There are several soft tissue management procedures around the implant such as acquiring keratinized tissue, papilla formation, gingival line leveling or esthetic gingival formation along with the prosthesis. This is no difference with natural teeth plastic surgery. Nowadays the patient's esthetic demand to the implant procedures are becoming high. Therefore, the fundamental procedures of periodontal microsurgery can be applied to the implant surrounding tissue and it will be quite beneficial to the patient.

Soft tissue augmentation around implant

Pre-ope

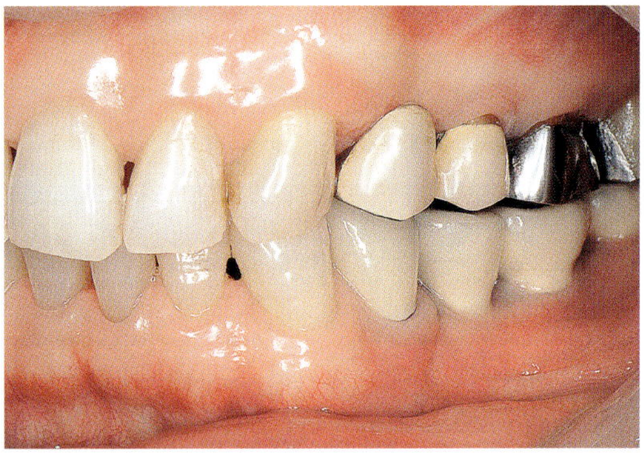

Fig 27a : Left buccal pre-ope view. Uneven occlusal plane on the molar region with unstable occlusion.

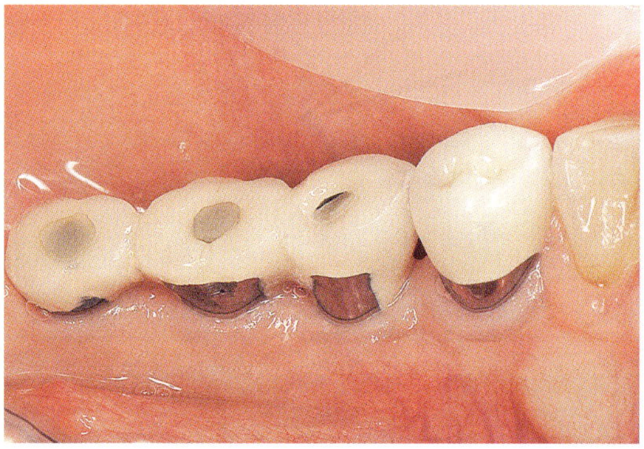

Fig 27b : Mandibular left posterior lingual pre-ope view. #18-19-20 have screw retained implant supported fixed partial denture.

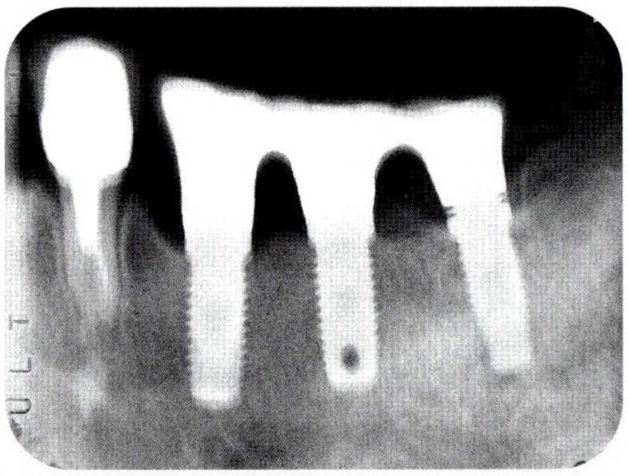

Fig 27c : Mandibular left posterior pre-ope x-ray. #18 unfitted prosthesis is appreciated.

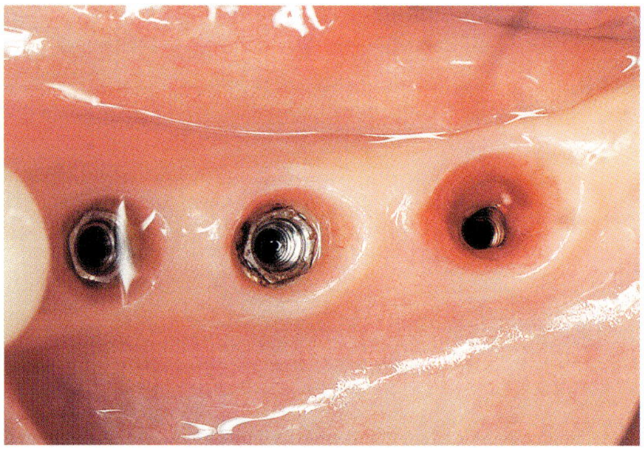

Fig 27d : Pre-ope view after removing abutments. #18 marginal gingival inflammation is appreciated.

Vertical gingival line	#22	#21	#20	#19	#18
Balance with adjacent teeth			X		
Balance with contra-lateral teeth			X	X	X
Horizontal gingival line	**#22**	**#21**	**#20**	**#19**	**#18**
Balance with adjacent teeth			X		
Balance with contra-lateral teeth			X	X	X

x is the problematic area

The important point of this case

Problem

- Horizontal gingival tissue thickness reduction and keratinized tissue reduction compared with contra lateral teeth have been appreciated.
- The fit of the prosthesis including abutments is poor and functionally unstable.

Purpose and technique of surgery

1. Posterior area doesn't have high esthetic demand but soft tissue reconstruction is required for functional reason. Free soft tissue graft is performed for gaining peri-implant keratinized tissue width and hight .

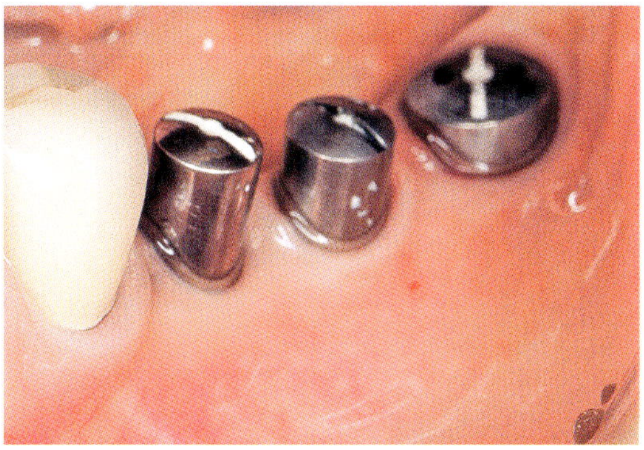

Fig 27e : Place healing abutments and wait for tissue healing.

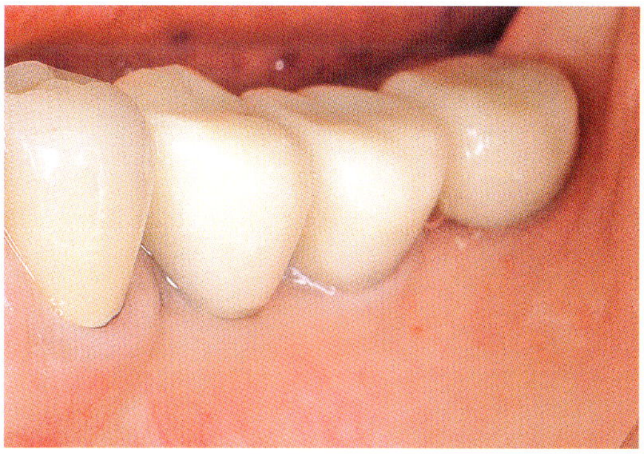

Fig 27f : First, the initial provisional restoration fitted to maxillary existing prosthesis is inserted. Then new maxillary and mandibular prosthesis will be inserted together.

Surgery (11/7/2000)

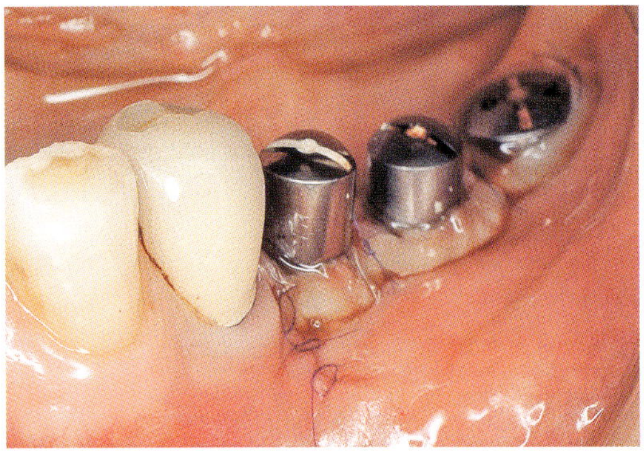

Fig 27g : Volume of the connective tissue harvested from the palate should be 30% more than the measurement in order to wrap around the implant.

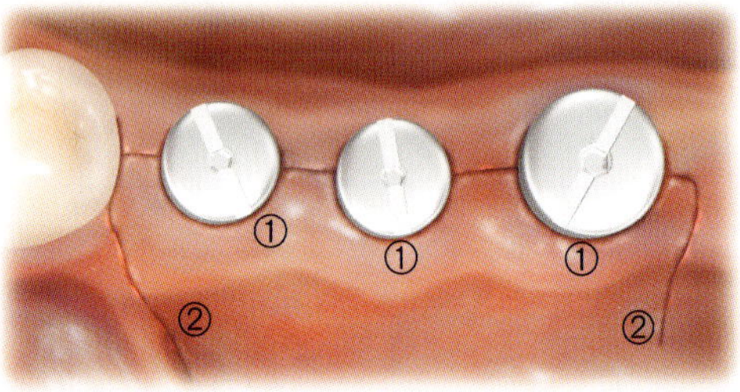

Incision : ① Crestal incision between implants is placed ② Then vertical incisions are placed on the distal of #21 and #18

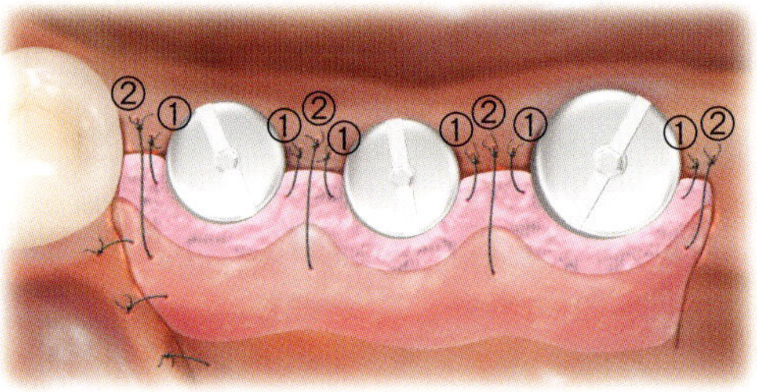

Suturing : ① Firstly, the connective tissue is sutured with lingual tissue ② Secondly, buccal tissue flap is sutured as if it covers up the connective tissue. If there is the area that should become keratinized tissue, this area should be exposed.

Point

Harvested connective tissue should be sutured to the lingual flap as if it enfolds around the implant. At that time, lingual flap is slightly lifted to construct papilla.

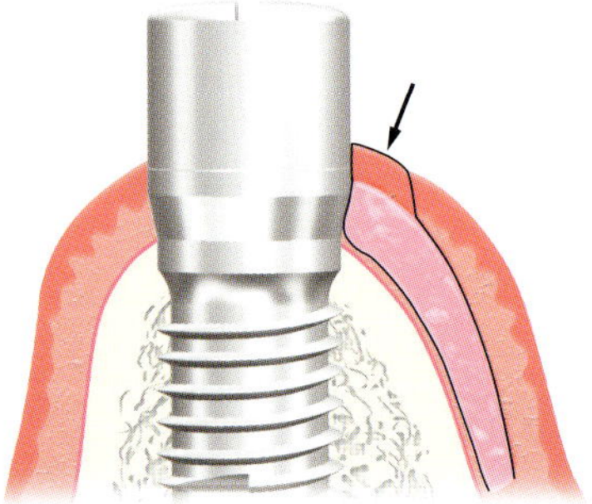

Sectional view at the time of the connective tissue graft. Thick connective tissue should be inserted and the area that needs to become keratinized tissue (indicated with an arrow) should be exposed. Flap should be moved apically and sutured to join this area.

2 months post-surgery

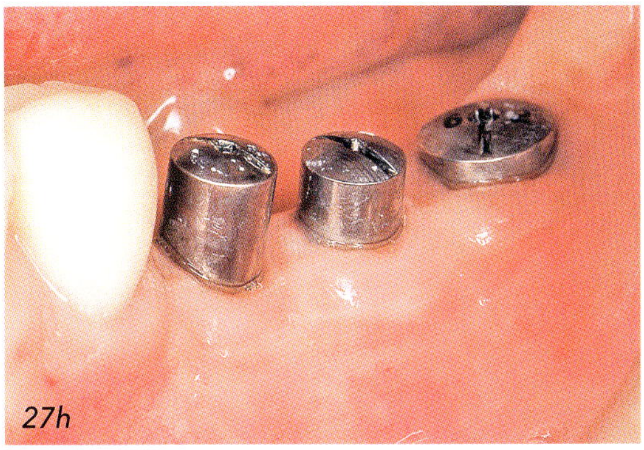

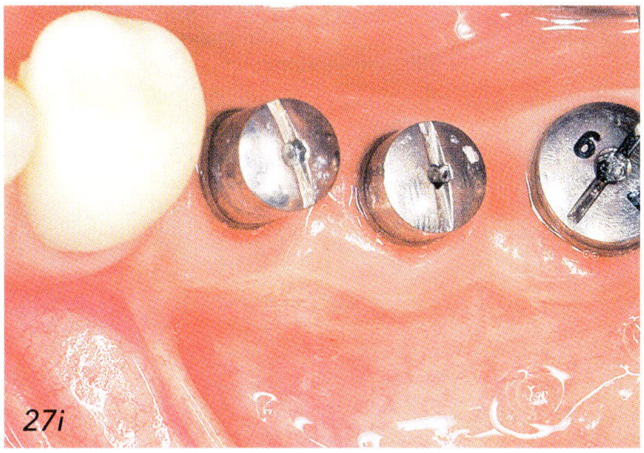

Fig 27h, i : Lower left buccal and occlusal views 2 months post-surgery. Peri-implant tissue looks beautiful and stable.

At the time of final restoration insertion / 15 years post-surgery

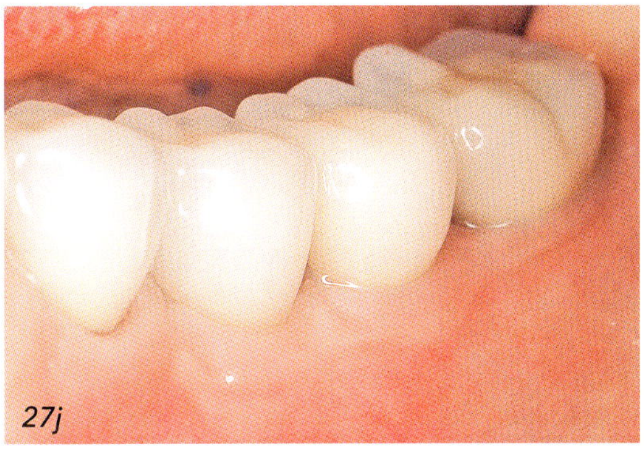

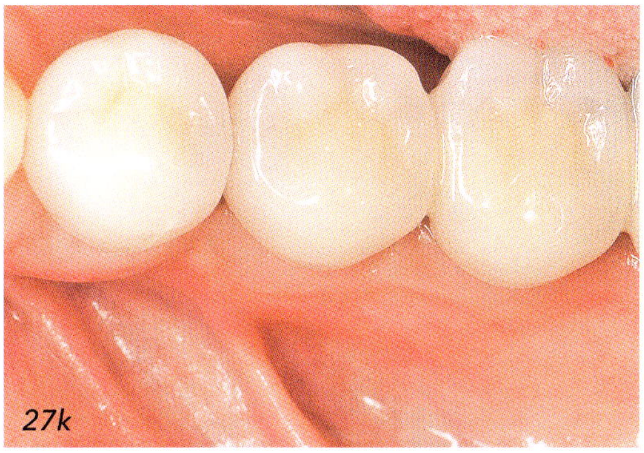

Fig 27j, k : 4 months post-surgery. Lower left buccal and occlusal views at the time of final restoration insertion.

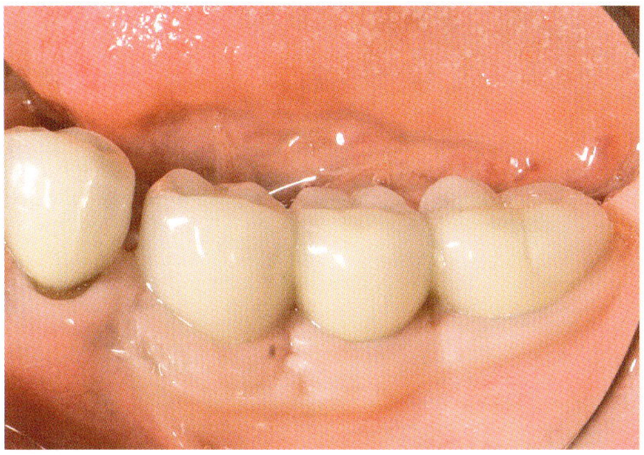

Fig 27l : 15 years post-surgery. The width of the keratinized gingiva is maintained, but the color tone is closer to the color tone of the palate side than before.

Evaluation

The fact that the connective tissue graft around the implant remains clinically stable after 10 years postsurgery encourages clinicians who perform implant procedures. However, this ongoing tissue color change should be taken into consideration.

Preventive connective tissue graft 1

Pre-surgery (12/4/2007)

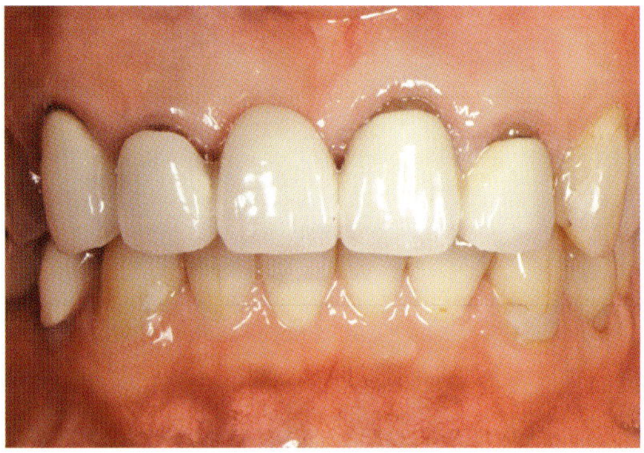

Fig 28a : Pre-operative facial view.

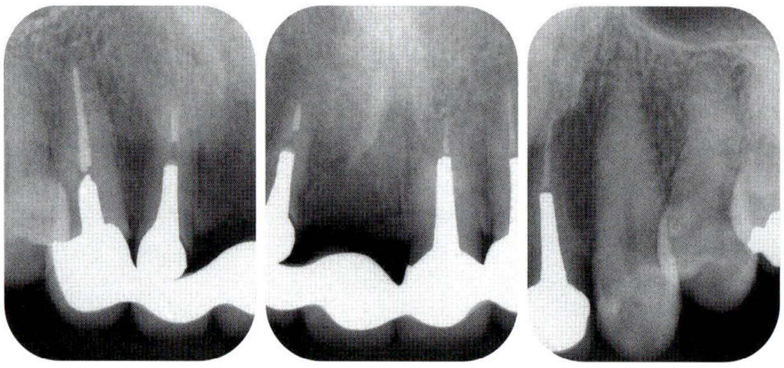

Fig 28b : Pre-operative dental X-rays of maxillary front tooth region.

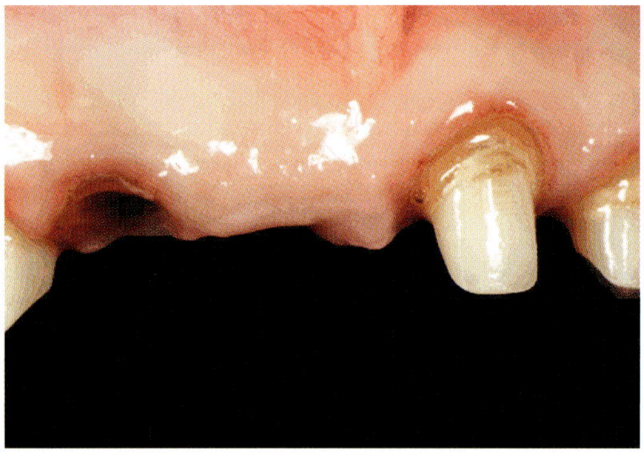

Fig 28c : Frontal view following removal of the prosthesis.

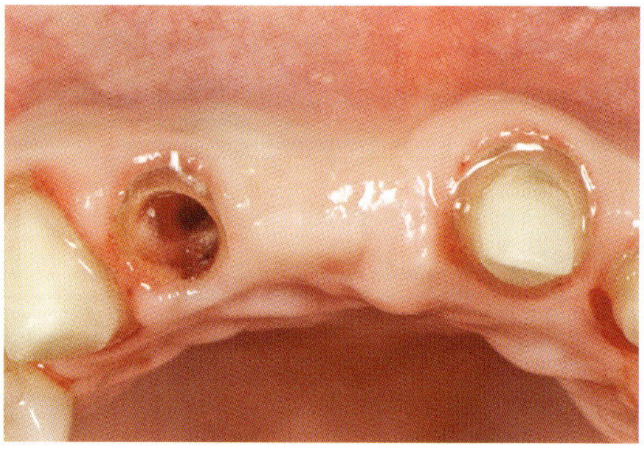

Fig 28d : A horizontal defect may be seen in the upper right alveolar ridge.

Vertical gingival line	#6	#7	#8	#9	#10	#11
Balance with adjacent teeth						
Balance with contra-lateral teeth						
Horizontal gingival line	**#6**	**#7**	**#8**	**#9**	**#10**	**#11**
Balance with adjacent teeth			X			
Balance with contra-lateral teeth			X			

X is the problematic area

Main points of the case

Problem

- Reduction of horizontal gingival level at upper right #1.
- Thin scallop-type gingiva.
- Multiple implant positioning at upper right #2, #1.
- High esthetic requirements of the patient.

Purpose and technique of surgery

The purpose was to perform esthetic implants in the upper right #2, #1 region with conservation of the peri-implant tissues. The implants were placed accurately using digital technology, and a sequential placement technique was used to minimize the reduction in tissue between them. A minor guided bone regeneration (GBR) procedure was used for the first implant placement, and CTG was used for the second implant placement immediately following extraction to maintain the gingival level on the labial side.

Diagnostic wax-up

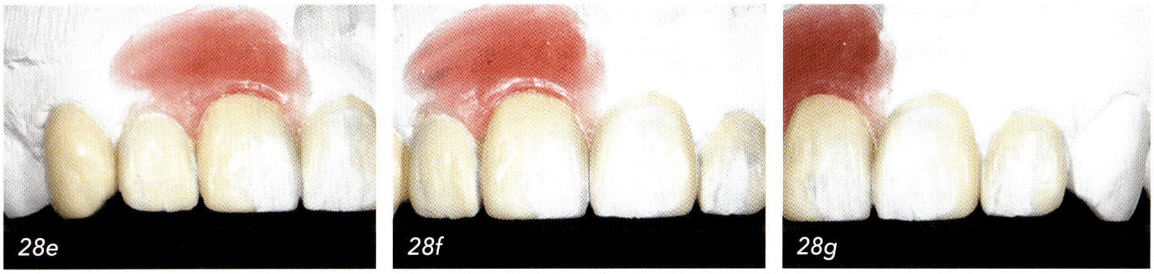

Fig 28e~g : The amount of soft tissue increase needed was checked using a diagnostic wax-up.

Upper right #1 implant placement and GBR (6/3/2008)

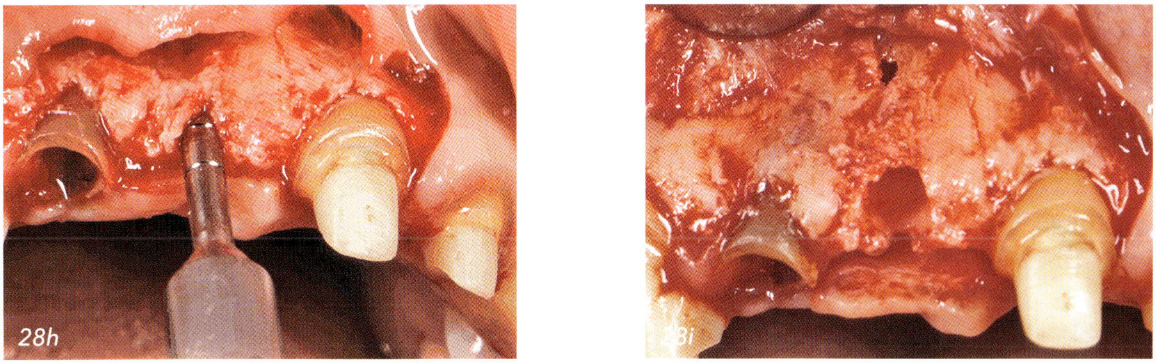

Fig 28h,i : Primary implant procedure. This was carried out using the osteotome technique, with the bone on the labial side maintained.

GBR and sutures

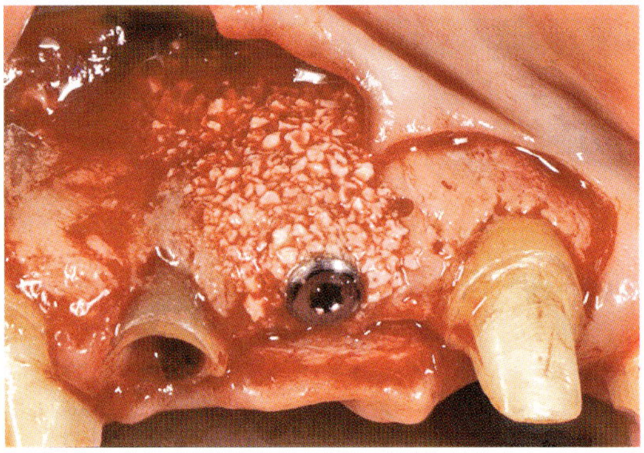

Fig 28j : GBR. The alveolar ridge was increased on the labial side using prosthetic material. A non-resorbable membrane was used.

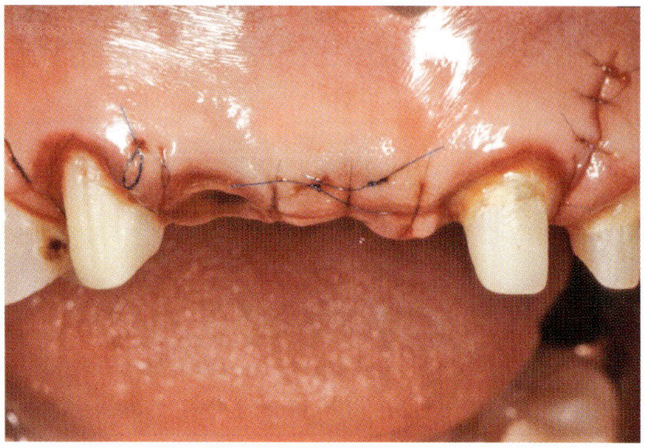

Fig 28k : Sutures.

Impression for the abutment following GBR

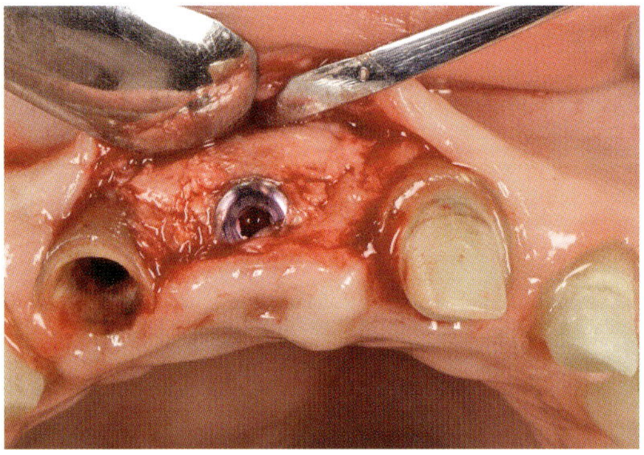

Fig 28l : The alveolar ridge following removal of the membrane. Increase in bone may be seen.

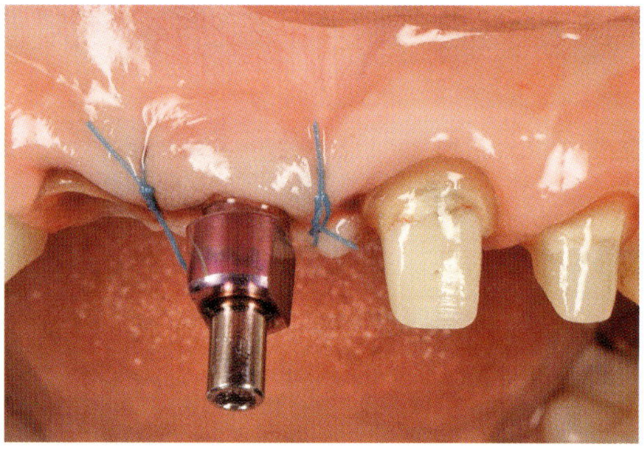

Fig 28m : Taking an impression for fabrication of the abutment.

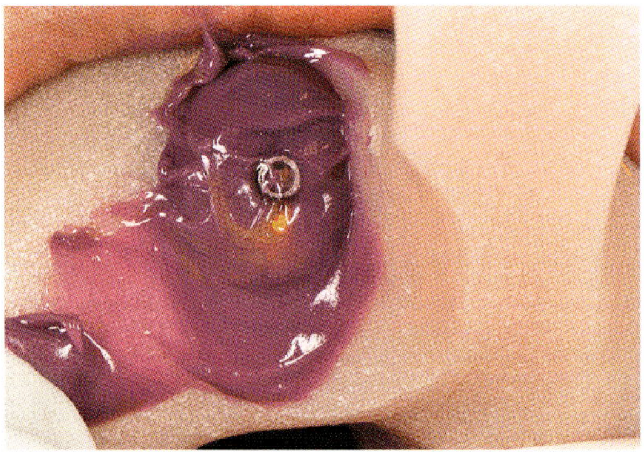

Fig 28n : The impression coping.

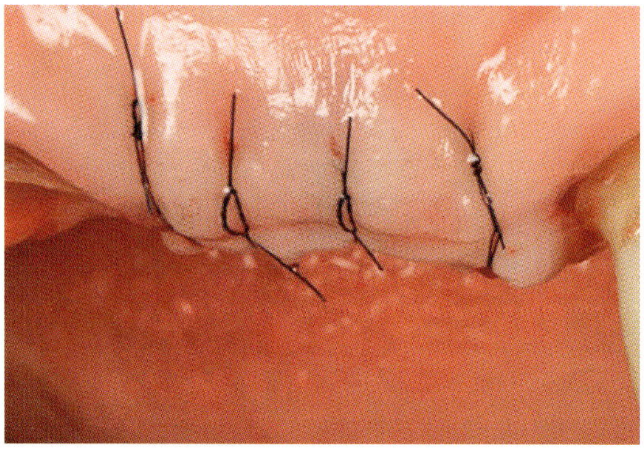

Fig 28o : After the impression was taken, the wound was sutured without using temporary healing abutment.

Abutment placement

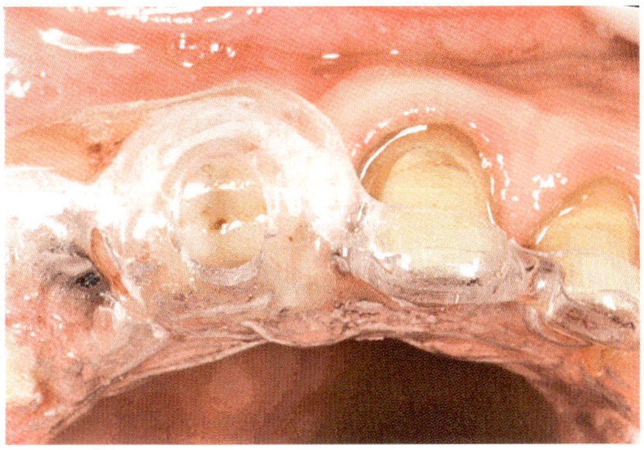

Fig 28p : In the secondary procedure, damage to the tissue between the implants was avoided by use of the punching technique.

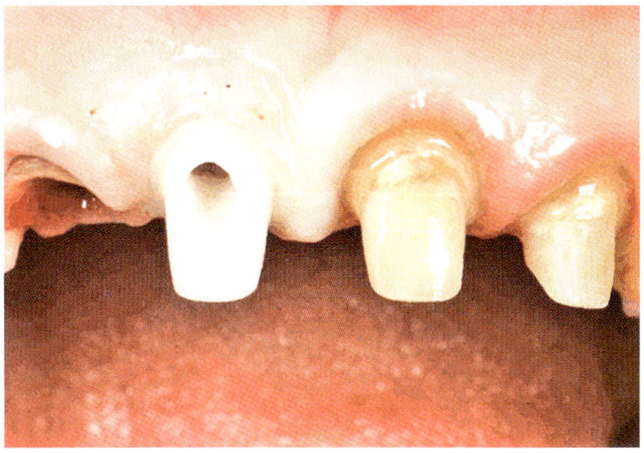

Fig 28q : Placement of a custom temporary abutment.

Upper right #2 implant placemen

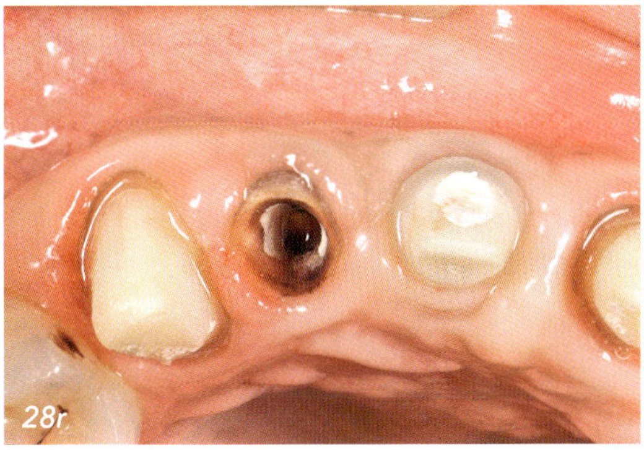

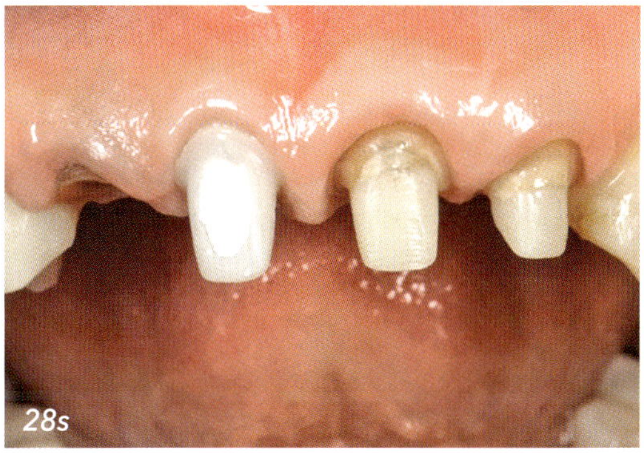

Fig 28r , s : Implant placement immediately following extraction was carried out at upper right #2, which had a poor prognosis. *r* : Occlusal view. *s* : Frontal view.

Provisional abutment fabrication

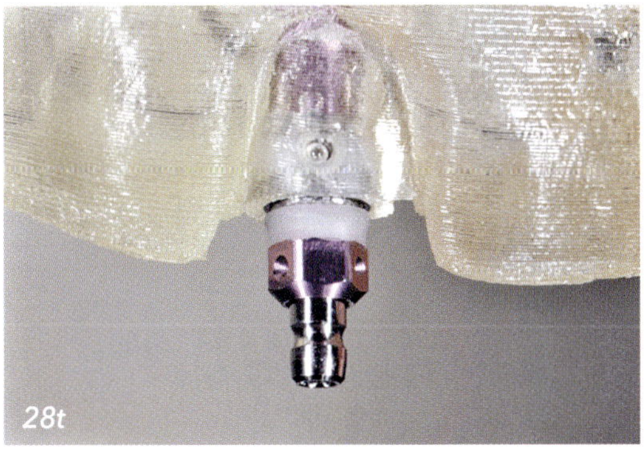

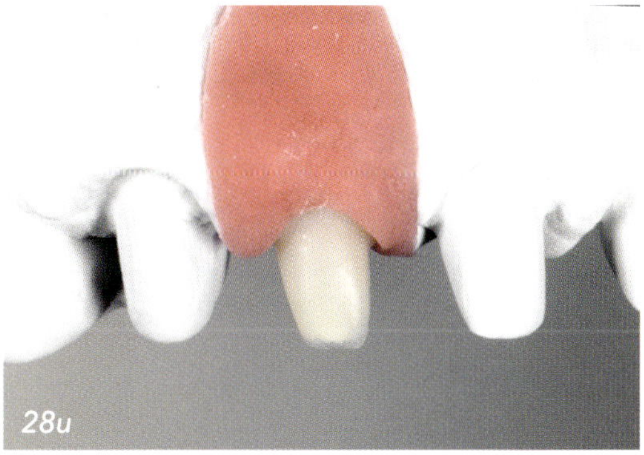

Fig 28t , u : Pre-surgery. A custom provisional abutment was fabricated using a surgical guide. *t* : A working model was fabricated by fitting the surgical guide with an implant adapter and attaching the implant analog. *u* : The custom abutment and provisional crown were fabricated on the working model.

Implant placement using a surgical guide

Fig 28v : Implant placement using a surgical guide system.

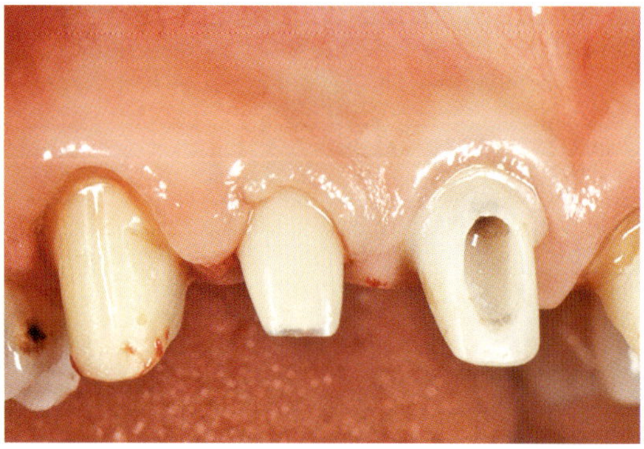

Fig 28w : A trial of the abutment was carried out following upper right #2 implant placement, and CTG was performed the same day.

Connective tissue grafting

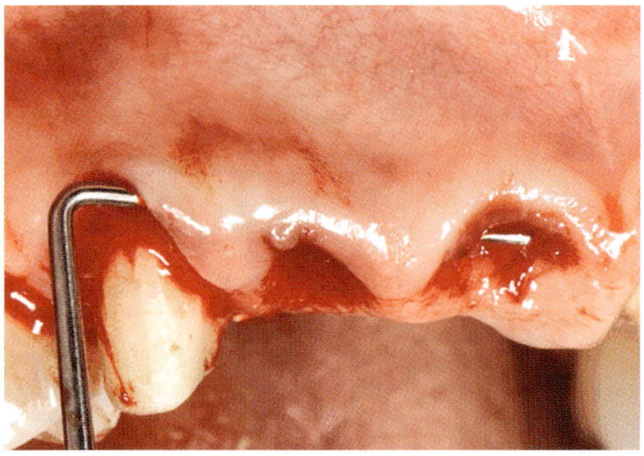

Fig 28x : A partial thickness gingival flap extending beyond the mucogingival junction (MGJ) was formed.

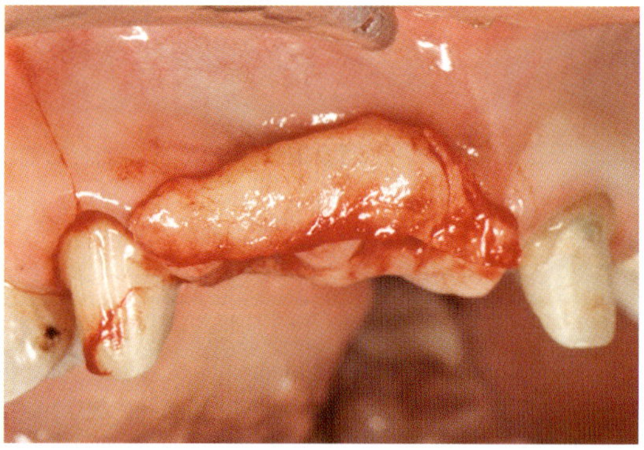

Fig 28y : Checking the size of the CTG taken from the palate. The size and shape of the CTG greatly affect the outcome.

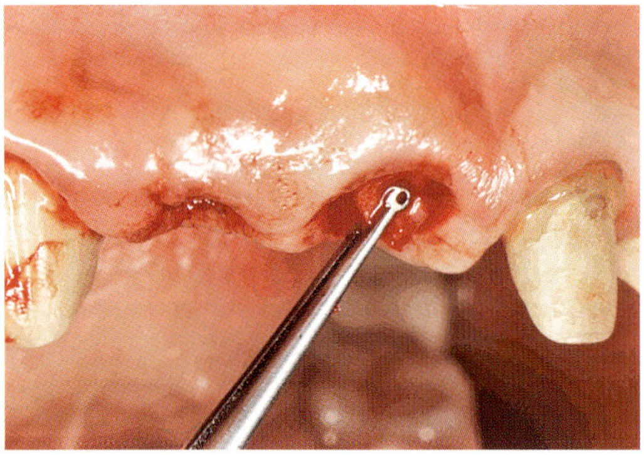

Fig 28z : A trial of the CTG was performed, and the contour on the labial side was checked.

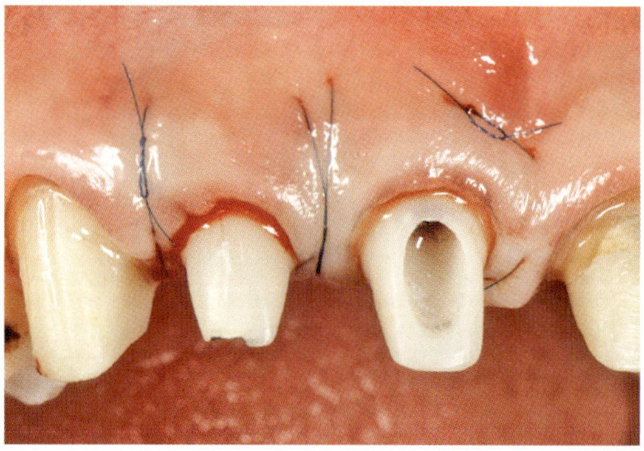

Fig 28aa : The important point is to refit the abutment when the CTG is sutured and secured.

Final abutment placement

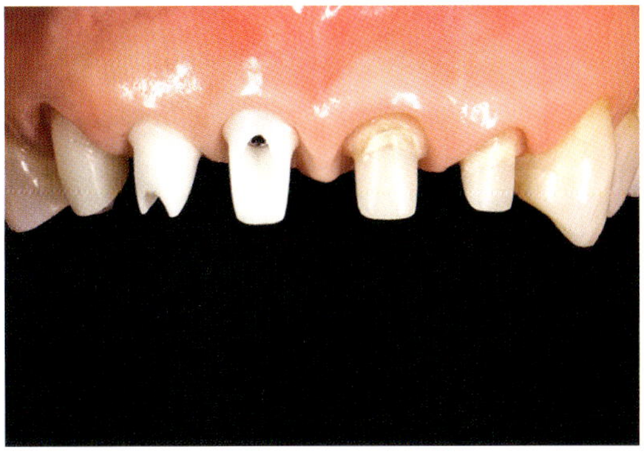

Fig 28bb : Frontal view. The peri-implant soft tissues are horizontally and vertically symmetrical, providing good balance.

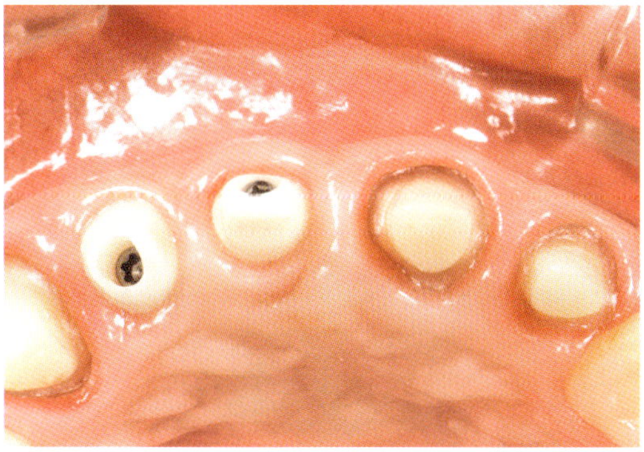

Fig 28cc : Occlusal view.

Final prosthesis fitting

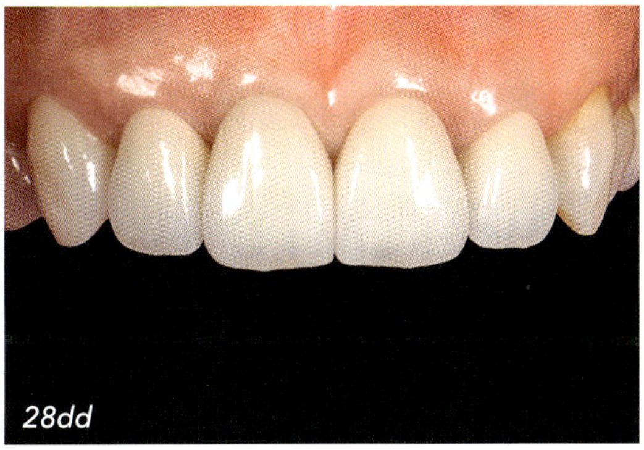

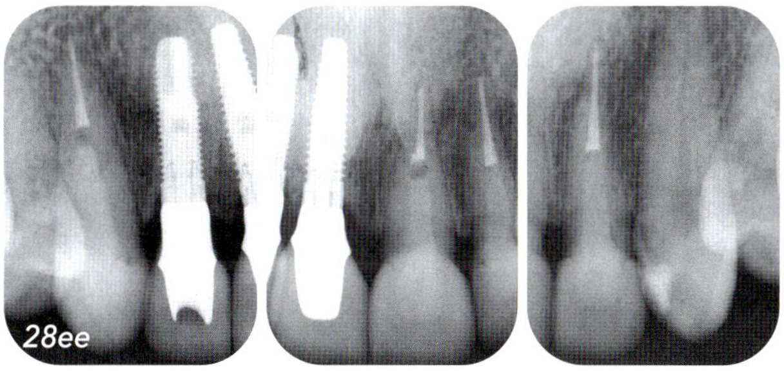

Fig 28dd, ee : Frontal view and dental X-rays of the final prosthesis at the time of fitting.

2 years after final prosthesis fitting

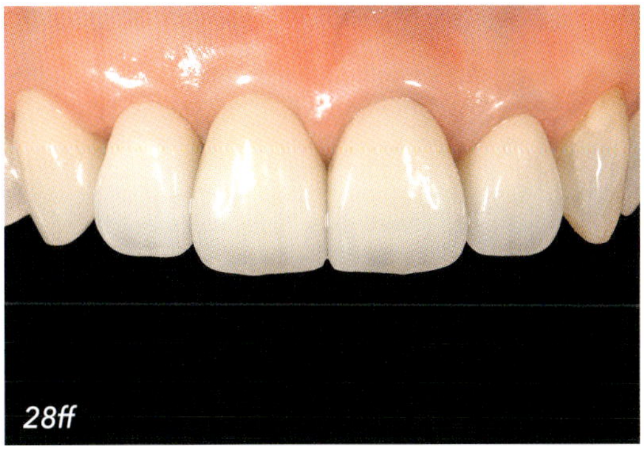

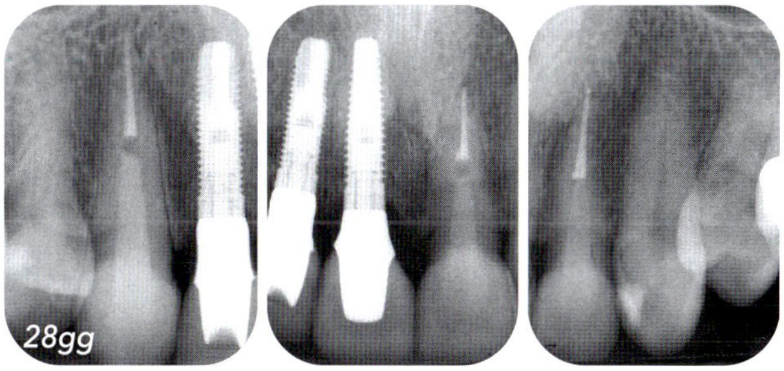

Fig 28ff, gg : Frontal view and dental X-rays of the final prosthesis 2 years after fitting. The peri-implant soft tissues have hardly changed over 2 years, maintaining a good condition. (Prosthesis by Dr. Masayuki Okawa.)

Evaluation

To ensure the success of the esthetic implant treatment, consideration needed to be given to how to maintain the level of the soft tissues in a high-risk patient. Furthermore, maintaining the interproximal space was the most important issue, since implants were placed successively in upper right #2 and #1. The treatment procedure gave fullest consideration to maintaining this space. Not placing the upper right #2 and #1 implants at the same time made it possible to maintain the height of the soft tissues in this region. With thin type soft tissues, the use of CTG from the start is helpful in patients with high esthetic requirements.

Preventive connective tissue graft 2

Pre-surgery (11/28/2011)

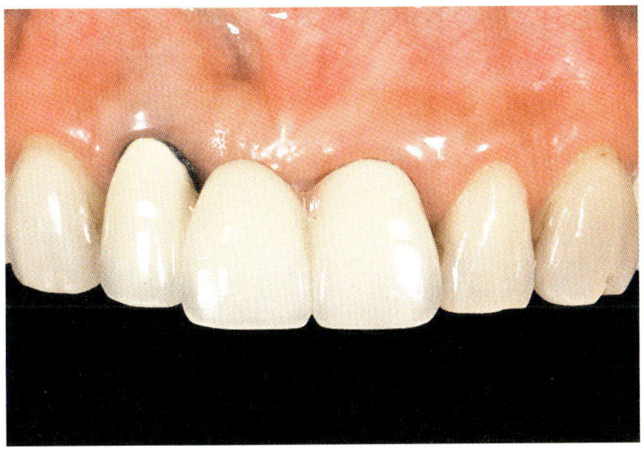

Fig 29a : Pre-operative facial view.

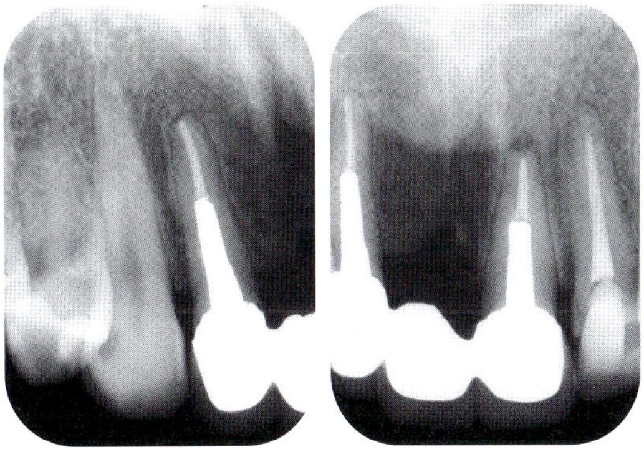

Fig 29b : Pre-operative dental X-ray of maxillary front tooth region

Vertical gingival line	#6	#7	#8	#9	#10	#11
Balance with adjacent teeth		X				
Balance with contra-lateral teeth		X				
Horizontal gingival line	**#6**	**#7**	**#8**	**#9**	**#10**	**#11**
Balance with adjacent teeth			X			
Balance with contra-lateral teeth			X			

X is the problematic area

Main points of the case

Problems

- Decrease in the labial side bone level due to root fracture of upper right #2.
- Decrease in the horizontal level of upper right #2 gingiva.
- Lack of mesiodistal alveolar width at upper right #1.
- Thin scallop type gingiva.
- High esthetic requirements of the patient.

Purpose and technique of surgery

An implant was used for root fracture of tooth #2. Implant placement in upper right #2 and #1 was considered at first, but the final plan was to extract upper left #1 and place implants at upper left #1 and upper right #2 due to the lack of mesiodistal alveolar width at upper right #1, the prognosis of instability in upper left #1, equivalent medical fees, etc. A surgical procedure had to be selected that took tissue preservation and growth into account, due to the high esthetic requirements of the patient. For this reason, the gap between the implant and the extraction socket was promptly filled with prosthetic material when the implant was placed. CTG was used to address the reduction in the level of soft tissue.

Upper right #2 implant placement immediately following extraction (2/3/2012)

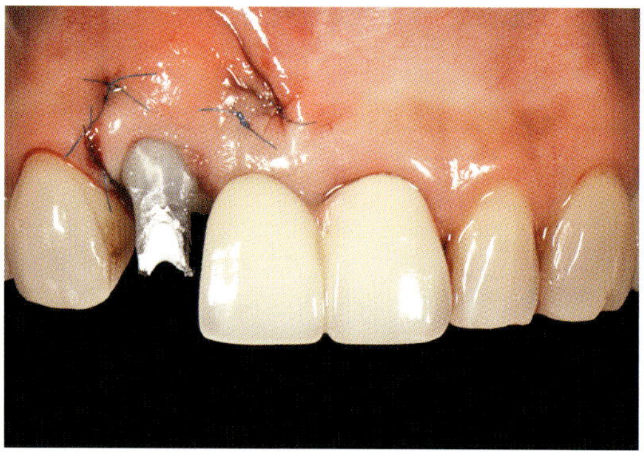

Fig 29c : Frontal view following implant placement.

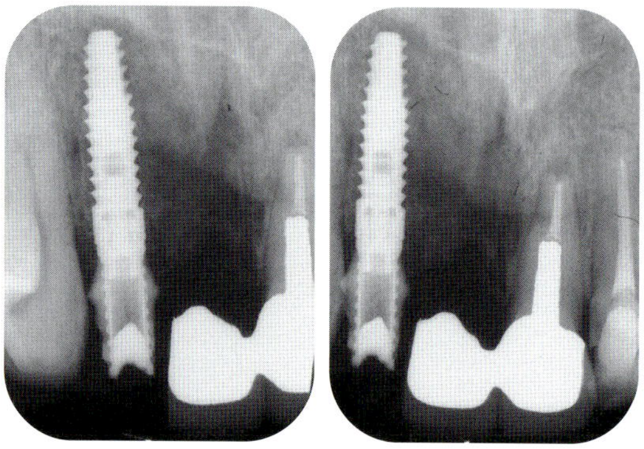

Fig 29d : Dental X-rays following implant placement. Because of the poor condition, only a single implant in upper right #2 was placed first.

Point

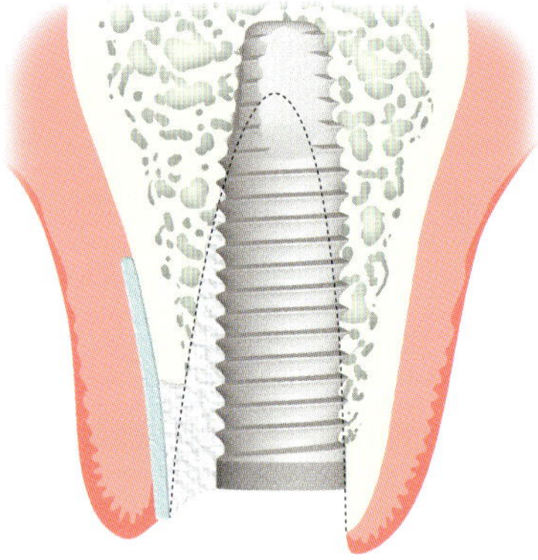

Implant placement immediately following extraction was used. However, because a bone defect was found on the labial side, an environment was created that could maintain the hard tissue on the labial side of the implant through the use of a resorbable membrane and prosthetic material. A custom provisional abutment was used.

2 months after implant placement

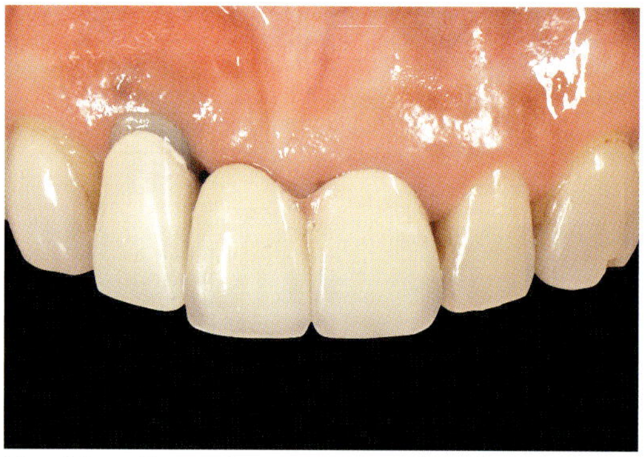

Fig 29e : Frontal view 2 months after implant placement. The peri-implant tissue level has shifted slightly toward the apex.

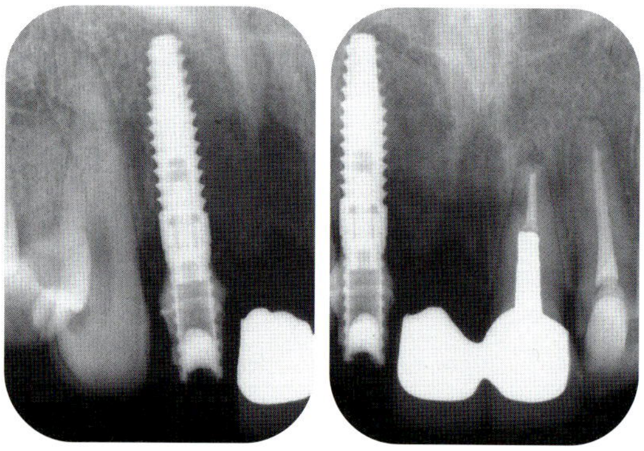

Fig 29f : Dental X-rays 2 months after implant placement

Upper left #1 implant placement immediately following extraction (9/8/2012)

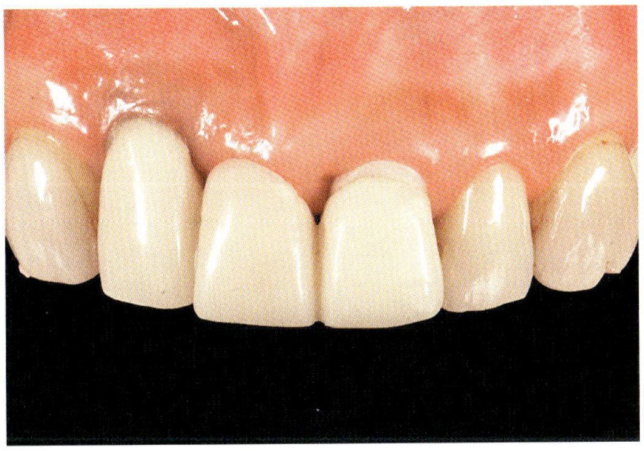

Fig 29g : After stability of upper right #2 was confirmed, implant placement of upper left #1 immediately following extraction was performed.

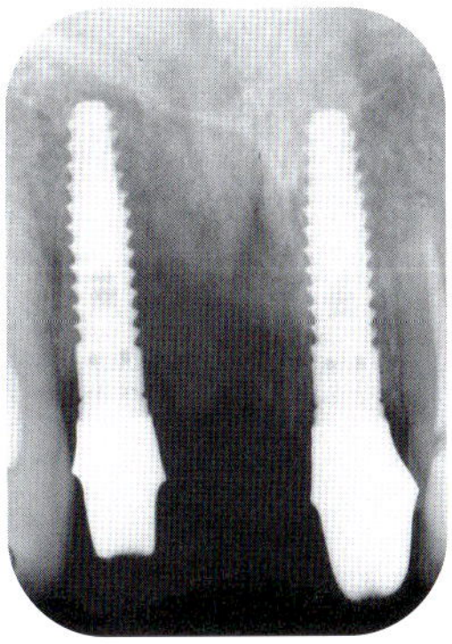

Fig 29h : Dental X-ray of upper left #1 after implant placement.

Connective tissue graft (7/19/2013)

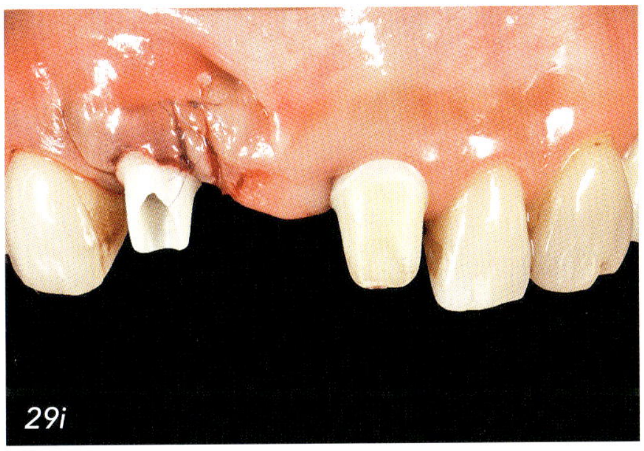

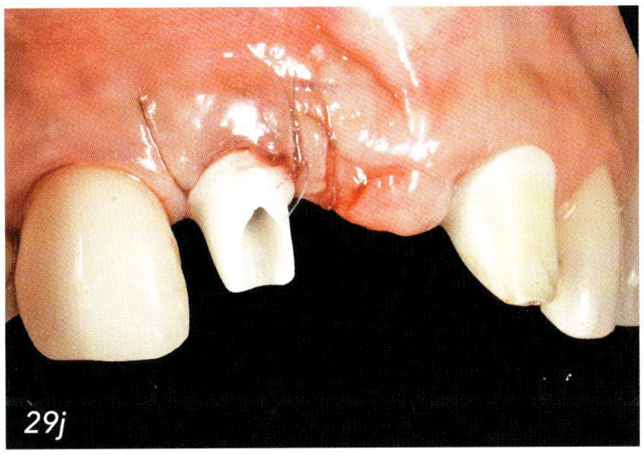

Fig 29i, j : CTG was performed in order to reconstruct the soft tissues on the labial side of upper right #2 and between upper right #1 and #2.

Point

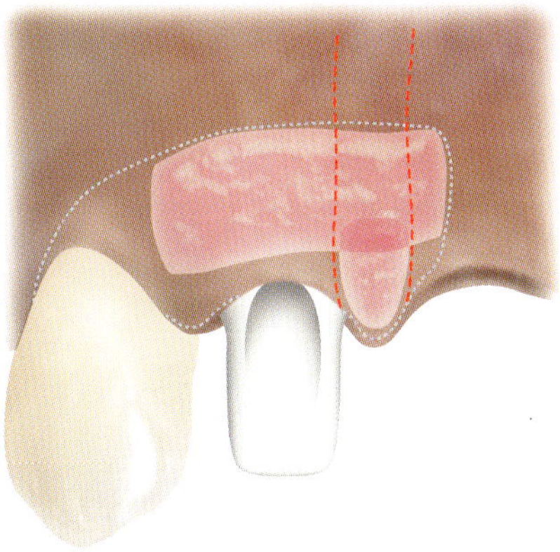

Diagram to show the CTG for reconstruction of the soft tissues on the labial side of upper right #2 and between upper right #1 and #2

Provisional restoration fitted four months after CTG

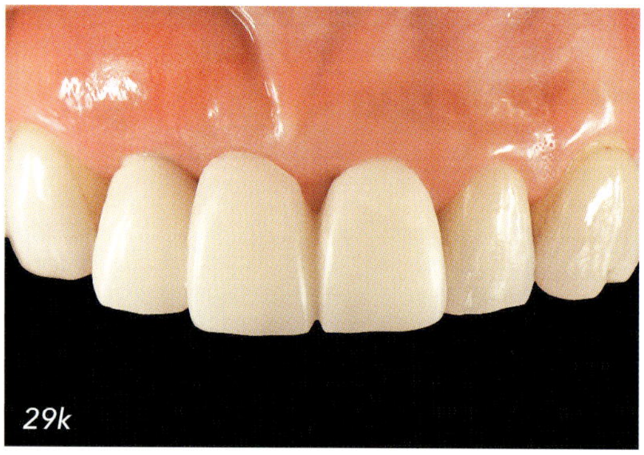

29k

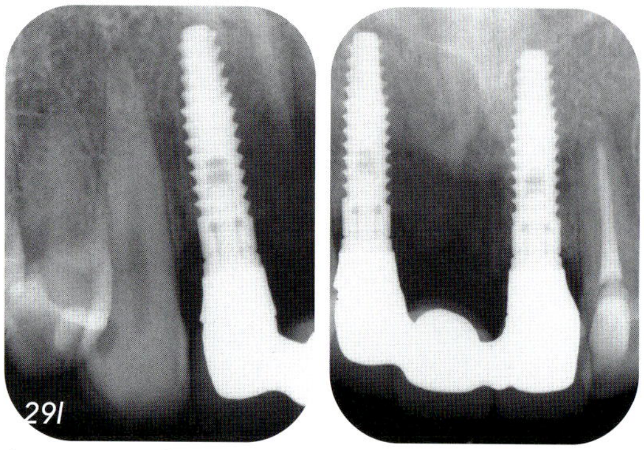

29l

Fig 29k, l : Frontal view and dental X-rays at the time of provisional restoration fitting.

Final prosthesis fitting

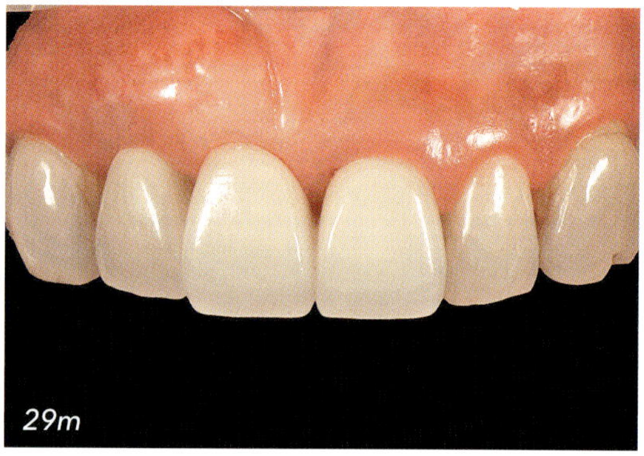

29m

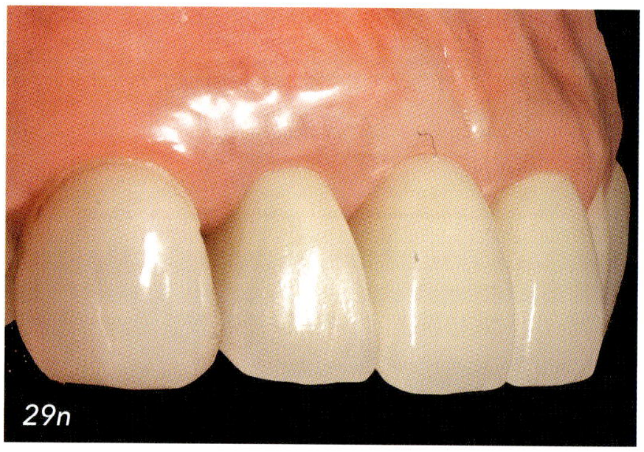

29n

Fig 29m, n : Frontal and lateral views at the time of final prosthesis fitting.

5 years after final prosthesis fitting

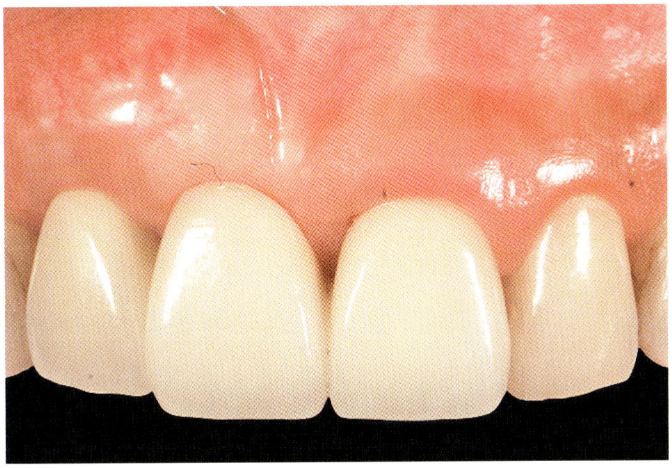

Fig 29o : Frontal view 5 years after final prosthesis fitting.

Evaluation

In the present case, management of the peri-implant tissue at upper right #2 was important. Labial side bone loss and gingival recession had been found at upper right #2 prior to extraction, therefore bone and soft tissue reconstruction was essential for the implant. It was difficult to judge the best way to carry these out. Implant placement of upper right #2 immediately following extraction and a simultaneous minor GBR procedure is technically very difficult, and this would not normally be the procedure of choice. However, this procedure was valid considering the fabrication of a provisional restoration during the treatment period due to the esthetic requirements of the patient. After the implant had stabilized, the morphology of the surrounding soft tissue was adjusted by CTG for esthetic purposes.

After 5 years of follow-up the peri-implant tissues are in good condition, and it appears that appropriate formation of hard and soft tissue has led to a satisfactory outcome.

References

1. Kokich VO Jr, Kiyak HA, Shapiro PA.Comparing the perception of dentists and lay people to altered dental esthetics. J Esthet Dent 1999 ; 11 (6) : 311-324.
2. Kokich VO, Kokich VG, Kiyak HA. Perceptions of dental professionals and laypersons to altered dental esthetics:asymmetric and symmetric situations. Am J Orthod Dentofacial Orthop 2006 Aug ; 130 (2) : 141-151.
3. Seibert JS. Reconstruction of deformed, partially edentulous ridges, using full thickness onlay grafts. Part I. Technique and wound healing. Compend Contin Educ Dent 1983 Sep-Oct ; 4 (5) : 437-453.
4. Wang HL, Al-Shammari K. HVC ridge deficiency classification:a therapeutically oriented classification. Int J Periodontics Restorative Dent 2002 Aug ; 22 (4) : 335-343.
5. Suzuki M, Ogata Y. Classification of single tooth edentulous ridges with augmentation recommendations for dental implant treatment. J Implant Advanced Clin Dent 2009 ; 1 (3) : 55-61.
6. Oösta F. Dohlman MD, Toronto : Carl Olof Nylen and the Birth of the Otomicroscope and Microsurgery. Arch Otolaryng 1969 ; 90.
7. Tibbetts LS, Shanelec DA. An overview of periodontal microsurgery. Curr Opin Periodontol 1994 : 187-193.
8. Tibbetts LS, Shanelec D. Current status of periodontal microsurgery. Curr Opin Periodontol 1996 ; 3 : 118-125.
9. Shanelec DA, Tibbetts LS. Recent advances in surgical technology, Treatment of periodontal disease, Clinical Periodontal 8th ed. WB Saunders Co 1996 : 677-684.
10. Tibbetts LS, Shanelec D. Periodontal microsurgery. Dent Clin North Am 1998 ; 42 (2) : 339-359.
11. Suzuki M. Efficacy of microscope for the periodontal surgery. Journal of Japan clinical periodontal society 2000 : 18
12. Fusino T, Tajima S, et al. Plastic surgery : Tokyo: Nanzando, 1996
13. Klopper P, Muller JH, van Hattum AH. Microsurgery and Wound Healing. Amsterdam, ExcerptaMedica. 1979 ; 280.
14. van Hattum AH, James J, Klopper PJ, Muller JH. A model for the study of epithelial migration in wound healing. Virchows Arch B Cell Pathol Incl Mol Pathol 1979 ; 30 (2) : 221-230.
15. Shanelec DA. Optical principles of loupes. J Calif Dent Assoc. 1992 ; 20 (11) : 25-32.
16. Suzuki M. Summary of Periodontal Microsurgery.- Efficacy and application for root coverage procedure-. The Quintessence 1999 ; 18 (12) : 49-56
17. Hegde R, Sumanth S, Padhye A. Microscope-enhanced periodontal therapy:a review and report of four cases. J Contemp Dent Pract 2009 Sep 1 ; 10 (5) : E088-96.
18. Nordland WP, Sandhu HS, Perio C. Microsurgical technique for augmentation of the interdental papilla:three case reports. Int J Periodontics Restorative Dent 2008 Dec ; 28 (6) : 543-549.
19. Cairo F, Carnevale G, Billi M, Prato GP. Fiber retention and papilla preservation technique in the treatment of infrabony defects:a microsurgical approach. Int J Periodontics Restorative Dent 2008 Jun ; 28 (3) : 257-263.
20. Francetti L, Del Fabbro M, Testori T, Weinstein RL.Periodontal microsurgery:report of 16 cases consecutively treated by the free rotated papilla autograft technique combined with the coronally advanced flap. Int J Periodontics Restorative Dent 2004 Jun ; 24 (3) : 272-279.
21. Shanelec DA. Periodontal microsurgery. J Esthet Restor Dent 2003 ; 15 (7) : 402-407.
22. Rossi R, Pilloni A, Morales RS. Qualitative assessment of connective tissue graft with epithelial component. A microsurgical periodontal plastic surgical technique for soft tissue esthetics. Eur J Esthet Dent 2009 Summer ; 4 (2) : 118-128.
23. Raetzke PB. Covering localized areas of root exposure employing the "envelope" technique. J Periodontol 1985 ; 56 (7) : 397-402.
24. Allen AL. Use of the supraperiosteal envelope in soft tissue grafting for root coverage. II . Clinical results. Int J Periodontics Restorative Dent 1994 ; 14 (4) : 302-315.
25. Langer B, Langer L. Subepithelial connective tissue graft technique for root coverage. J Periodontol 1985 ; 56 (12) : 715-720.
26. Bruno JF. Connective tissue graft technique assuring wide root coverage. Int J Periodontics Restorative Dent 1994 ; 14 (2) : 126-137.
27. Harris RJ. The connective tissue and partial thickness double pedicle graft : a predictable method of obtaining root coverage. J Periodontol 1992 ; 63 (5) : 477-486.
28. Nelson SW. The subpedicle connective tissue graft. A bilaminar reconstructive procedure for the coverage of denuded root surfaces. J Periodontol 1987 ; 58 (2) : 95-102.
29. Abrams L. Augmentation of the deformed residual edentulous ridge for fixed prosthesis. Compend Contin Educ Dent 1980-Jun ; 1 (3) : 205-213.
30. Langer B, Calagna L. The subepithelial connective tissue graft. J Prosthet Dent 1980 ; 44 (4) : 363-367.
31. Garber DA, Rosenberg ES. The edentulous ridge in fixed prosthodontics. Compend Contin Educ Dent 1981 ; 2 (4) : 212-223.
32. Suzuki M. Periodontal microsurgery overview — Application to alveolar ridge augmentation and papilla reconstruction. the Quintessence 2000 ; 19 (6) : 67-74.
33. Suzuki M. Periodontal microsurgery for implant therapy. Quintessence DENT Implantol 2001 ; 8 (6) : 50-57.
34. Wennström JL. Mucogingival considerations in orthodontic treatment.Semin Orthod 1996 Mar ; 2 (1) : 46-54.
35. Nozawa T, Enomoto H, Tsurumaki S, Ito K. Biologic height-width ratio of the buccal supra-implant mucosa. Eur J Esthet Dent 2006 Autumn ; 1 (3) : 208-214.

Index

Author : Dr. Masana Suzuki
1984 : Japan university Matsudo dental school graduate
1989 : Suzuki dental office at Katsushika-ku, Tokyo
2008 : Tsurumi university dental school, dept of orofacial implant, part-time lecturer
2009 : Japan university Matsudo dental school, visiting professor

Association : Japanese society of periodontology/ Periodontist
The Japanese academy of clinical periodontology/ Instructor
American academy of periodontology/ member
AMED/ board member

Study Group : SJCD (Society of Japan Clinical Dentistry) International : permanent director
Tokyo SJCD : Advisor
OJ : former chairman

Quintessence Publishing Co., Ltd.
3-2-6, Hongoh, Bunkyo-ku, Tokyo 113-0033, JAPAN
Tel: +81-3-5842-2270
Fax: +81-3-5800-7597
URL: www.quint-j.co.jp
Printing and Binding: Sun Art Printing Co., Ltd. Osaka
Printed in Japan
ISBN 978-4-7812-0906-7 C3047